Marguerite Patten
3000
RECIPE
COOKBOOK

Galley Press

Bridge House, Twickenham, Middlesex TW1 3SB, England

The material in this book has been previously published by The Hamlyn Publishing Group Limited in the '500 Recipes' series and by W H Smith in the *5000 Recipe Cookbook*. Published in this edition by Galley Press, an imprint of W H Smith and Son Limited. Registered No 237811 England. Trading as W H Smith Distributors, St John's House, East Street, Leicester LE1 6NE

ISBN 0 861 36615 8

Printed in Great Britain

Contents

How to Use This Book

For easy reference this book has been divided into eight self-contained sections, each with its own index, so that you can find exactly the right dish to fit the occasion. This means that certain dishes will be repeated in one or two sections to avoid the use of substantial cross-references, and for that reason well over 3,000 recipes have been included in this book to allow for necessary duplication.

Useful Facts and Figures

Notes on metrication

Solid measures

Exact conversion from Imperial to metric measures does not usually give very convenient working quantities and so the metric measures have been rounded off into units of 25 grams. The table below shows the recommended equivalents.

Ounces	Approx g to nearest whole figure	Recommended conversion to nearest unit of 25
1	28	25
2	57	50
3	85	75
4	113	100
5	142	150
6	170	175
7	198	200
8	227	225
9	255	250
10	283	275
11	312	300
12	340	350
13	368	375
14	396	400
15	425	425
16 (1 lb)	454	450
17	482	475
18	510	500
19	539	550
20 (1¼ lb)	567	575

Note: When converting quantities over 20 oz first add the appropriate figures in the centre column, then adjust to the nearest unit of 25. As a general guide, 1 kg (1000 g) equals 2.2 lb or about 2 lb 3 oz. This method of conversion gives good results in nearly all cases; although in certain pastry and cake recipes a more accurate conversion is necessary to produce a balanced recipe.

Liquid measures

Imperial	Approx ml to nearest whole figure	Recommended ml
¼ pint	142	150 ml
½ pint	283	300 ml
¾ pint	425	450 ml
1 pint	567	600 ml
1½ pints	851	900 ml
1¾ pints	992	1000 ml (1 litre)

Spoon measures All spoon measures given in this book are level unless otherwise stated.

Oven temperatures

The table below gives recommended equivalents.

	°F	Gas Mark	°C
Cool	225–250	¼–½	110–120
Very slow	250–275	½–1	120–140
Slow	275–300	1–2	140–150
Very moderate	300–350	2–3	150–160
Moderate	375	4	180
Moderately hot	400	5–6	190–200
Hot	425–450	7–8	220–230
Very hot	450–475	8–9	230–240

Notes for American and Australian users

In America the 8-oz measuring cup is used. In Australia metric measures are now used in conjunction with the standard 250-ml measuring cup. The Imperial pint, used in Britain, is 20-fl oz, while the American pint is 16 fl oz. It is important to remember that the Australian tablespoon differs from both the British and American tablespoons. The British standard tablespoon, which has been used throughout this book, holds 17.7 ml, the American 14.2 ml, and the Australian 20 ml. A teaspoon holds approximately 5 ml in all three countries.

British	American	Australian
1 teaspoon	1 teaspoon	1 teaspoon
1 tablespoon	1 tablespoon	1 tablespoon
2 tablespoons	3 tablespoons	2 tablespoons
3½ tablespoons	4 tablespoons	3 tablespoons
4 tablespoons	5 tablespoons	3½ tablespoons
5 tablespoons	6 tablespoons	4½ tablespoons
6 tablespoons	½ cup	½ cup
¼ pint	⅔ cup	⅔ cup
8 fl oz	1 cup	1 cup
½ pint	1¼ cups	1¼ cups
1 pint	2½ cups	2½ cups

Soups and Savouries

Making Your Own Soups

In this chapter you will find recipes for not only the most popular soups but also for some of the less usual ones. And don't forget that a home-made soup is not only delicious—it is also often extremely economical.

When preparing vegetable soups, take advantage of those vegetables that are in season and use them to give variety to your menus. Alternatively, often a meat bone or chicken carcase can be the basis of a really sustaining economical soup. By using the left-over bones, you need spend no further money on ingredients.

Because the ready-prepared soups are used so often by the busy housewife, you will also find a chapter on making the less usual and more interesting of these.

In soup-making there are certain terms which may need interpretation:

Bouquet garni The usual is a small bunch containing sprigs of parsley and thyme, and a bayleaf. You may also add 1–2 chives and any less usual herbs such as rosemary, marjoram, sage or fresh mint. The herbs are put into the stock (tied securely with cotton) and are either sieved with the other ingredients or removed before serving.

When fresh herbs are not available then use a good pinch of mixed dried herbs. Do not be too generous with dried herbs since they tend to give a musty flavour when used too lavishly.

Stock A white stock is made from the bones of chicken or veal: a brown stock from beef, mutton or game. When time does not permit using your own stock it is possible to use either yeast or beef extract or stock cubes with water.

Seasoning Whilst this normally means just salt and pepper, you will find that you can add considerable interest to soups by being rather more enterprising with seasoning—by using celery salt, garlic salt, paprika or cayenne pepper and pinches of spices from time to time.

A little white wine is often the secret of a really delicious soup. Use a light sherry or white wine for vegetable soups and a dark sherry or red wine in the rather heavier meat soups.

A soup that is sometimes lacking in richness tastes completely different if a knob of butter or tablespoon of cream is added to each portion just before serving.

Quantities to allow

It is very difficult to lay down hard and fast rules as to how much soup one should allow. If you are following the soup with a substantial main course, you generally allow $\frac{1}{3}$ pint of a clear soup, and $\frac{1}{4}$ pint of a more filling soup. If, however, the soup is to be the most filling part of the meal, increase these quantities.

Preparing stock

Cover bones with cold water, add a bay leaf, seasoning, and simmer gently for several hours.

Brown stocks are made from beef bones, mutton and game and are used mainly for meat soups.

White stocks are made from poultry bones (but do not include any giblets or meat from the bird) and from veal. They are used mainly for vegetable soups.

Fish stocks are made from the bones and skin of fish, or the shells of fish, and are used in fish soups.

Bacon stock: when you have stock left from boiling a piece of ham or bacon use it with such soups as pea (see page 21); you'll find the flavour excellent. A lentil or vegetable soup can be made with bacon stock too, with very good results.

Vegetable stocks are made by boiling vegetables and are used for many vegetable soups.

Note:

1 A stock pot should not be left in a warm kitchen where the liquid may go off. The stock should be used soon after making or kept in a refrigerator.

2 Potatoes and green vegetables are not good things to add to stock which is not being used

immediately because they cause it to deteriorate.

Stock cubes

If you find you haven't enough bones left over to use as the basis of stock, or if making stock takes up too much time, there are stock cubes on the market which give an excellent flavour to soups. They are dissolved in water, then added to the soup. You can buy both chicken and beef flavours, using the former for white stock and the latter for brown. Both yeast and beef extracts can be used for flavouring brown stock.

Cooking soups in a pressure cooker

No special recipes are given for pressure cooked soups because any recipe can be cooked this way. The time varies, of course, according to the type of ingredients but you need approximately a quarter of the amount of cooking time for most vegetables. Here are the points to remember about soup making in a pressure cooker.

Generally speaking, you will need to use approximately half the usual amount of water or stock for long-cooking soups. This is because you have little, if any, evaporation in a pressure cooker, which has been allowed for in the saucepan recipes. Where the ordinary saucepan method for soup takes only a few minutes decrease the amount of liquid by just under a third.

When making soup remember not to fill the cooker too full. You do not need the rack in the bottom of the pressure cooker.

Generally speaking soups should be cooked at a 15 lb. pressure and the pressure then allowed to return to normal at room temperature.

Where soups are sieved and thickened afterwards you will then treat the pressure cooker like an ordinary saucepan for thickening.

Using an electric blender

An electric blender or liquidiser is an admirable way of producing a purée soup without long cooking and without rubbing the ingredients through a sieve, and can be substituted whenever sieving is indicated in recipes. Vegetables and especially tomatoes, retain the maximum amount of flavour if lightly cooked, so you can produce a much better tomato soup if you purée the tomatoes in the electric mixer before cooking. Preparation of mixed vegetable soups in this way will reduce the cooking time by well under half but it has been found that onions which are cooked for such a short time tend to have a rather strong and, to some people, unpalatable flavour, so in any special recipe with a high percentage of onion it is better if ingredients are fully cooked before being put into the blender.

The parts of a blender are usually made of heat resisting materials but even so it is wise to warm them slightly for a minute or so before putting in a boiling soup.

To serve with soup

Croûtons

cooking time few minutes

you will need:

bread
hot fat for frying

1 Cut bread into really small dice or other shapes.
2 Toast or fry in hot fat until crisp and golden brown.
3 Drain on kitchen paper.

Caraway seed toast fingers

you will need:

crusts from slices of bread
butter
caraway seeds

1 Butter one side of the crusts only and sprinkle with caraway seeds.
2 Toast the buttered side to a golden brown and cut into fingers.
3 Serve at once.

Melba toast

Cut wafer-thin slices of stale bread and crisp them in the oven on a moderately low heat until golden brown.

10-Minute Soups

A really nourishing soup can turn a light snack into a complete and satisfying meal and the soups in this chapter all take a maximum of 10 minutes to prepare.

Asparagus soup

cooking time just under 10 minutes

you will need for 4 servings:

- 1 medium can asparagus
- 1 pint milk
- ½ oz. cornflour or 1 oz. flour
- 1 oz. butter or margarine
- extra seasoning

1. Open the can of asparagus and drain the liquid into a jug with the milk.
2. Chop the asparagus into tiny pieces.
3. Heat the butter or margarine, stir in the cornflour or flour.
4. Add the milk and asparagus stock.
5. Bring to the boil, taste and season.
6. Put in the pieces of asparagus.
7. Heat for a few minutes and serve.

Bean broth

cooking time under 10 minutes

you will need for 4 servings:

- 1 pint stock or water with one chicken stock cube or little yeast extract
- 2 skinned, chopped tomatoes
- 1 tablespoon chopped parsley
- 1 tablespoon chopped chives
- 1 medium can baked beans

1. Put all the ingredients into a saucepan and simmer for approximately 5 minutes.
2. This can be served topped with grated cheese if wished.

Beetroot soup

cooking time just under 10 minutes

you will need for 4 servings:

- 1 large cooked beetroot
- 2 chicken or beef stock cubes
- 1½ pints water
- seasoning
- squeeze lemon juice

To garnish:
chopped parsley

1 Skin the beetroot and grate.
2 Heat the water and stock cubes.
3 Add grated beetroot, lemon juice and seasoning, and heat for about 5 minutes.
4 Top with chopped parsley.

Carrot soup

cooking time 10 minutes

you will need for 4 servings:

8 small carrots
1 pint water
½ pint milk
1–2 chicken stock cubes
seasoning

To garnish:
chopped parsley or chives

1 Grate the carrots and simmer for about 8 minutes with the milk and water in which the stock cubes have been dissolved.
2 Season well and include a pinch of sugar if wished.
3 Pour into heated soup cups and garnish with the parsley or chives.

Variations:

Quick cream of carrot soup
Simmer the carrots with the water only. Meanwhile make a white sauce with ½ oz. butter, ½ oz. flour and ½ pint milk. Blend with the carrot mixture and season well.

Cheese and carrot soup
During the last 2 minutes of cooking of either the plain carrot soup or cream of carrot soup, stir in 4 oz. grated cheese. If overcooked it will become tough and stringy.

Corn-on-the-cob soup

cooking time just under 10 minutes

you will need for 4 servings:

1 oz. margarine or butter
½ oz. cornflour or 1 oz. flour
½ pint water
1 stock cube (preferably chicken)
1 pint milk
1 can sweetcorn or mixed sweetcorn and peppers
seasoning

To garnish:
little chopped chives or parsley

1 Heat the butter or margarine, stir in the cornflour or flour.
2 Cook gently for several minutes.
3 Add the water, stock cube, and milk and bring to the boil.
4 Cook until thickened.
5 Add the sweetcorn and heat for a few minutes.
6 Season well and garnish with chopped chives or parsley.

Fish soup

cooking time just under 10 minutes

you will need for 4 servings:

2 good-sized fillets plaice, whiting or sole
2 teaspoons grated onion
1 pint milk
½ pint water
½ oz. cornflour or 1 oz. flour
¼ pint white wine or ¼ pint water
1 oz. butter or margarine
seasoning

To garnish:
lemon slices
chopped parsley

1 Skin the fish and cut into tiny pieces with a sharp knife or kitchen scissors.
2 Simmer the fish with the onion in milk and water for about 5 minutes.
3 Blend the cornflour or flour with the wine or the water.
4 Add to the fish mixture.
5 Bring to the boil, stirring well.
6 Put in the butter or margarine and seasoning, and heat for 2–3 minutes.
7 Pour into soup cups and garnish with lemon and parsley.

Speedy green pea soup

cooking time just under 10 minutes

you will need for 4 servings:

1 pint water
1 chicken stock cube
1 small packet frozen peas or 1 can peas
seasoning
pinch dried mint or little chopped fresh mint
approximately 3 tablespoons top of milk or cream

1 Bring water in which stock cube is dissolved to the boil.
2 Put in frozen peas and cook for about 4 minutes. Canned peas need only about 2 minutes heating.
3 Rub through a sieve, return to the pan with the remaining ingredients and reheat.

Variation:
To make a soup with a stronger flavour, 1 or 2 finely diced rashers of bacon can also be cooked with the peas.

Potato soup

cooking time just under 10 minutes

you will need for 4 servings:

4 medium potatoes
1 small onion
½ pint milk
1 pint water
1–2 chicken stock cubes
seasoning

To garnish:
chopped chives or parsley

1 Grate the peeled potatoes and onion and simmer for about 8 minutes with the milk and water in which the stock cubes have been dissolved.
2 Season well and include a pinch of sugar if wished.
3 Pour into hot soup cups and garnish with the chives or parsley.

Variation:

Cheese and potato soup
Use either plain Potato soup or Cream of potato soup and in the last two minutes of cooking stir in 4 oz. grated cheese. Do not overcook or it will become tough and stringy.

Quick vegetable soup

cooking time 8 minutes

you will need for 4 servings:

approximately 1¼ lb. mixed vegetables
1½ pints stock or water
1 bouillon cube
seasoning

To garnish:
grated cheese
parsley

1 Peel and coarsely grate the vegetables.
2 Bring to the boil the stock or water to which the bouillon cube has been added, add the vegetables and seasoning and cook rapidly for about 5–8 minutes until the vegetables are just tender.
3 Pour into hot soup cups and sprinkle with lots of grated cheese and parsley.

Fish Soups

It is a pity that people are often so reluctant to try fish soups because they can be extremely good. Their great virtue lies in the fact that one can choose quite cheap fish as a basis for family soups or more luxurious fish for party fare. They are easily digestible and make a good choice to precede a meat course.

Basic fish soup

cooking time 55 minutes

you will need for 4 servings:

1 lb white fish*
8 oz. fish trimmings (skin, bones)
2 pints water
1 large onion or 2 leeks
1 oz. margarine
2 oz. flour
¼ pint milk
salt and pepper to taste
1 teaspoon chopped parsley

*Whiting gives a very delicately flavoured soup; fresh haddock gives a moderately strong flavour, while cod has a very definite flavour

1 Wash and clean fish and trimmings.
2 Simmer trimmings in water for 10 minutes. Strain.
3 Place fish in a pan with the stock and sliced onions or leeks. Bring to the boil and skim well. Cook gently for 10 minutes.
4 Lift out the fish and flake.
5 Cook the stock for 30 minutes longer. Strain and rinse the pan.
6 Melt the margarine, add the flour and cook without colouring for a few minutes. Add the stock and milk and cook until boiling, stirring continuously.
7 Add the flaked fish, season and boil gently for 5 minutes.
8 Add the chopped parsley and serve.

Variations:

Spiced fish soup
Add 2–3 cloves and/or a little grated nutmeg.

Brown fish soup
Use a brown meat stock. This seems a strange mixture but it is, in fact, very pleasant.

Tomato fish soup
Use either 1 pint water and 1 pint tomato juice or a thin sieved tomato purée.

Lobster bisque

cooking time 45 minutes

you will need for 4 servings:

- ½ large lobster or 1 small lobster
- 1 pint water or fish stock
- 1 teaspoon lemon juice
- 1 oz. flour
- ½ pint milk
- 2 oz. margarine or butter
- seasoning
- 2 tablespoons cream

To garnish:
paprika pepper
small pieces lobster

Remove the flesh from the lobster and cut into small pieces.
Put aside a few pieces for garnishing.
Put the shell, well washed and crushed, into a large saucepan.
Cover with the water or stock, add lemon juice and simmer gently for a good 30 minutes.
Strain carefully through a fine sieve and return liquid to the pan together with the lobster meat.
Blend the flour with the milk and stir this into the soup together with the margarine or butter, and season.
Bring slowly to the boil and cook, stirring all the time until thickened.
Add the cream, reheat and serve.
Garnish with paprika pepper and the small pieces of lobster.

Creamed haddock soup

cooking time 20 minutes

you will need for 4 servings:

- 1 small onion
- approximately 12 oz. fresh haddock
- small bunch parsley
- ½ pint water
- 1 oz. butter
- 1 oz. flour
- ½ pint milk
- seasoning

To garnish:
a little onion or red pepper or paprika pepper

1 Slice the onion and put with the haddock and parsley into the water.
2 Simmer gently until just soft.
3 Lift the fish out of the stock and flake very finely.
4 Make a thin sauce with the butter, flour, milk and a good ¼ pint of the fish stock.
5 Add the pieces of fish and heat gently.
6 Season.
7 Garnish with wafer-thin slices of raw or fried onion, or slices of pepper, or dust instead with a little paprika to give a contrasting colour.

Mussel soup

cooking time 30 minutes

you will need for 4 servings:

- 2 pints mussels
- 1 finely chopped onion
- 2 tablespoons finely chopped celery
- small bunch parsley
- seasoning
- 2 oz. rice
- 1 large skinned chopped tomato
- 1½ pints water
- squeeze lemon juice or little vinegar

To garnish:
chopped parsley

1 Scrub mussels, discarding any that are open and will not close when sharply tapped. Always remove the 'beard' (the rather stringy part).
2 Put into a large saucepan with onion, celery, parsley and seasoning and heat slowly until mussels open.
3 Remove mussels from liquid and take out of shells.
4 Meanwhile reheat liquid, add rice and cook until tender with chopped tomato.
5 Remove sprig of parsley, add mussels and lemon juice or vinegar, and reheat gently.
6 Garnish with chopped parsley.

Scallop bisque

cooking time 20–40 minutes

you will need for 4 servings:

- 2 tablespoons oil for frying
- 1 carrot
- 1 leek
- 1 clove garlic
- pinch of fennel (optional)
- 4 peppercorns
- 8 oz. white fish
- 2 *level* tablespoons cornflour
- 1 small can tomato purée
- ¼ pint dry white wine
- ¼ pint water
- 1½ pints milk
- 4 scallops
- 3 tablespoons cream
- salt

1 Heat the oil in a deep pan.
2 Chop the carrot, leek and garlic finely and add to the oil with fennel and peppercorns.
3 Sauté lightly.
4 Cut the white fish into small pieces.
5 Add to the vegetables.
6 Continue cooking gently for 2–3 minutes.
7 Add the cornflour and tomato purée.
8 Mix well, then add the wine and water.
9 Bring to the boil, then add the milk.
10 Cover, and cook gently for about 20 minutes or until the vegetables are tender.
11 Put through a sieve.
12 Cut the scallops into small pieces, add to the soup and return to gentle heat for about 10 minutes or until the scallops are tender.
13 Stir in the cream and season to taste.

Meat Soups

Bacon and barley soup

cooking time 1 hour 20 minutes

you will need for 6–8 servings:

1 bacon knuckle
2½ pints stock
2 oz. pearl barley
pepper
2 carrots
1 turnip
1 onion

To garnish:
chopped parsley

1. Soak the knuckle in cold water (6 hours if smoked, 2 hours if unsmoked).
2. Place in a saucepan with the stock.
3. Wash barley and add.
4. Season with pepper and bring to the boil.
5. Reduce heat, cover with lid and simmer gently for 40 minutes.
6. Add diced carrots, turnip and onion and simmer for further 40 minutes.
7. Remove knuckle from liquid and cut meat into small pieces.
8. Return these to the soup.
9. Taste and adjust seasoning if necessary.
10. Serve garnished with chopped parsley.

Kidney soup

cooking time 1½ hours

you will need for 4 servings:

8 oz. kidney (ox kidney can be used)*
1 small onion
2 oz. butter
1 oz. flour
2 pints stock or water
seasoning
parsley
little port or Burgundy

*If using lambs' kidneys the cooking time will be 30 minutes only so reduce the amount of stock to 1¼–1½ pints

1. Chop the kidney and onion very finely and fry in the hot butter for a minute or two, making sure not to harden the outside of the meat.
2. Blend in the flour, and gradually add the stock.
3. Bring to the boil, stir until smooth, add seasoning and a sprig of parsley, then simmer gently for about 1½ hours.
4. Remove the parsley, add wine and serve.

Chinese meat and vegetable soup

cooking time 12 minutes

you will need for 4 servings:

4 oz. greens*
4 oz. lean pork
1 pint stock
1 tablespoon sherry
1 teaspoon salt
⅓ teaspoon taste powder†

*You can use spinach, celery, cabbage, peas or green beans
†Sold in good grocers' shops—monosodium glutamate

1. Wash greens and cut into 1-inch lengths.
2. Slice meat and cut into ¼-inch dice.
3. Bring stock to the boil and slide meat in.
4. Boil ½ minute, then remove meat with a strainer or sieve.
5. Holding sieve over the pot of soup, pour sherry over meat and into soup.
6. Skim soup.
7. Add greens and simmer until tender.
8. Place meat with salt and taste powder in a bowl, pour soup over and stir well.

Mulligatawny soup

cooking time 1 hour

you will need for 4 servings:

1 apple
1 large carrot
2 onions
2 oz. fat or dripping
1 oz. flour
1 tablespoon curry powder
2 pints stock*
1 tablespoon chutney
1 oz. sultanas
pinch sugar
seasoning
little lemon juice or vinegar

*Made by simmering lamb or mutton bones or a small lamb's head

1. Chop the apple and vegetables into tiny pieces, toss in the hot dripping, then work in the flour and curry powder.
2. Add the stock, bring to the boil and cook until thickened.
3. Add remaining ingredients and cook together for about 45 minutes–1 hour.
4. Rub through a sieve and return to the pan to reheat.
5. Taste, adjusting seasoning if necessary, and add a little extra sugar or lemon juice if required.

Oxtail soup

cooking time 3¼ hours

you will need for 4 servings:

1 small oxtail
2 oz. cooking fat or margarine
1 small turnip
3 medium carrots
1 large onion
3 pints stock or water
good pinch mixed herbs
seasoning
2 oz. flour

Soak the cut-up oxtail for an hour or so then throw away the water.
Heat the fat, slice the vegetables and fry for about 5 minutes.
Add the stock, reserving 1 teacup, the oxtail, herbs and plenty of seasoning and simmer gently for about 3 hours.
Blend the flour with the teacup of cold stock or water and stir this into the soup.
Bring to the boil and cook for about 10 minutes.
Take out the pieces of oxtail, cut the meat from the bones, return to the soup and reheat.
As this soup will have a fair amount of fat it is best made the day before required, so that you can allow it to cool and then remove the fat from the top.

Scotch broth

cooking time 2¾ hours

you will need for 4 servings:

1 oz. pearl barley
8 oz. stewing beef or mutton
2 pints water
3 oz. sliced leeks or onion
8 oz. diced carrot
8 oz. diced swede
salt and pepper
2 oz. sliced cabbage

To garnish:
1 tablespoon chopped parsley

1 Blanch the barley by putting into cold water bringing to the boil, then pouring the water away.
2 Put the barley, diced beef* and water into a pan, bring to the boil, skim, and simmer gently for 1 hour.
3 Add all the prepared vegetables except the cabbage, plenty of seasoning and cook for a further 1½ hours.
4 Add the cabbage and allow another 15 minutes cooking.
5 Skim off any superfluous fat from the broth, pour into hot dish or soup cups and garnish with the parsley.

*If desired the meat can be left in one piece and removed from the soup whole so that it can be used for a separate dish

Sour-hot soup

cooking time 15 minutes

you will need for 4 servings:

4 oz. lean pork
½ square (1½ oz.) beancurd*
3 dried mushrooms, soaked*
1 pint stock
1 tablespoon sherry
1 tablespoon soya sauce
½ teaspoon pepper
1 tablespoon vinegar
2 teaspoons cornflour
1 tablespoon water
1 teaspoon salt
⅓ teaspoon taste powder†

*Optional—obtainable from shops selling Chinese food
†Sold in good grocers' shops—monosodium glutamate

1 Sliver pork, beancurd and mushrooms.
2 Bring stock to boil and add all three.
3 Simmer 5 minutes.
4 Add sherry, soya sauce, pepper, vinegar and cornflour blended with the water.
5 Cook until soup thickens.
6 Pour over seasoning and stir well.

Poultry and Game Soups

There is no greater waste of money than to discard any poultry or game carcase without using it as a basis for a soup.
The stock may not have enough flavour to make a soup by itself but it does give soup a first-class basis. If, however, there are pieces of flesh still left on the carcase you may find that you have sufficient 'body' without adding a lot of vegetables to detract from the flavour. Recipes on the following page are based on stock.

Cream of chicken soup

cooking time 3¼ hours

you will need for 12 servings:

1 small boiling fowl
water to cover
bouquet garni (see page 6)
seasoning
optional vegetables (1 carrot, 1 onion, piece celery)
2 oz. butter
2 oz. flour or 1 oz. cornflour
1 pint milk
¼ pint cream or evaporated milk
2 egg yolks

1. Cut up the fowl if wished or use whole. Cover with cold water, add *bouquet garni*, seasoning and a few vegetables if wished (but too many will kill the delicate flavour of the chicken).
2. Simmer for 2–3 hours until tender.
3. Take all the meat from the bones and rub it through a sieve.
4. Add to the stock to give a smooth thick mixture.
5. Make a sauce of the butter, flour and milk.
6. When thick and creamy add to the chicken mixture and reheat gently.
7. Beat the egg yolks with the cream and add to the soup, then cook gently until thickened again; this takes about 3 minutes. DO NOT BOIL.

Hare soup

cooking time 1¾ hours

you will need for 6–8 servings:

bones of a hare
2 pints water or stock
2 onions
2 bay leaves
2 small carrots
piece of turnip
bouquet garni (see page 6)
head and any other parts of hare flesh, such as liver, not used in main dish (blood can also be added to give richness of flavour)
⅛ pint port wine or Madeira (optional)
seasoning
pinch sugar
2 oz. dripping, margarine or butter

1. Put the bones, meat, diced vegetables, herbs and blood into pan with the water or stock.
2. Bring to the boil and continue cooking gently for 1½ hours.
3. Strain carefully; if any meat is left on the bones this should be sieved, minced or pounded until very fine and returned to the soup.
4. Blend the flour with a little water and add to the soup together with the margarine, butter or dripping.*
5. Bring slowly to the boil and cook until thickened, season then simmer for about 10 minutes.
6. Stir in the wine.

*The fat can be omitted if wished

Variations:

Rabbit soup

Substitute rabbit for hare in previous recipe.

Creamed rabbit or hare soup

Use 1½ pints stock, then make a white sauce with the flour, butter and ½ pint milk. Blend the stock into this.

Chicken soup (with carcase only)

cooking time 1½–2 hours

you will need:

one chicken carcase with a little flesh left on wings etc.
water to cover
bouquet garni (see page 6)
seasoning

1. Put the ingredients into a saucepan and simmer gently for approximately 2 hours.
2. Lift out the carcase and carefully cut any little pieces of meat away from the bones. Do not use the skin.
3. Reheat with the stock and serve.

Chicken soup and dumplings

cooking time 1½–2 hours

you will need for 4 servings:

1 chicken carcase
seasoning
water to cover
bouquet garni (see page 6)

For dumplings:
2 oz. flour (with plain flour ½ teaspoon baking powder)
1 oz. margarine, butter or shredded suet
water to bind

1. Simmer the ingredients for approximately 1½ hours.
2. Lift out from the stock, returning any pieces of meat to the pan with seasoning.
3. To prepare dumplings, sieve flour and seasoning then rub in butter or margarine or suet.
4. Mix to a fairly firm consistency with the water —you should be able to roll them in balls with slightly floured hands. (If the dough is too stiff the dumplings will be heavy and solid; if too soft, they will break.)
5. Make sure the liquid is boiling then add the dumplings. Cook steadily for 10–15 minutes.

Variation:

Herb dumplings

Add pinch of mixed herbs or 1–2 teaspoons fresh finely chopped herbs.

Turkey soup

Any of the suggestions for chicken soups could be used with a turkey carcase.

Using duck or goose in soups

It must be remembered that both duck and goose are very fatty and therefore it is better to make a stock, let it cool, lift off the excess fat which will have solidified and then proceed as for other meat or chicken soups. The flavour of the stock is excellent.

Game soups

The carcase of game, unless it has been hung for a very long time and is very 'high', produces a very good stock. For Hare soup it can be flavoured with various vegetables, or it can be used as the basis for a game soup prepared like chicken soup.

Curried poultry or game soups

By adding a little curry powder to the ingredients in either chicken or game stock you do give a very pleasant flavour to this type of soup.

Clear Soups

A clear soup is perhaps the most difficult to make because it must be clarified with the greatest of care. You will find the right way to make clear soup given in the recipe for Beef consommé (this page step 4). By putting in the egg shell and stiffly beaten egg white you collect any minute particles of vegetable, meat and fat which would spoil the clarity of the soup.
For family use, of course, the flavour is just as good whether the soup has been cleared or not.

Beef tea

cooking time 2 hours

you will need for 4 servings:

1 lb. lean beef
1 pint water
good pinch salt

After removing all fat, cut the meat into small pieces.
Put these into a stone jar or double saucepan, adding the water and salt; stand in a saucepan of water.
Bring the water in the saucepan just to the boil; then let it simmer very gently for a good 2 hours.
Strain the beef tea through muslin, then allow it to cool sufficiently to skim off the fat.
Reheat, without boiling, and serve with crisp toast.

Note:
Do not make large quantities of beef tea for it should not be kept for longer than a day.

Beef consommé

cooking time 1 hour

you will need for 4 servings:

12 oz. shin of beef
2 pints good stock
seasoning
1 onion
1 carrot
small piece celery
sprig parsley
bay leaf

To clear soup:
1 dessertspoon sherry, optional
1 egg white and shell

1 Cut the meat into small pieces and put these into a saucepan together with the other ingredients.
2 Simmer very gently for 1 hour, then strain through several thicknesses of muslin.
3 Add sherry if desired.
4 To clear consommé put in a stiffly beaten egg white and clean egg shell, gently simmer for a further 20 minutes, then re-strain.

Variations:

Consommé julienne
Add to the above quantity

1 good-sized carrot
½ medium-sized turnip
1 leek or onion
small piece cabbage
1 oz. margarine

Cut the vegetables into thin pieces about the size and thickness of a matchstick. Melt margarine in a saucepan and toss the vegetables in this until just turning brown. Add about ⅛ pint of the consommé and cook gently until the vegetables are quite tender. Take off any fat and add the remaining consommé, reheating gently.

Consommé Celestine

Make thin pancakes (see page 80) then cut into wafer-thin strips. Heat in the consommé.

Consommé au vermicelli

To the quantity of Beef consommé on page 15 add 2 tablespoons vermicelli. Cook gently for 7 minutes, then serve.

Veal consommé

Use same ingredients as Beef consommé plus 12 oz. stewing veal. Leave out the bay leaf and add a very light sherry to keep the pale colour.

Chicken consommé

Allow the stock in which chicken has been simmered to cool, remove the fat and reboil the stock with pieces of vegetable for about 30 minutes. Strain as Beef consommé.

Game consommé

Make a good stock by boiling the carcase of any game together with vegetables. Allow to cool, remove any fat, reheat, strain and flavour with sherry.

Clear chicken or turkey soup

cooking time 2 hours

you will need for 4 servings:

1 chicken or turkey carcase
2–3 peppercorns
salt and pepper
chopped parsley
1 carrot
1 onion
2 cloves

1. Remove any remaining small pieces of meat from the bones to keep on one side, then break up bones and put in a pan with cut-up vegetables, spices and seasoning.
2. Cover with water and simmer gently for about 2 hours.
3. Strain, add pieces of meat chopped small and chopped parsley; reheat.

Note:

If using a pressure cooker allow 25 minutes at 15 lb. pressure.

Clear mushroom soup

cooking time 10–15 minutes

you will need for 4 servings:

1 small onion (optional)
6–8 oz. mushrooms
1¼ pints white stock or water with 1 chicken stock cube
seasoning

1. Chop the onion very finely and slice the mushrooms.
2. Put into the stock, season and simmer for approximately 10–15 minutes.

Clear tomato soup

cooking time 25 minutes

you will need for 4 servings:

1½ lb. tomatoes
1 pint water or white stock
½ small beetroot, preferably uncooked
small piece celery
1 small onion, chopped
1 heaped teaspoon yeast extract
seasoning
2 bay leaves

1. Put all the ingredients in a large saucepan and cook gently until the tomatoes are very soft. This should take about 25 minutes.
2. Remove the beetroot and bay leaves; rub first through a sieve and then strain through muslin.
3. Reheat or serve cold.
4. If a slightly thickened soup is desired it will only be necessary to rub through the sieve, without straining afterwards.

Mock turtle soup

cooking time 3 hours

you will need for 8–10 servings:

small calf's head
water
sherry or Madeira
seasoning
bouquet garni (see page 6)
1 egg white and shell

1. Wash calf's head, split down the centre, remove brains if wished to use for a separate dish (also the tongue can be taken out).
2. Cover with cold water, bring to the boil, throw away the water and cover with fresh water. Add seasoning and herbs and simmer gently until tender—this takes 2–3 hours.
3. Strain off the stock and put into a pan.
4. Cut the meat from the head.
5. Clear the stock as described in Beef consommé (see page 15), add the meat diced; heat gently then put in sherry or Madeira just before serving.

Vegetable Soups

These are possibly the most popular of all soups in that they use reasonably economical ingredients and they can be varied according to vegetables in season. Try not to overcook vegetable soups as both colour and flavour tend to be lost. Although a good stock is often needed, this should not be too strongly flavoured or it will detract from the fresh flavour of the vegetables.

Borshch

cooking time 40 minutes–1½ hours

you will need for 4 servings:

1 large raw beetroot or slightly more cooked beetroot
1 carrot
1 onion
2–3 tomatoes
little chopped celery
clove garlic
2 pints water or stock*
seasoning
vinegar
little sour cream or cream cheese

*Use only 1½ pints with cooked beetroot

1 Grate the beetroot and put into pan with the grated or chopped carrot and onion, tomatoes, crushed garlic and celery.
2 Add the stock.
3 Simmer raw beetroot for 1½ hours or cooked beetroot for about 40 minutes.
4 Season and add a little vinegar.
5 Top with sour cream or cream cheese before serving.

Variations:

Jellied borshch
Dissolve about 1 level tablespoon powdered gelatine in the soup after cooking. Allow to cool, but not set, then stir in sour cream. Serve in soup cups and top with cream cheese.

Cranberry borshch
Follow the Borshch recipe above but use 6 oz. cranberries instead of beetroot and omit carrot and onion. You may need a little sugar to take away the 'bite' from the cranberry borshch. Cook for 25 minutes only.

Cream of artichoke soup

cooking time 45 minutes

you will need for 4 servings:

1½ lb. artichokes
1 pint water or white stock
¼ teaspoon vinegar
seasoning
2 oz. butter
½ oz. flour
¼–½ pint milk

To garnish:
paprika

1 Wash and peel the artichokes and, if large, cut into small pieces.
2 Remember to keep the artichokes in cold water, with a tablespoon of lemon juice to preserve a good colour, until ready to cook them.
3 Put into a saucepan with the water or stock, vinegar and seasoning.
4 Simmer gently for a good 30 minutes.
5 Rub through a sieve, then return the purée to the saucepan together with the butter.
6 Blend flour with the cold milk, stir into boiling purée and continue cooking, stirring all the time until it forms a smooth thick sauce.
7 Garnish with paprika and serve with toast.
8 A few of the artichokes can be saved and cut into tiny pieces to put into the soup as a garnish.

Variations:

Cream of beetroot soup
Use raw beetroot. Dice and simmer for approximately 1 hour. Continue as above.

Cream of carrot soup
Ingredients as Cream of artichoke soup, but add a pinch of sugar when cooking the carrots. Omit lemon juice and vinegar.

Cream of potato soup
Follow recipe for artichoke soup but add a little cream, if possible, just before serving.

Cream of turnip soup
All turnips, unless very young, tend to be rather strong in a soup so use ¾ lb. turnips and ¾ lb. potatoes and follow recipe for Cream of artichoke soup.

Cabbage soup

cooking time 1¼ hours

you will need for 4 servings:

2 oz. haricot beans
1 very small cabbage
2 leeks
small carrot
piece turnip
stick celery
1 potato
1 small onion
3 oz. butter
3 pints water
bouquet garni (see page 6)
seasoning
2–4 oz. fat bacon or pork

To garnish:
bread croûtons (see page 8)

1. Soak haricot beans for several hours in cold water.
2. Drain.
3. Dice vegetables and toss in the hot butter for about 10 minutes.
4. Add water and rest of ingredients.
5. Simmer for 1 hour.
6. Rub through a sieve and reheat.*
7. Garnish with bread croûtons.

*The pieces of pork can be removed before sieving and served separately

Cauliflower soup

cooking time 30–35 minutes

you will need:

1 medium cauliflower
1 onion
1 pint water or white stock
seasoning
1 oz. butter
1 oz. flour
½ pint milk

To garnish:
cayenne pepper

1. Cut up cauliflower stalk and some of the flowers, reserving the rest.
2. Put into a pan with the chopped onion, water and seasoning and simmer gently until tender.
3. Rub through a sieve.
4. Make white sauce from the butter, flour and milk; put in the cauliflower purée and reheat, adding a little extra milk if too thick.
5. Meanwhile divide the rest of the flowerets into very small pieces. Boil in salted water until just tender.
6. Put into the soup and garnish with cayenne pepper.

Variations:

Cream of cauliflower soup
Use a little less water and add cream after blending cauliflower purée with the sauce.

Cheese and cauliflower soup
Add 2–3 oz. grated cheese to the soup and heat until melted.

Golden ball cauliflower soup
Blend the yolk of 1 egg with a little cream. Stir into the soup just before serving and thicken without boiling. Garnish with hard-boiled egg yolk, rubbed through a sieve to look like mimosa balls.

Cream of celery soup

cooking time 30 minutes

you will need for 4 servings:

1 good-sized head celery
1½ pints stock or water
1 oz. flour
2 oz. butter
¼ pint milk
¼ pint cream or evaporated milk
seasoning, including celery salt

To garnish:
cayenne pepper

1. If you do not wish to sieve this soup, cut the celery into very tiny pieces.
2. Simmer celery with the water or stock until tender, then sieve if wished.
3. Meanwhile make a white sauce from the flour, butter and milk: this will be very thick, so the celery mixture or purée needs to be blended very slowly into this. Reheat, then add the cream and seasoning.
4. Garnish with cayenne pepper.

Chestnut soup

cooking time 1 hour 10 minutes

you will need for 4 servings:

1 lb. chestnuts
1 pint water or white stock
2 oz. margarine or butter
½ pint milk
good pinch salt, cayenne pepper, and sugar if liked

1. Split the skins of the chestnuts, cover with water and cook for 15 minutes.
2. Peel the nuts while still hot, then return to the saucepan with the water or stock.
3. Simmer gently for 45 minutes.
4. Rub the chestnuts through a sieve and put the purée into the pan, together with the butter or margarine, milk and seasoning.

5 Heat slowly, then serve with crisp pieces of toast or croûtons of bread.

Cucumber purée soup

cooking time 20 minutes

you will need for 4 servings:

1 large or 2 medium cucumbers*
1 onion
little celery
¾ pint white stock
1 oz. butter
1 oz. flour
½ pint milk
seasoning

To garnish:
parsley

*If all the skin is left on a cucumber it gives a very bitter flavour but a little should be included to give a slight green colour. Alternatively, the cucumber can be simmered in water for a few minutes before using for this recipe

1 Chop the cucumber and onion and mix with the chopped celery.
2 If celery is not obtainable chicory or celeriac can be used instead.
3 Put into a pan with the stock and simmer until tender.
4 Rub through a sieve.
5 Meanwhile make a white sauce with the butter, flour and milk, add the cucumber purée and reheat.
6 Season well.
7 A little lemon juice or vinegar can be added when heated but do not boil again.
8 Garnish with chopped parsley.

Lentil soup

cooking time 1½ hours

you will need for 4 servings:

8 oz. washed lentils
4 oz. bacon, chopped
1 onion, chopped
1 carrot
1 pint water or stock
seasoning
little chopped thyme or parsley
1 oz. butter
½ oz. flour
½ pint milk

To garnish:
chopped parsley

1 Put the lentils (these can be soaked overnight if wished), bacon, onion, carrots and stock into a casserole and add seasoning and herbs—the seasoning MUST be added at the very start of cooking.
2 Cover and simmer gently for about 1½ hours.
3 Meanwhile make a very thin sauce with the butter, flour and milk, add the lentil purée and reheat.
4 Check seasoning and serve garnished with chopped parsley.

Variations:

Lentil and celery soup
Use about 6 oz. lentils and 4 oz. chopped celery.

Lentil and tomato soup
Use 4 oz. lentils only and 8 oz. tomatoes.

Cream of mushroom soup

cooking time 15–20 minutes

you will need for 4 servings:

8 oz. mushrooms*
2 oz. butter or margarine
2 oz. flour
1 pint water or stock
¾ pint milk
seasoning

*Mushroom stalks can be used

1 Chop mushrooms finely unless you wish to strain the soup.
2 Melt margarine or butter in saucepan, fry mushrooms for 5 minutes, stirring to prevent their discolouring.
3 Stir in the flour and cook for 3 minutes.
4 Remove the pan from the heat and gradually add water and milk.
5 Bring to the boil and cook until soup thickens.
6 Season.

Cream of onion soup

cooking time 30 minutes

you will need for 4 servings:

8 oz. onions
1 oz. butter
2 tablespoons cornflour
2 pints milk
2 egg yolks
3 tablespoons cream
seasoning

1 Chop and gently fry the onions in the hot butter until tender, but do not brown.
2 Add the cornflour and mix in well, then cook for a further minute.
3 Add the milk and cook gently for about 20 minutes.
4 Mix egg yolks and cream together, add a little soup, then return all to the saucepan and reheat without boiling.
5 Season to taste.

Crème Olga

cooking time 35–40 minutes

you will need for 4 servings:

8 oz. spring onions
2 oz. mushrooms
2 medium potatoes
1 oz. butter
1½ pints milk
bayleaf
seasoning
1 egg yolk
4 tablespoons cream

To garnish:
croûtons (see page 8)

1 Slice onions, mushrooms and potatoes and cook slowly in the butter until soft but not coloured.
2 Add the milk, bayleaf and seasoning.
3 Simmer 20 minutes.
4 Rub through a fine sieve, return to the pan and stir until boiling.
5 Simmer a few minutes then remove from heat.
6 Add egg yolk blended with cream and reheat carefully.
7 Adjust the seasoning and serve with croûtons.

Low-calorie spinach soup

cooking time 30 minutes

you will need for 4 servings:

1 lb. fresh spinach or small packet frozen spinach
1 small onion
seasoning
½ pint water
½ pint milk (without cream)
a little grated nutmeg

1 Cook the spinach with onion, seasoning and water until tender.
2 Rub through a sieve, add to the milk with grated nutmeg and reheat.
3 Serve to those people who are watching their weight first, and stir in a knob of butter and one or two tablespoons of top of the milk or cream for the rest of the family.
4 This is a fairly filling soup and therefore small quantities are sufficient for most people.

Variation:

You can use ½ pint tomato juice instead of water or cook 1–2 tomatoes with the spinach.

Creamed spinach soup

cooking time 25 minutes

you will need for 4 servings:

1 lb. spinach or 1 small packet frozen spinach
1 oz. butter
1 small onion, sliced
1 oz. cornflour
1½ pints milk
2 egg yolks
3 tablespoons cream
nutmeg
seasoning

To garnish:
croûtons (see page 8)

1 Cook and sieve the spinach.
2 Heat the butter in a saucepan and sauté the onion until tender but not brown.
3 Add the cornflour, mix well and cook for a few minutes.
4 Add the milk, stir until boiling and boil for 3 minutes.
5 Strain the sauce on to the spinach, then return to the heat.
6 Mix the egg yolks and cream, add a little of the soup, then return all to the saucepan.
7 Add seasonings and reheat gently for several minutes before serving. DO NOT ALLOW TO BOIL.
8 Garnish with croûtons.

Minestrone soup

cooking time 2 hours 10 minutes

you will need for 4 servings:

3 oz. haricot beans
1 large onion
2 tablespoons olive oil
1 clove garlic
1–2 oz. diced bacon
seasoning
1½ pints water or stock
1 large diced carrot
2 tablespoons chopped celery
8 oz. tomatoes (bottled or fresh)
8 oz. finely shredded cabbage
2 oz. macaroni

To garnish:
1 tablespoon chopped parsley
grated Parmesan cheese

1 Soak the haricot beans overnight in water.
2 Chop onion finely and toss in the hot oil, together with the crushed garlic and bacon.
3 Add haricot beans, seasoning and water and simmer gently for about 1½ hours.
4 Put in rest of vegetables, with the exception of the cabbage, and cook for a further 20 minutes, adding a little more water if necessary.
5 Add cabbage and macaroni and cook until both are just tender.
6 Taste and add seasoning if necessary.
7 Serve with chopped parsley and top with the cheese.

Note:

A little red wine can be used in this recipe; put this in with the vegetables.

French onion soup

cooking time 40 minutes

you will need for 4 servings:

1–1½ lb. onions
1–2 oz. butter or good beef dripping
2 pints brown stock
seasoning
2 oz. grated cheese (preferably Gruyère)
4 slices toast or French bread

1 Melt the fat in a saucepan.
2 Slice the onions thinly and fry in the hot fat until a pale golden brown.
3 Add the liquid and seasoning.
4 Bring slowly to the boil, lower the heat and simmer gently for ½ hour.
5 Put each slice of hot toast on a soup plate; pour over the soup and sprinkle with cheese.

Variation:

French onion soup gratinée

Use ingredients for above recipe but put cheese-topped soup under grill for 2–3 minutes until cheese melts.

Pea soup

cooking time 35–40 minutes

you will need for 4 servings:

1½ lb. peas (including pods) or pods from 2 lb. fresh peas when young
1½ pints water or ham stock
small onion (if desired)
seasoning
small sprig mint
good pinch sugar
good knob butter

To garnish:
chopped mint or fried bread croûtons (see page 8) or peas, if required

1 Wash pods and shell.
2 Put pods and peas into a saucepan with stock (reserving few peas if required for garnish), onion, seasoning and mint, and simmer until tender.
3 Rub through a sieve; this must be done very vigorously, so that the flesh of the pods is pushed through and only the skins are left.
4 Return to the pan, reheat, adding a little sugar to taste and a good knob of butter. If the pods are very fleshy the soup may be a little thick when sieved so add a small quantity of extra stock or milk.
5 Serve garnished with a few freshly cooked peas or chopped mint or croûtons.

Spring soup

cooking time 40 minutes

you will need for 4 servings:

12 small spring onions
½ small lettuce
2 oz. margarine or butter
few small carrots
1 pint white stock or water
2 teaspoons flour
3 tablespoons milk
seasoning
1 egg

1 Slice the onions and shred the lettuce.
2 Heat 1 oz. of the margarine or butter in a saucepan and toss in half the onion and all the lettuce and carrots.
3 Add the stock and simmer gently for 30 minutes.
4 Rub through a sieve, then return to the pan.
5 Blend the flour with the milk and add this together with seasoning.
6 Bring slowly to the boil and cook until slightly thickened (the amount of thickening is very small in this recipe).
7 Heat the remaining 1 oz. margarine or butter and fry the rest of the onions.
8 Take the soup off the heat for a few minutes and stir in the well-beaten egg—do not cook again.
9 Serve garnished with the fried onions.

Cream of tomato soup

cooking time 1¼ hours

you will need for 4 servings:

1 lb. tomatoes
1 onion
1 carrot
1 stick celery
little fat bacon
1½ pints stock
salt
pepper
bouquet garni
¾ oz. cornflour
¼–½ pint milk
pinch sugar

To garnish:
chopped white of egg or croûtons (see page 8)

1 Slice the vegetables.
2 Fry the bacon slowly to extract the fat, then add the vegetables and fry for about 10 minutes.
3 Add the stock (or water), seasoning and *bouquet garni*, bring to the boil and simmer gently until tender—about 1 hour.
4 Remove the *bouquet garni* and bacon, rub the soup through a fine sieve, and add the cornflour blended with the milk.
5 Return to the pan, bring just to the boil, stirring well, and cook gently for 2–3 minutes.
6 Check seasoning, add the sugar and serve with your chosen garnish.

Variation:

Tomato soup

Ingredients as Cream of tomato soup but omit cornflour and milk. Cook the tomatoes and vegetables. Rub through a sieve, return to the pan and garnish with parsley or fried bread croûtons (see page 8).

Tomato and rice broth

cooking time 25–30 minutes

you will need for 4 servings:

$1\frac{1}{2}$ pints tomato juice or 8 oz. tomatoes and 1 pint water
2 oz. rice
1 diced onion
little diced celery or celeriac
1 diced carrot
salt
pepper

To garnish:
grated Cheddar cheese

1 If using tomatoes they should be simmered in the water or stock, then the liquid strained off, the tomatoes sieved and added to liquid.
2 Add the rice to boiling tomato liquid together with the diced vegetables.
3 Season well and cook for about 20 minutes until rice and vegetables are tender.
4 Serve with the grated cheese.

Tomato and vegetable soup

cooking time 10 minutes

you will need for 4 servings:

1 small packet mixed frozen vegetables (or tin mixed vegetables or 1 grated potato, 2 grated carrots, 1 grated onion, few peas)
seasoning
1 bottle or tin tomato juice
$\frac{1}{2}$ pint water (or liquid from tinned vegetables)

To garnish:
little grated cheese

1 Put all ingredients, except cheese, into pan and simmer until tender.
2 Serve topped with cheese.

Cream of vegetable soup

cooking time 45 minutes

you will need for 4 servings:

$1\frac{1}{4}$–$1\frac{1}{2}$ lb. mixed vegetables*
1 pint water or white stock
$\frac{1}{4}$ teaspoon vinegar
seasoning
2 oz. butter
$\frac{1}{2}$ oz. flour
$\frac{1}{4}$–$\frac{1}{2}$ pint milk

To garnish:
paprika and/or parsley

*Choose a good selection: because only a small amount of flour is used include 1 or 2 vegetables like potatoes and carrots which give thickening. Tomatoes and/or carrots will give colour. A small quantity of green vegetables can be added but avoid too many very strongly flavoured vegetables such as turnips—a mixed vegetable soup should have a good balance of flavours

1 Wash and peel the vegetables and, if large, cut into small pieces. Keep them in cold water as you prepare them until they are ready to cook: if you have included any artichokes add 1 tablespoon lemon juice to keep colour.
2 Put into a saucepan with water or stock, vinegar and seasoning.
3 Simmer gently for a good 30 minutes.
4 Rub through a sieve, then return purée to saucepan, adding the butter.
5 Blend the flour with the cold milk, stir into the boiling purée and continue cooking, stirring all the time, until it forms a smooth thick soup.
6 Garnish with paprika and/or parsley.

Vichyssoise

cooking time 40 minutes

you will need for 4 servings:

2 oz. butter
2 large onions, chopped
8 medium leeks, chopped
$1\frac{1}{2}$ pints chicken stock or water with 2 chicken stock cubes
2 medium potatoes, chopped
1 tablespoon parsley, chopped
2 eggs or egg yolks
$\frac{1}{4}$ pint cream or milk
seasoning

To garnish:
chopped chives or parsley

1 Heat the butter and fry chopped onions and leeks until golden but not brown.
2 Add stock, or water with chicken stock cubes, chopped potatoes and parsley.
3 Simmer for 30 minutes, rub through a sieve and return to the pan.
4 Blend the eggs with the cream, add to soup and cook WITHOUT BOILING for a few minutes.
5 Season.
6 Serve topped with chives or parsley.

Watercress soup

cooking time 11 minutes

you will need for 4 servings:

2 bunches watercress (about 4 oz.)
1 tablespoon corn oil
2 good teaspoons yeast extract
1 pint water
$\frac{1}{2}$ oz. cornflour
5 tablespoons milk

1 Wash the watercress thoroughly, reserve few sprigs for garnish, and remove leaves from stalks of remainder.
2 Sauté gently for 2–3 minutes in heated oil.
3 Add yeast extract and the water.
4 Bring to the boil, stirring, then simmer for about 5 minutes.
5 Sieve if required.
6 Mix cornflour and milk smoothly, add to the purée and cook for 3 minutes, stirring all the time.
7 Garnish with sprigs of watercress.

Soups that Make a Meal

To save preparing an elaborate meal, make a really satisfying and sustaining soup that can be a meal in itself. The British broths, American chowders and Continental bisques are all satisfying soups that are almost too filling for the first course of a meal. Served with cheese and fruit they are the answer to a one-course meal.

Vegetable soups

Celery chowder

cooking time 30–35 minutes

you will need for 4 servings:

8–10 oz. celery
1 onion
2 medium potatoes
½ pint white stock or water
seasoning
1 oz. butter
½ oz. flour
½ pint milk

To garnish:
celery tips or croûtons (see page 8)

1 Chop the celery into very tiny pieces, chop or grate the onion and cut the potatoes into small dice.
2 Simmer together in the stock or water until tender, seasoning well.
3 Meanwhile make a thin sauce of the butter, flour and milk, add vegetable mixture to this.
4 Heat thoroughly, check seasoning and serve garnished with tiny celery tips or croûtons.

Vegetable chowder

cooking time 23 minutes

you will need for 4 servings:

1 can or packet vegetable soup
2 potatoes

To garnish:
little chopped parsley
little grated cheese

1 Make up soup as directed on packet or heat contents of tin.
2 When the mixture begins to boil add the diced potatoes and cook for 20 minutes.
3 Top with chopped parsley and grated cheese before serving.

Fish soups

Fish soups are really at their best if not sieved, but served like a chowder (which is almost a stew). They are then a perfect dish for a main meal. You will get a better flavour if you simmer the bones and skin of white fish, or the shell of lobster, crab, prawns, etc. to give you stock.

Lobster chowder

cooking time 25–30 minutes

you will need for 4 servings:

1 small lobster
1 pint water
1–2 rashers bacon
1 teaspoon finely chopped onion
1½ oz. flour
1 medium potato, diced
⅜ pint milk or cream
good pinch sugar
salt
pepper
crisp toast fingers

1 Remove flesh from lobster, cut in small pieces and put aside.
2 Put shell only into pan with the water and simmer gently for about 15 minutes.
3 Strain and add enough water to make up to 1 pint again.
4 After removing rind, cut bacon into narrow strips.
5 Put into a pan and fry lightly; add the onion and flour and cook gently without colouring.
6 Gradually add the lobster stock, stirring all the time.
7 When the sauce has come to the boil and thickened, add lobster, cut into small pieces, and the rest of the ingredients.
8 Either reduce heat under pan to cook very gently or put in double saucepan and cook until it forms a thick creamy mixture.
9 Serve with crisp fingers of toast.

New England clam chowder

cooking time 30 minutes

you will need for 4 servings:

8 oz. salt pork, chopped
3 small onions
1½ pints boiling water
12 oz. potatoes, diced
⅛ teaspoon pepper
2 cans clams
1½ pints milk
6 water biscuits

1 Chop the pork and fry in a large saucepan.
2 Add the onions and sauté until browned.
3 Add boiling water, potatoes and pepper and boil about 15 minutes, or until potatoes are soft.
4 Mince and heat clams and any liquor; add with milk to mixture and bring to the boil.
5 Pour chowder over crumbled water biscuits in soup dishes.

Variation:

Oyster chowder

Approximately 16–20 oysters could be used in place of clams.

Salmon chowder

cooking time 20 minutes

you will need for 4 servings:

1 packet tomato or tomato and vegetable, or vegetable soup
1½ pints water
2 oz. tiny shell pasta or noodles
1 clove garlic, crushed (optional)
1 green pepper, finely chopped
1 medium can salmon

1 Make up the soup with 1½ pints of water (or as directed on the packet) and bring to boil.
2 Add the pasta and crushed garlic and simmer gently until pasta is tender.
3 Add the finely chopped green pepper and flaked salmon then heat together.

. . . but watch the waistline

Low-calorie fish chowder

cooking time 25–30 minutes

you will need for 4 servings:

8 oz. white fish
1–2 rashers bacon
1 onion, finely chopped
1 pint fish stock or water
1 medium potato, diced
¼ pint milk
good pinch sugar
salt
pepper

To garnish:
parsley
paprika

1 Cut the fish into neat cubes, using any skin and bones for stock as described on page 7.
2 Remove the rind from the bacon and cut into small pieces.
3 Fry with the chopped onion without allowing it to colour.
4 Add the fish stock, the pieces of fish, potato, milk and seasoning, and sugar.
5 Simmer gently for about 15 minutes, then serve topped with parsley and paprika.

Variations:

To make a richer chowder, add an egg blended with a little of the milk for the last 5 minutes and cook WITHOUT BOILING until thickened. A little corn-on-the-cob (which is fairly high in calories) makes a most attractive addition to this soup. Diced cucumber, which is low in calories, can be added to give extra texture as well as flavour.

Slimmer's chowder

cooking time 35 minutes

you will need for 4 servings:

1 oz. margarine
1 large onion
1–2 small rashers bacon
2 large tomatoes
2 sticks celery
½ large or 1 small green pepper
very few mushrooms (optional)
2 medium carrots
seasoning
2 pints water with little yeast extract to flavour
¼ small cabbage

To garnish:
chopped parsley

1 Melt the margarine and fry diced onion until just changing colour, then put in the chopped bacon and continue to cook for a few minutes.
2 Skin and chop tomatoes and add with all the other diced vegetables (except the cabbage) and the water mixed with the yeast extract cube—the tomatoes will become part of the liquid with cooking.
3 Cook steadily for approximately 20 minutes.
4 Add the finely chopped cabbage and cock for a further 10 minutes.
5 Garnish with chopped parsley.

Note:

To make a more satisfying dish for non-slimming members of the family, add a thick layer of grated cheese on top before serving.

Soups to Serve Cold

All too often soup is considered only as a hot dish, but in hot weather, or if you have a hot main course, a really delicious cold soup is an excellent start to the meal. Make sure your cold soups have a slight bite about them for their purpose is to sharpen one's appetite.

Jellied and thin soups

Jellied consommé

cooking time 1 hour

you will need for 4 servings:

12 oz. shin of beef
2 pints strong stock
seasoning
1 onion
1 carrot
small piece celery
sprig parsley
bayleaf

To garnish:
cucumber or lemon or smoked salmon

1 Make consommé using method on page 15 and allow to cool, when it will set into a light jelly.
2 If the weather is hot and you have no refrigerator, dissolve 2 level teaspoons powdered gelatine in consommé to help it to set.
3 Beat lightly before putting in soup cups.
4 Garnish with slices of cucumber or lemon or smoked salmon.

Jellied two-tone consommé

cooking time 1 hour

you will need for 4 servings:

1 pint beef consommé (see page 15)
1 pint chicken consommé (see page 16)
2 level teaspoons powdered gelatine
little sherry

1 Put the consommés to heat in two separate pans.
2 Soften the gelatine in a small amount of sherry and add half to the beef and half to the chicken consommé.
3 Allow to dissolve.
4 Let the two kinds of soup set lightly.
5 Whisk, and put a layer of light and a layer of dark consommé in separate cups or cut into cubes and arrange in the soup cups.
6 Serve very cold.

Consommé Florida

cooking time 1½ hours

you will need for 4 servings:

1½ pints consommé (see page 15)
2 large firm tomatoes
1–2 oranges
1 small green pepper

1 Peel oranges and add most of flesh to the consommé together with most of the chopped flesh of the green pepper and the skinned and seeded tomato pulp, reserving some of each for garnish.
2 Simmer gently for 30 minutes, then strain.
3 Serve very cold, garnished with tiny pieces of orange, raw tomato and tiny strips of green pepper.

Iced cucumber soup

cooking time 15 minutes

you will need for 4 servings:

1 medium cucumber
1 small onion, chopped
½ oz. butter
½ pint stock
seasoning
⅛ pint milk or evaporated milk

To garnish:
lemon

1 Cut cucumber into pieces, leaving on some of the peel.
2 Fry onion in butter, add cucumber, half the stock, seasoning and simmer gently for about 15 minutes.
3 Put through sieve.
4 Add milk and rest of stock to purée; when cold pour into freezing tray and leave until lightly frosted.
5 Serve in soup cups garnished with lemon.

Jellied gazpacho

cooking time 5–8 minutes

you will need for 4 servings:

- 1 beef or chicken bouillon cube
- ¾ pint boiling water
- 1 15-oz. can tomato juice (¾ pint)
- ½ oz. gelatine
- 2 tomatoes, peeled and chopped
- ½ green pepper, seeded and chopped
- ½ cucumber, peeled, seeded and chopped
- 1 small onion, chopped
- 2 tablespoons corn oil
- 2 tablespoons vinegar

To garnish:
lemon slices

1. Dissolve the beef or chicken bouillon cube in the boiling water.
2. Put into a pan with tomato juice and gelatine, and heat until the gelatine has dissolved.
3. Leave to cool.
4. Meanwhile steep the vegetables in the corn oil and vinegar.
5. When the liquid is almost set, strain through a very fine sieve or muslin.
6. Pour on to the vegetables and chill until jellied.
7. Break up with a fork, pile into glasses and garnish with lemon slices.
8. Serve with French bread.

Thick soups

Gazpacho

no cooking time

you will need for 4 servings:

- water
- 1 lb. tomatoes
- 1 medium cucumber
- 1 onion or several spring onions
- 1 or 2 cloves garlic
- 1 small green pepper
- seasoning
- little olive oil
- lemon juice or white wine vinegar

1. Put the water in the refrigerator to become very cold.
2. Skin the tomatoes as this helps when the mixture is sieved, or blended in an electric blender, to give a smooth mixture.
3. Peel the cucumber and cut into very small dice, saving a little as garnish.
4. Chop the tomatoes, onion and garlic; add to the cucumber and either pound until smooth or rub through a sieve; the pepper can also be sieved or chopped very finely, after removing all the seeds and core. (If using an electric liquidiser you will need to add a little water so none of the thick mixture is wasted.)
5. Put the purée into basin, then gradually beat in seasoning, olive oil and enough cold water to give a flowing consistency.
6. Taste to check seasoning and add lemon juice or vinegar.
7. Serve garnished with remaining cucumber.
8. This soup must be very cold so put in the refrigerator until ready to serve and serve in ice-cold soup cups.

Chilled mushroom soup

cooking time 15 minutes

you will need for 4 servings:

- 1 packet mushroom soup powder
- 1¼ pints water
- ¼ pint cream or evaporated milk
- 1 tablespoon white wine
- green food colouring, optional

To garnish:
lemon slices

1. Make up the soup powder with 1¼ pints water, cooking as directed.
2. Leave until completely cold, then add the cream or milk, white wine, and food colouring if desired.
3. Garnish with lemon slices.

Summer soup

cooking time 20–25 minutes

you will need for 4 servings:

- 1–2 medium potatoes
- 4–5 inches cucumber, chopped but not peeled
- 2–3 sprigs parsley
- salt
- pepper
- pinch dry mustard
- ¾ pint chicken stock, or water and bouillon cube
- 1 small onion, sliced
- ¼ pint milk or thin cream

1. Cook all the ingredients except the milk or cream in the chicken stock until potatoes are tender.
2. Force everything through a medium sieve, add the milk or cream and season.
3. This soup is equally good hot or cold, but if it is to be served cold it should be well chilled for at least 2–3 hours.

Iced tomato soup

cooking time 20 minutes

you will need for 4 servings:

- 1½ lb. tomatoes
- 1 pint water or white stock
- ½ small beetroot
- 1 small piece of celery
- 1 small chopped onion
- few drops Worcestershire sauce
- 1 teaspoon vinegar or lemon juice
- seasoning
- 2 bay leaves

To garnish:
lemon slices

1 Put all the ingredients into a pan and cook until the tomatoes are soft.
2 Removing beetroot, rub rest of mixture through a sieve and pour into the freezing tray of the refrigerator.
3 Leave for a short time until iced, then serve in cold cups topped with lemon rings.

Chilled vegetable chowder

cooking time 15 minutes

you will need for 4 servings:

1 packet thick vegetable soup
1 pint water
¼ pint milk
¼ pint cream or yoghourt

To garnish:
chopped chives or parsley

1 Blend the thick vegetable soup powder with the water.
2 Put into a pan and cook until tender.
3 Allow to cool, then stir in the milk, cream or yoghourt, and put into the refrigerator until very cold.
4 Put into cups and garnish with chives or parsley.

Watercress cream soup

cooking time 20 minutes

you will need for 4–6 servings:

4 oz. watercress
1 small onion
1 oz. margarine or butter
3 medium potatoes
1¾ pints chicken stock or water and 2 chicken bouillon cubes
little whipped cream

1 Coarsely chop watercress (reserving few leaves for garnish), chop onion and fry both in the margarine until the onion is pale golden.
2 Add the peeled, sliced potatoes and stock.
3 Bring to the boil, cover and simmer until the potatoes are soft.
4 Rub through a sieve and return to pan.
5 Add the cream, season if necessary, chill and serve in soup cups garnished with leaves of watercress.
6 Dredge lightly with paprika and serve with Melba toast (see page 8).

Note:
This may be served hot on a cold day.

Fruit soups

In hot weather a cold fruit soup is a most delicious beginning to a meal. It should have enough bite to make one feel hungry, so do not oversweeten the fruit. It is customary to serve fruit soups cold but they can be heated if preferred.

Apple soup

cooking time 20 minutes

you will need for 4 servings:

1 lb. fairly sharp cooking apples
1 pint water
½ pint white wine
sugar to taste

To garnish:
lemon rings

1 Chop the apples but do not peel or core.
2 Simmer in the water until tender then rub through a sieve.
3 Add to the white wine.
4 Taste and stir in required sugar while the apple mixture is still sufficiently warm to make it dissolve completely.
5 Serve really cold in soup cups, garnished with lemon rings.

Variations:

Apple and lemon soup
Add the grated rind and juice of 1 lemon to the apples.

Apple and orange soup
Add the grated rind and juice of 2 oranges to the apples.

Spiced apples
Add 1 teaspoon mixed spice to the apples when cooking.

Lemon soup

cooking time 8 minutes

you will need for 4 servings:

1 pint chicken stock or water and 2 chicken stock cubes
2 tablespoons lemon juice
1 egg
seasoning

1 Heat the stock.
2 Beat the lemon juice and egg.
3 Whisk into the stock together with seasoning and simmer without boiling for a few minutes.

Iced cherry soup

cooking time 25 minutes

you will need for 4 servings:

1½ lb. or 1 can cherries
juice 1 lemon
water
sugar to taste

To garnish:
mint

1 Cover fruit with water.
2 Simmer gently, adding lemon juice and sugar to taste.
3 Reserving few cherries for garnish, rub through sieve and pour into freezing trays to lightly freeze.
4 Serve in soup cups decorated with remaining whole cherries and mint leaves.

Variations:

Cherry plum soup
Use the rather 'sharp' small plums known as cherry plums. A very little white wine added to the mixture gives an excellent flavour.

Crab apple soup
This is made like the Iced cherry soup. Add a little cider if wished and garnish with wedges of lemon.

Cranberry soup
Substituting cranberries, use method for Iced cherry soup—you will need extra sweetening. Mixed soft fruits such as red currants and raspberries can also be used.

Soups that are Different

These soups are not based on vegetable or fish but depend on ingredients one does not normally use as a basis for soup. They are, however, easily made and extremely delicious.

Red wine soup

cooking time 10 minutes

you will need for 4–6 servings:

1 pint inexpensive red wine
good pinch ground cinnamon
1 teaspoon sugar
4 whole cloves
½ pint water
3 egg yolks
little pepper

1 Bring the wine, cinnamon, sugar, cloves and water to the boil and simmer without boiling for about 8 minutes.
2 Pour over the beaten egg yolks, stirring well, and add a little pepper to taste.
3 Serve at once, hot.

Note:
This can be chilled if liked, and served with 1 tablespoon yoghourt or sour cream on each plate or soup cup.

Variation:

White wine soup
Use an inexpensive white wine instead of red. This must be dry, not sweet, and it is nicer served cold.

Hollandaise cream soup

cooking time 12–15 minutes

you will need for 4 servings:

1 oz. butter
scant 1 oz. cornflour
1½ pints chicken or veal stock or water with 1 chicken bouillon cube
3 egg yolks
¼ pint cream
seasoning
½ teaspoon chopped tarragon
½ teaspoon chopped parsley

To garnish:
few peas

1 Melt the butter in a pan, add the cornflour and cook for several minutes.
2 Gradually add the stock, bring to boil and boil for 3 minutes, stirring all the time.
3 Beat together the egg yolks and cream and stir carefully into the soup: cook WITHOUT BOILING for a few minutes, stirring all the time.
4 Lastly add the seasoning, tarragon and parsley, and if liked garnish with cold peas.

Variations:

Hollandaise rice soup
Cook 1½ oz. rice in the stock for approximately 10 minutes then proceed as above.

Hollandaise lemon soup
Method as above but add ½ teaspoon very finely grated lemon rind and 2 tablespoons lemon juice at stage 4, taking care that the soup does not boil.

Cheese soup

cooking time 25 minutes

you will need for 4 servings:

1 onion, finely chopped
2 oz. butter
1½ oz. flour
1 pint milk
1 pint stock
2 teaspoons salt
pinch pepper
8 oz. grated Cheddar cheese
3 carrots, finely chopped or grated
2 sticks celery or piece of celeriac, finely chopped or grated

1 Sauté the onion in the butter until tender.
2 Add the flour and cook slowly for a minute, stirring well.
3 Add the milk, stock, and seasoning gradually, stirring continually, and bring to the boil.
4 Add the grated cheese and stir until melted.
5 Add carrots and celery, and cook until the vegetables are tender.
6 Serve hot with caraway seed toast fingers (see page 8).

Using Ready-prepared Soups

There is a great variety of soups on the market today, the main groups being:

1 *Canned* soups that need little, if any, diluting.
2 *Concentrated* or, as they are often called, condensed soups which need to be diluted with an equal quantity of liquid—the soup can be varied by using either milk, water, stock or a mixture of stock and milk, or even, in some cases, a little wine. (These soups can also be used as sauces or for gravy.)
3 *Dehydrated soups* which need a considerable amount of liquid which can be varied to give individual flavour—these need cooking for a long time as the ingredients are not pre-cooked.
This chapter gives ideas on mixing prepared soups, the way in which additional ingredients can be put in and suggests how to garnish them to give a 'home-made' look.

Asparagus soup

To serve hot

Heat or cook the canned or packet soup, then try one of the following ideas:

1 Stir in an egg beaten with 2–3 tablespoons cream and heat WITHOUT BOILING. Garnish with paprika.
2 Float tiny balls of soft cream cheese and chopped parsley on the soup just before serving.
3 Top with finely grated Parmesan cheese and a very small amount finely grated lemon rind.

To serve cold

This is delicious before a hot main course, even in winter. Add little lemon juice or white wine and cream to the cold cooked soup. Float wafer-thin lemon rings on top.

Note:

Asparagus is not a good soup to mix with other soups, except chicken or a creamed chicken soup, as its delicate flavour is easily lost.

Celery soup

To serve hot

Add finely diced ham or top with grated cheese or, to give colour, add a few strips of red or green pepper.

To serve cold

Top with balls of soft cream cheese and paprika, stir in celery salt and a little cream or mayonnaise. This is delicious if slightly iced.

Consommé or clear soup

To serve hot

Prepare with stock cube and water. Then serve with any of the traditional additions and garnishes; tiny matchsticks (julienne) of vegetables—very fine cooked spaghetti—or wine.

5-minute borshch:

It makes a splendid basis for Borshch. To approximately 1¼ pints consommé allow 1 large cooked beetroot, a little garlic salt and a squeeze lemon juice. Grate beetroot coarsely and put into consommé with lemon juice and garlic salt. Pour into soup cups and top with soured cream, or a spoonful of cream cheese, or fresh cream.

To serve cold

See Jellied and Iced consommé recipes, page 25.

Chicken soup

To serve hot

Add interest by using one of the following:

1 Blanched shredded almonds.
2 Equal amount of asparagus or mushroom soup mixed with chicken and topped with fried bread croûtons.
3 Make a little thinner than usual then cook a small packet frozen vegetables and 1 oz. rice with it to give Chicken broth.
4 Turn it into a creamed curry soup: fry 1 small chopped onion and 1–2 teaspoons curry powder in little margarine or butter until onion is tender. Add enough chicken soup for 4 and heat or cook in usual way.
5 Top with chopped watercress.

To serve cold

Blend with little cream and mayonnaise (see page 36), top with lightly whipped cream flavoured with little grated lemon rind.

Green pea soup

To serve hot

1 The soup can be curried in same way as the preceding Chicken soup.
2 It is also excellent mixed with very fine strips of cooked ham or crisply fried snippets of bacon, and topped with croûtons of toasted bread.
3 Mix with a tomato soup. Use rather more green pea than tomato—or mix with equal quantity of mixed vegetable or celery soup.

To serve cold

Not as successful as some soups but quite palatable if a little cream is added. Top with chopped fresh mint.

Kidney soup

To serve hot

Add just a little sherry or port wine. Made rather thinner than usual this soup can be turned into a sustaining dish if dumplings the size of an acorn are cooked in it (see recipe page 14).

This is not particularly suitable to serve cold.

Meat soups

These have very definite flavour which is inclined to predominate if mixed with other soups. They are better therefore if served by themselves. Add to them a little red wine—a garnish of cooked rice—croûtons (see page 8)—cheese straws (see page 42)—potato crisps—put on immediately before serving.

Mushroom or Cream of mushroom soup

To serve hot

Give this a little extra flavouring with mushroom ketchup or Tabasco sauce. Garnish with croûtons of fried bread and chopped parsley.

To serve cold

Add a little sherry and cream.

Onion soup

To serve hot

Top with toast or French bread and grated cheese and put under the grill for a few minutes. Onion soup can be mixed with tomato, chicken, or vegetable soups to give additional flavour.

To serve cold

A really good onion soup, if blended with a little cream and white wine, is not unlike a Vichyssoise.

Tomato soup

This makes an excellent basis for chowders (see page 31). As it is a soup so many people enjoy, it can also be served with one of the following flavourings to prevent it becoming monotonous.

To serve hot

1 Fry thinly sliced rings onion in a little margarine or butter until tender. Add to the tomato soup before serving.

2 Make rather thinner than usual and cook 2 medium grated raw carrots and add 1 oz. rice to each pint liquid for a Tomato carrot broth.
3 Pour into soup cups, top with a thick layer grated cheese and brown under grill for a moment or so.
4 Mix with celery soup and top with snippets of crisply fried bacon.

To serve cold
Blend with little cream or mayonnaise and top with freshly chopped mint.

Turtle soup

This is always improved by adding just a little sherry and often cheese straws (see page 42) are served with it.

To serve cold
Add sherry and gelatine as for consommé (see page 25) but as it is fairly gelatinous use only half the amount of powdered gelatine.

Vegetable soups

There is a variety of these—Cream of vegetable, Thick vegetable, etc., but all are generally improved if a little cream or top of the milk is added. The colour is sometimes rather dull so freshly grated carrot, diced tomato and parsley cooked for a few minutes in the soup add interest.

To serve cold
If there are pieces of vegetable in the soup it is better when sieved. Add a little cream and white wine, chill thoroughly and top with slices of lemon.

Making chowders with ready-prepared soups

Potato chowder

you will need:

1½ pints cooked packet or canned tomato, celery or chicken soup
½ lb. potatoes, peeled
1 carrot, scraped
little celery (when in season)
chopped parsley
seasoning

1 Cut all vegetables into small dice and put into hot soup.
2 Cook for 10–15 minutes until vegetables are soft but unbroken.
3 Season well and top with parsley.
4 Serve with crisp toast.

Potato and corn chowder
Ingredients as above, but use about 4 tablespoons canned or frozen corn instead of celery and carrot, plus small amount of grated onion.

Potato and fish chowder
Ingredients as above, but use 3 oz. shellfish or 6 oz. raw white fish instead of celery and carrot. Cut fish into tiny pieces and cook for about 6 minutes (allow less cooking time for shell fish). Garnish with lemon slices and cayenne or paprika.

Vegetable cheese chowder

you will need:

1½ pints cooked packet or canned celery, asparagus or mushroom soup
1 large packet mixed frozen vegetables
3 tablespoons milk
4 oz. grated cheese
paprika

1 Tip frozen vegetables into hot soup.
2 Cook until just soft, add milk and cheese and heat gently until cheese has melted. DO NOT OVERCOOK or cheese will become 'stringy'.
3 Garnish with paprika.

Fish bisque

you will need:

1½ pints cooked packet or canned tomato, celery, asparagus or mushroom soup
4 oz. shellfish or 8 oz. diced raw white fish
seasoning
1 hard-boiled egg
little parsley

1 Put the fish into hot soup and cook for about 6 minutes (allow little less cooking time for shell fish).
2 Season very well.
3 Chop hard-boiled egg and parsley and sprinkle over soup before serving.

Time Savers for the Store Cupboard

All too often recipes depend on a pinch of herbs or rather unusual seasoning to make them interesting. Ready-chopped dried herbs give flavour to a soup or savoury when you haven't time to chop fresh ones—this does not mean they are better than fresh herbs but just more convenient. Since these keep well it is well worth while purchasing some, if not all of the following.

HERBS

Basil for soups and stews
Balm used in stuffings
Bay leaves for soups and stews
Borage flavouring fruit and other drinks
Caraway for cakes
Celery for pickles
Coriander for curries and cakes
Mint for fruit drinks, salads
Parsley as a stand-by when fresh parsley not obtainable
Rosemary—use a very little inside a roasting fowl when fresh not available
Sage for stuffing or savoury dishes
Thyme for soups and stuffings

SAUCES

Worcestershire sauce for Tomato juice cocktails and adding bite to savoury dishes
Tabasco sauce can also be used for the same purpose, but gives a much hotter result
Chilli sauce same use but very hot indeed
Tomato sauce for adding to certain soups and savoury dishes
Soy sauce if you like Chinese cooking: also for sour-sweet sauce

SEASONINGS

English mustard
French mustard
Salt—both table and cooking
Celery salt for giving a celery flavour that is delicious in cooking
Garlic salt a mild garlic flavour
White pepper for table use
Black pepper stronger—for cooking
Paprika a sweet Hungarian pepper for goulash, garnishes
Cayenne a more hot red pepper to be used sparingly for cooking and garnishes
Vinegar brown or white malt for general purposes, pickling
White wine vinegar for fish recipes
Red wine vinegar for stronger dishes
Also obtainable are flavoured vinegars, such as sage, tarragon and garlic

DRIED MILK

It is now possible to purchase very good quality dried milk and a tin enables you to make a home-made soup or sauce even if you are short of milk.

Hors-d'œuvre

An hors-d'œuvre creates a very pleasant beginning to a meal and these easily prepared savouries help to make a meal more of a special occasion. If you have a fairly light main course they can make the meal more sustaining.
There is a great variety of foods that can be served as hors-d'œuvre and the following chapter gives some suggestions.

Method of serving

Unless you have an hors-d'œuvre dish it is better to arrange the hors-d'œuvre on individual plates. Alternatively you can arrange a selection of ingredients on little dishes on a trolley or tray so that people can help themselves.

Size of portions

It must be remembered that an hors-d'œuvre is meant to be only the beginning or 'appetizer' to a meal so do not make the portions too large.

Adding dressings and sauces

If you are serving a salad it is usual to put a mayonnaise or French dressing on this. If you are uncertain of people's likes and dislikes, it can be served separately.

Salad hors-d'œuvre

A light salad is a very good choice, either by itself or mixed with other ingredients, and in this chapter will be found several unusual as well as favourite salads. In addition the following make a good start to the meal.

Eggs

- Hard-boil, shell, then coat with mayonnaise and garnish with strips of green or red pepper or chopped parsley and paprika. Serve on a bed of lettuce.
- Hard-boil and serve as part of a mixed hors-d'œuvre.

Fish

- Shellfish, white fish and, of course, salmon, make an excellent basis for a salad. Toss in mayonnaise and arrange on lettuce or water-cress.

Chicken

- A chicken salad is rather substantial for an hors-d'œuvre but the following makes a light and interesting dish.

- Chicken and walnut salad

Add enough cream to mayonnaise to make it rather thin. To each $\frac{1}{4}$ pint mayonnaise add 2 oz. very finely chopped walnuts and 4–6 oz. finely shredded chicken. Allow to stand and serve with a garnish of watercress.

Meat

- Most meats are too substantial for hors-d'œuvre, but a salad can be served with Parma ham or pâté.

Avocado and grapefruit salad

no cooking time

you will need for 4 servings:

1–2 avocado pears
green pepper
grapefruit
tomato
watercress
endive
other salad plants as liked
French dressing (see page 90)

1. Cut avocado pears into slices, divide the grape-fruit into sections, and finely slice the green pepper.
2. Place on the prepared salad.
3. Serve with French dressing.

Avocado salad

no cooking time

you will need for 4 servings:

3 avocado pears
2 tomatoes
1 onion, finely chopped
2 tablespoons oil
1 teaspoon ground coriander, optional
2 teaspoons Tabasco sauce
lettuce

To garnish:
2 sliced tomatoes

1. Peel avocado pears and remove stones.
2. Peel tomatoes; chop pears and tomatoes coarsely, and stir in onion.
3. Fold fruits into blended oil, coriander and Tabasco, pile on bed of lettuce in a salad bowl and garnish with sliced tomatoes.
4. Chill if possible before serving.

Caesar salad

no cooking time

you will need for 4 servings:

$\frac{1}{2}$ clove garlic (optional)
1 lettuce
little sliced cucumber
2 tomatoes
1 hard-boiled egg
2 tablespoons grated cheese (optional)
4 anchovy fillets
mayonnaise (see page 36)
bread croûtons

1. Rub round a wooden salad bowl with the garlic, then arrange lettuce in the bowl with sliced cucumber, egg and tomatoes.
2. Sprinkle with the grated cheese and top with mayonnaise, anchovy fillets and croûtons.

Princess mushrooms

cooking time 10 minutes

you will need for 4 servings:

8 oz. mushrooms
1 oz. margarine or butter
seasoning

For the filling:
3 oz. margarine or butter
2 egg yolks
2 tablespoons finely grated cheese
seasoning

1 Choose small mushrooms. Peel and separate stalks.
2 Put the mushrooms and stalks into a casserole together with seasoning and margarine.
3 Cook gently in a moderate oven (375°F.—Gas Mark 4) for 10 minutes.
4 Drain thoroughly and cool.
5 Cream margarine and add finely chopped or sieved egg yolks and cheese.
6 Season well.
7 Pipe or pile into the middle of each mushroom and decorate with the stalk.

Oriental chicken and rice salad

cooking time 20 minutes

you will need for 4 servings:

6 oz. rice
cut clove garlic, optional
3 tablespoons salad oil
1 tablespoon vinegar (wine or tarragon for preference)
salt and pepper
1 tablespoon currants
1 large tomato, skinned, seeded and chopped
1 green pepper, finely sliced
2 tablespoons chopped walnuts, optional
8 oz. cooked chicken, cut into bite-size pieces

1 Cook rice in boiling, salted water and drain very thoroughly.
2 Meanwhile rub a large bowl with garlic and in it mix together the oil, vinegar and seasoning.
3 Add the hot rice and mix thoroughly.
4 Stir in the remaining ingredients and lastly the chicken.
5 Cover and set aside in a cool place for the flavours to blend.
6 When cold transfer to a serving dish.

Rice hors-d'œuvre

cooking time 20 minutes

you will need for 4 servings:

3 oz. rice
1 tablespoon oil
1 tablespoon vinegar
3–4 oz. shrimps or prawns
1 teaspoon chopped gherkins
1 teaspoon chopped chives or onion
seasoning
lettuce

1 Cook rice in boiling, salted water until just soft and drain well.
2 To the rice add the oil, vinegar, shrimps or prawns, gherkins, chives and seasoning, and mix everything together.
3 Pile on to the lettuce and serve thoroughly chilled.

Potato salad

cooking time 20–25 minutes

you will need for 4 servings:

1 lb. potatoes
$\frac{1}{4}$ pint mayonnaise or French dressing (see page 90)
2 teaspoons finely chopped onion
3 tablespoons finely chopped parsley
seasoning

1 Cook the potatoes in salted water until just cooked, making sure that they do not become over-soft.
2 Strain and leave until just cool enough to handle—BUT NOT COLD. (The secret of a good potato salad is to mix it when warm, then serve it when very cold.)
3 Cut into neat dice and toss in the mayonnaise, adding onion, parsley and seasoning.
4 Leave until cold, then if desired garnish with a little more chopped parsley.
5 If preferred, toss in oil and vinegar instead of mayonnaise.

Variations:
Add little diced cucumber or gherkin.
Add finely chopped celery and capers.
Add finely chopped celery, diced eating apple and raisins.

Heavenly potato salad

Method and ingredients as Potato salad but add:

a little finely chopped crisp bacon
a little diced celery and/or green pepper
chopped hard-boiled eggs

To garnish:
parsley and eggs

Russian salad

no cooking

you will need for 4 servings:

8 oz. cooked potatoes
8 oz. cooked carrots
8 oz. cooked peas
8 oz. runner or French beans*
4 oz. cooked turnips*
seasoning
2 tablespoons oil
1 tablespoon vinegar
lettuce, optional
mayonnaise (see page 36)

*Or use cooked mixed frozen vegetables

1 Cut all the vegetables into neat dice.
2 Put into a large bowl and pour over the oil and vinegar, then season well.
3 Leave for several hours, turning gently round in the dressing from time to time, so that the vegetables are not broken.
4 When ready to serve, pile on to a dish—on lettuce bed if desired—and form into pyramid.
5 Pour over just enough mayonnaise to coat.

Salad nicoise

no cooking time

you will need:

1 can tuna fish
1 lettuce
1 small can anchovy fillets
3–4 tomatoes
2 hard-boiled eggs
1 small green pepper or can red or green pepper
black olives

For the vinaigrette dressing:
1 level teaspoon made mustard
2 teaspoons sugar
½ teaspoon salt
black pepper
little garlic juice or pinch garlic salt
little chopped fresh herbs, chervil, parsley, chives, etc., or pinch dried herbs when out of season
¼ pint corn oil
2 tablespoons wine vinegar
1 tablespoon tarragon vinegar
1 tablespoon lemon juice

1 Drain off the oil from the tuna fish.
2 Put the lettuce into a salad bowl or arrange on a platter.
3 Put the tuna in the centre and arrange all the other ingredients round it.
4 Garnish with the pepper, cut into strips, and the olives.
5 Serve with vinaigrette dressing made as 6.
6 Mix all the seasonings and herbs together, stir in the corn oil ana finally beat in the vinegar and lemon juice.

Spanish salad

no cooking

you will need for 4 servings:

4 oz. cooked rice
2 oz. cooked peas (approximately)
1 thinly sliced tomato
2 teaspoons capers
2 sliced gherkins
1 chopped red pepper
seasoning
finely chopped garlic clove or few chopped spring onions

Mix all together and toss in mayonnaise.

Stuffed apples

no cooking time

you will need for 4 servings:

4 large red apples
2 sticks celery
2 oz. raisins
2 oz. stoned dates
1 oz. walnuts
few blanched almonds
mayonnaise (see page 36)

1 Cut the tops of the apples and carefully remove the core and a little of the pulp.
2 Mix together the chopped celery, raisins, dates, walnuts and enough mayonnaise to bind.
3 Pile into the apple cases.
4 Pipe a little mayonnaise around the edge and arrange spiked almonds on top.

Summer mould

cooking time few minutes

you will need for 4 servings:

6 oz. button mushrooms
little salt
3 tomatoes
3 tablespoons cider vinegar
1 tablespoon gelatine
2 tablespoons hot water
1 large apple, peeled and chopped
4 oz. peeled prawns
2 hard-boiled eggs, chopped
3 sliced tomatoes

1 Sprinkle mushrooms with salt.
2 Cover with water and simmer for 3 minutes.
3 Skin and seed tomatoes, then crush tomato pulp.
4 Mix the crushed tomatoes with the vinegar.
5 Dissolve the gelatine in 2 tablespoons hot water.
6 Stir into the mixture and add water to make 1 pint.
7 Mix together the apple, prawns, mushrooms and eggs.
8 Put this mixture into the mould (individual moulds could be used if preferred).
9 Top with the sliced tomato.
10 Pour over the gelatine mixture and allow to set.
11 Serve on a bed of chopped lettuce or salad vegetables.

Tomato and ham creams

no cooking time

you will need for 4 servings:

8 tiny firm tomatoes	2 tablespoons cream cheese
seasoning	1 tablespoon mayonnaise (see below)
1 teaspoon capers	lettuce
2 teaspoons chopped gherkins	cucumber slices
4 oz. ham, finely chopped	

1 Halve tomatoes, remove centre pulp, chop finely then mix with seasoning, capers, gherkins and ham.
2 Pile back into tomato cases.
3 Mix together cheese and mayonnaise and pile or pipe on top of each halved tomato.
4 Arrange on a bed of lettuce and garnish with slices of cucumber.

Mayonnaise

no cooking

you will need:

1 teaspoon sugar	1 egg*
1 teaspoon dry mustard	approximately $\frac{1}{4}$–$\frac{1}{2}$ pint oil (salad, olive or corn)
$\frac{1}{2}$ teaspoon salt and pinch pepper	3 tablespoons vinegar

*For a richer mayonnaise use only egg yolk

1 Combine the sugar, mustard, seasoning and egg and beat well with a rotary beater.
2 Add two-thirds of the oil VERY GRADUALLY, beating all the time, then stir in 1 tablespoon vinegar.
3 Add remaining one-third of the oil, beating all the time.
4 Finally mix in the remaining vinegar.

Using fruit and vegetables

Both fruit and vegetables make a very pleasant beginning to a meal; they are refreshing, not too filling and enable one to choose those foods that are in season and so at their best.

Asparagus

● Cooked or canned asparagus served with melted butter. Remember to provide finger bowls for people as it is eaten with the fingers—soup cups with a small flower floating in the cold water could be used instead.

● Serve hot or cold with hollandaise sauce (see page 90).

● Served cold with vinaigrette dressing (see page 37).

● *Au gratin:* arrange the hot asparagus in individual dishes, top with breadcrumbs and melted butter and brown under the grill. Finely grated cheese could be put on top as well.

● *Polonaise:* top cooked asparagus with crisp fried breadcrumbs, chopped hard-boiled egg, parsley and melted butter. In this method, as for *au gratin*, you will serve the asparagus with knife and fork.

Avocado pear

● Halve, remove stone and fill cavity with French dressing or with shrimps or prawns in mayonnaise (this page) or French dressing (page 90).

● Serve in a salad—see Avocado and grapefruit salad, page 33.

Artichokes

● Cook as page 37 and serve with hollandaise sauce or hot melted butter.

● Serve cold with vinaigrette dressing (page 37). You need finger bowls, as for asparagus.

● Cook small artichokes, remove the leaves, crush the lower fleshy part of the leaves, blend with chopped hard-boiled egg, put on a bed of lettuce and top with the artichoke hearts from which you have scooped out the hairy centre. Pour over mayonnaise or vinaigrette dressing.

Note:

The fleshy leaves are left whole, to be dipped in a vinaigrette dressing, and can be eaten with the fingers. A small knife and fork will be needed for the heart.

Beans

Young French beans make a delicious salad if tossed in oil, vinegar and seasoning and garnished with chopped chives or spring onions.

Carrots

One would not serve these separately but they can make a very attractive part of an hors-d'œuvre. If young use raw, grated. If older, dice and cook.

Chicory

Cook lightly in lemon and salt flavoured water. Serve with a cheese sauce (see page 89).

Leeks

Young leeks can be cooked and used as asparagus.

Mushrooms

Cooked or diced raw mushrooms can be put in a mixed hors-d'œuvre or served as a salad with vinaigrette dressing (see below).

Tomatoes

● When tomatoes are at their best one of the simplest hors-d'œuvre is to slice and toss them in oil and vinegar and seasoning, adding a little garlic or chopped chives or spring onions. Serve with a garnish of watercress as a salad.

● They can be stuffed with eggs, fish, meat, cottage cheese and served raw or lightly cooked.

Artichokes with vinaigrette dressing

cooking time 30–40 minutes

you will need for 4 servings:

4 globe artichokes
vinaigrette dressing (see below)

1 Wash artichokes and cut off the stems and the outer layer of leaves.
2 Simmer steadily for 30–40 minutes until tender.
3 Drain well and allow to cool.
4 Serve on small plates with the dressing.

Vinaigrette dressing

you will need:

2 dessertspoons vinegar (wine vinegar, cider vinegar or tarragon vinegar)
5 dessertspoons olive oil
good pinch salt
pepper to taste

Mix all the ingredients thoroughly together.

Fish hors-d'œuvre

On the following pages are suggestions for serving smoked or cooked shellfish as an hors-d'œuvre. Good choice for the busy cook for they need little cooking or elaborate preparation, and yet give a touch of luxury and interest to a meal. Other fish also make excellent hors-d'œuvre or light savouries.

Anchovies

● Top slices of fried bread or toast with chopped hard-boiled egg and anchovy fillets. Spread toast with anchovy butter (see page 55) before topping with the egg and fillets. Serve on a bed of lettuce or watercress.

● This is also a good savoury to end a meal. Take the tops off firm tomatoes, scoop out the centre pulp, chop finely and mix with chopped anchovy fillets and hard-boiled egg. Pile this mixture back into tomato cases. Serve on a bed of lettuce with sliced cucumber.

● Use the same recipe as for Scotch woodcock but serve the egg—when cold—on a bed of salad (see page 47).

● Rollmop or Bismarck herrings can be served as part of a mixed hors-d'œuvre or as a separate salad. Garnish with plenty of sliced onion, gherkins and serve with diced beetroot, diced dessert apple, lettuce, etc.

● The canned herring tit-bits can also be served as a salad.

Sardines, Sild, Pilchards

● These canned fish are best as part of mixed hors-d'œuvre or served separately as the basis of a salad. Serve with hard-boiled egg, watercress, etc.

● Fill patty case with the mashed fish. Top with chopped hard-boiled egg.

Prawns, Shrimps, Scampi, Lobster, Crab

● Prawns and shrimps are excellent in cocktails —see page 39—or lobster and crab could be used instead.

● Fried—the larger scampi are generally used for this. Coat with egg and crumbs and fry for a few minutes only in hot fat. Drain and serve with tartare sauce, page 91. Frozen scampi should be defrosted, dried well then coated.

● Meunière—toss the fish in hot butter until just cooked (in the case of the frozen uncooked scampi) or just hot. Lift on to a hot dish, then add a little lemon juice, chopped parsley and seasoning to the butter and continue heating until golden brown. Pour over the fish and garnish with lemon, parsley.

● Serve all shellfish as the base for salads with mayonnaise (see page 36).

Oysters
Serve on half the shell with lemon and cayenne pepper—some people like a little vinegar as well. Serve with brown bread and butter.

Serving smoked fish

There is a great variety of smoked fish today that can be served as an hors-d'œuvre or, if a more generous quantity is given, as a light savoury.

Smoked eel
Allow approximately 2 inches per person or 3–4 pieces of fillet. Remove the black skin and serve on a bed of lettuce with wedges of lemon, accompanied by horseradish sauce (see page 90) and brown bread and butter.

Smoked trout
Can be served as smoked eel.

Smoked salmon
Serve with lemon, paprika or cayenne and brown bread and butter.

Smoked sprats
As smoked salmon.

Uncooked kipper fillets
Can be served as an inexpensive substitute for smoked salmon. Marinade in a little oil and vinegar, with pepper and a little chopped onion and leave for several hours.

Antipasto

no cooking

you will need:

fillets of anchovies
rolled anchovies
small mushrooms—cooked in a very little vinegar
pickled beetroot, cut into tiny shapes
pickled onions
hard-boiled eggs
pimentos
sliced tomatoes
sardines
olives—both green and black

Arrange these either on individual plates or on one large serving dish, so that the colours form as attractive a picture as possible.

Scampi meunière

cooking time about 6 minutes

you will need for 4 servings:

1 large packet frozen scampi
3 oz. butter
little lemon juice
seasoning
1 tablespoon chopped parsley

1 Allow scampi to defrost sufficiently to separate easily.
2 Heat the butter in a frying pan and cook the scampi for about 4–5 minutes.
3 Lift out the fish and put on to hot dish.
4 Add lemon juice and seasoning to butter and cook until brown in colour. This takes only about 1–2 minutes, and care must be taken that it does not darken too much.
5 Add parsley and pour over the fish.

Mock smoked salmon

no cooking

you will need:

frozen kipper fillets
little oil
little vinegar
seasoning

1 Let kipper fillets defrost, then put on a flat dish (allowing one per person).
2 Cover with a little oil, vinegar and seasoning, particularly a good shaking of pepper.
3 Leave for several hours, lift out of the dressing and serve in the same way as smoked salmon with lemon and brown bread and butter.

Tabasco cocktail sauce

no cooking

you will need:

½ pint tomato ketchup
½–1 teaspoon Tabasco sauce
2 tablespoons lemon juice
¼ teaspoon salt
1 tablespoon horse-radish cream
2 tablespoons finely chopped celery
1 teaspoon grated onion, optional

Mix all ingredients and chill before serving.

White fish cocktails

no cooking

you will need for 4 servings:

8–12 oz. cooked fish*
Tabasco cocktail sauce (see above)
little lettuce
slices of lemon

*This can be a mixture of white fish—tuna—salmon—or use cooked white fish and little shellfish

1 Flake the cooked fish.
2 Shred the lettuce finely, enough to be eaten with fork or spoon.
3 Blend the fish with enough of the cocktail sauce to moisten well.
4 Arrange lettuce in glasses or on dishes and top with the fish.
5 Garnish with slices of lemon.

Note:
The stronger tasting cocktail sauce is more suitable for this cocktail as it gives greater interest, colour, etc. to white fish.

Prawn cocktail

no cooking

you will need for 4 servings:

picked prawns or shrimps
lemon
lettuce

For the cocktail sauce:
3 tablespoons thick mayonnaise (see page 36)
1 tablespoon tomato ketchup, or thick tomato purée, or skinned tomatoes
1 tablespoon Worcestershire sauce
2 tablespoons full cream or evaporated milk
seasoning
little celery salt (or chopped celery)
little finely chopped onion (optional)
little lemon juice

To make the sauce:

1 Mix all the sauce ingredients together, and taste to check seasoning and lemon juice.

To make the cocktail:

2 This can be arranged in glasses or flat small dishes. Shred the lettuce very finely, so it can be eaten with a spoon or small fork.
3 Top with the prawns or shrimps and cover with the sauce.
4 Garnish with lemon.
5 Serve as cold as possible.

Anchovy potatoes

no cooking

you will need for 4 servings:

6 cooked new potatoes
2 oz. butter or margarine
few drops lemon juice
1 teaspoonful anchovy essence

To garnish:
filleted anchovies
watercress

1 Cream the butter or margarine, add the lemon juice and anchovy essence.
2 Cut the potatoes in halves and pipe a large rosette of the anchovy mixture on top of each half.
3 Decorate with tiny pieces of anchovy and sprigs of watercress.

Stuffed peppers

cooking time 30 minutes

you will need for 4 servings:

4 green peppers
1 clove garlic
4 large tomatoes
2 tablespoons oil
1 can anchovy fillets
4 oz. cooked rice
little parsley
seasoning

1 Cut tops of peppers and remove core and seeds.
2 Cook for 5 minutes in boiling salted water.
3 Chop the garlic and skin and chop the tomatoes.
4 Fry in the hot oil.
5 Chop the anchovies.
6 Add rice, anchovies, parsley and seasoning to the tomato mixture.
7 Fill peppers with this mixture, and put back the tops.
8 Put into a greased dish and cover with greased paper.
9 Bake for 25 minutes in a moderately hot oven (400°F—Gas Mark 5).
10 Serve with tomato sauce (see page 91).

Egg dishes

Because an egg is a light and easily digestible food, egg dishes are ideal at the beginning of the meal. You can serve small omelettes (see page 57), hard-boiled eggs in salads, as well as savoury eggs (see recipes below).

Egg florentine

cooking time 30 minutes

you will need for 4 servings:

- 1½ lb. spinach
- ½ oz. butter
- 1 tablespoon cornflour
- ¼ pint milk
- 3–4 tablespoons cream
- pinch nutmeg
- seasoning
- 4 poached eggs

To garnish:
toast

1. Wash and cook the spinach in the usual way then rub through a sieve.
2. Make a sauce with the butter, cornflour and milk then stir in the spinach.
3. Add the cream, nutmeg and seasoning to taste.
4. Reheat, then put in four cocottes or individual serving dishes and carefully place a poached egg on the top of each.
5. Decorate with triangles of toast.

Stuffed eggs with martinique dressing

no cooking

you will need for 4 servings:

- mayonnaise (see page 36)
- pinch cayenne
- 4 hard-boiled eggs
- 2 large tomatoes
- 1 oz. cheese
- seasoning

To garnish:
watercress

For the dressing:

- 3 fl. oz. corn oil
- 1 fl. oz. vinegar
- ¼ teaspoon salt
- 1 teaspoon sugar
- 1 teaspoon chopped parsley
- a little chopped green pepper

1. Make mayonnaise, adding pinch cayenne to ingredients.
2. Remove a small piece from the top of each egg and scoop out the yoke.
3. Cut the tomatoes in halves and remove the pulp.
4. Place egg white in the tomato halves.
5. Mix together yolks, tomato pulp, cheese and seasoning to taste and use sufficient mayonnaise to bind.
6. Pile the egg mixture into the eggs and garnish with watercress.
7. To prepare dressing, put corn oil, vinegar, salt and sugar into a screw top jar and shake well; add parsley and pepper.
8. Serve with the stuffed eggs.

Meat hors-d'œuvre

Most meat is too heavy to serve as an hors-d'œuvre but the following are light, unusual and very delicious:

Parma or smoked ham

Can be served with slices of ripe melon, dessert or canned figs or a ripe dessert pear. Do not put sugar on the melon but offer sugar and a little cayenne separately.

Salami

Choose a variety of salami and serve very thin slices on crisp lettuce.

Garlic sausages

Very good with tomato salads and green salad.

Chopped liver

cooking time 5 minutes

you will need for 4 servings:

- 8 oz. calf's or chicken's liver
- 1 medium onion
- seasoning
- 1½ oz. melted fat (chicken fat is ideal)
- 1 hard-boiled egg

1. Fry the liver and chopped onion in the fat for about 5 minutes.
2. Lift out and chop both on a board very finely or put through a mincer.
3. Add seasoning.
4. Moisten with a little fat from the frying pan.
5. Arrange on a dish and cover with chopped hard-boiled egg.

Make Your Own Pâté

A pâté is probably one of the most popular hors-d'œuvre and, although you can buy very good pâté, a home-made one is both simple to make and particularly delicious to eat.

Crème à la Grecque

no cooking

you will need for 4 servings:

$\frac{1}{2}$ lb. smoked cod's roe
4–6 oz. unsalted butter
juice 1 lemon
1 tomato

1 Skin the cod's roe.
2 Cream the butter.
3 Pound the roe, adding butter, lemon juice, tomato juice and pulp.
4 When very light and creamy serve with black olives and hot toast or water biscuits.

Fish pâté

cooking time 20 minutes

you will need for 4 servings:

approximately 1 lb. salt smoked cod's roe
clove garlic, crushed
2 oz. butter
pepper
very little cream (optional)

1 Remove the skin from the cod's roe and put into a basin.
2 Add the very finely crushed garlic (garlic salt could be used instead), the butter and pepper.
3 Blend together very thoroughly and add the cream.
4 Cook very gently in another dish of cold water for about 20 minutes in a moderate oven (375°F.—Gas Mark 4), covering the top so it does not dry.

Creamed liver pâté

cooking time 55 minutes

you will need:

For the sauce:
1 oz. margarine
2 oz. flour
$\frac{1}{2}$ pint milk

8 oz. bacon, either shoulder or middle rashers
1 lb. lamb or pork liver
$\frac{1}{2}$ teaspoon sugar
2 teaspoons salt
pinch black pepper
1 teaspoon cinnamon
1 teaspoon ginger
2 eggs
$\frac{1}{4}$ pint cream

To cover the pâté while cooking:
4 oz. bacon rashers

To garnish:
gherkins, lemon, parsley, hot toast

1 Heat margarine, stir in flour, cook for 1 minute.
2 Gradually add milk.
3 Bring to the boil.
4 Cook until thickened.
5 Mince bacon and liver until it is very smooth. Stir into sauce.
6 Add all other ingredients.
7 Press mixture firmly into a greased shallow fireproof dish.
8 Arrange the bacon rashers across the top.
9 Stand in a water bath (another dish, partly filled with cold water) and cook for 45 minutes in the centre of a very moderate oven (350°F.—Gas Mark 3).
10 Allow to cool, then serve garnished with gherkin, lemon, parsley and hot toast.

Variations:

For a coarser pâté put the meat and bacon through a coarse mincer and allow only $\frac{1}{3}$ pint of milk.
For a less creamy pâté omit or reduce the cream.
For a chicken liver pâté use half the quantity of bacon to the quantity of chicken livers.
For a pâté with more bite add chopped gherkins and a little chopped onion.

End-of-Meal Savouries

A number of dishes can be served at the end of a meal but remember that this is not a main course and portions, therefore, should be small; a Welsh rarebit which would normally serve 4 people will be plenty for 8 if used as a light supper savoury at the end of a meal. Here are some suggestions.

Cheese

- Toasted on bread—put slices of Gruyère or

Cheddar cheese on hot buttered toast and brown under a grill.

- As one of the various kinds of Welsh rarebit. A Buck rarebit is a little substantial but the other varieties are all extremely good.
- As a fried savoury such as cheese aigrettes or cheese fritters (see below).
- As a soufflé (see page 61).
- As a cold dish—cheese mousse (page 44).
- A really creamy Camembert cheese is delicious if slightly iced and served with crisp lettuce and biscuits or bread.
- To give a combination of sweet and savoury—serve a cheese cake (page 44).

Bacon

- You will find a number of classic bacon savouries on page 64 and any of these make a very satisfying end to the meal.

Mushrooms

- Fry mushrooms and serve on fried bread or toast—a favourite after-dinner savoury.
- Vary by sprinkling grated cheese over them just before serving or spread the toast with a soft pâté rather than butter.

Fish

- Sardines on hot buttered toast can be varied by sprinkling with chopped parsley and grated cheese. They can also be put on top of a curry-flavoured butter (see page 55).
- Cod's roe can be fried with bacon and served on fingers of fried bread or toast.
- Soft herring roes can be steamed with butter, seasoning, and a little milk or cream between two plates over a pan of hot water. Or they can be fried in butter or margarine, or simmered in a little milk. They are then drained, put on hot buttered toast and garnished with cayenne or paprika.

Savouries with cheese

Cheese straws

cooking time 7 minutes

you will need:

4 oz. plain flour	2½ oz. butter
salt and cayenne	2 oz. grated cheese
little dry mustard	1 egg yolk

1. Sieve the flour, seasoning and mustard together, rub in the butter.
2. Add the cheese and bind with the egg yolk. If necessary add a little water as well.
3. Roll out firmly and cut into thin fingers.
4. Use a little of the pastry to make circles, so that when cooked the cheese straws can be threaded through these.
5. Brush with a very little egg white to give them a gloss.
6. Bake on lightly greased tins in a hot oven (450°F.—Gas Mark 7) for approximately 7 minutes.
7. Allow to cool slightly on the tin as the mixture is brittle and could very easily break.

Variation:

Cheese twists

Make pastry as above, roll out into a thin oblong strip and cut in halves. Spread one half with yeast extract and place the other half on top. Roll lightly together, cut into ¼-inch strips, twist and bake as above for about 10 minutes.

Cheese whirls

Make pastry as for straws, roll into a thin oblong, spread with yeast extract, roll up like a Swiss roll and cut into slices. Cook as from step 5 for about 10 minutes.

Cheese and tomato whirls

Make pastry as above, roll out into an oblong, spread with 2½ oz. can tomato paste, roll up from the long side and cut into ¼-inch slices. Cook as step 6 for 12 minutes.

Cheese aigrettes 1

cooking time 12 minutes

you will need for 4 servings:

⅛ pint corn oil	pinch of salt
¼ pint water	2 eggs
2½ oz. plain flour and ½ oz. cornflour, or 3 oz. plain flour	2 oz. Cheddar cheese
	pinch cayenne

1. Heat corn oil and water to boiling point in a saucepan.

2 Remove from the heat, add flour, cornflour and salt sifted together.
3 Mix well, return to the heat and cook until the mixture forms a ball and leaves the sides of the pan clean.
4 Remove from the heat, cool a little, then beat in the eggs one at a time.
5 Lastly add the grated cheese and cayenne.
6 Drop teaspoonsful into corn oil heated moderately and fry till well puffed and golden brown.

Variations:

Cheese and tomato aigrettes
Use ¼ pint tomato juice in place of water.

Cheese and bacon aigrettes
Use 1 oz. finely diced, cooked bacon as well as the cheese.

Savoury aigrettes
Use 1 teaspoon yeast extract with the water. Omit the salt.

Cheese aigrettes 2

cooking time 12 minutes

you will need for 4 servings:

1 oz. butter
⅛ pint water
2 oz. plain flour
2 eggs
pinch salt and cayenne
1½ oz. grated cheese (mixed Cheddar and Parmesan)

1 Bring butter and water to boiling point.
2 Toss in all the flour at once and beat until smooth.
3 Cool, then add the eggs gradually, beating the mixture very well after each addition.
4 Stir in the cheese and seasoning.
5 Drop small teaspoons of the mixture into a pan of hot deep fat (350°F.) and fry to a golden brown, taking 7–10 minutes.
6 Drain and serve hot, sprinkled with a little grated cheese.

Variations:

Nutty cheese aigrettes
Add ½ oz. salted chopped almonds to the mixture together with the grated cheese.
Variations given above with Cheese aigrettes 1 can also be used with this recipe.

Cheese puffs 1

cooking time 10 minutes

you will need for 4 servings:

3 oz. margarine or butter
¼ pint water
4 oz. plain flour
pinch salt
3 eggs
3½ oz. Cheddar cheese, grated
pepper
pinch cayenne
¼ teaspoon made mustard
oil for frying
parsley

1 Boil water in a saucepan; add butter. When melted, remove from heat and add flour and salt all at once.
2 Return to the heat and beat until mixture forms a soft ball and no longer sticks to the sides of the pan.
3 Cool.
4 Beat in eggs one at a time, then work in 3 oz. of cheese, the pepper and cayenne and mustard.
5 Put teaspoons of the mixture into deep, hot oil and cook for about 7 minutes until well puffed out and firm to the touch.
6 Drain and serve hot, sprinkled with remaining ½ oz. grated cheese.
7 Garnish with parsley.

Cheese puffs 2

cooking time 3–4 minutes

you will need for 4 servings:

4 oz. finely grated Cheddar cheese
pinch cayenne
½ teaspoon salt
1 egg
fat for frying

1 Mix the cheese, seasoning, and stir in the beaten egg yolk.
2 Fold in the stiffly beaten egg white and shape lightly in the hands into small balls.
3 Fry a few at a time in hot, deep fat (350°F. approximately or until a cube of bread turns brown in 1 minute) to a golden brown, taking 3–4 minutes.
4 Drain and serve as a savoury snack or on cocktail sticks for a party.

Variations:

Use 3 oz. grated cheese and 1 oz. chopped nuts.
Use 3 oz. grated cheese and 1 oz. diced ham.
Use 3 oz. grated cheese and 1 oz. very finely chopped green pepper.

English monkey

cooking time few minutes

you will need for 4 servings:

1 oz. butter
¼ pint evaporated milk
2 oz. breadcrumbs
4 oz. grated cheese
1 egg
mustard
Worcestershire sauce
4 slices toast
1 tomato

1 Heat butter in a pan, add milk and breadcrumbs.
2 When very hot add the grated cheese and beaten egg.
3 Season well, adding a little made mustard and few drops of Worcestershire sauce.
4 Stir together until thick and creamy.
5 Pour on to toast with sliced tomato.

Lemon cheese cake

cooking time 1¼ hours

you will need for 4 servings:

For lining baking dish:
4 good tablespoons cornflakes
little margarine

For the filling:
3 oz. margarine
3 oz. sugar
2 large or 3 small eggs
grated rind 1 lemon
juice 1 lemon
12 oz. cream or cottage cheese
2 tablespoons cream or evaporated milk*

1 Crush the cornflakes finely.
2 Rub the dish with margarine and press most of the cornflakes against this.
3 Cream the margarine and sugar, separate the eggs and add the egg yolks and the lemon rind. Then work in the cheese, the cream* and lemon juice until the mixture forms a really smooth consistency.
4 Fold in the stiffly beaten egg whites.
5 Put into the cornflake-lined dish and sprinkle the remaining cornflakes as a border round the cheese cake.
6 Bake for approximately 1¼ hours in a very slow oven until set (250—275°F.—Gas Mark 1–2).

*The cream is incorporated with the lemon juice and gives a softer and more delicate cheese cake. For a firmer consistency to cut into squares for a party, omit the cream

Piquant cheese crunchies

no cooking time

you will need:

bread slices
a little butter
cream cheese
yeast extract
cornflakes

1 Butter the bread and sandwich slices together with yeast extract.
2 Cut into neat fingers or cubes, spread outside with soft cream cheese, then roll in the crisp, crushed cornflakes.

Tomato cheese moulds

no cooking time

you will need for 4 servings:

¼ pint tomato juice
4 oz. cream cheese or grated cheese
2 teaspoons powdered gelatine
4 tablespoons hot water
1 teaspoon chopped parsley
1 teaspoon chopped gherkins
seasoning

1 Beat tomato juice very gradually into cheese until mixture is smooth.
2 Dissolve the gelatine in the hot water.
3 Add to cheese with seasoning, parsley and gherkins.
4 Pour into tiny moulds and turn out when set. Serve with salad.

Cheese mousse

cooking time 10 minutes

you will need:

1 oz. butter
1 oz. flour
¼ pint water
¼ pint evaporated milk
4 oz. Cheddar cheese
1 heaped teaspoon tomato purée
1 heaped teaspoon mustard
pinch salt and cayenne pepper
2 eggs
1 heaped teaspoon powdered gelatine

1 Prepare a 5-inch soufflé case by tying a wide double band of greaseproof paper round the outside so that it extends above the rim.
2 Melt the butter in a pan, stir in the flour and cook for a minute.
3 Add the water and milk gradually, bring to the boil and boil for one minute, stirring well.
4 Add the pieces of cheese, seasonings, tomato purée, egg yolks, and cook for another two minutes until smooth.
5 Soften the gelatine in 1 tablespoon cold water and dissolve in 2 tablespoons boiling water.
6 Add to the cheese mixture and allow to cool.
7 When just beginning to stiffen fold in the stiffly beaten egg whites.
8 Cool, stirring occasionally.

9 Pour into the soufflé case and put in a cool place to set.
10 Serve with a lettuce salad tossed in French dressing.

Celery and cheese soufflé

cooking time 33–43 minutes

you will need for 4 servings:

2 oz. butter	¼ pint milk
2 oz. flour	4 eggs
1 can celery soup* or mushroom or tomato or chicken	seasoning
	4 oz. grated cheese

*If using condensed soup, add little more milk

1 Melt butter in saucepan, stir in flour and cook steadily for a minute.
2 Add celery soup and milk, bring to boil and cook for 2–3 minutes.
3 Allow to cool slightly.
4 Separate eggs, add beaten egg yolks, seasoning and cheese.
5 Whisk egg whites until thick and fold into mixture.
6 Pour into a 7 inch greased soufflé or pie dish and bake in a hot oven (400°F.—Gas Mark 5) for 30–40 minutes.
7 Serve at once.

Cheese soufflé

cooking time approximately 30 minutes

you will need for 4 servings:

1 oz. butter	4 eggs, or 3 yolks and 4 whites
1 oz. flour	4 oz. cheese, finely grated
¼ pint milk	
seasoning	

1 Make a thick sauce with the butter, flour and milk.
2 Add seasoning and beat in yolks and cheese.
3 Fold in the stiffly beaten egg whites.
4 Put into greased 6–7 inch soufflé dish (with a 6 inch soufflé dish put a band of buttered paper round the top to support the mixture as it rises).
5 Bake in the centre of a moderately hot oven (400°F.—Gas Mark 5) for approximately 30 minutes.
6 Serve at once.

Variations:

For a more creamy result add 4 tablespoons of cream or extra milk to the sauce.
For a sharper result use nearly all Parmesan cheese. Use 3 oz. finely flaked smoked haddock and 2 oz. grated cheese.

10 ways with Welsh rarebit

A Welsh rarebit or 'rabbit' is a delicious tasty cheese snack that can form a complete meal, particularly if served with a really good salad, for the amount of cheese used in it is sufficiently high to produce a nourishing as well as appetising savoury.
Although this makes an excellent choice for a main savoury dish, it is one of the classic after-dinner savouries and, if serving it at the end of a meal, you'll find that the following quantities will be enough for twice the portions since only a small slice is offered. With every recipe you use for Welsh rarebit, be very careful not to over-cook the cheese in the mixture, otherwise it will be stringy and tough instead of creamy and delicious. Have the grill piping hot so that the mixture bubbles and browns quickly.
It is well worth while making a large quantity of the Welsh rarebit mixture and keeping the surplus in a jar in a cold place.

Welsh rarebit

cooking time 12 minutes

you will need for 8 after-dinner servings*:

1 oz. butter	pepper
1 oz. flour	8 oz. Cheddar cheese
¼ pint milk	1 tablespoon beer or ale
1 teaspoon made mustard	4–6 slices of buttered toast
salt	

1 Heat the butter in a saucepan, stir in the flour and cook steadily for several minutes, then gradually add the cold milk.
2 Bring to the boil and cook until smooth and thick.
3 Add the mustard, salt and pepper, most of the cheese, and the beer.

(continued on next page)

*This gives 4 portions as a main savoury, or can be cut into about 32 bite-size cocktail savouries

4 Heat steadily, without boiling too quickly, until the cheese has melted.
5 Spread over the hot buttered toast, sprinkle with the remaining cheese and brown under a hot grill.
6 Serve with green salad and French dressing (see page 90).

Variations:

Creamy Welsh rarebit
Ingredients and method as for Welsh rarebit, but use processed or Dutch cheese instead of Cheddar cheese.

Welsh rarebit with a 'bite'
Ingredients as for Welsh rarebit, but use 6 oz. Lancashire and 2 oz. Parmesan cheese instead of 8 oz. Cheddar cheese. Method as for Welsh rarebit.

Eggy Welsh rarebit
Ingredients and method as for Welsh rarebit, but add a well beaten egg or egg yolk after stage 4.

Soufflé Welsh rarebit
Ingredients and method as for Welsh rarebit, but add 2 egg yolks and finally 2 stiffly beaten egg whites after stage 4.

Tomato Welsh rarebit
Ingredients and method as for Welsh rarebit, but use $\frac{1}{4}$ pint tomato juice or purée instead of milk.

Celery Welsh rarebit
Ingredients and method as for Welsh rarebit, but use either canned celery hearts or cooked celery. Put the hot celery on buttered toast and use celery stock instead of milk in the mixture.

Corn rarebit
Ingredients and method as for Welsh rarebit, but add approximately 4 oz. cooked corn after stage 3. A little corn stock can be used in place of some of the milk.

Buck rarebit
Ingredients and method as Welsh rarebit, but top each portion with a poached egg.

York rarebit
Ingredients and method as Welsh rarebit, but put a thick slice of cooked ham on each piece of toast and cover with the cheese mixture.

Fish and meat savouries

Angels on horseback

cooking time few minutes

you will need for 4 after-dinner servings*:

4 large or 8 small oysters
seasoning
squeeze lemon juice
4 long rashers bacon

1 Season the oysters and add lemon juice.
2 Wrap a rasher of bacon round each oyster securing with a cocktail stick (if using small oysters, cut the rashers of bacon in halves).
3 Cook under the grill until the bacon is crisp and brown. Do not over-cook as this toughens the oysters.
4 Serve on hot buttered toast.

*Or 8 cocktail savouries

Canapés Diane

cooking time few minutes

you will need for 4 after-dinner servings*:

4 chicken livers
seasoning
squeeze lemon juice
4 rashers streaky bacon
8 tiny toast fingers

1 Cut chicken livers into halves.
2 Season and flavour with lemon juice.
3 Cut each rasher of bacon into halves.
4 Wrap each chicken liver in half rasher and secure with a cocktail stick.
5 Grill until bacon is crisp and brown.
6 Serve on pieces of hot buttered toast.

*Or 8 cocktail savouries

Devils on horseback

cooking time few minutes

you will need for 4 servings:

8 large juicy cooked prunes
4 long rashers bacon
8 toast fingers
butter
paprika

1 Stone the prunes, cut each rasher of bacon into halves and wrap round the prunes, securing with cocktail sticks.
2 Cook under the grill until the bacon is crisp and brown.
3 Serve on toast dusted with paprika.
4 If wished, a little liver pâté (see page 41) can be inserted into the centre of the prunes.

Little devils on horseback

cooking time few minutes

you will need for 4 after-dinner servings*:

4 rashers long streaky bacon, preferably green (unsmoked)
12 anchovy fillets
12 squares hot buttered toast

1 Divide each rasher of bacon into 3.
2 Remove the rind.
3 Put an anchovy fillet on each piece, roll firmly and secure with cocktail stick.
4 Grill until crisp and golden brown.
5 Put on to squares of hot buttered toast.

*Or 12 cocktail savouries

Breton fingers

cooking time few minutes

you will need for 4 servings:

1 small tin sardines in oil
½ teacup breadcrumbs
seasoning
1 teaspoon Worcestershire sauce
3 oz. Cheddar cheese, grated
little margarine or butter, if necessary
½ teaspoon made mustard
4 slices buttered toast

To garnish:
1 tomato

1 Mash the sardines very well and season.
2 Mix the oil from the sardine tin with the breadcrumbs, seasoning, Worcestershire sauce and cheese. If there is not sufficient oil to give a soft mixture then add a little margarine or butter and cream well.
3 Spread the mashed sardines on the slices of toast and cover with the crumb mixture.
5 Put under a hot grill for a few minutes until crisp and golden brown. Garnish with small pieces of tomato, and serve hot or cold.
If serving hot the fingers can be prepared earlier and just heated in oven.

Shrimp toast

cooking time few minutes

you will need for 4 servings:

4 oz. picked shrimps
2 oz. butter
seasoning
8 toast fingers
little nutmeg

1 Chop the shrimps and bind with 1½ oz. of the butter and seasoning.
2 Use the rest of the butter to spread on the toast the moment it is cooked.
3 Cover with the shrimp butter.
4 Top with little grated or powdered nutmeg.
5 Heat for a few minutes under the grill.

Scotch woodcock

cooking time few minutes

you will need for 4 after-dinner servings*:

4 small slices of bread
butter
3–4 eggs
seasoning
little milk
8 fillets anchovy

1 Toast the bread and butter, having removed any crusts.
2 Beat the eggs with the seasoning and a very little milk, and scramble in the hot butter. Put on the hot toast.
3 Top with anchovy fillets arranged on each portion.

*For a supper snack double the egg quantity and use large slices of toast

Bengal canapés

cooking time 12 minutes

you will need for 4 servings:

For the sauce:
½ oz. margarine
½ oz. flour
¼ pint milk
seasoning
1 tablespoon cream
2 tablespoons sweet chutney or finely chopped pickles
2 tablespoons grated cheese

4 slices bread
butter or margarine
4 oz. cooked ham

To garnish:
parsley and tomato

1 To make the sauce, heat the margarine, stir in the flour and cook for 2–3 minutes, then gradually add the milk, bring to the boil and cook until thickened.
2 Season well.
3 Toast or fry the bread, remove crusts and butter.
4 Chop the ham finely and heat for several minutes in the white sauce, adding the cream.
5 Spread over the toast, then add the chutney.
6 Cover with grated cheese and put under a hot grill for a few minutes until crisp and golden brown.
7 Garnish with parsley and strips of tomato.

Variations:

Use flaked smoked haddock in place of ham.
Use finely diced cooked liver in place of ham.

Devilled mushrooms and eggs

cooking time few minutes

you will need for 4 servings:

2 oz. butter	1 teaspoon Worcestershire sauce
4 oz. mushrooms, sliced	1 teaspoon mushroom ketchup
good pinch curry powder	3 hard-boiled eggs
$\frac{1}{2}$–1 teaspoon made mustard	4 rounds toast

1 Heat the butter.
2 Toss the mushrooms in this, then add all the flavourings.
3 Mix in the quartered hard-boiled eggs.
4 Heat and serve at once on toast.

Savoury choux

Choux pastry

you will need:

$\frac{1}{4}$ pint water	2 whole eggs and yolk of 1 egg or 3 small eggs
1 oz. margarine or butter	pinch salt, pepper, mustard
3 oz. flour (plain or self-raising)	

1 Put the water, margarine or butter and seasonings into a saucepan.
2 Heat gently until the margarine or butter has melted.
3 Stir in the flour.
4 Return the pan to a low heat and cook very gently but thoroughly stirring all the time, until the mixture is dry enough to form a ball and leave the pan clean.
5 Remove the pan from the heat and gradually add the well beaten eggs. Do this slowly to produce a perfectly smooth mixture.
6 Allow to cool, then use as individual recipes.

Bun cases

cooking time 35–40 minutes

for 4 servings:

1 There are several ways of making bun cases from choux paste. Either
 a grease and flour individual patty tins and put in a spoonful of the mixture or,
 b pile some of the mixture on to well greased and floured baking trays or,
 c put the mixture into piping bags and force through a large plain pipe on to floured and greased baking tray.
2 If you have a deep tin which can be put right over the cases while in the oven, this will help to give a better shape to the buns. The tin should be light in weight and several inches high to allow room for the buns to rise.
3 Put the tray of cakes into the centre of a hot oven (450°F.—Gas Mark 7) for 35 minutes if uncovered, 40 minutes if covered. Reduce the heat for the last 20 minutes to 400°F.—Gas Mark 5.
4 The buns should be a pale gold in colour and feel very firm and crisp. If you find there is some uncooked pastry in the centre of the buns, remove this and return the buns to the oven for a few minutes to dry. The oven should be cool.
5 Cool the buns gradually and away from a draught.
6 For after-dinner savouries or cocktails use only $\frac{1}{2}$ teaspoons of the mixture and you will find these need only approximately 25 minutes baking.
7 Fill as suggested on page 48.

Éclair cases

cooking time 25 minutes

you will need:

choux pastry (see recipe left)

1 Pipe the mixture into finger shapes on well greased and floured baking trays or put into greased and floured finger tins.
2 Bake, without covering, in the centre of a hot oven (450°F.—Gas Mark 7) for 25 minutes.
3 Fill as suggested below.

12 ways of filling savoury choux

Cheese
Make a really thick cheese sauce with 1 oz. butter, 1 oz. flour, $\frac{1}{2}$ pint milk, seasoning, 4 oz. cheese. Add a little whipped cream or mayonnaise. Put into éclair or bun case and dust tops with grated cheese and chopped parsley.

Sardine
Fill with mashed sardines and chopped hard-boiled egg yolks.

Vegetable
Fill with thick cheese sauce (see Cheese filling) mixed with cooked vegetables.

Prawns, shrimp or fish
Make a thick white sauce with 1 oz. flour, 1 oz. butter, $\frac{1}{3}$ pint milk. Add seasoning and approximately 4 oz. chopped prawns, shrimps or flaked cooked fish.

Chicken
Make a thick white sauce (see page 91) but in place of all milk use a little milk and chicken stock. Add approximately 6 oz. finely diced chicken.

Harlequin
Blend diced red and green peppers, tomatoes, cucumber and chopped hard-boiled egg with thick mayonnaise.

Salmon
Blend flaked, cooked or canned salmon with thick mayonnaise.

Ham
Blend finely chopped ham with either thick white sauce (see page 92), mayonnaise or scrambled egg.

Egg
Blend lightly scrambled egg with a little cream and chopped chives.

Savoury cream
Whip cream until fairly stiff. Add a few drops of lemon juice, seasoning, and a little finely chopped chives.

Cream cheese
Blend soft cream cheese with a little milk or cream, chopped parsley and chives.

Cottage cheese
Blend cottage cheese lightly with chopped nuts or chopped pineapple or chopped dates.

Cocktail Savouries and Snacks

The savouries for a cocktail party can be varied—and served either hot or cold. There is, however, one thing they should have in common—they must be small enough for people to pick up and eat without needing a plate. Ideally they should be small enough to be eaten in one mouthful.
If serving hot savouries they must be well drained so they do not make peoples' fingers greasy or sticky.

For a well planned cocktail party menu have
1 some savouries with cheese (see pages 50–51)
2 something with fish (see page 51)
3 something with bacon and/or other meat (see page 53)
4 something hot—although this is not essential (see page 51)
5 low-calorie 'titbits', for people watching their weight, such as radishes, gherkins, onions
6 salted nuts, crisps, etc.

Base for cocktail savouries
In order to balance the small pieces of food easily you need a base and this can be made from

Toast
This has the disadvantage of becoming 'soggy' in a relatively short time, but it is generally used for the basis of aspic savouries.

Fresh bread and butter
This is ideal for tiny pieces of smoked salmon, herring, etc.

Biscuits

Use either cheese biscuits or some of the great variety of cocktail-size biscuits available today.

Fried bread

Excellent since it can be prepared earlier in the day and either reheated for hot savouries or drained well and kept ready for cold savouries —it does not become soft for some hours.

Pancakes

Use the recipe for Scotch pancakes (see page 81) and make them the size of a halfpenny; this makes very good base for rather soft pâté, which will make even fried bread soften in a short time.

Choux pastry

Use this as a filling case (see page 48).

Pastry

As well as making miniature pastry cases (see savoury horns, page 86), you can make penny-sized tartlet cases to be filled, or just roll out the pastry and cut into rounds about the size of a halfpenny or penny, bake and use as the base for savouries; or make vols au vent (see page 83).

Canapés or small savouries

The quickest way to make savouries, particularly if serving on bread, toast or fried bread, is to cut large slices, butter them, then cover the whole slice with the topping. Cut into bite-size pieces and garnish each piece. Try to arrange ingredients, etc. in order of working; this is not only quicker, but more efficient. Cover the cocktail savouries with foil or polythene to keep them fresh and moist.

To make aspic savouries or canapés

Aspic canapés look most attractive, and the aspic jelly topping is practical, since it ensures that the food below is kept moist.

you will need:

aspic jelly
base (either toast, biscuits, bread)
topping—this can be:

- eggs—hard-boiled, sliced or firmly scrambled
- fish—sardines, smoked or fresh-cooked salmon, sild, pieces of herring
- meat—pâté, tongue, ham, salami
- vegetables—asparagus tips, tiny shapes or cooked carrot, beetroot, peas, beans

1. Make the aspic jelly according to packet directions, and allow to become lightly set but still soft enough to spread or brush over the food.
2. Arrange the food on long slices of the chosen base to give good colour and flavour contrast.
3. Lift the slices on to flat, clean trays or pastry board, so that any surplus jelly can be picked up and used again.
4. Either spread the jelly over the food with a warm palette knife or brush over, using a dry pastry brush; if using a pastry brush, do this several times to give a good layer.
5. Some of the jelly will drip down the sides—pick this up and use again.
6. For perfect results you may find it best to allow the jelly to set then brush over with a liquid layer of cold jelly to give a final smooth result.
7. Allow to set firmly, then cut into desired shapes with a sharp knife dipped in hot water.

Uncooked cheese savouries

By using different kinds of cheese you can provide a considerable variety of cocktail savouries with the minimum of preparation.

With fruit

Choose a fairly firm cheese that can be cut into small dice without crumbling. Put on cocktail sticks with:

- cubes or balls of melon (cut the balls with a vegetable scoop)
- ripe green or black grapes
- segments of well drained canned mandarins, or diced canned or fresh pineapple
- slices of banana—sprinkled with lemon juice to keep the colour
- firm Cheddar, Derby, Double Gloucester, Wensleydale, Dutch or processed cheese—all blend excellently with fruit

With ham

- Arrange small cubes of ham on buttered

biscuits and top with a teaspoon or piped rosette of cream cheese and a dusting of paprika.
● Put cubes of ham and of a fairly sharp cheese—Lancashire, Leicester—on to cocktail sticks with small onions.

With fish

● Use the same kinds of cheese as for fruit and put on to cocktail sticks with prawns or shrimps.
● Arrange tiny cubes or slices of cheese on buttered biscuits and top with rolled anchovy fillets.

With vegetables

● Blend either Danish blue, Stilton, cream cheese, grated Cheddar or other firm cheeses, with a little butter or mayonnaise and use as a filling for the centre of celery stalks—or the base of chicory.
Cut into ½–1 inch lengths and top with chopped parsley and/or a dusting of paprika.
If the mixture is very soft and smooth it can be piped on to the pieces of celery.
● Grate equal quantities of cheese—or use soft cream cheese—and young carrots. Blend well; if using a firm cheese add a small amount of butter to give a consistency you can roll into balls. Make the balls about the size of a hazel nut and roll in chopped parsley or chopped nuts—various seasonings can be added as wished.
● Put cubes of cheese on cocktail sticks with tiny gherkins or halves of gherkin and cocktail onions.

With nuts

● Sandwich walnut halves with soft cream cheese or grated cheese blended with a little butter or margarine.
● Mix soft cream cheese with chopped salted peanuts and roll in balls.

Cooked cheese savouries

Since cheese toughens with over-cooking, timing of the savouries is important. If you have no help in the kitchen, put the savouries on to oven proof dishes, heat or brown as required, and serve on the same dish.

With bacon or sausage

● Wrap tiny cubes or fingers of cheese in small pieces of bacon, secure with wooden cocktail sticks and cook in the oven until the bacon is crisp.
● Insert a thin finger of cheese into tiny cooked cocktail or Frankfurter sausages and heat in the oven for a few minutes until the cheese melts.

As toasted snacks

● Make Welsh rarebit recipes (see page 45), brown under the grill or in the oven and cut into tiny cubes before serving.
● Or put the Welsh rarebit mixture on to fried bread or pancakes and heat for a few minutes.

Fried

● Coat cubes of cheese with egg and crumbs and fry for a few minutes until crisp and golden brown.
● Make very tiny Cheese fritters (see page 80), or Cheese meringues (see page 79).

Savouries with fish

Some of the tinned fish make a most suitable cocktail savoury—anchovies, herring titbits, pieces of rollmop herring, sardines, for example. Or try the following:

Smoked fish, eel, trout, kipper, salmon.
Shellfish, crab, lobster, prawns, shrimps.
Fresh cooked fish, white fish, salmon.
Fish roes, caviare, cod's roe.

Anchovies

● Chop the fillets and blend with chopped hard-boiled egg and enough butter or mayonnaise to make a thick paste. Pile on to rounds of buttered bread or biscuits. Garnish with capers or parsley.
● Twist fillets of anchovy round stuffed olives and arrange on buttered biscuits or flat dishes.
● Make miniature portions of Scotch Woodcock (see page 47).
● Use tiny pieces for aspic canapés.

Herring titbits

● Arrange on a bed of lettuce and put a pile of cocktail sticks beside the dish.
● Put on brown bread and butter with little watercress.
● Garnish with little butter flavoured with mustard and piped into small stars; serve either on bread (with no butter) or crisp bread.

Rollmop herring

Can be served as herring titbits and on cocktail sticks with tiny cocktail onions.

Sardines

● Mash and pipe on top of rings of hard-boiled egg on rounds of buttered bread or biscuits.
● Serve miniature portions of Breton fingers (see page 47).
● Mash, season well with pepper and a little lemon juice, and pile into centre of celery sticks.
● Serve very tiny pieces of hot sardine on buttered toast.

Eel

● Remove the dark skin, cut into tiny pieces and serve on buttered brown bread garnished with scrambled egg or horseradish cream.
● Put tiny pieces on top of bread covered with watercress butter (see page 55).

Trout

● Flake the flesh from the skin and bones and mix with little horseradish cream; serve on toast.
● Put tiny pieces on buttered brown bread and garnish with horseradish sauce (see page 90) and watercress.

Kipper

● Flake pieces of cooked kipper and mix with hard-boiled egg and chopped watercress. If necessary blend with little oil and vinegar and season well. Put on buttered bread.
● Blend the flaked kipper flesh with finely diced cocktail onions and gherkins and spread on fingers of bread and butter.

Salmon

● Wrap pieces of smoked salmon round asparagus tips and cut into about $\frac{1}{2}$-inch pieces.
● Put salmon on slices of buttered bread and garnish with horseradish sauce (see page 90) and watercress.
● Blend with scrambled egg, put on top of crisp toast or fried bread and garnish with parsley and a dusting of paprika.

Crab or lobster

● Flake flesh, blend with mayonnaise (see page 36) and little lemon juice and spread on buttered bread or biscuits.
● Blend with a little tomato purée and finely diced cucumber. Season well and pile on fingers of pastry or bread and butter; garnish with lemon.
● Choose hen lobster and blend the red roe (coral) with butter and seasoning. Spread on bread and top with lobster meat.

Prawns or shrimps

● Put on buttered bread and garnish with mayonnaise and watercress.
● Coat with beaten egg and crumbs, fry for a few minutes in hot fat, drain and serve on cocktail sticks. Serve with a dish of tartare sauce as a dip (see page 91).
● Arrange fresh shrimps or prawns on lettuce and serve with cocktail sticks and a dip of tomato flavoured mayonnaise (for this blend either a sieved tomato to each $\frac{1}{4}$ pint mayonnaise [see page 36] or use 1 tablespoon tomato ketchup or purée. Season with Tabasco, soy or Worcestershire sauce).
● Use under aspic jelly as canapés.

Cooked white fish or salmon or tuna.

● Blend equal quantities of cooked fish and creamy mashed potato together, bind with egg yolk and season well. Form into fish cakes the size of a penny, coat in egg white and crumbs and bake or fry until crisp. Stick cocktail sticks through them and serve while hot.
● Blend fish with little mayonnaise (see page 36) and chopped egg white. Form into pyramid shapes on buttered biscuits or rounds of bread and garnish with chopped or sieved egg yolk and parsley.
● Choose the tiniest tomatoes available. Halve, remove the centre flesh and chop this with flaked fish, gherkin and onion. Blend with thick mayonnaise (see page 36) and return to cases. Garnish with capers or gherkins.

Caviare

● Cover slices of brown bread and butter with a ring of hard-boiled egg and top with 1 teaspoon caviare.

● Hard-boil eggs, halve, remove the yolks and blend this with caviare. Pile back into white cases and cut each half through centre.

Cod's roe

● When smoked, blend with little butter and cayenne pepper and put on watercress butter (see page 55) spread on fingers of bread.

● When fresh add mayonnaise (see page 36) and seasoning and use as a filling for pieces of celery, or bind with egg yolks.

● Cut into small cubes and wrap in pieces of bacon rashers. Secure with wooden cocktail sticks and heat in the oven until bacon is crisp.

Mussel titbits

cooking time 8 minutes

you will need:

- 1–1½ pints mussels
- 18 small rounds of toast, or biscuits
- 2 oz. margarine or butter
- small quantity of finely chopped watercress
- few drops lemon juice
- anchovy paste
- paprika

1. Put the mussels into a large saucepan, adding just enough water to cover bottom of pan.
2. Heat gently until mussels open.
3. Remove them from shells, discarding beards.
4. Spread toast or biscuit with mixture made by creaming margarine or butter and adding finely chopped watercress and lemon juice.
5. Put a mussel on each round, then pipe a ring of anchovy paste round it. Dust with paprika.

Haddock pyramids

no cooking

you will need for 24 savouries:

- 24 small rounds toast, or biscuits
- 4 oz. cooked haddock
- seasoning
- 1 tablespoon mayonnaise (see page 36)
- sieved white of 1 hard-boiled egg
- gherkins or stuffed olives

1. Mince or flake the fish very finely, mixing with the mayonnaise and egg white.
2. Season well, then form into a pyramid and decorate with a ring of gherkin or olive.

Variation:

Lobster pyramids

Substitute flaked lobster for haddock.

Anchovy fingers

cooking time 10 minutes

you will need for 12–18 savouries:

- 4 oz. short crust pastry (see page 82)
- 1 tin anchovies
- egg or milk to brush pastry

1. Roll the pastry into a neat oblong shape and cut into 6 strips about 1½ inches wide.
2. Arrange anchovies along these strips, then fold as though making sausage rolls.
3. Cut into lengths of about 2–3 inches.
4. Put on to a baking tin, brushing the pastry with milk or egg.
5. Bake for a good 10 minutes just above the middle of a hot oven (450°F.—Gas Mark 7).
6. Serve plain or, when the fingers are cold, twist another fillet of anchovy in a spiral round the outside.

Anchovy and egg canapés

no cooking

you will need:

- 24 cocktail biscuits
- little butter or mayonnaise (see page 36)
- 3 hard-boiled eggs
- 1 can rolled anchovy fillets

1. Cover the biscuits with butter or thick mayonnaise.
2. Cut the eggs into thin slices.
3. Put on the buttered biscuits and top with anchovy fillets—the neat roll fits well into the centre of the egg yolk.

Savouries with meat

The most useful meats to buy for cocktail savouries are salami, liver sausage or pâté, sausages or sausage meat, tongue and ham.

Salami

● Cut into tiny strips and arrange on fingers of bread and butter with scrambled egg.

● Roll strips round cocktail onions and secure with cocktail sticks.
● Chop salami and blend with chopped hard-boiled egg, mayonnaise (see page 36) and chopped parsley. Spread on toast, fingers of bread and butter, or biscuits.

Liver sausage or pâté

● If using liver sausage, blend with a little butter to give the consistency of pâté. Spread on buttered bread or tiny Scotch pancakes (see page 81) and top with capers or slices of gherkin.
● Remove stones from soaked cooked prunes and fill with liver pâté. Put on to cocktail sticks.
● Fill centre of celery sticks with liver pâté and cut into ½-inch lengths.

Sausages

● Tiny cocktail sausages can be grilled, fried or baked until crisp and golden brown. Put on to cocktail sticks and serve hot or cold. To make them more interesting put one of these savoury dips in the centre:
Blend equal quantities of mayonnaise (see page 36) and ketchup together and flavour with little made mustard.
Make a white sauce and flavour with tomato ketchup and mustard.
● Cut cooked sausages into small pieces and put on cocktail sticks with pieces of pineapple and gherkin.
● Blend sausage meat with little finely chopped cocktail onion and gherkin. Form into balls about the size of a hazel nut. Roll in egg and breadcrumbs and cheese mixed, or chopped nuts, and bake in the oven for about 10 minutes until crisp and brown and cooked.

Tongue and ham

● Cut tiny strips and roll into a cornet shape round soft cream cheese or cream cheese mixed with chopped gherkins, capers and parsley.
● Dice ham and put on cocktail sticks with pieces of fresh or canned pineapple or melon.
● Roll strips of tongue round tiny pieces of mustard pickle. Secure with cocktail sticks.

Bacon

● Roll small pieces of bacon round pieces of seasoned chicken liver. Secure with a cocktail stick and cook in a hot oven until the bacon is crisp.
● Make miniature portions of Devils on horseback or Angels on horseback (see page 46).
● Roll small pieces of bacon round cocktail-size cooked sausages or Frankfurter sausages—which have been split and filled with chutney or mustard pickle. Secure with cocktail sticks and cook until crisp and brown.
● Fry bacon rinds very slowly, until they are as crisp as possible. Cut or break into small lengths, toss in Parmesan cheese and serve little dishes of these instead of potato crisps.

Quick cocktail snacks with vegetables

Vegetables not only give colour but can provide a good variety of quick cocktail savouries.

Asparagus

● Lay cooked or well drained asparagus tips on slices of fresh brown bread and butter then roll firmly and cut into ½–1 inch lengths. The bread must be fresh and have the crusts removed.
● Arrange tiny tips on scrambled egg or chopped hard-boiled egg blended with mayonnaise (see page 36).

Beetroot

● Use as the basis of aspic canapés.
● Tiny pieces of beetroot can be used as garnish on cheese savouries or on small pieces of herring on biscuits or bread and butter.

Corn on the cob

● The cooked corn can be blended with cream cheese and Parmesan cheese as a filling for tiny pastry cases.
● Corn is delicious blended with ham butter (see page 55) as a topping for bread and butter.

Carrots

● Thin strips of carrot or tiny washed carrots can be served either by themselves or round a dish of cream cheese dip (see page 55).

For Cream cheese dip: blend 8 oz. soft cream cheese with 2 tablespoons cream, seasoning, and a little chopped gherkin and onion, put into small dish.

Celery

● Pieces of celery can be filled with soft cheese mixtures, or with ham, or with fish blended with mayonnaise or liver pâté (see pages 36, 41).

● Use celery curls as garnish for many savouries—very thin long strips of celery, put into very cold water for a few hours, will curl tightly. Dry well before serving.

Mushrooms

● Tiny cooked mushrooms can be reheated on crisp fried bread—do this on the serving plate.

Stuffed mushrooms can be made to look most attractive. Cook and allow mushrooms to cool. Carefully remove the stalks and pipe rosettes of cream cheese, or put cheese or ham butter (see this page), or scrambled egg in the centres. Lift on to biscuits, rounds of toast or buttered bread. Garnish with paprika or chopped parsley and put stalks back in position.

● Neat slices of lightly cooked or raw mushrooms can be used on aspic canapés.

Tomatoes

● Halve tiny tomatoes and mix the centre pulp with cream cheese and diced gherkin. Pile back into tomato cases and top with a rose shape of cream cheese.

● Halve tiny tomatoes and mix centre pulp with mayonnaise (see page 36) and chopped prawns. Pile into cases and garnish with prawns.

● Halve tiny tomatoes and mix centre pulp with minced meat or chicken. Season well and blend with beaten egg. Heat for about 5–8 minutes in the oven so tomatoes and filling are hot but tomato cases are unbroken. Serve at once.

Flavoured butters

The flavour of toasted snacks can be made much more interesting by mixing the butter with any of the following:

Anchovy Add a little anchovy essence or few chopped anchovies.

Cheese Allow 1–2 oz. finely grated cheese to the same amount of butter. Add a little mustard and seasoning.

Curry Add ½–1 teaspoon curry powder or curry paste to each ounce of butter.

Ham Add 1–2 oz. finely chopped ham to each ounce of butter.

Lobster Blend the red coral (roe of a hen lobster) to 2 oz. butter.

Parsley Add 1–2 teaspoons chopped parsley to each oz. butter with a little lemon juice.

Watercress Add 1–2 tablespoons finely chopped watercress to each oz. butter, season and add little lemon juice.

Savouries for Suppers and Light Meals

In the following pages are a selection of savouries that can be served as light meals. Some of them can be used as hors-d'œuvre, if a smaller portion is prepared.

Egg dishes

There is probably no more versatile food than an egg, which can be combined with other ingredients, or can make the basis of a good savoury by itself.

Whatever method you choose, do not overcook, for both flavour and texture are easily spoiled.

Baked eggs

cooking time 10–12 minutes

you will need for 4 servings:

1 oz. butter
4 eggs
seasoning
2 tablespoons cream

1 Grease 4 individual baking dishes with butter.
2 Break an egg into each, season well and cover with cream.
3 Bake slowly for about 10–12 minutes in a very moderate oven (350°F.—Gas Mark 3) until the eggs are just set.
4 Alternatively, steam in a pan of hot water.

Boiled eggs

cooking time 3½–10 minutes

you will need:

eggs
water

1. Put sufficient water into a saucepan to cover the eggs.
2. Bring the water to the boil, then lower the eggs gently into it.
3. Time carefully, and boil either 3½–4 minutes if you require a soft egg, 7–10 minutes for a firm egg.

10 ways of using boiled eggs

● Put hard-boiled eggs into cold water for 1 minute, then remove the shells. Coat with cheese sauce (see page 89) and grated cheese and brown under the grill.

● Follow instructions above, but put the eggs on a bed of cooked, sieved spinach.

● Shell soft-boiled eggs carefully by putting immediately into cold water for 1 minute, very gently tapping the shell and peeling. Coat with cheese sauce (see page 89) and put under the grill for just 1 minute.

● Shell the soft-boiled eggs as described above, coat with mushroom sauce, a layer of crumbs, and a little margarine; brown under the grill.

● Put layers of sliced hard-boiled egg and cooked sprigs of cauliflower into a shallow dish. Top with cheese sauce (see page 89) and brown under the grill.

● Make a quick tomato sauce (see page 91), put the shelled hard-boiled eggs in this and heat for just 1 minute. Serve on top of cooked rice.

● Halve hard-boiled eggs, remove yolks and mash them with a little butter, curry powder and chutney. Pipe or pile back again into white cases and serve on bed of lettuce.

● Halve hard-boiled eggs, remove yolk, mash with sardine, seasoning and a little lemon juice. Pile back again into white cases and serve on bed of lettuce.

● Hard-boiled eggs can also be served on spinach with a cheese sauce (see page 89).

● Shell hard-boiled eggs and arrange on crisp rounds of fried bread. Brush with a little melted butter, spread with a smooth chutney blended with a little curry powder. Sprinkle with crumbs, and put for 1 minute under a hot grill.

Egg and banana curry

cooking time 1 hour

you will need for 4 servings:

For the sauce:
1 onion, chopped
1 clove garlic, finely chopped
1 tablespoon oil or 1 oz. fat
2 dessertspoons curry powder
1 teaspoon curry paste
1 oz. cornflour
1 chicken stock cube
¾ pint water
1 apple, finely chopped
1 dessertspoon redcurrant jelly
juice ½ lemon
1 oz. sultanas

4 bananas
1 dessertspoon oil or ½ oz. fat
squeeze lemon juice
6–8 oz. long grain rice

To garnish:
3 eggs, hard-boiled
watercress

1. Fry the onion and garlic in the heated oil.
2. Stir in the curry powder, curry paste, cornflour and crumbled stock cube.
3. Cook for 3–4 minutes.
4. Add water, apple, jelly, lemon juice and sultanas.
5. Bring to the boil, stirring, and simmer gently for 1 hour.
6. Place the bananas loosened from but still in their skins in an ovenproof dish.
7. Brush each banana with the oil and sprinkle with lemon juice.
8. Bake for about 15 minutes in a moderate oven (375°F.—Gas Mark 4).
9. While the curry is cooking, boil the long grain rice by one of the methods given on page 70. Arrange on a hot dish with the curry on top, garnish with the hard-boiled eggs and watercress and serve the baked bananas separately.

Fried eggs

cooking time few minutes

you will need:

fat
eggs

1 Heat a little fat in the frying pan.
2 Break eggs into a saucer and slide into pan. Tilt the pan slightly as each egg goes in to keep the white a good shape.
3 If you like a crisp skin at the bottom of the eggs, turn the heat very low so that you get this without over-cooking the yolk.
4 If you like the top of the yolk covered with white, spoon a little fat over the yolk as it cooks.

10 ways to serve fried egg

1 The favourite and obvious way is *with bacon,* frying the bacon in the pan first, pushing to one side so that the eggs are actually fried in the bacon fat.

2 *On fried potato cakes*—make these by mashing potato with a little parsley, margarine, and seasoning, forming into cakes. Coat with flour, fry in pan until crisp and brown on either side. Top with a fried egg.

3 *On savoury fried rice*—fry a chopped onion in a little fat together with 2 chopped, skinned tomatoes, add 3 oz. cooked rice and seasoning. When hot, put into serving dish. Top with fried eggs.

4 *In a nest*—cut a circle in the centre of a slice of bread; fry one side until crisp and golden brown. Turn, carefully pour the egg into the centre hole, then fry the eggs and the second side of bread together.

5 *On sausage cakes*—form sausage meat into tiny cakes, adding mixed herbs if wished, then fry until crisp and golden brown, and top with fried eggs.

6 *Top cooked spaghetti* with fried eggs.

7 *Top baked beans* with fried eggs.

8 *Top fish cakes* with fried eggs.

9 *Top slices of fried corned beef* or luncheon meat with fried eggs.

10 *Tomato fried eggs*—fry tomatoes until just soft in pan, break eggs on to hot purée and fry gently until the white and yolk are just set.

Omelettes and fillings

For a substantial omelette allow 2 eggs per person; if making omelettes for a number of people do not try to cook too many eggs at a time—it is better to use a maximum of 4–6 (enough for an omelette for 2–3 people) in a 7–8 inch pan. If you cook a larger number the process is too slow and the eggs tend to toughen.

For a plain (or French) omelette, whisk the eggs lightly with seasoning, adding a little water if wished (allowing about 1 dessertspoon to each egg).

Heat a good knob of butter or spoonful of oil in the omelette pan, put in the eggs and allow to set lightly on the bottom, then work the mixture by loosening the omelette from the sides of the pan and tilt so that the liquid flows underneath. Put in the filling, fold or roll away from the handle and tip on to a hot dish.

For a soufflé omelette the whites and yolks are separated and the stiffly beaten whites folded into the beaten egg yolk. This tends to give a drier but of course thicker and lighter omelette and can be set more satisfactorily if given a minute or so cooking in the usual way and then set under a moderately hot grill, or finished cooking in the oven if the handle of the pan permits.

Adding filling to an omelette

There are two ways of doing this:

1 Cook the filling (i.e. bacon and tomato, or mixed vegetables, or fish) in a separate pan, add this to the eggs before folding the omelette.

2 The mixture can be cooked in the omelette pan in extra butter or oil. This has the advantage that you allow the eggs to absorb all the interesting flavour and use one pan only, but the omelette may stick and it is not easy to keep the omelette pan immaculate.

10 omelette fillings without cooking

1 *Anchovy* Add approximately 2 chopped anchovies per person to the beaten eggs. Be sparing with the salt. When the omelette has been folded, garnish with a lattice of anchovy fillets.

2 *Cheese* Allow 1–2 oz. grated cheese per person. Either mix with the beaten eggs (TAKE CARE THE OMELETTE IS NOT OVERCOOKED, OR IT WILL BECOME VERY TOUGH) or put the cheese in before folding.

3 *Beetroot* Allow approximately 1 tablespoon grated cooked beetroot per person. Put on top of the eggs when half set.

4 *Cream cheese* Put spoonfuls of cream cheese on to the half-set eggs and continue cooking.

5 *Cottage cheese* Put spoonfuls of cottage cheese on to the half-set eggs and continue cooking.

6 *Herb* Allow a good ¼ teaspoon dried herbs or 1–1½ teaspoons chopped fresh herbs per person. Add to the eggs when beaten.

7 *Prawns* Allow approximately 1–2 oz. finely chopped prawns per person. Add to the eggs when beating.

8 *Shrimps* Allow approximately 1–2 oz. finely chopped shrimps per person. Add to the eggs when beating.

9 *Smoked salmon* Allow ½–1 oz. smoked salmon per person. Add to the eggs when beating.

10 *Parsley* Allow 1–2 teaspoons chopped parsley per person and add to the eggs when beating.

10 luxury ways to serve an omelette

These are equally suitable for an hors-d'œuvre or a main dish:

1 *Asparagus* Fill the omelette with cooked fresh or canned asparagus tips and garnish with asparagus.

2 *Brandy omelette* Add a little brandy to the beaten eggs and serve the omelette sprinkled with a little warm brandy. This is particularly delicious if you also fill with chopped hot prawns or shrimps.

3 *Caviare* Put either black or red caviare into the omelette just before serving.

4 *Ham* Toss diced York ham and red peppers or smoked Parma ham in a little hot butter. Put into the omelette just before serving.

5 *Liver pâté* Put liver pâté into the omelette just before serving. Garnish with lemon.

6 *Mushrooms* Either add chopped fried mushrooms to the beaten eggs before cooking, or fill with mushrooms or a really creamy mushroom sauce.

7 *Prawns* Either toss the prawns in hot butter and a little brandy, or sherry, or heat in a really creamy sauce. Put into the omelette before folding.

8 *Smoked salmon* Add strips of smoked salmon to the omelette just before it is set.

9 *Omelette provençale* Fry diced aubergines, diced red peppers and/or green peppers and tomatoes in a little hot butter. Put into the omelette just before folding.

10 *Savoury cream* Beat a little Parmesan cheese into whipped cream, together with seasoning and finely chopped fresh herbs. Put into the omelette just before serving.

10 ways to make an omelette go further

1 *Bread* Allow approximately ½ slice of bread per person. Cut into small dice. Fry until crisp and golden brown in extra hot butter or oil. Pour the eggs over the crisp bread and cook in the usual way.

2 *Beans* Allow approximately 1 tablespoon cooked haricot or baked beans per person. Heat in a little hot butter or oil. Pour the eggs over the beans and cook in the usual way.

3 *Bacon* Use cheap pieces of bacon. Dice and fry in pan. Add the butter or oil. Heat and make the omelette in the usual way.

4 *Potato* Allow 1 sliced cooked potato per person. Fry in extra hot butter or oil. Pour the eggs over the crisp potatoes and cook in the usual way.

5 *Lyonnaise* Allow ½ onion, sliced, and 1 cooked potato per person. Fry steadily in hot oil or butter until the onion is transparent and tender. Add extra butter or oil if necessary. Pour on the eggs and cook in the usual way.

6 *Tomato* Allow 1–2 tomatoes per person. Cook tomatoes separately as they are inclined to make the omelette sticky. Add to the half-set omelette or to the beaten eggs and cook in the usual way.

7 *Mixed vegetable* Allow 1–2 tablespoons mixed cooked vegetables per person. Either heat in hot butter or oil in the omelette pan or heat separately. Add to beaten eggs or pour eggs over the hot vegetables. Cook in the usual way.

8 *Medley omelette* Fry a small quantity of diced cooked potato, onion, bacon and tomato. When soft, either put in the centre of egg mixture, or add to the beaten eggs.

9 *Add cornflour* Blend 2 teaspoons cornflour with a little milk or water and beat eggs into it.

10 Add a little *cooked pasta* or *cooked rice*.

Scrambled eggs

To scramble eggs

cooking time few minutes

you will need:

butter or margarine
eggs
seasoning
a little milk if desired*

*For a softer but less rich scrambled egg

1 Allow 1–2 eggs per person and up to 1 tablespoon milk.
2 Heat a good knob of butter or margarine in a saucepan, pour in the eggs beaten with the seasoning, and cook steadily, stirring well from the bottom until the mixture starts to thicken.
3 Turn the heat very low and continue cooking until set as firm as you like.

Note:

A very good way to cook scrambled egg with minimum waste and a very creamy consistency is in the top of a double saucepan or in a basin over hot water.

10 ways to make a scrambled egg savoury

1 *In bacon nests* Twist rashers of bacon into circles and grill or fry while scrambling the eggs. Put creamy scrambled egg in the centre and serve at once.

2 *With cheese* Add 1 oz. of grated cheese to each 1–2 eggs. Put in the cheese as the mixture starts to thicken.

3 *With ham* Heat finely diced ham in butter or margarine, then add eggs.

4 *With chicken* Heat finely diced cooked chicken in butter or margarine then add eggs and continue as for scrambled egg.

5 *With prawns or shrimps* Blend these with beaten eggs and cook gently in hot butter or margarine.

6 *With finnan haddock* Heat flaked fish in hot butter or margarine. Add beaten eggs and continue as scrambled egg.

7 *With vegetables* Heat 1–2 tablespoons cooked vegetables per person in hot butter or margarine. Add eggs and continue as for scrambled eggs.

8 *With crisp crumbs* Use rather more butter or margarine than usual and fry about 1 tablespoon crumbs per person in this until they are crisp and golden but not too brown. Add the eggs and continue as for scrambled eggs.

9 *With potato* Use rather more butter or margarine than usual and toss 1 diced potato in this for each person. Add scrambled eggs with a little chopped chives or parsley and cook in the usual way.

10 *With mixed vegetables* Allow 1 skinned tomato, 1 teaspoon chopped onion, a little chopped red or green pepper per person. Do not use milk with the egg. Put in rather more butter or margarine than usual. Toss the vegetables in this then add beaten and seasoned eggs and scramble in the usual way.

How to use poached eggs

To poach an egg

cooking time 3 minutes

you will need:

eggs
butter
seasoning

1 If using a poacher, put a piece of butter into each cup and allow to melt.
2 Carefully slide an egg into the cup and season.
3 Put the lid on the pan and allow the water to boil steadily for about 3½–4 minutes.
4 Slide the egg on to buttered toast.
5 If not using a poacher, bring a good ½ pint water to boil in a saucepan or frying pan.
6 Add 1 dessertspoon vinegar to prevent the egg whites spreading.
7 Add salt and slide the eggs into the boiling water.
8 Leave for 3 minutes, or until egg whites are set.
9 Carefully remove eggs with fish slice and put on toast.

10 ways with poached egg supper snacks

1 *Poached eggs Florentine* Put the poached eggs on to a bed of cooked spinach.

2 *Poached eggs mornay* Put the poached eggs on to buttered toast, coat with cheese sauce (see page 89) and brown for 1 minute under a hot grill.

3 *Poached egg au gratin* Put the poached eggs on to hot buttered toast, top with a good layer of breadcrumbs and grated cheese, then brown for 1 minute under the grill.

4 *Savoury poached eggs* Make a ratatouille (see page 76) and add just a little extra liquid. Cook the ratatouille mixture in a rather wide pan or deep frying pan. Drop the eggs into this and allow to set, or poach separately and serve on top of each portion of mixed vegetables.

5 *Poached eggs in wine* Heat cheap red wine in a shallow pan and poach the eggs in this.

6 *Poached eggs on gammon* Grill slices of gammon, top with grilled tomatoes and poached eggs.

7 *Poached eggs on haddock* Cook portions of finnan haddock in water or milk and top each with a poached egg.

8 *Tomato poached eggs* Put either tomato juice, tomato soup or tomato purée into a wide pan or deep frying pan. Break the eggs into this and poach in the usual way. Serve with crisp toast or French bread.

9 *Poached egg in consommé* Although this is generally served as a soup, it can also be a light savoury. Make the consommé (see page 15), adding a little sherry, but cooking in either a wide saucepan or deep frying pan. Poach the eggs in this and serve in soup cups with French bread.

10 *Scotch pancakes topped with poached egg* Make Scotch pancakes (see page 81) and top with poached eggs.

Soufflés can be easy

A soufflé sounds extremely difficult but it is, in fact, very easy. Here are the rules to follow:

For a hot soufflé When adding the egg yolks make sure the sauce or other purée is sufficiently cool so the yolks will not curdle.

Fold the egg whites in very gently so you do not lose the fluffy texture.

Preparing dish for hot soufflé Providing the mixture only comes about two-thirds of the way up the dish before being cooked, there is no need for any special preparation. You can, however, put band of buttered paper to support the weight of the mixture as it rises, if the dish is to be filled very lavishly. It does, as a matter of fact, make a very attractive looking soufflé if it has risen high above the top.

Serving hot soufflés Time the cooking of a soufflé so it can be served the moment it comes out of the oven.

Cold soufflés When adding the egg whites in a cold soufflé, make absolutely certain that the jellied mixture is partially set so that it will hold the egg whites in position. If it is very runny, the egg whites float to the top and you will not have an even texture.

Preparing the dish for cold soufflés This should, of course, be done as suggested above, by putting a band of paper round the top (see Ham and mushroom soufflé, page 62).

Cheese and potato soufflé

cooking time 55 minutes

you will need:

1 lb. potatoes
2–3 oz. grated cheese
1 oz. margarine
2 tablespoons milk
1 teaspoon finely chopped chives or grated onion
seasoning
2 eggs or 1 egg and 1 teaspoon baking powder

1 Cook, drain and mash the potatoes well.
2 Beat in the margarine, milk, chives and cheese, then season well.
3 Stir in the well-beaten egg yolks and, when the mixture is cool, FOLD in the stiffly beaten egg whites and the baking powder, if this is being used.
4 Put into a well-greased soufflé dish and bake in the centre of a moderately hot oven (400°F.—Gas Mark 5) for 30 minutes until well risen and crisp and brown on top.

Corn cob soufflé

cooking time 45 minutes–1 hour

you will need for 4 servings:

2–3 corn cobs or frozen or canned corn on the cob
½ pint milk
1 teaspoon flour
1 teaspoon cornflour
1 oz. margarine
seasoning
2–3 eggs
4 oz. grated cheese
a little chopped parsley or chives

1 Boil cobs until tender and scrape corn from the cobs.
2 Make the white sauce from the milk, flour, cornflour and margarine, season and remove from the heat.
3 Add the beaten egg yolks, 3 oz. of the cheese, chopped parsley or chives and corn.
4 Fold in the stiffly beaten whites of eggs.
5 Put into an ovenproof dish, sprinkle with the rest of the cheese, dot with margarine.
6 Bake in a very moderate oven (350°F.—Gas Mark 3) for 30–45 minutes until light brown.

Ham soufflé

cooking time 35–40 minutes

you will need:

4 oz. cooked ham
1 oz. butter or margarine
¾ oz. flour
¼ pint milk
1 oz. grated cheese, optional
4 eggs or 3 yolks and 4 whites
seasoning
good pinch herbs

1 Chop the ham into small pieces, heat the butter then stir in the flour.
2 Cook for a few minutes then gradually add the milk.
3 Bring to the boil and cook until smooth and thick.
4 Add the grated cheese, ham, seasoning, herbs and egg yolks.
5 Whisk the egg whites until stiff.
6 Fold egg whites into the ham mixture.
7 Put into a prepared soufflé dish and bake for approximately 25–30 minutes in the centre of a moderately hot oven (400°F.—Gas Mark 5).

Note:

This soufflé is an excellent main dish, for the ham makes it filling as well as nourishing.

Salmon rice soufflé

cooking time 40 minutes

you will need for 4 servings:

1 oz. margarine
1 oz. flour
½ pint milk
1 medium can pink salmon
2 oz. long-grain rice, cooked
3 eggs
seasoning

1 Make a sauce of the margarine, flour and milk.
2 Add can of salmon, the rice, then stir in the egg yolks and the stiffly beaten egg whites. Season.
3 Put into the prepared soufflé dish and bake for approximately 30 minutes in the centre of a moderate oven (375°F.—Gas Mark 4).

Spinach soufflé

cooking time 40–50 minutes

you will need for 4 servings:

8 oz. cooked spinach
1½ oz. butter
½ oz. flour
2½ tablespoons milk
salt and pepper
pinch nutmeg
5 tablespoons sieved breadcrumbs
6 eggs
¼ pint whipped cream

1 Drain the spinach as dry as possible and chop very finely.
2 Make a thick cream sauce of the butter, flour and milk.
3 Add seasonings and nutmeg and cool.
4 Add spinach and half the breadcrumbs and mix thoroughly.
5 Beat egg yolks lightly and the egg whites stiffly.
6 Add the yolks and cream to the spinach mixture, then fold in the egg whites.
7 Butter a soufflé dish and scatter with remaining crumbs.
8 Pour in the mixture which should fill two-thirds of the dish.
9 Bake for 30–45 minutes in a pan of hot water in a moderate oven (375°F.—Gas Mark 4).

Ham and mushroom soufflé

cooking time 15 minutes

you will need for 4 servings:

1 packet mushroom soup
½ pint water
4 oz. finely chopped ham
½ oz. powdered gelatine
2 egg whites
2 hard-boiled eggs
1 tablespoon chopped parsley
2 tablespoons whipped cream
seasoning

1 Make up mushroom soup with only ½ pint water.
2 Simmer as detailed on the packet.
3 Soften the gelatine in 1 tablespoon water then dissolve in the hot mushroom soup; cool and fold in cream, chopped ham, seasoning and the stiffly beaten egg whites.
4 Pour into 1 pint soufflé dish prepared with a band of buttered paper tied firmly round the outside, and which should stand up several inches above the top of the dish.
5 Leave until firm.
6 Remove paper.
7 Chop 1 hard-boiled egg and sprinkle this with the chopped parsley round edge of soufflé.
8 Cut remaining egg into 8 fingers and arrange in centre.

Light cheese snacks

Cheese is such an adaptable savoury in that it is particularly suitable for the end of a meal or for a cocktail party and you will find most of the cheese recipes in this section are equally suitable for a main dish savoury if served in rather larger quantities.

Cheese kabobs

cooking time approximately 3 minutes

you will need:

Cheddar cheese
pieces of tomato
small squares of buttered bread
bacon
pickled onions

1 Put cubes of cheese, pieces of tomato, buttered bread, bacon, and pickled onions alternately on to skewers.
2 Cover wire rack on grill pan with foil.
3 Place kabobs on foil and grill approximately 3 minutes, turning once.

Cheese and shellfish kabobs

cooking time few minutes

you will need:

Cheddar cheese
large prawns or shrimps
butter
quarters of lemon

1 Put cubes of cheese, large prawns or shrimps, and quarters of lemon alternately on skewers.

2 Brush the prawns or shrimps with a little melted butter.
3 Cover wire rack on grill pan with foil.
4 Place kabobs on foil and grill approximately 3 minutes, turning once.

Fruit cheese kabobs

cooking time approximately 3 minutes

you will need:

Cheddar cheese
cubes dessert or fairly sweet apple
banana
pineapple
butter

1 Put cubes of cheese, apple, banana and pineapple alternately on to skewers.
2 Brush with a very little melted butter.
3 Cover wire rack on grill pan with foil.
4 Place kabobs on foil and grill for approximately 3 minutes, turning once.

Spanish cheese kabobs

cooking time approximately 3 minutes

you will need:

Cheddar cheese
pieces green pepper
banana
tomato

1 Put cubes of cheese, pieces of green pepper, banana and tomato alternately on to skewers.
2 Cover wire rack on grill pan with foil.
3 Place kabobs on foil and grill approximately 3 minutes, turning once.

Cheese and prawn moulds

cooking time few minutes

you will need for 4 servings:

½ pint aspic jelly
6 oz. peeled prawns
6 large radishes
8 oz. grated Cheddar cheese
½ lb. skinned tomatoes
pinch pepper
¼ teaspoon salt
few drops Tabasco sauce
3 tablespoons cream

1 Pour enough aspic jelly into bottom of fish-shaped jelly mould (or 1¾-pint ring mould) to cover bottom thinly.
2 Allow to set.
3 Arrange some of the prawns in bottom of mould to represent scales of fish and place slices of radish for eyes, set in a little more aspic jelly.
4 Chop remaining radishes and prawns and add to cheese.
5 Remove seeds from tomatoes and chop pulp finely.
6 Stir into cheese mixture with salt and Tabasco sauce.
7 Fold in remaining aspic and cream.
8 Spoon into mould and allow to set, preferably chilling in refrigerator.
9 Warm mould slightly and turn out sharply on to serving dish.
10 Serve with crisp green salad.

Cheese charlotte

cooking time few minutes

you will need for 4 servings:

2 oz. Cheddar cheese
few slices thinly cut brown and white bread and butter
3 eggs
2 teaspoons powdered gelatine
3 tablespoons water
¼ pint cream or evaporated milk
2 oz. cream cheese
½ teaspoon French mustard
pinch salt and cayenne

To garnish:
almonds
watercress

1 Grate Cheddar cheese.
2 Line a buttered charlotte mould or 5-inch cake tin with the bread, using alternate fingers of white and brown.
3 Whisk the egg yolks until thick and add the gelatine first soaked then dissolved in the very hot water.
4 Stir in the cream or evaporated milk, cheeses and seasonings, then fold in the stiffly whipped whites.
5 Turn the mixture into the charlotte mould and chill.
6 Turn out and serve garnished with watercress and decorated with almonds.

Fish and meat snacks

These will not be as substantial as a main dish, but pieces of left-over chicken, meat, or bacon can be used to make a very good savoury.

To cook cod's roe

cooking time 20 minutes

1 Wash the roe and steam or boil this for approximately 20 minutes.
2 Cut into slices and fry in a little fat until brown.
3 After steaming the roe, skin it, add seasoning, and spread on the slices of bread and butter.

Fried herring roes

cooking time few minutes

you will need:

herring roes (fresh, canned or frozen)
flour
seasoning
fat for frying

To garnish:
parsley
paprika or cayenne

1 Allow the roes to defrost, then dry well on plenty of kitchen paper.
2 Roll in enough flour to coat thoroughly, seasoning this flour well.
3 Fry for a few minutes only in hot fat.
4 Garnish with parsley and paprika or cayenne; serve with vegetables or on hot buttered toast.

Fish sticks mornay

cooking time approximately 10 minutes

you will need:

1 packet frozen fish sticks
little grated cheese
tomatoes
fat for frying

1 Separate the fish sticks and roll in grated cheese.
2 Halve the toamtoes.
3 Fry the cheese coated fish sticks, then the tomatoes in hot fat.*

*If preferred, these can be baked on a greased tin in the oven or brushed with melted fat after coating with cheese and cooked under a hot grill, turning over then coating with more cheese and melted fat

Bacon buntings

cooking time 4 minutes

you will need for 3 servings:

6 sausages, cooked
1 tablespoon chutney
6 middle rashers bacon

1 Split the cooked sausages and fill with chutney, pickle or mustard.
2 Trim the bacon rashers and stretch.
3 Wind each rasher spirally around the sausages and hold in place with a small wooden cocktail stick.
4 Put under the grill.
5 Cook and turn about four minutes.

Bacon and cheese

cooking time few minutes

you will need:

rashers bacon
slices of cheese—preferably Cheddar

1 When frying bacon a slice of cheese is a very delicious accompaniment—add when the bacon is nearly cooked, and fry for a moment or so until the cheese starts to melt.
2 Then lift out and serve on top of the rashers of bacon.

Bacon medallions

cooking time 15–20 minutes

you will need for 4 servings:

4 thick middle rashers bacon
3 oz. margarine or bacon fat
1 8-oz. can mushrooms
1 red pepper
4 oz. runner beans
4 tomatoes
3 oz. cooked rice

To garnish:
hard-boiled egg
parsley
lemon

1 Remove rind from bacon and cut fat at $\frac{1}{2}$-inch intervals.
2 Put on grid of grill pan with halved tomatoes in the pan.
3 Brush with melted fat or margarine and cook under grill until tender and the fat golden brown.
4 Meanwhile, heat rest of fat in pan and cook mushrooms and thinly sliced red pepper until tender.
5 Add beans.
6 Saving a small amount of this mixture for garnish, bind rest with the cooked rice. Heat well and form into ring on hot dish.
7 Chop egg and parsley together.
8 Arrange slices of bacon and halved tomatoes in centre of rice ring.
9 Top one end of each bacon slice with slice lemon and the egg mixture and the other end with mushroom mixture, but leave centre clear as the pink of the bacon is so inviting.

Bacon and mushroom batter

cooking time 40 minutes

you will need for 4 servings:

4 oz. medium mushrooms
1 oz. butter
8 rashers lean bacon
½ pint batter (see page 80)
seasoning

1 Put the mushrooms into an ovenproof dish, a dab of butter on each, and season well.
2 Roll the rashers, arrange in the dish and cook in a hot oven (450°F.—Gas Mark 7) for 10 minutes.
3 Pour in the batter and return to the oven for about 30 minutes.
4 Serve at once.

Hot bacon and oat cobbler

cooking time 30 minutes

you will need for 4 servings:

1 packet vegetable soup
scant 1 pint water
3–4 rashers bacon (cut small and well fried)
6 oz. self-raising flour
2 oz. rolled oats
salt and pepper
2 oz. butter or margarine
1 egg
milk (to make ¼ pint with egg)
little grated cheese

1 Cook the vegetable soup as instructed on the packet but using just under 1 pint of water.
2 Prepare bacon.
3 Sieve flour and seasonings into basin.
4 Add oats and mix thoroughly.
5 Rub butter in lightly.
6 Add bacon.
7 Beat egg and milk together and pour over dry ingredients, mixing with a broad-bladed knife.
8 Roll out on floured board to about ½ inch thick and cut into rounds.
9 Put the vegetable soup into a casserole and heat for about 10 minutes in a moderately hot oven (400°F.—Gas Mark 5).
10 Arrange rounds of scone on top and sprinkle with grated cheese to give an attractive glaze.
11 Bake for approximately 12–15 minutes in a hot oven (450°F.—Gas Mark 7).

Bacon and pineapple loaf

cooking time 1 hour

you will need for 4 servings:

12 oz. bacon
2 oz. fine breadcrumbs
salt and pepper
pinch mixed herbs
1 egg
1 15-oz. can pineapple slices

To garnish:
watercress

1 Mince or chop bacon finely.
2 Add breadcrumbs, seasoning, a very small pinch of mixed herbs, the egg and about a tablespoon pineapple syrup from the can.
3 Blend well and put into a well-greased loaf tin.
4 Cover with greased paper and bake for approximately 1 hour in the centre of a moderate oven (375°F.—Gas Mark 4).
5 Turn out carefully and garnish with pineapple slices—replace for a few minutes in the oven to heat the pineapple then top with sprigs of watercress.

Peas with bacon

cooking time 20 minutes

you will need for 4 servings:

4 rashers bacon
2 lb. peas
½ teaspoon salt

1 Dice bacon and fry in medium pan with tightly fitting lid over low heat until crisp.
2 Remove from heat and drain all but 1 tablespoon fat from the pan.
3 Add peas and remaining ingredients.
4 Cook, covered, over medium heat for 10–15 minutes, or until peas are just tender.

Savoury bacon dip

no cooking

you will need:

10 oz. cottage or cream cheese
8 oz. minced or chopped cooked bacon
½ grated or minced onion
1 tablespoon chopped parsley
¼ teaspoon garlic salt
¼ teaspoon pepper
¼ teaspoon salt

1 Sieve the cottage cheese or mash the cheese into a basin and add all the ingredients.
2 Blend well and allow to stand for about an hour.
3 Re-season to taste.
4 Serve with potato crisps, small biscuits or celery sticks.

Poultry snacks

Chicken cream

cooking time 15 minutes

you will need for 4 servings:

1 packet cream of chicken soup powder
¾ pint milk
¼ oz. powdered gelatine
1 tablespoon water
⅛ pint water or white stock
1 lb. cooked chicken (as much breast as possible)
1–2 eggs
¼ pint evaporated milk
1 tablespoon sherry
seasoning

1 Blend the soup with the milk and cook gently.
2 Dissolve the gelatine in the hot stock, first softening it in the tablespoon of water.
3 Mix together the soup and the gelatine liquid, allow this to cool and then add the chicken, beaten egg, evaporated milk and sherry.
4 Taste and season well.
5 Pour into rinsed mould or basin and allow to set.
6 Serve with plain green salad and fingers of toast.

Chicken flan

cooking time 50 minutes

you will need:

6–8 oz. flan or short-crust pastry (see page 82)
1 onion, chopped
1 small red or green pepper, finely chopped
little fat
6 oz. minced chicken
4 oz. coarsely grated Cheddar cheese
2 tablespoons chopped parsley
salt and pepper
1 egg
¼ pint milk

1 Prepare the flan case and bake it 'blind' (see page 84).
2 Toss the onion and pepper in a little hot fat.
3 Mix with the chicken, cheese and parsley.
4 Turn into the pastry case after thoroughly seasoning.
5 Beat the egg into the milk, season and pour into the flan case.
6 Bake in a moderate oven (375°F.—Gas Mark 4) for approximately 30 minutes.

Fricassée of chicken breasts

cooking time 45 minutes–1 hour

you will need for 4 servings:

4 frozen chicken breasts
1 oz. butter or margarine
1 oz. flour
¾ pint milk
seasoning
2 tablespoons cream

1 Allow chicken breasts to defrost at room temperature.
2 Make the sauce with the butter, flour and milk; season well.
3 Put in the chicken breasts and cook very slowly in a covered pan for approximately 35–45 minutes until tender.
4 Stir in the cream and re-season if wished.
5 Serve with cooked rice or crisp toast.

Variations:

Chicken and mushroom fricassée
As recipe above but use 2 oz. butter or margarine and fry 2–4 oz. chopped mushrooms before making the sauce—this gives a slightly darker mixture. If you prefer a lighter sauce, follow the above recipe, cooking the chicken breasts in the sauce, then fry the mushrooms SEPARATELY and stir into the sauce just before serving.

Golden chicken fricassée
Follow instructions for Fricassée of chicken breasts, but blend the yokes of 2 eggs or 2 whole eggs with the cream, add to the sauce and cook very gently WITHOUT BOILING for a few minutes.

Chicken à la King

cooking time 10–15 minutes

you will need for 4 servings:

1 sliced red pepper
2 oz. mushrooms, sliced
2 oz. butter
½ pint white sauce (see page 92) made partly with chicken stock
12 oz. diced cooked chicken
seasoning
1 tablespoon olives
4 slices toast

To garnish:
olives

1 Fry pepper and mushrooms in butter or cook under grill until soft.
2 Stir into sauce with other ingredients.
3 Pile on to toast.
4 Garnish with olives.

Chicken medley nest

cooking time 35 minutes

you will need for 4 servings:

1 lb. potatoes
knob butter
2 tablespoons milk
salt and pepper

For the filling:
2 tablespoons oil or 2 oz. butter
1 onion, chopped
½ oz. cornflour or 1 oz. flour
½ pint milk
salt and pepper
8 oz. cooked chicken
4 oz. cooked ham
4 oz. sweet corn or cooked carrots
1 dessertspoon chopped parsley

1 Cook the potatoes in boiling salted water until tender.
2 Mash with butter, milk and seasoning to taste.
3 Pipe a thick border of creamed potato round the edge of a large fireproof dish. Brush with a little milk and brown under the grill.
4 To prepare the filling, heat the oil or butter and fry the onion until tender.
5 Add flour or cornflour and cook 1 minute.
6 Add milk, bring to the boil and cook 3 minutes, stirring all the time. Season to taste.
7 Add chicken, ham, sweet corn or carrots, and parsley and mix well.
8 Cook a further 3 minutes to heat through.
9 Pile into the potato shell and serve.

Turkey or chicken creole

cooking time 20 minutes

you will need for 4 servings:

4 oz. rice
1 oz. fat
1 green pepper, sliced
¼ pint turkey or chicken stock
1 head celery (or can celery)
about 12 oz. sliced cooked turkey or chicken meat
seasoning

To garnish:
3 large tomatoes, sliced

1 Cook rice in boiling salted water.
2 Heat fat and toss in it the sliced pepper and celery cut in large pieces.
3 Add stock.
4 Simmer until vegetables are nearly cooked.
5 Add turkey and season well.
6 When thoroughly hot, arrange on bed of the cooked rice.
7 Garnish with sliced tomato.

Snacks with meat

Baked corned beef with barbecue sauce

cooking time 30 minutes

you will need for 4 servings:

1 12-oz. can corned beef
a little dripping or margarine

For the sauce:
¼ pint boiling water
1 teaspoon curry powder
1 teaspoon Worcestershire sauce
4 teaspoons tomato sauce
seasoning
1 teaspoon brown sugar
2 tablespoons tiny cocktail or pickling onions, optional

1 Grease a baking dish and put the corned beef into this, covering the top with greased paper.
2 Heat for about 15 minutes in a moderately hot oven (400°F.—Gas Mark 5), then remove the paper.
3 Meanwhile, blend all the ingredients for the sauce together.
4 Pour this over the corned beef and cook for a further 15 minutes, basting the meat several times with the sauce.

Corned beef scotch eggs

cooking time 15–20 minutes

you will need for 4 servings:

For the sauce:
1 oz. margarine
1 oz. flour
¼ pint milk or stock
3 oz. breadcrumbs
1 12-oz. can corned beef
seasoning
6 hard-boiled eggs
1 egg, beaten
fat for frying

1 To make the sauce, heat the margarine in the pan, stir in the flour and cook for 2 minutes, then add the liquid.
2 Bring to the boil and cook until thick.
3 Add most of the breadcrumbs and the flaked corned beef.
4 Season well.
5 Press the mixture round the outside of the shelled hard-boiled eggs.
6 When neatly shaped, brush with beaten egg, toss carefully in remaining breadcrumbs and fry until crisp and golden brown.

Hamburgers

cooking time 10–30 minutes

you will need for 4 servings:

1 lb. minced beef
1 large or 2 medium onions, grated
seasoning
½ teaspoon mixed herbs
1 heaped teaspoon chopped parsley
1 teaspoon Worcestershire sauce
1 large potato

1 Put meat into a basin, add grated onion, seasoning, herbs, parsley and sauce.
2 Grate in raw peeled potato.
3 Mix thoroughly together. There will be no need to add liquid as the potato binds the mixture together.
4 Form into large cakes* and either fry steadily in hot fat for about 10 minutes or bake on a well greased tin for about 25–30 minutes in a moderately hot oven (400°F.—Gas Mark 5).
5 Serve hot and, if wished, with a fried egg on top.

*The cakes can be floured or tossed in crisp breadcrumbs before cooking—don't try to turn into a neat rissole shape

Hamburger 'hot pot'

cooking time 15 minutes

you will need:

1 large packet mixed frozen vegetables
1 can tomato soup
1 large packet frozen hamburgers
seasoning

To garnish:
chopped parsley
4 slices toast

1 Put the frozen vegetables into about ¼ inch salted water and cook for about 4 minutes.
2 Add the tomato soup and heat for a few minutes, stir briskly, then add the hamburgers, cook gently for about 8 minutes and season. If possible use a fairly large saucepan or even a frying pan, so that the hamburgers do not get broken in cooking.
3 Serve on a hot dish with a border of triangles of crisp toast, and topped with chopped parsley.

Hamburgers and sauce

cooking time 10 minutes

you will need for 4 servings:

8 oz. minced beef
1 chopped onion
2 oz. rolled oats
1 egg
2 oz. dripping or fat
salt and pepper
tomato sauce (see page 91)

To garnish:
green pepper, cut in rings
tomatoes, cut in halves

1 Mix together the mince, onion, oats, egg and seasoning and divide into 4–8 round cakes.
2 Score the tops with the back of a knife.
3 Heat the dripping in a frying pan and cook the hamburgers for a few minutes on both sides.
4 Reduce the heat and cook gently for 5 minutes until they are cooked through.
5 Garnish with some gently fried pepper rings, tomato halves and serve with tomato sauce.

Ham loaf de luxe

cooking time 35 minutes

you will need for 4 servings:

approximately 10 oz. cooked ham
2 teaspoons grated onion or chopped chives
2 teaspoons chopped parsley
1 can corn, or corn and peppers
1 egg to bind or thick sauce made from ½ oz. flour ½ oz. butter ⅛ pint milk
1 tablespoon cream or top of milk
seasoning
2 hard-boiled eggs

1 Mince the ham with the onion, parsley, drained corn or corn and peppers, and the egg or sauce and cream.
2 Season lightly and press half the mixture into a greased loaf tin.
3 Arrange the 2 shelled eggs on top of this and cover with the rest of the mixture.
4 Put a piece of foil or greaseproof paper over the mixture and bake for approximately 35 minutes in the centre of a moderate oven (375°F.—Gas Mark 4).
5 Turn out and serve hot.

Savoury pruneburgers

cooking time 10 minutes

you will need for 4 servings:

seasoning
12 oz. minced beef
2 oz. butter or margarine
1 oz. flour
⅓ pint milk
1 tablespoon onions, finely chopped
2–3 cooked prunes, chopped
1–2 oz. almonds, toasted and slivered
8 fingers toast

To garnish:
8 prunes
parsley

1 Add seasoning to meat.
2 Melt butter in pan.
3 Add beef, cook for 2 minutes.

4 Push meat to one side.
5 Add flour to hot butter; stir until blended.
6 Add milk gradually, stirring constantly until sauce is thick and smooth.
7 Add onion and stir well.
8 Just before serving, stir in prunes and almonds.
9 Serve on hot toast or the curry-buttered bun halves (see recipe below).
10 Garnish with sprigs of fresh parsley and hot plumped prunes.

Curry-buttered buns

cooking time few minutes

you will need:

4 soft rolls
2 oz. butter or margarine
⅛ teaspoon curry powder

1 Halve and toast buns.
2 Combine butter and curry powder, spread on buns.

Sausage croquettes

cooking time about 8 minutes

you will need for 4 servings:

1 lb. pork sausage meat
4 oz. chopped bacon
salt
pepper
1 beaten egg
breadcrumbs
3 oz. lard or fat
2 large cooking apples

1 Mix the sausage meat with the bacon and seasoning.
2 Form into 8 cork shapes.
3 Dip in the beaten egg and toss in breadcrumbs.
4 Fry in hot fat for about 8 minutes.
5 Core but do not peel the apples, cut into slices about ⅓ inch thick and fry.
6 Serve with potato croquettes.

Devilled sausages

cooking time few minutes

you will need for 4 servings:

1½ oz. butter or margarine
1 teaspoon curry powder
1 tablespoon chutney
seasoning
8 oz. beef sausages
fried bread or toast fingers

1 Cream butter, add curry powder, chutney and seasoning.
2 Spread over sausages.
3 Put under grill and heat thoroughly.
4 Serve on hot toast or fried bread fingers.

Sausages splits

cooking time 20–30 minutes

you will need for 4 servings:

1 lb. pork sausages
8 oz. mashed potato
½–1 tablespoon horseradish sauce
1 tablespoon tomato ketchup
garlic salt
cayenne

To garnish:
chopped parsley

1 Cook sausages by boiling, grilling or frying. Allow to get cold.
2 Cook potatoes and mash.
3 Beat in the horseradish sauce, ketchup, garlic salt and cayenne.
4 Put this into a forcing bag.
5 Cut each cold sausage down its length but not quite into 2 parts and open out flat on a serving dish.
6 Pipe the savoury mixture down the centre of each sausage and top with chopped parsley.
7 Serve on a salad platter.

Surprise sausages

cooking time 30 minutes

you will need for 4 servings:

4 pork sausages
½–1 tablespoon made mustard
2 oz. Cheddar cheese
4 rashers bacon
salt and pepper

1 Slit the sausages lengthways but do not cut through.
2 Spread each slit with mustard.
3 Cut cheese into wedges and stuff a piece into each sausage.
4 Wrap each sausage in a bacon rasher, season and fasten in place with a cocktail stick.
5 Put in roasting tin, season and cover with lid or foil.
6 Bake in a moderate oven (375°F.—Gas Mark 4) for 30 minutes.
7 Serve with salad.

Savouries with Rice and Pasta

Rice and pasta are extremely sustaining, so they make a good basis for interesting and economical savouries. There are certain rules in cooking both rice and pasta which give a very much better result.

How to cook rice

1 Allow 2 pints water, 1 teaspoon salt to each 4 oz. rice. Bring the water to the boil. Add salt and rice. Cook steadily until tender. This will depend on the type of rice but test after about 12–15 minutes. Strain and if you wish to separate the grains pour either boiling or cold water through them, then spread on a flat tray to dry.

2 To each oz. of rice allow 2 fluid oz. of water (or to 1 cup rice allow 2 cups water). Put the rice, water and salt to taste in a saucepan. Bring to the boil. Stir briskly. Cover with a tightly fitting lid, lower the heat and allow to simmer for approximately 14–15 minutes, by which time the water will all be absorbed and the grains quite separate.

To cook pasta

Always allow plenty of water—you need a minimum of 2 pints to each 4 oz. pasta—with approximately 1 teaspoon salt. Add the pasta to the boiling water. Do no overcook—it is ready when it just yields to a fork against the side of the pan. Naturally tastes vary as to how soft the pasta should be, but it has more flavour if it is not too soft.

Brown rice and cheese

cooking time 35 minutes

you will need for 4 servings:

2 eggs
½ pint milk
4 oz. grated cheese
seasoning
4 oz. cooked brown rice

To garnish:
paprika
chopped parsley

1 Beat the eggs.
2 Pour on the milk, add the grated cheese and seasoning and bake for approximately 35 minutes in the centre of a moderate oven (375°F.—Gas Mark 4).
3 Garnish with chopped parsley and paprika. Serve with rice.

Cream cheese noodles

cooking time 50 minutes

you will need for 4 servings:

6 oz. noodles
seasoning
6–8 oz. cottage or cream cheese
1 oz. grated Parmesan cheese
2 oz. butter
2 tablespoons parsley
1 small onion, chopped
3 eggs

1 Cook the noodles until tender in boiling salted water.
2 Strain.
3 Add all the other ingredients.
4 Bake in a greased casserole for approximately 30 minutes in the centre of a moderate oven (375°F.—Gas Mark 4).

Egg and savoury rice

cooking time 20 minutes

you will need for 4 servings:

3 oz. long-grain rice
salad cream (see page 91)
1 oz. sultanas
1 teaspoon capers
lemon juice
4 hard-boiled eggs

To garnish:
watercress
2–4 oz. shrimps
3 tomatoes

1 Cook the rice (see this page).
2 When hot mix with salad cream, sultanas, capers and lemon juice.
3 Cool.
4 Place in shallow dish after blending with capers and lemon juice.
5 Garnish with watercress, sliced tomatoes and shrimps.

Harlequin rice

cooking time 50 minutes–1 hour

you will need for 4 servings:

2 onions, sliced
1 oz. dripping or fat
1 large can tomatoes
½ pint apple juice or stock
pinch salt
pinch pepper
few drops hot sauce (chilli or Tabasco)
½ clove garlic, minced
6 oz. rice, uncooked
2 tablespoons olives, sliced

1. Brown onions in dripping or fat.
2. Add remaining ingredients and pour into shallow baking pan.
3. Cover.
4. Bake in a very moderate oven (350°F.—Gas Mark 3) for 40–50 minutes until rice is tender.
5. Toss rice mixture lightly with fork twice during last 20 minutes of cooking.

Kedgeree

cooking time 25–30 minutes

you will need for 4 servings:

6–8 oz. rice
12 oz. flaked cooked white or smoked fish
a little cream or milk
2 oz. butter
2 hard-boiled eggs
seasoning

1. Cook the rice until just tender (see page 70).
2. Strain and put into the pan with the fish, the cream and the butter.
3. Heat gently, seasoning well, then add the chopped hard-boiled egg white, pile in a hot dish, and top with the chopped yolk.

Macaroni alla bebe

cooking time 25–30 minutes

you will need for 4 servings:

6 oz. macaroni
about 4 oz. chopped cooked tongue*
4 oz. chopped cooked chicken
2–4 oz. mushrooms
1 oz. butter
½ pint béchamel or white sauce (see page 91)
1–2 tablespoons cream (optional)
little grated cheese

*Small lambs' tongues excellent in this recipe—you can use all ham or all tongue

1. Boil the macaroni in salted water until tender.
2. Meanwhile prepare the meat mixture.
3. Fry the chopped mushrooms in the butter, add the chopped tongue and chicken, then stir in the béchamel or white sauce.
4. Heat together, stirring well, and take care the mixture is not too thick—if necessary, add a little milk.
5. Mix with the strained macaroni, stir in a small quantity of the grated cheese and the cream.
6. Taste and re-season if necessary.
7. Put into a shallow entrée dish, sprinkle grated cheese on top and brown under a hot grill.

Macaroni with bacon and wine sauce

cooking time 15 minutes

you will need for 4 servings:

6 oz. quick-cooking macaroni
4 oz. bacon
⅛ pint white wine
salt and pepper
1 egg yolk
⅛ pint cream
Parmesan cheese

1. Cook macaroni in boiling salted water until tender.
2. Strain.
3. Meanwhile dice and fry the bacon until just crisp, add the wine and good shake of pepper.
4. Stir in the cooked macaroni, then the well beaten egg and cream.
5. Mix thoroughly, heat gently, taste and re-season as necessary.
6. Serve with grated Parmesan cheese.

Macaroni and mushroom loaf

cooking time 50 minutes

you will need for 4 servings:

4 oz. cooked macaroni or spaghetti
2 oz. margarine
1 small onion
2 large tomatoes
4 oz. mushrooms
seasoning
1 egg
few breadcrumbs
2 tablespoons grated cheese

To garnish:
cooked peas
mushrooms

1. Chop the spaghetti into small lengths—the quick-cooking macaroni is an ideal length.
2. Heat the margarine and fry the finely chopped onion, sliced tomatoes and chopped mushrooms until soft.
3. Mix with the macaroni or spaghetti, seasoning, egg and enough breadcrumbs to make a sticky consistency.
4. Press into a greased loaf tin and bake in the centre of a moderate oven (375°F.—Gas Mark 4) for 40 minutes.
5. Turn out and sprinkle the grated cheese on top.
6. Garnish with peas and mushrooms.

Economical paella

cooking time 30 minutes

you will need:

1 large onion
little oil or butter
2 large tomatoes, sliced
8 oz. rice
1 pint stock, or water and chicken stock cube
little cooked chicken
1 jar mussels
seasoning
chopped parsley

1 Peel and chop the onion finely, then fry in the hot butter or oil until transparent looking.
2 Add the sliced tomatoes, but do not cook further.
3 Put in the rice and the stock, or water and chicken stock cube.
4 Bring to the boil, then lower the heat, put a lid on the pan and cook gently for 15 minutes.
5 Remove the lid, add diced chicken and mussels —the liquid can be added if wished.
6 Heat gently with the rice for a few minutes, adding extra seasoning and parsley.

Note:

If wished about 1 teaspoon powdered saffron may be put in with the rice when cooking.

Risotto

cooking time about 40 minutes

you will need for 4 servings:

1 oz. margarine
1 onion, finely chopped
1 clove garlic, crushed (optional)
6 oz. rice
1¼ pint chicken stock or water with bouillon cube
salt
ground black pepper
4 oz. cooked chicken
2 oz. cooked ham*
2 tomatoes
1 medium can peas
Parmesan cheese

*If chicken omitted, allow 6 oz. ham

1 Melt the margarine in a frying pan.
2 Fry the onion and garlic lightly.
3 Add the rice and cook until all the fat is absorbed.
4 Stir in the stock and simmer gently for about 30 minutes until the rice is just cooked.
5 Season.
6 Add the chicken and ham cut into strips, the tomato, skinned, seeded and cut into strips, and drained peas.
7 Heat through and serve immediately accompanied by grated Parmesan cheese.

Rigati in creamed meat sauce

cooking time 30 minutes

you will need for 4 servings:

4–6 oz. bacon, diced
1 onion, finely chopped
1 oz. butter
beef or chicken bouillon cube
¼ pint hot water
¼ pint thick cream or ¼ pint thick white sauce
seasoning
6 oz. rigati or long-cut macaroni
grated cheese

1 Fry the onion and bacon in the hot butter until golden brown.
2 Dissolve the bouillon cube in the hot water, add to the sauce or cream, stir in the bacon and seasoning and heat together.
3 Meanwhile, cook the rigati or macaroni in boiling salted water until tender, drain and mix with the sauce and some grated cheese.
4 Put into hot dish, top with more grated cheese and brown under the grill if wished.

Salmon and rice croquettes

cooking time 35–40 minutes

you will need for 4 servings:

2 tablespoons rice
1 medium can salmon
salt
pepper
2 teaspoons lemon juice
1 egg
2–3 tablespoons crisp breadcrumbs

To garnish:
watercress
lemon

1 Cook rice (see page 70).
2 Flake salmon with fork.
3 Add seasoning and lemon juice.
4 Blend well together, form into croquettes and allow to stand for 15 minutes (to settle firmly into shape).
5 Brush with egg and roll in crumbs.
6 Place in buttered ovenware dish and bake for 15–20 minutes in a moderate oven (375°F.—Gas Mark 4).
7 Garnish with watercress and lemon slices.

Spaghetti bolognese

cooking time 1 hour

you will need for 4 servings:

6–8 oz. spaghetti
grated cheese

For the sauce:
1–1½ oz. butter and 1 tablespoon olive oil or 2 oz. butter
½–1 clove garlic (optional)
1 onion, finely chopped
4 oz. mushrooms
1 carrot, shredded
approx. 6 oz. minced beef
1 can tomatoes or 1 tube or small can tomato purée or 4 fresh tomatoes
seasoning
½ pint good brown stock if using tinned tomatoes or ⅝ pint if using fresh tomatoes or purée
1 wineglass red wine

1 Heat the butter and oil in a pan, then gently fry the crushed garlic, onion, mushrooms and carrot for several minutes.
2 Add the meat and the rest of the ingredients and simmer until the sauce has thickened.
3 Cook the spaghetti in boiling salted water—the quick cooking variety takes 7 minutes.
4 Strain.
5 Pour the sauce on top and serve with grated cheese.

Note:

Although not correct, you could include a sliced red or green pepper in this sauce. A little chopped parsley can be added just before serving.

Southern casserole

cooking time 40 minutes

you will need for 4 servings:

8 oz. Cheddar cheese
8 oz. sausages
4 oz. spaghetti
can creamed sweet corn
4 oz. butter
seasoning

1 Slice cheese thinly.
2 Grill, fry or bake the sliced sausages until golden brown.
3 Meanwhile, cook the spaghetti until tender, strain, chop into neat lengths, and mix with the creamed sweet corn.
4 Season well.
5 Put a layer at the bottom of a casserole, cover with a layer of cheese, then a layer of corn mixture.
6 Top with a thick layer of cheese.
7 Cook for 15 minutes in a moderately hot oven (400°F.—Gas Mark 5).
8 Arrange hot sausages on top.

Spaghetti marinara

cooking time 20–25 minutes

you will need for 4 servings:

6 oz. spaghetti

For the sauce:
1–2 large onions
1–2 cloves garlic
tablespoon olive or corn oil
¼–½ pint shrimps or prawns
¼ pint Riesling or Graves white wine
3 large tomatoes
seasoning

To garnish:
little chopped parsley

1 Put the spaghetti into boiling salted water and boil until tender.
2 To prepare the sauce, chop the onions finely, grate or crush the garlic.
3 Fry steadily in the hot oil until golden brown.
4 Add the chopped prawns or shrimps to the onions and brown delicately—DO NOT OVERCOOK OTHERWISE THEY TOUGHEN.
5 Add the wine and tomatoes, skinned and chopped, to the prawn mixture, season and heat throughly.
6 Stir in the drained spaghetti.
7 Serve garnished with chopped parsley.

Spanish rice au gratin

cooking time 30 minutes

you will need for 6 servings:

8 oz. long-grain rice
2 oz. butter
6 oz. onion, chopped
4 oz. celery, chopped
2 small green peppers, seeded and sliced
1 lb. ripe tomatoes, skinned and sliced
salt, sugar and pinch chilli powder
1 teaspoon Worcestershire sauce
2 tablespoons tomato ketchup
4 oz. cheese

1 Cook rice in boiling, salted water for 14 minutes (see page 70).
2 Meanwhile, cook onions, green pepper and celery in butter.
3 Add tomatoes, salt, sugar, chilli powder, Worcestershire sauce and ketchup.
4 Add cooked rice and simmer until thick.
5 Pour into a buttered casserole and top with cheese.
6 Place under grill and melt.

Savoury Vegetable Dishes

Vegetables are all too often considered as an accompaniment to meat or fish but in fact they make a good savoury dish by themselves, quite the best way to appreciate the true flavour of vegetables when they are in season.

Aubergines with tomatoes

cooking time 30 minutes

you will need for 4 servings:

2 large aubergines
3 large tomatoes
seasoning
2 tablespoons breadcrumbs
2 tablespoons milk or stock
1 oz. butter

1 Cook whole aubergines in boiling salted water until just tender.
2 Slice aubergines and tomatoes and fill a dish with alternate slices of each, seasoning well and ending with aubergines.
3 Cover with crumbs, stock or milk, and butter.
4 Bake for 15 minutes in a moderately hot oven (400–425°F.—Gas Mark 5–6).

Stuffed aubergines

cooking time 30 minutes

you will need for 4 servings:

2 medium aubergines
½ teaspoon salt
2 teaspoons corn oil
3 oz. breadcrumbs
2 oz. cooked ham, diced
1 hard-boiled egg, chopped
1 tomato
4 oz. grated Cheddar cheese
½ pint cheese sauce (see page 89)
1 oz. extra grated Cheddar cheese

1 Wash the aubergines and remove the stalks, then cut in half lengthwise.
2 Loosen the flesh in each aubergine half from ¼ inch from the skin and then lightly make criss-cross cuts across the surface to ensure even cooking.
3 Sprinkle with salt and corn oil.
4 Put on a greased baking tin in a moderately hot oven (400°F.—Gas Mark 5) until the centre is nearly cooked.
5 Blend breadcrumbs with all the other ingredients.
6 Scoop out about half the flesh from the centre of the cooked aubergines, chop up and add to the stuffing.
7 Fill the aubergine cases with the stuffing, sprinkle with grated cheese and return to the oven for a further 15 minutes.
8 Serve hot with cheese sauce.

Note:
When aubergines are not available, the same stuffing is delicious in red or green peppers.

Boston baked beans

cooking time 5½ hours

you will need for 4–6 servings:

1 lb. dried haricot beans
cold water
8 oz. fat salt pork
1 large onion
1 oz. brown sugar
2 tablespoons black treacle
2 teaspoons dry mustard
1 teaspoon salt
pepper

1 Wash beans, cover with cold water and soak overnight.
2 Drain, put into a large pan and cover with water.
3 Bring to the boil and simmer for 10 minutes.
4 Drain, reserving ½ pint of the liquid.
5 Chop rind of pork into 1-inch squares and cut rest of meat in half.
6 Place half the pork and the onion, peeled and sliced, in a heatproof casserole, cover with the beans and add rest of pork.
7 Blend remaining ingredients with the drained liquor and pour into casserole.
8 Cover and cook in a very slow oven (275°F.—Gas Mark 1) for about 5¼ hours.
9 Stir occasionally and add more water if beans seem too dry.

Cauliflower au gratin

cooking time 30–35 minutes

you will need for 4 servings:

1 cauliflower
4 oz. grated cheese
2 oz. butter
seasoning
little milk or cream

1 Cook cauliflower in boiling salted water until tender.
2 Drain well and beat until a soft purée.
3 Put half in a dish and cover with half the cheese, butter and seasoning.
4 Add rest of cauliflower, cheese, butter, seasoning and 2 or 3 tablespoons milk or cream.
5 Bake for 10–15 minutes near the top of a fairly hot oven (425°F.—Gas Mark 6).

Cauliflower garnished with egg and crumbs

cooking time 20–25 minutes

you will need for 4 servings:

1 cauliflower
4 heaped tablespoons breadcrumbs
2 oz. butter
1 hard-boiled egg, chopped
1 tablespoon chopped parsley

1 Break cauliflower into sprigs and boil in salted water until just tender.
2 Drain and arrange in a hot dish with all the white flowers uppermost.
3 Toss crumbs in butter until brown and crisp.
4 Mix with egg and parsley.
5 Sprinkle over cauliflower.

Creamy cauliflower with ham

cooking time 25 minutes

you will need for 4 servings:

1 large cauliflower
1 oz. butter
1 oz. flour
¾ pint milk
salt
pepper
1 small onion, finely grated
4 thick slices ham, diced
4 tablespoons cream
2 tablespoons mayonnaise (see page 36)

1 Trim outer leaves from the cauliflower. Boil, whole, in salted water until tender.
2 Meanwhile, to make the sauce, melt the butter in a pan, sprinkle in the flour and gradually add the milk stirring all the time.
3 Season with salt, pepper and add onion.
4 Blend in the diced ham, cream and mayonnaise.
5 Reheat very gently, WITHOUT ALLOWING TO BOIL.
6 Drain the cauliflower well.
7 Arrange on a dish and cover with the ham sauce.
8 Serve with peas and boiled rice.

Stuffed mushrooms

cooking time 35–40 minutes

you will need for 4 servings:

8 medium mushrooms
2 oz. long-grain rice
1 tablespoon oil
1 small onion, chopped
2–3 rashers streaky bacon, chopped
pinch saffron (optional)
2 oz. grated cheese
1 egg
4 slices bread
oil for frying

1 Skin the mushrooms, if necessary, but do not remove the stalks.
2 Cook the rice in boiling salted water until tender (see page 70).
3 Drain well.
4 Heat the oil and fry the onion and bacon, add rice and cook a further 2–3 minutes.
5 Remove from the heat and add saffron, cheese and egg.
6 Mix well.
7 Pile the stuffing mixture on to the mushrooms, arranging evenly around the stalks.
8 Place on a baking tray and bake for approximately 20 minutes in a moderate oven (375°F. —Gas Mark 4).
9 Cut the bread to the same size as the mushrooms and fry until golden brown in the heated oil.
10 Drain well on soft paper.
11 Place mushrooms on fried bread and serve.

Barbecued potatoes

cooking time 1¼–1½ hours

you will need for 6–12 servings:

6 large potatoes
12 middle rashers bacon
knob butter
seasoning
3–4 oz. grated Cheddar cheese
1 oz. butter or bacon fat
1 large or 2 medium onions, very thinly sliced
3 large tomatoes
dash of Worcestershire sauce
little made mustard

To garnish:
watercress

1 Cook the potatoes in their jackets until soft.
2 Halve carefully and remove centre potato pulp.
3 Mash pulp, add some of seasoning, knob butter and nearly all the cheese.
4 Pile or pipe back again into potato cases, leaving a large well in the middle.
5 Sprinkle rest of cheese on top of potato.

continued on next page

6 Make 6 of the rashers into 12 small bacon rolls and put these on a skewer.
7 Put the bacon rolls and potato cases in a moderately hot oven (400°F.—Gas Mark 5) for about 10 minutes until crisp and brown.
8 Meanwhile, heat fat in pan and fry sliced onions until nearly tender.
9 Add rest of bacon—cut into thin strips—and continue frying until bacon and onions are cooked.
10 Stir in sliced tomatoes, seasoning, mustard and Worcestershire sauce, and cook gently until a soft moist mixture is formed.
11 Pile into each potato case, top with bacon rolls, garnish with watercress.

Savoury potatoes

cooking time 1¼ hours

you will need for 4 servings:

4 large potatoes

For the filling:
4 oz. raw ham
1 small onion
3 oz. grated cheese
1 egg
salt and cayenne pepper
made mustard
1½ oz. butter or margarine

1 Cook the potatoes by washing, drying, pricking with a fork and baking for about 1 hour in a hot oven (425–450°F.—Gas Mark 6–7).
2 Put the ham and onion through a mincer and mix in 2 oz. of the cheese, the beaten egg and seasonings.
3 Cut the potatoes into halves, scoop out the pulp and mix first with the fat then with the savoury mixture.
4 Put the mixture into the potato cases.
5 Sprinkle with the rest of the cheese.
6 Wrap each potato in foil to completely cover it, then bake for another 15 minutes in the hot oven.
7 Serve at once in the foil containers.

Tomato and mushroom towers

cooking time 15 minutes

you will need for 4 servings:

8 tomatoes
2 onions
1 oz. butter
seasoning
5 oz. grated Cheddar cheese
8 large button mushrooms

1 Cut tops off the tomatoes and remove pulp.
2 Chop the onions and lightly fry in some of the butter.
3 Season well and mix the cheese to a paste with the tomato pulp.
4 Remove the mushroom stalks, chop and mix with the cheese paste, setting aside the whole mushrooms.
5 Place tomatoes in a fireproof dish putting cooked onion inside them.
6 Spread cheese mixture on undersides of mushrooms.
7 Sit a mushroom on top of each tomato and cover with the tomato lids.
8 Brush over with remaining butter.
9 Bake in hot oven (425–450°F.—Gas Mark 6–7) for about 15 minutes.
10 Serve immediately.

Ratatouille

cooking time 45 minutes–1 hour

you will need for 4 servings:

2 onions
1 lb. tomatoes
salt
1 medium marrow
4 small aubergines
1 red or green pepper
a little fat bacon
1–2 cloves garlic
pepper

To garnish:
little chopped parsley

1 Chop the onions, skin the tomatoes and cut them in half, sprinkle with salt and leave upturned to drain.
2 Peel the marrow, cut in large chunks, remove the stalks of the aubergines and cut in chunks.
3 Seed and slice the pepper.
4 Heat the bacon fat in a strong pan and gently fry the onions and the crushed garlic.
5 Add the aubergines, marrow, tomatoes and pepper.
6 Season well and simmer slowly, with well-fitting lid on the pan, until vegetables are tender.
7 Serve sprinkled with parsley.

Making Salad Savouries

For salads, you need not adhere strictly to quantities. They provide an opportunity for mixing together those ingredients that one particularly likes. But to be sustaining, a salad should contain a protein food such as egg, cheese, meat or fish. It should also have a good selection of colourful ingredients.

Chicken almond salad

cooking time 5 minutes

you will need for 4 servings:

- 6 oz. seedless raisins
- 12 oz. cooked chicken
- 4 oz. toasted almonds
- 1 tablespoon grated onion
- 1 tablespoon chopped parsley
- 1 teaspoon salt
- pepper
- 1 tablespoon lemon juice
- 2 tablespoons mayonnaise
- ¼ pint thin cream

1 Plump seedless raisins by covering with cold water.
2 Bring to the boil, cover and leave to stand for 5 minutes.
3 Cut chicken into long shreds, place with all the other ingredients in a mixing bowl and mix with mayonnaise and cream just before serving.
4 Serve on a bed of lettuce with cranberry sauce.

Curried chicken salad

no cooking

you will need for 4 servings:

- 12 oz. cooked chicken
- 3 oz. celery, diced
- 4 oz. sharp apple, diced
- 2 teaspoons finely grated onion
- 2 teaspoons curry powder
- ¼ pint salad cream (see page 91)
- 2–3 tablespoons cream
- salt and pepper
- 2 oz. almonds, toasted and chopped

1 Cut chicken into large pieces.
2 Mix with the celery, apple and onion.
3 Blend the curry with the salad cream and cream.
4 Season to taste and add the almonds.
5 Stir the chicken and vegetables into the dressing.
6 Chill before serving with lettuce and tomatoes.

Emerald salad

cooking time few minutes

you will need for 4 servings:

- 1 lime jelly
- ½ pint water
- juice ½ lemon
- 12 oz. cottage cheese
- ½ lettuce, shredded
- 1 small fresh pineapple or ½ large pineapple
- 1 grapefruit
- 1 orange
- 1 box cress
- 5–6 radishes

1 Dissolve lime jelly in ¼ pint of the water, heated to very hot.
2 When thoroughly dissolved stir in lemon juice and remaining ¼ pint cold water, mixing well.
3 When mixture begins to thicken, lightly fold in half the cottage cheese, but do not mix too thoroughly.
4 Fill a lightly oiled ring mould with the mixture and chill.
5 Line centre of salad platter with shredded lettuce.
6 Turn lime shape out on top, cover base of centre with shredded lettuce and fill up with cottage cheese.
7 Arrange overlapping slices of radishes round the cheese piled in the centre of the lime mould.
8 Border the mould with pieces of prepared fruit, placing a posy of cress between each little pyramid of fruit sections.

Gammon and pineapple salad

no cooking time

you will need for 4 servings:

- 4 oz. cooked gammon or ham
- 1 15-oz. can pineapple slices
- vinaigrette dressing (see page 37)
- lettuce

To garnish:

- pineapple
- radishes
- cucumber
- anchovy fillets

1 Dice gammon and pineapple.
2 Toss in dressing to which you have added a little pineapple syrup.
3 Serve on bed of crisp lettuce.
4 Garnish with pineapple, radishes, cucumber and anchovy fillets.

Harlequin salad

no cooking time

you will need for 4 servings:

6 oz. cooked macaroni
little mustard
mayonnaise (see page 36)
4 hard-boiled eggs
3 oz. chopped ham or shelled shrimps
4 tomatoes
small piece cucumber or few chopped gherkins
1 green pepper
lettuce

To garnish:
watercress
little chopped parsley
lemon

1 Rinse cooked macaroni in cold water.
2 Allow to dry well.
3 Blend a little mustard with mayonnaise and toss macaroni in this.
4 Add chopped eggs, ham or shrimps, 2 of the tomatoes sliced thickly, the diced cucumber and sliced pepper.
5 Pile on a bed of lettuce and garnish with watercress, parsley, remaining tomatoes and lemon.

Hot potato salad

cooking time 20–25 minutes

you will need:

1½ lb. new potatoes
8 oz. French beans
2 tablespoons oil
1 tablespoon vinegar
3 tablespoons hot chicken stock
1 tablespoon finely chopped onion
4–6 rashers streaky bacon

1 Cook potatoes and beans separately.
2 Make a dressing from the oil, vinegar, stock and onion.
3 Dice the rashers and fry lightly.
4 Slowly add the dressing to the bacon and heat.
5 Pour this mixture over the hot, drained, sliced potatoes and beans.
6 Serve hot with cold ham, meat or poultry and a green salad.

Sundowner's hat salad

no cooking

you will need for 6 servings:

1 can pineapple slices
8 oz. grated Cheddar cheese
¼ teaspoon salt
⅛ teaspoon paprika
1 green pepper
1 red pepper
1 lettuce
2 tomatoes

1 Drain juice from pineapple.
2 Mix cheese and seasonings with 1 tablespoon of the juice.
3 Mould into egg cups.
4 Unmould each on to a slice of pineapple and mark top to represent dent in the crown of a hat.
5 Arrange a strip of red pepper for hatband and use green pepper for a bow.
6 Serve on lettuce leaves, garnished with tomato quarters and salad cream (see page 91).

Fried Savouries

There is a great variety of fried savouries one can make but generally speaking the rules for success are:

1 make sure the fat is sufficiently hot to set the outside of the savoury quickly. This prevents the mixture from being soggy.
2 Drain well on either kitchen paper or crumpled tissue paper.
3 Serve as quickly as possible after cooking.

Bacon beignets

cooking time few minutes

you will need for 6–8 portions:

1 lb. cooked bacon (forehock, collar or gammon)
8 oz. plain flour
2 eggs
seasoning
1 teaspoon basil or marjoram
¼ pint milk
⅛ pint beer or water

1 Cut the bacon into 1-inch cubes.
2 Sieve the flour and seasoning into a bowl and add the eggs and herbs.

3 Gradually mix in the milk, then the beer or water.
4 Beat well and allow to stand for at least 1 hour.
5 Dip pieces of bacon into the batter.
6 Fry in deep, hot fat until golden brown.
7 Drain on crumpled kitchen paper.

Cheese brochettes

cooking time 3–4 minutes

you will need for 4 servings:

6 medium-thick slices bread
1 lb. Cheddar cheese
$\frac{1}{4}$ pint milk
2 oz. seasoned flour
fat for frying
1 lb. cooked spinach
$\frac{1}{2}$ pint cheese sauce (see page 89)

For the egg dip:
2 egg yolks
$\frac{1}{4}$ teaspoon salt
pinch cayenne
1 tablespoon water

1 Take six 1-inch squares of bread and five 1-inch squares of Cheddar cheese, approximately $\frac{1}{4}$ inch thick, and spear alternately on to a small skewer so that they just touch.
2 Mix together ingredients for egg dip.
3 Soak the brochettes in milk, roll in seasoned flour and then in the egg dip.
4 Fry in deep fat at a very moderate heat (i.e. when a cube of bread turns golden brown in 1 minute) until golden brown.
5 Drain and serve hot, on a bed of spinach, covered with cheese sauce.

Cheese meringues

cooking time 2–3 minutes

you will need for 4 servings:

2 egg whites
seasoning
2 oz. finely grated cheese, preferably Parmesan
fat or oil for frying

To garnish:
parsley
watercress

1 Whisk egg whites until very stiff.
2 Fold in seasoning and cheese.
3 Drop spoonfuls into hot oil or fat and fry until crisp and brown.
4 Drain and serve at once.
5 Garnish with parsley or watercress.

Fried cheese sandwiches

cooking time few minutes

you will need for 4 servings:

8 large thin slices wholemeal bread
8 oz. Cheddar cheese, thinly sliced
4 teaspoons chutney
2 oz. butter for frying

To garnish:
2 tomatoes

1 Cover the bread slices with the cheese, and spread over a little chutney.
2 Put two cheese-covered slices together and press firmly.
3 Cut into neat shapes and fry to a crisp golden brown on both sides in butter.
4 Serve hot, garnished with tomato slices.

Making fritters

Fritters are quick to prepare and cook, and can easily be varied. Here are some suggestions:

Diced ham Mix approximately 8 oz. diced ham with batter (see Corned beef, page 80) and fry in spoonfuls.

Cheese Dip slices or portions of cheese in batter, fry for 1 minute (see page 80).

Fish Mix about 6–8 oz. well drained flaked cooked fish in batter, fry in spoonfuls for few minutes.

Roe Separate cooked soft or hard herring roes or dice cod's roe. Coat in batter and fry until crisp and golden brown.

Carrot Cooked young carrots can be coated in plain or cheese-flavoured batter and fried steadily until crisp and golden brown.

Cauliflower fritters

cooking time few minutes

you will need for 4 servings:

1 cooked cauliflower
1 egg
$2\frac{1}{2}$ tablespoons milk and water
2 oz. flour
seasoning
paprika
1 oz. melted butter
oil or fat for frying

To garnish:
chopped parsley

1 Divide cooked cauliflower into sprigs.
2 Make batter by mixing egg yolk and milk with seasoned flour, then fold in the melted butter and stiffly beaten egg whites.
3 Dip cauliflower sprigs in this.
4 Fry in hot fat until crisp and golden brown.
5 Drain and garnish with parsley.

Corned beef fritters

cooking time 5–8 minutes

you will need for 4 servings:

For the batter:
4 oz. flour (plain or self-raising)
1 egg
$\frac{1}{4}$ pint milk
seasoning

12 oz. corned beef
fat for frying

1 Make the batter by blending the egg with the seasoned flour then adding the milk gradually.
2 Slice the corned beef thinly and coat carefully with the batter.*
3 Put into hot fat and fry steadily until the fritters are crisp and brown on the outside and the meat very hot inside.
4 Serve the fritters with salad or with fried onion rings and vegetables.

*If preferred the corned beef can be flaked and mixed with the batter, then drop spoonfuls of the mixture into the hot fat

Cheese fritters

cooking time 8 minutes

you will need for 4 servings:

4 oz. flour (with plain flour use 1 teaspoon baking powder)
1 egg
$\frac{1}{4}$ pint milk
seasoning
4 oz. finely grated cheese
oil or fat for frying

1 Make a thick batter with the flour, egg and milk.
2 Season well and add the grated cheese.
3 Drop in small spoonfuls in hot oil or fat and fry until crisp and golden brown.

Quick macaroni fritters

cooking time 5 minutes

you will need for 4 servings:

2 oz. macaroni
3 eggs
4 oz. grated cheese
seasoning
little fat for frying
1 packet mushroom soup
$\frac{1}{4}$ pint water
$\frac{1}{2}$ pint milk

1 Cook macaroni in plenty of boiling salted water until tender.
2 Drain well.
3 Beat together eggs, cheese and seasoning.
4 Mix in macaroni.
5 Heat fat in frying pan and drop in spoonfuls of the mixture.
6 Fry until crisp and golden, turn and brown other side.
7 Drain and serve with a mushroom sauce made by heating mushroom soup with water and milk.

Cheeseolettes

cooking time few minutes

you will need for 4 servings:

3 eggs
2 oz. flour (with plain flour use $\frac{1}{2}$ teaspoon baking powder)
4 oz. grated Cheddar cheese
1 tablespoon grated onion
2 tablespoons chopped parsley
seasoning
fat or oil for frying

1 Blend all the ingredients together.
2 Heat the fat in pan and drop in spoonfuls of this mixture.
3 Fry until crisp and golden brown.
4 Turn, brown on the other side.
5 Drain well and serve with a dish of sliced tomatoes and another of crisp lettuce.

Pancake dishes to make

Pancake batter

cooking time few minutes

you will need for 4 servings:

4 oz. flour, preferably plain
pinch salt
2 eggs
$\frac{1}{2}$ pint milk, or milk and water
oil or fat for frying

1 Sieve flour into a bowl and add salt.
2 Make a well in the centre and stir in one egg and half the milk beaten together.
3 Beat lightly with a wooden spoon for a few minutes.
4 Add the remaining egg whisked together with the rest of the milk and mix well until batter is perfectly smooth.
5 Cover bowl and allow to stand in a cool place for 1 hour before using if possible.
6 Melt the oil or fat in a thick frying pan to coat bottom and when very hot pour off any excess.
7 Pour about 2 tablespoons of the batter into the pan and cook over medium heat until set.
8 Turn and cook other side until a golden brown.
9 Repeat until all batter is used.

18 simple fillings for pancakes

- thick cheese sauce (see page 89)
- diced bacon and tomatoes
- diced ham heated in white, cheese or tomato sauce (see pages 89–91)
- diced chicken heated in white, béchamel, or cheese sauce (see pages 89–91)
- prawns, or shrimps, heated in white, cheese, béchamel or hollandaise sauce (see pages 89–91)
- creamy spinach purée
- cooked asparagus tips
- hot sausages
- mixed cooked vegetables in thick white, cheese or tomato sauce (see pages 89–91)

Prawn and mushroom pancakes

cooking time 15 minutes

you will need for 4 servings:

½ pint pancake batter (see page 80)
fat or oil for frying

For the filling:
1½ oz. butter
1 oz. flour
½ pint milk
seasoning
little lemon juice
2–3 oz. shelled prawns
2 oz. button or chopped mushrooms
little butter for frying

1. Prepare pancake batter.
2. Heat fat or oil and cook pancake quickly until the underside is golden brown. Toss and cook the other side.
3. Put on to a piece of greaseproof paper.
4. Keep the pancakes in a warm place between layers of greaseproof paper* until the filling is ready.
5. For the filling melt the butter in a saucepan over a low heat, add the flour and cook gently for a minute stirring all the time.
6. Gradually add the liquid, still stirring, until the mixture thickens.
7. Season and add lemon juice, prawns, and lightly fried mushrooms.
8. Cook for a few minutes more, then spoon on to pancakes, roll them up, and warm them in a cool oven if necessary.
9. Serve with lemon slices and garnish with more prawns.

Variation:
Vary the filling by adding chicken, sweet corn, peppers or ham to the basic sauce.

* On uncovered dish in a slow oven or over pan boiling water

Savoury Scotch pancakes

cooking time 4 minutes

you will need for 4 servings:

4 oz. flour (with plain flour use either 2 teaspoons baking powder or ½ small teaspoon bicarbonate of soda and 1 small teaspoon cream of tartar)
pinch salt, pepper and mustard
1 egg
¼ pint milk
1 oz. melted margarine (optional)

1. Sieve together all the dry ingredients.
2. Beat in first the egg, then the milk.
3. Stir in the melted margarine if used.
4. Grease and warm the griddle, electric hot plate or frying pan. It is best to use the middle of the pan—the part that touches the heat.
5. To test for correct temperature, drop 1 teaspoon of the mixture on to this; if it goes brown within 1 minute, the plate is ready.
6. Drop spoonfuls of the batter on to the plate.
7. Cook for about 2 minutes.
8. Turn with a palette knife and cook the other side.
9. Press firmly with the back of a knife; if no batter comes from the sides and the pancakes feel firm, they are ready.
10. Cool on a wire tray.

These are delicious topped with butter and cheese, with cream cheese and jam, or with hot sausages and crisp bacon.

Variations:

Caraway pancakes
Add 1 teaspoon caraway seeds—particularly good topped with cream cheese.

Tomato Scotch pancakes
Blend with tomato juice instead of milk.

Cheese Scotch pancakes
1–2 oz. finely grated Parmesan cheese can be added.

Onion Scotch pancakes
Fry 1 grated onion in a little hot margarine. Add to flour and omit 1 tablespoon milk.

Savouries with Pastry

A savoury flan, tart or pastry is likely to be an extremely popular dish and as such is ideal for a number of occasions, including picnics, so I have included, at the end of this chapter, tips for carrying savouries on picnics.

How to make the pastry

Flaky pastry

cooking time — as individual recipe

you will need for 4 servings:

- 8 oz. plain flour
- pinch salt
- 5–6 oz. fat ($\frac{1}{3}$ cooking fat and $\frac{2}{3}$ margarine, or all butter or all margarine)
- water

1. Sieve flour with salt.
2. Mix fat and divide into 3 portions.
3. Rub one portion into flour in the usual way and mix to rolling consistency with cold water.
4. Roll out to oblong shape.
5. Take the second portion of fat, divide it into small pieces and lay them on surface of $\frac{1}{3}$ of dough, leaving remaining $\frac{2}{3}$ without fat.
6. Fold $\frac{1}{3}$ without fat on to $\frac{1}{3}$ with fat, then fold other $\frac{1}{3}$ over—to form an open envelope.
7. Turn pastry at right angles, seal open ends and 'rib' it (press with the rolling pin at intervals to give a corrugated effect and equalize the distribution of trapped air). This makes sure that the pastry will rise evenly.
8. Repeat the process again using the remaining fat and turning pastry in same way.
9. If the consistency is still firm, roll out pastry once more, but should it begin to feel very soft and sticky first put it into a cold place for 30 minutes to become firm before rolling out.
10. Fold pastry as before, turn it, seal edges and 'rib' it. Altogether the pastry should have 3 foldings and 3 rollings.
11. Then stand in a cold place for a little while before baking, since the contrast between the cold and the heat of the oven makes the pastry rise better.
12. To bake use a very hot oven (475°F.—Gas Mark 8) then lower heat to Gas Mark 6 or turn the electric oven off to finish cooking for remaining time at lower temperature.

Puff pastry

cooking time — as individual recipe

you will need:

- 8 oz. plain flour
- 7–8 oz. butter or margarine or $\frac{2}{3}$ margarine and $\frac{1}{3}$ whipped up cooking fat
- cold water to mix
- good pinch salt
- few drops lemon juice

1. Sieve the flour and salt together.
2. Mix to rolling consistency with cold water and lemon juice.
3. Roll to oblong shape.
4. Make fat into neat block and place in centre of pastry.
5. Fold over first the bottom section of pastry to cover the fat, then the top section over this.
6. Turn the dough at right angles, seal the edges and 'rib' carefully (press with the rolling pin at intervals to give a corrugated effect and equalize distribution of trapped air). This makes sure that the pastry will rise evenly.
7. Roll out the pastry.
8. Fold into envelope again, turn to right again, seal edges, 'rib' and roll.
9. Repeat 5 times, making 7 rollings and 7 foldings in all. It will be necessary to put the pastry to rest in a cold place once or twice between rollings to prevent it becoming sticky and soft.
10. Always put it to rest before rolling for the last time, and before baking.
11. Bake in a very hot oven (to make it rise, and keep in the fat).
12. Bake for the first 10–15 minutes in a very hot oven (475–500°F.—Gas Mark 8–9) then lower to moderately hot (400°F.—Gas Mark 5). Well made puff pastry should rise to 4–5 times its original thickness.

Short crust pastry

cooking time — as individual recipe

you will need:

- 8 oz. flour
- good pinch salt
- 4 oz. fat (equal quantities margarine or butter and cooking fat or lard)
- approximately 2 tablespoons cold water

1 Sieve flour and salt together and rub in fat until mixture looks like fine breadcrumbs.
2 Using first a knife and then fingertips so that you can feel the texture of the pastry, gradually add enough of the cold water to mix the dough to a rolling consistency.
3 Lightly flour the rolling pin and pastry board —if a great deal of flour is necessary to roll out the pastry, then you have used too much water.
4 Roll out to required thickness and shape, lifting and turning it to keep light.
5 Exact cooking times for pastry are given in the recipes, but as a general rule it should be cooked in a hot oven (425–450°F.—Gas Mark 6–7).

Vol au vent cases 1

cooking time 15–30 minutes

you will need for 6–8 large cases*:

1 1-lb. packet frozen pastry or puff pastry made with 8 oz. flour (see page 82)

1 Roll out the puff pastry to ½ inch thickness, keeping the rolling pin straight across. If the pastry is in just the right condition for rolling, you will need little, if any, flour on the board or rolling pin.
2 Cut into rounds.
3 Cut the centres out of half the rounds to form rings.
4 Place these rings on top of complete rounds.
5 Seal edges and put on to DAMP baking trays.
6 Glaze with beaten egg.
7 Bake in a very hot oven (475°F.—Gas Mark 8) until well risen and brown, then reduce heat slightly to make sure pastry is cooked—this will vary from 15–30 minutes according to size.

*Or 12 medium, or 36 cocktail cases

Vol au vent cases 2

cooking time 15–30 minutes

you will need for 6–8 large cases*:

1 1-lb. packet frozen puff pastry or puff pastry made with 8 oz. flour (see page 82)

1 Roll out the puff pastry as in Vol au vent 1 but to ¾–1 inch thickness, and cut into rounds.
2 Put on to DAMP baking trays.
3 With a smaller cutter press half way through pastry.
4 Glaze with beaten egg.
5 Bake in a very hot oven (475°F.–Gas Mark 8) until well risen and brown, then reduce heat slightly to make sure pastry is cooked.
6 Lift out the centre portion—this is quite easy to do with the point of a sharp knife—and return to the oven for a short time to dry out.

*Or 12 medium, or 36 cocktail cases

Fillings for vols au vent

Fill with either fish, chicken, mushrooms or a selection of vegetables mixed in a thick white sauce or mayonnaise.

To serve vols au vent hot

1 Bake the pastry cases and keep warm.
2 Make the fillings and keep warm.
3 Put the 2 together and serve at once.

To serve vols au vent cold

1 Allow both pastry and filling to become cold.
2 Put together and serve.

How to make a flan case

1 Use either a proper flan ring on a baking sheet, or a sandwich tin, or a deep pie plate.
2 Use either short crust pastry, or cheese pastry, using the short crust recipe (see page 82) and adding 4 oz. grated cheese.
3 It is traditional for a savoury flan to be made in a plain and not a fluted flan case, although this is not very important.
4 Roll out the pastry to slightly larger than the ring or tin.
5 Lift it without breaking by folding over the rolling pin.
6 Put flan ring on to the upturned baking tin—this makes flan easier to slide off—grease ring or tin very lightly.
7 Place the pastry over the ring or case. Press down gently but firmly at the bottom and then at the sides.
8 Cut away surplus pastry at the top being careful not to drag and stretch the pastry. Alternatively roll over with a rolling pin—if you do this firmly, and the edge of the tin is reasonably sharp, you can cut away any surplus pastry quickly and efficiently.

To bake 'blind'

To bake a pastry case 'blind' means to bake it without a filling. As there is a tendency for the pastry to rise if not weighted down by a filling, it is advisable to use plain flour. Also you can either prick the pastry well with a fork, or put a piece of greased greaseproof paper or foil inside, and cover with crusts of bread or dry haricot beans to weight down the bottom. Bake for about 15 minutes in a hot oven (425°F.—Gas Mark 6) then lift out the beans and paper and, if using a flan ring, take this away, so the outside edge of the pastry will crisp. Allow a further 5–10 minutes in the oven.

Asparagus and hollandaise flan

cooking time 25 minutes

you will need for 4 servings:

Onion pastry:
3 oz. butter or margarine
6 oz. plain flour
½ teaspoon salt
1 tablespoon grated onion
2 tablespoons cold water

For the filling:
4 hard-boiled eggs
8 oz. cooked asparagus or 1 can asparagus tips

mock hollandaise sauce:
1 oz. butter
1 oz. flour
½ pint milk
salt and pepper
2 egg yolks
3 oz. butter
1 tablespoon lemon juice

1. Make the pastry by rubbing fat into sifted flour and salt.
2. Add onion and mix to stiff paste with the water.
3. Knead and roll out slightly larger than 8 or 9-inch pie plate.
4. Fit into plate, trim and flute edges.
5. Bake 'blind' (see above) in centre of a hot oven (425–450°F.—Gas Mark 6–7) for 20–25 minutes, until inside is golden and crisp.
6. Roll out trimmings, cut into small rounds and bake for 10 minutes only to use for garnish.
7. While flan is cooking make the white sauce with butter, flour and milk. Then while still warm and just before serving, stir in the two beaten egg yolks, the 3 oz. butter, a teaspoon at a time, and finally the lemon juice.
8. Season well.
9. Fill baked pastry case with thoroughly chopped hard-boiled eggs.
10. Pour sauce over chopped eggs and garnish with the cooked or canned asparagus placed like spokes of a wheel, tips outwards.
11. Place little pastry rounds between the asparagus groups and serve at once. A crisp green salad will make a good accompaniment.

Variations:

Salmon and hollandaise flan
Use medium can of salmon and put this in flan case with hard-boiled eggs.

Broccoli and hollandaise flan
Use cooked broccoli instead of asparagus.

Bacon and cheese flan

cooking time 40–45 minutes

you will need for 4 servings:

4 oz. short crust pastry (see page 82)
6–8 rashers streaky bacon
1 egg
3 oz. grated cheese
pinch salt
pinch cayenne
¼ pint top of milk or evaporated milk

1. Line a 7-inch flan ring or tin with the pastry.
2. Remove the rind from the bacon, cut 4 rashers into thin strips and fry lightly.
3. Beat the egg, add the cheese, seasonings and milk.
4. Place some cooked bacon in the flan and pour the cheese mixture over.
5. Bake in moderate oven (375°F.—Gas Mark 4) for 30 minutes.
6. Remove from the oven and garnish with the remaining bacon.
7. Return to oven and cook for further 10 minutes.
8. Serve hot or cold.

Beef and vegetable flan

cooking time 25 minutes

you will need for 4 servings:

8-inch short crust flan case (see page 82)
1 can stewed steak, or stewed steak and vegetable casserole
1 teaspoon cornflour

To garnish:
1–2 tomatoes
1 hard-boiled egg

1 Cook the flan case until crisp and golden brown.
2 Meanwhile, heat the casserole, blending in the cornflour to thicken gravy.
3 Pile into hot case.*
4 Garnish with slices of tomato and hard-boiled egg.
5 Serve hot.

* If you prefer to serve cold, put the casserole mixture into cold pastry case. In this way you keep the pastry crisp. For special occasions, make up a small quantity of savoury jelly (see below) and brush over the top of the flan to give an attractive glaze

To make savoury jelly:

Add enough beef bouillon cube to $\frac{1}{4}$ pint water to give good beef flavour. Dissolve 1 teaspoon gelatine in the very hot liquid. Allow to set lightly, then spoon over the cold meat filling.

Cheese and onion roll

cooking time 35–40 minutes

you will need for 4 servings:

1 large onion, finely chopped
2 oz. butter
2 oz. white breadcrumbs
4 oz. grated Cheddar cheese
1 teaspoon chopped parsley
salt and pepper
4 oz. flaky or puff pastry (see page 82)
1 egg

1 Cook the onion in butter until transparent.
2 Stir in the breadcrumbs, toss in pan until crisp and remove from heat.
3 Add the cheese, parsley and seasoning to taste.
4 Roll out pastry to an oblong about 10 inches by 6 inches.
5 Brush edges with beaten egg.
6 Spread filling over pastry, roll up from short side and seal the edges.
7 Brush over with egg.
8 Bake in a hot oven (450°F.—Gas Mark 7) for 15 minutes.
9 Reduce heat to moderate (375°F.—Gas Mark 4) for 15 minutes.
10 Serve hot or cold.

Cheese soufflé tarts

cooking time 12–15 minutes

you will need for 4 servings:

4 oz. short crust pastry (see page 82)
2 eggs
2 oz. finely grated Cheddar cheese
pinch cayenne
good pinch salt
pinch pepper
$\frac{1}{2}$ teaspoon chopped parsley

To garnish:
watercress

1 Roll out the pastry very thinly and line 9–12 patty tins.
2 Beat the egg yolks with the cheese and seasonings, add the parsley and lastly the stiffly beaten egg whites.
3 Put into the pastry cases and bake for approximately 12–15 minutes in the centre of a very hot oven (475–500°F.—Gas Mark 8–9).
4 Serve hot or cold garnished with watercress.

Corned beef pasties

cooking time 45 minutes

you will need for 4 servings:

1 12-oz. can corned beef
large potato
large onion
seasoning
a little stock, flavoured with beef or chicken bouillon cube
12 oz. short crust pastry
little milk or beaten egg

To serve:
salad
beetroot

1 Flake the corned beef and mix with GRATED raw potato and GRATED raw onion.
2 Season well and add enough stock to give a moist texture (do not make it too wet otherwise the pastry will be spoiled).
3 Roll out the pastry and cut into large rounds.
4 Put a good spoonful of the mixture into the centre of each round, fold over and flute edges firmly together. The pasties should have the traditional Cornish pasty shape.
5 Brush the pastry with milk or a little beaten egg, lift carefully on to baking tins and cook for 20 minutes in the centre of a hot oven (425–450°F.—Gas Mark 6–7).
9 Lower the heat and cook for a further 20 minutes to make sure the filling is hot and the potato and onion cooked.
7 Serve with salad and sliced beetroot.

Harlequin flan

cooking time 40–45 minutes

you will need for 4 servings:

6 oz. short crust pastry (see page 82)
2 eggs
$\frac{3}{8}$ pint milk
seasoning
selection of cooked vegetables—diced young carrots, turnips, beans, peas, beetroot and raw tomato, cucumber
4 oz. grated cheese

1. Line a deep flan ring or oblong tin with pastry, bake 'blind' for 10–15 minutes in a hot oven (425–450°F.—Gas Mark 6–7).
2. Meanwhile beat the eggs, add warm milk and seasoning.
3. Arrange the vegetables in the flan.
4. Stir cheese into custard and pour over the vegetables.
5. Bake for about 30 minutes in moderate oven (375°F.—Gas Mark 4) until filling is firm.
6. Serve hot or cold.

Quiche Lorraine or cheese flan

cooking time 30–35 minutes

you will need for 4 servings:

4 oz. bacon rashers
6 oz. short crust or flaky pastry (see page 82)
6 oz. grated cheese
$\frac{1}{4}$ pint milk
$\frac{1}{4}$ pint cream
2 eggs
seasoning

1. Chop bacon finely and fry very lightly.
2. Line a really deep flan tin with pastry.
3. Beat eggs, add cream, milk, grated cheese, bacon and seasoning.
4. Pour in to flan carefully and bake in centre of a moderately hot oven (400°F.—Gas Mark 5) until the pastry is brown and the filling firm.

Note:

For a more economical flan, use more milk and egg yolks only.

Nutty Cheddar horns

cooking time 17 minutes

you will need for 9 horns:

1 lb. plain flour
$\frac{1}{4}$ teaspoon salt
1 teaspoon baking powder
2 oz. butter
scant $\frac{1}{2}$ pint milk
1 egg

For the filling:

8 oz. grated Cheddar cheese
1$\frac{1}{2}$ tablespoons mayonnaise (see page 36)
pinch cayenne
4 pickled walnuts

1. Sieve flour, salt and baking powder into bowl.
2. Rub in butter and mix to a fairly stiff dough with the milk.
3. Roll into oblong 12×9 inches and cut into strips 1×12 inches.
4. Damp edge of strips and coil round cream horn tins.
5. Brush with beaten egg and stand on greased baking sheet.
6. Bake in a moderately hot oven (400°F.—Gas Mark 5) for 12 minutes.
7. Remove tins and bake for a further 5 minutes.
8. Allow to cool.
9. Blend grated cheese, mayonnaise and cayenne pepper.
10. Chop walnuts coarsely and fold into cheese mixture.
11. Fill horn cases with cheese filling.

Leek flan

cooking time 30–40 minutes

you will need for 4 servings:

1 lb. leeks

For the pastry:

1 oz. butter
4 oz. flour
seasoning
1 egg
2 tablespoons milk
2 tablespoons cream
seasoning
4 rashers streaky bacon
4 oz. cheese

1. Chop the leeks and boil until tender.
2. Rub the butter into the flour sifted with the seasoning.
3. Stir in the beaten egg and enough milk to make a soft dough.
4. Roll out and press the dough into a greased 6-inch sandwich tin or flan ring.
5. Mix the cream with the leeks and seasoning and spread over the dough.
6. Lay the bacon strips on top and cover with the cheese.
7. Bake in centre of a moderately hot oven (400°F.—Gas Mark 5) for 30 minutes.

Savoury egg flan

cooking time 25 minutes

you will need for 4 servings:

6 oz. short or cheese crust pastry (see page 82)
$\frac{1}{2}$ pint water and 1 beef stock cube or $\frac{1}{2}$ pint stock
$\frac{1}{4}$ oz. gelatine
squeeze lemon juice
3 hard-boiled eggs
3 tomatoes

To garnish:

lettuce

1 Roll out pastry, line a 7-inch flan ring and bake 'blind' in hot oven (425–450°F.—Gas Mark 6–7) for about 20 minutes—until crisp and golden brown.
2 Crumble beef extract cube and dissolve in $\frac{1}{4}$ pint hot water.
3 Add gelatine and when completely dissolved, add lemon juice and $\frac{1}{4}$ pint cold water; leave in a cool place.
4 Fill flan case with quartered hard-boiled eggs and skinned and quartered tomatoes.
5 When savoury jelly is just setting, spoon mixture over the eggs and tomatoes, filling the flan.
6 Allow any surplus jelly to set and serve chopped with the flan on a lettuce bed.

Soufflé tarts

cooking time 15 minutes

you will need for 4 servings:

4 oz. short crust pastry (see page 82)
3 tablespoons Gruyère or Parmesan cheese, grated
2 teaspoons finely chopped parsley
3 eggs
1 teaspoon grated onion
seasoning

1 Line tins with thin pastry.
2 Mix well beaten eggs with most of the cheese, the onion, parsley and seasoning.
3 Put spoonfuls of the filling into the pastry, scatter more grated cheese over the top and bake in centre of a hot oven (450°F.—Gas Mark 7) for 15 minutes.

Savoury flan

cooking time 30–35 minutes

you will need for 4 servings:

7 oz. plain flour
2 oz. soya flour
salt
2 tablespoons soya oil
2 oz. grated cheese
little egg
water

For the filling:

$\frac{1}{2}$ large onion, chopped
$\frac{1}{2}$ green or red pepper
2 oz. mushrooms
2 oz. chopped bacon
2 oz. tomatoes
seasoning
1 large egg
4 tablespoons milk
1 oz. grated cheese

1 Make the pastry by placing the flours and salt into a mixing bowl and adding the soya oil and cheese.
2 Mix together, add a little beaten egg and enough water to form into a pastry dough.
3 Roll the pastry out thinly.
4 Grease an 8–9 inch flan ring or pie plate and line with pastry.
5 Mince or chop together coarsely the onion, pepper, mushrooms, bacon and tomatoes.
6 Add seasoning, egg and milk and pour this mixture into the pastry case.
7 Sprinkle with grated cheese and cook for 30–35 minutes in a moderately hot oven (400°F.—Gas Mark 5).
8 This flan can be served either hot or cold.

Bread and scone dishes

Pizza

cooking time 1 hour

you will need for 4 servings:

$\frac{1}{2}$ oz. yeast
1 dessertspoon tepid water
1 lb. plain flour
$\frac{1}{4}$ pint water
4 tablespoons olive oil
1 lb. or 1 can tomatoes
1 clove garlic, chopped
1 can anchovies
4 oz. Parmesan or Cheddar cheese
salt and pepper
few black olives

1 Dissolve the yeast in tepid water.
2 Mix the flour with 1 tablespoon of the olive oil, then add the dissolved yeast and water.
3 Knead until dough is smooth.
4 Leave it in a covered bowl for 2 hours.
5 Peel and chop the fresh tomatoes, or drained canned tomatoes, and put them in a pan with rest of oil and garlic.
6 Season with salt and pepper and simmer gently for 30 minutes.
7 Add the anchovies and most of the cheese when tomatoes are almost cooked.
8 When the dough has risen, roll it until it is very thin and spread it over a large, well oiled baking tin.
9 Cover it with tomato mixture and bake in centre of a hot oven (425–450°F.—Gas Mark 6–7) for approximately 25 minutes.
10 Top with rest of grated cheese and black olives.

Cocktail pizza tarts

1 Mix up half the quantity of the tomato mixture (step 5).
2 Roll out 6 oz. quantity of short crust pastry (see page 82) and make about 24 tiny tartlet cases, baking until crisp and brown.
3 Fill with the tomato mixture, top with cheese and tiny pieces of olive or anchovy fillets.

5 minute pizzas

cooking time 1 minute

you will need for 4 servings:

4 soft rolls
butter, optional
8 slices cheese
16 anchovy fillets
few olives

1 Halve the soft rolls, butter if wished.
2 Put the slices of cheese on top with the anchovy fillets in a cross and decorate with sliced olives.
3 Put under the grill for 1 minute only.

Quick pizza scones

cooking time 30 minutes

you will need for 4 servings:

For the dough:
1 lb. self-raising flour
1 teaspoon salt
2 teaspoons baking powder
3 oz. margarine
2 medium eggs
$\frac{1}{2}$ pint less 4 tablespoons milk

For the sauce:
2 tablespoons oil
1 medium onion, finely chopped
1 clove garlic, finely chopped
4 tablespoons tomato purée
$\frac{1}{2}$ teaspoon dried oregano (optional)
salt and pepper
3 oz. finely grated cheese*
anchovy fillets
halved stuffed olives

*Parmesan will give extra strong flavour

1 Sift dry dough ingredients into bowl.
2 Rub in fat to fine breadcrumbs consistency.
3 Mix to a soft dough with lightly beaten egg and milk and knead lightly until smooth.
4 If scones are not wanted until later, place dough in a polythene bag and keep in refrigerator or cool larder until ready to bake.
5 Heat oil, add onion and garlic and cook slowly till soft but not brown.
6 Stir in tomato purée and seasonings and remove from heat.
7 Turn the dough on to a lightly floured board and roll out to $\frac{1}{2}$–$\frac{3}{4}$ inch thick.
8 Cut into 8 rounds with a 3-inch cutter.
9 Place the rounds on a greased and floured baking tray, allowing room between each for spreading.
10 Make a 'well' in each round with the floured base of a jam jar or tumbler about $2\frac{1}{2}$ inches across.
11 Fill each 'well' with the tomato sauce and cover with grated cheese.
12 Top with anchovy fillets and halved stuffed olives.
13 Bake near the top of a hot oven (425°F.—Gas Mark 7) for about 20 minutes and serve at once.

Potato cheese scones

cooking time 10–15 minutes

you will need for 4 servings:

1 teaspoon yeast extract
6 fl. oz. milk and water
2 oz. instant mashed potato powder or 4–6 oz. cooked potato
4 oz. plain flour and 2 teaspoons baking powder, or 4 oz. self-raising flour and 1 teaspoon baking powder
2 oz. melted butter or margarine
2 oz. processed cheese, finely diced
1 egg

1 Heat the yeast extract with the milk and water, then stir in the instant mashed potato powder.
2 Cool slightly, add the flour, melted butter and cheese.
3 Mix well, then add enough beaten egg to give a stiff mixture.
4 Roll out to about $\frac{3}{4}$ inch thick on a well floured pastry board.
5 Cut into rounds or triangles.
6 Brush with rest of egg to give an attractive glaze, and bake near the top of a hot oven (450–475°F.—Gas Mark 7–8) for approximately 10–12 minutes.
7 These are delicious sandwiched together with butter and processed cheese, and served with a salad.
To reheat: split, top with processed sliced cheese and put under grill for 1 minute.

10 Tips for Carrying Food on Picnics

- Make use of foil or plastic bags to keep food intact, and to prevent containers becoming sticky and heavy.
- Don't plan too 'starchy' a meal. Have such foods as fruit and salad and avoid over-sweet 'sticky' buns, cakes and things that break easily, otherwise the family will become sleepy and slightly irritable.
- Make use of waxed cartons with tightly fitting lids (or washed ice cream cartons) for potato or Russian salad, fresh fruit salad, etc.
- Wide-topped vacuum flasks can turn a picnic into a feast. Use them for hot dishes such as soups, stews (fricassée of veal, curry, etc.), milk puddings for younger children, baby's dinner. They are also useful for cold dishes such as stewed fruit, fruit salad, mixed salads and ice cream, or for cold drinks. Never put lumps of ice in vacuum flasks, as shaking might cause the flask to break. Chill the drink and blend with crushed ice, then pour into vacuum flask.
- Carry meat and fruit patties or pies in the tin in which they were cooked, or bake in aluminium foil dishes which are light AND give excellent cooking results.
- Use tubes of mustard and mayonnaise which take up little space in the hamper.
- For a picnic that you travel to by bus or on foot, pack food in individual plastic bags, so each member of the family carries his own; shell hard-boiled eggs and season all food well so you need not take seasoning.
- For a car picnic be more ambitious with savoury galantines, pies and flans, which can be transported in foil containers or UNBREAKABLE MOULDS—pack articles round with paper so they do not tip and spill.
- Take damp face flannels or sponge in plastic bag to 'freshen up' after the meal.
- Take all your left over bags, bottles and containers HOME if you can't find waste bins.

Sauces for Savoury Snacks

Anchovy sauce

cooking time 8 minutes

you will need:

1 oz. butter
1 oz. flour
½ pint milk
chopped anchovies or 1 teaspoon anchovy essence
salt and pepper

1. Heat the butter gently.
2. Remove from the heat and stir in the flour.
3. Return to the heat and cook without browning.
4. Again remove the pan from the heat and gradually blend in the cold milk.
5. Bring to the boil and cook, stirring with a wooden spoon, until smooth; if any lumps have formed remove by whisking sharply.
6. Add the chopped anchovies or anchovy essence, taste and season well.

Cheese sauce

cooking time 8 minutes

you will need:

1 oz. butter
1 oz. flour
½ pint milk
3–6 oz. grated cheese
little dry mustard
salt and pepper

1. Heat the butter gently.
2. Remove from the heat and stir in the flour.
3. Return to the heat and cook gently for a few minutes so that it does not brown.
4. Again remove the pan from the heat and gradually blend in the cold milk.
5. Bring to the boil and cook, stirring with a wooden spoon until smooth, whisking sharply to prevent any small lumps forming.
6. Add the grated cheese, mustard and seasoning. Serve with vegetable dishes.

Béchamel sauce

cooking time 18 minutes

you will need:

- ingredients as for white sauce (see page 91)
- small piece carrot
- small piece celery
- small piece very finely chopped onion

1 Soak the vegetables in the warm milk for 10 minutes. Strain.
2 Follow method for white sauce, using the flavoured milk.

Cranberry sauce

cooking time 10–15 minutes

you will need:

- 12 oz. cranberries
- 3 oz. sugar
- 2 tablespoons water
- 1 tablespoon port or sherry, optional

1 Heat water and sugar together.
2 Add the fruit and cook until tender.
3 Add port or sherry if wished.

French dressing

no cooking

you will need:

- ½–1 teaspoon English or French mustard
- pinch sugar, salt and pepper
- 1 tablespoon finely chopped parsley or chives
- 1 tablespoon salad oil
- 1 dessertspoon vinegar

1 Mix the dry ingredients together in a basin or on a saucer.
2 Add the oil and vinegar and mix together very thoroughly.

Hollandaise sauce

cooking time 10–15 minutes

you will need:

- 2 egg yolks
- pinch cayenne
- salt and pepper
- 1–2 tablespoons lemon juice or white wine vinegar
- 2–4 oz. butter

1 Use a double saucepan if possible. If not a basin can be used. Put the egg yolks, seasonings and vinegar into the top of the pan, or basin.
2 Whisk over hot water until sauce begins to thicken.*
3 Add the butter in very small pieces, whisking in each pat until it has completely melted before adding the next. DO NOT ALLOW TO BOIL or it will curdle.
4 If too thick add a little cream.

*Cooking time for this varies. If a double saucepan or large basin is used over hot water, the cooking will be quicker, but take special care that sauce does not curdle

Horseradish sauce

cooking time 8 minutes

you will need:

- ingredients as white sauce (see page 91)
- 1 dessertspoon vinegar
- 2 tablespoons grated horseradish
- little cream
- pinch sugar

1 Make white sauce (see page 91).
2 Whisk in the vinegar and horseradish.
3 Add the cream and sugar.

Mexican sauce

no cooking

you will need:

- 2 large tomatoes
- 1 large onion
- 2 tablespoons finely chopped parsley
- 2 tablespoons olive oil
- 2 teaspoons Tabasco sauce
- ½ teaspoon salt

1 Chop tomatoes and onion finely, and add parsley.
2 Combine oil, Tabasco sauce and salt and mix with the chopped vegetables.
3 Serve with cold meats or cheese.

Mustard sauce

cooking time 8 minutes

you will need:

- ingredients as for white sauce (see page 91)
- ½–1 teaspoon dry mustard
- extra milk or cream

1 Blend the dry mustard with the flour.
2 Make the white sauce.
3 Stir in the extra milk or cream.

Onion sauce

cooking time 40 minutes

you will need:

8 oz. onion
water to cover
1 teaspoon salt
1 oz. butter or margarine
1 oz. plain flour
$\frac{1}{4}$ pint milk
seasoning to taste

1 Cover onions with water, add salt and cook for 30 minutes or until tender.
2 Drain (reserving a $\frac{1}{4}$ pint liquor for the sauce) and chop onions finely.
3 Melt fat in a pan, add flour and cook without browning for 2 minutes.
4 Remove from heat, gradually add onion water and milk and reheat, stirring until sauce comes to the boil and thickens.
5 Add onions and simmer for 5 minutes.
6 Taste, season and pour into warmed sauceboat.

Parsley sauce

cooking time 8 minutes

you will need:

ingredients as for white sauce (see below)
1–2 teaspoons chopped parsley
squeeze lemon juice

1 Make white sauce and add the chopped parsley.
2 Blend in the lemon juice.

Salad cream

cooking time 12 minutes

you will need:

1 tablespoon cornflour
$\frac{1}{2}$ pint milk
2 oz. butter or 2 tablespoons olive oil or corn oil
seasoning
1 teaspoon sugar
pinch dry mustard
2 eggs
$\frac{1}{4}$ pint vinegar

1 Blend cornflour with milk, put into a saucepan with butter or oil and plenty of seasoning and sugar.
2 Bring to the boil and cook until thickened.
3 Let it cool slightly, add beaten eggs and cook WITHOUT BOILING for several minutes.*
4 Cool again slightly, then whisk in the vinegar. Allow to get cold before using.

*If wished the cornflour mixture can be transferred to a double saucepan or basin over hot water so the eggs can be cooked with the sauce without fear of curdling

Tartare sauce

no cooking

you will need:

mayonnaise (see page 36)
2 teaspoons chopped parsley
2 teaspoons chopped gherkins
2 teaspoons chopped capers
little chopped tarragon, if available or few drops tarragon vinegar

1 Make the mayonnaise and add chopped parsley, gherkins and capers.
2 If available add also a very little chopped tarragon or a few drops tarragon vinegar.

Tomato sauce

cooking time 40 minutes

you will need:

1 oz. butter
1 small onion
1 carrot
1 rasher bacon
5 large fresh or canned tomatoes
1 bay leaf
$\frac{1}{2}$ oz. flour or $\frac{1}{4}$ oz. cornflour
$\frac{1}{2}$ pint stock or liquid from canned tomatoes
good pinch salt, pepper and sugar

1 Heat the butter and toss the diced onion, carrot and bacon in this—do not brown.
2 Add tomatoes and bay leaf and simmer.
3 Blend the flour with the stock, add to the ingredients and simmer gently for about 30 minutes, stirring from time to time.
4 Rub through a sieve, add seasoning and sugar and reheat.

White sauce

cooking time 8 minutes

you will need:

1 oz. butter or margarine
1 oz. flour
salt and peppers
$\frac{1}{2}$ pint milk to give coating consistency, or $\frac{1}{4}$ pint milk to give panada or binding consistency, or 1 pint milk for thin sauce

1 Heat the butter gently.
2 Remove from the heat and stir in the flour.
3 Return to the heat and cook gently for a few minutes without browning.
4 Again remove the pan from the heat and gradually blend in the cold milk.
5 Bring to the boil and cook, stirring with a wooden spoon, until smooth.
6 Season well.
7 If any small lumps have formed, whisk sharply.

Index

Fish Dishes

Helpful Hints

How to tell if fish is fresh
Firstly, by its smell; this may not be easy to identify in a shop full of fish, but stale fish has a very definite smell of ammonia.

Fresh white fish
These should be quite firm and the eyes and scales should look bright and clear.

Oily fish
Herrings and mackerel have a bright silvery look about the scales and skin, which are dull and the eyes cloudy when stale.

Smoked fish
Haddock keeps well, but if it is stale, it looks dry and dull.

Shellfish
These are fresh if they are a bright colour. With lobsters and prawns, if the tails spring back after being pulled out, they have been freshly caught and cooked. Shellfish is of good quality if it feels weighty for the size.

Apart from the freshness, fish have the best flavour if eaten in season and the Fish Buying Guide on page 40 gives the best times to buy.

To clean fish
If the fish is already filleted, the fishmonger will have washed it. Even so, it is better to wash it again, in plenty of cold water, and pat it dry on kitchen paper.

Rounded fish (mackerel, herring, whiting etc.)

1 Use either a pair of scissors or a sharp kitchen knife.
2 Slit from the belly to the head, then push the knife firmly into the slit to open it sufficiently to be able to remove the intestines. Retain an wash roe.
3 Sometimes fish is cooked with the head on, bu to remove it, cut away just behind the gills.

Flat fish (sole, plaice, etc.)

1 Cut away the belly of the fish, which is jus behind the gills, and clean out thoroughly.
2 If the head is to be removed, cut this off givin a semi-circular shape to the top of the body.

To scale fish
1 Hold it by the tail and scrape very firmly wit the back of the knife towards the head.
2 Remove loosened scales with cold water.

Filleting
1 Cut off the head with a sharp knife (for fis stock, the head provides a great deal of flavour)
2 Make a deep incision down the back of the fish i.e. on the side with the dark skin.
3 Make a shallow cut round the edge of the flesh avoiding the bones and fins.
4 Insert the tip of the knife in the flesh an gradually loosen it away from the backbone folding it over gently. Don't hurry or pull otherwise some of the flesh may be left on th bone.
5 Having removed 1 fillet from the back, tur the fish over and repeat this process, workin this time from the tail rather than the head.
6 Now remove the second fillet from the blac side, then the white.

Skinning
1 Take the fillet in the left hand, holding it by th tip.
2 Make a firm cut with a sharp knife just at th tip, then lift the flesh with the knife away fror the skin; continue until all the flesh is free.
3 Dip the edge of the knife in a little salt for better cutting edge.

This is the correct way to skin fish, but if yo are in a great hurry, put the fillets under a ho

grill for a moment and the skin will come away easily.
Most fishmongers will fillet and skin on request.

Rolling

Fillets of white fish, plaice, whiting, sole, look very attractive if rolled when cooked. Often fillets are stuffed before rolling, but even when served plain with a sauce, they look interesting if neatly rolled.

1 When rolling fish, skin it first (see this page).
2 Season each fillet of fish adding a squeeze of lemon juice and a spread of butter or margarine.
3 Roll loosely from the head to the tip of the tail, into a nice neat shape.
4 Roll so that the skinned side is inside the roll.

Folding

1 Fold fillets in half before putting into the dish.
2 The skin is generally removed before doing this, but if it is left on, this should be folded inwards.

Quantities

These depend a great deal on individual appetites. As a general rule allow:

Fillets. Either 1 large or 2 smaller fillets per person—total weight approximately 5 – 6 oz.

Cutlets. 1 7 – 9 oz. cutlet per person. Some of this weight is accounted for by the fairly large bone.

Whole. A whole fresh haddock or codling approximately 2½ lbs. for 4 people. The extra weight is caused by the heavy head.

Smoked. 1 large or 2 smaller kippers per person. A really good sized smoked haddock should be enough for 4 people.

Cooking Methods

Fish must never be over-cooked as the delicate flavour is lost so easily.

1 *Poaching.* This method is advocated where people must have no fat, and where the fish itself like salmon, turbot etc., has a fairly strong flavour.
2 *Steaming.* This is often recommended for invalids because the fish is so easy to digest.
3 *Frying.* Either shallow or deep fat frying is suitable. The former does not give such a crisp evenly browned cover, but is easier.
4 *Grilling.* An excellent method since it retains the maximum flavour. Keep the fish well basted with margarine or butter.
5 *Baking.* Bake the fish either plain with various ingredients, or stuffed, in a covered dish, or cover with greased paper or foil. Ideally suited for whole fish or pieces.
6 *Roasting.* This is rarely used for fish, but in the case of sturgeon, it can be roasted in a little fat, as meat.
7 *Casseroling.* Fish is first class in a casserole and it is a particularly suitable dish when entertaining, as it can be cooked and served in the one container.
8 *In soups.* An excellent ingredient in soup and particularly good way of using cheaper pieces of fish or, for special occasions, shellfish.

Whichever method you choose, test to see that the fish is adequately cooked. The flesh should have just shrunk away from the bone or skin, or in the case of fillets, the flakes should separate easily.

Poaching

One hears of 'boiled' fish but in fact it should never be boiled—only simmered. Rapid boiling destroys both flavour and texture—the fish is inclined to break and will become very dry.
Simmering or poaching means cooking very gently in either salted water or in a fish stock

made from the bones and skin of the fish and flavoured with bay leaf, onion and carrot. Allow 7 minutes per lb. for thin fillets of fish and 10 minutes for thick cutlets.

If poaching in one piece, allow 12 minutes first lb. and 10 minutes for second lb.

For very large fish allow 7 – 8 minutes per lb. for any weight after first 2 lb.

Court-bouillon

This is the liquid often used for poaching fish. It can be varied according to personal taste, but generally consists of:

1 pint water
1 tablespoon lemon juice
few peppercorns
1 sliced onion
1 teaspoon salt
bouquet garni (see below)

Allow sufficient of the above ingredients to cover the fish and poach as above.

Bouquet-garni

This term is used to describe a small bunch of mixed herbs. For fish this should consist of a small bunch of parsley, thyme, lemon thyme, rosemary (if possible) and fennel (if possible). Add a little sage and chives if wished.

When fresh herbs are unobtainable, use a small quantity of dried herbs.

Frying

SHALLOW

Coat fish in seasoned flour or in egg and breadcrumbs.

Heat the fat, oil or butter in a pan. Allow enough to give a depth of at least ¼ inch and preferably ½ inch.

It is the right temperature when a small cube of bread turns golden brown in 1 minute. Put in the fish, fry fillets for approximately 3 minutes on one side, turn and cook for the same time on the other. Drain.

For cutlets, allow 4 – 5 minutes on either side, reducing the heat after the fish begins to brown.

DEEP

Coat with seasoned flour, egg and breadcrumbs or batter (see page 9). Use oil or cooking fat sufficiently hot to turn a cube of bread golden brown in just under 1 minute. Put the frying basket into the hot oil to heat so the coated fish will not stick. Lower in the fish and cook fillets for approximately 4 minutes—thick cutlets or whole fish approximately 7 minutes, lowering the heat as the fish begins to turn brown. Take out and drain.

Oven fried

Use seasoned flour or egg and breadcrumbs coating. Brush the baking tin with a little oil and put it into oven to get really hot. Put in the prepared fish. Brush with more oil or melted butter or margarine and bake in moderately hot oven (400°F.—Gas Mark 5) allowing 12 – 15 minutes for fillets—approximately 20 minutes for cutlets.

To drain

So that fish is really dry and crisp after frying, it must be well drained.

Put crumpled tissue paper, kitchen paper or kitchen roll on a hot dish and put the fish on to this. Do not use greaseproof paper because this holds the fat rather than absorbs it.

Egg and breadcrumb coating

you will need:

To coat 4 large or 8 small fillets or 4 steaks
1 egg
very little milk or water
approximately 2 oz. crisp breadcrumbs or soft breadcrumbs for bigger pieces of fish which take longer to cook

1. Add little water or milk to egg and beat slightly.
2. Dip fish into this or brush it over.
3. Put breadcrumbs into paper bag or on sheet of paper and turn fish in this, pressing on crumbs firmly.

Seasoned flour coating

you will need:

To coat 4 large fillets or steaks or 8 small fillets
approximately 1 oz. flour
¼ teaspoon salt
celery salt, cayenne pepper, paprika pepper, pinch of mixed herbs, little grated lemon rind (optional), pinch pepper

1 Mix the flour and seasonings.
2 Put seasoned flour on to greaseproof paper or into a greaseproof paper bag.
3 Put fish in this and shake gently in the flour.

Fritter batter

you will need:

To coat 4 steaks or large fillets or 8 small fillets	4 oz. flour seasoning 1 egg ¼ – ½ pint milk and water

1 Sieve flour and seasoning.
2 Add egg, gradually beat in liquid.

For fillets, use larger quantity of liquid, for more solid cod etc., ¼ pint only.

Grilling

Most fish is suitable for grilling. Fillets, unless very thick, can be grilled without turning. Whole fish should be turned so both sides are cooked. Make sure the grill is pre-heated and keep the fish well brushed with melted butter.

For fillets: allow approximately 4 minutes, turning the heat down after the first 2 – 3 minutes.

For thicker fish: grill quickly for 2 – 3 minutes on both sides, then reduce heat for a further 3 – 4 minutes.

Grilled mushrooms are an ideal accompaniment and can be cooked at the same time.

Baking

Care should be taken with fillets to keep them moist. Butter the dish well, put in the seasoned fish, add a little stock, milk or white wine and cover with buttered paper (use the stock in sauces).
Bake fillets of plaice, sole etc., for approximately 12 – 20 minutes, cutlets of white fish for approximately 20 minutes, whole fish for approximately 12 minutes per lb. (if stuffed, weigh with stuffing).
The oven should be moderate to moderately hot (375° – 400°F.—Gas Mark 4 – 5).

White Fish

Buying and Cooking Tables

FISH IN SEASON	TO BUY AND COOK
BASS **May - Sept**	Sea bass the best of the various bass, a striped fish that can be cooked like salmon.
BRILL **May - Aug**	Large flat fish, only small supplies available. Use like turbot.
BREAM **July - Dec**	Generally a freshwater fish. Buy whole or in fillets. Not very plentiful, but a good flavour. Bake with a savoury stuffing or grill. Per person, allow 6 – 8 oz. on bone, 4 – 6 oz. filleted.
COD **all year best Oct - Mar**	Excellent all-purpose fish because of its definite flavour: particularly good in made-up dishes. Poach, fry, bake or grill. It has large flakes, so when frying is inclined to break unless floured well before being coated with egg and breadcrumbs or batter
FLOUNDER **Nov - Mar**	Not quite such a delicate flavour as sole or plaice, but very much like them. Can be used in the same way. Allow 8 oz. per person or 1 small fish, or 4 – 6 oz. when filleted.
HADDOCK **Oct - Feb**	Can be used in every way like cod. Buy fillets, cutlets or whole fish. May be slightly dry when cooked unless kept well moistened. 8 oz. per person when whole, 4 – 6 oz. in fillets or steaks.
HAKE **June - Jan**	Not unlike cod, but a more delicate flavour. Best fried or baked. Buy steaks or fillets, 4 – 6 oz. per person. Good with various sauces.

FISH IN SEASON	TO BUY AND COOK
HALIBUT **July - April**	More expensive fish, though generally cheaper than turbot. Excellent poached, grilled or baked. Small halibut under 3 lb. should be baked whole. A 'filling' fish, so allow 4 – 6 oz. per person when buying steaks or a good 6 oz. when buying whole.
DOG FISH or HUSS **Sept - May**	Will be skinned and filleted. Best baked or fried. Not very fleshy, so allow 6 – 8 oz. per person. Best with good flavoured sauce.
JOHN DORY or DORY **Sept - early Jan**	Good flavour, but ugly appearance. Buy fillets and cook in any way suitable for sole or turbot. Allow 6 oz. per person.
PLAICE **Late May - Dec**	One of the most popular fish easily distinguished from other flat fish by yellow or reddish brown spots on the dark skin. Bake, fry, grill, steam, poach or serve in the same way as sole. 1 small fish per person or approximately 6 oz.
SKATE **Nov - May**	An ugly but undoubtedly delicious fish. Generally sold in rather triangular-shaped pieces. Fry, bake or poach or use cold in salads. Best when steamed a few minutes before being fried. Because of the large heavy bones, allow about 10 oz. per person.
SOLE **Some kind available all year**	Considered by many people the finest fish of all and certainly the one that has produced more delicious fish dishes and sauces. Dover sole does not mean it

FISH IN SEASON	TO BUY AND COOK
	comes from Dover, but is so called to distinguish it as the finest sole. Others, lemon, Torbay, witch, dabs are all good. Bake, fry, poach, steam or grill and serve with lemon, melted butter or other sauces. Allow 1 fish or 8 oz. per person.
TURBOT April - early Sept	Can be distinguished from halibut by the spots on its skin. Bake, grill, fry or poach and serve with sauce. Excellent cold in salads. It is a substantial and expensive fish. Per person, allow 4 – 6 oz. as fillets, or 6 oz. in steaks or whole.
WHITING Oct - April	An ideal fish for children and invalids since it has a very fine delicate flavour and is small-flaked. Much less expensive than sole or plaice, and can be filleted and served in the same way. Poach, bake, grill or fry. Allow 1 fish or 8 oz. when filleted, per person.

Cooking bass

This fish is all too rarely seen, but it is delicious when freshly caught, so do take every opportunity of buying it when you find it in stock. Its distinctive flavour is not lost when served with a sauce.

Baked bass

cooking time 25 – 30 minutes

you will need for 4 servings:

4 fillets bass
1 tiny onion
small knob butter or margarine
lemon
parsley
seasoning
sauce duglére (see page 84)

1. Season the fillets and put into a buttered dish.
2. Cover with finely chopped onion and a little more butter.
3. Cook in a moderate oven (375°F.—Gas Mark 4)
4. Make the sauce.
5. To serve lift fish on to a hot serving dish removing the onion, and coat with sauce.
6. Garnish with lemon and parsley.

Bass in cheese and wine sauce

cooking time 30 – 35 minutes

you will need for 4 servings:

seasoning
4 fillets bass
1 oz. margarine or butter
2 – 3 tablespoons wine or sherry
2 tablespoons grated cheese
½ pint cheese sauce (see page 81)
croûtons fried bread, optional

1. Season fillets and put into a greased dish.
2. Top with butter and wine, cover with foil or lid, and cook in a moderate oven (375°F.—Gas Mark 4) for approximately 30 – 35 minutes.
3. Meanwhile make the cheese sauce using slightly less milk than in the recipe.
4. Lift fish on to a hot serving dish.
5. Mix liquid from the dish into sauce.
6. Coat fish with sauce.
7. Top with cheese and put for one or two minutes under a hot grill.
8. Garnish with croûtons.

Cooking brill

Brill is very firm fleshed and has a good flavour when served cold in salads. It can also be substituted for plaice, sole or turbot in hot dishes.

Grilled brill

cooking time 8 – 10 minutes

you will need for 4 servings:

4 fillets brill*
seasoning
squeeze lemon juice
approximately 2 oz. butter or margarine

* Because of its firm texture, brill is particularly good when grilled. It has a fairly dry flesh, so keep it moist with plenty of butter or margarine

1. Season fillets and add lemon juice.
2. Brush the grid of the grill pan with a little melted margarine or butter and put on the fillets.
3. Grill until golden, turn, brush with more margarine or butter and grill.

Brill Portugaise

cooking time 35 – 40 minutes

you will need for 4 servings:

4 large fillets brill
1 large onion
2 – 3 large tomatoes
approximately 4 tablespoons fish stock or white wine
seasoning
2 oz. margarine or butter
chopped parsley
lemon

1 Put fillets into a buttered dish and cover with wafer thin onion slices.
2 Skin and slice tomatoes fairly thickly and arrange over the top.
3 Add the liquid.
4 Season well and top with butter or margarine.
5 Cover dish with paper or foil.
6 Bake in the centre of a moderate oven (375°F. —Gas Mark 4) for approximately 35 – 40 minutes.
7 Serve in the cooking dish, garnished with parsley and lemon.

Note:

As an additional sauce with this, either a tomato (page 84) or a white wine sauce (page 84) would be suitable and any liquid left in the serving dish could be incorporated in it.

Variations:

Brill mornay

Recipe as above but add a thick layer grated cheese on top of the tomatoes before cooking. Do not cover the dish.

Potato pie

Use recipe as above but top with very creamy mashed potato and a little margarine.
Increase the cooking time to 45 – 50 minutes until the potato is very crisp and golden brown

Cooking bream

This fish is ideal for grilling or frying, as it has not a very strong flavour and is easily spoilt by being combined with anything with a pronounced taste. Stuffings should be kept fairly delicate.

Stuffed whole bream

cooking time 30 minutes

you will need for 4 servings:

4 small bream
stuffing as previous recipe, parsley stuffing (see page 87), or mushroom stuffing (see page 86)
1 – 2 oz. butter or margarine

1 Split bream and remove heads.
2 Skin fish (see page 7) and stuff.
3 Brush generously with melted butter.
4 Put into a well-buttered dish, cover and cook for approximately 30 minutes in the centre of a moderate oven (375°F.—Gas Mark 4).

Baked stuffed bream

cooking time 20 – 25 minutes

you will need for 4 servings:

seasoning
8 small fillets bream
squeeze lemon juice
little butter

For stuffing:
2 oz. soft breadcrumbs
1 oz. butter or margarine
1 hard-boiled egg
1 tablespoon chopped parsley
seasoning
squeeze lemon juice
1 teaspoon grated lemon rind

lemon slices for garnish

1 Season fillets, adding lemon juice.
2 Mix all stuffing ingredients together and spread on the fish.
3 Roll or fold, dot with butter and put into a buttered dish.
4 Cook, covered, for approximately 20 – 25 minutes in a moderate oven (375°F.—Gas Mark 4).
5 Serve garnished with lemon slices.

Grilled stuffed fillets of bream

cooking time 10 – 12 minutes

you will need for 4 servings:

seasoning
8 small fillets bream
squeeze lemon juice
little butter

For stuffing:
2 oz. soft breadcrumbs
1 oz. butter or margarine
1 hard-boiled egg
1 tablespoon chopped parsley
seasoning
squeeze lemon juice
1 teaspoon grated lemon rind

1 Season fillets, adding lemon juice.
2 Mix stuffing ingredients together and spread on fish.
3 Roll or fold fillets and brush generously with melted butter.
4 Grill steadily for approximately 10 – 12 minutes, turning halfway through.

Cooking cod

This is possibly the most versatile fish of all, as it lends itself to every cooking method. As it is a large fish, a whole fillet is generally sufficient for 2 – 3 servings and when absolutely fresh, is very sweet and succulent.

Cod and macaroni casserole

cooking time 20 – 25 minutes

you will need for 4 servings:

3 oz. macaroni
1½ – 2 lb. cod fillet
2 onions
2 carrots
little chopped dill, fennel or parsley
seasoning
water

For the sauce:
2 oz. margarine
1½ oz. flour
½ pint fish stock (see page 72)
salt
pepper
⅛ pint cream or milk
⅛ – ¼ pint white wine or cider
grated cheese
breadcrumbs
little margarine

1. Cook macaroni until tender in 2 pints boiling salted water.
2. Drain thoroughly.
3. Put fish into pan with onions, carrots and dill.
4. Season, add enough cold water to cover.
5. Simmer, covered, until tender.
6. Drain fish, but retain ½ pint stock for the sauce.
7. Chop fish and fill a casserole with alternate layers of fish and macaroni, finishing with macaroni.

To make sauce:

1. Heat margarine.
2. Stir in flour and cook gently for several minutes until the roux is dry.
3. Gradually stir in fish stock, bring sauce to boil and cook until thick.
4. Season well after stirring in milk and white wine.
5. Pour over macaroni, then cover with grated cheese, breadcrumbs and margarine.
6. Make sure both macaroni and fish are hot, then pour on very hot sauce, cover top as directed and brown under a pre-heated grill.

Note:

To cook slowly, put into centre of a moderate oven (375°F.—Gas Mark 4) and leave for about 1 hour, or a little longer at a lower temperature.

Variations:

Cod and potato cheese

Use 12 oz. boiled potatoes, cut into thick slices, in place of the cooked macaroni.

Cod and vegetable cheese

Substitute 12 oz. to 1 lb. cooked mixed vegetables for macaroni. Add peas, beans, sliced carrot, sprigs of cauliflower.

Cod fillets Portugaise

cooking time 20 – 30 minutes

you will need for 4 servings:

4 cod fillets
1 Spanish onion
2 – 3 tomatoes
salt
pepper
1 oz. grated cheese
1 oz. butter

1. Place fillets in a greased fireproof dish.
2. Slice onion and tomatoes very thinly and place on top.
3. Sprinkle over salt, pepper and grated cheese.
4. Dot with butter.
5. Bake 20 – 30 minutes in moderate oven (375°F. —Gas Mark 4).

Cod in cider

cooking time 30 minutes

you will need for 4 servings:

4 cod cutlets
salt, pepper
1 tablespoon olive or vegetable oil
2 small onions or shallots
½ pint dry cider
½ oz. flour
1 oz. butter
2 oz. chopped mushrooms
2 teaspoons chopped parsley

1. Put cutlets into a fireproof dish.
2. Season and pour oil over.
3. Sprinkle with finely chopped onion or shallot, and add cider.
4. Cover* and bake in a moderately hot oven (400°F.—Gas Mark 5) for 20 minutes.
5. Remove from oven, skin fish and remove bone if unlikely to destroy the shape of the fish.
6. Take out a little cooking liquor and blend thoroughly with flour and butter.
7. Pour back over the fish, making sure it is evenly distributed.
8. Add mushrooms and parsley and cook, uncovered, for a further 10 minutes at moderate heat, or a little longer if cutlets are thick.

Note:

If more liquid is needed when you thicken the sauce, add extra cider.

* The lid must fit well or the liquid will evaporate.

Cod Italienne

cooking time 30 minutes

you will need for 4 servings:

4 6-oz. cod steaks
2 medium onions
1 oz. butter
8 oz. can tomatoes
2 teaspoons made mustard
2 teaspoons brown sugar
2 tablespoons finely chopped parsley
½ teaspoon mixed herbs
2 teaspoons salt
sprinkle cayenne pepper

1 Wash steaks and wipe dry.
2 Arrange in a greased casserole dish, cover with sliced onions fried in butter.
3 Heat together tomatoes, mustard, sugar, parsley, herbs, salt and pepper, then pour over fish and onions.
4 Cover dish with a fitting lid or aluminium foil and bake in the centre of a moderate oven (400°F.—Gas Mark 5) for 25 minutes.
Serve with potatoes.

Savoury cod with mushroom stuffing

Illustrated on the cover

cooking time 20 – 30 minutes

you will need for 4 servings:

For the stuffing:
4 oz. crustless white bread
milk
1 tablespoon chopped parsley
finely grated rind 1 lemon
1 egg yolk
salt and pepper
4 mushrooms

4 cod fillets, 1-inch thick
1 oz. margarine

1 Crumble bread into bowl and pour over milk to moisten, leave to soak.
2 Squeeze any surplus milk from bread so it is fairly dry.
3 Stir in chopped parsley, lemon rind, egg yolk, salt and pepper.
4 Wash mushrooms, remove stalks, chop finely and add to stuffing. Keep mushroom caps on one side.
5 Wipe fish with damp cloth. Fill centres with stuffing and wrap side pieces firmly around, tie in position with string.
6 Put into fireproof dish or baking tin, sprinkle with pepper and salt.
7 Brush melted margarine over cod fillets and mushroom tops.
8 Cover fish with greaseproof paper or foil and bake in moderate oven (375°F.—Gas Mark 4) for 20 – 30 minutes.
9 After 10 minutes, put mushrooms in the dish with fish.

Serve with green peas.

Cod fillets with creamed tomato sauce

cooking time 30 minutes

you will need for 4 servings:

4 cod fillets
¼ pint milk
1 oz. butter
½ pint white sauce (see page 83)
chopped parsley for garnish

For the sauce:
½ lb. tomatoes
1 small onion
1 small bunch herbs
1 blade mace
2 peppercorns
1 oz. lean ham, sliced
½ oz. butter
½ tablespoon vinegar
¼ pint white fish stock (see page 72)
few drops cochineal

1 Wash the fish, put into greased dish with milk and dot with butter.
2 Bake, covered, for 20 minutes in a moderate oven (375°F.—Gas Mark 4).
3 While it is cooking make a sauce with all ingredients, except cochineal.
4 Cook slowly until tender.
5 Rub through a sieve.
6 Add to white sauce. Mix in cochineal, and pour over fillets.
7 Garnish with parsley.

Stuffed cod cutlets and tomato sauce

cooking time 30 – 35 minutes

you will need for 4 servings:

4 cod cutlets
tomato sauce (see page 84)

For stuffing:
2 tablespoons oil or 2 oz. butter
1 small chopped onion
4 oz. fresh white breadcrumbs
4 oz. grated cheese
2 tablespoons chopped parsley
1 egg
parsley and tomatoes for garnish

1 Heat oil or butter and fry onion until tender.
2 Add breadcrumbs, 2 oz. cheese and parsley.
3 Mix well and bind with beaten egg.
4 Remove bones from cutlets, fill centres with stuffing.
5 Put remaining cheese on top.
6 Place in a greased dish and bake in a moderate

oven (375°F.—Gas Mark 4) for 25 - 30 minutes.

7 When cooked remove skin and place cutlets on a serving dish.
8 Garnish with parsley and tomato wedges and serve with croquette potatoes and tomato sauce.

Baked potatoes with cod stuffing

cooking time approximately 2½ hours

you will need for 4 servings:

4 large potatoes
knob margarine
seasoning
about ½ lb. cod fillet
squeeze of lemon juice

1 Bake potatoes in their jackets.
2 Slice tops off, scoop out centres.
3 Mash pulp with margarine and seasoning.
4 Skin cod and cut into 4 pieces.
5 Put a piece into each potato case.
6 Add seasoning and lemon juice. Pipe or pile potato on top of fish and bake in a moderate oven (375°F.—Gas Mark 4) until fish is cooked and potatoes brown and crisp on top.

Variation:

On 2 pieces of cod put sliced tomato and a little veal stuffing (see page 87), on the others, a small spoonful of horseradish cream (see page 82). Salmon can be substituted for cod.

Cod scallops

cooking time 15 minutes

you will need for 4 servings:

12 oz. flaked cooked cod
¼ pint thick white sauce (see page 83)
seasoning
1 oz. grated cheese
8 oz. mashed potatoes

To garnish:
little parsley

1 Stir fish into sauce and season thoroughly.
2 Put on to escallop shells and sprinkle with cheese.
3 Pipe a border of potato around the edge of the shells.
4 Put under a hot grill for a few minutes until crisp and brown on top.
5 Serve garnished with parsley.

Variations:

Fish scallops
Any cooked white fish may be used.

Lobster scallops
Flaked canned lobster can be used instead of, or with, white fish.

Prawn scallops
Whole or chopped prawns may be used instead of white fish—or use half quantity prawns and half white fish.

Cod bake

cooking time 40 minutes

you will need for 4 servings:

1 lb. potatoes
seasoning
2 large grated onions
2 tablespoons chopped parsley
1½ lb. flaked cooked cod
1 gill milk

1 Grease a shallow casserole.
2 Put a layer of grated potato on the bottom, season well, add a sprinkling of the onion and parsley, then a layer of fish. Continue filling the casserole like this, finishing with a potato layer.
3 Pour milk over.
4 Cover with greased paper, then the lid.
5 Bake in the centre of a moderately hot oven (400°F.—Gas Mark 5) for 40 minutes.

Serve hot or cold.

Fish roast

cooking time 30 minutes

you will need for 4 servings:

2 lb. middle cut cod or fresh haddock
8 oz. tomatoes*
2 oz. fat or butter
1 teaspoon salt
pinch pepper

* Thinly sliced onion may be substituted

1 Remove any fins and make about 4 shallow slashes across the back.
2 Slice 1 tomato thickly and place 1 slice in each slash.
3 Dot fish with fat or butter, sprinkle with salt and pepper and put into an oven dish.
4 Put remaining tomatoes around fish and bake in a hot oven (425 - 450°F.—Gas Mark 6 - 7) for about 30 minutes until the fish is cooked. Baste once or twice during the baking.

Fish cream

cooking time approximately 1 hour

you will need for 4 servings:

- 1 lb. cod, skinned
- ¼ pint thick creamy white sauce (see page 83)
- 2 teaspoons finely grated onion
- 1 teaspoon finely chopped parsley
- seasoning
- 3 tablespoons soft fine breadcrumbs
- 2 tablespoons cream (optional)

1 Put fish through a mincer, or chop finely.
2 Mix well all ingredients. Always make sauce mixture very soft to give a creamy consistency.
3 Put into a greased mould.
4 Either steam gently for 1 hour or bake for just under 1 hour in a very moderate oven (300 – 350°F.—Gas Mark 2 – 3).
Turn out and serve hot or cold, with mayonnaise, olives or a green salad.

Variations:

Use tomato sauce (see page 84) instead of a white sauce. Add chopped olives instead of onion.

Steamed fish cream

cooking time 45 minutes

you will need for 4 servings:

- ½ lb. flaked cooked fish—cod, hake, fresh haddock
- 1 egg
- seasoning
- few drops anchovy essence
- few drops vinegar
- ¼ pint thick white sauce (see page 83)
- 2 tablespoons breadcrumbs
- 2 tablespoons cream from the top of the milk, or evaporated milk

1 Mix all ingredients together.
2 Put into a greased basin.
3 Cover thoroughly and steam for 45 minutes.
4 Turn out and serve hot or cold.

Fish and tomato bake

cooking time about 30 minutes

you will need for 4 servings:

- 1 lb. tomatoes
- 1 teaspoon sugar
- ¼ teaspoon pepper
- 1 teaspoon salt
- 1 bay leaf
- few drops lemon juice
- 4 steaks cod, haddock or turbot

To garnish:
- lemon slices
- parsley

1 Skin and slice tomatoes and put into an ovenproof dish with sugar, seasoning, bay leaf and lemon juice.
2 Place fish on top and cover dish with buttered greaseproof paper.
3 Bake in a moderate oven (375°F.—Gas Mark 4) for about 30 minutes.

Serve hot or cold, garnished with lemon slices and chopped parsley.

Chutneyed fish

cooking time 25 – 30 minutes

you will need for 4 servings:

- 1 lb. fish—fresh haddock, cod or hake
- 1 egg
- ½ teacup milk
- 2 tablespoons chutney
- few slices cucumber or gherkin
- 1 teaspoon grated onion
- few drops vinegar
- seasoning
- 2 tablespoons crisp breadcrumbs
- 2 tablespoons grated cheese (optional)
- 1 oz. margarine

1 Put fish into a greased dish.
2 Mix egg, milk, chutney, cucumber, onion, vinegar and seasoning together.
3 Pour over fish.
4 Sprinkle top with breadcrumbs and cheese, and dot with margarine.
5 Bake in the centre of a moderately hot oven 400°F.—Gas Mark 5) for 25 – 30 minutes, depending on the thickness of the fish.

Cooking flounder

A substitute for sole or plaice, although flounder has not such a good flavour, but is worth buying when really fresh.

Stuffed fillets of flounder with Béarnaise sauce

cooking time 20 – 25 minutes

you will need for 4 servings:

- seasoning
- 4 large or 8 small fillets flounder
- parsley stuffing (see page 87)
- approximately ⅛ pint white wine
- Béarnaise sauce (see page 80)
- 1 tablespoon tomato purée

1 Season fillets and spread with parsley stuffing.
2 Fold or roll and put into a dish with the wine.
3 Cover tightly with greased paper, foil or a well fitting lid, and cook for approximately 20 - 25 minutes in a moderate oven (375°F.—Gas Mark 4).
4 Make the Béarnaise sauce and, when thick, add tomato purée.
5 Lift fillets on to a hot serving dish and strain a very little of the liquid into the sauce.
6 Mix well and pour over the fish.

Serve at once.

This looks most attractive in a border of browned Duchesse potatoes (see page 88).

Cooking haddock

This is one of the nicest cheaper white fish, with a very fine texture and a particularly delicate and sweet flavour. It lends itself to all methods of cooking and is especially good fried, baked or grilled.

Baked haddock

cooking time 20 minutes

you will need for 4 servings:

- 4 large or 8 small fillets fresh haddock
- seasoning
- good knob butter
- 2 teaspoons parsley
- ¼ pint cream

1 Skin the fillets (see page 7).
2 Season them and lay flat in an ovenproof serving dish.
3 Add remaining ingredients and cook for approximately 20 minutes in a moderate oven (375°F.—Gas Mark 4).

Note:

The cream forms an almost golden crust over the fish which is absolutely delicious. This dish can be made more colourful by garnishing with paprika pepper, more chopped parsley and lemon, when cooked.

Variations:

1 Add very finely chopped mushrooms, lightly fried in butter, to the cream before cooking.
2 Put a thick layer of grated cheese or thin slices of cheese over the cream before cooking.
3 Put fish, cream etc., into a fairly deep dish and top with a layer of very creamy mashed potato. Allow approximately 30 minutes' cooking time.

Fish cutlets continental

cooking time 25 - 30 minutes

you will need for 4 servings:

- 4 cod or fresh haddock cutlets
- 1 small can red peppers or 1 red pepper
- 1 oz. margarine
- 1 small packet frozen peas

For stuffing:

- 4 tablespoons white breadcrumbs
- 1 tablespoon finely chopped parsley
- seasoning
- finely grated rind and juice 1 lemon
- 1 small egg
- ½ oz. melted margarine

For parsley sauce:

- 1 oz. margarine
- 1 oz. flour
- just under ¾ pint milk
- 2 tablespoons finely chopped parsley
- seasoning

1 Wash the fish.
2 Remove centre bone from each cutlet with a sharp knife.
3 Place cutlets in a fireproof dish, previously brushed inside with melted margarine.
4 Stuff centre of each cutlet (see below).
5 Cut peppers into ¼-inch wide strips.
6 Arrange over fish in a lattice design.
7 Put small knobs of margarine on top and cover dish completely with foil.
8 Bake in the centre of a pre-heated moderately hot oven (400°F.—Gas Mark 5) for 25 - 30 minutes.
9 Cook peas in boiling salted water.
10 Lift fish on to a hot serving dish and pour sauce (see below) over.
11 Drain peas and arrange around fish.

To make the stuffing:

Mix all ingredients together.

To make parsley sauce:

1 Melt margarine over a low heat.
2 Stir in flour and cook until it bubbles.
3 Remove from heat and gradually stir in milk.
4 Return to heat, bring to the boil and cook gently for 2 - 3 minutes stirring all the time.
5 Stir in parsley and season well.

Paprika fish

cooking time 35 minutes

you will need for 4 servings:

1 - 1½ lb. fillets plaice, whiting or haddock	1 oz. flour
2 teaspoons paprika pepper	1 - 2 teaspoons salt
8 tablespoons milk	pinch pepper
extra milk	2 teaspoons made mustard
	1 tablespoon vinegar

1 Skin fish and cut into 3-inch pieces. Place in layers in a greased casserole, sprinkling each layer with paprika.
2 Add milk. Cover and cook in a moderate oven. (375°F.—Gas Mark 4) for 30 minutes.
3 Drain fish, putting on to hot dish, keeping the liquid and making it up to ½ pint with extra milk.
4 Blend dry ingredients with a little fish liquid and made mustard. Boil remaining liquid and, when boiling, add to blended ingredients. Return to pan and stir until boiling. Boil gently for 5 minutes.
5 Stir in vinegar and pour sauce over fish.

Serve hot.

Haddock with wine sauce

cooking time 20 minutes

you will need for 4 servings:

4 large or 8 small fillets haddock	½ pint white wine
2 shallots or small onions	¼ pint water or fish stock (see page 72)
salt, pepper	*For sauce:*
2 teaspoons chopped parsley	1 oz. butter
	1 oz. flour

1 Fold the fillets.
2 Put into a buttered dish with chopped shallots, parsley, seasoning, ¼ pint wine and water or fish stock.
3 Cover with buttered paper and bake in a moderate oven (375°F.—Gas Mark 4) for approximately 20 minutes.
4 Meanwhile heat butter, stir in flour and cook gently for several minutes.
5 Add remaining wine and cook until smooth.
6 Lift fillets on to a hot dish.
7 Add unstrained liquid from the dish to sauce and cook until smooth and thick.
8 Pour over the fish.

Cooking hake

It can be compared to cod but has a slightly less definite flavour. Because of its firm texture, hake is extremely good when grilled.

Cheese stuffed hake

cooking time 20 - 30 minutes

you will need for 4 servings:

4 cutlets hake	½ teaspoon dry mustard
2 oz. breadcrumbs	salt, pepper
2 oz. grated cheese	2 oz. butter

1 Wipe cutlets and remove central bone.
2 Mix breadcrumbs with cheese, mustard, salt, pepper and 1 oz. melted butter.
3 Divide into four and stuff cutlets.
4 Tie each with string.
5 Place in a buttered ovenproof dish and bake in a moderate oven (375°F.—Gas Mark 4) for 20 - 30 minutes, until tender.
6 Top each cutlet with a knob of butter. Serve with peas and carrots.

Grilled hake

cooking time 10 minutes

you will need for 4 servings:

4 cutlets hake	1 - 2 oz. butter or margarine
seasoning	squeeze lemon juice

1 Season fish and brush with melted butter or margarine and lemon juice.
2 Because this fish is fairly thick, it can go into the grill pan, not on the grid, so brush the bottom of the grill pan with a little melted butter or margarine.
3 Put under a hot grill and cook for approximately 4 - 5 minutes until golden brown.
4 Turn and brush with a little extra butter or margarine and cook the other side.

Variations:

Anchovy grilled hake
Blend either a little anchovy essence or chopped anchovy fillets with the butter before cooking.

Devilled grilled hake
Add pinch curry powder and few drops

Worcestershire sauce to the butter before grilling.

Curried hake

Add ½ to 1 - teaspoon curry powder to butter and when the fish is turned, brush with the curried butter and top with a little chutney before grilling second side.

Grilled hake mornay

Sprinkle a good layer of grated cheese on to fish after it has been turned, then brush with melted butter.

Spanish hake

cooking time 20 – 25 minutes

you will need for 4 servings:

2 oz. margarine
4 medium-sized cutlets hake
3 large tomatoes
1 oz. grated cheese
1 large grated onion
seasoning
crisp breadcrumbs

1 Grease a dish with margarine and put in the fish.
2 Mix chopped tomatoes, cheese, onion and seasoning.
3 Pile mixture on to fish.
4 Sprinkle breadcrumbs over.
5 Dot each cutlet with remaining margarine.
6 Cover dish with a lid or paper.
7 Bake for 20 – 25 minutes in the centre of a moderately hot oven (400°F.—Gas Mark 5).

Cooking halibut

This is one of the more luxurious fish and is delicious when grilled, fried or poached. Because of its firm texture, it is excellent served cold, so can be used in any of the fish salads. It is usually cheaper than turbot, which it resembles, so can be substituted for it in any recipe.

Fried halibut

1 Halibut can be coated with egg and breadcrumbs, with batter (see page 9) or seasoned flour.
2 Fry steadily in shallow fat for 3 – 4 minutes on either side until golden brown, then, if rather thick, lower the heat for a few extra minutes to make sure the fish is cooked right through the centre.

Canadian style halibut

cooking time 35 minutes

you will need for 4 servings:

4 halibut steaks
salt
1½ oz. margarine or butter
½ pint milk
1 oz. flour
2 hard-boiled eggs

1 Carefully remove skin from steaks and lightly rub flesh all over with salt.
2 Place in an ovenproof dish, dot with ½ oz. margarine or butter and add milk.
3 Cover and bake in a moderately hot oven (400°F.—Gas Mark 5) fo4 20 – 25 minutes.
4 Strain off milk and keep fish hot while making the sauce.
5 Melt remaining margarine or butter, add flour and cook for 1 to 2 minutes.
6 Gradually stir in milk in which fish was cooked and bring to the boil, stirring.
7 Boil gently for 5 minutes, then add chopped eggs.
8 Coat steaks with sauce and serve at once, with baked, halved tomatoes.

Halibut au Parmesan

cooking time 8 – 10 minutes

you will need for 4 servings:

4 portions halibut
seasoning
approximately ½ oz. flour
1½ oz. grated Parmesan cheese
1 whole egg or 1 egg white
oil or butter
chopped parsley
lemon slices

1 Season the fish. Mix flour with a little extra seasoning and cheese.
2 Brush fish lightly with beaten egg or egg white, then roll in the cheese coating.
3 Put enough oil or butter into a frying pan to give a good ½-inch depth.
4 Fry the fish for approximately 8 – 10 minutes, turning until crisp and golden brown.
5 Top with parsley and garnish with lemon slices.

Halibut maltesa

cooking time 30 – 40 minutes

you will need for 4 servings:

1¼ – 1½ lb. halibut
½ teaspoon salt
¼ teaspoon pepper
2 tablespoons olive oil or fat
1 – 2 cloves garlic, minced or crushed (optional)
4 tomatoes or 1 medium can tomatoes
2 oz. blanched almonds

1. Cut fish into 4 neat pieces.
2. Season with salt and pepper.
3. Heat olive oil, add garlic and peeled and chopped tomatoes.
4. Cook until tomatoes are sauce consistency.
5. Add salt to taste.
6. Place fish in shallow casserole, cover with tomato sauce.
7. Bake in moderate oven (375°F.—Gas Mark 4) for 20 – 25 minutes.
8. Just before serving, sprinkle sliced almonds over.

Halibut meunière

cooking time 15 minutes

you will need for 4 servings:

4 halibut steaks
1 oz. seasoned flour
3 oz. butter
juice ½ small lemon
little chopped parsley

1. Wipe and dry the steaks and coat each lightly with seasoned flour.
2. Gently fry them in butter for 12 – 15 minutes, turning once.
3. When cooked, lift steaks on to a warmed serving dish. Reheat the butter until nut brown in colour.
4. Stir in the lemon juice and parsley and pour over the fish.
5. Serve at once.

Halibut en papillote

cooking time 40 minutes

you will need for 4 servings:

4 half halibut steaks, ¾ inch thick

For sauce:
1 oz. margarine
1 oz. flour
¼ pint milk
2 tablespoons white wine
2 – 3 sliced mushrooms
2 tablespoons cream
salt, pepper

1. Trim steaks and place on a piece of foil, large enough to wrap them completely.
2. Melt margarine, add flour and cook gently for 2 – 3 minutes.
3. Stir in milk and bring to the boil.
4. Add wine and mushrooms and cook for a further 3 – 4 minutes, stirring continuously.
5. Remove from heat and stir in cream. Season to taste.
6. Divide sauce over steaks and seal in the foil, twisting the ends securely.
7. Place on a baking sheet and bake in a moderately hot oven (400°F.—Gas Mark 5) for 30 minutes.

Cooking huss

This is a very popular fish, but has a rather unusual appearance. It can be fried, grilled or baked in butter and is also good in made up dishes like fish pies.

Baked huss with tomatoes

cooking time 30 – 35 minutes

you will need for 4 servings:

4 portions huss
4 large tomatoes
seasoning
squeeze lemon juice
knob butter or margarine

1. Put fish into a greased baking dish and top with lemon juice, skinned sliced tomatoes, margarine or butter, and seasoning.
2. Cover dish with lid, greaseproof paper or foil.
3. Bake approximately 30 – 35 minutes in the centre of a moderate oven (375°F.—Gas Mark 4).

Cooking dory (John Dory)

A rather rare fish but worth trying. It is good baked and because of its excellent taste, needs the minimum of other flavours.

Baked dory

cooking time 25 – 30 minutes

you will need for 4 servings:

4 portions dory
2 oz. butter
seasoning
squeeze lemon juice
2 teaspoons chopped parsley

1. Put fish into a buttered dish.
2. Add melted butter, seasoning, lemon juice and parsley.
3. Bake for approximately 25 – 30 minutes in a moderate oven (375°F.—Gas Mark 4), basting

once or twice or covering the dish before cooking.

Variations:

1 Add ¼ pint white wine and use to make a wine sauce.
2 Add ¼ pint milk or cream and make into a white sauce to serve with the fish.
3 Add ¼ pint fish stock (see page 72) and use as part of the liquid to make cheese sauce to serve with the fish.

Cooking plaice

Almost the most popular fish and rarely as expensive as sole. It can be cooked by all methods and any of the classic recipes for sole is equally suitable for plaice. Its flavour deteriorates when full of roes and in the Spring, when a plaice appears large, much of the size is caused by very big roe.

Plaice Florentine

cooking time 25 minutes

you will need for 4 servings:

4 large fillets plaice
2 tablespoons white wine or lemon juice
1 lb. spinach
3 oz. grated cheese
½ pint white sauce (see page 83)

1 Fold fillets in half, place in a greased baking dish.
2 Sprinkle with wine or lemon juice, cover with buttered paper and bake in a moderate oven (375°F.—Gas Mark 4) for 10 minutes.
3 Cook spinach, drain well, sieve or chop.
4 Add half the cheese to sauce.
5 Place spinach in a heatproof dish, put fish on top, cover with sauce.
6 Sprinkle with remaining cheese and brown under the grill.

Plaice and tomato fillets

cooking time 10 – 15 minutes

you will need for 4 servings:

8 plaice fillets
4 medium-sized tomatoes
2 oz. margarine or butter
4 tablespoons milk
seasoning

1 Skin the fillets and tomatoes.
2 Put half a tomato on each fillet; add a little seasoning and a dab of margarine and roll fish around the tomato.
3 Put on to a plate with the milk and remaining margarine.
4 Cover with another plate, and steam over a pan of boiling water for about 10 minutes.

Fillet ballerina

cooking time 12 minutes

you will need for 4 servings:

4 fillets Dover sole or plaice
seasoned flour
2 oz. butter
lemon juice
2 bananas
2 tablespoons sweet or sour cream
lemon juice, optional

1 Dry fillets, coat with seasoned flour.
2 Fry on both sides in 1 oz. butter until golden brown.
3 Sprinkle with lemon juice, cover with sliced bananas.
4 Baste with juices from the pan and place under a hot grill for 3 or 4 minutes.
5 Remove fish and bananas and keep warm.
6 Add 2 tablespoons sour cream (if sweet is used, add a lemon juice) and remaining butter to pan juices.
7 Stir until hot and pour over the fish.

Plaice or sole in wine sauce

cooking time 25 minutes

you will need for 4 servings:

2 medium-sized sole or plaice (filleted and skinned)
salt, pepper
¼ pint white wine
¼ pint water
few peppercorns
1 medium-sized onion, sliced
1 small bay leaf

For sauce:
1 oz. butter
1 oz. flour
¼ pint milk
salt and pepper

To garnish:
lemon, parsley

1 Rinse and dry fillets, sprinkle with salt and pepper and roll lightly from tail to head.
2 Place in a buttered shallow ovenproof dish.
3 Pour wine and water over.
4 Add peppercorns, onion and bay leaf and cover closely with buttered paper or foil.
5 Cook in a very moderate oven (350°F.—Gas Mark 3) for 20 minutes.
6 Drain fish and place on dish. Keep hot.
7 Melt butter, add flour and cook, stirring, for a few minutes.
8 Strain liquid from fish into milk and stir into

pan a little at a time, cooking gently. Season and pour over fish.

9 Garnish with lemon slices and parsley.

Rolled plaice with gherkin tartare sauce

cooking time 10 minutes

you will need for 4 servings:

8 fillets plaice
1 egg
2 oz. fresh white breadcrumbs
fat

For the sauce:
1 oz. butter
1 oz. flour
½ pint milk
3 tablespoons mayonnaise (see page 86)
salt, pepper
6 – 8 gherkins

1 Skin the fillets.
2 Roll up and secure with small skewers or cotton.
3 Brush rolls with beaten egg and coat with breadcrumbs.
4 Fry in deep fat until golden brown, approximately 7 – 10 minutes.
5 Drain and keep hot.

To make the sauce:

1 Melt fat in a saucepan.
2 Add the flour.
3 Cook for 1 minute.
4 Add milk and stir over a low heat until boiling.
5 Simmer for 5 minutes.
6 Remove from the heat, stir in the mayonnaise.
7 Season with salt and pepper and add the chopped gherkins.
8 Pour sauce over fish or serve separately.

Cooking skate

This fish is absolutely delicious when fresh and has a texture slightly similar to lobster which makes it most suitable for fish salads. One of the tastiest ways of serving it is in browned butter for which a recipe is given.

Fried skate in browned butter

cooking time 12 – 15 minutes

you will need for 4 servings:

4 portions skate
seasoning
3 oz. butter
1 tablespoon lemon juice or 1 tablespoon white, brown or wine vinegar

1 Steam the skate for about 5 minutes.
2 Dry well.
3 Fry seasoned fish in butter until tender, turning to cook both sides.
4 Lift on to a hot dish and continue cooking the butter until golden brown, adding lemon juice or vinegar.
5 Pour over the skate and serve at once.

Variations:

1 Add little chopped parsley to the butter.
2 Tiny snippets of fresh lemon added to the butter.
3 Add a few capers and diced gherkins to the butter.

Skate with cream sauce

cooking time 15 minutes

you will need for 4 servings:

4 portions skate
salted water
sprig parsley
seasoning
onion

For sauce:
1 oz. butter
1 oz. flour
½ pint milk
2 tablespoons cream
1 hard-boiled egg
2 teaspoons chopped cloves or spring onions
½ teaspoon grated lemon rind
little lemon juice

1 Put skate into cold salted water. Bring to simmering point then skim.
2 Add sprig parsley, seasoning and onion and simmer for 10 minutes.
3 Meanwhile make sauce of butter, flour and milk. Add cream, chopped egg and other ingredients.
4 Strain fish and cover with sauce.

Cooking sole

There are more recipes and methods of cooking this fish than any other, from the classic dishes to frying or grilling. The only criticism of sole that can be made is that it can become a little dry, so great care should be taken to keep it really moist.

Grilled sole

1 When grilling sole it is usual to cook the fish whole rather than filleted.
2 Pre-heat the grill thoroughly.
3 Brush the fish with melted butter, grill until

tender on one side, turn, brush again with melted butter and cook the second side.

4 Seasoning and lemon juice can be added as required.

Sole Americaine

cooking time 15 minutes

you will need for 4 servings:

seasoning
4 large or 8 small fillets sole
2 tablespoons water
1 – 2 oz. butter

For sauce:
1 oz. butter
1 grated onion
3 large tomatoes
¼ pint water or white wine
seasoning

1 Season fillets well, then roll tightly.
2 Put into well-greased dish with water and a knob of butter.
3 Cover with greased paper and cook for 15 minutes in a moderate oven (375°F.—Gas Mark 4).

To make the sauce:

1 Heat butter, add onion and cook gently.
2 Add skinned, sliced tomatoes, water or wine and seasoning.
3 Cook until a smooth paste.
4 Put sole on to hot plate, pour sauce over.

Note:

If sauce becomes a little too thick, thin it with liquid in which fish was cooked.

Sole and salmon fillets

cooking time 20 minutes

you will need for 4 servings:

8 small fillets sole
2 oz. margarine or butter
4 oz. cooked or canned salmon
seasoning
few drops lemon juice
4 tablespoons milk

1 Skin fillets; cream margarine; work in the salmon and a little seasoning, together with lemon juice.
2 Spread this mixture over fillets, roll and secure them tightly.
3 Put on a plate and pour milk over.
4 Cover with a second plate and steam over a saucepan of boiling water for 10 minutes; or put into a buttered dish, cover with buttered paper and bake for 20 minutes in a moderate oven (375°F.—Gas Mark 4).

Sole au gratin

cooking time 20 minutes

you will need for 4 servings:

8 small fillets sole
1 oz. butter
1 tablespoon chopped onion (optional)
3 tablespoons flour
½ pint milk or fish stock (see page 72) and milk
1 dessertspoon chopped parsley
1 teaspoon vinegar
1½ teaspoons salt
¼ teaspoon pepper
browned breadcrumbs

1 Place fillets in a greased fireproof dish.
2 Melt fat, fry onion until brown.
3 Stir in flour, then gradually stir in liquid.
4 Boil sauce for a few minutes, then stir in parsley, vinegar and seasoning. Pour over the fish.
5 Sprinkle with breadcrumbs and bake for about 20 minutes in a moderately hot oven (400°F.—Gas Mark 5) or cook under the grill.

Sole Bercy

cooking time 30 – 40 minutes

you will need for 4 servings:

4 large or 8 small fillets sole
2 shallots or small onions
2 teaspoons chopped parsley
salt, pepper
½ pint white wine
¼ pint water or fish stock (see page 72)
1 oz. butter
1 oz. flour

1 Fold fillets, put into a buttered dish with chopped shallots, parsley, seasoning, ¼ pint white wine and water or fish stock.
2 Cover with buttered paper and bake in a moderate oven (375°F.—Gas Mark 4) for approximately 20 minutes.
3 Heat butter, stir in flour and cook gently for several minutes. Add remaining wine and cook until smooth.
4 Lift fillets on to a hot dish. To the sauce add unstrained liquid from the dish.
5 Cook until smooth and thick. Pour over the fish.

Sole bonne femme

cooking time 20 minutes

you will need for 4 servings:

4 large or 8 small fillets sole
seasoning
little chopped parsley
¼ pint white wine
1 oz. butter
1 oz. flour
½ pint milk
2 – 3 oz. mushrooms
extra butter

1 Butter an ovenproof dish and put fillets in.
2 Add seasoning, parsley and wine.
3 Cook steadily in a moderate oven (375°F.—Gas Mark 4) for approximately 20 minutes until just tender.
4 Make a thick sauce of butter, flour and milk.
5 Fry sliced mushrooms in extra butter.
6 Lift fillets on to a hot dish and arrange mushrooms around them and strain the wine liquid into the sauce.
7 Stir briskly until very smooth, then pour over the fish.

Serve in a border of mashed potato.

Sole in creamed tomato sauce

cooking time 20 – 25 minutes

you will need for 4 servings:

8 small or 4 large fillets sole
3 oz. finely chopped mushrooms
3 tablespoons chopped parsley
1½ tablespoons finely chopped onion
1 can condensed cream tomato soup or tomato sauce (see page 84)
little lemon juice
mushrooms
2 large onions
1 oz. butter
thyme
pinch pepper
parsley

1 Wash and dry fillets.
2 Mix mushrooms, parsley and onion with 1 tablespoon tomato soup or sauce.
3 Put 1 spoonful stuffing on each fillet and fold over.
4 Place in a lightly buttered ovenproof dish, sprinkle with lemon juice.
5 Cover closely and bake in a moderate oven (375°F.—Gas Mark 4) for 15 – 20 minutes.
6 Fry few sliced mushrooms and onions slowly and separately in melted butter until tender.*
7 Heat remaining tomato soup or sauce, thyme and pepper, and simmer gently for 2 – 3 minutes.
8 Add onions.
9 Coat fillets with sauce and garnish with mushrooms and parsley.

* This could be done earlier in the day and the mushrooms and onions reheated in the oven.

Sole Espagnole

cooking time 15 minutes

you will need for 4 servings:

4 large or 8 small fillets sole
3 oz. butter or oil
1 onion
1 red pepper
4 tomatoes
salt, pepper

1 Season fillets and fry in some of the fat.
2 In a separate pan, fry thinly sliced onion and pepper.
3 Keep hot and add skinned sliced tomatoes to the pan.
4 Cook until very soft.
5 Season well.
6 Cover fillets with vegetables and juices.

Sole with lobster butter

cooking time 12 – 15 minutes

you will need for 4 servings:

4 large or 8 small fillets sole
salt, pepper
½ pint cider
2 oz. butter
little extra butter
lobster coral (roe)
1 oz. flour
lemon slices

1 Fry or bake the seasoned fillets in butter.
2 If baking, add a little of the cider.
3 Blend the coral with 1 oz. butter until smooth.
4 Heat remaining butter, stir in the flour and cook for a few minutes.
5 Add the cider, bring to the boil and simmer, stirring until smooth.
6 Stir in the lobster butter.
7 Arrange fillets on a hot dish adding any liquid to the sauce.
8 Pour over sauce and garnish with lemon slices.

Sole rachel

cooking time 50 minutes

you will need for 4 servings:

- 4 large or 8 small fillets sole, skinned (reserve skin and bones)
- 1½ – 2 oz. peeled onion
- 1 bay leaf
- 3 peppercorns
- 1 teaspoon salt
- water
- 6 oz. mushrooms
- 1 oz. butter
- 3 tablespoons cream
- seasoning
- ¼ pint dry white wine
- ¾ oz. flour
- 1 egg yolk
- fleurons of puff pastry (see page 60), optional

1. Place fish skin and bones in a pan with onion, bay leaf, peppercorns and salt.
2. Cover with water and boil for 20 – 30 minutes.
3. Wipe or wash the mushrooms, reserve some for garnish, chopping remainder finely.
4. Gently cook, covered, in ¼ oz. butter, 1 tablespoon cream and seasoning, for 4 – 5 minutes.
5. Strain.
6. On to each fillet place a little of this mixture.
7. Fold and place in a heat-proof dish.
8. Pour over wine and ¼ pint fish stock.
9. Cover with buttered paper and bake in a moderate oven (375°F.—Gas Mark 4) for approximately 20 minutes.
10. Melt remaining butter and blend with flour.
11. Add strained liquor from the fish and bring to the boil, stirring with a wire whisk.
12. Boil for 1 – 2 minutes.
13. Remove from heat and beat in remaining cream and yolk.
14. Adjust seasoning, heat through and then pour over the fish.
15. Garnish with mushroom slices and fleurons of pastry.

Sole ribbons or *soles en goujons*

cooking time 4 – 5 minutes

you will need for 4 servings:

- 2 medium soles
- 1 tablespoon seasoned flour
- 1 beaten egg
- browned breadcrumbs
- fat
- little cayenne pepper

1. Skin the soles, fillet, wash and dry them well.
2. Cut fillets across into ½-inch ribbons.
3. Roll in seasoned flour, dip into beaten egg and coat with breadcrumbs.
4. Fry in fat for 4 – 5 minutes until crisp and golden brown.
5. Drain well and serve sprinkled lightly with a little cayenne pepper.

Sole veronique

cooking time 45 minutes

you will need for 4 servings:

- 2 medium-sized soles
- 2 – 3 peppercorns
- few parsley stalks
- 1 small onion, optional
- ½ pint water
- seasoning
- 3 tablespoons white wine
- 1 finely chopped shallot, optional
- 1 small can evaporated milk OR ¼ pint cream
- 1 oz. butter
- 1 oz. flour
- 4 oz. green grapes

1. Have the soles skinned and filleted.
2. Put heads, skin and bones into a pan with peppercorns, parsley stalks, onion and water.
3. Simmer for 30 minutes.
4. Strain off the liquor.
5. Season fillets, roll them skinned side in and place upright on a buttered deep plate or dish.
6. Add stock, wine and shallot, cover and poach in a moderate oven or over a pan of boiling water until cooked.
7. Keep fish hot and strain off liquor.
8. Make up to just over ½ pint with evaporated milk or cream.
9. Make a white sauce with butter, flour and milk.
10. Skin and stone grapes.
11. Coat fish evenly with the sauce and garnish with grapes.

Sole Walewska

cooking time about 20 minutes

you will need for 4 servings:

- salt, pepper
- 4 large or 8 small fillets sole
- ¼ pint white wine
- little butter
- Hollandaise sauce (see page 82)
- flesh of 1 small cooked lobster
- lobster butter (see page 85), optional

1. Season fillets, put into an oven dish, add wine and a little butter.
2. Bake in a moderately hot oven (400°F.—Gas Mark 5) for approximately 15 minutes or until tender.
3. Make the sauce.
4. Lift fillets on to a hot dish and strain liquid gradually into the sauce, reheating gently to thicken.
5. Add lobster pieces, then pour over the fish.

Note:

The lobster butter can either be stirred into the sauce, or put on top of it just before serving.

Cooking Turbot

This is a luxury fish but not as expensive as it may appear at first, as it is so solid in texture and sustaining that a little goes a long way. While often served with elaborate sauces, turbot has such a good flavour it can be fried, baked or grilled.

Turbot Florentine

cooking time 15 minutes

you will need for 4 servings:

approximately ½ lb. cooked spinach
4 tablespoons cream
seasoning
2 oz. margarine or butter
4 portions turbot
2 oz. grated cheese
2 tablespoons soft breadcrumbs

1 Sieve or chop spinach very small.
2 Mix with cream, a little seasoning and 1 oz. margarine.
3 Put spinach in the bottom of a deep scallop shell or a dish, with the turbot on top.
4 Sprinkle over cheese and breadcrumbs, pinch salt and dot with margarine.
5 Bake near the top of a moderately hot oven (400°F.—Gas Mark 5) for a good 15 minutes.

Serve with creamed or Duchesse potatoes (see page 88).

Turbot mornay

cooking time 15 – 20 minutes

you will need for 4 servings:

4 portions turbot
seasoning
½ pint milk
½ lemon
1 – 2 oz. margarine or butter
1 oz. flour
2 oz. grated cheese

1 Put the fish into a dish.
2 Add seasoning, ¼ pint milk and sliced lemon.
3 Bake in the middle of a moderate oven (375°F. —Gas Mark 4) for 15 – 20 minutes.
4 Melt the margarine.
5 Stir in flour and cook for 3 minutes.
6 Remove pan from heat and gradually stir in remaining milk.
7 Bring slowly to the boil, stirring.
8 Put turbot on to a hot dish and strain liquid into sauce, stirring well to keep it smooth.
9 Simmer sauce for a further minute, then add cheese and cook until dissolved.
10 Season well, pour over the fish and serve with creamed spinach.

Creamed fish

cooking time 10 – 15 minutes

you will need for 4 servings:

2 oz. margarine or butter
1 oz. flour
½ pint milk
1 lb. cooked white fish – whiting, plaice, turbot or fresh haddock
seasoning
2 tablespoons cream or evaporated milk

1 Heat margarine, stir in flour and cook for several minutes.
2 Stir in milk, bring gradually to the boil, stirring all the time, and cook until the sauce has thickened.
3 Add flaked fish, seasoning and cream; then heat thoroughly.

Serve on crisp toast or with creamed potatoes.

Cooking whiting

A versatile fish, it can be substituted for sole or plaice and is excellent when baked as its maximum flavour is retained. Its fine texture also makes it ideal for serving to invalids or children.

Whiting Bretonne

cooking time 15 – 20 minutes

you will need for 4 servings:

4 large or 8 small fillets whiting
salted water
1 or 2 sliced onions
butter

For sauce:
¼ pint Hollandaise sauce (see page 82)
¼ pint tomato purée or sauce (see page 84)

1 Poach whiting in salted water.
2 Fry onion rings in butter.
3 Drain fish well and arrange on a hot dish.
4 Whisk the hot sauces together (away from the stove) taking care they do not curdle.
5 Coat the fish with this.
6 Garnish with onion rings.

Whiting with cheese topping

cooking time 12 – 15 minutes

you will need for 4 servings:

8 small or 4 large whiting
flour
seasoning
2 – 3 oz. butter
2 oz. grated cheese

1 Wash and dry fish.
2 Split them and remove backbones.
3 Season flour, put into a paper bag and shake fish in it.
4 Melt butter in grill pan and fry one side of fish.
5 When fish is nearly cooked underneath, sprinkle liberally with cheese and brown under preheated grill.
6 Pour over the fish any butter in the grill pan. Serve with broccoli or asparagus tips and creamed potatoes.

Whiting in wine sauce

cooking time about 20 minutes

you will need for 4 servings:

salt, pepper
8 small or 4 large whiting
1 sherry glass white wine
¾ pint water
½ pint white sauce (see page 83)
parsley

1 Season fish and put into a saucepan or fish kettle and pour wine over.
2 Bring water to the boil and pour over fish seasoning and wine.
3 Simmer for 10 – 12 minutes depending on the size of the fish.
4 Remove fish carefully to hot dish and keep warm.
5 Turn up heat under stock and boil fast until reduced to about 5 tablespoons.
6 Add white sauce to stock and pour over whiting.
7 Garnish with parsley.

Baked fish and cheese

cooking time 35 minutes

you will need for 4 servings:

4 fillets white fish
1 small onion, chopped
2 oz. butter or margarine
salt, pepper, cayenne pepper
4 oz. grated cheese
¼ teaspoon mustard powder
¼ pint milk
2 oz. fresh breadcrumbs

1 Skin, wash and dry fillets. Place in a greased fireproof dish.
2 Fry onion in 1 oz. butter very slowly until almost cooked.
3 Sprinkle fillets with salt, pepper and onion.
4 Mix together cheese, mustard, milk and seasonings, and heat slowly until cheese has melted.
5 Pour over fish.
6 Melt remaining butter and mix with breadcrumbs.
7 Sprinkle on top and cook for 25 minutes in moderately hot oven (400°F.—Gas Mark 5).

Variation:

Add a chopped hard-boiled egg to the cheese mixture after the cheese had melted or place slices of hard-boiled egg on the fillets.

Fish pasties

cooking time 30 minutes

you will need for 4 servings:

8 oz. short crust pastry (see page 61)
8 – 10 oz. white fish
4 oz. cooked diced potato
1 tablespoon chopped parsley
2 tablespoons chopped onion
¼ teaspoon salt
pinch pepper

1 Cut pastry into four 8-inch circles.
2 Mix fish with other ingredients and pile ¼ on each pastry piece.
3 Moisten pastry edges and fold each circle half.
4 Bake in centre of a hot oven (425 – 450°F.—Gas Mark 6 – 7) for 30 minutes.

Serve hot or cold with salad.

Pickled fish

cooking time 30 minutes

you will need for 4 servings:

3 – 4 lb. white fish
1 lemon
2 onions
2 cloves
1 bay leaf
1 – 2 chilli peppers
approximately ½ pint vinegar
½ pint water
seasoning

1 Cut fish into neat pieces.
2 Rub with a little lemon and put into an oven-proof dish.
3 Cover with sliced onions, cloves, bay leaf, chilli peppers, vinegar and water.
4 Add seasoning and lemon juice.
5 Cook in moderate oven (375°F.—Gas Mark 4) for 30 minutes, standing the container in a pan of hot water.

Serve hot or cold.

Fish bake

cooking time 15 minutes

you will need for 4 servings:

4 fillets white fish
salt, pepper
butter
2 – 4 oz. mushrooms
1 finely chopped onion
few capers
8 tablespoons cream

1 Skin the fish and lay each fillet on a double thickness of foil.
2 Season and dot with butter.
3 Lay slices of mushrooms and a little onion along each fillet.
4 Add capers and pour cream over fillets, dividing it equally between them.
5 Wrap tightly and place on a greased baking tray.
6 Bake for about 15 minutes in a moderately hot oven (400°F.—Gas Mark 5). Unwrap just before serving.

Fish and bacon bake

Ingredients as previous recipe, but add 2 rashers bacon, which goes extremely well with either fresh haddock or cod.

1 Cut the bacon into small pieces and fry until just crisp and golden.
2 Continue as for Fish bake, adding chopped bacon with mushrooms and onion.

Fish sticks au gratin

cooking time about 15 minutes

you will need for 4 servings:

4 cutlets white fish
little butter
4 slices Cheddar cheese
1 large sliced tomato

To garnish:
4 olives
8 fillets anchovy
lemon slices
little watercress

1 Fry cutlets in butter until golden brown.
2 Put into a hot ovenproof dish. Top each cutlet with a slice of cheese and tomato.
3 Put under the grill for a few minutes.
4 Garnish with sliced olives, a lattice of anchovy fillets, lemon and watercress.

Fish in wine and mushroom sauce

cooking time about 30 minutes

you will need for 4 servings:

4 fillets or cutlets white fish
¼ pint water
¼ pint white wine
seasoning
2 oz. mushrooms
2 oz. margarine or butter
1 oz. flour
⅜ pint milk

To garnish:
chopped parsley

1 Put fish into a greased casserole and pour over water and wine. Add seasoning, and cover dish.
2 Bake in the middle of a moderately hot oven (400°F.—Gas Mark 5) for 15 minutes.
3 Fry chopped mushrooms in margarine or butter until just soft.
4 Blend flour with milk, add to mushrooms and seasoning, and bring slowly to the boil, stirring all the time.
5 When fish is cooked, put on to a hot dish, strain wine liquid into sauce and continue simmering for a further 5 minutes.
6 Pour over fish and garnish with parsley.

Fish and potato hash

cooking time 15 minutes

you will need for 4 servings:

1 medium-sized finely chopped onion
1 oz. fat
¾ lb. cooked, mashed potatoes
1 lb. cooked, flaked white fish
1 teaspoon vinegar
1 teaspoon salt
pepper
chopped parsley

1 Fry onion in fat until tender.
2 Blend potatoes and fish. Add to onion and fry until brown underneath.
3 Sprinkle with vinegar, salt, pepper and parsley. Serve hot.

Fish curry

cooking time 5 – 10 minutes (after making sauce)

you will need for 4 servings:

1 lb. cooked fish
1 pint curry sauce (see page 81)

1 Add the flaked fish to the hot sauce and heat gently for 5 – 10 minutes without boiling.
2 Serve with boiled rice or creamed potatoes.

Variation:

Use raw fish—cut into neat pieces and cook for 15 minutes.

Fish timbales

cooking time 30 minutes

you will need for 4 servings:

12 oz. flaked cooked white fish
½ pint white sauce (see page 83)
2 eggs
few drops of lemon juice
seasoning
extra white sauce or melted butter

1 Pound the fish until smooth.
2 Mix all the ingredients together.
3 Grease small moulds and divide mixture between them, pressing well down.
4 Cover each mould with greased paper, and steam for ½ hour.
Serve with white sauce or melted butter.

Fish cakes

cooking time about 15 minutes

you will need for 4 servings:

12 oz. flaked cooked fish*
8 oz mashed potato
¼ pint thick white sauce (see page 83) or 1 egg
seasoning
crisp breadcrumbs or flour
1 egg
fat

To garnish:
parsley
lemon

* Cod, fresh haddock, turbot or hake are best, because of more definite flavour

1 Mix fish, potato, sauce or beaten egg together. Add seasoning.
2 Form into flat cakes and brush with egg, cover with breadcrumbs or flour.
3 Fry in hot fat until crisp and brown on both sides and very hot right through.
4 Drain carefully on kitchen paper.
5 Garnish with parsley and lemon slices.

Variations:

Anchovy fish cakes
Add either a few chopped anchovy fillets or anchovy essence to the sauce or egg. Put the essence in with the sauce or egg and beat it well. It is very strong and must be evenly blended.

Cheese fish cakes
Add 1 – 2 oz. finely grated cheese to the mixture and/or coat in very finely grated dry cheese as well as breadcrumbs.

Fish croquettes

cooking time 15 – 20 minutes

you will need for 4 servings:

¼ pint thick white sauce (see page 83)
¾ lb. flaked cooked fish
seasoning
½ teaspoon mixed herbs
1 teaspoon chopped parsley
2 tablespoons soft breadcrumbs
1 teaspoon grated onion
egg or milk and breadcrumbs for coating
fat

1 Make sauce, mix with all other ingredients and allow to cool.
2 Form mixture into rolls. Dip them first in a little egg or milk, then into breadcrumbs.
3 Fry or grill until crisp and brown.

Fish in savoury custard

cooking time 45 minutes

you will need for 4 servings:

4 small fish fillets or cutlets
1 egg
½ pint milk
seasoning
1 teaspoon chopped parsley
small pinch mixed herbs

1 Arrange rolled fillets or boned cutlets in a greased dish.
2 Beat egg, pour on milk.
3 Add seasoning, parsley and herbs.
4 Pour over fish and bake in a very moderate oven (350°F.—Gas Mark 3) for approximately 45 minutes, standing the dish in another containing cold water.

Fritters

cooking time 10 – 15 minutes

you will need for 4 servings:

4 oz. flour (with plain flour add 2 teaspoons baking powder)
1 teaspoon salt
¼ teaspoon pepper
2 eggs
¼ pint milk (approx.)
6 oz. cooked flaked fish or canned fish
1 tablespoon chopped parsley
fat

1. Mix flour, baking powder if used, salt and pepper together.
2. Mix to a stiff batter with the eggs and milk.
3. Beat well, add fish and parsley.
4. Fry tablespoons of mixture until golden brown on both sides.
Serve at once.

This quantity makes about 8 fritters.

Pan hash

cooking time 15 minutes

you will need for 4 servings:

8 oz. cooked mashed potatoes
8 oz. cooked vegetables, chopped
8 oz. flaked cooked fish or canned fish
salt and pepper
1 oz. fat

1. Mix all the ingredients, except fat, together.
2. Genty fry the mixture in hot fat until well browned on both sides—about 15 minutes—turning like a pancake after 7 minutes.

Note:

If no cooked vegetables are available, use 1 lb. cooked mashed potatoes.

Sturgeon

This is known as a 'Royal fish' as it is the property of the Crown and therefore rarely available.

It has a very firm texture and a taste rather more like veal than anything else. When fresh, the flesh should be white and the veins clear blue. It can be baked either in butter, or butter and white wine.

Allow approximately 20 minutes per lb. in a moderate oven (375°F.—Gas Mark 4).

It is excellent with a stuffing—either veal or sage and onion stuffing.

Sturgeon can also be sliced and fried, grilled or poached in a *court-bouillon* (see page 8).

Cutlets or pieces of sturgeon can be roasted, as a joint of meat, in a little hot fat or butter. Baste during cooking to keep it moist and allow approximately 20 minutes per lb. in a moderately hot oven (400°F.—Gas Mark 5).

Oily Fish

This type of fish varies from luxurious salmon to the economical and nutritious herring. Because it contains a high percentage of oil, a great deal of fat is not necessary in cooking.

FISH IN SEASON	TO BUY AND COOK
HERRINGS Obtainable from various sources throughout year, from Britain in season June – February	Buy whole but most fishmongers will bone and fillet if asked. Make sure herrings are very firm and bright-eyed. Can be grilled, fried, baked, stuffed, or pickled and soused to serve with salads. Most economical. 1 – 2 herrings per person.
MACKEREL **Mar – July**	Looks like a larger, more silvery herring. Make sure they are fresh, since stale mackerel can be particularly dangerous. Cook as herrings, particularly good served with a thick gooseberry purée as sauce. 1 per person.
MULLET **April – Oct.**	Both grey and red. Bake or grill with plenty of butter. Red mullet is delicious baked in buttered paper bags. Always put liver back into fish after cleaning, as it has a particularly good flavour. 1 grey or 2 red (smaller) mullet per person.

FISH IN SEASON	TO BUY AND COOK
SALMON Mar – Aug	Serve hot or cold. Make sure not to dry it in cooking and lose oily texture, flavour and colour. A substantial fish. Allow approximately 6 oz. per person.
SALMON TROUT April – Aug	Cook as salmon, but generally best to buy a small salmon trout and cook it whole. Allow 8 oz. per person.
SPRATS Oct – Mar	These tiny fish can be baked or fried. Remove heads, dust with seasoned flour before cooking. Very easily digested and quite delicious. Allow 6 – 8 oz. per person.
WHITEBAIT May – Aug	The tiniest fish. Leave heads on, dust well in seasoned flour and cook in deep fat until crisp and tender. Drain well and serve either as a main course or an hors-d'œuvre with cayenne pepper, lemon and brown bread and butter. Allow 4 – 8 oz. per person.

Crispy oat herrings

cooking time 10 minutes

you will need for 4 servings:

4 herrings
1 beaten egg
4 oz. oatmeal
4 oz. cooking fat

To garnish:
lemon
parsley

For the sauce:
¼ pint tomato ketchup
4 pickled gherkins, chopped
1 tablespoon capers

1. Clean and fillet herrings, (see page 7 and this page) wash and dry thoroughly.
2. Dip in beaten egg, then coat thoroughly with oatmeal.
3. Heat fat in a frying pan until hot.
4. Cook herrings on both sides over a gentle heat for 4 – 5 minutes
5. Heat the tomato ketchup and stir in gherkins and capers.
6. Garnish fish with lemon and parsley and serve with sauce.

Devilled herrings No. 1

cooking time 10 minutes

you will need for 4 servings:

4 medium-sized herrings
½ oz. margarine
1 teaspoon mustard
1 teaspoon vinegar
1 teaspoon Worcestershire sauce
pinch salt
¼ pint water
1 grated onion
½ teaspoon pickling spice
1 tablespoon sugar

1. Split herrings and remove backbones (see this page).
2. Cream margarine, add mustard, vinegar, Worcestershire sauce and salt.
3. Spread this paste on the herrings.
4. Roll tightly.
5. Put into a saucepan with the water, onion, spice and sugar.
6. Simmer gently for 10 minutes.
7. Serve hot or cold.

Note:
Mackerel may be cooked in the same way, but will take slightly longer.

To fillet herrings:

1. Scale, if necessary, by scraping with a knife from tail to head.
2. Cut off head, slit along stomach.
3. Remove the intestines, and roe which should be kept. Roe can be cooked with the fish or separately. Wash.
4. Open the herring and put cut side downwards on to a board.
5. Run your thumb very firmly along the centre, feeling the backbone; do this several times.
6. Turn fish over; you will find the backbone completely loosened and easy to remove.
7. Trim fins and tail.

Devilled herrings No. 2

cooking time about 15 minutes

you will need for 4 servings:

3 dessertspoons dry mustard
2 tablespoons sugar
2 dessertspoons vinegar
4 herrings, cleaned and filleted (see pages 7, 31)
1 medium chopped onion
1 bay leaf
6 cloves
1 oz. margarine or butter
$\frac{1}{8}$ pint water

1 Mix mustard and sugar to a paste with vinegar.
2 Open herrings flat, spread mustard mixture on the inside and roll up from the tail end.
3 Fry onion, bay leaf and cloves in margarine or butter until well browned.
4 Add herrings and water and cook very gently for 10 minutes. Baste herrings occasionally with the liquid. Serve with sweet chutney.

Note:
Can be allowed to cool in liquid and served cold with salad.

Grilled herrings and mustard sauce

cooking time about 15 minutes

you will need for 4 servings:

4 large or 8 small herrings
little butter
1 tablespoon mustard
1 teaspoon vinegar
pinch salt

For the sauce:
2 oz. butter
1 oz. flour
$\frac{3}{8}$ pint water

For garnish:
parsley
lemon

1 Trim and clean herrings (see page 7).
2 Butter lightly and grill on both sides.

To make the sauce:
1 Heat 1 oz. butter, stir in flour and cook for several minutes.
2 Blend mustard with water until smooth, add to butter and flour and bring to the boil slowly, stirring until smooth.
3 Add vinegar, remaining butter and salt.
4 Garnish fish with parsley and lemon and serve with sauce.

Herrings fried in salt

cooking time 8 – 9 minutes

you will need for 4 servings:

herrings
salt

There is so much oil in the flesh of a herring that it can be fried without additional fat. Use only a strong thick frying pan, as a thin one will burn.

1 Sprinkle the pan with salt.
2 Heat gently at first, shaking the pan occasionally. Continue heating until pan is very hot, then lay in the herrings, previously scaled, cleaned, washed and dried (see page 7).
3 Fry on each side 4 – 5 minutes until golden brown and crisp. Serve at once.

Marinierte herring (pickled) (Jewish)

cooking time few minutes

you will need for 4 servings:

3 medium or 2 large cleaned, filleted herrings (see pages 7, 31)
1 large thinly sliced onion
just over $\frac{1}{4}$ pint vinegar
2 tablespoons water
1 tablespoon brown sugar
3 bay leaves
12 peppercorns
1 teaspoon mixed whole spice (optional)
6 thin slices lemon
1 milt, mashed
2 tablespoons sour cream (optional)

1 Place whole herrings or sections in quart jar. Add onion.
2 Bring vinegar, water and sugar to a quick boil, then cool till lukewarm.
3 Add liquid to jar with bay leaves, spices, lemon slices.
4 Combine mashed milt with sour cream and stir in lightly, or shake jar to distribute.
5 Cover and let stand 24 hours before serving.

Raw spiced herrings

no cooking

you will need for 4 servings:

4 large salted herrings
$\frac{1}{2}$ pint vinegar (preferably tarragon)
2 – 3 tablespoons sugar
$\frac{1}{4}$ pint tomato juice
4 cloves
4 allspice
2 gherkins
1 onion
2 bay leaves

1 Soak herrings in cold water overnight.
2 Mix other ingredients to make a marinade and leave to stand for a few hours.
3 Dry and clean, then fillet herrings (see pages 7, 31); cut in ½-inch slices.
4 Pour marinade over them. Leave for 24 hours.

Serve chilled.

Soused herrings No. 1

cooking time 1½ hours

you will need for 4 servings:

6 or 8 herrings
1 tablespoon mixed pickling spice
3 pickled onions
1 bay leaf (optional)
1 teaspoon salt
¼ pint vinegar
¼ pint water

1 Cut off the heads, scale and clean fish.
2 Arrange in a baking dish (not a tin) alternately thick end to thin end. Scatter pickling spice over, add sliced onions and bay leaf.
3 Sprinkle in salt, pour in vinegar and water mixed together.
4 Bake in a very slow oven (275°F.—Gas Mark 1) for 1½ hours. Serve cold.

Soused herrings No. 2

cooking time 1 hour

you will need for 4 servings:

4 herrings
1 teaspoon pickling spice
1 teaspoon sugar
¼ pint water
1 small onion
1 teaspoon sweet spice
¼ pint vinegar
2 bay leaves

1 Split the herrings.
2 Take backbones out.
3 Roll the fish.
4 Put into a covered casserole together with all other ingredients and cook in a very moderate oven (300°F.—Gas Mark 2) for 1 hour.

Mackerel may be cooked in the same way.

Stuffed herrings

cooking time 30 – 35 minutes

you will need for 4 servings:

2 heaped tablespoons rolled oats
2 oz. shrimps or prawns
½ teaspoon anchovy essence
4 tablespoons milk
seasoning
4 herrings
4 tablespoons malt vinegar
2 oz. fat

1 Mix oats, shrimps, anchovy essence, milk and seasoning thoroughly together.
2 Cut each boned and cleaned herring into 2 fillets and spread a little of the mixture on to each fillet, then roll up from head to tail.
3 Brush the inside of a 1½-pint ovenproof dish with melted fat. Place in the stuffed fillets, add vinegar and cover with small knobs of fat.
4 Bake on the middle shelf of a moderate oven (350°F.—Gas Mark 4) for 30 – 35 minutes.

Serve immediately.

Swedish herrings

cooking time 25 – 30 minutes

you will need for 4 servings:

4 large herrings
1 – 2 level teaspoons salt
2 tablespoons vinegar
2 tablespoons water
1½ tablespoons sugar
¼ teaspoon pepper
pinch ground cloves
2 tablespoons brown breadcrumbs

1 Clean herrings and divide into 8 fillets.
2 Rub the fillets well with salt and place, overlapping slightly, into a flat dish.
3 Mix vinegar, water, sugar, pepper and cloves and pour over herrings.
4 Sprinkle with breadcrumbs and bake in a moderate oven (375°F.—Gas Mark 4) for 20 – 25 minutes

Mackerel and gooseberry sauce

cooking time 20 – 30 minutes

you will need for 4 servings:

4 large mackerel
1 oz. butter or margarine
seasoning
8 – 12 oz. green gooseberries
2 – 3 oz. sugar
about ¼ pint water

1 Cut heads from mackerel, split them and remove backbones.
2 Brush with a little butter or margarine and season well.
3 Bake for approximately 20 – 30 minutes, depending on the size, in a moderately hot oven (400°F.—Gas Mark 5).
4 Simmer gooseberries with sugar and water.
5 Sieve, or beat until smooth, then add remaining butter or margarine.
6 Pour sauce over fish and serve.

Baked mackerel with prune and fennel stuffing

cooking time 25 – 30 minutes

you will need for 4 servings:

4 mackerel
4 tomatoes

Stuffing:
4 oz. cooked rice
2 oz. melted butter
8 plumed prunes, chopped
2 – 3 dessertspoons chopped fennel or 2 – 3 fennel seeds
grated rind ½ lemon
chopped parsley
salt, pepper
lemon juice

1 Split and clean mackerel, halve tomatoes.
2 Mix stuffing ingredients together.
3 Put into mackerel and tie or secure edges.
4 Lift fish on to buttered dish, surround with tomatoes.
5 Bake for 25 – 30 minutes in moderately hot oven (400°F.—Gas Mark 5).

Mackerel with paprika sauce

cooking time about 35 minutes

you will need for 4 servings:

4 medium-sized mackerel
2 oz. chopped mushrooms
1 large skinned and chopped tomato
2 oz. breadcrumbs
½ oz. margarine or butter
few drops lemon juice
seasoning

For the sauce:
1 oz. margarine or butter
½ pint milk
1 oz. flour
little salt
2 teaspoons paprika pepper

1 Split mackerel and take backbones out.
2 Mix mushrooms, tomato, breadcrumbs, margarine, lemon juice and seasoning. Put into mackerel and secure well with small cocktail sticks.
3 Bake in a well-greased dish covered with greaseproof paper for 15 – 20 minutes in the middle of a moderate oven (375°F.—Gas Mark 4).

To make the sauce:

1 Heat margarine, stir in flour and cook for 3 minutes.
2 Take pan from heat and gradually add cold milk. Bring gently to the boil, stirring until sauce thickens.
3 Whisk in salt and paprika pepper.

Serve with fish.

Note:

Paprika is an acquired taste, so if uncertain whether it will be well liked, cut down the quantity—but it is surprisingly mild.

Mullet meunière

cooking time 10 – 12 minutes

you will need for 4 servings:

4 grey or red mullet
little flour
3 oz. butter
squeeze lemon juice
little chopped parsley
few capers, optional

1 Cut heads from fish, clean, and put livers back into fish.
2 Lightly coat fish with flour.
3 Heat butter and fry mullet steadily for about 10 minutes.
4 Lift out and put on to a hot dish.
5 Add lemon juice and a little chopped parsley to the butter.
6 Heat until golden brown and pour over the fish.

Mullet Niçoise

cooking time 20 – 25 minutes

you will need for 4 servings:

4 red or grey mullet
seasoning
4 skinned tomatoes
1 lemon
1½ oz. butter
8 – 12 anchovy fillets

1 Clean fish and cut heads off. Season lightly.
2 Slice tomatoes and extract lemon pulp.
3 Melt butter—pour ½ into a casserole.
4 Put in fish, tomatoes and lemon pulp.
5 Cover with remaining butter and foil or a lid, and cook in a moderately hot oven (400°F.—Gas Mark 5).
6 Just before serving, top with anchovy fillets.

To poach salmon slices

1 Season salmon, add a little lemon juice and tie carefully in a neat 'parcel' of buttered paper.
2 Put into cold salted water with a little lemon and oil in the water.
3 Bring slowly to the boil, simmer gently and allow 10 minutes per lb.
Alternatively, bring just to boiling point, cover with tightly fitting lid, turn heat off and leave until water is quite cold.

This is an ideal way of poaching salmon if it is to be served cold.

To poach whole salmon

1 Scale and clean fish carefully.
2 Put into cold salted water, adding several slices of lemon, 1 small bunch parsley and 1 or 2 tablespoons olive oil.
3 Bring water fairly quickly to boiling point, then immediately turn heat very low so liquid simmers very gently.
4 Allow 10 minutes per pound cooking time for the first 6 lb., i.e. a 5 lb. fish would take 50 minutes. Allow 5 minutes per pound cooking time for the next 6 lb., i.e. a 10 lb. fish would take 1 hour 20 minutes. Allow 2 minutes per pound for the next pound over 12 lb., i.e. a 15 lb. fish would take 1 hour 36 minutes (6 lb. at 10 minutes per pound, 6 lb. at 5 minutes per pound and 3 lb. at 2 minutes per pound).
5 Remove pan from heat and allow salmon to remain in the water for a short time to cool slightly before lifting out.

To serve cold salmon

The cooled cooked salmon should be lifted on to a dish and garnished with plenty of lemon, green salad and cucumber.
Never leave salmon exposed to the air for any length of time. Cover with foil or greaseproof paper, as it dries very easily and this spoils both colour and texture.

Salmon cream

cooking time few minutes

you will need for 4 servings:

¼ pint aspic jelly (make according to packet directions)
1 level teaspoon powder gelatine
¼ pint mayonnaise (see page 86)
2 tablespoons cream
½ – ¾ lb. flaked cooked salmon
2 hard-boiled eggs
2 sliced gherkins
seasoning

1 When making aspic jelly, dissolve the extra teaspoon powder gelatine in it.
2 Allow to cool, then mix with mayonnaise, cream, salmon and 1 chopped hard-boiled egg and 1 gherkin.
3 Season well.
4 Put into a rinsed mould and allow to set.
5 Turn out and decorate with remaining egg and gherkin.

Serve with salad.

Variations:

Fish and cucumber cream
Substitute 8 oz. cooked white fish for salmon and add 4 oz. coarsely grated cucumber.

Fish cream
Use 12 oz. flaked cooked white fish instead of salmon. This should be cooked carefully so fish does not become too moist. Either poach or steam it between 2 plates.

Lobster cream
Use flesh from 1 medium-sized lobster. Flake body flesh finely and cut claw meat into fine pieces. Garnish with lobster claws.
For a decorative main course for 2 people, use this recipe but only 1 small lobster and put mixture into well-washed and dried halved lobster shells.

Shrimp cream
Substitute 8 oz. chopped shrimps for salmon.

Salmon croquettes

(also suitable for pilchards or sardines)

cooking time 10 – 15 minutes

you will need for 4 servings:

1 oz. flour
¼ teaspoon ground mace or nutmeg
pinch pepper
pinch salt
⅓ pint salmon stock and milk
2 teaspoons vinegar
8 – 12 oz. cooked salmon

To coat:
1 egg
breadcrumbs
fat

1 Blend flour, spice and seasoning with a little cold liquid.
2 Bring remainder to the boil, pour on to blended flour and mix well. Return to pan, bring to the boil, stirring all the time, and boil gently for 5 minutes.
3 Beat in vinegar and fish and turn on to a wetted plate. When cold and firm, divide into 4 or 8 portions and form into sausage shapes.
4 Coat in beaten egg. Roll in breadcrumbs and grill for a few minutes until golden brown, or fry in hot fat.

Serve hot or cold with mixed salad.

Fish scallops

cooking time 10 – 15 minutes

you will need for 4 servings:

- ¾ lb. flaked cooked fish—salmon, fresh haddock or hake
- seasoning
- ¼ pint thick white sauce (see page 83)
- 4 escallop shells
- 1 oz. grated cheese
- 8 oz. mashed potatoes
- parsley to garnish

1. Stir fish into sauce and season thoroughly.
2. Beat well and put on to the escallop shells, sprinkle with cheese.
3. Carefully pipe round a border of mashed potato.
4. Put under a hot grill for a few minutes until top is crisp and brown.
5. Serve garnished with parsley.

Baked sprats

cooking time 10 – 15 minutes

you will need for 4 servings:

- sprats
- seasoning
- fat
- parsley
- lemon

1. Cut heads off sprats and season lightly.
2. Heat a small quantity of fat in a baking tin.
3. Arrange sprats in a layer in the tin and cook for approximately 10 – 15 minutes in a moderately hot oven (400°F.—Gas Mark 5).
4. Garnish with parsley and lemon and serve.

Fried sprats

cooking time 5 minutes

you will need:

- sprats
- seasoning
- flour
- little fat
- lemon
- parsley

1. Wash sprats, dry very thoroughly and remove heads.
2. Dust lightly with seasoned flour.
3. Fry for about 5 minutes in a little hot fat.
4. Drain well and serve with lemon and parsley.

Deep fried sprats

cooking time 4 minutes

you will need:

- sprats
- seasoned flour
- deep fat or oil

1. Prepare sprats as in previous recipe. Cook in frying basket in oil or fat until crisp and golden brown.
2. Drain well.

Freshwater Fish

FISH IN SEASON	TO BUY AND COOK
CARP Oct – Feb	Unless very small, this fish is too tough for grilling or frying. Is best baked rather slowly, preferably with onions and tomatoes, in a covered casserole. Allow 8 oz. per person.
EEL Sept – May	Must be purchased alive. The fishmonger will cut and skin them. Stew, or make into a jelly. 6 – 8 oz. per person.
TROUT April – Sept	Buy whole, grill, fry or bake. Delicious fried and served with brown butter sauce, i.e. meunière (see page 22). Keep well basted when cooking as the fish is rather dry. Ideal to cook almost immediately after being caught.
PERCH May – Feb	Generally small enough to serve 1 fish per person. Be careful of the sharp spikes in the dorsal fine. Is difficult to scale, so plunge for a minute in boiling water then scale. Delicious flavour. Best fried and serve with meunière sauce (see page 22).

FISH IN SEASON	TO BUY AND COOK
BREAM	see White Fish table (page 10).
SMELT Sept – Mar	Becoming rare. Can be poached, grilled, fried, baked or cooked in white wine or cider. To prepare, remove fins, but leave head. When fresh has a delicate smell—very like violets.

Baked carp

cooking time 40 minutes

you will need for 4 servings:

1 carp or part of a carp, about 2 lb.
2 oz. melted butter
1 onion
4 tomatoes
seasoning

1. Season fish very well.
2. Put 1 oz. butter into the dish with half the sliced onion and tomatoes.
3. Lay fish on top and cover with remaining onion, tomatoes and butter.
4. Bake for approximately 40 minutes in a moderately hot oven (400°F.—Gas Mark 5).

To poach carp

cooking time 20 minutes

you will need for 4 servings:

court-bouillon (see page 8)
1 carp about 2½ – 3 lb.
white sauce (see page 83)

1. Prepare *court-bouillon.*
2. Put in the carp.
3. Simmer steadily for approximately 20 minutes.
4. Drain well and serve with sauce made with half stock and half milk.

Collared eel

cooking time 1 hour 30 minutes

you will need for 5 – 6 servings:

1 large eel
parsley stuffing (see page 87)
good pinch ground cloves, mace, allspice, mixed herbs, sage
salt, pepper
3 tablespoons vinegar

1. Cut off head and tail of the eel, remove skin and backbone. Keep these for stock.
2. Mix spices and herbs with stuffing.
3. Spread eel flat and cover inner side with mixture.
4. Roll up, beginning with the broad end, bind in shape with strong white tape.
5. Make stock by simmering backbone, head and tail in water to cover for about 20 minutes.
6. Season well, add 1 tablespoon vinegar and put eel in.
7. Simmer gently for about 40 minutes, then lift out.
8. Press eel between two dishes or boards until cold.
9. Add remaining vinegar to eel stock.
10. Simmer gently for ½ hour, then strain.
11. When eel is cold, return to liquid and leave until required.

Jellied eels

cooking time 45 minutes – 1 hour

you will need:

eels
water
salt
lemon juice
gelatine

1. Cut skinned eels into 2-inch lengths.
2. Put into enough cold water just to cover, add a little salt and squeeze of lemon juice.
3. Simmer very gently for approximately 45 minutes to 1 hour, until flesh is tender.
4. Lift out fish and arrange in mould or dish.
5. Measure liquid and, if a very firm jelly is required, add 1 teaspoon powder gelatine to each ½ pint stock.
6. Strain over eels and allow to set.

Note:

If liquid is boiled down, not only does it have a better flavour, but gelatine is unnecessary. Bay leaf or spice can also be added for flavour.

Eel with parsley sauce

cooking time 45 minutes

you will need for 4 servings:

2 lb. eels
sprig parsley
2 slices lemon
parsley sauce (see page 83)

To garnish:
lemon
parsley

1. Skin eel and cut into 2 – 3-inch lengths.
2. Put into cold salted water, adding sprig parsley and lemon slices.
3. Simmer gently for approximately 45 minutes.
4. Drain and serve with parsley sauce, garnished with lemon and parsley.

Perch meunière

cooking time 10 – 12 minutes

you will need:

1 perch per person
3 oz. butter
lemon juice
few capers, optional
chopped parsley

1. Fry perch steadily for 10 minutes in butter.
2. Lift out and put on to a hot dish.
3. Add good squeeze lemon juice, capers and a little parsley to the butter.
4. Heat until golden brown and pour over the fish.

Trout Grenoblaise No. 1

cooking time 13 – 15 minutes

you will need for 4 servings:

4 medium-sized trout
2 oz. mushrooms
2 tablespoons coarse breadcrumbs
seasoning
3 – 4 oz. butter

1. Take backbones out of trout.
2. Thinly slice mushrooms and mix with breadcrumbs.
3. Season fish lightly and fry for about 10 minutes in butter.
4. Lift out and put on to a hot dish.
5. Cook mushrooms and breadcrumbs for about 5 minutes.
6. Pour over the fish and serve.

Trout Grenoblaise No. 2

cooking time 13 – 15 minutes

you will need for 4 servings:

4 medium-sized trout
seasoning
3 – 4 oz. butter
2 oz. blanched almonds

1. Take backbones out of trout.
2. Season fish lightly and fry for about 10 minutes in butter.
3. Lift out and put on to a hot dish, then fry almonds for about 5 minutes.
4. Pour over the fish.

Trout in Chablis

cooking time 15 minutes

you will need for 4 servings:

4 medium-sized trout
seasoning
approximately ⅓ pt. white wine
½ oz. flour
1 oz. butter

To garnish:
lemon
parsley

1. Take backbones out of trout; put into a casserole; season well and pour over enough wine to cover.
2. Bake in the middle of a moderate oven (375°F.—Gas Mark 4) for 15 minutes, or simmer gently in a large saucepan for 10 minutes.
3. Lift on to a hot dish.
4. Stir flour into hot butter and cook for several minutes, then gradually add the wine left from cooking the fish.
5. Heat for a few minutes, pour over fish and garnish with lemon and parsley.

Trout meunière

cooking time 10 – 12 minutes

you will need:

1 medium-sized trout per person
3 oz. butter
squeeze lemon juice
little chopped parsley
few capers, optional

1. Clean trout and cut off head.
2. Heat butter and fry trout steadily for about 10 minutes.
3. Lift out and put on to a hot dish.
4. Add lemon juice, parsley and capers to butter.
5. Heat until golden brown and pour over fish.

Fried smelts

cooking time 5 minutes

you will need for 4 servings:

about 1½ lb. smelts
seasoning
flour
little milk
fat

For garnish:
parsley
lemon

1 Clean fish and dry well.
2 Mix seasoning with flour.
3 Dip fish in milk and roll in flour.
4 Fry for about 5 minutes in hot fat.
5 Drain and garnish with fried parsley and lemon.

To fry parsley:
Put well-dried parsley sprigs in hot fat and fry them for about 30 seconds until they are crisp, but still green.

Roes

There is a great deal of goodness in the fish roe although if there is a lot of roe in plaice, for example, the flavour of the fish itself tends to deteriorate.
Herring roes, because they are so light and easily digestible, are an excellent food for children and the elderly. They also have the advantage of being very cheap.
The table below gives an idea of how roes are best used:

FISH TYPE	TO COOK
COD ROE **fresh**	These should first be steamed. Allow approximately 10 – 15 minutes per lb. and the roe is then ready to use in a variety of ways. Many fishmongers sell cooked roe. Fry cod's roe either in a little butter or margarine or in bacon fat. If in fairly thin slices, it will only take a few minutes to heat and fry. Or blend slices with melted butter, grill. Serve in a fish pie (see page 62) in place of white fish, cutting the roe into neat fingers. If mashed with butter and well seasoned, it makes a delicious pâté.
smoked	Excellent as an hors-d'œuvre or pâté. Serve on crisp lettuce with hot toast and butter. For a more elaborate type of pâte see directions for Crème à la Grecque and variations (page 40).
HERRING ROES **soft**	Separate and dry the roes, coat in a little flour and fry for a few minutes in butter or margarine. Or put on a plate with butter, margarine, a little seasoning and cream or milk. Cover with a second plate and steam over a pan of rapidly boiling water for approximately 10 minutes. Serve on hot toast garnished with paprika, butter and/or chopped parsley. Steam, put into a white sauce and serve instead of white fish in a fish pie (see page 62).
hard	Coat in seasoned flour or egg and cream, then fry in butter or margarine. Brush with melted butter or margarine and grill steadily. Steam as soft roes, omitting the milk, then pound with seasoning, and use as a sandwich filling or pâté.
STURGEON'S ROE (Caviare)	One of the most expensive delicacies although there is cheaper caviare than the Russian which is considered the finest. Serve on brown toast or brown bread and butter topped with finely chopped hard-boiled egg and a squeeze of lemon. As an hors-d'œuvre, serve on a bed of lettuce with lemon and hot brown toast.

Devilled roes

Cooking time few minutes

you will need for 4 servings:

8 oz. herring roes (cooked)
2 oz. butter
1 teaspoon made mustard
1 teaspoon Worcestershire sauce
salt, pepper
4 slices toast
anchovy fillets

1 Drain cooked herring roes.
2 Cream with melted butter, made mustard, Worcestershire sauce, and sprinkle of pepper and salt.
3 Spread on toast.
4 Top with anchovy and grill.

Pâté from cod's roe

no cooking

Use ingredients as Crème à la Grecque (see this page) but add finely crushed garlic for a strong flavoured pâté, together with cayenne pepper.

Variations:

Cream pâté
Work in a little thick cream.

Herb paté
Add a little finely chopped fresh parsley and lemon thyme.

Crème à la Grecque

no cooking

you will need for 4 servings:

8 oz. smoked cod's roe
4 – 6 oz. unsalted butter
juice 1 lemon
1 tomato
black olives
toast or water biscuits

1 Skin the roe.
2 Cream the butter.
3 Pound roe, adding butter, lemon juice, tomato juice and pulp.
4 When very light and creamy, serve with black olives and hot toast or water biscuits.

Shellfish

There are a great variety of shellfish available in Great Britain, ranging from the very expensive lobster to the really quite cheap cockles and winkles.

There is, however, one basic rule about shellfish. Buy it fresh, for it is not only very unpleasant when stale, but also extremely dangerous.

FISH IN SEASON	TO COOK
CLAM Sept – April	Smaller than oyster, but can be served in the same way and are particularly good in a chowder.
COCKLES Sept – April	Tiny shellfish served cold. To cook, wash thoroughly, put into salted water, then into either roasting tin in moderate oven or saucepan containing very little water. Heat until shells open. Take out and serve with seasoning and a little vinegar. Excellent added to sauces.
CRAB May – Aug	Dress, making sure to remove the stomach bag and grey brown fingers, serve hot or cold. To cook, put into boiling salted water, simmer for 20 – 25 minutes, rinse in cold water. The male crab is best, and it has larger claws.
CRAWFISH (Langouste) May – Aug	Although no large claws, use as lobster.
CRAYFISH (Écrevisse) Oct – Mar	Small freshwater shellfish, similar to lobster. If caught fresh, cook for 10 minutes only, but otherwise treat it in the same way as lobster.

FISH IN SEASON	TO COOK
LOBSTER Feb – Oct	Serve hot or cold. To cook wash well, tie claws and put into boiling water. Simmer for 20 – 25 minutes according to size BUT NO MORE, then put into cold water. Hen lobster has wide tail and red coral which is delicious. If buying ready-cooked lobster, make sure it has been freshly cooked. The lobster should feel heavy for the size and the tail should spring back when tested. Be sure to take out intestinal vein and the 'fingers'.
MUSSELS Sept – April	Serve as oysters, raw or in sauce.
OYSTERS Sept – April	Generally served raw as hors-d'œuvre, can be used in sauces or as main dish, delicious as filling for omelettes. Imported oysters now cover 'closed season'.
PRAWNS small Feb – Oct large Mar – Dec	Excellent fresh or frozen small prawns, or large prawns known as scampi; can be served throughout the year. Delicious hot or cold, in main dishes or with hot sauce.
SHRIMPS Feb – Oct	See prawns.
SCALLOPS or ESCALLOPS Oct – Mar	Use in sauces, or main dishes. The roe (coral) should be firm and bright in colour. Remove the black part and gristly fibre. Save shells to use in scalloped dishes.
WHELKS Sept – April	Buy when alive, clean in plenty of water. Boil steadily in salted water for approximately 1 hour. Take out of shells with pin and serve with seasoning and vinegar.
WINKLES Sept – April	Like small whelks.

NEVER OVER-COOK SHELLFISH AS IT BECOMES TOUGH AND TASTELESS.

To dress crab

One medium-sized crab is enough for two people, a large one for four. Weigh the crab in your hand, when buying, and avoid any that feel light for size. The lightweights have very little meat.

1 Pull off all claws and wipe the shell.
2 Turn crab on its back and take the body from the main shell.
3 Remove and discard the stomach bag and grey fingers. These must not be eaten.
4 Take out all meat, putting dark and white into separate basins, then crack the top of the shell and remove pieces so there is a flat cavity to fill.
5 Crack claws and remove the meat, adding it to the light meat.
6 Arrange dark and light meat alternately in the shell and garnish with parsley.

Crab pilaff

cooking time 10 minutes

you will need for 4 servings:

4 oz. butter or margarine
8 oz. cooked long grain rice
4 tomatoes, peeled and chopped
4 oz. sultanas
2 large cooked crabs OR $1\frac{1}{4}$ lb. crab meat
salt
ground black pepper
grated Parmesan or dry Cheddar cheese, optional

To garnish:
strips anchovy fillets

1 Melt butter or margarine and add rice.
2 Stir until fat is absorbed, then add tomatoes, sultanas, crab meat and seasonings.
3 Stir until heated through.
4 Divide mixture between two shells or, if crab meat is used, pile on to a heated dish.
5 Generously sprinkle cheese on each portion, decorate with anchovies and serve with a tossed green salad.

To boil cockles

Fresh cockles must be washed at least three times to get rid of all the sand. They should then be put into salted water (1 teaspoon salt to each pint of water). Drain, and put into a saucepan with enough water to cover the bottom.
Cover the pan with a tightly fitting lid, foil or cloth, and heat very gently for approximately 5 – 8 minutes, shaking the pan from time to time until the shells open. Remove the little fish and put into a white sauce (see page 83) or allow to cool and serve with a little vinegar and brown bread and butter.

Clam fritters

cooking time 5 – 6 minutes

you will need for 4 servings:

- 16 clams
- ¼ pint fritter batter (see page 9)
- deep fat or oil for frying
- parsley
- lemon

1 Open clam shells and remove the fish.
2 Coat with batter and fry in the hot oil or fat until crisp and golden brown.
3 Drain and serve with parsley and lemon slices.

Devilled crab No. 1

cooking time 25 minutes

you will need for 8 servings:

- 2 oz. breadcrumbs
- 1 oz. butter
- 1½ – 2 lb. crab meat, fresh, frozen or canned
- 1 finely chopped onion
- 1 finely chopped green pepper
- 1 tablespoon chopped parsley
- 1 teaspoon Worcestershire sauce
- salt, pepper
- 1 – 2 tablespoons dry mustard
- ½ pint double cream
- few drops Tabasco or pinch chilli powder or cayenne pepper

1 Toss breadcrumbs in hot butter.
2 Mix crab meat with half the breadcrumbs, reserving the rest for topping
3 Add onion, green pepper, parsley, sauce and seasoning.
4 Mix mustard with cream and stir into crab meat mixture, then add Tabasco. Taste after every drop of Tabasco so as not to make the mixture too hot.
5 Pile into crab shells or buttered shallow casserole dish.
6 Cover with remaining breadcrumbs, well seasoned, and bake in a hot oven (425 – 450°F.— Gas Mark 6 – 7) for 20 minutes or until well browned.

Serve at once.

Devilled crab No. 2

cooking time 10 minutes

you will need for 2 servings as main dish, 4 as hors-d'œuvre

- 1 large crab or 2 small crabs
- seasoning
- 1 teaspoon curry powder
- 1 teaspoon Worcestershire sauce
- 1 oz. fine breadcrumbs
- 1 oz. butter

1 Take the crab meat from the shell and flake.
2 Mix with seasoning, curry powder, sauce and ½ oz. breadcrumbs.
3 Fry remaining breadcrumbs in butter.
4 Put the crab meat into the shell.
5 Cover with breadcrumbs and heat under the grill.

Crab au gratin

cooking time 6 minutes

you will need for 4 servings:

- 1 large crab
- 4 oz. grated cheese
- shake pepper
- made mustard
- 1 oz. butter
- cream, optional
- breadcrumbs

1 Remove crab meat from shells and mix dark and light.
2 Blend with 2 oz. cheese and seasoning and heat for a few minutes with ½ oz. butter and cream.
3 Put into 4 individual dishes or crab shell.
4 Top with remaining cheese and butter and breadcrumbs, and brown under a very hot grill for about 6 minutes.

Lobster with wine sauce

cooking time 15 – 20 minutes

you will need for 4 servings:

- 1 onion or 2 shallots
- 2 oz. butter
- 3 tomatoes
- ¼ pint white wine
- ¼ pint brandy
- salt, pepper
- 1 large or 2 medium lobsters

1 Dice onion finely and fry in butter.
2 Add skinned tomatoes, wine and brandy and

simmer for about 10 minutes, seasoning to taste.

3 Remove lobster meat from shell and claws, dice and add to the tomato mixture.
4 Heat for about 5 minutes and serve with crisp toast or rice.

Lobster au gratin

cooking time 15 minutes

you will need for 4 servings:

2 – 3 mushrooms
1 onion
1 oz. butter
½ oz. flour
¼ pint evaporated milk
seasoning
1 cooked lobster or tin lobster
1 oz. sieved Swiss cheese (processed Gruyère)
1 teaspoon browned breadcrumbs
paprika
parsley or watercress

1 Peel and slice mushrooms and onion.
2 Fry in butter but do not brown.
3 Add flour and stir milk in gradually, simmer until thickened and vegetables tender, season to taste.
4 Remove meat from shell and claws or drain tinned lobster.
5 Add to sauce and heat through.
6 Pile into the shell or into individual dishes and sprinkle with cheese and breadcrumbs.
7 Grill until brown and decorate with lines of paprika pepper and parsley sprigs.

Lobster cutlets

cooking time 15 – 20 minutes

you will need for 4 servings:

1 oz. margarine
1 oz. flour
¼ pint milk
seasoning
1 medium-sized lobster
3 – 4 oz. fine breadcrumbs
1 egg
1 teaspoon finely grated onion
fat
egg and browned breadcrumbs

1 Melt margarine, stir in flour and cook for 3 minutes.
2 Remove pan from the heat and stir in cold milk; bring to the boil, stirring all the time, until a thick sauce is formed, and add seasoning.
3 Let this cool, then mix in the lobster meat, breadcrumbs and the well beaten egg and onion.
4 Form into cutlet shapes, brush with egg and coat in breadcrumbs.
5 Heat fat and fry cutlets until brown and crisp on both sides; then lower heat and cook gently for a further few minutes to make sure cutlets are heated right through.

Serve with fried or creamed potatoes, peas or creamed spinach and a piquante sauce (see page 83).

Lobster mornay

cooking time 10 – 15 minutes

you will need for 4 servings:

1 large lobster
½ pint cheese sauce (see page 81)
2 tablespoons cream, optional
2 tablespoons sherry, optional
grated cheese (Cheddar, Parmesan, Gruyère)

1 Prepare lobster, removing all meat from the body and large claws.
2 Save small claws for garnish.
3 Make cheese sauce, add cream, sherry and lobster meat and heat very gently for about 3 – 4 minutes.
4 Pile into a serving dish or into halved lobster shells.
5 Sprinkle with cheese and put for a few minutes under the grill.

Lobster with brandy sauce

cooking time 15 minutes

you will need for 4 servings:

1 large or 2 medium lobsters
2 oz. butter
¼ pint cream
2 egg yolks
¼ pint milk
¼ pint brandy or sherry
seasoning

1 Dice lobster meat and toss in butter.
2 Add cream, egg yolks blended with milk, brandy or sherry and seasoning.
3 Heat very gently, taking care not to boil until the sauce has thickened. A double saucepan is ideal.
4 Serve at once, garnished with small lobster claws.

Variation:

Use ½ pint white sauce (see page 83), add diced lobster, sherry and a little cream or an egg yolk and heat gently.

Lobster with savoury jelly

cooking time a few minutes

you will need for 4 servings:

For the jelly:
½ oz. powder gelatine
½ pint water
¼ pint vinegar
2 tablespoons lemon juice
seasoning

1 prepared lobster
1 small lettuce
cucumber
tomatoes

1. Soften the gelatine in a little cold water.
2. Heat remaining water with vinegar, lemon juice and a little seasoning.
3. Pour the hot liquid over the gelatine and stir until dissolved.
4. Allow this jelly to set, then chop into cubes.
5. Arrange on a shallow dish to surround the halved lobster.
6. Surround with a border of small lettuce leaves, sliced cucumber and tomatoes.

Lobster Thermidor No. 1

cooking time 15 minutes

you will need for 4 servings:

3 oz. butter
1 oz. flour
⅜ pint milk
2 tablespoons cream
mustard
seasoning
1 large or 2 medium lobsters
1 small onion or shallot
2 tablespoons white wine or sherry
2 oz. grated cheese

1. Make the sauce with 1 oz. butter, flour, milk, cream, a little mustard and season well.
2. Add diced lobster meat and heat gently.
3. Fry very finely chopped shallot or onion in remaining butter.
4. Add to mixture together with wine or sherry.
5. Pile into lobster shells, cover tops with grated cheese and brown under a hot grill.

Lobster Thermidor No. 2

cooking time 15 minutes

you will need for 4 servings:

8 oz. tomatoes
4 oz. sliced mushrooms
1 oz. flour
2 oz. butter or margarine
⅜ pint milk
2 medium-sized lobsters
mustard
seasoning
⅜ pint sherry or white wine
1 - 2 oz. grated cheese

1. Fry the chopped, skinned and sliced tomatoes until tender.
2. Add mushrooms.
3. Stir in flour and cook for 3 minutes, then gradually add milk.
4. Bring to the boil and cook until thickened.
5. Stir in the flaked lobster meat, a little mustard and season well.
6. Add sherry or wine.
7. Pile into the halved lobster shells, sprinkle cheese on top and brown under a hot grill.

Lobster Thermidor No. 3

cooking time 20 minutes

you will need for 4 servings:

2 medium-sized lobsters
¼ pint white wine
¼ pint fish stock
½ pint béchamel sauce (see page 84)
approximately 1 tablespoon made mustard
1 chopped shallot
little tarragon
little chervil
1 oz. finely grated Parmesan cheese

1. Split lobster shells and remove all meat.
2. Simmer wine, stock, sauce, mustard, shallot and herbs together.
3. Strain carefully and reheat sauce mixture with the lobster pieces.
4. Pile back into lobster halves and top with a light sprinkling of cheese.
5. Brown under a hot grill.

This recipe originally required live lobsters—which are split while still alive.
The meat is removed from the claws, piled on to the halved lobster.
Dust lightly with salt, brush well with melted butter or oil, then bake for 15 minutes in a moderate oven (375°F.—Gas Mark 4).
Continue then as from Step 2 onwards.

Mussels marinière

cooking time 10 minutes

you will need for 4 servings:

2 pints mussels
1 small onion
2 or 3 pieces celery
seasoning
1 bunch parsley
1 tablespoon tarragon vinegar
little wine, optional*
chopped parsley

* A good dry white wine, Graves, is excellent. If not using white wine add 1 tablespoon white wine vinegar as well as the tarragon vinegar

1 Scrub mussels well, discarding any that are open and will not close when sharply tapped. Put into a large saucepan together with water, onion, celery, a good pinch of salt and pepper, parsley, vinegar and wine.
2 Heat slowly until mussels open. Sometimes you will find a small growth, looking like a weed, in the mussels—this must be taken out and the beards removed.
3 Leave the mussels on ½ shells. Reboil the liquid and strain over them.
4 Garnish with chopped parsley.

Fried oysters

cooking time 6 minutes

you will need:

oysters
¼ pint fritter batter (see page 9) OR 1 egg and breadcrumbs
deep oil or fat for frying

1 Remove oysters from shells.
2 Coat with batter or egg and breadcrumbs.
3 Fry in oil or fat until crisp and golden brown.
4 Drain and serve.

Creamed oysters

cooking time 12 minutes

you will need for 4 servings:

½ pint white or béchamel sauce (see page 84)
2 tablespoons cream
little lemon juice or white wine or sherry to flavour
approximately 16 oysters

To garnish:
lemon slices
parsley sprigs
fingers crisp toast

1 Make the sauce.
2 Add cream, wine and oysters and heat gently for a very few minutes.
3 Pour into serving dish and garnish.

Coquilles St. Jacques

cooking time approximately 20 minutes

you will need for 4 servings:

4 medium-sized scallops
½ pint milk
little mashed potato
2 oz. butter
1 oz. flour
seasoning
1 tablespoon white wine or sherry
few crisp breadcrumbs
1 oz. grated cheese

1 Simmer the scallops in milk for approximately 10 minutes until quite soft.*
2 When cooked, put scallops on to their shells.
3 Pipe a border of mashed potato around each.
4 Melt butter, stir in flour and cook gently for 3 minutes.
5 Gradually add milk, made up to ½ pint.
6 Cook sauce until thick, adding seasoning and wine.
7 Carefully mask the tops of the scallops with this.
8 Sprinkle with breadcrumbs and cheese and put into a hot oven or under the grill until heated through and crisp and brown on top.

* This must be done slowly, for too quick cooking makes them tough.

Coquilles St. Jacques bonne femme

cooking time 25 minutes

you will need for 4 servings:

4 scallops
½ pint milk
4 tablespoons white wine
1 oz. margarine
2 oz. mushrooms
¾ oz. flour
salt, pepper
creamed potato
sprigs parsley

1 Slice scallops and simmer in milk and wine until tender—about 10 minutes.
2 Drain carefully and place in the deep shells and keep hot.
3 Melt margarine and fry sliced mushrooms until soft, about 3 – 4 minutes.
4 Add flour and cook for a further 1 – 2 minutes.
5 Stir in the fish liquor and bring to the boil, stirring all the time.
6 Boil gently for 5 minutes, then season to taste.
7 Pipe a firm border of creamed potato around the edge of each scallop shell and pour the sauce over the fish.
8 Reheat under the grill until lightly browned and garnish with parsley.

Fried scallops

cooking time 5 minutes

you will need for 4 servings:

4 scallops
little flour or thin batter (see page 9)
seasoning
fat for frying

1 Lift scallops from shells.
2 Dry and coat in well seasoned flour, or batter.
3 Put into deep or shallow fat and fry steadily for approximately 5 minutes.

Scallops and bacon

cooking time 5 minutes

you will need for 4 servings:

4 scallops
seasoning
little lemon juice
4 small rashers bacon

1 Lift scallops from shells.
2 Season, add a little lemon juice.
3 Wrap each in a bacon rasher, secure with a skewer.
4 Fry or grill for 5 minutes.

Scallops provençale

cooking time 12 minutes

you will need for 4 servings:

8 scallops
salted water
1 large peeled sliced tomato
1 small finely chopped onion
¼ lb. finely chopped mushrooms
salt, pepper
2 oz. butter
⅛ pint béchamel sauce (see page 84)

1 Wash scallops, cover with cold salted water, bring to the boil and simmer for 7 or 8 minutes until soft.
2 Drain and chop white and red parts together and mix with tomato, onion, mushrooms, salt and pepper.
3 Cook in butter for 3 minutes.
4 Add sauce, mix and fill 4 shells.
5 Brown under a hot grill for a few minutes.

Seafood curry

cooking time 35 – 40 minutes

you will need for 4 servings:

2 tablespoons oil or
2 oz. butter
1 finely chopped onion
4 level dessertspoons curry powder
1 oz. cornflour
1½ pints water*
1 medium-sized chopped apple
4 tablespoons coconut
2 chicken stock cubes, optional
2 tablespoons lemon juice
seasoning
few sultanas
8 oz. canned or frozen seafood (scampi, prawn, shrimp or lobster)

* Or fish stock from simmering shells

1 Heat the oil.
2 Add onion and fry for a few minutes, then add curry powder and cornflour.
3 Cook over low heat for 1 minute.
4 Add water, apple, coconut and stock cubes and simmer gently for about ½ hour, stirring occasionally.
5 Add lemon juice and correct seasoning.
6 Add sultanas and fish and heat through.

Serve with boiled rice.

Paella

cooking time approximately 1 hour

you will need for 4 servings:

4 pieces cooked or raw young chicken
1 onion
1 clove garlic
2 tablespoons olive oil
2 pints water
4 tomatoes
4 oz. rice
2 chicken *bouillon* cubes
little saffron
1 small cooked lobster or tin lobster
4 Dublin Bay prawns, or 8 – 10 smaller prawns
6 – 8 mussels
8 oz. frozen peas
½ tin pimento or 1 red pepper

1 Cut up chicken, onion and garlic and fry in oil until golden.
2 Add 1 pint water and simmer for 15 minutes.
3 Add tomatoes, skinned and chopped.
4 Add rice, remaining water and *bouillon* cubes.
5 Simmer for 5 minutes, stir in saffron.
6 Add lobster pieces, prawns, mussels, peas and pimentos.
7 Simmer until rice is cooked and has absorbed most of the liquid, 15 – 20 minutes.

Variation:

Substitute pieces of white fish for chicken.

Curried prawns No. 1

cooking time about 1 hour

you will need for 4 servings:

1 oz. margarine or oil
1 small onion
½ apple
1 dessertspoon curry powder
1 teaspoon curry paste
1 dessertspoon flour
pinch ginger
pinch cinnamon
1 pint fish stock (see page 72) or water
1 teaspoon vinegar or lemon juice
1 teaspoon sugar
good pinch salt and pepper
1 dessertspoon sweet chutney
1 pint prawns

1 Heat margarine, fry finely chopped onion and apple until nearly soft.
2 Then work in curry powder and paste, flour, ginger and spices and cook for 3 minutes, stirring all the time.
3 Gradually add stock or water and all other ingredients except prawns.
4 Bring slowly to the boil, lower the heat and cook gently for approximately ¾ hour in a COVERED pan.
5 Add shelled prawns and heat for a further 10 minutes.

Serve with cooked rice, more chutney and, if available, a little grated coconut.

Curried prawns No. 2

cooking time approximately 1 hour

you will need for 4 servings:

- 1 medium-sized onion
- 1 cooking apple
- 1 oz. butter
- 1 tablespoon curry powder
- 1 teaspoon curry paste
- 1 tablespoon cornflour
- ½ pint stock (see page 72) or water
- 1 dessertspoon chutney
- 1 tablespoon dessicated coconut
- 1 dessertspoon sultanas
- 1 teaspoon lemon juice
- salt
- 1 - 2 tablespoons milk or cream, optional
- 8 oz. frozen or freshly shelled prawns

1 Chop onion and cooking apple.
2 Sauté in butter.
3 Add curry powder, paste and cornflour.
4 Stir until blended, cook a few minutes.
5 Stir in stock.
6 Bring to the boil, stirring all the time.
7 Add chutney, coconut and sultanas.
8 Cover and simmer for at least 1 hour.
9 Stir in lemon juice, salt, and milk or cream.
10 Put in prawns and heat for a few minutes.

Potato and prawn mornay

cooking time 35 minutes

you will need for 4 servings:

- 1 - 1½ lb. creamed potatoes
- margarine
- ½ pint white sauce (see page 83)
- 3 oz. grated cheese
- 2 hard-boiled eggs
- ½ pint picked prawns
- 2 oz. breadcrumbs

1 Line the bottom and sides of a casserole with potato.
2 Brush with a little melted margarine and put into hot oven (425 - 450°F.—Gas Mark 6 - 7) for about 10 minutes until crisp.
3 Make the sauce.
4 Add most of the cheese, chopped eggs and prawns.
5 Pour into potato-case and top with breadcrumbs and cheese and dot with margarine.
6 Return to oven for about 10 - 15 minutes.

Prawn and corn bake

cooking time 35 minutes

you will need for 4 servings:

- ½ pint cheese sauce (see page 81)
- 4 oz. fresh, canned or frozen prawns
- 1 large can corn or 10 - 12 oz. cooked corn
- 1 stick celery
- salt, pepper

1 Make the cheese sauce and add most of the prawns, (reserving a few for garnish), corn and finely chopped celery.
2 Season to taste and turn into a greased casserole.
3 Cook for 25 minutes in a moderate oven (375°F.—Gas Mark 4).
4 Garnish with remaining prawns and serve with rice or vegetables.

Prawns in soya sauce

cooking time 10 - 15 minutes

you will need for 4 servings:

- 8 oz. prawns
- 3 slices ginger
- 1 spring or small onion
- 3 tablespoons soya sauce
- 2 tablespoons sherry
- 4 teaspoons sugar
- 4 teaspoons salt
- 2 teaspoons cornflour
- 1 tablespoon cold water
- 3 tablespoons oil

1 Wash prawns thoroughly, do not shell but clip whiskers and legs.
2 Slice ginger and cut onion into 1-inch lengths.
3 Mix soya sauce, sherry, sugar and salt. Add cornflour, blend with water.
4 Heat oil until it smokes.
5 Add prawns, ginger and onion.
6 Stir to coat with oil.
7 Add sauce.
8 Simmer giant prawns for 10 minutes, small prawns for 5 minutes.

Cheese and shrimp or prawn ramekins

cooking time 7 minutes

you will need for 4 servings:

- 4 eggs
- ½ pint white sauce (see page 83)
- 4 oz. grated Cheddar cheese
- 2 – 3 oz. shelled shrimps or prawns
- 2 teaspoons chopped parsley
- pinch cayenne pepper and salt

1. Boil eggs for 7 minutes, then plunge into cold water for 1 minute.
2. Remove the shells and roughly chop eggs, add to sauce.
3. Add 2 oz. cheese, shrimps or prawns and parsley, and heat through without boiling.
4. Season and pour into buttered ramekin dishes.
5. Sprinkle with remaining cheese and brown under a hot grill.

Serve at once with crisp toast.

Shellfish risotto

cooking time 40 – 45 minutes

you will need for 4 servings:

- 1 onion
- 1 small green pepper
- 2 oz. margarine or oil
- 8 oz. long grain rice
- 1 pint stock or water
- 8 oz. canned or frozen or fresh prawns
- salt, pepper

To garnish:

- 6 prawns (not shelled)
- watercress

1. Peel and coarsely chop onion, halve pepp remove the seeds and chop.
2. Melt 1 oz. margarine or oil.
3. Add onion and pepper and fry gently un cooked.
4. Remove vegetables and keep warm.
5. Melt remaining oil or margarine, stir in ri and cook gently for 3 – 4 minutes.
6. Add boiling stock or water.
7. Cover saucepan and simmer gently, witho stirring, until all stock is absorbed (appro mately 15 – 20 minutes).
8. Add vegetables and prepared prawns and he through.
9. Season well and pile into a hot dish.
10. Garnish with unshelled prawns and watercres

Potted shrimps

cooking time few minut

you will need for 4 servings:

- 2 pints or 2 lb. peeled shrimps
- 3 – 4 oz. butter
- ½ – 1 teaspoon grated nutmeg
- little pepper
- toast
- lettuce
- lemon slices

1. Pack shrimps loosely in individual containe or into a small basin.
2. Heat butter, add flavourings and pour over.
3. Allow to cool.
4. Serve with crisp hot toast on a bed of lettu with lemon to garnish.

Smoked Fish

This group covers a very wide range, many of which are served as hors-d'œuvres.

Because of the smoking process, the fish kee well, but the flavour is lost if kept too long.

	TO SERVE
COD	This is filleted then cured. Cook as smoked haddock. Allow 8 oz. per person.
HADDOCK	Either filleted and smoked or cured whole. Poach in water or milk and serve with butter or a sauce, or top with poached egg. Take care not to overcook. Very good as Kedgeree (see page 50 allow 8 – 10 oz. per person.
HERRING	Kippers can be fried, grille baked or boiled. Bloaters are best grilled or fried Buckling are served as smoke trout.
SALMON	Serve as hors-d'œuvre.

	TO SERVE
SPRATS	Unusual but very good. Grill or fry. Allow 8 oz. per person.
TROUT	An excellent hors-d'œuvre. Serve with horseradish sauce, lemon and brown bread and butter. Allow 1 fish per person.

	TO SERVE
WHITING	Cook as haddock, generally called 'golden fillets'. Allow 2 fillets per person.
EEL	An unusual but excellent hors-d'œuvre. Serve as smoked trout, removing tough skin. Allow 3 – 4 per person.

Grilled bloaters

cooking time 7 – 8 minutes

you will need:

bloaters as required
little margarine or dripping to fry roes

1 Break off the heads.
2 Split open the backs, remove roes and backbone.
3 Toss roes in a little hot margarine or dripping until golden brown.
4 Pre-heat the grill, grease grid in grill pan, place fish on it, insides to the heat.
5 When brown, turn and grill outsides.

Serve very hot with the fried roes.

Fried bloaters

cooking time 6 minutes

you will need:

bloaters
little fat

1 Break off the heads.
2 Heat the fat.
3 Put in the bloaters and fry on both sides until crisp and golden brown.

Curried kedgeree

cooking time 40 minutes

you will need for 4 servings:

1 large onion, thinly sliced
1 oz. fat
4 teaspoons curry powder
1 tablespoon flour
1 pint water
1 teaspoon sugar
2 teaspoons vinegar
2 teaspoons salt
4 oz. rice
12 oz. smoked haddock

1 Fry onion in fat until golden brown.
2 Stir in curry powder, cook for 5 minutes, then add flour.
3 Again cook for 5 minutes, then slowly add water and bring to the boil.
4 Stir in sugar, vinegar, salt and rice. Boil gently until rice is tender, about 20 minutes.
5 Add flaked fish and cook for a further 10 minutes.

Serve piled on a hot dish.

Note:

Cooked white fish may be substituted for smoked haddock.

Haddock eggs

cooking time 12 minutes

you will need for 4 servings:

6 – 8 eggs
water
3 – 4 oz. cottage cheese
1 teaspoon lemon juice
6 oz. flaked cooked smoked haddock
seasoning
lettuce
12 – 16 small gherkins

1 Place eggs carefully in boiling water, turn after a few minutes to centralize the yolks and boil for 12 minutes.
2 Place in cold water and break shells.
3 Peel eggs when cold and cut in halves lengthways.
4 Extract yolks and mash them. Gradually cream in cheese, lemon juice and fish.
5 Add seasoning to taste and pile mixture into halved hollows of egg whites.
6 Serve on lettuce, garnishing tops of eggs with fans of sliced gherkin.

Irish fishboats

cooking time 1½ – 1¾ hours

you will need for 4 servings:

- 4 large potatoes
- 1 oz. butter
- 1 egg yolk
- 4 teaspoons mixed mustard
- 6 oz. cooked flaked smoked haddock
- salt, pepper
- finely chopped parsley

1. Bake potatoes in their jackets for approximately 1¼ – 1½ hours in moderate oven (375°F.—Gas Mark 4).
2. Cut off tops, take out pulp.
3. Mash pulp with butter and egg yolk, add mustard.
4. Add haddock and season well.
5. Return mixture to potato shells and heat through in the oven for 15 – 20 minutes.
6. Garnish with parsley before serving.

Haddock quenelles

cooking time 20 minutes

you will need for 4 servings:

- 8 oz. cooked fresh or smoked haddock
- 2 oz. margarine or butter
- 2 eggs
- 4 tablespoons breadcrumbs
- seasoning
- ½ pint milk

1. Stir fish into melted margarine, add breadcrumbs and seasoning.
2. Cool mixture and beat in egg yolks.
3. Form into 4 fingers or quenelles.
4. Bring milk to the boil; lower quenelles and cook gently for 10 minutes.
5. Drain and keep hot; then use milk as foundation for a white sauce (see page 83) to serve with the quenelles.

Kedgeree

cooking time 10 minutes

you will need for 4 servings:

- 2 oz. butter
- 12 oz. cooked flaked smoked haddock
- 6 – 8 oz. cooked rice
- 2 hard-boiled eggs
- 1 – 2 beaten eggs
- ⅛ pint cream
- seasoning

1. Melt the butter.
2. Put fish in and shake over the fire until thoroughly hot.
3. Add rice, chopped hard-boiled eggs and seasoning.
4. Shake and stir over the heat with a fork for a few minutes.
5. Add beaten eggs and cream.
6. Reheat, stirring with a fork and, while still creamy, turn into a dish and serve very hot.

Variations:

For a less extravagant recipe, omit cream and raw eggs, and bind with a small quantity of milk.
Garnish with fried rings of onion.
Serve with crisp fried bacon rolls.

Mushroom kedgeree
Fry 3 – 4 oz. sliced mushrooms in extra 1 oz. butter, add to rice and fish at the last minute.

Salmon kedgeree
Use flaked canned salmon or flaked cooked salmon in place of smoked haddock.

Jugged kippers

cooking time 5 minutes

you will need:

- kippers
- boiling water

1. Roll up the kippers.
2. Put into a jug and pour in enough fast boiling water to cover.
3. Cover jug and let it stand for 5 minutes in a hot place (beside the hot plates on the stove for instance).
4. Remove the fish, drain.
5. Serve with a pat of butter on top.

Kippers maître d'hôtel

cooking time 20 minutes

you will need for 2 servings:

- 2 kippers
- paprika
- lemon juice
- maître d'hôtel butter (see page 85)
- parsley

1 Remove heads from kippers.
2 Dust inside of each with paprika, then sprinkle with lemon juice.
3 Put kippers together and wrap in greaseproof paper.
4 Place in baking tin in moderate oven (375°F.—Gas Mark 4) for about 20 minutes.
5 Turn out on to hot serving dish and pour juices from wrapping paper over top.
6 Blend ingredients for maître d'hôtel butter and mould into small squares, placing one on each fish before serving.
7 Garnish with parsley and serve with plain or French mustard.

Kipper pâté

cooking time 5 minutes

you will need for 4 servings:

4 kippers
good shake pepper
little paprika pepper
2 oz. butter
toast
1 hard-boiled egg

1 Cook kippers, preferably by the jugged method (see page 50).
2 Flake the flesh, discarding skin.
3 Mix with seasoning and butter.
4 Serve on toast, or with toast as an hors-d'œuvre, garnished with sliced or chopped egg.

Fried kippers

cooking time 6 minutes

you will need:

fat
kippers

1 Heat the fat.
2 Put kippers in and cook on either side until crisp and golden brown.

Note:

Do not over-fry, as this dries the flesh.

Grilled kippers

cooking time 5 minutes

you will need:

kippers
butter or margarine

1 Brush kippers with plenty of butter or margarine.
2 Cook under a hot grill and keep well basted with fat.

Mock smoked salmon with kipper fillets

no cooking

you will need:

kippers
oil
vinegar
chopped onion (optional)

1 Choose really thick, moist kippers and divide into neat fillets.
2 Cover with a little oil and vinegar and chopped onion.
3 Leave for several hours, then lift out.

Note:

Raw kippers are a good substitute for smoked salmon in hors-d'œuvre and sandwich fillings.

To serve smoked salmon

1 Arrange slices of smoked salmon on a plate with wedges of lemon and serve with brown bread and butter and paprika pepper.
2 Wrap each piece of smoked salmon round a well drained cooked, or canned asparagus tip. Serve either as a hors-d'œuvre or with salad as a main course.
3 Cook spinach until tender. Sieve and reheat with a little cream. Arrange on individual dishes and top with smoked salmon.
4 Top each slice of smoked salmon with shrimps or prawns, and serve with a thick mayonnaise (see page 86) and salad.
5 Cut the smoked salmon into thin strips and put into a Hollandaise sauce (see page 82). Serve with fresh salmon or white fish.

Smoked sprats

Follow directions for fresh sprats (page 36) but keep moist during cooking.

Frozen Fish

During the past years the supply and selection of frozen fish has increased, so now good fish can be obtained throughout the year—and people living in small towns away from the coast can choose from a wide variety.
Remember that frozen fish, like other frozen foods, is stored by the retailer in cabinets that are either set at 0 or minus 0 degrees F., so when once bought, fish must either be used as soon as possible or stored in a similar temperature in the home.
In an ordinary domestic refrigerator, it can be left in the freezing compartment for 1 – 3 days only—depending on the instructions on the packet. It is only in those cabinets with special deep-freeze compartment, or in hom deep-freeze cabinets, that fish can be ke longer. The minimum time should elaps between buying the frozen fish and storing correctly.
Once defrosted or partially defrosted, fish mu NOT be re-frozen.
The processors of frozen fish claim it is ver fresh, for in many cases the fish is frozen o board ship immediately after it is caught.
The table below gives some of the most usu types of frozen fish and the best ways of de frosting and cooking.

Frozen White Fish

FISH TO BUY AND COOK	TO DEFROST
COD Obtainable both as long 'blocks' of fish (often without bone and skin) or in portions ready coated for cooking. The uncoated fish is suitable for any method of cooking suggested for fresh cod, but it tends to be a little more 'watery'.	No need to defrost—fry or grill portions as fresh fish allowing a little longer cooking time than fresh since the cold of freezing takes some of the heat from fat. Larger pieces can be cut into convenient slices and cooked while frozen.
HADDOCK as cod	
PLAICE Obtainable both as whole fish or fillets. Cook as fresh plaice.	To keep fillets a good shape, defrost before starting to cook Leave at room tem perature, althoug the process can b hurried by standin the packet in COLI water. Hot water wi spoil both flavou and texture of fish Whole plaice nee NOT be defrosted be fore cooking.
SOLE Use and cook as plaice.	
WHITING Rarely obtainable—but use as fresh whiting.	defrost as plaice.

Frozen Oily Fish

FISH TO BUY AND COOK	TO DEFROST
HERRINGS Not often frozen and sold in packets but a whole catch is often frozen and sold loose by the fishmonger. Fish seems to lose a little of its firm texture so while it can be cooked as fresh, baking rather than frying or grilling is best for this fish.	As plaice at room temperature.
MACKEREL as herrings	
SALMON Sold as frozen cutlets and often obtainable as whole fish. While of good quality, it tends to lose both colour and flavour. Cook as fresh salmon but keep well moistened during cooking period and serve with a sauce.	As plaice at room temperature.
WHITEBAIT More often sold frozen than fresh. When defrosted dry well, then coat thoroughly. Cook as fresh whitebait.	Defrost carefully at room temperature.

Frozen Freshwater Fish

FISH TO BUY AND COOK	TO DEFROST
TROUT Generally sold 2 in a packet. Once defrosted, cook as fresh fish, although it can be cooked from frozen state. A little flavour is lost in freezing, so serve with plenty of sauce or seasoning.	Either at room temperature or cook when frozen.

Frozen Shellfish

FISH TO BUY AND COOK	TO DEFROST
CRAB Frozen as crab meat. Sometimes both light and dark meat frozen together. Use as fresh dressed crab, but a little flavour is lost, so season well.	Room temperature NEVER STORE AFTER DEFROSTED.
PRAWNS Sold loose, in packets or bags. Use as fresh prawns when once defrosted but the flesh tends to be somewhat tougher in most cases. Always allow to defrost completely before heating. Good in sauces, but if defrosted SLOWLY can be used any way.	As plaice at room temperature or in cold water.
SHRIMPS as prawns	
SCAMPI As prawns if serving cold but for frying the UNCOOKED FROZEN SCAMPI can be cooked when frozen.	If cooked, defrost as ordinary prawns, but often frozen uncooked, giving better texture. There is no need to defrost completely. Thaw out sufficiently to separate the fish.

Frozen Smoked Fish

FISH TO BUY AND COOK	TO DEFROST
HADDOCK Sold in portions or small fish in polythene bags—sometimes complete with little margarine or butter. Cook as directed by immersing in boiling water.	No need to defrost.
KIPPERS Sold either as whole kippers or boned kipper fillets — sometimes in bags. Cooking in the bag is ideal as there is no strong smell.	Cook from frozen.

Other Frozen Fish or Fish Products

FISH TO BUY AND COOK	TO DEFROST
HERRING ROES Can be bought in packets or loose. When defrosted, cook as fresh herring roes. Very little difference in texture or taste.	On plate at room temperature. Do not leave too long after defrosted as they become very watery.
POTTED SHRIMPS Sold in small containers often only enough for one person, so can be turned out of the container in a neat shape. Do not serve even slightly frozen or the taste is spoiled. Serve as home-made potted shrimps.	At room temperature or stand containers in COLD water.
FISH CAKES Various flavoured frozen fish cakes obtainable. Best fried or grilled and served as fresh fish cakes. Cook when frozen.	Since the fish cakes are firmer and very much easier to handle while still frozen, do not allow to defrost too much.
FISH STICKS or FISH FINGERS Name depends on the brand, but these fingers of fish—often cod or cod and haddock mixed—are coated. Excellent for children who like the neat appearance and that they are free from bone and skin. Can be fried, grilled, baked as ordinary fish. Follow cooking time recommended by the manufacturer.	Better cooked while still frozen.

SCAMPI

During the past few years scampi has become extremely popular.

It is delicious served either as the start of a meal or a main course.

The real scampi are the large Mediterranean prawns, the size of the Dublin Bay prawns more easily obtained in this country. All the recipes, which serve 4 people, assume you are using these, which allows 4 – 5 per person. If serving as a first course you will need only about 3. These large prawns are often very difficult to get and those sold as scampi are much smaller, in which case you will need about 8 per person. Scampi is often sold frozen and uncooked so after buying, it should go straight into the freezing compartment of the refrigerator. Do not store for more than 2 or 3 days unless the

refrigerator has a deep-freeze compartment. Other scampi is sold already cooked and any reheating must be done quickly as overcooking will cause this, like all other shellfish, to toughen.
SCAMPI, LIKE ALL SHELLFISH, DETERIORATES VERY QUICKLY SO NEVER STORE ANY LEFT FROM A MEAL.

To defrost:
Ideally the packet should be left at room temperature for 2 or 3 hours. This ensures it is defrosted gently but has not been standing in a defrosted state. If you need to hurry the defrosting process, stand the packet in COLD water which will not spoil or toughen it.
Strain off any liquid before using.

NEVER RE-FREEZE SCAMPI.

Scampi provençale

cooking time 5 – 6 minutes

you will need for 4 servings:

1 small onion
1 clove garlic
2 or 3 tomatoes
2 tablespoons olive oil
about 18 large prawns, cooked or raw
little white wine
chopped parsley
seasoning

For garnish:
extra chopped parsley

1 Fry chopped onion, garlic and tomatoes in oil.
2 If using raw scampi, add these together with parsley and wine. Cook steadily for about 5 – 6 minutes.
3 If using cooked prawns, add wine, parsley and seasoning to onion mixture and get this very hot before heating the prawns for 2 – 3 minutes.
4 Serve garnished with parsley.

Scampi Americaine

cooking time 7 – 9 minutes

you will need for 4 servings:

4 – 5 good-sized tomatoes
2 tablespoons olive oil
pinch garlic salt
about 18 large prawns, cooked or raw
chopped parsley
little white wine

1 Fry the tomatoes in oil and garlic salt.
2 If using raw scampi, add these together with chopped parsley and wine. Cook steadily for about 5 – 6 minutes.
3 If using cooked prawns, add wine, parsley and seasoning before heating the prawns for 2 – 3 minutes.

Serve on a bed of boiled rice.

Fried scampi

cooking time few minutes

you will need for 4 servings:

about 18 large prawns, cooked or raw
coating batter (see page 9) or egg and breadcrumbs
fat for frying

To garnish:
lemon
parsley

1 If using frozen scampi, defrost at room temperature.
2 Dry well before coating with egg and breadcrumbs or dipping in batter.
3 Heat the fat to approximately 365°F.—a cube of bread will turn golden brown within about 1 minute.
4 Put in the fish and fry steadily.

Fried scampi with curry mayonnaise

cooking time 3 – 5 minutes

you will need for 5 – 6 servings:

about 20 – 24 prawns
oil for frying

For mayonnaise:
1 teaspoon sugar
1 teaspoon dry mustard
½ teaspoon salt
pinch cayenne pepper
1 egg
¼ pint oil
3 tablespoons vinegar
2 – 3 teaspoons curry paste
2 teaspoons capers

1 Defrost frozen scampi; shell fresh prawns.
2 Heat the oil to 375°F. (until cube bread turns golden brown in ½ minute) and deep fry prawns 3 – 5 minutes.
3 Drain on kitchen paper.
4 To make mayonnaise, combine sugar, mustard, salt, pepper and egg and beat well with a rotary beater.
5 Add ⅔ oil very gradually, beating all the time.
6 Stir in 1 tablespoon vinegar.
7 Add remaining oil, beating all the time.
8 Finally mix in remaining vinegar, curry paste and capers.

Serve with salad.

Scampi meunière

cooking time 5 – 6 minutes

you will need for 4 servings:

3 oz. butter
about 18 large prawns, cooked or raw
seasoning
little lemon juice
1 dessertspoon chopped parsley
few capers, optional

To garnish:
lemon slices

1 Heat butter and add prawns. If using cooked prawns, they need just be heated, but with raw prawns, cook steadily for about 4 minutes.
2 Lift on to a hot dish and continue cooking butter until it is dark brown.
3 Add seasoning, lemon juice, parsley and capers, and pour over the scampi.
4 Garnish with lemon slices.

Devilled whitebait

When whitebait is cooked, toss in salt and pepper, then serve sprinkled liberally with Worcestershire sauce and wafer thin slices of fried onion.

Whitebait

cooking time 3 – 4 minutes

you will need for 4 servings:

1 lb. whitebait
flour
fat for frying
salt
cayenne pepper
slices lemon
brown bread and butter

1 Defrost whitebait.
2 Dry carefully, then dredge in flour.
3 Fry until crisp and brown in boiling fat, drain and dust with salt and cayenne pepper.
4 Serve with sliced lemon and brown bread and butter.

Double fried whitebait

cooking time 3 – 4 minutes

1 Fry in hot fat for about 1 – 2 minutes until very pale coloured.
2 Lift out the frying basket containing the fish and reheat fat.
3 Lower whitebait into the fat for the second time.

Canned Fish

Before the cans are opened, the fish keeps indefinitely, provided they are stored in a cool dry place. Once open, the fish must be used as soon as possible.

FISH	WAYS TO USE
ANCHOVY FILLETS	These are sold flat or rolled. A garnish for salads and fish dishes, as part of a hors-d'œuvre or as a stuffing (see page 57) or on scrambled eggs.
BRISLING	Very like sardine and can be used in any sardine recipes.
COD'S ROE	As freshly smoked cod's roe (see page 39).
COD	As fresh or frozen cod.
CRAB	For sandwich filling, in salads or as fresh.
HERRINGS	In tomato sauce, heat gently and serve on toast or with vegetables, or use cold in salads; in mustard sauce, makes an excellent fish pie if topped with creamed potato and browned in the oven.
HERRING ROES	Serve as fresh (see page 39).
LOBSTER	As a spread on hot buttered toast, as sandwich filling, in salads or as fresh (see pages 43).
PASTES	Various fish pastes are sold in cans or jars. Use on hot buttered

FISH	WAYS TO USE
	toast, as sandwich filling or quick stuffings for fish fillets.
PILCHARDS	As canned herring.
PRAWNS	Add to sauces, mix with scrambled eggs, make into cocktails (see page 78), add to salads as fresh (see page 79).
SALMON	As fresh (see pages 35); excellent in salmon fish cakes (see page 58), salmon fish pie (see page 59). Choose red salmon for cold dishes, the pink for hot.
SARDINES	Either in tomato sauce or oil. Serve as sandwich filling, as part of a salad or hors-d'œuvre, as a savoury on hot buttered toast.
SCAMPI	As prawns or scampi (see pages 46, 54).
SHRIMPS	As prawns.
SILD	As sardines.
'TIT BITS'	These are tiny pieces of raw herring in brine, served with toast or bread as cocktail snacks.
TUNA	As salmon.

GENERALLY SOLD IN JARS

FISH	WAYS TO USE
MUSSELS	As cooked mussels.
HERRINGS	Rollmop or Bismarck. Use as part of an hors-d'œuvre or salad.

Anchovy eggs

cooking time 10 minutes

you will need for 4 servings:

6 – 8 eggs
1½ oz. butter or margarine
1 can anchovy fillets
pepper
lettuce

1 Boil eggs for 10 minutes.
2 If serving hot, plunge into cold water for 1 minute only, cracking the shells, then peel carefully. If serving cold, leave in cold water.
3 Halve eggs and remove yolks.
4 Mash and mix with butter and half the fillets, chopped. Keep remainder for garnish. Season to taste.
5 Pile into egg whites, top with rolled, halved fillets and serve on a bed of lettuce.

Friday fish casserole

cooking time 30 minutes

you will need for 4 servings:

1 can condensed cream mushroom soup
¼ pint yoghourt
1 16-oz. can salmon*
1 can sweet corn
2 hard-boiled eggs
¼ teaspoon dry mustard
salt, pepper

* Pink salmon can be used

1 Blend soup with yoghourt and liquid from salmon.
2 Combine with drained sweet corn, flaked salmon, chopped eggs and seasoning.
3 Pour into greased casserole and bake in a moderate oven (375°F.—Gas Mark 4) for 25 – 30 minutes.

Sardine Welsh rarebit fingers

cooking time few minutes

you will need for 4 servings:

2 oz. butter
12 oz. grated Cheddar cheese
2 teaspoons made mustard
pinch cayenne pepper, salt
4 tablespoons milk
4 large slices toast
12 sardines

To garnish:
parsley

1 Cream butter, add cheese, seasoning and milk, and mix to a stiff paste.
2 Spread thickly over toast and grill to a golden brown.
3 Lay 3 sardines on each slice and heat through under the grill.
4 Cut into fingers, garnish and serve hot.

Scotch woodcock

cooking time 10 minutes

you will need for 4 servings:

6 eggs	1½ oz. butter or margarine
milk	4 slices buttered toast
seasoning	8 anchovy fillets

1. Beat eggs with milk and seasoning.
2. Heat butter.
3. Add egg mixture and cook lightly and slowly, stirring from time to time until set.
4. Pile on to hot buttered toast.
5. Garnish with anchovy fillets.

Tuna bacon bowl

cooking time 8 – 10 minutes

you will need for 4 servings:

4 bacon rashers	1 teaspoon salt
3 hard-boiled eggs	dash pepper
½ cucumber	
6 oz. flaked tuna	*For piquant sauce:*
2 tablespoons mayonnaise	1 carton cultured cream
	6 gherkins

1. Grill and fry bacon until crisp, allow to cool, then crumble finely.
2. Chop eggs.
3. Peel cucumber, cut half into small pieces, thinly slice remainder and keep for garnish.
4. Mix all ingredients and garnish with cucumber.
5. Serve with piquant sauce made by mixing cream and chopped gherkins.

Tuna luncheon casserole

cooking time 1 hour

you will need for 4 servings:

4 oz. noodles	dash cayenne pepper
2 oz. butter or margarine	1 tablespoon chopped parsley
1 small packet frozen peas	1 tablespoon chopped onion
4 eggs	4 oz. grated Cheddar cheese
½ pint milk	
1½ teaspoons salt	1 7-oz. can tuna

1. Cook noodles until tender, then drain them.
2. Heat butter in pan with tightly fitting cover.
3. Add peas and cook, covered, over medium heat for 10 – 15 minutes, or until just tender. Do not add water.
4. Combine remaining ingredients in large bowl. Add noodles, peas and butter from pan, and mix well.
5. Turn into a baking dish and set in pan containing 1 inch hot water.
6. Bake for 40 – 45 minutes in a moderate oven (375°F.—Gas Mark 4) or until a silver knife inserted in the centre, comes out clean.

Tuna espagnole

cooking time 40 minutes

you will need for 4 servings:

2 large cans tuna	1 oz. margarine
1 green pepper	½ pint white sauce (see page 83)
1 large onion	
3 tomatoes	seasoning

1. Drain fish, keeping oil.
2. Slice pepper, onion and tomatoes.
3. Heat margarine with oil and fry vegetables gently until soft.
4. Make white sauce and season well.
5. Put fish mixture into an ovenproof dish and pour sauce over.
6. Cook in a moderate oven for 25 minutes (375°F.—Gas Mark 4).

Salmon fish cakes

cooking time 10 minutes

you will need for 4 servings:

8 – 12 oz. salmon	fat or oil for frying
8 oz. mashed potatoes	seasoning
1 egg	
½ oz. flour	*To garnish:*
approximately 2 oz. crisp breadcrumbs	lemon slices
	watercress

1. Drain salmon and flake.
2. Add potatoes, some of the salmon liquid and bind with egg yolk.
3. Season to taste.
4. Form into about 8 flat cakes and coat with flour.
5. Brush with egg white, roll in breadcrumbs.
6. Fry steadily in shallow fat until crisp and golden brown on both sides.
7. Drain on crumpled tissue or kitchen paper and serve with lemon slices and watercress.

Variations:

Herb fish cakes

Add 1 teaspoon freshly chopped lemon thyme and 2 teaspoons chopped parsley.

Curried fish cakes

Add 1 teaspoon curry powder to fish and work in well before adding potato.

Rice fish cakes

Use 6 oz. cooked and well-drained rice instead of potatoes.

Salmon and rice croquettes

cooking time 30 – 35 minutes

you will need for 4 servings:

2 oz. rice
¼ pint water
1 medium can salmon
salt, pepper
2 teaspoons lemon juice
1 egg
crisp breadcrumbs
butter
watercress
lemon slices

1. Add rice to briskly boiling water, stir well, cover pan, allow to return to the boil, reduce heat and cook until rice is tender (approximately 15 minutes).
2. Flake salmon and mix with well-drained rice.
3. Blend with salt, pepper and lemon juice.
4. Form into croquettes and stand for 15 minutes to settle firmly into shape.
5. Egg and breadcrumb the croquettes.
6. Put in buttered ovenware dish and bake for 15 – 20 minutes in a moderate oven (375°F.—Gas Mark 4).
7. Serve with crisp watercress and lemon slices.

Salmon ring

cooking time few minutes heating only

you will need for 4 servings:

2 eggs
¼ pint mayonnaise (see page 86)
2 teaspoons powder gelatine
1 tablespoon vinegar or lemon juice
⅛ pint water
8 – 12 oz. canned or flaked cooked salmon
2 tablespoons cream from top of milk
salt, pepper
olive oil

To garnish:
lettuce
8 oz. potatoes, cooked and diced
2 sliced tomatoes
½ cucumber
chopped parsley
1 – 2 sliced olives
mayonnaise (see page 86)

1. Beat egg yolks into mayonnaise.
2. Soften gelatine in vinegar, add very hot water and stir until dissolved. Add to egg mixture.
3. Fold in the fish, cream, stiffly beaten egg whites and season well.
4. Pour into a ring mould, rinsed in cold water or brushed with olive oil.
5. When set, turn on to a bed of lettuce and garnish with tomato and cucumber slices.
6. Fill centre with a potato and cucumber salad made by mixing potatoes, 4 oz. diced cucumber, parsley, olives and mayonnaise.

Salmon loaf

cooking time 40 – 45 minutes

you will need for 4 servings:

12 oz. canned salmon*
2 oz. breadcrumbs
2 eggs
1 tablespoon vinegar
pinch ground mace, grated nutmeg
pepper, salt

* Tuna can be substituted

1. Flake fish and mix it thoroughly with other ingredients.
2. Turn into well-greased loaf or cake tin and bake in a moderate oven (375°F.—Gas Mark 4) for 40 – 45 minutes.
3. Turn out carefully and serve hot with parsley sauce (see page 83) or cold with salad.

Salmon pie

cooking time 30 minutes

you will need for 4 servings:

8 – 12 oz. salmon
½ pint white sauce (see page 83)
12 oz. mashed potato
margarine

1. Flake fish and blend with sauce, adding fish liquid.
2. Put into a pie dish and top with potato and dot with margarine.
3. Bake in the centre of a moderately hot oven (400°F.—Gas Mark 5) for 30 minutes.

Variations:

Luxury salmon pie

Use slightly less sauce and add 3 – 4 tablespoons cream and 2 chopped hard-boiled eggs.

Salmon and vegetable pie

Blend fish and sauce with 4 oz. cooked peas, 2 – 3 sliced gherkins, 2 sliced carrots.

Salmon and asparagus pie

Arrange well-drained cooked or canned asparagus tips on top of fish and sauce, then cover with potato or flaky pastry (see page 61).

If using pastry, brown in a very hot oven (475°F.—Gas Mark 8) for first 20 minutes, then lower heat to moderate (375°F.—Gas Mark 4).

Pies and Flans

Here is a selection of fish pies, pastries and flans. The combination of fish and crisp pastry is extremely good and makes tasty picnic dishes as well as hot savouries.

Short crust pastry

cooking time — as individual recipe

you will need:

8 oz. flour
good pinch salt
4 oz. fat
approximately 2 tablespoons cold water

1 Sieve flour and salt and rub in fat until mixture looks like fine breadcrumbs.
2 Using first a knife and then the fingertips to feel the pastry, gradually add enough cold water to make the dough into a rolling consistency.
3 Lightly flour the rolling pin and pastry board. If a great deal of flour is necessary to roll out the pastry, it is too wet.
4 Roll pastry to required thickness and shape, lifting and turning it to keep it light.
5 Exact cooking times and temperatures are given in the recipes, but as a general rule it should be baked in a hot oven (425 – 450°F.—Gas Mark 6 – 7).

Suet crust pastry

cooking time — as individual recipe

you will need:

8 oz. self-raising flour, or plain flour with 2 teaspoons baking powder
pinch salt
2 – 4 oz. finely shredded suet
water

1 Sieve flour, salt and baking powder.
2 Add suet and mix to a rolling consistency with cold water.
3 Roll out thinly, as this pastry rises.
4 Line a pudding basin with the dough, keeping enough for the cover.
5 Put in the filling and put on the pastry cover.
6 Cover top with greased greaseproof paper an[d] wrap in a pudding cloth.
7 Steam or boil rapidly for 2 – 3 hours, dependin[g] on filling.

Note:
Make sure the water is boiling rapidly when th[e] pudding goes on and always replenish wit[h] boiling water.

Cheese pastry No. 1

cooking time — as individual recip[e]

you will need:

8 oz. plain flour
1 level teaspoon dry mustard
4 oz. vegetarian fat, margarine or butter
2 – 3 oz. finely grated cheese
cold water

1 Sieve flour and mustard.
2 Rub in fat until mixture resembles fine breadcrumbs.
3 Add cheese and mix to a dry dough with water

Cheese pastry No. 2

cooking time — as individual recip[e]

you will need:

2 oz. plain flour
$1\frac{1}{2}$ oz. margarine or butter
$1\frac{1}{2}$ oz. finely grated cheese
seasoning
egg yolk or milk

1 Rub margarine or butter into flour.
2 Add cheese and plenty of seasoning.
3 Make to a firm dough with egg yolk or milk.
4 Bake in a really hot oven (450°F.—Gas Mark 7 and cool for a few minutes on baking trays, a[s] this pastry is very brittle.

Puff pastry

cooking time approximately 30 minutes

you will need:

8 oz. flour
salt
cold water
lemon juice
7 – 8 oz. butter or margarine

1 Sieve flour and pinch salt.
2 Mix to rolling consistency with water and a few drops lemon juice. Roll into oblong.
3 Make fat into neat block and place in centre of pastry. Fold over it, first, bottom section of pastry, then top, so fat is covered.
4 Turn dough at right angles, seal edges, 'rib'* carefully and roll out.
5 Fold dough into envelope shape, turn, seal edges, 'rib' and roll again.
6 Repeat 5 times, making total of 7 rollings and foldings.
7 Rest pastry in cold place once or twice between rollings so it does not become soft and sticky, and always rest it before the last rolling and before baking.
8 Bake in very hot oven (475 – 500°F.—Gas Mark 8 – 9) for first 10 – 15 minutes, then lower to Gas Mark 5 – 6 or turn electric oven off, or re-set to 400°F. until pastry is cooked.

* Press pastry several times along its length, making a corrugated pattern which traps air inside.

Puff pastry should rise to 4 or 5 times its original thickness.

Flaky pastry

cooking time as individual recipe

you will need:

8 oz. plain flour
pinch salt
5 – 6 oz. fat
water

1 Sieve flour with salt.
2 Divide fat into 3 portions.
3 Rub 1 portion into flour in usual way and mix to rolling consistency with cold water.
4 Roll out to oblong shape.
5 Take the second portion of fat, divide it into small pieces and lay them on ⅔ of the dough Leave remaining ⅓ without fat.
6 Take 2 corners and fold back over second ⅓ so that the dough looks like an envelope with its flap open.
7 Fold over top end of pastry, so closing the 'envelope'.
8 Turn pastry at right angles, seal open ends of pastry and 'rib' it. This means depressing it with the rolling pin at intervals, so giving a corrugated effect and equalizing the pressure of air, which makes certain the pastry will rise evenly.
9 Repeat the process again, using remaining fat and turning pastry in same way.
10 Roll out pastry once more. Should it begin to feel very soft and stickly, put into a cold place for 30 minutes to become firm before rolling out.
11 Fold pastry as before, turn it, seal edges and 'rib' it. Altogether the pastry should have 3 foldings and 3 rollings.
12 Stand in a cold place for a little while before baking, since the contrast between the cold and the heat of the oven makes the pastry rise better.
13 Baking times and temperatures are given in the individual recipes but, as a general rule, bake in a very hot oven (475°F.—Gas Mark 8) for the first 15 minutes, then lower to Gas Mark 5 – 6, or turn an electric oven off to finish cooking for remaining time.

Cheese and fish pie

cooking time 30 – 45 minutes

you will need for 4 servings:

1½ lb. mashed potatoes
4 oz. grated cheese
¾ – 1 lb. cooked fish
¾ pint white sauce, coating consistency (see page 83)
3 tablespoons chopped parsley
salt, pepper
lemon to garnish

1 Mix potato and cheese, and line a greased pie dish with it, leaving enough to cover the top.
2 Mix flaked fish, sauce and parsley and season to taste.
3 Pour into the dish and cover with remaining potato mixture.
4 Bake in a moderate oven (375°F.—Gas Mark 4) for 30 – 45 minutes.
5 Serve hot, garnished with lemon slices.

Crumble topped fish pie

cooking time 35 minutes

you will need for 4 servings:

4 oz. onion
2 oz. butter or margarine
2 oz. flour
1 – 2 teaspoons dry mustard
¾ pint milk
seasoning
1 dessertspoon lemon juice or 1 teaspoon vinegar
1½ lb. smoked haddock
3 hard-boiled eggs

For crumble topping:
4 oz. flour
large pinch salt
good shake pepper
2 oz. butter or margarine
2 – 3 oz. finely grated Cheddar cheese

To garnish:
anchovy fillets

1 Finely chop onion and fry in butter or margarine until pale golden.
2 Stir in flour and mustard and cook for 2 minutes.
3 Remove from heat and gradually add milk. Bring to the boil and cook until smooth and thickened.
4 Add seasoning, lemon juice and flaked fish and heat without boiling for several minutes. Then add chopped eggs.
5 Put into a hot shallow ovenproof dish and top with crumble mixture (see below) and garnish with anchovies. Heat towards the top of a moderately hot oven (400°F.—Gas Mark 5) for approximately 20 minutes until the crumble is golden brown.

To make the crumble:

1 Sift flour and seasoning together.
2 Rub in fat finely, add cheese and toss lightly together to mix.

Cod's roe pie

cooking time 20 – 40 minutes

you will need for 4 servings:

¾ lb. cod's roe*
½ pint white sauce or anchovy sauce (see pages 80 and 83)
1 lb. cooked potatoes
2 tablespoons grated cheese

* Cod's roe is available already cooked

1 Wash roe and boil or steam for approximately 20 minutes.
2 Cut into slices, put in a pie dish and pour sauce over.
3 Mash potatoes, pile or pipe on top of roe.
4 Sprinkle with cheese and bake in a hot oven (450°F.—Gas Mark 7) for 20 minutes.

Curried fish pie

cooking time 30 – 40 minutes

you will need for 4 servings:

1 – 1½ lb. white fish
1½ tablespoons curry powder
1 oz. flour
1 – 2 oz. sultanas
1 large onion, chopped
1 teaspoon salt
pinch pepper
just under ½ pint milk
6 oz. short crust pastry (see page 61)

1 Skin and cube fish.
2 Dip cubes into curry powder and flour mixed together.
3 Place fish, sultanas, onion and seasoning in alternate layers in a greased 1½ pint pie dish.
4 Sprinkle any remaining curry powder and flour over and pour milk over.
5 Cover with pastry, decorate with trimmings cut in leaves and make a 1-inch slit in the pastry cover.
6 Brush with milk to glaze.
7 Bake in a moderately hot oven (400°F.—Gas Mark 5) for 30 – 40 minutes.

Double-crust fish Normandy

cooking time 30 minutes

you will need for 4 servings:

Cream pastry:
10 oz. plain flour
½ teaspoon salt
pinch pepper
1 teaspoon paprika
3 oz. butter or margarine
3 oz. vegetable fat
2 egg yolks
1 tablespoon lemon juice
about 4 tablespoons cold water
milk or beaten egg

For filling:
1 lb. smoked cooked haddock, well flaked
2 chopped hard-boiled eggs
1 tablespoon chopped parsley
1 cooking apple, peeled and chopped
½ pint thick white sauce (see page 83)
1 egg yolk
1 dessertspoon lemon juice
pinch pepper

1 Sift flour and seasonings twice.
2 Rub in the fat.
3 Beat egg yolks, lemon juice and water together and stir in, mixing to a dry dough.
4 Turn out on to lightly floured board.
5 Roll out about ⅜ and put on 8-inch pie plate.
6 Mix filling ingredients together and spoon into pie plate.
7 Moisten pastry edges, top with remaining pastry, pressing edges to seal, then trim and flake up edges with the back of a knife.
8 Decorate top centre with pastry leaves.
9 Brush with milk or beaten egg.

10 Bake above centre in hot oven (450°F.—Gas Mark 7) for 10 minutes. Reduce heat to moderate (375°F.—Gas Mark 4) for about 20 minutes.

Serve hot.

Gala fish pie

cooking time 40 minutes

you will need for 4 servings:

10 oz. flaky pastry (see page 60)

For the filling:
1 lb. fresh haddock, cod or halibut
2 scallops, optional
2 oz. fresh or frozen prawns
¾ pint milk
2 oz. butter or margarine
2 oz. flour, self-raising or plain
2 teaspoons anchovy essence
2 hard-boiled eggs

To glaze:
beaten egg

1 Make flaky pastry.
2 Poach haddock and scallops very gently in milk. Drain off the liquid and keep for sauce.
3 Flake fish, chop scallops.
4 Melt butter, add flour, cook for a few minutes, gradually add fish liquid. Bring to the boil, boil for a few minutes.
5 Add anchovy essence, fish and sliced eggs.
6 Roll pastry into an oblong, 3 inches wider and longer than a 1¼ – 1½ pint pie dish. Trim edges, then cut off strips to line the edge of the pie dish.
7 Brush edge with beaten egg, and put strips in place, joining them with beaten egg where necessary.
8 Pour fish mixture into lined dish.
9 Cover pie with remaining pastry. Do this carefully to avoid stretching. Trim the edges. Flake edges with the back of a knife, decorate with pastry leaves, make a hole in the centre.
10 Brush with beaten egg.
11 Bake in centre of very hot oven (475°F.—Gas Mark 8) for approximately 10 minutes, then lower heat to moderately hot (400°F.—Gas Mark 5) for further 20 minutes.

Herring pie

cooking time 30 – 40 minutes

you will need for 4 servings:

8 oz. grated raw potato
8 oz. grated apple
1 grated onion
¼ teaspoon grated nutmeg
2 teaspoons salt
pinch pepper
1 teaspoon lemon juice
4 herrings, cleaned and filleted (see page 7)
6 oz. short crust pastry (see page 61)

1 Arrange ½ potato, apple and onion in a pie dish.
2 Sprinkle with nutmeg, seasoning and lemon juice.
3 Lay the filleted herrings on top. Cover with remaining potato, apple and onion mixture. Season well.
4 Roll out pastry and cover pie dish, decorate and bake in the centre of a moderately hot oven (400°F.—Gas Mark 5) for 30 – 40 minutes.

Russian fish pie

cooking time 45 – 50 minutes

you will need for 4 servings:

12 oz. white fish or smoked haddock
¼ pint milk
¼ pint water
1 bay leaf
8 oz. flaky pastry (see page 60) or frozen pastry
½ oz. butter
½ oz. flour
2 oz. grated cheese
1 dessertspoon finely chopped parsley
salt, pepper
beaten egg

To garnish:
parsley

1 Wash fish and poach gently in milk, water and bay leaf until cooked.
2 Roll pastry into 9-inch square and place on a baking tray.
3 Drain fish, reserving ¼ pint liquor.
4 Skin, bone and flake fish.
5 Melt butter, add flour and gradually stir in the liquor.
6 Bring to the boil and cook for 2 – 3 minutes.
7 Add fish, cheese and parsley.
8 Season with salt and pepper.
9 Pile mixture into the centre of the pastry square.
10 Moisten edges, fold each corner to the centre forming an envelope.
11 Seal, leaving a small central incision for the steam to escape.
12 Cut leaves from pastry trimmings for decoration.
13 Brush with beaten egg.
14 Bake in a very hot oven (475 – 500°F.—Gas Mark 8 – 9) for 10 minutes, then lower heat to moderately hot (400°F.—Gas Mark 5) for a further 30 minutes.

Serve immediately, garnished with parsley.

Fish mornay flan

cooking time 45 minutes

you will need for 4 servings:

4 oz. short or cheese crust pastry (see pages 60 and 61)

For the filling:

8 – 10 oz. cooked smoked haddock or 1 medium can of tuna fish or salmon

1 oz. flour

1 oz. margarine

fish stock

approximately $\frac{3}{8}$ pint milk

salt, pepper

3 oz. grated cheese

To garnish:

1 hard-boiled egg

parsley

1 Line 7-inch flan tin or sandwich tin with pastry and bake blind for approximately 20 minutes in centre of hot oven (425 – 450°F.—Gas Mark 6 – 7) for short crust, or 25 minutes in moderately hot oven (400°F.—Gas Mark 5) for cheese pastry.
2 Allow to cool for a few minutes, then transfer flan case to an ovenware serving dish.
3 Arrange the well drained cooked or canned fish in pastry case. Place in a slow oven (275 – 300°F. —Gas Mark 1 – 2) to heat the filling.
4 Measure fish stock from can or allow $\frac{1}{8}$ pint for haddock. Make up to $\frac{1}{2}$ pint with milk. Melt margarine, add flour, cook for a few seconds. Slowly stir in the liquid.
5 Bring to the boil, boil for 2 minutes, stirring all the time.
6 Add salt and pepper to taste and cheese, stir well.
7 Pour sauce over the filling and decorate with sliced egg and parsley.

Flan mornay

cooking time 35 minutes

you will need for 4 servings:

For flan:

6 oz. short crust pastry (see page 61) or 10 oz. well mashed potatoes

For filling:

1 lb. cooked flaked cod

$\frac{1}{4}$ pint cheese sauce (see page 81)

few capers

2 teaspoons chopped parsley

2 rashers bacon

To garnish:

lemon slices

1 Make a flan shape either of pastry or potatoes. Bake pastry blind until just golden coloured, but take particular care not to overcook.
2 Put fish into flan case.
3 Cover with sauce, into which has been stirred the capers and parsley.
4 Arrange narrow strips of bacon on top.
5 If all the ingredients are very hot, the flan can be cooked for a few minutes under a hot grill, but if they have cooled, put at the top of a hot oven (450°F.—Gas Mark 7) for about 10 minutes until the bacon is crisp and the sauce golden brown.
6 Garnish with lemon and serve piping hot.

Savoury fish pasties

cooking time 25 minutes

you will need for 4 servings:

12 oz. short crust pastry (see page 61)

For filling:

8 oz. cooked smoked haddock

$\frac{1}{2}$ oz. butter

$\frac{1}{2}$ oz. flour

$\frac{1}{4}$ pint milk

seasoning

3 teaspoons capers

2 sliced hard-boiled eggs

2 sliced tomatoes

1 Roll out pastry and cut into four large squares about $\frac{1}{4}$ inch thick.
2 Make a sauce of butter, flour and milk.
3 Season well, then add flaked fish, capers, eggs and tomatoes.
4 Put mixture in the centre of each pastry square.
5 Bring the corners of the pastry to the centre—making an envelope shape.
6 Moisten the edges with water and press together firmly.
7 Lift carefully on to baking trays and bake for approximately 25 minutes in the centre of a hot oven (450°F.—Gas Mark 7).
8 Lower heat to 400°F.—Gas Mark 5 for a further 10 minutes.
9 Serve hot or cold.

Variations:

Omit eggs and add 2 oz. grated cheese.

Omit tomatoes and add 2 oz. chopped fried mushrooms.

Fish flan

cooking time 25 minutes

you will need for 4 servings:

6 oz. short crust pastry (see page 61)
¼ pint white sauce, panada consistency (see page 83)
¾ lb. flaked cooked fish
seasoning
1 teaspoon anchovy essence
1 tablespoon grated cheese, optional
sliced tomato
parsley

1 Line a sandwich tin or flan ring with pastry.
2 Put beans or crusts of stale bread on a piece of greased paper in the centre of the pastry to stop it rising. Now bake the pastry blind for 20 – 25 minutes in centre of a hot oven (450°F.—Gas Mark 7).
3 Make sauce, add fish, season well and stir in anchovy essence.
4 Put into pastry case, sprinkle with cheese and return to oven for 5 minutes.
5 Garnish with tomato and parsley

Serve hot or cold.

Omelettes and Pancakes

Fish is an excellent filling for either crisp pancakes or creamy omelettes. As the crispness of a pancake is spoiled by prolonged waiting, have the fish filling ready to put in, then roll and serve the pancake immediately. When making a large quantity of pancakes, keep them hot on a flat dish in the oven and the filling hot in a pan.

Creamy fish omelette

cooking time 15 – 20 minutes

you will need for 4 servings:

8 oz. cooked flaked fish (white fish, salmon or shellfish)
½ pint white sauce (see page 83)
3 oz. butter
6 – 8 eggs
seasoning
parsley

1 Add fish to sauce in the top of a double saucepan.
2 Heat 1½ oz. butter in an omelette pan.
3 Beat 3 – 4 eggs with seasoning and pour into butter.
4 Allow to set in a thin skin at the bottom of the pan, then tilt pan and at the same time work the edges of egg mixture towards its centre, so the liquid egg runs underneath to set.
5 When omelette is set, put in half the filling and fold or roll omelette away from the handle and tip on to a hot dish.
6 Repeat with remaining ingredients.
7 Garnish with parsley and serve.

Variations:

Luxury fish omelette
Use Hollandaise (see page 82) instead of white sauce and blend with a little cream.

Fish and cheese omelette
Use cheese (see page 81) instead of white sauce.

Fish omelette au gratin
Use cheese sauce, fill and fold omelette, sprinkle with breadcrumbs and grated cheese, then brown for 1 minute under a hot grill.

Pancake batter

cooking time few minutes

you will need:

4 oz. flour (preferably plain)
pinch salt
1 egg
½ pint milk

1 Sieve flour and salt together.
2 Drop in egg and mix well.
3 Gradually beat in just enough liquid to make stiff, smooth batter. Be sure there are no lumps.

4 Allow to stand for a few minutes, then gradually whisk or beat in the rest of the liquid.

Note:

This mixture can be allowed to stand some time before cooking. If possible put into a refrigerator or really cool place. Give final beat or whisk before using.

Fish omelette

cooking time 15 minutes

you will need for 4 servings:

2 medium onions
3 oz. butter
2 cooked beetroots chopped
4 – 6 oz. flaked cooked fish
seasoning
8 eggs
4 tablespoons cold water

1 Chop onions finely and fry in 1 oz. butter until tender.
2 Add beetroot and fish.
3 Season, lift out and keep hot.
4 Beat eggs well with water and seasoning. Add a little more butter to the pan and pour in a quarter of the beaten egg. When egg begins to set, top with a quarter of the filling.
5 When completely set, turn omelette and cook the other side.
6 Make 3 more omelettes in the same way.

Pancakes with shrimp sauce

cooking time 10 – 15 minutes

you will need for 4 servings:

For sauce:
¾ oz. butter
¾ oz. cornflour
½ pint milk
1 dessertspoon tomato purée or juice
squeeze lemon juice
anchovy essence
seasoning
4 oz. canned or fresh shrimps

For pancakes:
3 oz. plain flour } or 4 oz.
1 oz. cornflour } flour
pinch salt
1 egg
½ pint milk
corn oil for frying

For garnish:
lemon slices
parsley

1 Melt butter and add cornflour.
2 Mix well and cook for 1 minute, stirring.
3 Remove from heat, add milk, then return to heat and boil for 3 minutes, stirring constantly.
4 Add tomato purée, lemon juice, anchovy essence and season to taste.
5 Finally add drained shrimps and keep hot till required.
6 Sift together flour, cornflour and salt.
7 Make a well in the centre and break in the egg.
8 Add some of the milk and beat all well together till a smooth batter is formed.
9 Finally stir in remaining milk.
10 Heat a little oil, and fry pancakes in the usual way.
11 Put some of the shrimp sauce in the centre of each pancake, roll up and serve garnished with lemon slices and parsley.

Salmon pancakes

cooking time 15 minutes

you will need for 4 servings:

For pancakes:
3 oz. plain flour
1 oz. cornflour
pinch salt
1 egg
½ pint milk
oil for frying

For filling:
1 oz. margarine
½ oz. cornflour
½ pint milk
1 diced stick celery
1 chopped hard-boiled egg
4 oz. cooked or canned salmon
1 teaspoon chopped parsley
seasoning

For garnish:
parsley

1 Sieve flour, cornflour and salt.
2 Make a well in the centre, add egg and some of the milk.
3 Beat until a smooth batter is formed.
4 Stir in remaining milk, then leave batter to stand for as long as possible.
5 Heat a little oil in a small frying pan and cook the pancakes in the usual way.
6 Place spoonfuls of the salmon filling (see below) into each pancake and fold.
7 Garnish with parsley.

To make the filling:

1 Heat margarine, add cornflour and cook for 1 minute.
2 Stir in milk, bring to the boil and boil for 3 minutes, stirring all the time.
3 Add remaining ingredients, and cook for a further 1 minute to heat through.

White fish pancakes

cooking time 15 minutes

you will need for 4 servings:

- batter with cornflour (see page 66) or basic pancake batter (see page 65)
- 1 oz. margarine
- 1 oz. flour
- ½ pint milk or milk and fish stock (see page 72)
- 12 oz. cooked flaked white fish
- seasoning
- lemon slices
- parsley

1. Make pancake mixture.
2. Make a creamy white sauce with margarine, flour and milk, add fish and season well.
3. Cook pancakes and keep hot on an uncovered dish in the oven or over a pan of boiling water.
4. Fill each pancake with the hot fish mixture, and roll. Serve with lemon and parsley.

Variations:

Anchovy pancakes

Omit salt in the sauce and add either the contents of a small can of chopped anchovies, leaving some for garnish, or flavour with anchovy essence.

Fish pancakes au gratin

Make ¾ pint white sauce (see page 83). Blend fish with approximately ½ the sauce only and use as a filling. Arrange rolled pancakes in a serving dish, coat with remaining sauce, fine breadcrumbs and a little butter or margarine, then brown for a few minutes in the oven or under the grill.

Fish pancakes mornay

Make ¾ pint white sauce and stir 3 oz. grated cheese into it. Heat fish in ½ sauce and fill pancakes with it. Then pour remaining sauce over the rolled pancakes.

Cover with breadcrumbs and grated cheese, and brown under a grill or in the oven.

Cucumber fish pancakes

There are 2 ways of making these. Add 2 or 3 tablespoons diced cucumber to the white sauce after heating the fish, or heat cucumber and fish gently in a Hollandaise sauce (see page 82).

Fish and egg pancakes

Add 2 hard-boiled eggs to the sauce with the fish.

Mousses and Soufflés

A hot soufflé should be served as soon as possible after it is removed from the oven, since it begins to 'flop' very rapidly.

Make sure the mixture is beginning to stiffen before folding in the egg whites in a cold soufflé or mousse—then it will have a light texture.

Lobster mousse

cooking time few minutes

you will need for 4 servings:

- 2 eggs
- ¼ pint well seasoned white or béchamel sauce (see pages 83 and 84)
- 1 dessertspoon powder gelatine
- just over ⅛ pint water
- 2 tablespoons cream
- seasoning
- 1 – 2 tablespoons lemon juice or sherry
- 8 – 12 oz. minced or finely chopped lobster

To garnish:

- cucumber
- lemon
- lobster claws
- salad

1. Separate egg whites from yolks and cook yolks with sauce for few minutes without boiling.
2. Dissolve gelatine in very hot water, add to sauce, together with cream and seasoning.
3. When cooler add lemon juice or sherry, and fish or meat.
4. When mixture is cool and just beginning to thicken slightly, FOLD in stiffly beaten egg whites.
5. Pour into prepared mould or dish.
6. When set, decorate with cucumber, lemon, lobster claws and salad.

Note:

This is a basic recipe, so flaked cooked fish, chopped ham or chicken can be substituted for lobster.

Tuna soufflé

cooking time 35 minutes

you will need for 4 servings:

2 medium cans tuna
milk
1 oz. margarine
¾ oz. cornflour
1 bay leaf
2 peppercorns
1 tablespoon chopped parsley
1 tablespoon capers
2 eggs
2 oz. grated cheese
lemon slices
parsley

1 Flake fish and with milk make the liquid from the cans up to ½ pint.
2 Heat margarine, add cornflour and cook for 1 minute.
3 Add fish liquor, bay leaf and peppercorns and stir until boiling, boil for 3 minutes stirring all the time. Remove bay leaf and peppercorns.
4 Add parsley.
5 Use ½ sauce to moisten fish, add capers and put this mixture in a pie dish.
6 Add egg yolks and 1 oz. cheese to remaining sauce.
7 Beat egg whites stiffly and fold into sauce.
8 Spread mixture on top of fish, sprinkle with remaining cheese and bake for about 25 minutes in moderate oven (375°F.—Gas Mark 4).
9 Garnish with lemon and parsley.

Hake soufflé

Illustrated on the cover

cooking time approximately 35 minutes

you will need for 4 servings:

1 oz. butter or margarine
1 oz. flour
¼ pint milk or fish stock (see page 72)
8 oz. hake*
seasoning
3 egg yolks
1 tablespoon tomato sauce (see page 84)
4 egg whites
shrimp, mushroom or cheese sauce (see pages 81 and 84)

* While any fish can be used, fresh haddock or hake, turbot or halibut are excellent.

A better and stronger flavour is given in this recipe if raw fish is used. This should be put through a mincer twice to give a very fine texture. If the fish is cooked it should be flaked well and no skin used.

1 Heat butter, stir in flour and cook for several minutes.
2 Gradually work in milk, bring to the boil and cook until thickened and smooth.
3 Add fish, seasoning and egg yolks.
4 Mix well, then stir in sauce and stiffly beaten egg whites.
5 Pour into a soufflé dish, to a little more than ¾ full. Tie a band of paper round the outside, buttering this well where it comes above the dish.
6 Bake for approximately 35 minutes in the centre of a moderate oven (375°F.—Gas Mark 4).
7 Serve at once with sauce.

Variations:

1 Add a small amount of chopped gherkin or cucumber, parsley or capers.

2 Use salmon or shellfish and a few drops anchovy essence.

3 Use milk instead of fish stock and add 2 oz. finely grated Cheddar cheese at Stage 4.

Cod soufflé

cooking time about 35 minutes

you will need for 4 servings:

8 oz. cod
1 oz. butter or margarine
1 oz. flour
¼ pint milk or fish stock (see page 72)
seasoning
3 egg yolks
2 tablespoons cream
4 egg whites
shrimp, mushroom or cheese sauce (see page 84)

A better and stronger flavour is given if raw fish is used. This should be put through the mincer twice to give a very fine texture. If the fish is cooked, it should be skinned and flaked.

1 Heat butter, stir in flour and cook for several minutes, then gradually work in milk.
2 Bring to the boil and cook until thickened and smooth, add fish, seasoning, and egg yolks.
3 Mix well, then stir in cream and stiffly beaten whites.
4 Put into a soufflé dish, ¾ filling it. Tie a band of buttered paper round the outside, so it comes well above the dish.
5 Bake for approximately 35 minutes in the centre of a moderate oven (375°F.—Gas Mark 4).
6 Serve at once with sauce.

Variations:

Smoked haddock soufflé
Use cooked smoked haddock or roe and add a little grated Parmesan cheese.

Turbot soufflé
Substitute turbot for cod.

Add a small amount of chopped gherkin or cucumber, parsley or capers.

Use salmon or shellfish and a few drops anchovy essence. Try tomato juice instead of milk.

Cream cheese and prawn soufflé

cooking time approximately 10 minutes

you will need for 4 servings:

2 egg yolks
6 oz. cream cheese
¼ pint milk
salt, pepper, mustard
1½ dessertspoons gelatine
½ gill water or white stock
4 oz. prawns
¼ pint cream
3 egg whites

To garnish:
watercress
prawns

1 Beat egg yolks.
2 Blend cream cheese with milk, pour gradually on to egg yolks and cook gently till mixture thickens. Season.
3 Dissolve and melt gelatine in water.
4 Add to cheese mixture, cool and add prawns, fold in whipped cream and stiffly beaten egg whites.
5 Pour into prepared soufflé dish or into individual dishes.
6 Garnish with prawns and watercress when set.

Salmon mousse

cooking time about 15 minutes

you will need for 4 servings:

2 eggs
¼ pint white sauce (see page 83)
1 dessertspoon powder gelatine
1 tablespoon vinegar or lemon juice
⅛ pint water
¾ lb. flaked cooked fresh salmon
seasoning
1 dessertspoon sherry, optional
2 tablespoons cream from top of milk

1 Separate yolks from whites of eggs.
2 Stir beaten egg yolks into sauce.
3 Cook very slowly for several minutes WITHOUT BOILING, then allow to cool, stirring from time to time to prevent a skin from forming.
4 Soften gelatine in vinegar, pour on the very hot water. Allow to cool, then add to egg sauce mixture, with fish, seasoning, sherry and cream.
5 Lastly FOLD in stiffly beaten egg whites and pour into a damp mould to set.

Serve with a salad.

Puddings and Moulds

These are delicious for buffet meals as well as more formal occasions.

Fish loaf

cooking time 50 minutes

you will need for 4 servings:

1½ lb. flaked cooked white fish
2 eggs
2 tablespoons chopped gherkins
2 oz. breadcrumbs
3 tablespoons milk
seasoning

To garnish:
½ pint white sauce (see paga 83)
1 sliced hard-boiled egg
olives

1 Mix all ingredients together.
2 Put into very well-greased loaf tin.
3 Cover with buttered paper or foil.
4 Stand in a tin of water and bake in a very moderate oven (350°F.—Gas Mark 3) for approximately 50 minutes.
5 Serve hot with sauce poured over and arrange egg and olives on top.

Variations:
Minced raw fish instead of cooked and 4 tablespoons milk.

Anchovy loaf
Add 2 teaspoons anchovy essence to milk.

Salmon mould

no cooking

you will need for 4 servings:

- ¼ pint aspic jelly (made according to packet instructions)
- 1 teaspoon powder gelatine
- ¼ pint mayonnaise (see page 86)
- 2 tablespoons cream from the top of the milk
- 8 – 12 oz. flaked cooked salmon
- 2 hard-boiled eggs
- 2 sliced gherkins
- seasoning

1. When making aspic jelly, dissolve gelatine in it.
2. Allow to cool.
3. Mix with mayonnaise, cream, flaked salmon, chopped egg and 1 gherkin.
4. Season well.
5. Put into a rinsed mould and allow to set.
6. Turn out and decorate with remaining egg and gherkin.

Variations:

Fish and herb mould

Use flaked cooked white fish and green mayonnaise (see page 86) in place of salmon and ordinary mayonnaise.

White fish mould

Substitute 12 oz. flaked cooked white fish for salmon. Poach or steam fish between 2 plates, and break into rather large flakes. A few drops anchovy essence can be added to the mayonnaise.

Fish pudding No. 1

cooking time 45 minutes

you will need for 4 servings:

- ¾ lb. flaked cooked fish
- 1 egg
- 4 tablespoons milk or cream
- seasoning
- 1 teaspoon grated onion
- 1 teaspoon finely chopped parsley
- ¼ lb. mashed potato
- few drops vinegar
- parsley
- pinch mixed herbs

1. Mix all ingredients together.
2. Put into a greased basin and steam for 45 minutes.
3. Serve hot or cold.

Fish pudding No. 2

cooking time 30 – 45 minutes

you will need for 4 servings:

- 1½ – 2 lb. hake or cod
- 2 oz. margarine or butter
- 2 eggs
- seasoning
- 1 oz. flour
- 3 tablespoons milk or cream from top of milk
- shrimp or mushroom sauce (see page 84)

1. Fillet raw fish and put through a mincer twice until fine and smooth.
2. Melt margarine, add to fish.
3. Beat eggs, add one at a time to other ingredients and mix with fish.
4. Put mixture into a well greased basin and cover with margarined paper and a cloth.
5. Either steam for 45 minutes, or stand pudding in a dish of cold water in a moderate oven (375°F.—Gas Mark 4) and cook for 30 minutes.

Variation:

For an even lighter pudding, separate the eggs, add yolks first, then FOLD in stiffly beaten egg whites.
Serve with shrimp or mushroom sauce.

Prawn and rice mould

cooking time 1 hour

you will need for 4 servings:

- 5 oz. rice
- 8 oz. cottage cheese
- 1 dessertspoon minced onion
- 2 eggs
- salt, pepper

For sauce:

- 4 oz. peeled frozen prawns
- 1 dessertspoon cornflour
- ½ oz. butter
- ⅓ pint milk
- anchovy essence

1. Cook rice in boiling salted water for 12 minutes.
2. Drain through a sieve and rinse with boiling water.
3. Shake well and allow to dry for a few minutes in a warm oven.
4. Sieve cottage cheese.
5. Add rice and onion.
6. Mix in well beaten eggs and season well.
7. Turn into an oiled ring mould.

8 Stand in a pan of hot water and bake in a moderate oven (375°F.—Gas Mark 4) for 1 hour or until set.
9 Turn on to a dish and fill centre with prawn sauce (see below).

To make the sauce:

1 Melt butter.
2 Remove from heat and stir in cornflour, blending well.
3 Gradually add warmed milk.
4 Return to heat and allow to thicken, stirring continuously.
5 Add anchovy essence to taste and prawns and simmer gently for 2 – 3 minutes.

White fish and prawn mould

cooking time 16 minutes

you will need for 4 servings:

Ingredients as Smoked haddock mould (see this page) but use ¾ lb. white fish, turbot, cod, hake or haddock, and 4 oz. cooked prawns

1 Cook the white fish as in previous recipe.
2 Add the prawns at Stage 5, chopped if large.
3 Continue as Smoked haddock mould recipe.

Cheese and prawn moulds

no cooking

you will need for 4 servings:

½ pint aspic jelly (made according to packet instructions)
6 oz. peeled prawns or shrimps
6 large radishes
8 oz. grated Cheddar cheese
3 medium skinned tomatoes
¼ teaspoon salt
pinch pepper
few drops Tabasco sauce
3 tablespoons cream

1 Cover bottom of fish-shaped jelly mould (or 1¾ pint ring mould) thinly with aspic jelly.
2 Allow to set.
3 Arrange most of the prawns or shrimps in bottom of mould to represent scales of fish, with radish slices for eyes and set in a little more aspic jelly.
4 Chop remaining radishes and prawns, add to cheese.
5 Seed and finely chop tomatoes.
6 Stir into cheese mixture with seasoning and Tabasco sauce.
7 Fold in remaining aspic and cream.
8 Spoon into mould and allow to set, preferably in refrigerator.
9 Warm jelly mould slightly and turn out sharply on to serving dish.

Serve with crisp green salad.

Smoked haddock mould

cooking time 16 minutes

you will need for 4 servings:

1 lb. smoked haddock
½ pint milk
1 oz. margarine
1½ oz. flour
salt, pepper
2 hard-boiled eggs
1 tomato

To garnish:
cucumber
1 hard-boiled egg

1 Wash and trim fish and gently poach in milk until tender, approximately 7 – 8 minutes. Strain off milk and keep.
2 Skin and flake fish.
3 Melt margarine, stir in flour and cook for 2 – 3 minutes.
4 Gradually add milk, stirring continuously, bring to boil and cook for a further 3 – 4 minutes.
5 Add flaked fish and seasoning, mix well.
6 Arrange neat slices of 1 egg and strips of skinned tomato in a pattern at the bottom of a 1 pint basin or mould, adding any spare pieces of egg and remaining egg to filling.
7 Spoon filling into basin and allow to set.
8 When firm, turn on to a serving dish and garnish with cucumber slices and wedges of egg

Soups, Stews and Casseroles

The following recipes are basic ones which can be followed according to the fish in season. Care must be taken where slower cooking ingredients such as onions and other vegetables are included in a stew or casserole, that these are partly cooked before adding the fish, then it does not become overcooked.
If fish is cooked too long in a casserole it not only loses its flavour but becomes very unattractive in appearance and the pieces break rather badly.
Fish looks more attractive if the skin is removed for a casserole dish but take care the portions do not break.

Fish soup should be served more often for it is both nourishing and delicious. It should be served as soon as ready, particularly when shellfish is included as this toughens with prolonged heating

Fish stock

Cover the bones, skin and head, if available, of the fish with cold water, add seasoning and simmer gently for 10 – 15 minutes. Strain and use.
For more delicate flavoured fish stock, add a *bouquet garni* (see page 8) or just a sprig of parsley. A bay leaf can be added or an onion, or for a really strong flavour, use onion, carrot and a small piece of celery. Never make the stock too strong or it will take away the delicate flavour of the fish.

Fish soup

cooking time 55 minutes

you will need for 4 servings:

1 lb. white fish (haddock if possible)
8 oz. fish trimmings (skin, bones)
2 pints water
1 large onion or 2 leeks
2 cloves
1 oz. margarine
2 oz. flour
¼ pint milk
salt and pepper
1 tablespoon chopped parsley

1 Wash and clean fish and trimmings.
2 Simmer trimmings in water for 10 minutes. Strain.
3 Add fish to stock, onion or leeks and cloves. Bring to the boil and skim well. Cook gently for 10 minutes.
4 Lift out the fish and flake.
5 Cook stock for 30 minutes longer. Strain stock and rinse pan.
6 Melt margarine, add flour, cook without colouring for a few minutes, add stock and milk and stir until boiling.
7 Add flaked fish, season, then boil gently for 5 minutes.
8 Add parsley and serve.

Bouillabaisse—thick fish soup

cooking time 25 minutes

you will need for 4 servings:

2 – 3 tablespoons olive oil or 2 – 3 oz. butter
1 large onion
1 – 2 cloves crushed garlic
2 tomatoes
approximately 1½ lb. white fish—if possible a mixture of sole, red mullet, eel, hake*
pinch saffron
2 teaspoons salt
¾ teaspoon pepper
1 bay leaf
2 pints boiling water
flesh of 1 small lobster or equal weight cooked prawns
¼ pint white wine
toast and chopped parsley to garnish

* The greater the mixture of fish, the better the flavour

1 Heat the oil or butter in a large pan, then fry the sliced onion, the garlic and sliced tomatoes until just soft.
2 Put all the other ingredients except the wine and the shellfish into the pan, cutting fish into neat pieces.
3 Pour boiling water over and boil briskly for 12 – 15 minutes.
4 Remove lobster from shell, cut into small pieces and add, with wine, 5 minutes before end of boiling time.
5 Remove bay leaf.
6 Pour into a hot dish and garnish with toast and parsley.

Cream of mussel soup

cooking time 15 minutes

you will need for 4 servings:

2 pints mussels
1 onion
sprig parsley
1 pint water
seasoning
2 oz. butter
2 oz. flour
1 pint milk
little white wine, optional
extra parsley

1 Prepare the mussels and inspect them carefully (see page 45).
2 Put into pan with onion, parsley, water (slightly less water if adding wine) and seasoning.
3 Take off shells and be careful to remove the 'beard', i.e. the rather stringy part, from mussels.
4 Meanwhile make a white sauce of the butter, flour and milk. Strain mussel liquid into this, add white wine and heat.
5 Put in mussels, heat gently, and serve garnished with chopped parsley.

Mussel soup

cooking time 25 minutes

you will need for 4 servings:

2 pints mussels
1 finely chopped onion
2 tablespoons finely chopped celery
small bunch parsley
seasoning
1½ pints water
2 oz. rice
1 large skinned chopped tomato
squeeze lemon juice or vinegar

1 Scrub mussels well, discarding any that are open and will not close when sharply tapped.
2 Put into large saucepan with onion, celery, parsley, seasoning and water and heat slowly until mussels open.
3 Remove mussels, take off shells.
4 Reheat liquid, add rice and cook until tender with tomato and seasoning.
5 Remove parsley, add mussels and lemon juice or vinegar, and reheat gently.
6 Garnish with chopped parsley.

Note:

Always remove the 'beard', i.e. the rather stringy part, from mussels.

Fish chowder No. 1

cooking time 30 minutes

you will need for 4 servings:

1 lb. white fish
1 large onion
2 bacon rashers
1 oz. fat or butter
8 oz. potatoes
8 oz. carrots
1 pint water
2 tablespoons flour
½ pint milk
pepper
½ teaspoon salt
chopped parsley

1 Cut fish into small pieces.
2 Fry onion and bacon in fat or butter.
3 Add the diced potato, carrots and water. Simmer for 10 minutes, then add fish. Cook until potato is tender.
4 Add flour mixed with a little milk and stir until boiling; cook 5 minutes.
5 Add remaining milk and reheat without boiling.
6 Season and sprinkle with parsley before serving.

This makes a thick soup, suitable for lunch or supper.

Fish chowder No. 2

cooking time 45 minutes

you will need for 4 servings:

1 lb. white fish
½ pint water
1 rasher bacon
1 oz. butter or margarine
1 small onion
2 potatoes
1 pint milk
1 teaspoon salt
shake of pepper
2 tablespoons crisp breadcrumbs

1 Wash fish and put it into a saucepan with half the water.
2 Bring to the boil, lower heat and simmer for 10 minutes.
3 Drain thoroughly, keeping the stock.
4 Cut bacon into neat squares and fry until just brown; add butter and, when this is very hot, put in the finely chopped onion and continue cooking until nearly soft.
5 Add the diced potatoes and remaining water, bring to the boil and cook for 10 minutes.
6 Put in fish, stock, milk, seasoning and simmer very gently for another 20 minutes.
7 Before serving, sprinkle breadcrumbs over the top.

This chowder is a favourite American soup dish and very appetizing for a light supper.

Lobster chowder or thick lobster soup

cooking time 35 – 40 minutes

you will need for 4 servings:

1 small lobster	pinch sugar
1 pint water	seasoning
1 – 2 bacon rashers	about ¾ pint milk or evaporated milk
little fat for frying	1 medium-sized potato, diced
1 teaspoon finely chopped onion	toast
1½ oz. flour	

1 Remove flesh from lobster. Put shell into pan with water and simmer gently for about 15 minutes.
2 Strain and add enough water to make up to 1 pint.
3 Take rind from bacon and cut into narrow strips.
4 Put into pan and fry lightly, add onion and flour and cook gently without colouring.
5 Gradually add lobster stock, stirring all the time.
6 When sauce has come to the boil and thickened, add lobster, cut in small pieces, and remaining ingredients.
7 Either reduce heat under pan or transfer to double saucepan and cook until a rich creamy texture.
8 Serve with crisp fingers of toast.

Clam chowder

Follow directions for previous recipe but substitute approximately 12 – 16 chopped clams for lobster.

Lobster bisque

Illustrated on the cover

cooking time 40 minutes

you will need for 4 servings:

½ large lobster or 1 small lobster	½ pint milk
1 pint water or fish stock (see page 72)	2 oz. margarine
1 teaspoon lemon juice	seasoning, including paprika pepper
1 oz. flour	2 tablespoons cream

1 Remove flesh from lobster and cut into small pieces. Save a few pieces for a garnish.
2 Put the shell—well washed and crushed—into a large saucepan. Cover with water or stock, add the lemon juice and simmer gently for a good 30 minutes.
3 Strain carefully through a fine sieve and return to the pan, with the lobster meat.
4 Blend flour with milk and stir into the soup, with margarine and seasoning. Bring slowly to the boil and cook, stirring all the time until thickened.
5 Add the cream and reheat.
6 Serve garnished with paprika pepper and lobster pieces.

Tuna chowder

cooking time 15 – 20 minutes

you will need for 4 servings:

1 packet mushroom soup	1 can tuna
1 pint water	3 hard-boiled eggs
12 oz. diced vegetables (carrots, celery, onion and few peas)	1 lemon

1 Blend soup with water.
2 Put into a pan, add vegetables and cook for about 15 – 20 minutes.
3 Put into the flaked tuna fish and the sliced hard-boiled eggs, heat for a few minutes. Serve with lemon slices.

Salmon chowder

Ingredients as tuna chowder, substituting canned salmon for tuna.

Lobster and fish stew

cooking time 35 – 40 minutes

you will need for 4 servings:

1½ tablespoons olive oil
1½ oz. butter
8 oz. halibut or other white fish
4 oz. shelled shrimps
1 medium lobster tail
2 tablespoons brandy (optional)
1 medium onion
2 garlic cloves
4 tomatoes or 1 lb. can tomatoes
salt
4 tablespoons white wine
1 teaspoon lemon juice
extra olive oil
croûtons
1 tablespoon chopped parsley

1 Heat olive oil and butter in heavy pan until sizzling: add fish, shrimps and lobster, then fry, turning occasionally, until lobster shell is bright red and fish lightly browned.
2 Transfer to casserole: heat brandy in small pan, set aflame and pour over seafood.
3 In first pan, add minced onion and crushed garlic, cook slowly until tender.
4 Add tomatoes and salt, cook until mushy.
5 Add with wine to casserole: simmer for 5 minutes.
6 Just before serving sprinkle with lemon juice and additional olive oil.
7 Garnish with croûtons and parsley.

Note:

This assumes you can obtain uncooked lobster: otherwise, add after fish has cooked for 10 minutes.

White fish stew

cooking time 30 – 45 minutes

you will need for 4 servings:

3 – 4 oz. butter
4 large onions
4 large potatoes
3 lb. assorted white fish, cod, plaice, sole, turbot, red mullet, brill, hake, haddock
2 bay leaves
sprig thyme
salt, pepper
2 – 3 wine glasses white wine*

* Red wine can be used especially with cod

1 Melt the butter in a fireproof dish large enough to hold all the ingredients.
2 Put in the roughly chopped onions and let them become gold, but not brown.
3 Add the chopped potatoes and cook for a few minutes.
4 Add the skinned, boned fish, sliced into serving-sized pieces.
5 Throw in the crumbled bay leaves and thyme, season to taste.
6 Pour on the wine and cover the dish.
7 Cook gently on top of the stove or in a very moderate oven (300 – 350°F.—Gas Mark 2 – 3) for 30 – 35 minutes.

Note:

Check that the dish does not dry out and both potatoes and fish are soft.

Haddock casserole

cooking time 35 minutes

you will need for 4 servings:

1½ lb. haddock*
few shrimps or prawns
lemon juice
⅛ pint white wine
butter
salt, pepper
1 bay leaf
about ½ pint milk
¾ oz. cornflour
cooked carrots
2 tablespoons cooked peas
grated nutmeg
parsley

*Other white fish could be used

1 Wash fish and cut into fairly large portions.
2 Place in a baking dish with the shrimps, squeeze lemon juice, wine, a few knobs of butter, seasoning and bay leaf.
3 Cover and bake in a slow oven (300°F.—Gas Mark 2) until the fish is tender—about 25 minutes.
4 Remove bay leaf, then carefully strain off the liquor.
5 Put fish into a casserole and keep hot.
6 Make liquor up to ¾ pint with milk.
7 Blend cornflour smoothly with a little of the liquor and put the rest on to heat.
8 Add mixed cornflour and boil for 3 minutes stirring constantly.
9 Remove from heat, add carrots and peas, then pour over fish.
10 Sprinkle with a little grated nutmeg and garnish with parsley.

Salads

Fish provides a good basis for a salad and it is not necessary to use expensive lobster or crab. Many kinds of white fish can be used in salads, including skate, because of its firm almost shellfish-like texture; halibut or turbot, because both these fish have a strong flavour and plaice or sole, if rolled, cooked in white wine and then drained and cooled.

The cheaper white fish, hake, haddock, cod, look more attractive if the fish is flaked and blended with other ingredients.

Chaud-froid of fish No. 1

cooking time approximately 10 minutes

you will need for 4 servings:

- 1 lb. fish—fillets of sole or plaice, or 1 large fillet of fresh haddock
- ¼ pint aspic jelly
- ⅛ pint mayonnaise (see page 86)
- tomatoes, gherkins, radishes
- salad or mashed potato

1. Steam or simmer fish carefully, being careful not to break it. If using sole or plaice roll the fillets.
2. Make the aspic jelly, following instructions on the jar or packet.
3. When cold and beginning to set, fold into the mayonnaise.
4. Carefully mask the cold fillets of fish.
5. Garnish with tomatoes, gherkins and radishes.
6. Serve either on a bed of salad or surrounded with a border of piped mashed potato.

Chaud-froid of fish No. 2

Ingredients as above, but instead of mayonnaise use ½ pint béchamel sauce (see page 84) and 1 teaspoon powdered gelatine which should be dissolved in the hot aspic jelly.

Caprice salad

no cooking

you will need for 4 servings:

- 4 heads chicory
- 1 large apple
- 4 oz. diced celery
- 4 – 6 fresh mushrooms
- 1 tablespoon olive oil
- few drops lemon juice
- ¼ teaspoon salt
- 1 can drained grapefruit sections
- 1 can tuna
- mayonnaise (see page 86)

1. Separate leaves of chicory, soak in cold water, pat dry.
2. Dice cored apple, combine with celery and diced mushrooms.
3. Toss with olive oil, lemon juice and salt.
4. Pile into chicory leaves, arrange with grapefruit sections and flaked tuna on salad plates.
5. Garnish with mayonnaise.

Crab salad

no cooking

you will need for 4 servings:

- 1 large dressed crab
- 2 – 2½ oz. cooked rice
- 1 – 1½ oz. finely chopped celery
- 1 teaspoon chopped parsley
- 2 teaspoons chopped gherkins
- 1 dessertspoon lemon juice or vinegar
- 1 tablespoon oil
- seasoning
- lettuce

1. Mix together all the ingredients except the lettuce and small crab claws.
2. Season well.
3. Serve on individual dishes on a bed of lettuce—garnish with crab claws.

Curried haddock salad

cooking time 10 minutes

you will need for 4 servings:

- 1 oz. butter
- 1 small onion
- 1 small sweet apple
- 1 dessertspoon curry powder
- 3 tablespoons mayonnaise (see page 86)
- 1 lb. cooked fresh haddock
- lettuce

To garnish:

- watercress
- tomatoes
- gherkins or cucumber

1 Heat the butter.
2 Chop onion very finely and fry in butter until soft.
3 Peel the apple and chop or grate finely.
4 Mix curry powder with the fried onion and heat for a minute or so—this takes away the 'raw' flavour of the powder.
5 Put onion, curry and apple into the mayonnaise and mix thoroughly.
6 Flake the fish—but not too finely. Arrange this on lettuce leaves and pour over the sauce.
7 Garnish with watercress, sliced tomatoes and gherkins or cucumber.

Fish potato salad

no cooking

you will need for 4 servings:

2 egg yolks
salt and pepper
1 teaspoon lemon juice
1 teaspoon vinegar
¼ pint olive oil
12 oz. flaked cooked fish
12 oz. hot cooked thinly-sliced potatoes
4 sprigs chopped mint
4 sprigs chopped parsley
¼ chopped onion

1 Mix the egg yolks, salt, pepper, lemon juice and vinegar.
2 Now add drop by drop the oil, beating constantly. As the dressing beings to form the oil can be added more rapidly.
3 Put all the other ingredients into a dish and mix well with the dressing.
4 Leave to cool and toss gently before serving.

Galician seafood salad

no cooking

you will need for 4 servings:

1 medium cooked lobster or 2 cooked rock lobster tails
2 chopped hard-boiled eggs
2 chopped gherkins
1 medium onion, thinly sliced
4 oz. cooked shrimps
1 tablespoon vinegar
½ teaspoon made mustard
salt and pepper
2 tablespoons olive oil

To garnish:
lettuce
2 pimentos
1 or 2 hard-boiled eggs
lemon

1 Remove lobster meat from shell and cut in slices.
2 Add remaining ingredients except olive oil and toss to blend.
3 Chill.
4 Just before serving add olive oil, toss lightly.
5 Serve on lettuce, garnished with strips of pimento and sliced hard-boiled egg and lemon.

German salad

no cooking

you will need for 4 servings:

2 apples
2 medium cooked potatoes
4 sweet gherkin pickles
16 oz. pickled Bismark herring fillets
1 tablespoon minced onion
1 tablespoon chopped parsley
3 tablespoons olive oil
2 hard-boiled eggs
1 teaspoon salt
¼ teaspoon black pepper
1 tablespoon vinegar
2 – 3 small cooked beetroot
lettuce

1 Core and thinly slice apples; slice potatoes.
2 Combine apples, potatoes, pickles, chopped herring, onion and parsley.
3 Toss with 1 tablespoon olive oil.
4 Mash egg yolks, add salt and pepper, beat in remaining olive oil, then add vinegar.
5 Add ½ quantity sauce to potato mixture with some of the finely minced beetroot.
6 Arrange on lettuce with remaining beetroot and chopped egg whites.
7 Serve remaining sauce as garnish.

Herring salad

cooking time 10 minutes

you will need for 4 servings:

4 large herrings
4 large cooked potatoes
1 cooked beetroot
1 small onion or equivalent in spring onions
2 sweet apples
4 gherkins
2 tablespoons vinegar
seasoning

To garnish:
1 or 2 hard-boiled eggs
parsley

1 Remove backbones from herrings, cover with greaseproof paper and bake for 10 minutes in a moderately hot oven (400°F.—Gas Mark 5).
2 When the fish is cold, cut into small pieces, taking off the skin and any other bones. Mix with diced potatoes, beetroot, grated onion or onions, apples, chopped gherkins, vinegar and seasoning.
3 Form this into an attractive shape, or pack tightly into a mould and put into a cold place for 1 hour. Then turn it out.
4 Garnish with egg cut into shapes and parsley.

Lobster salad

no cooking

you will need for 4 servings:

2 medium-sized lobsters
lettuce
approximately ¼ pint mayonnaise (see page 86)
lemon
sliced tomatoes
cucumber

1 Split lobster down the centre.
2 Take out the intestinal vein and grey 'fingers'.
3 Crack the large claws. If you have special lobster picks, leave the meat in the cracked shells, otherwise carefully take out the meat. Do this with a fine skewer and crack the claws with a light hammer or weight.
4 Serve the claw meat in the shell with the body meat, or lift it out of the shell and dice neatly. If body meat is diced, pile this back into the halved shells, polished with a very little salad oil. Put meat from the large claws on top or neatly beside the body.
5 Arrange shells and meat on a bed of lettuce, top with mayonnaise, or serve it spearately. Garnish with lemon slices, tomatoes and cucumber.

Note:

This can be varied by adding hard-boiled eggs and meat piled neatly in the centre of the lettuce. For economy, mix diced lobster meat with diced cooked white fish.
For a more glamorous looking salad, make a little aspic jelly and, when set, whisk and arrange round the lobster. The tiny lobster claws make an attractive garnish. When serving the meat in large claws, have finger bowls available.

Peas and crab salad

no cooking

you will need for 4 servings:

1 large crab or 1 can crab meat
4 oz. cooked peas
3 oz. cooked rice
½ teaspoon salt
¼ teaspoon curry powder
mayonnaise or salad dressing (see page 86)
crisp lettuce

1 Flake crab meat, removing any membrane.
2 Add rest of ingredients, except lettuce and mix gently.
3 Serve piled on lettuce leaves.

Niçoise salad

no cooking

you will need for 4 servings:

8 oz. fresh or 1 packet frozen green beans
1 medium can tuna
little chopped celery
4 tomatoes, quartered
3 medium cooked and quartered potatoes
vinaigrette sauce (see page 86)
6 fillets anchovy, chopped
1 tablespoon capers
2 – 3 tablespoons chopped olives

1 Arrange beans, flaked tuna, celery, tomatoes and potatoes on individual salad plates.
2 Top with sauce.
3 Combine anchovies, capers and olives and sprinkle over the top.

Oriental salad

no cooking

you will need for 4 servings:

4 oz. cooked macaroni or rice
8 oz. coarsely flaked cooked white fish
few sliced gherkins or cucumber
⅛ pint oil
2 tablespoons vinegar
seasoning
1 tablespoon capers
1 dessertspoon Worcestershire sauce
½ pint prepared shrimps or prawns
lettuce

To garnish:
1 or 2 hard-boiled eggs
parsley

1 Mix macaroni or rice, fish, gherkins, oil, vinegar, seasoning, capers, Worcestershire sauce and most of the shrimps.
2 Pile in small mounds on lettuce leaves.
3 Chop egg yolks and whites separately and garnish with these, chopped parsley and remaining shrimps.

Turbot salad

Illustrated on the cover

cooking time 15 – 20 minutes

you will need for 4 servings:

4 cutlets turbot or halibut
seasoning
¼ pint cider
lettuce

To garnish:
tomatoes
watercress
lemon

olive oil

1 Put the fish in a shallow dish, cover with seasoning and cider, and put a piece of paper on top.

2 Cook for about 15 – 20 minutes in moderately hot oven (400°F.—Gas Mark 5).
3 Leave in the liquid until cool.
4 Lift fish on to a bed of crisp lettuce.
5 Garnish with tomatoes, watercress and lemon.
6 Mix 1 or 2 tablespoons of the cider liquid with equal quantity of olive oil. Season well and serve separately.

Smoked haddock salad

no cooking

you will need for 4 servings:

8 oz. cooked potatoes
2 hard-boiled eggs
12 oz. flaked cooked smoked haddock
1 dessertspoon capers
1 small finely chopped onion or few spring onions
⅛ pint mayonnaise or cream cheese dressing (see page 86)
watercress

1 Dice potatoes and quarter the hard-boiled eggs.
2 Mix with all other ingredients except watercress.
3 Pile on to a bed of watercress.

Prawn or shrimp cocktail

no cooking

you will need for 4 servings:

For the sauce:
5 tablespoons thick mayonnaise (see page 86)
1 tablespoon tomato ketchup or thick tomato purée
1 tablespoon Worcestershire sauce
1 tablespoon lemon juice
1 teaspoon finely chopped onion
1 teaspoon finely chopped celery or ¼ teaspoon celery salt
salt to taste

lettuce
1 pint pickled fresh shrimps or prawns, or frozen or canned fish
lemon slices

1 Mix all ingredients together for the sauce.
2 If serving on flat dishes, choose small lettuce leaves and arrange prawns or shrimps on these and coat with sauce. The correct way of serving these cocktails, though, is to use glasses, when the lettuce should be shredded very finely, put at the bottom of the glasses, then covered with prawns or shrimps and sauce.
3 Garnish with lemon and serve as cold as possible.*

* Or arrange the glasses in container of crushed ice.

Variations:

Crab meat cocktail
Use flaked crab meat instead of prawns mixing dark and light meat together, or having dark meat in centre of glass with white meat around. Garnish with lemon.

Lobster crab meat cocktail
Mix flaked lobster and crab meat together—this is particularly good with canned fish.

Lobster cocktail
Use lobster meat, divided into small pieces, instead of prawns. Garnish with the tiny claws and lemon.

White fish cocktail
Use flaked white fish instead of prawns and, for added flavour and a more 'biting' sauce, put in a little anchovy essence.

Seafood cocktail
This generally means a mixture of shellfish.

Creamed cocktail
Use any type of fish and, instead of mayonnaise, use whipped cream, which gives a more delicate flavoured sauce.

Fish and Hollandaise cocktail
Use any type of fish with Hollandaise sauce (see page 82) in place of mayonnaise.

Prawn salad

no cooking

you will need for 4 servings:

1 tablespoon oil
2 tablespoons vinegar
1 tablespoon cream from top of milk
1 pint prawns
seasoning
approximately 4 oz. diced celery
2 teaspoons capers
2 teaspoons chopped parsley
1 tablespoon chopped gherkin
lettuce
sliced potatoes

1 Pour the oil, vinegar and cream over the prawns.
2 Add a sprinkling of seasoning and leave for about 30 minutes.
3 Mix in the celery, capers, parsley and gherkin.
4 Serve on a bed of lettuce with potatoes.

Rollmop herrings

cooking time few minutes

you will need for 4 servings:

4 oz. kitchen salt
2 pints water
approximately 1 pint pure malt vinegar
8 herrings
1 – 2 onions
2 – 3 bay leaves
2 – 3 gherkins
2 – 3 chillipeppers
1 – 2 tablespoons pickling spices
extra vinegar

1 Make brine of kitchen salt and water.
2 Soak the herrings in the brine for 2 hours if filleted, twice as long if whole.
3 Lift out of the brine and put into a large shallow dish.
4 Cover with vinegar and leave for several hours.
5 Take the fish out of the vinegar, lay flat on a wooden board, then roll each fish or fillet round a small tablespoon of finely shredded onion and secure with a small cocktail stick.
6 Put into jars with bay leaves, gherkins and chillis and cover with cold spiced vinegar (see below).

Spiced vinegar:

1 Measure the vinegar in which the herrings have been soaking and make up to 1 – 1½ pints (depending on the size of the jars) with more vinegar.
2 Allow 1 tablespoon pickling spice to each pint vinegar, boil together and allow to cool.

Note:

Rollmops will keep in a cool place for 2 – 3 weeks.

Pickled cucumber

you will need:

1 large cucumber
3 tablespoons vinegar
2 tablespoons water
2 tablespoons sugar
¼ teaspoon salt
dash white pepper
1 tablespoon chopped parsley

1 Wipe cucumber, slice without peeling and place in glass dish.
2 Mix vinegar, water, sugar, salt and pepper thoroughly, pour over the cucumber and sprinkle with parsley.
3 Allow to stand 2 – 3 hours in refrigerator before serving.

Sauces, Butters, Dressings, Stuffings

There are a number of sauces which blend well with cooked fish of various kinds. A good sauce makes a great deal of difference to the flavour and imaginative sauces transform quite simple fish dishes into interesting ones.
Flavoured butters, put on the top of fish just before serving, give a luxury finish to an inexpensive dish.

Anchovy and egg sauce

cooking time 15 minutes

you will need:

1 oz. butter
1 oz. flour
½ pint water
3 hard-boiled eggs
8 anchovy fillets
2 tablespoons vinegar
1 tablespoon oil
seasoning
2 tablespoons fine breadcrumbs
1 tablespoon chopped parsley

1 Heat butter, then stir in flour. Cook for several minutes, then add water, bring to the boil and cook until thickened.
2 Shell the eggs and chop with anchovies until very fine.
3 Add to sauce, together with the rest of the ingredients and mix well.

Béarnaise sauce

cooking time 20 – 25 minutes

you will need:

2 egg yolks
salt, pepper
pinch cayenne pepper
vinegar
1 – 2 tablespoons lemon juice or white wine
2 – 4 oz. butter
finely chopped shallot
chopped parsley
tarragon vinegar

1 Put egg yolks, seasoning and vinegar into the top of a double saucepan.
2 Whisk over hot water until sauce begins to thicken.
3 Add lemon juice or wine and butter in very small pieces, whisking in each pat and allowing it to melt before adding the next. Do not boil or it will curdle.
4 Add shallot and extra pepper, then parsley and little vinegar.

Chaud-froid sauce

cooking time 20 minutes

you will need:

- ½ pint béchamel sauce (see page 84)
- ¼ pint chicken jelly* or aspic jelly (made according to packet instructions)
- 3 tablespoons thick cream
- seasoning

* Made by boiling chicken carcase, then allowing the stock to simmer for some time until strong enough to jelly

1 Allow sauce to cool slightly, stirring well to prevent a skin forming on the top.
2 Whisk in chicken or aspic jelly and stir until a smooth mixture.
3 Add lightly whipped cream and seasoning.

For coating pieces of meat or poultry, use while still slightly warm.

For coating fish,well strained chicken stock can be used, but fish stock is better. If boiled for a long time this will form a jelly, but if in a hurry, add 1 teaspoon powder gelatine or aspic jelly crystals to each ½ pint stock.

Cheese sauce

cooking time 6 – 8 minutes

you will need:

- 1 oz. butter
- 1 oz. flour
- ½ pint milk
- seasoning, including mustard
- 3 – 6 oz. grated cheese

1 Melt butter.
2 Stir in flour and cook for a few minutes.
3 Remove pan from heat and gradually add milk, bring to the boil and cook until thickened.
4 Add seasoning and cheese, then heat gently, stirring until smooth.

Curry sauce

cooking time 1½ – 2½ hours

you will need:

- 2 oz. butter fat*
- 1 large onion
- 1 or 2 tomatoes
- 1 tablespoon curry powder†
- 1 teaspoon curry paste
- 1 tablespoon flour
- ¾ pint brown stock‡
- little sugar
- 1 oz. dried fruit
- seasoning
- 1 tablespoon grated coconut or desiccated coconut
- 1 tablespoon lemon juice

* In Indian dishes the butter is first heated, then allowed to cool to make pure butter fat
† Or make a blend of turmeric, chilli powder, mace, ginger, cummin
‡ Use fish stock for a fish curry

1 Heat butter fat and fry chopped onion, tomatoes, curry powder and paste.
2 Work in flour, and cook for several minutes.
3 Add stock, bring to the boil and cook until thickened.
4 Add remaining ingredients and simmer steadily until thick and smooth.

Devilled sauce

cooking time 20 minutes

you will need:

- ½ pint Espagnole sauce (see page 82)
- 1 tablespoon Worcestershire sauce
- cayenne pepper
- 2 teaspoons French mustard
- chopped parsley

1 Add all ingredients except the parsley to Espagnole sauce.
2 Simmer gently for a few minutes, then add parsley.

Dill sauce

cooking time 15 minutes

you will need:

- 1½ oz. butter
- 1½ oz. flour
- ½ pint plus 1 tablespoon stock
- 1½ tablespoons vinegar
- ½ – 1 tablespoon sugar
- salt
- 1 egg yolk
- 2 tablespoons chopped dill

1 Melt butter, add flour and stir well until blended.
2 Gradually add stock, vinegar, sugar and salt, stirring continuously.
3 When well blended and thickened, pour a little of the sauce over beaten egg yolk, return to pan and reheat carefully.
4 Stir in chopped dill.

Egg and lemon sauce

cooking time few minutes

you will need:

- 4 egg yolks or 2 whole eggs
- 4 tablespoons lemon juice
- 3 tablespoons stock*
- seasoning

* This can be fish, meat or poultry stock, depending on the dish

1. Whisk eggs until thick, then gradually beat in lemon juice.
2. Gradually whisk in stock.
3. Heat gently, WITHOUT BOILING, then season to taste.

Espagnole sauce

cooking time 10 – 15 minutes

you will need:

- 2 oz. cooking fat or dripping
- salt, pepper
- 1 oz. flour
- 1 pint brown stock
- 3 – 4 mushrooms
- 2 rashers bacon
- 1 small onion
- 1 carrot
- 2 large tomatoes, skinned and pulped
- sherry

1. Heat fat and fry chopped vegetables, except tomatoes, and chopped bacon.
2. Mix in flour and cook steadily until brown.
3. Add stock, stirring all the time, bring to the boil, season and simmer until vegetables are tender and sauce very thick.
4. Sieve and reheat, adding tomato pulp and sherry to taste.

Fish sauce

cooking time 15 – 20 minutes

you will need:

- 2 oz. butter
- 1 oz. flour
- ½ pint fish stock*
- 1 teaspoon made mustard
- bay leaf
- grated nutmeg
- 1 tablespoon lemon juice
- seasoning
- 2 teaspoons chopped parsley

* Simmer the bones and skin of the fish until a good flavoured stock results

1. Heat 1 oz. butter, stir in flour and cook for several minutes.
2. Gradually add stock, bring to the boil and cook until thickened.
3. Add all other ingredients, except parsley and simmer for about 10 minutes.
4. Strain and add parsley.

Gooseberry sauce for mackerel

cooking time 20 minutes

you will need:

- gooseberries
- water
- sugar
- small knob margarine

1. Simmer fruit in water until tender.
2. Sieve.
3. Return to pan.
4. Reheat with sugar to taste and margarine.

Hollandaise sauce

cooking time 20 – 25 minutes

you will need:

- 2 egg yolks
- salt, white pepper
- pinch cayenne pepper
- 2 tablespoons vinegar
- 2 – 4 oz. butter
- 1 – 2 tablespoons lemon juice or white wine

1. Put egg yolks, seasonings and vinegar into the top of a double saucepan.
2. Whisk over hot water until sauce begins to thicken.
3. Add butter in very small pieces, whisking in each pat and allowing it to melt before adding the next. DO NOT ALLOW TO BOIL.
4. Add lemon juice and, if too thick, a little cream.

Variation:

Mousseline sauce
Use 1 oz. butter to 2 egg yolks and add a little cream and grated nutmeg.

Horseradish cream

no cooking

you will need:

- 1 tablespoon grated horseradish
- ½ teaspoon vinegar
- 2 – 3 tablespoons cream
- seasoning

1. Mix all together.

Note:

This cream is very strong.

Lobster sauce

cooking time 10 minutes

you will need:

- 1 oz. butter
- 1 oz. flour
- 3 tablespoons cream
- ½ pint lobster stock
- 1 small boiled lobster
- salt, pepper

1. Melt butter, add flour, stir well until blended.
2. Add cream and stock gradually, stirring constantly.
3. Simmer 10 minutes, stirring occasionally.
4. Add lobster meat, cut in pieces, and season. Reheat.

Mild curry sauce

cooking time 15 minutes

you will need:

- 1 onion
- 1 teaspoon curry powder
- 1 oz. butter
- béchamel sauce (see page 84)

1. Fry the chopped onion and curry powder in the butter until soft.
2. Add to sauce and simmer for a few minutes.
3. Strain and reheat.

Mustard sauce No. 1

cooking time 15 minutes

you will need:

- 3 teaspoons mustard (preferably French)
- 2 egg yolks
- ¼ pint white stock
- 2 oz. butter
- 1 tablespoon lemon juice
- seasoning

1. Put the made mustard and egg yolks into a basin over hot water or the top of a double saucepan.
2. Whisk until thick and creamy.
3. Gradually whisk in stock and continue to whisk until thickened again.
4. Add butter gradually as in Hollandaise sauce (see page 82).
5. Lastly whisk in lemon juice and seasoning.

Mustard sauce No. 2

cooking time 15 minutes

you will need:

- 2 oz. butter
- 1 oz. flour
- ⅜ pint water
- 1 tablespoon mustard
- 1 teaspoon vinegar
- salt

1. Melt 1 oz. butter.
2. Stir in flour and cook for several minutes.
3. Blend mustard with water until smooth, add to butter and flour and bring to the boil slowly, stirring until smooth.
4. Add vinegar, remaining butter and pinch salt.

White sauce

cooking time 10 minutes

you will need:

- 1 oz. butter or margarine
- 1 oz. flour
- ½ pint milk for coating consistency OR ¼ pint milk for panada or binding consistency, OR 1 pint milk for thin white sauce for soups
- salt, pepper

1. Heat butter gently, remove from heat and stir in flour.
2. Return to heat and cook gently for a few minutes, so that the '*roux*' as the butter and flour mixture is called, does not brown.
3. Again remove pan from heat and gradually blend in the cold milk.
4. Bring to the boil and cook, stirring with a wooden spoon until smooth.
5. Season well.

If any small lumps form, whisk sharply.

Variations:

Anchovy sauce
Stir in chopped anchovies or 1 teaspoon anchovy essence.

Caper sauce
Use ¼ pint milk and ¼ pint stock. Add 2 teaspoons capers and a little caper vinegar.

White fish sauce
Use ¼ pint fish stock and ¼ pint milk.

Parsley sauce
Add 1 – 2 teaspoons chopped parsley and squeeze lemon juice if wished.

Creamed tomato sauce
Whisk a thick tomato purée (which should be hot but not boiling) into hot white sauce. Do not boil.

Cucumber sauce
Whisk ¼ pint thick cucumber purée into white sauce, add little lemon juice, green colouring and cream.

Mustard cream sauce
Blend ½ – 1 teaspoon dry mustard with flour. Proceed as white sauce, stirring in little extra milk or cream.

Horseradish sauce (hot)
Whisk 1 dessertspoon vinegar and 2 tablespoons grated horseradish into white sauce. Add small amount of cream and pinch sugar.

Béchamel sauce
Simmer finely chopped onion, carrot, celery in milk. Strain and make as white sauce.

Economical Hollandaise sauce
Make white sauce, remove from heat and whisk in 1 egg, 1 dessertspoon lemon juice or vinegar. Cook gently, without boiling, for a few minutes.

Maître d'hôtel sauce
As white sauce, but use half fish stock. Use 2 teaspoons chopped parsley and 3 tablespoons thick cream just before serving.

Mushroom sauce
Cook 2 oz. mushrooms, chopped, in the milk, then use milk to make white sauce. Add mushrooms and reheat.

Oyster sauce
Make white sauce, add about 12 oysters and a little cream just before serving. Do not overcook.

Prawn or shrimp sauce
Make white sauce, add 2 – 3 oz. chopped prawns or shrimps and a little anchovy essence just before serving. If using fresh prawns or shrimps, simmer shells and use ¼ pint stock instead of milk.

Tartare sauce (hot)
Make white sauce, then whisk in 2 egg yolks, 1 tablespoon cream, 1 tablespoon capers, 1 teaspoon chopped gherkin, 1 teaspoon chopped parsley and a squeeze lemon juice. Cook gently for a few minutes without boiling.

White wine sauce

cooking time 15 minutes

you will need:

1 oz. butter
1 oz. flour
½ pint white wine*
bouquet garni (see page 8)
seasoning
2 tablespoons cream

* A cheap Sauternes or Graves is ideal

1. Melt butter.
2. Stir in flour and cook for several minutes.
3. Gradually add wine, bring to the boil and cook until thickened.
4. Simmer with *bouquet garni* for about 10 minutes, seasoning well,
5. Remove *bouquet*, add cream and simmer for 2 – 3 minutes.

Sauce duglére

cooking time approximately 20 minutes

you will need:

2 oz. butter or margarine
1 small onion
4 large tomatoes
1 oz. flour
½ pint fish stock (see page 72) fish stock and white wine, or white wine
seasoning

1. Heat butter and in it toss finely chopped onion and skinned chopped tomatoes.
2. Stir in flour and cook for several minutes.
3. Gradually add the liquid, bring to the boil and cook for approximately 10 – 15 minutes.
4. Rub through a sieve.
5. Reheat and season.

Tomato sauce No. 1

cooking time 15 – 20 minutes

you will need:

1 lb. tomatoes
1 small onion
1 pint water
½ oz. cornflour
1 teaspoon dry mustard
2 oz. soft brown sugar
salt
½ teaspoon paprika
1 dessertspoon vinegar
1 tablespoon Worcestershire sauce
dash Tabasco sauce

1 Peel and chop tomatoes and onion, add water and simmer gently for 15 – 20 minutes.
2 Mix together smoothly remaining ingredients and add to tomatoes and onion.
3 Simmer gently for 3 minutes stirring constantly.
4 Correct seasoning if necessary.

Tomato sauce No. 2

cooking time 15 minutes

you will need:

- 2 rashers bacon, optional
- 1 small onion
- ½ lb. sliced tomatoes or 1 tin tomato puree
- seasoning
- good pinch sugar
- squeeze lemon juice
- small bunch parsley

1 Fry bacon until just cooked.
2 Fry finely sliced onion in bacon fat until tender, but not browned.
3 Add remaining ingredients and simmer until a smooth pulp.
4 Rub through a sieve, then reheat gently—add a little water or stock for a thinner sauce—or serve the sauce without sieving it, but remove parsley.

Tartare sauce

cooking time dependent on sauce used

Ingredients as either mayonnaise (see page 86) or Hollandaise sauce (see page 82) and

- ½ – 1 tablespoon chopped parsley
- 1 – 2 tablespoon chopped gherkins (or fresh cucumber)
- 1 – 2 teaspoons chopped capers

Make the sauce and add the extra ingredients.

Flavoured Butters

Anchovy butter
To 2 oz. butter, work in 1 teaspoon anchovy essence or 1 tablespoon finely chopped anchovies. For spreading on cocktail biscuits, etc., or if for decoration or canapés, sieve before piping.

Cheese butter
To 2 oz. butter add good pinch salt, pepper and dry mustard and 1 oz. finely grated cheese. For spreading or piping.

Egg butter
To 2 oz. butter add sieved or mashed yolk of 1 egg and seasoning. For spreading or piping.

Lobster butter
To 2 – 3 oz. butter allow the red coral from a hen lobster, a little seasoning and squeeze lemon juice. Beat well. For spreading and piping.

Sardine butter
To 3 oz. butter add skinned and boned contents of 1 small can of sardines. Do not use the oil. For spreading or piping.

Tomato butter
To 2 oz. butter allow 1 teaspoon concentrated tomato purée or ketchup. If using fresh tomatoes, skin and purée them, strain away juice. Fresh tomato is better for spreading.

Watercress butter
To 2 oz. butter allow 1 tablespoon chopped watercress and squeeze lemon juice.

Maître d'hôtel or parsley butter

no cooking

1 Add chopped parsley, seasoning and squeeze lemon juice and work into butter.
2 Chill and cut into neat pieces.

Lemon butter baste

no cooking

you will need:

- 4 oz. butter
- 1 tablespoon lemon juice
- 1 tablespoon French or mild mustard
- 1 teaspoon paprika
- ¼ teaspoon salt

Blend all ingredients together.

Dressings

Vinaigrette dressing

you will need:

1 teaspoon made mustard
2 teaspoons sugar
½ teaspoon salt
black pepper
little garlic juice or pinch garlic salt
little chopped fresh herbs, chervil, parsley, chives, etc., or pinch dried herbs
¼ pint oil
2 tablespoons wine vinegar
1 tablespoon tarragon vinegar
1 tablespoon lemon juice

1. Mix all the seasonings and herbs together.
2. Stir in the oil.
3. Beat in vinegars and lemon juice.

Cheese mayonnaise

no cooking

you will need:

4 oz. blue cheese
pinch salt and pepper
1 teaspoon made mustard
2 tablespoons olive oil
2 tablespoons milk or cream
2 tablespoons vinegar

1. Beat cheese until smooth.
2. Work in seasoning, then oil.
3. Lastly add milk and vinegar.

Serve with potato salad.

Mayonnaise

no cooking

you will need:

1 egg yolk
good pinch salt, pepper and mustard
⅛ – ¼ pint oil
1 dessertspoon vinegar or lemon juice
1 dessertspoon warm water

1. Put egg yolk and seasonings into a basin.
2. Gradually beat in oil, drop by drop, stirring all the time, until mixture is thick. Once it is creamy, stop adding oil, as too much curdles the mixture.
3. Beat in vinegar gradually, then warm water. Use when fresh.

Note:

With an electric blender, put egg, seasoning and vinegar into goblet. Switch on for a few seconds, then pour oil in steadily.

Cream cheese dressing

no cooking

you will need:

4 oz. cream cheese
2 tablespoons olive oil
pinch salt and pepper
1 teaspoon made mustard
2 tablespoons milk
2 tablespoons vinegar

1. Beat cheese until smooth.
2. Work in oil and seasoning.
3. Add milk and vinegar.

Green mayonnaise

you will need:

mayonnaise (see this page)
chopped parsley
chives
sage
thyme

To the mayonnaise add parsley, chives, sage and thyme.

Stuffings

Mushroom stuffing

cooking time 10 minutes

you will need:

2 oz. margarine
1 small onion
4 oz. mushrooms
4 oz. soft breadcrumbs
2 teaspoons chopped parsley
seasoning

1. Melt margarine and fry finely chopped onion.
2. Add finely chopped mushrooms, breadcrumbs parsley and seasoning.

Onion stuffing (for baked herrings, mackerel, whiting)

no cooking

you will need for 4 servings:

2 oz. stale bread, soaked and squeezed
2 oz. finely chopped onion
1 tablespoon chopped parsley
2 teaspoons mixed dried herbs
1 teaspoon salt
¼ teaspoon pepper
½ oz. melted dripping or other fat
2 teaspoons vinegar

1. Mix bread, onion, parsley, herbs and seasoning together.
2. Add fat and vinegar and mix well.

Parsley stuffing (for white fish)

no cooking

you will need:

- 4 oz. fine breadcrumbs
- 4 tablespoons chopped parsley
- 2 teaspoons mixed dried herbs
- salt and pepper
- 2 oz. melted butter
- few drops lemon juice
- milk to mix

1. Mix ingredients together to a stiff consistency.
2. Use to stuff fish, or as stuffing balls.

Veal stuffing

cooking time as individual recipe

you will need:

- 4 oz. breadcrumbs
- 1 egg
- ½ teaspoon mixed herbs
- 2 oz. shredded suet or melted margarine
- 2 – 3 teaspoons chopped parsley
- grated rind and juice of ½ lemon
- seasoning

1. Mix all ingredients thoroughly together.

Vegetables

While many vegetables are excellent with fish there are certain types that blend rather better.

Asparagus fresh or canned	An excellent accompaniment to any fish dish.
Beans either fresh, frozen or canned	Blend well with fried, grilled or other fish.
Broccoli fresh or frozen	First-class vegetable to serve with fried or grilled fish or with fish salads.
Chicory or Celery	Both blend well with fish either alone or with a cheese sauce.
Corn on the cob	Can be added to fish stew or casserole or served separately.
Green vegetables	Cabbage, sprouts, etc., are not particularly good as the rather strong flavour of a green vegetable can detract from delicate flavours of fish.
Haricot Beans fresh or canned	Good in fish stews or casserole dishes.
Peas fresh or frozen	Excellent with all fish and especially with fresh salmon.
Potatoes creamed, mashed, Duchesse potatoes (see this page), fried	Blend well with any type of fish dish and the best accompaniment for fried or grilled fish are, of course, beautifully fried chipped potatoes.
Roast potatoes	When cooked in a vegetable fat or oil, blend well.
Spinach	Creamed spinach, although it has such a strong flavour, is a first-class accompaniment. A complete meal can be made with white fish on a bed of spinach, coated with cheese sauce and browned.

Duchesse potatoes

cooking time 20 – 25 minutes

you will need:

- 1 or 2 eggs
- 1¼ lb. well-mashed potatoes
- 2 oz. butter

To garnish: parsley

1. Mix beaten egg and butter with potatoes.
2. Pipe on to greased baking tins, or as border on dish, and bake for about 20 – 25 minutes in a moderately hot oven (400°F.—Gas Mark 5).
3. Serve garnished with parsley.

Index

T

HONEY
Ginger

Main Meals

Hors-d'oeuvre

Serving hors-d'oeuvre

If you are planning to serve a selection of hors-d'oeuvre, it is best to use one of the special hors-d'oeuvre trays which has a number of divisions, so that there is a separate section for each type of food. If this is not possible, you can make up individual plates on which the various types of food are attractively arranged. Since most hors-d'oeuvre are coated, during preparation, with either oil and vinegar or mayonnaise, it will not be necessary to serve these separately.

Spiced grapefruit

cooking time: 3–5 minutes

1 Halve the grapefruit in the usual way and separate the segments of fruit.
2 Spread a little butter on top, and sprinkle with spice and sugar.
3 Either heat for a few minutes under the grill or in a hot oven.

Sherry and ginger grapefruit

Put a thin slice of preserved ginger between each segment of grapefruit, sprinkle with sherry, blended with 1–2 teaspoons preserved ginger syrup; serve heated, as above, or chilled.

Melon cocktail

no cooking

you will need:

melon
fresh orange segments
sugar (optional)

1 Dice the melon or make balls of the pulp with a vegetable scoop.
2 Arrange in glasses with segments of fresh orange.
3 Sprinkle with sugar if wished.

Summer melon

Mix melon balls or diced fruit with halved fres[h] cherries, strawberries, and other summer fruit[s]. Sprinkle with lemon juice rather than oran[ge] juice, to give a refreshing flavour, and add a ve[ry] little sugar.

Florida basket

no cooking

you will need:

2 large grapefruit
2 rings pineapple
sugar
4 cherries
sprig mint

1 Prepare the grapefruit by halving and removin[g] the segments of fruit.
2 Mix with chopped pineapple and sugar, and pi[le] back into the halves of grapefruit.
3 Top with cherries and mint.

Melon and raspberry cocktail

no cooking

you will need:

melon
fresh raspberries
little kirsch

1 Dice the melon or make balls of the pulp with vegetable scoop.
2 Mix with raspberries and a little kirsch.
3 Pile into glasses.

Pineapple and lemon juice

no cooking

you will need:

canned pineapple juice
fresh lemon juice
sprigs mint or lemon slices

1 Mix canned pineapple juice with a little fres[h] lemon juice.
2 Serve in cocktail glasses, topped with sprigs o[f] mint or slices of lemon.

Tomato orange cocktail

no cooking

you will need:

canned tomato juice
canned or fresh orange juice
sprigs mint
orange slices

1 Mix the juices together, using two parts tomato juice and one part orange juice.
2 Chill thoroughly with a few bruised sprigs of mint.
3 Serve in small glasses topped with orange slices.

Grapefruit and prawns

no cooking

you will need:

grapefruit
few prawns (or shrimps)
mayonnaise
lettuce
lemon to garnish

1 Halve grapefruit, and remove the segments of fruit.
2 Mix with a few prawns (or shrimps) and a little mayonnaise.
3 Arrange shredded lettuce in the grapefruit halves.
4 Put the fruit and fish on top, garnishing with lemon.

Avocado and prawns

no cooking

you will need:

avocado pears
prawns (or shrimps)
oil
vinegar
seasoning

1 Halve avocado pears and remove the stones.
2 Fill the centre with shrimps or prawns, tossed in oil and vinegar.
3 Serve with small forks and spoons, topping with more well seasoned oil and vinegar if wished.

Grapefruit and avocado salad

Halve and skin ripe avocado pears, then cut into slices; arrange on a bed of lettuce with segments of fresh or canned grapefruit. Top with a few prawns in mayonnaise or oil and vinegar dressing.

Prawns mornay

cooking time: 15 minutes

you will need:

½ pint cheese sauce (see page 88)
8 oz. prawns
lemon
parsley

1 Make the cheese sauce.
2 Add the prawns, and heat for a few minutes.
3 Divide into 4 small dishes, top with chopped parsley.
4 Garnish with wedges of lemon.

Prawns Milanaise

Make the tomato sauce, page 87, heat the prawns in this. Put in small dishes and top with grated cheese.

Smoked eel and horseradish

no cooking

you will need:

smoked eel
lettuce
lemon
horseradish sauce
brown bread and butter

1 Buy the smoked eel, allowing 2–3 oz. per person.
2 Remove the skin and arrange on crisp lettuce.
3 Garnish with lemon and serve with horseradish sauce and brown bread and butter.

Smoked salmon and spinach

cooking time: 15 minutes

you will need:

4 tiny tartlets cases (short crust pastry, see page 75)
approximately 8 oz. cooked spinach (frozen ideal)
little butter
1 tablespoon cream
4–6 oz. smoked salmon
lemon

1 Bake the tartlet cases in a hot oven (450°F. – Gas Mark 7) until crisp and brown.
2 Reheat the spinach with the butter and cream.
3 Arrange in the hot tartlet cases.
4 Put the smoked salmon on to cold plates, garnish with lemon.
5 At the last minute arrange the tartlet cases on the plates.

Sardines gratinées

cooking time: 5 minutes

you will need:

fingers fried bread or toast
sardines
curry powder
chopped parsley
Worcestershire sauce

1 Fry or toast bread.
2 Arrange sardines in oil on fingers of bread.
3 Brush with oil from can, or with melted butter.
4 Sprinkle with curry powder and chopped parsley together with a few drops Worcestershire sauce.
5 Heat under the grill, and serve with crisp salad.

Crab mornay

cooking time: 15 minutes

you will need:

½ pint cheese sauce (see page 88)
2 medium sized crabs
lemon
parsley

1 Make the cheese sauce, and put half of this at the bottom of 4 small dishes.
2 Cover with flaked crab meat and rest of the sauce.
3 Heat under the grill and serve with lemon and chopped parsley to garnish.

Variations:

Lobster mornay – recipe as for Crab mornay above, using flaked lobster meat.
Canned lobster could be used instead.

Seafood scallops – recipe as Crab mornay above, but use a selection of cooked or canned fish and shellfish; put into the dishes and top with tiny croûtons of fried bread.

Anchovy olives

no cooking

you will need:

anchovies
green olives
brown bread and butter

1 Wrap fillets of anchovies round olives.
2 Serve on thin fingers of brown bread and butter.

Salmon pyramids

no cooking

you will need:

8 oz. cooked or canned salmon
2 hard-boiled eggs
little mayonnaise
salad to garnish

1 Blend the flaked salmon with the chopped hard-boiled egg white.
2 Bind with mayonnaise.
3 Form into pyramid shapes and serve on crisp lettuce with sliced tomatoes, cucumber etc.
4 Sprinkle the finely chopped yolk over the top.

Cod's roe pâté

cooking time: 20 minutes

you will need:

cod's roe
butter or margarine
lettuce
pepper
chopped chives (optional)

1 If cod's roe is uncooked, steam in butter paper for about 20 minutes and allow to cool.
2 Remove from the skin and blend with a little butter or margarine and pepper.
3 Serve on crisp lettuce with brown bread and butter, or crisp toast and butter.
4 Chopped chives can be added if wished.

Variation:

Salmon pâté – use cooked salmon instead of cod's roe, but give the pâté additional flavour with lemon juice and garlic salt.

Ham rolls

no cooking

you will need:

2 oz. cream cheese
2 teaspoons chopped gherkins
2 teaspoons chopped capers
2 teaspoons chopped parsley
8 small strips cooked ham
lettuce
tomatoes
mayonnaise (optional)

1 Mix cheese with gherkins, capers and parsley.
2 Spread over the ham and roll up.
3 Serve on bed of salad, covering with little mayonnaise if wished.

Spiced tongue

no cooking

you will need:

1 small onion or few cocktail onions
4–6 oz. cooked tongue
1 teaspoon Worcestershire sauce
1 tablespoon chutney
watercress

1 Chop the onion very finely.
2 Cut the tongue into neat pieces.
3 Mix with onion, sauce, and chutney.
4 Serve on bed of watercress.

Variation:

Spiced sausage – recipe as spiced tongue, above, but use cooked sausage or frankfurters.

Chicken walnut salad

no cooking

you will need:

cooked chicken
mayonnaise
chopped walnuts
strips of red or green peppers

1 Moisten small strips of cooked chicken with mayonnaise.
2 Add coarsely chopped walnuts.
3 Garnish with strips of pepper.

Variation:

Curried chicken hors d'oeuvre – blend a little curry powder with the mayonnaise, toss cooked rice in this, then add the chicken etc. as recipe above for chicken walnut salad.

Croque monsieur

cooking time: few minutes

you will need:

bread and butter
5 slices of cheese and ham
beaten egg
little milk
fat

1 Make sandwich of bread and butter, with slices of cheese and ham.
2 Dip in beaten egg, mixed with a little milk.
3 Fry steadily in hot fat until crisp and golden brown on either side.
4 Serve at once.

Carrot salad

no cooking

you will need:

carrots
mayonnaise
parsley
chives
shredded cabbage

1 Grate good sized raw carrots coarsely.
2 Blend with mayonnaise, chopped parsley and chopped chives.
3 Serve on bed of shredded cabbage.

Beetroot salad

no cooking

you will need:

cooked beetroot
oil
vinegar
chives or spring onions
watercress

1 Dice beetroot.
2 Blend, without making too moist, with little oil and vinegar.
3 Add finely chopped chives or spring onions.
4 Serve on bed of watercress.

Variation:

Beetroot and apple salad – use equal quantities of cooked beetroot and dessert apple. Dice the beetroot and apple (peel this if wished) then proceed as recipe above.

Asparagus salad

cooking time: 20–25 minutes (if using fresh asparagus)

you will need:

asparagus tips (cooked or canned)
oil
vinegar
lettuce
chopped hard-boiled egg

1 Toss the cooked or canned asparagus tips in well-seasoned oil and vinegar.
2 Arrange on a bed of crisp lettuce and garnish with chopped hard-boiled egg.

Mixed vegetable or Russian salad

cooking time: 10–25 minutes

you will need:

vegetables (carrots, turnips, potato, also peas, beans etc. if possible)
mayonnaise
chopped parsley

1. Dice vegetables finely.
2. Cook steadily in boiling water.
3. Drain and blend with mayonnaise while still hot.
4. Garnish with chopped parsley when cold.

Celery salad

no cooking

you will need:

crisp celery
chopped walnuts
chopped parsley
mayonnaise

1. Chop celery finely.
2. Mix with walnuts, parsley and mayonnaise.

Variation:

Danish celery salad – crumble a little Danish Blue cheese, add to mayonnaise as recipe.

Cucumber salad

no cooking

you will need:

cucumber
vinegar and seasoning or oil and vinegar or lemon juice
chopped parsley

1. Slice cucumber thinly.
2. Blend with vinegar and seasoning or oil and vinegar or lemon juice.
3. Lift from the dressing just before serving, and top with chopped parsley.

Potato salads

cooking time: 10–25 minutes

you will need:

old or new potatoes
mayonnaise or oil and vinegar
chopped chives or grated onion
parsley
paprika pepper

1. Cook potatoes steadily until just soft – dice if wished for speedy cooking, but be careful they do not break.
2. Drain carefully, and blend – WHILE STILL HOT – with mayonnaise or oil and vinegar.
3. Blend with chopped chives or finely chopped or grated onion and chopped parsley.
4. Garnish with more parsley and paprika pepper.

Variations:

Mix dressed potatoes with:
(a) Chopped gherkins, capers and celery.
(b) Chopped celery, grated dessert apple and sultanas.
(c) Chopped celery and diced cucumber.

Tomato salad

no cooking

you will need:

tomatoes
oil
vinegar
seasoning
chopped chives or spring onions

1. Slice tomatoes thinly, and blend with oil and vinegar, season well.
2. Garnish with chopped chives or spring onions.

Variation:

Tomato and pepper salad – use 1 green and 1 red pepper to each 3 tomatoes. Prepare the tomatoes as above, then cut the peppers into thin rings, discarding core and seeds. Arrange on long dishes and garnish as above.

Cole slaw

no cooking

you will need:

crisp cabbage
sultanas
chopped nuts
mayonnaise
lemon juice

1. Shred cabbage finely.
2. Mix with sultanas, chopped nuts, mayonnaise and a little lemon juice.

Spiced cole slaw

no cooking

you will need:

crisp cabbage
lemon juice
oil
1 teaspoon chilli sauce or Worcestershire sauce
shredded red pepper
chopped gherkins
capers
chopped celery (optional)

1. Shred cabbage finely.
2. Blend with lemon juice, little oil, chilli sauce or Worcestershire sauce.
3. Mix with finely shredded red pepper, chopped gherkins, capers and chopped celery when in season.

Soups

Among the recipes which follow, you will find several of the easier-to-make soups, as well as a number of more substantial recipes, which can turn a light snack into a good main meal. When making and serving soup, remember:

1 Take a little time and trouble to garnish soups to make them look more colourful.
2 Light coloured soups, such as cream soups look attractive if both chopped parsley or paprika pepper are sprinkled over the top, or you can use very finely chopped egg yolk.
3 Dark coloured soups, such as meat soups need a light garnish. Grated cheese, chopped egg white, fried croûtons of bread are effective.
4 Always make sure the soup is very hot before serving. If you wish to keep it hot for an extended period of time, without it becoming too thick or burning on the bottom of the pan, transfer it to the top of a double saucepan.
5 A pressure cooker is an ideal way of making stock or soups, particularly those which normally need prolonged cooking. I have therefore, included recipes for pressure cooked soups.

Lentil soup

cooking time: 2 hours

you will need:

8 oz. lentils
seasoning
3 oz. onions
3 pints cold water
1–2 cloves (optional)
1 teaspoon salt
small bacon bone
strips of streaky bacon
croûtons

1 Soak lentils overnight in water. Season.
2 Put lentils into pan with sliced onion, water, cloves, salt and bacon bone. Cook steadily.
3 When lentils are soft, sieve.
4 Rinse pan, return the purée which you can thin with stock or thicken as necessary. Season.
5 Garnish with croûtons of fried bread and crispy streaky bacon when serving.

Variations:

Curried lentil soup – blend the lentils at stage 2 in the recipe above, with 2–3 teaspoons curry powder or curry paste. Return to the pan, adding 2 oz. sultanas, pinch sugar, piece of apple and ingredients as lentil soup, continue as recipe.

Green pea soup – as recipe for lentil soup using split peas instead of lentils and omitting cloves. Cooking time 1½–2 hours.

Vegetable chowder

cooking time: 1¼ hours

you will need:

2 large potatoes
2 large onions
small piece swede
small piece celeriac
½ clove garlic
finely diced celery
pinch mixed herbs
seasoning
good pinch celery salt
bay leaf
2 pints water or white stock

to garnish:

chopped watercress
little grated cheese
paprika pepper

1 Dice all vegetables very finely, and crush garlic.
2 Put into casserole with seasoning, bay leaf and liquid.
3 Cover with lid and allow about 1¼ hours in slow oven (300°F. – Gas Mark 2).
4 Garnish with watercress, cheese and pepper.

Variations:

Vegetable cream chowder – as above but use only 1¾ pints water or stock, and add ¼ pint thin cream before serving.

Vegetable ham chowder – as for vegetable chowder above, but add 2–3 oz. finely chopped ham or boiled bacon.

Fish and vegetable chowder – continue as recipe above and cook for about 45 minutes at stage 3, then add 8–10 oz. skinned, diced, raw white fish and continue cooking. Garnish as above, but serve with wedges of lemon.

Speedy chowders – use any of the recipes above, but grate, rather than dice the vegetables, and cook in a saucepan for about 20 minutes only. In the fish and vegetable chowder, add the fish 10 minutes before serving.

Beef and onion soup

cooking time: 1½ hours

you will need:

4 medium sized onions
1¾ pints good beef stock (or water with beef bouillon cubes)
seasoning
2 slices bread
2 oz. butter

1 Chop onions finely.
2 Put into casserole with stock and seasoning.
3 Cover with lid and cook for 1½ hours in slow oven (300°F. – Gas Mark 2).
4 Dice bread, fry in butter. Serve on soup.

Variation:

Paprika soup – use the recipe for beef and onion soup before, but blend 2–3 skinned, chopped tomatoes and 2 teaspoons paprika with the onions etc. at stage 2.

Chicken broth

cooking time: 2 hours

you will need:

1 large onion	2 pints water with 2 chicken bouillon cubes, or 2 pints chicken stock
2 carrots	2 oz. rice
2 large tomatoes	little chopped parsley
small pieces uncooked chicken	seasoning

1 Dice vegetables and chicken very finely.
2 Put into casserole with other ingredients.
3 Cover with a lid and cook for 2 hours in a very slow oven (275°F. – Gas Mark 1).

Variation:

Creamed chicken broth – follow directions above, cooking either in the oven for 2 hours or for 1 hour in a covered saucepan. Sieve the soup or emulsify in a warmed liquidiser goblet, put into a pan and reheat; then add about ¼ pint thin cream and a little extra seasoning.

Minestrone soup

cooking time: 2 hours

you will need:

3 oz. haricot beans	1 dessertspoon chopped parsley
2 oz. quick cooking macaroni	8 oz. tomatoes (fresh or canned)
1 oz. dripping or oil	8 oz. chopped cabbage
1 finely chopped or grated onion	water
piece chopped celery	seasoning
	1 oz. grated cheese

1 Soak the beans for 24 hours.
2 Simmer in about 1½ pints water until soft.
3 Boil macaroni for 7 minutes in salted boiling water.
4 Heat dripping and fry the onion, celery and parsley for 5 minutes.
5 Add chopped tomatoes, cabbage and 1 pint water and bring to the boil.
6 Put in the beans, macaroni and seasoning.
7 Simmer for 30 minutes.
8 Serve sprinkled with grated cheese.

Note: This soup is very thick.

Summer soup

cooking time: 20 minutes

you will need:

1 pint bottled or canned tomato juice	about 12 oz. mixed vegetables
	seasoning

1 Simmer the vegetables in the tomato juice un just tender, adding a little extra water if t mixture becomes too thick.
2 Season well and serve with cheese flavour biscuits.

Variations:

Tomato and cucumber soup – add 1 medium siz peeled cucumber to the tomato juice. Cut tl into thin shreds and simmer until just tender.

Turkish cucumber soup – simmer very thin slic of peeled cucumber in the tomato juice un tender. Allow to cool, then serve topped wi natural yoghourt.

Onion soup

cooking time: 15 minutes

you will need:

2 medium potatoes	½ oz. butter
bunch spring onions (not too large) **or** 2 good-sized onions	seasoning
	1½ pints stock or wat
	little cream

1 Chop both potatoes and onions very finely ar toss in the butter for about 5 minutes.
2 Add seasoning, stock or water and simmer f about 5 minutes.
3 Stir well so that you break up the potatoes t thicken soup, but there is no need to sieve it.
4 Add a little cream and serve at once.

To serve: Excellent topped with grated cheese

Cream of tomato soup

cooking time: 30–40 minutes

you will need:

1 lb. tomatoes	½ pint water
1 onion	seasoning
2 bay leaves	1 pint thin white sau (see page 88)
4 peppercorns	

1 Simmer the tomatoes and chopped onion t gether with bay leaves and peppercorns in tl water until quite soft. Season.
2 Rub through a fine sieve.
3 Heat the sauce and reheat the tomato purée.
4 Take both pans off the heat and make sure tl contents are not boiling.
5 Whisk together. This method stops the so curdling.

Cream of asparagus soup

cooking time: 25–30 minutes

you will need:

1 lb. asparagus
1 oz. butter or margarine
1 pint water
1 onion
seasoning
¾ pint thin white sauce (see page 88)

1 Cut the asparagus into small pieces.
2 Toss in the melted butter or margarine and cook for 5 minutes.
3 Add the water and chopped onion.
4 Simmer steadily until the asparagus is very soft. Season.
5 Rub through a fine sieve.
6 Reheat the asparagus purée and add to the hot sauce.
7 Continue as with cream of tomato soup.

Creamy potato soup

cooking time: 25 minutes

you will need:

approximately 1 lb. potatoes
½ pint water
seasoning
1 pint milk
2 oz. butter
little cream if wished
chopped chives **or** spring onion stems

1 Grate the peeled potatoes (this saves sieving).
2 Put into saucepan with the water and seasoning and cook for about 20 minutes until very soft (watch they don't become too thick and burn).
3 Add the milk, butter, cream and lots of seasoning.
4 Bring to the boil and stir until smooth consistency.
5 Garnish with the chives or onion stems.
6 Serve with fried bread cut into small pieces.

Variation:

Onion and potato soup – grate 2 large onions and add to the potatoes at stage 1 in the soup above.

Cream of mushroom soup

cooking time: 12 minutes

you will need:

8 oz. mushrooms*
2 oz. butter or margarine
2 oz. flour
1 pint water or stock
¾ pint milk
seasoning

* The stems of mushrooms could be used if wished.

1 Chop mushrooms, finely, unless straining the soup.
2 Melt butter or margarine in saucepan.
3 Fry mushrooms for 5 minutes, stirring to prevent them discolouring.
4 Stir in the flour and cook for 3 minutes.
5 Remove from the heat and gradually add water and milk.
6 Bring to the boil and cook until soup thickens.
7 Season and serve.

Cheese soup

cooking time: 10 minutes

you will need:

1 small thinly sliced onion
1 oz. butter
1 oz. plain flour
½ pint milk
½ pint stock or water
½ level teaspoon salt
pinch pepper
4 oz. Cheddar cheese (diced small)

1 Cook the onion in the butter for a few minutes.
2 Add the flour and cook for another minute.
3 Stir in the milk and stock or water, and bring to the boil.
4 Season and simmer gently for about 5 minutes.
5 Toss in the cheese and stir without boiling until melted.
6 Serve piping hot. Cheese soup can be reheated and used the next day.

Variation:

Carrot and cheese soup – use the recipe above, but add 2 large grated carrots at stage 4. Cook for only 5 minutes so the carrots remain fairly firm in texture then continue as the recipe.
If reheating the cheese soup do not allow to boil as this would make it curdle.

Artichoke soup

pressure cooking time: 20 minutes

you will need:

1½ lb. artichokes
½ pint water or white stock
¼ teaspoon vinegar
seasoning
½ oz. flour
¼ pint milk
½ oz. margarine or butter

1 Wash and peel the artichokes, if large cut into halves.
2 Put into the pressure cooker with the water, vinegar (to preserve the colour) and seasoning.
3 Put on the lid and bring steadily up to pressure.
4 Lower the heat and cook for 15 minutes.
5 Allow pressure to drop then remove lid.
6 Mix the flour with the milk, sieve or mash the artichokes.

continued

7 Return to the pan, together with the milk mixture, and bring slowly to the boil.
8 Add the margarine and any additional seasoning if necessary.
9 Cook for 2–3 minutes.

Celery soup

pressure cooking time: 20 minutes

you will need:

1 good head celery
¾ pint white stock or water
1 small onion
bunch fresh herbs (tied in muslin) or pinch dried herbs
seasoning
1 oz. flour
½ pint milk
1 oz. margarine

1 Cut the celery into small pieces and put into cooker with the stock, onion, mixed herbs and seasoning.
2 Put on the lid and bring steadily up to pressure.
3 Lower heat and cook 15 minutes.
4 Continue as with recipe for artichoke soup thickening in the same way.

Haricot bean soup

pressure cooking time: 35 minutes

you will need:

8 oz. haricot beans
1 pint water
2 onions
seasoning
1 oz. flour
½ pint milk
knob of butter

1 Soak the beans overnight.
2 Put into cooker with 1 pint of water in which they were soaked, chopped onions and seasoning.
3 Put on the lid and bring steadily to pressure.
4 Lower heat and cook for 30 minutes. If beans are very large, cook for 35 minutes.
5 Allow pressure to drop and remove lid.
6 Rub beans through a sieve and return to cooker.
7 Blend the flour with the milk.
8 Add to soup and bring to the boil.
9 Boil steadily for 3–4 minutes.
10 Add a knob of butter before serving.

Lentil soup

pressure cooking time: 17 minutes

you will need:

8 oz. lentils
2–3 sticks celery
2 medium sized potatoes
2 onions
1½ pints water
seasoning
bunch herbs, or good pinch dried herbs
¼ pint milk

1 Put all the ingredients except milk into pressure cooker.
2 Add salt, bring steadily to pressure.
3 Lower heat and cook for 15 minutes.
4 Allow pressure to drop.
5 Rub through a sieve.
6 Return to the cooker with the milk and reheat.

Fish Dishes

Choosing and cooking fish

Whatever method of cooking is used for fish, there are certain basic rules which are most important to remember:

1 DO NOT OVERCOOK fish. The moment the flesh breaks away from the skin or bones, the fish should be served.
2 DO NOT keep fish dishes waiting, since this will again overcook the fish, with a consequent loss of flavour and moisture.
3 TAKE GREAT CARE when choosing fish. When fresh, it should be firm, with no strong smell. The eyes should be bright, and scales firm and clear.
4 Shellfish should feel heavy for the weight. If they are surprisingly light, then it is certain they contain a high percentage of water, and you are not receiving good value for your money.
5 DO NOT STORE FISH FOR TOO LONG A PERIOD, EVEN IN A REFRIGERATOR.

Shallow frying fish

1 Coat the fish, if desired. For this type of frying, it is better to use seasoned crumbs and an egg, rather than a batter.
2 Make sure the fat is really hot before putting in fish.
3 Fry quickly on either side to brown the fish.
4 Then in the case of cutlets or thick pieces of fish, lower the heat to make sure it is done right through to the centre.

5 Drain well on absorbent or tissue paper before serving.

Sole meunière

cooking time: 10–15 minutes

you will need:

8 fillets sole
seasoning
squeeze lemon juice
very little flour
4 oz. butter

to garnish:

lemon rings
chopped parsley

1 Season the fish and give a squeeze lemon juice.
2 Dust lightly with the flour.
3 Heat the butter in a pan and fry fish carefully until golden brown, BUT DO NOT OVER-COOK.
4 Lift on to hot dish.
5 Heat remaining butter in pan until really golden brown, adding little extra lemon juice if wished.
6 Pour over the fish and top with lemon and parsley.

Lemon plaice

cooking time: 8–10 minutes

you will need:

8 small fillets plaice
seasoning
1 oz. flour
1 lemon

to fry:

2–3 oz. fat

1 Wash and dry the plaice, then coat in the seasoned flour blended with the grated rind of the lemon.
2 Fry steadily in the hot fat until crisp and golden brown, then drain on absorbent paper.
3 Remove the rest of the peel from the lemon and sprinkle tiny pieces of the pulp over the fish just before serving.

Deep frying fish

1 You can use either seasoned flour, egg and bread crumbs or batter for coating.
2 Make sure the fat is really hot before the fish goes in.
3 Brown the fish quickly in the hot fat.
4 Lower the heat to make sure it is done through to the centre.

Grilling fish

1 Make certain the grill is really hot before putting the fish underneath.
2 Brush both the grid of the grill pan with fat and brush the top of the fish with fat also.
3 Cook quickly until golden brown, turning thicker pieces of fish. Always keep fish very well 'basted' with butter or fat during the grilling period.

Grilled herring and mustard sauce

cooking time: 10–15 minutes

you will need:

4 large or 8 small herrings
little butter
lemon
parsley

1 Butter the herrings well.
2 To make sure the grill pan does not smell too much of the fish, it is a good idea to put greased foil over the grill pan and put the herrings in this.
3 Grill on both sides of the fish.
4 Serve with mustard sauce, garnished with lemon and parsley.

for the sauce:

2 oz. butter
1 oz. flour
½ pint water
1 tablespoon mustard
1 teaspoon vinegar
salt

1 Heat 1 oz. of the butter in a pan.
2 Stir in the flour and cook for several minutes.
3 Blend the mustard with the water until very smooth.
4 Add to the butter and flour and bring to the boil SLOWLY, stirring until smooth.
5 Add the vinegar, extra butter and pinch salt.

Grilled fish au gratin

Grill any chosen fish and when nearly cooked press a thick layer of grated cheese over the top of the fish, together with a few soft or crisp breadcrumbs. Return to the grill and cook until the cheese melts and browns.

Steaming fish

Most fish can be steamed, if wished, but one generally chooses flat fish, such as plaice, sole, fillets of haddock etc. One of the most popular methods of steaming fish is as follows:

1 Put the fish on a large plate, add seasoning, a squeeze of lemon juice, knob of butter, then cover with a second plate. *continued*

2 Stand over a pan of boiling water, and cook steadily for approximately 10–12 minutes for thin fillets of fish, up to 20 minutes for whole fish or thick fillets.
3 If wished, milk can be poured over the fish before cooking, and this could be used as a basis for a sauce.
4 This method of cooking is recommended for invalids, since the fish is so easily digested. It does however look rather colourless, so that a garnish of chopped parsley, lemon etc. (if allowed), makes it more appetising.

Savoury steamed fish

Put the fish on a large plate as stage 1 above, but instead of adding seasoning and butter, cover with several tablespoons hot soup, e.g. cheese, mushroom or tomato, or any of the shellfish soups. Continue as recipe above.

Boiling or poaching fish

While the term 'boiling' is used to describe the method of cooking fish in water, the word BOIL is actually incorrect, since the fish should be cooked in water BELOW BOILING POINT. If you boil the fish it breaks and becomes dry in texture. It is therefore better to poach it gently in well-seasoned water, or fish stock. The stock is made by first cooking the bones and skin of the fish with seasoning and a bay leaf. All white fish as well as salmon and mackerel can be cooked by this method. White fish should be poached as follows:

1 Put the fish into the cold, seasoned water or stock.
2 Allow to come to about 180°F. (the point when one or two bubbles can be seen on the surface of the water).
3 Simmer steadily, allowing about 7 minutes per lb. (10 minutes if about 1 lb. only).
4 Drain carefully, and serve with melted butter or sauce.

To poach salmon

In order to keep the particular moist texture and colour of fresh salmon, it is best to wrap it in buttered or oiled paper before the poaching process. Poach salmon as follows:

1 Oil or butter a good sized sheet of greaseproof paper.
2 Put the salmon on this, adding seasoning and a squeeze of lemon juice.
3 Tie the paper round the salmon, making a neat parcel.
4 Put into a pan of cold water, with a little oil or butter and lemon juice in the water (vinegar could be used instead).
5 Bring steadily to the boil.
6 With a very small piece of salmon, remove from the heat at once.
7 Put a lid on the pan and allow the fish to cool in the liquid.
8 If cooking a larger piece of salmon, continue to simmer gently, allowing 10 minutes per lb. When cooked, allow the salmon to stand in the water for a short time, then lift out, and unwrap.

Skate with cream sauce

cooking time: 15 minutes

you will need:

4 portions of skate
1 oz. butter
1 oz. flour
½ pint milk
2 tablespoons cream
hard-boiled egg
2 teaspoons chopped chives or spring onions
parsley
½ teaspoon grated lemon rind
little lemon juice

stock for cooking fish:

seasoning
parsley
onion
water

1 Put skate into cold salted water.
2 Bring to boil and skim.
3 Add sprig of parsley and onion.
4 Simmer for just 10 minutes.
5 Meanwhile, make sauce of butter, flour and milk.
6 Add cream, chopped hard-boiled egg and other ingredients.
7 Strain fish and put on to hot dish.
8 Cover with sauce.
9 Serve with creamed or new potatoes and young carrots.

Variation:

Fish pie – follow the recipe for Skate with cream sauce, but cook any white fish you like. Put the fish and sauce into a pie dish, top with creamy mashed potato and bake.

Mock lobster salad

cooking time: 10 minutes

you will need:

approximately 1½ lb. skate
mayonnaise
little tomato ketchup
2–3 drops anchovy essence (optional)
lettuce
tomatoes
radishes, etc.

1 Boil fish as in recipe for skate with cream sauce making certain you do not overcook fish.
2 Blend a little tomato ketchup (or purée) into mayonnaise to give a faint pink colour.
3 Add anchovy essence if wished.
4 Coat flaked fish with mixture.
5 Serve on a bed of lettuce garnished with tomatoes, radishes, etc.

Variation:

Italian fish salad – recipe as above, using any white fish, but cook this in seasoned white wine at stage 1 instead of water and cook until tender. Use any white wine left over instead of tomato purée to add to the mayonnaise stage 2. Serve garnished with olives, green pepper and tomatoes.

Table for baking fish

Baking fish is a simple and tasty way of cooking it, but DO NOT overcook, as so much of the flavour will be lost. Correct times and oven temperatures for baking fish are given below.

Type of fish	Cooking time
Fillets, thin	approximately 15 minutes in moderate to moderately hot oven (375°F.–400°F. – Gas Mark 4–5)
Thicker cutlets	approximately 20–25 minutes, oven temperatures as above
Whole fish:	
Herrings	25 minutes
Codling, Haddock etc.	up to 40 minutes, oven temperatures as above

Plaice with mushroom cheese sauce

cooking time: 15–20 minutes

you will need:

8 fillets plaice
salt and pepper
1 oz. butter
juice ½ small lemon
1 can condensed cream of mushroom soup
¼ can liquid (made from fish stock and water)
3 oz. grated cheese
pinch pepper

to garnish:
paprika pepper
parsley

1 Season each fillet and roll into a curl.
2 Place in a well-buttered fireproof dish, and sprinkle with lemon juice.
3 Cover and bake in a moderate oven (375°F. – Gas Mark 4) for 15–20 minutes.
4 To make the sauce, empty the mushroom soup into a saucepan, add stock and mix well. Heat thoroughly.
5 Add cheese and pepper, and coat fish.
6 Decorate with a thin line of paprika pepper and a sprig of parsley.

Fish mornay

cooking time: 20 minutes

you will need:

4 fillets white fish (filleted sole, plaice, whiting—or, for economy, fillets fresh haddock or cod)
½ pint cheese sauce (see page 88)
little extra butter

to garnish: lemon and parsley

1 Either bake the fish in a little of the milk and butter from sauce and seasoning, until tender, or grill it.
2 Make the sauce, adding the stock from the fish at the last minute.
3 Arrange the fillets of fish on a dish.
4 Pour over the sauce and garnish with lemon and parsley.

Stuffed cod or haddock with mushroom stuffing

cooking time: 30–35 minutes

you will need:

1 fish weighing about 2½ lb.

for stuffing:

4 oz. mushrooms
1 oz. butter or margarine
2 teaspoons chopped parsley
grated rind 1 lemon
1 dessertspoon lemon juice
1 egg
4 oz. breadcrumbs
seasoning

to serve:

½ pint white, parsley or cheese sauce (see page 88)
few extra mushrooms

1 Remove head from fish.
2 Split it down the under-side (or get the fishmonger to do this for you).
3 Chop the mushrooms for the stuffing and mix with all the other ingredients. *continued*

4 Press into fish and tie or skewer into position.
5 Put into a greased dish, cover with greased paper.
6 Bake for approximately 30 minutes in the centre of a moderate oven (375°F. – Gas Mark 4) DO NOT OVERCOOK.
7 Test, and if fish is just coming away from skin it is cooked.
8 Lift on to a hot dish and garnish with grilled or fried mushrooms.
9 Serve with the hot sauce and fried potatoes, green peas or cauliflower.

Stuffed mackerel with paprika sauce

cooking time: 20 minutes

you will need:

4 medium sized mackerel

for stuffing:

2 oz. mushrooms
2 oz. breadcrumbs
2 teaspoons suet, margarine or butter
1 large skinned and chopped tomato
few drops lemon juice
seasoning

for sauce:

1 oz. margarine or butter
1 oz. flour
½ pint milk
salt
2 level teaspoons paprika pepper

1 Split the mackerel and take out the backbone.
2 Make the stuffing by mixing the finely chopped mushrooms, with the other ingredients, lemon juice and seasoning.
3 Put into the mackerel and secure with small cocktail sticks.
4 Bake in a well greased dish covered with greased paper for 15 minutes in centre of a moderate oven (375°F. – Gas Mark 4). If the fish are fairly large, they will take 20 minutes.
5 While the fish is cooking, prepare the sauce. Heat margarine in a saucepan.
6 Stir in the flour and cook for 3 minutes.
7 Remove pan from heat and gradually add cold milk.
8 Bring gently to the boil, stirring all the time, until the sauce thickens.
9 Add a little salt and paprika pepper, whisking to make sure it is thoroughly mixed.
10 Serve with the fish.

Note: Paprika is an acquired taste so if uncertain whether it will be liked cut down the quantity – but it is surprisingly mild.

Lenten fish pudding

cooking time: 3 hours

you will need:

for suet crust:

8 oz. plain flour
2 level teaspoons baking powder
½ teaspoon salt
pinch pepper
4 oz. finely shredded suet
cold water to mix

for filling:

1 oz. margarine
1 oz. flour
¾ pint milk
1 lb. cooked flaked cod
salt and pepper
2 tablespoons chopp[ed] parsley
little grated nutmeg

1 Well grease an 8-inch pudding basin.
2 Sieve plain flour, baking powder, salt and pepper.
3 Rub in suet lightly and mix to a light and spong[y] dough with cold water.
4 Turn on to floured board, cut off ⅔ of pastr[y] roll out to a round about ½ inch thick, dust wi[th] flour, fold in two and gather top edges to form bag, slip into pudding basin and work into plac[e].
5 Melt fat, add flour and cook without brownin[g].
6 Slowly add milk to form a smooth sauce.
7 Add fish, seasoning, parsley and nutmeg, pou[r] into lined basin.
8 Roll out remaining pastry to ½ inch thickne[ss] and cover right over rim of basin, pressing we[ll] round edges.
9 Trim the edge, cover with greaseproof paper an[d] a pudding cloth.
10 Boil or steam for 3 hours.

Variation:

Fish and vegetable pudding – follow recipe above but put 2 thinly sliced cooked carrots and chopped raw onions into the sauce at stage 7.

Picnic pasty

cooking time: 40–45 minutes

you will need:

1 can condensed green pea soup
8 oz. cooked cod **or** 4 hard-boiled eggs
3 tablespoons mashed potato
1 teaspoon chopped parsley
salt and pepper
8 oz. short crust pastry (see page 75)
little milk

1 Empty green pea soup into a pan.
2 Flake the fish and add to the soup (or choppe[d] hard-boiled eggs).
3 Add potato, parsley and seasoning, and hea[t] thoroughly.
4 Roll out pastry on a floured board in a larg[e] round about 9 inches in diameter.

5 Place soup mixture on to one half of the pastry.
6 Brush round the edge with milk, fold pastry over, seal edges and brush with milk.
7 Place on a greased baking sheet and bake in a moderately hot oven (400°F. – Gas Mark 5) for 40–45 minutes.

Variation:

Harvest pasty – use condensed mushroom soup instead of green pea soup; add 1 tablespoon chopped chives in addition to ingredients listed.

Lobster vol-au-vent

cooking time: 25–30 minutes

you will need:

8 oz. puff pastry (see page 76)
egg or milk to glaze
1 medium sized lobster
little cream
seasoning
lemon to garnish

for sauce:

1 oz. butter
1 oz. flour
$\frac{1}{3}$ pint milk

1 Roll out the pastry to make a large circle or oval.
2 Make a smaller circle or oval in the centre pressing half-way through the pastry.
3 Brush the top with a little milk or egg if possible.
4 Bake for a good 10 minutes in the centre of a very hot oven (475°F. – Gas Mark 8).
5 Lower the heat for a further 10–15 minutes until the pastry is crisp and golden brown.
6 Meanwhile, make a sauce with the butter, flour and milk.
7 Remove pastry from the oven and with the tip of a sharp knife, remove the middle circle of pastry.
8 Return to the oven for a few minutes to dry out.
9 Flake the lobster meat and add to the sauce, together with the cream and seasoning.
10 Put hot filling into the hot pastry case and garnish with lemon, small lobster claws.
11 If serving cold, make sure that both pastry and filling are cold before they go together.

Shrimp or prawn mould

cooking time: 1 hour 10 minutes

you will need:

1 lb. cooked white fish
$\frac{1}{2}$ pint shelled shrimps or prawns
$\frac{1}{2}$ pint white sauce (see page 88)
2 eggs
seasoning

1 Chop fish and shrimps – mix with sauce, egg yolks and seasoning.
2 Fold in stiffly-beaten egg whites.
3 Put into buttered mould (choose fancy shape if possible).
4 Cover with buttered paper.
5 Either steam for 1 hour or stand in dish of water and cook in very moderate oven for 1 hour.
6 Turn out and serve hot with parsley or hard-boiled egg sauce, and garnish with mixed vegetables.
7 OR serve cold with mayonnaise, which can be delicately flavoured with anchovy, or tomato or horseradish cream. Garnish with lettuce, tomatoes, cucumber.

Fisherman's pie

cooking time: 40 minutes

you will need:

1–1$\frac{1}{4}$ lb. cooked white fish
2 onions – boiled and chopped
$\frac{1}{2}$–$\frac{3}{4}$ pint white sauce (see page 88)
seasoning
1 lb. mashed potatoes
little margarine
grated cheese
few prawns or shrimps

1 Mix flaked fish and onions into sauce.
2 Season and put into dish
3 Cover with lattice work of piped potatoes.
4 Brush with melted margarine and cover with grated cheese.
5 Bake for 25–30 minutes in moderately hot oven (400°F. – Gas Mark 5).
6 Garnish with the prawns and shrimps.

Fish medley flan

cooking time: 25 minutes

you will need:

6 oz. short crust pastry (see page 75)
2 large tomatoes
seasoning
about 8 oz. cooked fish **or** use canned tuna or salmon
about $\frac{1}{4}$ pint thick white sauce (see page 88)
3 tablespoons mayonnaise
1 can anchovy fillets
few shrimps or prawns
2 hard-boiled eggs
parsley

1 Bake pastry 'blind' in a flan tin until golden in colour.
2 Arrange the sliced and seasoned tomatoes over the bottom of the flan.
3 Flake the fish and blend with the sauce, mayonnaise and half the chopped anchovy fillets and prawns.
4 Add 1 of the chopped hard-boiled eggs.
5 Spread over the sliced tomatoes, and top with

remaining anchovy fillets, prawns, chopped hard-boiled egg and parsley.

Variation:

Economy fish flan – omit the anchovy fillets and shrimps or prawns from the recipe before, and used diced cooked carrots, cooked peas and diced cooked potatoes instead.

Casserole dishes with fish

This method of cooking fish, is perhaps less usual than grilling, frying etc.; however, you should try it as it does result in a dish with a great deal of flavour.

Often it is not necessary to make a sauce, since the ingredients cooked with the fish provide their own liquid.

Here is one very simple way of making a **casserole dish with white fish:**

1 Put fish into buttered casserole.
2 Pour over a good flavoured soup – such as asparagus, cream of tomato, mushroom, etc.
3 Cover with foil or a lid and cook until the fish is tender.

Cod steaks with celery and bacon

cooking time: 35–40 minutes

you will need:

3 or 4 cod steaks (approximately 1 inch thick)
1 small head celery
4 oz. streaky bacon
1 teaspoon chopped parsley
little milk
1 oz. butter or margarine
1½ level tablespoons flour
salt and pepper

1 Sprinkle fish steaks with salt and leave for 30 minutes.
2 Wash and chop celery and cook in boiling salted water until tender.
3 Strain, saving stock.
4 Dice and fry bacon lightly.
5 Arrange the fish steaks in a greased ovenproof casserole dish and add any fish liquid to the celery stock.
6 Mix bacon, celery, parsley and pile on to the cod steaks.
7 Cover with lid or greased paper and bake in a moderate oven (375°F. – Gas Mark 4) for 35 minutes.
8 Add milk to the celery liquid to give ½ pint.
9 Make a sauce of the butter, flour, pepper and liquid.
10 Pour over fish and serve.

Variation:

Spanish cod – use 1 green pepper and 1 red pepper instead of celery, cut the peppers into rings and cook at stage 2 until tender. Flavour the sauce with garlic salt at stage 9.

Cod casserole

cooking time: 30–35 minutes

you will need:

1½ lb. cod fillets
1 small onion
1–2 cloves (optional)
1 bay leaf
salt and pepper
2 oz. margarine
2 oz. flour
½ pint milk
1 tablespoon chopped parsley
2 oz. cheese
2 hard-boiled eggs
3 tomatoes
little parsley for garnish

1 Put fish in pan with onion stuck with cloves, bay leaf and salt.
2 Cover with water and cook gently until tender.
3 Remove fish, extract any skin or bones, and cut into large pieces.
4 Melt fat in pan, stir in the flour and add milk and strained fish liquor to make a smooth sauce.
5 Add parsley, grated cheese, chopped hard-boiled egg and seasoning.
6 Grease a deep casserole.
7 Arrange alternate layers of fish and sauce, ending with a layer of sauce.
8 Decorate the top with quartered tomatoes and bake in a hot oven (425°F.–450°F. – Gas Mark 6–7) for 10–15 minutes.
9 Garnish with finely chopped parsley.

Haddock and mushroom casserole

cooking time: 40 minutes

you will need:

4 pieces fresh haddock
seasoning

for the mushroom stuffing:

2 oz. margarine
1 small onion
4 oz. mushrooms
8 tablespoons soft breadcrumbs
2 teaspoons chopped parsley
seasoning

1 First make stuffing. Heat margarine and fry very finely chopped onion in this.

2 Add finely chopped mushrooms (stalks as well), crumbs, parsley, seasoning.
3 Work together then press this on top of each piece of fish.
4 If you like a sauce, pour a little milk in the casserole.
5 Cover with a lid and bake for 40 minutes in moderate oven (375°F. – Gas Mark 4).
6 Use the milk to make a white or parsley sauce (see page 88). A cheese sauce also blends well with this dish (see page 88).

Variation:
Haddock and anchovy casserole – omit the mushrooms from the stuffing and use a can of anchovies instead, chop finely and add to the crumbs etc. Use the oil from the can and omit 1 oz. margarine.

Cod and onion Portugaise

cooking time: 1 hour

you will need:

4 portions of cod (fillet or steaks)
seasoning
4 medium sized tomatoes
2 large onions
¼ pint cider
2 teaspoons chopped parsley

for topping:

2 tablespoons grated cheese
2–3 tablespoons soft breadcrumbs
1 oz. margarine

to garnish:

parsley
lemon

1 Put seasoned cod into casserole.
2 Skin and slice tomatoes thickly, but slice onions very thinly.
3 Put cider into dish, then add onions, parsley and finally tomatoes.
4 Cover casserole with lid and cook for 1 hour in a very moderate oven (350°F. – Gas Mark 3).
5 Lift off lid and put cheese, crumbs and margarine on top.
6 Brown for a few minutes under a grill.
7 Garnish with lemon and parsley.

Cod Creole

cooking time: 50 minutes

you will need:

1 lb. filleted cod
salt and pepper
juice 1 lemon
1 oz. butter

for sauce:

1 oz. butter
1 oz. flour
¾ pint fish stock, or water with few drops anchovy essence
3 cloves
pinch mixed spice
½ teaspoon chilli sauce
4 tomatoes
parsley

to garnish:

paprika pepper
strips of red or green pepper

1 Lay the fillets in a greased casserole, season and sprinkle with lemon juice.
2 Dab 1 oz. butter on top, cover loosely with greased paper and bake slowly for 30 minutes.
3 Melt the butter in a pan, sprinkle in the flour and blend well.
4 Add fish stock, cook until smooth sauce.
5 Add cloves, spice and chilli sauce.
6 Peel and chop the tomatoes, and add them with the parsley.
7 Simmer for about 20 minutes.
8 When ready, pour over the fish, cover loosely again, and continue to bake in moderate oven for about 20 minutes.
9 Just before serving, sprinkle lightly with paprika pepper to add colour, and garnish with strips of red or green peppers.

Tomato and haddock casserole

cooking time: 30 minutes

you will need:

2 onions
3 oz. butter
2 tablespoons parsley
6 good-sized tomatoes
seasoning
1½–2 lb. fresh haddock
4 oz. breadcrumbs

1 Chop the onions very finely.
2 Spread some butter at the bottom of the dish.
3 Cover with half the chopped onion, parsley and sliced tomatoes. Season.
4 Arrange the fish, cut into convenient-sized pieces, on the tomatoes.
5 Cover with a layer of the remaining tomatoes, onion and parsley. Season.
6 Put crumbs over the top with rest of butter.
7 Cover with greased paper or foil.
8 Bake for approximately 25–30 minutes in the centre of a moderately hot oven (400°F. – Gas Mark 5).

Meat Dishes

Roasting meats

In the tables which follow, you will find instructions for the proper methods of roasting the most popular types and cuts of meat. However, it is also possible to roast some of the cheaper joints, providing you use a very LOW temperature, and allow at least twice to three times the normal period per lb.
There is also the question of the amount of fat to be used when roasting. During the past few years a great deal of emphasis has been placed on the fact that using a lot of fat is neither good nor necessary. Only a minimum amount is required to roast successfully, and in some cases none at all. The following tables indicate the amount necessary for different types of meat.

Tables for roasting meat

Beef

Do not put too much fat on beef since it will harden the outside of the roast. If cooking a sirloin cut in a covered roaster, or in foil, you will need no fat at all, and only a little fat is required for very lean pieces like topside.

Cut to choose Sirloin, Ribs, Fillet, Aitch-bone (good quality), Topside, Rump.

Cooking time 15 minutes per lb. plus 15 minutes over.

Well done: 20 minutes per lb., plus 20 minutes over, **or** 40 minutes per lb. in very slow oven.

Mutton or lamb

Lamb should be roasted with a small amount of fat. Mutton however, does not require any extra as there is generally a fair amount of fat on the joint.

Cut to choose Leg, Loin, Best end of neck (lamb), Shoulder, Breast, stuffed and rolled.

Cooking time 20 minutes per lb. plus 20 minutes over.

Pork

Do not put fat on pork when roasting, but to produce a crisp crackling, rub the skin with a little oil and sprinkle lightly with salt.

Cut to choose Loin, Leg, Bladebone, Spare rib.

Cooking time 25 minutes per lb. plus 25 minutes over.

Veal

Since this meat is very lean, it must have fat with it when being cooked, unless it is wrapped in greased paper or foil. Otherwise cover the top of the joint with a little fat and baste during cooking.
For a large joint, buy very fat bacon, and cut this into narrow strips. Insert these into a larding needle (a large carpet needle can be purchased, if the former is not available) and thread the strips through the joint. In this way, the meat will be kept tender and moist as it cooks.

Cut to choose Shoulder, Breast, Best end of neck, Loin, Fillet, Chump end of loin.
Cooking time 25 minutes per lb. plus 25 minutes over.

To make gravy for roast meat

cooking time: 5–10 minutes

1. When the meat has been roasted, lift on to a hot dish.
2. Pour away the surplus fat from the tin, leaving a good tablespoon, blend this with a little stock or water flavoured with a bouillon cube or gravy flavouring.
3. Bring to the boil.

Note: This makes a THIN gravy which is correct for a joint that is not stuffed.
For a THICK gravy, a good tablespoon of flour should be added to the fat and cooked for 2–3 minutes before adding stock.

Pot roast pork and cabbage

cooking time: 2 hours

you will need:

- 1 oz. butter
- 2 large onions
- 2 lb. pork (take this from leg or loin)
- seasoning
- pinch sage
- 1 good sized cabbage

1 Heat the butter and toss the thinly sliced onions in this.
2 Add the joint of pork and cook steadily in the pan until golden brown on all sides.
3 Add seasoning, sage and just about ¼ pint water.
4 Put a tightly fitting lid on the pan (or foil or greaseproof paper under the lid) and cook over a slow heat for about 1¼–1½ hours.
5 If worried about the water evaporating completely, you can lift lid and add more, but it should be just the right amount.
6 Add the finely shredded cabbage, toss in the fat and liquid at the bottom of the pan.
7 Continue cooking for a further 30 minutes until the cabbage is tender and the pork cooked.
8 Drain the cabbage from the liquid in the pan.
9 Arrange with the onion on a hot dish with the pork in the centre.
10 Use the fat, etc., at the bottom of the pan for gravy.
11 Serve with mashed turnips and boiled potatoes.

Variation:

Pot roast beef and vegetables – use the same method as for pork, but use a rolled piece of beef instead. Use water as in the recipe for pork or use red wine, at stage 3. Instead of cabbage at stage 6, add sliced potatoes and carrots.

Rolled pork

cooking time: 2½ hours

you will need:

3 lb. piece of pork belly

for stuffing:

2 oz. slice of bread, diced	½ teaspoon chopped thyme
1 oz. seedless raisins	8 oz. pork sausage meat
1 stick celery or chicory	salt and pepper
1 small chopped onion	1 beaten egg

1 Bone and flatten the pork.
2 Mix together all the stuffing ingredients, spread over the pork, roll up and tie securely.
3 Place the bones on top.
4 Bake in an open roasting tin in a very moderate oven (350°F. – Gas Mark 3) for 2½ hours.

Stuffed breast of lamb

cooking time: 1¼ hours

Breast of lamb is very economical to buy, although many people dislike the fact that it is rather fat. If, however, you use a stuffing that absorbs some of the fat content, it will be a great help and the flavour of the meat is excellent. If boning and rolling, ask the butcher to remove the bones. They can be used as a base for stock when making soup or gravy. This stuffing is economical and very good.

you will need:

1 good-sized breast of lamb

for stuffing:

8 tablespoons breadcrumbs	1 tomato
1 oz. rolled oats	1 egg
2 large onions	little chopped parsley
	seasoning

1 Mix all the ingredients together. The onion should be chopped very finely and the tomato skinned and chopped.
2 Spread over the lamb and roll firmly.
3 Roast for approximately 1–1¼ hours in a moderately hot oven (400°F. – Gas Mark 5).

To vary:

Instead of the stuffing above try:

Sausagemeat and kidney – blend about 12 oz. sausagemeat with 1–2 chopped lamb's kidneys, good pinch sage and seasoning.

Sage and apricot – use a packet of sage and onion stuffing instead of breadcrumbs in the recipe and add about 4 oz. chopped canned apricots instead of the onions and tomato, bind with the egg, parsley, seasoning and a little apricot juice.

Roast stuffed breast of lamb

cooking time: depending on size of joint

you will need:

1 breast lamb (boned)
1 oz. dripping or lard

for stuffing:

8 oz. sausagemeat	salt and pepper
1 small onion, chopped	2 oz. fresh breadcrumbs
1 dessertspoon chopped parsley	

1 Wipe the meat with a damp cloth.
2 Trim away any excess fat.
3 Mix together the sausagemeat, onion, parsley, seasoning and breadcrumbs.
4 Spread the stuffing on the meat.
5 Roll up loosely and tie securely with string.
6 Place in a roasting tin with the dripping.
7 Roast in a moderate oven (375°F. – Gas Mark 4) allowing 40–45 minutes per pound.

Gourmet-style roast leg of lamb

cooking time: depending on size of joint

you will need:

1 leg lamb
1 clove garlic
cooking oil
salt and pepper
2 tablespoons flour
1 oz. dripping or lard
¼ pint orange juice
3 tablespoons demerara sugar

1 Wipe the joint with a damp cloth.
2 Rub the joint with a cut clove of garlic then make small incisions in the skin of the joint and insert slivers of garlic.
3 Brush the skin over with oil, then dust with seasoned flour.
4 Place the joint in a roasting tin with the dripping and roast in a moderate oven (350°F. – Gas Mark 3) allowing 25–30 minutes per pound.
5 When half cooked, sprinkle the meat with half the orange juice.
6 Repeat ten minutes later, then ten minutes before the end of the cooking time sprinkle the meat with sugar.
7 Remove garlic before serving.

Variations

Pineapple glazed lamb – use canned pineapple juice with a little fresh lemon juice instead of orange juice.

Tomato glazed lamb – use canned or bottled tomato juice instead of orange juice and only 1 tablespoon sugar.

Crown roast

cooking time: approximately 1¼–1½ hours

you will need:

loin of lamb 4–4½ lb. shaped into a crown (the butcher will do this for you)

for stuffing:

2 oz. dried apricots
3 oz. prunes
4 oz. breadcrumbs
1 cooking apple
1½ oz. nuts
grated rind and juice ½ lemon
1 tablespoon oil

for gravy:

¼ oz. cornflour
½ pint stock
seasoning

to garnish:

1 small can halved apricots
8–10 cherries
parsley

1 Soak apricots and prunes overnight.
2 Protect the tip of each rib bone with foil or greaseproof paper.
3 Brush the whole of the loin with a little oil.
4 Mix all the ingredients for the stuffing togeth and bind with the lemon juice and oil.
5 Place in the centre of the loin and cook for 1¼–1 hours in a moderately hot oven (400°F. – Ga Mark 5).
6 When cooked, remove the foil or greaseproc paper.
7 Place the crown roast in a serving dish and kee warm while making gravy.
8 Drain any excess oil from the roasting tir leaving about a dessertspoon.
9 Add the cornflour and cook for 1 minute.
10 Add the stock, bring to the boil and boil for minutes stirring all the time.
11 Season to taste.
12 To serve, place a cutlet frill on each rib, an garnish the crown roast with apricots, cherrie and parsley.
13 Serve the gravy separately.

Mint-glazed shoulder of lamb

cooking time: depending on size of joint

you will need:

1 shoulder lamb
salt and pepper
1 oz. dripping or lard
3 tablespoons honey
1 tablespoon chopped mint

1 Season joint with salt and pepper and place in a roasting tin with the dripping.
2 Roast in a moderate oven (375°F. – Gas Mark 4) allowing 25–30 minutes per pound (or as given in table, page 22).
3 Mix the honey and mint together.
4 30 minutes before the end of cooking time remove the joint from the oven and coat with the honey mixture.
5 Return to the oven to finish cooking.

Gammon steak and pineapple

cooking time: 30 minutes

you will need:

4 thick slices gammon 1 inch thick
1 small can pineapple slices
4 cloves
little oil
1 level teaspoon dry mustard
1 level teaspoon cornflour

1 Trim the rind from the gammon and arrange 4 slices pineapple on top.
2 Spike the gammon fat with the cloves.
3 Brush with oil, sprinkle with mustard and cornflour, then place in an ovenproof dish.

4 Pour over the pineapple juice from the can.
5 Bake for 20–30 minutes in a moderately hot oven (400°F. – Gas Mark 5).
6 When cooked, remove cloves and put gammon and pineapple on serving dish.

Variations:

With glazed apple rings – top with cored, but not skinned rings of dessert apple at stage 1 and use either apple or orange juice at stage 4.

With sweet sour onion rings – cover each gammon steak with several thin onion slices at stage 1. Add the ingredients as recipe above at stage 3, plus a good sprinkling of brown sugar. Spoon over tomato juice at stage 4 instead of pineapple juice.

Roast stuffed shoulder of lamb

cooking time: depending on size of joint

you will need:
shoulder of lamb

for stuffing:
1 good-sized onion
2 rashers bacon (or 2 oz. bacon fat)
chopped celery or use diced raw potato and add ½ teaspoon celery salt)
6 tablespoons soft breadcrumbs
seasoning
1 tablespoon chopped parsley
good sized grated carrot

1 Ask the butcher to bone the shoulder and use the bone for stock. Wipe meat, sprinkle salt and pepper into 'pocket' where the bone was.
2 Fry finely chopped onion with chopped bacon or bacon fat.
3 Add all other ingredients.
4 Mix well and press into pocket of the meat.
5 Roast and serve with braised onions.

Stuffed lamb roll

cooking time: 2 hours

you will need:
1 large piece middle neck of lamb or 2 small pieces per person (your butcher will cut these for you)
mixed vegetables

for stuffing:
1½ teacups breadcrumbs
1 oz. rolled oats
2 large onions
1 tomato
1 egg
little chopped parsley
seasoning

1 Mix all stuffing ingredients together; the onion should be chopped very finely and the tomato skinned and chopped.
2 Press a little of the stuffing on to each piece of meat.
3 Put into a dish on a bed of finely sliced vegetables.
4 Cover with foil or buttered paper and cook for about 2 hours very slowly at 300–325°F. – Gas Mark 2.

Stuffed leg of lamb with spring vegetables

cooking time: depending on weight of lamb

you will need:
good-sized leg of lamb

for stuffing:
8 oz. breadcrumbs
4 oz. rather fat bacon
2 oz. chopped mushrooms
1 large finely chopped onion
little chopped mint or parsley
egg
seasoning

for serving:
young carrots
parsley, chopped
turnips
nutmeg
small onions
tomatoes
roast potatoes

1 Either get your butcher to bone the leg, or slit it down the side.
2 Mix the crumbs with the finely chopped bacon, mushrooms, onion, mint and egg.
3 Season well and press into the slit or cavity where the bone was.
4 Tie securely.
5 Roast in the usual way (see page 22).
6 Serve with whole carrots tossed in butter and chopped parsley, small turnips or mashed turnips formed into pyramid shapes and dusted with a little nutmeg, and boiled onion, baked tomatoes and roast potatoes.

Stuffed shoulder of lamb

cooking time: depending on size of joint

you will need:
1 shoulder lamb (boned)

for mushroom stuffing:
8 oz. mushrooms
1 small onion
2 oz. dripping or lard
4 oz. fresh breadcrumbs
1 tablespoon chopped parsley
salt and pepper
1 teaspoon Worcestershire sauce
1 egg

1 Wipe the joint with a damp cloth. *continued*

2 Prepare and chop the mushrooms and onion.
3 Sauté in 1 oz. of the dripping until tender.
4 Add the breadcrumbs, parsley, seasoning and Worcestershire sauce.
5 Bind together with beaten egg.
6 Stuff the joint with this mixture, then roll up and tie securely with string.
7 Place in a roasting tin with the remaining 1 oz. of dripping and roast in a moderate oven (375°F. – Gas Mark 4) allowing 35–40 minutes per pound, or as in tables, page 22.

Roast veal with creamed sauce

cooking time: 1 hour 40 minutes

you will need:

joint veal (approximately 3 lb.)
fat, bacon fat or butter for keeping moist
seasoning
2 tablespoons cream
¾ pint rather thin white sauce (see page 88)

1 Season veal and cover with plenty of fat and paper or foil (or insert strips of fat through meat with 'larding' needle).
2 Allow 25 minutes per lb. and 25 minutes over in a moderately hot oven (400°F. – Gas Mark 5).
3 30 minutes before the end of cooking time, take joint out of oven.
4 Remove paper and pour off most of the fat from the tin, leaving about 1 tablespoon.
5 Blend cream with sauce, pour into meat tin.
6 Baste joint with this.
7 Continue cooking as before, but lower heat to moderate, basting several times with the sauce.
8 Serve with mixed vegetables.

Variations:

Roast veal with paprika sauce – blend 2 teaspoons paprika with the cream and the sauce at stage 5, and when heated add about 3 tablespoons tiny cocktail onions.

Devilled roast veal – follow directions for roast veal with creamed sauce but add 1 tablespoon Worcestershire sauce, 2 teaspoons made mustard and good shake cayenne pepper to the sauce and cream at stage 5.

Roast stuffed bacon

cooking time: 2 hours

you will need:

about 2½ lb. piece bacon (long back is ideal)
knob margarine or butter

for stuffing:

8 oz. sausage meat
4 oz. breadcrumbs
grated rind 1 lemon
1 teaspoon mixed herbs
1 small chopped onion
1 tablespoon chopped parsley
1 egg

for the glaze:

1 teaspoon made mustard
1 tablespoon lemon juice
2 tablespoons brown sugar
1 tablespoon water

1 Soak bacon overnight, then dry.
2 Combine ingredients for stuffing, then spread on inner side of bacon and roll round.
3 Tie with string.
4 Put into covered roaster with little margarine or butter on the lean part of the bacon, or cover with buttered paper or foil.
5 Cook for 1½ hours in centre of moderately hot oven (400°F. – Gas Mark 5).
6 Take off lid or foil, remove rind of bacon.
7 Mix mustard, lemon juice, sugar and water.
8 Score the fat of the bacon and brush this glaze over it.
9 Continue cooking for a further 30 minutes.
10 Serve with baked apples or apple sauce, roast potatoes and a green vegetable.

Rice-stuffed roast cutlets

cooking time: 55 minutes

you will need:

4 cutlets
extra butter for paper bags
4 greaseproof paper bags or sheets of paper

for stuffing:

2 oz. cooked rice
1 tablespoon chopped parsley
2 tablespoons chopped onion
grated lemon rind
1 oz. butter or 1–2 rashers chopped bacon
egg
seasoning

1 Mix rice, parsley, onion, lemon rind, melted butter or chopped bacon together.
2 Add egg and seasoning.
3 Spread on top of each 4 cutlets.
4 Insert into 4 buttered bags, or wrap sheets of well buttered paper round cutlets.

5 Roast for approximately 35–45 minutes in moderately hot oven (400°F. – Gas Mark 5).

Variation:

Lemon raisin stuffed cutlets – use the recipe above, but add 3 oz. seedless raisins and the grated rind of 1 extra lemon to the rice at stage 1; use butter to blend.

Frying meat

Frying is a very popular way of cooking meat, and either a small amount of fat or deep fat can be used. Here are a few points to be kept in mind.

1 When SHALLOW FRYING always put the meat into HOT fat to seal the outside, then lower the heat for the remainder of the cooking time, in order to make sure it is cooked through to the centre.
2 Thick chops, steaks, etc. will need turning once or twice during cooking.
3 If you like a golden brown coating, you can either cover with well seasoned flour or coat with egg and crumbs. Fillets (i.e. slices) of veal or lamb cutlets, are often coated in this way.
4 DEEP FRYING methods are the same as for shallow frying. Make sure the fat is very hot before putting in the meat, then lower it at once to give the meat time to cook through to the centre.
5 When frying bacon, gammon, etc., you will find a better result is obtained if the meat is put into a cold pan. Unless frying very lean gammon, there is no need to add extra fat.

Parmesan cutlets

cooking time: 25 minutes

you will need:

8 small cutlets of lamb or mutton
1 egg
2 oz. grated Parmesan cheese
approximately 1 oz. crisp breadcrumbs
fat for frying
tomato sauce (see page 87)

1 Simmer the cutlets very gently for about 15 minutes in salted water or stock.
2 Drain and dry.
3 Coat with beaten egg and the cheese mixed with the crumbs.
4 Fry steadily until crisp and golden brown.
5 Drain and serve with tomato sauce, page 87, new or creamed potatoes and peas.
6 Garnish with cutlet frills.

Garnished lamb cutlets

cooking time: 15–20 minutes

you will need:

8 lamb cutlets
egg
breadcrumbs
fat for frying
8 rashers streaky bacon
4 lambs' kidneys
watercress

1 Coat the cutlets in egg and breadcrumbs.
2 Fry gently in hot fat until tender.
3 Fry the bacon rashers.
4 Cut the kidneys in half and coat in egg and breadcrumbs.
5 Fry until golden.
6 Arrange the cutlets on a dish.
7 Cover with the bacon and top with the kidneys.
8 Garnish with sprigs of watercress.

Variations:

Lamb cutlets Portuguese – do not coat the cutlets, just fry until *nearly* tender. Lift on to a plate, then add a medium can tomatoes, 1–2 chopped or grated onions and a crushed clove garlic to the fat in the pan (pour out any surplus fat if wished). Heat well, then return the cutlets to this sauce and complete cooking.

Lamb cutlets in creamed mushroom sauce – do not coat the cutlets, fry until just tender. Keep hot, pour away all fat except about ½ tablespoon, add 2–3 oz. thinly sliced mushrooms, ¼ pint thin cream, 3–4 tablespoons stock and seasoning. Simmer gently for 5 minutes then pour over the cutlets.

Peppered lamb cutlets – crush about 1 tablespoon peppercorns, press into both sides of the cutlets before frying; do not coat, just fry in fat until tender.

Luxury cutlets – do not coat the cutlets, fry in hot butter until nearly tender, then add 3 tablespoons dry sherry, 2 teaspoons chopped parsley, 2 oz. cooked ham (cut into thin strips). Heat with the meat for a few minutes then serve.

Cheese coated cutlets – fry the uncoated cutlets. Make a thick cheese mixture of 1 oz. butter, 1 oz. flour, ¼ pint milk, 3 oz. grated cheese, 2 oz. soft breadcrumbs and seasoning. Press on the cutlets then heat for a few minutes in the pan until the mixture starts to melt and serve at once.

Sausage-stuffed cutlets

cooking time: 20 minutes

you will need:

4 cutlets of lamb or mutton

for stuffing:

grated rind 1 lemon	1 egg
little chopped parsley	crumbs
8 oz. sausage meat	fat

1 Add grated lemon rind and parsley to sausage meat.
2 Press this over the top of each cutlet, keeping the shape intact.
3 Coat with beaten egg and crumbs.
4 Fry until crisp, brown and cooked.

Pork chop Milanaise

cooking time: 25–30 minutes

you will need:

2–3 oz. short-cut macaroni	1 onion
4 loin chops	3–4 tomatoes
seasoning	little stock
2 oz. margarine or butter	4 oz. breadcrumbs
	2–3 oz. grated cheese

1 Cook macaroni for approximately 7 minutes in boiling salted water.
2 Fry seasoned pork chops steadily in most of the hot butter or margarine.
3 When tender lift on to a hot dish and keep warm.
4 Fry the thinly sliced onion, then the tomatoes in the fat remaining in the pan, add a little stock.
5 When tender mix with the cooked and drained macaroni.
6 Arrange in a serving dish, topped with the pork chops, breadcrumbs and cheese and a little butter.
7 Brown under the grill. Serve with green salad.

Veal escalopes

cooking time: 10–15 minutes

you will need:

4 thin fillets veal	1 tablespoon chopped parsley
seasoning	olives
4 oz. butter	
juice 1 lemon	

1 Fry the seasoned fillets of veal in hot butter for about 4–5 minutes on either side.
2 Lift on to hot dish.
3 Cook butter left in pan with lemon juice until golden brown, add parsley.
4 Pour over meat. Garnish with olives.

Veal escalopes or fillets in cream sauce

cooking time: 15–20 minutes

you will need:

Ingredients as before, plus ⅓ pint thin cream	mushrooms

1 Cook the fillets veal as before.
2 Lift on to hot dish.
3 Add cream to butter remaining in pan and cook steadily until golden brown.
4 Whisk in lemon juice (do not boil) and add parsley.
5 Pour over meat and garnish with fried mushrooms.

Veal and ham fritter with fried eggs

cooking time: 15 minutes

you will need:

8 oz. veal	pinch sage
8 oz. ham or boiled bacon	2 eggs
8 oz. breadcrumbs	fat for frying
1 tablespoon chopped onion	4 eggs

1 Mince veal and ham.
2 Mix with half breadcrumbs, onion and sage.
3 Bind with a beaten egg.
4 Form into 4 flat cakes.
5 Roll in the second egg and crumbs.
6 Fry steadily in hot fat.
7 Fry the 4 eggs and serve on top of the 4 cakes.

Variations:

Veal and ham rissoles – as before but use cooked veal instead of uncooked veal, and to prevent the fritters becoming too dry use only 2 oz. crumbs to bind. Cooking time: 10 minutes.

Beef and ham rissoles – use minced beef instead of veal and flavour with 1–2 teaspoons made mustard.

Fried ham

cooking time: 10 minutes

you will need:

sprinkling of flour	1 teaspoon made mustard
4 thick slices cooked ham	2 tablespoons water
2 oz. butter	little brown sugar

1 Flour the ham lightly.
2 Heat the butter and toss the ham in this until piping hot.
3 Lift on to hot dish.
4 Add mustard, water and sugar to fat remaining in pan.
5 Pour over ham and serve.
6 Delicious with mushrooms, fried potatoes and eggs.

Corned beef cutlets

cooking time: 15 minutes

you will need:

4 oz. breadcrumbs
1 12-oz. can corned beef
seasoning
1 egg
crisp breadcrumbs
fat for frying

for sauce:

1 oz. margarine
1 oz. flour
¼ pint milk or stock

1 Make the sauce by heating the margarine in the pan, stirring the flour into the margarine and cooking for 2 minutes, then adding the liquid.
2 Bring to the boil and cook until thick.
3 Add the breadcrumbs and flaked corned beef.
4 Season well and form into cutlet shapes.
5 Coat with beaten egg and crisp breadcrumbs.
6 Fry in hot fat until crisp and golden brown.
7 Serve hot with fried tomatoes, peas and sauté potatoes or cold with salad.

Grilling meat

Many people prefer grilling meat to frying, particularly when cooking steaks. For successful grilling, keep in mind the following points:

1 Make sure the grill is hot before putting meat underneath.
2 Keep LEAN meat, such as steaks or fillets, well brushed with melted fat during the cooking process. Kidneys, liver etc. also need frequent brushing with fat, to prevent them from becoming too dry. Chops however, require very little.
3 Seal the outside of the meat under a high grill, then turn heat low to cook through to centre.
4 When grilling thick bacon rashers or slices of bacon or gammon DO NOT pre-heat the grill. Put the meat under the cold grill, then heat. This method prevents the fat from curling at the edges. Snip it with kitchen scissors to encourage it to become crisp.

Grilled lamb cutlets with Gruyère cheese

cooking time: 15–20 minutes

you will need:

8 small lamb cutlets
little butter
4 slices Gruyère cheese
parsley

1 Brush the lean part of the cutlets with a little melted butter.
2 Put on the grid on the grill pan and cook under the hot grill until brown and tender, turning as necessary.
3 Divide each slice of cheese in half then put on top of the cooked cutlets.
4 Put under the grill for a few minutes to melt the cheese.
5 Garnish with chopped parsley.

Grilled veal cutlets

cooking time: 15–20 minutes

you will need:

4 cutlets veal (cut from loin)
little melted butter or margarine
mushrooms
tomatoes
watercress

1 Heat grill, brush cutlets with melted butter.
2 Cook steadily under the grill, standing meat on grid.
3 Cook mushrooms and tomatoes in grill pan at the same time.
4 Garnish with watercress.

Variations:

Veal cutlets au gratin – grill as above, and when cutlets are cooked roll in a mixture of crisp crumbs and grated cheese and brown under grill on either side. Delicious served with creamy onion sauce (see page 87).

Veal cutlets mornay – grill the cutlets as above, arrange on hot dish and coat with cheese sauce (see page 88). Garnish with asparagus tips.

Veal cutlets in lemon sauce – grill as above and, when cooked, top each cutlet with soured cream, blended with grated lemon rind. Heat for 1–2 minutes only under the grill.

Piquant veal cutlets – blend the butter, at stage 1, with 1 tablespoon chutney, 1 teaspoon chilli sauce and 1 teaspoon made mustard.

Grilled stuffed kidneys with rice

cooking time: 15–20 minutes

you will need:

8 medium sized kidneys
8 rashers streaky bacon
little melted butter
4 oz. rice

for stuffing:

1 thick slice bread (crust removed)
1 small onion
1 can condensed tomato soup
pepper

1 Crumble bread and mix with chopped onion and $\frac{1}{4}$ can tomato soup. Season well.
2 Halve and stuff each of the kidneys and wrap securely in a rasher of bacon.
3 Switch grill on to high, brush grill pan with a little butter, place on kidneys and brush with butter.
4 Grill for 15–20 minutes, turning once during cooking.
5 Cook the rice in boiling salted water until tender, drain and dry.
6 Serve kidneys on the cooked rice.
7 Heat remaining tomato soup and serve separately as a sauce.

Variation:

Mushroom stuffed kidneys – use mushroom soup instead of tomato. Serve with pickled walnuts, as well as remaining mushroom soup.

Grilled gammon and pineapple

cooking time: 15 minutes

you will need:

4 slices of gammon
1–2 oz. butter
light sprinkling of sugar (if wished)
4 pineapple rings
parsley

1 Snip round the edges of the gammon, having removed the skin, at $\frac{1}{2}$-inch intervals.
2 Arrange on the grid of the grill pan, brushing the lean with melted butter.
3 Put under the grill, and light, then cook steadily, turning after about 5 minutes.
4 After 10 minutes cooking, sprinkle the meat with a little sugar, then arrange pineapple rings under the grill with the bacon.
5 Brush the pineapple with butter and sprinkle with sugar then continue cooking until both gammon and pineapple are golden brown and tender.
6 Garnish with parsley.

Variation:

Grilled gammon and peaches – follow previous recipe, but use peaches instead of pineapple. Garnish with glacé cherries.

Grilled tournedos of steak

cooking time: 6–12 minutes

you will need:

4 steak tournedos
butter
garnish (see below)

1 If the butcher has not made the fillets of steak into tournedos, you can do it yourself. Form them into neat rounds and tie them with fine string.
2 Heat the grill*, and brush the steaks liberally with melted butter, putting them on the greased grid of the grill pan.
3 Cook according to personal taste, allowing about 3 minutes on either side for underdone thick tournedos – up to about 6 minutes on either side for medium well done. For well done steaks, lower the heat slightly after the first few minutes.
4 Dish up the tournedos and garnish as below. The tournedos are generally served on crisp rounds of fried bread.

*The steaks can be fried in butter instead of grilled if wished.

Garnishes for tournedos:

Tournedos Africaine – serve with fried bananas and horseradish sauce.

Tournedos Dumas – cover cooked steak with onion sauce (see page 87) and grated cheese, then top with slices of ham and brown again under the grill. Serve with croquette potatoes.

Tournedos Othello – top with poached or fried egg.

Tournedos d'Orsay – top with olives and cooked mushrooms.

Variations:

Peppered steaks – either sprinkle both sides of the steak with black pepper or press crushed peppercorns against the meat before frying.

Steaks au poivre – this is a more elaborate version of the peppered steak above. Prepare and fry the peppered steaks, lift on to a hot dish, then add cream and brandy to the butter remaining in the pan. Heat and pour over the meat.

Steak Diane

Toss a finely chopped onion in about 3 oz. butter; flavour this with a little chopped parsley and Worcestershire sauce. Fry 3–4 very thin steaks in this mixture, lift out. Add a little brandy to the pan if wished, heat and pour over the meat and serve.

Baked meat dishes

The following recipes give a variety of baked meat dishes. The difference between baking and roasting is that in a baked dish, the meat is frequently pre-cooked, and then combined with other ingredients, as in Shepherd's pie. Or the meat may be cooked in with other ingredients in order to give it more flavour. This keeps it moist.

Beef Braemar

cooking time: 25 minutes

you will need:

2 sliced onions
2 oz. butter
4–8 oz. mushrooms
1 lb. diced roast beef
8 tablespoons fresh breadcrumbs
4 oz. grated Cheddar cheese
salt and pepper

1 Fry the onions in butter until golden.
2 Then add the mushrooms, cook for 2 minutes.
3 Arrange the meat, onion and mushrooms in an ovenproof dish.
4 Sprinkle with the breadcrumbs.
5 Top with the cheese, add salt and pepper.
6 Pour any remaining fat over the top and bake in oven (450°F. – Gas Mark 7) for about 15 minutes.

Variation:

Highland lamb – use diced cooked lamb instead of beef and add a little chopped mint at stage 3.

Curried shepherd's pie (1) (with uncooked meat)

cooking time: 1¼ hours

you will need:

2 onions
1 oz. fat
½ oz. flour
1 tablespoon curry powder
½ pint stock* (or small can tomatoes and little stock)
12 oz. freshly minced beef
seasoning
1 tablespoon chutney
1 lb. mashed potatoes

*less stock can be used if wished

1 Fry the onions (finely chopped) in the hot fat.
2 Add flour and curry powder.
3 Then add stock or tomatoes and stock.
4 Bring to the boil and cook until thickened.
5 Add the minced beef and cook gently stirring from time to time to 'break up' any lumps in the mince.
6 Add seasoning and chutney.
7 When the meat is tender, put into a pie dish.
8 Cover with the mashed potatoes (and little margarine and grated cheese if wished).
9 Brown in the oven until crisp.

Variations:

Curried shepherd's pie (2) (with cooked meat) – method as above, but at step 5 add the minced or diced cooked meat, heat for a few minutes only, then proceed with remainder of recipe. Cooking time approximately 30 minutes.

Tomato shepherd's pie – omit the curry powder in either of the two recipes and fry 3–4 skinned sliced tomatoes with the onions at stage 1. Use stock at stage 3.

Beef and tomato loaf

cooking time: 1½ hours

you will need:

12 oz. tomatoes
1½ lb. minced beef
3 rashers bacon
3 oz. rolled oats
seasoning
1 tablespoon chopped parsley or chives

1 Skin tomatoes and chop coarsely.
2 Mix with beef, finely chopped bacon and other ingredients.
3 Put into well greased loaf tin, and cover with greased paper.
4 Bake in the centre of a very moderate oven (350°F. – Gas Mark 3) for 1½ hours.
5 Turn out after standing for 15–20 minutes.

Devilled lamb fillets

cooking time: 35 minutes

you will need:

4 slices lamb cut from top of leg
seasoning
2 oz. butter
1 teaspoon made mustard
1 tablespoon Worcestershire sauce
3 tablespoons water
3–4 pickled walnuts
few pickled onions

1 Fry the seasoned slices of lamb in the hot fat for a few minutes on either side. *continued*

2 Transfer to shallow dish.
3 Blend mustard and sauce with boiling water.
4 Pour over meat adding chopped walnuts and onions.
5 Cook for about 25 minutes in a moderately hot oven.
6 Serve with rice, chutney and green vegetables.

Kidney and lamb toad-in-the-hole

cooking time: 45 minutes

you will need:

4 small lamb chops or cutlets
2 lamb's kidneys
4 small tomatoes
knob fat

for batter:

4 oz. plain flour
pinch salt
1 egg
½ pint milk and water

1 Sieve flour and salt.
2 Gradually beat in egg, milk and water.
3 Put cutlets into good sized baking dish and cook for 10 minutes in a really hot oven.
4 Add halved kidneys, tomatoes and fat and heat for further 5 minutes.
5 Pour over batter and cook for 15–20 minutes until well risen.
6 Reduce heat slightly and cook for further 10–15 minutes.

Variation:

Sausage toad-in-the-hole – use about 1 lb. sausages at stage 3, instead of meat. Cook for 10 minutes if large sausages, 5 minutes if small; then proceed as recipe.

Veal and vegetable cottage pie

cooking time: 1 hour 35 minutes

you will need:

1 oz. flour
approximately 1 lb. stewing veal
2 oz. dripping
stock or water with yeast extract
seasoning
8 oz. diced root vegetables
2 hard-boiled eggs
1½ lb. mashed potatoes
little margarine

1 Flour the diced veal well then fry in the hot dripping.
2 Add stock or water flavoured with yeast extract, to cover. Season.
3 Bring to the boil and cook until thickened.
4 Add vegetables and simmer gently for about 1¼ hours until the meat is tender.
5 Transfer to a pie dish – the mixture should be fairly stiff by this time – if not, spoon out some of the gravy, which can be served separately.
6 Cover the meat mixture with sliced hard-boiled eggs, then the potatoes.
7 Put knobs of margarine on top and brown for about 20 minutes in a moderately hot oven.

Savoury baked tripe

cooking time: 1 hour 40 minutes

you will need:

1 lb. dressed tripe
1 small onion
2 eggs
½ pint milk
little chopped parsley
pinch herbs
seasoning

1 Blanch the tripe (see below).
2 Cut the onion into small pieces and the tripe into narrow fingers.
3 Simmer gently together for about 1 hour until tender.
4 Strain and keep about ½ pint of the stock.
5 Beat the eggs, add milk and tripe stock.
6 Put the tripe in a casserole.
7 Cover with egg mixture, parsley and herbs.
8 Season well.
9 Bake for about 40 minutes in the centre of a very moderate oven (325°F.–350°F. – Gas Mark 2–3), standing the dish in another of cold water.

To blanch tripe: put into cold salted water, bring to the boil. Throw water away and continue cooking as indicated in individual recipes.

Variation:

Creamed tripe – proceed as stages 1–4 in recipe above. Make a white sauce as page 88 with ½ pint milk etc. and 2–3 tablespoons cream. Stir the tripe and onions in this with ¼ pint tripe stock and season well. Heat and serve with crisp toast or creamed potatoes.

Tongue rolls

cooking time: 15–20 minutes

you will need:

4 large slices tongue or 8 smaller thinner slices
4 large rashers bacon

for filling:

2 oz. breadcrumbs
2 tomatoes (chopped)
2 chopped gherkins
seasoning
little chopped parsley
1 egg

1 Halve the large slices of tongue and halve the rashers of bacon.
2 Mix all the ingredients for the stuffing together.
3 Spread over the pieces of tongue.
4 Roll firmly, then wrap round in the bacon.
5 Put into 4 greaseproof paper bags or 3 pieces of paper or foil.
6 Bake for 15–20 minutes in a hot oven (450°F. – Gas Mark 7) until the bacon is cooked and the tongue is really hot.
7 Serve with mixed vegetables.

Variation:

Curried tongue rolls – use the filling above, but blend ½–1 teaspoon curry powder and a small grated onion with the ingredients. If wished, fry the onion and curry powder in ½ oz. margarine first, to give a softer texture to the filling.

Ham and beef galantine

cooking time: 1½ hours

you will need:

12 oz.–1 lb. minced beef
4 oz. chopped ham
2 eggs
1 dessertspoon chopped chives
3–4 oz. breadcrumbs
seasoning

to glaze:

3 tablespoons mayonnaise
¼ pint aspic jelly
tiny pieces of gherkin
tomato
radish

1 Mix all ingredients together.
2 Place on greased tin or mould and cover top of tin with greased paper.
3 Either steam, or bake for approximately 1¼–1½ hours in a very moderate oven (350°F. – Gas Mark 3).
4 Turn out and cool.

To make glaze:

5 Stir the thick mayonnaise into the aspic jelly when cold.
6 Allow to stiffen slightly and coat the galantine.
7 Spread with knife dipped in hot water.
8 When firm, make a pattern of gherkin, tomato and radish.
9 Serve with salad platter of spring onions, halved tomatoes, sliced cucumber and potato salad.

Casseroles

Stewing meat in the oven

I have included a great variety of casserole dishes in this section because I think most people will agree that they are probably one of the easiest and most delicious ways of serving meat, poultry and even fish. And the great variety of attractive casseroles available today makes it possible to use the same dish for both cooking and serving.

When preparing a casserole, DO remember NOT to hurry things up by trying to cook it any more quickly than the recipe states. It is the long, slow cooking which produces the particularly pleasant flavour.

Beef and pepper ragoût

cooking time: 2¼ hours

you will need:

12 oz. potatoes
12 oz. chuck steak
12 oz. onions
1 green pepper
2 oz. butter
1 dessertspoon flour
½ pint stock (or water and bouillon cube)
3 tablespoons cheap red wine
3 large sliced tomatoes
salt and pepper
breadcrumbs

1 Butter a large casserole dish and line with sliced potatoes.
2 Lay the chuck steak over this.

continued

3 Prepare a sauce by finely slicing onions and green pepper and browning in butter.
4 Stir in the flour and add stock.
5 Add the wine.
6 Pour the sauce over the meat and cover with sliced tomato. Season.
7 Sprinkle with breadcrumbs, dot with butter and cook in a very moderate oven (350°F. – Gas Mark 3) for 2 hours. Turn the heat up to 400°F. – Gas Mark 5 for the last 20 minutes to brown the breadcrumbs.

Variation:

Pork and apple ragoût – use the recipe above, but substitute about 1 lb. lean pork (cut from the leg) for beef and use 2–3 skinned sliced dessert apples and a sprinkling of sage instead of the pepper.

Tomato beef casserole

cooking time: 3 hours

you will need:

little butter
2–3 lb. topside beef
6 onions
6 carrots
1 lb. tomatoes (skinned)
2 meat extract cubes
½ pint hot water
8 oz. spaghetti or macaroni
butter
grated cheese

1 Melt butter in a saucepan or casserole.
2 Add beef, browning on all sides.
3 Add sliced onions, carrots, tomatoes, beef cubes dissolved in water.
4 Cover and cook either on top of the stove or in a slow oven (300°F. – Gas Mark 2) for 3 hours.
5 Cook spaghetti or macaroni in boiling salted water until tender; drain, toss in a little butter and add a little grated cheese.
6 Serve round the joint and vegetables.

Beef and corn stuffed marrow

cooking time: 1 hour

you will need:

1 medium sized marrow
3 tomatoes
2 tablespoons oil or butter
1 finely chopped onion
1 lb. minced beef
1 heaped tablespoon flour
½ pint of beef stock
seasoning
1 can of corn

1 Wipe the marrow and scoop out the seeds.
2 Skin, chop and remove pips from tomatoes.
3 Melt oil or butter.
4 Add onion and fry gently.
5 Add mince and fry for 3–4 minutes.
6 Mix in the flour.
7 Add stock, seasoning and bring to the boil.
8 Simmer for 5 minutes.
9 Add corn and tomatoes and reseason if necessary.
10 Pile into marrow halves.
11 Place in a fireproof casserole and cover with a lid or foil.
12 Bake in a moderate oven (375°F. – Gas Mark 4) for 45 minutes or until cooked.
13 To serve, cut across the marrow into thick slices.

Spiced beef casserole

cooking time: 3 hours

you will need:

1–1¼ lb. stewing beef
1 oz. flour
½ teaspoon curry powder
½ teaspoon paprika pepper
½ teaspoon mixed spice
seasoning
2 oz. fat
¾ pint stock
1 clove garlic (optional)
1 tablespoon Worcestershire sauce
1 tablespoon vinegar
8 small onions
6 oz. diced celery

1 Cut the meat into 1-inch squares.
2 Mix flavourings with the flour and roll meat in this.
3 Fry in a hot fat for a few minutes, then lift into casserole.
4 Add stock, garlic, sauce and vinegar to residue of fat and flour left in pan. Season.
5 Bring to boil and cook for several minutes.
6 Put onions and celery into casserole and cover meat and vegetables with the sauce.
7 Put on lid and cook for approximately 3 hours in a slow oven (300°F. – Gas Mark 3).

Countryman's bacon casserole

cooking time: 1¼ hours

you will need:

1½ lb. potatoes
8 oz. onions
8 oz. cooking apples
½–1 oz. sugar
12 oz. lean cooked bacon
seasoning
good pinch chopped sage
1 oz. margarine

1 Peel and slice the potatoes and onions very thinly.
2 Peel and slice the apples fairly thickly, sprinkle with sugar.
3 Cut the cooked bacon (this can either be fried rashers or boiled bacon) into neat pieces.

4 Put half the well-seasoned potatoes and onions at the bottom of the casserole.
5 Top with the apples, bacon and sage then the rest of the onions. Cover with the potatoes and the margarine.
6 Cook in the centre of a very moderate oven (325–350°F. – Gas Mark 3–4) for approximately 1¼ hours.

Variations:

With stock – the above recipe gives a fairly 'dry' texture; if wished add about ¼ pint stock.

Tomato bacon casserole – add a thick layer of sliced tomatoes instead of the apples.

Chuck steak and mushroom casserole

cooking time: 2 hours

you will need:

4 chuck steaks (4–6 oz. each)
salt and pepper
1 oz. flour
8 oz. thinly sliced onion
4 oz. mushrooms
1 beef extract cube
¼ pint hot water

1 Ask your butcher for steaks cut 1 inch thick.
2 Roll the steak in seasoned flour.
3 Put the sliced onions and mushrooms into a casserole and place the steaks on top.
4 Dissolve the beef extract cube in hot water and pour over steaks.
5 Cover dish with foil or a well-fitting lid and cook in a slow oven (300°F. – Gas Mark 2) for 2 hours.

Lamb and butter bean casserole

cooking time: 3–4 hours

you will need:

1 small shoulder lamb
2 large onions
2 oz. flour
1 large can tomatoes
1 beef extract cube
½ pint hot water
seasoning
1 large can butter beans

1 Ask butcher to remove blade bone from shoulder and roll meat into neat shape.
2 Put with the sliced onions in ovenproof casserole.
3 Blend flour with can of tomatoes, add the beef cube dissolved in the hot water.
4 Pour over the onions in the casserole, season.
5 Cook in a slow oven (300°F. – Gas Mark 2) for 3–4 hours.
6 Ten minutes before serving, add drained butter beans.

Ragoût of pork

cooking time: approximately 1¼ hours

you will need:

1 beef extract cube
½ pint hot water
½ oz. lard
4 onions
4 pork chops
¾ oz. flour
salt and pepper
1 bay leaf
1 small can tomato purée

1 Crumble and dissolve beef extract in hot water.
2 Melt the fat and cook the chopped onions for a few minutes.
3 Add the pork chops and brown on both sides.
4 Remove and stir the flour into the fat.
5 Add salt, pepper, bay leaf and tomato puree.
6 Replace the chops in the sauce and cook in a moderate oven (375°F. – Gas Mark 4) for 1 hour.
7 Remove the bay leaf and serve the chops with boiled potatoes.

American lamb casserole

cooking time: 2 hours 20 minutes

you will need:

8 scrag end lamb chops
seasoning
little flour
fat or margarine
2 large onions
clove garlic
4 skinned tomatoes
1–1½ lb. potatoes
about 3 tablespoons stock

1 Fry the lamb chops, after coating with seasoned flour, for a few minutes, then lift out of pan.
2 If necessary, add little extra fat and fry thinly sliced onions, garlic and tomatoes for a few minutes.
3 Fill casserole with layers of meat, onions and tomatoes and thinly sliced potatoes, ending with potatoes.
4 Add seasoning and stock and put small amount of fat or margarine over top layer of potatoes.
5 Cover and cook for about 2 hours in a very moderate oven (350°F. – Gas Mark 3).
6 Take off lid and allow 15–20 minutes to brown potatoes.

Variation:

Minted lamb casserole – omit the tomatoes in the recipe above, but use 3 onions instead. When the onions and garlic have been fried at stage 2, sprinkle with a generous amount of freshly chopped mint. About 4 oz. uncooked peas could be added at stage 3.

Summer casserole

cooking time: 1½ hours

you will need:

- 2 lb. scrag end neck lamb
- fat for frying
- 1 onion
- 1 small turnip
- 3 new carrots
- 1 pint water
- salt and pepper
- 2 sprigs mint
- 1 sprig thyme
- 4 oz. shelled peas (or 1 small package frozen peas)

1. Prepare the lamb and cut into pieces removing all gristle.
2. Fry meat in a little fat till lightly brown with finely chopped onion.
3. Drain and place the meat and onion in a casserole.
4. Dice the turnip and slice the carrot and add to the casserole with water.
5. Season with salt and pepper and add the mint and thyme.
6. Cover the casserole and place in a moderate oven (375°F. – Gas Mark 4) for about 1½ hours.
7. If fresh peas are used, cook them separately and stir into casserole just before serving.
8. If frozen peas are used, stir them into the casserole about 15 minutes before serving.

Lancashire hot-pot

cooking time: 2 hours

you will need:

- 12 oz. lean best neck of mutton or stewing steak
- 1 lb. potatoes
- 2 large onions
- salt and pepper
- hot water
- 1 oz. margarine

1. Cut the meat into neat pieces.
2. Peel and slice the potatoes and onions to about ¼ inch thick.
3. Fill a casserole with alternate layers of meat, potato and onion, ending with a layer of potato.
4. Sprinkle salt and pepper over each layer.
5. Half fill the casserole with hot water, put the margarine on top in small pieces.
6. Put on the lid and bake in the coolest part of the oven for 2 hours (350°F. – Gas Mark 3), or if baking a pudding in the oven at the same time, cook for 1½ hours (375°F. – Gas Mark 4).
7. Take the lid off for the last 20 minutes to brown the top.

Thrifty hot-pot

cooking time: 2½ hours

you will need:

- 2 lb. scrag end neck lamb
- 1 oz. dripping
- 2 onions
- 1 teaspoon mixed herbs
- salt and pepper
- 1 lb. potatoes
- ½ pint stock
- chopped parsley

1. Prepare, trim and cut the neck into pieces.
2. Fry the meat in a pan in the dripping.
3. Remove the meat and lightly fry the sliced onions.
4. Place a layer of meat, then a little of the onion and a sprinkling of the herbs and seasoning in a casserole dish.
5. Then cover with a layer of potatoes.
6. Repeat this process until all the ingredients have been used, finishing with a layer of potatoes.
7. Pour in the stock, cover with a lid and cook at 350°F. – Gas Mark 3 for about 2½ hours.
8. Half an hour before the end of the cooking time remove the lid and allow potatoes to brown.
9. Sprinkle chopped parsley on top and serve.

Lamb and rice casserole

cooking time: approximately 1 hour

you will need:

- 3 oz. butter
- 2 good sized onions
- 4 oz. rice
- 1½ pints water flavoured with yeast extract or stock
- salt and pepper
- cooked lamb
- pinch nutmeg or cinnamon
- ½ pint tomato sauce or purée

1. Heat 2 oz. butter in a pan.
2. Add the finely chopped onions and when tender add the rice.
3. Toss with the onion and butter, then pour in the stock or water.
4. Season well and cook for about 10 minutes until the rice has absorbed most of the liquid.
5. Add the lamb, cut into neat fingers, and the nutmeg and an extra 1 oz. butter.
6. Put into casserole.
7. Cover with lid and heat gently for about 40 minutes.
8. Serve with tomato sauce (see page 87) or puree of tomatoes.

Leg of mutton or cut of beef with broad beans

cooking time: 3 hours

you will need:

2 oz. butter
3 lb. piece leg mutton or cut beef (shoulder piece or vein piece)
1–2 meat extract cubes
½ pint hot water
1 lb. potatoes
1 large can broad beans

1 Melt butter in a casserole or large saucepan.
2 Add joint and brown the outside.
3 Remove joint.
4 Place 3 meat skewers in the bottom of the pan and place the joint on these.
5 Crumble beef cubes into the hot water.
6 Pour this gravy over the joint.
7 Cover the dish with a well-fitting lid and place in a very moderate oven (350°F. – Gas Mark 3). Cook for 2½–3 hours.
8 40 minutes before the end of the cooking time place potatoes around the joint. To obtain browned potatoes remove lid from casserole 15 minutes before the end of cooking time.
9 This pot-roast may be cooked on the top of cooker for same time.
10 Serve with broad beans.

Barbecued spare ribs

cooking time: 1¼ hours

you will need:

1 beef extract cube
½ pint hot water
1 small onion
2 tablespoons lemon juice
1 level tablespoon brown sugar
2 level tablespoons dry mustard
1 level teaspoon salt
2 teaspoons tomato paste
1 tablespoon Worcestershire sauce
4 thick chops or ribs pork
½ oz. butter or oil

1 Dissolve beef cube in the water.
2 Peel and chop the onion.
3 Add lemon juice.
4 Mix sugar, mustard and salt with the tomato paste, sauce and the liquids.
5 Place the chops in a wide shallow casserole and bake uncovered for about 30 minutes or until well browned in a moderately hot oven (400°F. – Gas Mark 5).
6 Pour off any fat.
7 Meanwhile, fry the onion in the butter or oil until brown.
8 Add remaining ingredients, pour over chops.
9 Cover and continue baking for about 45 minutes.

Tomato rolls

cooking time: 2¼ hours

you will need:

4 thin slices leg veal
1 oz. butter
seasoning
1 finely chopped onion
little chopped parsley
grated lemon rind

for sauce:

small onion
tiny piece eating apple
1 oz. butter or margarine
1 rounded teaspoon cornflour
generous ½ pint water (or white stock)
small can tomato purée
seasoning

1 Spread each slice of veal with butter and sprinkle with seasoning, onion, parsley and lemon rind.
2 Roll firmly with the onion mixture inside – secure with skewers.

To make sauce:

3 Grate onion and apple and toss in butter for a few minutes, taking care they do not brown.
4 Blend cornflour and water, pour into saucepan.
5 Add tomato purée.
6 Bring to boil and cook until clear and smooth.
7 Season well.
8 Put the veal rolls into a casserole – cover with sauce and lid or foil.
9 Cook for approximately 2 hours in a slow oven (300°F. – Gas Mark 2).

Variations:

Veal rolls Provençal – fry 2 oz. chopped mushrooms and 2 chopped onions and a chopped clove of garlic in 2 oz. butter. Add tomato purée, water and cornflour as before.
Veal birds – spread slices of veal with your favourite stuffing, then roll. Cover with the tomato sauce or brown sauce. Cook as before. Serve with bacon rolls and diced root vegetables.
Veal and bacon rolls – spread stuffing on veal and roll, then roll rashers of bacon round each piece of veal. Tie and continue as for veal rolls. If bacon is reasonably fat, you can reduce the amount of dripping.

Italian pot pie

cooking time: 1 hour 10 minutes

you will need:

1 beef extract cube
½ pint hot water
4 lamb's kidneys
4 large onions
1 oz. butter
1 oz. flour
parsley to garnish

1 Dissolve beef extract cube in the hot water.

continued

2 Peel, wash and core kidneys.
3 Peel onions, and remove the centres until the cavity is large enough to hold a kidney.
4 Place onion centres in a casserole and put the stuffed onions on top.
5 Add gravy.
6 Bake in moderate oven (375°F. – Gas Mark 4) for 1 hour.
7 Strain off the liquid around the onions.
8 Melt the butter, stir in the flour and blend in the stock carefully.
9 Bring to the boil and cook until the sauce thickens.
10 Pour this round the cooked onions in the casserole and serve garnished with parsley.

Spanish rice with frankfurters

cooking time: 1 hour 25 minutes

you will need:

1 green pepper
1 large onion, sliced
3 tablespoons bacon fat or oil
large can tomatoes
1 tablespoon sugar
1½ teaspoons salt
pinch ground cloves
1 bay leaf
8 oz. uncooked rice
water
8–10 split frankfurters

1 Chop pepper finely.
2 Fry onion in fat until tender.
3 Add the tomatoes, green pepper and seasonings.
4 Simmer for 10 minutes.
5 Stir in the rice, cover and simmer for about 45 minutes, adding water gradually to keep the mixture moist.
6 Arrange alternative layers of the rice mixture and frankfurter halves in a greased casserole and cover.
7 Bake in a moderate oven (375°F. – Gas Mark 4) for about 30 minutes.

Variations:

Family paella – an economical paella can be made by adding a few shelled prawns to the Spanish rice at stage 7, just before serving.

Party paella – use the recipe for Spanish rice, but only 3–4 frankfurters, then add 8–12 oz. diced raw chicken and fry with the onions at stage 2. Stir shelled prawns or other shellfish into the very hot rice at stage 7, just before serving.

Welcome home hot-pot

cooking time: 20 minutes, plus time of cooking stew

you will need:

your favourite stew recipe

for topping:

8 oz. plain flour
¼ teaspoon salt
2 level teaspoons baking powder
4 oz. lard and margarine mixed
about 5 tablespoons milk
egg and milk to glaze

1 Make your favourite stew the way you always do, but 20 minutes before it is cooked, remove casserole lid and put on this exciting scone mix topping.
2 Sieve plain flour, salt and baking powder.
3 Rub in fat until mixture resembles fine bread-crumbs.
4 Bind to a stiff dough with milk.
5 Knead lightly and roll out to ½ inch thickness.
6 Cut into rounds with a 2-inch cutter.
7 Place rounds on top of stew, brush with beaten egg or milk.
8 Return to moderately hot oven (400°F. – Gas Mark 5) for the last 20 minutes.

Gammon casserole

cooking time: 1 hour

you will need:

4 slices gammon
2 eating apples
4 tomatoes
1 onion
1 oz. seedless raisins (optional)
¼ pint cider
pepper (no salt)

1 Remove skin from gammon and arrange in the casserole.
2 Core, but do not peel apples.
3 Cut each apple into half through the centre.
4 Arrange apples and whole tomatoes round gammon.
5 Cover with thinly sliced onion, raisins, and cider and a good pinch of pepper.
6 Put lid on casserole and cook for about 1 hour in centre of a moderate oven (375°F. – Gas Mark 4).

Bacon with raisin sauce

8–10 servings

cooking time: $2\frac{1}{2}$ hours

you will need:

piece collar or hock bacon approximately $2\frac{1}{2}$–3 lb.
about 12 tiny onions or 24 cocktail onions
2 sliced apples (sharp apples in a dessert variety are ideal)

for sauce:

1 good teaspoon mustard powder
1 tablespoon brown sugar
$\frac{1}{2}$ pint cider
seasoning
4 oz. stoned raisins

1 Blend the mustard, sugar and cider together.
2 Add the seasoning and the raisins.
3 Put the piece of bacon into a casserole with the onions.
4 Cover with the sliced apples and pour the sauce round the side.
5 Put on lid or cover with aluminium foil.
6 Cook for approximately $2\frac{1}{2}$ hours in a moderate oven (375°F. – Gas Mark 4).

Variation:

Bacon with sour sweet sauce – use the recipe for raisin sauce above, but add 2 tablespoons chopped vinegar pickles and a tablespoon honey as well as the sugar. In view of the extra sweetening in this sauce, you may need to reduce the heat after $1\frac{1}{4}$ hours to make sure the mixture does not burn.

Bacon and beans casserole

cooking time: 2–$2\frac{1}{2}$ hours or longer on lower heat

you will need:

8 oz. dried butter beans
$1\frac{1}{2}$ lb. forehock bacon
4 tomatoes
2 green peppers (optional)
1 stick celery
1 onion
2 carrots
seasoning
$\frac{1}{2}$–1 pint stock, or water with bouillon cube

1 Soak butter beans overnight.
2 Strain off water.
3 Cut bacon into chunks.
4 Slice tomatoes and de-seeded peppers.
5 Chop the celery, onion and carrots.
6 Place all ingredients into a large casserole and season well.
7 Add the stock and cover tightly.
8 Cook for 2–$2\frac{1}{2}$ hours in a very moderate oven (325°F. – Gas Mark 3) or on lower marks for 4–5 hours.
9 Delicious served with jacket potatoes.

Barbecued bacon

5–6 servings

cooking time: $1\frac{1}{2}$ hours

you will need:

$1\frac{1}{4}$–$1\frac{1}{2}$ lb. collar bacon
2 sliced dessert apples
2 very thinly sliced onions
4 thickly sliced tomatoes
$\frac{1}{4}$ pint cider
seasoning
parsley to garnish
1 lb. mashed potatoes

1 Put the bacon into casserole with sliced apples (leaving skins on), onions and tomatoes.
2 Cover with cider, season well.
3 Bake in a covered dish for $1\frac{1}{4}$–$1\frac{1}{2}$ hours, in the centre of a very moderate oven (375°F. – Gas Mark 3–4).
4 Garnish with parsley. Serve with piped creamed potatoes and green vegetables.

Stews

As stated in the introduction to the meat chapter, many of the cheaper cuts of meat are NOT suitable for roasting, frying, etc. However, they are excellent for stews, as well as casserole dishes, and cooked in this way, are both delicious and economical. When making stews, do remember the following points:

1 In some recipes you will find the meat, vegetables etc., are first gently fried in fat. This gives added richness of flavour and should not be omitted.
2 NEVER hurry the cooking time, and make sure the lid of the pan fits tightly when stewing, as if too much moisture escapes from the pan the stew could burn, through lack of liquid.
If you are not entirely happy to leave the saucepan unattended, transfer the stew to the top of a double saucepan.

Beef Provençale

cooking time: 3¼ hours

you will need:

- 2 tablespoons olive oil
- 2 large onions
- 3 rashers bacon
- 1¼ lb. chuck steak, cut into neat fingers
- seasoning
- 1 oz. flour
- ¼ pint cheap white wine*
- approximately ½ pint water
- bunch mixed herbs (or good pinch dried herbs)
- 3 or 4 tomatoes
- few olives to garnish

*This helps to tenderise the meat.

1. Heat the oil in the pan and fry the sliced onions and bacon.
2. Add the meat coated with well seasoned flour and toss in the oil for a few minutes.
3. Add all the other ingredients, except the olives.
4. Bring to the boil and cook for a few minutes until a fairly thick liquid.
5. Taste and re-season if desired.
6. Reduce the heat, put a lid on the pan and simmer gently for approximately 3 hours.
7. Remove bunch of herbs and pour on to a hot dish.
8. Garnish with olives and serve in a border of freshly cooked vegetables or cooked rice.

Variation:

Somerset beef – omit the white wine in the recipe above and use fairly dry cider instead. If you can obtain crab apples use about 12 of these or 2 cooking apples in place of olives. Either the whole crab apples or sliced cooking apples should be added at stage 6, after cooking the beef etc. for 1½ hours.

Brisket roundabout

cooking time: 2½–3 hours

you will need:

- 1 stock cube
- ¼ pint hot water
- 3 lb. boned brisket of beef
- 8 oz. sliced onions
- ½ oz. dripping or margarine
- 8 oz. skinned tomatoes
- salt and pepper
- 1 large can butter beans

for stuffing:

- 2 oz. white bread-crumbs
- 2 teaspoons chopped parsley
- ½ teaspoon mixed herbs
- salt and pepper
- 1 oz. chopped suet
- grated rind ½ lemon
- beaten egg to bind

to garnish:

chopped parsley

1. Dissolve beef cube in water.
2. Make stuffing by mixing all dry ingredients together and binding with a little beaten egg.
3. Spread stuffing on the meat, roll and tie firmly with fine string.
4. Fry onions in hot dripping until soft.
5. Add meat and tomatoes and pour over the liquid.
6. Season well, cover and cook slowly on the top of the stove or in a slow oven (300°F. – Gas Mark 2) for 2–3 hours.
7. 15 minutes before the end of cooking add the canned butter beans.
8. Serve sprinkled with freshly chopped parsley.

Flemish beef stew

cooking time: 2¼ hours

you will need:

- 1 lb. diced flank of beef or stewing beef
- 2 sliced onions
- 2 oz. dripping or fat
- 2 sliced carrots
- water
- bay leaf
- good pinch mixed herbs
- 1 thick slice bread
- seasoning
- mustard

1. Fry well seasoned meat and onions in the hot fat until golden brown.
2. Add carrots and 1¼ pints water.
3. Put in herbs and bay leaf. Season.
4. Simmer in a covered saucepan until meat is tender (this will take about 2 hours).
5. Remove crusts from slice of bread.
6. Spread both sides of bread with mustard and drop on top of the stew.
7. Cook for a further 5 minutes.
8. Then beat the bread into the stew.

Variation:

Hasty beef stew – use minced beef and grated onions and carrots in the recipe above. Fry the beef and onions as stage 1, add the carrots and 1 pint stock or use tomato juice then simmer, stirring from time to time, for about 45 minutes. Continue as stage 5 onwards.

Greek beef stew

cooking time: 2½ hours

you will need:

- 1½ lb. lean stewing beef
- 3 tablespoons oil or fat
- 1 pint water
- 6 oz. can tomato paste
- 3 tablespoons cider vinegar
- 2½ teaspoons salt
- ½ teaspoon black pepper
- 2 2-inch sticks cinnamon
- 1 onion, stuck with 8 whole cloves
- 2 lb. small white onions

1 Cube the meat and brown on all sides in hot oil or fat.
2 Combine the water, tomato paste, vinegar, salt and pepper.
3 Heat to boiling point and pour over the meat.
4 Add the cinnamon and onion stuck with the cloves.
5 Cover and simmer until meat is tender.
6 Add the onions about 35 minutes before cooking time is up.

Beef in red wine

cooking time: 2¼ hours

you will need:

1½ lb. stewing beef, cut into cubes
½ oz. seasoned flour
1 oz. dripping
2 rashers streaky bacon, cut in pieces
12 small onions
2 oz. mushrooms, peeled and sliced
pinch sugar
¼ pint red wine (scant measure)
½ pint stock
seasoning
bouquet garni

1 Roll cubes of beef in seasoned flour.
2 Melt dripping and add meat.
3 Brown well on all sides.
4 Remove meat and add bacon, onion, mushrooms, pinch sugar and brown gently again.
5 Take out mushrooms and onions.
6 Return meat.
7 Heat the wine and add it to meat.
8 Add stock to cover, seasoning and *bouquet garni.*
9 Cover and cook slowly for 1 hour.
10 Add onions and mushrooms and continue cooking for another hour.
11 Serve with chopped parsley and creamed potatoes.

Jugged beef

cooking time: 2½–3 hours

you will need:

2–3 meat cubes
¾ pint hot water
1½ lb. shin beef
2 oz. seasoned flour
4 oz. chopped bacon
2 onions
2–4 cloves
grated rind ½ lemon
bouquet garni
6 small mushrooms

1 Dissolve meat cubes in water.
2 Cut meat into 2-inch pieces and roll in the seasoned flour.
3 Chop bacon and fry in a saucepan.
4 Add the meat, browning lightly.
5 Add onions, cloves, lemon rind, *bouquet garni*, mushrooms and liquid.
6 Cover and cook slowly either on top of the stove or in a casserole in a slow oven (300°F. – Gas Mark 2) for 2½ to 3 hours.
7 Remove *bouquet garni*, onion and cloves before serving.

Goulash

cooking time: 2 hours

Use ingredients as for pressure cooked goulash on page 57, but cook in a saucepan for 1½ hours. Then add potatoes and continue cooking for further 30 minutes. You will need at least ½ pint stock.

Variation:

With veal – a mixture of beef and veal can be used.

Mexican mince

cooking time: 1¼ hours

you will need:

1 tablespoon olive oil
2 chopped onions
2 crushed cloves garlic
1 lb. minced beef
¾ oz. flour
6 tomatoes, skinned
2 teaspoons Worcestershire sauce
4 oz. kidney beans or haricot beans, soaked overnight
1 meat extract cube
¼ pint hot water
salt

1 Heat olive oil in a saucepan and fry onions and garlic.
2 Add meat and brown lightly.
3 Sprinkle on the flour and then add tomatoes cut into quarters, sauce, beans, meat cube dissolved in water and salt to taste.
4 Cover and cook slowly either on top of the stove or in a casserole in a slow oven (300°F. – Gas Mark 2) for 1 hour.

Savoury mince with chestnuts

cooking time: 1¼ hours

you will need:

8 oz. cooked meat
1 lb. chestnuts
1 onion
4 cloves
stock
1 oz. fat for sauce
1 oz. flour
salt and pepper
fat or butter

1 Mince the meat.
2 Cut a small piece of skin off each chestnut, place in cold water and bring to the boil. *continued*

3 Skin them while warm and put in a saucepan with the onion, cloves and stock to cover.
4 Simmer gently for 1 hour, and strain, keeping the liquid. If necessary add water to make ½ pint.
5 Melt the fat, fry the flour until brown, add the liquid, and boil.
6 Reheat the minced meat in the sauce, season, and dish up in a border of chestnuts, tossed in a little fat or butter.

Oxtail ragoût

cooking time: 4 hours

you will need:

1 medium-sized oxtail
cornflour or flour for coating
salt and pepper
little fat
4 oz. bacon – diced
1 medium onion
4 cloves
bouquet garni
1 clove garlic, crushed
4 small carrots, thickly sliced
1 small turnip, in large dice
2 sticks celery, in large dice
14 oz. can tomatoes
¾ pint water
1 beef extract cube
1–2 leeks, sliced

1 Remove any excess fat from oxtail and cut into serving pieces.
2 Blanch in boiling water, drain and dry.
3 Coat the pieces in cornflour or flour to which salt and pepper have been added.
4 Heat the fat in a pan and sauté the pieces of oxtail and bacon till golden.
5 Pour off any excess fat in the pan.
6 Add the onion stuck with cloves, *bouquet garni*, garlic and all vegetables except the leeks.
7 Add the tomatoes, water and crumbled beef cube.
8 Simmer for 3–4 hours.
9 30 minutes before end of cooking time, add the sliced leeks.

Panned pork chops

cooking time: 1¼ hours

you will need:

4 pork chops
2 oz. butter
1 pint sieved tomato
about ¼ pint of water
1 level tablespoon brown sugar
1 teaspoon Worcestershire sauce
seasoning

1 Trim the chops and brown on both sides in butter with all other ingredients.
2 Cover the pan and simmer gently for 1 hour or until the meat is tender.
3 Serve with creamed potatoes and Brussels sprouts.

Winter beef stew

cooking time: 1½–2 hours

you will need:

1 skirt of beef
8 oz. minced pork or sausage meat
1 egg
1 teaspoon chopped parsley
1 oz. grated cheese
salt and pepper
1 potato
1 onion
1 beef extract cube

1 Slit the beef down the middle, taking care that only one side is opened. (The butcher will do this for you.)
2 In a bowl, mix the pork, egg, parsley and cheese.
3 Add salt and pepper.
4 Mix all ingredients thoroughly.
5 Fill up the skirt with this mixture.
6 Using white cotton, sew up the slit in the skirt.
7 Put the skirt with a sliced potato, a sliced onion and a crumbled beef extract cube in a saucepan.
8 Just cover with water.
9 Bring the water to the boil.
10 Lower the heat and simmer for 1½ hours or until the meat is tender.
11 When ready, take the skirt out of the soup and cut into slices.
12 To serve: First serve the soup with fried or toasted bread cut into cubes. Serve the sliced skirt with sauté potatoes and fried onions.

Oxtail

cooking time: 2½ hours

Recipe as for pressure cooked oxtail, see page 57, but simmer in saucepan in 1½ pints water for 2½ hours.
Some people find this dish over 'fatty' in which case cook previous day and allow to cool. Then remove the fat from the top of the dish.

Brawn

cooking time: 3 hours

you will need:

1 pig's head or 6 pig's trotters
8 oz. stewing beef (not essential)
2 bay leaves
seasoning
pinch mixed herbs
small bunch parsley

1 After washing pig's head or trotters well, put into a large saucepan and cover with water.
2 Simmer gently for 1 hour.
3 Remove from the stock which should be saved.
4 Cut all meat from head or trotters, removing any gristle and bones.

5 Cut meat and stewing beef into neat small dice.
6 Return the meat to the stock, adding bay leaves, seasoning, pinch herbs and the bunch of parsley.
7 Simmer gently for 1½–2 hours until the meat feels quite tender.
8 Take out the parsley and pour into a rinsed mould or large basin. Allow to set.

Variation:

Tongue brawn – omit the stewing beef in the recipe above and simmer 1 or 2 small lamb's tongues with the pig's head or trotters. Cut these in neat pieces, skinning and removing bones, and mix with the meat from the head or trotters at stage 6. If preferred, buy about 6–8 oz. cooked tongue (in one piece), dice and add to the rest of the ingredients at stage 8.

Haricot mutton

cooking time: 2½ hours

you will need:

4 oz. haricot beans
1 oz. lard or dripping
1 large onion
1 sweet red pepper
1 lb. stewing mutton
1 oz. flour
1 pint water or stock
salt and pepper
few potatoes
parsley to garnish

1 Soak haricot beans overnight in cold water, leaving plenty of room in the container for the beans to swell.
2 Heat the lard in the saucepan and fry the sliced onion, chopped pepper and meat, cut into neat pieces, for a few minutes.
3 Stir in the flour and cook this gently for about 5 minutes, stirring all the time.
4 Gradually add the cold stock or water.
5 Bring to the boil, stirring well until the stock has boiled and thickened slightly.
6 Add haricot beans, well drained, and seasoning.
7 Simmer gently for nearly 2 hours.
8 Slice the potatoes on top of the mutton stew adding a good pinch of salt and pepper.
9 Cook for a further 25 minutes until the potatoes are tender.
10 To dish up, lift the sliced potatoes carefully from the stew, put these on a hot dish, pour the haricot mutton on top.
11 Garnish with sprigs of parsley.

Boiled breast of lamb

cooking time: 1¼–1½ hours

you will need:

breast lamb
stuffing (see page 88)
1–2 meat extract cubes
1 pint hot water
1 onion

1 Ask the butcher to leave breast in one piece. Remove small bones and any surplus fat.
2 Make stuffing – spread on lamb.
3 Roll it up and tie firmly with string.
4 Crumble and dissolve meat cubes in 1 pint hot water.
5 Place meat and a chopped onion in a saucepan and pour over liquid.
6 Cover the pan and boil until the meat is tender – about 1¼–1½ hours.
7 Remove meat.
8 Serve hot with mixed vegetables and the gravy, or cold with salad.

Lamb soubise

cooking time: 1¾ hours

you will need:

piece best end neck of lamb
1 oz. butter
1½ lb. onions
2 carrots
1–2 meat extract cubes
1 pint hot water
salt and pepper
4 oz. rice
parsley, to garnish

1 Ask your butcher to bone and roll the meat.
2 Melt butter in a thick saucepan.
3 Add the meat and brown the outside for a few minutes.
4 Peel and chop 1 onion and the carrots.
5 Crumble and dissolve beef cubes in 1 pint hot water.
6 Add the vegetables and bones and gravy to the meat and simmer slowly for 1¼ hours. Season.
7 Remove the meat and strain the stock.
8 Wash the saucepan, then return the meat and stock to it.
9 Put in rice and remaining chopped onions and cook until the rice is soft, about 15 minutes.
10 Serve the meat cut into rounds.
11 Sieve the rice and onions, which will have absorbed most of the stock in the saucepan.
12 Serve separately in a sauceboat.
13 Sprinkle chopped parsley on the soubise sauce.

Fricassée of lamb or mutton

cooking time: 2 hours

you will need:

8 pieces middle or scrag end lamb or mutton
4 carrots
2 onions
seasoning
2 oz. butter
2 oz. flour
½ pint milk
few cooked peas
4 oz. Patna rice
2 large slices bread
little fat for frying bread
chopped parsley
paprika pepper

1 Simmer lamb with halved carrots and chopped

onions until just tender – about 1½ hours.
2 Season well.
3 Make a thick sauce of the butter, flour and milk.
4 Add ½ pint of the meat stock and stir until quite smooth.
5 Add the meat, carrots and peas to this.
6 Heat gently.
7 Serve in a border of boiled rice and garnish with triangles of fried bread, chopped parsley and paprika pepper.

Variation:

Fricassée of chicken – use a small jointed chicken instead of lamb or mutton. Shorten cooking time at stage 1 to 1 hour. Cook with the same vegetables as for lamb, but flavour with grated lemon rind at stage 4. This is delicious garnished with hot cooked prunes instead of fried bread.

Stewed breast of lamb

cooking time: 1¼ hours

you will need:

1 onion
1 carrot
1 stick celery
1 breast of lamb, boned
2 tablespoons flour
salt and pepper
1 oz. dripping or lard
1½ pints stock or water
1 medium potato
2 tablespoons pearl barley

1 Chop onion and slice other vegetables.
2 Wipe the meat with a damp cloth.
3 Trim away any excess fat and cut the meat into pieces about 2 inches square.
4 Toss the meat in seasoned flour.
5 Melt the fat and lightly fry the onion, carrot and celery.
6 Add meat and continue frying for a few minutes.
7 Add stock, potato and seasoning.
8 Bring to the boil and sprinkle in the pearl barley.
9 Reduce the heat and simmer for about 1 hour.
10 Reseason if necessary.

Pork sausage casserole

cooking time: 40 minutes

you will need:

2 large onions
2 oz. lard
2 large carrots, grated
3 large tomatoes
1 oz. flour
½ pint water or stock
seasoning
1 lb. pork sausages
little chopped parsley
bacon (optional)

1 Fry the very thinly sliced onions in the hot lard.
2 Add the grated carrots and sliced skinned tomatoes.
3 When soft, work in the flour.
4 Cook for a minute or so, then add the stock gradually.
5 Bring to the boil and cook until smooth and thickened.
6 Season well.
7 Add sausages and simmer gently for about 25 minutes.
8 Serve sprinkled with the parsley and top with bacon rolls if wished.

Variations:

Beef sausage casserole – follow recipe as above but use beef sausages instead of pork and beer instead of water or stock.

Sausage and leek casserole – use 1 lb. leeks in place of onion and carrots. Wash and slice the leeks, fry in the hot lard as stage 1 above, then add the sliced skinned tomatoes and continue as the recipe for the pork sausage casserole.

Osso bucco

cooking time: 1½ hours

you will need:

2 veal hocks
1 oz. olive oil
1 carrot
2 onions
1 small can tomatoes
bouquet garni
2 meat extract cubes
1 pint water
salt and pepper
grated rind ½ lemon
parsley
Parmesan cheese

1 Cut veal into 3-inch pieces.
2 Heat the olive oil and fry the meat, carrot and onions until browned.
3 Add the tomatoes, *bouquet garni* and the 2 meat cubes, crumbled and dissolved in hot water.
4 Season with salt and pepper.
5 Cover and cook until tender – about 1½ hours.
6 Remove the *bouquet garni* and serve sprinkled with lemon rind and parsley.
7 Serve with boiled rice and grated Parmesan cheese sprinkled on top.

Fricassée of veal

cooking time: 1¾ hours

you will need:

1¼ lb. stewing veal
1 pint white stock or water with chicken bouillon cube
seasoning
1–2 onions
lemon
2 oz. butter
2 oz. flour
½ pint milk

1 Cut the veal into neat fingers.
2 Put in a pan with water and chicken bouillon cube, or stock, seasoning, onion and thinly-pared lemon rind.

3 Simmer steadily for 1¼ hours.
4 Make a thick sauce of the butter, flour and milk.
5 Add ½ pint veal liquid and when the sauce is quite smooth add the veal.
6 Heat gently, whisk in lemon juice before serving.
7 Serve with creamed potatoes or boiled rice.

Veal Marengo

cooking time: 1¼ hours

you will need:

1 lb. neck veal	½ pint white stock or water
little flour	8 oz. skinned tomatoes
seasoning	2 oz. mushrooms
3 oz. butter or 3 tablespoons oil	4 slices bread
2 finely chopped onions or shallots	fat for frying
	parsley
	lemon

1 Cut the meat into neat pieces.
2 Coat with a thin layer of seasoned flour and fry until pale golden brown in the hot butter or oil.
3 Add finely diced onions and fry until transparent.
4 Add stock, chopped tomatoes and mushrooms.
5 Season well.
6 Simmer gently for approximately 1 hour.
7 Serve garnished with croûtons of fried bread, parsley and lemon.

Fried veal with rice

cooking time: 1 hour

you will need:

4 neck of veal cutlets	1 stick celery
seasoned flour	1 tomato
1 small onion	3 oz. fat or oil
1 small green sweet pepper	¼ pint stock
	8 oz. rice

1 Toss the cutlets in seasoned flour.
2 Peel and chop the onion and chop other vegetables.
3 Melt 2 oz. fat and fry the veal until brown on both sides.
4 Add the stock, or water and meat cube.
5 Simmer the meat until it is tender (45 minutes).
6 Boil the rice.
7 Melt 1 oz. fat and fry the onion, green pepper and celery.
8 Stir in the cooked rice and add the tomato.
9 Serve the cutlets on top of the rice mixture and pour over the juices from the frying pan.

Variation:

Parmesan veal and rice – continue as the recipe above; arrange the cutlets on the bed of rice, top with a thick layer of grated Parmesan (or other cooking cheese). Heat for a few minutes under the grill, then add the juices from the frying pan and serve.

Liver pilaf

cooking time: 25 minutes

you will need:

½ aubergine	1 oz. seasoned flour
1 large tomato	4 oz. mushrooms
6 oz. Patna rice	¾ pint boiling salted water
1 meat cube	1 oz. butter
1 lb. calves' liver	

1 Slice aubergine and tomato.
2 Put rice, tomato, aubergine and meat cube into a saucepan and cover with boiling water.
3 Cover and cook gently on the top of the stove for 20–25 minutes or until the rice has absorbed all the water.
4 Meanwhile, cut liver into small pieces and toss in seasoned flour.
5 Peel and slice mushrooms.
6 Melt the butter and fry the liver for a few minutes.
7 Add mushrooms and liquid.
8 Cover and simmer gently for 15–20 minutes.
9 Make a ring of rice and vegetables on a hot serving dish and pour the liver and mushrooms in the centre.

Variation:

Lamb pilaf – dice about 1 lb. lean lamb (cut from the leg) and use in place of the liver. The cooking time at stage 8 should be extended to 35 minutes, use a little extra liquid so meat does not dry.

Bacon stew with kidney dumplings

cooking time: 1½ hours

you will need:

2–3 meaty bacon bones	1 parsnip
	2 small onions

for dumplings:

4 oz. sheeps' kidney	salt and pepper
1 oz. butter	1½ oz. shredded suet
4 oz. self-raising flour	cold water to mix

1 Place the bacon bones in a pan with cold water, bring to the boil, then discard water.
2 Add fresh water to cover and add the chopped parsnip and onions.
3 Simmer gently for 1½ hours.
4 Cook the kidneys in butter, chop finely or put through mincer.

continued

5 Mix together the flour, seasoning and suet, stir in the kidney and mix to a fairly soft dough with water.
6 Form into small balls, add these to the stew and continue cooking for 10–20 minutes.

Variation:

Bacon and herb dumplings – use the recipe above, but omit the kidney. Instead dice 2–3 rashers of bacon, fry until crisp then add to the flour etc. at stage 5, together with a teaspoon of freshly chopped herbs.

Ham in Cumberland sauce

cooking time: 15 minutes

you will need:

8 thin or 4 thicker slices cooked ham

for sauce:

¼ pint water
grated rind and juice 1 lemon
grated rind and juice 2 oranges
1 teaspoon cornflour or arrowroot
2 tablespoons water (or port wine for special occasions)
3 tablespoons red-currant or apple jelly

1 Put the water and grated fruit rinds into a saucepan and simmer for about 5 minutes.
2 Strain if wished, then return the liquid to pan, but if you grate the rinds finely they are very soft and look attractive in the sauce.
3 Add the fruit juice and the cornflour or arrowroot blended with the 2 tablespoons water or wine.
4 Bring to the boil and add jelly.
5 Cook until clear.
6 Put in ham and heat gently for a few minutes only so that the meat remains a pleasant pink colour.
7 Serve at once with garden peas and cooked corn on the cob.

Variation:

With mustard – the sauce can be varied in flavour by adding made mustard to taste, or pepper or a little salt.

Braised Dishes

Braising meat

The term 'braising' means a combination of roasting and stewing. In most of the following recipes, you will find that the meat is first cooked in fat, then simmered in a thick rich sauce, thus giving a rather more succulent result than in an ordinary stew or casserole dish.

Beef olives

cooking time: 2 hours

you will need:

1 lb. stewing meat or top side beef
1 onion
1 carrot
2 oz. fat
seasoning
1 bay leaf
¾ pint stock or water with meat cube
1 oz. flour

for veal forcemeat:

2 oz. fresh breadcrumbs
1–2 oz. suet
1 tablespoon chopped parsley
1 level teaspoon dried thyme or savory
½ level teaspoon grated lemon rind
pinch salt
salt and pepper
1 egg
milk to mix

1 Ask your butcher to thinly slice top rump or chuck steak into pieces about 4 × 3 inches.
2 Prepare the forcemeat by combining all ingredients.
3 Spread some on each piece of flattened, beaten meat, roll up and secure with thick white cotton or very fine string.
4 Peel and slice the onion and carrot.
5 Heat the fat and fry the onion and beef olives in it; add the carrot and seasoning, bay leaf and stock.
6 Stir in flour and cook until thickened.
7 Cover and simmer until tender, or transfer to a covered casserole.
8 Remove string before serving.

Variation:

Sausage stuffed olives – instead of the stuffing above blend 8 oz. pork or beef sausagemeat with 2 teaspoons chopped parsley, ½ teaspoon chopped sage and bind with an egg.

Apple spare rib

cooking time: 10–15 minutes

you will need:

4 spare rib pork chops
1 egg
sage and onion stuffing*
(see page 88)
1 oz. lard
¼ pint stock, or water and meat cube
2 Bramley apples

*or packet stuffing.

1 Dip the chops in the beaten egg, then the sage and onion stuffing.
2 Melt the lard, fry the chops on both sides until golden brown.
3 Add the meat cube and water, or stock, and leave on a low heat for 10–15 minutes until the chops are cooked through.
4 Remove chops and place on one side to keep warm.
5 Add the peeled, cored and chopped apples to the frying pan and cook until they are reduced to pulp.
6 Place a spoonful of the apple mixture on each chop and pour extra juice around the chops.

Braised hand of pork

cooking time: 3 hours

you will need:

1 lb. onions
1 lb. carrots
8 oz. tomatoes
1 oz. dripping
3–3½ lb. hand of pork
salt and pepper
2 meat cubes
½ pint hot water

1 Peel the onions and carrots and cut them into pieces with the tomatoes.
2 Melt the dripping in a saucepan and brown the meat.
3 Remove from the pan and put in the vegetables.
4 Fry for a few minutes.
5 Turn the vegetables into a casserole and place the meat on top.
6 Season well.
7 Crumble and dissolve the meat cubes in the hot water and pour this gravy over the joint.
8 Cover the casserole.
9 Cook in moderate oven (375°F. – Gas Mark 4) for 2½–3 hours.
10 Serve the sliced meat surrounded by vegetables, and hand gravy separately. This may be thickened by blending in 1 oz. flour and bringing to the boil.

Barbecued lamb

cooking time: 2 hours

you will need:

2 pieces middle neck lamb
2 tablespoons oil or 2 oz. fat
¾ pint water
3 tablespoons vinegar
½ pint canned orange juice
2 teaspoons Worcestershire sauce
1 teaspoon salt
pinch each pepper, dry mustard, paprika
½ teaspoon each celery seed, basil, oregano
5 whole cloves
2 teaspoons sugar

1 Brown pieces of lamb in hot corn oil, or fat, in pan.
2 Add water and vinegar; simmer for 1 hour.
3 Remove lid and boil rapidly until liquid is reduced to about ½ pint.
4 Cook and skim.
5 Meanwhile combine the orange juice, Worcestershire sauce, seasonings and sugar in small saucepan.
6 Simmer for 10 minutes.
7 Add to the lamb, stirring carefully to blend with the broth.
8 Cover and simmer a further 45 minutes, or until lamb is tender.
9 Serve with boiled rice.

Braised best end of neck

cooking time: 2 hours

you will need:

1 best end of neck lamb or mutton
2 onions
2 carrots
1 turnip
1 stick celery
2 oz. dripping or lard
stock
salt and pepper

1 Remove the chine bone and flap from the joint and wipe the meat with a damp cloth.
2 Prepare and roughly dice the vegetables.
3 Melt the dripping in a pan and brown the meat quickly.
4 Remove the meat and add the vegetables.
5 Brown them gently, then place the joint on top.
6 Add sufficient stock to just cover the vegetables.
7 Season, cover the pan and cook gently for about 1½ hours.
8 Place the pan uncovered in a moderately hot oven (400°F. – Gas Mark 5) for about 30 minutes to brown and crisp the fat.
9 Serve on a dish with additional assorted root vegetables cut into strips, and boiled.

Note:

The joint may also be cooked with the vegetables in a very moderate oven (350°F. – Gas Mark 4) for the whole of the cooking time, about 1¾ hours.

Devilled pork and beans

cooking time: 2 hours

you will need:

- 4 oz. haricot beans*
- approximately 1¼ lb. belly of pork
- 1 oz. margarine
- 2 good sized onions
- 1 oz. flour
- ½ pint stock or water
- good pinch curry powder
- ½–1 tablespoon Worcestershire sauce
- 1 tablespoon tomato ketchup
- 2 teaspoons mustard seasoning

*or use canned haricot beans in tomato sauce and omit tomato ketchup.

1 Soak beans overnight (unless using canned haricot beans).
2 Simmer until nearly tender.
3 Dice pork and fry gently in the margarine.
4 Add chopped onions and cook gently in the hot margarine and pork fat.
5 Stir in flour and cook again for several minutes.
6 Add stock, sauces, beans, flavourings and seasonings.
7 Bring to boil and when thickened transfer to casserole.
8 Cover well and cook gently for 1½–2 hours.

Braised breast of mutton

cooking time: 2–2¼ hours

you will need:

- breast mutton
- flour
- seasoning
- 2 onions
- approximately 1 lb. diced mixed vegetables
- 2–3 large skinned tomatoes

1 Coat breast of mutton – which need not be boned – with a good layer of seasoned flour.
2 Fry steadily in a large pan until golden brown on both sides.
3 If pan is not large enough, cut into pieces, also add a little fat.*
4 Lift out of pan into casserole.
5 Toss sliced onions in fat in the pan.
6 Spread over meat in casserole.
7 Add all vegetables, chopping tomatoes coarsely.
8 Cover with about ½ pint boiling water and put on lid.
9 Cook steadily for about 1½–2 hours in a very moderate oven (325°F.–350°F. – Gas Mark 2–3).

*Most breasts of mutton are sufficiently fat, but you need enough fat coming from the meat to brown it well and fry the onions.

Variation:

Braised pork chops – use 4 good sized pork chops instead of the breast of mutton, continue as stages 1–2. Add a little sage to the onions at stage 6 and 1 large thinly sliced apple or about 8 soaked, but not cooked, prunes at stage 8.

Braised heart

cooking time: 2 hours

Follow recipe for pressure cooked heart on page 58, allowing 1 pint stock, and instead of pressure cooking, put into a casserole and cover.

Allow 2 hours in a very moderate oven (350°F. – Gas Mark 3) or simmer for about 1¾ hours in a covered saucepan.

Sausage jambalaya

cooking time: 1 hour 20 minutes

you will need:

- 1 lb. sausages
- 2 onions, chopped finely
- 1 clove garlic
- 1 medium can tomatoes or 8 oz. skinned tomatoes
- 1 red pepper
- salt and pepper to taste
- few oysters (optional)
- 6–8 oz. rice
- 8 oz. shrimps or prawns

1 Fry the sausages steadily until brown.
2 Add onions and chopped garlic and cook in fat until clear.
3 Add tomatoes and chopped pepper and simmer slowly for 1 hour, adding water as needed. Season.
4 Add oysters and 1½ pints water and raw rice.
5 Bring to boil.
6 Cover tightly and simmer for 20 minutes.
7 Add shrimps or prawns at the last 10 minutes.
8 Serve immediately.

Braised veal and ham

cooking time: 2 hours

you will need:

- 1 onion
- 3 tomatoes
- 2 oz. lard
- 12 oz. stewing veal
- 1 oz. flour
- seasoning
- ¾ pint stock (or water with yeast extract)
- 6 oz. boiled bacon or ham

1. Fry the sliced onion and skinned sliced tomatoes in the hot lard until tender, but not browned.
2. Add the veal rolled in the seasoned flour and cut into neat fingers.
3. Gradually cook until golden coloured.
4. Stir in the stock.
5. Bring to the boil and cook until thickened and smooth.
6. Season well.
7. Simmer gently for 1 hour.
8. Add fingers of the boiled bacon or ham and cook for a further 45 minutes.
9. Serve with creamed potatoes.

Poultry and Game Dishes

Choosing and cooking poultry

Due to improved methods of breeding, it is possible to purchase a much cheaper and wider range of poultry today. A great variety of chickens of all possible types are available – small birds for frying and grilling, large ones for roasting, and older fowls for steaming, boiling and so on.

A great deal of this poultry is frozen, and it is most important to remember that it MUST be defrosted before cooking. This should be done slowly at room temperature.

Tables for cooking poultry

Chicken

Method	Cooking time
Roasting: All chickens, whether small or large, need covering with fat over the breast. Use cheap fat bacon, cooking fat, or butter. Cover breast of bird with buttered paper, if you wish it to be golden brown.	15 minutes per lb. and 15 minutes over (weight to include stuffing). Start in hot oven then reduce to moderate.
Boiling: For older birds, allow 2½–3 hours depending on size. The water must simmer very gently.	For older birds, allow 2½–3 hours, depending on size.
Frying and Grilling	Approximately 20 minutes cooking time.

Turkey

Method	Cooking time
Roasting: As for chicken, but if not stuffing turkey, put a piece of butter inside body cavity to keep flesh moist.	As for chicken, but use moderate oven. Large birds need only 12 minutes per lb. for any weight above 12 lb.

Duck and duckling

Method

Roasting: A little fat is sometimes used in early stages of roasting a young duckling, but is not really necessary. To reduce fat, prick skin gently with a fine skewer, after the duck has been roasting about 30 minutes. If wished, brush skin with melted honey about 10 minutes before serving, to encourage a golden brown crisp skin.

Cooking time

As for chicken.

Goose

Method	Cooking time
Roasting: Prick two or three times during cooking. If a great deal of fat is flowing, pour it off during the cooking process. This helps to crisp outside of bird, and protect oven.	As for chicken.

Game

Method	Cooking time
Roasting: Cover with plenty of fat, as most game tends to be rather dry.	Roast in moderately hot oven. **Pheasant,** and **guinea fowl** are cooked as for chicken. **Rabbit** requires 20 minutes per lb. and 20 minutes over. **Small birds,** such as partridge require a total cooking time of about 30 minutes.

Stuffed roast chicken

(illustrated on the cover)

cooking time: depending on weight of chicken

you will need:

1 chicken, 5–6 lb. in weight
butter or bacon fat

for stuffing:

1 oz. blanched almonds
1 medium raw onion
4 oz. mushrooms
uncooked liver from chicken
8 oz. white breadcrumbs
1 egg
seasoning

1 Toast the almonds until golden brown. Chop coarsely.
2 Peel and chop the onion and mushrooms finely. Chop the liver.
3 Put breadcrumbs into a basin. Pour over enough warm water to cover. Leave for 30 minutes. Drain off excess water.
4 Mix all the other ingredients with the bread. Add the beaten egg. Season well.
5 Put into chicken and roast for 15 minutes per lb. and 15 minutes over in a hot oven *or*
6 Allow 25 minutes per lb. at 350°F. – Gas Mark 3.

Note:

Cover the breast of the chicken well with butter or bacon fat before roasting and if using a covered roaster or foil, remove for the last 15 or 20 minutes to brown.

Variations in stuffing:

Giblet stuffing – add the chopped **cooked** giblets to the stuffing mixture above.

Sausage, raisin and walnut stuffing – add 2–3 oz. seedless raisins and 3–4 oz. chopped walnuts to 12 oz. pork sausagemeat.

Roast rabbit

cooking time: 1½ hours

you will need:

1 rabbit
either sage and onion or veal stuffing (see page 88) or 8 oz. sausage meat
fat
about 4–5 rashers streaky bacon

1 Wash rabbit as described in devilled rabbit (see page 56) and dry well.
2 Stuff the body of the rabbit (the head can be left on, although most people today like to remove this before cooking).
3 Heat knob of fat in roasting tin and spoon the hot fat over the rabbit.
4 Cover top with the bacon and put on lid or cover with foil over the tin.
5 Cook for about 1½ hours in the centre of a moderately hot oven (400°F. – Gas Mark 5), turning the heat down for the last 15 minutes if necessary.
6 Serve with roast potatoes and a green vegetable.
7 The liver, etc., of the rabbit can be simmered to give stock for gravy.

Note:

If you are not using sage and onion stuffing, an onion sauce (see page 87) is excellent with roast rabbit.

Ducks with apricot sauce

cooking time: depending on size of duck

you will need:

2 small ducklings or 1 larger duck
very little honey

for sauce:

1 medium sized can apricot halves
squeeze lemon juice
3 level teaspoons arrowroot or cornflour
2–3 tablespoons apricot brandy

to garnish:
watercress

1 Roast the ducks for approximately 1¼–1½ hours, depending on size, in a hot oven.
2 After they have been cooking for just about 45 minutes take out of the oven.
3 With a fine skewer break the skin only to enable any surplus fat to run out. BE VERY CAREFUL NOT TO INSERT THE SKEWER TOO DEEPLY FOR IF YOU DO YOU WILL FIND THE FAT RUNS INTO THE DUCK RATHER THAN OUT.

4 Brush over the birds with a little warm honey to make sure you have a really crisp brown skin.
5 Put back again into hot oven and continue cooking.
6 A little time before the ducks are ready to dish up, make the sauce. Strain the liquid from the can of apricots.
7 Add the juice of the lemon and, if necessary, enough water to give just under ½ pint liquid.
8 Blend with the arrowroot.
9 Put into the saucepan and cook until smooth, thickened and clear.
10 Taste and if necessary add a small amount of sugar or honey for the sauce should be slightly sweet but not sticky.
11 To give a shine to the sauce, you can either add a spoonful of strained fat from the ducks, or a small knob of butter.
12 Dish up the ducks.
13 Put the apricot halves into the sauce and heat for just a few moments.
14 Stir in the apricot brandy and heat but do not boil.
15 Pour over the ducks. Garnish with watercress.

Variation:

Ducks with cherry sauce – use canned black or Morello cherries in place of apricots and flavour with cherry brandy at stage 14.

Rôtisserie cooked chicken

Many modern cookers have a rôtisserie spit, either in the oven, or under the grill. The chicken is put on the rod, brushed with melted butter or fat, and cooked on the turning spit. Timing as for roasting (see tables, page 49).

Frying chicken

The small spring chickens, or broiler chickens as they are often called, can be grilled or fried.

To fry in shallow fat:

1 Coat the jointed chicken (to joint chicken, see right), with seasoned flour or with a little flour then egg and breadcrumbs.
2 Heat the fat in a pan – allowing about ½ inch fat or oil.
3 Fry the joints steadily until golden brown on the under side, then turn other side.
4 Lower the heat to make sure the flesh is cooked through to the bone.
5 Serve with fried mushrooms, tomatoes, and crisp green salad.

To fry in deep fat:

1 If wished, coat the jointed chicken with egg and crumbs or with batter.
2 Make sure fat is hot to ensure quick browning and a crisp outside.
3 Brown chicken on both sides.
4 Lower the heat and cook steadily until crisp and golden and cooked through to the middle. With deep fat the chicken will be cooked within 15 minutes.
5 Drain well on absorbent paper, and serve with salad.

To joint a chicken for frying or grilling

1 Use a sharp, not too long knife or large kitchen scissors. First cut away the thighs and drum sticks, you will find this quite easy if you 'locate' the bone that joins the thigh to the body of the bird.
2 Cut down the centre – very slightly to one side of the breast bone – making two joints of breast and wings.
3 Cut away the rest of the body, there is so little meat on this that it is not worth grilling or frying, but can be used for stock.
4 If wished the thighs and drum sticks can be divided and the wings could be cut away from the breast to give a total of 8 pieces, but most people prefer 4 good sized joints.
5 If the birds are very small just divide into halves, so each half consists of breast, wing, one thigh and drum stick – flatten slightly for easy cooking.

Chicken Cordon Bleu

cooking time: 15–20 minutes

you will need:

2 small frying chickens*
4 slices ham
4 slices Gruyère or Cheddar cheese
little seasoned flour
egg and breadcrumbs for coating
fat for frying

*make sure they have nice meaty breasts

1 Use a sharp knife and cut away the breasts from the 2 chickens.
2 Slit them in half lengthways and sandwich together with ham and cheese.
3 Dip first in a little seasoned flour and then in egg and breadcrumbs.
4 Fry until crisp and golden brown in hot fat, then lower the heat and cook steadily for about 15–20 minutes.

Fried chicken and almonds

cooking time: 20 minutes

you will need:

1 jointed frying chicken	4 tablespoons soft breadcrumbs or crushed cornflakes
little flour	3 oz. butter or oil
seasoning	1–2 oz. blanched shredded almonds
egg	

1. Coat the chicken in seasoned flour, then beaten egg and crumbs.
2. Fry the chicken steadily in the hot butter or oil until golden brown.
3. Lower the heat and continue cooking for approximately 15 minutes until quite tender. Turn the chicken to brown evenly.
4. Transfer to hot serving dish.
5. Add extra knob of butter to pan and when hot toss the almonds in this.
6. Pour over the chicken and serve with vegetables or a salad.

Variation:

With lemon and parsley – almonds can be omitted and a little grated lemon rind and chopped parsley tossed in butter can be used instead.

Spiced chicken

cooking time: 40–45 minutes

you will need:

3 lb. young chicken	1-inch stick cinnamon
3 oz. butter	1–2 cloves garlic
1–2 teaspoons powdered turmeric	3 large onions
1 teaspoon ground ginger	salt
6 cloves	rice or noodles, to serve

1. Cut the uncooked chicken in about 12 joints, i.e. 4 from breast, 4 from wings, 4 from legs.
2. Skin the chicken and dry it thoroughly after washing.
3. Heat the butter and add the turmeric to it.
4. Put in the chicken pieces.
5. Raise the heat and fry the chicken for 7–8 minutes.
6. Add the ginger, cloves and splintered cinnamon.
7. Stir, then add chopped garlic and onions.
8. Sprinkle with salt and put on the lid of the pan.
9. Raise the heat to high for 10 seconds, then lower to medium.
10. Shake the pan, return to the heat and cook, without uncovering it, but shaking the pan from time to time, for about 25 minutes – longer if the broiler is older or seems tough.
11. Uncover, leave for another minute.
12. Serve with rice or noodles.

Grilling poultry

While a very young jointed duckling could be grilled, the most suitable poultry to choose is a young broiler chicken. Buy a bird which has already been jointed, or joint it yourself (see page 51). Cook as follows:

If wished, coat the joints with seasoned flour. Put the joints on to the greased grid of the grill pan, brush with plenty of oil or melted butter. Put under a hot grill – but not too near the heat. Grill quickly until the skin is golden brown, turn and brush the under side with more butter or oil, and continue browning.

Either move further away from the grill heat, or lower this and cook steadily until cooked through to the centre.

Mushrooms, tomatoes, etc., can either be put round the joints half way through cooking or can be cooked in the grill pan under the chicken. Use any juices that drop into the pan as the basis for a sauce if wished.

Grilled chicken with parsley butter

cooking time: 20 minutes

you will need:

grilled chicken	grated lemon rind
butter	chopped parsley

Cook the chicken as above, and serve with pats of butter flavoured with grated lemon rind and chopped parsley.

Curried grilled chicken

cooking time: 20 minutes

you will need:

jointed chicken	celery salt
flour	melted butter
curry powder	lemon wedges
cayenne pepper	

1. Sprinkle the joints of chicken with flour, mixed with little curry powder, cayenne pepper and celery salt.
2. Brush with melted butter, then roll again in curry flavoured flour.
3. Cook as grilled chicken.
4. Serve with wedges of lemon.

Variation:

Lemon grilled chicken – omit the curry powder and seasonings as previous recipe and blend the finely grated rind of 1–2 lemons with the flour. Add the juice of 1–2 lemons, pinch paprika and pinch salt to the butter at stage 2, and continue as the recipe.

Grilled chicken with golden sauce

cooking time: 20 minutes

you will need:

4 chicken joints	2 oz. melted butter

for sauce:

1 oz. butter	salt and pepper
1 oz. plain flour	2 hard-boiled eggs
½ pint milk	watercress, to garnish
1 egg yolk	

1 Brush chicken joints with melted butter, grill for 3 minutes on each side.
2 Reduce heat and grill for 8–10 minutes each side.
3 Make sauce by melting butter, stirring in flour, and adding milk.
4 Cook until sauce thickens and remove from heat.
5 Beat in the egg yolk, seasoning and the very finely chopped hard-boiled eggs.
6 Serve chicken with sauce poured over, garnished with watercress.

Variation:

Grilled chicken and creamed corn – follow the directions for the recipe above, but omit the hard-boiled eggs from the sauce. Make the sauce to stage 4, add a medium can corn kernels or cooked corn kernels and heat, then continue as the rest of the recipe.

Devilled turkey legs

cooking time: 10–15 minutes

you will need:

1 leg or 2 drum sticks turkey (if bird is large*)

for coating:

3 oz. turkey fat	squeeze lemon juice
6 oz. breadcrumbs	1 tablespoon chutney
1–2 level teaspoons curry powder	pinch each of salt, pepper, mustard, sugar
½–1 teaspoon Worcestershire sauce	

*or if preferred, small thick pieces of turkey meat.

1 Mix all coating ingredients together.
2 Spread over pieces of turkey meat.
3 Brown on both sides under hot grill.
4 Lower heat and cook more slowly to heat through.
5 Serve with potatoes and peas.

Devilled chicken (1)

cooking time: 10–12 minutes

you will need:

12 oz. cold chicken	½ teaspoon black pepper
2 teaspoons tomato ketchup	2 teaspoons made mustard
2 teaspoons vinegar	2 tablespoons olive oil
pinch cayenne pepper	

1 Cut the chicken into neat pieces.
2 Blend all the other ingredients together.
3 Brush over the chicken.
4 Grill until browned on both sides.
5 Serve hot with boiled rice, vegetables and sweet chutney, or cold with salad.

Making terrines and loaves etc. with poultry and game

The following two recipes are basic ones for making a terrine and a loaf. They can however be varied according to the ingredients available. For example try duck instead of chicken in the terrine, mixing a little chopped sage with seasoning. Or use chicken instead of rabbit in the loaf, or grouse or pigeons.
Either of these recipes is an easy to serve and an economical way of using poultry and game. Also, because they can be carved so effortlessly, they are ideal for entertaining.

Chicken terrine

cooking time: 1¼–1¾ hours

you will need:

1 small chicken	seasoning
6 rashers streaky bacon or bacon pieces	1 tablespoon sherry (if desired)
	3 tablespoons stock

1 Cut the breast away from the bones, slicing this carefully.
2 Remove all the rest of the meat from the bones.
3 Put this, together with the giblets and bacon,

through a mincer, using all the skin; or chop the chicken meat, giblets and bacon very finely.

4 Grease a good sized basin or mould.
5 Put one third of the minced chicken at the bottom.
6 Cover this with half the sliced chicken breast, seasoning each layer well.
7 Continue with another third of the minced chicken, then the rest of the breast and finally the remainder of the minced chicken.
8 Mix the sherry with the chicken stock and seasoning.
9 Pour over the meat.
10 Cover with buttered paper and cook for approximately 1¼ hours in the centre of a very moderate oven (350°F. – Gas Mark 3). If the chicken is not very young, allow up to 1¾ hours.

Variation:

Game terrine – use 1 large pheasant, 2 grouse or 4 pigeons instead of the chicken in the recipe above. Use sherry as stage 8 or brandy.

Rabbit loaf

cooking time: 1–2 hours

you will need:

- 1 rabbit
- 4 oz. bacon pieces
- 1 oz. fat
- 1 large onion
- 8 oz. pork sausage meat
- seasoning
- 3 tablespoons milk or stock
- little margarine
- crisp breadcrumbs if baking or soft crumbs if steaming

1 Cut all the meat from the rabbit bones with a sharp knife and use these to give stock to serve with the rabbit loaf for a hot dish.
2 Put the rabbit flesh and bacon through a mincer. Fry the onion in the fat.
3 Add to the sausage meat and mince.
4 Other flavourings can be added if wished – chopped parsley, little sage, garlic or garlic salt, chopped celery or celery salt.
5 Blend and season well.
6 Gradually moisten with the milk or stock from simmering the bones with the liver of the rabbit.
7 Grease a mould or tin with the margarine and coat with the crumbs.
8 Put in the rabbit mixture, and cover with foil or greased paper.
9 Either steam for about 2 hours or bake for 1–1¼ hours, in the centre of a moderate oven (375°F. – Gas Mark 4).
10 Turn out and serve hot with gravy and mixed vegetables, or cold with salad.

Variation:

Chicken loaf – use a plump young chicken instead of the rabbit in previous recipe. Flavour with parsley, lemon and celery salt at stage 4.

To casserole poultry or game

The following recipes are meant primarily to tenderise rather older poultry or game, but each one can also be used as a basic recipe to adapt to other poultry or game. This method of cooking is ideal when entertaining, as it requires no last minute 'dishing up'. For such occasions, however, rather younger birds could be selected.

Devilled chicken (2)

cooking time: 1½–1¾ hours

you will need:

- 1 small young fowl (weighing about 2–2½ lb.)
- 2–3 oz. margarine or oil
- ½ teaspoon curry powder
- 1 tablespoon Worcestershire sauce
- little vinegar
- 1 teaspoon dry mustard
- good pinch salt and pepper
- 1 dessertspoon lemon juice
- ½ teaspoon sugar
- 2 oz. fine breadcrumbs

for sauce:

- giblet stock
- seasoning
- 1 onion
- a little flour

1 First divide the uncooked fowl into neat joints.
2 Put the giblets into a saucepan, cover with water, add seasoning and the whole onion.
3 Cover the pan and simmer gently for good 30 minutes.
4 While these are simmering, prepare the chicken as follows: cream the margarine, add the curry powder, Worcestershire sauce, vinegar, mustard, salt, pepper, lemon juice and sugar.
5 Spread this paste over the joints of the chicken.
6 Roll in the soft breadcrumbs.
7 Grease a casserole thoroughly, put in the pieces of chicken and cover with any left-over crumbs, a piece of greased greaseproof paper, then lid of the casserole.
8 Bake for 1–1¼ hours in the middle of a very moderate oven (350°F. – Gas Mark 3).
9 During the cooking time take off the lid and add 2 tablespoons of the giblet stock if the chicken appears to be drying at all.
10 Put the cooked joints on a hot dish and pour round a sauce made by thickening the giblet stock with a little flour and cooking until smooth.

Country chicken

cooking time: 2–3 hours

you will need:

1 boiling fowl
2 oz. fat
2 oz. flour
seasoning
8 carrots
3 onions
1 pint water
pinch powdered thyme
squeeze lemon juice
bay leaf
½ pint milk
1–2 tablespoons cream

1 Cut the fowl into neat pieces. If large, make 9 joints (2 drum sticks, 2 thighs, 4 pieces breast and wing and the back). If small divide into 5 (halve breast and include wings on each side – leave thigh and drum sticks as one joint).
2 Heat fat in pan.
3 Flour the chicken with 1 oz. only of seasoned flour and toss in fat until pale gold.
4 Slice carrots and onions and add to the chicken, together with the giblets if wished.
5 Cover with water, add a little extra seasoning, the thyme, lemon juice and bay leaf.
6 Put lid on the pan and simmer for 2 hours with small bird, 3 hours with larger bird.
7 Remove bay leaf, blend rest of flour with the milk and add to stock.
8 Bring steadily to the boil and cook until thickened.
9 Stir in the cream.
10 Taste and reseason if wished.
11 Serve either with vegetables or to provide a contrast in texture, with orange salad and savoury scones.

Variation:

Country duck casserole – use the previous recipe for country chicken, but instead of milk use extra stock or cheap red wine, and omit the cream. Instead of carrots use about 8 oz. shelled chestnuts.

Boiled chicken

cooking time: 2½ hours

you will need:

boiling chicken (approximately 3 lb.)
2–3 sticks celery
2 small onions
½ pint water
seasoning

1 Simmer chicken with celery, onions, etc., for approximately 2½ hours until tender.
2 Serve with one of the following sauces:

White sauce – see recipe page 88, but use half chicken stock, and half milk.

Parsley sauce – see recipe page 88, but use half chicken stock, and half milk.

Hard-boiled egg sauce – see recipe page 88.

Turkey Creole

cooking time: 20–25 minutes

you will need:

4 oz. rice
1 oz. turkey fat
1 green pepper
1 head celery (or can celery)
¼ pint turkey stock
about 12 oz. sliced cooked turkey meat
seasoning
3 large tomatoes

1 Cook rice in boiling salted water.
2 Heat fat and toss in sliced pepper and large pieces of celery.
3 Add turkey stock.
4 Simmer until vegetables are nearly cooked.
5 Add turkey and season well.
6 When thoroughly hot, arrange on bed of cooked rice.
7 Garnish with sliced tomato.

Pigeon casserole

cooking time: 2¼ hours

you will need:

2 good sized pigeons
1 oz. flour
2 oz. fat
1 onion
4 carrots
½ swede
½ pint stock
seasoning
4 tomatoes
bay leaf

1 Fry the floured pigeons in the hot fat for a few minutes.
2 Lift out and put into a casserole.
3 Fry the chopped onion, carrots and diced swede in the fat and cook for a few minutes.
4 Gradually add the stock.
5 Bring to the boil and cook until thickened and smooth.
6 Season well.
7 Pour over the pigeons, adding the tomatoes, bay leaf and cover with a lid or foil.
8 Cook gently for about 2 hours in the centre of a very moderate oven (325°F.–350°F.–Gas Mark 2–3).
9 Remove bay leaf before serving.

Variations:

Grouse casserole – cook as for pigeon casserole above allowing 1 good sized grouse or 2 smaller ones. Diced bacon can be added if wished.

Casserole of hare – use a jointed young hare in

place of pigeons or grouse. Since this is larger (it would serve 6–8 people) double all the ingredients in previous recipe. Add a glass of port wine and 2 tablespoons redcurrant jelly to the sauce at stage 5.

Devilled rabbit

cooking time: 1½ hours

you will need:

1 rabbit
little vinegar
4 oz. fat bacon
large onion
about 8 oz. diced mixed root vegetables
1 teaspoon curry powder
1 teaspoon Worcestershire sauce
1 pint water
seasoning
1 oz. flour
¼ pint milk
chopped parsley

1. Wash the rabbit in cold water, to which a little vinegar is added to whiten the flesh.
2. Cut the meat into pieces.
3. Dice the bacon and put into a pan with chopped onion, vegetables, rabbit, curry powder and sauce.
4. Fry for a few minutes, then add water and bring to the boil.
5. Season well.
6. Put on the lid and simmer gently for about 1½ hours until the rabbit is tender.
7. Blend the flour with the milk and stir into the liquid.
8. Bring to the boil, stirring well and cook until smooth and thickened.
9. Taste and reseason if necessary.
10. Garnish with chopped parsley.

Jugged rabbit

cooking time: 2½–3 hours

you will need:

1 rabbit
1½ oz. clarified dripping
1 oz. flour
1 onion
2 cloves
¼ pint claret (optional)
1 teaspoon lemon juice
bouquet garni
1 pint stock
salt and pepper
8 peppercorns
1 oz. butter
1 scant oz. flour
veal stuffing (see page 88)

to serve:

redcurrant jelly

1. Wash and dry rabbit, divide into joints and fry in hot fat until browned, sprinkling with the flour.
2. Add onion stuck with cloves, claret, lemon juice, *bouquet garni* and stock to cover.
3. Season with salt and peppercorns.
4. Cover and simmer for 2½–3 hours.
5. 30 minutes before serving, thicken the sauce with 1 oz. butter worked with a little less flour and add more wine if desired for a fuller flavour.
6. Veal stuffing makes a good garnish and redcurrant jelly should be served separately.

Variation:

Jugged hare – this is almost more delicious than rabbit. Since the hare is larger you will need slightly more ingredients for the sauce, so use: 1½ pints stock at stage 2 with just over ¼ pint claret (or port wine). When thickening the sauce at stage 5, use 1½ oz. butter and 1½ oz. flour.

Rich rabbit stew

cooking time: 1¾–2¼ hours

you will need:

1 rabbit
4 oz. streaky bacon
18 button onions
2 oz. butter
1½ oz. flour
1 pint stock
bouquet garni (parsley, thyme, bay leaf)
3–4 cloves
6 peppercorns
salt
¼ pint claret (optional)

1. Divide rabbit into small joints, dice the bacon, peel the onions.
2. Fry onions and bacon in butter until brown, and set aside.
3. Fry rabbit joints until lightly browned, add flour and cook until joints are well browned.
4. Replace onions and bacon, and add hot stock, *bouquet garni*, cloves, peppercorns and salt to taste.
5. Cover closely and simmer until rabbit is tender (approximately 1½–2 hours).
6. Shortly before serving add the claret and the rabbit liver finely chopped, letting it simmer for 10 minutes before serving.

Pressure Cooking of Meat, Poultry and Game

A pressure cooker is an excellent means of producing a first class meal in a remarkably short time. It also enables you to make the tougher and cheaper variety of meats and poultry really tender without having to cook them for hours. However, when using a pressure cooker, do remember the following points:

1 Do NOT allow longer cooking time than given in the recipes, since a few minutes in a pressure cooker corresponds to a considerably longer period of ordinary cooking.
2 Make sure the pieces of meat, poultry, etc. are cut to a uniform size.

Goulash

pressure cooking time: 20–25 minutes

you will need:

1 lb. stewing meat (preferably beef)
1 oz. fat
1 medium sized onion
¼ pint tomato pulp or canned tomatoes
¼ pint stock or water
seasoning (include 1–2 teaspoons paprika pepper)
1 lb. potatoes

1 Cut the meat into neat cubes.
2 Heat the fat at the bottom of the cooker and fry the meat and onion until brown.
3 Add tomato pulp, stock, seasoning and paprika.
4 Fix the lid and bring to pressure.
5 Allow pressure to drop then add the sliced potatoes.
6 Re-fix the lid, and bring once again to pressure.
7 Lower the heat and cook for 10 minutes.

Note: This should be a very thick stew.

Oxtail

pressure cooking time: 20 minutes

you will need:

1 oxtail
1 oz. dripping
¾ pint water
2 onions
2 carrots
1 stick celery
seasoning
4 cloves (optional)
1 oz. flour
parsley, to garnish

1 Cut the oxtail into sections.
2 Melt the dripping in bottom of the cooker and fry oxtail until just brown.
3 Add the water, vegetables, seasoning and cloves.
4 Fix the lid, bring to pressure.
5 Then lower the heat.
6 Cook for 20–25 minutes.
7 Allow pressure to drop then remove the lid.
8 Blend the flour with a little cold water or stock.
9 Add to the liquid and bring to the boil.
10 Boil until thick.
11 Serve sprinkled with parsley.

Galantine of rabbit

pressure cooking time: 15 minutes at 15 lb. pressure

cooking time: 1¾–2 hours

you will need:

1 medium sized rabbit
2 tomatoes
½ teaspoon chopped or powdered dried sage
½ teaspoon grated lemon rind
1 egg
seasoning
vegetables for making stock (optional)
milk or stock to bind

to coat:

little flour
1 teaspoon breadcrumbs

1 Remove all the meat from the bones.
2 Put the meat, including liver and heart of rabbit through a mincer.
3 Mix the rabbit meat with all other ingredients, skinning tomatoes and chopping them finely.
4 Add just enough milk or stock (made from rabbit bones) to make a sticky consistency.
5 Form into a roll, flouring the outside lightly.
6 Put either into greased paper, a floured cloth or greased mould.
7 Put ½ pint water into the pressure cooker, then stand the galantine on the rack.
8 Bring rapidly to pressure, then maintain at pressure for 15 minutes.
9 Allow pressure to drop gradually.
10 Coat the galantine with crisp breadcrumbs.
11 If preferred, steam for 1¾–2 hours.

To make stock:

1 Put the rabbit bones with seasoning into the cooker just covering them with water.
2 Vegetables, such as sliced onion or carrot, can be added if wished. Do not use rack.
3 Bring the cooker to pressure, then maintain at pressure, for 20 minutes.

Braised heart

pressure cooking time: 25 minutes

you will need:

1 lb. ox heart or sheep heart
1 oz. dripping
2 onions
2 carrots
1 small turnip
seasoning
bunch herbs or 1 teaspoon mixed herbs
½ pint stock, **or** water flavoured with meat **or** vegetables extract
1 oz. flour plus little extra flour for coating

1 Cut ox heart into thick slices.
2 Heat fat in bottom of pressure cooker.
3 Flour the hearts and season well.
4 Fry in the hot fat until brown.
5 Add all the other ingredients, except the 1 oz. flour.
6 Fix the lid and bring to pressure.
7 Lower heat and cook for 25 minutes.
8 Blend the flour with very little cold stock.
9 Add to the liquid.
10 Bring to the boil and boil for 3 minutes.

Savoury Pies and Puddings

Baking meat or poultry in a pastry crust or in a steamed or boiled pudding helps to retain much of the flavour. Whenever possible, do NOT precook meat, although in some recipes this is essential.

Hot water crust pastry (or raised pastry)

cooking time: according to recipe

you will need:

12 oz. plain flour
pinch salt
3–4 oz. fat
¼ pint water

1 Sieve flour and salt.
2 Melt fat in warm water and add to flour.
3 Mix with knife and knead gently with fingers.

Note: Unlike other pastry, this should be used when warm.

Beef flan

cooking time: 25–30 minutes

you will need:

6 oz. short crust pastry (see page 75)
either 8 oz. diced, cooked meat **or** flaked corn beef
¼ pint **thick** brown sauce or tomato sauce (see pages 87, 88)
or 1 can stewing steak or steak and vegetables and 1 teaspoon cornflour to thicken liquid from can

to garnish:

3 skinned tomatoes
1–2 hard-boiled eggs

1 Bake pastry in flan case 'blind' until crisp and golden.
2 Heat the meat and liquid together, blending in the cornflour, if necessary.
3 Garnish with sliced tomatoes and hard-boiled egg or eggs, arranging these alternately round the flan.
4 Serve hot or cold. If serving hot, wait until meat mixture is very hot, then pour into hot flan and garnish. Do not heat together, otherwise the pastry becomes soggy.
For a cold flan, put cold meat mixture into cold cooked pastry case and garnish.

Croustade of beef

cooking time: 45 minutes–1 hour

you will need:

4–6 oz. short crust pastry (see page 75)
2–3 oz. mushrooms
1 oz. butter
seasoning
approximately 1 lb. fillet rump or other grilling steak CUT IN ONE PIECE

1 Roll out the pastry very thinly to a neat oblong.
2 Chop the mushrooms finely and blend with the butter and seasoning to form an almost paste-like consistency.
3 Spread this over the centre of the pastry, leaving the ends quite bare.
4 Put the piece of steak on top, season lightly and wrap it up in the pastry dough.
5 Tuck in the ends and seal the edges with water.
6 Put on to a lightly greased baking tin.
7 If you like it rare, allow 20–25 minutes in a hot

oven (475°F. – Gas Mark 8), then lower the heat to moderate and allow a further 20 minutes.
If you like it medium, when the heat is lowered to moderate allow 30–40 minutes.
If you like it well done, allow a good 40 minutes after turning down to moderate.

8 Serve with mushroom sauce or brown sauce (see page 88).

Variation:

Lamb cushions – use lean lamb chops in place of steak. Make up 8 oz. pastry to cover 4 good sized lamb chops. Roll out the pastry and cut into 4 squares, then continue as the recipe to the end of stage 3. Cook the chops for 15 minutes and cool. Put on the pastry, wrap carefully, then bake as stage 7.

Hasty steak pie

6 servings

cooking time: 45 minutes

you will need:

- 6 oz. short crust pastry (see page 75)
- 1 oz. butter
- 1 onion
- 1 green pepper
- 2 tomatoes
- 1 16-oz. can stewed steak
- 1 packet peanuts (optional)

1 Divide pastry in half.
2 Roll out one piece and line an 8-inch pie dish.
3 Melt butter in saucepan.
4 Chop onions and pepper finely and fry in butter.
5 Chop tomatoes and add them when onion has just started to turn colour.
6 Add can of steak and mix all ingredients well together.
7 Transfer into pastry case when cool.
8 Roll out remaining pastry and cover pie, marking edge with a fork.
9 Prick top, brush with a little milk and toss peanuts onto it.
10 Bake in centre of a hot oven (425°F. – Gas Mark 6) for 30–35 minutes.

Meat and vegetable roll

cooking time: 1 hour

you will need:

- 8 oz. plain flour
- 2 level teaspoons baking powder
- pinch salt
- 1½ oz. margarine or lard
- cold water to mix
- 8 oz. minced beef
- 1 finely chopped carrot and onion
- salt and pepper
- 2 tablespoons stock
- milk to glaze

1 Sieve together plain flour, baking powder and salt.
2 Rub in fat until mixture resembles breadcrumbs.
3 Add sufficient cold water to give a dry dough.
4 Mix together minced beef, finely chopped carrot and onion.
5 Season well with salt and pepper.
6 Add stock to moisten.
7 Roll pastry out to a large rectangle and trim edges.
8 Cover with filling, leaving ½-inch pastry edge.
9 Brush this with a little water and roll up as for Swiss roll.
10 Seal ends, prick the top with a fork and decorate with pastry leaves.
11 Brush with a little milk and bake in a moderately hot oven (400°F. – Gas Mark 5) for 1 hour.
12 Serve with chipped potatoes and a green vegetable.

Lamb pies

cooking time: 1½ hours

you will need:

- 8 oz. lamb
- 1 small onion, finely chopped
- ½ oz. dripping
- 1 tablespoon parsley
- 1 dessertspoon tomato ketchup
- 1 dessertspoon thick gravy
- seasoning
- 6 oz. short crust pastry (see page 75)
- little beaten egg

1 Mince the lamb.
2 Fry onion lightly in the melted dripping and add to the meat, parsley, ketchup and gravy.
3 Season well.
4 Line deep patty tins with rounds of pastry and damp edges.
5 Fill with the meat mixture and cover with a second round of pastry.
6 Seal and crimp the edges and make a small slit in the top to allow steam to escape.
7 Decorate if liked and brush with beaten egg.
8 Bake in a moderate oven (375°F. – Gas Mark 4) for 25 minutes.
9 Reduce heat to a slower oven (300°F. – Gas Mark 2) and cook for a further 1 hour.

Variation:

With cooked lamb – if liked this recipe can be made using cooked lamb, in which case the cooking time is 25 minutes in a moderate oven (375°F. – Gas Mark 4).

Lamb slices

cooking time: 1 hour

you will need:

8 oz. short crust pastry (see page 75)
12 oz. fresh lamb
2 onions
2 tomatoes
1 oz. dripping or lard
pinch chopped mint
seasoning

1 Roll out the pastry to a neat oblong shape.
2 Mince or chop the lamb finely.
3 Chop and fry the onions and tomatoes in the hot dripping until very soft.
4 Mix with the lamb, add mint, seasoning.
5 Spread over pastry.
6 Roll like a Swiss roll, then bake in the centre of a hot oven (425°F.–450°F. – Gas Mark 6–7) for approximately 25 minutes.
7 Lower the heat to moderate (375°F. – Gas Mark 4) for a further 30–40 minutes.
8 Cut into slices and serve hot or cold.

Variation:

Beef slices – use 12 oz. canned corned beef in place of lamb. Flake this and mix with the ingredients as stages 3 and 4. A more appropriate flavouring for beef is chopped parsley and a little made mustard, so omit the mint.

Mutton pie

cooking time: 2 hours

you will need:

8 small mutton cutlets
8 small onions
2 oz. fat
1 oz. flour
¾ pint water
seasoning
8 small tomatoes
few capers
6 oz. flaky or short crust pastry (see page 75)

1 Brown meat then onions in the fat.
2 Stir in the flour and cook for a few minutes.
3 Add water, bring to the boil and stir until smooth.
4 Season well.
5 Put lid on pan and simmer for 1 hour.
6 Lift onions and meat out of stock.
7 Arrange in pie dish so that all the bones are standing upright in the centre of the dish.
8 Put in tomatoes, capers and some of the gravy.
9 Cover with pastry, allowing bones to pierce this in the centre.
10 Bake for approximately 45 minutes in a really hot oven, then reduce heat for 20–25 minutes.

Meat and egg pasty

cooking time: 45 minutes

you will need:

for pastry:

8 oz. plain flour
½ teaspoon salt
½ teaspoon baking powder
2 oz. lard
2 oz. butter
4 tablespoons cold water

for filling:

1 can corned beef
½ pint can mushroom soup
4 eggs

1 Firstly, make the pastry. Sieve the dry ingredients.
2 Rub in the fat and butter until mixture is crumbly.
3 Mix to a soft dough with water.
4 Divide into 2 pieces and roll out.
5 Line a 7- or 7½-inch ovenproof dish (1½–2 inches deep) with 1 piece of pastry.
6 Make the filling – open the can of corned beef and tip into a bowl.
7 Mash with a fork and stir in half the mushroom soup.
8 Put mixture into the dish.
9 Make 4 hollows in the meat mixture and drop an unbeaten egg into each.
10 Carefully cover with the rest of the meat. If possible keep the yolks whole, but if they break it doesn't matter.
11 Cover with pastry, neaten edges and decorate.
12 Bake for 45 minutes in a moderately hot oven (400°F. – Gas Mark 5).
13 Heat rest of soup and serve as a sauce.

Veal and ham pie

cooking time: 2¼ hours

you will need:

12 oz. raised pastry (see page 58)
1 lb. fillet veal
6 oz. ham
salt and pepper
½ level teaspoon grated lemon rind
1–2 hard-boiled eggs
7 tablespoons water or bone stock
beaten eggs for glazing
1 level teaspoon gelatine
½ level teaspoon meat extract

1 Make pastry and keep warm in basin until ready to use.
2 Remove pastry from basin and with two-thirds of the dough line a 6-inch cake tin or 1 lb. loaf tin.

3 Wash and dry the meats, removing any skin, and cut into 1-inch cubes.
4 Roll the meat together in salt and pepper and lemon rind.
5 Place half the meat in the bottom of the pastry-lined tin.
6 Cut the eggs into halves.
7 Place on top of the meat and cover with remaining meat.
8 Pour into the pie 3 tablespoons of the water or stock.
9 Turn the top edges of pastry lining in over the meat, damp it all around.
10 Roll out the remaining third of pastry to make a lid.
11 Press down well all round edges and cut at ½ inch intervals with a sharp knife to secure.
12 Make a hole in the centre, brush over with beaten egg, decorate with pastry 'leaves' and again brush with beaten egg.
13 Place in the centre of a moderate oven (375°F. – Gas Mark 4) for 2–2¼ hours.
14 Leave to cool.
15 Melt the gelatine in remaining water or stock and stir in the meat extract.
16 When the pie is cool and the gelatine mixture just setting, pour into the pie through the hole in the centre.
17 Leave to set before serving.

Variations:

Chicken and ham pie No. 1 – use about 1 lb. diced raw chicken instead of veal. Have half light and half dark meat to give a variety of flavour.

Pork pie – use 1½ lb. lean pork (cut from the leg of pork) instead of veal and ham. Omit the hard-boiled eggs, if wished.

Ulster flan

cooking time: 1 hour

you will need:

for pastry:

6 oz. plain flour, sifted
3 oz. butter
salt
1 oz. grated cheese

for filling:

6 oz. bacon, streaky or back
bare ½ pint milk
salt and pepper
2 large eggs

1 Make the pastry by rubbing butter into the flour and salt.
2 Add the cheese and mix with water until normal pastry consistency is obtained.
3 Roll out, line an 8-inch flan ring with it, then bake blind (see page 74) for approximately 20 minutes, until pale golden brown.
4 Prepare the filling. First remove bacon rind.
5 Cut up the bacon, lightly grill or fry and put into the pastry case.
6 Add milk and seasonings to the beaten eggs.
7 Strain into the pastry case.
8 Bake in very moderate oven (350°F. – Gas Mark 3) for about 40 minutes.

Chicken and bacon pie

cooking time: 2 hours for chicken, 45 minutes for pie

you will need:

small boiling fowl, or half a large one (with giblets)
seasoning
pinch mixed herbs
little lemon rind
2–3 rashers bacon or piece ham
2 hard-boiled eggs
⅓ pint chicken stock
6–8 oz. short crust or flaky pastry (see page 75)

1 Simmer the fowl until tender. Cook giblets as well.
2 When cooking add seasoning, pinch mixed herbs and lemon rind.
3 Remove meat from bone and cut into small pieces.
4 Mix the light and dark meat together with the giblets.
5 Chop the uncooked bacon into small pieces.
6 Slice the hard-boiled eggs.
7 Season meat well.
8 Put a layer of chicken meat, then egg and bacon into pie dish, fill like this.
9 Cover with chicken stock.
10 Put on pastry lid and bake for about 45 minutes in centre of oven. Start with hot oven (425°F.–445°F. – Gas Mark 6–7) then lower to moderate (375°F. – Gas Mark 4).
11 Serve hot or cold.

Variations:

With potato – mashed potatoes could be used instead of pastry for the pie.

With beef – beef, simmered gently, could be used instead of chicken; add sliced tomatoes and mushrooms as well as the bacon.

Chicken and ham pie No. (2)

cooking time: approximately 1½ hours

you will need:

for hot water crust pastry:

scant ¼ pint water
4 oz. cooking fat or lard
large pinch salt
10 oz. flour (with plain flour 1½ level teaspoons baking powder)

1. Put water, lard and salt into pan.
2. Heat together until lard has dissolved.
3. Pour over the flour, knead well, use while warm and keep warm.

for filling:

small cooked boiling fowl or ½ larger fowl
bay leaf
seasoning
pinch mixed herbs
4 oz. bacon or cooked ham
egg or milk, to glaze
1 teaspoon powdered gelatine
3 tablespoons chicken stock plus stock to moisten

1. Cut all the bones away from the chicken and simmer these with bay leaf, seasoning and herbs.
2. Dice the chicken meat and ham and mix together keeping the stock separately.
3. Make a round or oval of pastry and long strip and line the bottom and sides of a 6 or 7-inch tin, fill with chicken mixture and a very little stock.
4. Make a round of pastry to cover the filling.
5. Lay this on top, it is important to seal the edges firmly.
6. Do not press down the pastry too hard since there must be room to pour in the jellied stock after cooking.
7. Make a slit in the centre of the top pastry and use any pieces left to form leaves, a rose or tassel.
8. Brush with the milk or beaten egg and milk to glaze the pie.
9. Bake for about 1¼–1½ hours in the centre of a moderately hot oven (400°F. – Gas Mark 5). If the pie is becoming too brown reduce heat slightly.
10. Allow to cool before removing from tin. Or if you have a special raised pie tin, unlock this carefully.
11. When the pie is cool, fill with the jellied stock.
12. To make this, dissolve the powdered gelatine in the 3 tablespoons chicken stock and pour through the split in the top of the pie.
13. Make a small greaseproof paper funnel for easy pouring.

Picnic roll

cooking time: 1 hour

you will need:

1 onion
1½ oz. butter
1 oz. flour
¼ pint milk
12 oz. minced cooked chicken, veal or beef
4 oz. chopped or minced ham
2–3 tablespoons breadcrumbs
seasoning
2–3 hard-boiled eggs
8–10 oz. short crust pastry (see page 75)
egg or milk, to glaze

1. Chop the onion and fry in the butter.
2. Stir in the flour.
3. Cook for several minutes.
4. Remove from heat and add milk.
5. Bring to boil, cook until very thick.
6. Add the veal or chicken, ham, crumbs and seasoning.
7. Press mixture on to floured board and form into oblong shape.
8. Put eggs on this then mould mixture round them. Form into a neat roll.
9. Roll out pastry into oblong shape.
10. Lift meat and egg roll onto this – wrap up in a neat parcel sealing top and ends.
11. Lift on to greased baking tin with sealed side on tin.
12. Slit along top to allow steam to escape. Brush with egg and milk or milk and bake for 40 minutes in centre of moderately hot oven (400°F. – Gas Mark 5).

Variation:

Seafood roll – use flaked canned tuna or salmon in place of the chicken or beef and ham. Flavour with the grated rind and juice of 1 lemon at stage 6.

Turkey vol-au-vent

cooking time: 35 minutes

you will need:

8 oz. turkey pieces from carcase and wings
4 oz. mushrooms
1 oz. butter
1 oz. flour
½ pint stock or milk
salt and pepper
8 oz. puff pastry
egg, to glaze

1. Cut the turkey off the bones and divide into evenly sized pieces.
2. Wash and slice the mushrooms.

3 Melt the butter in a saucepan and add the flour.
4 Pour in the stock, bring to the boil and stir until the sauce is thick.
5 Add the pieces of turkey and the mushrooms and heat gently for 5 minutes. Season.
6 In the meantime, roll out the pastry and cut into a large round. With a small cutter or saucer press a circle into the middle of the pastry, pressing half way through pastry.
7 Glaze the top and sides with a little beaten egg.
8 Bake in centre of very hot oven (475°F. – Gas Mark 8) for 10 minutes, then lower heat to moderately hot (400°F. – Gas Mark 5) for 10–12 minutes.
9 Carefully cut off the lid of the vol-au-vent and remove the dough.
10 Return the shell and the lid to the oven to dry out for 5–8 minutes.
11 Fill the shell with the hot turkey mixture and replace the lid.
12 Serve immediately.

Variation:

Game vol-au-vent – use cooked game in place of turkey. Either heat in a white sauce as the recipe above or make a brown sauce instead. Add the mushrooms and game to this sauce, flavour with a little brandy or sherry.

Turkey pie

cooking time: 35 minutes

you will need:

short crust pastry (see page 75)
12 oz. cooked turkey meat
4 oz. bacon
seasoning
scant ¼ pint turkey stock (made by simmering giblets)
1 hard-boiled egg
1 egg yolk
1 teaspoon powder gelatine

1 Roll out pastry and line deep oval, round or square tin with two-thirds of it.
2 Arrange sliced meat and bacon in this, adding seasoning and about 1 dessertspoon only of stock.
3 Place hard-boiled egg in centre.
4 Cover with pastry and decorate with pastry leaves. Do not press pastry 'lid' down too tightly on to meat.
5 Brush with beaten egg yolk.
6 Cook for about 25 minutes in centre of hot oven (425°F.–450°F. – Gas Mark 6–7), then lower heat to moderate (375°F. – Gas Mark 4) for further 10 minutes.
7 Cool slightly and turn out of tin.
8 If sides are not really brown, put into oven on flat baking tray for few minutes.
9 Allow pie to cool again.
10 Meanwhile, dissolve gelatine in turkey stock, allowing this to become quite cold and slightly stiffened.
11 Then pour through hole in top of pie.

Steak and liver pudding

cooking time: 4–5 hours

you will need:

for the pastry:

8 oz. plain flour
1 level teaspoon baking powder
little salt
4 oz. suet (chopped finely)
cold water to mix

for filling:

1 lb. stewing steak
4 oz. liver
flour, seasoned with salt and pepper
chopped onion (optional)
beef stock or cold water

1 Sieve together plain flour, baking powder and salt.
2 Mix in suet and bring to a stiff paste with cold water.
3 Knead slightly.
4 Cut off one third of pastry and retain for pudding lid.
5 Roll out remaining pastry into a circle ⅛ inch thick.
6 Line a greased 2-pint basin with this.
7 Cut steak into cubes, slice liver and coat each piece with seasoned flour.
8 Turn meat into lined basin.
9 Add a chopped onion to meat if desired.
10 Add enough stock or water to come half way up the meat.
11 Roll out pastry for top and seal onto pastry in basin.
12 Cover with foil or paper and steam for 4–5 hours.

Mushroom steak and kidney pudding

cooking time: 4–6 hours

you will need:

1 lb. beef steak, shin, blade or chuck
8 oz. ox kidney
1 oz. seasoned flour
4 oz. mushrooms
8 oz. suet crust pastry (see page 76)
½ oz. butter
little water or stock

1. Cut the steak into small cubes.
2. Wash, skin and cut the kidney into similar sized cubes, removing the core.
3. Roll in the well seasoned flour.
4. Wash and chop the mushrooms.
5. Make suet crust pastry.
6. Line buttered basin with suet crust pastry.
7. Fill the basin with the steak, kidney and mushrooms and pour in sufficient water or stock to come three-quarters of the way up.
8. Put the dough lid on top and seal to the lining with water.
9. Cover first with greaseproof paper, then with foil, and tie down covers securely.
10. Steam for 4–6 hours.
11. Turn out carefully.

Mutton pudding

cooking time: 4–5 hours

you will need:

8–10 oz. suet crust pastry (see page 76)
little flour
seasoning
8 pieces scrag end neck mutton
8 small onions
2 lambs' kidneys

1. Line basin with suet crust pastry rolling this out thinly and keeping back enough for a lid.
2. Fill with floured and seasoned meat, onions, chopped kidney and water to come two-thirds up basin.
3. Put on a suet pastry 'lid' and seal edges. Cover with greased paper, foil or a cloth. Steam or boil for about 4–5 hours.

Variation:

Chicken and vegetable pudding – choose a small boiling fowl, and cut this into joints. Remove bones if possible and roll the chicken meat in well-seasoned flour, at stage 2. Put into the lined basin with 2 oz. button mushrooms, the onions and 2–3 sliced raw carrots. Add water or use chicken stock (made by simmering the giblets in salted water) as stage 2, continue as recipe.

Vegetable and Salad Dishes

A well planned vegetable dish can be served as a main course, particularly if used in conjunction with cheese, or a small amount of meat or poultry. Take advantage of the more unusual vegetables, and try serving them with satisfying sauces or stuffings as your main dish. Many of the following recipes are suitable for this sort of meal.

Stuffed aubergines

cooking time: 1 hour

you will need:

4 aubergines
1 small onion
1 tablespoon olive oil
4 oz. minced beef
1 oz. breadcrumbs
chopped parsley
1 egg
¼ pint hot water
1 meat extract cube

to serve: tomato sauce (see page 87)

1. Halve the aubergines – remove centre pulp and mix it with chopped onion.
2. Fry onion and centre pulp in olive oil.
3. Add meat, breadcrumbs, parsley, egg, water and meat cube.
4. Fill the aubergines with the mixture and place on a greased baking dish.
5. Bake for about 1 hour in a moderate oven (375°F. – Gas Mark 4).
6. Serve with tomato sauce.

Stuffed sweet peppers or capsicums

cooking time: 1 hour

you will need:

3–4 peppers
1 small onion
1 tablespoon olive oil
4 oz. minced beef
1 oz. breadcrumbs
1 egg
chopped parsley
¼ pint hot water
1 meat extract cube

to serve:

tomato sauce (see page 87)

1 Cut peppers in half and remove seeds.
2 Fry chopped onion in olive oil.
3 Add meat, breadcrumbs, egg, parsley, water and meat cube.
4 Fill the peppers with the mixture and place on a greased baking dish.
5 Bake for about 45 minutes in a moderate oven (375°F. – Gas Mark 4).
6 Serve with tomato sauce.

Stuffed marrow

cooking time: 1¼ hours

you will need:

small marrow
1 small onion
1 tablespoon olive oil
4 oz. minced beef
1 oz. breadcrumbs
1 egg
chopped parsley
¼ pint hot water
1 meat extract cube

to serve:

tomato sauce (see page 87)

1 Halve marrow lengthways, remove seeds.
2 Fry chopped onion in olive oil.
3 Add meat, breadcrumbs, egg, parsley, water and meat cube.
4 Fill each half of marrow with the mixture and place on a greased baking dish.
5 Bake in a hot oven for about an hour.
6 Serve with tomato sauce.

Variation:

Stuffed green peppers – use the recipe above as a stuffing in green peppers. Halve large peppers, remove core and seeds and simmer peppers in boiling, salted water for 5 minutes. Drain and cool and pack with the stuffing. Bake on a greased dish for approximately 35 minutes in a hot oven.

Stuffed onions

pressure cooking time: 6 minutes

cooking time: 1½ hours

you will need:

4 medium sized Spanish onions
3 tablespoons breadcrumbs
1 oz. grated cheese
1 egg
1 oz. margarine or butter
seasoning

to serve:

white or cheese sauce (see page 88)

1 Wash the onions and remove the outer skins.
2 Put on the rack in the cooker with ¼ pint water and salt.
3 Fix the lid and bring to pressure.
4 Lower the heat and cook for 2 minutes.
5 Reduce the pressure immediately and open the cooker.
6 Take out the onions. These will not be cooked, but it will be possible to remove the centre core.
7 Chop this part of the onion finely.
8 Add to the other ingredients and pile this stuffing back into the centre cavity.
9 Put the onions into a greased container and stand on the rack with the same liquid.
10 Re-fix the lid and bring to pressure again.
11 Lower the heat and cook for a further 4 minutes.
12 Allow pan to return to normal pressure gradually.
13 Serve with white or cheese sauce.
14 This dish can also be cooked in an ordinary casserole for 1½ hours.

Vegetable pie

cooking time: 50 minutes

you will need:

1 lb. mixed diced vegetables
hard-boiled eggs (optional)
½ pint cheese sauce (see page 88)
1 lb. mashed potatoes
1 tablespoon grated cheese

1 Put the vegetables into a greased pie dish.
2 If using hard-boiled eggs, slice and arrange on top of vegetables.
3 Pour over the sauce and cover with the mashed potato.
4 Sprinkle on the grated cheese and bake for 30 minutes in the centre of a moderately hot oven (400°F. – Gas Mark 5) until crisp and brown.

Summer casserole au gratin

cooking time: 35–40 minutes

you will need:

8 oz. cooked young carrots
1–2 cooked diced turnips
4–6 cooked diced new potatoes
about 12 spring onions
2 oz. butter
2–3 tomatoes

for sauce:

$1\frac{1}{2}$ oz. butter
$1\frac{1}{2}$ oz. flour
$\frac{1}{2}$ pint milk
2 eggs
seasoning
3 oz. grated cheese

Toss all the vegetables in the butter, except the tomatoes, which should be sliced and added afterwards.
2 Put into casserole.
3 Make thick sauce of butter, flour, milk; add egg yolks and seasoning, the grated cheese, and stiffly beaten egg whites.
4 Pour over vegetables and put into centre of moderately hot oven (400°F. – Gas Mark 5) for about 25 minutes until well risen and firm.

A summer salad sandwich

cooking time: 25–30 minutes

you will need:

for cheese scone mixture:

8 oz. plain flour
$\frac{1}{2}$ level teaspoon salt
$\frac{1}{2}$ level teaspoon dry mustard
1 level teaspoon baking powder
pinch pepper
$1\frac{1}{2}$ oz. butter
8 oz. grated Cheddar cheese
scant $\frac{1}{4}$ pint ice cold water

for filling:

2 oz. butter
1 rounded teaspoon chopped capers
2 level teaspoons anchovy paste
3 tomatoes
cucumber

1 Sieve dry ingredients into a large bowl, rub in butter and mix in cheese.
2 Mix to a stiff dough with ice cold water, knead slightly and turn onto floured board.
3 Form into oblong and roll to $\frac{1}{2}$ inch thickness.
4 Wrap dough in greaseproof paper and enclose in aluminium foil.
5 Store in chill tray of refrigerator until required.
6 Cut dough into six fingers, place on baking sheet and bake in a hot oven (425°F. – Gas Mark 6) for 25–30 minutes, until golden brown.
7 Cool on a rack.
8 When cold split each scone in three.
9 For the filling cream butter and beat in capers and anchovy paste.
10 Spread bottom layer of scones with anchovy butter.
11 Place middle layer on top and cover with sliced tomatoes or cucumber.
12 Cover with top layer of scone and garnish with slices of tomato or cucumber.

Cheese and plum salad

no cooking

you will need:

1 lb. ripe plums
4 oz. grated Cheddar cheese
2 level teaspoons mayonnaise
good pinch cinnamon
lettuce leaves
watercress

1 Wash and dry plums; cut in half and remove stones.
2 To make filling, mix grated cheese, mayonnaise and cinnamon to soft paste and form into small balls, allowing one ball to each plum.
3 Sandwich filling and plums together and stand on a bed of lettuce.
4 Garnish with watercress.

Variations:

Cheese and apricot salad – use the same filling for well-drained, canned apricots, or for ripe halved apricots.

Cheese and apple ring salad – core, but do not peel dessert apples, sprinkle either with lemon juice or an oil and vinegar dressing. Put on a bed of lettuce, then top with balls of the cheese mixture and garnish with dates or walnuts.

Moulded chicken salad

cooking time: few minutes

you will need:

about 1 lb. cooked chicken or chicken and ham
1 pint chicken stock or use can chicken soup and make up to 1 pint with milk or water
1 oz. gelatine
3 tablespoons mayonnaise
2 hard-boiled eggs
3–4 oz. cooked diced vegetables, peas, carrots, cucumbers, etc.
seasoning
lettuce, tomatoes

1 Chop chicken fairly finely, but do not mince.
2 Heat most of the chicken stock.
3 Soften gelatine in remaining liquid.
4 Add to hot stock and stir until thoroughly dissolved.
5 Cool, then stir in chicken, mayonnaise, chopped eggs, vegetables and seasoning.
6 Pour into mould or basin and leave to set.
7 Serve with lettuce and tomatoes.

Salmon cream

cooking time: 10 minutes

you will need:

¼ pint aspic jelly
1 level teaspoon powdered gelatine
¼ pint mayonnaise
2 tablespoons cream
8–12 oz. cooked salmon
2 hard-boiled eggs
2 sliced gherkins
seasoning

1 When making the aspic jelly, dissolve the extra teaspoon gelatine powder in the liquid.
2 Allow to cool.
3 Mix with the mayonnaise, cream, flaked salmon and 1 of the chopped hard-boiled eggs and 1 of the gherkins.
4 Season well.
5 Put into a rinsed mould and allow to set.
6 Turn out and decorate with the other egg and gherkin. Serve with salad.

Tossed cheese salad

no cooking

you will need:

2 medium sized onions
2 large tomatoes
1 small lettuce
1 bunch watercress
few chives
8 oz. diced Cheddar cheese
1 tablespoon olive oil
1 tablespoon vinegar
salt and pepper
1 teaspoon lemon juice

1 Slice onions thinly and cut tomatoes in 8 pieces.
2 Shred lettuce coarsely.
3 Place in salad bowl with half watercress, tomatoes, chopped chives and cheese.
4 Whisk olive oil in vinegar a little at a time with seasoning and lemon juice.
5 Pour over salad ingredients and toss well.
6 Arrange sliced onion around edge of bowl and place remaining watercress in a bunch in centre. Chill for 30 minutes before serving.

Orange salad (to serve with cold duck, goose, etc.)

no cooking

you will need:

lettuce
2 large oranges
small teaspoon mustard
good pinch salt, pepper and sugar
1½ tablespoons oil
1½ tablespoons vinegar

1 Wash and dry lettuce and arrange on small plates.
2 Peel oranges and remove outside pith.
3 Then, using a very sharp knife, cut sections from the oranges.
4 Arrange on the lettuce.
5 Put the mustard on to a flat plate and add the seasonings.
6 Gradually blend in the oil and vinegar.
7 Pour over the salad. Arrange round sliced duck.

Hot Puddings

In this chapter you will find a variety of hot puddings, some of them old favourites, others quite new suggestions.
An attractive pudding completes a good meal, and often when people are not particularly hungry and do not eat much of the other courses, they will derive most of their food value from the pudding. It is therefore important that you frequently use recipes which contain milk, fruit etc., so that as well as tasting pleasant, they contain ingredients which will provide real food value.

Pear upside-down cake

(illustrated on the cover)

cooking time: 1¼–1½ hours

you will need:

for topping:

1 oz. butter	8–10 canned pear halves
2 oz. brown sugar	

for cake mixture:

6 oz. flour (with plain flour 1½ level teaspoons baking powder)	6 oz. butter or margarine
1 oz. cornflour	6 oz. castor sugar
1 oz. cocoa powder	few drops vanilla essence
	2 eggs
	2 tablespoons milk

1. Melt butter and blend with brown sugar.
2. Spread over base of greased 8-inch cake tin.
3. Arrange pear halves on top, cut sides down.
4. Sift together dry ingredients.
5. Cream margarine, sugar and vanilla essence till light and fluffy.
6. Beat in eggs gradually.
7. Fold in dry ingredients alternately with milk.
8. Spoon mixture over pears.
9. Smooth with a knife.
10. Bake in centre of oven at 350°F. – Gas Mark 3 for 1¼–1½ hours.
11. Serve warm with cream.

Variation:

Peach and cherry upside-down cake – use about 4–5 halved peaches and glacé cherries in place of pears. Add the grated rind of 1 lemon to the butter and brown sugar and the juice of the lemon in place of milk at stage 7.

Apple and lemon croquettes

cooking time: 1¼ hours

you will need:

4 large cooking apples	2 oz. sugar
6 tablespoons fine breadcrumbs	1 egg
grated rind 1 lemon	crisp breadcrumbs
	fat for frying

1. Bake apples in skins, skin and mash while hot, adding crumbs, lemon rind and sugar.
2. Leave until cold, then make into finger shapes.
3. Roll in beaten egg and crisp crumbs.
4. Fry until golden brown.
5. Serve with custard or with lemon marmalade sauce (see below).

Variations:

Apple and rice croquettes – use recipe above, but use 2 oz. cooked rice in place of crumbs.

Apple and ginger croquettes – use either of the previous recipes, i.e. either adding cooked rice or crumbs to the apple mixture. Add 3–4 oz. chopped preserved ginger at stage 1 while the apples are still warm.
Stir about 1 tablespoon preserved ginger syrup into the lemon marmalade sauce or add 1–2 oz. chopped preserved ginger.

Lemon marmalade sauce

cooking time: about 10 minutes

you will need:

juice 1 lemon	1 rounded teaspoon cornflour or arrowroot
3 tablespoons orange or lemon marmalade	
¼ pint water, blended with	

1. Combine all ingredients in saucepan.
2. Boil until clear, stirring well. Taste and sweeten if desired.

Arabian pudding

cooking time: 1 hour

you will need:

- 1 large cooking apple
- 4 oz. fat
- 4 oz. soft brown sugar
- 2 eggs
- 4 oz. flour (with plain flour 1 teaspoon baking powder)
- 1 level teaspoon mixed spice
- ¼ level teaspoon salt
- 1 tablespoon milk
- 1 glacé cherry

1. Peel and core the apple.
2. Cream the fat and sugar together in a bowl, until light and fluffy.
3. Beat in eggs thoroughly, one at a time.
4. Fold in the sieved flour, mixed spice, salt and milk.
5. Brush a 6-inch deep cake tin or soufflé dish with melted fat and line bottom with greaseproof paper.
6. Cover this with thinly sliced apple to form a circular pattern and place a glacé cherry in the centre.
7. Place the cake mixture over the fruit evenly.
8. Bake on the middle shelf of a very moderate oven (350°F. – Gas Mark 3) for 1 hour.
9. Turn out on to a hot serving dish.
10. Serve with custard or cream.

Bread and butter pudding

cooking time: 45 minutes

you will need:

- 3 slices very thin bread and butter
- 1 egg
- ½ pint milk
- 1 good tablespoon sugar
- 2 tablespoons dried fruit

1. Divide the bread and butter in neat triangles and arrange in a greased pie dish.
2. Beat the egg and pour the warmed milk over it.
3. Add half the sugar and the dried fruit.
4. Pour over the bread and butter and dust the top with sugar.
5. Cook for about 45 minutes in a very moderate oven (350°F. – Gas Mark 3), when the custard should be set.
6. For the last 15 minutes move the dish to top of oven so that the pudding browns and becomes crisp.

Variations:

Orange bread and butter pudding – omit dried fruit, add grated rind of an orange and 1–2 oz. crystallised peel.

Luxury bread and butter pudding – add 2–3 tablespoons cream to egg and milk. Increase amount of dried fruit slightly, add few chopped glacé cherries and a little crystallised peel.

Fruit crisp

cooking time: 30 minutes

you will need:

- 1 lb. fruit – apples, rhubarb, plums or soft fruit
- little water
- sugar to taste
- 1 oz. sugar
- 1 oz. fat
- 2 oz. flour
- 2 oz. crisp breadcrumbs or coarse oatmeal

1. Put the fruit with very little water and sugar into a pie dish and heat thoroughly in the oven.
2. Cream the fat and sugar.
3. Add the flour and breadcrumbs or oatmeal. The mixture should now look like sticky crumbs.
4. Sprinkle this on top of the hot fruit and bake in the centre of a moderate oven (375°F. – Gas Mark 4) for a good 30 minutes.

Fruit crumble

cooking time: 35–40 minutes

you will need:

- 1 lb. fruit*
- sugar to sweeten fruit
- 3 oz. sugar
- little water
- 2 oz. butter or margarine
- 4 oz. flour (plain or or self-raising)

*this recipe is suitable for all fruit.

1. Put the fruit with sugar and very little water into a fairly large pie dish. Soft fruits like raspberries need no water.
2. Heat for about 10–15 minutes.
3. Rub the butter into the flour and add the 3 oz. sugar.
4. Sprinkle the crumbs evenly over the fruit pressing down fairly firmly. This makes certain the crust can be cut into neat slices.
5. Bake in the centre of a moderate oven (375°F. – Gas Mark 4) for about 25 minutes until crisp and golden brown.
6. Serve hot or cold.

Cornflake crumble

you will need:

- 2 oz. butter
- 1 oz. golden syrup
- 2 oz. sugar
- 4 oz. VERY CRISP cornflakes
- 1 lb. fruit

Method as for fruit crumble but cream the butter with the golden syrup and sugar. Work in cornflakes. This is particularly good with rhubarb and soft fruits.

Fruit sponge flan

cooking time: 15 minutes

you will need:

for flan:

- 2 eggs
- 2 oz. castor sugar
- 2 oz. flour (with plain flour ½ teaspoon baking powder)
- 1 dessertspoon water

for filling:

- about 12 oz. cooked or canned fruit
- ¼ pint sweetened juice
- 1 teaspoon arrowroot

1 Grease and flour an 8-inch, deep flan tin (or 9-inch shallow flan tin).
2 Whisk eggs and sugar until very thick and creamy.
3 FOLD IN the sieved flour and the water.
4 Pour into the flan tin and bake for approximately 10 minutes in a hot oven (425°F.–450°F. – Gas Mark 6–7), until firm and golden brown, just above middle of the oven.
5 Turn out carefully and when cold fill with the well drained fruit.
6 Blend the arrowroot (cornflour could be used instead) with the juice and boil until thick and clear. Spread over fruit.
7 If this looks very colourless, you may like to add 1–2 drops edible kitchen colouring.
8 Decorate with cream if desired.

Lemon apples

cooking time: 1 hour 10 minutes

you will need:

- 4 good sized cooking apples
- 1 large lemon
- 1–2 tablespoons brown sugar
- ¼ pint water
- 1 slightly rounded teaspoon cornflour or arrowroot
- ½ oz. almonds

1 Core apples and slit skin round centre.
2 Put in casserole.
3 Mix grated rind of lemon with sugar and press into centre of each apple.
4 Cover with lid and cook until tender – about 1 hour in moderate oven (375°F. – Gas Mark 4).
5 Remove apples and take off top skin.
6 Scrape any juice and sugar from dish into saucepan.
7 Add lemon juice and water blended with cornflour.
8 Boil together until smooth sauce.
9 Pour over apples and decorate with blanched chopped almonds.

Redcurrant apples

cooking time: 1 hour

you will need:

- apples
- sugar
- butter
- redcurrant jelly
- thick cream for serving

1 Core and split the skins on large baking apples and fill the centres with a little white sugar and a knob of butter.
2 Bake for approximately 45 minutes at 375°F. – Gas Mark 4.
3 Remove top skins and fill holes with plenty of redcurrant jelly.
4 Put back into the oven for a further 15–20 minutes, during which time the redcurrant jelly will melt and run down the outside of each apple making it pale pink.
5 Pour a little thick cream over each apple before serving.

Rhubarb batter

cooking time: 40 minutes

you will need:

- 8 oz. plain flour
- 2 eggs
- 1 pint milk
- water
- 12 oz. rhubarb
- good knob fat
- little sugar

1 Make a smooth batter with the flour, egg and milk and water.
2 Wipe rhubarb and cut into small lengths.
3 Heat good knob of fat in Yorkshire pudding tin.
4 Add rhubarb to the batter.

5 Pour into the hot fat and bake for approximately 15 minutes in a very hot oven (450°F.–475°F. – Gas Mark 7–8).
6 Lower the heat and cook for a further 25 minutes until firm and brown.
7 Dredge with plenty of sugar when serving.

Orange custard

cooking time: 1½ hours

you will need:

3 eggs
1 oz. sugar
grated rind and juice 1 orange
1 pint milk
1 small can mandarin oranges
1 teaspoon cornflour
sugar

1 Beat the eggs and sugar.
2 Heat the rind with the milk.
3 Pour over the eggs and strain into a shallow dish.
4 Bake for approximately 1½ hours, standing the custard in another dish of cold water, in a very cool oven.
5 Decorate with the orange sections.
6 Serve with thick sauce made by blending the orange syrup from the can of oranges, orange juice with a heaped teaspoon cornflour. Boil until thick and clear, sweeten to taste.

Plum meringue

cooking time: 40 minutes

you will need:

1 lb. plums
½ pint water
4 oz. sugar
extra water
2 oz. rice
2 eggs, separated

1 Put the plums in a saucepan with the water and 2 oz. sugar.
2 Simmer until fruit is soft.
3 Remove plum stones and measure pulp.
4 Add enough water to give 1¼ pints.
5 Add rice and cook steadily until rice is soft, stirring from time to time.
6 Remove from heat and add the beaten egg yolks.
7 Put into oblong baking dish.
8 Whisk egg whites until very stiff and fold in the rest of the sugar.
9 Put into piping bag with ½-inch rose pipe and make lattice work on top of the sweet.
10 Set for approximately 20 minutes in centre of a very moderate oven (350°F. – Gas Mark 3).

Rhubarb charlotte

cooking time: 45 minutes

you will need:

3 oz. margarine
10 oz. stale breadcrumbs
2 oz. sugar
little grated lemon or orange rind (or pinch spice)
12 oz. rhubarb
sugar to taste

1 Heat the margarine and fry the crumbs until golden brown.
2 Mix with the sugar and fruit rind.
3 Put one-third at the bottom of a dish.
4 Cover with half the chopped rhubarb – no water – but sugar to taste.
5 Cover with next third of crumbs, rest of the rhubarb and sugar and a final layer of crumbs.
6 Bake for about 40 minutes in the centre of a moderate oven (375°F. – Gas Mark 4).
7 Turn out if wished.
8 Serve with cream or custard sauce.

Variations:

With apple – mix rhubarb with thinly sliced apples.

With orange – mix rhubarb with sections of orange.

With cereal – use half crumbs and half puffed wheat or cornflakes.

Apple charlotte – use either thinly sliced apples or thick apple purée instead of rhubarb.

Plum charlotte – use either halves plums or thick plum purée instead of rhubarb.

Caramel sauce

cooking time: 10 minutes

you will need:

2 oz. sugar*
4 tablespoons water

*granulated sugar may be used, but it does not brown so quickly as loaf sugar. It is essential to use a really strong pan.

1 Put the sugar and half the water into the pan.
2 Stir until sugar has quite dissolved.
3 Boil without stirring until sauce is brown.
4 Take the pan off the heat and add remainder of water.
5 Return to the heat and continue boiling and stirring until smooth again.

Semolina and caramel crisp

cooking time: 20–25 minutes

you will need:

- 1 pint milk or milk and water
- 3 oz. semolina
- 1 tablespoon marmalade
- 2–3 oz. dried fruit – dates, sultanas
- 1 good tablespoon crisp breadcrumbs
- caramel sauce (see page 71)

1. Bring the milk to the boil.
2. Whisk in the semolina and add the marmalade and dried fruit.
3. Cook gently, stirring from time to time, for 15 minutes.
4. Meanwhile, make the caramel sauce.
5. Pour the cooked semolina into a hot greased pie dish and sprinkle over the breadcrumbs.
6. When quite brown, pour the caramel sauce over the pudding.

Variation:

Rice caramel crisp – cook 2 oz. round (Carolina) rice in the milk etc. instead of the semolina. This will take about 20–25 minutes. Continue as the recipe.

Rhubarb crunch

cooking time: 30 minutes

you will need:

- 1½–2 lb. rhubarb*
- 2 tablespoons sugar
- ½ teaspoon cinnamon
- 6 oz. flour (with plain flour use 1½ level teaspoons baking powder)
- 4 oz. butter or margarine
- 4 oz. brown sugar
- 1–2 oz. chopped nuts

*When rhubarb gets older, cook for short time before adding topping.

1. Chop rhubarb into 1-inch slices and put into a well greased pie dish.
2. Sprinkle with the sugar and cinnamon to taste.
3. Mix the flour, butter and brown sugar until like breadcrumbs.
4. Stir in the chopped nuts and smooth down over the rhubarb.
5. Place in the centre of a hot oven (425–450°F. – Gas Mark 6–7) for 30 minutes until brown and crisp.
6. Serve hot or cold. Rhubarb crunch is excellent with ice cream.

Vanilla creams

cooking time: 30 minutes

you will need:

- packet vanilla flavoured blancmange or 1¼ oz. cornflour and a few drops vanilla essence (or vanilla pod)
- 1 pint milk
- 2 oz. sugar
- 3 eggs, separated
- 2 tablespoons cream or evaporated milk
- icing sugar

1. If using vanilla pod, put this into pan with the milk.
2. Heat together.
3. Take out pod and rinse in cold water then put back into jar of sugar.
4. Blend cornflour or blancmange with a little cold milk.
5. Bring rest to the boil with vanilla essence or pod, pour over cornflour.
6. Return to the pan with sugar and bring to the boil, stirring from time to time until thick and smooth.
7. **Remove from the heat** and add egg yolks beaten with cream, and lastly stiffly beaten egg whites.
8. Put into 4 or 5 ovenproof dishes and bake for approximately 20 minutes in a moderate oven (375°F. – Gas Mark 4).
9. Dust with sieved icing sugar and serve at once.

Variations:

Chocolate – use either chocolate blancmange or 1 oz. cornflour and 1 dessertspoon cocoa.
Coffee – use ¼ pint strong coffee and ¾ pint milk.
Rum – omit vanilla flavouring, add 1–2 tablespoons rum, or a little rum essence.

Bananas au rhum

cooking time: 20 minutes

you will need:

- 1 oz. butter
- 8 medium bananas
- juice 1 lemon
- 2 tablespoons water
- 2 oz. brown sugar
- 3 tablespoons rum

1. With the butter, grease a shallow dish and arrange the halved bananas in this.
2. Blend the lemon juice and water and pour over the fruit.
3. Cover with sugar, and bake for 20 minutes in a moderately hot oven (400°F. – Gas Mark 5); add rum 5 minutes before end of cooking.
4. Serve hot with cream.

Steamed Puddings

A light steamed pudding is quickly and easily made. It is, however, important to remember the following points:

1 Have the water really boiling when the pudding goes into the steamer, except in those cases where the recipe indicates the water should NOT boil.
2 Always fill up with boiling water.
3 Allow plenty of space in the basin for the pudding to rise.

Apple pudding

cooking time: 2–3 hours

you will need:

8 oz. suet crust pastry (see page 76)
1½ lb. apples
sugar
water
dried fruit can be added if wished

1 Line a well greased basin with part of the suet crust.
2 Peel, core and slice the apples.
3 Put into the pastry with a good sprinkling of sugar and enough water to half cover the fruit.
4 Roll out the rest of the dough to form a cover.
5 Damp edges of the pastry lid and press on to the pudding.
6 Cover well.
7 Steam over boiling water for 2½–3 hours, or boil for 2 hours. Steaming gives a lighter pudding.

Variations:

Apple and blackberry pudding – as for apple pudding, but mix apples and blackberries.
Blackcurrant pudding – as for apple pudding, but use all blackcurrants instead of apples. Add sugar, but no water.
Cherry pudding – as for apple pudding, but use really ripe cherries, sugar and about 2 tablespoons water.
Damson and apple pudding – as for apple pudding, but use half damsons and half apples, sweetening well.
Plum pudding – as for apple pudding, but use halved plums, sugar and a little water.
Rhubarb pudding – as for apple pudding, but use chopped rhubarb, sugar and no water. Chopped dates can be added.

Old-fashioned lemon suet pudding

cooking time: 2–3 hours

you will need:

8 oz. suet crust pastry (see page 76)
2 lemons
2 oz. butter
2–3 oz. brown sugar

1 Line a pudding basin with suet crust pastry as described on page 63.
2 Put in the lemons, cutting top and bottom of these so that the juice can flow.
3 Add butter and sugar.
4 Cover with a 'lid' of suet crust pastry and cook as apple pudding.

Halfpay pudding

cooking time: 1½–2 hours

you will need:

3 oz. suet or margarine
4 oz. breadcrumbs
2 oz. flour (with plain flour use 1 level teaspoon baking powder)
2 tablespoons golden syrup
3 oz. sultanas
3 oz. currants
milk or egg and milk to mix

1 Mix together the suet, crumbs and sieved flour. If using margarine, melt this and add in place of the suet.
2 Put in the golden syrup, dried fruit and stir thoroughly.
3 Add the milk or milk and egg to give a sticky consistency.
4 Half-fill a greased basin, cover with greased paper.
5 Steam for 1½–2 hours.

Variation:

With golden syrup – if wished 2–3 tablespoons golden syrup can be put at the bottom of the basin to give a sauce.

Mocha pudding

cooking time: 2½ hours

you will need:

4 egg yolks
2 egg whites
2 oz. sugar
2 oz. chocolate powder
¾ pint milk
¼ pint very strong coffee
2 oz. chopped glacé cherries
2 oz. chopped nuts (optional)
1 oz. finely chopped crystallised peel
2 tablespoons sherry (optional)
2 oz. sultanas

1 Beat the eggs, sugar and chocolate powder together.
2 Pour over the milk and coffee.
3 Add the rest of the ingredients.
4 Pour into a greased basin and steam gently WITHOUT BOILING for approximately 2½ hours, or bake for about the same time in a slow oven (275°F. – Gas Mark 2) standing the dish in another of warm water.
5 Cover the pudding with well-buttered paper or foil.
6 If serving cold decorate with a little cream and pieces of chocolate.

Variation:

Chocolate orange pudding – omit the coffee in the mocha pudding and use an extra ¼ pint milk instead. Add the very finely grated rind of 2–3 oranges and 3 oz. chopped crystallised orange peel in place of 1 oz. crystallised peel. Decorate with fresh orange, cream and chocolate.

Finger pudding

cooking time: 1 hour

you will need:

3 oz. castor sugar
2 eggs, separated
3 oz. ground almonds
½ teaspoon grated lemon rind
good pinch ground cloves
¾ teaspoon cinnamon
1½ oz. butter
1 oz. Savoy or finger biscuits

1 Blend sugar and egg yolks until creamy.
2 Add almonds, lemon rind, cloves, cinnamon, melted butter and crushed biscuits.
3 Fold in stiffly beaten egg whites.
4 Turn into greased mould and steam gently for 1 hour. Do not allow water to boil rapidly, otherwise pudding will curdle.

Pies and Tarts

The following recipes cover easy-to-make desserts using pastry. To be really successful with your pastry and pastry recipes, keep in mind the following points:

1 Make certain that the pastry is not too thick.
2 If making a covered plate pie, dust the bottom of the pastry with a little flour and sugar, cornflour or semolina. This absorbs the juice from the fruit and prevents the bottom layer of pastry becoming soggy.
3 To give an attractive appearance to your cooked pie or tart, dust with icing sugar, castor sugar or brush with egg white, or a little water and sugar before baking.
4 If you want to keep the pastry, wrap it in paper or foil and put it in the refrigerator, or you can prepare the pie or tart and leave it in a cool place a day before cooking. Always cover with paper while storing.

Baking pastry 'blind'

Where a recipe states that the pastry should be baked 'blind', it means without any filling. To prevent the bottom of the tart or flan from rising, either put crusts of stale bread or haricot beans on a piece of greased greaseproof paper, removing these about 5 minutes before the flan is quite baked.

Short crust pastry

for all general purposes

cooking time: according to recipe

you will need:

8 oz. flour
good pinch salt
4 oz. fat*
approximately 2 tablespoons cold water to mix

*there are many fats and combinations of fat to use.

Choose between:
Modern whipped light fat – use only 3½ oz. only as it is very rich
Pure cooking fat or lard
Margarine – for best results use a table margarine, a superfine or luxury margarine
Butter
Margarine and fat – perhaps the favourite of all – 2 oz. margarine and 2 oz. cooking fat

1 Sieve flour and salt and rub in fat until mixture looks like fine breadcrumbs.
2 Using first a knife and then the fingertips to feel the pastry, gradually add just enough cold water to make the dough into a rolling consistency.
3 Lightly flour the rolling pin and pastry board.
4 If a great deal of flour is necessary to roll out the pastry, then you have made it too wet.
5 Roll pastry to required thickness and shape, lifting and turning it to keep it light.
6 Exact cooking times for pastry are given in the recipes, but as a general rule it should be cooked in a hot oven (425°F.–450°F. – Gas Mark 6–7).

Variation:

Sweet short crust – add about 1 oz. sugar to the flour at stage 1. This pastry can be used in tarts etc. in place of short crust pastry.

Flaky pastry

cooking time: according to recipe

you will need:

8 oz. plain flour
pinch salt
5–6 oz. fat*
water to mix

*use all butter, all margarine, or ⅔ margarine and ⅓ cooking fat.

1 Sieve flour with salt.
2 Divide fat into 3 portions.
3 Rub 1 portion into flour in usual way.
4 Mix to rolling consistency with cold water.
5 Roll out to oblong shape.
6 Now take the second portion of fat, divide it into small pieces and lay them on surface of ⅔ of dough.
7 Leave remaining ⅓ without fat.
8 Take its 2 corners and fold back over second ⅓ so that the dough looks like an envelope with its flap open.
9 Fold over top end of pastry, so closing the 'envelope'.
10 Turn pastry at right angles, seal open ends of pastry and 'rib' it. This means depressing it with the rolling pin at intervals, so giving a corrugated effect and equalising the pressure of air. This makes certain that the pastry will rise evenly.
11 Repeat the process again, using the remaining fat and turning pastry in same way.
12 Roll out pastry once more, but should it begin to feel very soft and sticky, put it into a cold place for 30 minutes to become firm before rolling out.
13 Fold pastry as before, turn it, seal edges and 'rib' it.
14 Altogether the pastry should have 3 foldings and 3 rollings. It is then ready to stand in a cold place for a little while before baking, since the contrast between the cold and the heat of the oven makes the pastry rise better.
15 To bake, use a very hot oven (475°F. – Gas Mark 8) for the first 15 minutes, after this lower the Gas Mark to 5 or 6, or turn the electric oven off to finish cooking for remaining time at a lower temperature.

Flan pastry or biscuit crust (for sweet flans and fruit tarts)

cooking time: according to recipe

you will need:

4 oz. fat*
2 dessertspoons sugar
8 oz. flour
pinch salt
cold water or yolk 1 egg to bind

*margarine or butter is excellent for this pastry.

1 Cream fat and sugar together until light in colour.
2 Sieve flour and salt together and add to creamed fat, mixing with a knife.
3 Gradually add enough cold water, or egg and water, to make a firm rolling consistency.
4 Use fingertips to feel the pastry as in short crust pastry.
5 To line flan, put pastry over case and press down base and sides firmly, then roll over top with rolling pin for a good edge. Decorate edge if wished.
6 Bake in a hot oven (425°F.–450°F. – Gas Mark 6–7) or as stated in individual recipe.

To fill a pastry flan

Make flan as previous recipe. You need pastry made with 6 oz. flour etc. to fill a 7–8 inch flan ring or sandwich tin. If using a flan ring put this on an upturned baking tin, so making it easier to remove when cooked.

Bake the pastry 'blind', see page 74, for about 15 minutes, then remove paper from the inside and you can remove the flan ring too so the outside browns. Lower the heat slightly if wished and bake for a further 5–8 minutes. Allow to cool, then prepare the fruit as for the Fruit sponge flan on page 70. Put the cold fruit into the cold pastry and continue as step 6 in recipe on page 70.

Puff pastry

cooking time: according to recipe

you will need:

- 8 oz. plain flour
- good pinch salt
- cold water to mix
- few drops lemon juice
- 7–8 oz. butter

1. Sieve flour and salt together.
2. Mix to rolling consistency with cold water and lemon juice.
3. Roll to oblong shape.
4. Make butter into neat block and place in the centre of pastry and fold up first the bottom section of pastry and then the top section, so that the butter is quite covered.
5. Turn the dough at right angles, seal edges and 'rib' carefully and roll out.
6. Fold dough into envelope, turn it, seal edges, 'rib' and roll again.
7. Repeat 5 times, so making 7 rollings and 7 foldings in all.
8. Put the pastry to rest in cold place once or twice between rolling it for the last time, and before baking.
9. Bake in very hot oven (to make it rise and keep in the fat). Bake for the first 10–15 minutes at 475°F.–500°F. – Gas Mark 8–9, then lower to Gas Mark 5–6 or turn electric oven right out or re-set to 400°F. to finish cooking at lower temperature.
10. Puff pastry should rise to 4 or 5 times its original thickness.

Suet crust pastry

(for savoury or sweet puddings)

cooking time: according to recipe

you will need:

- 8 oz. flour (with plain flour 2 level teaspoons baking powder)
- pinch salt
- 2–4 oz. finely shredded suet
- water to mix

1. Sieve flour, salt and baking powder.
2. Add suet.
3. Mix to rolling consistency with cold water.
4. Roll out thinly, as this pastry rises.
5. Line a pudding basin with the dough, leaving some over for the cover.
6. Proceed as individual recipes.

Apple raisin fingers

cooking time: 40 minutes

you will need:

- 8 oz. short crust pastry (see page 75)
- 3 large cooking apples
- 1 oz. fine cake crumbs or chopped nuts
- 3 oz. raisins
- 1–2 oz. sugar

1. Line square tin or round flan ring with half the pastry.
2. Grate apples rather coarsely and mix with other ingredients.
3. Spread over pastry.
4. Cover with rest of the pastry.
5. Bake for approximately 20 minutes in hot oven (425–450°F. – Gas Mark 6–7) then further 20 minutes in moderate oven.
6. Cut into fingers.

Variations:

Apple date fingers – recipe as above, but add 4 oz. chopped dates.

Apple cheese fingers – recipe as in apple raisin fingers above, but add 4 oz. grated Cheddar cheese to the ingredients.

Cinnamon apple fingers – recipe as in apple raisin fingers, above, but sieve 1 teaspoon powdered cinnamon with flour when making pastry, and add further teaspoon to the cake crumbs.

Lattice apple tart

cooking time: 40 minutes

you will need:

- 1½ lb. apples, weight after peeling
- little golden syrup
- 3 oz. sultanas
- grated rind 1 lemon
- 8 oz. short crust pastry (see page 75)

1. Cook the apples with the golden syrup and very little, if any, water, until a thick purée.
2. Add the sultanas when cooked and the grated lemon rind.
3. Line the bottom and sides of a tin or dish, about 1½ inches in depth, with the pastry.
4. Bake this case 'blind' (see page 74) for about 10 minutes in a hot oven (425–450°F. – Gas Mark 6–7).
5. Fill with the apple mixture.
6. Roll out the remaining pastry very thinly and make a lattice design over the top.
7. Continue cooking for approximately 30 minutes in the centre of the oven, but 10 minutes before the end of cooking time, brush the lattice top with a syrup made by diluting a good dessertspoon of golden syrup with the same amount of water.

Apple star pie

cooking time: 40–45 minutes

you will need:

- 10 oz. short crust pastry (see page 75)
- 1 lb. apples (weight after peeling and coring)
- 3 oz. currants or sultanas
- 1 oz. crystallised lemon peel
- sugar to taste
- 2 tablespoons apricot jam or lemon marmalade
- icing sugar to decorate

1. Roll out the pastry and use half to line pie plate.
2. Cover with thinly sliced apples, half the currants, lemon peel and a sprinkling of sugar.
3. Roll out the rest of pastry to cover top.
4. Cut out 4 or 5 star shapes with tiny cutter.
5. Put over fruit, etc.
6. Bake for 20–25 minutes in centre of a hot oven (425–540°F. – Gas Mark 6–7), then lower the heat and cook for further 20 minutes.
7. Heat remainder of currants and apricot jam together and put into star shapes.
8. Dust top lightly with icing sugar.

Spiced apple pie

cooking time: 40 minutes

you will need:

- 1½ lb. apples (weight after peeling and coring)
- 2 oz. sultanas
- 2 oz. currants
- 2 oz. butter
- grated rind and juice 1 lemon
- golden syrup to sweeten
- 1 teaspoon cinnamon and ginger
- 6 oz. flaky or short crust pastry (see page 75)
- little sugar

1. Slice apples fairly thinly.
2. Put into pie dish with the fruit, melted butter, lemon rind and juice, golden syrup and spices.
3. Add very little water.
4. Cover with the pastry, brush with water and sprinkle with sugar.
5. Bake for approximately 20 minutes in the centre of a hot oven (425–450°F. – Gas Mark 6–7).
6. Then lower the heat for a further 20 minutes to make sure apples are cooked.

Pear dumplings

cooking time: 30–40 minutes

you will need:

- 12 oz. short crust pastry (see page 75)
- 4 good sized fairly ripe pears
- little apricot jam, mincemeat, marzipan, chopped nuts or brown sugar
- little sugar

1. Roll out the pastry and cut into 4 squares.
2. Peel and core pears, but try to keep the stalks on.
3. Fill core with one of the fillings.
4. Put on pastry and gather together to completely cover the pear, with the stalks showing.
5. Lift on to greased baking tray and bake for 30–40 minutes until pastry is crisp and golden brown.
6. Sprinkle with sugar.
7. If the pears were 'stalkless' put stalks of angelica in place.

Apricot and pear flan

cooking time: 30 minutes

you will need:

approximately 6 dessert pears
1 cooked pastry flan case, using short crust pastry (see page 75)
¼ pint water
1 teaspoon arrowroot
2 heaped tablespoons apricot jam
few blanched almonds

1 Peel and core the pears, keeping them in a weak brine until ready to coat them with the sauce. (For the brine use 1 level dessertspoon of salt to 1 pint water.)
2 Drain and dry the pears well and arrange in the flan case.
3 Blend the arrowroot with water and put into a saucepan together with the apricot jam.
4 Bring slowly to the boil, stirring all the time, and cook gently until thickened and clear.
5 Cool slightly, then pour over the pears and decorate with the almonds.

Blackcurrant whirl

cooking time: 35 minutes

you will need:

6 oz. short crust pastry (see page 75)
1 large can black-currants or about 12 oz. cooked fresh fruit
1 teaspoon cornflour or arrowroot
1 pint really thick sweetened custard

1 Bake pastry 'blind' in flan tin until crisp and brown.
2 Drain the blackcurrants from the juice.
3 Measure out ¼ pint of juice.
4 Blend with the cornflour and boil until thick and smooth.
5 Mark out flan into 6 or 8 equal sized portions and fill them with alternative portions of custard and blackcurrants.
6 Spoon or brush the flan filled with the black-currants with the glaze.

Variations:

With cherries – use canned or cooked cherries and blancmange instead of custard.
With apple and blackberries – omit the custard and fill with alternate sections of apple purée and cooked blackberries.
With mixed fruit – try mixed fruit – or soft fruits – or bilberries instead of blackcurrants.

Lancashire fig pie

cooking time: 1 hour 40 minutes

you will need:

8 oz. figs
½ pint water from soaking figs
1 level tablespoon cornflour
1 level tablespoon golden syrup or treacle
2 oz. sultanas or currants
pinch mixed spice
6 oz. short crust pastry (see page 75)

1 Soak figs overnight in water to cover.
2 Simmer gently until tender.
3 Lift the figs out of the liquid.
4 Measure ½ pint of this and blend with the corn-flour.
5 Put into the saucepan with the syrup and cook until thickened.
6 Blend with the figs, currants and spice.
7 Line a deep pie plate with the pastry and bake 'blind' (see page 74) for approximately 15 minutes in a hot oven (425–450°F. – Gas Mark 6–7) until golden, but not brown.
8 Put in the fig filling and finish cooking in just a moderate oven (375°F. – Gas Mark 4) for a further 25 minutes.

Lemon meringue pie

cooking time: 1 hour 10 minutes

you will need:

6 oz. short crust pastry (see page 75)
3 level dessertspoons cornflour or custard powder
½ pint water
2 oz. margarine
3–4 oz. sugar
2 large egg yolks
2 lemons

for meringue:

2 large egg whites
2 oz. sugar

1 Line a pie dish with the pastry and bake 'blind' (see page 74) for 25 minutes in a hot oven (450°F. – Gas Mark 7).
2 Blend the cornflour or custard powder with the cold water.
3 Put into a saucepan and cook gently until thickened.
4 Add the margarine and sugar. Remove from heat.
5 Add the egg yolks to the cornflour mixture and the very finely grated zest of the lemon rind and lastly the juice. Return to stove at low heat for a minute or two, to allow eggs to set.
6 Pour into the pastry case.

7 Whip the two egg whites very stiffly and fold in nearly all the sugar.
8 Pile this on top of the lemon filling and dust with the remaining sugar.
9 Bake for 45 minutes in a very slow oven (250°F. – Gas Mark ½), when the meringue should feel firm to touch. Do not bake the meringue more quickly otherwise it will not stay crisp when cold.

Orange flan

cooking time: 25 minutes

you will need:

4 oz. short crust or flan pastry (see page 75)
3 large oranges
½ pint thick custard (made with custard powder, or eggs and milk)
2–3 tablespoons apple jelly

1 Line a flan case with the pastry and bake 'blind' (see page 74) for about 20–25 minutes until crisp and golden brown.
2 Add finely grated orange rind to the custard and spread over the bottom of the flan.
3 Divide the orange into sections, cutting away pith and removing pips.
4 Arrange on top of the custard.
5 Melt the jelly with about 1 tablespoon water and pour over the oranges.

Breton pears

cooking time: 40 minutes

you will need:

4 large ripe pears
8 oz. short crust pastry (see page 75)
little apricot jam
4 cloves, if liked

1 Peel and core the pears.
2 Roll the pastry out thinly and cut into 4 squares.
3 Put a pear in the centre of each square of pastry, filling the hole with apricot jam and a clove.
4 Gather the corners of the pastry up to the top of the pear.
5 Put on to a greased baking sheet and bake for 20 minutes in the centre of a hot oven (450°F. – Gas Mark 7), then lower the heat to moderate for a further 15–20 minutes.

Note: If the pears are very hard, they should be simmered first.

Prune flan

cooking time: 1½–2½ hours

you will need:

6 oz. prunes
½ oz. margarine
1 tablespoon golden syrup
½ teaspoon mixed spice
½ teaspoon cinnamon
few drops lemon essence or lemon juice
1 tablespoon breadcrumbs
5–6 oz. short crust pastry (see page 75)

1 Soak the prunes in a very little water overnight or for several hours.
2 Simmer until soft.
3 Then cut with a pair of scissors into small pieces.
4 Put the margarine, syrup, prunes, spices and lemon flavouring into a pan and heat gently for a few minutes until all mixed together.
5 Add the breadcrumbs.
6 Line a 7-inch flan ring or sandwich tin with the pastry.
7 Fill with the prune mixture.
8 Put in the centre of a hot oven (450°F. – Gas Mark 7) and bake for 30 minutes, lowering the heat after 20 minutes.

To make a prune sauce – any prune juice that might be left could be thickened with a little cornflour, i.e. 1 teaspoon to each ¼ pint juice, and served with the flan.

Rhubarb amber flan

cooking time: 45 minutes–1½ hours

you will need :
for flan:
5–6 oz. short crust pastry (see page 75)

for filling:

12 oz. rhubarb
about 2 tablespoons water
2 oz. sugar
2 egg yolks

for meringue:

2 egg whites
2–4 oz. sugar

1 Make and bake the flan case 'blind' until crisp and PALE golden brown.
2 Cook the rhubarb with just the two tablespoons water and sugar until very soft.
3 Mash or sieve and mix with the beaten egg

yolks – do this while still hot so that the egg yolks get slightly cooked.

4 Put into the flan case.
5 Whisk egg whites until very stiff.
6 Fold in the sugar and pile over the filling.
7 For a hot sweet you need only use the 2 oz. sugar for the meringue and bake for approximately 20 minutes in the centre of a moderate oven until the meringue is golden brown.
8 If you wish to serve this sweet cold, then use the larger amount of sugar for the meringue and set for about 1–1¼ hours in the centre of a very slow oven (250°–275°F. – Gas Mark ½–1). This makes sure the meringue will be crisp when cold.

Variations:

Apple amber flan – recipe as above, using 1 lb. apples instead of rhubarb.

Plum amber flan – recipe as above, using 1 lb. plums instead of rhubarb.

Almond flan

cooking time: 35 minutes

you will need:

6 oz. short crust pastry (see page 75)
jam

for filling:

1 oz. margarine
1½ oz. sugar
1 teaspoon almond essence
1½ oz. flour
1 level teaspoon baking powder
1½ oz. semolina
1 egg
3 tablespoons milk or milk and water

1 Line a flan ring or sandwich tin with the pastry.
2 Spread lightly with jam.
3 Cream together the margarine, sugar and almond essence.
4 Mix together the dry ingredients.
5 Add to the margarine mixture alternately with the egg and milk.
6 Pour the filling onto the pastry case and bake in the centre of a hot oven (450°F. – Gas Mark 7) for approximately 15 minutes.
7 Lower heat for further 20 minutes.

Bakewell tart

cooking time: 35 minutes

you will need:

6 oz. short crust pastry (see page 75)
little jam
2 oz. margarine
2 oz. sugar
2 teaspoons almond essence
2 oz. flour
2 oz. ground almonds or semolina
2 oz. breadcrumbs
1 egg
2 tablespoons milk

1 Line a large pie plate or 8-inch flan ring with the pastry.
2 Spread over the jam.
3 Cream the margarine and sugar together.
4 Add the almond flavouring.
5 Mix all the dry ingredients together and add these alternately to the margarine with the egg and milk.
6 Spread this mixture over the pastry and jam, dust with a very little sugar.
7 Bake in the centre of a hot oven (450°F. – Gas Mark 7) for 15 minutes, then lower the heat for further 20 minutes.

Autumn medley pie

cooking time: 35–45 minutes

you will need:

5–6 oz. short crust pastry or flaky pastry (see page 75)
approximately 1½ lb. mixed fruit (try apples, plums, greengages, damsons)
sugar to taste
very little water

1 Make the pastry as directed.
2 Put fruit into a pie dish or pie plate.
3 Add sugar and very little water.
4 Put the pastry on top, decorating the edges.
5 Bake just above centre of hot oven (425–450°F. – Gas Mark 6–7) lowering the heat if necessary.

Pancakes and Fritters

Pancakes and fritters make a delicious sweet, and are popular with nearly everybody. Pancake batter also has the added advantage that it can be made ahead of time. If stored in a screw topped jar in the refrigerator, or in a cool place, it will keep for a day or so, but do NOT whisk hard before cooking. Another time-saving method is to cook the pancakes, then keep them in foil in the refrigerator. When ready to serve them, re-heat in very hot fat on either side.

When making pancakes, keep the following points in mind:

1 TRY and keep one pan for pancakes (or pancakes and omelettes).
2 This should NOT be washed, but seasoned well when new, and then wiped out with soft paper or cloth after use. In this way it will not stick.
3 Put a small knob of fat, or little oil into the pan and allow this to get really hot – there should be just enough to cover the bottom of the pan.
4 Pour in enough of the batter to give a layer over the pan – this means tilting it so the batter runs easily.
5 Only JUST COVER the pan – do not have it too thick.
6 Cook rapidly on the bottom side, then turn with a broad palette knife or spatula, or toss.
7 Cook on the second side.
8 Serve as individual recipes.
9 Add more fat for each pancake.

To toss a pancake

1 Hold the pan loosely in your hand, leaving your wrist very flexible.
2 Flick the pan upwards quite briskly – the pancake should rise, turn in the air and drop back again into the pan with the cooked side uppermost.

The secret of a good pancake

1 Using really thin batter, so the pancakes are crisp and not soggy.
2 Quick cooking in a really hot pan.
3 Serving while they are very hot.

Basic pancake batter

cooking time: few minutes

you will need:

4 oz. flour (preferably plain)
good pinch salt
1 egg
½ pint milk
3 tablespoons water
fat for cooking

1 Sieve the flour and salt into a basin.
2 Add the egg and beat well.
3 Add enough liquid to give a sticky consistency and whisk very hard until smooth.
4 Add the rest of the liquid. Always whisk hard before cooking, unless batter has been kept for a day or so.

Rich pancake batter

cooking time: few minutes

you will need:

4 oz. flour (preferably plain)
good pinch salt
2 eggs
½ pint milk
just under 3 tablespoons water
1 oz. melted butter or 1 tablespoon olive oil
fat for cooking

Method as for basic pancakes (see above) but add the butter or oil just before cooking.

Buttered pancakes

cooking time: few minutes each pancake

you will need:

basic pancake batter (see above)

for filling:

3 oz. butter
3 oz. sieved icing sugar
juice 1 orange
1 teaspoon grated orange rind
sugar to garnish

1 Combine ingredients for filling.
2 Make pancakes.
3 As they are cooked, pile them upon a hot plate, spreading some of the butter filling between each and ending with a pancake.
4 Sprinkle with sugar.
5 Serve very hot while the pancakes are soaked in the orange butter.

Lemon pancakes

cooking time: few minutes

you will need:

basic pancake batter
sugar
lemon

1 Make the pancakes in the usual way.
2 Turn each one on to sugared paper.
3 Roll or fold.
4 Serve on a hot dish with slices of lemon and sugar.

Variations:

Fruit pancakes – make the pancakes and put on sugared paper. Fill with hot fruit purée, roll, put on a hot dish and top with icing sugar.

Dutch pancakes – make the pancakes and keep hot. Do not roll them. Just before serving, fold a stiffly beaten egg white into ½ pint whipped cream. Whip lightly. Spread pancakes with jam and the cream mixture. Fold up and top with whipped cream and grated chocolate.

Crêpes Suzette – add an extra egg to the basic pancake mixture. Fill each pancake with an orange mixture made by creaming together 4oz. butter and 3–4 oz. sugar then adding the grated rind of 2 oranges and a little curaçao. Fold pancakes into four over the filling and place in a hot dish. Mix together juice 2 oranges, 2–3 tablespoons curaçao and a little sugar and heat in a pan. Pour over the hot pancakes.

Ice cream pancakes – make the pancakes and keep hot until ready to fill. Fill each pancake with freshly sugared fruit and ice cream or just with ice cream. Serve with cream or with hot chocolate sauce.

Chocolate sauce

Put 4 oz. plain chocolate, ½ oz. butter and 2 tablespoons water into a basin over a pan of hot water and heat until melted.

Apple fritters

cooking time: 10 minutes

you will need:

3 large cooking apples
4 oz. flour (with plain flour add 1 teaspoon baking powder)
pinch salt
1 teaspoon sugar
1 egg
¼ pint milk or water and milk
1 oz. cooking fat or dripping

1 Peel, core and slice the apples into rings about ½ inch thick.
2 Mix the flour, salt, sugar, baking powder and egg together.
3 Add the water and milk.
4 Flour the rings of apple **before** dipping them into the thick batter. This is most important, otherwise the batter is likely to come away from the fruit when being cooked.
5 Heat the fat in the frying pan and when this is really hot, drop in the fritters.
6 Cook quickly for a good minute on one side, turn them over and cook quickly on the other side.
7 Turn the heat down and cook more slowly for nearly 10 minutes to make sure the apples are cooked in the middle.
8 Serve hot, dusted with sugar.

Variations:

Banana fritters – recipe as above, but use bananas in place of apples and cook for 6–7 minutes.

Pineapple fritters – drain rings of canned pineapple well, then flour as stage 4 in apple fritters. Continue as apple fritters, but the cooking time can be shortened slightly, since the pineapple does not require cooking.

Orange fritters – recipe as above, but use oranges in place of apples. Peel thickly to remove the pith and slice into rings.

Plum fritters (and other stoned fruit) – recipe as above. The stone can be removed from the fruit and the cavity filled with soft cream cheese.

Peach fritters – as recipe above, using halved fresh peaches or well drained canned peaches.

Cold Desserts

The following recipes give a good selection of cold sweets. When a sweet is to be served cold, it has the great advantage that it can be prepared beforehand. Indeed, in many cases, the flavour of a cold sweet will be better if it is prepared well ahead of the time it is to be used.

Marshmallow kissel

(illustrated on the cover)

cooking time: approximately 20 minutes

you will need:

1–1½ lb. fruit
little sugar to taste
½ pint water
1 level tablespoon cornflour
further ¼ pint water
4–6 oz. marshmallows

1 Simmer fruit with ½ pint water and sugar until tender.
2 Blend cornflour with the rest of the water.
3 Add to the fruit mixture and cook steadily until thickened and clear.
4 Pour into shallow dish and allow to cool.
5 Top with marshmallows.

Note: Since marshmallows give added sweetness to this dish, do not be too lavish with the sugar in cooking the fruit. Cherries, cherry plums, plums, are ideal for this dish.

Banana and apple whip

no cooking

you will need:

2 bananas
juice ½ lemon
3 dessert apples
large block ice cream
nuts

1 Skin and mash the bananas with the lemon juice to prevent the fruit discolouring.
2 Halve, core, but do not peel the apples.
3 Grate apples coarsely.
4 Mix fruit with the ice cream.
5 Pile into glasses and top with chopped nuts.

Note: This should be done just before the meal, so the mixture does not become too soft.

Peach royale

cooking time: 5 minutes

you will need:

4 whole peaches or 8 canned halves
2 oz. sugar
3 tablespoons water (with fresh peaches)
1 tablespoon lemon juice or brandy

for filling:

¼ pint cream
approximately 8 oz. fresh raspberries or strawberries*
little icing sugar
few blanched almonds

*frozen fruit can be used, in which case omit icing sugar.

1 If using fresh peaches, heat the sugar and water until a syrup.
2 Poach the halved peaches in this for approximately 5 minutes.
3 Stir in the lemon juice or brandy at the end of cooking time.
4 Allow to become quite cold.
5 Whip the cream very lightly and fold in the fruit and sugar if desired.
6 Pile into the peach halves and decorate with blanched almonds.

Butterscotch puddings

cooking time: 6 minutes

you will need:

2 oz. butter
3 oz. demerara sugar
6 level tablespoons fine semolina
½ pint milk
chocolate
walnuts
cream to decorate

1 Melt butter in saucepan over gentle heat.
2 Add sugar and fine semolina and stir.
3 Cook gently for 3 minutes.
4 Add milk gradually, stirring all the time.
5 Continue stirring until mixture boils and thickens.
6 Simmer 2–3 minutes.
7 Pour into 6 sundae glasses or individual dishes rinsed in cold water.
8 Chill.
9 Decorate to taste with grated chocolate, chopped walnuts, whipped cream.

Pineapple and lemon soufflé

cooking time: 5 minutes

you will need:

3 eggs
½ teaspoon lemon rind
4 oz. castor sugar
1 medium can pineapple (retain syrup)
¼ oz. gelatine
2 tablespoons lemon juice
¼ pint cream

to decorate:

little angelica
cream

1. Separate the eggs and put the yolks, lemon rind and sugar into a basin.
2. Beat until thick and creamy.
3. Measure the pineapple syrup (you need just ¼ pint).
4. Heat this and dissolve the gelatine in it.
5. Add the lemon juice.
6. Cool and add to the egg mixture together with the chopped pineapple, leaving a little pineapple for decoration.
7. Allow to cool and become slightly stiff.
8. Fold in lightly whipped cream and stiffly beaten egg whites.
9. Prepare your soufflé dish by tying a band of buttered paper above the top.
10. Pour the mixture carefully into this and leave to set.
11. Remove the paper with a knife dipped in hot water.
12. Decorate with a little cream, angelica and pineapple.

Fruit crispies

cooking time: 1¾ hours

you will need:

4½ oz. butter
3 oz. sugar
6 oz. flour (with plain flour use ¾ level teaspoon baking powder)

for meringue:

2 egg whites
4 oz. sugar (either all castor sugar or ½ castor and ½ icing sugar)
fruit in season

1. Cream butter and sugar.
2. Work in flour.
3. Knead well and roll into balls. If mixture very firm add few DROPS milk.
4. Put on to ungreased baking tins – allowing room to spread and flatten.
5. Bake for approximately 12–15 minutes in moderate oven (375°F. – Gas Mark 4) until pale golden in colour (do not allow to leave cooking any longer).
6. Remove from oven – reduce heat to 225°–250°F. – Gas Mark 0–¼. Leave oven door open for a time to lose the heat.
7. Whisk egg whites and fold in sugar.
8. Put mixture into piping bag with plain or rose nozzle and pipe rings of meringue round edge of each biscuit. If you haven't a pipe then do this with a teaspoon.
9. Return to the very cool oven for about 1–1½ hours until meringue is very firm.
10. These can be stored in an airtight tin for a day or so until ready to use.
11. Fill with autumn fruits, as suggested below.

Fillings for fruit crispies

1. **Blackberries** added at the last minute to an apple purée so that they are softened slightly but keep their shape.
2. **Diced peaches,** covered with melted redcurrant jelly and cream.
3. **Diced dessert pears,** topped with cream and pieces of ginger.

Meringue apples

cooking time: 2 hours

you will need:

4–5 peeled and cored apples

for syrup:

1 pint water
about 2 good tablespoons golden syrup
a little lemon rind

for filling:

mixed dried fruit
OR apricot jam
OR honey and cinnamon

for meringue:

3 egg whites
6 oz. sugar

1. Combine ingredients for syrup.
2. Poach apples in this.
3. Cook gently for about 30 minutes until just tender.
4. Drain and put in flat dish, filling centres of apples with any of the mixture suggested.
5. Make the meringue by beating egg whites and gradually adding sugar, until mixture stands in peaks.
6. Pile over apples.
7. Set in a very slow oven (250–275°F. – Gas Mark ½–1) until meringue is crisp. Serve with syrup.

Tipsy cake

(a pleasant change from trifle)

cooking time: 10–12 minutes

you will need:

1 deep sponge cake
2–3 kinds jam
2 teaspoons sugar
$\frac{1}{4}$–$\frac{1}{2}$ pint sherry or port wine
3 oz. crumbled macaroon biscuits
1 pint custard sauce*
cherries, nuts, etc., for decoration

*made with custard powder or egg and milk.

1 Cut cake into about 4 slices, cutting across sponge.
2 Put 1 slice into a dish, spread with 1 kind of jam.
3 Add sugar to sherry or port wine and moisten with this.
4 Sprinkle macaroon crumbs on top.
5 Put on second slice of cake, spread with different flavoured jam, the sprinkling of sherry, etc. Continuing like this, using all slices of cake.
6 Pour very hot custard over and leave until cold.
7 To prevent skin forming as custard cools, cover with a deep basin.
8 Decorate with cherries, fruit, nuts, etc.

Rhubarb snow

cooking time: 10–15 minutes

you will need:

rhubarb
water
sugar
egg whites

1 Cook the rhubarb with very little water and sugar until a very smooth purée – sieve if wished.
2 When quite cold fold in stiffly whisked egg whites (allowing 1 egg white to each $\frac{1}{2}$ pint purée).
3 Pile into glasses and serve very cold.

Variations:

Apple snow – recipe for above but use thick apple purée instead of rhubarb purée. Flavour the apples with either grated lemon rind or finely chopped crystallised ginger or powdered cinnamon.

Blackcurrant snow – recipe as above, but use thick sieved blackcurrant purée instead of rhubarb purée.

Sherry plum compote

cooking time: 5 minutes

you will need:

$1\frac{1}{2}$ lb. plums
3 oz. sugar
$\frac{1}{2}$ pint water
2 tablespoons sherry

1 Halve plums.
2 Remove kernels and crack them.
3 Boil sugar and water for several minutes.
4 Add sherry and kernels.
5 Pour over halved plums while hot and allow to become very cold.
6 Serve with whipped cream.

Caramelled pears

cooking time: 15–20 minutes

you will need:

3 oz. sugar
$\frac{1}{3}$ pint water
4 good sized firm, but not too hard, pears
6–8 almonds

1 Put 3 tablespoons of the water and sugar into a pan.
2 Stir until the sugar has dissolved, then boil until dark brown.
3 Add the rest of the water and bring to the boil.
4 Peel, core and slice pears.
5 Put them into caramel and cook for about 10 minutes.
6 Serve in glasses topped with blanched shredded almonds.

Spring time pudding

no cooking

you will need:

approximately 6 slices bread
$1\frac{1}{4}$–$1\frac{1}{2}$ lb. stewed fruit

1 Line a basin with thin pieces of bread – make sure there are no gaps in this.
2 Fill the centre with stewed rhubarb and juice, sweetening this well.
3 Put thin slices of bread over the top and a weight.
4 Leave for 24 hours.
5 Turn out and serve with cream or custard.

Note: Make sure you add the juice of the fruit in this sweet since this soaks through the bread or sponge colouring it a delicate pink and making it moist. If you have never made this pudding, you will be surprised just how difficult it is to realise that bread has been used.

Variations:

With raspberries – for a more luxurious sweet, mix the rhubarb with frozen raspberries and line the basin with sponge cake rather than bread.

Summer pudding – follow the previous recipe, but use summer berry fruits, such as raspberries and redcurrants, black and redcurrants, loganberries, etc. Top with plenty of cream when serving.

Winter pudding – recipe as Spring time pudding, but use cooked apples, flavoured with crystallised ginger, seedless raisins, lemon rind and juice.

Chocolate mousse

cooking time: 5 minutes

you will need:

4 oz. bar chocolate
2 tablespoons milk
2 egg whites

1. Melt the chocolate and milk in a saucepan over a low heat.
2. Allow to cool.
3. Add stiffly beaten egg whites.
4. Put into a dish and chill.

Variation:

With orange juice – this is also delicious with orange juice instead of milk.

Using a Pressure Cooker for Puddings

With any pudding containing flour, it is better to steam WITHOUT pressure for the first third of the cooking time, then put on the 5 lb. pressure weight, and allow two thirds of the total cooking time at this pressure. This is to make sure that the raising agent will rise properly.

Coffee pudding

cooking time: 15 minutes

pressure cooking time: 30 minutes

you will need:

2 oz. margarine
4 oz. flour (2 teaspoons baking powder if using plain flour)
2 oz. breadcrumbs
2 oz. sugar
$\frac{1}{4}$ pint strong coffee (just under)
1 egg
few drops vanilla essence

1. Rub margarine into the flour.
2. Add baking powder, crumbs and sugar.
3. Mix with the coffee, egg and vanilla essence.
4. Put into a greased basin, stand basin on rack in cooker in 2 pints **boiling** water and cover well.
5. Fix the lid, but do not put on pressure weight.
6. Steam rapidly for 15 minutes then put on pressure weight.
7. Bring to pressure at 5 lb.
8. Lower the heat and cook for 30 minutes.
9. Reduce pressure at once.
10. Serve with chocolate sauce.

Egg custard

pressure cooking time: 10 minutes at 5 lb. pressure

It is an extraordinary fact that an egg custard, which normally requires such slow careful cooking, can actually be made in a pressure cooker. The following recipe shows how it is done.

you will need:

2 small eggs
$\frac{1}{2}$–$\frac{3}{4}$ pint milk (depending how firm you like the custard)
1 good dessertspoon sugar
few drops vanilla essence, or vanilla pod

1. Beat the eggs lightly.
2. Heat the milk with the sugar and vanilla essence or vanilla pod (remove this when the milk is heated).

3 Pour over the eggs, then strain into basin or mould.
4 Heat ½ pint water in the cooker, then stand the custard on the rack.
5 Bring up to 5 lb. pressure.
6 Maintain at pressure for 10 minutes, then allow it to drop gradually.

Variations:

Caramel custard – make the caramel sauce (see page 71) and pour into the bottom of the mould, then pour the custard on top when the caramel is cold. Cook at pressure as above.

Coffee custard – flavour the custard with a little strong coffee.

Chocolate custard – blend 1 oz. chocolate powder with the beaten eggs and sugar.

Fig pudding

cooking time: 15 minutes

pressure cooking time: 30 minutes

you will need:

3 oz. chopped figs
2 oz. margarine or suet
2 oz. flour (with plain flour use ½ teaspoon baking powder)
2 oz. breadcrumbs
1 oz. sugar
little grated nutmeg
milk to mix

1 Soak the figs overnight, then strain.
2 Rub margarine into the flour or add suet.
3 Mix all ingredients together with enough milk to make a sticky texture.
4 Put into greased basin and cover well.
5 Stand on the rack in the cooker with 2 pints boiling water.
6 Cook as for coffee pudding (see page 86).

Savoury Sauces and Stuffings

There is nothing more delicious than a good sauce as an accompaniment to a main dish, or to vegetables. And a stuffing will not only add to the flavour of a dish, it will also help to make it go further. A number of savoury sauces and stuffings are included in the following section. Several of the basic sweet sauces are to be found in other parts of the book, where they appear with individual recipes.

Tomato sauce

cooking time: 10 minutes

you will need:

1 oz. butter or margarine
1 small onion
1 small apple
1 small tube or can tomato purée
2 level teaspoons cornflour
½ pint water
salt and pepper
good pinch sugar

1 Heat the butter and fry the chopped onion for a few minutes, then the grated peeled apple.
2 Add the purée, the cornflour blended with the water and seasoning.
3 Bring to the boil and stir until smooth.
4 Simmer gently for about 10 minutes, taste and reseason adding sugar if wished.

Creamy onion sauce

cooking time: 25–30 minutes

you will need:

3 medium-sized onions
water
1 oz. butter
1 oz. flour
¼ pint milk
2 teaspoons cream
seasonings

1 Boil the onions in salted water until soft.
2 Lift out of water and chop onions finely – save ¼ pint onion stock.
3 Make sauce with butter, flour, milk and onion stock.
4 Add chopped onions, cream and seasoning.

Apple sauce

cooking time: 10–15 minutes

you will need:

apples
water
sugar
knob of butter

1 Simmer apples with water and sugar to taste.
2 Sieve or beat until smooth.
3 Reheat with knob of butter.

White sauce

cooking time: 5–8 minutes

you will need:

1 oz. butter or margarine
1 oz. flour
salt and pepper
½ pint milk for coating consistency (i.e. to use as sauce)
OR ¼ pint milk for panada or binding consistency (to make croquettes etc.)
OR 1 pint milk for thin white sauce (for soups)

1 Heat the butter gently, remove from the heat and stir in the flour.
2 Return to the heat and cook gently for a few minutes so that the 'roux', as the butter and flour mixture is called, does not brown.
3 Again remove from the heat and gradually blend in the cold milk.
4 Bring to the boil and cook, stirring with a wooden spoon until smooth.
5 Season well. If any small lumps have formed, whisk sharply.

Variations:

Cheese sauce – recipe as above, but stir in 3–6 oz. grated cheese when sauce has thickened and add a little mustard.

Parsley sauce – recipe as above but add 1–2 teaspoons chopped parsley.

Hard-boiled egg sauce – make white sauce as above, add chopped hard-boiled eggs.

Mushroom sauce – recipe as above, but before making sauce simmer 2–4 oz. chopped mushrooms in the milk until tender.

Brown sauce

(coating consistency)

cooking time: 5–8 minutes

you will need:

1 oz. cooking fat or dripping
1 oz. flour
½ pint brown stock
salt and pepper

Method as in white sauce (see above). For a better flavour, fry about 2 oz. chopped onion and other vegetables in the dripping or fat first. Strain if wished.

Variation:

Tomato brown sauce – use ¼ pint stock and ¼ pint tomato juice or purée, instead of ½ pint brown stock.

Mushroom stuffing

cooking time: 5–6 minutes

you will need:

2 oz. margarine
1 small onion
4 oz. mushrooms
4 oz. soft breadcrumbs
2 teaspoons chopped parsley
seasoning

1 Heat margarine and fry finely chopped onion in this.
2 Add finely chopped mushrooms (stalks as well), crumbs, parsley, seasoning.
3 Work together and spread on slices of meat, or as directed in recipe.

Veal stuffing

no cooking

you will need:

2 oz. shredded suet or melted margarine
½ teaspoon mixed herbs
grated rind and juice ½ lemon
4 oz. breadcrumbs
1 egg
seasoning
2–3 teaspoons chopped parsley

1 Mix all the ingredients together thoroughly.
2 The cooked meat from the giblets can be added to make a richer stuffing, if wished.

Note: Make 2–3 times this quantity for a large turkey.

Sage and onion stuffing

cooking time: 20 minutes

you will need:

2 large onions (peeled)
4 oz. breadcrumbs
1 oz. suet
1 teaspoon dried sage
1 egg
good pinch salt and pepper

1 Put the onions into a saucepan, adding about ½ pint water.
2 Simmer steadily for about 20 minutes, when the onions will be partly cooked.
3 Remove from the water on to chopping board and chop up into small pieces.
4 Transfer to basin.
5 Add all other ingredients.

Variation:

With onion stock – some onion stock may be used instead of the egg.

Index

Puddings and Sweets

Quantities of puddings to allow:

As stated in the introduction, most recipes are for four people but of course it is not easy to be dogmatic about quantities as appetites vary so much. You can, however, use the following as a general guide:

Milk puddings
1 pint milk gives enough for four average servings.

Egg custards
A baked custard made with 1 pint milk and 2 eggs for a soft custard or up to 4 eggs for a firm custard, is enough for four people.

Blancmanges and moulds
A blancmange made with 1 pint of milk is enough for four average servings. If served with another sweet, such as a jelly, it can make five to six servings.

Jellies and jellied sweets
1 pint fairly clear jelly, i.e. either a fruit jelly or one containing a little cream etc. is enough for four servings. If many extra ingredients are added, such as fruit purée, cream, egg whites, etc. while one generally assumes that it makes four large servings, it could be stretched to six smaller ones.

Ice cream and frozen desserts
Allow 2 heaped tablespoons per person.

Pastry
For a fruit pie, i.e. pastry plus fruit—1 oz. of flour and fat accordingly, should be sufficient for one average serving. Where, however, the pastry is used for a jam tart, i.e. where the filling is not particularly substantial, it is safer to allow 1½ oz. of flour and fat accordingly. There are occasions, however, in dumplings, turnovers, etc. where a high proportion of pastry has to be made in order to give an adequate covering for the fruit.

Steamed puddings
If the pudding is a rather plain one, allow 1½ oz. flour, fat, sugar, etc. per person. If, however, it is a rich recipe, in which you have a high percentage of dried fruit, eggs, etc., 1 oz. of flour per person should be enough.

Baked puddings
Allow quantities as for steamed puddings (see above). If the pudding mixture is covering a generous amount of fruit, 1 oz. of flour or crumbs should be adequate per person.

Pancakes
A pancake batter made with 4 oz of flour etc. should make enough pancakes for four people.

Fritters
Allow quantities as for pancakes (see above).

Fruit
This will vary a great deal according to the type of fruit but 1 lb. of fruit gives four fairly small servings. In recipes such as Fruit fool or foule, allow ¼ pint purée i.e. a mixture of fruit and custard or cream, per person.

Trifles containing sponge cake
1 pint custard, cream etc. will give four very large or six small servings.

Sauces
½ - ¾ pint of sauce should be enough for four servings.

Boiled and Steamed Puddings

Six points for a perfect steamed pudding

1 Fill the basin no more than two-thirds full with the sponge pudding mixture, as it will rise during cooking.
2 Always cover the pudding well with either greaseproof paper, foil or a pudding cloth. Grease one side of a round of greaseproof paper, or on both sides since this will stop any water penetrating.
3 Tuck the edges very firmly so that the paper really is a good fit over the top of the basin.
4 Ensure that the pudding is placed over boiling water when the pudding goes into the steamer. To ensure that the pudding rises and will be light, boil rapidly for the first hour.
5 Make certain that the lid of the steamer fits very tightly so no steam escapes.
6 Make sure the water used for filling up the pan under the steamer is boiling.

To cover a basin with greaseproof paper

1 Make a large ring of greaseproof paper, 2 - 3 inches bigger than the top of the basin.
2 Grease it well.
3 Place over the top of the basin.
4 Start to twist the ends of the paper under as close to the edge of the basin as possible. Do this all the way round until you have a firm fit.
5 Unless you wish to make a handle (see below) there is no need to tie this on.

Boiled puddings

1 It is a good idea to make a 'handle' over the top of the basin.
2 Tie paper round with a string, make a firm knot, and cut.
3 Insert piece of string into this band at one side then pass over top loosely and fit in at other side. Do this several times to give firmness. Finally twist string over the strands. The pudding can then be lifted in and out of the pan with ease.
4 Half fill a pan with boiling water.
5 Stand the basin on an upturned saucer in pan.
6 Make sure the water boils rapidly and always replenish with boiling water. Be careful that the level of the water is not so high that it boils into the pudding.
7 Boil for same length of time as for steaming.

Steamed almond pudding (1)

cooking time 1½ - 2 hours

you will need:

2 oz. margarine
2 oz. sugar
2 oz. flour (with plain flour 2 level teaspoons baking powder, with self-raising flour 1 level teaspoon baking powder
2 oz. breadcrumbs
1 oz. ground almonds
2 eggs
1 teaspoon almond essence
milk

1 Cream the margarine and sugar thoroughly.
2 Sieve flour and baking powder.
3 Mix in the breadcrumbs and ground almonds.
4 Beat the eggs with the almond essence.
5 Add these to the margarine alternately with the flour. Do not overbeat.
6 Add enough milk to make the consistency of very thick cream.
7 Steam for 1½ - 2 hours.

Steamed almond pudding (2)

cooking time 1 hour

you will need:

3 oz. castor sugar
2 eggs
3 oz. ground almonds
½ teaspoon lemon rind
¾ teaspoon ground cinnamon
good pinch ground cloves
1½ oz. butter
1 oz. crushed biscuits

1 Beat sugar and egg yolks together until smooth and creamy.
2 Add almonds, lemon rind, cinnamon, cloves, melted butter and crushed biscuits.
3 Whisk whites stiffl and fold in to the mixture.
4 Pour into well greased mould and steam gently for 1 hour.

Apricot sponge pudding

cooking time 1½ hours

you will need:

4 oz. dried apricots
4 oz. flour (with plain flour 1 level teaspoon baking powder)
2 - 4 oz. margarine or butter
2 - 4 oz. sugar
1 - 2 eggs
little milk

1 Soak apricots over night.
2 Drain well and place at the bottom of well greased basin.
3 Sieve flour with baking powder.
4 Cream margarine or butter with the sugar.
5 Gradually beat in the egg or eggs, the flour and enough milk to make a soft consistency.
6 Put into a well greased basin and cover with greased greaseproof paper.
7 Steam for approximately 1½ hours.

Variations:

Cherry

Omit apricots and add 2 - 4 oz. chopped glacé cherries to the mixture.

Jam

Any jam can be put at the bottom of the basin and serve with extra jam or jam sauce (see page 85).

Lemon

Add the finely grated rind of a lemon to the fat and sugar and mix with lemon juice instead of milk. Omit apricots and serve with lemon sauce (see pages 85, 87).

Bread pudding

cooking time 2 - 3 hours

you will need:

boiling water
8 oz. bread
2 oz. suet or margarine
1 oz. sugar
1 tablespoon marmalade
2 - 4 oz. dried fruit
½ teaspoon cinnamon or nutmeg
milk

1 Pour boiling water over the bread and allow it to stand for a few minutes.
2 Squeeze out all the water.
3 Mix in all the other ingredients, with enough milk to make a sticky consistency.
4 Pour into a greased pudding basin and cover well. Steam for 2½ - 3 hours.
5 For baking put into a greased Yorkshire pudding tin and bake in a very moderate oven (300°F.—Gas Mark 2) for approximately 2 hours.

Brigade pudding

cooking time 2½ hours

you will need:

suet crust pastry (see page 32)
2 apples
4 oz. breadcrumbs
2 oz. currants
1 tablespoon marmalade
3 tablespoons golden syrup

Roll out the suet crust pastry and line the sides of a greased pudding basin, keeping some of the pastry for the top.
Slice the apples finely or grate them.
Mix with all the other ingredients.
Put into the pastry case and cover with the remaining pastry.
Put on greased paper and a pudding cloth and steam for 2½ hours.

Apple Brown Betty pudding

cooking time 1½ - 2 hours

you will need:

4 oz. brown bread-crumbs
1 lb. cooking apples
2 oz. dried fruit
½ teaspoon mixed spice
1 oz. sugar
2 oz. margarine
1 tablespoon golden syrup
2 teaspoons warm water

Grease a pudding basin and sprinkle some of the breadcrumbs round the inside.
Fill the basin with alternate layers of thinly sliced apples, dried fruit, breadcrumbs, spice and sugar, ending with breadcrumbs.
Put the margarine in tiny pieces on top.
Mix the syrup with the water and pour over the pudding.
Steam for 1½ - 2 hours.

Chocolate pudding

cooking time 1 hour 45 minutes

you will need:

2 oz. flour (with plain flour 1 level tea-spoon baking pow-der)
2 tablespoon cocoa
2 oz. breadcrumbs
2 oz. suet
2 oz. sugar
egg and milk or milk to mix
few drops vanilla essence

Sieve the flour, baking powder and cocoa.
Add the other ingredients except mixing liquid and mix thoroughly.
Beat egg, egg and milk or milk, adding vanilla essence.
Stir in sufficient liquid to the mixture to give a slightly sticky consistency.
Grease and flour basin and put in mixture.
Cover with greased greaseproof paper and steam or boil for approximately 1 hour 45 minutes.
Serve with chocolate or custard sauce (see page 84).

Variations:

Fruit

Add 4 - 12 oz. dried fruit. If using the larger quantity steam for 2 hours. Omit cocoa.

Ginger

Sieve 1 - 2 level teaspoons powdered ginger with the flour instead of the cocoa. Small pieces of chopped crystallised ginger can be included. Serve with golden syrup or custard.

Jam

Any flavoured jam can be put at the bottom of the basin and serve with jam sauce (see page 85).

Plain

Omit cocoa from chocolate pudding recipe and serve with hot jam, golden syrup or any of the sweet sauce on pages 83 - 87.

Christmas pudding

cooking time 6 - 8 hours

you will need:

2 oz. flour — plain or self-raising
1 level teaspoon mixed spice
1 level teaspoon cinnamon
½ level teaspoon nutmeg
4 oz. mixed candied peel
4 oz. chopped blanched almonds
1 tablespoon golden syrup or black treacle
4 oz. fine breadcrumbs
4 oz. shredded or grated suet or melted mar-garine
4 oz. brown sugar
4 oz. grated apple
1 small grated carrot
1 lb. mixed dried fruit—½ lb. raisins, 4 oz. sul-tanas, 4 oz. currants
grated rind and juice 1 1 large lemon
2 eggs
¼ pint stout, ale, beer or milk or use nearly ¼ pint of these and 2 tablespoons rum

1 Mix all the ingredients thoroughly together.
2 Stir well and leave the mixture for 24 hours to mature.
3 Press into a large basin and cover with greased paper.
4 Cover, if wished, with a paste made from 6 oz. flour and water to give a firm dough—this keeps the pudding very dry.
5 Steam or boil for 6 - 8 hours.
6 Remove the damp covers and when cold put on dry paper.
7 Steam for a further 2 - 4 hours on Christmas Day.

Economical Christmas pudding

cooking time 6 - 7 hours

you will need:

- 1 lb. seedless raisins
- 4 oz. sultanas
- 8 oz. breadcrumbs
- 8 oz. flour
- 2 level teaspoons baking powder
- 1 teaspoon mixed spice
- ½ grated nutmeg
- 6 oz. chopped or shredded suet
- 8 oz. brown sugar
- 8 oz. apples (grated)
- 8 oz. carrots, grated
- 1 tablespoon marmalade
- 1 tablespoon black treacle
- ¼ pint milk or ale
- 2 eggs

1. Wash and prepare fruit.
2. Mix breadcrumbs with sieved flour, baking powder, spices, suet and sugar.
3. Add apple and carrot and mix in raisins and sultanas.
4. Mix together marmalade, treacle, milk and eggs.
5. Add to dry ingredients and mix thoroughly to soft dropping consistency.
6. Thoroughly grease two 1½-pint pudding basins and divide mixture equally between them.
7. Place a round of greaseproof paper on top of each basin and cover with aluminium foil.
8. Steam for 6 - 7 hours over gentle heat, replenishing water as required.
9. Drain puddings well and store in cool, dry larder.

Note:
Do not make this pudding more than 2 weeks before required.
When ready to use steam for 2 hours.

Coffee pudding

cooking time 1½ - 2 hours

you will need:

- 2 oz. margarine
- 4 oz. flour (with plain flour 2 level teaspoons baking powder)
- 2 oz. breadcrumbs
- 2 oz. sugar
- just under ½ pint strong coffee
- 1 egg
- few drops vanilla essence

1. Rub the margarine into the flour.
2. Add the baking powder, breadcrumbs and sugar.
3. Mix with the coffee, egg and vanilla essence.
4. Put into a greased basin and steam for 1½ - 2 hours.
5. Serve with chocolate or coffee sauce (see page 84, 87).

Eggless sponge pudding

cooking time 2 hours

you will need:

- 2 oz. margarine
- 6 oz. flour (with plain flour 2 level teaspoons baking powder)
- 2 oz. sugar
- 1 tablespoon golden syrup
- 1 dessertspoon vinegar
- 1 level teaspoon bicarbonate of soda
- milk to mix

1. Rub the fat into the flour previously sifted with the baking powder.
2. Add the sugar and the golden syrup.
3. Mix the vinegar and bicarbonate of soda together.
4. Add this to the other ingredients and add enough milk to make a soft consistency.
5. Put the mixture into a greased pudding basin and steam or boil for nearly 2 hours.

Fatless sponge pudding

cooking time approximately 1 hour

you will need:

- 2 eggs
- 3 oz. sugar
- 4 oz. flour (with plain flour 3 level teaspoons baking powder, with self-raising flour 1 level teaspoon baking powder)
- 2 tablespoons milk or water

1. Beat the eggs and sugar in a basin over a pan of boiling water until thick.
2. Sieve the flour and baking powder together.
3. Fold into the eggs and lastly fold in the liquid.
4. Pour into a well-greased basin and steam or boil for a good hour.

Note:
This pudding is very good when eaten straight away.

Fig pudding

cooking time 1½ - 2 hours

you will need:

- 3 oz. chopped figs
- 2 oz. margarine or suet
- 2 oz. flour (with plain flour ½ level teaspoon baking powder)
- milk to mix
- 1 oz. sugar
- little grated nutmeg

1 Soak the figs overnight.
2 Rub margarine into the flour or add the suet.
3 Mix all together with enough milk to make a sticky consistency adding all the other ingredents.
4 Put into greased basin and cover well.
5 Steam for 1½ - 2 hours.

Steamed fruit roll

cooking time 1½ - 2 hours

you will need:

6 oz. flour (with plain flour 1½ level teaspoons baking powder)
3 oz. sugar
3 oz. suet
6 oz. dried fruit
milk to mix

1 Sieve flour and baking powder together.
2 Add sugar, suet, fruit and mix to a fairly firm consistency with the milk.
3 Form into a long roll and wrap loosely in greased greaseproof paper or foil and then in a pudding cloth or more foil.
4 Steam for approximately 1½ - 2 hours.

Golden pudding

cooking time 1½ - 2 hours

you will need:

2 oz. flour (with plain flour 1 level teaspoon baking powder)
½ teaspoon bicarbonate of soda
½ teaspoon mixed spice
½ teaspoon ginger
1½ – 2 oz. suet or margarine
2 oz. breadcrumbs
2 tablespoons golden syrup
milk to mix

1 Sieve together flour, baking powder, bicarbonate of soda, mixed spice and ginger.
2 Rub margarine into flour or add suet.
3 Add breadcrumbs, golden syrup and enough milk to make a sticky consistency.
4 Put into greased basin and cover well.
5 Steam for 1½ - 2 hours.

Golden fruit roll

cooking time 2 hours

you will need:

6 oz. flour (with plain flour 1½ level teaspoons baking powder)
pinch salt
3 – 4 oz. suet
4 oz. dried fruit — sultanas, currants, etc.
¼ pint milk
3 tablespoons golden syrup
2 oz. soft breadcrumbs

1 Sift together flour, salt and baking powder.
2 Add suet and sultanas, etc.
3 Mix to a soft dough with the milk.
4 Turn out on to a lightly floured board and roll out to a rectangle approximately 8 x 10 inches.
5 Moisten the edges with water and spread the centre with golden syrup.
6 Sprinkle soft breadcrumbs over the syrup to prevent syrup seeping out during cooking.
7 Roll up like a Swiss roll and wrap **loosely** in greased aluminium foil.
8 Steam for 2 hours over rapidly boiling water.
9 Serve with warmed golden syrup.

Individual sponge puddings

cooking time 25 - 35 minutes

1 Any of the sponge or light mixtures can be used.
2 Grease dariole moulds or castle pudding tins.
3 Fill the moulds or tins with about two-thirds of the mixture.
4 Cover with paper. It is a good idea to 'pleat' the paper in case the puddings rise above the top of the tins.
5 Steam for approximately 25 minutes in the case of sponge puddings or 35 minutes for suet puddings.

Jam roly poly

cooking time 2 hours

you will need:

6 – 8 oz. suet crust pastry (see page 32)
6 – 8 oz. jam

1 Make pastry and roll out into a neat oblong about ¼ inch thick.
2 Spread with jam, being careful not to take jam right to the edges.
3 Turn in side edges and roll lightly like a Swiss roll.
4 Wrap lightly in greased greaseproof paper and then in a floured cloth.
5 Put into a steamer and cook for 2 hours over rapidly boiling water.

Lemon pudding

cooking time 1½ - 2 hours

you will need:

1½–2 oz. margarine
2 tablespoons golden syrup
4 oz. breadcrumbs
2 oz. sultanas
1 large lemon
1 tablespoon marmalade
1 egg

1. Mix margarine and syrup together, beating until margarine is soft.
2. Add the breadcrumbs, fruit and the grated lemon rind.
3. Stir in the marmalade, lemon juice and egg.
4. Put into a greased basin and cover well.
5. Steam for 1½ - 2 hours.
6. Serve with lemon sauce (see pages 85, 87).

Lemon curd pudding

cooking time 2 hours

you will need:

Crust:
6 oz. flour (with plain flour 1½ level teaspoons baking powder)
pinch salt
3 oz. shredded suet
cold water to mix

Filling:
2 oz. butter
6 oz. castor sugar
2 eggs
grated rind and juice 1 large lemon

1. Grease a 1½-pint pudding basin.
2. Sift the flour, baking powder and salt together and stir in the suet.
3. Mix to a stiff dough with cold water.
4. Roll out two-thirds of the pastry thinly and use to line the greased basin.
5. Roll out the remainder into a circle to fit top.
6. Prepare the filling by creaming the butter and sugar together.
7. Mix in the beaten eggs, the finely grated lemon rind and the lemon juice.
8. Spoon into centre of pudding.
9. Damp edges of pastry and fit the circle into the top, pressing edges firmly together.
10. Cover pudding with greased kitchen foil or double greaseproof paper.
11. Steam for 2 hours.

Marmalade pudding

cooking time 1½ hours

you will need:

4 oz. flour (with plain flour 2 level teaspoons baking powder)
2 oz. suet, margarine or cooking fat
2 oz. breadcrumbs
2 oz. sugar
2 tablespoons marmalade
milk to mix

1. Sieve together the flour and baking powder.
2. Add suet or rub the margarine or fat into the flour.
3. Put in the breadcrumbs and sugar.
4. Mix with the marmalade and enough milk to make a sticky consistency.
5. Put into a greased basin and cover well.
6. Steam for 1½ hours.

Mocha pudding

cooking time 1½ - 2 hours

you will need:

2 oz. margarine
3 oz. flour (with plain flour 2 level teaspoons baking powder)
1 oz. cocoa
2 oz. breadcrumbs
2 oz. sugar
¼ pint strong black coffee
few drops vanilla essence

1. Rub margarine into the flour.
2. Add the baking powder, cocoa, crumbs and sugar.
3. Mix with the coffee and vanilla essence.
4. Put into greased basin and cover well.
5. Steam for 1½ - 2 hours.

Boiled suet plum dumplings

cooking time 15 - 20 minutes

you will need:

4 oz. suet crust pastry (see page 32)
8 large plums
cream cheese
little sugar
water
pinch salt

1. Roll out pastry and cut into 8 rounds or squares.
2. Remove stones from each plum and. if wished, put a little cream cheese in the centre.
3. Put the plum on the pastry, dust lightly with sugar.
4. Roll pastry to form a good-shaped dumpling.
5. Cook in boiling salted water for about 15 - 20 minutes.
6. Drain and dust with sugar.

Steamed plum pudding

cooking time 1½ hours

you will need:

6 large plums
2 oz. crystallized peel
4 oz. soft bread-crumbs
3 oz. sugar
3 eggs
1 teaspoon vanilla essence
1 tablespoon water

1. Halve and stone the fruit and chop into small pieces.
2. Put into a basin with the peel, breadcrumbs and sugar.
3. Whisk the eggs very well with the vanilla essence blended with the water.
4. Pour over the plum mixture.
5. Stir together thoroughly and pour into a buttered basin.
6. Cover with buttered paper and steam steadily for 1½ hours.
7. Turn out and serve with vanilla flavoured custard sauce (see page 84).

Rainbow pudding

cooking time 15 - 25 minutes

you will need:

3 oz. butter or margarine
3 oz. sugar
5½ oz. flour (with plain flour 1½ level teaspoons baking powder)
¼ pint milk
vanilla essence
pink colouring
2 level teaspoons instant coffee powder
½ oz. custard powder

1. Grease 8 dariole or castle pudding tins.
2. Cream butter and sugar.
3. Fold in the flour, baking powder and milk.
4. Divide into 3 equal portions.
5. Add vanilla essence and pink colouring to 1 portion, instant coffee powder to the second portion, and custard powder to the third.
6. Pour a little of each into each tin, alternating with spoonfuls until all the mixtures are used.
7. Cover with greased paper and steam for 15 - 25 minutes until firm.
8. Turn out and serve with coffee sauce (see page 87).

Spiced pudding

cooking time 2½ hours

you will need:

4 oz. prunes
4 oz. figs
2 oz. margarine, cooking fat or suet
3 oz. flour (with plain flour 1 teaspoon baking powder)
2 oz. sugar
1 teaspoon mixed spice
¼ teaspoon cinnamon
¼ teaspoon nutmeg
3 oz. breadcrumbs
1 egg
milk to mix

1. Wash the prunes and figs thoroughly.
2. Cut into small pieces.
3. Rub fat into flour, or add suet.
4. Mix all the ingredients together, adding sufficient milk to make a sticky mixture.
5. Put into a greased basin and cover well.
6. Steam for 2½ hours.
7. Serve with custard sauce (see page 84).

Steamed sponge pudding

cooking time 1½ hours

you will need:

3 oz. margarine
3 oz. castor sugar
2 eggs
4 oz. flour (with plain flour 1 level teaspoon baking powder)
1 tablespoon milk

1. Cream margarine and sugar together until soft and light.
2. Add eggs gradually.
3. Stir in sieved flour and milk.
4. Grease a 1½-pint pudding basin and pour the mixture into the basin.
5. Cover with greaseproof paper or foil and put in a steamer over saucepan of rapidly boiling water.
6. Steam for a good 1½ hours.
7. Turn on to a hot dish and serve immediately with any sauce (see pages 83 - 87).

Variations:

Raspberry or blackcurrant

Place 2 tablespoons raspberry or blackcurrant jam at the bottom of a greased basin.

Fruit

Add 4 - 6 oz. mixed dried fruit and omit the milk. Serve with custard (see page 84).

Ginger

Sieve 1 level teaspoon powdered ginger with the flour and add 1 - 2 oz. diced crystallised ginger with the flour.

Syrup

Put golden syrup at the bottom of the basin and serve with golden syrup sauce (see page 85).

Apricot

Put 2 tablespoons apricot jam at the bottom of the greased basin and add the finely grated rind of 1 lemon to the margarine and sugar.

Lemon

Add finely grated rind of a lemon to the margarine and sugar and mix with 1 tablespoon lemon juice instead of milk. Put lemon curd or lemon marmalade at the bottom of the basin and serve with lemon sauce (see page 85).

Orange

Add finely grated rind of 2 oranges to margarine and sugar and mix with 1 tablespoon orange juice instead of milk. Put orange marmalade at the bottom of the basin and serve with orange sauce (see page 86) or hot marmalade.

Suet pudding

cooking time 2½ - 3 hours

you will need:

- 6 oz. flour (with plain flour 2 level teaspoons baking powder)
- pinch salt
- 2 oz. suet or cooking fat
- water to mix

1. Mix flour, baking powder and salt together.
2. Add suet or rub in cooking fat.
3. Mix to a fairly stiff dough with water.
4. Put into a greased basin and cover well.
5. Steam for 2½ - 3 hours.

Sussex pond pudding

cooking time 2 hours

you will need:

Crust:

- 6 oz. flour (with plain flour 1½ level teaspoons baking powder)
- pinch salt
- 3 oz. shredded suet
- 1 heaped tablespoon currants
- cold water to mix

Filling:

- 6 oz. demerara sugar
- 3 oz. butter

1. Grease a 1½-pint pudding basin.
2. Sift the flour, baking powder and salt together and stir in the suet and currants.
3. Mix to a stiff dough with cold water.
4. Roll out to ¼ inch thickness and line the greased basin, pressing the crust firmly to the sides.
5. Mix the butter and sugar for the filling together to form a ball and place in centre of pudding.
6. Damp edges of crust and draw over the filling pressing together to seal securely.
7. Cover basin with greased kitchen foil or double greaseproof paper.
8. Steam for 2 hours.
9. Be sure to turn pudding out into a deep dish as when cut a delicious buttery sauce will run from the pudding.

Toffee apple pudding

cooking time 2 hours

you will need:

- 3 – 4 oz. margarine
- 2 tablespoons brown sugar
- 6 oz. flour (with plain flour 2 level teaspoons baking powder)
- pinch salt
- 1 teaspoon sugar
- milk to mix
- 12 oz. apples
- little extra sugar for apples
- little water

1. Spread 1 oz. of the margarine all round the inside of a basin and sprinkle over the brown sugar.
2. Sieve the flour, baking powder and salt together.
3. Rub in the margarine and the sugar.
4. Mix to a rolling consistency with the milk.
5. Roll out thinly and line the sides of the basin, leaving some of the dough for the top of the pudding. Fill with sliced apples.
6. Add a little sugar—you will not need very much as the outside mixture is very sweet.

7 Pour over a little water, and cover with the remaining pastry.
8 Put a piece of greased paper, then a pudding cloth over the pudding.
9 Steam for 2 hours over rapidly boiling water.
10 Serve with custard sauce (see page 84).

Note:
This pudding is very popular with children, for when turned out it has a layer of a soft toffee flavoured mixture on the outside.

Pressure Cooker Puddings

Using a pressure cooker for puddings

A pressure cooker is not suitable for every type of pudding, but it does save a lot of cooking time for those mixtures that normally need to steam for some hours. Note the instructions about steaming for part of the time before pressure cooking. This allows the raising agent in the flour to "work" and gives you a light pudding.

Almond pudding

pressure cooking time 40 minutes

1 Use the recipe for steamed Almond pudding (see page 8).
2 Stand basin on the rack in the cooker with 2 pints boiling water.
3 Fix the lid, but do not put on the pressure weight.
4 Steam rapidly for 20 minutes.
5 Put on weight, bring to 5 lb. pressure.
6 Lower the heat and cook for 20 minutes.
7 Reduce pressure at once.

Bread pudding

pressure cooking time 40 minutes

1 Use the recipe for steamed Bread pudding (see page 8).
2 Stand the basin on the rack in the cooker with 2 pints boiling water.
3 Fix the lid, but do not put on the pressure weight.
4 Steam rapidly for 20 minutes.
5 Put on the weight and bring to 5 lb. pressure.
6 Lower the heat and cook for 20 minutes.
7 Reduce pressure at once.

Brigade pudding

pressure cooking time 50 minutes

1 Use the recipe for steamed Brigade pudding (see page 8).
2 Put the basin on the rack in the cooker with 2 pints boiling water.
3 Fix the lid, but do not put on the pressure weight.
4 Steam for 20 minutes.
5 Bring to 5 lb. pressure, lower the heat and cook for 30 minutes.
6 Reduce pressure immediately.

Brown Betty pudding

pressure cooking time 45 minutes

1 Use the recipe for steamed Apple Brown Betty pudding (see page 9).
2 Stand the basin filled with the mixture on the rack in the cooker with 2 pints of boiling water.
3 Fix lid and steam for 30 minutes at 20 lb. pressure.

Fig pudding

pressure cooking time 45 minutes

1 Use the recipe for steamed Fig pudding (see page 10).
2 Stand basin on the rack in the cooker with 2 pints boiling water.
3 Cook as for Coffee pudding (see page 16).

Coffee pudding

pressure cooking time 45 minutes

1 Use the recipe for steamed Coffee pudding (see page 10).
2 Stand basin on rack in cooker with 2 pints boiling water.
3 Cover well and fix the lid, but do not put on pressure weight.
4 Steam rapidly for 15 minutes.
5 Put on pressure weight and bring to pressure of 5 lb.
6 Lower the heat and cook for 30 minutes.
7 Reduce pressure at once.

Golden pudding

pressure cooking time 30 minutes

1 Use the recipe for steamed Golden pudding (see page 11).
2 Put basin on rack in cooker with 2 pints boiling water.
3 Cook as for Coffee pudding (see above).

Lemon pudding

pressure cooking time 45 minutes

1 Use the recipe for steamed Lemon pudding (see page 12).
2 Stand basin on rack in cooker with 2 pints boiling water.
3 Cover well and fix the lid, but do not put on pressure weight.
4 Steam rapidly for 15 minutes.
5 Put on pressure weight and bring to pressure of 5 lb.
6 Lower the heat and cook for 30 minutes.
7 Reduce pressure at once.
8 Serve with Lemon sauce (see pages 85, 87).

Marmalade pudding

pressure cooking time 40 minutes

1 Use the recipe for steamed Marmalade pudding (see page 12).
2 Stand on the rack in the cooker with 2 pints boiling water.
3 Cook as for Coffee pudding (see above).

Mocha pudding

pressure cooking time 40 minutes

1 Use the recipe for steamed Mocha pudding (see page 12).
2 Stand on the rack in the cooker with 2 pints boiling water.
3 Cook as for Coffee pudding (see above).

Suet pudding

pressure cooking time 1 hour

1 Use the recipe for steamed Suet pudding (see page 14).
2 Stand on the rack in the cooker with 2 pints boiling water.
3 Fix lid, but do not put on pressure weight.
4 Cook as for Brigade pudding (see page 15).

Viennoise pudding

pressure cooking time 25 - 30 minutes

you will need:

2 oz. loaf or granulated sugar
1 tablespoon water
$\frac{1}{4}$ pint milk
3 oz. bread
1 dessertspoon marmalade
2 oz. dried fruit
1 oz. granulated or castor sugar
little grated lemon or orange rind
2 eggs

1 Put the loaf sugar into a saucepan with the water.
2 Stir until the sugar has dissolved.
3 Boil steadily, without stirring, until the mixture turns into a dark brown caramel sauce.
4 Add the milk and heat **slowly** until the caramel dissolves.
5 Cut the bread into small squares, pour over the caramel liquid.
6 Add all the other ingredients.
7 Allow to stand for 15 minutes and put into a greased basin.
8 Cover well and stand on rack in cooker with approximately $\frac{1}{2}$ pint hot water.
9 Bring to pressure and allow 15 minutes (20 minutes if deep container).
10 Allow pressure to drop without putting under cold tap, but remove lid **at once** when dropped.
11 Serve hot or cold.

Baked Puddings

In this chapter there is a wide selection of baked puddings including a variety of delicious charlottes and ambers.

Apple amber

cooking time 1 hour 10 minutes

you will need:

1 - 1¼ lb. apples	4 - 5 oz. sugar
very little water	2 eggs

1. Simmer the apples with very little water and 2 - 3 oz. of the sugar.
2. When a thick smooth pulp add the beaten egg yolks.
3. Pour into a dish and set for approximately 30 minutes in the centre of a moderate oven (375°F.—Gas Mark 4).
4. Whisk egg whites until very stiff.
5. Fold in the remaining 2 oz. sugar and pile on top of the apple mixture.
6. Return to the oven to brown the meringue for 20 minutes if serving hot. If wishing to serve cold place in a cool oven for about 1 hour.

Variations:

Gooseberry

Use 1 - 1¼ lb. 'topped and tailed' gooseberries.

Plum

Use 1 - 1¼ lb. plums.

Biscuit

Grease the edge of the dish and press about 4 oz. sweet biscuit crumbs against the greased dish.

Crumb

Add 2 oz. fine cake crumbs to the fruit mixture.

Greengage

Use the method for apple amber but sieve the fruit to get rid of the skins.

Rhubarb

Use the method for apple amber. Take care in cooking the rhubarb that it does not become too watery. It is a good idea to cook it in a double saucepan with just sugar and no water.

Amber flan

Bake a pastry flan case 'blind' (see page 30) until it is very pale gold. Put in the mixture and cook until set, then top with the meringue and crisp as before.

Apple charlotte (1)

cooking time 50 - 60 minutes

you will need:

6 oz. white breadcrumbs	2 tablespoons water
3 oz. shredded or chopped suet	1½ lb. cooking apples
2 oz. granulated sugar	¼ level teaspoon cinnamon or spice
1 oz. butter	2½ oz. brown sugar
	little extra brown sugar

1. Mix the breadcrumbs, suet and granulated sugar well together.
2. Press ¾ of this mixture in a well greased pie or soufflé dish, covering the bottom and sides.
3. Melt butter in a pan and add water.
4. Peel, core and cut in neat dice the apples and add to the melted butter together with the cinnamon or spice and brown sugar.
5. Pour into pie dish and top with remaining crumb mixture, pressing down firmly.
6. Sprinkle crumbs with a layer of brown sugar.
7. Bake in the centre of a moderate oven (375°F. —Gas Mark 4) for 50 - 60 minutes until golden brown.

Apple charlotte (2)

Ingredients as for Apple charlotte (see above) but use approximately 4 oz. margarine instead of suet. Make the crumbs rather large. Fry in the hot margarine until thoroughly coated. Add the sugar, and proceed as before.

Variations:

Apricot

Use a large can of well drained apricots or dried appricots soaked overnight.

Blackberry and apple
Use 1 lb. cooking apples and 8 oz. blackberries.

Apple and orange
Use either of the Apple charlotte recipes but add the grated rind of 1 - 2 oranges and the orange juice when cooking the apples. Omit water and cinnamon.

Apple sultana
Use either of the Apple charlotte recipes adding 2 oz. sultanas to the apples when cooked.

Gooseberry
'Top and tail' the gooseberries and if ripe cook gently with no water, but if unripe use 3 tablespoons water for cooking. Proceed as for either of the Apple charlotte recipes.

Plum
If using ripe plums use no water; but with unripe plums add 2 - 3 tablespoons water. Proceed as for either of the Apple charlotte recipes.

Rhubarb
Crumb mixture as either of the Apple charlotte recipes. If using forced rhubarb cut into small pieces and cook with sugar but no liquid. If using older rhubarb, cook with the sugar and about 1 tablespoon water only.

Raspberry and redcurrant charlotte

cooking time 50 minutes

you will need:

8 oz. redcurrants
8 oz. raspberries
thin slices bread
3 – 4 oz. butter
sugar to taste

1. Remove crusts from bread — cut pieces to fit bottom of a small round dish or cake tin and enough to line sides and for a 'lid'.
2. Fry gently in the butter until golden but NOT crisp, then arrange at bottom and sides of the tin.
3. To give an attractive 'sugary' look to the sweet the tin can be greased and sprinkled with sugar BEFORE putting in the bread.
4. Fill lined tin with the raspberries and currants, sweetening them well.
5. Cover with more fried bread and a sprinkling of sugar.
6. Bake for approximately 45 minutes in centre of a very moderate oven (350°F—Gas Mark 3) until golden brown.
7. Turn out carefully on to a hot dish and serve with cream or custard sauce (see page 84).

Note:
Fruit that is sound but a little soft can be used in this.

Apple Brown Betty
(illustrated on cover)

cooking time 50 minutes - 1 hour

you will need:

ingredients as for steamed Apple Brown Betty pudding (see page 9)

1. Method as for Brown Betty pudding.
2. Put into a soufflé or pie dish and bake for 50 minutes - 1 hour in the centre of a moderate oven (375°F.—Gas Mark 4).
3. If wished decorate with slices of apple, dipped in a little sugar.

Upside-down pudding

cooking time 1 - 1¼ hours

you will need:

ingredients for Steamed sponge pudding, Fatless sponge or Eggless sponge (see pages 10, 13)
1 lb. fresh fruit or large can fruit
1 oz. butter
1 – 3 oz. sugar (preferably brown)

1. Melt the butter and put in the bottom of the greased dish.
2. Add the brown sugar. Use the smaller amount with canned fruit.
3. Arrange the fruit in the brown sugar and butter in the dish.
4. Make the sponge mixture and place over top.
5. Cook for 1 - 1¼ hours, depending on the richness of the mixture, in the centre of a moderate oven (375°F.—Gas Mark 4).
6. Turn out and serve with cream or ice-cream.

Note:
An upside-down pudding should not be cooked too quickly as you have fruit as well as the cake mixture. Always bake in the centre of the oven to make certain it is done right the way through.

Variations:

Apple

Arrange rather thick slices of cooking apple in the glaze with glacé cherries or pieces of ginger.

Apricot

Arrange halved apricots in the glaze.

Banana

Arrange rather thick sections of banana in the glaze with pieces of angelica or cherries. While preparing the banana, sprinkle with a little lemon juice so it does not discolour.

Coffee upside-down puddings

cooking time 15 - 35 minutes

you will need:

To decorate:
1 oz. margarine or butter
16 pieces cherry
16 small sections canned or fresh pineapple
2 oz. brown sugar

Filling:
2 oz. margarine
3 oz. sugar
1 egg
4 oz. flour
1 dessertspoon instant coffee powder
1 level teaspoon baking powder
little milk

1 Melt the 1 oz. margarine or butter in the bottom of greased individual moulds.
2 Arrange 4 pieces of cherry and pineapple to decorate and sprinkle with sugar.
3 Cream fat and sugar together.
4 Beat in the egg.
5 Lightly fold in the sieved flour, instant coffee and baking powder, adding milk to make a soft dropping consistency.
6 Pour into the moulds and cover with greased paper.
7 Bake in a moderately hot oven (400°F.—Gas Mark 5) for 15 - 35 minutes until firm.
8 Turn out and serve with coffee sauce (see page 87) or cream.

Eve's pudding

cooking time 45 - 50 minutes

you will need:

1¼ lb. cooking apples
2 oz. sugar
⅛ pint water
3 oz. margarine
3 oz. castor sugar
2 eggs
4 oz. flour (1 level teaspoon baking powder with plain flour)

1 Peel, core and slice the apples.
2 Put into a pie dish with the sugar and water.
3 Bake in the centre of a moderate oven (375°F. —Gas Mark 4) for approximately 10 minutes.
4 Cream together the margarine and sugar.
5 Beat in the eggs gradually and stir in the flour.
6 Spread over the hot apples and return to the oven for 35 - 40 minutes.
7 Sprinkle with sugar before serving.

Variations:

Dried fruit

Add a mixture of dried fruit to the apples.

Plum

Use plums in place of apples.

Soft fruit

Soft fruits can be used, in which case do not heat first, but put the sponge mixture over the top and allow approximately 40 minutes cooking time.

Fruit crumble

cooking time 25 minutes

you will need:

1 lb. fruit
sugar to taste
water

Topping:
4 oz. flour (plain or self-raising)
2 oz. butter or margarine
3 oz. sugar

1 Put the fruit with sugar and very little water into a fairly large pie dish. Soft berry fruits, such as raspberries and currants will need no water at all.
2 Heat for about 10 - 15 minutes.
3 Sieve the flour and rub the butter into it.
4 Add the sugar and sprinkle the crumbs evenly over the fruit pressing down fairly firmly. This makes certain the crust can be cut into neat slices.
5 Bake in the centre of a moderate oven (375°F. —Gas Mark 4) for about 25 minutes until crisp and golden brown.
6 Serve hot or cold.

Variations:

Coconut

Use 2 oz. flour and 2 oz. coconut instead of all flour. This is particularly good with gooseberries and currants.

Cornflake

Cream 2 oz. butter with 1 oz. golden syrup and 2 oz. sugar. Work in 4 oz. **very crisp** cornflakes. This is particularly good with rhubarb and soft fruits.

Spice

Use 3 oz. flour only, sieved with 1 teaspoon mixed spice and 1 oz. chopped walnuts. This is excellent with apples, rhubarb and plums.

Fruit cobblers

A fruit cobbler is rather similar to a fruit pie but it has a mixture on the top which takes the place of pastry and is considerably more economical.

Use approximately 1 oz. of fat to 4 oz. of self-raising flour (with plain flour add 1 level teaspoon baking powder). Rub the fat into the flour in the usual way, add 1 - 2 oz. of sugar and milk to mix. Roll out to about ½ inch in thickness and cut into 2-inch rounds or triangles.

Apple cobbler

cooking time 40 minutes

you will need:

1¼ lb. cooking apples
very little water
sugar to taste
8 oz. self-raising flour
2 oz. sugar
2 oz. margarine
milk to mix

1. Cut the apples into fairly large pieces. Put into a pie dish with water and sugar to taste.
2. Cook for approximately 25 minutes in a moderately hot oven (375-400°F.—Gas Mark 4-5).
3. Take out of oven and raise heat to 450°F.—Gas Mark 7.
4. Rub the margarine into the flour, add the sugar.
5. Mix to a fairly soft dough with the milk.
6. Roll out to about ½ inch thick. Cut into 2-inch rounds or triangles.
7. Arrange on top of the fruit. Return to the centre of the oven for a further 15 minutes.

Variations:

Apple and date

As above using approximately 4 oz. chopped dates.

Apple ginger

As above adding 2 oz. chopped crystallised ginger.

Cherry

As above using a good 1 lb. of cooking cherries, very little water, sugar to taste. Cook for only 15 minutes.

Gooseberry

Add water and sugar and cook for only 15 minutes before adding the cobbler mixture.

Greengage

As for Gooseberry cobbler, if using ripe greengages.

Plum

As for Gooseberry cobbler, cooking for only 15 minutes if plums are ripe.

Crunchy apple cobbler

(illustrated on cover)

cooking time 30 - 35 minutes

you will need:

8 oz. brown sugar
grated rind ½ lemon
1 level teaspoon cinnamon or powdered ginger
3 – 4 oz. seedless raisins
½ pint water
1½ lb. tart eating apples

Butterscotch topping:
½ lb. self-raising flour
pinch salt
2 oz. butter or margarine
water to mix
1 oz. softened butter or margarine
2 oz. brown sugar

1. Put the sugar, lemon rind, cinnamon or ginger, raisins and water in a saucepan. Stir until sugar is dissolved.
2. Bring to the boil.
3. Peel, core and quarter the apples and simmer in the syrup until just tender.
4. Turn into a shallow ovenware dish.
5. To make the topping, sift the flour and salt,

rub in the 2 oz. butter and mix to a soft dough with the cold water.

6 Roll out lightly on a well-floured board to oblong shape just under ½ inch thick.
7 Spread with the 1 oz. softened butter, sprinkle with brown sugar and roll up like a Swiss roll.
8 Cut into six even slices. Arrange on top of the apples.
9 Bake just above centre in a hot oven (425°F.—Gas Mark 6) for 20 minutes until well risen and golden brown.
10 Serve with cream or custard.

Fruit crunch

cooking time 40 minutes

you will need:

1 lb. fruit	2 oz. butter or margarine
very little water	2 oz. sugar
sugar to taste	4 oz. cornflakes

1 Put fruit with very little water and sugar to taste into a dish.
2 Cook slowly until nearly tender and a thick mixture.
3 Cream butter and sugar together.
4 Add cornflakes and press on top of the fruit.
5 Continue cooking in a moderate oven (375-400°F.—Gas Mark 4-5) for 25 minutes until top is crisp.
6 Serve with cream or custard.

Note:
Do not have fruit too juicy otherwise mixture on top will 'sink' in.

Crunch variations:

Apple date

As Fruit crunch (see above) using 1 lb. apples, 2 oz. dates.

Greengage

1 lb. greengages, little water, sugar to taste. Soften the fruit only. Do not allow it to become pulpy. Press the crunch on top and proceed as Fruit crunch (see above).

Rhubarb

As Fruit crunch (see above) using a good pound of rhubarb, sugar to taste, and very little water.

Strawberry shortcake

cooking time 15 minutes

you will need:

4 oz. margarine	approximately 1 lb. strawberries
4 oz. sugar	little extra sugar
2 eggs	whipped cream
6 oz. flour (with plain flour 2 level teaspoons baking powder)	

1 Cream the margarine and sugar until light and fluffy.
2 Beat the eggs and add gradually to the creamed margarine alternately with the flour.
3 Divide into 2 well greased and floured sandwich tins.
4 Bake for a good 15 minutes near the top of a hot oven (450°F.—Gas Mark 7).
5 Cool for a few minutes and turn out.
6 Arrange halved strawberries on 1 layer and sprinkle with sugar.
7 Put on the other round and pile the rest of the strawberries on top.
8 Serve with more sugar and cream.

Milk Puddings

The secret of a good milk pudding is generally in the slow cooking and wherever possible this should not be hurried. An extra rich flavour is given if a little butter or suet is added when baking rice, etc. see recipe for Rice pudding on page 23. Choose Carolina rice (round grain) for milk puddings. The short—elbow length—macaroni is particularly good for milk puddings as it is easier to serve.

Almond pears

cooking time 1½ hours

you will need:

4 fairly firm pears
2 oz. ground almonds
2 oz. apricot jam
2 oz. Carolina rice
1 pint milk
little sugar to taste

1. Peel and halve the pears and remove cores.
2. Fill centre with mixture of ground almonds and apricot jam.
3. Put the filled side downwards in the casserole.
4. Heat the rice and milk together in a saucepan with sugar to taste until thickening.
5. Pour over the pears and cook for a further hour in a slow oven (300°F.—Gas Mark 2).

Macaroni pudding (1)

cooking time 1 hour 5 minutes

you will need:

1 pint milk
3 oz. macaroni
1 oz. butter
2 oz. sugar
nutmeg
grated rind ½ lemon
1 oz. almonds
3 eggs

1. Boil milk.
2. Stir in macaroni and cook for 5 minutes.
3. Take from heat and add butter, sugar, flavouring, almonds chopped finely and egg yolks.
4. Fold in the stiffly beaten whites.
5. Steam in buttered and sugared plain mould for 1 hour. It should be cooked slowly but steadily.
6. Turn out and serve with fruit or lemon sauce (see pages 85, 87).

Note:

A cheaper pudding is made by omitting the almonds and 1 egg.

Macaroni pudding (2)

cooking time 30 - 40 minutes

you will need:

8 oz. macaroni
2 oz. sultanas
¾ pint sweetened custard
2 oz. coconut
2 oz. margarine or butter

1. Cook and drain macaroni as directed on packet.
2. Mix with sultanas and custard.
3. Pour into greased fireproof dish and sprinkle with coconut and dot with margarine or butter.
4. Bake in a moderate oven (375°F.—Gas Mark 4) for 20-30 minutes.

Macaroni milk pudding

cooking time 1 hour 35 minutes - 1 hour 40 minutes

you will need:

1 pint milk
3 oz. macaroni
1 – 2 oz. sugar
1 egg (optional)
little extra milk

1. Bring the milk to the boil.
2. Add macaroni and sugar and cook for about 5-10 minutes.
3. Stir in the egg, beaten with a little cold milk, and transfer to a pie dish.
4. Bake for approximately 1½ hours in the centre of a cool oven (250°F.—Gas Mark ½), stirring after about 30 minutes' baking.

Harlequin macaroni pudding

cooking time approximately 1 hour

you will need:

1 pint milk
rind 1 lemon
pinch salt
3 oz. castor sugar
3 oz. quick cooking macaroni
2 eggs
different coloured jams

1. Pour milk into saucepan and add lemon rind, salt and 1 oz. of the sugar.
2. Bring to the boil and sprinkle in the macaroni.
3. Simmer for 7 minutes, stirring regularly.
4. Remove from heat and allow to cool slightly.
5. Separate whites from yolks of eggs.
6. Lightly beat yolks and stir into macaroni mixture.
7. Pour into a flat oven-proof dish and bake in a moderate oven (375°F.—Gas Mark 4) for 30 minutes.
8. Remove from oven, whisk egg whites stiffly and sprinkle in remaining sugar.
9. With a star meringue pipe, pipe this meringue on to the pudding in straight lines, first across this dish one way, and then in the opposite direction to form a lattice pattern.
10. Fill spaces between lattice with coloured jams and return to oven for a further 15 - 20 minutes until golden brown.

Rice pudding

cooking time 2 - 3 hours

you will need:

2 – 3 oz. Carolina rice
1 pint milk
sugar to taste
little butter or suet

1 Soak the rice in the milk for a while before cooking, or cover with a little water (put into a hot oven for about 10 - 15 minutes until the rice has absorbed the water) or pour over the milk and cook slowly.
2 Add knob of butter or suet to give extra creaminess and sugar to taste.
3 Cook for about 2 - 3 hours in a very slow oven (275°F.—Gas Mark 1).

Note:
Instead of fresh milk use some evaporated or condensed milk to give extra creaminess and flavour.

Coffee rice pudding

Use recipe for Rice pudding as above but add a little instant coffee, coffee essence or strong black coffee to the milk.

Chocolate rice pudding

Use recipe for Rice pudding as above but add 1 oz. chocolate powder or ½ oz. cocoa to the milk by blending this with a little cold milk until dissolved. Add rest of the milk and continue as above.

Fruit rice pudding

Use recipe for Rice pudding as above but cook the rice in a very thin fruit purée or syrup instead of milk.

Orange rice pudding

Use recipe for Rice pudding above but add grated rind of 1 or 2 oranges and 2 oz. crystallised orange peel—allowing this to stand for a time in warm milk to soften it. Pour milk and peel over the rice and continue as before.

Caramel rice pudding

Use recipe for Rice pudding as above, plus 2 extra oz. sugar and 2 tablespoons water. Put the sugar and water into a pan and stir until sugar has dissolved then add pint milk and heat with the caramel, taking care not to boil rapidly. Pour over rice, add sugar, etc., and continue as before.

Crisp topped caramel rice

Use recipe for Rice pudding (see above) and when cooked sprinkle the top with brown sugar, crumbs and a little melted butter. Brown under a steady grill until crisp.

Sago pudding

cooking time 2 hours if baked in oven, 15 minutes on top of stove

you will need:

2 – 3 oz. sago
1 pint milk
1 – 2 oz. sugar

1 Wash the sago and put into a pie dish.
2 Cover with the milk and sugar.
3 Cook gently for approximately 2 hours in a very cool oven (250°F.—Gas Mark ½).
4 Or cook for 10 - 15 minutes on top of the stove stirring all the time.

Tapioca milk pudding

cooking time 2 hours if baked in oven, 15 minutes on top of stove

you will need:

2 – 3 oz. tapioca
1 pint milk
1 – 2 oz. sugar

Method as for Sago pudding (see above).

Semolina pudding

cooking time 45 minutes if baked in oven, 10 minutes on top of stove

you will need:

1 pint milk
1 – 2 oz. sugar
2 – 3 oz. semolina

1 Bring the milk to the boil.
2 Add the sugar and gradually whisk in the semolina.
3 Stir very briskly until thickened and smooth.
4 Cook for about 10 minutes on top of the stove or transfer to a pie dish and allow approximately 45 minutes in a cool oven (250°F.—Gas Mark ½).

Semolina and caramel crisp

cooking time 15 - 20 minutes

you will need:

1 pint milk
3 oz. semolina
1 tablespoon marmalade
2 – 3 oz. dried fruit, sultanas, dates
1 good tablespoon crisp breadcrumbs
Caramel sauce (see page 83)

1 Bring the milk to the boil.
2 Whisk in the semolina, add the marmalade and dried fruit.
3 Cook gently, stirring from time to time, for 15 minutes.
4 Meanwhile, make the caramel sauce.
5 Pour the cooked semolina into a hot greased pie dish.
6 Sprinkle over the breadcrumbs and crisp under a hot grill.
7 When quite brown, pour the caramel sauce over the pudding.

Egg Custards

A good custard and any sweets based on custard, need careful cooking, otherwise the mixture will curdle.

Follow the directions for timing most carefully and if you intend to steam the custard do not let the water boil, which will cause curdling. Keep it just under simmering point.

If you are baking your custard in the oven, place the pie dish in a container of cold water to stop it from boiling.

If your custard is allowed to boil, holes will form in the custard which spoils the appearance and flavour.

Bread and butter puddings and Queen of puddings are types of egg custards and should therefore have the same care in cooking.

Baked egg custard

cooking time 1¼ - 1½ hours

you will need:

4 eggs or egg yolks
1 – 2 oz. sugar
1 pint milk
grated nutmeg

1 Beat the eggs and sugar together.
2 Pour over the hot, but not boiling milk.
3 Pour into a pie dish and top with grated nutmeg.
4 Stand in another container of cold water. Bake for approximately 1¼ - 1½ hours in a very slow oven (275°F.—Gas Mark 1) until quite firm.

Note:
For a less firm custard use only 2 - 3 eggs.

Bread and butter pudding

cooking time 1 hour

you will need:

ingredients as egg custard (see above)
2 large or 4 small slices bread
little butter
2 oz. dried fruit
little extra sugar

1 Make the egg custard as directed on page 24.
2 Remove the crusts from the bread and butter thinly.
3 Cut into neat squares or triangles and arrange in a piedish.
4 Add the dried fruit and pour the egg custard over the top.
5 Allow to stand for 30 minutes.
6 Sprinkle the top with a little sugar and bake for approximately 1 hour in the centre of a very moderate oven (325°F.—Gas Mark 3).
7 If the pudding appears to be cooking too quickly after 45 minutes, lower the heat.

Caramel cream de luxe

cooking time 2½ - 3 hours

you will need:

4 oz. sugar
3 tablespoons water
½ pint milk
½ pint cream
4 egg yolks
2 egg whites
3 oz. blanched almonds
brown or icing sugar

1 Heat 3 oz. of sugar and water until brown caramel.
2 Add milk and cream and heat gently.
3 Beat eggs with the remaining sugar until creamy.
4 Pour the caramel mixture over the eggs, put into dish, and cook very slowly in a cool oven (250°F.—Gas Mark ½).
5 When set top with a thick layer of blanched almonds and brown or icing sugar.
6 Heat for a few minutes under the grill.

Chocolate crumb pudding

cooking time 1¼ - 1½ hours

you will need:

3 eggs
1 – 2 oz. sugar
1 oz. cocoa
4 oz. breadcrumbs
1 pint milk
1 oz. chocolate

1 Beat the eggs, sugar and cocoa together.
2 Add breadcrumbs and pour over the hot, but not boiling milk.
3 Allow to stand for about 30 minutes.
4 Cook as for Baked egg custard (see page 24).
5 Top with grated chocolate.
6 If serving cold top with lightly whipped cream.

Coconut custard

cooking time 1¼ - 1½ hours

you will need:

3 eggs
1 – 2 oz. sugar
1 pint milk
4 oz. coconut

To decorate:
little raspberry jam
extra coconut

1 Make custard as in Baked egg custard (see page 24).
2 Add coconut.
3 Allow to stand for about 30 minutes.
4 Put into pie dish and bake as for Baked egg custard.
5 When set cover the top with jam and sprinkle with coconut.
6 Serve hot or cold.

Caramel mould

cooking time 1½ hours

you will need:

2 oz. loaf or granulated sugar
2 tablespoons water
1 pint milk
4 egg yolks
2 egg whites
1 oz. castor sugar
2 oz. almonds, blanched

To decorate:
whipped cream

1 Put the sugar and water into a thick saucepan and brown slowly until sugar has dissolved, stirring all the time.
2 Add the milk and heat gently, stirring all the time, but do not allow to boil as caramel will cause it to curdle.
3 When the caramel has been absorbed into the milk pour over the beaten eggs.
4 Brown almonds under the grill and chop finely.
5 Add 1 oz. of the almonds and castor sugar to the mixture and pour into a greased mould.
6 Place a piece of buttered paper on top and steam gently for about 1¼ hours until firm.
7 Cool slightly and turn out carefully.
8 When quite cold decorate with whipped cream and remaining almonds.

Fruity caramel pudding

cooking time 2 hours 40 minutes

you will need:

3 oz. loaf sugar
3 tablespoons water
1 pint milk
4 oz. bread
2 oz. sultanas
2 oz. chopped glacé cherries
1 oz. finely chopped crystallised peel
4 egg yolks
2 egg whites

1 Put the loaf sugar and water into a strong pan and stir until sugar has dissolved.
2 Boil steadily until dark brown.
3 Allow to cool slightly, then add the milk.
4 Heat without boiling until the milk has absorbed the caramel.
5 Remove crusts from bread and cut into neat dice.
6 Pour the caramel liquid over the bread and allow to soak for at least 30 minutes.
7 Add all the other ingredients, beating the eggs very well.
8 Pour into a greased basin and steam gently **without boiling** for approximately 2½ hours.

Baked mocha pudding

cooking time 1¼ hours

you will need:

2 oz. sugar
1 oz. chocolate powder
4 oz. cake crumbs
3 eggs
⅜ pint milk
⅜ pint strong coffee

1 Put sugar, chocolate powder and cake crumbs into a basin.
2 Beat eggs with the milk and coffee.
3 Pour over the dry ingredients and allow to stand for about 15 minutes.
4 Transfer to a greased pie dish and stand in another container of cold water.
5 Cook for about 1¼ hours, in a very slow oven (275°F.—Gas Mark 1 or 2) until firm.
6 Cool for a minute or two before turning out and serve hot or cold with cream.

Fruity caramel custard

cooking time 12 - 15 minutes

you will need:

3 tablespoons golden syrup
1 pint milk
3 level tablespoons custard powder
1 oz. sugar
2 bananas
2 ripe eating apples
canned or whipped cream

1 Put the golden syrup into a saucepan and heat steadily until the syrup is a golden brown caramel.
2 Add most of the milk and bring to the boil.
3 Blend the custard powder with the rest of the milk and sugar.
4 Return to pan and cook until thickened.
5 Pour into serving dish and allow to cool.
6 Top with sliced bananas, apple and whipped cream.

Fruit custard

cooking time 1¼ - 1½ hours

you will need:

4 eggs
1–2 oz. sugar
1 pint milk
8 oz. mincemeat (little less if desired)

Use the method for Baked egg custard (see page 24), adding mincemeat.

Macaroon caramel custard

cooking time 15 minutes

you will need:

3 egg yolks
3 oz. sugar
1 pint milk
2 or 3 tablespoons water
2 macaroon biscuits
little cream

1 Beat the eggs with 1 oz. sugar.
2 Pour over the milk and cook very gently until the custard is thick enough to coat the back of a wooden spoon.
3 In another pan make a caramel with the rest of the sugar and water, stirring until sugar has dissolved.
4 Boil steadily without stirring until golden brown.
5 Cool slightly, and pour the custard into the caramel.
6 Heat together for a minute until the custard has absorbed all the caramel.
7 Crumble the macaroons at the bottom of a serving dish.
8 Pour the caramel custard on top and leave until quite cold.
9 Decorate with cream.

Macaroni custard

cooking time 15 minutes

you will need:

4 oz. quick cooking macaroni
1 tablespoon cornflour
¼ pint milk
1 egg
1½ tablespoons castor sugar
knob butter
nutmeg

1 Cook macaroni as directed on packet.
2 Blend cornflour with a little milk.
3 Add beaten egg and the remainder of the milk and castor sugar.
4 Add cooked macaroni and knob of butter and stir gently over heat until mixture thickens, taking care not to let it boil.
5 Pour into serving dishes and sprinkle with grated nutmeg.

Macaroon custard

cooking time $1\frac{1}{4}$ - $1\frac{1}{2}$ hours

you will need:

3 eggs
1 – 2 oz. sugar
1 pint milk
2 large macaroon biscuits or about 12 tiny ratafia biscuits
1 oz. blanched almonds
little apricot jam
little water

1 Beat the eggs and sugar together.
2 Pour over the hot but not boiling milk.
3 Add the broken macaroon biscuits or the whole ratafia biscuits.
4 Cook as for Baked egg custard (see page 24).
5 When ready top with blanched shredded almonds—which can be browned under the grill.
6 Dissolve about 2 tablespoons apricot jam with a little water and pour over the top of the custard before serving.
7 Serve hot or cold.

Queen of puddings

cooking time 55 minutes - 1 hour

you will need:

1 – 2 eggs
3 oz. sugar
$\frac{1}{2}$ pint milk
2 oz. fine cake or breadcrumbs
1 lemon
little jam

1 Beat the egg yolk or yolks with 2 oz. of the sugar.
2 Pour on the hot milk.
3 Put the crumbs and finely grated lemon rind into a basin and strain the egg and milk liquid over them.
4 Put a little jam at the bottom of a piedish and pour in the mixture.
5 Bake for 35 - 40 minutes in a very moderate oven (350°F.—Gas Mark 3) until firm.
6 Spread with jam over the top.
7 Whisk up the egg white or whites until stiff and fold in the remaining sugar, spread over the jam.
8 Return to the oven for approximately 20 minutes.

Variations:

Chocolate

Blend $\frac{1}{2}$ oz. cocoa or 1 oz. chocolate powder with eggs and sugar.

Coffee

Blend dessertspoon of instant coffee with eggs and sugar.

Coconut

Add 1 - 2 oz. desiccated coconut to eggs and sugar. Fold 1 oz. desiccated coconut into the egg white and sugar for the meringue.

Fruit

Use thick sweetened fruit purée, apple, rhubarb, plum are particularly good, in place of jam.

Lemon

Add grated rind of 2 lemons and use lemon curd instead of jam.

Orange

Add grated rind of 1 - 2 oranges and use orange marmalade or orange curd instead of jam.

Swiss roll

Instead of breadcrumbs use slices of Swiss roll. Arrange in the dish and proceed as before. You may like to use a little less sugar.

Sultana macaroni custard

cooking time 50 minutes - 1 hour

you will need:

3 oz. quick cooking macaroni
2 tablespoons golden syrup
2 eggs
1 oz. castor sugar
about $\frac{3}{4}$ pint milk
2 oz. sultanas
$\frac{1}{2}$ oz. chopped mixed peel

1 Cook macaroni according to instructions on packet and drain.
2 Put syrup in measuring jug and add eggs and sugar.
3 Beat thoroughly and make up to $\frac{3}{4}$ pint with milk, stirring well.
4 Place macaroni in greased pie dish.
5 Add sultanas and mixed peel and pour custard mixture on top.
6 Place in roasting tin filled with cold water to come half way up the side of the piedish.
7 Bake on middle shelf in a moderate oven (375°F.—Gas Mark 4) for 40 - 50 minutes until lightly set.

Raspberry snow ring

cooking time 1½ hours

you will need:

3 egg yolks
1 egg
1 oz. sugar
1 pint milk
1 lb. raspberries
3 egg whites
little sugar

1 Beat egg yolks, whole egg and sugar together.
2 Pour over the warmed milk and mix thoroughly.
3 Pour into a greased ring mould or stand a tin in the centre of a large one to give a ring shape.
4 Bake until set in a very slow oven (250 - 275°F.—Gas Mark ½ - 1).
5 Cool slightly and turn out.
6 Mash the raspberries and add the stiffly beaten egg whites, and sweeten.
7 Pile in the centre of the custard ring.

Variations:

Blackcurrant

Use 1 lb. blackcurrants instead of raspberries cooking them with sugar to taste, until soft.

Strawberry

Use 1 lb. strawberries instead of raspberries.

Toffee pudding

cooking time 1 hour 40 minutes

you will need:

4 oz. castor sugar
3 tablespoons water
¾ pint milk
2 large slices stale bread about ½-inch thick
3 egg yolks
2 oz. sultanas
To decorate:
glacé cherries
little cream

1 Put 3 oz. of the sugar and water into a pan and stir until sugar has dissolved.
2 Boil steadily until brown.
3 Add milk and heat gently until the caramel has dissolved in the milk.
4 Remove crusts from bread and cut into neat dice.
5 Pour liquid over this.
6 Beat eggs with remaining sugar and add to the mixture together with sultanas.
7 Leave to stand for 30 minutes.
8 Stir briskly and pour into greased basin and cover with greased paper.
9 Steam gently for about 1½ hours until firm.
10 Serve hot or cold decorated with glacé cherries and cream.

Steamed egg custard

cooking time 1¼ hours

you will need:

2 eggs
1 level tablespoon sugar
¾ pint milk
little grated nutmeg

1 Beat eggs with a fork.
2 Add sugar and the warmed milk. The milk must not boil or it will curdle the eggs.
3 Pour into a greased pie dish or basin and top with grated nutmeg.
4 Put basin into a steamer over very hot water and cook steadily for about 1¼ hours, being careful that the water does not boil as this will curdle the custard.
5 Cool slightly and turn out if wished.

Variations:

Almond custard

Add almond essence and top with chopped almonds.

Coffee custard

Add coffee essence to eggs and sugar.

Chocolate custard

Add little sieved cocoa to eggs and sugar.

Apricot mould

4 – 6 oz. dried apricots (the cheaper quality may be used)
2 oz. fine cake or breadcrumbs
2 eggs
½ pint milk
2 oz. sugar

1 Soak the apricots overnight in cold water, then simmer gently until tender, adding half the sugar.
2 Strain, but keep the juice. Beat the eggs with the remaining sugar, add milk, crumbs and some of the apricots.
3 Put into a greased mould or basin, cover the top of the pudding with buttered paper and steam very gently for about 1½ hours.
4 Turn out carefully. Pour hot juice round and decorate with rest of apricots.

Pies and Tarts

How to make good pastry

It is often thought good pastry cooks are born and not made. This may to a certain extent be true because some people have the ability to make pastry even though they do not weigh or measure very accurately, perhaps because they have good judgment about quantities. Do not be depressed if your first efforts at pastry making are not a great success. Persevere and you will find in time that your pastry will be first class. Here are some essential rules which it is wise to follow:

1 Because over-sticky pastry is difficult to handle and is therefore inclined to make one use too much flour, try to start off with everything as cold as possible. This means if you have a refrigerator it is a good idea to put the water in this for a short time before you begin to make the pastry.

2 Your choice of flour is not quite as important as people imagined some time ago. While experts will tell you you must use plain flour, many people make first-class pastry using self-raising. The fact does remain, however, that you get a shorter pastry with plain flour and the full quantity of fat and that your puff and flaky pastries rise because you have handled the mixture correctly and incorporated air rather than by the raising agent.

3 When making short crust or any pastry where the fat is incorporated in the bowl, chose a big bowl to allow plenty of air space.

4 In any pastry where you rub in the fat or you blend the flour into the creamed fat, handle it gently and lift it in the air as much as you can (a) to keep it cool and (b) to incorporate air.

5 Even if you are sure the flour is free from lumps, it is a good idea to sift it because as the flour drops into the bowl, it has become lightened with air.

6 When starting to make pastry use the recommended amount of fat—4 oz. fat to 8 oz. flour in short crust pastry.
If you increase the fat in flaky or puff pastry it becomes rather greasy. Should you decrease the fat the pastry must be eaten when hot and fresh.
If you increase the fat too much in short crust pastry, it becomes so rich that it is too difficult to handle. When you cut down on fat it is advisable to use self-raising flour or 2 level teaspoons of baking powder to each 8 oz. flour.
It is quite good to eat when fresh but it becomes stale more readily. As it is a firmer pastry it is more suitable for carrying on picnics.

7 The amount of liquid you use in pastry is very important, so do put this in gradually in short crust pastry, feeling the dough as you do so. Too much liquid gives you a sticky pastry and you need to flour the rolling pin and pastry board over much. It does give a rather tough pastry. Too little liquid on the other hand, means your pastry is difficult to roll since it is inclined to break and it also is difficult to cut when cooked since it will crumble badly. A very good test of the right amount of liquid (from 2 - 3 tablespoons of water to 8 oz. flour when using 4 oz. fat is the average amount—it varies according to the flour) is when your pastry board and rolling pin need only the lightest dusting of flour.

8 In flaky or puff pastry where little or no fat is put into the flour, your dough should feel fairly elastic. If you make it too dry it is very difficult to roll out into the shape necessary to incorporate the rest of the fat.

9 While baking times and temperatures vary according to the use of the pastry, on the whole it is baked quickly or even very quickly for the richer crusts. This sets the pastry and in the case of puff or flaky makes it rise well and prevents fat oozing out.

10 Having blended the pastry, the way you roll it is very important. If you think about the

crust as a piece of material and handle it in the same way, your pastry will keep a good shape. Always keep your rolling pin straight ahead of you. Roll out the pastry to a neat oblong and if it is getting too long and thin, lift the pastry, turn at right angles and roll straight ahead again. Do not turn your rolling pin in all directions otherwise it is like stretching a piece of material—your pie or tarts will be a very bad shape.

11 Lift the pastry from time to time. This keeps it cool and allows the air to get underneath.

12 If you can spare the time, it is always a good thing to let the pie, tarts, flan, etc., stand in the coldest place possible for a while before baking. In this way you set the shape of the pastry.

Calculating quantities of pastry

Where a recipe says '4 oz. of pastry' it means short crust, flaky, puff or whatever type of pastry is mentioned, made with 4 oz. of flour and the appropriate amount of fat. **It does not mean** a total weight of 4 oz.

4 oz. of short crust pastry will make a 6-inch flan or cover a 1-pint pie dish giving a rather thin crust. Or it will line 9 shallow or 6 deep patty tins. The same amount of flaky or puff pastry will go slightly further because of the higher percentage of fat. This of course, is only an approximate guide as the thickness of pastry is very much a matter of personal taste.

Baking pastry 'blind'

In many of the recipes using pastry, the term "bake 'blind' " is used. This means that the pastry should be baked without a filling, this being added once the pastry is cooked.

As, of course, pastry has a tendency to rise, it is advisable to use plain flour and to use one of the following methods to 'weight' the pastry down.

1 Prick the pastry well with a fork.

2 Put a piece of greased greaseproof paper, or foil, inside the pastry case. Cover this with bread crusts or dry haricot beans.

The pastry should be baked for about 15 minutes in a hot oven with short crust or flan pastry and then the beans and paper and flan ring, if used, removed. Return to the oven for a further 5 - 10 minutes for the inside pastry to brown and the outside edge to crispen. If using a rich flan pastry, this should be baked in a moderately hot oven (400°F.—Gas Mark 5) for approximately 25 - 30 minutes.

To store pastry

If storing tarts, flans, etc., keep in an air-tight tin away from bread, biscuits or cakes.

To reheat pastry

Heat through rather gently so the pastry does not become too brown before it is thoroughly hot.

Storing uncooked pastry

In order to save time, you may like to make and store pastry ready to bake when needed. Short crust pastry can be stored either as the rubbed-in crumbs and the liquid added later or as the made pastry. It must be wrapped in foil if moistened, otherwise it dries on the outside and cracks badly.

Flaky or puff pastry should be formed into a neat shape and covered in foil or put into a polythene bag.

The refrigerator is the ideal place for storing uncooked pastry.

To use frozen pastry

Follow the directions for storing and using as given on the individual packets. When once the frozen pastry has thawed out, it should be used as soon as possible and should not be kept for any length of time.

Biscuit crust

cooking time as individual recipe

you will need:

6 oz. plain flour
2 oz. cornflour
1 level tablespoon castor sugar
4 oz. butter
1 egg yolk
water to mix

1 Sieve flour, cornflour and sugar together.
2 Rub in the butter.
3 Mix to a firm dough with egg yolk and cold water.

Corn oil pastry

cooking time — as individual recipe

you will need:

5 tablespoon corn oil
2½ tablespoons cold water, preferably iced water
8 oz. flour
pinch salt

1 Blend the corn oil and water together well with a fork in a mixing bowl.
2 Gradually add the flour and salt sifted together.
3 Mix with a fork or palette knife to form a rollable dough (a little more or less flour may be required).
4 Roll out between 2 sheets of greaseproof paper.
5 Exact cooking times for pastry are given in the recipes, but as a general rule it should be cooked in a moderately hot to hot oven (400 - 425°F.—Gas Mark 5 - 6).

Flaky pastry

cooking time — as individual recipe

you will need:

8 oz. flour
pinch salt
5–6 oz. fat
water to mix

1 Sieve flour with salt.
2 Divide fat into 3 portions and rub 1 portion into flour.
3 Mix to a rolling consistency with cold water.
4 Roll out to oblong shape.
5 Cut the second portion of fat into small pieces and lay on ⅔ of the dough, leaving remaining ⅓ without fat.
6 Fold 2 of the corners over second ⅓ to make an envelope with its flap open.
7 Fold over top end of pastry so closing the 'envelope'.
8 Turn pastry at right angles and seal open ends.
9 'Rib' at intervals with a rolling pin to give a corrugated effect, thus equalising the pressure of air and so making certain the pastry will rise evenly.
10 Repeat the process using the remaining fat and turning pastry in same way.
11 Roll out once more and put into a cold place for 30 minutes if it feels very soft and sticky.
12 Fold pastry as before, turn, seal edges and 'rib' again.
13 Altogether the pastry should have 3 foldings and 3 rollings.
14 Stand in a cold place for a little while before baking to make the pastry rise better.
15 Cooking temperatures and times are given in individual recipes, but as a general rule bake in a very hot oven (475°F.—Gas Mark 8) for the first 15 minutes.
16 Lower the heat to Gas Mark 5 - 6, or turn an electric oven off to finish cooking.

Puff pastry

cooking time — as individual recipe

you will need:

8 oz. plain flour
good pinch salt
cold water to mix
few drops lemon juice
7–8 oz. fat

1 Sieve flour and salt together.
2 Mix to rolling consistency with cold water and lemon juice.
3 Roll to oblong shape and place neat block of fat in centre of pastry.
4 Fold over the bottom section of pastry and then the top so that the fat is quite covered.
5 Turn the dough at right angles, seal edges and 'rib' as Flaky pastry (see above).
6 Roll out and fold dough into an 'envelope' shape.
7 Turn, seal edges and 'rib' again.
8 Repeat 5 times, so making 7 rollings and 7 foldings in all.
9 Put pastry in a cold place once or twice between rollings to prevent it becoming sticky and soft and always leave in a cold place before rolling for the last time and before baking.
10 Bake for the first 10 - 15 minutes at 475 - 500°F.—Gas Mark 8 - 9, then lower to Gas Mark 5 - 6 or turn electric oven right out or re-set to 400°F. to finish cooking.
11 Puff pastry should rise to 4 - 5 times its original thickness. It is used for vanilla slices, vol-au-vent cases, etc.

Short crust pastry

cooking time — as individual recipe

you will need:

8 oz. flour
good pinch salt
2 oz. margarine
2 oz. cooking fat
approx. 2 tablespoons cold water to mix

1 Sieve flour and salt together.
2 Rub in margarine and fat until mixture looks like fine breadcrumbs.
3 Gradually add enough cold water to make the dough into a rolling consistency, using first a knife and then the fingertips to feel the pastry.
4 Lightly flour the rolling pin and pastry board.
5 Roll pastry to required thickness and shape, lifting and turning to keep it light.
6 As a general rule pastry should be cooked in a hot oven (425 - 450°F.—Gas Mark 6 - 7), but exact cooking times and temperatures are given in individual recipes.

Rich short crust pastry

Use the recipe for Short crust pastry (see above), using 5 oz. margarine, in place of margarine and cooking fat.

Sweet short crust pastry

Use the recipe for Short crust pastry (see above), adding 1 - 2 teaspoons castor sugar to the flour.

Suet crust pastry

cooking time — as individual recipe

you will need:

8 oz. flour (with plain flour 2 level teaspoons baking powder
pinch salt
2 – 4 oz. finely shredded suet
water to mix

1 Sieve flour, baking powder and salt.
2 Add suet.
3 Mix to rolling consistency with cold water.
4 Roll out thinly as this pastry rises.

Preparing the fruit for pies and tarts

Apples

For pies etc. they should be peeled, cored and cut into slices. Since apples discolour easily, drop them into a basin of cold water to which a very little salt can be added, i.e. no more than a teaspoon to a quart of water. Rinse the fruit before cooking and keep a plate over the top if there is any delay when they are once prepared.

Apricots

Wash and dry. If wished, cut into halves and remove the stone. Unless the apricots are very unripe, this is easily done. The stone gives a slightly almond taste, which some people do not like.

Bananas

Though rarely used in cooking, these are very delicious. They do discolour badly so should be sprinkled with lemon juice.

Blackcurrants

Remove from the stalks and some people like to 'top and tail' i.e. remove the little pieces of stalk and flower ends, but this takes a very long time and when cooked they are hardly discernable. Rinse in cold water. Allow to drain.

Cherries

These are more comfortable to eat if the stones are removed. The easiest way to remove them is to insert the bent end of a new fine hair pin into the fruit, pushing until you feel the bend of the hair pin hooking firmly round the stone. Pull sharply and you take the stone with you. As a certain amount of juice comes out, hold the cherries over the pie dish or basin while doing this. Rinse in cold water and allow to drain.

Damsons

Should just be wiped or washed and dried. It is not possible to stone before cooking.

Peaches

One rarely uses fresh peaches in pies but if they are very cheap they make a delicious tart filling. Skin by lowering very gradually into boiling water, leaving for ½ minute. Remove and put into cold water, then pull off the skin. Halve or quarter and remove stone.

Gooseberries

Wash and drain, either before or after 'topping and tailing' i.e. cutting away the little bits at the flower and stalk ends. A pair of kitchen scissors are the easiest way of doing this.

Quinces

These are very hard and need peeling and either dicing or grating. Some people like them cooked by themselves but they are a very excellent partner to apples in pies or tarts. Use equal quantities or twice as many apples as quinces.

Soft fruit

Arrange the soft fruit carefully on a fine sieve if possible. Run cold water gently over. In this way you clean but do not damage the delicate fruit.

To make a fruit pie

1 Use short, sweet short, flaky or puff pastry.
2 Roll out the pastry until it is the size of the top of the pie dish plus a little extra all round which you will need for the strips of pastry.
3 Cut narrow strips of pastry the width of the rim of the pie dish.
4 Brush the rim of the pie dish with water and then put on the strips of pastry.
5 Lift the remaining dough over the rolling pin and using the rolling pin as a support, lay over the fruit etc. in the pie dish.
6 Slip away the rolling pin, then press the pastry cover to the strips of pastry very firmly. You can brush the strips with water on top if wished, to make sure the two layers of pastry seal.
7 Cut away the surplus pastry. To make sure you do not stretch or pull the dough, lay your left fore-finger along the top and cut behind it in a clockwise direction.
8 The rim of the pastry is now ready to decorate and suggestions for decorating are given below. Traditionally one does not decorate a sweet pie with leaves etc. You just brush it if wished with a little egg white or water and dust with sugar before baking.

To bake a fruit pie

In order to make certain that the fruit and pastry are perfectly cooked, the pie should really be baked in the centre of the oven. If this does not fit in with the other food being cooked and you have to bake towards the top of the oven, you will probably find it better to lower the heat when the pastry begins to brown, as you have to keep the pie in for a longer period to thoroughly cook the fruit. You can, however, put a sheet of greaseproof paper or foil over the top to make sure it does not become scorched.

While many people do not consider it essential to make a hole or a slit in the pastry to allow the steam to escape, if you are using fruit which produces a lot of juice, this will help the pastry to become crisp.

To decorate edges

In order to encourage a crisp light edge to pastry, particularly if flaky pastry is used, one cuts the edges with a knife. Lay your left fore-finger against the rim of the pastry. Hold a knife horizontally and cut into the double rim of pastry to within $\frac{1}{10}$ inch so that you form a number of layers. You are then ready to decorate the edge.

1 Fluted

With your fore-finger and thumb pull the pastry away from the edge at regular intervals.

2 Picked up edge

Using your fore-finger and thumb, pinch the pastry at regular intervals so you have a 'standing-up' ridge as opposed to the fluted.

3 Forked edge

Fork round the top with the prongs making a neat and even depression.

4 Scalloped edge

Cut the pastry to a depth of $\frac{1}{2}$ - $\frac{3}{4}$ inch at intervals of about $\frac{1}{2}$ - $\frac{3}{4}$ inch. Pick up alternate sections of pastry and roll towards the centre of the pie. **(Continued overleaf.)**

5 Use any little bits of pastry that are left and roll out very thinly and using the tiniest fluted cutter you possess, cut tiny rounds. These can be arranged (a) over-lapping
(b) curled round to look like a flower bud
(c) standing up slightly

Apple pie

cooking time 30 - 40 minutes

you will need:

- 1 – 1½ lb. cooking apples
- sugar to taste
- very little water
- little lemon juice
- few sultanas, chopped dates, or other dried fruit (optional)
- 6 oz. short crust or flaky pastry (see pages 32, 31)

1 Peel, core and slice the apples.
2 Put the fruit into a pie dish with sugar to taste, little water, lemon juice and dried fruit if used.
3 If the fruit does not come far enough up the dish, put in a pie funnel or egg cup.
4 Roll out the pastry to about 1 - 1½ inches bigger all round than the pie dish.
5 Cut off a long narrow strip and moisten the edges of the pie dish.
6 Press the pastry strip on to the rim and lay the remaining pastry over the top of the pie, pressing the edges firmly together.
7 Flake the edges and if wished brush with a little water and sprinkle with sugar.
8 Bake in the centre of a hot oven (425 - 450°F —Gas Mark 6 - 7), until golden brown.
9 Reduce the heat to moderate for a further 15 minutes to ensure that the apples are cooked.

Variations:

Blackberry

Use half apples and half blackberries, omitting the dried fruit.

Plum

Use 1 - 1½ lb. plums. For a slightly almond flavour do not stone the plums, and do not use too much water.

Gooseberry

Use 1 - 1½ lb. gooseberries 'topped and tailed'. If ripe do not use too much water.

Raspberry

Add no water and pile the dish very high.

Rhubarb

Use 1 - 1½ lb. rhubarb, chopped into neat pieces and very little water.

Apple cream pie

cooking time 45 minutes

you will need:

- 6 oz. short crust pastry (see page 32)
- 4 oz. soft brown sugar
- 1 oz. flour
- ¼ teaspoon cinnamon
- ¼ teaspoon grated nutmeg
- pinch salt
- 1½ oz. butter
- 8 cooking apples
- 2 teaspoons lemon juice
- 2 tablespoons thick cream

1 Line a pie dish or flan ring with the pastry.
2 Put the sugar, flour, cinnamon, nutmeg and salt into a bowl and mix well together.
3 Rub in the butter.
4 Peel, core and slice the apples and sprinkle with lemon juice.
5 Add most of the sugar mixture, leaving about a quarter.
6 Toss apples in the sugar mixture to coat evenly.
7 Arrange in pastry case and sprinkle with remaining sugar mixture.
8 Bake in a hot oven for 10 minutes (450°F.—Gas Mark 7).
9 Reduce heat to moderate (375°F.—Gas Mark 4) for a further 25 minutes until apples are tender.
10 Pour cream over the apple mixture and bake for a further 10 minutes.
11 Serve at once.

Apple mallow pie

cooking time 45 minutes

you will need:

- 6 oz. short crust pastry (see page 32)
- 1¼ oz. cornflour
- 2 – 3 sugar
- ¾ pint apple pureé (see pages 63, 64)
- marshmallows

1 Line an 8-inch pie plate with the short crust pastry, keeping a little of the pastry for decoration.
2 Mix the cornflour and sugar with a little of the cold apple purée until smooth.
3 Put the rest on to heat.
4 Add mixed cornflour and stir until boiling.
5 Boil for 1 minute, stirring constantly.
6 Pour into the pie plate.
7 Roll out the remaining pastry and cut into narrow strips.
8 Twist each strip and arrange on the apple mixture to form a lattice-work.
9 Bake for about 35 - 40 minutes in centre of a moderately hot oven (400°F.—Gas Mark 5).
10 Put the marshmallows on top and return to the oven for a few minutes.

Lattice cherry pie

cooking time 45 minutes

you will need:

8 oz. short crust pastry (see page 32)
1 lb. cherries
3 oz. sugar
½ oz. cornflour
1 tablespoon water
squeeze lemon juice
knob butter

1 Line an 8-inch pie plate with the pastry.
2 Wash and remove the stems from the cherries and pierce with a sharp knife or skewer.
3 Put the sugar, cornflour, water, lemon juice and butter into a saucepan with the cherries and mix well together.
4 Bring to the boil and cook gently for 1 minute.
5 Allow to cool slightly, then pour into the pastry case.
6 Make a lattice top with the pastry trimmings and bake in a hot oven (425°F.—Gas Mark 6) for about 40 minutes.

To make plate tarts

1 For a 6-inch plate or pie plate, allow approximately 8 oz. pastry, ¾ - 1 lb. fruit. Little or no water. Sugar to taste.
2 To prevent the base becoming soggy you need **either** a little extra flour or cornflour and sugar **or** a little semolina.
3 Roll out the pastry. Using a good half, line the bottom of the pie plate.
4 Sprinkle this bottom layer of pastry with a very light dusting of flour and sugar, or semolina and sugar. This absorbs the juice from the fruit and prevents it soaking into the bottom pastry and making it soggy.
5 Arrange the fruit over the bottom layer of pastry, keeping it slightly away from the very edge.
6 With very hard plums or apples, add 1 - 2 tablespoons of water and sugar to taste.
7 With soft fruit, or fruit like rhubarb that makes a lot of juice, use sugar to taste but no liquid at all.
8 Put on the top round of pastry.
9 Seal firmly (see directions for pies).
10 Because of the double thickness of pastry, baking of a plate tart is important. You will probably find if using oven-proof glass, you get a better bottom layer of pastry if you stand this on a browning sheet or baking tin.
11 Bake in or just above the centre of the oven. Use a hot oven (425 - 450°F.—Gas Mark 6 - 7) for short crust pastry or a very hot (475°F.—Gas Mark 8) for flaky pastry, for the first 15 minutes. This makes certain the pastry is set and it is then advisable to lower the heat to moderate or moderately hot depending on the thickness of filling to make certain that the tart will be adequately cooked.
12 Leave for about 45 minutes total cooking time.
13 Even with the greatest of care in not adding too much liquid, you may sometime find that the tarts tend to boil over. It is therefore a wise precaution to stand them on a baking tin or piece of foil so that the liquid does not burn on the oven.

Fillings for plate tarts

Apple and cloves plate tart

To about 1 lb. apples, allow approximately 6 cloves. Sugar to taste and little water.

Apple and date plate tart

To each pound of unpeeled apples allow 4 oz. of dates, a little brown sugar and a good sprinkle of cinnamon. Add 1 tablespoon water.

Apple and ginger plate tart
Either sprinkle ½ - 1 teaspoon of powdered ginger over the apples adding a tablespoon of water and sugar to taste, or chop up about 2 oz. crystallised ginger.

Apple and mincemeat plate tart
To each 1 lb. of apples allow 4 good tablespoons mincemeat, no extra water and a small amount of extra sugar. Spread half the mincemeat below the sliced apples and the rest over the sliced apples.

Apple and orange plate tart
Add the grated rind of 2 oranges and the segments of 2 - 3 large oranges free from pith and skin if possible. Use white sugar, and no extra liquid.

Blackberry and apple plate tart
Use equal quantities of apples and blackberries adding no water and sugar to taste.

Blackcurrant plate tart
Since blackcurrants produce rather a lot of juice, have a fairly generous layer of flour and sugar or semolina over the bottom pastry. Add no water and sugar to taste. Blackberries, blueberries and whortleberries can be used in place of blackcurrants.

Cherry and apricot plate tart
Use 8 oz. cherries, 8 oz. halved apricots with sugar to taste and no liquid.

Cherry and almond plate tart
To 1 lb. cherries add 2 oz. chopped blanched almonds. No water and sugar to taste.

Damson plate tart
Since damsons are bitter and rather full of stones, it is almost better to make a thick purée and remove some of the stones before putting into the pastry.

Fig and rhubarb plate tart
To 12 oz. chopped rhubarb, allow 4 oz. dried figs. These should be softened by pouring boiling water over them an hour or so before required, then chopped into neat pieces.

Ginger plate tart
you will need:

6 oz. golden syrup
½ – 1 teaspoon powdered ginger
2 tablespoons redcurrants
2 oz. sultanas

Mix all ingredients together.

Gooseberry plate tart
Use no water, but sugar to taste.

Greengage plate tart
If fruit is unripe use 1 tablespoon of liquid. If ripe, use no liquid. Sugar to taste.

Mixed fruit plate tart
A tart with a mixture of fruits, i.e. soft fruits or fresh and dried fruits, is not only a change but a very good way of using rather expensive fruits in an economical manner. Try:

Rhubarb and strawberries
Apricot and redcurrant
Apple and blackcurrant
Apple and peaches

Plum plate tart
The fruit can either be halved or left whole in the case of smaller plums. If unripe use 1 tablespoon of liquid. If ripe, no liquid. When ripe, plums give a lot of juice, so use a fairly thick layer of flour and sugar over the bottom layer of pastry.

Prune plate tart
you will need:

8 oz. prunes soaked overnight and well drained
grated rind of 1 lemon
1 tablespoon lemon juice
1 – 2 tablespoons chopped walnuts (optional)
golden syrup or sugar to sweeten

Or use the filling of the Prune flan (see page 44) in a plate tart

Any of the above suggestions can be used in a fruit pie but one should increase the amount of liquid.

Lemon curd plate tart

Because lemon curd is a fairly thin mixture you make a more substantial filling in a plate tart if the following are mixed:

you will need:

6 – 8 oz. lemon curd
2 good tablespoons fine bread or cake crumbs
grated rind 1 lemon

Lemon curd - tart filling

cooking time 30 minutes

you will need:

4 oz. butter
4 oz. sugar
juice 2 large lemons
grated rind 3 lemons*
2 eggs

*When grating the lemons be quite sure to use only the 'zest' or peel

1 Put the butter, sugar, lemon juice and grated rind into a double saucepan or basin over hot water.
2 Heat thoroughly, then add the well-beaten eggs.
3 Continue stirring until the mixture coats the back of a wooden spoon.
4 Pour into hot jars and cover as for jam.

Mincemeat

no cooking

you will need:

4 oz. shredded suet
4 oz. grated apple
1 lb. mixed dried fruit
1 level teaspoon mixed spice
½ level teaspoon cinnamon
4 oz. demerara sugar
4 oz. mixed peel
4 oz. blanched almonds
finely grated rind and juice 1 lemon
½ teaspoon grated nutmeg
4 tablespoons brandy, whisky or rum

1 Mix all the ingredients together.
2 Put into dry jam jars and cover carefully.
3 Leave in a cool dry place.

Note:
If you want the mincemeat to keep well, do not cut down on the quantities of sugar, fat or spirit. Make certain that the fruit is washed thoroughly and that fruit and almonds are absolutely dry.

Bakewell tart

cooking time 35 minutes

you will need:

6 oz. short crust pastry (see page 32)
little jam
2 oz. margarine
½ – 1 teaspoon almond essence
2 oz. sugar
2 oz. flour
2 oz. ground almonds
2 oz. breadcrumbs
1 egg
2 tablespoons milk
little extra sugar

1 Line a large pie plate or 8-inch flan ring with the pastry.
2 Spread with a little jam.
3 Cream the margarine and sugar together and add the almond essence.
4 Mix all the dry ingredients together.
5 Add these alternately to the margarine mixture with the egg and milk.
6 Spread this mixture over the pastry and jam.
7 Dust with a very little sugar and bake in the centre of a hot oven (450°F.—Gas Mark 7) for 15 minutes.
8 Lower the heat for a further 20 minutes.

Large jam tart

cooking time 20 - 25 minutes

you will need:

short crust pastry (see page 32)
jam or jams

1 Line a pie plate or flan ring with the pastry.
2 Put in the jam or jams. You may like to use all one jam or make a lattice design of very thin strips of pastry twisted criss-cross over the top of the main pastry. You can then put in various coloured jams to form an attractive design. If your lattice work gives rather small sections, the easiest and neatest way of putting in the jam is to make a greaseproof paper bag as if one were icing, cut ¼-inch hole in the bottom, put in spoonfuls of the jam and squeeze through the hole. In this way, you are not likely to get the jam on to the pastry lattice work.
3 Bake in a hot oven (425 - 450°F.—Gas Mark 6 - 7) for a total of 20 - 25 minutes, lowering the heat slightly after 15 minutes if the pastry is getting a little too brown.

Mince tart

cooking time 20 - 25 minutes

you will need:

6 oz. short, flaky or puff pastry (see pages 32, 31)
approximately 8 oz. mincemeat

1 Roll out pastry and line a sandwich or flan tin with the pastry.
2 Put in the mincemeat, spreading round the pastry.
3 Bake for 20 - 25 minutes just above the centre of a hot oven (450°F —Gas Mark 7), reducing the heat after 15 minutes if necessary.

Treacle tart

cooking time 30 minutes

you will need:

5–6 oz. short crust pastry (see page 32)
4 good tablespoons golden syrup
squeeze lemon juice
2 tablespoons bread-crumbs

1 Line a sandwich tin or flan ring with the pastry and bake 'blind' for 10 minutes only in a hot oven (425°F.—Gas Mark 6).
2 Mix the syrup with the lemon juice and pour into the flan case.
3 Cover with the breadcrumbs and return to the oven, lowering the heat to moderately hot (400°F.—Gas Mark 5) for a further 20 minutes.

Little tarts

To line small tartlet cases:

1 One should choose a fluted cutter for small tarts but a plain one can of course be used and the tartlets fluted round the edge like a flan (see page 41).
2 Measure the cutter against the patty tin and to fill the patty tins your cutter should be about $\frac{3}{4}$-inch - 1 inch bigger than the top of the tin depending on its depth.
3 Cut the rounds of pastry, press into the patty cases which need not be greased unless very new.
4 If baking 'blind', follow the directions for baking 'blind' (see page 30).
5 If putting in a filling do not put in too much at one time since it may boil over. This applies particularly to jam or golden syrup and it is better to add a little extra when the tarts come out of the oven.

Jam tarts

cooking time 10 - 15 minutes

you will need:

short or sweet short crust, or flaky pastry (see pages 32, 31)
jam

1 Line patty tins (see page 30) and put a small amount of jam in each.
2 Bake in a hot oven (425 - 450°F.—Gas Mark 6 - 7) for short crust pastry or a very hot oven (475°F.—Gas Mark 8) for flaky pastry, for 10 - 15 minutes. The best position for the small jam tarts is just above the middle.
3 If the amount of jam seems rather small when the tarts are cooked, add a little extra while hot and this gives a slightly less uncooked flavour to the filling.

Golden syrup tarts

cooking time 10 - 15 minutes

you will need:

short crust pastry (see page 32)
golden syrup
squeeze of lemon juice
few breadcrumbs, crushed cornflakes or rolled oats

1 Line the patty tins with Short crust pastry (see page 32).
2 Put in the golden syrup, adding squeeze of lemon juice to each tart and coating the top with crumbs, crushed cornflakes or rolled oats.
3 Bake as Jam tarts (see page 38).

Custard tartlets

Ingredients as for Custard flan (see page 43), but bake the pastry cases for 5 minutes in a hot oven, fill with custard and bake for a further 15 minutes in a moderate oven (375°F.—Gas Mark 4).

Mince pies

cooking time 20 - 25 minutes

you will need:

8 oz. short, flaky or puff pastry (see pages 32, 31)
approximately 6 – 8 oz. mincemeat

1 Roll out pastry fairly thinly.
2 Cut into rounds a little larger than the size of the patty tins, and line the tins.
3 Put spoonfuls of mincemeat into the pastry cases—do not put too much mincemeat into the pastry otherwise it will seep out during cooking.
4 Cover with rounds of pastry a little smaller than the cases and press the edges together.
5 Make a slit on top with a sharp knife and bake for 20 - 25 minutes just above the centre of a hot oven (450°F.—Gas Mark 7), if necessary lowering the heat after 15 minutes.

Apple Strudel

cooking time 35 - 40 minutes

you will need:

8 oz. plain flour
good pinch salt
2 oz. butter or margarine, or 1 – 2 tablespoons oil
1 egg or 2 egg yolks (optional)
milk or water to mix

For filling:
2 oz. melted margarine or butter
2 tablespoons breadcrumbs
1 lb. cooking apples
2 oz. sugar
1 teaspoon mixed spice
2 oz. chopped nuts
little icing sugar

1 Sieve flour and salt together.
2 Rub in butter or margarine or make a well in the centre of the flour and add the oil, gradually working in the flour.
3 Add egg and enough milk to make a firm dough.
4 Knead lightly then cover with a cloth and leave for 30 minutes.
5 Flour a large cloth on a table and roll and pull at the dough until it is as thin as paper.
6 Brush the pastry with a little of the melted margarine or butter.
7 Fry the breadcrumbs in remaining butter or margarine. Place over pastry.
8 Slice apples thinly and evenly and arrange over the pastry.
9 Spread all the ingredients remaining evenly over the apples and roll carefully as though rolling a Swiss roll. Put onto a greased baking sheet, forming into a horseshoe to fit the tin if necessary.
10 Brush with a little melted margarine and cook in the middle of a hot oven (450°F.—Gas Mark 7) for 20 minutes.
11 Reduce heat to 375°F.—Gas Mark 4 and continue cooking for a further 15 - 20 minutes.
12 Serve hot or cold liberally dredged with icing sugar.

Variations:

Apricot

Use 1 lb. fresh or drained canned apricots; the nuts could be omitted.

Cherry

Use 1 lb. fresh or large canned red cherries. Stone the cherries and flavour with a little almond essence.

Plum

Use 1 lb. stoned plums, omitting the nuts.

Jam

Fill with 1 lb. red jam, 2 oz. sultanas and 2 oz. chopped almonds.

Apple dumplings

cooking time 45 minutes - 1 hour

you will need:

for 4 small apples, 8 oz. sweet or short crust pastry (see page 32)
(for 4 medium apples, 12 oz. sweet or short crust pastry)
little sugar
butter

1 Peel and core apples.
2 Fill with a little sugar and knob of butter.
3 Cut pastry into four squares and make into neat shapes round the apples.
4 Bake as for plum dumplings for approximately 45 minutes - 1 hour, reducing heat after 20 minutes.

Iced apple dumplings

1 Cook apple dumplings as recipe above.
2 When cooked, decorate with a little icing, glacé cherries and angelica.

Pear dumplings

Use the method for apple dumplings cooking for approximately 40 minutes - 1 hour, depending on ripeness of pears.

Baked plum dumplings

cooking time 25 minutes

you will need:

4 oz. sweet short crust or short pastry (see page 32)
8 large plums
cream cheese (optional)
little sugar

1 Roll out pastry and cut into 8 rounds or squares.
2 Remove stones from each plum and, if wished, put a little cream cheese in the centre.
3 Put the plum on the pastry and dust lightly with sugar.
4 Roll pastry round to form a good shaped dumpling.
5 Brush with a little water or egg white if wished, and dredge with sugar before baking (If preferred, dredge with sugar after baking.)
6 Bake for 25 minutes in the centre of a hot oven (425 - 450°F.—Gas Mark 6 - 7), reducing heat after 15 minutes.

Breton pears

cooking time 40 minutes

you will need:

4 large ripe pears
8 oz. short crust pastry (see page 32)
little apricot jam
4 cloves (optional)

1 Peel and core the pears.
2 Roll out the pastry thinly and cut into 4 squares.
3 Put the pear in the centre of each square of pastry.
4 Fill the hole with apricot jam and the clove.
5 Gather the corners of the pastry up to the top of the pear.
6 Put onto a greased baking sheet and bake for 20 minutes in the centre of a hot oven (425 - 450°F.—Gas Mark 6 - 7).
7 Lower the heat to moderate for a further 20 minutes.

Note:

If the pears are very hard they should be simmered first.

Apple turnovers (1)

cooking time 25 minutes

you will need:

8 oz. short crust pastry (see page 0)
little flour or semolina
8 oz. cooking apples (weight when peeled)
sugar

1 Roll out pastry thinly and cut into large rounds.
2 Put on to baking trays and dust with very little flour or semolina.
3 Cover half the pastry with thinly sliced apple and sugar to taste.
4 Fold over uncovered part of pastry, damp edges and seal.
5 Bake for approximately 25 minutes in the centre of a hot oven (425°F.—Gas Mark 6).
6 Dust with sugar before serving.

Variations:

Plum

Using firm plums instead of apples and removing stones from the fruit.

Apricot

Soak 8 oz. dried apricots over night and proceed as for apple turnovers above.

Apple turnovers (2)

cooking time 20 - 30 minutes

you will need:

4 oz. plain flour
2 oz. cornflour
3 oz. butter or margarine
1 teaspoon castor sugar
1 egg yolk
1 lb. cooking apples
sugar to taste
little grated lemon rind

1 Sieve flour and cornflour together.
2 Rub in the butter or margarine.
3 Add the sugar and mix to a stiff dough with the egg yolk.
4 Roll the pastry out thinly and cut into strips approximately 4 inches wide and 8 inches long.
5 Peel, core and slice the apples thinly and put into a basin with sugar to taste and lemon rind.
6 Put spoonfuls of the apple mixture on each piece of pastry.
7 Fold over to form a square sealing the edges with water and pressing down well.

8 Mark with a fork and put on to a baking tray.
9 Bake for about 20 - 30 minutes in a hot oven (425°F.—Gas Mark 6).

Baked jam roll

cooking time 45 minutes - 1 hour

you will need:

6 – 8 oz. suet crust pastry (see page 32)
jam

1 Roll pastry into neat oblong ¼ inch thick.
2 Spread with jam, but do not take jam right to the edges.
3 Turn in side edges and roll lightly like a Swiss roll.
4 Put on to a greased baking tin and bake just above centre of a moderately hot oven for 25 minutes (400°F.—Gas Mark 5).
5 Reduce heat to moderate (375°F.—Gas Mark 4) for rest of cooking time.

Flans

To line a flan case

1 Choose short crust, sweet short crust or special flan pastry, see pages 32, 42.
2 Roll out the pastry to an approximate size. To measure whether you have the right size, place your flan ring or sandwich tin lightly on the pastry round and you should allow the diameter of the tin plus a good 1½ inches for an average depth tin all the way round.
3 If using a sandwich tin, you may like to grease this very lightly. With a flan ring, however, unless new, greasing is really not necessary.
4 You will find it easier to get the pastry flan out of the ring if you stand the ring on a baking tin turned upside down. This means all you need to do is lift off the ring and slide your flan case on to the wire tray or serving plate.
5 To take the pastry from the pastry board or table to the sandwich tin or flan ring, you will find with a little practice it is quite easy to lay this over the rolling pin. Your rolling pin acts as a support.
6 Arrange the pastry in position over the sandwich tin or flan case. Slide away the rolling pin.
7 Press the pastry down firmly into the base of the tin. This makes a lot of difference to the shape of the flan. You will probably find that your crooked fore-finger is the best way of doing this. Press the pastry firmly against the sides of the flan ring. If you do not do this, one is inclined to cut or roll the pastry so that it drops in cooking but if you have pressed it well against the sides, this will not happen.
8 Either use a knife for the edge of the pastry, in which case lay your left hand fore-finger along the top of the pastry and cut steadily behind it in a clockwise direction. This prevents the knife cutting into the edges and any stretching of the pastry.
9 Or, on the other hand, if the edge of the flan case is sharp, the quickest, easiest and most successful method of neatening the top of a flan case is to roll firmly over the pastry and you have a perfect edge, without stretching the pastry in any way.
10 You are then ready to make an edge on the flan to fill or to bake 'blind' (see page 30).

To make an attractive edge on a flan

It is possible to buy fluted flan rings and traditionally one should use a plain flan ring for a savoury flan and a fluted one for a sweet flan. It may well be, however, that you are baking a flan case in a sandwich tin or flan ring and a slightly decorated edge makes it look more attractive. You can do this in two ways for a flan:

1 A fluted edge
Pinch the pastry between the fore-finger and thumb at about ½-inch intervals and pull down the pastry about ⅛ inch to ¼ inch from the top so giving you this effect:
2 A pinch edge
Take the pastry between the fore-finger and thumb at regular intervals and pull towards the centre of the flan case which gives you an even line on the top but a slightly pulled in effect when the flan case is removed from tin.

Flan pastry

(for sweet flans and fruit tarts)

cooking time — as individual recipe

you will need:

4 oz. butter or margarine	pinch salt
2 dessertspoon sugar	cold water or egg yolk to bind
8 oz. flour	

1 Cream butter or margarine and sugar together until light and creamy.
2 Sieve flour and salt together and add to creamed fat, mixing with a knife.
3 Gradually add enough water or egg and water to make a firm rolling consistency, using fingertips to feel the pastry.
4 Line a flan ring by putting pastry over case and pressing down base and sides firmly, rolling over top with a rolling pin for a good edge.
5 Bake in a hot oven (425 - 450°F.—Gas Mark 6 - 7).

Rich flan pastry

cooking time — as individual recipe

you will need:

5 oz. butter or margarine	8 oz. flour
2 oz. sugar	pinch salt
	egg yolk to bind

Use the method as for flan pastry (see above), but bake in a moderately hot oven (400°F.—Gas Mark 5).

To make a sponge flan

cooking time — 12 - 15 minutes

you will need:

2 eggs	2 oz. plain flour
2½ oz. sugar	½ level teaspoon baking powder
1 oz. butter	

1 Whisk eggs and sugar in a basin until thick.
2 Melt butter in a saucepan and allow to cool.
3 Sieve flour and baking powder and fold into the egg mixture.
4 Fold in the melted butter.
5 Pour into a greased and floured 8-inch flan tin.
6 Bake just above centre of a moderately hot oven (400°F.—Gas Mark 5) for 12 - 15 minutes.
7 Allow to cool before turning out.

To make a sponge flan with Genoese pastry

Use the above recipe, but 2 oz. melted butter instead of 1 oz.
Allow a minute or so longer to cook.

To fill sponge flans

These are filled in exactly the same way as short crust pastry flans.

Almond flan

cooking time — 35 minutes

you will need:

6 oz. short crust pastry (see page 32)	1½ oz. flour
little jam	1 level teaspoon baking powder
1 oz. margarine	1½ oz. ground almonds
1½ oz. sugar	⅛ pint milk
1 teaspoon almond essence	1 egg

1 Line a flan ring or sandwich tin with the pastry.
2 Spread lightly with jam.
3 Cream together the margarine, sugar and almond essence.
4 Mix together the dry ingredients and add to the margarine mixture alternately with the milk and egg.
5 Pour into the pastry case and bake in the centre of a hot oven (450°F.—Gas Mark 7) for approximately 15 minutes.
6 Lower heat for a further 20 minutes.

Banana and apricot flan

cooking time — 40 minutes

you will need:

4 – 5 oz. short crust pastry or sweet short crust pastry (see page 32)	3 oz. castor sugar
apricot jam	1 egg
5 – 6 bananas	3 oz. flour (with plain flour good ½ teaspoon baking powder)
3 oz. margarine	

1 Line a flan ring or sandwich tin with pastry.
2 Spread with jam and sliced bananas using about 2 or 3 of the bananas.
3 Cream the margarine and sugar.
4 Beat in egg and 2 of the bananas.
5 Stir in the flour and spread over the bananas in the flan.

6 Bake for approximately 20 minutes in the centre of a moderately hot oven (400°F.—Gas Mark 5).
7 Reduce heat to moderate and cook for a further 20 minutes until pastry is crisp.
8 Remove from oven and decorate with hot sieved jam and a ring of sliced banana.

Coffee cornflake flan

cooking time 20 minutes

you will need:

4 oz. short crust pastry (see page 32)
little jam
2 oz. butter or margarine
1 oz. sugar
1 heaped teaspoon instant coffee powder
1 level tablespoon syrup
cornflakes
little cream

1 Line 8-inch flan ring or sandwich tin or pie plate with the pastry.
2 Spread with jam.
3 Cream butter or margarine, sugar and instant coffee powder with the syrup.
4 Fold in sufficient cornflakes to absorb the mixture.
5 Pile into the pastry case and bake in a moderate oven (375°F.—Gas Mark 4) for 20 minutes until crisp.
6 Decorate with cream and serve hot or cold.

Custard flan

cooking time 30 minutes

you will need:

6 oz. short crust pastry (see page 32)
1 or 2 eggs
½ pint milk
1 level tablespoon sugar

1 Line a 7-inch flan ring or sandwich tin with the pastry.
2 Bake 'blind' for 10 minutes in a hot oven (425 - 450°F.—Gas Mark 6 - 7). This does not completely cook the pastry, but sets the bottom and stops it becoming soft.
3 Beat the eggs lightly.
4 Pour over the milk and add the sugar.
5 Pour into the pastry case and bake for a further 20 minutes at 400°F.—Gas Mark 5.

Gooseberry butterscotch flan with cream

cooking time 40 minutes

you will need:

6 oz. short crust pastry (see page 32)
1 lb. gooseberries
2 oz. flour
1 oz. brown sugar
2 tablespoons golden syrup
1 egg
⅛ pint milk

To decorate:
desiccated coconut
little whipped cream
little chocolate

1 Roll out the pastry and line either a deep flan ring or a pie dish.
2 Bake 'blind' in a hot oven (425 - 450°F.—Gas Mark 6 - 7) for about 10 minutes, until pale golden colour.
3 When cooked cover pastry with chopped 'topped and tailed' raw gooseberries.
4 Blend the flour with other ingredients and when smooth, spread over gooseberries.
5 Bake for approximately 30 minutes in the centre of a moderately hot oven (400°F.—Gas Mark 5) until the mixture is firm and the pastry crisp.
6 Shake over coconut and serve hot, or allow to cool, and cover with whipped cream and grated chocolate.
7 Serve with cream.

Marrow and ginger flan

cooking time 35 minutes

you will need:

6 oz. sweet short crust pastry (see page 32)
2 large eggs
4 oz. sugar
1 medium sized marrow
½ pint milk
good pinch cinnamon, nutmeg or ginger

1 Line a deep flan ring with the pastry.
2 Beat the eggs and sugar together.
3 Add the diced marrow, milk and spices.
4 Pour into the pastry case and bake for about 15 minutes in a hot oven (425 - 450°F.—Gas Mark 6 - 7).
5 Lower the heat to moderate (375°F.—Gas Mark 4) for a further 20 minutes until pastry and filling are cooked.

Orange flan (1)

cooking time 30 minutes

you will need:

5 – 6 oz. short crust pastry (see page 32)	grated rind 1 orange
1 oz. margarine	2 tablespoons orange juice
2 good tablespoons marmalade	1 egg
	2 good tablespoons breadcrumbs

1 Line a 7-inch flan ring or sandwich tin with the pastry.
2 Cream the margarine and marmalade together.
3 Add the grated orange rind, juice, egg and crumbs.
4 Put into the pastry case and bake in the centre of a hot oven (425 - 450°F.—Gas Mark 6 - 7) for 30 minutes, lowering the heat after 20 minutes.

Lemon flan

Use lemon marmalade and the rind and juice of 1 lemon.

Prune flan

cooking time 1½ - 2½ hours

you will need:

6 oz. prunes	few drops lemon essence or lemon juice
little water	½ teaspoon cinnamon
1 tablespoon golden syrup	1 tablespoon bread-crumbs
½ oz. margarine	5 – 6 oz. short crust pastry (see page 32)
½ teaspoon mixed spice	

1 Soak the prunes in a very little water overnight or for several hours.
2 Simmer until soft, then cut with a pair of scissors into small pieces.
3 Put the syrup, margarine, prunes, spice, lemon flavouring and cinnamon into a pan and heat gently for a few minutes until all mixed together.
4 Add the breadcrumbs.
5 Line a 7-inch flan ring or sandwich tin with the pastry.
6 Fill with the prune mixture.
7 Put in the centre of a hot oven (450°F.—Gas Mark 6 or 7) and bake for 30 minutes, lowering the heat after 20 minutes.
8 Any prune juice that might be left could be thickened with a little cornflour, i.e. 1 teaspoon to each ¼ pint juice, and served with the flan.

To make and fill a cold fruit flan

you will need:

5 – 6 oz. short crust, sweet short crust or flan pastry (see pages 32, 42)	arrowroot or cornflour glaze
either 1 large can fruit or ¾ – 1 lb. fruit with a little water and sugar or frozen fruit	

1 Make the pastry and bake 'blind' (see page 30).
2 To prepare the fruit:
  a When using canned fruit, drain the fruit over a fine sieve so that it is quite dry and you have not wasted any of the syrup. To make sure it is very dry, the fruit could be put on kitchen paper before actually going into the flan.
  b When using cooked fruit, make a syrup of approximately ½ pint water and 2 - 3 oz. sugar. Bring to the boil and then put in the prepared fruit. Simmer very gently until just soft but not broken. Lift out and drain as for canned fruit. Cool.
  c When using frozen fruit, allow to defrost but not to become over defrosted. Drain as canned fruit but when making the glaze allow a little less liquid since there will be further defrosting while the fruit actually stands in the pastry case.
  d When using fruit that does not need cooking, such as strawberries, cherries, etc. In order to sweeten the fruit you can put it in the jelly glaze (see page 49) for a few minutes, then lift out, drain and proceed as for other fruit.
3 Arrange the well drained cold fruit in the cold pastry case.
4 Make the glaze
5 Allow to cool then spoon or brush over the fruit.

Banana and strawberry flan

cooking time 15 - 20 minutes

you will need:

5 oz. flan or rich flan pastry (see page 42)	4 bananas
	8 oz. strawberries
	apricot jam

1 Line a flan tin with the pastry and bake 'blind' until crisp and golden brown.
2 Cover with alternate layers of sliced bananas and halved strawberries, leaving a few for decoration.
3 Cover with a thin layer of apricot jam.
4 Decorate with a ring of strawberry halves on the rim of the flan.
5 Fill remaining space with banana slices and 1 or 2 strawberries in the centre.

Grape flan

cooking time 25 minutes

you will need:

8 oz. black grapes
1 7-inch baked flan case
½ jelly tablet
whipped cream

1 Slice grapes in half and remove pips.
2 Arrange in flan case.
3 Dissolve jelly in ½ pint water and cool.
4 When just beginning to set, pour over the grapes.
5 When set firm pipe freshly whipped cream round the edges to decorate.

Orange flan (2)

cooking time 30 minutes

you will need:

5 oz. short crust pastry (see page 32)
3 oz. margarine
3 oz. sugar
grated rind 1–2 oranges
2 small eggs
3 oz. flour (1 level teaspoon baking powder with plain flour)
1 large can mandarin oranges
1 level teaspoon arrowroot
1 tablespoon orange marmalade

1 Line a flan ring or pie plate with the pastry.
2 Cream margarine, sugar and orange rind until soft.
3 Add the beaten eggs and flour.
4 Spread over the pastry and bake for approximately 30 minutes in the centre of a moderately hot oven (400°F.—Gas Mark 5).
5 Drain mandarin oranges and arrange on top of the flan.
6 Blend ⅛ pint of the juice with the arrowroot and marmalade.
7 Boil until clear.
8 Strain and allow to cool.
9 Brush over top of the flan.

Orange chocolate flan

cooking time 25 minutes

you will need:

4–5 oz. short or sweet short crust pastry (see page 32)
1 packet chocolate blancmange powder
1 pint milk
2 oz. sugar
1 orange

1 Roll out the pastry and line a flan case.
2 Bake 'blind' in a hot oven (425°F.—Gas Mark 6) until crisp and golden brown.
3 Blend the blancmange powder with a little of the cold milk.
4 Bring the rest of the milk to the boil and pour over the blended chocolate mixture.
5 Return to the pan with the sugar and grated rind of the orange.
6 Cook until thick and very smooth.
7 Pour into the flan case and decorate with orange sections.
8 Serve at once.

Apricot cream flan

cooking time 20-25 minutes for flan

you will need:

8 oz. sweet short crust pastry (see page 32)
1 egg
1 oz. castor sugar
½ oz. plain flour
few drops vanilla essence
¼ pint milk
1 large can apricot halves
2 level dessertspoons apricot jam
1 scant dessertspoon water

1 Line a flan ring or pie plate with the pastry and bake 'blind' until crisp and golden brown.
2 Whisk egg and sugar over a basin of hot water until thick and creamy.
3 Fold in flour.
4 Gradually stir in the essence and milk.
5 Heat slowly until mixture boils, stirring all the time.
6 Remove from heat and allow to cool.
7 When quite cold spread thickly over the pastry base.
8 Drain juice from apricots and arrange apricot halves over the cream filling.
9 Heat the jam with the water until jam has melted.
10 Strain and reheat until liquid just boils.
11 Spoon or brush over the apricots to glaze.

Pineapple cream flan

cooking time 20 - 25 minutes

you will need:

6 oz. short crust pastry (see page 32)	1 small can pineapple
	¼ pint whipped cream
	cherries to decorate

1. Line a flan tin with the pastry and bake 'blind' for approximately 20 - 25 minutes in hot oven (425°F.—Gas Mark 6) until crisp and brown.
2. Remove from oven and allow to cool.
3. Mix the pineapple and cream together.
4. When the flan is quite cold fill with pineapple and cream mixture.
5. Decorate with cherries.

Raspberry cream flan (1)

cooking time 20 - 25 minutes

you will need:

6 oz. flan or rich flan pastry (see 42)	¾ pint sweetened raspberry purée
1 packet raspberry flavoured cornflour	2 eggs
	cream

1. Line a flan ring or pie plate with the pastry and bake 'blind' until crisp and golden brown.
2. Mix the flavoured cornflour together with a little of the puree until smooth.
3. Put rest of purée on to heat and add the mixed cornflour.
4. Boil for 1 minute stirring constantly.
5. Remove from heat and add egg yolks.
6. Return to heat and simmer without boiling for several minutes.
7. Beat egg whites stiffly and fold lightly into the cooked mixture.
8. Leave to cool, then pile into the baked pastry case.
9. Top with cream.

Raspberry cream flan (2)

cooking time 20 - 25 minutes

you will need:

6 oz. short crust pastry (see page page 32)	1 level tablespoon cornflour
approximately 12 oz. raspberries, fresh or frozen	¼ pint milk
1 – 2 oz. sugar	1 – 2 oz. butter
	1 egg yolk
	⅛ pint whipped cream

1. Line a flan ring with the pastry and bake 'blind' for approximately 20 minutes in a hot oven (425°F.—Gas Mark 6).
2. Remove from oven and cool.
3. Arrange raspberries on the bottom of the flan case, saving a few for decoration.
4. Dust with a little of the sugar.
5. Blend cornflour and milk.
6. Cook until thick and very smooth.
7. Add rest of the sugar and the butter gradually and egg yolk.
8. Cook **without boiling** for several minutes, then cool.
9. Beat cream into this when completely cold.
10. Spread over the fruit and top with remainder of the raspberries.

Rhubarb cream pie

cooking time 10 minutes

you will need:

For biscuit crust pastry:	*For filling:*
6 oz. wholemeal biscuits	12 oz. forced rhubarb
3 oz. butter	⅜ pint water
	sugar to taste
	¼ pint cream or evaporated milk
	½ lemon jelly
	angelica

1. Crush the biscuit crumbs, add the butter and form into the shape of a flan case in the serving dish. Allow to stand in a cool place until very firm.
2. Cook the rhubarb with the water and sugar to taste.
3. When very soft but unbroken lift from the syrup.
4. Dissolve the jelly in this and when cold, but not set, fold in most of the evaporated milk or cream (this need not be whipped).
5. Put into the biscuit crumb case when just beginning to set.
6. Smooth flat and arrange the cooked, drained rhubarb on top in a neat pattern.
7. Decorate with the whipped evaporated milk and angelica.

Blackcurrant chiffon crunchy flan

cooking time 15 minutes

you will need:

For crunchy crust:
6 oz. digestive biscuits
3 oz. butter or margarine
3 level dessertspoons golden syrup
1 oz. castor sugar

For filling:
¾ – 1 lb. blackcurrants
water
sugar to taste
2 eggs
1 level dessertspoon powdered gelatine

To decorate:
little cream
few blackcurrants

1 Crush the biscuits into crumbs.
2 Put the butter or margarine and golden syrup into a small saucepan.
3 Heat and bring almost to the boil.
4 Put the sugar and crushed biscuits into a mixing bowl and add the melted butter and syrup mixture.
5 Mix thoroughly and allow mixture to cool slightly.
6 Knead well and press into a 7-inch plain flan ring or pie plate.
7 Place in a refrigerator or cool place until firm.
8 Cook the blackcurrants with very little water and sugar to taste until tender.
9 Rub through a sieve or beat with a wooden spoon until a smooth purée.
10 Stir in the egg yolks and cook gently until the mixture thickens.
11 Dissolve gelatine in an ⅛ pint very hot water.
12 Add to the blackcurrant mixture and allow to cool.
13 Fold in the stiffly beaten egg whites.
14 Pour carefully into the crunchy crust flan and allow to set.
15 Decorate with cream and few blackcurrants.

Lemon chiffon flan

cooking time 25 minutes

you will need:

5 – 6 oz. short or rich short crust pastry (see page 32)
3 eggs
3 oz. sugar
finely grated rind 2 lemons
1½ level dessertspoons powdered gelatine
⅛ pint water
⅛ pint lemon juice
¼ pint whipped cream or evaporated milk

1 Line a flan case with the pastry and bake 'blind' until crisp and golden brown.
2 Whisk egg yolks with the sugar and grated lemon rind until thick.
3 Dissolve gelatine in the hot water and lemon juice and add to egg mixture.
4 When cool fold in lightly whipped cream or evaporated milk.
5 Leave until beginning to set.
6 Fold in stiffly beaten egg whites.
7 Pour mixture in pastry case.

Coffee chiffon flan

cooking time 25 minutes

you will need:

For chocolate pastry:
2½ oz. margarine
2 oz. sugar
4 oz. flour
1 egg yolk
little water
½ oz. cocoa or 1 oz. chocolate powder

For coffee chiffon:
1 level tablespoon powdered gelatine
½ pint strong coffee
2 oz. sugar
2 egg yolks
¼ pint cream or evaporated milk
2 oz. walnuts
3 egg whites

1 Cream margarine and sugar until light and fluffy.
2 Add flour, chocolate powder, egg yolk and enough water to bind.
3 Roll out and line a deep 8-inch flan ring and bake 'blind' for about 25 minutes in a hot oven (425°F.—Gas Mark 6).
4 Dissolve the gelatine in the hot coffee.
5 Beat sugar and egg yolks together until thick and creamy.
6 Add to the hot coffee mixture and allow to cool.
7 When just beginning to set fold in nearly all the very lightly whipped cream, 1 oz. of the chopped walnuts and the stiffly beaten egg whites.
8 Pour into the pastry when both are quite cold.
9 When set decorate with remainder of walnuts and cream.

Lemon chiffon dessert

no cooking

you will need:

Coconut crust:
3 oz. biscuits
3 oz. butter
3 oz. sugar
3 oz. desiccated coconut

1 large egg
1 oz. sugar
1 small can evaporated milk
grated rind and juice 1 lemon

For filling:
1 lemon jelly
¾ pint water

To decorate:
little whipped cream
glacé cherries

1 Crush the biscuits into crumbs and mix with the creamed butter and sugar and coconut.
2 Form into a flan shape and leave to harden for an hour or so.
3 Dissolve the jelly in the water.
4 Pour on to the egg yolk beaten with the sugar.
5 Add the evaporated milk, lemon rind and juice and leave to become lightly set.
6 Fold in the stiffly beaten egg white and pile into the biscuit case.
7 Decorate with cream and cherries.

French strawberry tart

cooking time 25 - 30 minutes

you will need:

For pastry:
3 oz. butter
1 oz. sugar
6 oz. flour (preferably plain)
1 egg yolk
little water

For filling:
approximately 12 oz. strawberries
4 tablespoons redcurrant jelly
2 tablespoons water
little cream

1 Cream butter and sugar, work in flour, egg yolk and water to bind.
2 Roll out and line flan ring or tin.
3 Prick, bake 'blind' in moderately hot oven (400°F.—Gas Mark 5) until golden brown.
4 Fill tightly with whole strawberries, arranging these so that they stand upright.
5 Boil jelly and water until a smooth liquid.
6 Cool slightly, but do not allow to set again, then pour over fruit. Serve with cream.

Strawberry meringue tart

As French strawberry tart, but whisk 2 egg whites until very stiff. Fold in 2 good tablespoons sugar. Pile over fruit and glaze, and set in a very moderate oven until golden brown.

Banana soufflé tart

cooking time 15 - 20 minutes

you will need:

6 – 8 oz. flaky or short crust pastry (see pages 31, 32)
1 lemon jelly
¾ pint water
2 eggs

2 oz. sugar
3 large bananas

To decorate:
little cream

1 Line a flan ring with the pastry and bake 'blind' until crisp and golden brown.
2 Dissolve the jelly in the water and pour on to the well beaten egg yolks and sugar.
3 Allow to cool and when beginning to set add 2 mashed bananas.
4 Fold in the stiffly beaten egg whites and pile into the cooked and cooled pastry case.
5 Leave to set and decorate with cream and sliced banana.

Peach cheese cake

cooking time 15 minutes

you will need:

For cornflake flan:
2 oz. butter
2 oz. castor sugar
¼ teaspoon nutmeg
4 oz. cornflakes

For filling:
3 oz. castor sugar
2 eggs
pinch salt

¼ pint evaporated milk
1 oz. powdered gelatine
2 tablespoons peach syrup from can
6 oz. cream cheese
1 tablespoon grated lemon rind
4 tablespoons lemon juice
1 teaspoon vanilla essence
1 medium sized can sliced peaches

1 For the cornflake flan cream butter and sugar together.
2 Add nutmeg and crushed cornflakes and press into 8-inch flan ring on plate or shallow glass dish.
3 Make the filling by cooking the egg yolks, half the sugar, salt and milk in a double saucepan over boiling water until thick and creamy —beating well.
4 Add gelatine softened in the peach syrup.
5 Remove from heat and add cheese, lemon rind, juice and vanilla essence.
6 When cool, whip egg whites stiffly, fold in sugar and fold into custard mixture.
7 Pour into pie shell and chill until set.
8 Top with chilled drained peaches.

Glaze with arrowroot or cornflour

cooking time 4 - 5 minutes

you will need:

- 1 pint liquid
- 1 level tablespoon cornflour or arrowroot
- 2 – 3 drops vegetable colouring (optional)

1. Blend ingredients together until smooth.
2. Put into a saucepan and boil until thickened and clear.
3. Add 2 - 3 drops vegetable colouring if the mixture looks very pale.

Redcurrant jelly glaze

cooking time 5 - 7 minutes

you will need:

- 1 level teaspoon cornflour or arrowroot
- ¼ pint water
- 1 oz. sugar
- 2 good tablespoon redcurrant jelly

1. Blend the arrowroot or cornflour with the water in a saucepan.
2. Add the sugar.
3. Finally mix in the redcurrant jelly.
4. Stir until jelly has dissolved.
5. Boil until thick and clear.

Glaze with flavoured jelly mixture or gelatine

you will need:

- ¼ pint liquid
- ¼ flavoured jelly tablet or 1 level teaspoon powdered gelatine
- few drops vegetable colouring

1. Dissolve the jelly tablet or gelatine in the very hot liquid.
2. Allow to cool and begin to stiffen slightly.
3. Add a few drops colouring if necessary.

Pancakes and Fritters

To make perfect pancakes

A perfect pancake should be very thin, although, of course, one's own personal preference has to be considered. Some people like a thicker and more substantial pancake. The basic pancake mixture provides you with a really thin batter and the way to make sure the pancake is thin and crisp is to transfer the batter to a jug, so that you can pour it quickly over the whole of the bottom surface of the pan, once the fat is hot. Fat is mentioned in the recipe. This can be cooking fat, lard or butter or oil.

Tossing a pancake is not as difficult as it sounds. Make sure the pancake is cooked on the bottom side. The way you test this is to shake the pan and if the pancake moves easily, you know it is ready. Hold the pan loosely in your hand with the wrist quite relaxed and the pan slightly pointing downwards. Give a sharp flip, and with practise you will find the pancake rises, turns in the air and drops back again into the pan with the cooked side uppermost. In order to practise this, it is, however, a good idea to try tossing the pancakes that are cooked on both sides to begin with. If the thought of tossing is alarming, then turn with the help of a palette knife or small fish slice. Insert this under the centre of the pancake so you have a really good support and turn it over carefully and gently.

To keep pancakes hot

Ideally pancakes should be eaten hot the moment they are cooked and come from the pan, but with a family this is rarely possible. It is therefore important to keep the early ones hot while you continue cooking and you can do this either on a dish over a pan of hot water which should not be covered, or on a hot dish in a cool oven.

To store pancakes

It is possible to make a whole batch of pancakes at a convenient time, to wrap them in foil and store them in the refrigerator. All you need to do then, is to warm them through for a few minutes.

Basic pancake mixture

cooking time few minutes

you will need:

4 oz. plain flour	½ pint milk
pinch salt	little fat for frying
1 egg	

1. Sieve flour and salt into a bowl.
2. Make a well in the centre.
3. Beat the egg and add to the flour.
4. Pour in half the milk and mix with a whisk to a smooth batter.
   Mix well to remove all lumps.
5. Add remaining milk.
6. Strain the batter and allow to stand for 1 hour.
7. Melt a little fat in the pan, using just enough to keep the pancake from sticking.
8. Pour sufficient batter to cover the pan very thinly and fry on one side for approximately 1 minute.
9. Turn or toss over and continue cooking for about ½ minute until pancakes are a golden brown colour.

Lemon pancakes

Use recipe above. Sprinkle each pancake with sugar and lemon juice, rolling up or folding into quarters. Serve with a slice of lemon.

Chocolate pancakes

Use recipe above. Fill the pancakes with ice cream just before serving and coat with hot Chocolate sauce (see page 84).

Walnut pancakes

Use recipe above. Finely chop 2 oz. shelled walnuts, mix with 2 oz. sugar and sufficient cream to make a stiff mixture, heat in a saucepan and spread on the pancakes. Roll up and dust with icing sugar and serve.

Fruit pancakes

Use recipe above. Fill the pancakes with hot sweetened fruit purée and serve with cream, ice cream or custard sauce (see page 84).

Jam pancakes

Use recipe above. Fill the pancakes with hot jam and dust with icing sugar.

Gil-blas

Use recipe above. Cream together 2 oz. butter and 3 oz. sugar, preferably icing sugar. Add a few drops lemon juice and 1 oz brandy. Spread this mixture over the hot pancakes and fold into quarters. Serve at once.

Crêpes aux fruits — fruit-filled pancakes

cooking time few minutes

you will need:

½ oz. butter, melted	½ pint milk
1 oz. cornflour	
3 oz. plain flour	*To fry:*
pinch of salt	oil or fat
1 egg and 1 yolk	

1. Melt butter and cool slightly.
2. Sieve the cornflour, flour and salt into a bowl.
3. Make a well in the centre, drop in the eggs and mix to a smooth batter with some of the milk.
4. When the mixture is smooth and creamy, beat thoroughly.
5. Stir in the butter and then the remaining milk.
6. Leave to stand before frying.
7. Cook as for Basic pancakes (see above).

For filling:	2 level teaspoons cornflour
3 tablespoons raspberry jam	squeeze lemon juice
4 tablespoons pineapple juice	1 teaspoon kirsch liqueur
	1 small can pineapple

1. Boil the jam and 3 tablespoons pineapple juice from can together for 5 minutes.
2. Strain and return to pan.
3. Mix the cornflour smoothly with 1 tablespoon pineapple juice.
4. Add to the syrup.
5. Stir until boiling and boil for 3 minutes.
6. Add lemon juice and kirsch.
7. Chop pineapple and add to sauce, then reheat.
8. Make small pancakes, spread with the hot fruit filling and roll up.
9. Serve as soon as possible.

Crêpes Suzette (1)

cooking time — few minutes

you will need:

- 4 oz. plain flour
- good pinch salt
- 2 eggs
- ⅛ pint milk
- ⅛ pint water
- oil or butter for frying
- redcurrant jelly
- brandy, rum or curaçao
- little extra sugar

1. Sieve the flour and salt together.
2. Add the eggs, one at a time, and beat the batter thoroughly.
3. Leave for 10 minutes.
4. Beat again and gradually add the milk and water.
5. Whisk again until the surface of the batter is covered with little bubbles.
6. Put a very small quantity of the oil or butter in the pan.
7. Cool quickly until brown on one side.
8. Toss or turn the pancake and cook quickly on the other side.
9. Turn out on to a hot dish.
10. Spread with the redcurrant jelly and roll tightly.
11. Dust with sugar and sprinkle over the brandy, rum or curaçao.
12. To serve Crêpes Suzette in the authentic manner the brandy should be poured over and ignited when serving.

Crêpes Suzette (2)

cooking time — few minutes

you will need:

- 4 cubes sugar
- 1 orange
- 1 lemon
- 2 oz. butter
- 2 tablespoons curaçao or orange liqueur
- 8 small pancakes (see above)
- 1 oz. castor sugar
- 2 tablespoons brandy

1. Rub 2 of the sugar knobs on the skin of the orange and the other two on the lemon so that they absorb some of the aromatic oils.
2. Squeeze the juice from the orange and lemon and blend it with the softened butter, adding it gradually until creamy.
3. Add the orange liqueur.
4. Put the sugar knobs into a frying pan over a medium heat and allow to caramelise.
5. Add some of the prepared sauce and the pancakes, one at a time, allowing them to absorb the sauce before folding into quarters.
6. Add more sauce as necessary until all the pancakes are ready in the pan.
7. Sprinkle with castor sugar, turn over the pancakes and sprinkle again.
8. Pour the brandy into the pan over the pancakes.
9. Allow it to ignite and serve them while still flaming.

To make perfect fritters

The fritter batter must be thicker than pancake batter as it has to 'stick' to the food being coated. Damp fruit, such as canned or juicy apples, should be well drained and coated with a little flour before being dipped into the batter. Make sure the fat is really hot so that you set the batter on either side, then lower the heat so that the fruit becomes thoroughly cooked or heated. In the case of rather slow cooking apples, these should be sliced fairly thinly.

Apple fritters

cooking time — 10 minutes each fritter

you will need:

- 3 large cooking apples
- 4 oz. flour (with plain flour 1 teaspoon baking powder)
- pinch salt
- 1 teaspoon sugar
- 1 egg
- ¼ pint milk
- fat or oil for frying
- sugar for dusting

1. Peel, core and slice the apples into rings about ½ inch thick.
2. Mix the flour, baking powder, salt, sugar and egg together.
3. Add the milk.
4. Flour the rings of apple before dipping them into the thick batter. This is most important otherwise the batter is very likely to come away from the fruit when being cooked.
5. Heat enough fat or oil in the frying pan to cover—or use pan deep fat and when really hot drop in the fritters.
6. Cook quickly for a good minute on one side.
7. Turn them over and cook quickly on the other side—with deep fat it is not necessary to turn.
8. Turn the heat down and cook more slowly for nearly 10 minutes to make sure the apples are cooked in the middle.
9. Serve hot, dusted with sugar.

Variations:

Banana

Halve the bananas, then proceed as Apple fritters, shortening the cooking time 2 - 3 minutes, as bananas are easily and quickly cooked.

Pineapple

Cut slices of fresh pineapple. Remove skin and centre core, or drain canned pineapple. Proceed as for Apple fritters.

Omelettes and Waffles

Sweet omelette

cooking time few minutes

you will need:

- 4 eggs
- 2 oz. sugar
- 2 tablespoons cream or top of milk
- 1 oz. butter

1. Separate the yolks from the whites of eggs.
2. Beat the yolks with the sugar and cream or top of the milk.
3. Fold in stiffly beaten egg whites.
4. Heat the butter in an omelette pan and pour in the egg mixture.
5. Cook steadily for several minutes until firm at the bottom.
6. Put under a medium grill or into the oven until top is golden brown.

Fillings for sweet omelettes

Apple

Fill with thick apple purée and fold. Top with a thick layer of sieved icing sugar and put under the grill to brown.

Apricot

Fill with canned apricots and serve with hot Apricot sauce (see page 83).

Ice cream

Fill with ice cream and serve with hot Chocolate sauce (see page 84).

Coffee

Add strong coffee made with milk and sprinkle with blanched almonds.

Chocolate

Add a little grated chocolate melted in the milk. Fill with grated chocolate.

Jam

Fill with hot jam and top with more jam or sieved icing sugar.

Orange

Add grated rind and juice of orange instead of cream to the egg yolks. Fill with sliced oranges.

Waffles

cooking time few minutes

you will need:

For basic waffle batter:

- 4 oz. plain flour
- pinch salt
- 1 egg
- $\frac{1}{3}$ pint milk
- 1 oz. melted fat
- 1 oz. sugar

1. Sieve the flour and salt together.
2. Make a well in the centre and drop in the egg.
3. Beat the batter thoroughly, then gradually add the milk, beating all the time, until a smooth, thick batter.
4. Put in the melted margarine, and sugar.
5. Grease and heat the waffle iron and pour in just enough of the batter to cover this.
6. Cook quickly until crisp and brown.
7. Serve with jam, fruit or maple or golden syrup.

FOR A RICHER WAFFLE BATTER INCREASE THE AMOUNT OF FAT TO 2 oz.

Fluffy waffle

A 'fluffy' waffle is made as above but use 2 eggs, separating the egg yolks from the whites. Add the yolks first and whip the egg whites until stiff, folding these in after the milk.

Trifles and Jellies

Making jellies

The popularity of flavoured jellies means that few people today make their own with fruit juices. Follow the directions on the packet carefully, the water is usually kept below boiling, as some jellies, if boiled, do not set properly. Fresh fruit can be added to the jelly WITH THE EXCEPTION OF FRESH PINEAPPLE. If this is added uncooked, its acidity prevents the jelly from setting. Make a syrup of sugar and water and cook the pineapple for a time in this. Drain and use in the jelly. If using rather juicy fruits, slightly lower the quantity of water for dissolving the jelly.
The jelly mould should be either rinsed in cold water or brushed with a little oil to make certain that the mould will turn out.
If you wish to set the fruit in layers in the jelly, pour a little of the jelly into the mould, allow to set while keeping the rest of the liquid jelly in a warm enough place to prevent this happening. When the jelly has set, dip the pieces of fruit in liquid jelly, arrange on top and cover with another thin layer of the liquid jelly. Allow to set. Continue like this until the mould is filled.

Charlotte Katrine

no cooking

you will need:

sponge finger biscuits (approximately 12–14)
4 oz. plain chocolate
4 oz. unsalted butter
4 oz. ground almonds
2 oz. castor sugar
¼ pint thick cream
⅛ pint milk

To decorate:
whipped cream
glacé cherries
mandarin oranges

1 Place a circle of greased greaseproof paper in the bottom of a cake tin with a loose base, using a 5½ - 6-inch tin.
2 Cut a strip of greaseproof paper for the sides to come about 2-inches above the tin.
3 Arrange biscuits neatly round the sides of the tin.
4 Melt the chocolate and add the softened butter, ground almonds and sugar.
5 Beat well.
6 Beat the cream until stiff and add the milk.
7 Fold into the chocolate mixture and pour into the tin.
8 Stand in a cold place for 8 - 12 hours, or a refrigerator for 2 - 3 hours. Turn out carefully.
9 Pipe cream round outside of mixture and arrange cherries and mandarin oranges facing towards the middle.

Mexican flan

cooking time 5 - 10 minutes

you will need:

4 trifle sponge cakes or about 12 sponge finger biscuits
1 orange
2 oz. plain chocolate
3 level tablespoons custard powder
1 small can evaporated milk
1½ oz. sugar
8 oz. chopped fruit (apricots, pineapple, cherries)

To decorate:
cherries
angelica

1 Line the sides of a pie plate with the sponge cut into thin strips, or the split sponge biscuits.
2 Grate the orange rind finely and chop the orange and chocolate.
3 Blend the custard powder to a paste with a little of the milk.
4 Add sufficient water to the remainder to make up to ¾ pint.
5 Bring to the boil and pour on to the custard, stirring well.
6 Return to the pan and cook until thick, stirring carefully.
7 Stir in orange rind and sugar.
8 When cool, stir in orange, chocolate and chopped mixed fruit.
9 Pour into prepared dish and decorate with cherries and angelica when cold.

Chocolate supreme

no cooking

you will need:

4 oz. plain chocolate
little butter
4 sponge cakes
little sherry or liqueur
1 large can fruit salad

To decorate:
little cream
grated chocolate

1. Melt the chocolate in a basin over hot water.
2. Lightly brush inside of a foil or paper baking case with melted butter.
3. Pour the chocolate into the case and spread evenly over the bottom and sides.
4. Leave until set and peel off case.
5. Fill with sponge cakes soaked in sherry or liqueur and fruit salad.
6. Decorate with cream and grated chocolate.

Raspberry cream delight

no cooking

you will need:

⅛ pint milk
sherry or vanilla essence
approximately 30 sponge finger biscuits
1 large packet frozen raspberries
½ pint cream
2 oz. sugar

1. Pour the milk into a shallow dish and add sherry or vanilla essence.
2. Dip approximately 10 of the sponge finger biscuits into this mixture very quickly to just moisten them.
3. Arrange at the bottom of an 8-inch cake tin with a loose bottom previously lined with greaseproof paper.
4. Slice or chop raspberries saving a few for decoration.
5. Whip the cream and fold most of it into the raspberries, adding the sugar.
6. Put half this mixture over the sponge finger biscuits.
7. Cover with a layer of sponge finger biscuits previously dipped in the milk and vanilla or sherry liquid.
8. Cover with remainder of strawberry mixture and a final layer of 'dipped' biscuits.
9. Put into refrigerator or a cool place for several hours.
10. Turn out and pile the rest of the cream on top and decorate with remainder of raspberries.

Redcurrant finger pudding

cooking time 10 - 15 minutes

you will need:

3 tablespoons redcurrant jelly
3 tablespoons water
8 oz. sponge finger biscuits or sponge cakes
½ pint milk
vanilla essence
2 oz. sugar
1 oz. cornflour
2 – 3 oz. butter
1 egg yolk

1. Heat the redcurrant jelly and water together.
2. Remove from heat and allow to cool slightly.
3. Moisten the sponge fingers in the redcurrant liquid and arrange a few round the sides and bottom of a greased mould.
4. Put most of the milk into a saucepan together with the vanilla essence and sugar.
5. Blend the cornflour with the rest of the cold milk and pour over the heated milk.
6. Return to the pan and cook until thickened.
7. Stir in the butter until thoroughly absorbed.
8. Allow to cool slightly and add the beaten egg yolk.
9. Use while warm, but allow to cool a little longer.
10. Pour ⅓ of the mixture into the mould over the sponge fingers.
11. Cover with a few more moistened sponge fingers, then another layer of the mixture.
12. Put another layer of moistened sponge fingers on top, then a further layer of the mixture and finally a layer of sponge fingers.
13. Cover with a weight and leave for at least 12 hours in a cold place.

Orange finger pudding

Use the recipe for Redcurrant finger pudding above, soaking the sponge fingers in the juice of 2 oranges, 1 tablespoon sherry and 2 tablespoons water.

Banana finger surprise

no cooking

you will need:

1 lemon jelly
8 bananas
few cherries
sponge finger biscuits
⅜ pint lightly whipped cream
1 teaspoon powdered gelatine

1. Make jelly as directed on packet and pour a little into a cake tin or plain round mould, keeping the remaining jelly hot.

2 Slice 4 of the bananas and arrange in the jelly together with the cherries.
3 When the jelly is cold and just beginning to set arrange the finger biscuits all the way around the tin, making sure they fit tightly together.
4 Mash the remaining bananas with a little of the cream.
5 Dissolve the gelatine in the remaining hot jelly and add the mashed bananas.
6 Allow to cool, but not set, then fold in the remaining cream.
7 Pour into the mould and leave until firm.
8 Turn out carefully and decorate with a little cream.

Raspberry finger surprise

Use recipe as above but use 12 oz. fresh raspberries instead of bananas, and raspberry jelly.

Uncooked redcurrant pudding

no cooking

you will need:

slices bread
1 lb. redcurrants
sugar to taste
cream

1 Remove crusts from thin slices of bread.
2 Line the sides and bottom of a basin with the bread.
3 Put in the sweetened fruit.
4 Cover with a thin layer of bread and put paper or a saucer on top.
5 Weigh down and leave overnight or for some hours.
6 Turn out and serve with cream.

Note:
For a really delicious sweet try a mixture of redcurrants or loganberries and raspberries.

Apricot cream

cooking time 1½ hours

you will need:

8 oz. dried apricots
water
1 lemon jelly
4 oz. lemon marmalade
1 oz. walnuts (optional)
¼ pint cream

1 Soak the apricots overnight.
2 Simmer until quite soft and rub through a sieve.
3 Measure the juice and if necessary add enough water to give about ¾ pint.
4 Heat and dissolve the jelly in this liquid.
5 Add the marmalade, the apricot pulp and half the walnuts, chopped into neat pieces.
6 Allow to cool and when beginning to set fold in half the lightly whipped cream.
7 Pour into a mould and turn out when firm.
8 Decorate with whipped cream and nuts.

Banana mould

cooking time 7 minutes

you will need:

3 oz. quick cooking macaroni
1 lemon jelly
2–3 bananas
little sugar
little whipped cream

1 Cook macaroni as directed on the packet, and drain well.
2 Make up jelly as directed.
3 Peel and slice bananas and arrange a few slices in the bottom of the mould.
4 Cover with a layer of jelly.
5 Mix remaining bananas and jelly into macaroni and sweeten if necessary.
6 When jelly in mould is firm, add macaroni mixture and leave to set.
7 Unmould in usual way and serve decorated with whipped cream.

Chocolate peppermint creams

cooking time few minutes

you will need:

½ pint hot water
1 tablespoon cocoa
1 tablespoon powdered gelatine
½ pint custard made with custard powder — pouring consistency
2–3 oz. sugar
¼ pint whipped evaporated milk or cream
few drops peppermint essence

To decorate:
whipped cream
grated chocolate

1 Blend the water and cocoa together and dissolve the gelatine in it.
2 Add the custard and sugar and allow to cool.
3 Fold in cream or evaporated milk and peppermint essence.
4 Pour into glasses and when set decorate with whipped cream and grated chocolate.

Milk jelly

no cooking

you will need:

1 fruit flavoured jelly	¼ pint water
	¾ pint milk

1 Dissolve jelly in boiling water.
2 Allow the jelly to cool and add the cold milk.

Chocolate milk jelly

no cooking

you will need:

1 level teaspoon powdered gelatine	1 teaspoon chocolate powder
⅛ pint water	⅞ pint milk

1 Soften the gelatine in a dessertspoon cold water.
2 Pour on the remaining water which should be boiling and stir well until dissolved.
3 Blend in the chocolate powder and allow to cool.
4 Stir in cold milk and pour into mould to set.

Variations:

Lemon

Use ⅛ pint lemon juice instead of water, making sure it is quite cold before adding milk which should be whisked sharply onto the lemon juice.

Coffee

Use ⅛ pint strong black coffee instead of water, omitting chocolate.

Vanilla

Add a few drops of vanilla essence omitting chocolate powder.

Mocha

Add ⅛ pint strong black coffee to the chocolate milk jelly above.

Fairy ring delight

cooking time 10 minutes

you will need:

1 pint milk or evaporated milk	about ¼ pint hot water or mandarin syrup
3 oz. quick cooking macaroni	sugar to taste
1 orange jelly	1 small can mandarin oranges
	little whipped cream

1 Pour the milk into a saucepan and bring to the boil.
2 Sprinkle in the macaroni and simmer for 7 minutes, stirring occasionally.
3 Dissolve the jelly in the water or mandarin syrup and mix into the macaroni mixture.
4 Sweeten to taste and leave until just setting.
5 Stir and pour into a ring mould and allow to set.
6 Unmould in the usual way.
7 Decorate the mould with mandarin oranges and whipped cream.

Fruit honeycomb

no cooking

you will need:

½ lime or lemon jelly	little canned or cooked fruit
1 jelly tablet of same or another flavour—if using lime as base, select lemon for main part, or orange — keep to fresh flavours and cool colours	2 eggs
	little extra sugar

1 Make up both jellies in separate containers using ½ pint water for one jelly and just over ¾ pint water for the second.
2 Pour half the lime or lemon jelly into a 2-pint mould, rinsed in cold water, adding very well drained fruit.
3 Allow to set.
4 Cover with rest of lime jelly and leave until firm.
5 Meanwhile, heat the second jelly with the beaten egg yolk.
6 Remove from heat and cool slightly.
7 Fold in the stiffly beaten egg whites. This gives a slightly 'curdled' or honeycomb look.
8 Taste and add extra sugar if wished.
9 When cold, but not set, pour over lime and fruit base.
10 Turn out and serve with cream or ice cream.

Honeycomb mould

cooking time 5 minutes

you will need:

¼ pint lemon juice	1 large egg
¾ pint water	½ oz. powdered gelatine
2 oz. sugar	2 extra tablespoons water

1 Put the lemon juice, water, sugar and egg yolk into a saucepan and heat well for about 5 minutes until very slightly thickened.
2 Remove from heat and cool slightly.
3 Soften the powdered gelatine in the 2 tablespoons cold water.
4 Pour on the lemon mixture.
5 When this is quite cold fold in the stiffly beaten egg white.
6 Pour into a rinsed mould to set.

Jelly custard mould

cooking time few minutes

you will need:

1 fruit jelly or crystals
¼ pint water
1 pint custard sauce (made with egg or custard powder)
little sugar

1 Dissolve the jelly in the water.
2 When quite dissolved add to custard sauce, with extra sugar if desired.
3 Pour into mould to set.

Lemon jelly

cooking time 5 minutes

you will need:

3 lemons
¾ pint water
2 level dessertspoons powdered gelatine
sugar to taste

1 Grate the yellow 'zest' from the lemons being careful not to use any white pith which will make the jelly bitter.
2 Put the lemon rind and water into a saucepan and simmer gently for a good 5 minutes.
3 Strain through muslin.
4 Soften the gelatine in the juice from the lemons.
5 Pour on to the boiling lemon liquid.
6 Measure the liquid and if necessary add extra water to make 1 pint.
7 Add sugar to taste and pour into a mould or individual glasses.

Lemon milk jelly

cooking time 5 minutes

you will need:

1 large lemon
¼ pint water
2 level dessertspoons powdered gelatine
sugar to taste
¾ pint milk

1 Grate the yellow 'zest' from the lemon being careful not to use any white pith which will make the jelly bitter.
2 Put the lemon rind with the water into a saucepan and simmer gently for a good 5 minutes.
3 Strain through muslin and add the lemon juice.
4 Measure and if necessary make up to ¼ pint with water.
5 Reheat with the gelatine stirring until dissolved.
6 Add sugar to taste and allow to cool slightly.
7 Whisk in the cold milk and pour into a large mould or individual moulds.

Orange milk jelly

As above using 1 large orange, and just under ¼ pint water.

Lemon snowmist pudding

no cooking

you will need:

½ oz. powdered gelatine
⅛ pint cold water
½ pint boiling water
4–6 oz. sugar
⅛ pint lemon juice
3 egg whites
rind 2 lemons

1 Soften the gelatine in the cold water and dissolve it in the boiling water.
2 Add the sugar and juice and rind of 1 lemon.
3 Set the mixture aside in a cool place to cool.
4 When the mixture is thick enough to hold the mark of a spoon or when it is the consistency of unbeaten egg white, whip it with a wire whisk or wire spoon to incorporate air and bubbles and make it froth up.
5 Beat egg whites until stiff.
6 Beat into gelatine mixture with the wire whisk and continue beating until the mixture is about stiff enough to hold in peaks.
7 Turn into a mould previously rinsed with cold water and chill.
8 Unmould on to a plate and sprinkle with rest of grated lemon rind.
9 Serve with Custard sauce (see page 84).

Orange snowmist pudding

Use recipe above but use orange juice and rind instead of lemons.

Macaroni orange mould

cooking time 10 minutes

you will need:

2 oz. macaroni
water
1 orange jelly
1 small can mandarin oranges
whipped cream or ice cream

1. Cook macaroni in boiling water until tender.
2. Rinse under cold tap and drain well.
3. Dissolve jelly in hot water and make up to 1 pint using syrup from oranges.
4. Add macaroni to slightly cooled jelly and allow to set.
5. Serve with orange segments and whipped or ice cream.

Melon and ginger ring

cooking time 5 minutes

you will need:

1 pint fresh or canned pineapple juice
4 oz. semolina
4 oz. castor sugar
½ oz. gelatine
1 tablespoon cold water
2 egg yolks
4 tablespoons single cream
4 egg whites
small melon
crystallised ginger

1. Heat pineapple juice in a saucepan and sprinkle the semolina and sugar into the liquid.
2. Bring to the boil and cook gently for 3 minutes, stirring constantly.
3. Soften the gelatine in the cold water and add to the liquid.
4. Heat for a further minute.
5. Allow to cool slightly and add egg yolks and cream, mixing thoroughly.
6. Fold in the stiffly beaten egg whites and pour into an 8-inch plain ring mould, previously rinsed in cold water.
7. Leave to set.
8. Turn out when firm and decorate with pieces of crystallised ginger and top with diced melon.

Melon mint jelly

cooking time 5 minutes

you will need:

1 small melon
¾ pint water
2 oz. sugar
1 – 2 tablespoons chopped mint
1 oz. powdered gelatine
1 pint ginger ale
2 tablespoons lemon juice
green colouring

To decorate:
melon
mint

1. Cut melon into balls or cubes, saving a few for decoration.
2. Boil together the water and sugar for 5 minutes.
3. Pour over the mint and leave until cold, then strain.
4. Add the gelatine dissolved in a little cold water, the ginger ale, lemon juice and colouring.
5. Add the melon balls or cubes.
6. Pour into a wet mould and leave to set.
7. Turn out and decorate with melon and mint sprigs.

Pineapple crème

cooking time few minutes only

you will need:

1 can pineapple
grated rind and juice 1 lemon
½ oz. powdered gelatine
½ pint cream
2 eggs
little sugar

1. Chop most of the pineapple, but save a little for decoration.
2. Warm the pineapple juice and lemon juice and if necessary add enough water to give ½-pint.
3. Dissolve gelatine in this.
4. Beat the egg yolks with 1 or 2 tablespoons sugar.
5. Add the gelatine mixture, lemon rind and chopped pineapple.
6. Allow to set lightly, then fold in most of the lightly whipped cream and stiffly beaten egg whites.
7. When set, decorate with the last of the cream and pineapple.

Pineapple creole

cooking time 35 minutes

you will need:

½ pint milk	*For sauce:*
1 oz. Carolina rice	4–8 oz. pineapple jam
½ oz. gelatine	2 oz. sugar
1 oz. sugar	⅛ pint pineapple juice
⅛ pint cream	*To decorate:*
1 egg white	slices pineapple
	angelica
	cherries

1 Boil milk and add rice.
2 Stir until re-boiled, cover with lid and simmer until rice is cooked, for approximately 30 minutes.
3 Stir in sugar and gelatine, soaked in 2 tablespoons cold water.
4 Place into bowl of cold water and stir until cold.
5 Whip cream and egg white separately.
6 When rice cream mixture is on point of setting, fold in egg white and cream.
7 Place mixture into mould to set.
8 When chilled, unmould and decorate with pineapple, angelica and cherries.
9 Leave in cold place until ready to serve and serve with the sauce.
10 To make the sauce, heat all ingredients together and allow to cool.

Pineapple delight

no cooking

you will need:

3 large eggs	*To decorate:*
2 oz. sugar	whipped cream
½ pint hot milk	glacé cherries
1 small can pineapple slices	angelica strips
½ oz. gelatine	

1 Beat egg yolks and sugar in a basin over hot water until creamy, and add hot milk.
2 Strain juice from can of pineapple and make up to ¼ pint with water and heat.
3 Dissolve gelatine in the ¼ pint juice.
4 Chop pineapple very finely, saving about half to decorate.
5 Add pineapple and gelatine to the egg and milk mixture and leave to cool.
6 Fold in stiffly beaten egg whites.
7 Pour into a mould and turn out when firm.
8 Decorate with remaining pineapple, whipped cream, glace cheries and strips of angelica.

Raspberry cream mould

no cooking

you will need:

½ raspberry jelly	½ pint cream
¼ pint hot water	8 oz. raspberries

1 Dissolve the jelly in the water and leave to cool.
2 When beginning to set whisk up until frothy.
3 Add half the cream and whisk again until well mixed.
4 Stir in the raspberries, leaving a few for decoration.
5 Pour into an 8-inch sandwich tin and leave to set.
6 Turn out and cover with remaining cream.
7 Decorate with remaining raspberries.

Variations:

Strawberry

Use ½ strawberry jelly and 8 oz. strawberries instead of raspberries.

Redcurrant

Simmer a good 8 oz. redcurrants in a little water until soft, and use in place of raspberries above.

Red and blackcurrant ring

cooking time 20 - 25 minutes

you will need:

8 oz. redcurrants	2–3 oz. sugar
8 oz. blackcurrants	1 pint milk
little water	½ pint cream or whipped evaporated milk
sugar to taste	½ oz. powdered gelatine
3 eggs	

1 Simmer fruit in a little water, with sugar to taste, until tender.
2 Strain, saving the juice.
3 Put egg yolks, sugar and milk into the top of a double saucepan or basin over hot water and cook gently until thickened.
4 Dissolve gelatine in ¼ pint hot fruit juice and allow to cool.
5 When cold whisk into the egg mixture and allow mixture to stiffen slightly.
6 Fold in stiffly beaten egg whites and pour into ring or mould to set.
7 Turn out when set and fill centre or top with very cold fruit.

Redcurrant whip

cooking time 15 minutes

you will need:

1 lb. redcurrants
¼ pint water
1 large lemon
sugar to taste
2 teaspoons powdered gelatine
3 egg whites

1 Put redcurrants into a saucepan with half the water, juice from the lemon and rind and sugar to taste.
2 Cook until a smooth pulp and sieve if wished.
3 Dissolve the gelatine in the remaining very hot water.
4 Stir into the fruit mixture until dissolved.
5 Allow to cool and begin to stiffen.
6 Fold in stiffly beaten egg whites and pile into glasses.

Gooseberry

Use 1 lb. gooseberries instead of redcurrants.

Plum

Use 1 lb. plums instead of redcurrants.

Rhubarb

Use 1 lb. rhubarb instead of redcurrants.

Rhubarb delights

cooking time 10 - 15 minutes

you will need:

½ lb. forced rhubarb
good ¾ pint water
little sugar
1 lemon jelly
¼ pint cream or evaporated milk

To decorate:
blanched almonds

1 Cook the rhubarb in ¼ pint water and a little sugar until very soft.
2 Mash or rub through a sieve.
3 Dissolve the jelly in just over ½ pint water.
4 Add the rhubarb puree.
5 When cold fold in the lightly beaten evaporated milk or cream (saving just a little for decoration).
6 Put into glasses and decorate with cream and nuts.

Note:
A strawberry or raspberry jelly can be used.

Uncooked Pavlova

no cooking

you will need:

¼ pint unsweetened evaporated milk
1 level tablespoon gelatine
¼ pint cold water
3 egg whites
4 oz. sugar
½ teaspoon vanilla essence

To decorate:
fruit
whipped cream

1 Put milk into top of double saucepan and heat.
2 Soak gelatine in the cold water for 10 minutes.
3 Pour onto boiling milk and stir until dissolved.
4 Add egg whites and sugar and vanilla essence and whisk until thick and white.
5 Pour into a greased ring tin and allow to set.
6 Unmould and serve with fruit and cream.

Fruit Desserts

Serving fruit as a dessert

Many people thoroughly enjoy fresh fruit as a dessert.

Apples

Serve as they are with a fruit knife and fork for peeling and coring.

Apricots

Although they have such a delicious flavour when cooked, they are really rather disappointing when fresh. If ripe, however, they make a pleasant addition to fruit salads.

Bananas
If served raw, provide a fruit knife and fork or slice and serve with cream, ice-cream or any custard sauce. Sprinkle the bananas with lemon juice if they are exposed to the air for any length of time not only to add flavour, but to prevent them discolouring.

Blueberries
These are better cooked in tarts although they can be added to fresh fruit jellies or served with sugar and cream.

Blackcurrants
Because they have such a strong flavour many people do not like them uncooked, but they are very rich in vitamin C and so are excellent for children if added raw to jellies (make sure the jelly is no longer hot when you put in the blackcurrants). When cooking, simmer for quite a time to make certain the skins are really soft.

Cherries
If ripe they are delicious served raw. On a formal occasion small finger bowls should be provided.

Figs
When ripe they are served as a dessert fruit or they can be stewed in sweetened syrup.

Grapes
These can be added raw to fruit salad, jellies, or served as a dessert. On formal occasions small finger bowls should be provided.

Grapefruit
Although more popular as an hors-d'oeuvre, grapefruit makes a very refreshing sweet. Sprinkle with sugar and a little sherry or top with ice-cream. To make it easy to eat, separate the segments as usual.

Greengages
If very ripe they can be quartered and added to fruit salads or served as a dessert. Small finger bowls should be provided.

Loganberries
These can be served uncooked like raspberries with sugar and cream but since they have a rather strong flavour, many people prefer them simmered in a little sugar and water.

Lychees
Remove the hard shell and eat the soft white centre.

Melon
Although melon is usually served as an hors-d'oeuvre, it does make a very delicious sweet either by itself or mixed with other fruit in a fruit salad. Slices of melon can be topped with sugar and cream.

Nectarines
Serve with a fruit knife and fork and a finger bowl.

Oranges
Serve with a fruit knife and fork and a finger bowl. When adding to fruit salads cut the fruit so you leave behind the pith and skin.

Passion fruit
Cut into half with a fruit knife and fork and eat the soft pulp with a teaspoon.

Pears
Serve with a fruit knife and finger bowls.

Peaches
Serve with a fruit knife and fork and a finger bowl.

Pineapple
Cut away the thick skin. Cut into slices, removing the centre rather tough core. Serve with sugar and cream or sprinkle with a little kirsch.

Plums
If ripe they can be quartered and added to fruit salads or served as a dessert. Small finger bowls should be provided.

Raspberries
Serve with sugar and cream or added raw to jellies with ice-cream.

Redcurrants
When ripe they can be served raw, although many people find them a little tart for this.

Strawberries
Serve with sugar and cream or add raw to jellies with ice-cream, etc.

Tangerines
Serve with a fruit knife and fork and a finger bowl. When adding to fruit salads cut the fruit so you leave behind the pith and skin.

Ugli
This is a cross between a grapefruit and an orange and can be used as either fruit.

White currants
A rarely seen dessert fruit tasting very similar to redcurrants.

To make a fruit salad

The easiest way to make a fruit salad is to open a can of fruit, i.e. choose a fruit such as peaches or pineapple. All you need to do then is to slice bananas, apples and pears into this. Pears and apples should be peeled and sliced and covered well with the syrup so they do not discolour. Grapes should be halved and pipped. Some people like to remove the skins but in many ways it is a pity because this gives colour. Fresh cherries should be stoned (see page 32). Oranges should be peeled, with a knife, sufficiently thickly so that you cut away the white pith. You then cut the segments of orange between the skin so that you leave this behind. Do this over a basin so no juice is lost.
If the fruit salad is standing for any length of time, apples should be added last so they retain their crispness.
For special occasions you can add a little kirsch or sherry to the syrup.
If you do not wish to open a can of fruit, then make a syrup by boiling 2 - 4 oz. of sugar to approximately ½ pint water and flavour this with a little orange or lemon juice. On the other hand, if you do not wish a sweetened syrup, put all the prepared fruit into a bowl and moisten with fresh orange juice.

Hints on stewing fruit

1. Do not use too much water. Raspberries, currants, rhubarb, etc., need practically no water. Other fruits should be half covered.
2. Always boil sugar and water together first and then drop in the fruit and simmer gently. This ensures that the fruit keeps a good shape.
3. Always cook fruit slowly, otherwise it will break before being softened through to the middle.
4. If preferred fruit can be cooked in the oven, allowing 30 - 50 minutes (depending on the fruit) in a very moderate oven (350°F.—Gas Mark 3).
5. Cover dish with a lid or foil.

To cook dried fruit

When fresh fruit is not available dried fruits are a good standby in the larder.

1. Wash the fruit thoroughly.
2. Soak overnight in cold water to cover.
3. Cook gently for 1½ - 2 hours, adding sugar to taste, in the same water in which the fruit was soaked.
4. Or allow approximately 12 minutes in a pressure cooker at 15 lb. pressure.
5. A little lemon juice can be added to apples or apricots.
6. Figs and prunes have a very good flavour if cooked in weak tea or coffee rather than water.

To poach fruit

This is the ideal way to cook the firmer types of fruit in order to keep their shape.
Make a syrup of sugar and water, allowing 2 - 8 oz. sugar to each pint of water—the latter amount of sugar will produce a very sweet syrup. When boiling put in the fruit and cook very gently. If the fruit is very ripe it may be necessary to place it in the syrup when boiling.

To cook fruit in a pressure cooker

Although the soft fruits, such as raspberries or redcurrants, do not require the rapid cooking of a pressure cooker, there are many others where cooking time can be saved with improved results. In particular, dried fruits and hard cooking pears, which are normally stewed for a very long period, can now be cooked in a pressure saucepan within minutes. Time is saved and the flavour of pressure cooked fruit is always excellent because such small quantities of liquid are used in cooking that the juice is never watery, but full of fruit flavour. Allow ¼ pint water to 1 lb. fruit. NEVER HAVE THE PRESSURE COOKER MORE THAN HALF FULL WHEN COOKING FRUIT PULP AND ALLOW PRESSURE TO DROP GRADUALLY.

To pressure cook dried fruit

1 Wash the fruit thoroughly.
2 Soak overnight in water.
3 Put into the cooker without rack, adding sugar to taste and lemon juice if wished.
4 Fix the lid and bring to 15 lb. pressure.
5 Lower the heat and cook for period stipulated below, reducing pressure at once.

Fruit	Amount of water	Cooking time
1 lb. apple rings	¼ pint	3 minutes
1 lb. apricots	½ pint	10 minutes
1 lb. figs	½ pint	12 - 15 minutes
1 lb. fruit salad	as individual fruits	
1 lb. peaches	½ pint	10 minutes
1 lb. prunes	⅓ pint	6 minutes

Apples

pressure cooking time 2 minutes

you will need:

1 lb. cooking apples
sugar to taste
¼ pint water
few drops lemon juice (if desired)

1 Peel, core and slice apples.
2 Put on to the rack, add sugar, water and lemon juice.
3 Fix lid and bring to 5 lb. pressure.
4 Lower the heat and cook for 1 minute or so depending on the type of apple.
5 Reduce pressure instantly.
6 If desired, after removing the fruit, the syrup can be boiled for a few minutes to thicken.

Gooseberries

pressure cooking time 2 minutes

you will need:

1 lb. gooseberries
¼ pint water
sugar to taste

1 Top and tail gooseberries.
2 Put into the cooker with the water and sugar.
3 Fix lid and bring to 5 lb. pressure.
4 Lower the heat and cook for 2 minutes.
5 Reduce pressure at once.

Plums

pressure cooking time 3 minutes

Cook as for gooseberries (see above).

Apple purée

pressure cooking time 3 minutes

you will need:

2 lb. cooking apples
sugar to taste
¼ pint water
little lemon juice (if desired)

1 Peel, core and slice the apples.
2 Put apples, sugar, water and lemon juice into the pressure cooker.
3 Do not use the rack.
4 Fix the lid and bring to 5 lb. pressure.
5 Lower the heat and cook for 3 minutes.
6 Let cooker stand 1 or 2 minutes before putting under cold water.

Gooseberry purée

pressure cooking time 4 minutes

Cook as for gooseberries (see above) but allow 4 minutes cooking time. The gooseberries will then be a smooth pulp. Let cooker stand for a minute or so before putting under the cold tap to reduce pressure.

Plum purée

pressure cooking time 4 minutes

Halve plums and cook as for Gooseberry purée (see above).

Rhubarb purée

pressure cooking time 4 minutes

Method as for Gooseberry purée (see above).

Fruit purée

cooking time until fruit is soft

you will need:

fruit
sugar
water—with soft fruit use only 1 – 2 tablespoons water to 1 lb. fruit. With hard fruit approximately ¼ pint water to 1 lb. fruit for soft purée, ⅛ pint water for firm purée

1. Simmer prepared fruit in the water until softening slightly.
2. Add sugar to taste.
3. Continue cooking until very smooth.
4. Sieve or beat.

Apple foule

cooking time 15 - 20 minutes as required for fruit

you will need:

½ pint thick apple purée
sugar to taste
½ pint thick custard

1. Sweeten apple purée to taste.
2. Whisk sweetened fruit purée with the custard, making sure that both fruit and custard are cool.
3. Pour into serving dish and serve topped with cream or ice cream.

Variations:

Blackberry and apple

Use ¼ pint thick apple purée and ¼ pint thick blackberry purée.

Blackcurrant

Use ½ pint thick blackcurrant purée and sieve well to remove seeds.

Gooseberry

Use ½ pint thick sieved gooseberry purée.

Plum

Use ½ pint thick plum purée.

Rhubarb

Use ½ pint thick rhubarb purée.

Rich fruit fools or foules

Follow the recipe for Apple fool or foule (see above) but instead of sweetened custard use ½ pint of thick lightly whipped cream, or use half custard and half whipped cream. Do not overwhip cream as it becomes difficult to incorporate.

Spiced fruit fools or foules

To many people an ordinary fruit fool is a little insipid. You can give extra flavour to this by adding one or two cloves when cooking apples, a pinch of cinnamon with plums, a pinch of nutmeg with gooseberries.

Apricot cream with fresh fruit

cooking time 20 - 25 minutes

you will need:

8 oz. apricots
⅛ pint water
2 – 3 oz. sugar
3 egg yolks
2 level tablespoons cornflour
1 pint milk
little cream if wished

1. Simmer the apricots with water and sugar until very soft and smooth.
2. Sieve or mash.
3. Blend cornflour with a little cold milk.
4. Bring rest of the milk to the boil.
5. Pour over the cornflour and return to pan to thicken, stirring well.
6. Add sweetened apricot purée whisked with egg yolks.
7. Continue cooking gently until thick, but do not boil as mixture will curdle.
8. Stir in 2 - 3 tablespoons cream if wished, adding extra sugar to taste if required.
9. Put into a rinsed mould.
10. When set turn out and top with halved apricots.

Gooseberry cream

Use the method and ingredients as for Apricot cream, using gooseberries instead of apricots and topping with grated chocolate.

Loganberry cream

Use the method and ingredients as for Apricot cream, using loganberries instead of apricots and topping with red or blackcurrants.

Blackcurrant crème

cooking time 50 minutes

you will need:

approximately 1 lb. blackcurrants
¼ pint water
2 – 3 tablespoons golden syrup
1 tablespoon cornflour

1 Simmer the blackcurrants with the water and golden syrup until soft.
2 Sieve well and measure, making up to 1 pint with water if necessary.
3 Blend with the cornflour and simmer until smooth.
4 Serve in individual glasses.

Variations:

Loganberry

Use 1 lb. loganberries in place of blackcurrants.

Raspberry

Use 1 lb. raspberries instead of blackcurrants.

Red and blackcurrant

Use 8 oz. redcurrants and 8 oz. blackcurrants.

Baked apples

cooking time 1 hour

you will need:

4 large cooking apples
little butter
1 tablespoon golden syrup
little water

1 Wipe apples thoroughly and slit the skin round the centre. Do not cut too deeply.
2 Put a tiny knob of butter on top of each apple.
3 Put golden syrup and a little water on a baking dish and put into the oven for a few minutes to melt the syrup.
4 Place the apples in the dish and bake in the centre of a moderately hot oven (375°F.—Gas Mark 4 - 5) for approximately 1 hour.
5 Baste once or twice during cooking with the syrup liquid.

Stuffed apples

cooking time 1 hour

you will need:

4 cooking apples
4 oz. mincemeat
little butter

1 Core apples and place on a baking tray.
2 Fill the centres with mincemeat and top with a knob of butter.
3 Bake for approximately 1 hour in a moderate oven (375°F.—Gas Mark 4).

Variations:

Golden syrup and breadcrumbs

Fill with a few breadcrumbs and golden syrup, top with a knob of butter.

Dried fruit and spice

Fill with a little mixed dried fruit, mixed spice, brown sugar and top with a knob of butter.

Redcurrant and blackcurrant jelly

Fill with redcurrant or blackcurrant jelly.

Apricot jam

Fill with apricot jam and serve with hot apricot jam.

Bananas in raisin sauce

cooking time 45 minutes

you will need:

3 oz. seedless raisins
½ pint water
2 dessertspoons honey
juice 1 large lemon
pinch salt
1 level dessertspoon cornflour
little cold water
4 bananas
½ oz. butter

1 Simmer the raisins in nearly all the water for 10 minutes.
2 Strain liquid from raisins into pan.
3 Stir in the honey, lemon juice and salt
4 Mix cornflour with a little cold water and add to the mixture.
5 Cook together for 10 minutes.
6 Peel bananas and cut in half lengthwise.
7 Melt butter in glass oven-proof dish and arrange bananas in it.
8 Sprinkle the raisins on top and pour the hot sauce over all.
9 Bake in a very moderate oven (350°F.—Gas Mark 3) for 25 minutes.

Caramel bananas

cooking time 25 minutes

you will need:

8 bananas
2 oz. butter
6 oz. brown sugar

1 Peel and cut bananas into halves and place in a baking dish.
2 Dot with knobs of butter and sprinkle with brown sugar.
3 Bake for approximately 25 minutes in the centre of a moderate oven (375°F.—Gas Mark 4).
4 Serve at once with cream or ice cream.

Caramelled oranges

cooking time 35 minutes

you will need:

2 tablespoons water
2 oz. butter
3 – 4 small oranges
6 oz. brown sugar
cream or ice cream

1 Put the water, butter and sugar into a dish in the oven to get hot.
2 Meanwhile, peel the oranges and cut into halves.
3 Put the orange halves into the hot butter and sugar mixture and turn round in this so they become coated with the golden brown sauce.
4 Return to a moderate oven (375°F.—Gas Mark 4) for a further 25 minutes until the oranges are very hot and have absorbed the sauce.
5 Serve with cream or ice cream.

Bird's nest pudding

cooking time 1 hour

you will need:

1 pint milk
2 – 3 oz. rice or sago
1 tablespoon sugar
1 oz. margarine or butter
4 small cooking apples
4 dessertspoons blackberry jelly

1 Bring the milk to the boil.
2 Add the rice or sago and cook gently for a good 5 - 10 minutes until beginning to thicken.
3 Add the sugar and margarine.
4 Peel the apples and remove the core.
5 Fill the centres with the blackberry jelly, put into dish.
6 Pour over the rice mixture and bake in the centre of a moderate oven (375°F.—Gas Mark 4) for 45 - 50 minutes until the apples are quite soft.

Fruit flambé

cooking time 3 minutes

you will need:

2 oz. butter
4 large fresh or 8 halves of canned peaches, or pears, or rings of pine-apple
little rum or brandy
2 oz. brown sugar

1 Heat the butter and add the fruit sprinkled with rum or brandy.
2 Cook steadily for 3 minutes, adding the sugar.
3 Serve when the sugar has melted and given a brown sauce.

Fruit snows

cooking time will be dependant on the type of fruit

you will need:

1 lb. cooked sweetened fruit
2 – 4 egg whites

1 If using cooking fruit such as rhubarb, apples, plums, etc., this should be simmered with the minimum of water and sugar to taste.
2 If using dessert fruit such as raspberries, ripe blackcurrants, strawberries, these should just be mashed and sweetened.
3 Beat the egg whites very stiffly, then fold into the fruit purée.

Grapes in grapefruit

no cooking

you will need:

2 grapefruit
4 oz. sweet grapes, halved and pipped
¼ pint whipped cream
sugar if desired

1 Remove fruit from the grapefruit, sweeten if wished.
2 Dice it and mix with the grapes.
3 Pile into half grapefruit cases and top with the whipped cream.

Heavenly ambrosia

no cooking

you will need:

oranges
fresh or desiccated coconut
sugar
cream

1. Arrange alternate layers of peeled and sliced oranges with coconut and sugar.
2. Chill for at least 2 hours.
3. Serve with whipped cream.

Cold Moulds and Easy Sweets

In this chapter are moulds made with cornflour and easy sweets, and junkets. They are economical enough for family meals and yet can be made interesting for special occasions. Do not exceed the amounts of cornflour, custard powder, etc. since a solid sweet is not nearly so interesting and appetising.

Cornflour moulds

An ordinary cornflour mould or blancmange is generally made with flavoured cornflour and the instructions are given quite clearly on the packet i.e. to each packet you use 1 pint of milk and 1 - 2 tablespoons sugar. Care must be taken to blend the cornflour very thoroughly with a little cold milk for this is the secret of keeping it smooth. Bring the rest of the milk to the boil, pour over the blended cornflour, return to the saucepan with the sugar and stir very thoroughly until thick.

Sometimes people underestimate the cooking time and this gives a rather powdery taste to the mould. Cook well for several minutes. Pour into a mould rinsed with cold water to facilitate turning out and then cover with a plate, foil or damped greaseproof paper to prevent a skin from forming. Allow to set and serve with cream, ice-cream or jam sauce.

If using plain cornflour from a large packet, allow 1¼ oz. i.e. 5 level dessertspoons to one pint milk with little vanilla or other flavouring. A richer mould can be made by using slightly under the pint of milk and when thickened whisking in a little cream or evaporated milk. A small knob of butter added to the mixture as it thickens gives a richer taste.

To bake:

Add a beaten egg, pour into a pie dish and bake in a very moderate oven for approximately 25 minutes.

Apple and blackberry mould

(illustrated on cover)

cooking time 30 minutes

you will need:

½ pint cream
½ pint thick sweetened apple purée
½ oz. gelatine
⅛ pint hot water
1 egg white
1 lb. hulled blackberries
2 – 3 tablespoons water
sugar to taste
1 teaspoon cornflour
1 egg yolk
extra water and sugar
3 apples

1. Whip cream and blend with apple purée.
2. Dissolve gelatine in the hot water, add to apple and cream mixture, stir well, leave to become partially set.
3. Then add stiffly beaten egg white.
4. Meanwhile simmer blackberries in the water.
5. Sweeten with sugar to taste.
6. Mix cornflour to a paste with 1 tablespoon cold water. Add hot blackberry liquor, stir well and return all to the pan. Cook until thickened.
7. Add a little of this hot juice to the egg yolk and mix well.
8. Return to the pan and cook over a low heat until thick, without allowing mixture to boil. Cool.
9. Line mould with apple mixture making hollow in the centre for blackberries.
10. Leave until set, then put in blackberry mixture and chill in refrigerator.
11. Make a syrup of sugar and water—put in apple halves and cook gently until soft but unbroken.
12. Just before serving, turn out mould and decorate with poached apple halves filled with remaining blackberries.

Fruit blancmange

cooking time 10 minutes

you will need:

1¼ oz. cornflour	¾ pint milk
sugar to taste	¼ pint thick fruit purée

1. Blend the cornflour with sugar to taste and a little of the cold milk.
2. Bring the rest of the milk to the boil and pour over the blended cornflour.
3. Return to the saucepan to thicken.
4. Remove pan from the heat and whisk in the fruit purée.

Almond blancmange

Use recipe above but omit the fruit purée and use 1 pint milk adding a little almond essence and a few chopped blanched almonds.

Coffee blancmange

Use recipe above and add 1 or 2 teaspoons instant coffee to the milk, using 1 pint, and add a knob of butter as the mould thickens to give extra shine.

Chocolate blancmange

Use recipe above using 1 pint milk and slightly less cornflour. Add 1 level tablespoon cocoa and a few drops vanilla essence. Add a knob of butter as the mould thickens to give extra shine.

Vanilla blancmange

Use recipe above, but use 1 pint milk and omit fruit purée. Add a few drops vanilla essence if liked.

Butterscotch brittle cream (1)

cooking time 10 minutes

you will need:

2 oz. butter	1 oz. sugar
2 oz. brown sugar	3 oz. nut brittle
1 pint milk	little cream
1 packet caramel flavour cornflour or 1 oz. cornflour	

1. Put the butter and brown sugar into a saucepan and heat together until a golden brown sauce.
2. Put in most of the milk and bring to boiling point.
3. Stir in the cornflour blended with the rest of the milk.
4. Return to the pan and thicken, adding the sugar, half the crushed nut brittle and cream, saving a little cream for decoration.
5. Put into 4 sundae glasses and decorate with more cream and nut brittle when cold.

Butterscotch brittle cream (2)

cooking time 15 minutes

you will need:

2 oz. quick cooking macaroni	½ pint milk
2 oz. butter	½ teaspoon vanilla essence
2 oz. soft brown sugar	1 small carton double cream
1 heaped dessert–spoon cornflour	3 oz. chopped nut brittle

1. Cook macaroni as directed and drain.
2. Melt butter in saucepan, add sugar and allow to melt slightly. Add macaroni.
3. Blend cornflour with a little of the measured milk.
4. Heat remainder of the milk.
5. Pour a little of the heated milk over blended cornflour and return to saucepan.
6. Bring to the boil, stirring continuously, and boil for 1 minute.
7. Remove from heat and stir in macaroni, vanilla essence and cream.
8. When nearly cold add nut brittle, saving a little for decoration.
9. Serve in individual dishes topped with remaining nut brittle.

Custard creams

cooking time 25 minutes

you will need:

1 pint milk	1½ dessertspoons powdered gelatine with 2 eggs (little more with 1 egg)
1 or 2 eggs or egg yolks	⅛ pint water
1 good dessertspoon sugar	⅛ pint evaporated milk or cream
½ teaspoon vanilla essence or vanilla pod	

1. Pour hot milk on to beaten eggs, adding sugar and vanilla essence or vanilla pod.

2 Cook gently in double saucepan until thickened.
3 Dissolve gelatine in water.
4 Add custard mixture—having removed vanilla pod.
5 When cool, stir in evaporated milk or cream.
6 Pour into rinsed moulds to set.

Orange creams

cooking time 10 minutes

you will need:

2 oranges
1 dessertspoon custard powder or cornflour
sugar to taste
few glacé cherries
little cream or evaporated milk

1 Cut oranges into halves lengthways.
2 Squeeze out juice carefully, then remove all remaining skin and pith. Take care not to damage orange skins.
3 Blend custard powder with orange juice.
4 Put into a saucepan and cook gently until mixture thickens and goes clear.
5 Take off heat and gradually add enough evaporated milk to make mixture like thick cream.
6 Stir in a little sugar, but do not use too much so that you retain the fresh flavour of orange.
7 Add cherries to mixture, then spoon it into 4 orange cases.
8 When quite firm sandwich 2 halves of each orange together. Put a rubber band round them to carry on a picnic.

Caramel macaroni

cooking time 15 minutes

you will need:

2 oz. quick cooking macaroni
3 good tablespoons golden syrup
1 pint milk
2 tablespoons cornflour

To decorate:
whipped cream
toasted almonds

1 Cook macaroni as directed on packet and drain.
2 Put syrup into strong saucepan and boil without stirring until a rich golden brown colour.
3 Blend cornflour with a little of the measured milk.
4 Add remaining milk to caramel.
5 Allow caramel to dissolve.
6 Add a little of the hot caramel milk to the blended cornflour.
7 Return to saucepan and boil for 1 minute.
8 Add macaroni.
9 When cold top with whipped cream and toasted almonds.

Orange fluff

cooking time 15 minutes

you will need:

2 oranges
$\frac{1}{2}$–$\frac{3}{4}$ pint milk
3 oz. quick cooking macaroni
2 eggs

To decorate:
orange jelly slices
little whipped cream

1 Finely grate the rind of oranges and place in saucepan.
2 Squeeze out juice and make up to 1 pint with milk.
3 Pour this onto orange rind and bring to the boil.
4 Sprinkle in macaroni and simmer for 7 minutes, stirring occasionally.
5 Remove from heat and cool slightly.
6 Separate whites from yolks of eggs.
7 Lightly beat yolks and stir into mixture.
8 Return to heat and cook without boiling for about 3 minutes.
9 Whisk egg whites stiffly and fold into mixture.
10 Pile into dishes and leave until quite cold.
11 Decorate with cream and orange jelly slices.

Junket

cooking time few minutes

you will need:

1 pint milk
sugar to taste
1 teaspoon rennet

1 Heat milk and sugar to blood heat only.
2 Stir in rennet and pour into a dish or glasses.

Coffee

Blend 1 or 2 teaspoons instant coffee with the milk and sugar. Top the junket with cream and chopped nuts.

Caramel junket

cooking time few minutes

you will need:

3 tablespoons sugar
3 tablespoons water
1 pint milk
1 teaspoon sugar
1 teaspoon rennet

1 Heat the 3 tablespoons sugar with the water until golden brown.
2 Allow to cool.
3 Stir in the milk and teaspoon sugar and heat together until the caramel has been absorbed with the milk.
4 Allow to cool to blood heat and stir in rennet.

St. Clement's cloud

cooking time 10 minutes

you will need:

¼ pint water
4 oz. sugar
1 oz. cornflour
¼ pint orange juice canned or fresh
1 large lemon
1 orange
2 eggs

To decorate:
small pieces orange

1 Boil the water and sugar together for 4 minutes.
2 Mix the cornflour smoothly with juice from the orange and lemon and the orange juice.
3 Add to the syrup and boil for 3 minutes.
4 Add egg yolks and simmer gently without boiling for a few minutes.
5 Stir in the grated lemon and orange rind.
6 Beat egg whites stiffly and fold lightly into the cooked mixture.
7 Pile into sundae glasses and serve cold, decorated with sections of orange.

Mousses

A mousse should be a very light fluffy sweet and in order to create this texture, it is important to measure the ingredients carefully. In some recipes egg whites are used and these should be folded into the mixture when it is half set in order to give an even texture.

Caramel mousse

cooking time 5 - 10 minutes

you will need:

4 oz. sugar
8 tablespoons water
¼ oz. or 1 dessert-spoon gelatine
6 egg whites

To decorate:
cream
nuts
angelica

1 Put the sugar with about 4 tablespoons water into a saucepan.
2 Stir until the sugar has dissolved, then boil steadily until brown.
3 Add the rest of the water and reheat until caramel has dissolved.
4 Stir the gelatine into the caramel, previously dissolved in a little water.
5 Allow the mixture to cool and just start to thicken, then whisk egg whites stiffly.
6 Fold into mixture.
7 Put into a mould and allow to set.
8 Turn out and decorate with whipped cream, nuts, angelica, etc.
9 Serve with Caramel sauce (see page 83).

Chocolate cream mousse

cooking time 5 - 8 minutes for thickening egg yolks

you will need:

2 eggs
2 tablespoons castor sugar
4 tablespoons grated chocolate
½ teaspoon vanilla essence
5 tablespoons cream or evaporated milk
¼ oz. gelatine
2 tablespoons water
1 dessertspoon brandy

To decorate:
little mock cream (see page 87)
little flaked chocolate

1 Separate the yolks from the whites of egg.
2 Put the yolks into a basin with the sugar, chocolate and vanilla essence.
3 Beat over hot water until thick and creamy.
4 Allow to cool.
5 Add the cream or evaporated milk.
6 Whip the whites stiffly.
7 Melt the gelatine in the water and stir it quickly into the chocolate mixture.
8 Fold in egg whites and brandy lightly.

9 Turn into individual glasses and leave in a cool place for 30 minutes before serving.
10 Decorate with mock cream and flaked chocolate.

Gooseberry mousse

cooking time 15 minutes

you will need:

- ¼–½ pint water
- 2–3 oz. sugar
- 1 lb. gooseberries
- 1 level dessertspoon powdered gelatine
- ¼ pint cream or evaporated milk
- 2 egg whites
- little cream to decorate

1 Heat most of the water and sugar, to make a syrup.
2 Poach the 'topped and tailed' gooseberries in syrup until tender.
3 Remove from ¼ of the fruit and rub rest through a sieve.
4 Reheat and add the gelatine softened in remaining water.
5 Stir until gelatine has dissolved.
6 Leave until just beginning to stiffen and fold in whole fruit, lightly whipped cream and stiffly beaten egg whites.
7 Pile into glasses and top with cream.

Variations:

Apricot

Use 1 lb. apricots in place of gooseberries.

Damson

Use 1 lb. damsons in place of gooseberries, stoning the fruit before poaching or removing stones when sieving.

Strawberry

Use 1 lb. strawberries in place of gooseberries, and poach in ¼ pint syrup, only, for about 4 minutes.

Orange mousse

cooking time 10 minutes

you will need:

- 2½ level dessertspoons cornflour
- 1 pint milk
- 1 dessertspoon powdered gelatine
- ⅛ pint orange juice
- 2–3 oz. sugar
- ⅛ pint whipped evaporated milk or cream (see page 87)
- 2 egg whites

1 Blend the cornflour with a little of the cold milk.
2 Bring the rest of the milk to the boil.
3 Pour over the cornflour and return to the pan to thicken.
4 Dissolve the gelatine in the hot orange juice.
5 Cool slightly and stir into the cornflour mixture with the sugar.
6 Cover the mixture with a plate as it cools to prevent a skin forming.
7 When cold, fold in milk or cream and stiffly beaten egg whites and allow to set.

Variation:

Lemon

Use ⅛ pint lemon juice in place of orange juice.

Quick chocolate cream mousse

cooking time 5-8 minutes

you will need:

- 4 oz. chocolate (preferably plain)
- 2 dessertspoons sugar
- 2 eggs
- 2 dessertspoons cream

1 Grate chocolate and put into a basin with the sugar and egg yolks over hot water.
2 Beat until smooth.
3 Cool slightly, then add cream.
4 When quite cold fold in stiffly beaten egg white.
5 Pour into glasses and serve with biscuits.

Soft fruit mousse

no cooking

you will need:

- 12 oz. soft fruit
- 2 oz. sugar
- ¾ pint thick cream
- 1 teaspoon vanilla essence

1 Rub fruit through sieve and combine with sugar mixing well.
2 Whip cream and lightly fold in the sweetened fruit pulp.
3 Add vanilla.
4 Put into freezing tray of refrigerator and freeze until quite firm.

Soufflés

Hot soufflé

cooking time 35 - 40 minutes

you will need:

$\frac{1}{2}$ oz. cornflour
$\frac{1}{2}$ pint milk
1 oz. butter
1 – 2 oz. sugar
1 teaspoon vanilla essence
3 eggs or 3 egg yolks and 4 egg whites

1 Blend the cornflour with the milk.
2 Put into a saucepan and add the butter.
3 Cook until a smooth sauce.
4 Add the sugar and vanilla essence and remove from the heat.
5 Add the lightly beaten egg yolks and the stiffly beaten egg whites.
6 Pour into greased soufflé dish and bake in the centre of a moderately hot oven (400°F.—Gas Mark 5) for approximately 25 - 30 minutes.

Variations:

Almond
Add almond essence in place of vanilla and 2 oz. blanched almonds.

Chocolate
Add 2 oz. melted chocolate and a little vanilla essence or $\frac{1}{2}$ oz. cocoa.

Coffee
Use strong coffee instead of milk.

Lemon
Add the grated rind of 2 lemons and lemon juice instead of milk.

Damson soufflé

cooking time 40 - 45 minutes

you will need:

1 lb. damsons
approximately $\frac{1}{2}$ pint water
4 oz. sugar
1 lemon
2 teaspoons cornflour
2 eggs

1 Put the fruit with about half the water into a pan and simmer until a soft purée.
2 Sieve, then add the sugar, finely grated lemon rind and lemon juice.
3 Blend cornflour with the remaining water and add to the damson mixture.
4 Bring slowly to the boil and cook until smooth and clear.
5 Remove from heat and allow to cool slightly.
6 Add the egg yolks and fold in the stiffly beaten egg whites.
7 Pour into greased soufflé dish and bake for approximately 25 minutes in the centre of a moderately hot oven (400°F.—Gas Mark 5).
8 Serve at once.

Variations:

Apricot
Use 1 lb. soaked dried apricots or fresh apricots in place of damsons.

Gooseberry
Use 1 lb. gooseberries in place of damsons.

Plum
Use 1 lb. plums instead of damsons.

Pineapple soufflé

cooking time 40 minutes

you will need:

1 large can pineapple pieces
8 oz. breadcrumbs
3 eggs
2 oz. butter or margarine
2 oz. sugar
little pineapple jam

1 Drain pineapple from the juice and chop finely.
2 Mix with the crumbs, egg yolks.
3 Cream butter or margarine and sugar and add to the pineapple mixture.
4 Stir well and fold in stiffly beaten egg whites.
5 Pour into a greased soufflé dish and bake for approximately 40 minutes in the centre of a moderate oven (375°F.—Gas Mark 4).
6 Heat the juice with little pineapple jam and serve as a sauce.

Variation:

Apricot
Use large can apricots—for a special occasion use half macaroon crumbs and half fine cake crumbs instead of breadcrumbs.

Pineapple soufflé pudding

cooking time 40 minutes

you will need:

2 oz. butter
2 oz. castor sugar
2 large eggs
2 oz. flour (with plain flour use ½ level teaspoon baking powder)
¼ pint pineapple juice from can pineapple
1 small can pineapple

1 Cream together butter and sugar.
2 Add egg yolks, flour and pineapple juice. The mixture will probably curdle but in this pudding it does not matter.
3 Fold in the stiffly beaten egg whites.
4 Pour into prepared soufflé dish and stand in another dish of cold water.
5 Bake for approximately 40 minutes in the centre of a very moderate oven (350°F.—Gas Mark 3).
6 Decorate with pineapple and serve hot.

Variations:

Apricot

Use juice from can of apricots in place of pineapple juice and decorate with apricot halves.

Lemon

Use juice of 2 good sized lemons and ⅜ pint milk instead of pineapple juice. Add the grated lemon rind with the milk.

Peach

Use juice from can of peaches in place of pineapple juice and decorate with sliced peaches.

Orange

As Lemon soufflé pudding, using oranges in place of lemons.

Quick prune soufflé

cooking time 20 minutes

you will need:

10 oz. cooked prunes
1–2 oz. sugar
2 egg whites
1–2 dessertspoons lemon juice

1 Sieve cooked prunes and add sugar.
2 Whisk egg whites to stiff peak and fold lightly into prune purée.
3 Add lemon juice to taste and pour into a greased soufflé dish.
4 Bake in a moderate oven (375°F.—Gas Mark 4) for 20 minutes, until set.

Cold soufflés

A cold soufflé is not unlike a mousse in that it is very light and fluffy. Take care that the purée mixture is fairly stiff before folding in the egg whites.
To prepare the soufflé dish to support the sweet, tie a band of greaseproof paper well above the top of the soufflé dish. Butter this lightly. The object of this is that when the soufflé is set, you can remove the band of paper with a warm knife and your cold soufflé, like a hot one, rises proudly above the top of the container.

Cold blackcurrant soufflé

no cooking

you will need:

¼ pint cream or evaporated milk
1½ teaspoons powdered gelatine
⅛ pint water
¼ pint thick blackcurrant purée
2 eggs
2 oz. sugar
few drops lemon juice
few drops vanilla essence

To decorate:
cream

1 Whip the cream or evaporated milk (see page 87).
2 Dissolve the gelatine in the water and add to the blackcurrant purée, and vanilla essence.
3 Whisk the cream into the blackcurrant mixture quickly and vigorously so that the mixture does not curdle.
4 Put the yolks of the eggs with the sugar and lemon juice into a basin over hot water and beat until thick and creamy.
5 Remove from heat and continue beating until cold.
6 Stir gently into the blackcurrant mixture and fold in the stiffly beaten egg whites.
7 Pour into soufflé dish and allow to set.
8 Decorate with cream.

Variations:

Apple

Use ¼ pint thick apple purée instead of blackcurrants.

Chestnut

Use ¼ pint chestnut purée instead of blackcurrants.

Raspberry

Use ¼ pint thick raspberry purée instead of blackcurrants.

Cold vanilla soufflé

cooking time 13 minutes

you will need:

3 eggs
3 oz. sugar
1 teaspoon vanilla essence
½ pint milk
1½ level dessertspoons powdered gelatine
3 tablespoons water
⅜ pint whipped cream or whipped evaporated milk (see page 87)

To decorate:
cream
nuts

1 Cook egg yolks, sugar, vanilla essence and milk gently until a smooth custard.
2 Dissolve gelatine in hot water and stir into custard.
3 When cool fold in stiffly beaten cream.
4 Allow to thicken very slightly, then fold in stiffly beaten egg whites.
5 Pour into a soufflé dish tied with a band of greased paper outside, standing several inches above level of dish.
6 When quite firm decorate with cream and nuts and remove paper.

Variations:

Chocolate

Add 1 - 2 oz. chocolate to egg yolks.

Coffee

Dissolve gelatine in slightly diluted coffee essence or very strong coffee.

Lemon

Add finely grated lemon rind to egg yolks. Dissolve gelatine in hot lemon juice instead of water.

Meringue Desserts

The secret of making meringues lies in the stiffness of the egg whites. Do make certain that these are beaten until really stiff so that you can turn the bowl upside down. Add sugar as directed in the recipes and if putting meringue on top of a pastry case, make sure it touches the edge of the pastry. If this is not done and there is a gap between the meringue and the pastry, you will find there is a tendency for the meringue to 'weep' and become rather wet.

You will notice that various methods are given for making meringues. Many cooks like to fold in the sugar gradually as they are whisking the egg white, others are more successful if they whisk in some of the sugar, then fold in the remainder. There is a third method where all the sugar is gradually whisked into the stiff egg white.

Where half icing and castor sugar are used a harder meringue results, which some people prefer.

Try each method and see which you like best. Two baking temperatures and times have been given for many of the meringue sweets. This is because a meringue, if eaten when it is cold should be set very slowly so it is thoroughly dried. If not it shrinks and becomes rather damp and sad in texture. If you are serving it hot it can be cooked more quickly because there is no time for it to 'sag'.

Hot apple trifle

cooking time 25 minutes

you will need:

12 oz. apples—weight when peeled and cored
little water
sugar to taste
4 small sponge cakes
3 level tablespoons custard powder
1 pint milk
2 egg whites
6 oz. castor sugar

1. Stew sliced apples in a little water with sugar to taste until just tender.
2. Cut the sponge cakes in half horizontally and line the bottom of a fireproof dish.
3. Drain the juice from the stewed fruit and pour over the sponge cakes.
4. Cover with the fruit.
5. Blend the custard powder with 2 tablespoons of the milk and boil the remainder with 3 oz. of the sugar.
6. When boiling pour over the blended custard powder and return to the saucepan.
7. Boil for 1 minute and allow to cool slightly.
8. Pour over the fruit and leave for about 5 minutes.
9. Whisk egg whites until stiff.
10. Fold in 1 oz. of the sugar and whisk again.
11. Fold in a further 1 oz. of the sugar and pile on top of the custard, sprinkling top with remaining sugar.
12. Bake in a slow oven (300°F.—Gas Mark 2) for 25 - 30 minutes until meringue topping is crisp and golden brown.

Variations:

Apricot

Use 12 oz. apricots in place of apples.

Blackberry and apple

Use 8 oz. apples and 4 oz. blackberries in place of apples.

Plum

Use 12 oz. stoned plums instead of apples.

Rhubarb

Use 12 oz. rhubarb instead of apples.

Chocolate meringue pie (1)

cooking time 1 hour 10 minutes

you will need:

5 oz. short crust pastry (see page 32)
1 level tablespoon cornflour
1 oz. chocolate powder
½ pint milk
1 – 2 oz. sugar
few drops vanilla essence
2 egg yolks

Meringue:
2 egg whites
2 oz. castor sugar

1. Line a deep 7-inch flan ring with the pastry and bake 'blind' until crisp and firm.
2. Blend cornflour and chocolate powder with a little for the cold milk.
3. Bring rest of the milk to the boil and pour over the chocolate mixture.
4. Return to the saucepan with the sugar and vanilla essence and cook until thickened.
5. Allow to cool slightly and add beaten egg yolks.
6. Pour into pastry case and bake in a moderate oven (375°F.—Gas Mark 4) for 10 minutes until filling is firm.
7. Whisk egg whites until stiff and fold in the sugar.
8. Pile on top of chocolate mixture and brown for 7 - 10 minutes in a moderate oven, or if serving cold, put into low oven (275°F.—Gas Mark 1) for 45 minutes.

Chocolate meringue pie (2)

cooking time 1 hour 10 minutes

you will need:

8 oz. short crust pastry (see page 32)
2 – 3 oz. plain chocolate
¾ pint milk
1½ oz. cornflour
sugar to taste
vanilla essence
2 eggs
4 oz. castor sugar

1. Line a 9- or 10-inch deep pie plate with the pastry, making a good firm edge.
2. Bake 'blind' until crisp and golden brown.
3. Dissolve the chocolate in the milk and blend the cornflour with a little of the chocolate mixture.
4. Bring the rest almost to the boil and add the blended cornflour.
5. Cook for 1 - 2 minutes, stirring all the time.
6. Add sugar to taste and vanilla essence.
7. Allow to cool slightly, then stir in egg yolks.
8. Pour into pie case.
9. Whisk egg whites with 3 oz. of the sugar until stiff.
10. Pile on top of the chocolate filling and sprinkle the remaining sugar on top.
11. Bake in a slow oven (275°F.—Gas Mark 1) until lightly coloured.

Coffee meringue pie

cooking time 1 hour 5 minutes

you will need:

5 oz. short crust pastry (see page 32)
1½ oz. cornflour
2 egg yolks
2½ – 3 oz. demerara sugar
¾ pint milk
2 level dessertspoons instant coffee
½ oz. butter
½ teaspoon vanilla essence
Meringue:
2 egg whites
pinch salt
2 oz. castor sugar

1 Line a deep 7-inch flan ring with the pastry and bake 'blind' until crisp.
2 Mix the cornflour, egg yolks and sugar together with a little of the cold milk until smooth.
3 Put remaining milk on to heat with the coffee.
4 When the coffee powder has dissolved add the blended cornflour mixture.
5 Boil for 3 minutes, stirring constantly.
6 Remove from the heat and stir in the butter and vanilla essence.
7 Pour into pastry case.
8 Whisk egg whites with the salt until stiff and beat in 1 oz. of the sugar.
9 Fold in remaining sugar and pile on top of coffee mixture.
10 Bake for about 10 minutes in a moderate oven (375°F.—Gas Mark 4) or if serving cold, put into low oven (275°F.—Gas Mark 1) for 45 minutes.

Cream pie

cooking time 27 minutes

you will need:

1 8-inch baked flan case (see page 41)
8 oz. sugar
3 level tablespoons cornflour
pinch salt
1¼ pints cold milk
3 eggs
2 tablespoons butter
1 teaspoon vanilla

1 Make flan case as directed on page 41.
2 Mix together 2 - 3 oz. of the sugar, cornflour and salt.
3 Blend with ¼ pint of the cold milk and cook for 10 minutes until mixture thickens.
4 Heat rest of milk and pour over cornflour mixture.
5 Stir small amount into slightly beaten egg yolks, then gradually pour this into thickened milk.
6 Cook for about 2 minutes without boiling, stirring constantly.
7 Add butter and vanilla and cool slightly.
8 Turn into baked pastry shell.
9 Make meringue by stiffly beating egg whites and folding in remaining sugar.
10 Bake in very moderate oven (350°F.—Gas Mark 3) for about 15 minutes or until delicately browned.

Note:

If desired omit meringue and serve with sweetened whipped cream.

Variations:

Coconut

Stir in 6 - 8 oz. desiccated coconut to the cream filling, cover with meringue and sprinkle more coconut over the top.

Grapefruit meringue tart

cooking time 35 - 40 minutes

you will need:

5 oz. short crust pastry (see page 32)
1 oz. cornflour
3 – 4 oz. sugar
¼ pint water
¼ pint grapefruit juice
1 oz. butter
1 egg yolk
Meringue:
1 egg white
pinch salt
1 oz. sugar
1 level teaspoon cornflour

1 Line a flan ring with pastry and bake 'blind' until crisp and golden brown.
2 Mix the cornflour and sugar together with a little of the cold water until smooth.
3 Put the grapefruit juice and rest of the water into a pan and heat.
4 Add the blended cornflour and boil for 3 minutes, adding the butter and stirring all the time.
5 Add the egg yolk and cook for several minutes without boiling.
6 Pour into the baked pastry case.
7 Beat egg white until stiff with a pinch of salt.
8 Fold the sugar and cornflour blended together into the beaten egg white and top the flan with the meringue.
9 Brown for about 10 minutes in a moderately hot oven (400°F.—Gas Mark 5) and serve hot.

Lemon meringue pie

cooking time 1 hour 5 minutes

you will need:

6 oz. short crust pastry (see page 32)
3 level dessertspoons cornflour or custard powder
½ pint water
2 oz. margarine
3 – 4 oz. sugar
2 large eggs
2 lemons

Meringue:
2 oz. sugar

1. Line a pie dish with the pastry and bake 'blind' for 20 - 25 minutes in a hot oven (450°F.—Gas Mark 6 - 7).
2. Blend the cornflour or custard powder with the cold water.
3. Put into a saucepan and cook gently until thickened.
4. Add the margarine and sugar, egg yolks, and the very finely grated 'zest' of the lemon rind and finally the lemon juice.
5. Pour into the pastry case.
6. Whisk the egg whites stiffly, fold in nearly all the sugar.
7. Pile on top of the lemon filling and dust with the remaining sugar.
8. Bake for 45 minutes in a very slow oven (275°F.—Gas Mark 1) when the meringue should feel firm to touch. Do not bake the meringue more quickly otherwise it will not stay crisp when cold.

Variation:

Orange

Use 2 oranges in place of the lemons.

Macaroni apple

cooking time 1½ hours

you will need:

4 oz. quick cooking macaroni
2 cooking apples
2 eggs
4 oz. castor sugar

1. Boil macaroni and stew apples.
2. Mix macaroni, apples and egg yolk, and sprinkle with sugar.
3. Make meringue by whisking egg whites and adding sugar gradually and spread on top of dish.
4. Put in oven until meringue is golden brown —see last point of Chocolate meringue pie, page 75.
5. Serve hot or cold.

Mandorle meringue

cooking time 25 minutes

you will need:

1 pint milk
1 packet flavoured cornflour
2 eggs
3 oz. sugar
little lemon curd
little raspberry jam
little greengage jam

1. Put most of the milk into a saucepan to boil.
2. Blend the cornflour with the rest of the milk.
3. Add the boiling milk and put back again into saucepan to thicken.
4. Take off the heat and add the 2 egg yolks and 1 oz. of the sugar.
5. Cook for another 2 or 3 minutes without boiling to prevent curdling.
6. Pour into a pie dish.
7. Whisk the egg whites until stiff.
8. Fold in remaining sugar and pile over the cornflour mixture.
9. Make about 6 small hollows and fill 2 with lemon curd, 2 with raspberry jam and 2 with greengage jam.
10. Set for approximately 15 minutes in a very moderate oven (350°F.—Gas Mark 3) and serve hot.

Meringue apples

cooking time 2 hours

you will need:

4 large cooking apples
2 tablespoons apricot jam
2 tablespoons chopped walnuts or toasted almonds
2 egg whites
2 oz. icing sugar

1. Core apples and fill with jams and nuts.
2. Slit skins round centre and bake for 1 hour in a moderate oven (375°F.—Gas Mark 4).
3. Carefully remove skins.
4. Whisk egg whites until stiff and fold in most of the sugar.
5. Pile over apples and dust with remaining sugar.
6. Allow meringue to dry out in a very slow oven (275°F.—Gas Mark 1) for 1 hour.

Pineapple meringue pie

cooking time 35 minutes

you will need:

6 oz. sweet short crust pastry (see page 32)
1½ oz. cornflour
2 oz. sugar
pinch salt
¼ pint pineapple juice
1 oz. butter
2 egg yolks
1 tablespoon cream or top of milk
1 medium-sized can pineapple pieces

Meringue:
2 egg whites
3 oz. castor sugar

1 Roll out pastry and line an 8-inch sandwich tin or flan ring and bake 'blind' until crisp and golden brown.
2 Mix cornflour, sugar and salt to a smooth paste with a little of the pineapple juice.
3 Heat remaining juice and pour on to the paste.
4 Return to pan and cook until mixture comes to the boil, stirring all the time.
5 When mixture thickens, simmer gently for 2 minutes.
6 Remove from heat and beat in butter, egg yolks and cream. Allow to get quite cold and pour into pastry case, with pineapple.
7 Whisk egg whites until stiff and fold in half the sugar.
8 Whisk again until stiff and fold in remaining sugar.
9 Pile on to pineapple mixture and bake in a very hot oven (475°F.—Gas Mark 8) for 1 - 3 minutes until crisp and golden brown.

Raspberry custard meringue

cooking time 1 hour 10 minutes

you will need:

5 oz. short crust pastry (see page 32)
8 oz. raspberries
2 eggs
4 oz. sugar
½ pint milk

1 Line an 8-inch flan ring with the pastry and bake 'blind' for about 10 minutes in a hot oven (425°F.—Gas Mark 6).
2 Arrange raspberries in bottom of pastry case.
3 Beat egg yolks with 1 oz. of the sugar and pour over the hot milk.
4 Strain on top of fruit.
5 Whisk egg whites until stiff and fold in remaining sugar.
6 Pile on top of the custard and return to a cool oven (250°F.—Gas Mark ½) for 1 hour.

Variations:

Apple

Use 8 oz. sliced apples, sweetened to taste in place of raspberries.

Gooseberry

Use 8 oz. 'topped and tailed' sliced gooseberries.

Redcurrant

Use 8 oz. redcurrants, sweetened to taste, instead of raspberries.

Strawberry meringue pie

cooking time 10 minutes plus time for baking flan

you will need:

¼ pint milk
3 oz. fine semolina
2 egg yolks
3 oz. castor sugar
1 lb. strawberries
1 8-inch baked flan case

Meringue:
2 egg whites
5 oz. castor sugar

1 Heat milk and add semolina.
2 Cook until mixture comes to the boil and thickens, stirring continuously.
3 Remove from heat and beat in egg yolks and sugar.
4 Crush 4 oz. of the strawberries and stir into the mixture.
5 Pour into prepared flan case.
6 Chill and cover with remaining strawberries, reserving a few for decoration.
7 Beat egg whites until stiff and peaky.
8 Stir in 1 oz. of the sugar and whisk hard until meringue stands in firm peaks.
9 Fold in remaining sugar and pile on top of strawberry mixture.
10 Brown quickly in a very hot oven (475°F.—Gas Mark 8) for 1 - 2 minutes.
11 Decorate with strawberries.

Variations:

Blackberry

Use 1 lb. blackberries instead of strawberries.

Raspberry

Use 1 lb. raspberries instead of strawberries.

Ice Cream Dishes

Home-made ice cream

no cooking

you will need:

½ pint custard (if made with eggs and milk use yolks only)
2 oz. sugar
¼ pint whipped cream or whipped evaporated milk (see page 87)
1 teaspoon vanilla essence

1 Turn the cold control indicator to the coldest position at least 30 minutes before freezing.
2 Mix all the ingredients together and if egg whites are left from the custard, whisk these and fold into the mixture.
3 Pour into freezing trays and freeze until firm.
4 Take out the whisk briskly.
5 Refreeze.

Variations:

Coffee

Use 1 tablespoon coffee essence in place of vanilla and cook with the custard.

Fruit

Add fruit purée to the mixture.

Chocolate

Cook 2 oz. chocolate with the custard.

Banana and apple whip

no cooking

you will need:

2 bananas
juice ½ lemon
3 dessert apples
1 large block ice cream
nuts

1 Skin and mash the bananas with the lemon juice to prevent the fruit discolouring.
2 Halve, core, but do not peel the apples, and grate coarsely.
3 Mix the apples and banana with the ice cream.
4 Pile into glasses and top with chopped nuts.

Note:

This should be done just before the meal, so the mixture does not become too soft.

Banana ice flan

no cooking

you will need:

1 7– or 8–inch baked flan case (see page 41)
raspberry or strawberry jam
3 – 4 bananas
lemon juice
raspberry or strawberry ice cream
few grapes

1 Spread the bottom of the flan case with jam.
2 Slice up the bananas to cover the bottom of the flan case and sprinkle well with lemon juice.
3 Cover with spoonfuls of ice cream.
4 Garnish with grapes that have been halved and pipped.
5 Chill well until ready to serve.

Blackberry water ice

cooking time few minutes for fruit

you will need:

1 lb. blackberries
¾ pint water
3 oz. sugar
1 egg white (optional)

1 Simmer the blackberries, water and sugar until fruit is tender.
2 Rub through a sieve and freeze until firm.
3 If preferred when lightly frozen add a stiffly beaten egg white.

Variations:

Blackcurrant

Use the method for Blackberry water ice using 1 lb. blackcurrants.

Cherry

Use the method for Blackberry water ice using black cherries. Mash fruit and remove stones —there is no need to sieve.

Raspberry

Use the method for Blackberry water ice using only ½ pint water.

Strawberry

Use the method for Blackberry water ice, using only ¼ pint water, or ⅜ pint if very firm.

Chocolate Alaska

cooking time 3 minutes

you will need:

1 sponge flan case (see page 42)	¼ level teaspoon cream of tartar
2–3 oz. plain chocolate	4–5 oz. castor sugar
1 block vanilla ice cream	*To decorate:*
2 egg whites	little fruit—raspberries, strawberries, cherries

1. Place the flan case on a baking tray.
2. Chop chocolate and quickly mix into the ice cream using a fork.
3. Pile into the flan case.
4. Whisk egg whites until stiff with the cream of tartar.
5. Add 2 oz. of the sugar and whisk again until stiff enough to stand in peaks.
6. Fold in another 2 oz. sugar and spread the meringue over and around the ice cream, taking care to cover both ice cream and sponge.
7. Dredge with remaining sugar.
8. Bake in a hot oven (450 - 475°F.—Gas Mark 7 - 8) for about 3 minutes until the meringue is crisp and lightly coloured.
9. Decorate with fruit and serve at once.

Chocolate ice cream

no cooking

you will need:

½ large can evaporated milk	1 tablespoon cold water
3 level tablespoons castor sugar	3 oz. plain chocolate
1 level teaspoon powdered gelatine	3 tablespoons cold water
	½ teaspoon vanilla essence

1. Set refrigerator at coldest setting before mixing ice cream.
2. Pour milk and castor sugar into ice cream tray.
3. Dissolve gelatine in cold water over gentle heat and stir into milk mixture.
4. Place in refrigerator and chill until crystals begin to form.
5. Pour into chilled mixing bowl and whisk until thick.
6. Dissolve chocolate in water over gentle heat.
7. Fold chocolate and essence into whipped mixture.
8. Pour into freezing tray and freeze rapidly.

Variations:

Coffee

Omit chocolate and blend 1 dessertspoon instant coffee with gelatine and water.

Vanilla

Omit chocolate and use 1 teaspoon vanilla essence.

Fresh berry ice pudding

you will need:

1 lb. very ripe blackberries, strawberries, raspberries	*Ice cream:*
	2–4 egg yolks
	3 oz. sugar
	¼ pint milk
Meringue:	¼ pint cream
2 egg whites	
4 oz. castor sugar	*Crème Chantilly:*
	2 egg whites
	¼ pint cream
	vanilla essence
	icing sugar to taste

1. Make the meringues.
   This should be done some hours beforehand so they can cool.
2. Make the ice cream as recipe (page 79).
3. When firm turn out and whip as stage 4 on page 79.
4. Add nearly all the sieved berries.
5. Freeze until firm.
6. Cover the bottom of a mould or basin with few crushed meringues.
7. Cover with spoonfuls of the berry ice cream and then a final layer of crushed meringue.
8. Replace in the freezing compartment of the refrigerator to set.
9. For the *Crème Chantilly,* whisk egg whites very stiffly.
10. Whisk cream lightly and fold into the egg whites.
11. Add vanilla essence and a little sieved icing sugar to taste.
12. Turn out the ice cream pudding and top with the *Crème Chantilly*.
13. Any meringues left over can be served with this sweet.

Frozen apricot coconut cream

no cooking

you will need:

1 lb. cooked sweetened apricots
¼ pint milk
3 tablespoons lemon juice
3 oz. sugar
⅛ pint cream
¼ teaspoon almond essence
3 oz. desiccated coconut, toasted until brown

1 Rub apricots through a sieve and add juice.
2 Combine the purée, milk, lemon juice, sugar together.
3 Stir until the sugar has dissolved.
4 Pour the mixture into the refrigerator tray and place the tray in the freezing compartment with the control set at the lowest temperature.
5 Freeze until firm.
6 Remove the mixture to a chilled bowl and beat until smooth and fluffy.
7 Whip the cream until stiff and add almond essence.
8 Fold into the frozen mixture together with the coconut.
9 Return to the freezing compartment and freeze to the desired consistency.

Iced orange pudding

no cooking

you will need:

4 oz. fine cake or biscuit crumbs
2 eggs
3 oz. castor sugar
grated rind and juice 2 oranges
½ pint cream (or whipped evaporated milk)
To decorate:
2 oranges

1 Turn indicator of refrigerator to coldest position 30 minutes before required.
2 Line the freezing tray with waxed or greaseproof paper.
3 Sprinkle half the crumbs evenly over this.
4 Beat eggs and sugar until thick and creamy.
5 Add grated rind and juice of oranges and most of the cream or whipped evaporated milk.
6 Put into freezing tray and top with remaining crumbs.
7 Freeze for about 1 - 1¼ hours or until firm.
8 Turn on to a long dish and remove paper.
9 Decorate with remaining cream and orange segments.

Orange and lemon sorbet

cooking time 10 minutes

you will need:

2 lemons
2 oranges
½ pint water
2 eggs
2 – 3 oz. sugar

1 Cut the rind from the fruit very thinly.
2 Put into saucepan with the water and simmer gently for about 10 minutes.
3 Strain and add enough water to give ½ pint liquid again.
4 Beat yolks of eggs with sugar and add to the liquid together with the juice from the lemons and oranges.
5 Pour into freezing tray of refrigerator and freeze for about 30 - 40 minutes.
6 Remove from tray and mix with stiffly beaten egg whites.
7 Return to freezing tray and leave until lightly frozen.

Frozen pineapple cream

no cooking

you will need:

1 pint cream
½ teaspoon vanilla
1 ripe pineapple
2 tablespoons sugar
4 oz. candied fruits or fresh strawberries to decorate

1 Whip the cream until stiff and add the vanilla.
2 Put into a mould, surround with ice and salt and freeze for 2 hours, or pack in the freezing tray of an automatic refrigerator and freeze until just firm, but not too hard.
3 Pare and slice the pineapple, remove dark eyes and core.
4 Arrange the pieces in a serving dish and sprinkle with the sugar.
5 Dip a large serving spoon in hot water, then into the frozen cream.
6 Arrange the large ovals of frozen cream round the pineapple.
7 Decorate with the candied fruits or strawberries.

Note:

The cream is not sweetened in this recipe, but could be so if wished.

Grape cream

cooking time 15 minutes

you will need:

2 oz. black grapes	1 egg
1 pint lemon jelly	¼ pint whipped cream
1 pint milk	sugar to taste
3 oz. quick cooking macaroni	brandy or sherry to taste

1 Cut the grapes in half and remove the pips.
2 Arrange some of them in the bottom of jelly mould and cover with some of the lemon jelly.
3 Allow to set.
4 Pour the milk into a saucepan and bring to the boil.
5 Sprinkle the macaroni into the milk and simmer for 9 - 10 minutes, stirring occasionally.
6 Allow to cool slightly.
7 Separate the yolk from the white of egg.
8 Beat the yolk and add to the macaroni mixture.
9 Return to the heat and allow to cook gently for 2 minutes. Cool.
10 Stiffly whisk the egg white and fold it into the macaroni mixture.
11 Half whip the cream and fold in with the remainder of the jelly.
12 Sweeten if necessary and add brandy.
13 Leave until just setting.
14 Stir and pour this mixture on to the fruit and jelly and leave to set.
15 Turn out in the usual way and serve decorated with a little whipped cream and the remainder of the grapes.

Peach meringue sponge

cooking time 5 - 6 minutes

you will need:

1 frozen cream sponge	1 block ice cream
2 tablespoons cointreau	2 egg whites
1 medium sized can sliced peaches	4 oz. castor sugar

1 Preheat the oven to very hot (500°F.—Gas Mark 9).
2 Place the sponge on an ovenproof dish.
3 Remove the top half of the sponge round and sprinkle with cointreau.
4 Strain the peaches, saving the syrup.
5 Arrange most of the peaches on the cream, reserving a few for the topping.
6 Spoon ice cream carefully over the peaches and replace the top sponge.
7 Whisk egg whites until stiff.
8 Fold in sugar and then fold in the remaining peaches, chopped coarsely.
9 Spread meringue mixture over the sponge to seal it completely, and dredge with a little extra castor sugar.
10 Bake for 2 - 3 minutes in a very hot oven (475°F.—Gas Mark 8).
11 Serve at once.

Rhubarb sherbert

cooking time 10 - 15 minutes

you will need:

12 oz. early rhubarb	1 level tablespoon powdered gelatine
1¼ pints water	1 lemon
3 oz. sugar	

1 Cook the rhubarb with ¼ pint water and sugar.
2 Rub through a sieve.
3 Dissolve the gelatine in a little hot water.
4 Add the rest of the water, rhubarb purée and grated rind and juice of the lemon.
5 Add a little more sugar to taste if necessary.
6 Pour into freezing tray and leave until lightly frosted.
7 Serve in tall glasses.

Variations:

Apple

Use the method for rhubarb sherbert above, using 12 oz. apples instead of rhubarb.

Lemon

Use some of the lemon pulp as well as the juice.

Sweet Sauces

A good sauce makes a great deal of difference to a sweet and in this section there are a variety of sauces. Some, like the Chocolate sauce, may be made beforehand and kept in a cold place to use as required. If you wish to keep a sauce hot without any worries about it boiling or sticking to the pan, make it in the top of a double saucepan or a basin over hot water.

To keep custard sauces hot, pour into a hot jug and stand this in a pan of hot water until required. To prevent a skin from forming on the top of hot sauces, cover with a piece of foil or damped greaseproof paper.

Apricot sauce

cooking time 10 minutes

you will need:

2 level teaspoons arrowroot or cornflour
½ pint syrup from fruit
little sugar
2 tablespoons lemon juice
8 oz. canned or cooked apricots

1 Blend the arrowroot with a little of the syrup from the can of fruit or the cooked fruit.
2 Put into a saucepan with lemon juice and sugar to taste.
3 Bring to the boil and cook until thickened and quite clear.
4 Add the halved apricots and just heat gently.
5 Add more sugar if wished.

Brandy butter or hard sauce

no cooking

you will need:

4 oz. unsalted butter
6 oz. icing sugar
4 – 8 dessertspoons brandy

1 Cream the butter until white and creamy.
2 Gradually add the icing sugar and the brandy.
3 Allow to stand for some hours in a cold place to get really hard.

Variation:

Rum

Use 4 - 8 dessertspoons rum in place of brandy.

Cold brandy sauce

cooking time 15 minutes

you will need:

2 eggs
⅓ pint milk
2 oz. sugar
2 tablespoons brandy

1 Beat the egg yolks with the milk and put into a saucepan with the sugar and brandy.
2 Cook until thick enough to coat the back of a wooden spoon.
3 Allow to cool, stirring from time to time.
4 Just before serving fold in the stiffly beaten egg whites.

Butterscotch sauce

cooking time 10 minutes

you will need:

2 oz. brown sugar
1 tablespoon golden syrup
1 oz. butter
⅛ pint water

1 Put the sugar, syrup and butter into a pan.
2 Heat gently and stir until the sugar has dissolved.
3 Boil steadily for a few minutes.
4 Add the water and bring back to the boil.
5 Cook steadily until water has blended with the ingredients.

Caramel Sauce

There are several ways of making a caramel sauce—

1 Using sugar and no water
2 Using sugar and a little water (see individual recipe)
3 Using golden syrup

The first way is the most difficult to make. You must use a good saucepan and stir the sugar constantly over a low heat. When the sugar has dissolved boil steadily until it is golden brown, without stirring. Remove from the heat. This makes a strong caramel, ideal when milk is added later, after the caramel has cooled. If the caramel has not cooled the milk will curdle. Heat the caramel and milk together gently. (Follow this method for golden syrup).

Caramel sauce

cooking time 30 minutes

you will need:

3 oz. sugar
3 tablespoons water
1 pint milk
4 egg yolks
extra 1 oz. sugar

1 Put sugar into a saucepan with the water and stir until the sugar has dissolved.
2 Boil until brown caramel.
3 Cook slightly, then add the milk.
4 Heat **gently without boiling** until the caramel has dissolved in the milk.
5 Pour on to the beaten egg yolks.
6 Add extra sugar and thicken gently until mixture coats the back of a wooden spoon. A double saucepan or basin over hot water is the best way of doing this.

Chocolate sauce (1)

no cooking

you will need:

4 tablespoons drinking chocolate powder
approximately 1 tablespoon boiling water

1 Put the chocolate powder into a basin or jug.
2 Add sufficient water to form a thick syrup and stir well.
3 Use hot or cold.

Chocolate sauce (2)

cooking time 8 minutes

you will need:

1½ oz. block plain chocolate
1 teaspoon cocoa
1 oz. sugar
¼ pint water
½ teaspoon vanilla essence
1 egg yolk

1 Put the chocolate broken into small pieces into a saucepan.
2 Add the cocoa, sugar and half the water.
3 Stir until dissolved and bring to the boil.
4 Simmer for 2 - 3 minutes.
5 Add rest of water and vanilla essence.
6 Bring back to the boil and cook until syrupy and thick.
7 Remove from heat and add egg yolk.

Chocolate sauce (3)

cooking time 5 minutes

you will need:

1 oz. cocoa
2 oz. butter
1 oz. sugar
2 tablespoons golden syrup or honey
⅛ pint water

1 Put all the ingredients into a saucepan.
2 Heat together until thickened.
3 Serve at once or keep hot over a pan of hot water; or if wishing to serve cold do not allow the mixture to cook too long and become too thick.

Crème Chantilly

no cooking

you will need:

¼ pint cream
1 – 2 teaspoons sugar
few drops vanilla essence

1 Put the cream into a basin and whip until **just** stiff enough to stand in peaks. Do not continue whisking.
2 Fold in sugar and a few drops vanilla essence.
3 Whisk again very lightly if wishing to pipe.

Note:

Never over-whip cream otherwise it becomes buttery and starts to separate.

Custard sauce

cooking time 20 minutes

you will need:

1 egg
1 tablespoon sugar
½ pint milk

1 Beat the egg and sugar together.
2 Pour on the milk.
3 Pour into a jug and stand in the top of a double saucepan or a basin over hot water.
4 Cook very gently until the mixture just coats the back of a wooden spoon, stirring nearly all the time.

Fudge sauce (1)

cooking time 10 minutes

you will need:

4 oz. sugar
1 oz. butter
2 tablespoons water
1 small can evaporated milk

1. Heat the sugar, butter and water until the sugar has melted.
2. Add the evaporated milk and cook steadily until the mixture is thickened, stirring from time to time.
3. Use at once, or if serving cold add 1 or 2 tablespoons extra milk or cream to prevent the sauce thickening too much.

Fudge sauce (2)

cooking time 8 minutes

you will need:

4 oz. fudge
1 – 2 tablespoons milk or cream

1. Put the fudge into a basin and stand over hot water.
2. Heat gently until melted.
3. Stir briskly then add milk or cream.
4. Serve at once, or add 2 - 3 tablespoons cream or milk to prevent mixture becoming too stiff.

Variations:

Chocolate

Add a little chocolate or cocoa powder with the milk.

Coffee

Add 1 teaspoon instant coffee with the milk.

Vanilla

Add $\frac{1}{4}$ - $\frac{1}{2}$ teaspoon vanilla essence or other essence with the milk.

Golden syrup sauce

cooking time few minutes

you will need:

3 tablespoons golden syrup
1 lemon
$\frac{1}{4}$ pint water

1. Put the syrup into a saucepan, together with the grated rind and juice of the lemon.
2. Add the water and heat gently for a few minutes.

Jam sauce

cooking time few minutes

you will need:

4 – 5 tablespoons jam
juice 1 lemon
$\frac{1}{8}$ pint water

1. Put all the ingredients into a saucepan.
2. Heat together until jam has melted.

Lemon marmalade sauce

cooking time 5 - 8 minutes

you will need:

1 teaspoon arrowroot
4 tablespoons lemon juice
2 tablespoons lemon marmalade
4 tablespoons water

1. Blend the arrowroot and lemon juice.
2. Add the marmalade and water and boil until thick and clear.

Orange marmalade sauce

Method as above, using orange marmalade and 4 tablespoons orange juice.

Lemon sauce

cooking time 8 minutes

you will need:

2 lemons
water
1 level dessertspoon arrowroot or cornflour
2 oz. sugar

1. Measure the juice from the lemons and make up to $\frac{1}{2}$ pint with water.
2. Mix arrowroot to a smooth paste with a little of the liquid.
3. Heat remainder in a saucepan.
4. Add sugar and stir until dissolved.
5. Pour over the paste and return to pan.
6. Cook until sauce thickens and becomes clear, stirring constantly.
7. Stir in the finely grated rind of one lemon and pour into a jug or sauceboat.

Melba sauce

cooking time few minutes

you will need:

- 1 teaspoon cornflour or arrowroot
- 2 tablespoons water or syrup from canned or frozen fruit
- 4–6 oz. fresh, frozen or canned raspberries
- sugar to taste
- 3 tablespoons redcurrant or apple jelly

1 Blend the cornflour with the water.
2 Put all the ingredients into a saucepan and heat gently until the jelly has melted and the mixture clear.
3 Rub through a sieve if wished.

Variations:

Melba de luxe

Use the recipe as above adding 2 tablespoons brandy to the mixture.

Economical

Use 4 good tablespoons jam instead of fruit omitting the sugar and using $\frac{1}{8}$ pint water to the cornflour and jelly.

Mocha sauce

Use any of the recipes for Chocolate sauce (see page 84) using strong coffee instead of water.

Orange sauce

cooking time 8 minutes

you will need:

- 1 small orange
- juice 1 lemon
- water
- 1 level dessertspoon arrowroot or cornflour
- 1 rounded tablespoon golden syrup

Use the method for Lemon sauce (see page 85) using golden syrup instead of sugar.

Peach syrup

cooking time 8 minutes

you will need:

- 2 level teaspoons arrowroot or cornflour
- $\frac{1}{4}$ pint syrup from can fruit
- 2 tablespoons lemon juice
- little sugar to taste
- 1 medium can peaches

1 Blend the arrowroot with a little of the syrup from the can of fruit.
2 Put into a pan with the rest of the syrup and the lemon juice, adding sugar to taste if wished.
3 Bring to the boil and cook until thickened and quite clear.
4 Add the halved peaches and heat gently.
5 Taste and add more sugar if wished.

Apricot syrup

Method as above using 8 oz. canned or cooked apricots instead of peaches.

Pineapple syrup

Method as above using can pineapple instead of peaches. Shred the pineapple and add to the sauce at the last minute.

Sweet mousseline sauce

cooking time 10 - 12 minutes

you will need:

- 2 large eggs
- 2 oz. sugar
- $\frac{1}{8}$ pint cream
- little white wine or light dry sherry

1 Beat the egg yolks and sugar together in the top of a double saucepan or basin over hot water until thick and creamy.
2 Take off the heat and fold in the cream, sherry and stiffly beaten egg whites.
3 Return to the heat but ensure that the sauce does not cook further.
4 Serve with rich steamed puddings.

Sweet white sauce

cooking time 8 minutes

you will need:

- 1 tablespoon cornflour
- $\frac{1}{2}$ pint milk
- 1 oz. sugar
- little vanilla essence
- $\frac{1}{2}$ oz. butter

1 Blend the cornflour with a little cold milk.
2 Bring the rest of the milk to the boil.
3 Pour over the cornflour and return to the pan with the sugar.
4 Cook steadily until smooth and thick.
5 Add the essence and the butter.

Variations:

Chocolate

Use just under 1 tablespoon cornflour and a dessertspoon cocoa, or chocolate flavoured cornflour.

Coffee
Add 1 teaspoon instant coffee to the cornflour.

Lemon
Add finely grated rind of 1 or 2 lemons at the end of cooking, allow sauce to cook very slightly, then whisk in lemon juice; or use lemon flavoured cornflour.

Vanilla cream sauce

no cooking

you will need:

- 2 tablespoons fresh or canned thick cream
- ½ pint sweet white sauce (see page 86)
- vanilla essence

1 Stir the cream into the sauce.
2 Add the essence to flavour.

Variations:

Almond
Add a few drops of almond essence.

Orange
Add the juice and rind of an orange and tint with orange colouring.

Lemon
Add the rind and juice of a lemon.

Peppermint
Add a few drops peppermint essence and tint with green colouring.

Rum
Add a few drops rum or rum essence and tint pink.

To whip evaporated milk

1 Boil the can of milk for about 15 minutes in a pan of water.
2 Chill thoroughly for several hours.
3 Turn into a large bowl and whisk firmly.

Note:
For a very thick cream turn the milk into a bowl after boiling and stir in 1 level teaspoon powdered gelatine dissolved in 2 tablespoons hot water. Cool as before and then whip.

Mock cream

cooking time 5-8 minutes

you will need:

- 1 level tablespoon cornflour
- ¼ pint milk
- 1–2 oz. butter
- 1 oz. castor sugar

1 Blend cornflour to a smooth mixture with the milk.
2 Put into a saucepan and bring slowly to the boil, stirring all the time.
3 Cook until thick and allow to become quite cold.
4 Cream the butter and sugar until very soft and creamy.
5 Gradually beat in spoonfuls of the cornflour mixture.
6 Beat thoroughly and use as required.

Note:
Do not heat the butter to soften it when creaming with the sugar.

Index

BUTTER

Quick Meals

Basic Methods of Cooking

Baking—Cooking in dry heat in the oven.
Boiling—Cooking by immersing the food in a pan of liquid, which must be kept boiling gently all the time.
Braising—Almost a combination of stewing and roasting. Meat is placed on a bed of vegetables with a little liquid surrounding, in a covered vessel, and cooked slowly in the oven.
Casserole—Cooking slowly in the oven in a covered casserole dish.
Frying—Cooking in a little hot fat in an open pan. Deep frying is cooking by immersion in a deep pan of smoking hot fat.
Grilling—Cooking quickly under a red-hot grill; used for small tender pieces of meat, fish, etc.
Poaching—Cooking gently in water which is just below boiling point; usually eggs or fish.
Pressure Cooking—Cooking at higher temperatures than usual, so that food is cooked much more quickly.
Roasting—Cooking with a little fat in a hot oven. Fat is poured from the baking tin over the meat or poultry from time to time, using a long-handled spoon; this is known as basting.
Simmering—The rate of cooking used for stews; just below boiling point, so that the liquid bubbles gently at the side of the pan.
Steaming—Cooking either in a steamer over a pan of boiling water, or in a basin standing in (but not covered by) boiling water.
Stewing—Cooking slowly until the food is tender. It is done in just enough liquid to cover the food, as the liquid is served with it and should be rich. Stews may be cooked in covered saucepans or casseroles, on a hot plate or in the oven, but always at a low temperature.

Ideas to Help Save Time

Stocking your larder

Convenience foods: an incredible amount of time will be saved by either stocking plenty of the convenience foods, or buying these for quick and easy meals. Obviously one cannot store frozen foods even in an ordinary refrigerator without a deep freeze compartment. However, as these are becoming rather more common, a very excellent range of frozen foods will be found invaluable.

Shopping for dairy produce

Cheese Remember that processed cheese keeps well, so you can always have some available. It is possible in some shops to buy already grated Cheddar and Parmesan cheese. However, drums of Parmesan can be stored for a very long time. Use only small quantities of this particular cheese because it is very strong. You should also occasionally buy canned continental cheeses for emergencies.

Cream This may be purchased in bottles or cans. Make sure that you have bought the type that will whip if you need it for decoration.

Eggs Keep a good supply available. It is quite a sensible plan when cooking eggs to hard-boil 1 or 2 extra, so you always have some on hand for quick meals or garnishes.

Milk — Supplies of canned, evaporated or condensed milk are an excellent substitute for fresh milk and cream. Or you can get the bottled milk which has been sterilised to keep well. Some people use the powdered milk (sold for babies) in sweets if they have not time to shop for fresh milk.

Shopping for fish

There is an excellent selection of canned fish which can be stored for quick and easy meals.

Anchovies —filleted or rolled, can be added to eggs, or used for quick savouries to serve with drinks.

Herrings, Herring roes —for heating as supper snacks.

Pilchards —these can be used on toast, or for quick fish cakes. Mix with equal quantities of potato, coat and fry in the usual way.

Salmon —the cheaper pink salmon is again good in fish cakes. The better quality is good for salads, sandwiches, etc.

Sardines —in oil or tomato, these are a very rich protein food, and as such, excellent for children, who generally enjoy them very much.

Shell fish —these can all be used in similar ways to fresh fish. Use immediately after opening the can.

Tuna —this is often described as the chicken of the sea. It has a rather firm, dry flesh which makes it more enjoyable if heated in creamy sauces.

Frozen fish —practically every variety of fish can today be obtained frozen. Much of it can be cooked while still frozen for speed. Look out for the fish fingers or sticks as quick supper dishes. The herrings, kippers and smoked haddock which have already been filleted are also useful, because they can be cooked more quickly and eaten more easily.

Shopping for fruit

Fresh fruit in itself is one of the most time saving of foods, for it makes a perfect dessert with no effort at all. There are, however, endless varieties in canned fruits which will also save a great deal of time.

Apple purée —excellent for sauce or sweets where one is told to sieve the fruit.

Canned fruit salad —this makes the basis of a sweet if you add sliced fresh apples, bananas, oranges.

Frozen fruits —these can be almost as good as fresh. The secret is to use them when they are still very slightly frozen. They lose both colour and taste if defrosted too much.

Dried fruits —apricots, apples, figs, prunes, etc., are an excellent standby in the larder. A thorough soaking in cold water shortens the cooking time.

Shopping for meat

Canned meat has become of very much higher quality during the past years. It is wise to store the following:

Bacon —pre-packed bacon in polythene bags is a good standby, and keeps longer than the unpackaged variety.
However, once the pack is opened, the bacon must be used in the normal time.

Corned beef—can be served hot, or cold with salad (see pages 35, 36, 52, 63).

Ham —small cans of ham or chopped ham can be used in place of the fresh variety.

Steak —cans of stewed steak can be made the basis of many quick and easy meals (see pages 34–5).

Tongue —ox tongue or small cans of calves' tongue can be served hot or cold. Be careful with this meat when once the can is opened as it deteriorates very easily.

Frozen meats and chickens —these should be de-frosted at room temperature before cooking. The ready chopped chicken saves time and can be used in a variety of ways. Look out for ready prepared steak or hamburgers (frozen meat cakes) that just need a few minutes' cooking.

Shopping for pasta

Canned Macaroni, Ravioli and Spaghetti —these are extremely popular, and with good reason, for they provide a quick meal and a sustaining one. The canning process tends to make the pasta very soft so do not overheat.

Frozen pasta foods —various ravioli and other types of pasta dishes can be purchased. Generally speaking they are better cooked in the frozen state.

Quick cooking macaroni —there are a number of quick cooking macaroni foods on the market. Do not think extra cooking improves them for they have been manufactured so that they need only a few minutes in boiling salted water. If you are accustomed to the old-fashioned variety which did take rather longer to prepare, you may feel you should automatically increase the cooking time. This, however, is unnecessary and unwise, since much flavour will be lost.

Shopping for spreads

Savoury spreads —the usual standbys include cheese mixtures, pâté, paste, potted meats and fish.

Sweet spreads —you will save a lot of time if you keep on hand a supply of chocolate spread as a quick filling in cakes, curd to go in tarts or sponges, and jams, jellies and syrup.

Shopping for sweets and puddings

If your family is fond of sweets and puddings there are many ways in which you can save time. Have a good supply of the following in stock:

Canned milk puddings —these are good hot or cold.

Jellies —the quick dissolving jellies take only a few moments to prepare.

Meringue and pastry cases —ready made cases can quickly be filled with cream or ice-cream.

Pudding mixes —the ones on sale today are of high quality. Also, they save you the bother of collecting the various ingredients and mixing them.

Miscellaneous (sweet)

Chestnut purée —as a sweet, served with ice-cream. It can be used as the basis for stuffing.

Chocolate or Cocoa —it can be used as a drink but also for quick chocolate sauce. Blend with a little golden syrup, butter and water.

Coffee —the instant coffee not only produces a quick drink but it can also be used as a flavouring. Dilute with a small amount of water or sieve with flour.

Cornflour —sauces, both sweet and savoury, which are made with cornflour, cook much more rapidly. Remember to use only ½ oz. cornflour for every oz. of flour.

Dried fruit —in order to save time, look for washed, already cleaned packs of fruit and chopped peel.

Nuts —it is possible to buy these already shelled and skinned. Make certain that they are kept in a dry place, since without their skins they are more easily affected by damp.

Miscellaneous (savoury)

Bouillon —or beef cubes or vegetable extract can all be used with water to take the place of stock.

Cereals —quick cooking rice saves a great deal of time. Ready cooked breakfast cereals served with milk are a meal in themselves.

Mayonnaise —not only useful for serving with salads but also the basis for a quick hot sauce to serve with fish. Heat gently in a double saucepan.

Sauces —**anchovy** (or anchovy essence) for flavouring fish sauces.

Sauces (cont.) —**tomato** to serve by itself, or for flavouring stews. Worcestershire adds bite to a number of savoury dishes.

Soups —both the canned and dried soups of today are of first rate quality. The concentrated canned soups, used undiluted, provide a gravy or sauce for a meat or fish meal.

Vegetables —although it is impossible to have on hand all the varieties of every canned, cooked vegetables here are some of the most useful. **Asparagus tips** for salads, hors-d'oeuvre and to put in omelettes. **Beans** both haricot, as a supper savoury, or green beans as a vegetable. **Carrots.** The whole, small ones are generally better in flavour. **Mixed vegetables** as a hot dish, used by themselves or added to soups. **Mushrooms.** The tiny ones are excellent to fry, grill or bake. **Onions.** The dried ones are excellent time-savers. They need a little soaking before frying or steady simmering in a stew or soup. **Tomatoes.** Small cans of tomatoes are very good for cooking, the Italian plum tomato having the best flavour. Concentrated tomato purée in tubes is one of the most reliable and quickest ways of adding flavour. Do not use too much.

Stuffings —as well as buying dried herbs, you can also avail yourself of the complete stuffings now on the market. These just require moistening before using.

Potatoes —canned new potatoes are available, and also potato powder. This is very good if re-constituted carefully, and directions as to the amount of liquid must be followed most strictly.

Tea-time specials

Making cakes is quite a leisurely business but you can produce really most appetising results with the cake and biscuit mixes on the market. In addition there are frozen sponges which just need defrosting and decorating.

There may be occasions when you have the oven on, and time available, in which case it is very wise to make such things as biscuits, meringues or a really rich fruit cake for all of these store very well and can be served without further decoration. All one needs to do is to put the meringues together with a little cream.

Cooking tips

1 Salad oil on a pastry brush is a quick, sure way to grease oven dishes, patty tins, etc.
2 Rubbing or cutting the fat into flour for cakes and puddings is a quicker method than creaming, and can give delicious light results (see cake mixture no. 1, page 78).
3 Pastry and biscuit doughs can be made ahead of time, wrapped in foil or jars and stored in the refrigerator, or a cool place, and used as required.
4 Green salads with hot meats, savoury puddings and pastries are often quicker than hot greens, and supply palatable crispness as well as the raw food required in your daily diet.
5 Covered roasting tins or foil on top of meat keep the oven clean.
6 A pressure cooker enables you to cook a variety of vegetables at one time or even to cook fish and vegetables at one time.
7 Use ice-cream as a sauce instead of a separate sweet. Allow this to half melt, then put in a little flavouring. Never try to de-freeze it.

Instead of making pastry, crumbled biscuit crumbs can be used to line a greased pie plate.

Saving time when working

1 Collecting utensils and ingredients on a tray before starting to make up the recipe saves footsteps and omissions.
2 Oven-to-table dishes cut down on the washing up and there are many to choose from.
3 As you prepare food, put saucepans, etc., to soak.
4 When you have finished the first course put forks, knives, etc., into jug filled with hot water. You will then find the washing up easy to finish.

Storing ready-made pastry or flans

Pastry can be mixed and stored either in air-tight jars, or in plastic bags in the refrigerator. Rub the fat into the flour and put the crumbs away. The next time you need pastry, simply add the required amount of water. You will find that pastry crumbs, if stored in a refrigerator, produce a lighter short crust. If you prefer, however, you can bake several

short pastry flans and store them in air-tight tins, filling them as wished. The pastry – if kept away from cakes, biscuits or bread – keeps remarkably well.
If it has become a little soft, then replace the flan in the oven for a few minutes before serving.
Here are some time-saving fillings for these ready-baked flans:

Savoury fillings

1 Fry diced bacon, sliced mushrooms and sliced tomatoes until very soft, then top with grated cheese and brown under grill or in the oven.
2 Fry thinly sliced onions and tomatoes until very soft, season well and top with anchovy fillets.
3 Scramble eggs lightly, top with sardines and thinly sliced tomatoes.
4 Fry grated onion and grated apple in hot margarine, add 2 or 3 teaspoons curry powder, 1 teaspoon cornflour and 1 gill stock. Simmer for 10 minutes, then add a few sultanas, and diced cooked meat, sliced hard-boiled eggs, or prawns.
5 Heat 1 oz. butter and add ½ pint shelled prawns, 1 gill milk and 2 eggs. Heat gently, adding a pinch of paprika pepper, salt and nutmeg. When lightly set, pile into flan case.
6 Arrange chopped, cooked meat on a very lightly baked flan case. Beat an egg, add 1 gill milk and plenty of seasoning and pour over the meat. Bake for 25–35 minutes in a very moderate oven (350°F.—Gas Mark 3). Garnish with sliced tomatoes or parsley.

Sweet fillings

1 Fill the flan with lemon curd. Top with a thick layer of desiccated coconut and brown under a low grill.
2 Spread flan with redcurrant jelly. Mash 3 or 4 bananas, mix with a little whipped cream, sugar and lemon juice. Spread on the jelly, top with more redcurrant jelly.
3 Grate 3 dessert apples, add a good tablespoon sugar and 2 stiffly beaten egg whites. Put into a crisp cooked flan and top with cream or ice-cream.

Soups and Hors-d'oeuvre

Soup is one of the most warming and satisfying first courses of a meal. Indeed, a really substantial soup served with crisp bread or rolls and butter and followed by cheese and fruit gives you a complete meal with the minimum of work.
Hors-d'oeuvre are also a very pleasant way of starting a dinner, particularly when entertaining. A simple hors-d'oeuvre gives a feeling of leisure to a meal and need not cause a lot of extra work.

Stock

Many recipes for soups (and other dishes) require stock. I have given the recipe for making stock in a pressure cooker. However, proper care of home-made stock is a necessary 'chore' even for the person with little time. *It must* stand in a cool place or be boiled daily.

Brown bone stock

Pressure cooking time 45 minutes

You will need:

2 lb. marrow bones
1 carrot
1 turnip
2 pints water
1 onion
1 teaspoon salt

1 Break the bones, put into cooker with all other ingredients.
2 Bring slowly to the boil and remove scum from the top.
3 Fix the lid and bring steadily to pressure.
4 Reduce heat and cook for 45 minutes.
5 Allow pressure to return to normal before removing lid.
6 When the stock is cold, lift off any fat from top.
7 Do not add potatoes or green vegetables to this stock otherwise it will not keep.
8 In hot weather store in a refrigerator or re-boil every other day.

Quickly made stock

The excellent meat or yeast extracts or beef and chicken bouillon cubes which are available give you good flavoured stocks within a minute. By combining small or larger quantities of the flavouring with water, you can give the strength desirable in a particular recipe. For example, if a recipe calls for 'white stock', use a chicken bouillon cube or a smaller quantity of yeast extract. In a stew where a stronger sauce is needed, be more generous with the beef extract or bouillon cubes.

Onion soup

Pressure cooking time 3 minutes

You will need:

1½ lb. onions
1 pint stock or water
seasoning
1 oz. margarine or butter
2 oz. grated cheese
slices of toast

1. Melt the butter in the cooker.
2. Cut the onion finely and fry in the hot fat until pale golden brown.
3. Add the liquid and seasoning.
4. Put on the lid, bring to pressure.
5. Lower heat and cook for 3 minutes.
6. Allow pressure to drop.
7. Arrange toast on soup plates.
8. Pour the soup over and sprinkle with grated cheese.
9. For leek soup substitute leeks.

Scotch broth

Pressure cooking time 12–25 minutes

You will need:

1 oz. pearl barley
3 oz. onions or leeks, sliced
8 oz. stewing beef
8 oz. diced swede
4 oz. sliced cabbage
salt and pepper
8 oz. diced carrot
1 pint water
1 tablespoon chopped parsley

1. Blanch the barley by pouring on boiling water, leaving it a minute or two then straining it.
2. Cut the meat into neat pieces.
3. Put into the pressure cooker with the water and barley.
4. Put on the lid and bring steadily to pressure.
5. Lower heat and cook for 20 minutes.
6. Cool the pan under water and when pressure has dropped open the lid.
7. Open the cooker and add the diced vegetables, sliced cabbage and seasoning.
8. Replace the lid.
9. Bring up to pressure again, lower the heat and cook for a further 5 minutes.
10. Put the chopped parsley into a tureen, pour in the broth (after skimming off any superfluous fat).
11. If the meat is left in, this soup can be served as a substantial main dish. Or the meat can be served as a separate course.

Minestrone soup

Pressure cooking time 30 minutes

You will need:

3 oz. haricot beans
1 dessertspoon chopped parsley
1 tablespoon grated onion
piece chopped celery
1 oz. grated cheese
¾ pint water
1 oz. dripping or oil
seasoning
8 oz. tomatoes
8 oz. chopped cabbage
2 oz. cooked macaroni

1. Soak the beans for 24 hours.
2. Put them into the pressure cooker with the water.
3. Put the lid on and bring steadily to pressure.
4. Lower the heat and cook for 25 minutes.
5. Allow pressure to drop.
6. Remove beans from cooker and retain ½ pint of the liquid.
7. Melt fat in the pan, fry the onion, celery and parsley for 5 minutes.
8. Add the chopped tomatoes, cabbage, beans, macaroni, seasoning and the ½ pint of water.
9. Put on the lid and bring to pressure again.
10. Cook for 3 minutes.
11. As soon as pressure has dropped take off lid.
12. Serve the soup sprinkled with the grated cheese. This is a very thick soup.

Fish chowder

Pressure cooking time 6 minutes

You will need:

1½ lb. fish – hake, cod or fresh haddock
2 onions
3 carrots
½ pint water
pinch mixed herbs
1 oz. flour
½ pint milk
seasoning
1 oz. margarine

1. Melt the margarine in the cooker.
2. Cut the onions, carrots and fish into neat pieces.
3. Fry the vegetables in margarine for 5 minutes, taking care they do not brown.
4. Add the water, the fish (cut into neat pieces), the mixed herbs and seasoning.
5. Fix the lid and bring to pressure.
6. Lower the heat and cook for 6 minutes.
7. Cool the pan under cold water.
8. When pressure has dropped to zero open lid.

9 Blend the flour and milk together, add to the chowder, bring slowly to the boil, then cook for 3 minutes.
10 Garnish with chopped parsley and serve with toast.

Summer vegetable soup

Cooking time 25 minutes

You will need:

12 oz. mixed summer vegetables (include peas, carrots, broad beans, spring onions)
1–2 oz. margarine
1 pint water
½ pint milk
1 level tablespoon flour

1 Heat the margarine in the pan.
2 Toss the vegetables in this, then add the water.
3 Cook until tender.
4 Blend the flour with the milk, add to vegetables.
5 Reheat until smooth, season.

Tomato and vegetable soup

Cooking time 15 minutes

You will need:

either 1 small packet mixed frozen vegetables (or can mixed vegetables or 1 grated potato, 2 grated carrots, 1 grated onion, few peas)
1 bottle or can tomato juice
½ pint water (less if using liquid from canned or frozen vegetables)
seasoning
little grated cheese

1 Put all ingredients, except cheese, into pan.
2 Simmer until tender.
3 Serve in hot bowls topped with cheese.

Vegetable soup

Pressure cooking time 3 minutes

You will need:

12 oz. cooked diced vegetables
½ oz. dripping
¾ pint water or stock
seasoning

1 Melt the fat in the cooker.
2 Fry the vegetables in this for 5 minutes without browning.
3 Add the liquid and seasoning.
4 Put on lid, bring steadily to pressure, then lower the heat and cook for 3 minutes.
5 This is one of the few soups where it is better to cool the pan quickly by putting it under the cold tap for a few seconds. Serve either with pieces of vegetable left whole or sieve the soup and reheat.

Cream of watercress soup

Cooking time 10 minutes

You will need:

1 oz. butter
1 onion
1 carrot
½ tablespoon chopped chives or tops of spring onions
1 oz. flour
1 pint milk
seasoning
squeeze lemon juice
2–4 oz. chopped watercress

1 Heat milk with sliced onion and carrot and allow to stand for some time so that milk absorbs flavour of the vegetables.
2 Then strain milk.
3 Heat the fat, stir in the flour.
4 Cook for several minutes, then gradually add the milk.
5 Bring to boil, add seasoning, watercress, chives (plus a little yeast extract if wished).
6 Add lemon juice and serve.

COLD SOUPS

A cold soup can be a very refreshing start to a meal *but* it must be *really* cold, not just cool. This means it should be put in a refrigerator. Methods for preparing cold soup and the ideal quick soups to serve cold are as follows:

Jellied soups

A jellied soup should be lightly set, but never too firm.

Consommé. This is nice if jellied. A good canned consommé and most home-made consommé will set lightly when chilled, and will therefore need no gelatine. However, if the clear soup is very liquid, heat and dissolve 1 teaspoon powder gelatine in each ½ pint liquid. Put into soup cups and serve very cold with wedges of lemon.

Asparagus, Cream of Chicken, Mushroom, Tomato. Make the soup up to normal consistency with milk. Season *very* well, and reheat. Dissolve 1½ level teaspoons powder gelatine in each pint of the soup. Serve in soup cups topped with seasoned cream and/or lemon.

Tomato juice can be jellied allowing 1 level teaspoon powder gelatine to each ½ pint of the juice.

Chilled soups

Remember, these must be thoroughly chilled. *Tomato.* If using canned soup, thin down with a little milk. Serve very cold, topped with watercress.

Chicken, Cream of Asparagus, Cream of Mushroom. When ready to serve top with a little well seasoned whipped cream.

Cream of Asparagus, Cream of Mushroom, Mulligatawny. Blend with a little cream and serve topped with tiny flowerets of raw cauliflower.

Cucumber. Thick cucumber purée is refreshing.

Iced soups

For iced tomato soup proceed as follows:

1 Add a little chopped mint and top of the milk to canned tomato soup.
2 Re-season as necessary.
3 Pour into freezing trays and when half-frozen, pile into chilled soup cups.
4 Decorate with sliced cucumber and mint.

USING PREPARED SOUPS

Ready prepared soups, both canned and packet types, are an enormous help to the busy housewife. These are produced from very fine ingredients and give an excellent flavour. If, however, more individual results are desired they make a good base to which you can add your own personal touches.

Bouillon Cubes. These are not only excellent for stock but also for consommé. Add a little sherry and individual garnishes.

Creamed soups – Asparagus, Celery, etc. These are improved by diluting them with a little cream or top of the milk. They can be used as a basis for creamed vegetable soups, by adding few extra fresh or frozen vegetables.

Green Pea Soup. This can be given extra flavour by simmering a little chopped mint and bacon in the soup.

Chicken Soups. These can be used in a variety of ways. Add diced cucumber and simmer until tender, or mixed diced vegetables to a chicken noodle soup and produce a quick minestrone. *Mushroom and Tomato Soup.* These two soups. mixed together are very good.

Frozen vegetables. These also help to simplify soup making. Use frozen spinach purée for soups, and the ready prepared macedoine or mixed vegetables.

QUICK HORS-D'OEUVRE

Asparagus Canned. Hot or cold served with melted butter or mayonnaise and brown bread and butter.

Broccoli Frozen. Cooked and served with grated cheese and melted butter.

Egg Salad. Hard-boiled eggs, coated with mayonnaise and served with green salad.

Fruit and Fruit Juice. Canned or fresh. Served very cold. Grapefruit. Halved with sugar. Melon. Cut into portions with sugar and ginger.
Smoked Fish. Salmon. Served with lemon, paprika pepper and brown bread and butter.
Shell Fish. Prawns, shrimps, lobster placed on bed of lettuce topped with mayonnaise or tomato-flavoured mayonnaise (add few drops tomato ketchup to mayonnaise).

Mixed hors-d'oeuvre

There are many other ingredients that can be used to provide a delicious and easy to make hors-d'oeuvre. Try to have as good a variety of colour and flavour as possible.

Ideally this should consist of:
Something with a fish flavour: Sardines, anchovies, rollmop herrings, mussels, prawns, smoked salmon, fresh salmon, fish salads of any kind, cod's roe, cooked roes. Dress the fish with mayonnaise or oil and vinegar and garnish it with chopped parsley, etc.

Salads: Potato, Russian, tomato, sliced cucumber, corn on the cob, lettuce, watercress, celery, rice mixtures, etc. The salad should be mixed with mayonnaise or French dressing.

Meat: Diced salami, chopped sausages, small cubes or rolls of ham, tongue, chicken; these to be mixed with some dressing.

Eggs: Sliced hard-boiled, hard-boiled and stuffed, mixed with anchovies or the yolks mixed with anchovy essence, etc.
In addition use some of the ready prepared savoury ingredients which are such a good standby in the cupboard: pickled gherkins, cocktail onions, olives, pickled walnuts, etc.

Grapefruit baskets

No cooking

You will need:

2 large grapefruits
sugar
mint leaves
1 teacup fresh fruit in season (except strawberries)

Halve grapefruits, remove pulp.
Cut strips from top of skin for 'handles'.
Mix grapefruit pulp with fruit and sugar.
Pile back into cases.
Chill, decorate with mint leaves and 'handles'.

Grapefruit cocktails

No cooking

You will need:

2 fresh grapefruit or small can grapefruit
mint
fresh fruit in season (diced melon, strawberries, etc.)

Remove sections from grapefruit or open tin.
Mix with other fruit. Pile into glasses.
Sprinkle with sugar to taste.
Decorate with mint.

Grapefruit and orange cocktail

No cooking

Remove pulp from 2 small grapefruit and 2 oranges.
Mix together, add sugar to taste.
Put into cocktail glasses.
Decorate with cherries.

Iced tomato cocktail

No cooking

Mix $\frac{1}{2}$–$\frac{3}{4}$ pint tomato juice with 1 or 2 tablespoons sherry, squeeze lemon juice, seasoning.
Put into the refrigerator until very cold.
Put a spoonful crushed ice in each cocktail glass.
Pour in tomato juice.

Mock smoked salmon

No cooking

You will need:

2 large kippers
pepper
2 tablespoons salad oil
1 very thinly sliced onion
juice of 1 large lemon

Remove the flesh from the kippers in large pieces (quite easy with a sharp knife).
Put into shallow dish with onion.
Pour over lemon juice and salad oil, add pepper to taste.
Leave several hours.
Serve with brown bread and butter.

Melon cocktail

No cooking

1. Dice melon, put into glasses and sprinkle with sugar.
2. Or cover with ginger syrup and mix with stem ginger.

Pâté

This makes an economical but interesting pâté.
No cooking

You will need:

8 oz. skinned liver sausage
2 oz. butter
pinch mixed herbs
pinch nutmeg
$\frac{1}{4}$ clove crushed garlic (or a little freshly chopped onion)

1. Cream all ingredients together.
2. Serve with freshly made toast.

Prawn and melon cocktails

No cooking

You will need:

4 oz. prawns
$\frac{1}{2}$ melon
paprika pepper
1 small lettuce
$\frac{1}{8}$–$\frac{1}{4}$ pint cream salad dressing or mayonnaise

1. Dice the melon or cut into balls with a vegetable scoop.
2. Place the prawns in a basin.
3. Add the cut up melon and 2–3 tablespoons of cream dressing.
4. Mix well together.
5. Line 4 glass sundae dishes with small lettuce leaves and place spoonfuls of the prawn mixture in each glass.
6. Pour an extra teaspoon of dressing over each portion before serving and sprinkle with paprika pepper.

Devilled sausage

No cooking

You will need:

8 frankfurter sausages
4 tablespoons chutney
4 tablespoons mayonnaise
1 teaspoon Worcestershire sauce
1 teaspoon lemon juice
lettuce

1. Cut sausages into thin slices.
2. Make dressing. Mixing chutney and mayonnaise, add Worcestershire sauce and lemon juice.
3. Toss sausages in dressing.
4. Serve on a bed of lettuce.

Fish Dishes

Fish is an ideal food to choose when you are in a hurry for it cooks very quickly; in fact it is spoiled by over-cooking.
As well as the fish dishes in this section smoked fish haddock, kippers, etc. lend themselves to quick and easy meals.

Frozen fish

There are many excellent varieties of frozen fish on the market. They are ideal when in a hurry, for they enable one to cook the fish immediately without filleting or cutting into pieces.
As well as the white fish, look out for frozen fish fingers or fish sticks, fish cakes and frozen shell fish.

Baked fish

Cooking time as below

Most fish can be baked – but care should be taken with fillets of fish to keep them moist.

1 Butter the dish well, put in the seasoned fish.
2 Cover with buttered paper.
3 Add a little stock, milk or white wine to keep fish moist. Use this stock in sauces.
4 Bake fillets of plaice, sole, etc., for approximately 12–20 minutes.
Bake cutlets of white fish for approximately 20 minutes. Bake whole fish for approximately 12 minutes per lb. (if stuffed, weigh with stuffing).
5 The heat of the oven should be moderate to moderately hot (375–400°F.—Gas Mark 4–5).
6 Put halved tomatoes, mushrooms, etc., into oven at same time, and cover with butter and buttered foil.

Cheese stuffed plaice

Cooking time 25–30 minutes

You will need:

4 large or 8 small fillets plaice

stuffing
2 oz. butter
8 oz. grated Cheddar cheese
4 oz. fresh white breadcrumbs
1 tablespoon chopped parsley
salt and pepper
4 sliced tomatoes

to garnish
parsley sprigs
lemon slices

1 Wash and skin fillets of plaice.
2 Dry well.
3 Cream butter, beat in 6 oz. cheese, 2 oz. breadcrumbs, parsley and seasoning.
4 Spread thickly on fillets and roll from tail.
5 Place in well buttered, shallow, ovenproof dish with sliced tomatoes.
6 Mix remaining breadcrumbs and cheese and sprinkle over fish and tomatoes.
7 Bake in a moderate oven (375°F.—Gas Mark 4) for 25–30 minutes.
8 Garnish with parsley and lemon.

Chutneyed fish

Cooking time 30 minutes

You will need:

approximately 1 lb. fish (fresh haddock, cod or hake)
few drops of vinegar
2 tablespoons crisp breadcrumbs
few slices cucumber or gherkin
2 tablespoons chutney
½ gill milk
1 teaspoon grated onion
2 tablespoons grated cheese (not essential)
1 egg
seasoning
1 oz. margarine

1 This is a particularly useful dish for, when cooked the fish is already in a thick sauce.
2 Put the uncooked fish into a greased dish.
3 Mix the egg, milk, chutney, cucumber, onion, vinegar and seasoning together.
4 Pour this mixture over the fish.
5 Sprinkle the top with breadcrumbs, cheese and small pieces of margarine.
6 Bake in the centre of a moderately hot oven (400°F.—Gas Mark 5) for 25–30 minutes, depending on the thickness of the fish.

Cod Portugaise

Cooking time 30 minutes

You will need:

4 cod cutlets
salt and pepper
nut of butter
1 chopped onion
1 clove garlic, if liked
little chopped parsley
sprig of thyme
12 oz. peeled tomatoes
1 tablespoon tarragon vinegar
1 tablespoon water

1 Season cod cutlets with salt and pepper and lay them in a well-buttered shallow fireproof dish.

2 Add the chopped onion and the crushed garlic, roughly chopped parsley and sprig of thyme, covering all with the chopped, peeled tomatoes.
3 Moisten with tarragon vinegar and water, cook in a moderate oven (375°F.—Gas Mark 4) for 30 minutes.
4 Arrange the cutlets in a serving dish, reduce the cooking liquor by rapid boiling, taste for seasoning, add a few bits of butter and pour over the fish.

Crab salad

No cooking

1 medium-sized crab is enough for 2 people 1 large one for 4 people. Feel the crab when you buy it and if it feels surprisingly light for its size, ask the fishmonger to break it open – for 'lightness' often indicates that it is 'watery' and you are not getting good solid crab meat.

1 Either ask fishmonger to dress crab or open the main part of the shell by pulling up the rounded part.
2 Take out the skin-like 'bag' and the greyish-brown fingers, both of which should be discarded.
3 Remove all white meat and mix with the meat from the claws.
4 Remove the brown meat and keep this separately.
5 To make the salad arrange crab meat on bed of lettuce. Top with mayonnaise and garnish with tomatoes and cucumber.

Crab scallops

Cooking time 15 minutes

You will need:

1 dressed crab (large enough for 4 people)
4 tablespoons mayonnaise or salad dressing
little grated cheese if wished
4 tablespoons Worcestershire sauce
½ teaspoon made mustard
about 2 tablespoons crumbs
butter

1 Mix the crab meat, mayonnaise, sauce and mustard together.
2 Put into scallop shells which should be buttered first.
3 Scatter crumbs on top with a little butter and grated cheese and heat until crisp in the oven.
4 Serve with crisp toast and salad.

Cod's roe and bacon

Cooking time 6–10 minutes

In order to save time buy the ready cooked cod's roe.

1 Cut roe into slices.
2 Fry rashers of bacon until just crisp. Lift on to hot dish.
3 Add a little extra fat if necessary, fry the cod's roe until golden and hot.
4 Serve with watercress or fried tomatoes.

Cod's roe pie

Cooking time 25–30 minutes

You will need:

12 oz. cooked cod's roe
2 tablespoons grated cheese
1 lb. cooked potatoes
½ pint white sauce or anchovy sauce (see page 21)

1 Cut roe into slices, arrange in a pie dish and pour the sauce evenly over the top.
2 Mash the potatoes thoroughly, pile or pipe on top of the dish.
3 Sprinkle grated cheese on top and bake in hot oven (450°F.—Gas Mark 7) for 20 minutes.

Shrimp salad

No cooking

You will need:

6–8 oz. fresh or frozen prawns or shrimps
mayonnaise
lettuce
tomatoes

1 If using frozen prawns or shimps allow these to de-frost very gradually.
2 Toss the shell fish in mayonnaise. Serve on a bed of lettuce garnished with tomatoes, etc.

Creamed shrimp curry

Cooking time 20 minutes

You will need:

small jar shrimps
4 hard-boiled eggs
3 oz. rice
1 oz. butter
2 tablespoons cream
1 can concentrated mushroom soup
1 level teaspoon curry powder

1 Boil rice in salted water.
2 Heat butter.
3 Fry onion gently.
4 Stir in curry powder then add soup and heat.
5 Stir in shrimps, cream and chopped and halved hard-boiled eggs.
6 Season sauce if necessary.
7 Serve curry mixture with the boiled rice on either side.

Crunchy-top fish casserole

Cooking time 15 minutes

You will need:

1½ oz. butter or margarine	½ pint milk
1 tablespoon tomato ketchup	8 oz. cooked, flaked, smoked haddock or other fish (canned if wished
seasoning to taste	
½ oz. flour	
topping	
6 medium slices (approximately 3–4 oz.) bread	2 oz. butter or margarine
	1½ oz. grated Cheddar cheese

1 Melt 1½ oz. butter or margarine in a pan.
2 Stir in flour and cook slowly, without browning, for 2 minutes.
3 Remove from heat, gradually add milk, then reheat, stirring, till sauce comes to the boil and thickens.
4 Simmer 3 minutes, then add fish and ketchup.
5 Season to taste.
6 Turn into a greased heatproof dish.
7 Meanwhile, make topping by melting 2 oz. butter in pan.
8 Cut bread into cubes and fry in butter.
9 Top fish mixture with fried bread cubes, and sprinkle with grated cheese.
10 Brown under the quick grill.
11 Serve with a green salad or French beans or peas and grilled tomatoes or hot baby beetroot for colour.

HOT LOBSTER DISHES

Hot lobster dishes make a delicious party or special occasion dish and the following are quick and easy adaptations of classic lobster recipes. Be extra fussy that your lobster is very fresh and do not over-cook, otherwise it can become tough. Use the small claws of the lobster to provide an attractive garnish and serve with plenty of lemon.

Lobster Américaine

Cooking time 20–25 minutes

You will need:

1 large or 2 medium lobsters	2–3 large tomatoes
2 oz. butter	1 onion or 2 shallots
salt and pepper	1 gill white wine
	1 gill brandy

1 Dice the onion finely and fry in the butter.
2 Add the skinned tomatoes, wine and brandy and simmer for about 10 minutes.
3 Remove all lobster meat from shell and claws, slice and add to the tomato mixture. Heat for about 5 minutes.
4 Serve with crisp toast.

Curried lobster

Cooking time 45 minutes

You will need:

1 really large lobster or 2 medium sized lobsters	1 teaspoon sugar
2 large onions	2 oz. margarine or oil
1 teaspoon mixed spice	rice and chutney
½ teaspoon cinnamon	6–8 oz. chopped cucumber
1 teaspoon curry powder	1–2 oz. grated or desiccated coconut
½ pint fish stock	½ teaspoon powdered ginger
1 tablespoon lemon juice	1 chopped clove garlic
1 dessertspoon turmeric powder	1–2 oz. dried fruit
	1 dessertspoon flour
	2 bay leaves

1 To make the fish stock put the very small lobster claws, the head of the lobster and ¾ pint water into a saucepan with bay leaves and a little seasoning.
2 Simmer gently for 20 minutes, strain and make liquid up to ½ pint if necessary.
3 Heat the margarine in a saucepan, then fry the sliced onion and garlic until just soft.
4 Add the flour, spices, sugar and stock and cook very gently for 5 minutes, stirring all the time.
5 Add the flaked lobster meat, the cucumber, coconut and dried fruit and bring to the boil, stirring well to keep a smooth sauce.
6 Lower the heat and cook very gently for just about 5 minutes.
7 Serve with rice and chutney.

Lobster Cardinal

Cooking time 15–20 minutes

You will need:

1 large and 2 medium hen lobsters*	1 tablespoon sherry
2 tablespoons cream	½ pint white sauce (see page 21)

* The hen lobster has a bright red roe or coral. The fishmonger will pick this out for you or you can tell a hen lobster by the fact that it has a very wide tail.

1 Remove the meat from the lobster. Dice this.
2 Mash the coral rather well.
3 Make the white sauce.
4 Add the coral and stir in well.
5 Add the lobster meat, cream and sherry. Heat gently.
6 Pile into 4 hot dishes or serve on a bed of rice.

Lobster salad

No cooking

Allow 1 small or ½ medium lobster per person. Either ask the fishmonger to prepare lobster or split the lobster, remove the intestinal vein, and the lady fingers. These are found where the small claws join the body and shouldn't be eaten.

Crack the large claws very carefully and remove the lobster meat.

One way of serving lobster for lobster mayonnaise or salad, is to leave the meat in the shells and serve a half shell on each plate, piled with lobster flesh and garnished with salad, mayonnaise, meat from the large claws and the small claws.

The second way of serving the salad is to remove all the meat from the body, dice this, mix with mayonnaise and arrange on a bed of salad.

Lobster mornay

Cooking time 15–20 minutes

You will need:

1 large or 2 medium lobsters
1 tablespoon cream
½ pint cheese sauce (see page 21)

Make the sauce.

Add the diced lobster meat and cream and heat gently.

Serve on a bed of rice or with crisp toast.

Devilled crab

Cooking time 5 minutes

You will need:

dressed crab for 4 people
1 teaspoon made mustard
seasoning
3 oz. breadcrumbs
2 teaspoons Worcester sauce
little top of milk
butter

Mix crab with about 2 oz. breadcrumbs, Worcester sauce, seasoning, mustard and enough top of milk to moisten.

Put either into 4 individual dishes or into 1 large dish or crab shell, top with remaining crumbs and butter and brown under grill.

Serve with new potatoes and peas.

Fish rarebit

Cooking time 12 minutes

You will need:

4 slices of toast
seasoning
4–6 oz. grated cheese
4 tomatoes
lemon
watercress
4 oz. flaked smoked haddock or canned crab meat or left over white fish or shelled prawns
dash of Worcester sauce

for the sauce

½ oz. flour
½ gill milk
1 oz. margarine or butter

1 Make the sauce which will be very thick and will, therefore, need stirring a lot.
2 Add Worcester sauce and cheese, heat for 1 minute, add fish.
3 Meanwhile cook whole tomatoes in grill pan.
4 Toast bread under the grill, butter if wished, cover with fish mixture and return to the grill, browning this on the grid while tomatoes complete cooking.
5 Serve each rarebit with a tomato on top.
6 Garnish with watercress and lemon.

Fish cream

Cooking time 45 minutes

You will need:

8 oz. flaked cooked fish (cod, hake, fresh or dried haddock are particularly good)
½ pint thick white sauce (see page 21)
2 level tablespoons cream from the top of the milk or evaporated milk
1 egg
few drops anchovy essence
few drops vinegar
seasoning

1 Mix all the ingredients together.
2 Put into a greased basin.
3 Cover thoroughly, tie down and steam for 45 minutes.
4 Turn out and serve hot or cold with peas and grilled tomatoes.
5 Garnish with lemon.

Creamed fish creole

Cooking time 10 minutes

You will need for 2–3 servings

½ pint white sauce (see page 21 (or can of cream of celery soup)
1 tablespoon lemon juice or dry sherry
3 tablespoons sweet pepper strips (or chopped canned pimento)
4 tablespoons cooked peas
3 slices bread, toasted or fried
3 tablespoons single or cultured cream (or extra sauce)
¼ teaspoon celery salt
good sprinkling white pepper
8 oz. flaked cooked fish

1 Heat gently together sauce, cream, lemon juice, seasoning, sweet pepper strips, peas and fish.

2 Turn into hot serving dish; garnish with triangles of toasted or fried bread.

Fish potato puffs

Cooking time 45 minutes

You will need:

12 oz. flaked cooked white fish seasoning
2 teaspoons finely chopped onion
3 eggs
hard-boiled egg sauce
8 oz. well mashed potato
squeeze of lemon juice
chopped celery (use a little extra onion if you have no celery
1 oz. butter

1 Toss onion and celery in the butter, mix with potato, fish, lemon, parsley and egg yolks.
2 Season well.
3 Fold in stiffly beaten egg whites.
4 Put into soufflé dish and bake for 40 minutes in moderately hot oven (400°F.—Gas Mark 5).
5 Serve with hard-boiled egg sauce made by mixing 2 hard-boiled eggs with ½ pint white sauce (see page 21).

Fried fish

Cooking time 4–8 minutes

This is one of the most popular ways of serving any fish. It is important to remember the following:–

1 Dry the fish well and coat very thinly with seasoned flour.
2 Dip in fritter batter (see next column) or in beaten egg and crumbs. Shake off surplus crumbs or allow excess batter to drain away.
3 For shallow frying make sure the fat (which can be oil, cooking fat, butter) is hot. Put in the fish, cook steadily until brown, turn and cook on the other side. If using deep fat make sure this is not too hot otherwise the outside browns before the fish is cooked.
4 For shallow frying allow 2–3 minutes on either side, for filleted fish. 4–5 minutes for thicker fish cutlets or whole fish.
5 For deep frying allow 3–4 minutes total cooking time for fillets—7–8 minutes for whole fish or cutlets.
6 Always drain fried fish. Use kitchen paper. The latest absorbent kitchen rolls are excellent, but never use greaseproof paper.
7 Do not overcook the fish.

The ideal accompaniment is beautifully fried chips.

Fish to fry whole. Most fish can be fried whole but it is correct to fry small codling, fresh haddock, sole, plaice, trout, herring or mackerel whole rather than fillet them.

To coat in egg and crumbs

1 Add little water or milk to egg to make it easier to brush over fish.
2 Put crumbs into paper bag or on sheet of paper and turn fish in this, pressing crumbs firmly on to fish.
3 Use either very fine soft white crumbs or dried breadcrumbs.

Fritter batter

You will need:

4 oz. flour
1 egg
1½–2 gills milk and water
seasoning

1 Sieve flour and seasoning. Add egg.
2 Gradually beat in liquid.
3 For fillets use large quanitity of liquid. For more solid cod, etc., you can use 1½ gills only.

Fried fish in cheese

Cooking time 6–10 minutes

1 An excellent way to vary fish and to add extra food value if the fish are small in size is to coat in egg and a mixture of breadcrumbs and grated cheese.
2 Fry in shallow fat until crisp and golden brown.

Fried fish meunière

Cooking time 6–10 minutes

1 Do not coat the fish with egg and crumbs or with batter but instead with a very light coating of seasoned flour.
2 Cook in butter until just tender.
3 Lift out of the butter and put on to a hot dish. Add the squeeze of lemon juice or few drops of vinegar to the butter, a few capers and a little chopped parsley and cook gently until the butter is a dark brown.
4 Pour over the fish.
5 The most suitable fish are fillets of plaice, sole, portions of skate or large prawns.

Grilled fish

Cooking time 4–10 minutes

Most fish is suitable for grilling. Fillets of fish, unless very thick, can be grilled without turning. Whole fish should be turned so that it is cooked on both sides.

1 Make sure that the grill is hot before you begin cooking and keep the fish well brushed with melted butter so that it doesn't dry.

Never over-cook grilled fish.
- For grilling the fillets of fish allow approximately 4 minutes, turning the heat down after the first 2–3 minutes if desired.
- For thicker fish grill quickly for 2–3 minutes on either side then reduce heat for a further 3–4 minutes.
- An ideal accompaniment for any grilled fish are grilled mushrooms and tomatoes which can be cooked at the same time.

Devilled grilled fish

Cooking time 4–10 minutes

Spread the fish with butter, to which you have added a little curry powder and a few drops of Worcester sauce.

Tomato grilled fish

Cooking time 4–10 minutes

1 Add 2 or 3 teaspoons of concentrated tomato purée to a knob of butter.
2 Spread over the fish and grill as before.

Maître d'hôtel sauce

No cooking

To serve with grilled fish.
1 As white sauce (see page 21) but use ½ fish stock.
2 Add 2 teaspoons chopped parsley and 3 tablespoons thick cream just before serving.

Maître d'hôtel butter or Parsley butter

1 Add chopped parsley, seasoning and squeeze lemon juice and work into butter.
2 Chill and cut into neat pieces.

Hasty salmon pie

Cooking time 10–15 minutes

You will need:

a good-sized can of pink or red salmon
small can evaporated milk
pinch celery salt
pepper
1 oz. butter
1 onion
1 can peas (or peas and carrots or frozen peas)

for biscuit crust
4 oz. flour (with plain flour add 1 teaspoon baking powder)
1 oz. margarine
salt
milk

1 First make biscuit crust. Sieve flour and salt, rub in margarine, add enough milk to bind.
2 Roll out, cut into small rounds.
3 Bake for 8–10 minutes on greased baking tray in hot oven (450°F.—Gas Mark 7).
4 Meanwhile, fry sliced onion in the butter, add the salmon, evaporated milk, well-drained peas and seasoning.
5 Heat thoroughly. Put mixture into dish and top with crisp biscuit rounds.

Jiffy grilled plaice

Cooking time 5–8 minutes

You will need:

2 oz. margarine or butter
juice of ½ lemon
chopped parsley
seasonings
1 large size (14 oz.) carton frozen plaice fillets—partially thawed, or 8 small fillets plaice

1 Melt the margarine in the grill pan.
2 Season the fish and lay it flesh-side down in the pan.
3 Cook for 1 minute.
4 Turn with flesh-side up and grill steadily until golden brown and cooked, about 5–8 minutes, depending on thickness.
5 Arrange on a hot serving dish, add lemon juice to the remaining fat in pan, reheat.
6 Pour over the fish.
7 Sprinkle liberally with chopped parsley.

Kedgeree of salmon

Cooking time 30 minutes

You will need:

8 oz. flaked cooked salmon or canned salmon
2–3 tablespoons cream or top of milk
toast
3 oz. rice
2 hard-boiled eggs
2 oz. butter or margarine
seasoning
parsley to garnish

1 Cook rice in boiling salted water, drain and shake dry.
2 Heat the butter in a pan, stir in the rice, cream, fish and the chopped hard-boiled egg white.
3 Heat gently.
4 Season well.
5 Pile on to a hot dish and garnish with triangles of toast, chopped egg yolk and parsley.

Oven 'fried' fish

Cooking time 15–25 minutes

Although it takes a little longer to cook fish this way in the oven it needs no attention and also far less fat is required.
1 Coat the fish in egg and breadcrumbs, not in batter.

2 Grease the baking tin. Put it into the oven to get very hot.
3 When hot put the fish on to this and brush with a little melted fat.
4 Cook in a moderately hot oven (400°F.—Gas Mark 5) for 15–25 minutes.

Prawns in tomato sauce

Cooking time 20 minutes

You will need for 1–2 servings:

1–2 dessertspoons thick tomato purée	1 dessertspoon mayonnaise
teaspoon lemon juice	2 oz. prawns
salt	2 oz. rice
sugar	paprika
lemon slices and parsley to garnish	powdered basil
	1 gill white stock or water

1 Season the tomato purée, mix in mayonnaise.
2 Add white stock and prawns.
3 Heat gently in a saucepan.
4 Cook the rice in boiling salted water until tender (for about 20 minutes).
5 Place rice on a hot dish and pour the prawn mixture over it.
6 Garnish with lemon slices and parsley.

Prawn and haddock casserole

Cooking time 10–15 minutes

You will need:

4–6 oz. shelled prawns	1 large smoked haddock, or smoked haddock fillet
½ pint tomato juice (bottled or canned)	pepper
½ oz. flour	1 oz. butter
parsley	

1 Heat the butter in a pan, stir in the flour then add the tomato juice.
2 Bring to the boil and cook until slightly thickened.
3 Cut the haddock into neat pieces, put into the tomato liquid and poach gently for 5 minutes.
4 Add the prawns and cook without boiling for a further 5–10 minutes.
5 Serve with frozen peas and crisp rolls.
6 Decorate with parsley.

Rice and fish ring

Cooking time 20–25 minutes

You will need:

6 oz. rice (preferably Patna rice)	1 can salmon or tuna fish
1–2 oz. grated cheese	2 eggs
1 oz. butter	½ gill milk
1 teaspoon anchovy sauce	seasoning
½ pint white sauce (see page 21)	hard-boiled eggs (optional)

1 Put rice in 3 pints boiling salted water and cook for 15 minutes.
2 Meanwhile make white sauce (see page 21) adding anchovy sauce and flaked salmon.
3 Keep sauce warm while you strain rice.
4 Put rice back in saucepan with beaten eggs, milk, cheese, butter and seasoning. Cook for several minutes until egg is just set.
5 Form into a ring and fill centre with fish mixture.
6 If wished, garnish with sliced hard-boiled egg.

Alternative fillings. Cooked mushrooms, chopped ham, corned beef, frozen (or canned) prawns and hard-boiled eggs. Mix with sauce as given in recipe above.

Rice and shrimp salad

Cooking time 20 minutes

You will need:

3 oz. rice	2 tablespoons chopped cucumber
1 pint prawns or shrimps	1 tablespoon vinegar
1 tablespoon oil	few capers (not essential)
seasoning	little chopped parsley
to garnish	
lettuce, cress, tomatoes	radishes

1 Cook the rice until just tender in boiling salted water.
2 Strain and mix with the prawns or shrimps and all the other ingredients.
3 Put into a basin or mould and leave until the mixture holds its shape and the rice is quite cold.
4 Turn out on to a bed of lettuce and garnish with sliced tomatoes, cress, water-lilies of radish.
5 Save a few shrimps to put on top of the salad.

Salmon and hard-boiled eggs au gratin

Cooking time 20 minutes

You will need:

1 can concentrated cream of mushroom soup	1 can (small size) pink or red salmon
3 oz. grated cheese	3 or 4 eggs
4 tomatoes	4 slices bread
	parsley and gherkin if wished

1 Put on the eggs to hard-boil, meanwhile heat the soup. Do not dilute it, and add the contents of the tin of salmon.
2 If desired a little chopped parsley and/or chopped gherkin can be added.
3 When the eggs are cooked put into cold water so that they can be shelled easily.
4 Halve the eggs, arrange in a dish, pour the salmon and mushroom mixture on top and cover with grated cheese.

5 Brown under a hot grill.
6 Meanwhile toast the bread and grill the tomatoes.
7 Arrange the tomatoes in a separate dish and cut the toast into triangles.
8 Put these round the edge of the fish dish.

Quick prawn curry

Cooking time 5–10 minutes

You will need:

8 oz. prawns
¼ pint mayonnaise
1 teaspoon curry powder

1 Blend the curry powder with the mayonnaise, add the prawns.
2 To serve cold arrange on a bed of lettuce.
3 To serve hot put into a pan and heat very gently for 5–10 minutes.

Salmon à la Mornay

Cooking time 20 minutes

You will need:

4 cooked potatoes
4 oz. grated Swiss cheese
buttered crumbs (crumbs tossed in melted butter)
1 egg yolk
½ pint white sauce (see page 21)
1 can salmon

1 Mash potatoes and line greased baking dish with them.
2 Add cheese and egg yolk to the white sauce and pour half of it over potatoes.
3 Add fish and cover with remaining sauce and buttered breadcrumbs.
4 Bake in a moderate oven for 20 minutes (375°F.—Gas Mark 4).

Quick sauces to serve with fish

White sauce Cooking time 5–8 minutes

1 oz. butter or margarine
½ pint milk for coating consistency i.e. sauce
1 pint milk for thin white sauce for soups
1 oz. flour
salt, pepper
¼ pint milk for panada or binding consistency

1 Heat the butter gently, remove from the heat and stir in the flour.
2 Return to the heat and cook gently for a few minutes, so that the 'roux', as the butter and flour mixture is called, does not brown.
3 Again remove the pan from the heat and gradually blend in the cold milk.
4 Bring to the boil and cook, stirring with a wooden spoon until smooth.
5 Season well. If any small lumps have formed whisk sharply.

Anchovy sauce Cooking time 5 minutes. Make white sauce as in preceding recipe, adding chopped anchovies or 1 teaspoon anchovy essence.

Cheese sauce Cooking time 5–8 minutes. Stir in 3–6 oz. grated cheese when sauce has thickened and add a little mustard.

Lemon sauce No cooking

¼ pint mayonnaise
juice of 1 lemon
grated rind of 1 lemon

Whisk lemon juice into mayonnaise. Add rind.

Shrimp sauce Cooking time 5–8 minutes. Make white sauce, add about ½–1 teacup chopped prawns and a little anchovy essence just before serving. If using fresh prawns simmer shells and use ¼ pint stock instead of the same amount of milk.

Tartare sauce No cooking

¼ pint mayonnaise
2 teaspoons chopped parsley
2 teaspoons chopped gherkins
1 teaspoon capers

Mix all ingredients together.

Scallops and bacon (Escallops)

Cooking time 10 minutes

You will need:

4 scallops
4 rashers bacon
squeeze lemon juice

1 Remove scallops from shells.
2 Add squeeze lemon juice.
3 Wrap round in bacon rashers and put on to a skewer, or on grid of grill pan.
4 Grill steadily until cooked.
5 Take care not to cook too quickly otherwise the bacon will be cooked before scallops.

Scallops in cream sauce (Escallops)

Cooking time 10–12 minutes

You will need:

4 scallops
1½ gills milk
seasoning
lemon juice
1 oz. butter
1 oz. flour
2 tablespoons cream
paprika pepper

1 Simmer the scallops in the milk for 5–6 minutes until just tender.
2 Lift out of the milk and put on to the shells or in a hot dish.

3 Blend flour with the cream, add to the milk together with butter and seasoning.
4 Bring to the boil and cook until smooth and thick. Add squeeze lemon juice.
5 Pour over the scallops. Garnish with red paprika pepper.
6 Serve with rice or toast.

Spiced fish loaf

Cooking time 50 minutes

You will need:

1¼ lb. flaked cooked white fish
2 eggs
2 tablespoons chopped gherkins
3 oz. breadcrumbs
½ gill milk
good grating of nutmeg
seasoning

1 Mix all the ingredients together.
2 Put into a very well greased loaf tin.
3 Stand this in a tin of water and bake in a very moderate oven (350°F.—Gas Mark 3) for approximately 50 minutes.
4 Serve hot with ½ pint white sauce poured over the top and arrange olives and sliced egg on top.

Stuffed fillets of fish

(1 helping)

Cooking time 15–20 minutes

You will need:

1 large or 2 small fillets of whiting, plaice or sole
margarine
tiny jar of lobster, prawn or shrimp paste for stuffing
seasoning
lemon juice (plastic lemons are most practical for you can use a few drops when required and the rest will keep)

1 Wash and dry the fish, season and squeeze a few drops of lemon juice over, spread with the paste.
2 Roll firmly or fold over and put on to a plate with a little margarine.
3 Cover with the saucepan lid or another plate.
4 Stand over a pan of boiling water and cook for 15–20 minutes.

Poultry and Meat

Poultry and meat cooked in a hurry

When short of time, there is a tendency to feel one must have a succession of grilled or fried meat or poultry. Certainly the more tender pieces of meat cook more quickly—most of them can be grilled and fried in about 15 minutes. However, they do tend to be expensive, and there are many other ways of making quick appetizing meals from more economical ingredients. In the following chapter I have provided you with a variety of new ideas which I trust will give you the basis for a number of new main meals.

With regard to steaks and chops, even these become rather monotonous if always served in the same way. However, with a little imagination and not much extra preparation you can cook your chops and cutlets in many different ways. In fact, if you try some of the recipes in the following pages, you will be able to make the family believe you have spent a long time in preparing them.

Jointed young chicken also lends itself to a variety of tasty recipes, and you will find a number of suggestions for serving it. Boiling chicken can also be delicious and much more economical, as you will see from some of my ideas. For recipes which require longer cooking time, a pressure cooker is a very wise investment for the hurried cook. The pressure cooked recipes which I include in this chapter will be a guide for boiling and stews, and can be varied in a number of ways.

Other quick cooking meats are liver (choose calves' or lambs'), kidneys, bacon and sweetbreads and sausages all of which can be cooked in a number of interesting ways.

Also included are a number of recipes using bacon, gammon and ham, and the latter part of the chapter is devoted to meals made from canned and ready-cooked or frozen meats, all of which can be transformed into quick and satisfying main dishes.

Fried chicken

1 To save time buy the jointed chicken—or if this is not available most shops will cut it up for you. Very small chickens are cut into 2 halves—1 per person; larger ones into 4 joints (2 leg joints—2 breast and wing).

2 For quicker frying deep fat is advisable, and one should allow 5–6 minutes at a fairly high heat then turn the heat down for further 10–15 minutes.
Either coat with egg and crumbs or with seasoned flour or batter.
3 For shallow frying do NOT use batter, but seasoned flour or egg and crumbs, and fry steadily in hot butter for 15–20 minutes. If preferred the chicken can be browned only in the fat then transferred to a moderately hot oven and roasted for 25 minutes.
4 Serve with: Fried vegetables and salad.
Fried bananas and canned or frozen corn.

Grilled chicken
This takes about the same time as frying. The poultry should be well brushed with plenty of hot butter.
Serve with grilled bacon, tomatoes, or tomato sauce (see page 38).

Mushrooms and grilled chicken

Cooking time 15–25 minutes

You will need:

very young chicken, jointed (either 1 large or 2 small)
3 oz. butter
breadcrumbs
8 oz. mushrooms
4 chopped shallots
1 crushed clove garlic
1 tablespoon chopped parsley

1 Heat butter in grill pan.
2 Add to that the thinly sliced mushrooms, the shallots, the garlic and the parsley.
3 Joint very young chicken—use 1 large or 2 smaller birds and brush the chickens with melted butter, cook in the grill pan, on top of the mushrooms, etc., turning frequently.
4 Just before serving, sprinkle each joint with breadcrumbs. Replace under grill and brown.

Chicken country style

Cooking time 35–40 minutes

You will need:

4 joints frying chicken
½ can milk
2 tablespoons chopped parsley
2 oz. butter
can concentrated vegetable soup
1 clove garlic (can be omitted) seasoning

1 Brown joints of chicken in hot butter in pan with crushed garlic.
2 Add vegetable soup.
3 Pour enough milk into can to half fill, then pour this into saucepan.
4 Stir well until soup has dissolved.
5 Bring to boil and simmer until tender. Season well.
6 Serve garnished with parsley.

Chicken biscaienne

Cooking time 30 minutes

You will need:

small young chicken
2 oz. bacon (green bacon being best)
1 oz. flour
1 or 2 leaves of sage
1 oz. butter
1 small onion
5 tomatoes
salt and pepper

1 Cut up the chicken into pieces for serving.
2 Fry these for 1–2 minutes with the chopped bacon.
3 Add butter.
4 Sprinkle with flour, stir well and add chopped onion.
5 Cook on for 2 or 3 minutes, then add peeled tomatoes and sage.
6 Season well with salt and pepper, put on the lid and cook gently for about 25 minutes, shaking the pan now and again.

Economical chicken pie

Cooking time 35 minutes

You will need:

8 oz. shortcrust pastry (see page 86)

filling
1 can condensed cream of chicken soup or ½ pint **thick** chicken stock
4 oz. cooked chicken (diced)
salt
pepper
1 teaspoon lemon juice
1 hard-boiled egg

to glaze a little milk

1 Line an 8-inch flan ring or sandwich tin with ⅔ of the pastry.
2 Mix the cream of chicken soup with cooked chicken, seasoning and lemon juice.
3 Spread the mixture in pastry case.
4 Arrange sliced hard-boiled egg on top.
5 Cover with remaining pastry, seal edges and flute.
6 Brush with milk and bake in a moderately hot oven (400°F.—Gas Mark 5) for 30–35 minutes.
7 Serve hot with vegetables or cold with salad.

Corn and chicken platter

Cooking time 10 minutes

You will need for 2–3 servings

1–5oz. packet quick-frozen sweet corn*
8 oz. cooked diced chicken

for the dressing

4 tablespoons oil
1 tablespoon vinegar
salt, pepper
sugar, salt
olives
chopped parsley

* Canned corn needs no cooking.

1 Cook the sweet corn according to directions on the packet and leave to get cold.
2 Marinade the chicken in the French dressing for about 1 hour.
3 Arrange on a dish with the sweet corn and garnish with olives and parsley.

Snacks with chicken left-overs

1

Stuff tomatoes with tiny untidy pieces of chicken chopped very finely and mixed with diced cucumber and mayonnaise.

2

Combine the pieces of chicken with a thick sauce.

3

Mix the chicken with scrambled egg as a filling for pastry cases, in sandwiches or on toast.

USING A BOILING CHICKEN WISELY

A boiling chicken is an excellent buy for you can use it in so many different dishes. For example:

Meal No. 1 (hot)

Chicken with Egg Sauce Slice the breast from the boiled chicken, then serve on rice or with vegetables with a hard-boiled egg sauce i.e. add chopped hard-boiled egg white to white sauce (see page 21, but make with half chicken stock and half milk). Garnish with crisp bacon rolls and the egg yolk and mixed vegetables.

Meal No. 2

Chicken Royal Another hot meal. Dice the meat from 1 leg and thigh. Add a wing if not enough. Make up ¾ pint white sauce—or to save even more time make up extra sauce and save ¾ pint from first dish. Add the diced chicken, a chopped pepper, the corn from a corn on the cob (gently cooked), 1 chopped slice of ham. Serve on buttered toast or with vegetables.

Meal No. 3 (cold)

Chicken mould Make 1 pint tomato flavoured jelly by dissolving ¾ oz. powder gelatine in 1 pint tomato juice (buy the tomato juice that hasn't a lot of Worcester). When cold, but not set, add 2 teacups diced cooked chicken, chopped hard-boiled egg, cup mixed vegetables. Pour into a mould and allow to set. Serve with salad.

Mixed grill

cooking time 10–30 minutes

The ingredients can vary but choose a selection of the following:

You will need:

a small cutlet
sausage
piece of steak
piece of lambs' or calves' liver
lamb or pigs' kidney
mushrooms
halved or whole tomatoes
rasher of bacon

1 Put the mushrooms and tomatoes in the grill pan, seasoning well.
2 Start these under a hot grill for a few minutes.
3 Put the meat (well seasoned), with the exception of the bacon, on the grid, brushing with plenty of melted butter, margarine or fat.
4 Cook quickly, turning as necessary.
5 Add bacon at the last minute so this will not be overcooked.
6 Arrange on hot dish and serve with peas, French fried potatoes, chipped or sauté potatoes.
7 Accompany with a crisp green salad if wished.

Grilled steak

Cooking time 5–15 minutes

1 Brush grid and steak with butter or olive oil.
2 Season steak and if wished break down tissues by 'banging' with rolling pin or meat tenderiser. Or you may care to marinade the meat by leaving it to stand for 1 hour in a mixture of oil and vinegar to which you add seasoning,

including a pinch garlic salt or crushed clove garlic.
Put on to grid of grill pan with tomatoes, mushrooms at bottom of pan.
Cook rapidly on either side under hot grill for a few minutes.
This is sufficient for people who like their steak 'rare' (underdone) in the centre, but if you like it well done, lower the heat and cook steadily.
Garnish with watercress, parsley butter (see page 19) perhaps adding a dash Worcester sauce instead of lemon, asparagus tips, fried onion rings, croûtons of bread.
Serve with mixed vegetables, potatoes, and try a really crisp salad with French dressing as an accompaniment.

The most popular steaks for grilling are:

Rump
An excellent flavour, a little less tender than steaks from fillet.

Fillet
Particularly tender. The fillet is limited so this is expensive, for it comes from the undercut of sirloin.

Minute
A thin steak, generally cut from fillet, which needs only ½–1 minute's cooking on either side.

Sirloin
A steak cut from the sirloin, not undercut, excellent flavour.

Porterhouse
Large piece of sirloin steak.

Chateaubriand
A very large fillet steak.

To fry steak

Cooking time 3–12 minutes

Choose same quality and cuts of steak as for grilling.

1 Heat a good knob of butter or olive oil in the pan and put in the steak.
2 Brown quickly on either side to seal in the flavour.
3 Lower the heat and cook gently for about 10–12 minutes for well done steak—about 6–8 minutes for medium cooked and 3–4 for underdone.
4 French or English mustard are the usual accompaniment. Some people like Worcester sauce. Tomatoes, mushrooms, watercress are the best garnish, or fried onion rings.

To fry onions

Cooking time 8 minutes

1 Peel and cut onions into rings.
2 Separate rings. Dip in milk and seasoned flour.
3 Shake off surplus flour and fry in shallow or deep fat.

Tournedos of steak

Buy fillet steaks and ask the butcher to tie them into rounds to form tournedos. If you prefer to use small wooden or metal skewers you can do so. To keep outer side of meat very moist wrap fat bacon around it. Fry or grill as preferred. Serve on rounds of fried bread.

Tournedos of

Steak Africaine

Grill or fry the steaks. Garnish with fried banana. Serve with horseradish sauce.

Tournedos of

Steak Artésienne

Fry the steak. Garnish with rounds of aubergine, tomatoes and/or celery. Top with rings of fried onion.

Tournedos of

Steak Belle-Hélène

Fry the steak, garnish with asparagus and truffle. Truffles are obtained in cans and are very expensive, so mushrooms can be substituted.

Fillet steaks

à l'Américaine

Cooking time 10–15 minutes

You will need:

4 fillet steaks
crisp breadcrumbs
creamed potatoes or potato crisps
1 egg
4 bananas
watercress
horseradish sauce

1 Peel and halve the bananas, dip them in beaten egg and roll in breadcrumbs.
2 Fry in a little butter.
3 Serve on top of the grilled fillet steaks.
4 Arrange on a hot dish with a border of piped potatoes or potato crisps and pour a little of the sauce round.

To make the horseradish sauce: Stir either 2 tablespoons fresh, grated horseradish or 2 tablespoons bottled horseradish into ½ pint creamy white sauce (see page 21). Add a little extra seasoning.

Steak Diane

Cooking time 3–4 minutes

1 Fry minute steaks (very thin steaks) in hot butter.
2 A little finely chopped shallot and parsley together with a few drops of Worcester sauce or brandy can be added to the butter before putting in the meat.
3 Serve at once.

Casserole of steak

Cooking time 15–20 minutes

You will need:

4 small fillet steaks	can vegetable soup
pinch herbs	water
slice bread	salt
pepper	made mustard

1 Heat soup and approximately ½ pint water in pan.
2 Put in steaks, herbs, salt and pepper.
3 Simmer gently for 10–15 minutes.
4 Spread a small slice crustless bread with mustard and cook for 5 minutes.
5 Beat into liquid so bread disintegrates to thicken sauce.

Speedy beef stroganoff

Cooking time 10 minutes

You will need:

1 large onion	pinch pepper
1 can button mushrooms, drained	½ teaspoon salt
1 lb. rump or fillet steak	⅛ teaspoon garlic salt
¼–½ teaspoon paprika	1 teaspoon diced parsley
¼ pint sour cream*	4 oz. cooked rice or noodles

* or thin cream and 1 tablespoon lemon juice

1 Sauté onion and mushrooms in butter or margarine very gently until onion is tender.
2 Add steak and cook very gently, stirring constantly, for about 5 minutes.
3 The meat should not brown and should be rare inside.
4 Add the pepper, salt, garlic salt, parsley and paprika.
5 Stir and simmer for 3 or 4 minutes longer.
6 Just before serving add the sour cream.
7 Heat briefly, serve over rice or noodles.

Hamburgers de luxe

Cooking time 10–12 minutes

You will need:

1 lb. minced rump steak	good pinch herbs
4 oz. soft crumbs	soft rolls
1 tablespoon chopped onion	seasoning
	1 egg

1 Make the patties by mixing meat, crumbs, onion, seasoning, herbs and egg together.
2 Form into 8 flat cakes.
3 Fry carefully on both sides.
4 If wished add a slice of cheese on top just before serving between the rolls.
5 Serve as well big bowls of crisp lettuce, chicory, watercress and quartered fresh tomatoes.
6 Have fresh fruit salad, or cheese and crust bread to follow.

Cheeseburger

Cooking time 10 minutes

You will need:

hamburger mixture

1½ oz. breadcrumbs	6–8 oz. fairly lean steak, minced
1 tablespoon minced or grated onion	pinch pepper and salt
½ egg to bind.	

cheese rarebit mixture

1 oz. butter or margarine	pinch salt and cayenne pepper
1 level teaspoon made mustard	6 oz. grated Cheddar cheese
4 hamburger buns or soft rolls	2 tablespoons milk

1 Make the hamburgers.
2 Mix together all the ingredients, divide into equal portions and shape into round flat cakes slightly larger than the buns.
3 Prepare the rarebit mixture.
4 Cream the butter or margarine with the seasonings, add grated cheese and milk and mix well.
5 Grill or fry the hamburgers 2 or 3 minutes on each side.
6 Spread a generous helping of the rarebit mixture over both sides of each split hamburger bun and grill to a golden brown.
7 Put a cooked hamburger on bottom of the grilled bun and close.
8 Serve hot with mustard or ketchup.

Beefburgers on baps

Cooking time 10 minutes

You will need for 10–12 beefburgers:

1½ lb. finely minced beefsteak	1 heaped tablespoon browned breadcrumbs
¼ teaspoon black pepper	2 teaspoons made mustard
1 medium onion, in wafer-thin slices	2 tomatoes, sliced
1 teaspoon salt	5 or 6 bap rolls
	little butter

1 Blend the minced meat, salt, pepper and mustard and shape into 10–12 flat cakes.

Place in grill pan, without the grid, and grill at medium heat for 5 minutes each side, or less if preferred rare.

Halve, toast and butter the bap rolls; top each with a beefburger and top these with a wafer slice of onion, slice of tomato and a sprinkle of crumbs.

Dot the top of each with butter and slip under the hot grill for about 3 minutes.

Viennese steaks

Cooking time 15 minutes

You will need for 6 servings

1–2 tablespoons tomato ketchup
1½–2 lb minced beef
1 dessertspoon chopped parsley
little grated nutmeg
black pepper
salt
½ level teaspoon finely crushed dried mixed herbs
2 eggs
1 or 2 onions
flour
butter or oil for frying
brown sauce (see page 37)

1. Mix the minced meat with parsley, nutmeg, seasonings and mixed herbs to taste.
2. Separate 1 egg and set white aside.
3. Beat yolk with another whole egg and use to bind meat mixture.
4. Divide into portions and shape each with floured hands to look like rather large slices of fillet steak.
5. Dredge with flour on all sides.
6. Fry in heated butter or oil until well browned on both sides, then drain and keep hot.
7. Peel and slice onion.
8. Coat with flour, dip into beaten white of egg, then into flour again, and fry until golden and crisp.
9. Serve as a garnish. Or cook a larger quantity and serve round the steaks.
10. Serve brown sauce separately.

Goulash

Pressure cooking time 20–25 minutes

You will need:

1 lb. stewing meat (preferably beef)
1 onion
seasoning (include 1–2 teaspoons paprika pepper)
1 oz. fat
1 gill tomato pulp
1 lb. potatoes
¼ pint stock or water

1. Cut the meat into neat cubes.
2. Heat the fat at the bottom of the cooker and fry the meat and onion until brown.
3. Add the tomato pulp, stock, seasoning and paprika.
4. Fix the lid and bring to pressure.
5. Lower heat and cook for a good 10 minutes.
6. Allow pressure to drop then add the sliced potatoes.
7. Re-fix the lid, bring once again to pressure, lower the heat and cook for 10 minutes.
8. This should be a very thick stew.

Braised heart

Pressure cooking time 25 minutes

You will need:

1 lb. either ox heart or sheep heart
bunch herbs or 1 teaspoon mixed herbs
½ pint stock or water flavoured with meat or vegetable extract
1 oz. flour
1 oz. dripping
2 onions
2 carrots
1 small turnip
seasoning

1. Cut the ox heart into thick slices.
2. Heat the fat in the bottom of the pressure cooker.
3. Flour the hearts and season well.
4. Fry in the hot fat until brown.
5. Add all the other ingredients except the 1 oz. flour.
6. Fix the lid and bring to pressure.
7. Lower the heat and cook for 25 minutes, allow pressure to drop.
8. Blend flour with a very little cold stock, add to the liquid. Bring to the boil and boil for 3 minutes.

Boiled brisket

Pressure cooking time 25–30 minutes

You will need for 6 servings:

2 lb. brisket of beef*
2 large carrots
2 onions
1 small turnip
½ pint water
seasoning
bunch of parsley

1. Cut the vegetables into fairly large pieces.
2. Put into the cooker with the meat, parsley, seasoning and water.
3. Fix the lid and bring to pressure.
4. Lower the heat and cook for 25 minutes.
5. Allow pressure to drop gradually.
6. Boiled beef is served with unthickened gravy.

* *Note:* If the meat is salted, soak for a good hour before cooking. Instead of brisket, topside or silverside of beef can be used.

Brisket salad

Cooked brisket is excellent served cold.

If cooking at home (see preceding recipe) allow to cool in the liquid.

If serving hot, first carve off required amount, then return meat to liquid.

Arrange on a bed of green salad and serve with pickles and mayonnaise.

Liver, fried or grilled

Cooking time 4–8 minutes

When frying or grilling liver, do remember that it should never be overcooked, otherwise instead of being moist and tender it becomes hard and dry. Coat with very little seasoned flour and fry with bacon or brush with melted butter and grill. Allow 2–4 minutes either side depending on thickness.

Devilled liver

Cooking time 6–10 minutes

You will need:

1 lb. calves' liver cut in thin slices
2 teaspoons chutney
salt
pepper
bacon
toast
2 oz. margarine or butter
1 teaspoon curry powder
2 oz. breadcrumbs
1 teaspoon Worcester sauce
pinch of cayenne pepper
tomatoes

1 Cream margarine with other ingredients and spread on both sides of slices of liver.
2 Heat the grill for a few minutes, put liver under this and cook for 3 minutes.
3 Turn liver over, arrange seasoned, halved tomatoes and rolled rashers of bacon round it.
4 Grill for a further 3 minutes.
5 If liver is thick, lower heat and cook for several more minutes.
6 Arrange liver, bacon and tomatoes on hot dish with triangles of toast.

Liver pancakes

Cooking time 15–20 minutes

You will need:

basic pancake mixture (see page 73)
1 large onion
2 or 3 mushrooms
6 oz. calves' liver
2 oz. butter or fat
2 large skinned tomatoes
butter or fat for cooking

to garnish
fried tomatoes
fried mushrooms
little parsley

1 Make pancake mixture, season it extra well.
2 Chop the liver finely, slice the onion very thinly and the tomatoes fairly thickly.
3 Heat the butter or fat and cook the onion, then the tomatoes, then add the liver and cook gently for about 4 or 5 minutes—or more.
4 Lastly add the finely chopped mushrooms and cook for a further 1 or 2 minutes.
5 Cook the pancakes and fill with the liver mixture.
6 Roll firmly and put on to a hot dish.
7 Meanwhile, fry mushrooms, tomatoes and parsley for garnish.
8 Serve pancakes with garnish and a good brown gravy.
9 Cooked minced meat can be used in the same way.

Liver casserole

Cooking time 20 minutes

You will need:

12 oz. calves' or lambs' liver*
1½ oz. butter or margarine
1 oz. flour
1 small chopped or grated onion
packet frozen mixed vegetables
just under ½ pint stock or water
seasoning

* Ox liver could be used but will need about 1½ hours cooking or 15 minutes in pressure cooker.

1 Cut liver into fingers and coat with seasoned flour.
2 Fry in hot butter with the onion for 2 minutes on either side.
3 Add liquid and seasoning.
4 Bring to boil and cook until thickened.
5 Add frozen vegetables and cook for about 10 minutes.
6 Serve with creamed potatoes or rice.

Sweetbreads en brochette

Cooking time 30 minutes

1 Sweetbreads can be served in the same way as lamb en brochette (see page 29).
2 Boil steadily in salted water until nearly tender. Strain, remove skin and gristle, cut into neat pieces.
3 Put a small roll of bacon, a piece of sweetbread, a small roll of bacon on the skewer and continue like this until the skewer is filled.
4 Season and cook until tender.
5 Serve with crisp toast.

To fry or grill lamb

Cooking time 12–15 minutes

Choose loin or best end of neck chops or cutlets.

1 Since lamb contains a reasonable amount of fat no extra fat need be added when frying or grilling.
2 Have the grill hot to begin with, and brown the meat on either side then lower to moderate to cook through to the centre.
3 Fry the chops or cutlets steadily rather than too quickly to give a pleasant crispness to the outside fat of lamb.
4 Serve with grilled or fried tomatoes—mushrooms—or with tomato sauce (see page 38).
Note: Generally speaking, mutton is not suitable for grilling or frying and even if tender will take considerably more time than lamb.

Lamb cutlets in mint jelly

Cooking time 10–15 minutes

You will need:

4 lightly grilled lamb cutlets—it will save time if you roast a loin of lamb and cut off 4 cutlets from this
seasoning
$\frac{3}{4}$ gill water
sugar
cooked peas
mayonnaise
1 teaspoon powder gelatine
1 tablespoon lemon juice (use the juice from a plastic lemon, if wished) OR
1 tablespoon vinegar
1 tablespoon chopped mint
cooked potatoes
chopped parsley

1 Put the cutlets into a shallow dish.
2 Dissolve the gelatine in the very hot water, then stir in the lemon juice or vinegar, seasoning and mint.
3 Add little sugar to taste.
4 Pour over the cutlets and allow to set.
5 Arrange the cooked potatoes, tossed in mayonnaise and chopped parsley, and the cooked peas round the edge of the dish.
6 The chops or cutlets keep beautifully moist covered with the mint mixture, so you can prepare this dish for the family well ahead, and they can help themselves.

Lamb en brochette

Cooking time 10 minutes

You will need:

several thick slices lamb from leg or shoulder
cocktail sausages
grilled tomatoes
$\frac{1}{2}$ lambs' or pigs' kidney (optional)
melted butter
crumbs
rice

1 Cut into neat squares of about 1 inch.
2 Put on a skewer together with sausages and lambs' or pigs' kidney.
3 Brush with melted butter, season and roll in crumbs.
4 Cook under the grill.
5 Serve still on the skewers, on a bed of rice, garnished with grilled tomatoes. French mustard should accompany this.

Grilled lamb cutlets with forcemeat stuffing

Cooking time 15 minutes

You will need:

4 lamb cutlets or lamb chops

for the stuffing
2 large or 4 small skinned sausages OR 4 oz. sausage meat
teaspoon grated lemon rind
1 egg yolk
2 teaspoons chopped parsley
pinch mixed herbs
seasoning

1 Mix ingredients for stuffing together.
2 Cut the meat away from the bone for 2–3 inches.
3 Press stuffing in the cavity making it flat and neat.
4 Put the stuffed chops under grill.
5 Cook on both sides until crisp and brown.
6 Serve with potato crisps, grilled tomatoes, peas and watercress.

Devilled lamb

Cooking time 15 minutes

You will need:

4 lamb chops
1 tablespoon chopped parsley
1 teaspoon Worcester sauce
2 oz. butter
pinch curry powder

1 Put chops under hot grill and brown well on one side.
2 Turn and cook on second side for 1 minute.
3 Blend butter, parsley, sauce and curry powder.
4 Spread over hot chops and cook steadily for about 8 minutes under grill.

Quick lamb hotpot

Cooking time 30 minutes

You will need:

4 lamb chops
$\frac{3}{4}$ pint water
1 small onion or little diced onion
1 beef bouillon cube
packet frozen vegetables
seasoning
caper sauce (see page 37)

1 Put water and bouillon cube into saucepan.
2 Add chopped or dried onion and lamb chops, season well.
3 Simmer gently for 20 minutes.
4 Add vegetables and cook for further 10 minutes. Make caper sauce using a little of the stock as well as milk.
5 Lift lamb and vegetables on to hot dish and serve with sauce.

Tomato lamb hotpot

As in preceding recipe but instead of water and bouillon cube use 1 can tomato soup and $\frac{1}{4}$ pint water. Serve with rice or cooked spaghetti.

Fried and grilled kidneys

Cooking time 10 minutes

Pigs' or lambs' kidneys are best for frying or grilling.

To fry

1 Halve kidneys, remove gristle.
2 Toss the meat in seasoned flour.
3 Fry steadily in hot margarine or butter.

4 Serve with toast, fried bacon and vegetables.

To grill

1 Prepare as for frying, except the kidneys need no flouring.
2 Brush with plenty of melted butter.
3 Grill steadily.
4 Serve with grilled mushrooms, tomatoes, etc.

Note. Allow 1–2 kidneys per person.

Kebabs

Cooking time 10–15 minutes

You will need:

4 lambs' kidneys
4 small mushrooms
little flour
cooked rice
4 sausages
2 rashers of bacon
seasoning
stock or thin soup

1 Halve the kidneys and sausages and rashers of bacon, dust lightly with seasoned flour.
2 Put the meat etc., and the mushrooms on to 4 skewers.
3 Leave these all ready, then all the family need do is to put them under a hot grill, turning once or twice until the kidneys are tender.
4 If wished have rice cooked in a double saucepan, so it does not burn. Moisten this with a little stock or thin soup, and it will keep hot to serve with the kebabs. Put kebabs on to a bed of crisp watercress.

Kidneys in port wine sauce

Cooking time 15 minutes

You will need for 3–4 servings:

6–8 lambs' kidneys
2 oz. butter
¼ pint water or stock
little chopped onion (can be omitted)
1 oz. flour
seasoning
¼ pint port wine
pinch mixed herbs

1 Cut each kidney into 4, removing gristle.
2 Toss in the seasoned flour.
3 Fry gently with the onion in the butter for 5 minutes.
4 Add stock, port wine, herbs, seasoning.
5 Bring to boil and cook until thickened.
6 Simmer for further 5 minutes.
7 Serve with rice, creamed potatoes or toast.

Kidneys and scrambled egg

Cooking time 12 minutes

You will need:

2 lambs' kidneys
seasoning
4 eggs
2 oz. butter
4 slices fried bread or buttered toast

1 Cut the kidneys into small pieces, season well.
2 Heat butter and cook kidneys in this for about 7–8 minutes, if necessary add a tablespoon water to prevent sticking.
3 Beat and season eggs lightly, add to kidney and continue cooking until firm.
4 Serve on toast or fried bread.

To fry and grill pork

Choose loin chops or cutlets for either frying or grilling. Cutlets should have the bone trimmed to look more attractive when served.

To fry

1 Brown chops on both sides lightly in the pan then lower the heat and cook steadily through to the centre.
2 Pork should be fried steadily so that you draw the fat from the meat and no extra fat is then required.

To grill

1 Make sure grill is hot before starting to cook pork chops.
2 Pork chops or cutlets need little basting with fat, since there is generally a good distribution of fat and lean.
3 When once the outside of the meat has been sealed turn the heat low to make sure they are well cooked through to the centre.
4 Serve with fried apple rings or sauce and orange salad or just with grilled tomatoes, mushrooms.

Grilled pork chops with orange slices

Cooking time 15 minutes

1 Season pork chops and brown on either side under hot grill.
2 Add thick slices of orange sprinkled with a little brown sugar and cook together until the chops are tender and the orange slices hot.
3 Serve with watercress, peas and creamed potatoes.

Barbecued pork

Cooking time 35–40 minutes

You will need:

4 pork chops
4 tomatoes
1 oz. fat
½ gill
2 onions
2 eating apples
seasoning

1 Slice onions very thinly.
2 Fry in the fat until fairly soft, using large pan or frying pan.
3 Add water, the thickly sliced tomatoes. Arrange chops on top and season well.
4 Core, but do not peel the apples. Slice and arrange on top of the chops.

Put lid on pan or plate over frying pan and cook steadily, adding little extra water if necessary.

Grilled gammon rashers

Cooking time 10 minutes

Grilled gammon or grilled thick back bacon rashers (bacon chops) are delicious served with tomatoes, mushrooms, etc., and try grilling eggs in the pan underneath. Heat a little fat in grill pan, drop in eggs, put bacon on the grid and cook together.

Or try:

Grilling thick gammon rashers and when nearly cooked, put rings of pineapple, brushed with a little melted butter under the grill.

Serve together with watercress.

Gammon and cheese with Lyonnaise potatoes

Cooking time 25 minutes

You will need:

about 1 lb. sliced cooked potatoes
4 thick slices gammon
lettuce
tomatoes
8–12 oz. thinly sliced onions
4 slices cheese
little margarine

Put margarine into a pan and heat.

Fry the onions in pan until nearly soft, mixed with sliced, cooked potatoes.

Put lid on frying pan and cook very gently until potatoes are very hot and golden brown and onions tender.

Meanwhile fry or grill thick gammon rashers.

Just before serving put a slice of cheese on each rasher of bacon and melt under grill. Or put the slices of cheese in the frying pan and when just melting lift on to bacon.

Serve with a dish of sliced raw tomatoes and crisp lettuce in addition to the potatoes.

Gammon rashers with Vinaigrette Beans

Cooking time 10–15 minutes

You will need:

4 gammon rashers
1 egg
1 tablespoon chutney
seasoning
1 teaspoon vinegar
2 tablespoons breadcrumbs
packet frozen beans or canned beans or 1 lb. fresh French beans
1 tablespoon chopped parsley
1 oz. butter (or use gammon fat)

Score the fat of the gammon rashers and put under the grill when not too hot (or cook in a frying pan).

2 By putting the bacon under a moderate grill you prevent the edges curling.
3 Meanwhile, either cook the frozen or fresh beans or heat the canned beans.
4 While bacon and beans are cooking, hard-boil and chop the egg.
5 Drain the beans and melt the butter in the pan, or use the bacon fat.
6 Toss the breadcrumbs in this, add parsley, chopped egg, chutney, vinegar.
7 Arrange gammon rashers on a dish surrounded by beans.
8 Garnish with the egg mixture.

Bacon and mushroom casserole

Cooking time 10–15 minutes

You will need:

6 oz. quick-cooking macaroni
1 onion (could be omitted)
1 oz. butter
4–6 oz. grated cheese
4 rashers streaky bacon
1 can concentrated mushroom soup
seasoning

1 Put the macaroni into boiling salted water, bring water to boil again for 7 minutes, making sure it is cooking fairly quickly.
2 Meanwhile dice and fry the onion in the butter, then add the diced bacon and fry this.
3 Add the concentrated mushroom soup, heat thoroughly.
4 Strain the macaroni, tip into a large hot dish, cover with the mushroom mixture and the cheese and brown under a very hot grill.

Variations: Use kidney soup instead of mushroom. Add can of crabmeat instead of bacon. Add can of tuna fish instead of bacon. Use tomato instead of the mushroom soup.

Bacon pancakes

Cooking time 25 minutes

You will need:

for the batter
4 oz. flour
½ pint milk and water
pinch salt
1 egg

for the filling
4–6 oz. streaky bacon
2 oz. mushrooms
little extra fat for cooking the filling and the pancakes
1 small onion
2 or 3 large tomatoes
parsley to garnish
cheese or tomato sauce

1 Make the batter by mixing the flour (sieved with the salt) with the egg and enough liquid to make a stiff batter.
2 Beat well until smooth then add the rest of the liquid.
3 Allow to stand.
4 Meanwhile prepare the filling.
5 Remove the bacon rinds and fry these to obtain the fat from them, lift the rinds from

the pan, add a little extra fat if necessary and fry the onion (finely chopped) then the bacon. chopped mushrooms and tomatoes.

6 Keep this hot and season well.
7 Cook the pancakes.
8 Fill each and roll firmly, or if preferred put 1 pancake on a hot dish, spread with the filling, cover with a pancake and so on until all are used.
9 Serve with cheese sauce or a tomato sauce (see pages 21, 38) and garnish with parsley.

Sausages *in sweet-sour sauce*

Cooking time 20 minutes

You will need:

1 lb. sausages
4 oz. spaghetti (macaroni, rice or noodles may be used instead)

for sauce

½ pint cider
little salt
pepper
1–2 tablespoons capers
1–2 oz. chopped celery or chopped green pepper
4 sliced tomatoes
1 good tablespoon sugar

1 Put sauce ingredients in pan and simmer for about 20 minutes.
2 Meanwhile fry or grill sausages and cook spaghetti in boiling salted water for 7–10 minutes (some spaghetti will take longer to cook than this).
3 Drain spaghetti and arrange on hot dish.
4 Arrange sausages round like spokes of a wheel, pour sauce in centre.

Sausages *with barbecue sauce*

Cooking time 10–15 minutes

You will need for 4–6 servings

12 sausages (or better still 12 Frankfurter sausages)
little cream cheese
1 loaf of bread
radishes

for the sauce*

4 tablespoons tomato ketchup or tomato chutney
shake of pepper and salt
2 teaspoons made mustard (French or English)
1 teaspoon sugar

*If wished, a little Worcester sauce can also be added to the tomato sauce mixture.

1 Cook the sausages until brown and tender. Frankfurter sausages need no cooking, but can be brushed with melted margarine and browned to look more attractive.
2 Cut slices of bread and arrange these with the sausages on a large dish or plate.
3 Blend all the ingredients for the sauce together and transfer this to a small dish in the centre of the plate.
4 Cut the radishes into the shape of flowers. Allow them to stand in cold water for several hours so the 'petals' open out.
5 Press a little soft cream cheese into the centre of each flower and put these on the same platter.
6 Everyone can just help themselves to bread and sausage and dip the sausages into the spicy, tomato flavoured sauce.

Sausage jambalaya

Cooking time 25 minutes

You will need:

6 oz. Patna rice
1 large onion
seasoning
2–3 oz. butter or margarine for frying
1 lb. chipolata sausages
1 clove of garlic
8 oz. or can tomatoes
pinch cayenne pepper
1 finely chopped red or green pepper when in season

1 Fry the sausages in a pan, then lift out and fry the finely chopped onion and garlic.
2 Add the tomatoes and pepper, simmer until soft.
3 Put the rice into a pan of boiling salted water and cook until just tender.
4 Strain, add to the onion mixture.
5 Season well, add the sausages, and if using fresh tomatoes stir in a little stock to keep the mixture moist.

Grilled frankfurters *on toast*

Cooking time 5–8 minutes

1 Brush Frankfurters with little margarine.
2 Put under grill allowing 2 Frankfurters and ½ rasher of bacon per person.
3 Serve with hot buttered toast spread lightly with mustard.

To fry or grill veal

Chops from loin or best end of neck, or fillets (thin slices cut from leg) are ideal for either frying or grilling.

To fry

1 If wished, coat with egg and crumbs, or flour. This helps to keep flavour of meat.
2 Keep moistened with plenty of fat while frying.
3 Fry steadily until tender and golden brown.

To grill

1 Brush with plenty of melted butter and margarine to prevent drying.
2 Grill steadily until done and serve with grilled bacon.

Escallopes of veal

Cooking time 10 minutes

Buy thin slices (cut from the leg), beat gently with rolling pin to flatten even more.

2 Fry steadily in shallow fat, oil or butter and oil mixed, until golden brown on both sides.
3 Garnish with wedges of lemon or, for a more elaborate garnish, top rings of lemon with freshly chopped hard-boiled egg and parsley, or egg and capers. Excellent with green salad.

Fillets of veal *in cream sauce*

Cooking time 10 minutes

1 Use thin slices of veal but do not coat with egg and crumbs.
2 Season and fry gently in hot butter or margarine until tender.
3 Lift on to hot dish.
4 Add small amount of cream to the butter left in pan.
5 Heat gently and pour over veal.

Swiss veal foldovers

Cooking time 30 minutes

You will need:

4 veal fillets
4 slices processed Swiss cheese
1 can condensed cream of mushroom soup
4 squares boiled ham
rice
¼ teaspoon paprika
2 oz. fat
½ pint light cream
½ gill cooking Sauternes
2 tablespoons flour

1 Pound each veal slice to a very thin rectangle (about 8 x 4 inches).
2 Cut cheese and ham slices in half.
3 Stack alternately in centre of each veal fillet.
4 Fold veal over to cover cheese and ham, roll carefully in mixture of flour and paprika.
5 Brown in hot fat.
6 Mix remaining ingredients, add to pan.
7 Cover, simmer, stirring occasionally, 30 minutes or till tender.
8 Serve with hot rice.

Veal rolls

Cooking time 30 minutes

You will need:

4 fillets veal
4 fingers Gruyère or Cheddar cheese
4 small pieces cooked ham
seasoning
1 can concentrated tomato soup
water

1 Put the ham and cheese on the seasoned fillets veal.
2 Roll firmly and skewer or tie.
3 Put soup and an equal amount of water into pan.
4 Bring to the boil, stir until smooth.
5 Simmer veal rolls in the liquid for 25 minutes.
6 Instead of cheese and ham the meat can be filled with stuffing and chopped fried mushrooms.

Paprika veal

Cooking time about 40 minutes

You will need for one serving:

1 veal chop
potatoes
tiny knob of margarine
seasoning
1 can tomatoes (small size)
1 teaspoon paprika pepper
1 can peas or small packet frozen peas if wished
½ gill water

1 Heat the margarine and fry the veal chop in this for a minute or so on both sides.
2 Open the can of tomatoes, add to the meat, together with the paprika pepper, blended with water.
3 Add the halved potatoes and seasoning and simmer steadily for about 30 minutes until the potatoes are tender.
4 You should have a tightly fitting lid for this.
5 Add the well-drained peas (or the frozen peas), and replace the lid.
6 Watch the liquid the first time you make this, as it might evaporate too quickly, and you will need to add just a little extra water. It should, however, be a thick mixture.

Veal milanaise

Cooking time 20 minutes

You will need:

4 veal chops
4 skinned tomatoes
seasoning
2 oz. butter
1 can spaghetti in tomato sauce
few capers

1 Fry chops in the butter for 15 minutes.
2 Put on to hot dish.
3 Add sliced tomatoes and spaghetti to fat in pan and heat.
4 Stir in capers and arrange round veal.

Veal gratinée

Cooking time 15 minutes

You will need:

4 veal chops
4 slices cheese
knob butter
seasoning

1 Season chops. Spread on 1 side with half the butter and cook until brown.
2 Turn and grill on other side until just cooked.
3 Put slices of cheese over veal and continue cooking until cheese has melted.
4 Serve with green salad.

Veal Imperial

Cooking time 30 minutes

You will need:

4 veal chops
1 oz. butter
seasoning
1 can cream of mushroom soup
$\frac{1}{4}$ pint milk
little sherry or lemon juice

1 Brown the veal lightly in the butter.
2 Add soup, milk and seasoning.
3 Cover pan and simmer gently for 25 minutes, adding little extra milk if required.
4 Stir in sherry or lemon juice and serve with rice or creamed potatoes and green salad.

To serve frozen steakburgers

Bean burgers. Fry or grill and top with baked beans.

Cheeseburgers. Fry or grill until nearly ready, then top with slices of cheese and brown until cheese melts.

Kebabs. Divide each steakburger into 4. Put on skewer with bacon rolls and grill.

Steakburgers Mornay. Grill steakburgers. Put on to bed of creamed frozen spinach. Coat with cheese sause (see page 21) and brown under grill.

Steakburgers and tomato. Grill steakburgers on one side. Turn and cover with sliced tomatoes and grill on second side.

To serve canned stewed steak

Canned stewed steak is generally high quality meat and provides a quick meal within minutes. By varying the way it is presented you can avoid monotony.

Steak au gratin

Cooking time 15 minutes

1 Put steak into pan and heat steadily for about 10 minutes.
2 Tip into pie dish.
3 Cover top with biscuit or breadcrumbs and grated or thinly sliced cheese.
4 Brown under grill for 5 minutes.
5 If preferred meat and topping can be heated together in oven for approximately 30 minutes.

Curried steak

Cooking time 15–20 minutes

1 Fry a sliced onion in a knob of fat.
2 Add 2–4 teaspoons curry powder and cook for few minutes.
3 Stir the canned steak into onion mixture.
4 Bring to boil and heat gently for 10 minutes.
5 Add 1 tablespoon chutney to sauce and few sultanas.

Hasty goulash

Cooking time 15 minutes

1 Put steak into pan and heat for 10 minutes.
2 Tip small can of tomatoes in with steak, together with 1 tablespoon paprika pepper blended with 1 tablespoon water.
3 Heat for further 5 minutes.

Steak and marrow

Cooking time 15–20 minutes

can stewed steak • little butter or margarine • small marrow • few breadcrumbs • seasoning

1 Peel marrow and cut into rings.
2 Steam or boil until just tender.
3 Meanwhile heat steak.
4 Strain marrow rings, put on to heat resistant dish.
5 Top each ring with steak and crumbs.
6 Dot with a little butter or margarine and brown under grill.

Steak and dumplings

Cooking time 20 minutes

1 Heat the canned steak with $\frac{1}{3}$ pint water.
2 Make tiny dumplings by adding 1 oz. shredded suet to 2 oz. self-raising flour and a pinch salt. Mix with water to rolling consistency.

3 Roll in tiny balls—drop into the liquid and cook for 15 minutes.

Pilaf of beef

Cooking time 25 minutes

1 can stewing steak • 2 oz. rice • seasoning • 2 tomatoes • can of frozen mixed vegetables • ¾ pint water with little yeast or vegetable extract to flavour • 1 oz. dripping or margarine • chopped parsley

1 Skin and slice tomatoes.
2 Heat dripping and fry tomatoes in this.
3 Add water, well flavoured with yeast or beef extract.
4 Bring to the boil.
5 Shake in rice and cook steadily, seasoning well.
6 When rice is tender and has absorbed all liquid add steak and drained vegetables.
7 Heat thoroughly.
8 Garnish with chopped parsley.

Curried corned beef

Cooking time 10–20 minutes

You will need:

12 oz. corned beef
chopped dessert apple
1 oz. margarine OR
1 tablespoon oil
1 tablespoon curry powder
few chopped spring onions (use scissors for speed)
1 tablespoon chutney

If serving cold you will need a little salad dressing, lettuce, sliced tomatoes, etc.
If serving hot then use a small can mulligatawny soup, some diced cooked potatoes or cooked rice.

1 Heat the oil or margarine, add the onions and apple, toss in the oil for a few minutes; there is no need to cook them until soft.
2 Work in the curry powder and cook for several minutes, then add the chutney and flaked corned beef.

To serve cold:

1 Stir in enough mayonnaise to make a moist consistency.
2 Put on a bed of crisp lettuce (covered with lettuce until the family come home), garnish with sliced tomatoes, radishes, etc.
3 Serve with crisp rolls.

To serve hot:

1 Add the can of soup, potatoes or rice. Make sure you have enough soup to give a moist consistency.
2 Either put the heat very low under the pan, or transfer to a casserole and keep hot in a very slow oven.
3 Put a dish of chutney on the table, some rolls in the oven, so they too are piping hot, and make a big bowl of crisp lettuce salad to serve with this quick curry.
4 If you wish, flaked fish could be used instead of corned beef, hard-boiled eggs (keep these whole), or chopped cooked meat.

Corned beef cutlets

Cooking time 15–20 minutes

You will need:

12 oz. can corned beef
good 2 oz. breadcrumbs
seasoning
1 egg
crisp breadcrumbs
fat for frying
1 oz. margarine
1 oz. flour
¼ pint milk or stock

1 Make the sauce by heating the margarine in the pan, stirring in the flour and cooking for 2 minutes, then adding the liquid.
2 Bring to the boil and cook until thick.
3 Add the breadcrumbs and the flaked corned beef.
4 Season well.
5 Form into cutlet shapes. Coat with beaten egg and crisp breadcrumbs and fry in hot fat until crisp and golden brown.
6 Serve with fried tomatoes, peas and sauté potatoes.
7 Garnish with cutlet frills.

Lattice beef pie

Cooking time 25 minutes

You will need:

1 can corned beef or left-over beef
3 or 4 spring onions

for cheese sauce

1 oz. butter
seasoning
4 oz. grated cheese
little extra grated cheese
1 oz. flour
1 gill milk
12 oz.–1 lb. mashed potato

1 Make thick cheese sauce.
2 Add seasoning, the chopped meat or flaked corned beef and the chopped spring onion. Use some of the green stems too.
3 Put into shallow dish and pipe the potato in a lattice design.
4 Sprinkle the grated cheese over the potato and brown for about 10–15 minutes in a hot oven (425°F.—Gas Mark 6).

Corned beef hash

Cooking time 10–15 minutes

You will need:

12 oz. can corned beef
approximately 8 oz. mashed potatoes
1 egg
1 oz. dripping for frying
sliced beetroot
parsley
seasoning

1 Flake the corned beef and mix with the potatoes and beaten egg.
2 Season well.
3 Heat the dripping in a pan and put in the mixture.
4 Spread this evenly and allow to cook slowly until the underside is golden brown and the mixture really hot.
5 Fold like an omelette and turn on to a hot dish.
6 Serve garnished with beetroot and parsley.

Ham casserole

As in casserole of steak (see page 26) but use thick slices of cooked ham instead of steak and cook for 5 minutes only before adding bread.
A little sherry is delicious in this recipe.

Ham and potato cakes

Cooking time 15 minutes

You will need:

1 lb. mashed potatoes
4 slices Gruyère cheese
seasoning
4 slices ham
few tomatoes
chopped parsley
fat

1 Add seasoning and little chopped parsley to the mashed potatoes. If the mixture is dry, then add a little milk and margarine to moisten.
2 Form into 4 large flat cakes, put a little fat on each and brown in a moderately hot oven (400 °F. – Gas Mark 5).
3 Top with a slice of ham and cheese and return to the oven until the cheese is beginning to melt.
4 Decorate with parsley and serve with baked tomatoes.

Cheese and ham pudding

Cooking time 35 minutes

You will need:

2 oz. breadcrumbs
3–4 oz. chopped ham
clove garlic or slice onion
¾ pint milk
2–3 oz. grated cheese
3 eggs
1 oz. butter
seasoning

to garnish
sliced cooked tomatoes
chopped parsley

1 Rub saucepan with cut clove of garlic or onion.
2 Put the milk into a saucepan, heat with the crumbs and butter, add cheese, ham, seasoning.
3 Add beaten eggs.
4 Pour into baking dish and cook for approximately 35 minutes in centre of moderate oven (375 °F. – Gas Mark 4) until golden brown and firm.
5 Quickly arrange garnish on top as this pudding is inclined to sink slightly.
6 Serve with crisp toast or creamed potatoes and a green vegetable.

Spiced ham and macédoine of vegetables

Cooking time 15 minutes

You will need:

8 oz. cooked ham
1 oz. butter
1 oz. brown sugar
3 tablespoons vinegar
potato crisps
watercress
1 packet frozen vegetables
2 tablespoons red currant or cranberry jelly
2 teaspoons made mustard
good shake pepper

1 Put the butter, vinegar, jelly, sugar and mustard into a saucepan.
2 Heat gently until jelly has melted.
3 Put in the ham and heat through.
4 Meanwhile, cook the mixed vegetables.
5 Serve the ham in its sauce with the vegetables, potato crisps and watercress.

Ham omelette

Cooking time 5 minutes

You will need for 1 person only:

2 eggs
seasoning
1 oz. ham*
good knob of butter

* Cheaper quality ham can be used in this or it is a good way to use up canned luncheon meat.

1 Chop the ham or luncheon meat and mix with the beaten eggs.
2 Heat the knob of butter and pour in the egg mixture.
3 Allow about ½ minute for it to 'set' in a skin at the bottom, then tilt the pan and push the egg liquid backwards and forwards so it drops to the bottom of the pan. Continue until set.
4 Fold or roll away from handle and tip on to hot dish.

Ham in Madeira sauce

Cooking time 10–15 minutes

You will need:

8 thin slices or 4 thick slices of cooked ham
1 oz. butter
1 LEVEL tablespoon flour

juice 1 orange and 1 lemon
½ gill water
1 gill Madeira
good pinch, salt, pepper
sugar

1 Heat ham under hot grill for a few minutes.
2 Make sauce blending flour with water, then put all other ingredients into pan and cook, stirring well until thick and clear.
3 Pour over ham and serve with heated canned vegetables.

Ham and egg casserole

Cooking time 15 minutes

You will need:

4 hard-boiled eggs
½ pint white sauce (see page 18) (or a can of cream of chicken or tomato soup)
lettuce
4 tomatoes
4 oz. cooked chopped ham (or luncheon meat or boiled bacon)
seasoning
4 slices toast
little grated cheese

1 Make white sauce or heat the soup.
2 Add sliced eggs and ham.
3 Season well.
4 Put 4 slices toast in dish. Top with ham mixture, halved tomatoes and cheese.
5 Brown under grill or in the oven.
6 Serve with lettuce.

Devilled ham fritters

Cooking time 20 minutes

You will need:

1 small can chopped ham or use about 4 oz. fresh ham
4 oz. flour
1 teaspoon curry powder
1 tablespoon chutney
seasoning
1 gill milk
2 eggs
2 or 3 spring onions or chives
1 teaspoon Worcestershire sauce
frying fat

1 Sieve flour and curry powder into basin.
2 Add eggs, milk, Worcestershire sauce, chutney and finely chopped spring onions (use some of the green stems) and ham.
3 Season well.
4 Heat little fat in the pan.
5 Pour in enough mixture to cover pan.
6 Fry steadily until golden brown.
7 Turn and cook on the other side.
8 Pile fritters on a hot dish and serve with salad and tomatoes.

Kidney and macaroni

Cooking time 15–20 minutes

You will need:

4 oz. quick-cooking macaroni
2 oz. grated cheese
parsley to garnish
1 can kidney soup
4 eggs

1 Cook the macaroni for 7 minutes in boiling salted water.
2 Strain and heat with the soup.
3 Put into a shallow casserole.
4 Fry or poach the eggs, arrange on the kidney mixture.
5 Top with grated cheese and brown under the grill.
6 Garnish with parsley.

Tongue in Burgundy sauce

Cooking time 10 minutes

You will need:

4 thick slices cooked tongue
1 gill water
seasoning
1 oz. butter
1 oz. flour
1 gill Burgundy

1 Heat butter, stir in flour.
2 Cook for several minutes then gradually add Burgundy, water and seasoning.
3 Bring to boil and cook until thickened.
4 Cut slices of tongue into halves, heat in sauce.
5 Serve with mixed vegetables.

Sauces to serve with meat

Brown sauce Cooking time 10 minutes

Coating Consistency

1 oz. cooking fat or dripping
salt and pepper
½ pint brown stock
1 oz. flour

Panada sauce. As above but use ¼ pint brown stock.
Thin sauce. As above but use 1 pint brown stock.

1 Heat the fat or dripping in a pan. For a better flavour fry a little chopped onion, celery, carrot, in which case use 2 oz. fat.
2 Add the flour and cook steadily in the fat until brown in colour. Be careful not to overbrown this.
3 Add stock, carefully stirring all the time, bring to the boil, season and cook until thick and smooth. If vegetables have been used, strain.

Caper sauce Cooking time 5–8 minutes. As above, but use ¼ pint milk and ¼ pint stock. Add 2 teaspoons capers and little caper vinegar.

Curry sauce Cooking time 30 minutes–1 hour

1 medium-sized onion
1 cooking apple
1 oz. butter
1 dessertspoon chutney
1 level tablespoon cornflour
1 teaspoon curry paste
1–2 tablespoons milk or cream*
½ pint stock or water
salt
1 level tablespoon curry powder
1 tablespoon desiccated coconut
1 dessertspoon sultanas
1 teaspoon lemon juice

* This can be omitted with meat curries

1 Chop the onion and cooking apple and sauté in the butter.
2 Add curry powder, paste and cornflour.
3 Stir until blended, cook a few minutes and then stir in stock.
4 Bring to the boil, stirring all the time.
5 Add chutney, coconut and sultanas.
6 Cover and simmer for at least 1 hour.
7 Stir in the lemon juice, add seasoning and the milk or cream.

Horseradish sauce No cooking. Beat bottled horseradish relish or horseradish cream into little cream from top of milk, add few drops lemon juice or vinegar and seasoning.

Tomato sauce Cooking time 10 minutes

1 small tube or can tomato purée
1 oz. butter or margarine
2 level teaspoons cornflour
1 small apple
1 small onion
½ pint water
good pinch sugar
salt and pepper

1 Heat the butter and fry the chopped onion for a few minutes then the grated, peeled apple.
2 Add the purée, the cornflour blended with the water, and seasoning.
3 Bring to the boil, and stir until smooth.
4 Simmer gently for about 10 minutes, taste and re-season, adding sugar if wished.

Savoury Dishes

In this chapter you will find a variety of savoury dishes suitable for light lunch or supper. Although quick and easy to make they contain the essential foods for a well balanced meal and will give you endless variety.

Egg dishes

A quick meal is provided by some form of egg, whether by boiling, frying, poaching, scrambling, or in more elaborate dishes.

Get into the habit of topping creamed potatoes with a chopped hard-boiled egg.

Add a beaten egg to a thickened white or cheese sauce, taking care it does not boil after the egg is added. Just simmer gently for 2 or 3 minutes.

An egg beaten into a glass of hot or cold milk gives one of the quickest and most easily digested meals.

Six new ways to serve scrambled eggs

Cooking time 5–15 minutes

Most people like scrambled eggs, so here are some easy ways of turning them into dishes for supper or breakfast. All are sufficient for 4 people.

Scrambled Eggs de Luxe. To 4 or 5 eggs add 4 tablespoons cream. Season well and cook gently in hot butter.

Scotch Woodcock. Scramble 4 or 5 eggs in the usual way. Serve on hot toast and put anchovy fillets on top.

Mock Crab. Add 2 oz. grated cheese and 1 teaspoon tomato ketchup to 4 beaten eggs. cook lightly. This is delicious as a sandwich filling.

With Vegetables. Heat 1 teacup diced cooked vegetables in hot butter or margarine. Add 4 or 5 well-seasoned and beaten eggs. Cook until just set, pile on toast or creamed potatoes. Sprinkle with grated cheese if wished.

Crisp Scrambled Eggs. Cut 1 or 2 thin slices of bread, remove crusts and cut into tiny dice. Fry in hot butter until golden brown and crisp. Add 4 beaten eggs and cook in usual way—the tiny pieces stay crisp. Add little grated cheese if wished.

With Chicken Liver. Take liver from chicken giblets, chop finely and fry lightly in hot butter or margarine. Add 4 or 5 seasoned eggs and cook in the usual way.
(More scrambled eggs recipes on page 57.)

Baked eggs

Cooking time 5 minutes

1 Butter small oven-proof dishes and break an egg into each.
2 Sprinkle with salt and pepper and grate about ½ oz. cheese on the top.
3 Cover with breadcrumbs and add a small knob of butter.
4 Bake in moderate oven (375°F.—Gas Mark 4) for about 5 minutes.
5 Serve hot.

Buckingham eggs

Cooking time 10 minutes

You will need:

4 slices of bread
4 eggs
2 heaped tablespoons grated cheese
2 tablespoons milk
little butter for toast
small jar of anchovy paste
1 oz. margarine or butter
seasoning

1 Heat knob of butter or margarine in pan.
2 Meanwhile toast the bread, butter and spread it with the paste.
3 Add beaten eggs, milk and seasoning to hot margarine.
4 Scramble lightly, spread on toast and top with the grated cheese.
5 Heat under the grill for a few minutes until the cheese is golden.
6 Serve garnished with watercress.

Cheddar Scotch eggs

Cooking time 15 minutes

You will need:

4 hard-boiled eggs
little chopped chives or spring onions
little flour
1 egg
fat for frying
3 oz. grated Cheddar cheese
tiny knob of butter
seasoning
12 oz. sausage meat
breadcrumbs for coating

1 Shell eggs. Cut into halves very carefully.
2 Remove yolk, put into basin, mash, and add cheese, butter, chives, seasoning.
3 Mix well and press back into white cases.
4 Press the 2 halves together.
5 Divide sausage meat into 4 portions.
6 Flatten on lightly floured board.
7 Put egg on to this then wrap round in sausage meat.
8 Seal 'joints' very firmly.
9 Coat with beaten egg, roll in crumbs.
10 Fry *steadily* in deep fat until golden brown.
11 Drain very well on kitchen paper.

Egg and vegetable cutlets

Cooking time 20 minutes

You will need:

4 or 5 hard-boiled eggs
¼ pint thick white sauce (see page 21)
breadcrumbs
egg to coat
1 lb. diced and cooked mixed vegetables
seasoning

1 Chop eggs, mix with other ingredients and form in 4 or 8 small cutlet shapes.
2 Brush with beaten egg, roll in crisp bread-crumbs and fry until golden brown.
3 Serve hot or cold with salad or cooked vege-tables.

Eggs in baked potatoes

1 Scrub and bake large potatoes, 1 for each person.
2 When cooked, take off a slice and scoop out the greater part of the inside, mash this and press back into case making a neat shape.
3 Break eggs carefully, allowing 1 per person.
4 Put an egg into each case.
5 Top with grated cheese and seasoning.
6 Sprinkle with breadcrumbs and add a few tiny pieces of butter.
7 Place in a hot oven until cheese is brown and the eggs set. This takes approximately 15 minutes.

Eggs royale

Cooking time 25 minutes

You will need:

5 hard-boiled eggs
1 onion
4 oz. grated cheese
little milk
olives
small packet frozen beans
1 can condensed chicken soup
2 oz. butter
1 green pepper (or use cooked peas)

1 Heat the soup with just a little milk, add the beans, which should be lightly cooked.
2 Slice and fry the onion in the butter, then add the chopped pepper or cooked peas.
3 When tender, stir into the soup mixture together with 4 of the chopped hard-boiled eggs.
4 Arrange in a casserole and serve garnished with the last egg and sliced olives.

MAKING AN OMELETTE

Cooking time 5–8 minutes

Allow 1½–2 eggs per person

1 Beat eggs in a basin. Break each separately in a cup before transferring to basin (in case any are bad).
2 Add a good pinch salt and pepper, and for each 1½–2 eggs 1 tablespoon of water.
3 Put knob of butter into omelette pan and when hot pour in eggs. Leave for about 1 minute over high heat to allow bottom to set, then loosen egg mixture from sides of pan and cook rapidly, tipping pan from side to side so that the liquid egg flows underneath and cooks quickly.
4 When egg is set as you like it (tastes vary) slip palette knife under omelette and fold it away from handle of pan.
5 Grasp handle firmly and tip on to a hot plate.

Cheese omelette. Add grated cheese just before folding the omelette or use soft cream cheese.

Fish omelette. Heat flaked cooked fish or shell fish with a little butter and cream from top of milk. Add to omelette just before folding.

Meat omelette. Chop cooked meat very finely and add to beaten eggs, together with a little mustard as well as salt and pepper.

Mushroom omelette. Fry chopped mushrooms in a little butter. Add to beaten eggs.

Vegetable omelette. Either add chopped cooked vegetables to beaten eggs before cooking or heat the vegetables with a little butter, white or cheese sauce and add to omelette before folding.

Spanish omelette and fried rice

Cooking time 25 minutes

You will need:

6 eggs
chopped parsley
4 oz. rice
2 oz. butter
little olive oil
extra butter
seasoning
small can mixed vegetables
small can tuna fish, prawns or shrimps, or use several rashers of bacon
1 small finely chopped onion

1 First put on the rice to cook in boiling salted water, strain when just tender.
2 Heat a little butter and oil together and fry the rice until golden.
3 Heat the butter in the omelette pan, fry the onion and chopped bacon.
4 Add the flaked fish and drained vegetables to the egg and pour into the pan.
5 Cook steadily on the underside and when this seems firm put under a warmed grill to set the top side.
6 Serve with the rice.

Piquante eggs

Cooking time 25 minutes

You will need:

4 hard-boiled eggs
½ pint white sauce (see page 21)
2 tablespoons breadcrumbs
1 oz. margarine
2 tablespoons tomato ketchup
2 thinly sliced onions
2 tablespoons grated cheese

1 Heat the margarine and fry the sliced onions until just soft.
2 Put at the bottom of a dish with the shelled and halved hard-boiled eggs on top.
3 Mix the tomato ketchup into the hot, but not boiling, white sauce.
4 Season well and pour over the eggs.
5 Top with grated cheese and breadcrumbs and brown in the oven or under the grill.
6 If wished a little chopped cooked bacon can be mixed with the onions.

POACHED AND FRIED EGGS

Method of poaching eggs and other suggestions, see page 57.

Tomato poached eggs Cooking time 8 minutes

1 Heat a can of tomato soup in a shallow pan adding little water if too thick.
2 Break 3 or 4 eggs into this and poach in usual way.
3 Serve with toast.

Curried poached eggs

1 Heat a can mulligatawny soup in a shallow pan, adding little water if too thick.
2 Break 3 or 4 eggs into this and cook in usual way.
3 Serve with rice.

Cheese topped fried egg

1 Fry eggs in usual way, but just before setting put slices of cheese into pan.
2 Serve eggs on toast topped with cheese.

Fried egg fingers

1 Beat eggs, season well and pour into shallow dish.
2 Cut fingers of bread and remove crusts.
3 Soak in the egg until this is quite absorbed. Lift egg fingers carefully into hot fat and fry. This often appeals to people who do not like ordinary fried eggs.

Surprise eggs

Cooking time 10 minutes

You will need:

6 eggs
12 rounds bread and butter

filling

seasoning
2 oz. finely chopped cooked mushrooms
4 oz. cooked ham (minced or chopped)
tomato to garnish

1 Hard-boil and halve the eggs.
2 Cut small thin slices off the bottom to make them stand and remove the yolks.
3 Make a purée of the ham, mix with egg yolks, and chopped mushrooms and season.
4 Fill egg cases with mixture.
5 Garnish with tomato.
6 Serve with brown bread and butter.

Swiss eggs

Cooking time 12–15 minutes

You will need:

4 or 5 oz. processed Gruyère cheese
2 or 3 tablespoons cream
little butter
triangles of fried bread
4 eggs
seasoning

1 Butter a shallow dish and line it with sliced Gruyère cheese.
2 Break the eggs carefully and slide on top of the cheese.
3 Cover with cream, seasoning and the rest of the Gruyère cheese, which should be grated or finely chopped.
4 Bake in a moderately hot oven (400 °F. – Gas Mark 5) for about 12 minutes until the eggs are set.
5 Serve at once, garnished with triangles of crisply fried bread.

WAYS TO SERVE CHEESE

Whether cheese is served uncooked or in a variety of cooked dishes it is a first class protein food.

Many people who find pieces of cheese indigestible will eat it more readily if grated. This is particularly suitable when serving cheese in salads.

Take care that cheese is NOT overcooked; when adding to a sauce it should be heated gently, not boiled.

Serve a variety of cheese, so it does not become dull and monotonous.

Cheese and carrot fingers

Cooking time 10 minutes

You will need:

4 slices of bread
butter
seasoning
4–6 oz. grated cheese
2 good-sized grated carrots
chopped parsley

1 Mix the grated carrot and most of the cheese together with enough butter to bind.
2 Season well. Toast the bread.
3 Spread on top of crisp toast.
4 Cover with the rest of the cheese and brown.
5 Garnish with chopped parsley.

Cheese Charlotte

Cooking time 30 minutes

You will need:

6–8 oz. grated cheese –use all Cheddar or $\frac{2}{3}$ Cheddar and $\frac{1}{3}$ Parmesan cheese
seasoning
tomato
3 large thin slices bread and butter
1 egg
$\frac{1}{2}$ pint milk
parsley

1 Cut triangles from the bread and butter.
2 Arrange half of these at bottom of pie dish.
3 Sprinkle with half the cheese.
4 Arrange remainder of bread and butter on top of this, cover with rest of cheese.
5 Beat egg, add milk and season well.
6 Pour over bread and cheese mixture.
7 Bake for about 30 minutes in moderate oven.

Cheese croquettes

Cooking time 30 minutes

You will need:

6–8 oz. grated cheese
3–4 oz. breadcrumbs
1 egg
seasoning
fat for frying
1 teaspoon grated onion
1 teaspoon chopped parsley
thick white sauce (made from 1 oz. margarine, 1 oz. flour, ¼ pint milk)

1 Add cheese, onion, parsley and half crumbs to the warm white sauce, together with the egg yolk.
2 When mixture is cool, form into 8 finger shapes.
3 Brush with egg white and roll in the rest of the crumbs.
4 Fry until crisp and golden brown.
5 Serve hot or cold.

Cheese and egg meringues

1 Toast slices of bread on 1 side only.
2 Place untoasted side uppermost, and butter.
3 Separate yolks from whites.
4 Beat whites until stiff and form into a ring on the bread.
5 Drop the yolk into the centre.
6 Season and cover with grated cheese.
7 Place in a moderately hot oven (400 °F. – Gas Mark 5) for about 10 minutes until set.

Cheese and egg ring

Cooking time 20 minutes

You will need:

4 eggs
1 oz. butter
1 oz. flour
scant ½ pint milk
8 oz. grated Cheddar cheese
8 oz. sliced cooked green beans (fresh or frozen)
4–6 oz. rice

1 Put rice into boiling salted water and cook for 15–20 minutes (until tender).
2 Meanwhile hard-boil the eggs.
3 Shell the eggs.
4 Cut into 8 lengthwise.
5 Melt the butter in small saucepan.
6 Stir in the flour and cook gently for 1 minute.
7 Add the milk a little at a time, stirring constantly until the sauce is creamy and has thickened.
8 Remove from heat, add 6 oz. grated cheese, half the sliced green beans and the hard-boiled eggs.
9 Stir gently until the eggs have heated through.
10 Pour into a ring of well drained rice.
11 Arrange rest of beans round rice.
12 Sprinkle with remaining cheese.
13 Serve at once.

Cheese frankfurters

Cooking time 10 minutes

You will need:

8 frankfurters
8 slices bacon
8 oz. cheese

1 Cut a lengthwise slit in each frankfurter.
2 Cut strip of cheese the length of frankfurter and about ¼ inch thick.
3 Fill slit with strip of cheese, wrap slice of bacon around each frankfurter and fasten ends with toothpicks.
4 Grill frankfurters slowly, turning often, until the bacon and frankfurters are cooked through and browned.

Cheese and marrow savoury

Cooking time 20 minutes

You will need:

1 or 2 young marrows
1 oz. butter
4 tomatoes
seasoning
8 oz. grated cheese
1 level tablespoon flour
½ gill water

1 Slice marrow into rings.
2 Take out seeds but do not remove peel if very young.
3 Sprinkle with salt.
4 Steam over boiling water until tender.
5 Meanwhile, fry sliced tomatoes in butter.
6 Blend flour with water, add to tomato mixture and cook until thick, but smooth.
7 Stir in 6 oz. cheese and seasoning.
8 Arrange marrow rings on dish, cover with cheese mixture.
9 Sprinkle with grated cheese and brown under grill or in oven.
10 Serve with young vegetables.

Cream cheese mould

No cooking – just dissolving gelatine

You will need:

¼ pint tomato juice or evaporated milk or milk according to taste
1 teaspoon chopped parsley
1 teaspoon chopped gherkins
½ gill water
4 oz. finely grated cheese or cream cheese
seasoning
2 tablespoons powder gelatine

1 Beat tomato juice or milk very gradually into cheese until smooth mixture.
2 Dissolve the gelatine in the *hot* water.
3 Add to cheese with seasoning, parsley and gherkins.
4 Pour into tiny moulds and when set, turn out and serve with salad.

Cheese and onion fritters

Cooking time 10 minutes

You will need:

4 eggs
4 oz. grated cheese
seasoning
$\frac{1}{4}$ pint white sauce (see page 21)
1 grated onion
2 oz. flour
1 oz. dripping or vegetable shortening
$\frac{1}{2}$ gill tomato ketchup
2 oz. dripping or vegetable shortening for frying

1 Fry onion until soft in 1 oz. dripping.
2 Add to beaten eggs with flour, grated cheese, seasoning.
3 Beat until smooth.
4 Heat some of the shortening in frying pan.
5 Drop in 3 separate spoonfuls of mixture and cook until golden on underside, turn and cook on other side.
6 Drain and put on hot dish.
7 Continue cooking like this until all mixture is used.
8 Meanwhile make white sauce, add ketchup and heat without boiling.
9 Arrange on flat dish, serve sauce separately.

Cheese pilaff

Cooking time 25 minutes

You will need:

4–6 oz. Patna rice
3 large tomatoes
2 large onions
seasoning
3 oz. butter
6 oz. mushrooms
6–8 oz. grated or diced cheese
1–1$\frac{1}{2}$ pints water

1 Heat half the butter in pan.
2 Fry sliced onions until nearly soft.
3 Add skinned sliced tomatoes.
4 Cook for several minutes, then add water.
5 Bring to the boil, shake in the rice, season well and cook until tender (approximately 15–20 minutes), stir well as mixture thickens.
6 Meanwhile, fry mushrooms in rest of the butter.
7 Stir cheese into rice mixture.
8 Pile on to hot dish surrounded with mushrooms.

Cheese and potato soufflé

Cooking time 30 minutes

You will need:

12 oz. mashed potato
2 eggs
1 oz. margarine or butter
3–4 oz. grated cheese
seasoning
2 tablespoons milk
1 teaspoon finely chopped chives or grated onion

1 Mash the potatoes well.
2 Add the margarine, cheese, milk and chives, then season well.
3 Stir in the well-beaten egg yolks and, when the mixture is cool, *fold* in stiffly beaten egg white.
4 Put into a well-greased soufflé dish, bake in the centre of a moderately hot oven (400 °F. – Gas Mark 5) for 30 minutes until well risen and crisp and brown on top.

Cheese rissoles

Cooking time 10–15 minutes

You will need:

1 oz. butter
1 oz. flour
$\frac{1}{4}$ pint milk
seasoning
1 egg
fat for frying
6 oz. grated cheese
2 teaspoons chopped parsley
pinch mixed herbs
2 oz. soft breadcrumbs
crisp breadcrumbs

1 Heat butter in pan, stir in flour and cook for several minutes.
2 Gradually add milk, bring to boil, cook until thick.
3 Season well, add crumbs, cheese, parsley, herbs.
4 Cool mixture, form either into rounds or finger shapes, coat in beaten egg and crumbs.
5 Fry in hot fat until crisp and brown.

Cheese scones

Cooking time 10 minutes

You will need:

6 oz. flour (with plain flour add 2 teaspoons baking powder)
1 oz. margarine or butter or cooking fat
pinch mustard
2–3 oz. grated cheese
seasoning
milk to mix

1 Sieve flour, baking powder and good pinch of salt, pepper, mustard.
2 Rub in margarine, add cheese and enough milk to make a soft, rolling consistency.
3 Roll out to about $\frac{1}{2}$–$\frac{3}{4}$ inch thick.
4 Cut into desired shapes and bake on lightly greased tins for about 10 minutes in a very hot oven (475°F.—Gas Mark 8).
5 When cool, split and butter.

Cheese rusks

Cooking time 14 minutes

1 Make as for cheese scones, but rather thinner, about $\frac{1}{4}$ inch thick.
2 Cook for a good 5–7 minutes until brown on outside in moderately hot oven (425°F.—Gas Mark 6).
3 Remove from trays and split carefully through middle.
4 Put CUT side downwards on the tray and cook for a further 5–7 minutes.

Cheese and salmon mould

Cooking time 1 hour

You will need:

2 oz. breadcrumbs
1 gill milk
1 medium can salmon
seasoning
little chopped parsley
2 oz. grated cheese
1 egg
1 small onion
1 oz. margarine

1 Fry the finely chopped onion in the margarine.
2 Flake the fish and mix with all other ingredients.
3 Put into well greased loaf tin.
4 Cover with greased paper and bake for approximately 45 minutes in centre of moderate oven (375°F.—Gas Mark 5).
5 Turn out and serve with baked tomatoes, peas and creamed potatoes.

Cheese and shrimp fritters

Cooking time 5 minutes

You will need:

4 oz. shrimps (frozen or canned)
6 oz. grated Cheddar cheese
fat for frying

fritter batter

4 oz. plain flour
¼ pint milk
salt and pepper
1 egg

1 Sieve flour and seasonings into a basin.
2 Gradually beat in milk and lightly beaten egg.
3 Stir in the cheese and shrimps.
4 Place in teaspoon in the hot fat.
5 Fry until crisp and golden brown.
6 Drain well and serve at once.

Cold cheese soufflé

Cooking time 10 minutes

You will need:

2 egg yolks
3 egg whites
¼ pint milk
salt and pepper
mustard
1½ dessertspoons powder gelatine
gherkins
6–8 oz. finely grated Cheshire or Cheddar cheese
¼ pint cream or evaporated milk
½ gill water or white stock
tomatoes

1 Beat egg yolks.
2 Add milk and cook gently until mixture coats back of spoon, add cheese while still hot.
3 Dissolve gelatine in very hot water or stock.
4 Add to cheese mixture.
5 Cool then fold in lightly whipped cream or evaporated milk, seasoning and lastly the stiffly beaten egg whites.
6 Pour into prepared buttered soufflé dish.
7 Leave until set.
8 Garnish with flower shapes in gherkin and tomato, serve with salad and thin bread and butter.

Cream cheese and prawn soufflé

You will need:

ingredients as in preceding recipe
but use
6 oz. cream cheese
½ pint chopped prawns
watercress

1 Blend cream cheese with milk until smooth.
2 Pour on to the egg yolks, continue as before.
3 Add the prawns before the cream.
4 Pour into 4 small dishes and when set garnish with prawns and tiny springs of watercress.

Cheese and spinach soufflé

Cooking time 35 minutes

You will need:

¼ pint thick white sauce (see page 21)
4 oz. grated cheese
seasoning
1 teaspoon oil
3 eggs
¼ pint cooked and chopped spinach (frozen spinach is ideal)
1 teaspoon finely chopped onion or chopped chives

1 Heat the oil and fry the onion in this then mix with the sauce, spinach, grated cheese, seasoning and the beaten egg yolks.
2 FOLD in the stiffly beaten egg whites.
3 Pour into a greased soufflé dish and bake in the middle of a moderate oven (375 °F. – Gas Mark 4) for 35 minutes.

Cheese and tomato ring

No cooking

You will need:

packet aspic jelly
¼ pint evaporated milk
salt
4 large tomatoes
¼ pint water
½ pint milk
8 oz. cream or grated cheese
pepper
mustard

garnish

radishes
lettuce
tomatoes

1 Dissolve the aspic jelly in the boiling water.
2 Cool slightly then whisk in milk, cheese and lastly, when cool, the lightly whipped evaporated milk.
3 Taste and season.
4 When the mixture is just beginning to thicken add chopped tomato pulp.
5 Put into ring mould.
6 When set turn out and garnish with water-lilies of radish and tomato and lettuce.

Cheese and vegetable cutlets

Cooking time 25 minutes

You will need:

1 oz. margarine or butter
1 oz. flour
¼ pint milk
4 oz. grated cheese
about 8 oz. cooked mixed vegetables—as many as possible
oil for frying if desired
egg or milk for coating the cutlets
approximately 2 tablespoons soft breadcrumbs
crisp breadcrumbs for coating

1 Heat the margarine in a saucepan, stir in the flour and cook for several minutes.
2 Take the pan off the heat and gradually add the cold milk.
3 Return to the heat and bring slowly to the boil, stirring all the time to keep the sauce smooth.
4 Add the seasoning and the vegetables which should be diced.
5 Next, add the grated cheese and enough of the soft breadcrumbs to make a mixture that is firm enough to handle without being too dry.
6 When cold, mould into about 6 cutlet shapes, brush with milk or a little beaten egg and coat in crisp breadcrumbs.
7 Heat the oil in a frying pan and fry the cutlets until crisp and brown.
8 Serve with green peas and creamed potatoes.
9 If preferred, the cutlets can be put on to a hot greased baking tin and crisped in a hot oven (450°F.—Gas Mark 7) for about 10–15 minutes.

Cheeseolettes

Cooking time 10 minutes

You will need:

3 eggs
2 oz. flour (with plain flour use ½ teaspoon baking powder)
fat, oil or shortening for frying
4 oz. grated cheese
1 tablespoon grated onion
2 tablespoons chopped parsley
seasoning

1 Blend all the ingredients together.
2 Heat fat in pan and drop in spoonfuls of this mixture.
3 Fry until crisp and golden brown.
4 Turn, brown on the other side.
5 Drain well and serve with a dish of sliced tomatoes and another of crisp lettuce.

These are a cross between pancakes and omelettes.

English monkey

Cooking time 10 minutes

You will need:

4 slices toast
1 oz. butter
½ gill milk
2 oz. soft breadcrumbs
2 tablespoons cream
4 oz. grated cheese
2 eggs
mustard
Worcestershire sauce
1 tomato

1 Heat butter in a pan.
2 Add milk and breadcrumbs.
3 When very hot add the grated cheese and beaten egg.
4 Season well, adding a little made mustard and few drops Worcestershire sauce.
5 Stir together until thick and creamy.
6 Pour on to toast, garnish with sliced tomatoes.

Gourmet macaroni cheese

Cooking time 10–15 minutes

You will need for 3–4 servings:

4 oz. quick cooking macaroni
1 can condensed tomato soup
salt and pepper to taste
½ can milk (or water)
6 oz. grated cheese
1 can crab meat (optional)

1 Cook macaroni for 7 minutes in boiling salted water.
2 Drain.
3 Heat soup and milk in saucepan.
4 Add crab meat and macaroni and half the grated cheese.
5 Season to taste.
6 Pour into serving dish.
7 Top with remaining cheese.
8 Brown under grill.

Macaroni ring

Cooking time 10–15 minutes

You will need:

6 oz. quick cooking macaroni
4 oz. cooked ham
seasoning
3 tomatoes
1 finely chopped onion
1 oz. butter

for the cheese sauce

1 oz. butter
½ pint milk
seasoning
1 oz. flour
6 oz. diced or grated cheese

1 Chop onion or grate it.
2 Put the quick cooking macaroni into boiling salted water and cook for 7 minutes only.
3 Meanwhile make the cheese sauce.
4 Strain the macaroni and melt the butter in the pan, fry the onion, add the sliced tomatoes, then the macaroni and diced ham.
5 Heat together and form into a round.
6 Fill with the cheese sauce and serve at once.

Pebbles on the beach

Cooking time 30 minutes

You will need:

3 hard-boiled eggs
½ pint white sauce (see page 21)
1–2 oz. butter
2 oz. breadcrumbs
6 cooked new potatoes
2–3 oz. grated Cheshire or Cheddar cheese
chopped parsley
seasoning

1 Cut eggs and potatoes in halves crosswise and arrange them flat side down, in a fireproof dish.
2 Season sauce well and add grated cheese.
3 Pour the sauce over the eggs and potatoes, heat through in moderately hot oven for about 20 minutes.
4 Decorate with crumbs fried in the butter and parsley.

Quick macaroni fritters

Cooking time 15 minutes

You will need:

2 oz. quick cooking macaroni
3 eggs
4 oz. grated cheese
seasoning
little fat for frying
can condensed celery or tomato soup

1 Cook macaroni in boiling salted water for 7 minutes.
2 Drain well.
3 Beat eggs and cheese and seasoning.
4 Mix in macaroni.
5 Heat fat in frying pan and drop in spoonfuls of this mixture.
6 Fry until crisp and golden, turn and brown other side.
7 Drain and serve with salad or can of undiluted soup.

Savoury celery rarebit

Cooking time 10–15 minutes

You will need:

1 medium-sized stick of celery or a can of celery hearts
1 oz. margarine or butter
1 gill milk—or celery stock
½ oz. flour
1 tablespoon of beer or ale OR 1 dessertspoon Worcestershire sauce
4 slices of toast
6 oz. grated cheese
seasoning (including mustard)

1 Melt margarine in pan, stir in flour and cook until roux is dry.
2 Add cold milk, bring to boil and cook until very thick.
3 Season well, adding sauce or beer and nearly all the cheese.
4 Cut the celery into neat pieces, cook in boiling salted water until just soft or heat thoroughly if canned.
5 Arrange the pieces on the hot slices of toast and put the rarebit mixture on top.
6 Sprinkle with remainder of cheese.
7 Brown under a hot grill.

Vermicelli with cream cheese sauce

Cooking time 15 minutes

You will need:

4–6 oz. vermicelli

for the sauce

3 tablespoons finely chopped parsley
3 oz. grated Cheddar cheese
seasoning
1¼ gills boiling water
2 oz. butter
8 oz. soft cream cheese
1 crushed clove garlic or chopped small onion

1 Cook the vermicelli in boiling salted water until just tender.
2 Meanwhile put all the ingredients for the sauce into a basin, except the boiling water.
3 Mix very thoroughly, then gradually blend in the boiling water and stir until smooth sauce.
4 Dish up the pasta and serve with the sauce and grated cheese.

Asparagus with mousseline sauce

Cooking time 25 minutes

You will need:

1 medium-sized bunch of asparagus–cooked and drained
½ gill cream from the top of the milk
1 oz. margarine or butter
either 1 large egg or the yolks of 2 eggs
1 dessertspoon lemon juice
seasoning

1 Cook asparagus.
2 Put all the ingredients for sauce into a basin over hot water.
3 Cook until thickened.
4 Serve at once poured over asparagus or in a sauce boat.

Baked soufflé potatoes

Cooking time 1¼ hours

You will need:

4 large potatoes
2 egg yolks
peas
1 tablespoon cream
seasoning
2 stiffly beaten egg whites

1 Wash the potatoes and bake until tender, about one hour.

2 Cut off tops, scoop out pulp and sieve or mash until soft.
3 Add the yolks of egg, cream or top of milk, seasoning and the stiffly beaten egg whites.
4 Pile back into the potato cases and cook for 15 minutes until just pale golden brown.
5 Serve garnished with peas.

Barbecued beans

Cooking time 10 minutes

You will need:

small can tomatoes
2 onions
4 rashers bacon
seasoning
2 large cans beans in tomato sauce
little chopped parsley
1 oz. butter

1 Chop onions finely and toss in the hot butter until tender.
2 Add diced bacon and cook until crisp, then stir in the can of tomatoes and cook for several minutes.
3 Add beans and heat thoroughly.
4 Keep very hot, adding parsley and seasoning before serving.

Beetroot cups

No cooking

You will need:

4 cooked beetroots
2 oz. cooked peas
2 oz. cooked diced young carrots
seasoning
sliced cucumber
2 tablespoons chopped radishes
1 tablespoon chopped spring onions
French dressing (see page 63)

1 Scoop out centre of beetroot and dice.
2 Moisten beetroot cases with French dressing.
3 Mix peas, carrots, radishes, onion and diced beetroot.
4 Season well, toss in French dressing and pile mixture in beetroot cases.
5 Put on dish with a border of sliced cucumber.
6 Serve at once so beetroot does not discolour the filling.

Cauliflower savoury

Cooking time 25 minutes

You will need:

1 large cauliflower
4 mushrooms
$\frac{1}{3}$ pint white sauce (see page 21)
4 oz. grated cheese
seasoning
4 large tomatoes
1 large onion
2 oz. butter or margarine
2 hard-boiled eggs

for sauce

1 oz. butter
$\frac{1}{3}$ pint milk
1 oz. flour
seasoning

1 Divide cauliflower into flowerets.
2 Boil in boiling salted water until only just tender.
3 Fry the sliced onion, tomatoes and chopped mushrooms in butter, season well.
4 Arrange half the cauliflower in hot dish.
5 Cover with mushroom mixture.
6 Arrange rest of flowerets over the top in a round cauliflower shape.
7 Cover with white sauce and cheese.
8 Brown in oven or under grill.
9 Garnish with quartered tomatoes and hard-boiled eggs.

Cauliflower and tomato fritters

Cooking time 20 minutes

You will need:

1 large cauliflower
1 egg
seasoning
fat for frying
4 oz. flour (preferably plain)
$\frac{1}{4}$ pint tomato juice or 2 tablespoons concentrated tomato purée diluted with enough water to make $\frac{1}{4}$ pint

1 Sieve flour, add egg, tomato liquid and seasoning.
2 Beat well.
3 Divide the cauliflower into fairly even flowerets.
4 Cook in a little boiling salted water until just tender.
5 Drain well, being careful not to let the flowerets break.
6 Coat each piece of cauliflower with the batter.
7 Lower into hot fat (shallow fat will be very satisfactory) and cook on both sides until crisp and golden brown.
8 Drain well.

Devilled mushroom and egg

Cooking time 15 minutes

You will need:

4 rounds toast
2 oz. mushrooms
3 hard-boiled eggs
2 oz. butter
1 teaspoon Worcestershire sauce
good pinch curry powder
$\frac{1}{2}$–1 teaspoon made mustard
1 teaspoon mustard ketchup

1 Heat butter.
2 Fry chopped mushrooms in it, add flavourings.
3 When mushrooms are cooked add quartered hard-boiled eggs.
4 Heat and serve at once on toast.

Noodle and mushroom ring

Cooking time 30 minutes

You will need:

8 oz. noodles
2 eggs
seasoning
¾ gill milk
2 oz. grated cheese

for the filling

½ pint milk
4–6 oz. mushrooms
1 oz. margarine or butter
1 oz. flour
seasoning

1 Put the noodles into boiling salted water and cook for 15 minutes.
2 Drain, then mix with well-beaten eggs, milk, seasoning and grated cheese.
3 Put this mixture either into a double saucepan or a basin over hot water and cook gently until eggs have set, stirring well.
4 This will take approximately 15 minutes, for it is important that the mixture does not boil.
5 Form into the shape of a ring.
6 Skin the mushrooms but leave them whole, put into the milk together with a little seasoning and simmer gently until mushrooms are just tender.
7 Take them out of the milk and keep hot.
8 Measure the milk and make it up to ½ pint again.
9 Blend it with the flour, put into the saucepan together with the margarine and seasoning and, stirring all the time, bring to the boil.
10 Cook until the sauce thickens, then replace the mushrooms in the saucepan.
11 Heat in the sauce and pour into the centre of the noodle ring.

Potato basket

Cooking time 45 minutes

You will need:

1½ lb. potatoes
1 lb. cooked vegetables (as varied a mixture as possible)
4 oz. grated cheese
milk
margarine
1 egg
½ pint thick white sauce (see page 21)

1 Beat the potatoes until light and fluffy, adding milk and margarine.
2 Pipe or mould into a square shape with a hollow centre and brush with well-beaten egg.
3 Add the vegetables and cheese to half the sauce and heat thoroughly.
4 Pile this mixture in the centre of the 'basket'.
5 Pour the remainder of the sauce over the top and garnish with 1 large, whole mushroom.

Savoury macaroni or spaghetti

Cooking time 15 minutes

This is an excellent alternative to potatoes when they are scarce.

You will need:

4 oz. quick cooking macaroni
2 teaspoons chopped parsley
2 oz. margarine
1 very thinly sliced onion
2 teaspoons capers

1 Cook macaroni, strain.
2 Meanwhile fry sliced onion in plenty of margarine in pan.
3 Add macaroni, parsley and capers.
4 Serve round meat.

Savoury stuffed onions

Cooking time 1¼ hours

You will need:

4 medium-sized onions
1 teaspoon sage
1½ oz margarine
4 oz. breadcrumbs
1 or 2 fresh eggs
3 oz. grated cheese
seasoning

1 Put the onions into salted water and boil steadily for 30 minutes. By this time they will not be completely cooked but it should be possible to remove the centre core.
2 Keep stock.
3 Chop the core of the onion finely, add the remaining ingredients and pile this stuffing back into the centre cavity.
4 Put the onions into a greased casserole.
5 Pour over ½ gill of the onion stock and put a small piece of margarine on top of each onion.
6 Bake for 45 minutes in the covered dish at 400 °F. – Gas Mark 5.
7 Serve with cheese sauce (see page 21). Garnish with parsley.

Spinach pancakes

Cooking time 15 minutes

You will need:

4 oz. flour
1–2 eggs
½ pint milk
seasoning
fat for frying
1 lb. cooked and well-drained spinach
1 oz. butter
½ pint white sauce (see page 21)
3 oz. grated cheese or 4 oz. chopped ham

1 Sieve or chop the spinach and reheat with the butter.

2 Mix the flour, eggs, milk and seasoning together.
3 Pour a little of this batter in hot fat in the pan and cook for several minutes until crisp and brown.
4 Turn or toss and cook on the other side.
5 Fill each pancake with some of the spinach.
6 Keep hot on a dish over a pan of water.
7 When all the pancakes are cooked, add cheese or ham to the white sauce and pour it over the top.

Note: If preferred, all the pancakes may be kept and spread with spinach, then piled on top of each other in which case cut large slices as you would a cake, to serve.

Spinach ring

Cooking time 30 minutes

You will need:

2 lb. spinach
1 egg
seasoning
2 oz. soft breadcrumbs
1 onion
2 oz. butter

1 Cook the spinach with only the water left on the leaves after washing and a little salt.
2 When cooked, drain well and either sieve or chop finely.
3 Meanwhile fry the chopped onion in the hot butter until tender, add the spinach, crumbs and egg.
4 Season well.
5 Form into a ring and set in a hot oven.
6 Fill the centre with 1 of the fillings below and garnish with a ring of chopped hard-boiled egg.

Hard-boiled egg sauce: Stir 3 chopped hard-boiled eggs into ½ pint white sauce, (see page 21). Pour into centre of spinach ring and garnish with sliced and chopped hard-boiled egg.

Cheese filling: Fill ring with ½ pint thick cheese sauce (see page 21). Garnish with tomato or bacon rolls.

Creamed ham: 6 oz. chopped ham heated in ½ pint white sauce (see page 21).

Creamed chicken: As above, using chicken instead of ham.

Creamed prawns: Use 1 pint prawns instead of ham.

Savoury egg: Fry 2 sliced onions and 2 skinned, sliced tomatoes until soft in a little butter or margarine. Add 3–4 beaten eggs, season and cook until eggs are lightly scrambled.

Stuffed baked beetroot

Cooking time 15 minutes

You will need:

4 medium-sized cooked beetroots
2 oz. grated cheese
2 oz. breadcrumbs
seasoning
tomato, watercress and hard-boiled egg for garnishing
2 oz. butter or margarine

1 Cut a slice off the bottom of each beetroot so that they stand well.
2 Scoop out a little from the centre of each one. These pieces can be used in salad.
3 Cream margarine, add seasoning, crumbs and cheese.
4 Press into the centre of the beetroot and stand in a well-greased dish.
5 Bake for 15 minutes in a moderately hot oven (400°F.—Gas Mark 5) until cheese melts slightly.
6 Garnish with watercress, tomato rings and sliced hard-boiled eggs.

Stuffed cauliflower

Cooking time 35 minutes

You will need:

1 medium-sized cauliflower
⅓ pint milk
1 small onion sliced very thinly
1 oz. breadcrumbs
new potatoes
2 oz. margarine or butter
1 oz. flour
4 or 5 chopped mushrooms
3 oz. grated cheese
seasoning
parsley

1 Cook the cauliflower whole in boiling salted water until just soft. Cut a piece off the bottom if necessary, to make sure it stands firm.
2 Scoop out part of the centre and chop it finely.
3 Heat 1 oz. margarine, add the flour and cook for several minutes, then gradually add the milk.
4 Bring to the boil, cook until thickened, add seasoning and 2 oz. cheese.
5 Fry onion and mushrooms in the remainder of margarine until soft, stir in crumbs, chopped cauliflower and enough sauce to bind.
6 Press in centre of cauliflower.
7 Pour rest of sauce over the top, sprinkle with the rest of the cheese.
8 Put in a moderately hot oven (400°F.—Gas Mark 5) for 15 minutes until golden brown.
9 Serve with new potatoes and garnish with parsley.

Stuffed mushrooms

Cooking time 10 minutes

You will need:

12 large mushrooms
3 eggs
little milk
$1\frac{1}{2}$ oz. butter
4 slices buttered toast
few capers if desired
seasoning
little fat for mushrooms

1 Fry the mushrooms in the fat.
2 Chop the stalks and cook in the butter, then add the eggs, beaten with the milk and seasoning.
3 Scramble lightly.
4 Add the capers, then pile into the mushroom caps.
5 Arrange on toast.

Stuffed tomatoes

Cooking time approximately 15 minutes

There are innumerable ways of using stuffed tomatoes as main dishes. Here are some of the most interesting. Remember to season the tomato case before putting in the filling.

Hot.

Spanish tomatoes. Remove pulp from large tomatoes, mix with diced ham, egg, little brown gravy, lots of seasoning and a little grated onion or crushed garlic. Bake for 10–15 minutes in moderately hot oven.

Indian tomatoes. Mix pulp with cooked rice, little curry powder and onion fried in hot fat. Bake for 10–15 minutes in moderately hot oven.

Provençale tomatoes. Mix pulp with fried onion, grated cheese, breadcrumbs and seasoning. Bake for 10–15 minutes.

Au gratin. Mix pulp with breadcrumbs, seasoning, grated cheese and an egg if wished. Top with breadcrumbs, grated cheese and a little butter or margarine. Bake for 10–15 minutes.

Cold.

With shrimps or prawns. Mix pulp with shrimps or prawns (or cooked white fish) add mayonnaise, seasoning, chopped parsley, also capers and chopped gherkin if wished. Serve with crisp lettuce leaves.

With meat. Mix pulp with minced or finely chopped cooked meat or poultry, add seasoning, little mayonnaise if wished.

With cheese. Mix pulp with grated cheese and mayonnaise.

Tomato quickies

Tomatoes on toast. Fried tomatoes to serve on toast should be well seasoned with salt and pepper and a good pinch of sugar.

Tomatoes au gratin. Sliced tomatoes, put into a shallow dish, seasoned and topped with breadcrumbs, grated cheese and margarine, then cooked under the grill or in the oven are delicious with fish, cold ham or an omelette.

Tomato salad. Slice tomatoes, add little oil and vinegar, chopped parsley, chopped chives and seasoning. Leave for an hour or so and serve in a salad, or as an hors-d'oeuvre.

Tomatoes Italienne. Halve 6 large tomatoes. Chop contents of a small tin of anchovies, mix with 2 hard-boiled eggs, 2 oz. breadcrumbs, little chopped parsley and seasoning and the oil from the anchovy fillets. Pile on the tomatoes. Top with little margarine or butter and bake for about 8 minutes in a hot oven (450°F.—Gas Mark 7).

Tomato toasts

Cooking time 10 minutes

You will need:

4 large tomatoes
4 oz. chopped ham or cooked meat
4 large slices buttered toast
1 small onion
2 oz. margarine (or butter)
2 eggs
seasoning
parsley

1 Slice tomatoes, skinning them if wished.
2 Chop onion and cook in hot margarine then add ham or meat, the tomatoes and cook all together until very soft.
3 Add beaten eggs, seasoning and continue cooking until eggs are very lightly set.
4 Pile on to hot pieces of toast and garnish with parsley.
5 This makes an excellent quick supper dish.

Tomato pie

Cooking time 1 hour

You will need:

2 large onions
2 oz. butter
1 lb. tomatoes
3–4 oz. breadcrumbs
salt and pepper
4 eggs

1 Peel the onions and put them into a bowl of boiling water and leave them there for 2 or 3 hours. This is not essential, but it does mean they cook more quickly and have a lovely transparent appearance.
2 Drain, dry and slice them and fry them lightly in butter.
3 Butter a fireproof dish and fill it with alternate layers of the onions and sliced peeled tomatoes, sprinkling each layer with a few breadcrumbs, seasoned with salt and pepper.
4 Finish with a good layer of the crumbs, dot with flakes of butter and bake in a moderate oven for about 1 hour (375°F.—Gas Mark 4).
5 Top with poached eggs.

Bacon and beef patties

Cooking time 30 minutes

You will need:

8 oz. short crust pastry (see page 86)
8 oz. minced or chopped cooked or flaked corned beef
½–1 teaspoon mixed herbs (use the smaller quantity if using dried herbs)
3 rashers bacon – streaky bacon can be used for these
1 egg
2 skinned and chopped tomatoes
seasoning
milk or a little egg

1 Roll out the pastry and cut into 8 rounds.
2 Chop the bacon and mix with all the other ingredients.
3 Put the mixture in the centre of 4 of the rounds.
4 Damp the edges of the pastry and put the other 4 rounds on top.
5 Seal the edges firmly and brush over the top with milk or a little egg.
6 Bake for approximately 25–30 minutes in the centre of a hot oven (450 °F. – Gas Mark 7), reducing the heat to moderate after the first 15 minutes.
7 Lift off the baking tin to cool.
8 To keep the pastry crisp remember to make a small air hole with the point of a knife before baking.
9 You can decorate the patties with leaves and a small tassel or rose of pastry.

Variations

Omit the tomatoes and add 2 oz. finely chopped mushrooms instead. Add a spoonful of chutney and a shake of curry powder to the mixture. Since the chutney makes the mixture more moist, use 2 small tomatoes only.

Baconburgers *with curry sauce*

Cooking time 20 minutes

You will need:

4 slices bacon
1 lb. minced beef
⅛ teaspoon pepper
½ teaspoon salt
¼ teaspoon garlic salt
2 tablespoons butter or margarine

sauce

1 oz. flour
¼ teaspoon garlic salt
¼ teaspoon salt
1½ oz. butter or margarine
2 teaspoons curry powder
½ pint milk
4 slices toast

1 Fry bacon until almost crisp.
2 Remove from pan and quickly curl each strip around the end of a wooden spoon.
3 Secure each with a tooth-pick.
4 Mix together the beef, pepper, salt and garlic salt.
5 Shape into 4 patties and sauté in the butter or margarine for 6 minutes.
6 For the sauce: Melt the butter or margarine in a saucepan.
7 Mix together the flour, curry powder, garlic salt and salt and thoroughly blend into the butter or margarine.
8 Gradually add milk, stirring until smooth.
9 Cook and stir until thickened and flavours blended.
10 Place each patty on a slice of toast.
11 Top with a bacon curl and pour sauce over each.

Beef cakes

Cooking time 8–10 minutes

You will need:

1 can corned beef
approximately 8 oz. mashed potatoes
1 egg
breadcrumbs to coat
fat for frying

1 Mix the beef and potatoes together and season well. If rather dry add either an egg or milk to bind.
2 Form into cakes, coat with beaten egg and crumbs.
3 Fry until crisp and brown.
4 Serve with fried tomatoes, mushrooms etc.

Beef pancakes

Cooking time 12 minutes

You will need:

for the batter

4 oz. flour
1 egg
pinch salt
½ pint milk and water
fat for frying

for the filling

2 thinly sliced onions
seasoning
2 oz. margarine
2 sliced tomatoes
2 rashers bacon
1 can finely chopped corned beef
4 tablespoons milk

1 First make batter by sieving flour and salt together, then add egg and a little of the liquid.
2 Beat very hard.
3 Gradually add rest of liquid and beat until batter is smooth.
4 Now prepare the filling by frying onions and tomatoes in margarine.
5 Add chopped bacon and cook until crisp.
6 Add corned beef, milk, seasoning and heat thoroughly.
7 Heat a small knob of fat in frying pan, pour a little of batter in this and cook until golden, toss or turn pancake and cook until brown on under side.
8 Slide on to a hot plate, cover with a layer of filling. Keep pancake hot by putting plate over saucepan of hot water.
9 Continue cooking pancakes and pile on top of each other with a layer of filling between each.
10 Fry tomatoes or mushrooms to garnish.
11 To serve, cut into 4 thick slices.

Casserole of sausage and corn

Cooking time 20 minutes

You will need:

8 small sausages
can corn
½ green pepper, chopped
salt and pepper
½ pint white sauce (see page 21)

1 Mix corn, green pepper, salt and pepper.
2 Place in casserole in alternate layers with white sauce.
3 Arrange sausages on top to radiate from centre.
4 Bake in moderate oven for 20 minutes (375 °F. – Gas Mark 4).

Corn and bacon fritters

Cooking time 5–15 minutes

You will need:

1 small size carton frozen sweet corn, or can of corn
⅛ pint milk (½ gill)
2 rashers bacon
2 oz. self-raising flour
fat for frying

1 Cook the corn according to the directions on the carton if using frozen variety. The canned variety should just be strained.
2 Cut the rashers of bacon into small dice.
3 Fry gently for a few minutes.
4 Remove from the pan.
5 Make a batter with the flour and milk.
6 Stir in the corn and bacon.
7 Heat a little more fat in the frying pan and fry tablespoons of the mixture, turning once, until golden brown on both sides, about 5 minutes.

Corned beef cakes

Cooking time 12 minutes

You will need:

1 can corned beef
1 egg
seasoning
fat for frying
1 tablespoon chopped parsley
1 tablespoon grated onion
2 tablespoons breadcrumbs
fried tomatoes and fried bread to garnish

1 Flake the meat and mix with other ingredients.
2 Heat a little fat in frying pan.
3 Fry bread and halved tomatoes and keep warm in oven.
4 Drop spoonfuls corned beef mixture into fat.
5 Fry on 1 side, turn carefully and brown other side.
6 Serve at once.

Corned beef fritters

Cooking time 10 minutes

You will need:

1 can corned beef
2 oz. flour
1 or 2 beaten eggs
1 gill milk
seasoning
little chopped parsley or grated onion to flavour
fat for frying

1 Open tin of corned beef, flake the meat.
2 Beat flour with eggs and milk and add meat etc.
3 Drop spoonfuls of the mixture into the hot fat, turning when crisp and brown.

Corned beef hamburgers

Cooking time 10 minutes

You will need:

1 can corned beef
1 teaspoon mustard
lettuce
watercress
1 tablespoon mustard pickle
2 chopped gherkins
4 large or 8 small rolls
tomatoes
butter

1 Chop the corned beef and mix with the chopped gherkins, chopped pickles and mustard.
2 Split and butter the rolls, spread with the corned beef mixture, then brush the outside of the rolls with a little butter.
3 Put into a fairly hot oven for about 10 minutes.
4 Meanwhile make a salad of lettuce, watercress and tomatoes.

Frankfurter rolls

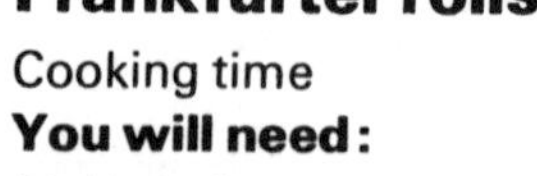

Cooking time 15 minutes

You will need:

4 bridge rolls
4 tomatoes
seasoning
butter
4 large or 8 small frankfurter sausages
mustard
cress

1 Split and butter the rolls.
2 Slice the tomatoes thickly and spread the slices over the bottom halves of the rolls.
3 Split the frankfurters and spread with made mustard, put on to the tomato slices and cover with the buttered tops of rolls.
4 Wrap in greaseproof paper or, better still, aluminium foil, and bake for about 15 minutes in a moderatley hot oven (425 °F. – Gas Mark 6).
5 Unwrap and serve at once with cress.

Crispy ham roll-ups

No cooking time except boiling eggs

You will need:

3 oz. coarsely crushed cheese biscuits
1 tablespoon chopped green peppers or 1 tablespoon chopped gherkins
8 oz. sliced boiled ham (6 or 7 slices)
2 hard-boiled eggs
1 teaspoon grated onion
1 tablespoon chopped parsley
pinch of salt
¼ cup mayonnaise
2 teaspoons prepared mustard

1 Chop eggs.
2 Blend crumbs with finely chopped eggs, onion, parsley, green pepper, salt and mayonnaise.
3 Spread each ham slice with mustard, then with biscuit crumb stuffing and roll up.
4 Serve with olives or gherkins.

Double decker Creole

Cooking time 5 minutes

You will need:

3 slices buttered toast, each cut across in 2 triangles

top layer filling

4 slices liver sausage spread lightly with mustard, warmed under grill and topped with 1 tablespoon finely chopped fried onion

bottom layer – Hot Slaw

3 oz. finely shredded cabbage boiled for 1 minute in 2 tablespoons vinegar then drained
a sprinkling of salt
1 teaspoon butter
1 teaspoon brown sugar

1 Sandwich buttered toast together with fillings.
2 Press down well, cutting across again, if liked.
3 Garnish with slices of tomato and pickled gherkin.

Note: Fillings for hot sandwiches vary according to taste, hunger, mood and what there is in the pantry. Cheese, eggs, canned fish and meats, peanut butter, pickles and relishes make interesting combinations for hot layer sandwiches. Seasonings are important and a salad accompaniment makes this type of snack a balanced meal.

Griddle cakes

with sausages and bacon

Cooking time 4–5 minutes

You will need for 12–14 cakes:

8 oz. self-raising flour
½ pint milk
½ level teaspoon salt
1 egg

1 Sift flour and salt together into a mixing bowl.
2 Make a well in the centre and add the milk and beaten egg and stir just until smooth.
3 Pour batter from the tip of a large spoon on to a lightly greased hot griddle, heavy frying pan or hot plate of an electric cooker.
4 Cook until bubbles begin to form on the surface, then turn and brown on the other side.
5 Serve warm with butter, sausages and bacon.
6 These are delicious also with fried tomatoes and bacon.

Ham soufflé

Cooking time 25–35 minutes

You will need for 2–3 servings:

¼ pint thick white sauce (see page 21)
4 oz. finely chopped ham
parsley to garnish
4 eggs
seasoning

1 Separate the eggs.
2 Blend egg yolks into sauce.
3 Add ham and seasoning and fold in stiffly beaten egg whites.
4 Pour into a prepared soufflé dish and bake in a moderate oven (375°F.—Gas Mark 4) for 25–35 minutes.
5 Serve at once, garnished with parsley.

Ham and tomato mould

Cooking time few minutes

You will need:

8 oz. cooked ham
seasoning
1 or 2 oz. cream or cottage cheese
4 hard-boiled eggs
½ pint tomato juice
1 dessertspoon powder gelatine

1 Dissolve the powder gelatine in the very hot tomato juice, softening it first in a tablespoon water.
2 When cold, but not set, stir in 2 sliced hard-boiled eggs and the diced ham.
3 Put into a rinsed mould and allow to set.
4 Turn out and serve on a bed of lettuce.
5 Halve the other 2 hard-boiled eggs, take out the centre yolk, mash, season and mix with a little cream cheese.
6 Pile back into the white cases and cut into quarters, so you have 8 portions, and arrange these round the mould.

Hot bacon and oat cobbler

Cooking time 25 minutes

You will need for 4–6 servings:

1 or 2 cans concentrated vegetable soup
2 oz. butter or margarine
salt and pepper to taste
little grated cheese
3–4 rashers bacon
6 oz. self-raising flour
2 oz. rolled oats
1 egg
milk to make ½ pint with the egg

1 Cut bacon into small pieces and fry.
2 Sieve flour and seasonings into basin.
3 Add rolled oats.
4 Mix thoroughly.
5 Rub margarine in lightly.
6 Add bacon.
7 Beat egg and milk together.
8 Pour over dry ingredients.
9 Mix with palette knife.
10 Roll out on floured board to about ½ inch thick. Cut into rounds.
11 Put the vegetable soup into a casserole and meanwhile heat for about 10 minutes in a moderately hot oven (400°F.—Gas Mark 5).
12 Arrange rounds of scone on top, sprinkle with grated cheese to give them an attractive glaze.
13 Bake for approximately 12–15 minutes in a hot oven (425–450°F.—Gas Mark 6–7). This makes a filling and economical meal.

Macaroni Valetta

Cooking time 15 minutes

You will need:

4–6 oz. quick-cooking macaroni
3–4 sliced tomatoes
3–4 oz. ham or corned beef
1 oz. fat
½–¾ pint white sauce (depending on amount of macaroni used) (see page 21)
3–4 oz. mushrooms cut in large slices

1 Put macaroni in boiling salted water.
2 Cook for 7 minutes.
3 Meanwhile heat fat in frying pan and cook mushrooms, then the tomatoes.
4 Make white sauce and, when boiled and quite smooth, heat chopped ham in this.
5 Drain macaroni, mix with sauce and fried mushrooms.
6 Pile into hot dish and decorate with fried tomatoes.
7 Spaghetti may be used instead of macaroni in this recipe.

Minced ham with eggs

Cooking time 10 minutes

You will need:

4 eggs
1 onion
1–2 tablespoons tomato purée
2 oz. butter
2–3 tablespoons chopped parsley
seasoning
stick celery
4–6 oz. minced or chopped ham

1 Trim and cut 1 large onion and a small stick of celery into cubes.
2 Fry in butter or margarine until tender.
3 Mix with the ham, add chopped parsley and tomato purée.
4 Put into individual ovenproof dishes, break an egg in the middle of each and bake in a moderate oven (375°F.—Gas Mark 4) for about 10 minutes, until the eggs are set.

Party platter

Cooking time 10 minutes to boil eggs

You will need:

4 eggs (hard-boil these in the morning, if possible)
little anchovy essence
chicory
tomatoes
gherkins
mayonnaise
4 slices ham
4 slices tongue
about 2 oz. cream cheese
chutney
lettuce
grated carrot

1 Mix the grated carrot with cream cheese, spread over the slices of ham and roll firmly.
2 Halve the eggs, mix the yolks with anchovy essence and mayonnaise and pile back into whites.
3 Spread the slices of tongue with chutney and chopped gherkins and roll.
4 Separate the pieces of chicory and fill with cream cheese.
5 Arrange all these on bed of lettuce and garnish with sliced tomatoes

Ragoût of kidney and tomatoes

Cooking time approximately 20 minutes

You will need:

4 lambs' kidneys
1 green pepper
seasoning
about ½ gill stock
large onion
4 large tomatoes
2 oz. butter
little flour
1 gill red wine
shake paprika pepper

1 Slice the onion and green pepper.
2 Halve the kidneys and roll in seasoned flour, then fry gently in the butter.
3 Add the onions and pepper and cook for about 5 minutes.
4 Put in the sliced tomatoes, wine, stock and more seasoning and cook until tender.

Rice cutlets

Cooking time 15 minutes

You will need:

2 teaspoons grated onion
2 teaspoons chopped parsley
4 oz. cooked rice
6–8 oz. cooked minced meat
crisp breadcrumbs
¼ pint thick white sauce (see page 21)
seasoning
1 tablespoon melted butter or margarine
brown or paprika sauce

1 Mix all ingredients but melted butter and crumbs together.
2 Form into cutlet shapes, brush lightly with butter, roll in crumbs.
3 Cook under grill until crisp. Turn and brown on the other side.
4 Serve with a good brown or paprika sauce. This is made by adding 1–2 teaspoons paprika pepper to ½ pint white sauce.

Sausage and egg galantine

Cooking time 55 minutes

You will need:

1 lb. sausage meat
2 or 3 hard-boiled eggs
little seasoned flour
pinch mixed herbs
1 beaten egg
few crisp breadcrumbs

1 Work half the egg and the herbs into the sausage meat.
2 Put flour on your pastry board and roll out sausage meat to a neat rectangle.
3 Put the hard-boiled eggs on this.
4 Roll firmly.
5 Brush with remainder of the egg and coat with breadcrumbs.
6 Bake for 45 minutes in a moderate oven (375 °F. – Gas Mark 4).
7 Serve hot or cold.
8 Instead of sausage meat you could use 12 oz. minced beef mixed with 4 oz. breadcrumbs and seasoning.

Savoury kidneys

Cooking time 10–15 minutes

You will need:

4 slices of bread
butter
small amount of flour
4 lambs' kidneys
4 small rashers of bacon
little butter
seasoning
2 tomatoes

1 Cut kidneys into small pieces and roll in seasoned flour.
2 Chop up bacon and fry lightly, add a little butter, then fry the kidneys and skinned sliced tomatoes until kidneys are soft.
3 Pile on hot buttered toast and garnish with parsley or serve on bed of cooked rice and serve with salad or peas.

Savoury beef mixture

If you have a cool larder or a refrigerator a good saucepan of a savoury minced beef mixture can be used in a number of ways but *never* attempt to keep this too long if you haven't a cool storage space.

You will need:

3 oz. fat
3 good sized onions
3 oz. flour
2 lb. minced beef
tube tomato purée (small size)
can of tomatoes
seasoning
stock of water

1 Heat the fat and fry the finely chopped or grated onions then work in the flour and cook for several minutes.
2 Add the tomato purée, can tomatoes and 1 pint of stock or water flavoured with yeast or meat extract.
3 Bring to the boil, season well, then add the minced beef.
4 Stir well to break up the meat then simmer gently for about 1 hour.

To batch No. 1. Serve as a hot sauce with cooked rice or spaghetti or vegetables. Use a good ¼ of this for 4 people.

To batch No. 2. Take about ¼ of this, add 4 oz. soft breadcrumbs, little mixed herbs and chopped parsley. Work together well and form into a loaf shape. Serve with salad. The loaf will slice if well chilled.

To batch No. 3. Cut the tops off tomatoes, scoop out the centre, pulp, mix with ¼ of the meat mixture. Pile this back into the tomato cases. Either bake for 15 minutes and serve hot with mixed vegetables or serve cold, topped with mayonnaise and garnished with salad.

To batch No. 4. Use the remaining ¼ for lining 4 scallop shells, making a hollow in the centre. Break an egg into each, season well and if liked top with grated cheese. Bake for 15 minutes in a moderate oven (375 °F. – Gas Mark 4). Serve with freshly buttered rolls and salad.

Spiced patties

Cooking time 10 minutes

You will need:

8 oz. minced rump steak
1 finely chopped onion
2 teaspoons capers
2 teaspoons chopped parsley
egg
tomatoes
8 oz. beef or pork sausage meat
1 clove of crushed garlic or use 1 tablespoon of chopped chives
2 teaspoons Worcestershire sauce
pepper and salt
soft breadcrumbs
fat for frying

1 Mix all the ingredients together, except egg and breadcrumbs.
2 Form into 8 patties.
3 Coat with egg and soft breadcrumbs.
4 Fry steadily in shallow hot fat.
5 Drain well. Serve hot on halved tomatoes.

Spanish potatoes

Cooking time 15 minutes

You will need:

- 1 tablespoon minced onion
- 2 tablespoons chopped green pepper
- 4 oz. chopped cooked ham
- ½ teaspoon paprika
- 3 oz. fat
- 4 diced boiled potatoes
- 1 teaspoon salt

1 Sauté onion, pepper, in fat until light brown.
2 Add potatoes, ham and seasonings and cook until heated through.

Southern luncheon bake

Cooking time 20 minutes

You will need:

- 4 ½-inch slices ham
- whole cloves
- 6 canned pineapple rings
- 2 tablespoons cranberry sauce or red currant jelly
- 2 tablespoons butter, melted
- ½ teaspoon salt
- 8 oz. mashed cooked potatoes
- 1 teaspoon grated orange peel
- 1 gill orange juice
- 1 tablespoon brown sugar

1 Arrange ham slices in shallow baking dish, stud sides with cloves.
2 Place a pineapple ring on each ham slice.
3 Beat butter and salt into potatoes and mount on pineapple rings.
4 Brown in oven 20 minutes (375 °F. – Gas Mark 4).
5 In saucepan, combine cranberry sauce, orange peel, juice and brown sugar.
6 Heat the ingredients together and serve separately.

Tongue and cream cheese rolls

No cooking time

You will need:

- 4 good-sized slices of tongue
- 2 tablespoons chopped cucumber
- 1 teaspoon chopped spring onion
- French dressing (see page 63)
- 3 oz. soft cream cheese
- 2 teaspoons capers
- little well-flavoured chutney or piccalilli

to garnish

- cooked peas
- beetroot
- potato salad

1 Spread each slice of tongue with chutney.
2 Mix the cheese, cucumber, onion and capers together.
3 Moisten with a very little French dressing.
4 Put on to the slices of tongue and roll, making sure the light filling shows at either end of each roll.
5 Arrange in a ring of sliced beetroot and garnish with potato salad and peas.

Snacks and Salads

In this chapter you will find a number of suggestions for delicious sandwiches, and other quick savouries, good enough to be served when you entertain, easy enough to solve all your problems when a hurried snack is required.

Your will also find a number of time-saving practical suggestions for the making of salads and some excellent salad recipes.

20 different savoury snacks

Cooking time 5–15 minutes

Toasted snacks are so easy and can be extremely appetising as well. They can be anything from a main meal to a dainty titbit to tempt the appetite.

Toast bread under a hot grill or in a toaster, or, where possible, over a red-hot coal fire. Trim the crusts if preferred. Butter well, and keep hot while making the topping.

1 Scrambled eggs: Beat the eggs, allowing 1 per person, season well, and for a softer mixture add 1 tablespoon milk to each 2 eggs. Heat a knob of butter in the pan and pour in the mixture. Cook as slowly as possible, stirring all the time until lightly set. Remove from heat while still a little liquid, since the eggs will stiffen slightly in the pan.

2 Scrambled eggs with chicken: Heat any tiny scraps of cooked chicken in the milk and butter, then add the beaten seasoned egg and cook as before.

3 Scrambled eggs with ham: As with chicken, but as ham is slightly salt, reduce quantity in seasoning.

4 Scrambled eggs with tomatoes: Allow a good-sized tomato for each 2 eggs. Skin and slice thinly and heat in the butter. Beat eggs, add to milk, season and cook as before.

5 Scrambled eggs with bacon, macaroni or spaghetti: Fry the bacon in the pan until really crisp, then add the cooked and well-drained macaroni. Heat for a minute, add the eggs and cook as before.

6 Scrambled eggs with fried bread and onions: Chop an onion finely and cook in the hot butter until soft then add a few cubes of bread and brown these. Add the beaten eggs and cook as before.

7 Tomatoes on toast: Halve or slice the tomatoes and fry steadily in butter or margarine. Season and add pinch sugar to taste. Garnish with chopped parsley, or serve with crisp bacon or poached or fried eggs on top.

8 English monkey: For 4 slices of toast. Heat 1 oz. butter in pan, add 1 gill milk, 2 oz. soft breadcrumbs. When very hot add 2 oz. grated cheese and a beaten egg. Season well, adding little made mustard and few drops Worcestershire sauce. Stir together until thick and creamy. Pour on to toast, garnish with sliced tomato.

9 Cheese and apple rings: Peel and core apples. Fry thick rings of apple in bacon fat. When apples are soft, add a slice of cheese and leave until beginning to melt. Put both apple and cheese slices on to toast.

10 Creamed haddock: Heat a good knob of butter in a pan, add little milk and flaked, cooked, smoked haddock. Heat together until a thick mixture. If wished, a beaten egg can be stirred into the mixture. Garnish with paprika pepper.

11 Roes on toast: Either fry the soft roes in hot butter or cook in milk and butter in a pan or on a dish over hot water. Drain well and garnish with paprika pepper.

12 Cod's roes: Cut the cooked cod's roe into slices and fry steadily in butter or, better still, use bacon fat, until pale golden brown. Put on to hot toast with a fried bacon rasher.

13 Kidneys on toast: Skin and halve the kidneys, season well and fry in hot butter until tender. OR quarter kidneys, coat in well-seasoned flour. Fry chopped bacon in a pan, add a little butter then the kidneys and cook steadily, adding little water or port wine to moisten. Excellent topped with a poached egg.

14 Poached eggs: Crack each egg, pour into a saucer. Season lightly. Butter a cup or poacher well and heat before pouring in the egg. Eggs can be poached in a special poacher, or in a cup in a pan of water, or lower the eggs into boiling water in a pan. When set, lift on to hot buttered toast.

15 Poached eggs with Welsh rarebit: Top Welsh rarebit or toasted cheese with a poached egg.

16 Poached eggs with mushrooms: Fry sliced mushrooms in hot butter, pile on toast then top with a poached egg.

17 Poached eggs in cheese sauce: Put the poached eggs on buttered toast, cover with a cheese sauce, sprinkle with grated cheese and brown very quickly under a hot grill.

18 Sardines on toast: Arrange well-drained sardines on hot buttered toast, season lightly, and heat for a minute under the grill.

19 Sardines on toast with tomatoes: Mash sardines, season well and spread on buttered toast. Cover with thickly sliced, skinned tomatoes, brush with little butter and cook under medium grill.

20 Sardines with cheese on toast: Mash sardines, season well and spread on toast. Cover with grated cheese and brown under the grill.

10 Savoury spreads for toast or sandwiches

1 Grated cheese, grated carrot and little chopped parsley, mixed together with mayonnaise.
2 Creamed butter, chopped watercress and a squeeze of lemon juice, seasoned well.
3 Creamed cheese and finely chopped celery; use a small amount of the green leaves too.
4 Creamed cheese and chopped boiled bacon or ham, then just a touch of chutney.
5 Chopped hard-boiled eggs, crisp chopped bacon and little mayonnaise to bind.
6 Chopped soft-boiled eggs, knob butter, little chopped parsley or watercress, pinch celery, salt and seasoning.
7 Chopped hard-boiled eggs, pinch curry powder and a little chutney.
8 Chopped tongue, chopped beetroot and little mayonnaise to bind.
9 Smoked cooked haddock, chopped lettuce and chopped gherkin. Bind together with butter.
10 Flaked cooked kippers (be careful to take out all the bones) little butter, squeeze of lemon juice and lots of pepper.

Toasted snacks under the grill

Cooking time 5–10 minutes

Toast 2 slices of bread for each person, butter. Meanwhile grill rashers of bacon (thin). Sandwich together and serve at once.

or put a slice of cheese on top of bacon rashers. Add chutney if wished.

or fill sandwich with grilled filleted herring or kipper.

or with mashed sardines. Spread over 1 slice of toast and heat for 1 minute then top with 2nd slice.

or with lean ham, heated for 1 minute under grill.

or with sliced or grated cheese mixed with chopped gherkins. Spread on 1 slice of toast, heat for 1 minute then top with second slice.

or butter bread and cover with a generous layer of beef paste. Roll each slice very firmly. Brush with melted butter or margarine and either crisp under a hot grill or in the oven. Other varieties of pastes can be used instead.

Fried hot sandwiches

Cooking time 5 minutes

Cheese dreams. Make sandwiches of bread and butter and your favourite cheese. Cut into fingers and fry until crisp and brown.

Croque monsieur. This is a slightly more sophisticated version of the cheese dreams. Cut slices of bread and butter (French bread is ideal for this), sandwich with sliced Gruyère cheese and ham and fry as before.

Supper sandwich

Cooking time 6 minutes

You will need for 1–2 servings:

1 Butter 4–5 slices of toast.
2 Place a layer of processed cheese on each.
3 Grill until cheese melts.
4 Heat 1 can tomato soup seasoned with 1 tablespoon chopped pickle.
5 Pour on sandwiches.

Three-decker club sandwich

Cooking time 5 minutes

You will need for 1–2 servings:

3 slices buttered toast
1 oz. Cheddar cheese
lettuce
tomato
1 slice boiled bacon or ham
mayonnaise
made mustard

1 Season mayonnaise with mustard.
2 On large slice of toast put sliced or minced boiled bacon or ham, moistened with a little mayonaise.
3 Top with second slice of toast, then with sliced or grated cheese, moisten with mayonnaise.
4 Top with third slice of toast.
5 Work quickly so that the toast is still warm when served.
6 Cut across and serve with lettuce and tomato.

Swiss toasts

Cooking time 5–10 minutes

You will need:

4 slices cheese
4 slices bread
1 large tomato
4 slices lean ham or other cold meat
little margarine
chutney

1 Toast the bread lightly, spread with a little margarine.
2 Put ham on each piece of toast, spreading it lightly with chutney.
3 Top with a cheese slice and a ring of tomato.

Put into a moderately hot oven (400°F.—Gas Mark 5) for 10 minutes until cheese just starts to melt.
Serve at once with crisp watercress.

Mock pizza pie

Cooking time 30 minutes

You will need:

4 large slices of bread
1 can tomatoes
few olives or parsley
grated cheese
little fat
1 large onion
can sardines or anchovies

1. Brush the large slices of bread with fat and arrange on a dish.
2. Fry the onions until tender, mix with the tomatoes and arrange on the bread.
3. Top with grated cheese and brown in the oven.
4. Garnish with anchovies or sardines and olives or parsley.

Mock vol-au-vent cases

Cooking time 10 minutes

Made of bread, these cases are an excellent substitute for puff pastry and, of course, far less trouble.
Cut slices of bread about ¾ inch thick, cut in rounds with pastry cutter.
With a small cutter, take a circle from centre of each, removing only about ¼ inch in thickness of the bread.
Fry until crisp and golden in hot butter or vegetable shortening.
Drain well and fill with savoury mixtures.

Easy savoury fillings:

Scrambled egg and grated cheese.
Thick cheese sauce and grated RAW carrot.
Chopped fried mushrooms.
Fried onions, tomatoes and chopped anchovies.
Left over meat, fish etc. in thick sauce.

Vol-au-vent cases

and fillings

Cooking time 15 minutes

You may not have time to do much baking so why not either buy ready-baked pastry cases or the made puff pastry which just needs rolling out and baking. For hot weather, nothing is nicer than these, filled and served with a good salad. Try some of these fillings:
Cream cheese and chopped ham. Mix 2–3 oz. cream cheese with the same amount of cooked ham. Moisten with mayonnaise. Garnish with radish waterlilies.
Savoury tongue. Mix chopped tongue with finely chopped chutney and a little mayonnaise.
Spiced beef. Mix chopped, cooked or corned beef with mayonnaise, chopped spring onions and a little horseradish.
Scrambled egg and anchovies. Lightly scramble eggs, adding chopped anchovies just before eggs are set. Garnish with rolled anchovies.
Fish filling. Mix flaked, canned or shell fish with mayonnaise, chopped cucumber and capers.

Savoury tarts

Cooking time 15 minutes

You will need to make some small tartlets of short crust pastry (see page 86). When crisp and cold, fill with any of the following:
Chopped hard-boiled eggs mixed with mayonnaise and a little chopped gherkin, OR
Canned or flaked cooked fish mixed with thick mayonnaise, chopped gherkins, parsley and capers.
Garnish with rings of radishes, strips of parsley and hard-boiled egg.

Savoury triangles

Cooking time 5 minutes for scrambled eggs

You will need:

6 large square slices of buttered white bread
3 eggs
6 oz. soft cream cheese
seasoning
few olives
knob of butter
3 large square slices of buttered brown bread
2 oz. ham
2 large tomatoes
about 2 inches cucumber
tiny piece gherkin or spring onion

1. Slice the tomatoes and cucumber thinly and season well.
2. Heat the knob of butter, beat and season the eggs and scramble lightly, adding the chopped ham.
3. Spread 3 of the slices of white bread and butter with the ham and egg mixture, cover with the brown slice.
4. Top this with the sliced tomatoes and cucumber, then the other white slices.
5. Beat the cream cheese until it is very soft, if necessary add a few drops of milk.
6. Cut each of the 3 large sandwich squares into 4 triangles—making 12 in all.
7. Coat top and sides with thin cheese, rather like icing little cakes.
8. Garnish on top with the slices of olive and leaves of gherkins or spring onions.

Welsh rarebit

Cooking time 5–10 minutes

You will need:

4–6 large slices of toast
8 oz. cheese
1 teaspoon made mustard
1 tablespoon beer or ale or Worcestershire sauce
butter for toast
salt
pepper
1 oz. butter
1 oz. flour
½ pint milk

1. Heat the butter in a saucepan, stir in the flour and cook steadily for several minutes, then gradually add the cold milk.
2. Bring to the boil and cook until smooth and thick.
3. Add the mustard, salt, pepper, most of the cheese and the beer.
4. Heat steadily, without boiling too quickly, until the cheese has melted.
5. Spread over the hot buttered toast, sprinkle with the remainder of the cheese and brown under a hot grill.
6. Serve at once.

SNACKS WITH FISH

Breton fingers

Cooking time 10 minutes

You will need:

1 small can sardines in oil
½ teaspoon made mustard
4 slices buttered toast
1 teaspoon Worcestershire sauce
2 oz. grated Cheddar cheese
seasoning
little margarine, or butter if necessary
1 tomato
1 heaped tablespoon breadcrumbs

1. Mash the sardines very well and season.
2. Mix the oil from the tin of sardines with the breadcrumbs, seasoning, Worcestershire sauce and cheese.
3. If there is not sufficient oil to give a soft mixture then add a little margarine or butter and cream well.
4. Spread the mashed sardines on the slices of toast and cover with the crumb mixture.
5. Put under a hot grill for a few minutes until crisp and golden brown.
6. Garnish with a small piece of tomato and serve hot or cold.
7. If serving hot the fingers can be prepared earlier and just heated in oven.

Mushroom and haddock fillets

Cooking time 10–15 minutes

You will need:

4–6 oz. quick cooking macaroni
1 good dessertspoon chopped parsley
1 can condensed mushroom soup
2 oz. butter
4 thin fillets of fresh haddock (about 3 oz. each)
¼ can milk

1. Place haddock in frying pan.
2. Heat soup and milk in pan, pour over fish.
3. Cook gently for 7–10 minutes.
4. Meanwhile cook macaroni for 7 minutes in boiling salted water, drain.
5. Melt margarine in saucepan, add macaroni and parsley.
6. Mix, heat thoroughly.
7. Place in serving dish, top with fish and sauce.

Neapolitan macaroni

Cooking time 25 minutes

You will need:

2 onions
2 oz. margarine
little grated cheese
1 lb. tomatoes
4–6 oz. macaroni
small can anchovies or sardines

1. Fry grated onion in the margarine until very soft.
2. Add the sliced tomatoes and simmer gently for 15 minutes.
3. Cook the macaroni in boiling salted water until tender.
4. Add to the tomato mixture.
5. When hot, add the can of anchovies or sardines.
6. Pile on to dish and garnish with grated cheese.
7. Serve with crisp toast.

Prawn cutlets

Cooking time 20 minutes

As egg and vegetable cutlets (see page 39) but use chopped prawns with a little anchovy essence to flavour.

Scrambled kipper on toast

Cooking time 10 minutes

You will need:

4–8 kipper fillets—frozen or fresh
4 slices bread
2 oz. margarine or butter
4 eggs
2 tablespoons milk
very little salt
pepper

1 Separate the kipper fillets and poach in water for 5 minutes.
2 When cooked, drain and flake the fish coarsely, removing the skin.
3 Break the eggs into a basin.
4 Add the milk and seasoning and beat lightly with a fork.
5 Meanwhile toast the bread, cut off crusts and spread with 1 oz. margarine.
6 Keep hot, melt the remaining ounce of margarine in a pan, add the eggs and cook gently, stirring occasionally.
7 When nearly set add the flaked kippers. Serve on toast.

MAKING A QUICK SALAD

A salad can be prepared in a very short time if you take advantage of the ready prepared or convenience foods available.

For green salads: It is time saving to wash and prepare lettuce, watercress etc. when purchased so they are all ready for use. Store them in the salad container or plastic bags in refrigerator or in a cool place.
Mustard and cress can often be purchased in containers, still growing, so cut and use as desired.
An unwashed lettuce keeps well in a biscuit tin or covered saucepan.
To prepare lettuce etc., in a hurry, wash in cold water, lay flat on tea towels and pat gently until dry, or shake well in salad container.

For Russian salads: Use the frozen prepared vegetables and cook as directed, drain well then toss in mayonnaise while still hot.
Canned Russian salad is a good standby. Top with a little paprika pepper and/or chopped parsley.

Potato salad: This can be bought ready for use in a tin. It is improved by adding little extra seasoning.

Canned beans, peas, asparagus: These all add interest to salads and use sliced apples, oranges etc., which are very easily prepared and combine well with all salad ingredients.

Salad specials

No cooking time

Stuffed celery salad: Mix cheese spread with a little soft mayonnaise. Fill centre of celery stick with this and dust with paprika pepper.

Stuffed chicory salad: Mix diced ham and hard-boiled eggs with equal quantities of salad cream and tomato ketchup. Fill centres of chicory hearts, garnish with hard-boiled egg yolk.

Cheese and pineapple: Mix diced pineapple chunks and diced cheese with mayonnaise. Pile on crisp lettuce or endive.

Winter specials: Arrange *raw* cauliflower, shredded cabbage, sprouts, spinach, sliced peppers, grated raw swedes, carrots, parsnip, nuts, apples, bananas, pineapple on a huge plate or in a large divided hors-d'oeuvre dish.

Apple cheese salad

No cooking

You will need:

4 dessert apples
2 oz. chopped dates
seasoning
juice of 1 lemon
4 oz. cream cheese
2 oz. chopped walnuts

1 Core but do not peel apples.
2 Cut each apple in 3 thick slices and sprinkle with lemon juice.
3 Mix cheese with nuts and dates, season well.
4 Spread on slices of apple and garnish with whole nuts.

French bean salad

No cooking

1 Mix 1 lb. cooked French beans (seasoned and flavoured with little lemon juice) with 2 chopped hard-boiled eggs, 1 thinly sliced green pepper.
2 Pile on lettuce and sprinkle with grated cheese.

Grapefruit and prawn salad

No cooking

You will need:

2 grapefruit
½ pint prawns
sliced cucumber
lettuce
mayonnaise

1 Halve grapefruit, remove sections of fruit and mix with mayonnaise and picked prawns (leaving 4 unpicked prawns for garnish).
2 Shred a little lettuce, put at bottom of grapefruit cases, pile prawn mixture on top.
3 Garnish with sliced cucumber and unpicked prawns.

Lettuce cups with salmon

No cooking time

You will need:

8 leaves from the heart of the lettuce
mayonnaise
cucumber
1 small can salmon
2 or 3 hard-boiled eggs
little horseradish cream

1 Arrange the lettuce leaves on a dish.
2 Chop the egg yolks and whites separately.
3 Put a spoonful of salmon in the middle of each lettuce leaf, with a ring of egg yolk round, then a ring of egg white.
4 Blend the horseradish with a little mayonnaise and put on the salmon.
5 Serve with thinly sliced cucumber.

Harlequin salad

Cooking time 10 minutes

You will need for 4–6 servings:

6 oz. quick-cooking macaroni
4 hard-boiled eggs
3 oz. chopped ham or shelled shrimps
1 green pepper
lettuce
little chopped parsley
little mustard
mayonnaise
4 tomatoes
small piece of cucumber or few chopped gherkins
watercress
lemon

1 Cook macaroni for 7 minutes in boiling salted water.
2 Rinse macaroni under cold water, allow to dry
3 Blend a little mustard with mayonnaise and toss macaroni in this.
4 Add chopped eggs, ham or shrimps, 2 of the tomatoes, sliced rather thickly, the diced cucumber and pepper.
5 Pile on a bed of lettuce and garnish with watercress, parsley, tomato and lemon.

Oriental chicken and rice salad

Cooking time 15–20 minutes

You will need for 3–4 servings:

6 oz. long grained rice
1 tablespoon vinegar, wine or tarragon for preference
1 tablespoon currants
1 large tomato, skinned de-seeded and chopped
cut clove of garlic (optional)
3 tablespoons salad oil
salt and pepper to taste
1 green pepper, finely sliced
2 tablespoons chopped walnuts (optional)
8 oz. cooked chicken cut into bite-size pieces

1 Cook rice until just tender in plenty of fast boiling, well salted water, then drain very thoroughly.
2 Meanwhile rub a large bowl with a cut clove of garlic and in it mix together the oil, vinegar and seasoning.
3 Add the hot rice and mix thoroughly.
4 Stir in the remaining ingredients and lastly the chicken.
5 Cover and set aside in a cool place for the flavours to blend.
6 When cold transfer to a serving dish.

Potato and bacon salad

Cooking time 30 minutes

You will need:

1 lb. new potatoes
2 or 3 rashers bacon
French dressing
1 tablespoon chopped onion
1 tablespoon chopped parsley
seasoning

1 Boil potatoes and fry bacon.
2 Dice and toss them with other ingredients while hot.
3 Serve on bed of lettuce when cold.

Sardine toadstools

Cooking time 10 minutes to hard-boil eggs

You will need:

4 hard-boiled eggs
can sardines
lettuce
2 firm tomatoes
mayonnaise
4 rounds bread and butter

1 Cut a fairly thick slice from each egg. It must be deep enough to enable you to remove the yolk without breaking the case.
2 Mash yolk with sardines. Season well and push back into white case.
3 Stand eggs on rounds of bread and butter.
4 Cut a slice off each end of the tomatoes. Balance this on the egg to make each look like a toadstool, put tiny dots of mayonnaise on top.
5 Arrange borders of lettuce round these, also using the 4 remaining slices of egg and the rest of the tomatoes.

Stuffed pear salad

No cooking

1 Peel, halve and core 4 dessert pears and toss in French dressing (see page 63).
2 Fill centres with cream cheese mixed with chopped glacé or fresh cherries.
3 Decorate with whole cherries and serve with watercress.

Summer salad

No cooking

1 Use an hors-d'oeuvre dish for a mixed salad.
2 In one section put potato salad garnished with rings of carrot, served on crisp lettuce.
3 In the second section, olives and carrots garnished with sliced carrot.
4 In the third a Russian salad.
5 In the fourth section, tiny beetroot.
6 Garnish each section with a 'waterlily' radish.

Summer platter

No cooking

You will need:

1 small lettuce
small piece cucumber
2 large tomatoes
few radishes
sliced strawberries
mayonnaise
French dressing
garlic clove (optional)
2 hard-boiled eggs
watercress
1 banana
1 orange
1 dessert apple
few red or black currants
chopped garlic or chives

1 Toss lettuce and thinly sliced cucumber lightly in French dressing.
2 Cut radishes into slices or 'water lilies'.
3 Arrange lettuce on flat dish which can be lightly rubbed with a cut clove of garlic, if wished.
4 Arrange other ingredients in rows.
5 Serve with mayonnaise to which chopped garlic or chives have been added.

Surprise loaf

No cooking*

You will need:

1 sandwich loaf
seasoning
2 skinned and chopped tomatoes
$\frac{1}{4}$ pint thick white sauce
4 oz. grated cheese
4 oz. chopped cooked ham or flaked corned beef or finely chopped cooked meat

*except for white sauce. (5–10 minutes) if serving cold, 35 minutes if serving hot (including white sauce).

1 Cut the crust off the loaf at 1 end, then scoop out the centre of the loaf.
2 This can be used for stuffings, or dried for breadcrumbs.
3 Mix all the ingredients together and press the moist filling into the centre of the loaf. Replace the crust.
4 If the weather is hot your family can just slice this stuffed loaf and eat it with salad. If cold, then you need only to rub the outside of the loaf with a little margarine paper, put it into a moderately hot oven, together with a dish of sliced or whole seasoned tomatoes, and bake for about 25 minutes.
5 The size of the loaf depends on the fondness of your family for bread.

Tomato fish mould

Cooking time 15 minutes

You will need:

1 small can tomato soup or tomato juice
2 hard-boiled eggs
seasoning
4 oz. flaked cooked fish or can of tuna fish or salmon
powder gelatine

1 Measure soup and to each $\frac{1}{2}$ pint allow 1 level dessertspoon powder gelatine (use slightly more gelatine with tomato juice as it is thinner than soup).
2 Dissolve gelatine in hot soup, add fish, sliced eggs and seasoning.
3 Pour into mould and allow to set.
4 Serve with salad.
5 For special occasions, add prawns to mould and garnish with prawns, whipped cream and cucumber. Serve with shredded lettuce.

Tomato and corned beef mould

Use the same recipe as tomato fish mould (see preceding recipe) but instead of the hard-boiled egg add sliced spring onions and 1 or 2 sliced gherkins or pieces of cucumber.

Tomato and salami salad

No cooking

1 Choose large, firm tomatoes.
2 Stand stalk side down and slice through nearly to the bottom 3 or 4 times.
3 Pack with slices of hard-boiled egg and salami.
4 Serve on a bed of cucumber, garnished with spring onions and served with mayonnaise.

Quick French dressing

No cooking

You will need:

6 tablespoons corn oil
seasoning
3 tablespoons vinegar
1 level tablespoon sugar

Put all ingredients into a screw-top jar and shake well.

Ways to flavour mayonnaise

Mayonnaise can form the basis of a number of new salad dressings; try the following:

Cheese mayonnaise: Cream 2 oz. soft cheese with 2 tablespoons milk. Add ¼ pint mayonnaise. Serve with vegetables, salads.

Curried mayonnaise: Blend 1–2 teaspoons curry powder with 1 or 2 tablespoons milk. Stir in ¼ pint mayonnaise. Serve with meat, salads.

Green mayonnaise: Add chopped fresh herbs to mayonnaise. Serve with fish salads, although if mint is used it is excellent with lamb salad.

Horseradish mayonnaise: Blend 1 tablespoon horseradish cream with ¼ pint mayonnaise. Serve with cold beef salad or canned salmon salad.

Lemon mayonnaise: Add grated rind and juice of 1 lemon to ¼ pint mayonnaise. Serve with cheese or fish salads.

Spiced mayonnaise: Add grated nutmeg and few drops Worcestershire sauce to ¼ pint mayonnaise. Serve with potato and vegetable salads.

Tomato mayonnaise: Add dessertspoon tomato ketchup or teaspoon tomato purée to ¼ pint mayonnaise. Serve with shell fish salad.

Puddings and Sweets

Many families feel a meal is not complete without some kind of pudding or dessert. However, this need not be too much of a problem if you follow my suggestions in Chapter I for stocking your larder and make sure you always have a good supply of canned, packaged or frozen fruits and puddings on hand.
In the following chapter you will find a number of easy ideas for delicious but quick home-made desserts.

Puddings in minutes

Many of the quick cooking foods of today give puddings and sweets in a matter of minutes.

Custard and cornflour puddings: Make packet custard or cornflour as directed. Add chopped fruit, chopped nuts, fine biscuit crumbs or chopped chocolate.
Put into a dish and top with fruit. Serve at once or serve cold.

Fritters: A thick batter is mixed quickly with an efficient whisk. Coat fresh or well-drained canned fruit with this OR add dried fruit to the batter OR flavour it with spice or cinnamon or add desiccated coconut. Cook as directed (see fruit fritters, page 69) and top with coconut.

Pancakes: These give endless variety. Fill with jam, fruit, ice-cream.

Rice or macaroni puddings: Quick cooking or canned creamed rice or macaroni is a very easy pudding. Heat or cook as directed, tip into hot dish and top with coconut, or with brown sugar, and crisp under a moderately hot grill.

Sponge puddings: The variety of pudding and sponge mixtures available today are worth buying when short of time, for you can steam individual sponge puddings in 15 minutes, then top with jam or curd. Try covering drained canned or cooked fruit with one of the sponge mixtures, then bake for approximately 30 minutes in a moderate oven.

Jellied sweets: These take time to set—but are so little trouble to make that a number have been included in this chapter. A jelly will set in a much shorter time if you dissolve in ¼ pint boiling liquid only, then make up rest of liquid with cold water, milk, etc.

Almond cream

Cooking time 5–10 minutes (longer if using egg custard)

You will need:

¾ pint thick custard – made with custard powder or yolks of 2 eggs and ¾ pint milk
few drops almond essence
3 average, sized macaroons, crumbled
1 dessertspoon powdered gelatine
1 gill water
2 oz. blanched almonds
few glacé cherries

1. Dissolve the gelatine in the water.
2. Add to the hot custard, together with almond essence and macaroon crumbs.
3. Put into mound and allow to set.
4. Split the almonds and brown under a grill or in the oven.
5. Turn out the cream and decorate with almonds and cherries.

Almond pancakes

Cooking time 30 minutes

You will need:

½ pint pancake batter (see page 73)
3 oz. almonds
1 egg white
fat or oil for cooking pancakes
apricot jam or apple purée
1 oz. sugar.

1. Make and cook the pancakes wafer thin, in the usual way, but instead of rolling, spread each pancake with apple purée or jam and chopped almonds.
2. Pile on top of one another.
3. When the last pancake has been added, whisk egg white, fold in sugar.
4. Spread on top of the pancakes, sprinkle with nuts and brown in the oven, for 10 minutes.
5. Serve in slices like a cake.

'Baked' apples

Pressure cooking time 3 minutes

You will need:

large cooking apples
¼ pint water
sugar to taste

1. Wash the apples well and with a sharp knife slit the skin round the fruit.
2. Put a piece of greased paper over the rack or trivet and stand the apples on this.
3. Put in the water, fix the lid and bring *gradually* to pressure.
4. Lower the heat and cook for 3 minutes (preferably at 5 lb. pressure).
5. Be very careful the pressure does not get too high, otherwise the apples will become 'fluffy' on the outside before being cooked through to the middle.
6. Reduce pressure immediately.
7. The water at the bottom of the cooker has a very good flavour and could be thickened, sweetened and served as a sauce.

Poached apples and ginger

Cooking time 25 minutes

You will need:

4 medium-sized perfect cooking apples
1–2 oz. crystallized ginger
2–3 oz. sugar
½ pint water

1. Put sugar and water into pan, heat until sugar has dissolved, then add the chopped ginger.
2. Peel the apples, halve and core.
3. Poach apples in the hot ginger syrup until soft but unbroken. This means cooking them very slowly indeed with the lid off the pan so that the syrup thickens.
4. Put into sundae glasses and decorate with more pieces of ginger.

Apple crunch

Cooking time 40 minutes

You will need:

1 lb. apples
2 oz. dates
little sugar to taste
water
2 oz. butter or margarine
2 oz. sugar
4 oz. cornflakes

1 Put sliced apples with dates, sugar and a very little water into dish and cook slowly until nearly tender and a thick mixture.
2 Cream butter and sugar, add cornflakes and press on top of apples.
3 Continue cooking in moderate oven (400 °F. – Gas Mark 4–5) until top is crisp.
4 Serve with cream or custard.
5 Do not have apples too juicy otherwise mixture on top will 'sink in'.
6 Any other fruit is equally good in this recipe and canned or bottled fruit can be used.

Banana blancmange

Cooking time 10 minutes

You will need:

1 packet vanilla-flavoured cornflour powder*
1 pint milk
1–2 oz. sugar
2 large or 3 small bananas

to decorate

little raspberry jam
sliced bananas

* or use 1¼ oz. plain cornflour and ½ teaspoon vanilla essence.

1 Blend cornflour with a little cold milk.
2 Bring rest of milk to boil.
3 Pour over cornflour, return to pan and thicken, adding sugar.
4 When quite thick, add mashed bananas.
5 Allow to set.
6 Turn out.
7 Pour little jam on top and arrange rings of bananas just before serving.

Banana meringue

Cooking time 7 minutes

You will need:

1 packet chocolate-flavoured blancmange
4 sliced bananas
2 eggs
cherries and angelica to decorate
1 pint milk
3 tablespoons sugar

1 Blend blancmange powder with little cold milk.
2 Put rest of milk in saucepan with 1 tablespoon sugar.
3 When boiling pour over blancmange mixture, return to pan and cook until thick and smooth, stirring well.
4 Add 2 beaten egg yolks and 3 sliced bananas and cook for several minutes *without boiling*. Pour into warm dish.
5 Whisk eggs whites until stiff, fold in rest of sugar, pile in a circle on chocolate mixture.
6 Brown for 1 minute under grill then decorate with sliced banana, cherries, angelica.
7 Serve cold.

Baked bananas

Cooking time 15 minutes

You will need:

4–6 good-sized bananas
lemon juice
knob of butter
2 tablespoons brown sugar

1 Slice bananas into shallow dish.
2 Squeeze lemon juice over the fruit, dot with butter and a layer of sugar.
3 Bake for about 15 minutes in hot oven (425°F. —Gas Mark 6).
4 Serve with cream.

Banana and red currant whip

No cooking

You will need:

4 large bananas
2 egg yolks
2 oz. sugar
½ pint whipped cream
squeeze of lemon juice
1 good tablespoon red currant jelly

1 Beat egg yolks and sugar until creamy and fold in the cream.
2 Mash the bananas with the red currant jelly and lemon juice, fold into the cream.
3 Put into 4 shallow glasses and top with red currant jelly.

Banana slices

Cooking time 10 minutes

You will need:

4 large bananas
little butter
4 fingers sponge cake
brown sugar

1 Melt the butter in a pan and brown the sponge cakes in this.
2 Divide each banana in half and split each portion.
3 Heat in pan for a moment.
4 Put 4 pieces of banana on each of the 4 fingers, brush with hot butter from the pan, coat lavishly with brown sugar.
5 Put under a moderate grill to melt the sugar.
6 Serve at once.

Orange and banana fingers

As in preceding recipe, but add 1 or 2 oranges. Peel orange, cut into wafer-thin slices, put on to sponge fingers under the bananas.

Black currant crumble

Cooking time 30 minutes

You will need:

1 lb. black currants
little sugar and water

for the crumble

4 oz. flour (plain or self-raising)
2 oz. margarine
3–4 oz. sugar

1 Put black currants into pie dish with little sugar and water.
2 Rub margarine into flour, add sugar.
3 Sprinkle over the fruit.
4 Bake for approximately 30 minutes in a moderately hot oven (400°F.—Gas Mark 5) until topping brown and fruit soft.

Caramel macaroni

Cooking time 12–15 minutes

You will need for 4–5 servings:

2 oz. quick cooking macaroni
1 pint milk
2 bananas
2 eating apples
3 good tablespoons golden syrup
2 level tablespoons cornflour
whipped cream and toasted almonds for decoration (could be omitted)

1 Cook macaroni for 7 minutes in boiling salted water.
2 Drain.
3 Put syrup into strong saucepan and boil without stirring until a rich golden brown colour.
4 Blend cornflour with a little of the measured milk.
5 Add remaining milk to caramel.
6 Allow caramel to dissolve.
7 Add a little of the hot caramel milk to the blended cornflour.
8 Return to saucepan, boil 1 minute.
9 Add macaroni.
10 When cold cover with sliced bananas and grated fresh apple or sliced apple, top with whipped cream and chopped toasted almonds.

Cherry layer creams

Cooking time 10 minutes

You will need for 6–8 servings:

2 pints milk
1 oz. gelatine, softened in 2 tablespoons cold water
4 oz. fine semolina
4 oz. castor sugar
1 teaspoon vanilla essence
2 medium cans red cherries, stoned and halved
2 egg yolks
2 egg whites

1 Gently heat milk and gelatine in a large saucepan until gelatine dissolves.
2 Gradually add semolina and cook, stirring, until mixture comes to the boil and thickens.
3 Cook gently for another 3 minutes; remove from heat and stir in sugar and egg yolks.
4 Whisk egg whites until stiff and fold into semolina mixture.
5 Fill glass dessert dishes with alternate layers of halved cherries and semolina cream.
6 Garnish with cherry halves. Chill until lightly set.

Chocolate and pineapple cream

Cooking time 5 minutes

You will need:

1 packet chocolate blancmange powder
pineapple and cream to decorate if wished
¾ pint only of milk
about 4 oz. chopped canned pineapple and little of the juice

1 Make the blancmange as directed on the packet, using only the ¾ pint milk.
2 Whisk in the pineapple and juice and put into glasses.
3 Top with pineapple and cream.
4 Serve hot or cold.

Coconut queen of puddings

Cooking time approximately 1–1½ hours

You will need:

raspberry jam
2 oz. desiccated coconut plus 1 level tablespoon for meringue
2 oz. breadcrumbs
angelica
1 pint milk
2 large eggs
3–4 oz. sugar
cherries

1 Spread raspberry jam at bottom of a pie dish.
2 Beat egg yolks with 1–2 oz. sugar, add the crumbs and coconut.
3 Heat milk, pour over egg mixture and put into dish.
4 Bake for approximately 45 minutes in very moderate oven (350°F.—Gas Mark 3) until just firm.
5 Spread raspberry jam on top.
6 Whisk egg whites stiffly, fold in 2 oz. sugar and coconut. Do this very carefully to keep fluffy texture of meringue.
7 Pile on sweet.
8 Decorate with cherries and angelica.
9 Set for 15–25 minutes in very moderate oven until just golden brown.
10 Serve hot.

Coffee and marshmallow foam

Cooking time few minutes

You will need:

8 oz. marshmallows
2 egg whites
1 good tablespoon chopped blanched almonds
¾ gill strong hot coffee
1 gill whipped evaporated milk (or creamy custard or cream)
1 good tablespoon chopped glacé cherries or pineapple
1 dessertspoon crystallized orange peel

1 Put the marshmallows, cut into halves, into a basin and stand this over a saucepan of hot water.
2 Pour the coffee over the marshmallows and leave until dissolved.
3 Allow the mixture to cool, but not become really stiff again.
4 Stir in the whipped cream, or evaporated milk or custard, the nuts, cherries and peel.
5 Lastly fold in the very stiffly beaten egg whites.
6 Pile into glasses and decorate with tiny pieces of cherry or pineapple.

Coffee pudding

Pressure cooking time 45 minutes

You will need:

2 oz. breadcrumbs
2 oz. margarine
few drops vanilla essence
4 oz. flour (2 teaspoons baking powder if using plain flour)
2 oz. sugar
1 egg
¼ pint strong coffee (just under)

1 Rub margarine into the flour, add baking powder, crumbs and sugar.
2 Mix with the coffee, egg and vanilla essence.
3 Put into a greased basin, stand basin on rack in cooker in 2 pints *boiling* water and cover well.
4 Fix the lid but do not put on pressure weight.
5 Steam rapidly for 15 minutes then put on pressure weight and bring to pressure of 5 lb.
6 Lower the heat and cook for 30 minutes.
7 Reduce pressure at once.
8 Serve with chocolate sauce or custard.

Duchess creams

Cooking time 5 minutes

You will need:

1 pint of sweetened custard (sauce consistency)
½ gill water
1 oz. sultanas
finely grated rind and juice of 2 oranges
½ oz. powdered gelatine
1 oz. crystallized orange peel
1 orange for decorating

1 Add grated rind to the custard while hot, then add gelatine dissolved in hot water.
2 Stir in the sultanas and crystallized peel and cool slightly, then add the orange juice. If this measures less than 1 gill add a little water.
3 Pour into sundae glasses and allow to set lightly.
4 Decorate with pieces of orange.

French pancakes

Cooking time 15 minutes

You will need:

2 oz. rice-flour or flour
2 oz. butter
2 oz. sugar
2 eggs
1½ gills milk
lemon rind
jam

1 Thoroughly grease 12 flat round tins (or saucers).
2 Cream the butter and sugar, beat in the yolks of the eggs with a little flour. Add the remainder of the flour with the milk and lemon juice.
3 Fold in the whites of the eggs, stiffly beaten, and pour into the tins.
4 Bake in a hot oven (450°F.—Gas Mark 7) until well risen, brown and firm—about 10 minutes.
5 Turn on to a sugared paper, put a little hot jam on each and sandwich 2 rounds together.
6 Pile neatly on a hot dish and dust with castor sugar.

Fruit fritters

Cooking time 7–10 minutes

You will need:

to make the fritter batter
4 oz. self-raising flour (or plain flour with 1 teaspoon baking powder)
1 oz. melted butter (or margarine or olive oil)
1 or 2 eggs
¼ pint milk
1 oz. sugar

1 Sieve the dry ingredients together, add the egg (or eggs) and the milk.
2 Lastly add the melted butter. This is not essential but helps to give a crisp fritter.
3 For a very light fritter the egg yolks should be put in first, and when you have a very smooth thick batter fold in the stiffly beaten egg whites at the very end.
4 Coat the fruit and fry *steadily* in shallow fat or in deep fat if preferred. This makes sure that the outside is brown and the fruit hot or well cooked, whereas if the fritters are fried too quickly you get the outside browning before the middle is cooked.
5 Drain on kitchen or crumpled tissue paper and dredge well with sugar. Fill with one of the following:

Apples. Choose good cooking apples. Peel, core and cut into thin slices. coat with the batter. It is a good idea to flour the apples before coating in the batter to help it 'stick' well.

Pineapple. Well-drain rings of pineapple, then proceed as for apples.

Bananas. Halve if wished and add a little rum or rum essence to the batter.

mixed
Fruit fritters

Cooking time 10 minutes

You will need:

- 4 large slices of bread
- butter for frying
- 2 oz. sultanas
- 2 or 3 tablespoons apricot jam
- 1 egg
- little milk
- 2 oz. glacé cherries
- 2 oz. walnuts or blanched almonds
- little sugar

1 Cut the bread into attractive shapes.
2 Beat the egg and milk together.
3 Add a little sugar.
4 Dip the bread in this and fry in the butter until golden brown.
5 Meanwhile heat the apricot jam in a pan, add the sultanas, cherries and nuts and pile on the fritters.

Fruit cups

Cooking time 30 minutes

You will need:

- 1 lb. fruit (apples, plums etc)
- 3 oz. soft breadcrumbs
- 2 tablespoons brown sugar
- 1½ oz. butter
- water and sugar
- juice and grated rind of 2 oranges

1 Simmer fruit with sugar, orange juice and very little water.
2 When fruit is just soft, but unbroken, put into fireproof dishes.
3 Toss crumbs in hot butter, add brown sugar and orange rind.
4 Sprinkle on top of each fruit cup and bake for 20 minutes in a moderately hot oven (400 °F.– Gas Mark 5).

Fruit pudding

Pressure cooking time 1 hour

You will need:

- 8 oz. suet crust pastry
- 1–1½ lb. fruit*
- 2 pints water
- sugar
- water

*This can be varied according to the season, apples, and blackberries, rhubarb, blackcurrants, etc. If using apples half fill the dish with water.

1 Line a well-greased basin with part of the suet crust.
2 Put the fruit into the pastry with a good sprinkling of sugar and a little water.
3 Roll out the rest of the dough to form a cover.
4 Damp edges of the pastry lid and press on to the pudding.
5 Cover well.
6 Stand on rack in cooker in 2 pints BOILING water.
7 Fix the lid but do NOT put on pressure weight.
8 Steam for 20 minutes.
9 Bring to 5 lb. pressure, lower the heat and cook for 40 minutes.
10 Reduce pressure.
11 Serve with a custard sauce.

Frosted chocolate pudding

Cooking time 25 minutes

You will need:

- 1 pint milk
- 3 eggs
- 1 oz. cornflour
- 4 oz. grated chocolate or 2 oz. chocolate powder
- 5 oz. sugar

1 Blend cornflour with a little cold milk.
2 Bring rest of milk, with grated chocolate, to the boil.
3 Add to cornflour and return to heat with 2 oz. of the sugar and cook until thick.
4 Cool slightly add egg yolks and complete cooking WITHOUT boiling for 10 minutes.
5 Pour into dish.
6 Whip egg whites, fold in last of the sugar.
7 Pile on chocolate mixture and set in a moderate oven (375°F.—Gas Mark 4) for 10 minutes.
8 Serve at once.

Orange chocolate pudding

Cooking time 25 minutes

1 Recipe as above, but add finely grated rind of 2 oranges to the cornflour mixture.
2 Skin the oranges and cut into wafer thin slices: arrange on top of the cornflour mixture, before putting on the meringue.
3 Set as before. This combination of orange and chocolate is delicious.

10 ways to dress up fresh fruit

Apples can be grated and added to lightly whipped cream or beaten into ice-cream. Top with grated chocolate.

Bananas can be fried in a little butter or baked in the oven (baked bananas, page 66), but they are also extremely good mashed with lemon juice and beaten into ice-cream. There are a number of quick banana recipes (see pages 66, 77, 88).

Blackcurrants can be added to jellies raw or they make a very good fresh blackcurrant fool by mashing and beating into ice-cream.

Grapefruit can be served as a sweet if the sections are mixed with a little sherry and sugar and piled on ice-cream.

Melon as well as being an excellent hors-d'oeuvre is a first class sweet. Divide into portions and mix the fruit with mandarin oranges or fresh oranges. Top with cream.

Oranges can be baked with sugar and butter (see page 67) but they make an excellent fruit compote. Peel the oranges, cut into rings and arrange them in a shallow dish. Sprinkle with sugar and add sherry or kirsch. Leave for several hours. Serve with cream or ice-cream.

Pears can be halved and coated with hot red currant jelly. When heating the jelly dilute with a little water. Or cover them with melted chocolate and serve with cream or ice-cream. When melting the chocolate do this in a basin over hot water, add just a little water.

Raspberries have such a delicious flavour that most people prefer them with sugar and cream. But if you want to make a very quick sweet, mash them to a pulp, and pile on rounds of sponge cake. Allow the raspberries to soak into the sponge a little, then top with whipped cream.

Red currants are an excellent dessert fruit. Arrange sprigs of these in a shallow dish and sprinkle with sugar so they become slightly frosted or crush the red currants with sugar and a few drops of vanilla essence or with vanilla sugar if this is obtainable in your store. Serve with yoghourt, cream or ice-cream.

Strawberries make an excellent filling for pancakes or can be served in salads with cream cheese. They also produce a delicious fruit salad, if halved and mixed with sliced banana.

Gooseberry and lemon jelly

Cooking time 15 minutes

You will need:

12 oz. green gooseberries
sugar to taste
cream to decorate
½ pint water
1 lemon-flavoured jelly

1 Make a syrup of the sugar and water and put in the gooseberries when the sugar has completely dissolved.
2 Simmer until the fruit is soft, lift out a few gooseberries for decoration and continue cooking the remainder until a pulp.
3 Rub through a sieve and measure the pulp and syrup.
4 Add enough water to give nearly 1¼ pints altogether.
5 Dissolve the lemon jelly in this hot mixture and put into a mould.
Turn out and decorate with cream and the whole fruit.

Grapefruit oat brûlée

Cooking time few minutes

You will need:

2 grapefruits
1 oz. butter
2 tablespoons rolled oats
2 tablespoons golden syrup

1 Halve and prepare grapefruit.
2 Melt butter in saucepan.
3 Add oats and syrup.
4 Mix thoroughly.
5 Divide oat mixture into 4.

6 Sprinkle over grapefruit.
7 Place under medium hot electric grill until lightly browned and crisp on top.

Hawaiian pie

Cooking time 10 minutes

You will need:

2 oz. butter or margarine (preferably unsalted)
2 oz. castor sugar
1 dessertspoon golden syrup
4 oz. crushed cornflakes

for filling

1 can pineapple rings
glacé cherries
whipped cream (if available)
2 tablespoons pineapple jam (apricot jam can be used)

1 Cream butter, sugar and syrup together, then work in cornflakes.
2 Form into flan shape.
3 Open can of pineapple rings and arrange fruit in flan case.
4 Blend 2 tablespoons pineapple syrup from can with pineapple jam, spread over fruit.
5 Decorate with glacé cherries and whipped cream.
6 Allow flan to harden before serving.

Ice-cream medley

Ice-cream is a sure favourite and enables you to give the family a popular sweet with little or no trouble. Here are some quick ideas.

1 Melt fudge in a double saucepan and pour over the ice-cream.
2 Beat well-drained chopped pineapple into the ice-cream and chopped walnuts to taste.
3 Add grated dessert apples to the ice-cream and put into glasses. Decorate with crystallized ginger.
4 Top ice-cream with cherry brandy and cream.

Jelly omelette

Cooking time 5–8 minutes

You will need:

3 large eggs
1 oz. butter
1 oz. sugar
½ teaspoon vanilla essence or cherry brandy
hot jam or jelly
icing sugar or castor sugar

1 Separate the eggs.
2 Whisk the egg yolks and sugar together.
3 Add the essence, then fold in the stiffly beaten egg whites.
4 Heat the butter in an omelette pan and pour in the egg mixture.
5 Cook steadily until set on the bottom then put under a medium grill to cook the top.
6 Fill with the jam or jelly.
7 Fold and serve at once, dusted with icing sugar or castor sugar.

Kissel

Cooking time 15 minutes

You will need:

1 lb. soft fruit
1 tablespoon cornflour
1 gill water
3 tablespoons golden syrup or honey

1 This delicious sweet is very simple to make. Put the fruit with water and syrup or honey into a pan.
2 Simmer until soft, then beat or sieve.
3 Stir on to cornflour and return to pan, cooking until smooth and clear.
4 Allow to cool.
5 Decorate with cream if possible.

Lemon and apricot mousse

No cooking time, just a few minutes to dissolve the jelly

You will need:

1 lemon-flavoured jelly
3 egg whites
1 medium-sized can apricots
¾ pint lightly whipped cream or evaporated milk

1 Open can of apricots and pour out the juice. Add enough water to give ¾ pint liquid.
2 Heat this and dissolve in it the lemon jelly.
3 When cold, add cream and stiffly beaten egg whites.
4 Put most of the apricots at the bottom of a shallow dish.
5 Pile the mixture on top.
6 When firm, decorate with the remaining apricots.

Lemon and coconut jelly

Cooking time few minutes

You will need:

juice of 2 lemons
½ pint water
little cream and sections of orange to decorate
2–3 oz. desiccated coconut
2–3 oz. sugar
1 tablespoon powdered gelatine
2 egg whites (the yolks can be used in almond cream, see page 65)

1 Soften the gelatine in the lemon juice, then pour on the very hot water, adding the sugar.
2 Allow to cool.
3 When just beginning to thicken, stir in coconut and stifly beaten egg whites.
4 Pour into a mould and when set turn out and decorate with whipped cream or fresh orange.

Lemon and coconut mould

Cooking time few minutes

You will need:

1 lemon jelly
2 oz. desiccated coconut
few pieces glacé cherry and blanched almonds
2 oz. sponge cake crumbs
2 eggs
1–2 oz. sugar

1. Dissolve jelly in just over ¾ pint boiling water.
2. Beat egg yolks and sugar until light.
3. Add coconut, crumbs and the lemon jelly.
4. Leave to set lightly, then fold in stiffly beaten egg whites.
5. Pour into mould and when quite firm, unmould and decorate with cherry and nuts.

Macaroon cream

Cooking time few minutes for custard

You will need:

¾ pint sweetened custard
1 gill water
2 oz. blanched almonds
few glacé cherries
1 dessertspoon powder gelatine
few drops almond essence
3 average-sized macaroons, crumbled

1. Dissolve gelatine in water, then add to hot custard, almond essence and crumbs.
2. Pour into mould and leave to set.
3. Split almonds and brown in oven or under the grill.
4. Turn out cream and decorate with almonds and cherries.

Melba sauce

Cooking time 10 minutes

You will need:

5 oz. raspberries*
2–3 oz. red currant or apple jelly
1 tablespoon sugar
1 teaspoon cornflour
2 tablespoons water

* fresh, frozen or canned – omit sugar with latter

1. Blend cornflour with water.
2. Put all ingredients into pan and cook gently until thickened.
3. Rub through a sieve if desired.

Economical

Melba sauce

Cooking time 10 minutes

You will need:

2–3 oz. raspberry jam
2–3 oz. red currant jelly
½ gill water
½ teaspoon arrowroot or cornflour

1. Blend the arrowroot or cornflour with the water.
2. Put into a saucepan with the other ingredients.
3. Cook until clear and slightly thickened.
4. Cool before using.

Mincemeat shortcakes

Cooking time 13 minutes

You will need:

8 oz. flour (with plain flour use 2 level teaspoons baking powder)
1 egg
mincemeat
2 oz. butter or margarine or vegetable shortening
3 oz. sugar
milk to mix

1. Sieve flour, rub in fat and add sugar, egg and enough milk to make a sticky dough.
2. Put spoonfuls of mixture on greased tin and bake for 10 minutes in really hot oven (450–475 °F. Gas Mark 7–8).
3. Top with mincemeat, re-heat for 2–3 minutes and serve at once.
4. Instead of mincemeat thick fruit purée can be used.

Mixed fruit Bavarian cream

Cooking time 8–10 minutes

You will need:

1 vanilla flavoured blancmange powder
1 pint milk
¼ pint whipped cream or evaporated milk
2 oz. sugar
2 oz. chopped glacé cherries
1 oz. chopped almonds
1 oz. chopped glacé pineapple (if wished)
2 oz. sultanas

1. Make blancmange in usual way, adding sugar and most of the fruit mixture.
2. Allow to cool, stirring well to prevent skin forming.
3. Fold in cream.
4. Pour into rinsed mould and allow to set.
5. Turn out and decorate with more cream and pieces of fruit.

Mocha meringue

Cooking time 10–15 minutes

You will need:

1 packet chocolate-flavoured blancmange powder
2 eggs
small piece of chocolate
½ pint milk
½ pint strong coffee
4 oz. sugar

1. Make the blancmange as directed on the packet, using milk and coffee instead of all milk.
2. Add 2 oz. sugar and the egg yolks and cook gently for a few minutes, without boiling.
3. Put into a dish.
4. Fold the rest of the sugar into the stiffly beaten egg whites, pile over the sweet and brown either in the oven or under a hot grill.
5. Decorate with grated chocolate.

Mocha walnut pudding

Cooking time 30 minutes

You will need:

1 chocolate flavoured blancmange powder
2 oz. chopped walnuts
2 eggs yolks
$\frac{3}{4}$ pint milk
$\frac{1}{4}$ pint strong coffee
1 oz. sugar
2 oz. fine breadcrumbs

for meringue
2 egg whites
2 oz. sugar
few halved walnuts

1 Blend the blancmange powder with a little cold milk, bring rest of milk to the boil, pour over the blended blancmange powder, return to pan with sugar and coffee.
2 Cook until thickened.
3 Stir in the nuts and crumbs, then the beaten egg yolks.
4 Put into a pie dish.
5 Whip egg whites until very stiff, fold in the sugar, pile over coffee and chocolate mixture, decorate with halved walnuts and set for about 20 minutes in a slow oven (300°F.—Gas Mark 2).

Orange and banana salad

Cooking time 5 minutes

You will need:

2 bananas, sliced
$\frac{1}{2}$ gill water
1 tablespoon sugar
juice and rind of 1 orange
2 oranges, sliced

1 Boil water, sugar and grated orange rind for 5 minutes.
2 Strain, add orange juice.
3 Peel and slice the remaining oranges and bananas, pour over the syrup.

Orange surprise

Cooking time 3 minutes

You will need:

4 oranges (or 2 very large ones)
2 oz. castor sugar
little ice-cream
2 egg whites

1 Cut tops off oranges and scoop out centre. Chop.
2 Put back into orange cases with ice-cream and a little sugar.
3 Whisk egg whites, fold in sugar.
4 Pile on top of ice-cream and oranges and brown for 3 minutes in a very hot oven (475°F. —Gas Mark 8).

Orange surprises

Cooking time 30 minutes

You will need:

4 good-sized oranges
2 eggs
3 oz. sugar
2 level tablespoons cornflour or custard powder
small pieces angelica

1 Cut the oranges into halves, squeeze out the juice very gently without breaking the cases, remove pith and pips:
2 Measure juice, add enough water to give $\frac{3}{4}$ pint liquid.
3 Blend the cornflour or custard powder with this, put into pan with 1 oz. sugar and thicken.
4 Remove from heat and cool slightly.
5 Add egg yolks, then thicken gently without boiling.
6 Make sure the 8 orange halves are standing firmly and fill them with mixture.
7 Whisk egg whites until stiff, fold in the rest of the sugar, pile on top of orange mixture and return to very moderate oven for approximately 20 minutes.
8 Decorate with leaves of angelica.

Pancake batter

You will need:

4 oz. flour
pinch salt
1 egg
$\frac{1}{2}$ pint milk or milk and water

rich pancake batter
4 oz. flour
pinch salt
1 tablespoon olive oil
2 eggs
just under $\frac{1}{2}$ pint milk or milk and water

1 Sieve flour and salt, add egg or eggs and enough milk to give sticky consistency.
2 Beat well then gradually add rest of liquid.
3 Add oil last if using this.

Hot peach Condé

Cooking time 35 minutes—1$\frac{1}{4}$ hours

You will need:

2 oz. rice or large can creamed rice
1 pint milk
little vanilla essence or vanilla pod
$\frac{1}{4}$ pint juice from canned peaches
1 teaspoon cornflour
2 egg whites
3 oz. sugar
sliced peaches

1 Cook the rice with the milk, 1 oz. sugar, vanilla flavouring, until just tender and soft. Remove vanilla pod.
2 Pour into hot dish.
3 If using canned rice pour into hot dish from can.
4 Whisk egg whites stiffly, fold in sugar, pile or pipe round edge of dish. Put into cool oven (275–300°F.—Gas Mark 1–2) for about 30–45 minutes until meringue is firm and golden brown.
5 Meanwhile thicken syrup with the cornflour, cooking until thick and clear.
6 Pile sliced peaches in centre of dish and cover with hot thickened syrup.
7 Serve at once.

Flapjack peach crumble

Cooking time 35 minutes

You will need:

3 oz. butter
1 oz. castor sugar
2 tablespoons golden syrup
6 oz. rolled oats
¼ teaspoon salt
1 medium-sized can of sliced peaches
1 oz. chopped blanched almonds

1 Cream butter and sugar until light and fluffy.
2 Add syrup, and cream a few minutes longer.
3 Gradually work in oats and salt until mixture is well blended.
4 Place drained sliced peaches and almonds in greased pie dish.
5 Spread flapjack mixture on top.
6 Bake on the middle shelf of a moderate oven (375°F.—Gas Mark 4) for 35 minutes.

Quick chocolate mousse

Cooking time 5 minutes

You will need for 2 servings:

4 oz. chocolate (preferably plain chocolate)
2 dessertspoons cream
2 eggs
2 dessertspoons sugar

1 Grate chocolate.
2 Put sugar, chocolate and egg yolk in a basin over hot water and beat together until smooth.
3 Cool slightly.
4 Add cream and when quite cold fold in stiffly beaten egg whites.
5 Pour into 2 small glasses and serve with biscuits.

Quick fruit dumplings

Cooking time 10–15 minutes

You will need:

4 oz. self-raising flour
½ oz. sugar
4 tablespoons milk
pinch salt
2 oz. finely chopped suet
large can peach slices or halves or apricots or plums or rhubarb

1 Sift flour and salt into a bowl and add suet and sugar.
2 Mix to a fairly stiff consistency with the milk, then, with floured hands, shape into 8 dumplings.
3 Drain fruit and pour syrup into a large, shallow pan.
4 Bring to boil then put in dumplings.
5 Reduce heat, cover pan and poach slowly for 10–15 minutes.
6 Transfer dumplings to a warm serving dish, coat with syrup and decorate with warmed canned fruit.
7 If you do not wish to open a can of fruit try poaching the dumplings in a mixture of water and lemon juice sweetened to taste. Dust them with sugar before serving.

Caramel pears

Cooking time 20 minutes

You will need:

4 good-sized, firm, but not too hard pears
6 or 8 almonds
3 oz. sugar
1½ gills water

1 Put 3 tablespoons of the water and the sugar into a pan, stir until the sugar has dissolved then boil until dark brown.
2 Add the rest of the water and bring to the boil.
3 Peel, core and slice pears, put them into caramel, and cook for about 10 minutes.
4 Serve in glasses topped with blanched shredded almonds.

Quick pineapple mousse

Cooking time few minutes

You will need:

½ can chopped pineapple*
1 dessertspoon powdered gelatine
cherries and angelica to decorate
2 eggs
1–2 dessertspoons castor sugar
3 dessertspoons water

*Pieces, cubes or slices can be used, in which case chop finely.

1 Dissolve the gelatine in the very hot water.
2 Put the pineapple, juice from can, sugar and egg yolks in a basin over hot water, beat together for about 5–10 minutes until creamy.
3 Leave to cool.
4 Add dissolved gelatine, then fold in stiffly beaten egg whites.
5 Put into fruit glasses and decorate with cherries and angelica.
6 Serve with biscuits or sponge cakes.

Raspberry mousse

Cooking time few minutes

You will need:

1 small can raspberries or 6 oz. fresh fruit
1½ gills milk
1 raspberry-flavoured jelly
¼ pint evaporated milk
2 egg whites

1 Drain the fruit and measure the juice.
2 If necessary add enough water to give ½ pint.
3 Dissolve the jelly in this thoroughly and when cool add the cold milk and the whipped evap-

orated milk, lastly fold in the stiffly beaten egg whites.
4 Pour into a rinsed mould and when firm turn out and decorate with the raspberries if wished.

Raspberry soufflé

Cooking time 12 minutes

You will need:

3 egg whites
2 tablespoons sugar
1 can raspberries or packet defrosted
raspberries (or use fresh raspberries and extra sugar)

1 Strain off juice from canned or frozen raspberries and mash the fruit.
2 Beat egg whites until very stiff, fold in the sugar and fruit.
3 Pour into buttered soufflé dish and bake for 12 minutes only in centre of moderately hot oven (400 °F. – Gas Mark 5).
4 Serve at once with the hot juice.

Rice creams

Cooking time 45 minutes

You will need:

3 oz. rice
1 pint milk
few tablespoons whipped cream
1 or 2 oz. sugar
little vanilla essence or grated orange or lemon rind to flavour

to decorate

jam or jelly
lightly whipped cream

1 Cook the rice with the milk, sugar and flavouring in the usual way until soft and tender.
2 Cool, then stir in the cream.
3 Put jam or jelly into 4 cups or small moulds and cover with rice.
4 Leave until quite cold and set, then turn out and top with whipped cream.
5 If preferred the jam can be warmed slightly with a little water to give a softer mixture and put over the rice moulds when turned out.

Strawberry croûtes

No cooking

You will need:

2 oblong sponge cakes
8 oz. fresh strawberries
little sugar
red currant jelly
cream

1 Cut sponge cakes through centre.
2 Put each half on small dish.
3 Spread liberally with red currant jelly.
4 Top with whipped cream and sweetened strawberries.

Strawberry Napoleons

Cooking time 8 minutes

You will need:

4 small square sponge cakes
4 large egg whites
8 oz. strawberries
6 tablespoons sugar

1 Crush most of the fruit, add a little of the sugar.
2 Spread over the 4 sponge cakes.
3 Whisk egg whites, fold in the rest of the sugar.
4 Pile over strawberry cakes, set for 5–8 minutes in a moderately hot oven (400 °F. – Gas Mark 5).
5 Decorate with rest of fruit.
6 Serve at once.

Strawberry-topped castle puddings

Cooking time 25–30 minutes

You will need:

4 oz. self-raising flour
4 oz. butter or margarine
2 eggs
strawberry jam
large pinch of salt
4 oz. castor sugar
few drops vanilla essence

1 Sift flour and salt together.
2 Cream fat, sugar and vanilla essence together until light and fluffy
3 Add eggs, 1 at a time, 1 tablespoon of the flour.
4 Fold in remaining flour.
5 Well-grease 6–9 individual pudding moulds (according to size) and $\frac{2}{3}$ fill with the mixture.
6 Cover each with greased paper or aluminium foil and steam for 25–30 minutes.
7 Turn out and top each pudding with a spoonful of strawberry jam.

Surprise pudding

Cooking time 10 minutes

You will need:

1 sponge cake
1 pint custard
1 lb. mixed summer fruit – black and red currants, raspberries, etc.

to decorate

whole fruit or glacé cherries

1 Cut a large circle from the middle of the sponge cake, leaving just a ring.
2 Stand on a serving dish.
3 Fill centre with the fruit and place part of the circle of sponge on top, making the cake look whole again.
4 Pour over the hot custard
5 Decorate with the fruit.
6 Serve hot or cold.

Sweet omelettes

Cooking time 10 minutes

You will need:

4 eggs	2 tablespoons cream from top of milk
2 oz. sugar	jam or other flavourings
1 oz. butter	

1 Separate the yolks from whites of the egg either by breaking the eggs carefully and tipping the white into a basin while retaining the yolk in the shell, or by breaking the whole egg on to a saucer, putting an egg-cup over the yolk and pouring the white into a basin.
2 Beat the yolks with the sugar and cream, then fold in stiffly beaten egg whites.
3 Heat the butter in the pan and pour in the egg mixture.
4 Cook steadily for several minutes until firm at the bottom.
5 Put under a medium grill or into the oven until the top is golden brown.
6 Fill with the hot jam and fold.
7 Top with more jam or sieved icing sugar and serve at once.

Suggestions for fillings

1 **Ginger marmalade omelette:** Fill with ginger marmalade and serve with cream.

2 **Almond macaroon omelette:** Add a crumbled macaroon biscuit, few drops of almond essence to the yolks and fill and top with warm apricot jam and chopped almonds.

3 **Apricot omelette:** Fill with canned apricots and serve with hot apricot syrup.

4 **Ice-cream omelette:** Fill with ice-cream and serve with hot chocolate sauce.

5 **Glazed omelette:** Fill with apple purée or other thick fruit purée, top with quite a thick layer of sieved icing sugar and put under the grill to brown. Watch it most carefully.

6 **Orange omelette:** Add grated orange rind and orange juice instead of cream to the egg yolks. Fill with sliced oranges.

Uncooked flan

No cooking

You will need:

2 oz. margarine or butter	cream or ice-cream
1 good teaspoon golden syrup	2 oz. sugar
	approximately 4 oz. cornflakes
	sliced fruit

1 To make flan, cream margarine, sugar and syrup.
2 Crush cornflakes slightly with a rolling pin.
3 Work into margarine mixture until firm texture.
4 Press into flan shape on plate.
5 Leave until ready to serve, then fill with sliced fruit and top with cream or ice-cream.

Vanilla soufflés

Cooking time 25 minutes

You will need:

1 packet vanilla-flavoured blancmange or 1½ oz. cornflour and a few drops vanilla essence (or vanilla pod)	2 tablespoons cream or evaporated milk
	1 pint milk
	2 oz. castor sugar
	3 eggs
	icing sugar

1 If using vanilla pod, put this into pan with the milk. Heat together.
2 Remove pod. Blend cornflour or blancmange powder with a little cold milk.
3 Bring rest of milk to the boil (add vanilla essence now, if using this), pour over cornflour, return to the pan with sugar and bring to the boil, stirring all the time until thick and smooth.
4 Remove from heat, add egg yolks beaten with cream and, lastly, stiffly beaten egg whites.
5 Put into 4 ovenproof dishes and bake for approximately 20 minutes in a moderate oven (375 °F. – Gas Mark 4).
6 Dust with sieved icing sugar and serve at once.

Chocolate soufflé
Use either chocolate-flavoured blancmange or 1 oz. cornflour and 1 dessertspoon cocoa.

Rum soufflé
Omit vanilla flavouring, add 1 or 2 tablespoons rum or a little rum essence.

Coffee soufflé
Use ¼ pint strong coffee and ¾ pint milk.

To whip evaporated milk

To whip evaporated milk with the greatest efficiency, boil the can of milk for about 15 minutes in a pan of water, then thoroughly chill for several hours. Turn into a large bowl and whisk firmly.
For very thick cream from evaporated milk, turn the milk out of the can after the 15 minutes boiling (open the can carefully so the milk does not spurt out) and stir on to a teaspoon powdered gelatine, dissolved in 2 tablespoons very hot water. Cool as before, then whip.
To save time it is a good idea to boil several cans of evaporated milk at one time and store

them in a cool place. They are then ready to whisk.
Some people omit the gelatine and add a little lemon juice to the evaporated milk instead.

Yoghourt and oat special

No cooking time
You will need for 3–4 servings:

2 bottles plain yoghourt
4 rounded tablespoons rolled oats
2 level dessertspoons golden syrup
2 oz. walnuts (roughly chopped)
glacé cherries for decoration
2 oz. seedless raisins
2 level dessertspoons castor sugar
2 eating apples (finely chopped)

1 Put yoghourt into mixing bowl.
2 Add rolled oats, raisins, castor sugar, syrup, apples and walnuts.
3 Mix thoroughly.
4 Leave a few hours.
5 Serve topped with glacé cherries.

Cakes and Biscuits

Many people feel when they are short of time they cannot produce home-made cakes, but do remember that modern cake mixes can be used as a basis for your home-made cakes and you can decorate them in any way you wish.
This saves you a great deal of time by cutting out preliminary preparations.
Another way in which time can be saved is to make up a batch of mixture and use it in several ways. As an example of this see cake mixtures 1 and 2, pages 78–9.

Almond cookies

Cooking time 12–15 minutes
You will need:

6 oz. flour
3 oz. ground almonds
6 oz. sugar
3 oz. margarine
egg yolks to mix
egg white to brush top
little sugar

1 Cream margarine and sugar until soft and light.
2 Add ground almonds, flour and enough egg yolk to bind.
3 Roll out to about $\frac{1}{3}$ inch thick, cut into squares, then make several slits in the dough.
4 Brush with egg white and little sugar.
5 Bake for 12–15 minutes in a moderate oven (375°F.—Gas Mark 4).

Almond shorties

Cooking time 15 minutes
You will need:

3 oz. butter
2 oz. sugar
3 oz. flour
$\frac{1}{2}$ oz. cornflour
1 oz. ground almonds

1 Rub butter into sieved flour and cornflour.
2 Work in sugar and ground almonds.
3 Roll out thinly on a floured board.
4 Cut into rounds and bake for 12–15 minutes in centre of moderate oven (375°F.—Gas Mark 4).
5 When cold, coat with almond-flavoured icing if wished and pipe lines of coffee icing.

Banana and rum pastries

Cooking time 15 minutes
You will need:

6 oz. short crust or sweet short crust pastry (see page 86)
3 bananas
3 teaspoons sugar
glacé cherries
little red currant jelly
$\frac{1}{4}$ pint whipped cream
2 teaspoons rum
icing sugar

1 Line 12 patty tins with the pastry.
2 Bake until crisp and brown in hot oven.
3 Spread with a little red currant jelly.
4 Mash bananas with rum and sugar.
5 Fold in whipped cream.
6 Fill tarts with this mixture, dust tops liberally with sieved icing sugar and decorate with glacé cherries.

Basic cake mixture number 1

This is 'rubbed in' mixture, and can be used for sweet pastry, biscuits, puddings and cakes. It is a wonderful standby as it can be used in so many different ways, and there is no need to use it all up on the day that it is made. It can be stored in a jar or plastic bag until required.

You will need:

1 lb. flour (with plain flour use 2 level teaspoons baking powder)
8 oz. margarine
4 oz. castor sugar

1 Sieve flour.
2 Rub in margarine.
3 Add sugar.

variations:

Jam or fruit fingers

Cooking time approximately 20 minutes

You will need:

¼ basic cake mixture
1 egg (optional)
a little water
cream
jam, or jelly with chopped fresh fruit, or canned fruit with glaze made by boiling 1 teaspoon cornflour or arrowroot with 1 gill fruit syrup

1 Add water, or egg and water to mixture, until of right consistency to roll.
2 Roll out and form into long oblong.
3 Flute the edges, prick, and bake 'blind' in a hot oven for about 20 minutes (450°F.—Gas Mark 7).
4 When crisp and golden brown, spread with jam and top with cream.
5 Or top with set jelly, to which is added chopped fresh fruit.
6 Or top with canned fruit, and cover with a glaze made by boiling the cornflour or arrowroot with the fruit syrup.
7 Decorate with whipped cream and cut into fingers.

Chocolate honey buns

Cooking time approximately 12 minutes

You will need:

¼ basic cake mixture
1 tablespoon honey
1 egg
bar of plain or milk chocolate (chopped)

1 Combine honey and egg with mixture.
2 Add chopped chocolate and mix thoroughly.
3 Put in little heaps on well greased baking tins, allowing room for the cakes to spread slightly.
4 Bake in a hot oven (450°F.—Gas Mark 7) for about 12 minutes.

Lemon and orange biscuits

Cooking time approximately 10 minutes

You will need:

¼ basic cake mixture
grated rind of 1 lemon and 1 orange
lemon and orange juice to bind
curd or icing for filling

1 Add sugar and grated fruit rind to basic mixture.
2 Add sufficient fruit juice to give proper rolling consistency.
3 Roll out as thinly as possible. The thinner the dough, the crisper the biscuits will be.
4 Cut into any desired shapes, or if in a hurry, into fingers.
5 If ¼ inch thick, bake for about 10 minutes in a moderate oven (375°F.—Gas Mark 4–5).
6 Cool on baking tin.

Apple or mixed fruit pudding

Cooking time 40 minutes

You will need:

¼ basic cake mixture
1 oz. brown sugar
¼ teaspoon mixed spice
1 oz. desiccated coconut
apples or other fruit
little water or sugar

1 Combine brown sugar, spice, coconut with basic mixture.
2 Put sliced apples or other fruit into a dish, adding a little water and sugar.
3 Cover with topping and cook in the centre of a very moderate oven (375°F.—Gas Mark 4) for approximately 40 minutes.

Basic cake mixture number 2

This is a creamed mixture, for lighter cakes, puddings, etc.

You will need:

12 oz. margarine
12 oz. sugar
6 eggs
1 lb. flour (with plain flour, use 4 level teaspoons baking powder)

1 Cream the margarine and sugar until soft and light.
2 Beat the eggs, and add gradually to the creamed mixture.
3 Sieve the flour and baking powder.
4 Stir gently into the egg and margarine mixture, taking care not to over-beat.

For greater economy use only 4 eggs and 4 tablespoons milk.

variations:

Coconut fruit loaf

Cooking time approximately 1 hour

You will need:

$\frac{1}{4}$ basic cake mixture	6 oz. dried fruit
for topping	
1 oz. brown sugar	1 oz coconut
1 oz. margarine	1 oz. walnuts

1 Add fruit to basic mixture. No extra liquid is required.
2 Put into loaf tin.
3 Make topping by creaming sugar with margarine, adding coconut and finely chopped walnuts.
4 Spread on top of loaf.
5 Bake for about 1 hour in the centre of a moderate oven (375 °F. – Gas Mark 4). This delicious loaf is excellent for carrying on a picnic.

Madeleines

Cooking time approximately 10 minutes

You will need:

$\frac{1}{4}$ basic mixture	cherries
jam or curd	OR whipped cream and few drops Tia Maria
coconut	

1 Half fill dariole moulds (castle pudding tins) with the basic mixture.
2 Bake for about 10 minutes in a hot oven (425–450 °F. – Gas Mark 6–7).
3 Turn out and when cold coat with jam or curd and roll in coconut. Top with a cherry.
4 For luxury Madeleines coat with whipped cream flavoured with a few drops Tia Maria and then roll in grated coconut. Top with whipped cream.

Ice-cream cake

Cooking time approximately 20 minutes

You will need:

$\frac{1}{4}$ basic mixture	fruit
1 tablespoon milk	whipped cream
ice-cream	

1 Add milk to basic mixture.
2 Bake in a fairly good sized square sandwich tin, or 9-inch round tin for about 20 minutes in a moderate oven (375–400°F.—Gas Mark 6–7).
3 Turn out and top with scoops of ice-cream, fruit and whipped cream. This makes a wonderful dessert.

Crisp shortbread cookies

Cooking time approximately 12–15 minutes

You will need:

$\frac{1}{4}$ basic mixture	1 oz. cornflour (flavoured if desired)
glacé cherries	

1 Add cornflour to basic mixture.
2 Roll into balls and top each with a piece of cherry.
3 Bake for approximately 12–15 minutes in a moderate oven (375°F.—Gas Mark 4). This mixture makes very crisp shortbread-like cookies.

Cheese cake

Cooking time 55 minutes

You will need:

	6 oz. rich short crust pastry (see page 86)
for the filling	
1 LEVEL tablespoon flour	8 oz. cream or cottage cheese
seasoning	2 eggs or 3 if rather small
2 oz. sugar	
1–2 oz. butter	2 oz. sultanas

1 Line a 7-inch flan ring with thin pastry, keep a little over.
2 Set 'blind' for about 10 minutes in a hot oven.
3 Cream butter and cheese and add all other ingredients gradually.
4 Put into pastry case.
5 Put a lattice work of very thin pastry on top and bake for about 45 minutes in the centre of a moderate oven (375 °F. – Gas Mark 4) until filling is brown and firm.

Cheese and almond cookies

Cooking time 15 minutes

You will need:

$2\frac{1}{4}$ oz. margarine	seasoning
$1\frac{1}{2}$ oz. grated cheese	egg white
1 oz. chopped almonds	1 tablespoon grated cheese
blanched almonds	
4 oz. flour (with plain flour use 1 level teaspoon baking powder)	

1 Cream margarine, $1\frac{1}{2}$ oz. cheese and seasoning.
2 Add chopped almonds and flour.
3 Roll into balls, put on lightly greased tins, allowing room to flatten.
4 Brush with egg white, sprinkle cheese on top, arrange almonds in a pattern, bake for 12–15 minutes in centre of moderate oven (375 °F. – Gas Mark 4).
5 Cool on tin.

Chestnut tart

Cooking time 25 minutes

You will need:

- 4 oz. short crust pastry (see page 86)
- can chestnut purée
- 2–3 oz. chocolate
- whipped cream
- 2 oz. margarine
- 3 oz. sieved icing sugar
- ½ teaspoon vanilla essence

1. Line a flan tin with pastry and bake until crisp and brown in hot oven, (425–450 °F. – Gas Mark 6–7).
2. Mix chestnut purée with creamed margarine and sugar.
3. Add vanilla.
4. Spread over the bottom of the flan.
5. Melt chocolate with a FEW DROPS only of water.
6. Pour on top of the chestnut purée when cold.
7. Decorate with rosettes of whipped cream.

Chinese 'chews'

Cooking time 25–35 minutes

You will need:

- 2 oz. margarine
- 2 oz. brown sugar
- 4 oz. self-raising flour
- 2 oz. chopped glacé cherries
- icing sugar
- 1 dessertspoon syrup or treacle
- 1 egg
- 4 oz. chopped dates
- 2 oz. chopped walnuts
- 2 oz. chopped peel
- grated lemon rind

1. Sieve flour, rub in the margarine.
2. Add all the other ingredients.
3. Grease and flour a square shallow tin, measuring 7 or 8 inches across.
4. Put in the cake mixture at 400 °F. – Gas Mark 5 for about 25–35 minutes.
5. Remove from tin.
6. Cut into fingers and dredge with icing sugar.

Chocolate almond tarts

Cooking time 20 minutes

You will need:

- 4 oz. sweet short crust pastry (see page 86)
- 2 egg whites
- 3 oz. sugar
- 2 oz. chocolate powder
- 3 oz. ground almonds
- little whipped cream
- cherries

1. Line patty tins with the pastry.
2. Prick and bake 'blind' in a hot oven (450 °F. – Gas Mark 7) about 8 minutes until set, but not browned.
3. Whisk egg whites, add other ingredients, put into pastry cases and bake for further 10–12 minutes in moderate oven.
4. When cold pipe border of cream, decorate with pieces of cherry.

Chocolate cake

Cooking time made in minutes

You will need:

- 4 oz. margarine
- 1 tablespoon cocoa
- few cherries and walnuts to decorate
- 4 oz. sugar
- 1 egg
- 8 oz. broken sweet biscuits

1. Crush the biscuits with a rolling pin.
2. Melt the margarine and sugar together in a saucepan.
3. Add the cocoa.
4. Remove from the heat and add the egg, mixing quickly.
5. Stir in the broken biscuits.
6. Turn into a greased loaf tin and press down.
7. Leave to set. Turn out and decorate with cherries and walnuts.

Chocolate cake

No cooking

You will need:

- 3 oz. butter
- 1 oz. castor sugar
- glacé icing
- 1 tablespoon golden syrup
- 4 oz. plain chocolate
- 8 oz. digestive biscuits

1. Crush biscuits into fine crumbs.
2. Brush a 7-inch flan ring with a little melted butter and place it on a flat dish.
3. Cream the butter, sugar and syrup, add melted chocolate and biscuit crumbs.
4. Pack mixture into ring, smoothing the top.
5. Chill for at least 3 hours.
6. Remove flan ring.
7. Coat cake with lemon or orange-flavoured glacé icing and decorate with grated chocolate.

Chocolate surprise cookies

Cooking time 12 minutes

You will need:

- 8 oz. flour (with plain flour use 2 level teaspoons baking powder)
- 2 oz. chocolate
- 4 oz. margarine
- 5 oz. sugar
- 1 egg
- little milk

1. Sieve flour, rub in margarine, add sugar, egg and enough milk to mix.
2. Put in small heaps in lightly greased and floured tins.
3. Make a hole in the centre of each cookie.
4. Put a piece of chocolate in each hole and almost cover with the cake mixture.
5. Bake for 10–12 minutes in hot oven (425–450°F.—Gas Mark 6–7).

Coffee japs

Cooking time 40 minutes

You will need:

3 egg whites
6 oz. castor sugar
6 oz. ground almonds

for the filling

1 tablespoon coffee essence
4 oz. butter or margarine
6 oz. sieved icing sugar

for the icing

1 tablespoon coffee essence
approximately 6 oz. sieved icing sugar
hazel nuts to decorate

1 Whisk the egg whites until stiff, add the sugar and the ground almonds.
2 Line a small Swiss roll tin with oiled paper, spread with the mixture and bake in the centre of a very moderate oven (350°F.—Gas Mark 3) until the cake begins to turn golden, approximately 20 minutes.
3 Take out of the oven, mark about 18 or 20 small rounds, as close together as possible so none of the cake is wasted.
4 Return to the oven and cook for about another 15 minutes.
5 Lift the rounds out carefully, and return the 'trimmings' to the oven for a further few minutes to brown more.
6 Make the filling by creaming butter and icing sugar and adding the essence very gradually, so the mixture does not curdle.
7 Sandwich the little cakes together with the coffee butter icing and spread some round the outside.
8 Crush the 'trimmings' to make crumbs and coat the sides of the cakes liberally.
9 Cover the tops with coffee icing and decorate with a hazel nut.

Continental cheese cake

No cooking

Another delicious continental cheese cake is made by splitting a sponge cake into 3 layers and spreading each layer with the following: 8 oz. cottage or cream cheese creamed with 2 oz. castor sugar, 2 oz. grated chocolate and a little maraschino or sherry.

Cornflake cookies

Cooking time 20 minutes

You will need:

2 egg whites
3 oz. desiccated coconut
5 oz. sugar
1 oz. ground almonds
2 oz. crumbled cornflakes
few cherries
rice paper

1 Whisk egg whites, add coconut, almonds, cornflakes, sugar and pile on to rice paper with a cherry on each.
2 Bake for 18–20 minutes in centre of very moderate oven (350°F.—Gas Mark 3).

Cornflake and coconut macaroons

Cooking time 15 minutes

You will need:

2 large egg whites
pinch of salt
2 oz. desiccated coconut
1 oz. crushed cornflakes
2 oz. ground almonds
3 oz. castor sugar
few drops almond essence

1 Whisk egg whites, add all other ingredients.
2 Knead well and put into small paper cases. This makes about 16–18 cakes.
3 Bake for 15 minutes in centre of moderate oven (375°F.—Gas Mark 5) until golden brown.

Cream layer cookies

Cooking time 10 minutes

You will need:

8 oz. flour
5 oz. margarine
5 oz. castor sugar
egg
little cochineal
whipped cream
angelica

1 Cream margarine and sugar until soft and light.
2 Add flour, knead well and work in enough egg to bind.
3 Colour $\frac{1}{3}$ of the dough pink, with cochineal.
4 Roll out until under $\frac{1}{4}$ inch thick, cut into rounds and bake on ungreased tins for about 10 minutes in moderate oven (375°F.—Gas Mark 4).
5 Cool on baking tins.
6 Sandwich 3 of these biscuits with whipped cream and decorate with whipped cream and angelica, putting a pink biscuit between 2 white ones.

Feather cream cakes

Cooking time 15 minutes

You will need:

3 oz. butter
3 oz. castor sugar
icing sugar to decorate
2 eggs
5 oz. flour (with plain flour use $1\frac{1}{4}$ teaspoons baking powder)
1 tablespoon cream (top of milk)

1 Cream butter and sugar very well indeed.
2 Gradually add well-beaten eggs, then fold in sieved flour and cream.
3 Put into greased and floured patty tins and bake for about 12–15 minutes in moderately hot oven (400°F.—Gas Mark 5).
4 Dust with icing sugar if wished.

Variations on previous recipe overleaf:

variations on Feather cream cakes

Queen Cakes: Add 1 oz. currants.

Coconut Cakes: Use 1 oz. coconut instead of 1 oz. flour.

Chocolate Cakes: Omit 1 oz. flour and use 1 oz. chocolate powder.

French cinnamon tea-cake

Cooking time 20–25 minutes

You will need:

1 egg
2 oz. castor sugar
1 tablespoon melted butter
4 tablespoons milk
few drops vanilla essence
4 oz. flour (with plain flour 1 teaspoon baking powder)

topping
melted butter
1 level teaspoon cinnamon (or alternatively spice)

1 Separate egg yolk from white.
2 Whisk egg white till stiff and peaky then gradually whisk in sugar, followed by yolk.
3 Fold in milk and essence and lastly flour and butter.
4 Turn mixture into well-greased 7-inch sandwich tin.
5 Bake towards top of oven (375°F.—Gas Mark 4) for 20–25 minutes.
6 Remove from oven, brush top with melted butter and sprinkle with cinnamon.
7 Serve warm with butter, clotted cream or cottage cheese and jam or honey.
8 Instead of the butter and spice top, this tea cake can be topped while warm with soft lemon icing and finely chopped walnuts.

Jiffy gingerbread

Cooking time 1 hour

You will need:

3 oz. cooking fat or margarine
8 oz. golden syrup or treacle (or mix these two)
1 LEVEL teaspoon bicarbonate of soda
4 oz. sultanas or raisins
2 oz. sugar (brown or white)
¾ gill of water or milk
8 oz. flour (with plain flour 1 teaspoon baking powder)
1–1½ teaspoons powdered ginger
1 egg

1 Heat fat, sugar, syrup and water in a large pan until fat has melted.
2 ALLOW TO COOL.
3 Sieve flour and all dry ingredients together.
4 Add to ingredients in saucepan and beat well.
5 Stir in egg and sultanas.
6 Pour into 7-inch tin lined with greased greaseproof paper and bake in the centre of a very moderate oven (350°F.—Gas Mark 3) for approximately 1 hour.
7 Cool in tin a short time before turning out.

Lemon jumbles

Cooking time 10 minutes

You will need:

4 oz. margarine
4 oz. sugar
1 egg
8 oz. flour (with plain flour use 2 level teaspoons baking powder)
grated rind of 2 lemons
lemon juice to mix

1 Sieve flour and baking powder together.
2 Rub in the margarine, add the sugar and lemon rind.
3 Mix in the egg and enough lemon juice to make a firm dough.
4 Roll out the dough until it is ¼ inch thick.
5 Cut into long strips and make these into bows.
6 Put on to a lightly greased and floured baking tin.
7 Bake for 10 minutes near the top of a very hot oven (475°F.—Gas Mark 8).
8 Brush top with a thin layer of lemon-flavoured water icing, made by mixing 4 tablespoons icing sugar with 1 tablespoon lemon juice.
9 Put cherries and angelica into centre.

Macaroon animals

Cooking time 20 minutes

You will need:

2 egg whites
6 oz. ground almonds
6 oz. castor sugar
about 2 teaspoons cornflour
little icing for decoration

1 Whisk egg whites lightly, add ground almonds, sugar and enough cornflour to make firm dough.
2 Roll out to thin dough, cut into shapes with animal cutters.
3 Put on rice paper or baking tins and bake for about 20 minutes in a very moderate oven (350°F.—Gas Mark 3).
4 Cut round paper when cold.
5 Decorate with icing.

Macaroon fingers

Cooking time 20 minutes

You will need:

whites of 2 eggs
6 oz. ground almonds
finely grated rind of 2 oranges
6 oz. sugar
few drops orange flavoured water
rice paper

1 Mix all ingredients together.
2 Form into finger shapes on rice paper on baking trays.
3 Bake for approximately 18–20 minutes in centre of moderate oven (375°F.—Gas Mark 4).
4 Cut around biscuits.
5 When cold they can either be covered with orange flavoured water icing and chopped nuts or left plain.

Mincemeat cookies

Cooking time 15 minutes

You will need:

4 oz. margarine
4 oz. sugar
icing sugar
8 oz. plain flour
little egg yolk
2 or 3 tablespoons mincemeat

1 Cream the margarine and sugar.
2 Work in flour and just enough egg yolk to bind it.
3 Cut into rounds and cut a circle from the centre of half the rounds.
4 Put the complete rounds on to baking trays, place the rings firmly on top.
5 Fill the centre with mincemeat.
6 Bake for about 15 minutes at 375°F.—Gas Mark 4.
7 Cool on the tin.
8 Dredge the outer ring with icing sugar.

Mocha flapjacks

Cooking time 25–30 minutes

You will need for 12 flapjacks:

2 oz. butter or margarine
2 oz. roughly chopped chocolate
4 oz. rolled oats
2 oz. golden syrup
2 oz. chopped walnuts
2 teaspoons coffee essence

1 Melt butter, syrup and coffee essence together in saucepan.
2 Add rolled oats.
3 Mix well and allow to cool slightly.
4 Fold in chopped nuts and chocolate.
5 Spread mixture evenly in lightly greased 7-inch square cake tin.
6 Cook on middle shelf, very moderate oven (350°F.—Gas Mark 3) for 25–30 minutes.
7 Cut in portions, while warm, allow to cool slightly. Remove carefully.

Orange tarts

Cooking time 15–20 minutes

You will need:

4–5 oz. short crust pastry (see page 86)
little marmalade

for filling

1 oz. butter
1 egg
3 oz. marmalade
3 oz. soft cake crumbs

1 Line patty tins with pastry and add a little marmalade.
2 Cream butter and marmalade, gradually beat in egg and crumbs.
3 Put mixture into tart cases and bake for 15–20 minutes in the centre of a moderately hot oven (400°F.–Gas Mark 5).
4 If desired, top with a little icing, made by combining icing sugar with enough orange juice to give spreading consistency.

Peanut butter cookies

Cooking time 10–12 minutes

You will need:

2 oz. self-raising flour
pinch of salt
2 oz. peanut butter
few drops vanilla essence
1 oz. fine semolina
2 oz. butter or margarine
2 oz. soft brown sugar
1 egg

1 Sift together flour, semolina and salt.
2 Cream fat, sugar, peanut butter and vanilla essence together until light.
3 Beat in egg, then stir in the dry ingredients.
4 Drop teaspoons of mixture, 1 inch apart, on to ungreased baking trays.
5 Bake in a moderate oven (375°F.—Gas Mark 4) for 10–12 minutes.
6 Cool on a wire tray. Store in an airtight container.
7 Makes approximately 24 cookies.

Pineapple cherry cookies

Cooking time 15 minutes

You will need:

3 oz. margarine
2 oz. sugar
1 oz. chopped glacé cherries
1 oz. chopped glacé pineapple
4 oz. flour (with plain flour 1 teaspoon baking powder)
cherries and pineapple to decorate

1 Cream margarine and sugar.
2 Stir in pineapple, cherries and sieved flour.
3 Roll into balls.
4 Put on to lightly greased and floured baking trays with room to spread.
5 Put a piece of cherry and pineapple on top.
6 Bake for 15 minutes in centre of moderate oven (375°F.—Gas Mark 4).
7 Cool on tin.

Pineapple Madeleines

Cooking time 15 minutes

You will need:

pineapple jam
coconut
glacé pineapple
2 eggs
3 oz. margarine
3 oz. castor sugar
4 oz. flour (with plain flour use 1 level teaspoon baking powder)
1 packet pineapple-flavoured cornflour

1 Cream margarine and sugar.
2 Add eggs and sieved flour and cornflour.
3 Half fill greased and floured dariole tins.
4 Bake for 15 minutes in centre of oven (400°F.—Gas Mark 5).
5 When cold, coat with pineapple jam and coconut and decorate with piece of glacé pineapple.

Raisin doughnuts

Cooking time 6 minutes

You will need:

4 oz. flour (with plain flour use 1½ level teaspoons baking powder)
½ gill milk
2–3 oz. lard for frying
2 oz. raisins
1 oz. sugar
1 egg
little castor sugar for coating

1 Sieve flour, add other ingredients and beat until a smooth, thick batter.
2 Heat lard in frying pan and drop in spoonfuls of mixture.
3 Cook steadily for about 3 minutes until golden, turn and cook other side.
4 Drain on crumpled tissue paper for 1 minute then roll in castor sugar.

Rock buns

Cooking time 10 minutes

You will need:

8 oz. flour (with plain flour use 2½ teaspoons baking powder)
6 oz. dried fruit
5 oz. margarine
5 oz. sugar
1 egg
2 oz. candied peel

1 Sieve flour and baking powder together.
2 Rub in margarine, add sugar, beaten egg and enough milk to make a stiff consistency. Be careful not to make the mixture too soft or the buns will spread badly.
3 Add the fruit and peel.
4 Grease and flour baking tins and put small heaps of the mixture on these, dusting lightly with sugar.
5 Bake for 10 minutes near the top of a hot to very hot oven (450–475°F.—Gas Mark 7–8). If the oven is inclined to be rather fierce, lower the heat after the first 5 minutes.

Variation
Omit dried fruit. Put in heaps on the baking trays. Make a small hole in the centre of each and put in a spoonful of jam—apricot or raspberry being the most suitable.

Sponge cakes

Cooking time 20–25 minutes

You will need:

6 oz. margarine
6 oz. castor sugar
little milk
2–3 eggs
8 oz. self-raising flour
few drops vanilla essence

1 Cream the margarine and sugar with the vanilla essence until soft and light.
2 Gradually beat in the eggs, stir in the flour, well sieved, and enough milk to make a soft consistency.
3 Put the mixture into a Swiss roll tin (lined with greaseproof paper, greased with margarine and lightly floured).
4 Bake for approximately 20–25 minutes in a moderate oven (375–400°F.—Gas Mark 4–5).
5 Serve plain, cut in fingers, or try the following variations:

Chocolate walnuts

You will need:

2 oz. margarine
3 oz. sieved icing sugar
chopped walnuts
2 teaspoons chocolate powder
walnut halves

1 Make icing by creaming margarine and sieved icing sugar with chocolate powder.
2 Coat sides and tops of sponge fingers.
3 Roll in chopped walnuts.
4 Decorate with piped border of chocolate icing and walnut halves.

Pineapple diamonds

You will need:

pineapple jam
whipped cream
crystallized pineapple

1 Cut cake into diamond-shapes, and cut these in half.
2 Spread with pineapple jam, sandwich together.
3 Coat and decorate the tops of the cake with whipped cream.
4 Decorate with crystallized pineapple.

Winter shortcake

Cooking time 20 minutes

You will need:

4 oz. margarine
4 oz. castor sugar
whipped cream
1 egg
6 oz. self-raising flour
fruit salad

1 Cream together the margarine and sugar.
2 Add the egg and sieved flour.
3 Divide the mixture between two 7-inch lightly-greased and floured sandwich tins.
4 Flatten the mixture with very slightly damped fingers.
5 Bake for about 20 minutes at 400°F.—Gas Mark 5.
6 Turn out and when cold, sandwich together and decorate with whipped cream and chopped canned fruit salad.

Bridge rolls

Cooking time 15 minutes

You will need:

8 oz. plain flour
½ oz. lard
½ level teaspoon salt
1 egg
4 level teaspoons baking powder
¼ pint milk (for use as required)

1 Sieve together plain flour, baking powder and salt.
2 Lightly rub in the lard.
3 Make a well in the centre, add the egg and some of the milk.
4 Fold in the flour gently to make an elastic dough, adding more milk if necessary.
5 Turn on to a floured board and divide into 8.
6 Shape into rolls.
7 Bake 15 minutes on lightly greased baking tin near top of hot oven (450–475 °F.—Gas Mark 7–8).
8 Cool on a wire tray.
9 Split open while hot and serve with butter and Cheddar cheese, or with a casserole of steak or ham.

Rich cheese scones

Cooking time 10 minutes

You will need:

8 oz. flour (with plain flour use 4 level teaspoons baking powder)
little milk to mix
good pinch salt, pepper, mustard
2 oz. butter
4 oz. grated cheese
1 egg

1 Sieve dry ingredients.
2 Rub in butter.
3 Add cheese, leaving a little to glaze scones.
4 Bind with egg and milk to soft rolling consistency.
5 Roll out dough to ½ inch thick and cut into shapes.
6 Brush with milk or egg and top with grated cheese.
7 Bake for good 10 minutes in hot oven (425–450° F.—Gas Mark 6–7).

Herb scones

Cooking time 12 minutes

You will need:

8 oz. self-raising flour
2 oz. margarine
½ level teaspoon salt
approximately 6 tablespoons milk
1 level teaspoon mixed herbs

1 Sift flour and salt into a bowl.
2 Rub in margarine.
3 Add herbs, then mix to a soft, but not sticky dough with the milk.
4 Turn out on a lightly floured board.
5 Knead quickly till smooth, then roll out to about ½ inch in thickness.
6 Cut into 4 rounds with a 3½–4 inch plain cutter or, pressing dough to round shape, cut across into 4 to 6 triangles.
7 Transfer to a greased baking sheet.
8 Brush tops with milk, then bake towards top of hot oven (450° F.—Gas Mark 7) for 12 minutes.

Quickie rolls

Cooking time 12 minutes

You will need:

8 oz. self-raising flour (with plain flour use 2 level teaspoons baking powder)
salt
1 oz. margarine
milk to mix

1 Sieve flour and salt, rub in the margarine and mix with enough milk to make a firm dough.
2 Roll out to smooth dough, a good ¼ inch thick.
3 Cut into long strips, then roll up each strip like a tiny Swiss roll.
4 Put these strips into greased patty tins, brush the tops with milk and bake for about 12 minutes in a hot oven (450° F,—Gas Mark 7).

Raisin and walnut scones

Cooking time 10 minutes

You will need:

6 oz. self-raising flour
salt
1 tablespoon brown sugar
milk to mix
1½ oz. margarine
2 tablespoons raisins
1 tablespoon chopped walnuts

1 Sieve flour and salt together.
2 Rub in the margarine, add all other ingredients, making a dough of a soft roll consistency.
3 Roll out to ½ inch thick.
4 Cut into small rounds, put on to a lightly greased baking tray and bake for 10 minutes (475° F.—Gas Mark 8).

Spiced Scotch pancakes

Cooking time 4 minutes

You will need:

1 oz. margarine
4 oz. self-raising flour
½ teaspoon mixed spice
1 egg
¼ pint milk

1 Sieve flour with spice, add the egg and gradually stir in the milk to make a smooth, thick batter.
2 Lastly, add the melted margarine.
3 Heat a griddle or frying pan and rub lightly with margarine.
4 Drop spoonfuls of the mixture on this and cook for about 2 minutes until the top side 'bubbles'.
5 Turn carefully and cook them for about the same time on the second side.

Short crust pastry

You will need:

8 oz. flour
4 oz. fat*
good pinch salt
cold water to mix—approximately 2 tablespoons

*There are many fats and combinations of fats that give a first class short crust pastry. Choose between:

Modern whipped light fat. Use $3\frac{1}{2}$ oz. only as it is very rich.
Pure cooking fat or lard.
Margarine—for best results use a table margarine, a superfine or luxury margarine.
Butter or perhaps the favourite of all—2 oz. margarine and 2 oz. cooking fat.

1 Sieve flour and salt and rub in fat until mixture looks like fine breadcrumbs.
2 Using first a knife and then the fingertips to feel the pastry, gradually add enough cold water to make the dough of a rolling consistency.
3 Lightly flour the rolling-pin and pastry board. If a great deal of flour is necessary to roll out the pastry then you have undoubtedly made it too wet.
4 Roll pastry to required thickness and shape, lifting and turning to keep it light.
5 Exact cooking times for pastry are given in the recipes but as a general rule it should be cooked in a hot oven (425–450°F.—or Gas Mark 6–7).

Rich short crust

As short crust pastry, but use butter and bind with egg yolk and a little water.

Sweet short crust

You will need:

8 oz. flour
5 oz. butter*
2 oz. sugar
pinch salt
egg yolk to bind

*Table, luxury or superfine margarine can be used.

1 Cream fat and sugar together until light in colour.
2 Sieve flour and salt together and add to creamed fat, mixing with a knife.
3 Gradually add enough water or egg and water to make a firm rolling consistency. Use fingertips to feel the pastry.
4 To line flan put pastry over case and press down base and sides firmly then roll over top with rolling-pin for a good edge.
5 Decorate edge as wished.

Entertaining

It is a great pity if lack of time stops one entertaining at home for 'easy to prepare' parties can be just as enjoyable as more ambitious ones. In this chapter are ideas for quick and easy sweet or savoury dishes which look attractive yet take a short time only to prepare.

Appetizers *for cocktail parties*

Made in a minute appetizers that need no cooking.

Raw cauliflower sprigs—well washed, are delicious if rolled in celery salt and grated Parmesan cheese.

Heat processed cheese in a colourful basin over hot water and serve with potato crisps.

Sardine fingers. Cut fingers of bread and spread with tomato butter, i.e. cream equal quantities of margarine and tomato ketchup. Top with sardines and garnish with grated Parmesan cheese and chopped parsley.

Liver sausage canapés. Mash liver sausage with tomato ketchup or chutney. Spread on small cocktail biscuits and pipe border of stars with cream cheese. Garnish with rings of gherkin.

Prawn canapés. Mix margarine with a little mayonnaise and a small quantity of finely chopped parsley or watercress. Spread on tiny rounds of bread or biscuits and press prawns on top.

Surprise cheese balls. Roll a little soft cream cheese round tiny cocktail onions, then toss in chopped parsley and red pepper. Put cocktail stick through each ball.

Asparagus fingers. Dip short canned or cooked frozen asparagus heads into a little mayonnaise. Put on thin slices of brown bread—spread with butter and roll firmly.

Cheese life-savers

Cooking time 15 minutes

You will need:

sliced white bread (day-old)
butter
finely grated cheese
pinch cayenne pepper
1 large carrot

1 Cut circles from the sliced bread using a $1\frac{3}{4}$-inch pastry-cutter and remove the centres using a 1-inch cutter.
2 Melt a little butter in a frying pan, dip the bread rings in the butter then toss in the finely grated seasoned cheese until well coated.
3 Use Cheddar to which a little Parmesan may be added for extra flavour.
4 Place the cheese-coated bread on a baking sheet and brown in a moderately hot oven (400°F.—Gas Mark 5) taking about 10 minutes.
5 Serve at once.
6 Trim the base of a large clean carrot and stand it upright with cocktail sticks prodded diagonally into the top part – hand the Life-savers on the sticks.

Cheese meringues

Cooking time 10 minutes

You will need:

2 egg whites
2 tablespoons finely grated cheese (preferably Parmesan)
little cooking fat for frying
good pinch each of salt, pepper, dry mustard

1 Whisk egg whites stiffly.
2 Fold in seasoning and cheese.
3 Make sure fat is really hot, then drop in small spoonfuls of cheese mixture.
4 Cook each meringue for 2 or 3 minutes until crisp and golden.
5 Drain on crumpled tissue paper and serve at once.
6 Delicious with a drink or as a light snack in the evening.

Cheese savouries

(Six hot savouries)

Cooking time 5–15 minutes

For these, you can use Cheddar cheese, or, even better, petit Gruyère triangles.

1 Dip triangles of cheese in fritter batter and fry.
2 Egg and crumb cheese triangles, then fry. Split, and put together again with a slice of ham or ham paste.
3 Sandwich cheese between slices of bread, soak in beaten egg for a few minutes, then fry.
4 Sandwich thin slivers of cheese between thinly rolled short pastry, seal the edges, brush pastry with beaten egg and bake for 15 minutes in hot oven.
5 Put slices of cheese on buttered bread spread with anchovy paste, and toast under grill.
6 Put slice of cheese on buttered bread, sprinkle with paprika and put in a hot oven until golden brown.

Cheese and salad platter

No cooking

You will need:

selection of cheese, Cheddar, Gruyère, Caerphilly
tomatoes
2 hard-boiled eggs
mayonnaise
parsley
vinegar
seasoning
tiny RAW cut cauliflower
cold new potatoes (left from another meal)
cooked carrots (or use canned carrots)
mint
lettuce
oil

1 Chop hard-boiled egg yolk.
2 Arrange cheese on bed of lettuce.
3 Divide cauliflower into neat sprigs, coat with mayonnaise and egg yolk.
4 Mix new potatoes with mint and mayonnaise.
5 Toss carrots in oil, vinegar, seasonings and chopped parsley.
6 Garnish with rings of egg whites.
7 Slice tomatoes, top with chopped parsley.

Cheese squares

No cooking time

You will need:

- bread
- butter
- cream cheese
- cornflakes

1. Cut fresh bread into 1-inch cubes.
2. Spread all sides first with butter, then with cream cheese.
3. Toss in cornflakes until completely covered.

Date and cream cheese delights

(makes 10–18, depending on size)

No cooking

You will need:

- 4 oz. cream cheese
- 1 oz. brown sugar
- 1 dessertspoon golden syrup
- 1–2 oz. crushed or chopped nuts for decoration
- 6 oz. dates (cut fine)
- 2 teaspoons grated orange rind
- 2 oz. rolled oats

1. Crush nuts.
2. Put cheese, sugar, syrup, orange rind, dates and rolled oats in mixing bowl.
3. Cream thoroughly together.
4. Chill (in a refrigerator if you like).
5. Shape into balls.
6. Roll in crushed nuts.
7. Place in paper cases.

Stuffed dates

Take stones out of firm dates and fill centres with soft cream cheese.

Stuffed prunes

Stone cooked and well-drained prunes and fill centres with cheese mixed with chopped nuts.

Meat popovers

Cooking time 15 minutes

You will need:

- 4 oz. flaked or chopped ham or corned beef or cooked bacon
- a batter made with 2 oz. flour
- 1 egg
- $\frac{1}{3}$ gill milk
- seasoning

1. Add the flaked or chopped ham, corned beef or cooked bacon to the batter.
2. Put a little fat in deep patty tins and get this very hot, pour in the mixture and bake for about 10–15 minutes near the top of a hot oven (450°F.—Gas Mark 7).
3. Serve hot with crisp salad.

Wine and cheese party

One of the easiest and most popular parties of today is a cheese and wine buffet.
Choose a good selection of cheeses on 1 or 2 plates or boards:
Fairly mild cheese: Cheddar, Cheshire.
A soft cheese like Camembert or Brie.
Cream cheese like Demi-sel or Cottage cheese.
Biting cheese: Danish blue, Stilton, Gorgonzola. Have plenty of French bread, crisp bread, biscuits, butter.
Dishes of celery and apples or crisp lettuce.
Serve a good red Burgundy—such as a Beaujolais or Maçon at room temperature and a white Burgundy—Chablis or white Bordeaux—dry Graves } slightly chilled

Autumn glory sundae

No cooking time

You will need:

- 1 family brick ice-cream
- a few blackberries
- angelica or small mint leaves to garnish
- 4–6 tablespoons blackberry brandy (or blackberry syrup)

1. Place spoonsfuls of ice-cream into 4–6 glasses.
2. Pour blackberry brandy over each portion then add more ice-cream.
3. Scatter blackberries over the top of each ice and add mint leaves or leaves of angelica by each berry.
4. Serve at once.

Baked oranges with ice-cream

Cooking time 15 minutes

- 1 block of ice-cream
- 2 oz. sugar
- little lemon juice or sherry
- 4 oranges
- 1 oz. butter

1. Peel and slice the oranges into rings.
2. Put into a shallow dish with the butter, sugar and lemon juice or sherry and bake for about 15 minutes in a moderately hot oven (400°F.—Gas Mark 5).
3. Arrange round the block of ice-cream.
4. The oranges should be very hot to form a good contrast to the ice-cream.

Banana fluff

No Cooking

You will need:

- 5 bananas
- $\frac{1}{4}$ pint cream
- 2 egg whites
- 2 tablespoons icing sugar
- about 12 sponge fingers
- little lemon juice

1 Whisk cream until stiff and egg whites until very stiff.
2 Mash 4 bananas with sugar and lemon juice. Fold cream into this, then add egg whites.
3 Line shallow dish with the sponge fingers and pile banana mixture on top.
4 Decorate with remaining banana.
5 Try this with fresh raspberries or strawberries when a luxury sweet is required.

Chocolate almond mousse

Cooking time 8–10 minutes

4 oz. plain chocolate
little cream or top of milk
2 eggs
2 oz. chopped blanched almonds
sponge cake

1 Chop the chocolate into small pieces.
2 Dissolve in a basin over hot water.
3 Add the yolks of the eggs and 2 tablespoons cream or milk.
4 Whisk or beat over hot water, until thick and creamy.
5 Cool, then add chopped almonds and whisked egg whites.
6 Put into glasses and serve with fingers of sponge.

And mocha mousse

Recipe as above but use strong coffee instead of cream and, if wished, add a little sugar.

Chocolate ice-cream pie

Cooking time 8–10 minutes

You will need for 6–8 servings:

approximately 8 oz. chocolate wholemeal biscuits
small piece of plain or milk chocolate
little whipped cream
4 oz. butter
1 vanilla ice-cream block
1 strawberry ice-cream block (both large size blocks)

1 Put the biscuits on a piece of greaseproof paper, cover with another piece of paper and roll firmly until fine crumbs.
2 Mix in a basin with the cool melted butter and form into a flan shape in a dish.
3 If wished you can put into a very moderate oven (350°F.—Gas Mark 3) for about 8–10 minutes to give added crispness, but the biscuit flan is perfectly all right if not cooked at all.
4 Allow to cool and when ready to serve, fill with vanilla and strawberry ice-creams, spreading these slightly so you have a 'streaky' effect.
5 Top with whipped cream and coarsely grated chocolate.
6 You can prepare the filling before your meal if you put the pie into the coldest part of the refrigerator.

Coupe Jacques mixed fruit sundae

No cooking

ice-cream
fruit salad—fresh or canned
whipped cream
Melba sauce (see page 72)
blanched almonds
canned or maraschino cherries

1 Chop and brown the almonds lightly under the grill or in the oven.
2 Arrange the fruit and ice-cream in individual glasses.
3 Top with a little Melba sauce, nuts, cream and cherries.

Delicious chestnut mousse

for a special occasion

Cooking time 10 minutes

You will need:

1 lb. chestnuts (or use chestnut purée)
½ gill water
2 oz. sugar
2 eggs
¼ pint cream
1 teaspoon powder gelatine

to decorate

little grated chocolate
vanilla essence
crystallized violet petals

1 Slit the skins so they do not burst, rub through sieve after boiling steadily for 10 minutes.
2 Separate eggs.
3 Beat egg yolks and sugar over hot water until thick, dissolve gelatine in the ½ gill very hot water, add to egg yolks.
4 Stir in chestnut purée and vanilla essence.
5 When stiffening, fold in cream and stiffly beaten egg whites.
6 Pile into glasses and top with crystallized violet petals and a little grated chocolate.

Fried peaches

Cooking time 3 minutes

You will need:

4 large fresh or 8 halves of canned peaches
little rum or brandy for special occasions
2 oz. butter
2 oz. sugar

1 Heat the butter and add the peaches sprinkled with rum or brandy.
2 Cook steadily for about 3 minutes, adding the sugar.
3 Serve when the sugar has melted and given a brown sauce.
4 Ice-cream or cream makes this a wonderful sweet.

Fruits flambés

Cooking time 5–10 minutes

1 Heat plenty of butter in a frying pan, then dust halves of skinned pears, peaches, etc., with brown sugar.
2 Toss in the hot butter until golden on the outside.
3 Lift on to a hot plate—pour over warmed brandy or Curaçao and ignite.
4 Serve at once.

Orange chocolate pie

Cooking time few minutes

You will need for 4–6 servings:

6 oz. digestive biscuits
3 oz. plain chocolate, grated
2 teaspoons lemon juice
1 oz. butter
½ orange jelly
1 small can evaporated milk
cream (optional)

1 Put the biscuits between 2 sheets of greaseproof paper or foil, crush them into fine crumbs with rolling pin.
2 Heat the butter and 2 oz. chocolate in a basin over a pan of hot water until melted.
3 Put the biscuit crumbs in a bowl, pour in the chocolate and butter and mix well with a fork.
4 Line the base and sides of a buttered 8-inch pie-plate or sandwich tin with the mixture. Press firmly into position.
5 Meanwhile, dissolve the jelly in a little hot water.
6 Make up to ¼ pint, leave in a cold place.
7 Whisk the milk with the lemon juice until thick.
8 When the jelly is almost setting, add it to the milk, whisking throughout.
9 Pile the mixture into the prepared case.
10 Leave to set. Decorate with remaining chocolate, and cream if used.

Peach surprise

No cooking

You will need:

2 large fresh peaches or 4 peach halves from canned fruit
small pieces of preserved or crystallized ginger
1 tablespoon ground almonds
4 thin slices of Swiss roll or pieces of sponge cake
little whipped cream
few maraschino cherries or canned cherries and syrup
whipped cream

1 Skin peaches by dipping them first into very hot water for a few seconds only, then into cold water.
2 Halve and remove stones.
3 Put the Swiss roll on to dishes and soak lightly with cherry syrup.
4 Mix about 2–3 tablespoons whipped cream with cherries, finely chopped ginger and ground almonds. Sweeten if wished.
5 Press into centre of peaches in place of the stones and turn upside-down on Swiss roll.
6 Pipe cream round fruit, decorate with cherries and serve with ice-cream.

Peach Melba

No cooking

Peach and other fruit Melbas are made in the same way as Strawberry Melba (see page 91). Use skinned fresh, or canned peaches. If using fresh peaches lower gently into boiling water for 30 seconds. Lift into cold water and skin. Do not skin too soon before serving or the fruit will turn a bad colour.

Raspberry sponge mould

No cooking

You will need:

1 packet frozen or 1 can raspberries
3 good-sized eating apples
6 sponge cakes (small sugar ones)
sugar to taste

1 Drain away surplus juice from canned raspberries; keep this to add to jellies or fruit drinks.
2 Line the sides and bottom of a mould with sliced sponge cake. Keep some for the top.
3 Peel and grate the apples, mix the raspberries and a very little sugar if wished.
4 Pack into the sponge-lined mould and cover with more sponge cake.
5 Put a saucer or small plate on top and a weight and leave overnight.
6 Top with remaining fruit.
7 This is excellent served with ice-cream.

Rum and coffee gâteau

No cooking

You will need:

1 sponge round about 7 inches in diameter (it can be a stale cake)
1 tablespoon rum
½ pint strong coffee
2–4 oz. split walnuts
4–5 oz. butter
4–5 oz. sugar (castor)
2 egg yolks
little water icing

1 Line a cake tin, the same size as the sponge cake, with greased paper.
2 Split the cake across to make about 4 layers.
3 Cream together the butter and sugar until very soft and light.
4 Work in the 2 egg yolks, 1 gill of the coffee and the rum.
5 The mixture will doubtless have a curdled appearance, but this does not matter.
6 Put 1 layer sponge cake in the bottom of the tin.
7 Pour over enough coffee to moisten this.
8 Spread with a thin layer of the coffee mixture.
9 Put the next layer of sponge over the top, moisten with coffee and spread with coffee mixture.
10 Continue in this way until you put on the top layer of sponge.
11 Simply moisten this with coffee.
12 Put a piece of paper over the top of the cake and put a weight on top. Leave overnight.
13 Remove the weight and paper and gently pour away any coffee that may have come to the top of the cake.
14 Turn out of tin.
15 Cover the top with a water icing and decorate with halved walnuts.

Strawberry Alaska

Cooking time 3–5 minutes

You will need:

1 sponge cake
5 egg whites
block of ice-cream
1 packet frozen strawberries
5 oz. castor sugar

1 Put the sponge cake into a dish and soak it well with strawberry syrup.
2 Arrange the strawberries on top with the firm ice-cream.
3 Put egg whites into a basin and whisk until very firm.
4 Fold in the sugar.
5 Pile the meringue over the top of ice-cream and fruit and bake for 3–5 minutes in a very hot oven (475–500°F.—Gas Mark 8–9).

Strawberry Melba

No cooking

You will need:

ice-cream
Melba sauce (see page 72)
strawberries
blanched almonds
whipped cream

1 Arrange the fruit and ice-cream in individual glasses.
2 Top with Melba sauce, rosettes of whipped cream and chopped blanched almonds.

Pears suprême

Cooking time 8 minutes

You will need:

8 canned pear halves
¼ pint pear syrup from can
2 tablespoons redcurrant jelly
2 oz. blanched almonds
¼ pint red wine
cream

1 Put the jelly, wine and syrup into a saucepan and heat until the jelly has melted.
2 Arrange the pears in a shallow dish, together with the almonds, pour over the wine sauce and allow to cool.
3 Serve with cream or ice-cream.

Frosted peaches

No cooking

You will need:

8 canned peach halves
1 oz. chopped nuts
1 oz. ground almonds
¼ pint thick cream
1 oz. chopped Maraschino cherries
8 Maraschino cherries to decorate

1 Whip the cream lightly, then add the ground almonds, cherries and nuts.
2 Put the halved peaches, together with the syrup from the can into the freezing trays of a refrigerator.
3 Fill with the cream mixture, and top with the cherries.
4 Frost for approximately 25 minutes, then serve with the lightly frozen syrup round the halved peaches.
5 DO NOT FREEZE for any longer, otherwise the fruit will be too hard.

Frosted pears

Recipe as above, but use chopped ginger instead of nuts.

BUTTER

Index

D

E

K

L

M

N

O

P

S

Refrigerator Dishes

Making the Most of your Refrigerator

Care of your refrigerator

With use, a layer of frost develops on the outside of the evaporator (frozen food compartment). This should never be allowed to become thicker than about ½ inch to keep the cabinet working at the correct temperature, otherwise you are not only consuming more gas, electricity or oil, but are slowing up the efficiency of the refrigerator. Some refrigerators have an automatic system, termed "automatic defrosters", which removes this ice.
With other cabinets, however, you have to either switch to defrost, or switch the refrigerator off until the snow has melted and then pour away the liquid. Do not try to chip this layer of frost off the evaporator, otherwise you may cause damage to the mechanism.
There is no maintenance of the mechanism in a refrigerator that has to be done by the housewife and in many cases the mechanism is completely sealed. In the event of any problems do call a refrigerator specialist.
Obviously a refrigerator must be kept spotlessly clean, but do not use strong smelling disinfectants or soap. Warm water with a few drops of vinegar or a little bicarbonate of soda added are quite sufficient to keep the refrigerator clean and pleasant smelling. As the rubber gasket comes into contact with one's hands, be very careful to wipe this well.
Remember that a refrigerator should not cause your ordinary foods to become excessively cold or frozen. If it does, the cold control is set at too low a temperature.

Using the frozen food compartment

Unless you have a refrigerator that combines a home freezer the frozen food compartment is not meant for indefinite storage of frozen foods—whether home or commercially frozen. Follow the directions on the packet for the correct time of storage.
Never try to re-freeze commercially frozen foods, for they have been frozen at a very low temperature and if they once thaw out must be used at once.
The frozen food compartment means that you have a plentiful supply of ice cubes to serve with drinks and that you can store frozen foods for several days. Always make certain that you have ice in the trays, ready for drinks, and renew this when the refrigerator is defrosted and cleaned.
Freezing, like cooking, alters the original state of food, and so in order to get the best result from the recipes in this section it is important to freeze at the speed suggested. If you have turned the cold control indicator to the coldest setting for making ice cream, do remember to turn back to the normal setting when you have finished, otherwise you will find the foods in the storage compartment becoming too hard.

Saving space in your refrigerator

No matter how large the refrigerator one has, there are occasions when one feels lack of space. Remember that polythene bags, foil and to a lesser extent greaseproof paper, are all good protections for the food and they take up less space than if they were kept in dishes. **NEVER PACK YOUR REFRIGERATOR SO TIGHTLY THAT THE AIR CANNOT CIRCULATE,** or you will get a very stale and unpleasant smell.

Wise storing of foods in a refrigerator

Never put steaming foods into a refrigerator. The steam causes an intermingling of smells and causes condensation in the cabinet.
The circulation of air is from the bottom to the top of a refrigerator, so always place strong-smelling foods, such as fish, near the top so there is far less possibility of other foods becoming affected.
The majority of foods should be covered, in particular those that give out strong smells and those which readily absorb strong smells.
The way in which you store foods in a refrigerator makes a tremendous amount of difference to their flavour and texture and the following is considered the best way to store individual items of food:

Bacon
Keep covered with foil or plastic bags and store towards the bottom of the refrigerator, because bacon readily dries.

Cheese
In many refrigerators there is a special cheese compartment, often in the door, and if cheese is placed in this it will not become too hard or dry. Ordinary cheese is not really suitable for refrigerator storing, but cream cheese should be kept in the cabinet. Place the cheese fairly low down in the refrigerator if there is no special compartment for it.

Eggs
In most modern refrigerators there is an egg rack in the door and if space permits eggs should always be kept in the refrigerator.

Fats
Many refrigerators have a special compartment to keep butter, etc., under the right conditions, at the same time keeping it sufficiently soft so it will spread easily. Always keep fats very well covered in their wrappings or foil.

Fruit
Never put bananas, melon or pineapple into the refrigerator for a long period since they do cause a rather unpleasant smell. Melons and pineapples can be placed in the refrigerator for an hour or so before serving since they taste better if slightly chilled. It is doubtful whether space will permit you to store all fruit in the cabinet, but fruit salads, etc., should be kept on the shelves to chill.

Meat
It is better to leave raw meat uncovered, but cooked meat should be placed in plastic boxes, bags or foil to prevent it becoming dry.

Fish
Fish should be stored as near the freezing compartment as possible because of its strong smell. An ideal place to put the fish is in the defrosting tray if this is large enough. Cover the fish with foil and you can put a few ice cubes round it if leaving it on a flat dish or plate.

Milk
It is essential to keep milk and cream covered when storing in a refrigerator. Replace the caps on milk bottles or put foil over the top of jugs.

Canned foods
Many canned foods, such as meat and fish, etc., have a better flavour if they are served cold and while there is no necessity to store canned foods they can be placed in the refrigerator for a short time before opening. When canned foods have been opened transfer them on to a plate or dish and keep in the refrigerator.

Salads
Green salads and green vegetables must be stored with great care. Unlike many foods they need a certain amount of humidity to keep them fresh. Salads should be stored in the special salad container of the refrigerator, or in plastic boxes. Store cucumbers, tomatoes and radishes in separate containers or boxes so they do not become too damp.

Vegetables
As for salads.

Wines, etc.
Always stand bottles of wine or soft drinks upright. White wines and drinks that should be served cold are best placed in the refrigerator just before serving, i.e., for a limited time only. Bottles of beer and lager can be kept in the refrigerator for some little time.

Storing frozen foods

Follow most carefully the instructions given by the manufacturers of frozen foods as to the length of time they should be stored in a refrigerator. If frozen food has been left in the warm air and allowed to defrost do not try and re-freeze it but use it straight away. Ensure you have a plentiful supply of ice in the frozen food compartment by keeping the ice trays filled with water.

To remove ice cubes

Many ice-making trays have a lever or method of removing ice cubes, but if not hold the tray of ice cubes upside down for a few minutes under the cold tap.

To serve the ice cubes transfer to a chilled bowl or a special ice container and serve with tongs.

When you desire an unusual number of ice cubes for a party, take the cubes from the ice trays, transfer to the defrosting tray under the freezing compartment, where they will keep for some time; then fill up the trays with fresh water.

Attractive ice cubes

The cubes you use for adding to drinks can be made most attractive in appearance and here are some suggestions:

1. Half fill the tray with water, putting the divider for ice cubes in position.
2. Allow this water to freeze, then arrange cherries, mint leaves and crystallised flowers on the ice, which should not be quite firm.
3. Cover with more water and continue freezing.
4. In this way you keep the mint leaves etc., in the centre of the ice cubes.

   or

   Colour the water with vegetable colourings.

   or

   Freeze diluted fruit juices or squash and use as an accompaniment to drinks.

To crush ice

The easiest way to crush ice is to put it on a clean tea cloth and crush with a rolling pin or small hammer.

Cocktails and Iced Drinks

Serving cocktails and iced drinks

As well as adding ice to your cocktail mixture make sure the glasses are pleasantly cold.

Where you wish the drinks to be *very* cold put the glasses in the refrigerator for a short time.

Frosting the rim of glasses looks most attractive for parties. Damp the rim of the glass with water or coat with a very little egg white, dip in fine castor sugar and put into the refrigerator to chill.

When wished the rim can be dipped in fruit juice which tends to slightly colour the sugar.

Cocktails with gin as a basis

Put cracked ice into a cocktail shake or mixer and shake or stir. Use a glass rod or silver spoon for blending and do not leave mixture too long in a metal container.

Martini (dry)

Use 1 part dry Martini to 2 parts gin. Serve with little cracked ice and top with lemon peel.

A dash of orange bitters can be added.

Martini (sweet)

Use I part sweet Martini vermouth to 2 parts gin. Serve with cracked ice and top with maraschino cherry.

Orange blossom

Use equal quantities of orange juice and gin, or orange squash and gin. Add to cracked ice and shake or mix.

Martinez

Mix a dash of orange bitters and a little maraschino to equal parts of dry Martini and gin. Serve with cracked ice and top with an olive and/or lemon rind.

Champagne cocktail

you will need for 1 glass:

1 lump sugar
2 - 3 dashes Angostura bitters
2 pieces lemon rind
ice cubes
champagne to fill glass

1 Put the lump sugar into glass with the bitters.
2 Squeeze 1 piece lemon rind firmly to extract oil of lemon into glass.
3 Add 1 ice cube to the cold glass then top with cold champagne.
4 Squeeze the other piece of lemon rind and decorate glass with this.
Some people like to use orange instead of lemon, and it is possible to use a dash of brandy with the bitters.

Mint julep

you will need for 1 glass:

1 large sprig mint
little sugar
crushed ice
whisky

1 Put the mint, sugar, ice and whisky into the glasses and leave in the refrigerator for some little time to become very cold.
2 Top with more crushed ice if wished.

Egg flip

you will need for 1 glass:

1 egg
$\frac{1}{4}$ pint cold milk
sugar to taste
little crushed ice

1 Whisk the egg, milk and sugar together until very fluffy.
2 Pour over crushed iced and serve in tall glass.

Brandy egg flip

you will need for 1 glass:

1 egg
1 tablespoon brandy
$\frac{1}{4}$ pint cold milk
sugar to taste

1 Whisk egg, brandy, milk and sugar together until very fluffy.
2 Pour over crushed ice and serve in a tall glass.

Creamy egg nog (1)

you will need for 1 glass:

1 egg
¼ pint cold milk
sugar to taste
1 tablespoon whipped cream or ice cream

1 Whisk egg, milk and sugar together until light and fluffy.
2 Put into an ice cold tumbler and top with the whipped or ice cream.

Creamy egg nog (2)

you will need for 1 glass:

1 egg
1 - 2 teaspoons sugar
1 tablespoon thick cream
⅜ pint cold milk

1 Put the egg and sugar into a basin and whisk until 'fluffy'.
2 Beat in the cream and milk.
3 Chill slightly.

Variations:

Top with grated nutmeg.
Add 2 teaspoons cocoa to the egg and sugar.
Use ½ coffee and ½ milk.

Claret cup

you will need for 18 - 24 glasses:

3 oz. sugar
¼ pint water
juice and rind 2 lemons
juice and rind 2 oranges
2 pints claret
ice cubes
little soda water
mint, borage, cucumber, apple and orange for decoration

1 Boil sugar and water with fruit rinds.
2 Strain over fresh fruit juices.
3 Add the claret.
4 Put into bowl over ice cubes and just before serving add soda water.
5 Decorate with the sliced cucumber, sprigs of borage or mint and the sliced apple or orange.

Cider cup

Recipe as for claret cup substituting 2 pints of cider for claret.

Fruit cup

Recipe as for claret cup substituting 1 pint apple juice and 1 pint ginger ale for claret.

Summer cream punch

you will need for 8 - 10 glasses

2 jars or cans thick cream or ½ pint cream
2 teaspoons sugar
½ pint Madeira or similar wine
soda water

1 Put the cream into a large jug.
2 Stir in the sugar and gradually blend in the wine.
3 Leave in a cool place until ready to serve.
4 Half fill the glasses with this mixture and top with soda water.
5 Add a little ice if wished.

Fruit punch

you will need for 8 - 10 glasses:

about 2 oz. mint leaves
1 - 2 oz. sugar
1½ pints strong China or Indian tea
¼ pint lemon squash
little crushed ice
1 large bottle lemonade

1 Crush the mint leaves and put into a large jug with the sugar.
2 Strain over the hot tea.
3 Add lemon squash and leave until cold.
4 Two-thirds fill tall glasses with the drained tea mixture.
5 Add little crushed ice and fill with lemonade.

Summer punch

you will need for 8 - 10 glasses:

4 oranges
3 lemons
1 grapefruit
4 oz. sugar
2 pints soda water or water
1 banana (optional)
fresh fruit — strawberries, orange slices, etc.

1 Squeeze the oranges, lemons and grapefruit.
2 Dissolve the sugar in a little boiling water and add to the juice.
3 Chill thoroughly.
4 Add the soda water, sliced banana and other fruit and serve.

Lemonade

you will need:

2 small lemons
1 pint boiling water
sugar or glucose to taste

1 Grate the rind from the lemons, being careful to use only the yellow 'zest'.
2 Put this into a jug and pour over the freshly boiling water.
3 Add lemon juice and sugar.
4 Leave until cold and strain.

Orangeade

(illustrated on the cover)

you will need:

2 oranges
1 pint boiling water
sugar to taste

1 Grate the rind from the oranges, being care ful to use only the orange 'zest'.
2 Put this into a jug and pour over the freshly boiling water.
3 Add the orange juice and sugar.
4 Leave until cold and strain.

Pineappleade

you will need:

1 large can pineapple chunks
rind and juice 3 lemons
$1\frac{1}{2}$ pints water
2 - 3 oz. sugar
soda water or water
crushed ice

1 Finely chop the pineapple, being careful that the juice is not wasted.
2 Put pineapple, lemon rind and juice, pineapple syrup, water and sugar into pan.
3 Bring to the boil, and simmer gently for 1 or 2 minutes only.
4 Cool.
5 Dilute with water or soda water when serving, and serve with crushed ice.

Rhubarbade

you will need:

1 lb. ripe rhubarb
2 sliced lemons
2 - 3 oz. sugar
$1\frac{1}{2}$ pints water
soda water

1 Wash and cut the rhubarb into 1-$1\frac{1}{2}$ inch lengths.
2 Put the rhubarb into a saucepan together with the sliced lemons and suga...
3 Add the water and bring to the boil.
4 Cook until tender.
5 Take off the heat and allow to cool. This drink is better left to stand for some little while for the flavour to come out.
6 Pour off the juice and dilute with a little extra water or soda water.
7 Serve in tall jugs with the rhubarb and lemons left in.

Gooseberry fluff

you will need for 6 - 8 glasses:

1 lb. gooseberries
2 lemons, sliced
2 - 3 oz. sugar
$\frac{3}{4}$ pint water
$1\frac{1}{2}$ pints soda water
mint to decorate

1 Wash, top and tail the gooseberries.
2 Put the gooseberries into a saucepan, together with the sliced lemons and sugar.
3 Add the water and bring to the boil.
4 Simmer for 1—2 minutes until the gooseberries just split.
5 Take off the heat and allow to cool.
6 Put a little of the liquid into the bottom of tumblers and top with soda water just before serving.
7 Decorate with some of the gooseberries, lemon and mint.

Grapefruit soda

you will need for 4 glasses:

2 grapefruit
sugar to taste
soda water
ice cream

1 Squeeze the juice from the grapefruit and sweeten to taste.
2 Divide between four tall glasses or tumblers.
3 When ready to serve, top up the fruit juice with soda water, leaving a little space for the ice cream.
4 Add spoonfuls of ice cream and serve.

Summertime soda

you will need for 1 glass:

juice 1 orange
juice 1 lemon
juice 1 grapefruit
soda water
1 tablespoon ice cream

1 Put the juice of the fruit in the bottom of a long tumbler.
2 Pour over soda water nearly filling the glass.
3 Add the ice cream.
4 Serve at once.

Banana ambrosia

you will need for 1 large or 2 small glasses:

1 banana
sugar to taste
lemon juice
$\frac{3}{8}$ pint milk
cinnamon (optional)

1. Mash the banana with a little sugar and lemon juice.
2. Beat in the cold milk.
3. Pour into a glass and top with a little cinnamon, if liked.

Banana frappé

you will need for 1 glass:

1 banana
squeeze lemon juice
little sugar
ice cream
$\frac{1}{4}$ pint milk
few chopped nuts to decorate

1. Mash $\frac{3}{4}$ the banana and put into a dish with the lemon juice and sugar.
2. Add a spoonful ice cream and the very cold milk.
3. Whisk together until frothy.
4. Pour into a tall glass and decorate with the remainder of the banana, sliced, and a few chopped nuts.
5. Serve with a spoon.

Blackcurrant and lemon frappé

you will need for 1 glass:

1 tablespoon blackcurrant syrup
squeeze lemon juice
1 tablespoon ice cream
good $\frac{1}{4}$ pint milk
lemon rings to decorate

1. Put the blackcurrant syrup into a basin, together with the lemon juice and the ice cream.
2. Add the milk.
3. Whisk until frothy.
4. Pour into tall glasses and decorate with lemon rings.

Mocha flip

you will need for 1 glass:

1 tablespoon mocha syrup (see page 16)
cracked ice
soda water
mint leaves to decorate

1. Put the syrup into the glasses over cracked ice.
2. Top with soda water, and decorate with mint leaves.

Mocha milk shake (1)

you will need for 1 glass:

1 tablespoon mocha syrup (see page 16)
$\frac{3}{4}$ tumbler cold milk
little cracked ice

1. Whisk syrup and milk together well.
2. Pour over cracked ice.

Mocha milk shake (2)

you will need for 1 glass:

1 tablespoon chocolate ice cream
$\frac{1}{4}$ tumbler coffee
$\frac{1}{2}$ tumbler cold milk
little sugar if wished

1. Whisk all ingredients together.
2. Pour into glass.

Orange milk shake

you will need for 2 glasses:

juice 2 oranges
$\frac{1}{2}$ pint milk
sprig mint and slice orange for decoration

1. Strain juice from oranges and chill.
2. Whisk with the very cold milk.
3. Pour into glasses and top with mint and orange slice.

Plantation milk shake

you will need for 2-3 glasses:

1 tablespoon peanut butter
3 tablespoons sugar
pinch salt
1 pint milk
$\frac{1}{4}$ teaspoon vanilla essence
pinch grated nutmeg

1. Place peanut butter, sugar and salt in a bowl.
2. Add 2 tablespoons milk.
3. Whip with beater until smooth.
4. Add remaining milk gradually and beat until smooth.
5. Add vanilla.
6. Chill in covered jar in refrigerator until ready to use.
7. When serving top with the grated nutmeg.

Iced chocolate (1)

you will need for 1 glass:

1 good teaspoon cocoa with 1 teaspoon sugar
or
2 heaped teaspoons chocolate with 1 teaspoon sugar
¾ tumbler cold milk
few drops vanilla essence
few crushed ice cubes
whipped cream (optional)

Whisk chocolate or cocoa and sugar with the milk until light and fluffy, add vanilla essence.
2 Pour over the crushed ice and if desired top with a little lightly whipped cream.

Chocolate milk shake

you will need for 1 glass:

1 tablespoon chocolate ice cream
¾ tumbler cold milk

Whisk ice cream and cold milk together until soft and light.

Iced chocolate (2)

you will need for 1 glass:

1 tablespoon chocolate syrup (see page 15)
¾ tumbler milk
little crushed ice

Whisk chocolate syrup and milk together until well blended.
2 Pour over crushed ice.

Chocolate soda

you will need for 1 glass:

1 tablespoon chocolate syrup (see page 15)
soda water
crushed ice (optional)

1 Put the chocolate syrup into each glass.
2 Top with soda water.
3 A little crushed ice could be added if wished.

Chocolate cocktail

you will need for 1 glass:

2 teaspoons chocolate syrup (see page 15) or 1 teaspoon chocolate powder
1 egg yolk
2 tablespoons Chartreuse
2 tablespoons port wine or maraschino
cracked ice

Put all the ingredients and ice into cocktail shake or mixer.

Cafe Borgia

(illustrated on the cover)

you will need for 1 glass:

2 teaspoons drinking chocolate
1 teaspoon coffee extract
1 slice orange
3 teaspoons boiling water
approx. ⅓ pint cold milk

1 Put the drinking chocolate and coffee into a container.
2 Add the boiling water and stir.
3 Add the milk and whisk well.
4 Serve with a slice of orange on the glass.

Chocolate milk shake

you will need for 1 glass:

1 dessertspoon chocolate powder or 1 good teaspoon cocoa
½ tumbler cold milk
sugar to taste
1 tablespoon ice cream

1 Whisk chocolate powder or sieved cocoa with cold milk until frothy.
2 Add sugar to taste.
3 Add the ice cream.

Chocolate peppermint milk shake

you will need for 1 glass:

¼ pint milk
1 tablespoon chocolate syrup (see page 15)
few drops peppermint oil
1 tablespoon vanilla ice cream (about 1 inch square)
1 small sprig mint for decoration

1 Put all the ingredients into a screw top jar with a well fitting lid and screw down firmly.
2 Shake briskly for about ½ minute.
3 Pour into a glass and serve immediately with drinking straws.
4 The sprig of mint should be placed over the edge of the glass.

Iced coffee

you will need:

coffee
crushed ice
mint
lemon slices
ice cream (optional)
lightly whipped cream (optional)

1 Make coffee in your favourite way and allow to get very cold in the refrigerator.
2 Pour over crushed ice and top with mint or slices of lemon.
3 If preferred, pour over ice cream or over crushed ice and top with a little lightly whipped cream.

Iced coffee de luxe

you will need for 4 glasses:

1¼ - 1½ pints strong coffee
ice cubes
sugar to taste
1 jar or can or ¼ pint thick cream

1 Make the coffee and allow to get really cold.
2 Put ice cubes at the bottom of 4 tall glasses and fill to within an inch of the top with the coffee.
3 Add a little sugar.
4 Whip the cream and pile or pipe on top just before serving.

Austrian iced coffee

you will need for 1 glass:

little cracked ice
1 tablespoon whipped cream
little sugar to taste
¾ tumbler hot coffee
little grated nutmeg if wished

1 Put the ice and whipped cream into tumbler, together with sugar to taste.
2 Pour over the hot coffee, and add grated nutmeg, then serve at once.

This combination of hot and cold flavours is delicious, but if wished the coffee can be ice cold instead of hot.

Frosted iced coffee

you will need for 1 glass:

egg white
sugar
little cracked ice
¾ tumbler ice cold coffee
1 tablespoon coffee or vanilla ice crea

1 First frost the rim of the glass by dippin in little egg white then castor sugar.
2 Put the ice in the tumbler, top with the coffee adding sugar to taste.
3 Top with the ice cream.

Hawaiian iced coffee

you will need:

½ pint very strong cold coffee
¼ pint chilled pineapple juice
1 pint soft coffee ice cream
walnuts

1 Mix the coffee, pineapple juice and ice crean with a beater.
2 Pour into glasses and decorate each with walnut.

Mocha coffee

you will need:

½ pint very strong cold coffee
5 tablespoons melted chocolate
1 pint coffee ice cream
little grated chocolat

1 Put coffee, chocolate and ice cream into bowl and beat to a smooth consistency.
2 Pour into glasses and sprinkle with chocolate

Viennese iced coffee

Recipe as for iced coffee de luxe, adding little grated chocolate over the top of th cream.

Spiced coffee

Recipe as for iced coffee de luxe, adding abou 1 teaspoon of mixed spice in the coffee whil hot. Grate a little nutmeg over the cream.

Coffee cream soda

Recipe as for iced coffee de luxe substituting 1 tablespoon of vanilla or coffee ice cream for the ice cubes at the bottom of the glass.

Viennese velvet

you will need:

vanilla flavoured ice cream
strong hot coffee
vanilla flavoured whipped cream

1 Fill several large glasses to near the top with vanilla flavoured ice cream.
2 Pour very strong hot coffee over the ice cream.
3 Top with whipped cream flavoured with vanilla.

Coffee milk shake

you will need:

coffee powder
milk
ice or ice cream
sugar

1 Mix together coffee powder and milk with a little sugar and ice or ice cream.
2 Whisk until frothy.

Coffee mint julep

you will need:

1 oz. sugar
1 pint moderately strong coffee
juice 1 lemon
juice 1 orange
mint leaves
crushed mint
sprigs mint to decorate

1 Dissolve the sugar in the coffee, then add to lemon and orange juice and cool by pouring over crushed mint leaves in a jug.
2 Put crushed ice into tall glasses, top with the strained coffee mint liquid.
3 Top with mint sprigs.

Making and storing fruit syrups, etc.

When fruit is plentiful and cheap it is worth while making your own fruit syrups and storing them for several days in the refrigerator.

Soft fruit syrup

you will need for each lb. fruit:

about 3 - 4 oz. sugar
juice 1 lemon
1 pint boiling water

1 Crush the fruit, cover with the sugar and lemon juice and leave for several hours.
2 Pour over the boiling water, stir well once or twice crushing the fruit as much as possible.
3 Cool, strain and keep in bottles or jugs in the refrigerator.

Hard fruit syrup

you will need for each lb. fruit:*

3 - 4 oz. sugar
juice and grated rind 1 lemon
1 pint water

* use ripe plums, damsons, rhubarb, gooseberries, etc.

1 Put all the ingredients into a pan and simmer gently for a few minutes.
2 Strain when the mixture is quite cold, and keep in bottles or jugs in the refrigerator.

Chocolate syrup

you will need:

1 oz. cocoa
3 - 4 oz. sugar
$\frac{1}{4}$ pint water
1 level teaspoon vanilla essence

1 Put all the ingredients into a saucepan, and heat gently for several minutes until slightly syrupy.
2 Put into a screw topped jar and use as required.

This can be stored in the refrigerator, and used as the basis for chocolate drinks.

Coffee syrup

you will need:

3 - 4 oz. sugar for caramel	½ pint very strong coffee*
3 tablespoons water	2 - 3 oz. sugar for sweetening

* If using freshly ground coffee make up with twice the usual amount of coffee, i.e. 2 tablespoons to ½ pint water.

1 Put the sugar and water for the caramel into a strong saucepan, and heat gently, stirring all the time, until the sugar has dissolved.
2 Boil steadily, without stirring until golden brown—not too dark.
3 Add the coffee and sugar and heat together until the caramel has been absorbed.

This can be stored in the refrigerator, and used as the basis for coffee flavourings.

Lemon syrup

This is much more concentrated than lemonade, and so can be used diluted with more water, soda water etc., and takes up less space in a refrigerator.

you will need:

6 large or 8 small lemons	8 - 12 oz. sugar

1 Squeeze the juice from the lemons and put into the saucepan with the pared rinds—do not use much white pith otherwise it is bitter.
2 Add the sugar, and stir carefully until dissolved, then boil until slightly thickened.
3 Strain and store in bottles—this is very strong and only a spoonful is required.

Orange syrup

Make as lemon syrup using 6 good sized oranges instead of lemons. To give more 'bite add the juice and rind of 1 lemon.

Lime syrup

As lemon syrup using about 8 limes instead of lemons.

Tangerine syrup

As lemon syrup using 6 tangerines and 2 lemons.

Grapefruit syrup

As lemon syrup using 1 good sized grapefruit and 1 lemon.

Mixed fruit syrup

you will need:

2 lemons	½ grapefruit
2 oranges	12 oz. sugar

Make like lemon syrup.

Mocha syrup

you will need:

1 oz. cocoa	1 level teaspoon vanilla essence
4 oz. sugar	
¼ pint strong coffee	

1 Put all the ingredients into a saucepan, and heat gently for several minutes until slightly syrupy.
2 Put into a screw topped jar and use as required.

This can be stored in the refrigerator, and used as the basis for cold drinks.

Appetisers and Hors-d'oeuvre

The following recipes are all suitable to serve at the first course of a meal. Make sure they are well chilled in the refrigerator, since this improves the flavour.

Grapefruit cocktails

you will need:

2 grapefruit	sugar to taste
2 oranges	cherries or grapes to decorate
juice 1 lemon	
little sherry	

1 Halve the grapefruit and remove the pulp.
2 Mix this with the slices of orange, lemon juice, sherry, if wished, and sugar.
3 Pile back into the grapefruit cases, and decorate with the cherries or grapes.
4 Serve as cold as possible.

Grapefruit melon cocktails

you will need:

2 grapefruit
¼ medium sized melon
sprinkling powdered ginger
sugar
little sherry or lemon juice
crystallised ginger to decorate

1 Halve the grapefruit and take out the pulp.
2 Mix with diced melon or balls of melon, made with a vegetable scoop, ginger, sugar and sherry or lemon juice.
3 Pile back into grapefruit cases and decorate with ginger.
4 Serve as cold as possible.

To make shellfish cocktails

1 These should be served in glasses, preferably on ice, but otherwise on flat dishes.
2 It is possible to obtain special containers that fit inside a larger container that should be filled with ice, in this way keeping the fish mixture very cold.
3 As you serve with small forks and teaspoons make sure the lettuce is shredded very finely.
4 Arrange a layer of shredded lettuce on the bottom of the dish.
5 Add fish etc., with the sauce.
6 Garnish with lemon, chopped parsley, cucumber etc.

Shrimp or prawn cocktail (1)

you will need:

5 tablespoons thick mayonnaise
1 tablespoon tomato ketchup or thick tomato purée
1 tablespoon Worcestershire sauce
1 tablespoon lemon juice
1 teaspoon finely chopped onion
1 teaspoon finely chopped celery when in season or ¼ teaspoon celery salt to taste

1 Mix all the ingredients for the sauce together.
2 Shred the lettuce finely and put at the bottom of glasses.
3 Cover with prawns or shrimps and the sauce.
4 Garnish with lemon if wished.
5 Serve as cold as possible, arranging the glasses in another container of crushed ice if available.

Cocktail sauce

A savoury cocktail sauce can be made and stored in the refrigerator to use as required. It enables you to produce shellfish and other cocktails for an hors-d'oeuvre within a short time.

you will need:

¼ pint mayonnaise or salad dressing
2-3 tablespoons tomato purée or ketchup*
few drops Worcestershire sauce
few drops Tobasco or chilli sauce
seasoning
little cream
lemon juice

1 Blend the mayonnaise with the tomato purée or ketchup.
2 Add the sauces, seasoning, then cream and lemon juice to taste.

* This does not refer to the concentrated tomato purée obtainable in tubes or cans—but fresh tomato purée. If wishing to use the canned use 1 tablespoon only and extra milk or cream.

Crab cocktail

you will need:

lettuce
crabmeat
lemon slices
cocktail sauce (see above)

1 Shred lettuce finely, arrange flaked crab meat on top.
2 If using canned crab meat then moisten slightly with some of the sauce.
3 If using fresh crab meat then arrange layers of cocktail sauce and meat.
4 Garnish with sauce and slices of lemon.

Lobster cocktail

As crab, but garnish with 1 or 2 tiny claws as well as lemon.

Prawn or shrimp cocktail (2)

As crab, but arrange one or two prawns or shrimps in their shells round the rim of the glass if possible.

Mock shellfish cocktails

Use white fish instead of the more expensive shellfish. Cooked skate, turbot or halibut are particularly good.

Iced tomato cocktail

you will need:

1 can tomato juice
squeeze lemon juice
pinch celery salt
cayenne pepper
twist lemon peel

1 Mix together the tomato and lemon juice, celery salt and cayenne pepper.
2 Chill thoroughly, pour into glasses and top with a twist of lemon peel.

Iced tomato juice

you will need:

½ pint tomato juice
pinch cayenne pepper
pinch celery salt
little sherry, if wished
few drops Worcestershire sauce
little crushed ice
lemon slices or mint to garnish

1 Mix the tomato juice, seasonings, sherry and sauce together.
2 Pour over a little crushed ice and leave in the refrigerator until ready to serve.
3 Top with lemon slices or sprigs of mint.

Cold Soups

A cold soup is a delicious start to a meal in hot weather and can either be served slightly jellied or iced. Make sure the soup cups are cold as well. These types of soup look better in a cup than a soup plate.

Jellied soups

you will need:

¼ oz. gelatine
⅛ pint cold water
1 pint clear, brown or white stock (or tomato or chicken soup)

1 Dissolve gelatine in water over low heat.
2 Stir all the time and add to the stock or soup.
3 Leave until cool, then chill in the refrigerator.
4 In hot weather it is frequently preferable to serve either jellied soups, consommés or ice cold fruit purées in glass or china cups.

Jellied consommé

you will need:

12 oz. shin of beef
2 pints good stock
seasoning
1 onion
1 carrot
1 small piece celery
sprig parsley
bay leaf
1 dessertspoon sherry (optional)

To garnish:

slices cucumber or
lemon or smoked salmon

1 Cut the meat into small pieces and put them into the saucepan together with the other ingredients.
2 Simmer very gently for 1 hour.
3 Strain through several thicknesses of muslin.
4 Add the sherry, if used.
5 Allow to cool.
6 Garnish with slices or cucumber or lemon or smoked salmon.

If a clear consommé is required add 1 dessertspoon sherry, if desired, and put in a stiffly beaten egg white and clean egg shell. Simmer gently again for 20 minutes and then re-strain.

Mushroom consommé

you will need:

8 oz. mushrooms
1 pint chicken stock or water with 2 chicken bouillon cubes
¼ oz. powder gelatine
seasoning
lemon wedges

1 Shred the mushrooms finely and simmer for a few minutes only in the chicken stock.
2 Add the gelatine, and stir until dissolved, seasoning well.

3 Allow to set lightly, then put into cold soup cups, whisking on top with a fork.
4 Serve with wedges of lemon.

This is a very thick mushroom mixture, so the amount of mushrooms can be cut down to 3-4 oz. if wished.

Jellied tomato consommé

you will need:

1 bouillon cube
¼ pint water or white stock
about 1½ pints canned or bottled tomato juice
1 tablespoon finely chopped onion or chives
1 level tablespoon powdered gelatine
seasoning
good pinch celery salt
sprigs mint
small lemon wedges

1 Dissolve the bouillon cube in the water or stock.
2 Add to the tomato juice and simmer with the onion for about 5-10 minutes.
3 Pour over the powdered gelatine, which can be softened in 1 tablespoon cold water.
4 Stir until thoroughly dissolved.
5 Season well.
6 Allow to cool and just begin to stiffen.
7 Whisk lightly with a fork and pile into very cold soup cups.
8 Garnish with sprigs of mint and serve with lemon wedges.

Iced cherry soup

you will need:

1½ lb. cherries or 1 can cherries
water
sugar to taste
juice 1 lemon
few whole cherries
mint leaves

1 Cover fruit with water.
2 Simmer gently, adding sugar to taste and lemon juice.
3 Rub through a sieve.
4 Pour into freezing trays and freeze lightly.
5 Serve in soup cups and decorate with cherries and mint leaves.

Variations:

Iced cherry plum soup

Use the small rather 'sharp' plums known as cherry plums. A very little white wine added to the mixture gives an excellent flavour.

Iced crab-apple soup

Follow the recipe for iced cherry soup above, using crab-apples instead of cherries, adding a little cider if wished. Garnish with wedges of lemon.

Iced mixed soft fruit soup

use redcurrants and raspberries following recipe as above.

Iced cucumber soup

you will need:

1 medium sized cucumber
1 small chopped onion
½ oz. butter
½ pint stock
seasoning
⅛ pint milk or evaporated milk
lemon

1 Cut cucumber into pieces—leaving on some of the peel.
2 Fry onion in butter.
3 Add cucumber and half the stock and seasoning.
4 Simmer gently for 15 minutes.
5 Put through sieve or into electric blender to make purée.
6 Add milk and rest of stock and when cold pour into freezing tray.
7 Leave until lightly frosted.
8 Serve in soup cups garnished with lemon.

Cold mushroom soup

you will need:

8 oz. mushrooms
1 tablespoon finely chopped chives or spring onion
1 pint white stock
1 tablespoon cornflour
¼ pint milk
seasoning
2 tablespoons cream
little chopped parsley

1 Very finely chop the mushrooms.
2 Put into a saucepan with the chives and stock and simmer for about 10 minutes only.
3 Blend the cornflour with the milk.
4 Stir into the soup and cook until thickened.
5 Season well, and allow to cool.
6 When quite cold stir in the cream.
7 Put into soup cups and garnish with parsley.

Chilled mushroom cream soup

you will need:

6 oz. mushrooms	2 egg yolks
¼ pint water	3 - 4 tablespoons cream
2 teaspoons cornflour	chopped parsley
¾ pint milk	paprika pepper
seasoning	

1 Cut up the mushrooms into small pieces and simmer in the water for 5 minutes.
2 Blend the cornflour with the milk, add to the mushrooms, together with seasoning, bring to the boil.
3 Cook for a few minutes until very slightly thickened, remove from the heat, add the egg yolks beaten with the cream and cook, without boiling, for several minutes.
4 Cool then put into the refrigerator to become very cold, and transfer to soup cups.
5 Garnish with chopped parsley and paprika pepper.

Chilled summer chowder

you will need:

1 large onion	¾ pint milk
1 oz. butter or margarine	seasoning
1 pint stock (or water and bouillon cube)	¼ pint double cream, yoghourt or top of milk
2 oz. fine semolina	chopped chives or parsley

1 Peel and very thinly slice onion.
2 Cook slowly in the fat until pale gold.
3 Add stock, sprinkle in semolina and continue cooking until mixture thickens, stirring all the time.
4 Cover pan and simmer gently for about 30 minutes or until onion is tender.
5 Remove from heat and stir in milk and seasoning to taste.
6 Rub through a sieve so that the mixture is like a smooth purée.
7 Allow to cool.
8 When cold blend in the cream or yoghourt.
9 Pour into soup bowls and chill.
10 Sprinkle with chives or parsley before serving.

Iced tomato soup

you will need:

1½ lb. tomatoes	1 small chopped onion
1 pint water, or white stock	few drops Worcestershire sauce
½ small beetroot, preferably uncooked	1 teaspoon vinegar or lemon juice
	seasoning
small pieces of celery*	2 bay leaves
	lemon to garnish

* or 1 good pinch celery salt

1 Put the ingredients all together in a large saucepan and cook gently until the tomatoes are very soft (about 25 minutes).
2 Remove the beetroot and bay leaves, then rub through a sieve and finally strain through muslin.
3 Pour into freezing tray of refrigerator and leave for a short time until slightly iced.
4 Serve garnished with lemon.

Gazpacho

you will need:

water	1 small capsicum (green pepper)
1 lb. tomatoes	seasoning
1 medium sized cucumber	little olive oil
1 onion or several spring onions	lemon juice or white wine vinegar
1 - 2 cloves garlic	

1 Put the water into the refrigerator to become very cold.
2 If wished skin the tomatoes as this makes sieving the mixture easier and if using an electric blender or liquidiser gives a smooth mixture.
3 Peel the cucumber and cut into very small dice, saving a little as a garnish.
4 Chop the tomatoes, onion, garlic and add to the cucumber.
5 Pound until smooth or rub through a sieve.
6 Add the chopped or sieved and de-seeded capsicum.
7 Put the purée into basin and gradually beat in seasoning, olive oil and enough cold water to give a flowing consistency.
8 Add lemon juice and seasoning to taste.
9 Put into refrigerator until ready to serve.
10 Serve in ice cold cups garnished with cucumber.

Vichyssoise

you will need:

2 oz. butter	2 tablespoons chopped chives or green tops of spring onions
8 medium sized leeks	1 tablespoon chopped parsley
1½ pints chicken stock	seasoning
2 medium sized potatoes	¼ pint cream

1 Heat the butter and toss the chopped leeks in this until pale golden colour, do not allow them to brown.
2 Add stock, the chopped and peeled potatoes, half the chopped chives and all the parsley.
3 Season well and simmer gently for 30 minutes.
4 Rub through a fine sieve, then gradually add the cream when the purée is quite cool.
5 Taste and when quite cold add seasoning as wished.
6 Serve very cold topped with the remaining chopped chives.

Cold and Frosted Savoury Dishes

Cold savoury dishes

With a refrigerator, any waste of food should be eliminated because small pieces of meat, fish, etc., are stored under perfect conditions. On the other hand, food does not last indefinitely. Cooked meat lasts several days whereas cooked fish doesn't last longer than 48 hours even when stored in the refrigerator. Many of the dishes in this section are made from small quantities of meat, fish, etc., that otherwise might have been wasted.

Fish cream

you will need:

¼ pint aspic jelly or use ½ oz. gelatine powder and ¼ pint fish stock	12 oz. flaked cooked white fish
1 teaspoon powder gelatine if using aspic jelly	½ pint white sauce (see page 29)
	¼ pint cream
	seasoning

1 Dissolve the gelatine powder in the fish stock or stir in the extra gelatine if using the hot aspic and allow to cool.
2 Flake the fish, and mix with the sauce, gelatine or aspic mixture and the lightly whipped cream. Season well.
3 Pour into a mould and allow to set.
4 Serve with lemon, mayonnaise and salad.

Salmon cream

Follow directions for fish cream, using fresh, cooked or canned salmon. If using canned salmon use the liquid from the can as part of the stock.

Fish mousse

you will need:

2 eggs	½ pint white sauce (see page 29)
½ oz. gelatine powder	12 oz. flaked cooked white fish
5 - 6 tablespoons water or fish stock	seasoning
	¼ pint cream

1 Separate the egg yolks from the whites.
2 Dissolve the gelatine in the hot stock or water, add beaten egg yolks.
3 Stir into the sauce, then add the flaked fish, seasoning.
4 Allow mixture to cool and just begin to stiffen slightly, then fold in the lightly whipped cream and stiffly beaten egg whites. Taste and re-season as necessary.
5 Put into mould and allow to set.
6 Serve with salad, mayonnaise and lemon.

Salmon mousse (1)

Follow directions for fish mousse, using fresh, cooked or canned salmon. If using canned salmon use the liquid from the can as part of the stock.

Fish and anchovy mousse

Follow directions for the fish cream, but add a small can of anchovies to the white fish, pounding these well. Season lightly both sauce and the mousse, since anchovies have a very pronounced flavour.

Chaudfroid of haddock

you will need:

- 1 medium sized whole haddock
- just under ¼ pint fish stock
- 1 teaspoon aspic jelly crystals
- ¼ pint mayonnaise
- 1 tablespoon cream

To garnish:

small pieces of gherkin, radish, lettuce, cucumber

1. Bone the haddock and open out flat.
2. Poach the fish in salted water until cooked, taking care not to overcook it.
3. Lift from the stock when cooked, and allow to drain, then transfer to dish.
4. Dissolve the aspic jelly in the hot fish stock, then stir into the mayonnaise with the cream.
5. When this mixture has stiffened slightly, spread over the fish with a palette knife dipped in hot water. Coat evenly.
6. Garnish with tiny shapes of gherkin and radish on top of the fish and arrange shredded lettuce, sliced cucumber round the fish.

Lobster mousse

you will need:

- 2 eggs
- ¼ pint white or béchamel sauce (see page 30)
- 1 level dessertspoon gelatine powder
- ⅛ pint water
- 2 tablespoons cream
- 1-2 tablespoons lemon juice or sherry
- 8-12 oz. minced or finely chopped lobster meat
- seasoning

To garnish:

cucumber, lemon, lobster claws and salad

1. Separate the egg whites from the yolks.
2. Cook the yolks with the sauce for a few minutes, being careful the mixture does not boil.
3. Dissolve the gelatine in the very hot water.
4. Add to the sauce, together with the cream.
5. When cooler add lemon juice or sherry and lobster meat and seasoning.
6. When the mixture is cool and just beginning to thicken slightly, fold in the stiffly beaten egg whites, and extra seasoning if wished.
7. Pour into prepared mould or dish.
8. When set decorate with cucumber, lemon, lobster claws and salad.

Ham mousse (1)

Method and ingredients as for lobster mousse above, using 8—12 oz. chopped ham instead of lobster meat.

Chicken mousse

Method and ingredients as for lobster mousse above, using 8—12 oz. chopped chicken instead of lobster meat.

Prawns in aspic

you will need:

- ½ pint aspic jelly
- 4 or 8 slices hard-boiled egg
- little mustard and cress
- 4-6 oz. shelled prawns (or shrimps)
- lettuce

1. Allow the aspic jelly to cool, and pour a small amount in the bottom of 4 or 8 moulds.
2. Put in the refrigerator to become lightly set, then arrange a slice of hard-boiled egg, dipped in liquid aspic, on this with a border of mustard and cress.
3. Put back into the refrigerator to become quite firm.
4. Blend the prawns with the rest of the aspic and spoon on to the set bottom layer.
5. Return to the refrigerator to set and become quite firm.
6. Turn out on to a bed of shredded lettuce.

Salmon aspic

you will need:

- ½ pint aspic jelly
- few slices cucumber
- 2 hard-boiled eggs
- 8 oz. cooked or canned salmon
- 2-3 tablespoons cooked peas

To garnish:

lettuce, cucumber, lemon

1. Pour enough aspic to give about ¼ inch at the bottom of a mould.

2 Put in the refrigerator to become lightly set, then arrange a few slices of cucumber and hard-boiled egg and peas in an attractive design over this. Leave to set firmly. It is easier to put the pieces of food in position on the jelly if they are dipped in liquid aspic.
3 Pour over another small amount of aspic jelly and allow to set.
4 Flake the salmon and mix with the rest of the sliced cucumber, hard-boiled eggs, peas and aspic jelly.
5 Put into the mould and set.
6 Turn out on to a bed of lettuce and garnish with cucumber and lemon.

Salmon cucumber mould

you will need:

few cooked peas
2 hard-boiled eggs
⅓ pint aspic jelly
1 teaspoon gelatine powder
cucumber
¼ pint mayonnaise
8 - 12 oz. flaked cooked salmon (or canned salmon)
lettuce

1 Put peas and sliced eggs in the bottom of 4 tiny moulds.
2 Just cover with aspic jelly.
3 Dissolve gelatine powder in remainder of aspic jelly, add to mayonnaise, then stir in the flaked salmon.
4 When set, turn on to bed of lettuce and garnish with sliced cucumber.

Salmon mousse (2)

you will need:

1 oz. butter
1 tablespoon finely chopped onion
1 oz. flour
½ pint milk
pinch thyme
bay leaf
little grated nutmeg
8 oz. salmon, canned or fresh
1 level dessertspoon gelatine
¼ cucumber and olives to garnish
2 tablespoons water
2 oz. stoned, chopped black olives
2 sticks diced celery, if available
1 lb. red eating apples
2 tablespoons tomato ketchup
3 tablespoons mayonnaise
salt and pepper
juice 1 lemon
watercress

1 Melt butter in a saucepan and gently fry the chopped onion until transparent, but not brown.
2 Stir in the flour and cook gently for 3 minutes.
3 Add milk gradually, stirring all the time.
4 Add thyme, bay leaf and nutmeg, and simmer over a low heat for 10 minutes.
5 Remove herbs and leave to cool.
6 Finely flake salmon and gradually beat into the sauce.
7 Add gelatine which has been dissolved in the water, olives, celery and 1 diced raw eating apple.
8 Stir in tomato ketchup and mayonnaise, and season to taste.
9 Pile into a serving dish and chill.
10 Just before serving, garnish with rest of apples, cut into slices and dipped in lemon juice to retain colour. Fill the centre of the dish with more black olives, cucumber finely sliced, and watercress.

Chicken and ham velouté

you will need:

8 oz. cooked chicken
8 oz. cooked ham
1 oz. butter or chicken fat
1 oz. flour
¼ pint chicken stock & ¼ pint milk (or ½ pint milk)
2 egg yolks
seasoning
3 level teaspoons gelatine powder
¼ pint chicken stock

1 Finely chop or mince the chicken and ham.
2 Make a sauce of the butter, flour and chicken stock and milk.
3 When thickened add the egg yolks, and cook without boiling for several minutes, seasoning well.
4 Blend the chicken and ham with the sauce, then add the gelatine dissolved in the very hot chicken stock.
5 Pour into a mould to set, and serve with various salads.

Chaudfroid of chicken

you will need:

5 - 6 tablespoons aspic jelly
1 teaspoon gelatine powder
5 - 6 tablespoons thick mayonnaise or thick sauce from chicken stock
seasoning
4 neat pieces cooked chicken
1 - 2 tablespoons cream or evaporated cream

To garnish:

peas, tomato, egg,
gherkin or stuffed olives, lettuce

1 Make the aspic jelly and, while still warm, dissolve gelatine in it, then whisk the mayonnaise or thick sauce into this.
2 Taste, season if necessary.
3 Allow the chaudfroid sauce to cool and be fairly thick.
4 Put the pieces of chicken on a wire sieve, then carefully coat with the sauce and leave to set.
5 Cut away any surplus sauce from the bottom of each joint, garnish each piece with peas, tiny pieces of tomato, egg, gherkin or stuffed olives.
6 If using leg and thigh joints of chicken, it is easier if you cut the bone with a sharp knife.
7 Arrange on a bed of lettuce.
8 If wished, the whole chicken can be coated with the chaudfroid sauce and decorated.

For special occasions make up a savoury butter by creaming a little tomato ketchup and paprika pepper into butter; season well. Pipe a border of this round each piece of chicken. This is an excellent party dish.

Chicken tomato mould

you will need:

¼ pint tomato juice
½ oz. gelatine powder
12 oz. cooked chicken
seasoning

1 Heat the tomato juice and dissolve the gelatine in this.
2 Cool, and allow to stiffen slightly, then add the diced or minced cooked chicken. Season to taste.
3 Pour into a mould and allow to set, then turn out.
4 Serve with various salads.

Ham and beef galantine

you will need:

12 oz. — 1 lb. minced beef
4 oz. chopped ham
2 eggs
1 dessertspoon chopped chives
1 oz. breadcrumbs
seasoning

To glaze:

⅛ pint thick mayonnaise
¼ pint aspic jelly
tiny pieces gherkin, tomato and radish

1 Mix all ingredients except those for the glaze, together.
2 Either steam or bake in a greased tin or mould for approximately 1¼-1½ hours in a very moderate oven (350°F.—Gas Mark 3).
3 Cover top of tin with greased paper.
4 Turn out and cool.

To make glaze:

1 Stir the mayonnaise into the aspic jelly when cold.
2 Allow to stiffen slightly and coat the galantine.
3 Spread with knife dipped in hot water.
4 When firm, make a pattern of gherkin, tomato and radish.
5 Serve with salad platter—spring onions, halved tomatoes, sliced cucumber and potato salad.

Ham and love-apple circle

you will need:

4 - 6 oz. soft cream cheese
1 tablespoon finely chopped cucumber or gherkins
parsley
2 teaspoons capers
few drops Worcestershire sauce
about 12 oz. cooked ham
½ oz. gelatine
1 pint tomato juice (use either the juice from fresh tomatoes when plentiful and cheap or canned or bottled tomato juice)
salt and pepper
celery salt

To garnish:

crisp lettuce, stuffed hard-boiled eggs and Russian salad

Mix together the cream cheese, cucumber, parsley and capers, with few drops Worcestershire sauce.

2 Spread very thinly on the slices of ham, which should all be about the same size.
3 Roll firmly and pack into a slightly oiled ring mould.
4 Dissolve the gelatine in the tomato juice and season well.
5 Allow to cool and then pour carefully over the ham rolls taking care not to disturb them.
6 For a lighter result omit about 4 tablespoons tomato juice and substitute the stiffly beaten whites of 2 eggs. These should be folded into the mixture when it is just beginning to stiffen and then the fluffy savoury jelly poured over the ham rolls.
7 Allow to set and turn out carefully.
8 Garnish with crisp lettuce, stuffed hard-boiled eggs and fill the centre with Russian salad.

Ham mousse (2)

you will need:

2 eggs
¼ pint white sauce (see page 29)
1 level dessert-spoon gelatine powder
⅛ pint water
8 oz. cooked and finely chopped ham
seasoning
1 tablespoon sherry or lemon juice
2 - 3 tablespoons cream or evaporated milk

To garnish:
lettuce

1 Separate the whites from the yolks of the eggs.
2 Stir the yolks into hot sauce and cook gently for a few minutes.
3 Add gelatine, which should be dissolved in the water.
4 When cool stir in ham, seasoning, sherry or lemon juice and cream.
5 Lastly fold in stiffly beaten egg whites.
6 Put into 4 individual dishes to become firm.
7 Garnish with lettuce and serve with potato and other salads.

Lamb cutlets in mint jelly

you will need:

4 lightly grilled lamb cutlets (it will save time if you roast a loin of lamb and cut off 4 cutlets from this)
1 teaspoon gelatine powder
6 - 7 tablespoons hot water
1 tablespoon lemon juice or vinegar
seasoning
1 tablespoon chopped mint
sugar to taste
cooked potatoes
mayonnaise
chopped parsley
cooked peas

1 Put the cutlets into a shallow dish.
2 Dissolve the gelatine in the very hot water, stir in the lemon juice or vinegar, seasoning and mint.
3 Add little sugar to taste.
4 Pour over the cutlets and allow to set.
5 Arrange the cooked potatoes, tossed in mayonnaise and chopped parsley and the cooked peas round the edge of the dish.

The chops or cutlets keep beautifully moist covered with the mint mixture, so you can prepare this dish for the family well ahead and they can help themselves.

Brawn

you will need:

1 pig's head or 6 pig's trotters
water
8 oz. stewing beef (optional)
2 bay leaves
seasoning
pinch mixed herbs
1 small bunch parsley

1 Thoroughly wash pig's head or trotters, put into a large saucepan and cover with water.
2 Simmer gently for 1 hour.
3 Remove from the stock, which should be saved.
4 Cut all meat from head or trotters, removing any gristle and bones.
5 The meat and stewing steak should be cut into neat small dice.
6 Return the meat to the stock, adding bay leaves, seasoning, pinch herbs and the bunch of parsley, and simmer gently for 1½—2 hours until the meat feels quite tender.
7 Take out the parsley and pour into a rinsed mould or large basin.
8 Allow to set.

Pork and veal ring

you will need:

1 lb. very lean pork
1 lb. stewing veal
1 onion
1 - 2 carrots
about 6 pepper-corns
2 bay leaves
seasoning
$1\frac{1}{2}$ - 2 pints water
1 tablespoon vinegar (white if possible)
little gelatine if necessary
Russian salad

1 Put all the ingredients, except vinegar, gelatine and Russian salad into a saucepan.
2 Add the water.
3 Put on a tightly-fitting lid and simmer for about 2 hours.
4 Lift out meat and, when cool enough, cut into small pieces and arrange in a ring mould.
5 Meanwhile, boil the stock in an open pan until it is just under half pint.
6 If using stewing veal dissolve a bare dessert-spoon of powdered gelatine in the stock; but if you have used knuckle of veal, there should be enough natural setting substance to dispense with the gelatine.
7 Add the vinegar and extra seasoning if desired and strain over the meat.
8 Fill centre with Russian salad and serve with beetroot and lettuce.

Cheese moulds

you will need:

$\frac{1}{2}$ pint tomato juice or milk
6 oz. cottage cheese or finely grated cheese
2 dessertspoons powder gelatine
$\frac{1}{4}$ pint hot water
seasoning
2 teaspoons chopped parsley
2 teaspoons chopped gherkins

1 Beat tomato juice or milk very gradually into cheese until a smooth mixture.
2 Dissolve the gelatine in the hot water.
3 Add the gelatine to the cheese with seasoning, parsley and gherkins.
4 Pour into 4 moulds and when set turn out and serve with salad.

Cream cheese soufflé

you will need:

3 eggs
8 oz. cream cheese
$\frac{1}{4}$ pint milk
$\frac{1}{2}$ oz. gelatine powder
$\frac{1}{4}$ pint water
$\frac{1}{4}$ pint cream
1 - 2 oz. grated Parmesan cheese
2 teaspoons chopped chives
seasoning

To garnish:
gherkins
tomato

1 Separate the egg yolks from the whites.
2 Blend the cream cheese with half the milk to give smooth mixture.
3 Dissolve the gelatine in the very hot water.
4 Beat the egg yolks with the rest of the milk until smooth, and add to the gelatine mixture stirring together very thoroughly.
5 Allow this to cool, then stir in the cream cheese mixture, lightly whipped cream, Parmesan cheese, chives and seasoning.
6 Lastly fold in the stiffly beaten egg whites, and put into a prepared soufflé dish.
7 When set garnish with a ring of thinly sliced gherkin, and a design of pieces of tomato.

Cream cheese and ham soufflé

Use the same recipe as cream cheese soufflé, but omit the Parmesan cheese and add 4 oz. finely diced ham to the cream cheese.

Cream cheese and tomato loaf

you will need:

Tomato layers:
1 pint tomato juice
$\frac{1}{2}$ oz. gelatine powder
squeeze lemon juice
3 tablespoons finely diced cucumber

Cheese layers:
8 oz. cream cheese
1 tablespoon chopped chives
2 teaspoons horse-radish cream

To garnish:
lettuce, cucumber,
hard-boiled egg

1 Heat the tomato juice and dissolve the gelatine in this.

2 Add the lemon juice and when the mixture is cold pour a little into a loaf tin, adding 1 tablespoon diced cucumber.
3 Let this layer set and prepare the cheese filling.
4 Blend cream cheese with the chives and horseradish.
5 Spread half this over the tomato layer, in the loaf tin.
6 Spoon most of the tomato liquid over the cheese, adding 1 tablespoon cucumber, leaving enough tomato mixture for a top layer. However, the loaf is more effective if you have a rather deeper tomato layer in the centre.
7 Put back into the refrigerator to set.
8 Spread the last of the cheese mixture over the the tomato jelly.
9 Cover with the remaining tomato liquid and cucumber.
10 When the loaf is completely firm turn out on to a bed of shredded lettuce and garnish with sliced cucumber and hard-boiled egg.

Tomato cheese creams

you will need:
½ oz. gelatine powder
¾ pint tomato juice
¼ pint cream
8 oz. grated cheese
seasoning

1 Dissolve the gelatine powder in the heated tomato juice.
2 Cool, and when just beginning to stiffen slightly, fold in the lightly whipped cream, grated cheese and a little seasoning.
3 Put into prepared moulds and leave to set.

Tomato cheese moulds

you will need:
½ oz. gelatine powder
1 pint tomato juice
8 oz. grated cheese

1 Dissolve the gelatine in the heated tomato juice.
2 Allow to cool, and stiffen very slightly, then add grated cheese.
3 Spoon into prepared moulds, and allow to set.

Tomato cheese mousse

you will need:
2 eggs
½ oz. gelatine powder
⅝ pint tomato juice
¼ pint cream or thick mayonnaise
8 oz. grated cheese
seasoning

1 Separate the egg yolks from the whites.
2 Dissolve the gelatine in the heated tomato juice, then pour the mixture on to the beaten egg yolks.
3 Allow mixture to cool, and begin to stiffen slightly, then fold in the lightly whipped cream or mayonnaise, grated cheese and stiffly beaten egg whites.
4 Add seasoning, although this may not be necessary when using mayonnaise.
5 Pour into moulds and allow to set.

Golden ring

you will need:
5 hard-boiled eggs
1 small packet frozen peas
½ oz. gelatine powder
1 pint tomato juice
seasoning
olive oil

To decorate:
lettuce
little cream cheese (optional)

1 Shell and cut the eggs into halves across the centre.
2 Cook and drain the peas.
3 Dissolve the gelatine powder in the hot tomato juice and season.
4 Pour little of this into a ring mould, brushed with olive oil.
5 When lightly set, arrange the halved eggs, cut side downwards to the jelly, and the peas to form an attractive pattern.
6 Spoon over a very little of the tomato gelatine mixture and when set add the rest of the tomato liquid.
7 Turn out when quite firm on to a bed of lettuce and decorate with cream cheese if wished.

In summer, garnish with thinly sliced cucumber and mixed fresh vegetables, served in mayonnaise.

In winter, grated carrot, grated cheese, chopped gherkins or olives makes a good filling for the centre of the ring.

Harlequin ring

you will need:

- ½ oz. gelatine powder
- 1 pint tomato juice
- 4 oz. chopped celery
- 3 hard-boiled eggs
- 4 oz. cooked, frozen or canned peas
- 2 oz. grated carrot
- seasoning
- olive oil

1 Dissolve the gelatine in the hot tomato juice.
2 When cold, but not set, add the other ingredients.
3 Pour into a ring mould previously rinsed in cold water or brushed with olive oil.
4 Allow to set.
5 Turn out and fill the centre with salad and serve with salad cream de luxe (see page 35).

Mushroom soufflé

you will need:

- 3 eggs
- ½ pint mushroom soup
- just under ½ oz. gelatine powder
- 3 tablespoons hot water
- ¼ pint cream
- seasoning
- 1 - 2 hard-boiled eggs
- parsley
- paprika pepper

1 Separate the egg yolks from the whites.
2 Heat the mushroom soup, pour on to the beaten egg yolks and blend thoroughly.
3 Dissolve the gelatine in the hot water, add to the hot soup and stir thoroughly until blended.
4 Cool this mixture, and let it begin to stiffen slightly, then fold in the lightly whipped cream, and stiffly beaten egg whites.
5 Taste and season as necessary.
6 Put into prepared soufflé dish and garnish with a ring of chopped hard-boiled egg white mixed with chopped parsley and a central ring of chopped egg yolk and paprika pepper.

Mushroom cheese soufflé

Make as mushroom soufflé.
Blend 4 oz. grated cheese with the mushroom soup.

Asparagus creams

you will need:

- 1 pint asparagus soup
- ½ oz. gelatine powder
- 1 tablespoon water
- few canned or cooked asparagus tips (optional)
- 3 tablespoons cream
- 2 egg whites
- seasoning

To garnish:
asparagus tips, lettuce, tomatoes

1 Heat the asparagus soup and pour over the gelatine, which should be softened in the water.
2 Allow to cool, and begin to stiffen very slightly, then add the chopped asparagus tips, cream, lightly whipped, and the stiffly whisked egg whites and seasoning.
3 Pour into 4 individual moulds, and allow to set.
4 Turn out on to a bed of lettuce, and garnish with asparagus tips and sliced tomatoes.

Mushroom creams

Make as asparagus creams adding 2—3 finely chopped cooked or raw mushrooms. Garnish with sliced raw mushrooms, tossed in oil and vinegar and well seasoned watercress.

Frosted savoury dishes

There are not a great number of savoury ingredients that can be served frosted, but the following are quite delicious and certainly unusual.

Iced camembert cheese

1 Mash a Camembert cheese with a little cream, put into the refrigerator freezing tray.
2 Leave until lightly frozen, then serve on a bed of lettuce with water biscuits etc.

If preferred the whole or portions of the cheese can be frozen instead of blending it with the cream.

Frosted cheese moulds

you will need:

2 oz. butter
8 oz. finely grated cheese
salt and pepper
1 teaspoon made mustard
¼ pint cream

1 Cream the butter with the cheese and seasonings.
2 Add the lightly whipped cream.
3 Fill very cold dariole moulds with the mixture.
4 Put into the freezing tray of the refrigerator, and freeze on the coldest position until firm.
5 Lower indicator to normal setting to store.
6 Serve with crisp lettuce, water biscuits etc.

Frosted salad rolls

you will need:

4 very large lettuce leaves
filling (see below)
little water or lemon juice

1 After washing and drying, break the centre stem of the lettuce leaves, so they roll well.
2 Put on a little of the filling, then roll firmly.
3 Sprinkle each roll with a few drops of water to encourage the frosted look—or lemon juice could be used instead.
4 Put into the freezing tray of the refrigerator and leave until faintly frosted (about 30 minutes).
5 Serve on thin fingers of bread and butter or crisp buttered savoury biscuits.

Care must be taken in freezing these, since if they are allowed to become too hard the lettuce is most unpleasant, but if lightly frosted they look interesting, and taste delicious.
Do not keep any length of time when once they come from the freezing compartment, since the lettuce will wilt and look tired.

Anchovy filling

Pound a can of anchovies with 2 hard-boiled eggs and 2 tablespoons fine breadcrumbs.

Crab filling

Flake a small can crab meat (or meat from small fresh crab), blend with little mayonnaise, diced cucumber, chopped parsley.

Egg filling

Hard-boil 3 eggs, then chop and blend with little mayonnaise, whipped cream (about 1 tablespoon each), chopped chives, parsley to taste.

Lobster filling

Add a little lemon juice to the ingredients in crab filling, using flaked, canned or fresh lobster meat.

Savoury cheese filling

Blend 4 oz. cream cheese, 4 oz. grated cheese, with chopped chives, parsley, seasoning and about a tablespoon mayonnaise.

Savoury tomato filling

Skin and chop 2 large tomatoes, blend with 6 oz. grated cheese, little chopped spring onion, seasoning.

Salmon filling

Flake canned or cooked salmon, add diced cucumber little mayonnaise or horseradish cream and seasoning.

Basic recipe for reference

White sauce

you will need:

1 oz. butter or margarine
1 oz. flour
salt and pepper
½ pint milk for coating consistency, i.e. sauce
¼ pint milk for panada or binding consistency
1 pint milk for thin sauce for soups

1 Heat the butter gently.
2 Remove from the heat and stir in the flour.
3 Return to the heat and cook gently for a few minutes so that the 'roux' as the butter and flour mixture is called, does not brown.
4 Remove pan from the heat and gradually blend in the cold milk.
5 Bring to the boil and cook stirring with a wooden spoon until smooth.
6 Season well.
7 If any lumps have formed whisk sharply.

Béchamel sauce

Simmer pieces of very finely chopped onion, carrot, celery in milk. Strain and make as white sauce.

Salad Dishes

There can be no argument about the fact that all salad ingredients taste better if stored in the refrigerator at the correct temperature.
As already mentioned on page 8 salads should not be left on the shelves of the refrigerator since the temperature is correct but the atmosphere too dry. Many refrigerators have special salad containers and your salad ingredients should be put in this.
To store a ready-made salad, make the salad on the serving dish, then cover completely with either damp kitchen paper or with kitchen foil. You will find the salad keeps crisp looking for many hours.

Tuna salad

you will need:

1 3½-oz. can tuna fish
little salad cream
1 dessertspoon lemon juice
2 tablespoons cream or top of milk
good sprinkle pepper

1 Remove tuna from can and mash very finely.
2 Mix with salad cream, lemon juice, cream or top of milk and pepper.
3 Beat well until fluffy.
4 Chill.
5 Serve with endive, tomato and hard-boiled egg.

Gammon and pineapple salad

you will need:

4 oz. cooked gammon or ham
1 can pineapple
French dressing (page 34)
lettuce

To garnish:
pineapple, radishes,
cucumber, anchovy fillets

1 Dice gammon and pineapple.
2 Toss in French dressing, adding a little pineapple syrup.
3 Serve on bed of crisp lettuce.
4 Garnish with pineapple, radishes, cucumber and anchovy fillets.

Ham, apple and blue cheese salad

you will need:

1 ½-inch thick slice ham
6 oz. Danish blue cheese
3 red eating apples
lemon juice
lettuce
chopped green pepper
parsley

1 Cut ham into ½-inch thick squares.
2 Roll cheese into small balls.
3 Dice apples, leaving peel on, and dip into lemon juice to keep their colour.
4 Line a dish with lettuce and make piles of cheese, ham and apple.
5 Sprinkle with chopped green pepper and garnish dish with parsley.
6 Serve with French dressing.

Cold chicken and salad

(illustrated on the cover)

The following ingredients blend very well with the delicate flavour of chicken:

1 Savoury rice salad, adding chopped peppers, onion, peas, grated carrot and mayonnaise to cooked rice.
2 Grated raw carrot with sultanas and mandarin oranges.
3 Beetroot diced and set in raspberry jelly flavoured with vinegar.

Chicken and rice salad

you will need:

6 oz. long grained rice
1 clove garlic (optional)
3 tablespoons salad oil
1 tablespoon tarragon or wine vinegar
salt and pepper
1 tablespoon currants
1 large tomato
1 green pepper
2 tablespoons chopped walnuts (optional)
8 oz. cooked chicken

1 Cook rice until just tender in plenty of salted boiling water.
2 Drain thoroughly.
3 Rub a large bowl with garlic and put the oil, vinegar and seasoning to taste into the bowl.
4 Add the hot rice and mix thoroughly.
5 Stir in the remaining ingredients and lastly the chicken.
6 Cover and set aside in a cool place for the flavours to blend.
7 When cold transfer to a serving dish.

Perfection salad

you will need:

¼ oz. gelatine
¼ pint boiling water
2 tomatoes
½ cucumber
chopped olives
2 oz. diced celery
seasoning
1 teaspoon lemon juice
1 tablespoon vinegar

To garnish:
1 oz. cream cheese,
lettuce leaves, olives

1 Dissolve the gelatine in the boiling water.
2 Slice the tomatoes and cucumber.
3 Add olives, celery, seasoning, lemon juice and vinegar.
4 Stir the above ingredients into the dissolved gelatine.
5 Place into individual moulds and put into the refrigerator to set.
6 When quite firm unmould on to crisp lettuce leaves.
7 Garnish on top with cream cheese and olives.

Sweet salad

you will need:

8 radishes
½ cucumber
1 tomato
1 banana
1 lettuce
1 hard-boiled egg
1 apple
1 small carrot
2 oz. stoned dates
2 oz. chopped nuts
1 tablespoon castor sugar

1 Slice all vegetables, egg and fruit and dice apple and carrot.
2 Shred the lettuce saving the heart for garnishing.
3 Place the shredded lettuce leaves into salad bowl with the rest of the ingredients, except the egg and nuts.
4 Toss them well together so that everything is well distributed.
5 Place heart in the centre, garnish with hard-boiled egg and sprinkle with chopped nuts.
6 Serve very cold with a light well-sweetened dressing.

Piquant egg salad

you will need:

hard-boiled eggs
diced cucumber
shredded mushrooms
chopped gherkins
capers
peppers
crisp lettuce

1 Coarsely chop hard-boiled eggs.
2 Put into a bowl and mix with the cucumber, the mushrooms, the gherkins, capers and peppers.
3 Arrange on a bed of crisp lettuce.
4 Serve with a vinaigrette dressing.

Cottage cheese and pineapple platter

you will need:

1 lb. cottage cheese
1 head chicory
4 medium sized tomatoes
8 chilled pineapple slices
sprigs parsley

1 Pile the cottage cheese in the middle of a platter.
2 Surround with chicory leaves and whole tomatoes and a semi-circle of pineapple slices.
3 Garnish with sprigs of parsley.

Cheese, grape and banana salad

you will need:

8 oz. grapes
2 sliced bananas
lemon juice
12 oz. cottage cheese

To garnish:
lettuce

1 Wash and seed the grapes.
2 Toss bananas in lemon juice to preserve the colour.
3 Arrange chilled cottage cheese in a circle on a serving plate or plates.
4 Fill the centre with the fruit.
5 Garnish with lettuce and serve with mayonnaise.

Iced cheese and pear salad

you will need:

3 level tablespoons mayonnaise
4 oz. Cheshire cheese
1 red pepper (capsicum), canned or fresh
¼ pint double cream
2 large pears
4 lettuce leaves
sprigs watercress

1 Turn refrigerator up to maximum.
2 Mix mayonnaise with Cheshire cheese, chopped red pepper and the cream, and spread in ice tray.
3 Place in freezing compartment of refrigerator and stir every ½ hour until mixture is lightly frozen.
4 Wipe pears (peel if skins are tough), cut in half and remove core.
5 Place each half pear on a lettuce leaf, pile iced cheese mixture on pear and garnish with watercress sprigs.
6 Serve immediately.

Fresh beet salad

you will need:

beetroot
olive oil
lemon juice
lettuce
chopped parsley

1 Well scrub and peel raw beetroot, then shred on fine shredder.
2 Add a little olive oil and fresh lemon juice and blend.
3 Pile on fresh lettuce, decorate with lettuce heart and fresh chopped parsley.

Stuffed cucumber salad

you will need:

cucumber
lemon juice
seasoning
lettuce leaves
8 oz. flaked, cooked or canned fish
mayonnaise

1 Skin the pieces of cucumber and cut into half lengthways.
2 Take out the centre part and chop this finely.
3 Squeeze lemon juice over it, add a little seasoning and let it stand for 1 hour before using.
4 Mix fish, chopped cucumber, mayonnaise and rest of seasoning together.
5 Press this into 2 halves of the cucumber and put these together again.
6 Wrap in lettuce leaves.

Grapefruit salad

you will need:

fresh grapefruit
cottage cheese
chives, or spring onions, chopped
mandarin orange sections
dessert apple, chopped
celery, diced
green pepper, chopped

French dressing:

3 tablespoons corn oil
1 tablespoon vinegar
¼ level teaspoon salt
1 level teaspoon sugar

1 Cut each grapefruit in half and carefully remove the grapefruit sections, cutting away the pith.
2 Remove any pith and skin from the centre of each half.
3 Combine the cottage cheese and chopped chives and place some in each grapefruit half.
4 Combine the grapefruit sections, mandarins, chopped apple, celery and pepper and toss together in the prepared chilled dressing.
5 Arrange this mixture in the grapefruit halves and serve with extra salad if liked.

6 Put all the ingredients for the French dressing in a screw top jar and shake well.

Potato salad

you will need:

1 lb. potatoes
¼ pint mayonnaise or salad dressing
2 teaspoons finely chopped onions
3 tablespoons finely chopped parsley
seasoning

1 Cook the potatoes in salted water but do not allow to become over-soft.
2 Strain and leave until just cool enough to handle *but not cold.*
3 Cut into neat dice and toss in the mayonnaise, adding onion, parsley and seasoning.
4 Leave until cold.
5 Garnish with a little chopped parsley.

Russian salad

you will need:

8 oz. cooked potato	4 oz. turnip
8 oz. cooked carrots	2 tablespoons oil
8 oz. cooked peas	1 tablespoon vinegar
French beans	seasoning
	lettuce (optional)
	mayonnaise

1. Cut all the vegetables into neat dice.
2. Put into a large bowl and pour over the oil and vinegar.
3. Season well.
4. Leave for several hours, turning round in the dressing from time to time, being careful to keep the vegetables in neat pieces.
5. Pile on to a dish on lettuce if desired and form into a pyramid.
6. Pour over just enough mayonnaise to coat.

Tomato potato salad

you will need:

tomatoes	chopped parsley or chopped onion or chives
seasoning	
potato salad	

1. Cut the tops off tomatoes, and scoop out the centre pulp.
2. This may be used for other purposes.
3. Drain and season the cases.
4. Fill with potato salad, flavoured with chopped parsley, onion or chives.
5. Serve very cold.

Tomato green pea salad

As tomato potato salad, using cooked green peas, tossed in mint sauce, instead of potatoes.

Tomato prawn cups

you will need:

large firm tomatoes	prawns
seasoning	mayonnaise
little lemon juice	lemon wedges to garnish
shredded lettuce	

1. Cut the tops off the tomatoes (when used as part of a mixed hors-dœuvre select small tomatoes).
2. Scoop out the centre pulp, use this for other purposes.
3. Drain and season the cases, and flavour with a little lemon juice.
4. Fill the cases with the finely shredded lettuce and prawns, tossed in mayonnaise.
5. Garnish with pieces of lemon and serve on a bed of lettuce.

Prawn meat cups

Make as above, using a mixture of prawns and finely chopped veal. This is a surprising, but very pleasant mixture.

Tomato meat cups

you will need:

large firm tomatoes	horseradish cream
seasoning	little chopped meat

1. Cut the tops off large firm tomatoes, scoop out the centre pulp.
2. Drain the cases, and season very well.
3. Chop the centre pulp, and mix with horse-radish cream in the case of beef and veal. In the case of lamb mix with mayonnaise and a little chopped mint. For pork mix with chopped chives and grated apple.
4. Pile back into tomato cases and serve on crisp lettuce with chicory and celery etc.

Avocado pear salad

you will need:

2 avocado pears	mayonnaise
8 oz. cooked, frozen or canned peas	lettuce
seasoning	1 tablespoon walnuts

1. Cut avocado pears lengthwise.
2. Remove stone and skin.
3. Cut the pulp into small dice.
4. Mix with the cooked peas and season.
5. Heap on a dish and cover with mayonnaise.
6. Surround with finely shredded lettuce and sprinkle this with very finely chopped walnuts.

Pineapple salad

you will need:

1 large can or packet of frozen pineapple
2 tablespoons mayonnaise
lettuce
1 oz. chopped walnuts
watercress
paprika pepper

1 Drain the syrup from the pineapple and blend 1 dessertspoon of it with the mayonnaise.
2 Arrange each slice of pineapple on a lettuce leaf and coat with a little of the dressing.
3 Sprinkle with the nuts and garnish with gherkins, pepper and watercress.

Salad Dressings and Sauces

Salad dressings and sauces can be made in larger quantities and kept in the safe temperature of a refrigerator.

French dressing

you will need:

1 dessertspoon vinegar
1 tablespoon salad oil
pinch sugar
1 tablespoon finely chopped parsley or chives
salt and pepper

1 Mix all the ingredients together in a basin.
2 Chill.

Economical salad dressing

you will need:

1 small can full cream or condensed milk
½ teaspoon salt
¼ pint vinegar
1 teaspoon dry mustard

1 Mix all the ingredients together and beat well.
2 Chill before serving.

Vinaigrette dressing

you will need:

2 dessertspoons vinegar (wine vinegar, cider vinegar or tarragon vinegar)
5 dessertspoons olive oil
good pinch salt
pepper to taste

Mix all ingredients together in a bowl.

Classic mayonnaise

you will need:

1 egg yolk
good pinch salt, pepper and mustard
⅛ - ¼ pint olive oil
1 dessertspoon vinegar
1 dessertspoon warm water

1 Put the egg yolk and seasonings into a basin.
2 Gradually beat in the oil, drop by drop, stirring all the time until the mixture is thick.
3 When it becomes creamy stop adding oil—too much will make the mixture curdle.
4 Gradually beat in the vinegar.
5 Beat in the warm water.

Magic mayonnaise

you will need:

1 small can full cream condensed milk
¼ pint salad oil or melted butter
2 egg yolks
½ teaspoon salt
1 teaspoon mustard
dash cayenne pepper
¼ pint vinegar or lemon juice

1 Place all the ingredients in a bowl.
2 Beat well with a whisk until the mixture thickens.

This mayonnaise can be stored in a refrigerator for a very long time.

Mayonnaise without eggs

you will need:

1 level teaspoon mustard
1 teaspoon sugar
½ teaspoon salt
large pinch pepper seasoning
1 small can evaporated milk
½ pint olive oil
2 - 3 tablespoons wine vinegar

1 Put the mustard into a bowl with sugar, salt and pepper.
2 Add the evaporated milk.
3 Mix and beat in the olive oil, drop by drop.
4 Add the vinegar.
5 Season to taste.

Curried mayonnaise

Add a little curry powder or paste to mayonnaise (see above recipe).

Green mayonnaise

Add finely chopped parsley, chives, sage and thyme to mayonnaise.

Family mayonnaise

you will need:

3 tablespoons flour
1 teaspoon dry mustard
cayenne or white pepper
1 teaspoon salt
1 tablespoon sugar
1 egg
½ pint water
4 tablespoons vinegar
3 tablespoons olive oil

1 Blend the flour, mustard, seasoning and sugar to a paste with the egg.
2 Gradually stir in the water.
3 Add the vinegar and cook over boiling water until thick.
4 Cook for a further 5 minutes.
5 Cool and beat in the oil.

Salad cream

you will need:

1 oz. flour
1 teaspoon sugar
½ teaspoon salt
good pinch pepper and dry mustard
½ pint milk
1 oz. butter or 1 tablespoon oil
1 egg
⅛ pint vinegar

1 Mix the flour and seasonings together with a little of the cold milk.
2 Bring the remainder of the milk to the boil and pour over, stirring thoroughly.
3 Put the mixture into the saucepan, adding the butter or oil and beaten egg and cook very slowly until the sauce coats the back of a wooden spoon.
4 Remove from the heat and whisk in the vinegar.
5 Pour at once into a screw topped bottle.

Salad cream de luxe

you will need:

good ½ teaspoon mustard
2 teaspoons water
good pinch salt and pepper
1 teaspoon sugar
1 tablespoon lemon juice or vinegar (preferably white vinegar)
1 jar or can ¼ pint thick cream

1 Blend the mustard with the water.
2 Put into a basin and add salt, pepper, sugar and vinegar.
3 Using a wooden spoon blend a teaspoon of cream at a time and stop stirring once it is smooth and blended.

Ice Cream and Water Ices

Making your own ice cream

To make your own ice cream is not at all difficult, as long as certain rules are followed:-

1 Most recipes for ice cream (not water ices or sorbets) should contain a fairly high percentage of fat in the form of cream or evaporated milk. This makes certain that the mixture is creamy when frozen. Where ice cream powder is used cream is not essential.
2 Ice cream (again not sorbets or water ices) MUST be frozen as quickly as possible to prevent the formation of ice crystals in the sweet. Turn the cold control indicator on the refrigerator to the coldest position 30 minutes before putting in the mixture.
3 There is no need to take the food out of the refrigerator during this period, since it will not become too hard or cold.
4 When once the ice cream is frozen, return the indicator to the normal setting position to store the ice cream.
5 Most recipes for ice cream have a better texture if the mixture is beaten half way through freezing—this introduces air and lightness into the mixture. In the same way the introduction of stiffly beaten egg whites lightens the mixture.

Using sugar in ice creams

When tasting the mixture before freezing you may consider it tastes a little too sweet.
Freezing does absorb sweetness though, and you will find the ice cream suits most palates when frozen.
While castor sugar can be used, icing sugar gives the smoothest ice cream.

Flavourings in ice cream

Freezing absorbs flavours, so use full amount of flavourings suggested in individual recipes.

Time to freeze ice creams

While no definite time is given in the recipes to freeze the ice creams, since refrigerators vary a great deal in their speed of operation, it is fairly certain that for the first freezing about 30 - 40 minutes will ensure that the ice cream is sufficiently frozen to whip air into the mixture.
If it is still very soft and liquid leave it for a longer period, since it must be of a thickish consistency to remove and whip.
For the final freezing about 45 minutes - 1 hour should give a sufficiently firm texture.
Ice cream becomes very hard when over frozen and therefore it is not so creamy and pleasant to eat. If this has happened, take the tray out of the refrigerator for a short time before serving the ice cream.

To make ice cream puddings

To make an ice cream pudding, you need an attractive mould or tin that fits into the freezing compartment of the refrigerator.
You may care to make two different kinds of ice cream, a plain one and perhaps a marshmallow ice cream, or two distinct flavours, or perhaps a cream and water ice.
Maybe you could be ambitious and combine three types of ice cream or frozen desserts, but the method is the same.

1 Make your ice creams or frozen mixtures, and freeze until just lightly frosted—where recipes ask for beating this should be done, and the mixture returned to the freezing trays for the second time.
2 While the ice cream is freezing chill the mould or tin very thoroughly.
3 Spread the first ice cream in position. You may decide you wish to have an outer layer of vanilla ice cream, so this should be spread thickly over the base and sides of the mould—leave enough for a top 'covering'.
4 Fill the centre with the second flavour or use the second flavour and then a third.
5 Top with the first flavour, and return the mould to the freezing compartment and leave until mixtures are very firm.
6 Chill serving dish, and invert the mould over this.
7 Leave in a warm place for a few minutes or wrap a cloth wrung out in hot water round the mould for a few minutes.
8 Serve, decorated with lightly whipped cream, fruit, etc.

Using cream in ice creams

While a certain amount of cream (or evaporated milk) must be used in ice cream to give sufficient fat content, *never* over-whip the cream, since this gives a rather solid, or buttery, taste to the sweet.
Whisk only until fairly stiff, and if the cream you buy is very rich, such as Jersey cream, dilute with a small amount of milk.

To whip evaporated milk

A better texture is given in many recipes where evaporated milk is used, if this is whisked first.
There are several methods of doing this.

Method 1

Boil the can of milk unopened for 15 minutes—no longer. Cool and put in the refrigerator and leave overnight. Open can and whisk until light and fluffy.

Method 2

Open can of milk, and add 2 teaspoons lemon juice to this. Whisk until light and fluffy.

Method 3

Boil can of milk for 15 minutes.
Meanwhile dissolve 1 level teaspoon gelatine powder in 2 tablespoons very hot water.
Open the can of milk while hot (be careful in doing this so that it does not 'spurt' out).

Pour on to dissolved gelatine, and stir well. Allow to become quite cold, then whisk until light and fluffy.

Evaporated milk ice cream

you will need:

1 level teaspoon gelatine powder	1 large can evaporated milk
1 tablespoon boiling water	2 - 3 oz. sugar
	flavouring

1. Dissolve the gelatine in the water.
2. Stir into the evaporated milk together with the sugar.
3. Pour into freezing tray and freeze on the coldest position for approximately 30 minutes.
4. Put into mixing bowl, add flavouring and whisk until light and fluffy.
5. Return to the freezing tray and freeze until firm, then return indicator to normal position to store.

Variations on evaporated milk ice cream

Chocolate

Dissolve 1½ oz. cocoa or 2 oz. chocolate powder and 1 teaspoon vanilla essence in 3 tablespoons milk, add to whisked evaporated milk.

Coffee

Dissolve 2 teaspoons instant coffee in 1 tablespoon milk and add to whisked evaporated milk.

Fruit

Make ¼ pint thick fruit purée, add to whisked evaporated milk. If needed add a little sugar.

Vanilla

Add 1—1½ teaspoons vanilla essence to the whisked evaporated milk.

Banana ice cream

you will need:

2 large ripe (but not discoloured) bananas	3 tablespoons milk or thin cream
1 dessertspoon lemon juice	¼ pint thick cream or whipped evaporated milk
2 oz. icing sugar	2 egg whites
½ teaspoon vanilla essence	few drops cochineal (optional)

1. Mash the bananas carefully, adding lemon juice and sugar.
2. When quite smooth (if wished sieve through a nylon sieve) add vanilla essence and milk or thin cream.
3. Lastly fold in the lightly whipped cream.
4. Put into freezing tray and freeze on coldest position for approximately 35 minutes.
5. Put into bowl and whisk lightly, then fold in the stiffly beaten egg whites.
6. Return to freezing tray and freeze until firm, then return indicator to normal setting to store.

If wished this ice cream can be coloured with a very few drops of cochineal.

Banana chocolate ice cream

Recipe as above, but add 2 oz. coarsely grated milk chocolate when adding the stiffly beaten egg whites.

Golden banana ice cream

Recipe as above, but beat two egg yolks with the banana purée, lemon juice and sugar.

Banana pecan ice cream

Recipe as banana ice cream, but add 2—3 oz. coarsely chopped pecan nuts to the bananas. Walnuts could be used instead of pecan nuts.

Honey ice cream

you will need:

3 tablespoons honey	⅜ pint cream or evaporated milk
2 eggs	
1 teaspoon vanilla essence	

1. Slightly warm the honey if very thick.
2. Separate the egg yolks from the whites and beat the yolks with the honey and vanilla essence until smooth mixture.
3. Stir in the cream or evaporated milk—which need not be whipped.
4. Pour into freezing tray and freeze on the coldest setting for about 30 minutes.
5. Remove to bowl, whisk, and add stiffly beaten egg whites.
6. Return to freezing tray and continue freezing on coldest position until firm, then return indicator to normal setting to store.

Honey walnut ice cream

Recipe as above, but add 2—3 oz. chopped walnuts with egg whites.

Honey macaroon ice cream

Recipe as honey ice cream but use ½ teaspoon almond essence instead of the vanilla essence. When adding the stiffly beaten egg whites add 2 broken macaroon biscuits.

Honey peanut ice cream

Recipe as honey ice cream, but add 4 oz. peanuts with stiffly beaten egg whites.

Orange ice cream

you will need:

2 eggs
3 - 4 oz. icing sugar
rind and juice 3 large oranges
rind and juice 1 small lemon
½ pint cream or evaporated milk

1. Separate the eggs.
2. Put the yolks of the eggs and sugar into a basin, and whisk until thick in texture.
3. Add to this the very finely grated rind and juice of the oranges and lemon.
4. Stir in half the whipped cream or evaporated milk.
5. Pour into freezing tray and freeze for approximately 40 minutes on coldest position.
6. Turn into bowl, and whip then add the rest of the cream and stiffly beaten egg whites.
7. Return to freezing tray and freeze until firm, then return indicator to normal setting to store.

Lemon ice cream

Recipe as above but use the grated rind and juice of 3 lemons instead of the oranges. Add about 1 oz. extra sugar.

Tangerine ice cream

Recipe as orange ice cream, but use 4 tangerines and 1 lemon.

Orange raisin ice cream

Recipe as orange ice cream, but soak 3 oz. seedless raisins in the orange and lemon juice for 1 hour before making the ice cream.

Orange, raisin and rum ice cream

Recipe as orange ice cream, but soak 3 oz. seedless raisins in the orange and lemon juice and 1 tablespoon rum for 1 hour before making the ice cream.

Orange brandy ice cream

Recipe as orange ice cream, but soak the grated orange rind and lemon rind with the orange and lemon juice and 2 tablespoons brandy or Curaçao for about 30 minutes before making ice cream.

Orange chocolate ice cream

Recipe as orange ice cream, but add 3 oz. coarsely grated or chopped milk or plain chocolate when folding in the whipped cream and egg whites.

Prune ice cream

you will need:

8 oz. dried prunes
1 dessertspoon lemon juice
2 oz. icing sugar
½ pint thick cream or evaporated milk or ¼ pint thick cream and ¼ pint thin cream

1. Soak the prunes overnight in cold water to cover.
2. If sufficiently soft there is no need to cook, just drain and rub through a sieve.
3. If not soft then simmer gently, until tender, drain and sieve.
4. Blend purée with lemon juice and sugar.
5. Add half the thick or the thin cream.
6. Pour into freezing tray and freeze on the coldest position for approximately 35 minutes.
7. Turn into a bowl and whisk then add the rest of the lightly whipped cream.
8. Return to the freezing tray and freeze until firm, then turn the indicator to normal position to store.

Fluffy prune ice cream

Recipe as above, but add 1 level teaspoon gelatine powder and 2 eggs together with an extra 1 oz. sugar.
Proceed as steps 1—3, then dissolve the gelatine in 2 tablespoons of the prune liquid (which should be very hot).

Add to the prune purée with beaten egg yolks, lemon juice and sugar. Continue as recipe to step 8, then add both the cream and stiffly beaten egg whites and complete freezing.

Raspberry ice cream (1)

you will need:

- 12 oz. raspberries
- 1 tablespoon lemon juice
- 4 tablespoons water
- 1 large can condensed milk (full cream quality)
- ¼ pint thin cream or evaporated milk

1 Mash or sieve the raspberries, and the lemon juice and water.
2 Stir in the condensed milk and cream.
3 Pour into freezing trays and freeze on coldest position for approximately 40 minutes.
4 Turn into bowl and whip, then return to freezing trays, and leave until firm, then return cold control to normal setting to store.

Raspberry ice cream (2)

you will need:

- 8 oz. fresh fruit or 1 packet frozen raspberries or 1 medium sized can
- 2 tablespoons sugar
- ¼ pint thick cream
- 2 egg whites
- few drops cochineal, if wished

1 Sieve or mash the fruit until smooth.
2 Add the sugar and lightly whipped cream.
3 Pour into freezing tray and freeze on coldest setting for approximately 30 minutes.
4 Put into bowl, whip lightly, then fold in the stiffly beaten whites of the eggs and cochineal. if desired.
5 Return to the freezing trays and freeze until firm, then turn cold control to normal setting to store.

Strawberry ice cream (1)

Use recipe for raspberry ice cream (1), but dissolve 1 level teaspoon gelatine powder in 4 tablespoons hot water, then proceed as for raspberry ice cream.

Strawberry ice cream (2)

Ingredients as raspberry ice cream (2), but add 1 level teaspoon gelatine powder dissolved in 3 tablespoons water to the fruit purée.

Note:
A better texture is obtained with a strawberry ice cream if this small amount of gelatine is used—it helps to prevent the mixture becoming 'chippy'.

Making ice cream with ice cream powder

Ice cream powders enable one to make the sweet very easily, and if wished, very economically too, for the powder blended with water or milk can be used as a basis for plain ice creams. They can also be used as a basis for really elaborate sweets.
Follow the directions for mixing and quantities as in the recipes, and freeze quickly.

Plain economy ice cream

you will need:

- 5 oz. ice cream powder
- ⅓ pint cold water

1 Set refrigerator to the coldest temperature.
2 Place the ice cream powder in a bowl and whisk in the water.
3 Put mixture into freezing compartment of refrigerator, and leave for about 30 minutes.
4 Take mixture out and whisk again thoroughly for 1 minute.
5 Return to freezing compartment for 1—2 hours then ice cream will be ready to serve.

Rich vanilla ice cream

For a slightly richer mixture, use evaporated milk instead of water.

Extra rich ice cream

you will need:

- 5 oz. ice cream powder
- 5 oz. water
- 4 oz. cream

To make a really de luxe mixture use cream instead of part of the water, keeping the proportions and method the same as for the economy recipe.

Banana ice cream

you will need:

3 bananas
little lemon juice
5 oz. ice cream powder
¼ pint evaporated milk
¼ pint water

1 Mash bananas and sprinkle with lemon juice.
2 Add ice cream powder, evaporated milk and water.
3 Whisk mixture to a smooth cream.
4 Freeze for 30 minutes.
5 Tip mixture from tray to bowl and whisk again.
6 Return mixture to tray and freeze until ready to serve.

Coconut ice

you will need:

5 oz. ice cream powder
1 6-oz. can evaporated milk (made up to ½ pint liquid with 4 oz. water)
2 oz. dessicated coconut
cochineal to colour (optional)

1 Blend ice cream powder and milk to a smooth paste and whisk thoroughly until smooth and creamy.
2 Fold in coconut and pour into freezing tray.
3 Leave until frozen ½ inch from sides of tray and then turn mixture into bowl and whisk again thoroughly for 1 minute.
4 Return to freezing tray and leave until firm (approx. 1½—2 hours).
5 Cochineal may be added to this ice cream to make variations in the colours.
6 To serve, spoon into individual glasses or cut into squares.

Cherry delight

you will need:

5 oz. ice cream powder
1 small can evaporated milk (made up to ½ pint liquid with 4 oz. water)
1 miniature bottle cherry brandy
2 - 3 tablespoons cream
2 oz. maraschino cherries, halved
2 oz. shelled Brazil nuts, roughly chopped
cochineal to colour

1 Blend the ice cream powder and the milk until smooth.
2 Stir in the cherry brandy and whisk together until creamy.
3 Lightly whip the cream and fold into the mixture.
4 Pour into containers and place in the freezing compartment of the refrigerator, having set the unit at the lowest temperature.
5 Leave for about 30 minutes.
6 Remove and place the mixture in a chilled bowl and beat well until creamy again, adding the cherries and pieces of nut and cochineal.
7 Replace in the container and freeze for a further 1½—2 hours.
8 To serve, pile into individual glasses and decorate with nuts and cherries.

Mocha ice cream

you will need:

2 eggs
5 oz. ice cream powder
1 - 2 oz. castor sugar
1 oz. cocoa
¼ pint strong coffee
¼ pint cream
grated chocolate for decoration

1 Set refrigerator at lowest temperature.
2 Separate the eggs.
3 Mix together ice cream powder, egg yolks, sugar, cocoa and coffee and whisk thoroughly until smooth and creamy.
4 Pour into freezing tray and freeze for 30 minutes or until mixture is frozen ½ inch from sides of tray.
5 Turn out of freezing tray into a basin, fold in stiffly beaten egg whites and cream. Whisk thoroughly for 1 minute.
6 Return to freezing tray and freeze for 1½ hours until ice cream is firm.
7 To serve, scoop into individual glasses and decorate with grated chocolate.

Chocolate peppermint ice cream

you will need:

- ½ pint evaporated milk
- 5 oz. ice cream powder
- 1½ teaspoons peppermint oil
- 1 packet chocolate buttons
- 1 packet chocolate vermicelli or bar grated chocolate

1. Set refrigerator to the coldest setting.
2. Blend the milk and ice cream powder to a smooth cream.
3. Add the peppermint oil and whisk until smooth and creamy.
4. Pour into freezing tray and when frozen ½ inch from the sides of the tray remove and place in a bowl.
5. Whisk thoroughly until smooth and gently fold in the chocolate buttons.
6. Return to the freezing tray and freeze for another 1½—2 hours.
7. To serve, turn out into individual dishes and scatter chocolate vermicelli on top.

Malt crunchy ice cream

you will need:

- 5 oz. ice cream powder
- ¼ pint milk (made with 1 part evaporated milk to 3 parts water)
- just over ¼ pint cream
- 4 slices malt fruit bread
- whipped cream to decorate

1. Set refrigerator to lowest temperature.
2. Mix together the ice cream powder with the milk and cream.
3. Whisk thoroughly until smooth.
4. Pour into freezing tray and leave until frozen ½ inch on both sides of tray.
5. Bake the four slices of malt fruit bread gently in the oven until crisp. Crush into very coarse crumbs with a rolling pin.
6. Turn out ice cream mixture into a bowl and whisk for 1 minute.
7. Stir in malt crumbs, return to freezing tray and allow to set firm.
8. To serve, scoop ice cream into individual glasses, pipe cream around ice cream and top with cream.

Marshmallow and pineapple ice cream

you will need:

- ½ pint milk
- 3 oz. pink marshmallows, finely chopped
- 3 oz. ice cream powder
- 4 oz. chopped canned pineapple
- marshmallows and whipped cream for decoration

1. Warm the milk.
2. Melt half the marshmallows in the milk and pour on to ice cream powder.
3. Whisk together until smooth.
4. Pour into freezing tray and leave until frozen ½ inch from sides of tray.
5. Turn mixture into bowl and whisk for 1 minute.
6. Fold in remaining marshmallow pieces and chopped pineapple.
7. Return to freezing tray and allow to set firm.
8. To serve, place spoonfuls of ice cream on a whole pineapple ring and decorate with chopped marshmallows and cream.

Orange and rum ice cream

you will need:

- 1 can mandarin oranges
- 16-oz. can evaporated milk (made up to ½ pint with 4 oz. water)
- 5 oz. ice cream powder
- 3 teaspoons rum essence, or 1 miniature bottle rum
- 1 oz. pistachio nuts (optional)
- whipped cream

1. Set refrigerator to lowest temperature.
2. Drain juice from mandarin oranges and add enough of the juice to the diluted evaporated milk to make ¾ pint liquid.
3. Blend with the ice cream powder and rum and whisk together until smooth and creamy.
4. Pour mixture into freezing tray and freeze for 30 minutes.
5. Turn out mixture into bowl and whisk thoroughly for 1 minute.
6. Gently fold in halved mandarin pieces and return mixture to refrigerator for 1½—2 hours, until firm.
7. To serve, scoop into individual glasses and decorate with pistachio nuts and whipped cream.

Orange ice cream

you will need:

2 oranges
water
5 oz. ice cream powder
orange slices for decoration

1. Thinly pare and shred rind of the oranges.
2. Simmer orange rind in water for 4 minutes.
3. Strain and add to the orange juice from the 2 oranges and make up to ½ pint with water.
4. Whisk in ice cream powder and freeze for 30 minutes.
5. Tip into bowl and whisk again.
6. Return to fridge and freeze until ready.
7. Serve in glasses and decorate with slices of orange.

Strawberry shortcake ice cream

you will need:

Shortcake:

4 oz. butter or margarine
2 oz. castor sugar
6 oz. plain flour
pinch salt

Ice cream:

1 medium sized can strawberries
5 oz. ice cream powder
milk
¼ pint cream

whipped cream for decoration

1. **Shortcake:** Cream fat and sugar until light and fluffy.
2. Fold in sieved flour and salt and knead gently until thoroughly mixed.
3. Roll out and bake in an 8-inch sandwich tin at (350°F.—Gas Mark 4) for approximately 45 minutes.
4. Leave to cool.
5. **Ice cream:** Set refrigerator to lowest setting.
6. Strain juice from strawberries and make up to ½ pint liquid with a little milk.
7. Put on one side 6 strawberries for decoration and mash remainder with a fork.
8. Mix together ice cream powder, mashed strawberries and liquid and whisk until smooth and creamy.
9. Pour mixture into freezing tray and leave until it is frozen ½ inch from sides of tray.
10. Turn out into bowl and whisk thoroughly for 1 minute.
11. Return to freezing tray and leave until firm (approx. 1½—2 hours).
12. To serve, pile ice cream on to shortcake base. Decorate with remaining strawberries or fresh ones when available and whips of thick cream.

Ice cream with added egg whites

you will need:

5 oz. ice cream powder
½ pint water
2 egg whites

1. Prepare the plain economy vanilla ice cream (see page 39) and freeze for 30 minutes.
2. Whip up the egg whites until stiff.
3. Turn the frozen ice cream into a basin and whip up until smooth.
4. Fold in the stiffly whipped egg whites and return to the freezing tray.
5. Freeze for another 2 hours.

This gives a very light texture and doubles the bulk of the ice cream.

Golden ice cream

you will need:

2 eggs
5 oz. ice cream powder
¼ pint evaporated milk
¼ pint water

1. Separate the egg yolks from the whites.
2. Whisk ice cream powder in a bowl with milk, water and egg yolks.
3. Freeze mixture for 30 minutes.
4. Tip mixture into bowl and fold in stiffly beaten egg whites.
5. Return mixture to tray and freeze until ready to serve.

Lemon and ginger fluff

you will need:

2 large lemons
4 teaspoons castor sugar
½ pint boiling water
wafer biscuit
5 oz. ice cream powder
3 large egg whites
3 - 4 oz. crystallised ginger

1. Set refrigerator to lowest temperature.
2. Grate 2 teaspoons of lemon rind from the whole lemons.

3 Halve lemons and squeeze out juice.
4 Slice remaining skins, add sugar and pour over the boiling water.
5 Leave to cool and strain.
6 Add lemon liquid and grated lemon rind to ice cream powder.
7 Whisk together until smooth and creamy.
8 Pour into freezing tray and leave until frozen ½ inch from sides of freezing tray.
9 Turn mixture out into bowl and whisk thoroughly for 1 minute.
10 Fold in stiffly beaten egg whites and return mixture to freezing tray.
11 Leave to freeze until firm, testing occasionally to see that the ice cream is fluffy and not too frozen.
12 To serve, scoop into individual glasses and decorate with pieces of ginger and a wafer biscuit.

Custard ice cream (1)

you will need:

1 level tablespoon custard powder
2 tablespoons sugar
½ pint milk
flavouring (see below)
¼ pint cream or evaporated milk

1 Make the custard in the usual way with the custard powder, sugar and milk.
2 Add flavouring.
3 When cold, stir from time to time to prevent a skin forming, add half the cream or whipped evaporated milk.
4 Pour into the freezing tray and freeze on coldest position for approximately 30 minutes.
5 Turn into a bowl and whisk, then add the rest of the cream or evaporated milk.
6 Return to freezing tray and continue freezing on coldest position until firm, then turn indicator to normal setting to store.

Custard ice cream (2)

you will need:

2 eggs
2 oz. sugar
½ pint warm milk
flavouring (see below)
¼ pint cream
whipped evaporated milk

1 Separate the egg yolks from the whites.
2 Beat the yolks with the sugar, pour on the warm milk, then cook gently using the top of a double saucepan or basin over hot water until thick enough to coat the back of a wooden spoon.
3 Allow custard to cool, stirring from time to time to prevent a skin from forming.
4 Add half the whipped cream or evaporated milk, and stiffly beaten egg whites and pour into a freezing tray and freeze on the coldest position for approximately 30 minutes.
5 Turn into a bowl, and whisk, then add flavouring and rest of cream or evaporated milk, continue freezing on coldest position until firm, then turn indicator to normal setting to store.

Variations in flavour for custard ice creams

Almond
Add 1—1½ teaspoons almond or ratafia essence and about 2 oz. chopped blanched almonds.

Burnt almond
Blanch and brown about 2 oz. almonds, then add to the custard.

Brown bread
Stir about 2 oz. fine brown breadcrumbs into the custard when cold.

Banana
Mash 3 bananas with 1 tablespoon lemon juice and add to the custard mixture.

Coffee
Blend 2 tablespoons instant coffee powder (3 for a strong flavour) with the custard powder in recipe 1. Dilute the powder with 1 tablespoon milk and add at step 5 in the second recipe.

Chocolate
Cook 1—1½ oz. cocoa or 2 oz. chocolate powder with the custard powder in recipe 1, or dilute this with 1—2 tablespoons milk and add at step 5 in the second recipe.

Fruit
Blend just over ¼ pint thick fruit purée with the custard when cold in either recipe.

French almond

Crush about 4 oz. French almond rock and add to the cold custard and cream.

Maple

Add 2 tablespoons maple syrup to the custard omitting 1 oz. sugar. When maple syrup is not available use 1 tablespoon golden syrup and 1 oz. brown sugar instead.

Peppermint

Stir about 8 peppermint creams into warm custard and reduce the amount of sugar.

Basic ice cream with gelatine

you will need:

- 1 teaspoon gelatine powder
- 2 tablespoons hot water
- ½ pint milk
- 3 oz. sugar
- ½ pint evaporated milk or cream
- flavouring (see below for details of flavouring and when this should be added)

1. Soften the gelatine in the hot water.
2. Put into a basin over hot water and add the milk and sugar.
3. Heat together until the gelatine is thoroughly dissolved.
4. Cool, then add the cream.
5. Pour into the freezing tray of the refrigerator.
6. Freeze in the coldest position (see page 6) for approximately 40 minutes, until lightly frozen.
7. Remove from the tray into a large cold bowl and whisk sharply.
8. Return to the tray and re-freeze until firm, then return indicator to normal position, to store.

Variations on ice cream with gelatine

Chocolate

Blend 2 oz. chocolate powder and 1 teaspoon vanilla essence to the milk.

Coffee

Blend 2—3 teaspoons powdered coffee with milk.

Mocha

Blend 1½ oz. chocolate powder and 1 teaspoon powdered coffee with milk.

Fruit

Make ¼ pint fruit purée—sieving strawberries, raspberries, blackcurrants, gooseberries.
Use only ¼ pint milk and when cool add the fruit purée.
Taste when the ice cream is frozen for the first time and if necessary add a little extra sugar.

Vanilla

Add 1½ level teaspoons vanilla essence to the milk.

Cream ice

you will need:

- 2 egg whites
- 2 level tablespoons icing sugar
- ¼ pint cream
- flavouring (see below)

1. Whisk the egg whites until very stiff.
2. Fold in the sugar and half the lightly whipped cream.
3. Put into freezing tray and freeze for approximately 30 minutes on the coldest setting.
4. Turn into a bowl, whip lightly, and fold in the rest of the cream and flavouring.
5. Return to freezing tray and continue freezing until firm, then turn cold control indicator to normal position to store.

Flavouring for ice cream

Almond

Add 1 teaspoon almond essence and 1—2 oz. browned blanched chopped almonds.

Coconut

Add 1 oz. desiccated coconut.

Coffee

Blend 1-2 teaspoons powdered coffee with 1 tablespoon milk, add to egg whites and cream.

Chocolate

Blend 1—1½ oz. chocolate powder with egg whites and cream.

Malt
Add 1½ oz. malt to egg whites and cream.

Peppermint
Add about 1 teaspoon peppermint essence to the mixture, or try 1 tablespoon *crème de menthe* instead.

Liqueur
Any of the rather sweet liqueurs, and in particular Tia Maria (coffee flavoured), apricot brandy or cherry brandy can be added to the ice cream mixture above.
Use a generous tablespoon, adding this with the second lot of cream.

Vanilla
Use 1 teaspoon vanilla essence.

Caramel ice creams

Most of the ice creams can be flavoured with caramel.

you will need:
3 oz. sugar
3 tablespoons water

1 Put the sugar into a saucepan with the water.
2 Heat gently, stirring well until the sugar has dissolved.
3 Boil steadily until the sugar mixture becomes golden brown.
In the custard ice creams allow the caramel to cool slightly, then add the milk and heat gently with the caramel, until thoroughly absorbed.

In the cream ice creams dilute the caramel with another tablespoon water, cool then add to the other ingredients.
If making caramel ice cream you will need to leave out just over half the sugar in the recipe.

Caramel nut ice cream
Add 2 - 3 oz. chopped nuts with the caramel.

Caramel sultana ice cream
When the caramel has been made add about 3 oz. sultanas and, if wished, 1 teaspoon sherry.

Chestnut ice cream
It is possible to add chestnut purée to most of the ice cream mixtures allowing 1 part purée to 2 parts ice cream mixture. The purée can be added when the ice cream is beaten, and should be sweetened, see page 48.
However since a chestnut purée has a rather uninviting colour you will probably find it better to serve the purée with the ice cream, rather than inside it. See the recipe for chestnut sundae on page 48.

Rich chocolate ice cream

you will need:
2 tablespoons milk
2 oz. grated chocolate or chocolate powder
2 eggs
2 oz. icing sugar
1 teaspoon vanilla essence
¼ pint thin cream (or use little milk with thick cream)
¼ pint thick cream

1 Warm milk and dissolve the chocolate in this.
2 Separate the egg yolks from the whites.
3 When cool add the well beaten egg yolks and icing sugar.
4 Stir in the vanilla essence, thin cream and pour into freezing tray.
5 Freeze on the coldest position for approximately 30 minutes.
6 Turn into cold mixing bowl and fold in lightly whipped thick cream and stiffly beaten egg whites.
7 Return to the freezing tray and freeze until firm, then return indicator to normal position to store.

Rich chocolate walnut ice cream
Recipe as above, but add 2 oz. finely chopped walnuts to the mixture at the same time as the sugar.

Rich chocolate and sultana ice cream
Recipe as above, but add 3 oz. sultanas to the warm chocolate and milk mixture.

Rich chocolate and cherry ice cream
Recipe as above, but add 3 oz. halved maraschino cherries to the chocolate mixture.

Using marshmallows in ice cream

The use of marshmallows in ice cream gives a particularly light texture. Because of the 'fluffy' consistency of marshmallows, which is present even when dissolved in milk, there is no need to beat this type of ice cream during freezing.

Banana marshmallow ice

you will need:

- 4 oz. marshmallows
- ¼ pint milk
- 4 ripe, but not discoloured, bananas
- 1 tablespoon lemon juice
- ½ pint cream or evaporated milk
- 1 oz. sugar

1. Put the marshmallows into a pan with the milk.
2. Heat for a few minutes, then remove from the heat, and allow the marshmallows to melt and cool.
3. Mash the bananas with the lemon juice.
4. Blend with the marshmallow liquid, and the lightly whipped cream or evaporated milk.
5. Taste the mixture and add the sugar if required.
6. Pour into freezing tray and freeze on the coldest setting until firm, then turn the indicator to normal setting to store.

Banana chocolate marshmallow ice

Recipe as above, but omit sugar, and add 2—3 oz. coarsely grated or chopped chocolate—plain or bitter chocolate makes a pleasant contrast in flavour.

Cherry walnut mallow

you will need:

- 6 oz. marshmallows
- ¼ pint milk
- 3 oz. chopped maraschino cherries
- 2 oz. chopped walnuts
- ⅜ - ½ pint cream

1. Put the marshmallows and milk into a saucepan and heat for a few minutes only then allow to cool, beating until smooth.
2. Add the cherries and nuts, then the lightly whipped cream.
3. Put into freezing trays and freeze on the coldest setting until quite firm, then return to normal setting to store.

Cherry macaroon mallow

Recipe as above, but use 2 chopped macaroon biscuits instead of walnuts.

Tutti fruitti mallow

Ingredients as cherry walnut mallow, but add 2—3 oz. chopped canned pineapple. If wished only 4 oz. of the marshmallows need be melted, the other 2 oz. being chopped finely, and added with the cherries, nuts and pineapple.

If desired a spoonful of sugar may be added in these recipes, but it is doubtful whether this is necessary.

Mocha mallow

you will need:

- 4 oz. white marshmallows
- ¼ pint milk
- ¼ pint very strong coffee
- 4 oz. chocolate, milk or plain
- ½ pint cream or evaporated milk

1. Put the marshmallows into a pan with the milk and heat for a minute or two only, then allow to cool.
2. Add the coffee and beat well until smooth.
3. Melt the chocolate in a basin over hot water, and add the marshmallow mixture to this.
4. When the mixture starts to stiffen a little fold in the lightly beaten cream.
5. Pour into freezing trays, or if the mixture is fairly thick spoon it into the trays and freeze on the coldest position until firm, then turn indicator to normal position to store.

Chocolate mallow

Recipe as above but use ½ pint milk and no coffee.

Mocha nut mallow

Recipe as mocha mallow, but add 3 oz. chopped nuts—hazel-nuts are particularly good—when adding the cream.

Mocha raisin mallow

Recipe as mocha mallow, but add the raisins (dates could be used instead) to the warm marshmallow mixture.

Strawberry mallow

you will need:

6 oz. marshmallows	8 - 10 oz. ripe strawberries
¼ pint milk	¼ pint cream

1 Put the marshmallows and milk into a pan and heat for a few minutes only, allow to cool.
2 Crush or sieve the strawberries, and add to the cold marshmallow mixture, beating well until thoroughly blended.
3 Fold in the lightly whipped cream.
4 Put into freezing trays, and freeze on the coldest position until just firm, then turn to normal setting to store.
It is very doubtful whether extra sugar will be needed in this recipe, but add accordingly to taste when all the ingredients are blended together.

Raspberry mallow

Ingredients as above, but use ripe raspberries or a mixture of raspberries and loganberries.

Making ice cream sundaes etc.

An ice cream sundae is one of the most delicious, and easy to make sweets. As it has to be made at the last minute have ready all the ingredients—the sauce in the refrigerator, the nuts chopped and the fruit well drained and prepared.

For a party, rather than having last minute rushes in the kitchen between courses, bring all the ingredients attractively arranged on dishes on to the table, and let your guests make their own sundaes.

The term 'coupe' is used to describe many of the sundaes.

Almond sundae

you will need:

vanilla or vanilla and honey ice cream	apricot and almond sauce (see page 58)
blanched almonds	whipped cream

1 Put a spoonful of vanilla ice cream in the glass.
2 Add spoonful of the sauce.
3 Top with more ice cream and sauce.
4 Decorate with whipped cream and blanched almonds.

Toasted almond sundae

Blanch almonds, split or shred them and put on trays in a moderate oven, leaving until dark brown in colour.

Recipe as almond sundae using the toasted instead of blanched almonds.

Almond and cherry sundae

you will need:

vanilla ice cream	apricot and almond sauce (see page 58)
maraschino or canned cherries	whipped cream

1 Put a spoonful of vanilla ice cream in a glass and top with well drained cherries.
2 Add more ice cream and coat with the almond and apricot sauce blended with a very little syrup from the maraschino or canned cherries.
3 Top with cream and cherries.

Almond coffee sundae

you will need:

coffee ice cream	whipped cream
coffee sauce (see page 58)	blanched or toasted almonds

1 Arrange the ice cream in glasses and top with sauce.
2 Decorate with whipped cream and a very thick layer of almonds.

Almond hedgehog sundae

you will need:

almond flavoured ice cream	1 tablespoon apricot almond sauce (see page 58) or apricot jam
blanched almonds	

1 Brown the almonds until golden in a moderate oven, and split in half lengthways, if wished.
2 Arrange a neat round of ice cream in glasses or dishes.
3 Stick in the almonds to look like the 'prickles' on a hedgehog.
4 Top with apricot sauce or jam.

Butterscotch sundae

you will need:

vanilla or banana ice cream
butterscotch sauce (see page 58)
little whipped cream

1 Top the ice cream with hot or cold butterscotch sauce.
2 Decorate with unsweetened whipped cream.

Butterscotch walnut sundae

you will need:

vanilla ice cream
chopped walnuts
butterscotch sauce (see page 58)

1 Arrange layers of ice cream, nuts and sauce in tall glasses.
2 Top with sauce and whole walnut.

Butter Brazil sundae

you will need for 4 glasses:

4 oz. butter Brazils
vanilla, coffee or chocolate ice cream
butterscotch sauce (see page 58)

1 Crush the butter Brazils rather coarsely.
2 Arrange layers of ice cream and the nut mixture in glasses.
3 Top with butterscotch sauce.

Butterscotch orange sundae

you will need:

fresh oranges
orange flavoured ice cream and/ or water ice
butterscotch sauce (see page 58)

1 Peel and divide oranges in slices, free from pith and skin.
2 Arrange layers of ice cream and oranges in glasses.
3 Top with the sauce and decorate with fresh orange slices.

Cardinal sundae

you will need:

raspberry or strawberry jelly
raspberries or strawberries
vanilla, or raspberry or strawberry ice cream
whipped cream

1 Arrange alternate layers of whisked jelly, fruit and ice cream in glasses.
2 Top with cream and fruit.

These tall sundaes are often given the name of parfaits, particularly where you have a mixture of jellies, etc., with the ice creams.

Cherry sundae

you will need:

canned or cooked cherries
vanilla or other flavoured ice cream
whipped cream
cherry brandy

1 Arrange layers of cherries, ice cream and a little syrup from the fruit in glasses.
2 Top with whipped cream and a generous spoonful of cherry brandy.

Chestnut (or marron) sundae

you will need:

Chestnut Purée
whipped cream
sugar to taste
marrons glacés
vanilla ice cream or chestnut ice cream

1 Fold a little chestnut purée into some of the cream and sweeten slightly.
2 Arrange layers of ice cream, chestnut cream, chestnut purée in glasses.
3 Top with plain whipped cream and marrons glacé.

To prepare chestnut purée

1 Boil chestnuts for about 10 minutes in water, having slit their skins to prevent them bursting.
2 Remove shells and skins while warm.
3 To each 1 lb. chestnuts make a syrup of ½ pint water, 3 oz. sugar and 1 teaspoon vanilla.
4 Cook the chestnuts steadily in the syrup for about 30 minutes.
5 Drain and sieve. The syrup can be used to serve with sweets.

Bought chestnut purée

It is possible to buy chestnut purée—either in cans or tubes. Generally the tubes are of sweetened purée—so do not add extra sugar to recipes.

The purée in cans is generally firm and unsweetened, so add sugar and a little vanilla essence to taste.

Chocolate sundae

(illustrated on the cover)

you will need:

chocolate or vanilla ice cream
chocolate sauce (see page 56)
flaked chocolate
whipped cream

1 Arrange layers of ice cream, sauce and flaked chocolate in glasses.
2 Top with whipped cream and chocolate.

Chocolate butterscotch sundae

you will need:

chocolate ice cream
butterscotch sauce (see page 58)
whipped cream (optional)

1 Arrange layers of the ice cream and sauce in glasses.
2 Top with whipped cream.

Chocolate and coffee sundae

you will need:

chocolate ice cream
coffee ice cream
chocolate sauce (see page 56)

1 Arrange alternately the two flavoured ice creams in glasses.
2 Top with plenty of hot or cold sauce.

Mocha sundae

you will need:

chocolate ice cream
coffee ice cream
whipped cream
coffee sauce (see page 58)

1 Arrange layers of the two flavoured ice creams in glasses.
2 Top with the sauce and cream.

Chocolate nut sundae

Make as chocolate sundae adding any chopped nuts—Brazil-nuts, hazel-nuts, almonds, etc.

Chocolate orange sundae (1)

you will need:

chocolate ice cream
fresh oranges
chocolate sauce (see page 56)

1 Arrange layers of ice cream and sliced oranges (free from pith and skin) in glasses.
2 Top with cold chocolate sauce.

Chocolate orange sundae (2)

you will need:

orange water ice
chocolate sauce

Arrange the water ice in tall glasses and at the very last minute top with hot or cold chocolate sauce.
The contrast of the richness of chocolate sauce, and the 'bite' of a not too sweet orange water ice is delicious.

Coffee sundae

you will need:

coffee ice cream
coffee sauce (see page 58)
Tia Maria
whipped cream
coarsely chopped nuts or grated chocolate

1 Arrange layers of the ice cream and sauce in glasses, and sprinkle with a few drops of Tia Maria.
2 Blend some of the Tia Maria into the whipped cream.
3 Decorate with the chopped nuts or the chocolate and whipped cream.

Coffee rum sundae

As above using rum instead of Tia Maria. Alternatively add rum to the coffee sauce so it is more evenly distributed.

Coffee fudge sundae

you will need:

coffee ice cream
fudge sauce (see page 56)
chopped nuts
whipped cream for decoration

1 Arrange layers of the ice cream, sauce and nuts in glasses.
2 Decorate with ice cream beaten until a little soft or with whipped cream.

Note:
Since fudge is a rich sauce many people will find extra cream too 'fatty', that is why I suggest beating a little ice cream to pile on top—(vanilla ice cream could be used for this).

Coupe Jacques

you will need:

fruit salad
vanilla ice cream
whipped cream

1 Arrange layers of the fruit and ice cream in glasses.
2 Top with the cream.

This is only one version of this very popular and delicious sweet—see below for other suggestions.

Variations:

1 For a luxury sweet soak the fruit in kirsch.
2 For a refreshing sweet use a lemon or orange water ice rather than ice cream.
3 For a more colourful sweet top with melted redcurrant jelly diluted with a little water.

Fruit and chocolate sundae

(illustrated on the cover)

you will need:

For the chocolate layer:

1 level tablespoon cornflour
1 level dessertspoon cocoa
½ pint milk
1 oz. sugar
2 or 3 tablespoons cream
fruit flavoured jelly
pineapple
grapes

1 Prepare chocolate layer by blending the cornflour and cocoa with the milk.
2 Put into saucepan, adding sugar and stir until smooth and thickened.
3 Allow to cool, stirring from time to time to prevent skin forming.
4 Fold in cream.
5 To prepare sundae, add layers of the cold chocolate cream, whisked jelly, pineapple and grapes.

Date and walnut sundae

you will need:

dessert dates
little orange juice
fresh oranges
orange or vanilla ice cream

1 Soak the dates for a short time in the orange juice to moisten, chopping them up if very large.
2 Skin and slice oranges, removing all pith and skin.
3 Arrange layers of the dates, oranges and ice cream in glasses and top with chopped nuts.

Date and orange sundae

As above omitting walnuts and topping with fresh oranges or orange curd.

Maple syrup sundae

you will need:

vanilla or almond ice cream
maple syrup
chopped nuts

Coat the ice cream with the syrup and decorate with chopped nuts.

Mock maple syrup

When maple syrup is not available a rather similar flavour can be obtained by heating together equal quantities of brown sugar (demerara) and golden syrup.

Pear ginger sundae

you will need:

dessert or canned pears
preserved ginger
vanilla or ginger flavoured ice cream
whipped cream

1 Arrange halved or sliced pears in glasses with a little chopped preserved ginger and ice cream.
2 Top with whipped cream, pieces of preserved ginger and some of the syrup from ginger.

Pear Hélène

(illustrated on the cover)

you will need:

canned or dessert pears
vanilla ice cream
chocolate sauce*

1 Drain canned pears or peel and core dessert pears.
2 Prepare the chocolate sauce.
3 Put block of ice cream on a cold serving dish with pears arranged on and around it.
4 If serving the sauce hot, do this at the very last minute pouring over the pears so they are well coated.
5 If serving the sauce cold, this can be put over the pears earlier and the ice cream arranged in the centre at the last minute.

* There are several recipes in this book, but below is a special American chocolate sauce which blends extremely well with ice cream and fruit.

American chocolate sauce

(illustrated on the cover)

you will need:

6 oz. brown sugar
3 oz. cocoa
½ pint milk
vanilla essence

1 Put all the ingredients into a saucepan.
2 Stir until the sugar has dissolved.
3 Boil for 2 minutes or longer if a thicker sauce is required.
4 Serve hot or cold.

Pineapple mint sundae

you will need:

chopped canned or fresh pineapple
vanilla ice cream
sugar, with fresh pineapple
mint leaves
pineapple jam

1 Chop some of the pineapple into neat pieces, and some very finely.
2 Blend the finely chopped pineapple with some of the syrup from the can and pineapple jam to give a sweet sauce.
3 If using fresh pineapple, add sugar and water and simmer for a minute or two, then add to jam.
4 Arrange layers of the ice cream and pineapple sauce in glasses.
5 Top with large pieces of pineapple and mint leaves.

Pineapple sundae

Arrange layers of ice cream with chopped fresh or canned pineapple—sweetening to taste—and flavouring with Curaçao or kirsch if wished. Top with cream and pineapple.

Raspberry sundae

you will need:

raspberries or raspberry jam
sugar to taste
raspberry ice cream
vanilla ice cream

1 If using fresh raspberries sprinkle with a little sugar and leave for a short time for the juice to flow slightly.
2 Arrange layers of the ice creams and fruit in glasses and top with fruit or slightly diluted jam.

Also try a combination of raspberry water and cream ices in sundaes.

There are many ways in which one can combine strawberries with ice cream. In order to have this delicious fruit at their best, chill for a short time only in the refrigerator.

Strawberry sundae (1)

you will need:

strawberries
sugar
strawberry ice cream
whipped cream

1 Halve or quarter some of the strawberries, sprinkle with a little sugar so the juice flows.
2 Arrange layers of ice cream and prepared fruit in glasses.
3 Top with whipped cream and whole sweetened fruit.

Strawberry sundae (2)

you will need:

strawberries
sugar
little kirsch
strawberry ice cream
strawberry water ice

1 Halve the strawberries and sprinkle with sugar and kirsch.
2 Arrange the cream and water ices and fruit in tall glasses.
3 Decorate with whole fruit.

Chocolate strawberry sundae

you will need:

chocolate ice cream
strawberry ice cream
whipped cream
grated chocolate
whole fruit

1 Arrange alternate layers of chocolate ice cream and strawberry ice cream or water ice with fruit in tall glasses.
2 Top with whipped cream, grated chocolate and whole fruit.

Chocolate and strawberry flavours blend unexpectedly well.

Making water ices

Water ices are not only easy to make, but are most refreshing to eat, and appeal to those people who do not like creamy frozen sweets. There are no problems about freezing water ices as they can be frozen at the normal setting.

Ideally they must not be served too cold, and should be beaten slightly with a fork just before serving.

To serve pile into chilled sundae glasses. Cream can be served with the ices.

Blackcurrant water ice

you will need:

12 oz. blackcurrants
1 egg white
½ pint water
3 oz. water

1 Simmer the blackcurrants with the water and sugar until soft.
2 Rub through a sieve, and if necessary add more water to give about ¾ pint purée.
3 Add the stiffly beaten egg white.
4 Put into freezing tray and freeze until firm, stirring lightly with a fork after about 40 minutes.

Blackberry water ice

Recipe as above, adding juice of 1 lemon to the fruit.

Blueberry water ice

Recipe as blackcurrant water ice, adding 1 tablespoon lemon juice to the fruit.

This fruit is also known as whortleberries or blaeberries.

Cranberry water ice

Recipe as blackcurrant water ice, but use ¾ pint water.

Gooseberry water ice

you will need:

1 lb. gooseberries
½ pint water
3 oz. sugar
juice and grated rind 1 lemon
1 egg white

1 Simmer the gooseberries with the water, sugar and lemon rind.
2 When soft rub through sieve, then add the lemon juice and cool.
3 Fold in the stiffly beaten egg white.
4 Pour into freezing trays and freeze until firm, stirring lightly after about 40 minutes.

Greengage water ice

Recipe as for gooseberry water ice. Choose rather firm under-ripe greengages to give the maximum amount of flavour.

Lemon water ice (1)

you will need:

rind 2 lemons
½ pint water
3 - 4 oz. sugar
¼ pint lemon juice
1 egg white

1 Pare the lemon rind finely, and simmer for about 5 minutes with the water.
2 Strain and dissolve the sugar in the warm liquid.
3 Cool, add lemon juice and stiffly beaten egg white.
4 Put into freezing tray and freeze for about 40 minutes then stir slightly with a fork, and leave until ready to serve.

The egg white helps to prevent the water ice becoming 'chippy' but could be omitted if wished.

Lemon water ice (2)

Recipe as above, but omit the egg white, and dissolve 1 level teaspoon gelatine powder in the hot water or use about 2 squares from a 1 pint lemon jelly tablet.

Note:
This gives a fairy strong flavoured water ice; if too strong when tasted at step 3, dilute with an extra ¼ pint water.

Loganberry water ice

you will need:

1 lb. loganberries	3 oz. sugar
¾ pint water	1 egg white

1. Simmer the loganberries with the water and sugar until soft.
2. Rub through a sieve and cool.
3. Add the stiffly beaten egg white, and put mixture into freezing tray.
4. Freeze for about 40 minutes, then stir lightly, and leave until ready to serve.

Raspberry water ice

Recipe as above, using ripe raspberries which should be sieved uncooked and added to the sugar and water syrup.
If the raspberries are not ripe simmer for a short time with the water and sugar.

Strawberry water ice

Recipe as loganberry water ice, but a better flavour is given if just under 1 lb. strawberries are used together with 4—6 oz. redcurrants.

Melon water ice

you will need:

½ pint water	1 ripe melon
grated rind and juice 2 lemons	1 egg white
3 oz. sugar	green colouring (optional)

1. Simmer the lemon rind and sugar in the water.
2. Remove all pulp from melon and rub through a sieve, and add to strained liquid and lemon juice.
3. Fold in the stiffly beaten egg white, add green colouring if desired and put into freezing tray and freeze for about 45—50 minutes, then stir lightly, and leave until ready to serve.

Orange water ice (1)

you will need:

rind 1 lemon	1 tablespoon lemon juice
rind 2 oranges	¼ pint orange juice
½ pint water	1 egg white
3 oz. sugar	

1. Pare the lemon and orange rinds thinly, and simmer with the water for 5 minutes.
2. Strain, and dissolve the sugar in the liquid. while it is still warm.
3. Cool, add lemon and orange juice and stiffly beaten egg white.
4. Put into freezing trays and freeze for about 40 minutes, then stir lightly with a fork, and leave until ready to serve.
   The egg white helps to prevent the water ice becoming 'chippy', but could be omitted if wished.

Orange water ice (2)

Recipe as above, but omit the egg white and dissolve 1 level teaspoon gelatine powder in the hot water or use about 2 squares from a 1 pint orange jelly tablet.

Note:
This gives a fairly strong flavoured water ice, if too strong, when tasted at step 3, then dilute with about ¼ pint more water.

Tangerine water ice

Recipe as orange water ice above, using rind from 3 tangerines instead of oranges.

Interesting ways to serve ice cream

The way you serve any food makes a great deal of difference to the appearance of the dish, and ice cream lends itself to rather spectacular methods of serving.

Apple rafts

you will need:

apples	apricot jam
ice cream	water

1. Bake apples in the usual way, then skin and stand on slices of ice cream.
2. Heat apricot jam with a little water and allow to cool.
3. Cover the apples and ice cream with the sauce.

Banana splits

you will need:

bananas	grated chocolate
strawberry or vanilla ice cream	Melba sauce (see page 73) (optional)
whipped cream	

1 Halve bananas lengthways, and arrange on either side of spoonfuls of ice cream.
2 Decorate with whipped cream, and grated chocolate.
3 Add a little Melba sauce, if wished.

Pear baskets

you will need:

canned pears	preserved ginger
vanilla ice cream	

1 Fill halved canned pears with vanilla ice cream.
2 Top with preserved ginger.

Melon basket

you will need:

1 melon	sugar
sherry	ice cream

1 Cut the top from a melon, remove all the centre seeds and discard.
2 Scoop out the pulp and dice neatly, or cut into circles with a vegetable scoop.
3 Pack the flesh back into the melon case, flavouring with sherry and sugar.
4 Top with ice cream—most flavours blend well with this.

Stuffed pineapple

you will need:

1 pineapple	sugar
vanilla ice cream	kirsch

1 Cut the stalk end from a pineapple, then remove all the centre pulp, dicing this finely.
2 Mix with vanilla ice cream, adding little extra sugar if wished and flavouring with kirsch.
3 Pile back into the pineapple case, and put back the top.
4 If your freezing compartment is sufficiently deep put pineapple in there for about 1 hour to freeze, if not serve as quickly as possible.

For a more luxurious sweet the pineapple and ice cream can also be mixed with chopped marrons glacés and crystallised fruits.

Ice cream shorties

you will need:

about 12 short-cake biscuits	whipped cream
vanilla ice cream	strawberries or other soft fruit

1 Cover the biscuits with ice cream.
2 Top with whipped cream and fruit.

Making sorbets

A sorbet is very similar to a water ice, except that a higher percentage of egg whites are used, so giving a more 'fluffy' texture.

When large formal dinners used to be served a sorbet was often given between courses to 'clear the palate', so the flavour must be refreshing and not too sweet.

A sorbet can be frozen at the normal setting of the refrigerator, so there is no need to turn to the coldest position.

Fruit sorbet

you will need:

½ pint thick sweetened soft fruit purée	2 egg whites

1 Mix fruit purée with the stiffly beaten egg whites.
2 Put into the freezing tray of the refrigerator and freeze until just firm. Stir lightly before serving.

Lemon sorbet

you will need:

2 eggs	½ pint water
rind and juice 2 large lemons	3 oz. sugar

1 Separate the yolks from the egg whites.
2 Peel strips of lemon rind from the fruit.
3 Simmer the rind with the water for 7—8 minutes.
4 Strain the liquid, pour over the beaten egg yolks and sugar.
5 Add the lemon juice.
6 Freeze until thickening slightly, then add to the stiffly beaten egg whites.
7 Return to the refrigerator and leave until firm.

Egg yolks can be omitted but they add additional food value. If yolks are not used, dissolve sugar in the liquid.

This is an ideal sweet for 'slimmers' if sugar substitute is used instead of sugar.

Fruit sherbets

A sherbet is not unlike a sorbet, except it has a little cream or ice cream powder added to give slightly more richness.
For good texture the mixture must be beaten during freezing, but it can be frozen on normal setting.

Apple sherbet (1)

you will need:

3 oz. ice cream powder
juice ½ lemon
¾ pint apple purée (made from 1 lb. apples and 2 oz. sugar)
2 egg whites
chopped pistachio nuts for decoration

1 Blend together ice cream powder and lemon juice with apple purée and whisk together until smooth.
2 Pour into freezing tray and allow to freeze for approximately ½ hour.
3 Turn mixture into bowl and whisk thoroughly for 1 minute.
4 Fold in the stiffly beaten egg whites and whisk again.
5 Return to freezing tray and allow to set firm.
6 To serve, scoop into individual sundae glasses and decorate with chopped pistachio nuts.

Apple sherbet (2)

Ingredients as previous recipe, but omit ice cream powder, and mix apple purée with ¼ pint thin cream or evaporated milk.

Rhubarb sherbet

Use either recipe for apple sherbet, substituting rhubarb for apple purée.
Cook the rhubarb with the minimum amount of water.

Loganberry sherbet

you will need:

2 - 3 oz. sugar
½ pint water
juice and grated rind lemon
1 lb. loganberries
2 egg whites

1 Heat sugar, water, lemon rind and loganberries, until soft.
2 Rub through sieve, add lemon juice and more sugar if desired.
3 Put into freezing tray, leave for 20—30 minutes until lightly frozen, then stir into the egg whites which should be stiffly beaten.
4 Re-freeze until firm.
5 Serve by itself or with vanilla ice cream.

Rosy sherbet

you will need:

12 oz. rhubarb
¼ pint water (for cooking rhubarb)
3 oz. sugar
1 level tablespoon gelatine powder
1 pint water
grated rind and juice 1 lemon

1 Cook the rhubarb with water and sugar and rub through a sieve.
2 Dissolve the gelatine in a little hot water, add the rest of the water, the rhubarb purée and lemon juice and rind.
3 Taste and add little more sugar if necessary, but the sherbet is nicer if rather sharp.
4 Pour into freezing tray and leave until light frosted.
5 Serve in tall glasses.

Sauces to Serve with Ice Cream

Hot sauces to serve with ice cream

A very quick and easy sweet is to serve commercial or home-made ice cream with an interesting sauce over the top.

A good contrast is to serve cold ice cream with a hot sauce.
To keep the sauce hot, transfer it to the top of a double saucepan over hot water.

Apricot lemon sauce

you will need:

6 tablespoons apricot jam
grated rind and juice 2 lemons
6 tablespoons water
1 - 2 oz. sugar
pulp from 1 lemon (optional)

1 Simmer the jam and lemon rind in the water for about 5 minutes.
2 Add the sugar and lemon juice and heat together.
3 Add the lemon pulp.

The 'bite' from the pieces of fresh lemon is very pleasing in contrast to the sweet sauce and ice cream.

Apricot orange sauce

Recipe as above, but use orange instead of lemon juice and only 4 tablespoons water.

Caramel sauce

Since even hot caramel sauce over ice cream becomes cold quickly a thinner mixture than usual must be used otherwise it will become too hard.

you will need:

4 oz. sugar
4 tablespoons water
To serve hot: further 4 tablespoons water
To serve cold: further 6 tablespoons water

1 Put sugar and water into a saucepan and stir until the sugar has dissolved, do not have the heat too high for this.
2 Boil steadily, there is no need to stir, until the mixture becomes golden brown.
3 Add the rest of the water and heat in the caramel.
4 Serve hot or cold.

Chocolate sauce (1)

you will need:

1 dessertspoon cornflour
1 dessertspoon cocoa
½ pint milk
1 tablespoon sugar
few drops vanilla essence
knob butter

1 Blend the cornflour and cocoa with a little milk.
2 Heat the remainder of the milk.
3 When nearly boiling pour on to the blended mixture.
4 Return to the heat and cook for 2 minutes, stirring continuously.
5 Add sugar, vanilla essence and butter.

Chocolate sauce (2)

you will need:

1 oz. margarine or butter
1 oz. cocoa
½ teaspoon vanilla essence
2 tablespoons water
2 oz. sugar or 1 oz. sugar and 1 tablespoon golden syrup

1 Put all the ingredients into a saucepan and heat gently until cocoa has quite dissolved.
2 Do not boil this sauce as it will spoil its shiny appearance.

Coffee sauce

you will need:

¼ pint strong coffee
1 oz. sugar
2 tablespoons golden syrup
few drops vanilla essence
½ oz. butter

1 Put all the ingredients in a saucepan and heat together until slightly thickened.
2 Serve hot.

Fudge sauce

you will need:

8 oz. sugar (brown or white)
1 oz. butter
¼ pint milk
3 tablespoons water
1 small can evaporated milk
flavouring (see below)

1 Put the sugar, butter, milk and water into a strong pan, and heat steadily until the sugar has melted, stirring well.
2 Continue cooking, stirring from time to time until the mixture forms a soft ball when tested in cold water.
3 Take off heat and gradually stir in the evaporated milk beating well.
4 Serve hot or cold.

To keep hot without becoming too thick stand over a pan of hot water until required.

To store and use cold put into a screw topped jar, and take out amount desired—the sauce should not be too thick, but does tend to thicken with keeping, so add a little milk, evaporated milk or cream if wished.

Coffee fudge sauce

Use recipe above, with strong coffee instead of water.

Chocolate fudge sauce (1)

Recipe as above, adding 1 oz. cocoa to the sugar, butter, etc., and ½ teaspoon vanilla essence.

Chocolate fudge sauce (2)

Recipe as above, but melt 2—3 oz. chocolate with the evaporated milk in a basin over hot water.
Add to the fudge mixture, beating well to blend after the sugar etc., has reached the soft ball stage.

Vanilla fudge sauce

Recipe as fudge sauce, but add I good teaspoon vanilla when mixture reaches soft ball stage.

Walnut fudge sauce

Recipe as fudge sauce, but add 3 oz. chopped walnuts and 1 teaspoon vanilla or ½ teaspoon vanilla and ½ teaspoon almond essence when mixture reaches soft ball stage.

Chocolate peppermint fudge

Use recipe for fudge sauce, but add 1 oz. cocoa to the sugar, butter etc., and a few drops peppermint essence
or
stir about 4 oz. chocolate peppermint creams into the mixture when it has formed a soft ball, but wait for a few minutes so it is not too hot, or the chocolate coating becomes dull and unattractive.

Easy fudge sauce

you will need:

- 4 oz. fudge (any flavour)
- 2 tablespoons milk, cream or evaporated milk

1 Put the ingredients into a basin and stand over a pan of boiling water.
2 Heat well, stir and serve hot or cold.
3 If storing a larger quantity allow rather more milk since this does stiffen with keeping.

Cold sauces to serve with ice cream

Keep these in the refrigerator before serving, so they are really very cold. Most of the sauces will keep for some time, so make a good quantity and store in air tight jars.

Apricot ginger sauce (1)

you will need:

- 6 tablespoons apricot jam
- 1 tablespoon syrup from preserved ginger
- 2 tablespoons chopped preserved ginger
- 3 tablespoons water

1 Heat all the ingredients together for sufficient time to melt the jam.
2 Stir well. If rather thick add little more water.

Apricot ginger sauce (2)

you will need:

- 4 tablespoons water
- 1 good tablespoon sugar
- 6 tablespoons apricot jam
- 2 oz. preserved ginger
- 2 tablespoons orange juice

1 Put the water, sugar and jam into saucepan and heat together until jam has melted.
2 Add preserved ginger and orange juice.

Apricot almond sauce

you will need:

6 oz. chopped canned or cooked apricots
4 tablespoons apricot syrup
1 tablespoon apricot jam
2 oz. blanched almonds

1 Heat the apricots, syrup and jam together until jam has melted.
2 Cool and add split blanched almonds.

Butterscotch sauce (1)

you will need:

8 oz. brown sugar
4 oz. butter
¼ pint water

1 Put the sugar and butter in a pan.
2 Stir until the sugar has dissolved, then boil steadily until darkened a little (about 3 minutes).
3 Add the water and heat thoroughly.
4 Allow to cool.

Butterscotch sauce (2)

you will need:

2 oz. butter
4 oz. brown sugar
4 oz. golden syrup
2 egg yolks
4 tablespoons water

1 Put the butter, sugar and syrup into a saucepan and heat until the sugar has dissolved, stirring well.
2 Draw to one side and cool slightly, then add the egg yolks beaten with the water and heat for a few minutes.
3 Serve very cold.

If preferred all the ingredients can be put in the top of a double saucepan or in a basin over hot water and stirred together until well blended.

Caramel cream sauce

you will need:

4 oz. sugar
4 tablespoons water
¼ pint cream or evaporated milk

1 Put the sugar and water into a pan, and stir until the sugar has dissolved over a steady heat.
2 Boil, without stirring, until the mixture becomes golden brown—*do not darken too much.*
3 Allow to cool—the sauce will probably set, but this does not matter—but you *must not* add cream or evaporated milk to hot sauce, otherwise it will curdle.
4 Add the cream or evaporated milk, and heat very gently, stirring from time to time until the milk and caramel have blended together.
5 Serve cold.

Chocolate cream sauce

you will need:

⅜ pint milk
1 teaspoon vanilla essence
4 oz. plain chocolate
½ oz. butter or 2 teaspoons oil
¼ pint cream
little sugar if wished

1 Put the milk, vanilla, and chocolate into a saucepan or the top of a double saucepan.
2 Heat gently until the chocolate has melted, allow to cool, stirring once or twice, and add the oil or butter.
3 Stir in the cream and beat well to mix, then taste and sweeten if wished.

This sauce can be stored for 1 or 2 days in the refrigerator.

Coffee sauce

you will need:

¼ pint strong coffee
1 oz. sugar
2 tablespoons golden syrup
2 tablespoons cream

1 Heat the coffee, sugar and syrup together for a few minutes.
2 Cool, then add the cream.
3 Chill thoroughly.

Coffee cream

you will need:

1 egg white
1 oz. sieved icing sugar
¼ pint cream
1 teaspoon instant coffee
1 teaspoon Tia Maria
chopped nuts for decoration

1 Whisk the egg white until very stiff, fold in the icing sugar.
2 Whip the cream until moderately stiff, then fold in the egg white mixture.
3 Add coffee and Tia Maria.
4 Pile over vanilla or chocolate ice cream and decorate with chopped nuts.

Fluffy golden sauce

you will need:

2 eggs
2 tablespoons sieved icing sugar
¼ pint cream
flavouring (see below)

1 Separate the egg yolks from the whites.
2 Put the yolks into a basin with the sugar and beat well until thick and creamy.
3 Blend with the lightly whipped cream and flavouring.
4 Lastly fold in the stiffly beaten egg whites.
5 Pile on top of ice cream.

This sauce keeps for an hour or so in the refrigerator, but should not be left too long, though it must be served very cold.

Brandy golden sauce

Gradually add 1—2 tablespoons brandy to the whipped cream and egg mixture.

Coffee golden sauce

Add ½—1 tablespoon Tia Maria to the cream and egg yolks.

Vanilla golden sauce

Use 1 teaspoon vanilla essence or substitute vanilla flavoured sugar for the icing sugar.

Kirsch cream

you will need:

¼ pint cream
2 tablespoons icing sugar
1 oz. blanched almonds, shredded
2 tablespoons kirsch

1 Whip the cream until just stiff enough to stand in peaks.
2 Gradually add the sugar, then the blanched almonds and kirsch.

Hard sauces

The combination of the hard sauce (normally used with Christmas pudding) and the soft sweetness of ice cream is very pleasant.

Basic recipe

you will need:

3 oz. unsalted butter
6 oz. sieved icing sugar
flavourings (see below)

1 Cream butter and icing sugar until smooth and white in colour.
2 Gradually beat in the flavouring, pile or pipe into dish.
3 Store in the refrigerator until very hard indeed.

Brandy hard sauce

Add about 2 tablespoons brandy.

Brandy orange hard sauce

Very gradually add 2 tablespoons brandy and grated rind and juice of 1 orange. Instead of fresh orange juice a little orange brandy could be used.

Cinnamon hard sauce

Gradually add 2 tablespoons brandy to butter and sugar mixture, then add 1 teaspoon powdered cinnamon.

Cherry brandy hard sauce

Gradually add 2 tablespoons cherry brandy to the butter and sugar mixture.

Lemon hard sauce

Gradually add grated rind and juice of 1 lemon to the butter and sugar mixture, then work in 1 tablespoon dry sherry.

Orange hard sauce

Add grated rind of 1 orange, then gradually add the juice and a tablespoon orange brandy. Stir in a tablespoon very finely chopped crystallised orange peel.

Rum hard sauce
Use brown instead of icing sugar, and add 2 tablespoons rum gradually to the butter and sugar mixture.

Sweets using Ice Cream

By adding ice cream to a quite ordinary sweet, you can transform it into something rather special. In many of the recipes below, the ice cream can be put into a dish and placed in the main part of the refrigerator just before the meal, as it is better with a slightly softened texture.

Baked Alaskas

This combination of ice cream, fruit and meringue sounds a very difficult sweet to serve in one's own home. In fact it is very simple, for everything can be prepared beforehand and the sweet put into the oven for a few minutes before serving the first course.
You will find that the meringue forms such a good 'insulation' round the ice cream that it will not melt while eating the first course of the meal.
Be very careful however to *completely cover* the ice cream with the meringue—and also to brown in a *very hot oven* so that the heat does not penetrate through to the ice cream.
This sweet is also known as a Norwegian omelette or soufflé surprise. In these recipes however one generally omits the sponge cake (see Baked Alaska recipes) and just uses ice cream and fruit.
Put these on to an overproof dish and coat with meringue, baking as an Alaska.

Basic method to make a Baked Alaska

you will need:
1 ice cream block
1 sponge cake the same size as the ice cream
fruit

Meringue:
4—5 egg whites
sugar*

* allow either 1 oz. sugar per egg white or if you have a very sweet tooth 2 oz. per egg white.

1. Choose an ovenproof dish, so the sweet can be served and baked on the same container.
2. Put the sponge cake on the dish, soaking with a little fruit syrup if wished.
3. Top with the *very firm* block of ice cream and fruit.
4. Make the meringue mixture by whisking the egg whites until *very stiff*, then folding in the sugar gradually.
5. Pile or pipe the meringue mixture over the whole of the sponge cake, and ice cream mixture—taking care no ice cream is left uncovered otherwise it will melt.
6. Put into a *very hot oven* (475°F. - 500°F. — Gas Mark 8 - 9) for about 3 minutes only, until golden brown.
7. Remove from the oven and serve at once or leave no longer than 30 minutes before serving.

Apple Alaska

Put cooked, well drained apple, flavoured with a little ginger, on to the sponge.
Use vanilla or coffee ice cream.

Blackberry Alaska (blackcurrants can be used in same way)

Use either sweetened ripe blackberries or well drained canned blackberries.
Crush the fresh fruit and put on to the sponge.
Use vanilla ice cream.

Cherry Alaska

Use vanilla or tutti fruitti ice cream.

Soak the sponge cake with syrup from the canned or cooked cherries.

Arrange most of the cherries round the sponge, but save a few for decoration.

Coat with meringue, putting cherries on top before baking.

Chocolate Alaska

This is rather nicer if no sponge cake is used, but if you wish for a more substantial sweet and include a sponge cake, moisten it with sherry or a little liqueur. Coat chocolate ice cream with the meringue and serve with hot or cold chocolate sauce (see page 56).

Chocolate walnut Alaska

Coat ice cream thickly with nuts.

Coffee pear Alaska

Arrange halved canned pears on the sponge and top with coffee ice cream.

This sweet can be served with coffee sauce if wished (see page 56).

Grapefruit Alaska

you will need:

- 2 large grapefruit
- little sugar for the fruit
- 1 block vanilla ice cream
- 3 egg whites
- 3 oz. sugar
- glacé cherries

1. Halve the grapefruit and remove the fruit carefully, cutting away the pith and skin.
2. Mix the fruit with a little sugar.
3. Pile back into the cases, topping with a spoonful of ice cream.
4. Whisk the egg whites until stiff.
5. Fold in the sugar.
6. Cover the grapefruit mixture with the meringue and put into a very hot oven for only 3 minutes.
7. Decorate with a cherry and serve at once.

Raspberry Alaska

Crush canned, frozen or fresh raspberries (sweetening these). Put on to the sponge cake and leave for a while, so this becomes moistened with the fruit purée.

Top with vanilla or raspberry ice cream and meringue.

Serve decorated with whole fruit. This is put on after baking.

Strawberry Alaska

As raspberry Alaska, using strawberry ice cream—although a combination of strawberries and chocolate or coffee ice cream is unusual and pleasant.

The above are just a few suggestions for this sweet, but it can be varied in so many ways.

Shortcake Alaska

Use a crisp round of shortcake or shortbread instead of sponge cake.

Alaska flan

This is made in the same way as a baked Alaska, but omitting the sponge cake.

The ice cream etc., is put into a baked flan case with the fruit, covered with ice cream, and baked as an Alaska.

Alaska pie

you will need:

- 5 oz. sweet short crust pastry (see page 81)
- 1 lb. well drained cooked or raw soft fruit
- 1 ice cream block
- 3 oz. sugar
- 3 egg whites

1. Make flan and bake until brown. Cool.
2. Half fill with fruit. If uncooked sweeten and mash slightly.
3. Slice firm ice cream and arrange on top, then cover with more fruit.
4. Finally, fold sugar into stiffly beaten egg whites.
5. Cover ice cream, fruit, etc., and bake for 3 minutes only in very hot oven (475°F. - 500°F. —Gas Mark 8 - 9).
6. Serve at once.

Apple and banana whip

You will need:

2 egg whites
1 large ice cream block
3 good apples for grating
3 oz. castor sugar
2 firm bananas
chopped nuts for decoration

1 Whisk the egg whites until very stiff.
2 Allow the ice cream to soften a little.
3 Grate the apples, cover with sugar and mix well.
4 Mash the bananas finely and fold into the stiffly beaten egg whites.
5 Chop up the ice cream and gradually beat into the fruit and egg white mixture.
6 When all the ingredients have been mixed together, whisk well.
7 Pour into an attractive bowl or individual glasses and chill.
8 Decorate with chopped nuts.

Blackberry ice pudding

you will need:

1 lb. fresh or frozen blackberries

Meringue:

2 egg whites
4 oz. castor sugar

Ice cream:

4 egg yolks
3 oz. sugar
¼ pint milk
¼ pint cream

Crème Chantilly:

2 egg whites
¼ pint cream
icing sugar to taste

1 Make the *meringue* by whisking the egg whites until very stiff.
2 Gradually fold in the sugar.
3 Pipe or put spoonfuls on to well oiled paper on an oiled tray.
4 Dry out very slowly in a very cool oven 225°F. - 250°F.—Gas Mark 0 - ½) for several hours until the meringue is crisp.
5 To make the *ice cream* turn the indicator of the refrigerator to the coldest position for 30 minutes before starting to freeze the mixture.
6 Beat the egg yolks and sugar until light and thick.
7 Fold in the milk and cook gently for a short time in a basin over hot water.
8 Cool and fold in the lightly whipped cream.
9 Put into freezing tray and freeze until just firm.
10 Turn out and whisk sharply.
11 Whip until light in texture folding in just under half of the sweetened blackberries.
12 Freeze until firm and then turn the indicator to normal position to store.
13 Cover the bottom of a ring mould with crushed meringues.
14 Cover with spoonfuls of the blackberry ice cream and then a final layer of crushed meringue.
15 Replace in freezing compartment of the refrigerator to set, or stand the ring mould on ice cubes in a large bowl until ready to serve.
16 Make the *Crème Chantilly* by whisking the egg whites very stiffly and the cream lightly.
17 Fold together and add whole blackberries and a little sieved icing sugar.
18 Turn out the ice cream ring and fill with the *Crème Chantilly*. Any meringues left over can be served with the sweet.

Note:
Fresh or frozen blackberries should be slightly cooked with sugar to taste. If fresh and very ripe, they can be used raw.

Fruit basket

you will need:

Pastry:

8 oz. flour (preferably plain)
4 oz. margarine
1 oz. sugar
2 egg yolks
little water to mix

Meringue:

2 egg whites
4 oz. sugar (preferably castor)

Filling:

ice cream
selection of summer fruits—ripe strawberries, raspberries, cherries, black and red currants, gooseberries (softened by simmering in a little sugar and water)

To decorate:

band angelica
little melted redcurrant jelly

1 Make the pastry in the usual way adding sugar and bind with the egg yolks and water.
2 Roll out thinly and line a 2-pint greased pie dish.
3 Bake 'blind' in the centre of a moderately hot oven (400°F.—Gas Mark 5) for approximately 25 minutes.
4 Cool slightly and turn out on an ovenproof dish.
5 Stiffly whisk egg whites and gradually fold in sugar.
6 Pipe or shape with a spoon to make a fluted band top and bottom of the pastry case.
7 Return to a slow oven (300°F.—Gas Mark 2) for about 30 minutes until meringue is crisp.
8 Allow to cool.
9 Fill with ice cream and fruit.
10 Glaze with a little redcurrant jelly melted with 2 tablespoons water or fruit syrup.
11 Press a band of angelica, softened by soaking in warm water, into the sides of the basket and serve.

Jamaican jiggers

you will need:

3 level tablespoons golden syrup
$\frac{3}{8}$ pint water
1 level dessert-spoon arrowroot
2 level tablespoons halved glacé cherries
2 level tablespoons chopped nuts
1 tablespoon demerara sugar
1 - 2 tablespoons rum
few drops lemon juice (optional)
1 block coffee ice cream
wafer biscuits

1 Heat the syrup in a strong saucepan until lightly caramelised.
2 Remove from the heat and carefully add half the water.
3 Blend the arrowroot with the remaining water and add to the caramel liquid.
4 Return to the heat, stirring all the time, until boiled.
5 Allow to boil for several minutes.
6 Cool slightly and add the remaining ingredients except the ice cream and wafer biscuits.
7 Chill.
8 Cut the ice cream into 12 cubes and place in 4 sundae glasses.
9 Pour a little sauce over each and serve at once decorated with wafer biscuits.

Raspberry meringue shortcake

you will need:

6 oz. plain flour
2 oz. castor sugar
4 oz. table margarine

Filling and topping:

2 egg whites (large eggs)
1 heaped table-spoon castor sugar
1 block vanilla ice cream
8 oz. raspberries
extra raspberries and redcurrants to decorate

1 Sieve the flour and sugar into a mixing bowl.
2 Rub in the margarine.
3 Knead together *very well* into a soft smooth ball.
4 Turn out on a lightly floured board.
5 Roll out fairly thinly, pressing the outside edges with the fingers to prevent cracking.
6 Cut into 3 rounds with a $5\frac{1}{2}$-inch cutter or saucepan lid and prick well with a fork.
7 Bake on the third shelf from the top of a pre-heated very moderate oven (325°F. - 350°F.—Gas Mark 3) for 30—40 minutes. Cool on a wire tray.
8 Whisk the egg whites until they stand in stiff peaks.
9 Add the sugar and whisk again.
10 Place the ice cream in a small basin.
11 Lightly chop up with a knife.
12 Sandwich the biscuit rounds with the ice cream and raspberries and place on a fireproof dish.
13 Cover the top and sides completely with meringue.
14 Bake on the third shelf from the top of a very hot preheated oven (475°F.—Gas Mark 8) for 3 - 4 minutes, until golden brown. Decorate with raspberries and redcurrants and serve immediately.

Sweet omelette glacé

you will need:

- 3 eggs
- 1 oz. sugar
- 2 - 3 tablespoons cream
- 1 crumbled macaroon biscuit (not essential)
- 1 - 2 oz. butter
- 3 tablespoons redcurrant jelly
- ice cream
- 1 tablespoon icing sugar
- 1 oz. blanched almonds

1. Beat eggs with sugar and cream.
2. Add macaroon biscuit if used.
3. Heat butter in pan, and pour in egg mixture.
4. Cook until just set.
5. Add redcurrant jelly and little ice cream and fold omelette in usual way.
6. Sprinkle with a little icing sugar and almonds.

Strawberry basket

you will need:

- 1 large packet frozen strawberries or fresh strawberries
- 1 sponge cake
- 1 large block vanilla ice cream
- little cream
- wafer biscuits
- angelica

1. Drain the syrup from the fruit.
2. Cut the sponge cake to the size of the block of ice cream and place on a plate.
3. Pour over a little of the fruit syrup.
4. Arrange the ice cream on the cake.
5. Pipe a band of cream round the top and press the wafer biscuits round the 4 sides so that they overlap each other.
6. Arrange the strawberries on top of the 'basket' and finish with a handle of angelica.
7. Serve at once.

Surprise banana tartlets

you will need:

- 6 oz. short or sweet short crust pastry (see page 81)
- 3 bananas
- squeeze lemon juice
- banana ice cream
- 2 egg whites
- 3 oz. castor sugar
- chocolate sauce (see page 56)

1. Roll out the pastry and line about 12 tartlet tins or 1 large flan ring.
2. Bake 'blind' for 15 minutes for small cases and about 25 minutes for the large flan, until crisp and golden brown, using a hot oven (425°F. - 450°F.—Gas Mark 6 - 7).
3. Allow pastry cases to cool thoroughly, then fill with bananas mashed with the lemon juice and top with the banana ice cream.
4. Whisk the egg whites until very stiff, fold in the sugar, and pile over the ice cream.
5. Bake for about 2—3 minutes in a very hot oven (475°F. - 500°F.— Gas Mark 9 - 10) to brown the meringue.
6. Serve with the chocolate sauce.

Cold Sweets

While a refrigerator is not essential for many of the dishes in this chapter, there is no doubt that it helps in making them easily and also it does give a better result because they will be served really cold. Never put the food into the refrigerator when steaming (see explanation under jellies) and if the mixture has a high percentage of cream, do not put too near the freezing compartment, as it will become rather hard and in consequence lose some of its rich flavour.

Apricot and pineapple sponge

you will need:

- 1 small can apricots, or 8 oz. cooked apricots
- 1 medium sized can pineapple
- juice 1 lemon
- water
- ½ oz. gelatine powder
- 2 egg whites

1. Drain liquid from apricots and pineapple, add lemon juice and enough water to give just over ¾ pint.
2. Dissolve gelatine in this, add chopped fruit.
3. When nearly set, fold in stiffly beaten egg whites.
4. Pile into large bowl or glasses.

Ananas Creole

you will need:

½ oz. gelatine	1½ oz. sugar
½ pint milk	⅛ pint cream
1 oz. rice	1 egg white

Sauce:

8 oz. apricot jam	⅛ pint pineapple juice
2 oz. sugar	

Decoration:

pineapple slices	cherries
angelica	sultanas

1. Soak gelatine.
2. Boil milk and add rice.
3. Stir until boiling and cover with lid.
4. Simmer until rice is cooked.
5. Stir in sugar and gelatine.
6. Place into bowl and stand in cold water and stir until cold.
7. Whip cream and egg white separately.
8. When rice mixture is on point of setting, fold in egg white and cream.
9. Place mixture into mould to set.
10. When chilled, unmould the mixture and decorate.
11. Leave in refrigerator until ready to serve.
12. Warm apricot jam with sugar in saucepan.
13. Add pineapple juice and mix well.
14. Decorate with pineapple slices, angelica, cherries and sultanas. Top with sauce.

Blackcurrant purée

you will need:

8 oz. blackcurrants	¾ pint milk, chilled
2-2½ oz. sugar to taste	

1. Cook fruit in a very little water until just tender.
2. Press through hair sieve or muslin.
3. Add sugar and milk.
4. Chill and serve very cold.

Alternatively this purée can be thickened with 2 level teaspoons arrowroot or cornflour blended and boiled with 1 pint of juice, flavoured with lemon juice and cooled before placing in the refrigerator. Serve garnished with a few whole fruits on top.

Cold caramel sponge

you will need:

4 oz. loaf or castor sugar	pinch salt
¼ pint water	whipped cream and nuts, or angelica and crystallised rose petals for decoration
2 rounded teaspoons gelatine	
6 egg whites	

1. Put the sugar with about 4 tablespoons water into a saucepan.
2. Stir until sugar has dissolved, then boil steadily until brown.
3. Add the rest of the water and reheat until caramel has dissolved.
4. Stir the gelatine, making sure it is thoroughly dissolved.
5. Allow the caramel mixture to cool and just start to thicken.
6. Whisk the egg whites stiffly with a pinch salt.
7. Fold into the caramel mixture.
8. Put into a mould and allow to set.
9. Turn out and decorate with whipped cream and nuts, or angelica, etc.

Orange whip

you will need:

1 egg	water
4 oranges	3 level tablespoons cornflour
juice 1 large lemon	sugar
1 can mandarin oranges	

1. Separate the egg yolk from the white.
2. Cut a slice from the top of each orange and remove the pulp.
3. Press out the juice, add the lemon juice, juice from the can of mandarins and enough water to make up to ¾ pint.
4. Mix the cornflour and egg yolk with a little of the fruit juice.
5. Put the rest on to heat.
6. Add the mixed cornflour and boil for 3 minutes, stirring.
7. Add sugar as required.
8. Stir in the butter and orange sections, leaving a few for decoration.
9. Fold in the stiffly beaten egg white.
10. Pile the mixture in the orange cases and chill.
11. Decorate with remaining orange sections.

Chocolate mice

you will need:

- 1 can creamed rice or 1 pint rice pudding
- 6 halves canned pears
- chocolate sauce (see page 56) or chocolate blancmange
- almonds

1. Arrange the rice in small dishes with the halved pears on top.
2. Put ingredients for sauce in pan, heat without boiling.
3. Pour over pears.
4. Put almonds in position for ears and tails.
5. Serve hot or cold.
6. The mice can be served on a bed of jelly instead of rice if preferred, or a block of ice cream.

Peach meringue sponge

you will need:

- 1 frozen cream sponge or fresh sponge filled with cream
- 2 tablespoons Cointreau
- 1 can sliced peaches
- 1½ level tablespoons custard powder
- 2 egg whites
- 4 oz. castor sugar

1. Preheat the oven to very hot (500°F.—Gas Mark 9).
2. Place the sponge on an ovenproof dish.
3. Remove the top sponge round from the cake and sprinkle with the Cointreau.
4. Strain the peaches and arrange on the cream part of the sponge, keeping back a few slices.
5. Chop these coarsely.
6. Blend the custard powder with the fruit syrup.
7. Bring to the boil, stirring, and simmer for 3 minutes.
8. Allow to cool and pour over the peaches, replace the top sponge on the peaches.
9. Whisk the egg whites until stiff, fold in the sugar then fold in the chopped peaches.
10. Spread over the sponge, dredge with castor sugar and bake for 2 - 3 minutes in a very hot oven (475°F.— Gas Mark 8).
11. Serve at once.

Melon fruit slice

(illustrated on the cover)

One of the nicest sweets is made by cutting slices of melon and topping each slice with green and black grapes, cherries and slices of fresh orange.

Make certain that this is chilled in the refrigerator before serving.

Pineapple and strawberries

An easy and delicious sweet is to serve rings of pineapple, canned or fresh, topped with fresh strawberries and cream.

For very special occasions soak pineapple in kirsch.

Leave in refrigerator for an hour or two before serving.

Plum fool

you will need:

- 1½ level tablespoons custard powder
- ½ pint milk
- 2 - 3 oz. sugar
- 1 lb. plums
- 2 - 3 tablespoons water
- few glacé cherries

1. Blend the custard powder with a little cold milk.
2. Bring the rest of the milk to the boil and pour over the custard powder, stirring all the time.
3. Return to the saucepan and cook until thickened, adding 1 level tablespoon of the sugar.
4. While the custard is being made, simmer the plums with the water and rest of the sugar.
5. Remove the stones and either rub through a sieve or beat into a smooth pulp.
6. When both fruit and custard have cooled slightly, beat together.
7. Pour into individual glasses and chill.
8. Decorate on top with cherries.

Rich fruit purée

Method and ingredients as for plum fool above, using whipped cream or part custard and part whipped cream.

Blackcurrant fool

Method and ingredients as for plum fool above, but use 12 oz. blackcurrants and simmer without water for a very thick fruit purée is needed for this recipe. Rub through a sieve and allow fruit to get quite cold before adding to custard as blackcurrants have so much acid that the mixture might curdle.

Damson fool

Method and ingredients as for blackcurrant fool above, substituting damsons for blackcurrants.

Gooseberry fool

Method and ingredients as for plum fool using rather green fruit to give a good flavour. Stir the fruit well to begin with so that it does not burn. Sieve to get rid of pips and skins.

Rhubarb fool

Method and ingredients as for plum fool above substituting rhubarb for plums but use 12 oz. fruit and simmer in a covered dish in a low oven, adding no water at all. Either sieve or beat with a wooden spoon to a smooth purée.

Raspberry cloud

you will need:

¼ oz. butter
approx. 10 - 15 narrow fingers sponge cake

Filling:

1 lb. raspberries
½ pint thin cream or evaporated milk
2 - 3 oz. sugar
¼ oz. gelatine powder
⅛ pint water
3 egg whites

1. Grease a plain mould or cake tin with the melted butter.
2. Arrange sponge cake fingers slightly diagonally.
3. Crush three-quarters of the raspberries and sieve if wished.
4. Blend with the cream, sugar and gelatine, previously dissolved in very hot water.
5. Allow mixture to cool and stiffen slightly.
6. Fold in stiffly beaten egg whites and pour into mould.
7. When set turn out and decorate with whole raspberries.

Raspberry cream pie

you will need:

6 oz. wholemeal biscuits
3 oz. butter

Filling:

⅜ pint water
2 oz. sugar
8 oz. raspberries
½ raspberry jelly
¼ pint evaporated milk

1. Make the pastry by crushing the biscuit crumbs.
2. Add the butter and form into the shape of a flan case in a serving dish.
3. Allow to stand in a cool place until very firm.
4. Make a syrup of the water and sugar and add 2 oz. mashed raspberries.
5. Dissolve jelly in this and when cold, but not set, fold in most of the evaporated milk (this need not be whipped).
6. Put into the biscuit crumb case when just beginning to set.
7. Smooth flat and arrange rest of raspberries on top.
8. Dust with a little sugar if wished.

Raspberry and orange cups

you will need:

2 oranges
1 - 2 level tablespoons castor sugar
1 large packet frozen raspberries or fresh raspberries

1. Peel the oranges and remove pith.
2. Divide in half and slice finely, removing pips.
3. Sprinkle with the sugar and leave to stand for several hours.
4. Just before serving mix the raspberries and oranges together.
5. Serve in sundae glasses.

Rhubarb rice cream

you will need:

1 lb. rhubarb	2 oz. short grain rice
¾ pint water	¼ pint cream
2 - 3 oz. sugar	angelica

1. Cook the rhubarb with the water and sugar until it becomes a pulp.
2. Add the rice and continue cooking for a further 15 - 20 minutes, stirring from time to time, until the rice is tender.
3. Stir briskly and put into glasses.
4. Chill thoroughly.
5. Top with whipped cream and angelica.

Rhubarb snow

you will need:

1 lb. rhubarb	4 oz. sugar
2 tablespoons water	2 or 3 egg whites

1. Cook the rhubarb with the water and sugar until a very smooth purée — sieve if wished.
2. When quite cold fold in stiffly whisked egg whites.
3. Pile into glasses and serve very cold.

Cold soufflés

you will need:

3 eggs	3 tablespoons water
3 oz. sugar	⅜ pint whipped cream or evaporated milk
1 teaspoon vanilla essence	nuts and whipped cream to decorate
½ pint milk	
1½ level dessert-spoons gelatine powder	

1. Separate the egg yolks from the whites.
2. Cook egg yolks, sugar, vanilla and milk gently until a smooth custard.
3. Dissolve gelatine in hot water.
4. Stir into custard then, when cold, fold in stiffly beaten cream.
5. Allow to thicken very slightly then fold in stiffly beaten egg whites.
6. Pour into a soufflé dish, with a band of buttered paper tied firmly round outside, standing several inches above level of dish so that soufflé mixture itself more than fills dish and does not overflow.
7. When quite firm decorate with nuts, cream etc.
8. Lastly carefully remove band of paper.

Lemon soufflé

Add finely grated rind of 1 lemon to egg yolks. Dissolve gelatine in hot lemon juice instead of water.

Chocolate soufflé

Add 1 - 2 oz. chocolate to egg yolk.

Coffee soufflé

Dissolve gelatine in slightly diluted coffee essence or very strong coffee.

St. Clement's Cloud

you will need:

2 eggs	grated rind and juice 1 lemon
¼ pint water	grated rind 1 orange
4 oz. sugar	1 orange to decorate
1 oz. cornflour	
¼ pint orange juice	

1. Separate egg yolks from the whites.
2. Boil the water and sugar together for 4 minutes.
3. Mix the cornflour smoothly with the orange and lemon juice.
4. Add to the syrup and boil for 3 minutes, stirring constantly.
5. Add the egg yolks and simmer gently without boiling for a few minutes.
6. Stir in the grated lemon and orange rind.
7. Beat the egg whites stiffly and fold lightly into the cooked mixture.
8. Pile into sundae glasses and chill.
9. Decorate with sections of fresh orange.

Strawberry condé

you will need:

3 oz. rice
1 pint milk
1 oz. sugar
¼ pint cream or evaporated milk
8 - 12 oz. strawberries
2 - 3 tablespoons redcurrant jelly
2 tablespoons water

1 Simmer rice, until very soft, in milk and sugar.
2 Cool, then beat in cream.
3 Pour into shallow dish.
4 Arrange strawberries on top, halving these if large.
5 Heat jelly and water together, cool slightly, then pour over fruit.
6 Chill well before serving.

Custard cream

you will need:

1 pint milk
1 or 2 eggs
1 dessertspoon sugar
½ teaspoon vanilla essence or vanilla pod
1½ dessertspoons gelatine powder with 2 eggs (little more with 1 egg)
⅛ pint water
⅛ pint evaporated milk if desired

1 Pour hot milk on to beaten egg, adding sugar and vanilla essence or broken vanilla pod.
2 Cook gently in double saucepan until thickened.
3 Dissolve gelatine in water.
4 Add custard mixture, having removed vanilla pod.
5 When cool, stir in evaporated milk.
6 Pour into rinsed mould to set.

Daffodil cream

you will need:

2 - 3 eggs
½ teaspoon lemon rind
8 oz. castor sugar
1 large can pineapple rings
2 tablespoons lemon juice
½ oz. gelatine
½ pint cream or evaporated milk
little angelica for decoration

1 Separate eggs and mix yolks, lemon rind and sugar together.
2 Drain and add finely chopped pineapple, leaving 1 or 2 slices for decoration.
3 Heat juice and melt gelatine in it.
4 Cool and add to egg mixture.
5 Fold in stiffly beaten egg whites and cream or evaporated milk, leaving a little for decoration.
6 When set, decorate with daffodils made by pineapple pieces and angelica for stems, leaves, etc.

Frosted marshmallow delight

you will need:

½ packet raspberry blancmange
½ pint milk
1 oz. sugar
1 oz. chopped glacé cherries
2 oz. chopped marshmallows
2 oz. chopped canned pineapple
¼ pint cream

1 Blend the blancmange with a little cold milk.
2 Bring the rest of the milk to the boil.
3 Pour over blancmange and thicken.
4 Allow to cool, adding sugar, cherries, marshmallows, pineapple.
5 When quite cold fold in cream.
6 Pour into freezing trays, and freeze until firm.

Frosted rice cream

you will need:

¼ pint cream
1 small can pineapple rings
4 oz. cooked rice
few glacé cherries
apricot or pineapple jam

1 Beat half the cream and enough syrup from the can of pineapple into the rice to give a consistency of thick cream.
2 Freeze lightly in the freezing tray of the refrigerator.
3 Arrange the rings of pineapple on each serving plate and top with the frozen rice cream.
4 Decorate with cherries, cream and a little jam.

Frosted stuffed peaches

you will need:

8 canned peach halves

Filling:

$\frac{1}{4}$ pint cream
2 oz. cooked rice
8 oz. frozen or fresh raspberries
1 oz. sugar (optional)
few blanched almonds

1. Arrange the peaches with some of the syrup in the freezing tray of the refrigerator.
2. Blend the whipped cream, rice, raspberries and sugar and fill each of the peach halves with the mixture.
3. Top with shredded blanched almonds.
4. Freeze lightly.

Frozen pineapple cream

you will need:

$\frac{1}{4}$ pint thick cream
$\frac{1}{2}$ teaspoon vanilla
1 large can pineapple slices
2 tablespoons sugar if wished
2 oz. candied cherries or fresh strawberries

1. Whip the cream until stiff.
2. Add the vanilla.
3. Pack into a mould and freeze for 2 hours.
4. Arrange the slices of pineapple on a serving dish and sprinkle with sugar to taste.
5. Dip a large serving spoon in hot water then into the frozen cream.
6. Arrange large ovals of frozen cream round the pineapple.
7. Decorate with cherries or strawberries.

Fruity mallow cups

you will need:

1 egg white
$\frac{1}{2}$ oz. sugar
$\frac{1}{4}$ pint cream
2 oz. rice
14 pink and white mallows
1 small can pineapple chunks
1 tablespoon pineapple juice

1. Whisk egg white and sugar until stiff and peaky.
2. Fold into whipped cream.
3. Combine with rice, quartered marshmallows, pineapple and pineapple juice.
4. Pile into individual glasses.
5. Chill and top with whole marshmallows.

Soft fruit kissel

you will need:

$\frac{1}{2}$ pint water
3 oz. sugar
8 oz. redcurrants
8 oz. blackcurrants
8 oz. raspberries
2 level teaspoons cornflour or arrowroot

1. Heat $\frac{3}{8}$ pint water with the sugar.
2. When the sugar has dissolved add currants and simmer gently until tender.
3. Add raspberries and arrowroot blended with rest of the water.
4. Bring to the boil and cook gently until thick and smooth.
5. Serve very cold with cream or yoghourt.

Lemon snow

you will need:

1 oz. cornflour
1 pint milk
3 oz. sugar
grated rind 1 or 2 lemons
1 teaspoon gelatine powder
$\frac{1}{8}$ pint water
2 egg whites

1. Blend cornflour with a little cold milk.
2. Bring rest of milk to boil.
3. Pour over the cornflour and return to pan to thicken with sugar and lemon rind, stirring well.
4. Dissolve gelatine in the hot water.
5. Add to cornflour mixture.
6. When mixture is beginning to cool, but not set, fold in stiffly beaten egg whites.
7. Put into a mould to set.
8. Turn out and top with soft fruit compote.

Honeycomb mould

you will need:

1 large egg
½ pint lemon juice
¾ pint water
2 oz. sugar
½ oz. gelatine powder
2 tablespoons cold water

1 Separate the egg yolk from the white.
2 Put the lemon juice, water, sugar and egg yolk into a saucepan and heat well for about 5 minutes until very slightly thickened, stirring continuously.
3 Remove from heat and cool slightly.
4 Soften the gelatine powder in the cold water.
5 Pour on the lemon mixture and add stiffly beaten egg white.
6 Pour into a rinsed mould to set.

Loganberry cream

you will need:

1 lb. loganberries
2-3 oz. sugar
½ pint water
½ oz. powdered gelatine (or enough to set 1 pint)
¼ pint cream
little extra cream to decorate
few whole loganberries

1 Simmer loganberries, sugar and water until very soft.
2 Either rub through sieve or beat well until smooth.
3 Measure purée and if necessary add a little extra water to make up to just over 1 pint.
4 Reheat and dissolve gelatine in this.
5 Allow to cool, just start to stiffen, then add lightly whipped cream.
6 Pour into shallow dish or dishes and when set decorate with cream and a few whole raw or cooked loganberries.

If desired, this can be set as a mould, in which case use just 1 pint purée. Turn out and decorate with whisked greengage or fresh lemon jelly and cream.

Strawberry whirl

you will need:

1 dessertspoon cornflour
½ pint thick strawberry purée
little sugar to taste
½ pint thick cream
strawberries to decorate

1 Blend cornflour with the purée and cook until thickened, add sugar to taste.
2 Chill.
3 Fold in whipped cream and pile or pipe into glasses.
4 Decorate with strawberries.

Refrigerator cake — date and nut roll

you will need:

⅔ can sweetened condensed milk
2 teaspoons lemon juice
8 oz. sweet biscuit crumbs
icing sugar
4 oz. finely chopped dates
2 oz. chopped nuts

1 Blend the milk and lemon juice.
2 Add the biscuit crumbs and mix well.
3 Lightly roll mixture into an 8- or 10-inch rectangle on a board sprinkled with icing sugar.
4 Mix the dates and nuts and spread on the crumb mixture.
5 Roll up like a Swiss roll.
6 Wrap in waxed paper and chill for 6 to 8 hours.
7 Slice and serve with hard sauce or mock cream.

Making mallobets

These desserts make use of marshmallows for sweetness and lightness of texture. They are *not* ice creams however, as no cream or evaporated milk is used.

Take care that the marshmallows are not melted for too long; they should be half melted only, so they remain 'springy' in texture.

Apricot mallobet

you will need:

- 4 oz. dried or 8 oz. canned or fresh apricots
- 1 oz. sugar with fresh or dried fruit
- 1 tablespoon lemon juice
- 6 oz. marshmallows
- 2 egg whites
- water with dried or fresh fruit

1. Soak the dried apricots overnight in cold water to cover.
2. Simmer with the sugar and lemon juice then put through a sieve.
3. If using canned apricots rub through a sieve and add to lemon juice and syrup from can.
4. Fresh apricots should be cooked with the sugar and just under ½ pint water, then sieved, and added to lemon juice.
5. Put the fruit into a basin with the marshmallows, and heat over hot water until the marshmallows are half melted, then beat well together.
6. Cool then fold in stiffly beaten egg whites.
7. Put into freezing trays and freeze on normal setting until firm.

Peach mallobet

Recipe as apricot mallobet above, using dried, canned or fresh peaches.

Orange mallobet

Recipe as above but use the juice and rind of 2 oranges, and add the juice and rind of 1 lemon as well.

Grapefruit mallobet

Recipe as lemon mallobet, but use the juice from 1 grapefruit and the finely grated rind from ½ the grapefruit only.

Tangerine mallobet

Recipe as lemon mallobet, but use the finely grated rind and juice of 3 tangerines and 1 lemon.

Plum mallobet

Recipe as apricot mallobet using fresh plums.

Lemon mallobet

you will need:

- ¼ pint water
- 4 oz. white marshmallows
- juice and finely grated rind 2 lemons
- 2 egg whites

1. Put the water and marshmallows into a pan, heat for a minute or two only, then remove from the heat.
2. Turn the marshmallows over in the liquid until half melted, but still very 'springy'.
3. Add lemon juice and rind, and when quite cold fold in the stiffly beaten egg whites.
4. Pour into freezing tray and freeze on normal setting until firm.

Fruit Melbas

This sweet has become very popular, and deservedly so, since it is delicious.

The recipe for Melba sauce is given below and this can be varied slightly — see individual recipes.

When ingredients for this sauce are not available a more economical variation can be made as follows:—

Economical Melba sauce

you will need:

- ½ teaspoon cornflour or arrowroot
- 3 tablespoons raspberry jam
- 3 tablespoons redcurrant jelly
- 1 tablespoon lemon juice
- 3 tablespoons water

1. Blend the arrowroot or cornflour with the water.
2. Put into the saucepan with all the other ingredients.
3. Heat gently, stirring from time to time until melted.
4. Allow to cool.

Melba sauce

you will need:

1 level teaspoon cornflour
2 tablespoons water or fruit syrup from can or frozen fruit
1 tablespoon castor sugar
6 oz. fresh, frozen or canned raspberries
3 tablespoons redcurrant or apple jelly

1. Blend cornflour with the water or syrup.
2. Put into a saucepan with the other ingredients.
3. Cook gently until thick.
4. Beat until smooth or rub through sieve.

Peach Melba

you will need:

ripe dessert peaches or canned peaches
sugar
water
vanilla or kirsch
Melba sauce
whipped cream (optional)

1. Skin ripe peaches and if wished sweeten by immersing for a minute or so in very sweet sugar and water syrup flavoured with vanilla or kirsch.
2. If using canned peaches drain well.
3. Arrange halves or quarters of the peaches in glasses with ice cream.
4. Top with Melba sauce and if wished, whipped cream.

Pear Melba

As peach Melba substituting pears for peaches.

Raspberry Melba

you will need:

sweetened raspberries
ice cream
Melba sauce
whipped cream (optional)

1. Arrange layers of sweetened raspberries and ice cream in glasses.
2. Top with Melba sauce and whipped cream, if desired.

Cherry Melba

you will need:

canned or very ripe stoned cherries
ice cream
Melba sauce
whipped cream and cherries for decoration

1. Arrange layers of cherries in glasses with ice cream. Do not use any syrup from the can.
2. If using not so ripe dessert cherries simmer them with a little sugar and water first.
3. Top with Melba sauce—this can be varied by using some of the cherry syrup in the sauce or a little cherry brandy.
4. Decorate with whipped cream and cherries.

Strawberry Melba

you will need:

sweetened strawberries
ice cream
Melba sauce
whipped cream (optional)

1. Arrange layers of sweetened strawberries and ice cream in glasses.
2. Top with Melba sauce and whipped cream if wished.

Note:
Strawberries can be mixed with the raspberries or used by themselves in the sauce in place of the raspberries, but there is much more flavour when raspberries are used.

Banana Melba

you will need:

sliced bananas
ice cream
Melba sauce
whipped cream

1. Arrange layers of sliced banana into glasses with ice cream.
2. Top with Melba sauce and whipped cream, if wished.

Jellies

Setting jellies in a refrigerator

Naturally, one of the most welcome points about a refrigerator is no matter how hot the weather outside you can be sure of a jelly sweet setting very quickly.
Do not put jellies or jellied moulds into the refrigerator when they are steaming for the steam causes condensation in the cabinet and also is inclined to create a mixture of smells which is undesirable.

For savoury jelly recipes see Cold and Frosted Savoury Dishes (pages 21-29).

Quick setting of jellies

As stated above, a refrigerator sets jellies in an unbelievably short time. If, however, you have left it until the last minute it is possible, when the jelly has finished steaming, to put the mould in the freezing compartment for a short time. Do not leave it too long otherwise it becomes iced.
The more shallow the mould the quicker your jelly will set.

Quick setting of jellies with ice cubes

Jelly can almost set instantaneously if the following method is used.

Crush ice cubes and put into a pint measure. Although the ice fills the pint measure, it only corresponds to about ¾ pint water. Dissolve the jelly in a ¼ pint very hot water and then stir in the crushed ice. You will find your jelly has set.

Setting fruit in layers in a jelly

1 Make up the jelly and get the fruit ready.
2 Pour enough jelly in the bottom of the mould to give a layer of about ½ inch.
3 Put into the refrigerator and allow it to set lightly.
4 Dip the fruit in a little of the liquid jelly, which should be kept in the kitchen so it does not set.
5 Arrange on top of the bottom layer of jelly.
6 Return to the refrigerator for a few minutes.
7 Pour over some of the cold but not set liquid jelly and set lightly.
8 Add more fruit dipped in liquid jelly and continue in this way until the mould is completely filled, and all the jelly and fruit used.
9 End with a layer of jelly.

To facilitate setting you can stand the mould on a bed of ice cubes in a refrigerator.

Preparing moulds for jellies

Sweet jelly

Rinse the mould with cold water.

Savoury jelly

Brush the mould with a very little oil.

To remove jellies from moulds

1 Wrap a warm cloth round the outside of the mould and leave for 2 - 3 minutes, or immerse in warm, but not too hot water for about 30 seconds.

2 Put the serving plate on top of the mould and turn over sharply.
3 If the serving dish is slightly dampened the jelly or mould will slide on this, so if you have not placed it in the very centre of the dish, or where desired, you can move it without any difficulty.

To pipe on jellies

One often wishes to pipe cream on a jelly and it is a little difficult to make it stick.
Blot the jelly with a piece of tissue or kitchen paper, which will take off the shine and slight stickiness from the outside. You will then find piping quite simple.

Charlotte Russe

you will need:

½-¾ pint lemon jelly
cherries and angelica
7 or 8 Savoy sponge fingers
egg white (optional)
2 tablespoons cold water
¼ oz. gelatine
¼ pint thick cream
⅛ pint fresh milk
1 oz. castor sugar
½-1 teaspoon vanilla essence

1 Use a 1-pint soufflé dish or similar straight-sided mould.
2 Prepare a jelly and cool and pour ¼ inch layer into the bottom of the mould.
3 Place in the freezer compartment or a cool place to set firm.
4 Decorate with rounds of cherries and small pieces of angelica.
5 Pour in more jelly to give a depth of about ½ inch.
6 Return to refrigerator to chill (or a cool place) until the jelly is nearly set.
7 Split the Savoy fingers and trim off the ends so that they will fit neatly round the edges of mould.
8 If liked, the sides of the Savoy fingers may be brushed with white of egg to help them stick together.
9 Put the cut ends into the jelly with the cut sides of the Savoy fingers inside.
10 Fit the fingers closely together leaving no gaps.
11 Allow to set firm.
12 Soak the gelatine in the cold water.
13 Whip the cream well and add the milk and sugar, vanilla essence to taste and continue whipping.
14 Dissolve the gelatine over hot water and add to the cream mixture, folding it in carefully.
15 Continue stirring gently until almost set.
16 Pour into the prepared mould and chill until set firm.
17 Trim off Savoy fingers level with the mixture.
18 Unmould on to a serving dish.
19 Decorate with chopped lemon jelly round the base of the charlotte.

Note:
It is not satisfactory to substitute evaporated milk for cream in this dish, owing to the very delicate flavour.

Orange Charlotte Russe

(illustrated on the cover)

Follow the directions for the Charlotte Russe, but use ½-¾ pint orange instead of lemon jelly.
1 Put the whole of the jelly in the bottom of the prepared mould and allow to set. Do not use glacé cherries or angelica.
2 Continue in exactly the same way from here onwards as Charlotte Russe.
3 When sweet is complete turn out and decorate with a ring of mandarin oranges and cream, or a flower as shown in the cover photograph.

Orange mousse ring

(illustrated on the cover)

you will need:

1 orange table jelly
⅝ pint hot water
¼ pint cream
2 egg whites
canned pineapple
glacé cherries
angelica

1 Dissolve table jelly in the hot water.
2 Allow to cool and just become slightly sticky.
3 Fold in lightly whipped cream and the stiffly beaten egg whites.
4 Taste and if necessary, add a little more sugar.
5 Pour into rinsed ring mould.
6 Allow to set.
7 Decorate as illustrated on the cover with pineapple, cherries and angelica.

Gooseberry boats

you will need:

12 oz. gooseberries
2 - 3 oz. sugar
½ pint water
1 lemon flavoured jelly
8 cocktail sticks
1 - 2 sheets rice paper

1 Simmer the gooseberries with the sugar and water until very soft.
2 Either sieve or beat well until a smooth purée.
3 If necessary add extra water to give 1 pint.
4 Reheat and dissolve jelly in this.
5 Pour into boat-shaped tins and allow to set.
6 Turn out and stand on small dishes.
7 Cut rice paper into the sails used on Chinese junks.
8 Thread a cocktail stick through each sail and press into the jelly.
9 If wished, arrange on top tiny sweets or a little cream or fresh fruit.

Jellied rice

you will need:

1 raspberry jelly
2 oz. cooked short grain rice
1 packet frozen raspberries
cream to decorate

1 Make the jelly in the ordinary way.
2 Cool and when beginning to thicken slightly add the cooked rice.
3 Stir in the fruit.
4 Chill and decorate with cream.

Melon mint jelly

you will need:

¼ pint water
2 oz. sugar
2 tablespoons chopped mint
1 oz. gelatine powder
¼ pint cold water
1 pint ginger ale
2 tablespoons lemon juice
green colouring
6 ice cubes
melon balls or cubes
mint to garnish

1 Boil together the water and sugar for 5 minutes.
2 Pour the liquid over the mint and leave until cold, then strain.
3 Add the gelatine dissolved in the cold water, the ginger ale, lemon juice and colouring.
4 Stir in the ice cubes until dissolved.
5 Add melon balls or cubes.
6 Pour into a wet mould and leave to set.
7 Turn out and garnish with melon and mint.

Milk jelly (1)

you will need:

1 packet jelly
¼ pint very hot water
¾ pint cold milk

1 Dissolve the jelly in the very hot water.
2 When cool, but not set, add the milk—in this way the jelly will not curdle.
3 Pour into mould and allow to set.

Milk jelly (2)

you will need:

½ oz. gelatine powder
2 tablespoons water
1 pint milk less 2 tablespoons
little vanilla or other flavouring (see below)
1 oz. sugar

1 Put the gelatine and water into a basin over a pan of hot water and heat together until the gelatine is dissolved.
2 Warm the milk with the flavouring, add to the gelatine, and stir until blended, stirring in the sugar.
3 Pour into mould and allow to set.

Flavourings:

Vanilla

Use either 1 teaspoon essence or use vanilla sugar instead of ordinary sugar or heat a vanilla pod with the milk.

Almond
Add 1 teaspoon almond or ratafia essence.

Coffee
Add a little instant coffee powder to the milk.

Chocolate
Blend 1 oz. chocolate powder with the milk.

Fruit flavours

Use about 1 teaspoon of essence and colouring or about 1 teaspoon cold fruit syrup (see page 15) which should be added when the milk and gelatine have cooled, but not set.

Raspberry ring

you will need:

Outer ring:

8 oz. raspberries
little sugar
water
1 raspberry flavoured jelly

Filling:

½ pint cream (or whipped evaporated milk)
2 or 3 meringue cases
8 oz. raspberries
little sugar

1 Prepare the outer ring first.
2 Mash raspberries, add sugar and enough water to make 1 pint.
3 Heat and dissolve jelly in this.
4 Pour into ring mould previously rinsed out in cold water.
5 Allow to set and turn out.
6 Whip cream lightly until it just holds its shape.
7 Crumble meringues, fold into cream together with whole raspberries and a little sugar.
8 Pile into centre of jelly ring.

Chocolate and pineapple delight

(illustrated on the cover)

you will need:

1 pineapple jelly tablet
½ pint hot water
1 tablespoon cocoa
3 tablespoons sugar
½ pint milk
1 small can pineapple rings or pieces
whipped cream
glacé cherries
angelica

1 Make the jelly using the hot water.
2 Blend the cocoa and sugar with a little of the milk.
3 Heat the remaining milk.
4 Add to the cocoa.
5 Return to the saucepan and boil for one minute.
6 When jelly and cocoa mixtures are cool whisk together.
7 *Do not mix while hot.*
8 Pour into a mould and stand in a cold place to set.
9 Turn on to a serving dish.
10 Fill the centre with whipped cream and decorate with pineapple, cherry and angelica as illustrated.

Frozen Mousses

Because of its firm consistency, and particularly light texture, a frozen mousse does not need beating during freezing. It is however advisable to freeze on the coldest setting for perfect success, then return the indicator to the normal setting to store.

While a mousse can be frozen in an ordinary refrigerator tray, it is possible to freeze in individual dishes, providing these can stand the low temperatures of the freezing compartment. For a large buffet party individual cartons can be used.

Apple mousse

you will need:

1 lb. apples	grated rind and juice
¼ pint water	1 lemon
3 oz. sugar	½ pint cream or evaporated milk

1 Peel the apples and cook with the water and sugar until a smooth thick purée. Sieve if wished.
2 Add the lemon juice and rind.
3 When quite cold fold in the lightly whipped evaporated milk or cream.
4 Spoon into the freezing trays, and freeze on coldest setting until just firm, then return control to normal setting to store.
If wished 1 or 2 stiffly beaten egg whites can be added *after* the cream, in which case you may care to add a little extra sugar.

Spiced apple mousse

Recipe as above, but omit lemon rind and juice and add ½ teaspoon powdered cloves, ½ teaspoon powdered nutmeg, and ½ teaspoon powdered cinnamon to the apple purée.

Apple ginger mousse

Recipe as above, but add 1 tablespoon ginger syrup when cooking apples and 1 - 2 oz. chopped preserved ginger.

Frozen chocolate mousse

you will need:

3 eggs	little extra sugar if
4 oz. chocolate	wished
⅜ pint cream	

1 Separate the egg yolks from the whites.
2 Put the egg yolks and chocolate into a basin over hot water.
3 Stir until the chocolate has melted, and then beat together until smooth consistency, do not overheat.
4 Allow to cool, then fold in the lightly whipped cream, and the stiffly beaten egg whites, add a little extra sugar if wished.
5 Put into freezing trays and freeze on coldest setting until firm, then return indicator to normal setting to store.

For a stronger flavour use 6 oz. chocolate and 1 teaspoon vanilla essence.

Frozen chocolate orange mousse

Use recipe above, but add finely grated rind of 1 or 2 oranges and 2 tablespoons orange juice, mixing this with the egg yolks and chocolate. A little Curaçao could also be added.

Frozen chocolate almond mousse

Use frozen chocolate mousse recipe, but add 4 oz. blanched split almonds which can be browned if wished for a more definite flavour.

Chocolate Bavaroise

you will need:

2 eggs	1 tablespoon icing sugar
4 oz. plain chocolate	¼ oz. gelatine
¼ pint milk	4 oz. butter

1 Separate the egg yolks from the white.
2 Melt chocolate slowly in milk.
3 Add icing sugar, egg yolks and melted gelatine.
4 Mix butter carefully into mixture.
5 Fold in stiffly beaten egg whites.
6 Turn into mould and chill.

Chocolate mousse

you will need:

2 eggs	scant ¼ pint cream or evaporated milk
2 tablespoons castor sugar	¼ oz. gelatine
4 tablespoons grated chocolate	2 tablespoons water
½ teaspoon vanilla essence	1 dessertspoon brandy
	whipped cream and flaked chocolate for decoration

1 Separate the yolks from the whites of eggs.
2 Put the yolks into a basin with the sugar, chocolate and vanilla essence.
3 Beat over hot water until thick and creamy.
4 Allow to cool.
5 Add the cream or evaporated milk.
6 Whip the whites stiffly.

7 Melt the gelatine in water and stir it quickly into the chocolate mixture.
8 Lightly fold in egg whites and brandy.
9 Turn into individual glasses and chill.
0 Decorate with whipped cream and flaked chocolate.

Quick chocolate mousse

you will need:

4 oz. chocolate, preferably plain
2 eggs
2 dessertspoons sugar
2 dessertspoons cream

1 Grate chocolate.
2 Separate the egg yolks from the whites.
3 Put sugar, chocolate and egg yolk in a basin over hot water and beat together until smooth.
4 Cool slightly.
5 Add cream and when quite cold fold in stiffly beaten egg white.
6 Pour into 2 small glasses and serve with biscuits.

Frosted coffee mousse

you will need:

2 - 3 oz. sugar
1 teaspoon gelatine powder
¼ pint very strong coffee
1 tablespoon Tia Maria (optional)
⅜ pint cream
2 egg whites

1 Dissolve the sugar and gelatine powder in the hot coffee.
2 Add the Tia Maria, if wished.
3 Allow to cool and stiffen slightly, then fold in the lightly whipped cream and stiffly beaten egg whites.
4 Put into the freezing trays and freeze on the coldest position until firm, then return indicator to normal setting to store.

Frosted coffee rum mousse

Recipe as above adding 1 - 2 tablespoons rum, and omitting the Tia Maria.

Peach mousse

you will need:

1 medium sized can peaches
lemon juice (optional)
½ pint cream
2 egg whites
little extra sugar, if wished

1 Drain the peaches and finely chop or sieve the fruit, adding lemon juice if used. Do not use the syrup from the peaches.
2 Whip the cream and blend with the purée.
3 Lastly fold in the stiffly beaten egg whites, taste and add little extra sugar if wished.
4 Put into freezing trays, and freeze on coldest setting until firm, then return indicator to normal setting to store.

If fresh ripe peaches are used add 2—3 oz. sugar.

Apricot mousse

Recipe as above using canned or fresh apricots instead of peaches. If it is necessary to cook apricots do so in the minimum amount of water, with sugar to taste, and drain from liquid before sieving or mashing.

Pineapple mousse

Use chopped canned pineapple instead of peaches.

Raspberry mousse (1)

Use 12 oz. fresh raspberries mashed or sieved with 3 oz. sugar or well drained canned or frozen fruit.

Strawberry mousse (1)

Use 12 oz. fresh strawberries mashed with 3 oz. sugar or well drained canned or frozen fruit.

Strawberry mousse (2)

You will need:

8 oz. strawberries
2 oz. sugar
¾ pint thick cream
1 teaspoon vanilla essence

1 Sieve or mash the strawberries.
2 Combine fruit pulp and sugar, mixing well.
3 Whip the cream and lightly fold in the sweetened fruit pulp.
4 Add vanilla.
5 Put into freezing tray of refrigerator and freeze until quite firm.

Note:
For savoury frozen mousses see pages 21-29.

Raspberry mousse (2)

Make as strawberry mouse above substituting 8 oz. raspberries for strawberries.

Saving Time with a Refrigerator

Your refrigerator is not really doing its job properly unless it enables you to save a great deal of time by allowing you to shop for larger quantities with the knowledge that the food will keep fresh. It also enables you to prepare certain foods and store them in the refrigerator ready for use.

Pastry for example can be prepared in the usual way and stored in the refrigerator until required. In the case of short crust pastry, it is easier to manage if you simply rub the fat into the flour and store in a plastic bag and then add the cold water at the last minute.

For the richer pastry, i.e. puff and flaky, these can be prepared, wrapped in foil and kept for some days in the refrigerator. Remember the cooler the ingredients for pastry, the better the result, so place a jug of water in the refrigerator before you start to make the pastry and use this for mixing.

Flaky pastry
(for sausage rolls, mince pies, etc.)

You will need:

8 oz. plain flour
pinch salt
5 - 6 oz. fat
water to mix

1 Sieve flour with salt.
2 Divide fat into 3 portions.
3 Rub 1 portion into flour in the usual way and mix to rolling consistency with cold water.
4 Roll out to oblong shape.
5 Take the second portion of fat and divide it into small pieces laying them on the surface of ⅔ of dough.
6 Leave remaining ⅓ without fat.
7 Take its 2 corners and fold back over second ⅓ so that the dough looks like an envelope with its flap open.
8 Fold over top end of pastry, so closing the 'envelope.'
9 Turn pastry at right angles, seal open ends of pastry and 'rib' it. This means depressing it with the rolling pin at intervals, giving a corrugated effect and equalising the pressure of air.
10 Repeat the process again using the remaining fat and turning pastry in same way.
11 Roll out pastry once more, but if it begins to feel very sticky and soft put it into a cold place for about 30 minutes to become firm before rolling out.
12 Fold pastry as before, turn it, seal edges and 'rib' it.
13 Altogether the pastry should have 3 foldings and 3 rollings. It is then ready to stand in a cold place for a little while before baking, since the contrast between the cold and heat of the oven make the pastry rise better.
14 Bake in a very hot oven (475°F.—Gas Mark 8) for the first 15 minutes, then lower the heat to (400°F. - 425°F.—Gas Mark 5 - 6) or turn the electric oven off to finish cooking for remaining time at a lower temperature.

Puff pastry
(for vol-au-vent cases, vanilla slices, cream horns, etc.)

you will need:

8 oz. plain flour
good pinch salt
cold water to mix
few drops lemon juice

1 Sieve flour and salt together.
2 Mix to rolling consistency with cold water and lemon juice.
3 Roll to oblong shape.
4 Make fat into neat block and place in centre of pastry and fold over it, first the bottom section of pastry, and then the top section, so that fat is quite covered.
5 Turn the dough at right angles, seal edges and 'rib' carefully as in flaky pastry (see page 80), and roll out.
6 Fold dough into envelope, turn it, seal edges, 'rib' and roll again.
7 Repeat 5 times, so making 7 rollings and 7 foldings in all.
8 It will be necessary to put pastry to rest in a cold place once or twice between rollings to prevent it becoming sticky and soft.
9 Always put it to rest before rolling it for the last time and before baking.
10 Bake in very hot oven (to make it rise and keep in the fat). Bake for the first 10-15 minutes at 475° - 500°F.— Gas Mark 8 - 9, then lower to 400°F. - 420°F.— Gas Mark 5 - 6 to finish cooking at lower temperature.
11 Well-made puff pastry should rise to 4 or 5 times its original thickness.

Short crust pastry
(for all general purposes)

you will need:

8 oz. flour
good pinch salt
4 oz. fat
about 2 tablespoons cold water to mix

1 Sieve flour and salt and rub in fat until mixture looks like fine breadcrumbs.
2 Using first a knife and then the fingertips to feel the pastry, gradually add enough cold water to make the dough into a rolling consistency.
3 Lightly flour the rolling-pin and pastry board. If a great deal of flour is necessary to roll out the pastry then you have undoubtedly made it too wet.
4 Roll pastry to required thickness and shape, lifting and turning it to keep it light.
5 As a general rule short crust pastry should be cooked in a hot oven (425°F. - 450°F.— Gas Mark 6 - 7).

Choux pastry
(for cream buns and eclairs)

you will need:

¼ pint water
1 oz. margarine or butter
pinch sugar
3 oz. flour (plain or self-raising)
2 whole eggs and 1 egg yolk or 3 small eggs

1 Put water, fat and sugar into a saucepan.
2 Heat gently until fat has melted.
3 Remove from heat and stir in flour.
4 Return pan to low heat and cook very gently, but thoroughly, stirring all the time until mixture is dry enough to form a ball and leave pan clean.
5 Remove pan from heat and gradually add well beaten eggs. Do this slowly to produce a perfectly smooth mixture.
6 Allow to cool.

Flan pastry or biscuit crust
(for sweet flans and fruit tarts)

you will need:

5 oz. butter or margarine
2 dessertspoons sugar
8 oz. flour
pinch salt
1 egg yolk
cold water

1 Cream fat and sugar together until light in colour.
2 Sieve flour and salt together and add to creamed butter or margarine, mixing with a knife.
3 Gradually add egg yolk and enough water to make a firm rolling consistency.
4 Use fingertips to feel the pastry as in short-crust pastry (see above).
5 Bake in a hot oven (425°F. - 450°F.— Gas Mark 6 - 7).

Cream buns

you will need:

choux pastry (see page 81)	cream or ice cream
	fruit (optional)

1. Put the choux pastry mixture into a piping bag and pipe on to floured and greased baking trays.
2. Alternatively put spoonfuls of the mixture into greased and floured patty tins or baking trays.
3. Put into the centre of a hot oven (450°F.—Gas Mark 7) for 35 minutes.
4. For the last 20 minutes reduce the heat to 400°F.—Gas Mark 5.
5. At the end of cooking time the buns should be pale golden in colour and feel very firm and crisp.
6. Cool away from a draught.
7. When quite cold split and fill with cream or ice cream. A little fruit can be added if wished.

Biscuit crust flans

you will need:

For the crust:

3 oz. butter	filling (see below)
2 oz. sugar	
6 oz. biscuit crumbs (see individual recipes)	

1. Cream butter and sugar.
2. Work in the crumbs and press into a flan shape.
3. Leave to harden for several hours, then fill.

Filling (1)

Fill with ice cream and top with fruit, chocolate sauce or Melba sauce (see pages 56, 73). Plain semi-sweet biscuit crumbs are ideal for this.

Filling (2)

Use ginger-nut crumbs in the crust. Fill with a fluffy jelly mixture, made by dissolving any fruit flavoured jelly in just under ¾ pint water. Pour on to 2 egg yolks, add 1 tiny can of evaporated milk and a little sugar to taste. When lightly set fold in the stiffly beaten whites of the eggs. Decorate with cream or fruit.

Filling (3)

Fill with fruit and jelly or glaze as described in the fruit sponge flan.

Use chocolate wholemeal biscuit crumbs with a pear filling.

Use ginger-nut crumbs with an apricot or apple filling.

Use ½ biscuit crumbs and ½ crushed breakfast cereal with any fruit filling.

Pancakes

A pancake batter can be stored in a screw top jar for several days in the refrigerator. Either whisk sharply before cooking, or shake the jar very vigorously to make sure the batter is well blended.

Cooked pancakes can be kept in the refrigerator.

Cook them in the usual way and wrap in foil or plenty of greaseproof paper.

Pancake batter

you will need:

4 oz. flour	½ pint milk or milk and water
pinch salt	
1 egg	

1. Sieve flour and salt.
2. Add egg and enough milk to give a sticky consistency.
3. Beat well, then gradually add rest of liquid.
4. Always whisk hard before cooking.

Rich pancake batter

you will need:

- 4 oz. flour (preferably plain)
- good pinch salt
- 2 eggs
- $\frac{3}{8}$ pint milk
- just under $\frac{1}{8}$ pint water
- 1 oz. melted butter or tablespoon olive oil
- fat for cooking

Method as for pancake batter but add the butter or oil just before cooking.

Fillings

1 Jam.
2 Ice cream coated with chocolate sauce (see page 56).
3 Soft fruit and ice cream.

Sandwich Making

A refrigerator will help you when preparing sandwiches—for if wanted early in the morning for a picnic or packed luncheon, they can be cut the night before and stored in the refrigerator.
Either wrap in foil or several layers of slightly damped kitchen paper, or wrap in greaseproof paper and put in polythene bags or put in the salad container of the refrigerator. In this way the bread remains fresh and the fillings moist.
Sandwich fillings or spreads can be made earlier and stored in containers in the refrigerator or wrapped in foil.

Cutting sandwiches in a hurry

Use the sandwich loaf lengthways, brush on softened (not melted butter) for greater economy or use a special small palette knife or butter spreader since this enables you to spread quickly and easily. Arrange the bread, butter and fillings in a definite order on the working table or surface so there is no muddle.
If working unaided cut all the bread required, butter, cover with filling and second slice of bread and stack in neat piles.
This is better than buttering all the bread first, since it tends to dry badly.
If working with 'helpers' have a definite flow of work: 1 person cuts bread, passes it on to the second to butter, who then passes it to the third person to fill and form into piles.
Made sandwich spreads or creams are quicker to use, and more economical than slices of meat etc.

A further savoury idea, and one that saves time also, is to use savoury butters—so incorporating both butter and filling together.

10 Savoury butters for Sandwich fillings

Anchovy

Cream chopped anchovies with the butter and chopped cress.

Carrot

Add grated raw carrot and grated cheese to the creamed butter.

Cheese

Blend equal quantities of cream cheese, butter, grated cheese together. Add seasoning and bind with a little mayonnaise.

Ham

Blend equal quantities of chopped ham and butter together, add chopped parsley, little made mustard and chopped cress.

Hard-boiled egg butter

Chop 3 hard-boiled eggs, and blend with 3 oz. creamed butter, little chopped chives, seasoning, chopped cress and mayonnaise to moisten.

Soft-boiled egg butter

Soft-boil 3 eggs, chop and mix with 2 oz. butter, seasoning and shredded lettuce.

Lemon butter
Add grated rind of 1 lemon to 3 oz. butter, together with 2 teaspoons lemon juice, shredded lettuce, and diced cucumber.

Lobster butter
Cream 3 oz. butter, then add contents of a medium sized can lobster or equal amount of freshly cooked lobster meat. Add paprika pepper, lemon juice and a little mayonnaise to taste.

Salmon butter
Cream 4 oz. butter with about 4 oz. flaked cooked or well drained canned salmon. Add 1 tablespoon shredded cucumber, little mayonnaise and chopped parsley.

Savoury butter
To 4 oz. butter add 1 teaspoon curry powder, few drops Worcestershire sauce, 2 teaspoons chutney. Add chopped watercress and 1 or 2 chopped gherkins.

Sandwich fillings

1 Chop hard-boiled eggs and mix with chopped diced crisp bacon and a little salad dressing or mayonnaise.
2 Chop hard-boiled eggs and mix with sweet chutney and chopped watercress.
3 Slice Gruyere or Cheddar cheese and spread lightly with made mustard and sprigs of watercress.
4 Grate cheese and mix with grated raw carrot and moisten with little mayonnaise.
5 Mash sardines, mix with finely diced or sliced cucumber, little lemon juice.
6 Spread canned well-drained salmon on crisp lettuce then spread lightly with horseradish cream, sprinkle with grated cheese. Top with more lettuce, then the bread and butter.
7 Cook kippers lightly, flake flesh from bones, season well, add little lemon juice or vinegar and mix with little butter and chopped watercress.
8 Flake corned beef, mix with little made mustard, mayonnaise, chopped spring onion.
9 Chop tongue finely, mix with a little mayonnaise, good pinch curry powder and chopped hard-boiled eggs.
10 Spread thin slices of cooked beef with horseradish cream and finely chopped beetroot.
11 Chop cooked ham or boiled bacon, mix with skinned chopped tomatoes and shredded lettuce. If necessary add little mayonnaise.
12 Chop cooked lamb finely, mix with sweet chutney and a little mint sauce.

Index

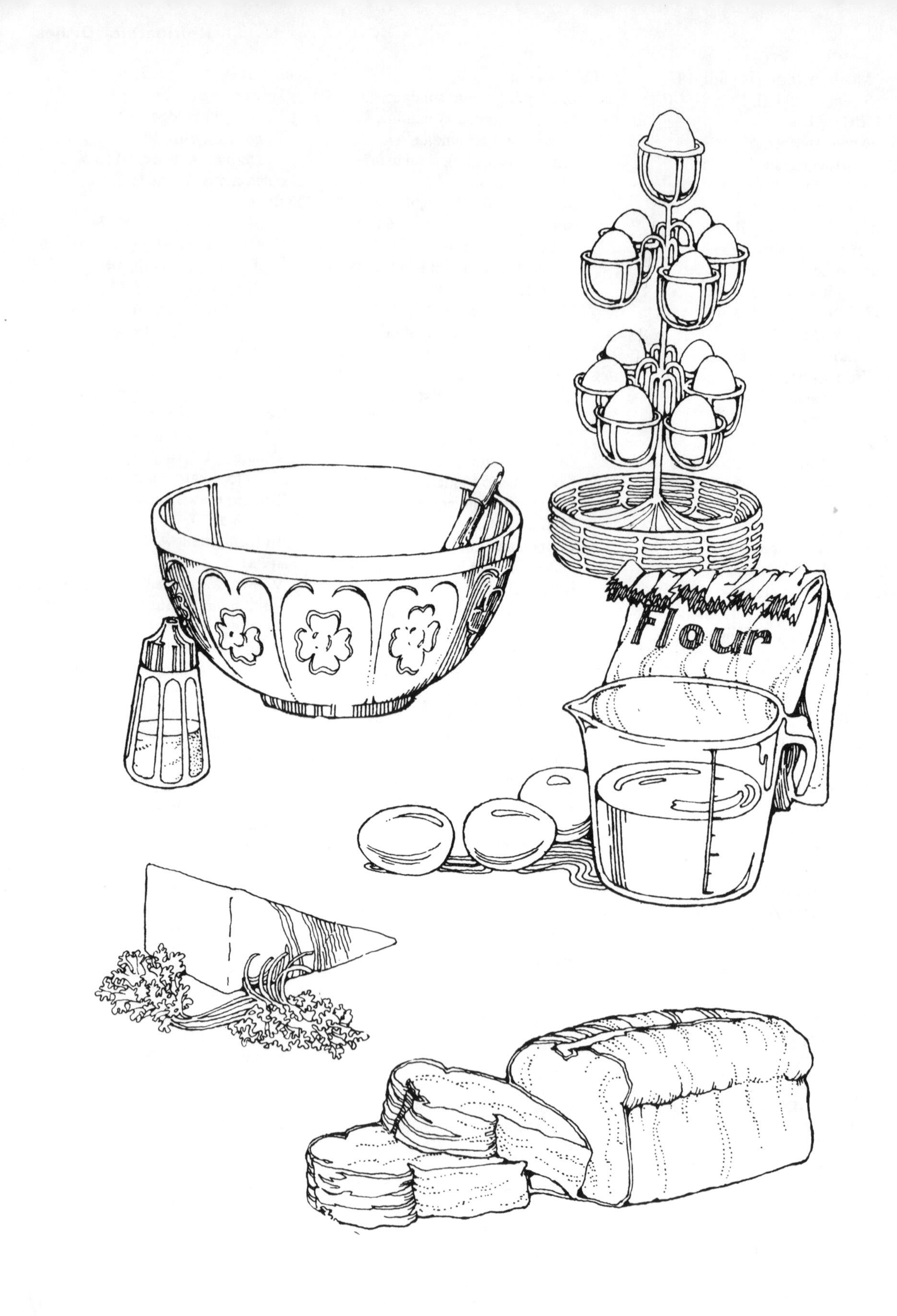
Flour

Bread and Scones

General Information about Bread Making

To choose the right bread recipe

There are a great variety of breads in this book, but some of the recipes may appear rather similar with perhaps the exception of more fruit, more fat, etc. In order to help you decide on which of the recipes to choose, remember the following:

Breads that contain a high percentage of fat, fruit or syrup are better if they are kept some little while before cutting, so this is not a recipe to make on the day you wish to eat the bread.

On the other hand, breads that contain a low percentage of these ingredients do not keep well, so are better eaten when fresh.

To use an electric mixer for kneading dough

Some electric mixers have a special dough hook for kneading yeast doughs, and other mixers recommend using the ordinary whisk. It must, however, be remembered that bread kneading is a slow, deliberate process, and that the mixer should be turned to the lowest speed in order to do this job well.

Yeast bread

In this section you will find basic bread doughs with variations according to the type of flour, ways of making the bread richer by adding milk, eggs, etc., and how to give crispness or softness to the dough so that you can produce exactly the sort of bread that you and your family like.

If you have never made bread before, read through the first section. It may sound rather difficult to start with, but in fact it is not difficult at all. It is just a case of understanding the various processes in bread making and the reasons for adding or omitting certain ingredients.

Some people are more successful by one method than another, so if you are new to bread making, try each method in turn and see which one gives you the best result.

Success with yeast cookery

1 Yeast is a living organism or plant, so it must have warmth and food so it can 'grow' and make bread or cakes. All ingredients and utensils should be kept comfortably warm to encourage gentle growth.

2 Never put yeast dough to rise in a very warm place otherwise you will kill the yeast too soon and the bread will not rise. The yeast should only be killed when the dough is put into the oven, see pages 8–9 for suggested places to put yeast to rise.

3 Fresh yeast should be putty coloured, crumble easily and have a sweet smell. If it is patchy in colour, very hard, and has a strong unpleasant smell, it is stale and should not be used.

4 Store fresh yeast, well wrapped, in the refrigerator if you want to use it several days ahead, an ordinary larder is too warm.

5 If you have no refrigerator then buy yeast freshly or use dried yeast.

6 There are two types of yeast :
Brewers yeast used in wine making
Bakers yeast used in bread making, this latter gives better results in baking.
In addition to the points stressed on page 8 there are certain other factors which give successful results.

7 Have all ingredients and utensils at a comfortable temperature, just warm, NOT TOO HOT and not very COLD.

8 Bake at the right temperatures. Most yeast cooking needs a hot oven at the beginning to kill the yeast directly the food is put into the oven.

9 Handle the dough firmly, but not too roughly.

10 The fact that in some recipes the quantity of water is given rather approximately is not a fault, for flours vary considerably in the amount of liquid they absorb, see page 10. An ideal bread dough is easy to handle yet not too stiff. You can always tell when it is sufficiently handled by testing with a firm pressure of your finger. If the mark comes out the bread is kneaded enough.

Read before using yeast

Cooking with yeast is very well worth doing, for it provides a more interesting variety of cakes, buns and bread at very economical prices. Don't be frightened by the terms used in yeast cookery, they are quite simple.

1 Sponge break through
This means that having creamed the yeast and sugar and added liquid and a sprinkling of flour, you put the mixture in a warm place until the surface is covered with small bubbles.

2 To prove
This means allowing the dough to rise, and this is done by putting the dough in a warm place, NOT TOO HOT, until it has increased its bulk to twice the original size. Never allow it to become more than twice the original size or the dough will be over-proved and its taste and texture spoiled.

3 To knock back
This means that when the dough has proved it is then kneaded gently but firmly until it regains its original size.

4 To knead
This is a vital process in bread making or in any recipes using yeast. If insufficient kneading is given to the dough you have a badly flavoured and textured loaf. If too much kneading is given, on the other hand, you have a too open textured dough and one that tends to be heavy due to overhandling.

5 Use the heel of your hand
While people vary in the way they knead dough it is quicker, easier and on the whole more satisfactory if the heel of the hand is used. This is the part of the palm near the wrist, and it means giving it first a push with this firm part of the palm, then with the help of the fingertips bringing it back again into shape.

Proportions of yeast

Some of the recipes may seem to have rather amazing discrepancies in the proportion of yeast allowed. A large percentage of yeast may have been allowed because of the high quantity of fruit, fat, etc. On the other hand, it may be that this particular bread is improved by a high percentage of yeast.

If you use half the quantity of any recipe, you do not necessarily halve the amount of yeast exactly. You use slightly above half the quantity of yeast to give you the best result.

On the other hand, if you are doubling the amount of ingredients in the recipe, use just under twice the amount of yeast, for you do not need quite so much to make this larger quantity rise.

To use dried yeast

When fresh yeast is not obtainable dried yeast can be used in any of these recipes.

You buy it in tins or packets, and in the case of large tins it is often stamped with the date up to which it should be stored. Keep dried yeast in a cool, dry place.

Use ½ oz. yeast (1 level tablespoon) instead of 1 oz. of fresh yeast. To reconstitute the dried yeast, put in a jug with a teaspoon sugar and a little of the warmed liquid quoted in the recipe. Leave for 10 – 15 minutes and whisk up with a fork. The dried yeast often acts more slowly than fresh, so it will take the dough longer to double its size – approximately half as long again, e.g. 1½ hours instead of an hour. The same applies to the time quoted for proving.

Dried yeast is suitable for the sponging method 1 and for method 2, but is not recommended for method 3. See below.

Various methods of incorporating yeast

Experiments have shown it is possible to incorporate yeast into the flour by several methods.

Method 1 *Because this is the most usual it is the one described in the majority of recipes in the yeast section of the book.*
Suitable for fresh and dried yeast
This method produces the best results in rich yeast breads as well as being a good method for all yeast mixtures. It does however take a little longer than methods 2 and 3 since you have the initial stage.

Either cream the yeast with a little sugar and then blend with part of the tepid liquid or just blend with the tepid liquid and omit the sugar. Dried yeast always needs the sugar for best results, but it has been found possible to leave out sweetening with fresh yeast if preferred.

When the yeast has been blended with the liquid (and sugar), either sprinkle the top with a layer of flour or make into a batter consistency with some of the flour in the recipe.

Leave the mixture in the basin or jug in a warm place until the surface is covered with bubbles, 'the sponge breaks through'. After this blend with the flour and other ingredients.

When making bread the yeast and liquid are often put into a 'well' made in the centre of the flour in the mixing bowl, the top of the liquid is sprinkled with a little of the flour then the bowl is covered and left in a warm place until 'the sponge breaks through'.

Method 2 Suitable for fresh and dried yeast

This is a quicker method than method 1 and while slightly less good in rich yeast doughs is excellent for all general yeast cookery including bread.

For fresh yeast, blend with a little tepid liquid then add to the flour, etc., with remaining liquid.

For dried yeast, dissolve 1 teaspoon sugar in a little tepid liquid, sprinkle the dried yeast on top. Leave in a warm place until frothy, then blend with the flour, etc.

Method 3 Suitable only for fresh yeast

Rub the yeast into the flour as one would fat into pastry then add liquid. You must knead very thoroughly by this method to make sure the yeast is well distributed.

This method can be used for bread, but does not produce the finest results. It is however quite suitable for buns, particularly the type where the dough is rolled out, like a Chelsea bun.

Warm places to put dough to rise

As you will see below there can be a great deal of difference in the time you allow yeast doughs to rise or prove, depending on how quickly you need to have the dough available for baking.

When you wish to prove in a warm place the following suggestions may be found helpful.

1 Cover the dough, see page 9.
2 Put in the airing cupboard well away from the hot water pipes or hot water tanks or heaters.
3 Put into the warming drawer (switched on) of the cooker—BUT DO NOT HAVE THE ELECTRIC OR GAS OVEN HEAT ON AS THIS WILL MAKE IT TOO HOT. The warming drawer must just be comfortably warm to the touch.
4 Stand the dough in a bowl in a steamer over a saucepan of warm water. The water must be about 110°F. only, so your hands can feel comfortably warm in it, no more.
5 Stand the dough in a bowl on the plate rack of the cooker and keep a pan of water gently simmering below.
6 Stand on top of the boiler provided this is not too hot. If it feels rather hot to the touch then put several layers of paper and tea cloths under the bowl or container.
7 Stand reasonably near to radiators or fires, but never allow to touch the heat.

The reason emphasis is laid on the fact that the yeast must not become too hot when rising or proving is that it will be killed with excess heat during the initial stages which will completely spoil the recipe.

Cold places to put dough to rise

You can put the dough into a cool place, which gives a slower and ultimately better result than a warm one.

This can be in a really cold cupboard, or refrigerator, but it must not be a very damp place, like a cellar, or outside shed. You will find timing for slow proving below.

To time the dough for rising

The richness of the dough is one factor that alters time of rising; do not expect very rich mixtures to rise quite as quickly as plainer bread doughs, so allow slightly longer than the times given below.

The heat of the surroundings however is the main factor in timing the rising of yeast doughs.

Remember that times given below are only very average and may vary a little.

The times are for about 4 – 5 lb. bread dough; a very small quantity will rise in a somewhat shorter time, a very large quantity will take a little longer.

In a warm place, see page 8	The dough will be ready within 45 minutes to just over 1 hour.
In an average room temperature, about 60°F.	The dough will be ready in about 2 – 2½ hours. To prolong rising put in the coolest part of the room.
In a very cold room or cupboard, about 45°F.	The dough can take up to 12 hours. This is very convenient for overnight rising; if you wish to hasten next day just move into a warmer place for final period.
In the storage compartment of an ordinary refrigerator, about 35°F.	The dough can be left for about 24 hours and could be left up to a maximum of 48 hours. Take out of the refrigerator and leave in room temperature for a period of up to 1 hour.

By making use of the various ways of proving yeast doughs you can ensure the dough is ready at a time to suit the cooking.

To cover the dough

Although recipes do not state that the dough MUST be covered while rising or proving this is a good idea since it prevents the surface becoming hard and dry.

Use either a clean tea cloth, which should be placed completely over the bowl allowing plenty of space at the top for the dough to rise or cover with lightly oiled foil or greaseproof paper.

One of the most satisfactory coverings however is to cover the top of the bowl with a sheet of polythene, which retains moisture better than cloth, foil or paper, or to put the dough INTO a large polythene bag. If inserting into a bag remember the dough will double its bulk and allow sufficient space.

Many people do not have very large mixing bowls in which case the dough can be put into lightly oiled covered saucepans, biscuit tins with well-fitting lids or plastic storage canisters.

Baking times

Please remember that the baking times in bread making are very approximate, for if you use a slightly larger loaf tin than the one given in the recipe, your bread will be shallower and therefore cook a little quicker.

Loaves put on to flat tins rather than *in* tins, tend to bake more quickly. If your flour has absorbed rather less liquid than the average it will also shorten the baking time.

To test yeast bread

To test whether bread is cooked, knock sharply on the bottom with your knuckles. The bread should have a hollow sound. If it does not, then it needs further cooking.

Faults in bread making

If you are disappointed with your bread, it can be because of the following reasons:

1. If the bread is very open, and not of a smooth even texture, it is generally caused by either too much liquid or over-handling in kneading.
2. If you have a rather grey crumb, which looks unattractive and causes the bread to taste slightly heavy, it can be due to over-proving or over-fermentation.
3. If there is a strong smell of yeast from the finished bread, it is either too high a proportion of yeast, or again, over-proving.
4. Tiny white spots on the crust of the loaf when baked means that the dough had a chance to form a skin while proving.
   This is avoided by covering carefully and allowing the bread to prove steadily rather than too rapidly.

To look after tins for bread or other yeast cooking

For loaves of bread, you will use the orthodox loaf tins and these should be looked after very

carefully, i.e. if they are washed after use, dry them most carefully, particularly in the corners where they could become rusted in time.
You may find that there is no need to wash the tins, for a loaf of bread should turn out without sticking in any way. If the tins are then wiped out with very soft or kitchen paper immediately after use, they can be cleaned perfectly and this keeps them in far better condition.
Flat baking tins which will be used for rolls and other shapes of bread should be looked after in the same way.
If you make bread only occasionally, there is no need to buy special bread tins. Your ordinary cake tins will do admirably and a round instead of an oblong loaf looks most attractive. You will, of course, look after the cake tins in the same way as the loaf tins.

To prepare tins for bread making

All tins for bread making should be lightly greased.
The best thing to use is either lard, cooking fat, very well clarified dripping, oil or butter.
Melt the solid fats, and brush over the tins lightly with a pastry brush. Shake a little flour over from a flour dredger or a spoon; tap this firmly over the tin, being extra careful with a loaf tin that it is getting into each of the corners. Tap the tin very firmly to shake away any surplus.

To use up surplus dough

Many of the basic breads in this book are based on a fairly large amount of flour, and you may find that this is too much for you. That is why a recipe has been given, see page 16, with a smaller percentage of flour.
If, however, you know you will be needing fresh bread within another 24 hours, it saves a great deal of time if you make up the large batch of dough, take out as much as you need and put the rest, very well covered in polythene or foil, in your refrigerator. It can be kept in there for a maximum of 48 hours, brought out, left in room temperature for at least an hour, kneaded, formed into loaves or rolls and baked in the usual way.

Deep freezing bread

Some people have their own home deep freeze or they have a deep freeze section to their domestic refrigerator and it is possible to freeze *COOKED* bread to use on a future occasion.
When the bread has been cooked, allow it to cool completely, wrap in polythene and put into the deep freeze at the correct temperature for speedy freezing.

Best results in proving

Although it is often more convenient to hasten the proving of the dough in a warm place, provided the heat is not too great, and this does not harm the dough in any way, it has been found that stronger and therefore better textured breads, etc., result from slower proving.

Bulk in proving

A plain bread dough will rise to just about twice its original bulk and is ready when it springs back when pressed firmly but gently with a lightly floured finger.
A moderately rich dough such as milk loaves or bread with a certain amount of fat and eggs in will rise rather less than twice its original bulk so you do not wait any longer if the finger test shows it is ready.
A very rich fruit loaf (almost as rich as a cake in fat and fruit) will rise decidedly less than twice its original bulk.

Flour to use in yeast cookery

Since yeast is the ingredient used to make the dough rise you do not want any other raising agents, so choose PLAIN FLOUR.
In bread making in particular you get the finest results if a STRONG PLAIN flour, normally called bread flour, is used. It is not always possible to get this, but try if you wish the very best bread.
The reason for choosing a strong flour is that it absorbs a greater quantity of water, and so gives a greater volume and lighter texture.
In rich buns and fruit breads where there is a high percentage of fat, ordinary plain flour can be used.

Stone ground or wholemeal flour will absorb considerably more liquid than white flour, so if substituting this for recipes in the book allow more liquid.

Liquid in yeast cookery

Water gives the lightest results so is advisable for plain breads.

Milk gives more flavour, food value and produces a better colour to both crust and crumb. It helps the bread to keep.

Eggs add food value, colour, flavour and also help to make the dough light.

As will be seen in various recipes a mixture of milk and water or eggs and milk can be used to give the total amount of liquid.

Good average amounts of liquid are given in the various yeast recipes in this book and you may find them quite satisfactory. On the other hand you may find you consistently need rather MORE liquid than given, this is because you are using the type of flour which absorbs a high percentage of liquid.

If you find the dough mixture is rather dry do not try to manage with exactly the amount stated in the recipe, add a little more to give a SOFT DOUGH.

If the flour you are using is the type that absorbs less liquid you may find the dough seems rather soft. This is easily rectified by using a generous amount of flour when kneading the dough.

Sugar in yeast doughs

Sugar is a food on which yeast (a living plant) thrives, but it is a mistake to imagine that you cannot get yeast to ferment unless you use sugar.

Recent experiments have shown that too much sugar in a recipe HINDERS the fermentation of the yeast, that is why very rich fruit breads take a long time to rise.

Once upon a time one always creamed the yeast with a teaspoon sugar to commence fermentation, but this is not really essential, in fact some people find they get best results with fresh yeast if the sugar is NOT used at all in the initial stage.

Fat in yeast doughs

By adding fat to yeast doughs you get a richer mixture that keeps better. Very rich fruit breads and cakes keep for some considerable time. Do not expect any yeast dough containing a reasonable amount of fat to rise as high as a plain dough.

Salt in yeast cookery

Salt is added in bread, etc., to improve the flavour, and bread without salt would be very unpalatable. Remember too much salt is not only unpleasant in flavour, but it does kill yeast, and so prevents the dough rising.

To serve the bread, bring it out and let it defrost at room temperature. You will then find the bread is perfect, although for some people it may be a little soft on the outside as the freezing process does destroy the crispness of the crust. You can then put it into the oven for just a short time and crisp it thoroughly.

To freshen bread that has become stale

There are several ways in which bread can be freshened if it has become stale.

1 Brush the outside very lightly with milk or water and crisp in the oven for a short time.
2 Have a bowl of water available and dip the bread quickly in and out of the water, so that it becomes completely moistened without being soggy. Put into the oven at a moderate temperature (375°F.—Gas Mark 4) and re-heat for about 15 – 20 minutes.
3 Put the bread into a metal biscuit tin with a tightly fitting lid. Make sure the lid is on firmly and put into a hot oven for a good 10 minutes. Allow to cool in the closed tin.

Although bread is possibly the yeast food you will wish to freshen more often than anything else, these methods are also suitable for other yeast cookery.

To steam bread

If you do not wish to put the oven on there is another way to make bread which does not, of course, produce a crisp outside, but is very suitable for some of the fruit breads, whether made with yeast or baking powder. You

grease cocoa or chocolate powder tins. Half fill with the yeast dough and allow to prove until it reaches the top of the tin.
Put on the greased lid.
With baking powder bread you can fill about ⅔ up the tin since the bread will not rise so drastically.
Put into a steamer over a pan of steadily boiling water and allow approximately the same cooking time as in the oven.

Pre-packed bread, scone mixes

There are on the market a range of bread and scone mixes.
These are particularly useful for the small family because the packet gives enough flour and yeast for one loaf.
The instructions on the packet should be followed very carefully.
All the other hints on bread making in this book are equally important for this type of bread as that made from an ordinary packet of flour. You should get good results from the mixes, since the flour is of the right type for bread and scones.

To cook a good shaped tin loaf

In order to have a really good shaped tin loaf, you can do one of two things. Either drop the piece of very well kneaded dough into the prepared loaf tin and then, with your knuckles, just press it into shape, OR you can knead the dough until an oblong shape, the length of the bread tin, but 3 times the width. You then fold the dough over, rather as if you were making a flattish Swiss roll, and put it into the loaf tin. This gives a smoother and more even top.

Crisp crust bread

In order to get a really crisp crust to your loaves of bread, brush with a little melted butter, margarine or oil before baking.
If baking in loaf tins, slip out of the tins at the end of the cooking time, brush the sides with a little melted butter or oil and replace in a hot oven on a flat baking tin for about 5 minutes.

Soft crust bread

Bake the bread without glazing in any way and towards the end of the cooking time, brush rather liberally with a little milk to soften the crust.

Flour topped bread

Many people like a very soft floury type of bread, and this is easily obtained by brushing the loaves rather generously with milk before putting into the oven and then dusting liberally with sieved flour.

How to shape bread

After you have experimented with ordinary tin loaves, i.e. baking in loaf tins, you will be anxious to make more ambitious shapes.

Shapes for bread

Bloomer loaf

1 Form the dough into a rather 'fat' roll.
2 Flatten the top slightly, then mark on top with a sharp knife before proving.
3 Bake on flat baking tins.

Cottage loaf

1 Form the dough into two rounds, one considerably smaller than the other.
2 Press the small round on top of the larger and make a deep thumb mark in the middle of the top round.
3 Bake on flat baking tins.

French stick

1 Form the dough into long 'stick' shape.
2 Score on top with sharp knife before proving.
3 Bake on flat baking tins.

Coburg

1 Form dough into large rounds.
2 Mark with wide cross on top before proving.
3 Bake on flat baking tins.

French or Vienna loaf

1 Form into a rather shorter and thicker 'stick' than the French stick.

Farmhouse or Danish loaf

1 If using basic bread dough, mix with rather more milk than water.
2 This can be baked in a loaf tin, but fill the loaf tin slightly fuller than usual, so you get the typical rounded edges.
3 Score well on top before final proving.
4 Brush with a little milk and sprinkle top with light dusting of flour before baking.

Fancy shapes for bread

In many shops you see most intriguing shapes for bread and with a little practice you can work out rather original loaves.
Here are suggestions you may like to try.

1 Plaited bloomer
Shape the dough as a bloomer loaf, but save a little bit of the dough. Make this into a plait and lay loosely across the top of the bloomer loaf, brushing with a little egg and milk or milk for a glaze.

2 Plaited loaves
Make one long strip of dough, rather as though you were making a bloomer loaf. Cut into three strips to within about 1 – 1½ inches from one end. Plait loosely.

3 Twist
As above, but make only into two strips and twist rather than plait.

4 Whirls
Make a long thin stick, like a French stick. Twist one end round, then continue with the rest of the stick, whirling it round the centre.
With every shape you make, remember the dough will spread a lot in proving, so do not plait or twist too tightly.

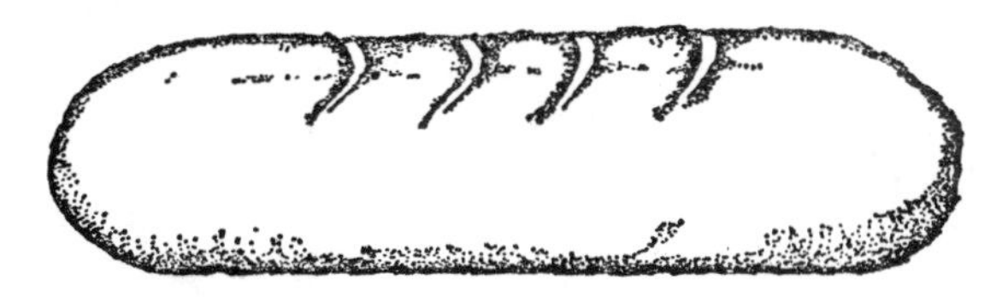

Bloomer loaf

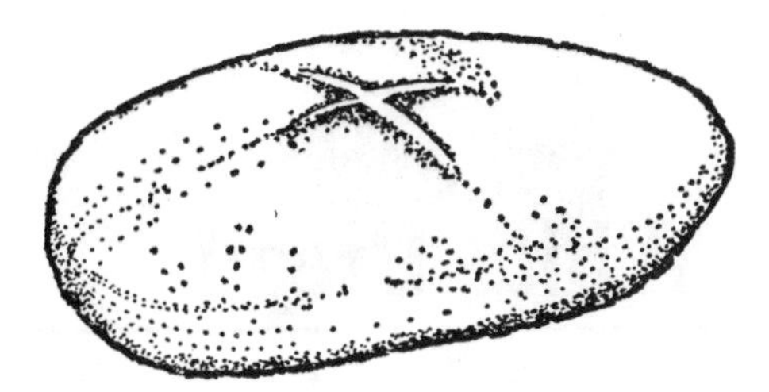

Coburg

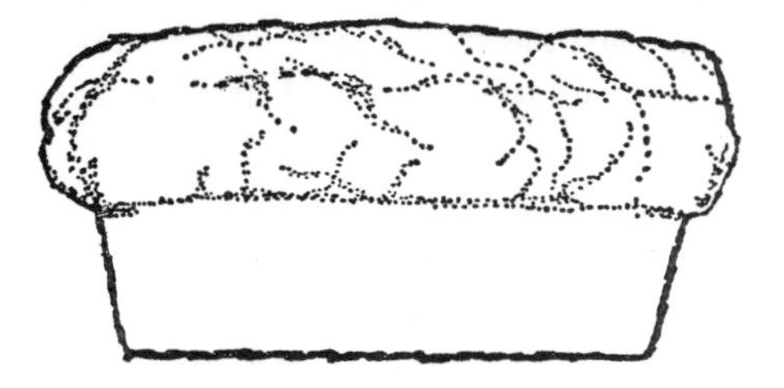

Farmhouse or Danish loaf

French or Vienna loaf

French stick

Cottage loaf

White Bread

White bread method I

cooking time — I hour

you will need:

3 lb. strong plain flour*	I teaspoon sugar (could be omitted with fresh yeast)
3 heaped teaspoons salt†	about $1\frac{1}{2}$ pints lukewarm milk and water mixed
I oz. yeast or $\frac{1}{2}$ oz. dried yeast	

* This is the flour which gives the very finest results in bread making, but as explained on page 10, ordinary white flour could be used

† Or according to taste, so use a little less on first occasion

1 Sieve the flour and salt into the bowl and put in a warm place until the flour is thoroughly warm This can be carried out on the plate rack of a cooker with a large saucepan of water boiling gently underneath, see pages 8–9 for suggestions for warming yeast, which are also suitable for warming flour. This stage is not essential but helps the rapid rising of the flour if you are in a hurry.

2 Put the yeast with the sugar, if liked, but see page 10 for the use of sugar in bread making. With dried yeast the sugar is essential. Mix with a teaspoon until liquid, then add up to $\frac{1}{3}$ of the warmed liquid.

3 Either sprinkle the top lightly with flour and allow to rise in a warm place
OR mix in enough flour to make a batter
OR make a well in the centre of the flour and pour in the yeast liquid, dust the top lightly with flour.

4 When the sponge breaks through, blend the yeast liquid with the flour and the rest of the liquid to make an elastic dough.

5 Turn the dough on to a floured board and knead well, for hints on kneading, see page 7. When you are satisfied the dough is smooth, put back in the bowl.

6 Cover, see page 9, and leave in a warm place for

about 1 hour until the dough is double its bulk. If wishing to prove more slowly, see page 9 and you will also find on page 10 hints for testing when the dough has risen sufficiently.

7 For ordinary loaves of bread, warm two 2 lb. loaf tins and grease and flour.
8 Turn the dough on to the floured board, re-knead and divide into two with a knife.
9 Re-knead, then press into the prepared loaf tins. Cover, see page 9, and prove in a warm place for about 20 minutes or until the dough has risen level with the top of the tin.
10 Bake in the centre of a very hot oven (475°F.—Gas Mark 8) for 15 minutes, then a further 40 minutes in a moderately hot oven (400°F.—Gas Mark 5). Remove loaves from tins and return to the oven for another 5 minutes, standing on the oven shelf to give a brown crust.
Loaves are cooked when they sound hollow when rapped on base with the knuckles.
For details as to the advantages of this method see page 8.

White Bread method 2

cooking time 1 hour

you will need:

3 lb. strong plain flour*
3 heaped teaspoons salt
1 oz. yeast or ½ oz. dried yeast
about 1½ pints lukewarm milk and water mixed
1 teaspoon sugar (to be used with dried yeast only)

* This is the flour which gives the very finest results in bread making, but as explained on page 10, ordinary white flour could be used

1 Sieve the flour and salt into the bowl and put in a warm place until the flour is thoroughly warm. This can be carried out on the plate rack of a cooker with a large saucepan of water boiling gently underneath, see pages 8–9 for suggestions for warming yeast, which are also suitable for warming flour. This stage is not essential but helps the rapid rising of the flour if you are in a hurry.
2 Blend the yeast with up to ⅓ of the warmed liquid.
3 Make a well in the centre of the flour, add the yeast, etc., and mix with the hand to an elastic dough, adding the remainder of the milk and water.
4 Turn the dough on to a floured board and knead well, for hints on kneading, see page 7. When you are satisfied the dough is smooth, put back in the bowl.
5 Cover, see page 9, and leave in a warm place for about 1 hour until the dough is double its bulk. If wishing to prove more slowly, see page 9 and you will also find on page 10 hints for testing when the dough has risen sufficiently.
6 For ordinary loaves of bread, warm two 2 lb. loaf tins and grease.
7 Turn the dough on to the floured board, re-knead and divide into two with a knife.
8 Re-knead, then press into the prepared bread tins. Cover, see page 9, and prove in a warm place for about 20 minutes or until the dough has risen level with the top of the tin.
9 Bake in the centre of a very hot oven (475°F.—Gas Mark 8) for 15 minutes, then a further 40 minutes in a moderately hot oven (400°F.—Gas Mark 5). Remove loaves from tins and return to the oven for another 5 minutes, standing on the oven shelf to give a brown crust.
Loaves are cooked when they sound hollow when rapped on base with the knuckles.
For details as to advantages of this method see page 8.

White bread method 3

cooking time 1 hour

you will need:

3 lb. strong plain flour*
3 heaped teaspoons salt†
1 oz. fresh yeast‡
1 teaspoon sugar (could be omitted)
about 1½ pints lukewarm milk and water mixed

* This is the flour which gives the very finest results in bread making, but as explained on page 10, ordinary white flour could be used
† Or according to taste
‡ *This method is not recommended for dried yeast*

1 Sieve the flour and salt into the bowl and put in a warm place until the flour is thoroughly warm. This can be carried out on the plate rack of a cooker with a large saucepan of water boiling gently underneath, see pages 8–9 for suggestions for warming yeast, which are also suitable for warming flour. This stage is not essential but helps with the rapid rising of the flour if you are in a hurry.
2 Rub the yeast into the flour, and sugar if liked, as one would for pastry, making sure it is evenly distributed.

3 Add the liquid gradually to make an elastic dough.
4 Turn the dough on to a floured board and knead very well with the hands until smooth. In this method, kneading is very essential as the yeast has to be evenly distributed.
5 Put back into the bowl and cover, see page 9, and leave in a warm place for about 1 hour until the dough is double its bulk. If wishing to prove more slowly see page 9 and you will also find on page 10 hints for testing when the dough has risen sufficiently.
6 For ordinary loaves of bread, warm two 2 lb. loaf tins and grease.
7 Turn the dough on to the floured board, re-knead and divide into two with a knife.
8 Re-knead, then press into the prepared bread tins. Cover, see page 9, and prove in a warm place for about 20 minutes or until the dough has risen level with the top of the tin.
9 Bake in the centre of a very hot oven (475°F.—Gas Mark 8) for 15 minutes, then a further 40 minutes in a moderately hot oven (400°F.—Gas Mark 5). Remove loaves from tins and return to the oven for another 5 minutes, standing on the oven shelf to give a brown crust. Loaves are cooked when they sound hollow when rapped on base with the knuckles. For details as to the disadvantages of this method, see page 8.
This is not the best way of making bread, but a very quick and easy one.

Cornflour bread

For a very fine textured bread, select the ordinary bread dough, see pages 14–16, but use 14 oz. flour, 2 oz. cornflour in place of 1 lb. flour. This does not make a great deal of difference to the proving time.

Starch reduced breads

It is possible to buy a flour made by a firm who produce starch reduced rolls and crispbreads. This is a flour that is higher in protein and somewhat lower in starch than most flours. It is a self-raising flour and so can be used in any of the baking powder breads and scones.
You will find that no extra liquid is required.
The flour does tend to be slightly creamier in colour than usual but produces a perfectly light result. If it is used to make yeast breads, be rather more sparing with the yeast than usual, because it contains a raising agent. You will then find you get a perfectly acceptable result.

White bread—small loaves

Many people do not wish to make as much bread as the basic recipe using 3 lb. flour, and since the yeast is not reduced in proportion, here is a recipe for a small quantity of bread.

cooking time 30 – 40 minutes

you will need:

½ oz. fresh yeast (or 2 level teaspoons dried yeast)
1 level teaspoon sugar
½ pint tepid water, OR milk and water
1 lb. flour
1 level teaspoon salt*
2 oz. lard or margarine

* Or according to taste

1 Blend yeast with sugar, add liquid and sprinkle lightly with little of flour, OR blend into batter with about ⅓ of flour. Leave for 15 minutes, or until the batter or surface is bubbling and frothy.
2 Sift the salt with the rest of flour. Lightly rub in lard or margarine.
3 Add rubbed in mixture to the batter and mix thoroughly to form an elastic dough, which will leave the sides of the basin clean.
4 Turn dough on to a lightly floured board, and knead well for about 5 minutes, see page 7.
5 Cover. Leave to rise until the dough springs back when pressed with a floured finger and is double original bulk—about 1 hour at average room temperature, see page 9. Proving the dough inside a greased polythene bag is recommended, see page 9.
6 Turn out risen dough on to a floured board. Divide into two and knead each piece lightly. Mould each piece by flattening with knuckles to form a rectangle, and then folding into three.
7 Place each piece in a greased 1 lb. loaf tin, cover lightly, see page 9, and leave until the dough rises to the top of the tin.
8 Bake on the centre shelf of a hot oven (450°F.—Gas Mark 7) for 30–40 minutes.

Note:

Methods 2 or 3, see page 15, could be used if preferred.

Brown Bread

One method only has been given for the following brown breads, but remember you can use either of the others, which are described on page 8. You will also find on the same page the types of breads for which these methods are most suited.

Brown Bread

cooking time 40 – 55 minutes

you will need:

- 1½ lb. plain or bread flour
- 1½ lb. stone ground flour (wholemeal flour)
- 3 – 7 level teaspoons salt (according to taste)
- 1 level teaspoon sugar
- 1 oz. yeast
- 1½ pints tepid water (at least)

1 Sieve the flours and salt into a warm basin, then put in warm place.
2 Cream yeast and sugar in another basin, add part of liquid.
3 Put this into a well made in the centre of the flour and give a light dusting of flour over the top.
4 Cover with a clean cloth and leave in a warm place until top is covered with bubbles, about 15 minutes.
5 Add rest of liquid, you may need a little more than this as a better result is obtained with brown bread if the dough is slightly slacker (moist) than usual.
6 Knead well until dough is smooth and leaves bowl clean.
7 Put in a warm place to rise for about 1½ hours, then knead again.
8 Form into two loaves and put into two 2 lb. loaf tins, warmed and lightly greased, half filling them.
9 To give a very crisp crust, brush with melted margarine or use milk or egg and water.
10 Prove for 20 minutes.
11 Bake in the centre of a hot oven (450°F.—Gas Mark 7) for 10 minutes, then reduce heat to moderate (375°F.—Gas Mark 4) for further 30 – 45 minutes.
12 Test by knocking on the bottom of the loaves, which should sound hollow.
13 Cool away from draught.

Note:
An ounce of lard or margarine rubbed into flour helps to keep bread moist.

Brown twin loaves

cooking time 40 – 55 minutes

you will need:

- 1 lb. white flour
- 1 lb. wholemeal flour
- 2 level teaspoons salt
- ¾ oz. yeast
- 1 teaspoon sugar
- approximately 1 pint tepid water

1 Sieve flours and salt into a warm basin, then put in warm place.
2 Cream yeast and sugar in another basin, add part of liquid.
3 Put this into a well made in the centre of the flour, and give a light dusting of flour over the top.
4 Cover with a clean cloth and leave for a good 15 minutes in a warm place until the top is covered with bubbles.
5 Add rest of liquid until you have a soft dough.
6 Knead well until dough is smooth and leaves bowl clean.
7 Put in a warm place to rise for about 1½ hours, then knead again.
8 Form into shape to fit into and half fill a large cake tin about 9 – 10 inches square. The tin should be greased and warmed.
9 Mark a very firm indentation down centre.
10 To give a very crisp crust, brush with melted margarine or use milk or egg and water.
11 Prove for a final time, about 20 minutes.
12 Bake in the centre of a hot oven (450°F.—Gas Mark 7) for 10 minutes then reduce heat to moderate (375°F.—Gas Mark 4) for further 30 – 45 minutes.
13 Test by knocking on the bottom of the loaf, which should sound hollow.
14 Cool away from draught.

Nutty wholemeal loaf

cooking time 40 – 55 minutes

you will need:

3 lb. stone ground flour
3 teaspoons salt
1 oz. yeast
1 level teaspoon sugar
1¾ – 2 pints tepid water

1 Sieve the flour and salt into a warm basin, then put into a warm place.
2 Cream the yeast and sugar in another basin, and add part of the liquid.
3 Make a well in the centre of the flour and pour in the yeast liquid.
4 Dust lightly over the top with flour and cover with a clean cloth.
5 Leave in a warm place until the top is covered with bubbles, a good 15 minutes.
6 Add the rest of the liquid, adding a little more if necessary to make a soft consistency, but firm enough to handle.
7 Knead well until the dough is smooth and leaves the bowl clean.
8 Put into a warm place to rise for about 1½ hours.
9 Knead again. Form into loaves, this amount will make three loaves, and put into three warmed and lightly greased 7-inch cake tins.
10 Prove for a final time, about 20 minutes, then bake in the centre of a hot oven (450°F.—Gas Mark 7) for the first 10 minutes.
11 Reduce heat to moderate (375°F.—Gas Mark 4) for a further 30 – 45 minutes.
12 This is another method of making wholemeal bread where the dough is dry enough to knead. For a recipe where kneading is not carried out see below.

Note:

If wished, you can sprinkle the top with medium ground or coarse oatmeal or cracked wheat before proving.

Wholemeal bread

cooking time 40 – 55 minutes

you will need:

3 lb. stone ground flour
3 – 7 teaspoons salt (according to taste)
1 oz. yeast
1 teaspoon sugar
2 – 2½ pints tepid water

1 Sieve flour and salt into a warm basin, then put in a warm place.
2 Cream yeast and sugar in another basin, add part of liquid.
3 Put this into a well made in centre of flour, giving a light dusting of flour over top.
4 Cover with a clean cloth and leave in a warm place for a good 15 minutes until top is covered with bubbles.
5 Add enough water to give a very soft dough that is much too slack to knead.
6 Beat well with a wooden spoon.
7 Allow to prove in a warm place for approximately 1 hour, 30 minutes.
8 Beat again and half fill two 2 lb. warmed bread tins.
9 Prove for the final time, about 20 minutes, then bake in the centre of a hot oven (425° – 450°F. —Gas Mark 6 – 7) for the first 10 minutes.
10 Reduce heat to moderate (375°F.—Gas Mark 4) for a further 30 – 45 minutes, depending on size of loaves. To test, knock on bottom of loaves; they should sound hollow. Cool away from draught.
11 With dried yeast, mix with the sugar and a little tepid liquid.
12 Allow to stand in warm place until soft, approximately 20 minutes, then cream. Continue after this as for fresh yeast.

Note:

Makes of dried yeast vary, so follow instructions for each particular make—generally speaking 1 oz. fresh yeast is equivalent to 1 level tablespoon dried yeast.

Varieties of White and Brown Bread

Rye bread

Rye flour can be obtained occasionally in shops selling continental flour.

The best result is obtained by following the directions for white bread, see page 14, but using 2 – 2½ lb. rye flour and ½ – 1 lb. white flour, so you have a total of 3 lb. of flour.

If you use all rye flour, you do get a very dark

and, to some people, slightly bitter loaf of bread.

You can vary the flavour of your rye bread as follows

1 Because it is rather a bitter flour, increase the amount of sugar to 1 tablespoon.
2 Leave out the sugar and instead add 1 – 2 tablespoons syrup, honey or treacle, the latter giving a rich dark colour and moist texture. Molasses could be used instead.
3 For a more moist bread, a little fat could be rubbed into the flour.

Methods 1 and 2, see pages 14–15, should be used for rye bread. It is less suitable for method 3.

Add the liquid steadily. You will probably find you need rather more liquid than with the basic bread dough.

Soya flour bread

Soya flour is a rich source of protein and a little can be added to basic bread doughs, see pages 14–15, instead of some of the flour.

Allow 14 oz. flour, 2 oz. soya flour in place of 1 lb. flour. The soya gives a very pleasant flavour to the bread and will not make a great deal of difference in the amount of liquid required. It may take a few minutes longer to bake. The bread will be richer, not quite so light, and a pleasant colour.

Milk bread

Use the recipe for white bread, see page 14, but blend with tepid milk instead of water. This gives a softer texture to the bread and it does make it very delicious in flavour.

Egg or farmhouse bread

Use the basic bread recipe, see page 14, but to each 1 lb. of flour allow 1 egg. This means using a little less liquid to mix. The egg should be blended with the flour before adding the rest of the liquid. Save just a small amount of the egg to brush over the bread before baking.

Caraway seed bread

The basic white bread, see page 14, milk bread and egg bread can all be flavoured with caraway seeds.

Use approximately 1 tablespoon caraway seeds to each 1 lb. of flour. If wished, the bread can be brushed with a little egg or milk, and sprinkled with caraway seeds halfway through the baking. If they are put on at the beginning, it makes them too hard.

French bread

cooking time 1¼ hours

you will need:

1 lb. white flour
1 oz. fresh yeast
½ pint warm water

1 Sieve the flour into a bowl. Make a well.
2 Cream the yeast very carefully and thoroughly with some of the water and pour it into the well. Add the rest of the water.
3 Mix and knead until all the water has been absorbed.
4 Then cover the bowl with a dry cloth and put it in a warm place to rise for about 3 hours or overnight in a cool place, see page 9.

Stage 2

you will need:

½ oz. salt
½ pint warm water, and the dough see above
1 lb. flour

1 Dissolve the salt in the water and pour it all over the dough, which will have a crusty skin on it. Mix up well until you have got rid of the skin.
2 Then gradually add the flour and knead for as long as you like. The longer the better, for the object is to make the dough as light as possible, but 10 or 15 minutes will be sufficient.
3 Then lift the dough and slap it down into the bowl, again and again; go on doing this for a few minutes, as long as you can stand it. Cover the bowl with a damp cloth and put it back in a warm place to rise for at least 2 hours.

Stage 3

1 Divide the dough into four equal portions.
2 Roll each piece into a ball and leave for 15 minutes covered with a dry cloth, on a floured board.
3 Now spread a clean tea cloth on a baking sheet and sprinkle it liberally with flour.
4 When the 15 minutes are up shape each ball into a long strand sausage by rolling and pulling, as long and as thin a strand as your baking sheet will take comfortably.

5 Then lay the loaves you have thus fashioned on the cloth, pulling the cloth well up between the loaves and at each side, to prevent the bread from expanding outwards.
6 Cover the whole with another cloth and allow to prove in moderate warmth for 1 hour.
7 Then roll the loaves very gently off the cloth, one by one, on to the baking sheet. Touch them as little as possible—they shouldn't stick to the cloth if it is well floured, but if they have, a wooden spoon is better than fingers for removing them.
8 Make two or three shallow cuts on each loaf with a very sharp knife (a razor blade knife is best) and bake in a hot oven (425 – 450°F.—Gas Mark 6 – 7) for first 15 minutes, reducing heat to moderate (375°F.—Gas Mark 4) for 1 hour.
9 The oven door should not be opened for the first 30 minutes and then the loaves will probably need turning and the crusts can be brushed with melted butter or margarine or milk to make a crisp crust.

Jewish Sabbath bread twists (*Chalahs*)

cooking time 30 minutes

you will need:

2 lb. flour
1 teaspoon salt
1 oz. Kosher margarine
¾ pint tepid water
2 eggs
1 oz. yeast
1 teaspoon sugar
little egg to glaze
poppy seeds

1 Mix the flour and salt in a large basin.
2 Melt the margarine in a saucepan, add ½ pint of water and warm to blood heat.
3 Beat the eggs and add the water and margarine.
4 Cream the yeast and sugar and add the ¼ pint water and the margarine mixture.
5 Make a hole in the centre of the flour and pour the yeast liquid into it.
6 Work together to form a light dough.
7 Sprinkle some flour on the top, cover with a cloth and leave in a warm place to rise until double its bulk.
8 Turn on to a well floured board and work lightly.
9 Cut off two fairly large pieces and shape each for the lower portion of the two twists.
10 Brush over with beaten egg.
11 Divide the remainder into six pieces, knead and shape each into a long strand, then make two plaits and place one on top of each twist.
12 Brush over with egg and sprinkle with poppy seeds.
13 Leave to rise for about 20 minutes and bake for about 30 minutes in centre of hot oven (450°F.—Gas Mark 7).

Huffkins

Huffkins are an East Kent tea bread. They are simply thick flat oval cakes of light bread, with a hole in the middle.

cooking time 20 – 25 minutes

you will need:

½ pint tepid milk and water, mixed
1 teaspoon sugar
1 oz. fresh yeast or ½ oz. dried yeast
1 lb. flour
1 level teaspoon salt
1 oz. lard

1 Mix liquid and sugar in a jug and crumble the fresh yeast, or sprinkle the dried yeast on top.
2 Stand in a warm place until frothy, about 10 minutes.
3 Mix flour and salt into a bowl, and rub in the fat.
4 Add yeast liquid to flour and work well to form a firm dough. Cover.
5 Put to rise in a warm place until double in bulk.
6 Turn the dough on to a floured board and knead lightly.
7 Divide into twelve equal pieces.
8 Roll each piece into a ball and flatten with the hand.
9 Place the dough pieces onto greased and floured baking sheets and make a hole in the centre of each one by drawing the dough apart with the two first fingers.
10 Sprinkle with flour and cover.
11 Return to a warm place to rise for 20 – 30 minutes.
12 Bake in the centre of a hot oven (425 – 450°F.—Gas Mark 6 – 7) for 20 – 25 minutes or until golden brown.
13 Remove from oven and wrap in a cloth until cool.

Oatmeal bread I

Oatmeal bread, known as Clapbread in Lancashire, is an old English bread variety and goes particularly well with cheese. It keeps fresh and moist for several days and is good toasted.

cooking time 1 hour

you will need:

1/8 pint warm water	1/2 pint milk
1 teaspoon sugar, if using dried yeast	12 oz. plain flour, strong if possible
1/2 oz. fresh yeast or 2 teaspoons dried yeast	1 level tablespoon salt
8 oz. oatmeal, fine, medium or rolled	2 tablespoons oil or melted margarine

1 Mix water and sugar in a jug and crumble the fresh yeast, or sprinkle the dried yeast on top.
2 Stand in a warm place until frothy, about 10 minutes.
3 Soak the oatmeal in the milk for 30 minutes.
4 Mix flour and salt in a bowl, add the soaked oatmeal, the oil or margarine and the yeast liquid.
5 Work to a firm but soft dough, adding extra flour if needed, until the dough leaves the bowl clean.
6 Turn the dough on to a lightly floured board and knead until smooth and elastic.
7 Cover and put to rise in a warm place until double in bulk.
8 Turn the dough on to a floured board and knead lightly.
9 Divide into two.
10 Flatten each piece and roll up like a Swiss roll, shaped to fit a 1 lb. bread tin.
11 Place each roll of dough in a greased 1 lb. bread tin, cover and leave to rise until the dough rises to the top of the tins.
12 Brush the top of the loaves with milk and sprinkle with oatmeal.
13 Bake on the middle shelf of a hot oven (425 – 450°F.—Gas Mark 6 – 7) for 30 minutes. Lower heat to very moderate (300 – 350°F.—Gas Mark 2 – 3) for a further 30 minutes.
14 Remove from tins and cool on a wire tray.

Alternative shapes:

Shape the two pieces of dough to form large buns, flatten slightly, brush with milk and dredge with flour or oatmeal and cook on a floured baking sheet as above.

Flatten the bun shapes to 1-inch thickness, cut in six, brush with milk and dredge with flour or oatmeal. Bake on a baking sheet dredged with flour or oatmeal as above.

Note:

These shapes may not require quite such a long baking time.

Oatmeal bread 2

Use the basic recipes, see pages 14–15, for bread, but instead of 1 lb. flour, use 13 oz. flour and 3 oz. rolled oats, or 14 oz. flour, 2 oz. oatmeal. This gives a very pleasant nutty flavour to the bread. You may find it takes a little longer to prove, but the actual baking time should not vary a great deal.

If using rolled oats, add dry to the flour.

If using oatmeal, it is better if this is soaked with some of the liquid for about 30 minutes in the same way as recipe on this page.

Potato bread

Follow the directions for the basic bread, see page 14, but instead of 1 lb. flour use 13 oz. flour, 3 oz. of very dry, floury, cooked potato. The best way to achieve this is to bake old potatoes in their jackets and scoop out and sieve the floury potato before adding to the flour.

You may find that you need a little less water than usual with this bread but it is very pleasant for a change.

Quick rolled oat bread

cooking time 55 minutes – 1 hour, 10 minutes

you will need:

3/4 oz. yeast	7 oz. quick cooking rolled oats
1 tablespoon brown sugar	8 oz. plain flour
approximately 1/4 pint tepid water	1/2 teaspoon salt

1 Cream yeast with 1 teaspoon sugar and add 2 tablespoons water.
2 Mix dry ingredients, make a well in centre and pour yeast into it.
3 Leave until bubbles appear in the yeast.
4 Add sufficient warm water to make a light dough.
5 Knead well and leave in a warm place to rise.
6 Knead again.
7 Place in a greased, floured 2 lb. tin.
8 Cover and leave to rise.
9 Bake in a hot oven (425 – 450°F.—Gas Mark 6 – 7) for 10 minutes, then reduce heat to moderate (375°F.—Gas Mark 4) and bake for a further 45 minutes – 1 hour.

Rice breads

Use the basic bread recipes, see pages 14–15, but instead of 1 lb. flour use 14 oz. flour and 2 oz. boiled rice. The round Carolina type rice gives best results.

In plain breads, boil rice in water until just tender. In sweeter, richer breads boil in milk.

The rice makes no difference to the cooking time, but because it is moist when cooked you may need a little less liquid in recipes. It can be added to flour while hot, but care should be taken not to put in yeast liquid until rice has cooled.

Rich Vienna bread

cooking time 35 – 40 minutes

you will need:

2½ lb. white flour
½ oz. salt
4 oz. butter or margarine
1 oz. fresh yeast or ½ oz. dried yeast
1 pint warm milk, plus warm water as required

1. Use methods 1 or 2 for white bread, see pages 14–15, but rub butter or margarine into flour. Special attention should be paid to the shaping of the loaves and the crusts should be brushed with rich milk when the loaves are turned round.
2. To shape
   Divide dough into four pieces. Shape each piece into a ball and roll into a wide triangle. Starting with top of triangle, roll dough to form a roll with pointed ends. Put on flat baking tray, seams downwards.
3. Follow general directions for proving and baking in methods 1 or 2, see pages 14–15, making three deep diagonal cuts with sharp knife across loaf just before baking.

Saffron bread

An interesting flavour is given to the basic bread dough, see page 14, if a little saffron is added.

To each 1 lb. of flour, allow approximately ¼ teaspoon of saffron, which should be dissolved in the tepid liquid before adding to the flour.

Wholemeal bap

cooking time 20 minutes

you will need:

8 oz. stone ground flour
½ teaspoon salt
just over ¼ oz. yeast
½ teaspoon sugar
scant ¼ pint water

1. Follow the method for Nutty wholemeal loaf, see page 18, to the end of stage 8.
2. Knead again. Form into one loaf and put into a warmed and lightly greased 8-inch sandwich tin.
3. Prove for a final time, about 20 minutes, then bake in the centre of a hot oven (425°F.—Gas Mark 6) for 20 minutes.

York Mayne bread

This is one of the oldest traditional breads and it became, in the late 16th century, the subject of a minute passed by the City Corporation to say that a certain amount of this bread must be baked.

cooking time 25 minutes

you will need:

½ oz. yeast
good ½ pint warm milk and water
12 oz. plain flour
6 – 8 oz. sugar
1 teaspoon coriander seeds
1 good teaspoon caraway seeds
3 egg yolks
2 teaspoons rose water (obtainable from chemists)
2 egg whites

1. Blend the yeast with the tepid milk or milk and water.
2. Mix together the flour, sugar, coriander and caraway seeds.
3. Add the egg yolks, rose water and yeast liquid and blend together, adding any extra tepid liquid to give a fairly soft dough.
4. Lastly add the stiffly beaten egg whites.
5. Knead, cover and allow to prove.
6. Knead again and make into the desired shape, either a tin or a round loaf.
7. Cover and prove until double its size, then bake in a moderately hot oven (400°F.—Gas Mark 5). If baking in a loaf tin, it will take approximately 25 minutes. If baking in a round on a flat baking tin, it will take a little less cooking time.

Long bread rolls

cooking time 25 – 30 minutes

you will need:

1 lb. white, brown or wholemeal bread dough,* see pages 14–18

* 1 lb. flour will give good sized loaf

1 Make dough, allow to prove, then form into a long neat shape.
2 Lift on to a warmed greased baking tray and make several cuts on top of the loaf with a sharp knife.
3 Prove again and bake as white bread twists, see below, brushing the loaf with milk or a little egg and milk to give a shiny top.

Note:

These are quick and easy to make and an ideal shape if you are short of loaf tins as they are baked on flat trays.

White bread twists

cooking time 25 – 30 minutes

you will need:

3 lb. plain or bread flour
3 level teaspoons salt
1 oz. yeast
1 level teaspoon sugar
1½ pints tepid water (at least)

1 Sieve flour and salt into a warm basin, then put in a warm place.
2 Cream yeast and sugar in another basin, adding part of liquid.
3 Make a well in the centre of the flour and pour the yeast liquid in, giving a light dusting of flour over the top.
4 Cover with a clean cloth and leave for a good 15 minutes in a warm place until the top is covered with bubbles.
5 Add rest of liquid until you have a soft dough.
6 Knead well until dough is smooth and leaves bowl clean.
7 Put in a warm place for about 1½ hours to rise, then knead again.
8 You can make one twist and use remaining dough for loaves or rolls.
9 If you are using all the dough to make twists, divide into three parts and each will give a good sized loaf. Knead each portion of dough lightly, then divide into three and form these into strips of equal length.
10 Plait loosely and put on to warmed and lightly greased baking tray, allowing room for the twist to spread as well as rise.
11 Allow to prove for approximately 20 minutes in a warm place.
12 Bake the twists of bread in centre of hot oven (450°F.—Gas Mark 7) for about 10 – 15 minutes, then reduce heat to moderate (375°F. —Gas Mark 4) for further 15 minutes.

Rolls, Brioches, Croissants and Baps

In this section you will find small rolls which are very often easier to make to begin with than a large loaf of bread.
You will also find some of the continental rolls, such as brioches and croissants, which are not nearly so difficult to make as one might imagine. It is just a case of following the basic principles of bread making, but using rather richer ingredients.

Assorted rolls

Use white, brown or wholemeal dough, see pages 14–18.
For a very soft milk roll use the 'pan' bread scone dough omitting sugar, see page 28.
For rich rolls use brioche dough, see page 25.
For flaky rolls use croissant dough, see page 25.

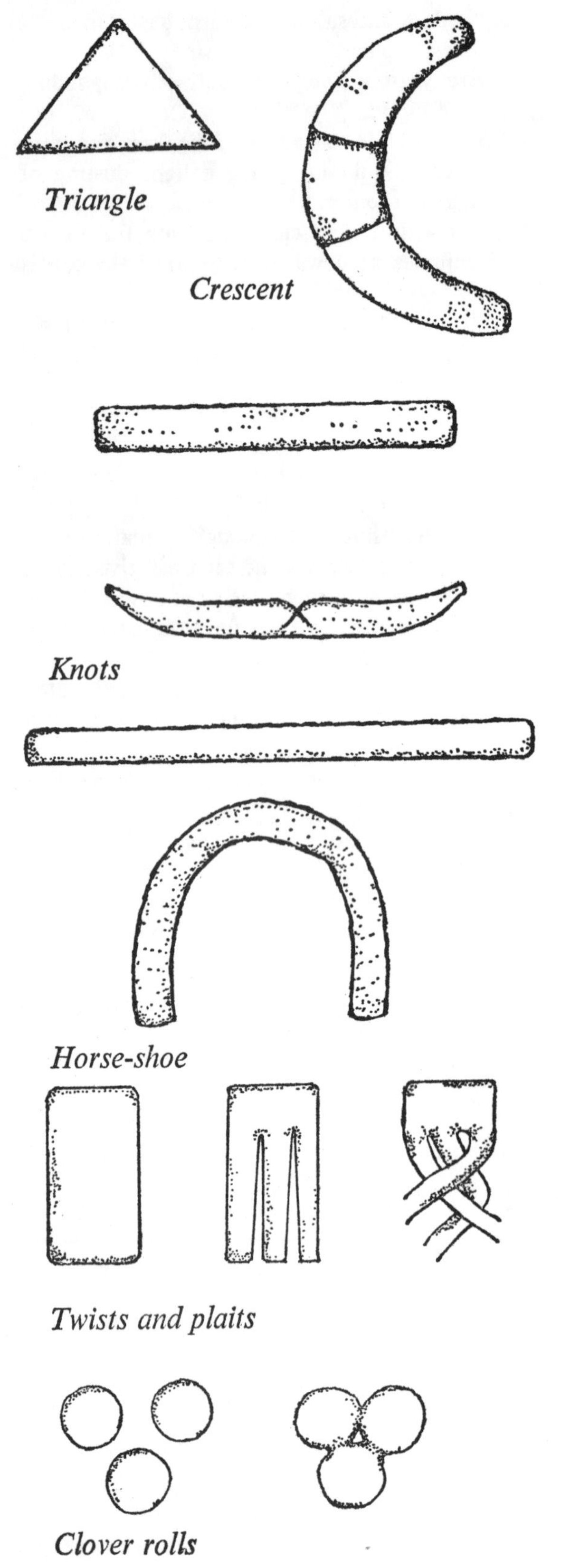
Triangle

Crescent

Knots

Horse-shoe

Twists and plaits

Clover rolls

1 Make and prove dough as given in the recipes, then divide into small pieces—1 lb. flour will give you about fourteen to sixteen rolls.

2 Knead each roll lightly then form into shapes.

3 *Triangles*
Cut into triangles.

4 *Crescents*
Cut into triangles.
Roll from long end towards point, shape round to make a crescent.

5 *Knots*
Form into long roll.
Knot lightly in centre.

6 *Horseshoe*
Form dough into long strip.
Make into horseshoe.

7 *Twists and plaits*
Make dough into long, fairly fat strips.
Cut up to form two or three strips.
Twist or plait.

8 *Clover rolls*
Divide the dough for each roll into three balls.
Put three balls into each deep warmed and greased patty tin.

9 *Batons*
Make dough into neat baton shapes.
Score once or twice on top after proving.

Batons

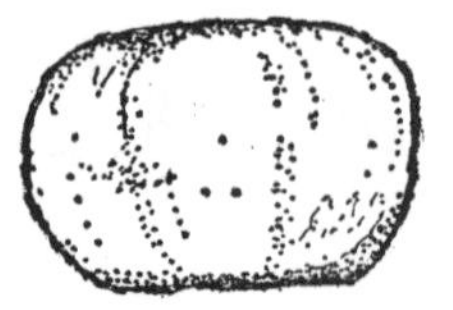

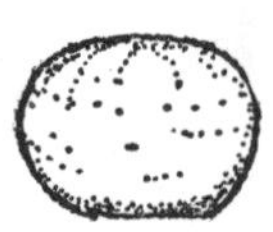

Miniature cottage loaves

10 *Miniature cottage loaves*
Divide dough into two pieces, one being twice as big as the other.
Place the smaller one on top of the other to form miniature cottage loaf.

To top rolls

1 For a crisp top, brush with melted butter before baking.
2 For a glaze, brush with egg and milk or water or milk before baking.
3 For floury rolls, brush with milk and sprinkle with flour.
4 Top with poppy seeds.

To bake rolls

Having shaped the rolls, and if you have time, it looks most attractive to shape a selection of rolls, put on to warmed, greased baking trays.
Allow to prove until nearly double their original size.
Bake for 10 – 15 minutes towards the top of a hot—very hot oven (450 – 475°F.—Gas Mark 7 – 8).
Test to see if cooked in exactly the same way as for a loaf of bread.

Brioches

cooking time 12 minutes

you will need:

½ oz. yeast
1 oz. sugar
just over ⅛ pint tepid milk
12 oz. plain flour
pinch salt
5 oz. margarine
2 eggs

1 Cream yeast with teaspoon sugar.
2 Add tepid milk and enough flour to make thick batter.
3 Put into warm place for 15 minutes.
4 Sieve flour and salt into warm bowl.
5 Rub in margarine and add rest of sugar.
6 Work in yeast mixture and lastly beaten eggs.
7 Put this dough to prove for 2 hours.
8 Knead lightly until smooth. Divide into 8 – 10 pieces.
9 Put the brioches into greased and floured fluted tins, then prove for 10 – 15 minutes.
10 Bake in hot oven (450°F.—Gas Mark 7) for about 12 minutes.

Croissants

cooking time 12 – 15 minutes

you will need:

8 oz. plain flour
pinch salt
good ½ oz. yeast
1 teaspoon sugar
¼ pint tepid milk
3 – 4 oz. butter
little egg for brushing

1 Sieve flour and salt.
2 Cream yeast and sugar, add the tepid milk and strain on to the flour.
3 Mix together well, then prove for an hour. Have a warm, but not too hot, place for this.
4 Turn on to a floured board, knead lightly then roll out to an oblong shape.
5 Put 1 – 1½ oz. butter over the dough in small pieces as though making flaky pastry.
6 Fold, turn and roll out again.
7 Repeat twice using the rest of the butter.
8 Roll out, cut into triangles and twist.
9 Turn into horseshoe shapes and put on to warmed, lightly greased baking trays.
10 Brush with beaten egg and bake after proving for 15 minutes.
11 Allow 12 – 15 minutes in a hot oven (450°F.—Gas Mark 7).

Note:

These may also be made into brioche shapes.

Croissants from bread dough

You may find that you have a little ordinary bread dough left over, see page 14, and you can turn this into croissants.
Method 1 is to use 8 oz. bread dough to 4 – 8 oz. puff pastry. The more puff pastry you use, the larger and flourier they will be.

1 Knead the bread dough with a little extra flour so you can roll it out to an oblong shape.
2 Roll out the puff pastry to an equal size shape and place on top of the bread dough.
3 Fold in three like an envelope.
4 Roll again and repeat two or three times.
5 Then continue as detailed instructions for shaping croissants, see above.

Method 2 is to roll out the 8 oz. bread dough and then continue from stage 5 of croissants, see above.

Crispbreads

cooking time 45 minutes

you will need:

- 4 oz. soft white plain flour
- 2 oz. brown flour
- 1 teaspoon sugar
- 1 teaspoon salt
- 1 level tablespoon dried yeast OR 1 oz. fresh yeast
- ½ pint warm water
- 1 tablespoon olive oil or corn oil

1. Sieve the flours with the sugar and salt.
2. Rub the yeast into the flour.
3. Make a rather thin smooth batter with the water.
4. Stand till frothy, about 10 minutes, in warm place.
5. Stir in oil.
6. Pour the light, frothy batter in a circle on to baking sheets, greased and thickly floured with brown flour. (Thin baking sheets are better than thick heavy ones.)
7. Tilt the baking sheets to run the batter thinly over.
8. Stand aside until the surface looks bubbly.
9. Dredge tops with brown flour.
10. Bake in a very slow oven (250 – 275°F.—Gas Mark ½ – 1) on top shelf.
11. After 15 minutes take the baking sheets out and mark the crispbread in pieces with a pastry wheel or serrated knife. Prick with a fork.
12. Return to middle shelf of oven for about 30 minutes. The crispbreads will be more evenly cooked if the side ones are moved to the middle halfway through cooking time.
13. Turn off the heat and leave to dry off in the oven with the door ajar.

Variations:

Substitute 1 oz. rolled oats for 1 oz. flour.
Add 1 teaspoon caraway seeds.

These are light and crisp and taste very good. Appearance improves with practice.

Wholemeal crispbreads

Use the recipe for crispbreads, but use 6 oz. wholemeal flour. You may find you need just a very little more liquid.

Scottish baps 1

cooking time 15 minutes

you will need:

- ¼ oz. yeast
- 1 level teaspoon sugar
- ⅜ pint tepid milk and water
- 12 oz. plain flour
- ½ teaspoon salt
- 1 – 1½ oz. lard

1. Cream yeast and sugar, blend with liquid.
2. Sieve flour and salt, rub in lard.
3. Make a well in centre of flour mixture and pour in yeast liquid.
4. Leave to prove for 15 minutes.
5. Knead dough until it is a smooth ball, cover and leave for about 1 hour.
6. Knead and form into small ovals and place on warm, greased baking trays allowing for spreading.
7. Brush with milk, dust with flour and leave for 15 minutes.
8. Dust again with flour and press tops firmly.
9. Bake near top of hot oven (450°F.—Gas Mark 7) for 15 minutes.

Scottish baps 2

Baps are served for breakfast in Scotland and should be hot from the oven. The dough may be put to rise overnight in a cool place away from draughts. In this case, use the smaller amount of yeast.

cooking time 15 – 20 minutes

you will need:

- 1 lb. plain flour
- ½ teaspoon salt
- 2 oz. lard or butter
- ½ – 1 oz. yeast
- 1 teaspoon castor sugar
- ⅛ pint tepid milk and water mixed

1. Warm the flour.
2. Sieve it with the salt into a warm bowl.
3. Rub in the fat and make a well in the centre.
4. Cream the yeast in a small basin with the sugar.
5. Add the tepid liquid and pour into the flour.
6. Mix into a soft dough.
7. Stand the dough in a warm place until it has doubled its size (about 1 hour, although it will take longer if the small amount of yeast is used).

8 Knead lightly.
9 Roll out and cut into six to eight square pieces.
10 Dust with flour.
11 Place on a greased and floured baking sheet.
12 Put in warm place for 20 minutes covered with a cloth.
13 Bake in the middle of a hot oven (450°F.—Gas Mark 7) for 15 - 20 minutes.

Variations:

Brown baps
Use ½ wholemeal flour and ½ white flour and a little more liquid.

Wholemeal baps
Use 1 lb. wholemeal flour and little more liquid.

You can use the rather high percentage of yeast, which gives an exceptionally light, highly risen result. You may find, however, for some people that it is a little too 'yeasty' in flavour.

Scotch butteries

cooking time 15 minutes

you will need:

1 oz. yeast
1 level tablespoon castor sugar
just under ¾ pint tepid water
6 oz. lard
6 oz. butter or margarine
1 lb. flour
1 level tablespoon salt

1 Cream yeast with 1 teaspoon sugar, add tepid water and a sprinkling of flour.
2 Put on one side and allow to rise.
3 Meanwhile rub 2 oz. lard, 2 oz. butter into flour, and salt, blend with yeast liquid and roll out to a neat oblong, on floured board.
4 Mix remainder of lard and butter together. Put half of this on to dough in small pieces exactly as if making flaky pastry.
5 Fold, turn and roll out again, doing exactly the same thing with rest of lard and butter.
6 Re-roll thinly and cut neatly into about 3-inch squares to make your butteries. Place on a baking sheet.
7 Allow individual shapes to prove.
8 Bake in hot oven for approximately 15 minutes (425 - 450°F.—Gas Mark 6 - 7).

Note:

Although recipe states ¾ pint tepid water, use only ½ pint to begin with and add a little more, *if needed*, when you mix into flour.

Shamrock rolls

cooking time 10 - 12 minutes

you will need:

1 oz. fresh yeast or ½ oz. dried yeast
5 tablespoons lukewarm water
2 oz. castor sugar
5 oz. mashed potatoes
2 oz. butter or margarine
1½ rounded teaspoons salt
¾ pint hot milk
1 egg, slightly beaten
1½ lb. flour

1 Sprinkle the dried, or crumble the fresh, yeast into the warm water and allow to stand 5 - 10 minutes until frothy, adding 1 teaspoon of the sugar with dried yeast.
2 Mix the potatoes, butter, sugar, salt and hot milk together. Allow to cool.
3 Add the yeast and egg, mixing well, then gradually work in flour.
4 Turn on to a lighly floured board and knead until the dough is elastic.
5 Cover dough and leave to rise in a warm place until dough has doubled its size, about 1 hour.
6 Knock back dough, shape into twenty-four balls and place the balls on to well greased baking trays.
7 For the shamrock 'leaves' use scissors to snip balls almost to the centre in three places, then make a short snip in the middle edge of each 'leaf'.
8 Cover and allow to rise in a warm place for 10 minutes.
9 Brush shamrocks with beaten egg and bake on top shelf in hot oven for 10 - 12 minutes (425°F.—Gas Mark 6)

Variations:

Poppy seed shamrock rolls
Before the rolls go into the oven, sprinkle with poppy seeds.

Nut shamrock rolls
Sprinkle tops with chopped nuts.

Fruit shamrock rolls
Add 2 - 3 oz. dried fruit to dough.

Vienna rolls

cooking time 15 – 20 minutes

you will need:

1 lb. plain flour	½ oz. yeast
1 teaspoon salt	1 teaspoon sugar
2 oz. butter or margarine	¼ pint tepid milk
	1 beaten egg

1. Sieve together the flour and salt.
2. Warm slightly, then rub in the margarine.
3. Make a well in the centre of the mixture, cream yeast and sugar, add milk and beaten egg and pour into well.
4. Form into an elastic dough and beat thoroughly by hand.
5. Leave to rise, covered, in a warm place until the dough has doubled in bulk, then turn on to a floured board.
6. Knead well and divide into twelve pieces.
7. Shape into plaits, round rolls, crescents and miniature loaves, see page 24, and place on to well greased baking trays.
8. Leave to rise again for 15 – 20 minutes.
9. Brush with beaten egg and bake in hot oven (425 – 450°F.—Gas Mark 6 – 7) for 15 to 20 minutes.

Vienna bread

Use recipe for Vienna rolls but form into large loaves, allow to rise for 20 minutes, brush with beaten egg and bake for about 35 – 40 minutes, slightly reducing the heat after first 15 minutes.

Yeast milk 'pan bread' scones

cooking time 15 minutes

you will need:

½ oz. yeast	1 level teaspoon salt
2 oz. sugar	2 oz. butter or margarine
approximately ½ pint warm milk	1 beaten egg
1 lb. plain flour	

1. Cream yeast with a teaspoon of sugar, add a little warm milk and sprinkling of flour.
2. Stand in a warm place until mixture bubbles.
3. Put flour, salt, rest of sugar into bowl and rub in butter or margarine.
4. Make a well in the centre and put in the yeast mixture, beaten egg and sufficient milk to make an elastic dough.
5. Knead thoroughly by hand, cover bowl with a clean cloth, then leave in a warm place to rise. Dough should double in bulk.
6. Turn on to a lightly floured board, knead lightly and roll *lightly* until about ½ – ¾ inch in thickness.
7. The dough should be very soft. Cut into about sixteen squares.
8. Put on to lightly greased and warmed baking trays, allowing room to spread as well as rise.
9. Prove for approximately 15 minutes in warm place.
10. To give a shiny top brush with little egg and milk, or for floury top sieve flour lightly over the scones after brushing with little milk.
11. Bake just above centre of a hot to very hot oven (450 – 475°F.—Gas Mark 7 – 8) for approximately 15 minutes.

Variations:

Fruit 'pan bread' scones

Add about 3 oz. dried fruit.

Cheese 'pan bread' scones

1. Use only 1 teaspoon sugar.
2. Sieve good pinch salt, pepper, celery salt and dry mustard with flour.
3. Add 3 – 4 oz. finely grated cheese to flour mixture after rubbing in butter.

Lemon or orange 'pan bread' scones

1. Add finely grated rind of 1 or 2 oranges to flour.
2. Blend with the fruit juice made up to ½ pint liquid with milk.
3. Brush top of scones lightly with milk, then sprinkle with very little sugar and finely grated fruit rind before baking.

Fruit Breads with Yeast

In almost every country there is a tradition of making fruit breads. Some of these are so rich that they are almost like a cake. This means that the loaves keep extremely well and so may be made in rather larger quantities. You can always have a good fruit bread made well before it is needed.
Because the dough is much richer than an ordinary plain bread dough do not expect it to rise as quickly.

Almond and orange plait

cooking time 30 minutes

you will need:

- 1 oz. yeast
- 3 oz. sugar
- ¼ pint fresh orange juice
- 12 oz. flour, preferably plain
- 2 oz. butter or margarine
- 2 egg yolks
- grated rind of fresh orange
- good pinch salt
- 4 oz. candied orange peel
- few finely chopped almonds

1. Cream yeast with 1 teaspoon sugar.
2. Add orange juice and a sprinkling of flour.
3. Leave in warm place to rise for about 20 minutes, until surface is covered with little bubbles.
4. Cream butter and rest of sugar, add egg yolks and grated orange rind.
5. Work in flour, sieved with pinch salt, and yeast liquid. It should be a soft yet pliable mixture.
6. Add peel.
7. Knead lightly but firmly with hands until a smooth dough.
8. Return to bowl, cover with cloth, leave in warm place for about 1 hour until nearly double its original size.
9. Knead again and form into three long equal-sized strips. Plait these *loosely*—this is important to allow dough to rise.
10. Lift on to warmed and greased baking tray, cover with chopped almonds.
11. Allow to prove for approximately 20 minutes.
12. Bake for approximately 30 minutes in centre of oven. Use hot oven (450°F.—Gas Mark 7) for first 20 minutes, then lower heat slightly for final 10 minutes.

Variation:

Orange rye bread

Use the recipe for almond and orange plait, but instead of 12 oz. ordinary white flour, use 8 oz. rye flour, 4 oz. white flour. This gives a very delicious flavour.

Apricot bread

cooking time 35 - 45 minutes

you will need:

- just ¾ oz. yeast
- 1 tablespoon sugar
- 3 tablespoons apricot syrup
- just under ½ pint tepid milk and water
- 1 lb. plain flour
- 4 oz. dried apricots, weight after cooking, (or canned fruit)
- good pinch salt
- 1 oz. butter

1. Cream yeast with 1 teaspoon sugar.
2. Add apricot syrup, some of the tepid milk and water and sprinkling of flour.
3. Allow to stand in warm place until mixture bubbles; this will take approximately 20 minutes.
4. Chop apricots.
5. Sieve flour and salt together, add sugar and rub in butter.
6. Stir in chopped fruit, the yeast liquid and rest of tepid milk, adding this gradually. The mixture must not be too soft; it must be firm enough to handle.
7. Knead well and put into a warmed greased 2 lb. loaf tin, allowing mixture to come halfway up tin.
8. Bake in centre of a really hot oven (475°F.—Gas Mark 8) for 15 minutes, then lower heat to moderate (375°F.—Gas Mark 4) for further 20 - 30 minutes.

Note:

To give 4 oz. cooked dried apricots only about 1½ oz. need be soaked and cooked until just tender. DO NOT OVERCOOK. If using canned apricots choose very firm ones, or you can use raw apricots and little extra sugar and water to take place of syrup.

Apricot twist

cooking time 45 minutes

1 Follow the recipe for bara brith, see page 31, but instead of raisins use 4 oz. chopped dried, uncooked apricots and 4 oz. sultanas.
2 Make the dough firm enough to knead, divide into two equal-sized pieces and twist lightly after proving.
3 Put on to a warmed baking tin and allow to prove once again for about 15 minutes.
4 Bake for approximately 45 minutes at the temperature given for bara brith.

Apricot and walnut bread

cooking time 40 – 45 minutes

you will need:

3 oz. dried apricots
½ pint cold water
just ¾ oz. yeast
3 teaspoons sugar
3 oz. shelled walnuts
1 lb. plain flour
1 teaspoon salt
1 oz. margarine
1 egg
2 tablespoons milk

To glaze:
3 – 4 oz. sugar
4 – 6 tablespoons water

1 Soak apricots for several hours in the cold water. Strain very well and keep the liquid.
2 Cream yeast and 1 teaspoon of sugar, and add just under ½ pint of the apricot liquid, *warmed.*
3 Chop apricots and walnuts.
4 Sieve flour, salt and remaining sugar into bowl, rub in margarine, stir in apricots and walnuts, yeast and apricot liquid, add egg and milk mixture. Knead well, adding little extra warm liquid if needed.
5 Grease a 2 lb. loaf tin, half fill with the dough and leave to rise until double bulk, brush over with melted margarine.
6 Bake in hot oven (425 – 450°F.—Gas Mark 6 – 7) for 30 minutes, then lower heat to moderate (375°F.—Gas Mark 4) for further 10 – 15 minutes. This bread needs to be baked *just below the middle shelf* of the oven.
7 To glaze, melt sugar in water, boil 2 – 3 minutes, brush over finished loaf.

Note:

If apricots are very soft and moist they need not be soaked, in which case use milk and water instead of apricot liquid.

Variations:

Prune and walnut bread
Use 3 – 4 oz. dried prunes instead of the apricots, soaking and using in exactly the same way.

Fig and walnut bread
Use 3 oz. dried figs instead of the apricots, soaking and using in exactly the same way.

Peach and walnut bread
Use 4 oz. dried peaches but as peaches have very little flavour add the finely grated rind of 1 lemon to give more taste to the bread.

Bannock

A type of fruit bread or cake

cooking time 1 – 1¼ hours

you will need:

½ oz. yeast
8 oz. sugar
just under 1 pint water
2 lb. plain flour
good pinch salt
4 oz. butter or margarine
4 oz. lard
12 oz. sultanas
4 oz. candied peel

1 Cream the yeast with a teaspoon sugar.
2 Add about ½ pint TEPID water and a sprinkling of flour.
3 Put into a warm place for 15 minutes until the surface is covered with bubbles.
4 Add this yeast mixture to the rest of the sieved flour and salt and work in enough of the rest of the tepid liquid to give a pliable dough.
5 Knead well, then allow to prove or rise in a warm place. This will take at least an hour, and cover the bowl with a cloth so the dough does not dry.
6 Knead again, then add the butter and lard, which should be warmed slightly, but not oiled, the sugar and the rest of the ingredients.
7 Put into a well greased 3 – 4 lb. loaf tin, allow to prove once again in a warm place for about 30 minutes, until well risen in the loaf tin.
8 Bake for 1 hour—1 hour, 15 minutes in the centre of a moderate oven (375°F.—Gas Mark 4), reducing the heat after about 50 minutes if the loaf is becoming too brown.
9 Test to see if cooked by tapping on the bottom, and the loaf should sound hollow.

Note:

In the old days one could buy the bread dough from the baker, and you would then buy 2 lb. bread dough instead of making your own, and proceed as from stage 5.

Bara brith I

cooking time 1½ - 2 hours

you will need:

12 oz. lard or butter
3 lb. flour
1 teaspoon salt
12 oz. sugar or syrup
½ teaspoon mixed spice
1 lb. stoned raisins
1 lb. currants
4 oz. candied peel
2 eggs
1 pint milk
1 oz. yeast

1 Rub the fat into the flour.
2 Add salt, sugar, spice and dried fruit and mix well together.
3 Form a well in the centre of the mixture, add eggs and the warmed milk and 1 oz. yeast.
4 Mix well into a soft dough consistency.
5 Place in a warm place, after covering, until it rises to double its original size. Turn the dough on to a floured board.
6 Place in a 9½ - 10½-inch greased tin and bake in centre of a moderately hot oven (400°F.—Gas Mark 5) for 1½ or 2 hours, depending on the size of the cake, reducing heat to very moderate (300 - 350°F.—Gas Mark 2 - 3) after first 30 minutes.

Note:

In order to preserve the characteristic flavour of the bara brith on no account must the stoned raisins be omitted or substituted. The bara brith when cold is cut and buttered in exactly the same way as bread and is delicious.

Bara brith 2

cooking time 1 - 1¼ hours

you will need:

½ oz. yeast
4 oz. sugar
⅜ pint tepid milk
1 small egg
1 lb. plain flour
¾ teaspoon salt
4 oz. lard
2 oz. candied peel
4 oz. currants
pinch mixed spice
6 oz. raisins

1 Cream yeast with a teaspoon of sugar, add ¼ pint tepid milk and egg.
2 Sieve flour and salt, rub in lard, add sugar, peel, currants, spice and raisins.
3 Make a well in centre of mixture, pour in yeast liquid, sprinkling a light dusting of flour on top.
4 Leave in a warm place for about 20 minutes.
5 Mix yeast with the flour, adding extra milk until you have a soft dough.
6 Put back in a warm place to prove for at least an hour.
7 Turn on to a floured board and mix lightly with a warm knife.
8 Put into a well greased and floured 8-inch cake or 2 lb. loaf tin and bake for 1 - 1¼ hours in the middle of a moderately hot oven (400°F.—Gas Mark 5).
9 Reduce heat to very moderate (350°F.—Gas Mark 3) after 30 minutes.

Barm Brack

Fruit loaf or speckled bread

cooking time 2 - 2½ hours

you will need:

1 oz. barm or yeast
8 oz. brown sugar
3 lb. flour
1½ pints warm milk
4 oz. butter
4 oz. lard
good pinch salt
1 lb. currants
8 oz. stoned raisins
4 oz. candied peel
3 eggs

1 Cream yeast with a teaspoon sugar and a sprinkling of flour and milk or make a light soft dough of the flour, salt, barm and milk.
2 Cover and set to rise in a warm place for 45 minutes.
3 Then melt fats and when slightly cooked pour into the dough.
4 Add the rest of flour, salt, sugar, fruit and beaten eggs and mix thoroughly with the hands or a wooden spoon.
5 Cover and allow to rise in a warm place until the size is doubled, about 1 - 1½ hours.
6 Fill three large greased 2 lb. bread tins three-quarters full, put them to stand in a warm place for 20 minutes.
7 Bake in centre of a hot oven (425 - 450°F.—Gas Mark 6 - 7) for 30 minutes, then decrease the heat to very moderate (300 - 350°F.—Gas Mark 2 - 3) and bake slowly for 1½ - 2 hours more.
8 This should not be eaten fresh, and will keep 2 or 3 weeks.

Cherry Twist

cooking time 35 – 40 minutes

you will need:

12 oz. plain flour
pinch salt
2 teaspoons yeast
1 teaspoon sugar
2 oz. margarine
warm milk or water

For icing:
6 oz. sieved icing sugar
3 – 4 dessertspoons warm water
2 – 3 glacé cherries

1 Sieve the flour and salt into a warmed mixing bowl.
2 Cream the yeast and sugar together in a small basin.
3 Rub the margarine into the flour then add the creamed yeast.
4 Pour in sufficient warm milk or water to form a soft dough.
5 Beat with the hand until smooth.
6 Stand in a warm place to prove for about 1 hour.
7 Knead lightly and cut into three equal-sized pieces.
8 Roll this into long strips, then plait loosely to allow room to rise.
9 Put on to warmed greased baking tin. Prove for 20 minutes, then bake in the centre of a hot oven (450°F.—Gas Mark 7) for approximately 20 – 25 minutes, then lower the heat to moderate (375°F.—Gas Mark 4) for a further 15 minutes, until the bread sounds hollow.
10 When cool, cover with very thin glacé icing, and glacé cherries.

Coconut twist

cooking time 40 – 45 minutes

you will need:

½ oz. yeast
1 oz. sugar
½ pint milk and water
1 lb. flour
2 level teaspoons salt
3 oz. desiccated coconut, 1 oz. sugar OR 4 oz. sweetened coconut

1 Cream yeast with sugar and add tepid milk and water.
2 Mix flour, salt, coconut and sugar in a bowl.
3 Add yeast liquid and mix to a firm dough, adding more flour if necessary.
4 Turn on to a lightly floured board and knead until the dough feels smooth and elastic.
5 Cover the dough and put to rise to double size.
6 When risen, turn the dough on to a board lightly dusted with flour and coconut and knead.
7 Divide the dough into three even pieces.
8 Roll the pieces out into long strips and plait together.
9 Form into a circle on a greased and floured baking sheet.
10 Cover and allow to rise to double size. To keep a good shape this recipe is best risen slowly in a cold place, see page 9.
11 Bake on the middle shelf of a hot oven (425 – 450°F.—Gas Mark 6 – 7) for 40 – 45 minutes until golden brown, lowering heat if liked.
12 While still warm glaze with a wet brush dipped in honey or golden syrup. Cool on a wire tray. This is delicious served with butter and lemon curd.

Variations:

Coconut cherry twist

Add 2 – 3 oz. chopped glacé cherries.

Iced coconut twist

Make the coconut twist and allow to cool. Cover with a thin layer of lemon glacé icing made by blending 4 tablespoons icing sugar with 1 dessertspoon lemon juice. Spread this over the twist. Then decorate either with toasted coconut or chopped almonds.

Sweet coconut rolls

Follow the recipe for coconut twist to stage 6. Divide the dough into about twelve small pieces and form into balls. Roll each ball in coconut, then put on to a greased and floured baking sheet. Cover and allow to prove. Bake for approximately 15 minutes in a hot oven (425 – 450°F.—Gas Mark 6 – 7).

Coconut loaf

Follow the recipe for coconut twist to stage 6. Then form into a loaf shape and put into either a 2 lb. loaf tin or two 1 lb. loaf tins. Allow to prove as before. The 1 lb. loaves will take approximately 35 minutes to cook, the 2 lb. loaf about 45 minutes. These can be covered with coconut before baking or coated with lemon glacé icing after baking, see above.

Currant bread

cooking time 45 minutes

you will need:

- 1 lb. plain flour
- ½ teaspoon salt
- 4 oz. butter or margarine
- 4 oz. castor sugar
- ¾ oz. yeast
- 1 egg
- ½ pint tepid milk and water mixed
- 6 oz. currants

1. Sieve the flour and salt into a bowl and put in a warm place.
2. Rub in fat.
3. Stir in sugar, except 1 teaspoonful.
4. Cream yeast with 1 teaspoon sugar.
5. Beat egg and add it, also warmed milk and water.
6. Make a well in the flour.
7. Add liquids, work into a dough using a wooden spoon.
8. Beat well.
9. Cover with cloth and stand in warm place for 1¼ hours.
10. Beat in fruit with the hand.
11. Divide into two.
12. Place in two warmed greased 1 lb. loaf tins.
13. Cover with a cloth, put in warm place for approximately 25 minutes.
14. Bake in centre of moderately hot oven (400°F.—Gas Mark 5) for 45 minutes, reducing heat slightly after 30 minutes.

Sweet potato bread

Follow the recipe for currant bread, but instead of 1 lb. flour use 12 oz. flour, 4 oz. floury cooked potato.
The best way to cook the potato is in its jacket, then sieve it and add to the flour. Continue as for currant bread.

Dutch Easter bread

cooking time 55 minutes

you will need:

- ½ oz. yeast
- 1 teaspoon sugar
- ½ pint milk
- 12 oz. plain flour
- 1 level teaspoon mixed spice
- 6 oz. currants and sultanas
- 1 oz. chopped candied peel
- 1 oz. melted butter

For almond paste:

- 3 oz. ground almonds
- 3 oz. castor sugar
- 1 egg yolk
- 1 teaspoon lemon juice

1. Cream yeast and sugar together and add the tepid milk. Mix into warmed sieved flour and spice from a well in the centre.
2. Knead together, put into a bowl and cover with a damp cloth, put to rise in a warm place for approximately 30 minutes.
3. Knock back the dough, work in dried fruit and peel and melted butter. Shape into an oblong 10 inches × 5 inches and lay a sausage shape of almond paste, 9½ inches long, on top of the dough. Press the dough round the almond paste, tucking the join underneath the loaf.
4. Place on a baking sheet and prove until double its bulk.
5. Glaze with milk and bake in a hot oven (425 – 450°F.—Gas Mark 6 – 7) for 10 minutes, and then bake for a further 45 minutes at 350°F.—Gas Mark 3, or until evenly brown and a hollow sound is obtained when the loaf is tapped on the underside.
6. Allow to cool. Slice and serve with plenty of butter.

Fig and treacle bread

cooking time 40 – 45 minutes

you will need:

- good ½ oz. yeast
- approximately ½ pint tepid water
- 1 lb. white or wholemeal flour OR use 8 oz. wholemeal and 8 oz. white flour
- 1 level teaspoon salt
- 2 oz. sugar, preferably brown
- 4 – 6 oz. chopped figs
- 2 tablespoons black treacle
- 1 oz. melted margarine OR 1 tablespoon oil

1. Blend the yeast with half the tepid water.
2. Mix together the flour, salt, sugar and chopped figs, then add the black treacle and melted margarine or oil.
3. Put in the yeast liquid and mix lightly together, adding enough of the extra tepid water to give a really soft scone-like dough.
4. Knead together thoroughly.
5. Cover and put the dough to prove until double its size.
6. Knead again and form into either a tin loaf shape, putting into a 1½ – 2 lb. loaf tin, or put in a 7-inch square cake tin.
7. Cover and prove again, then bake in the centre of a moderately hot oven (400°F.—Gas Mark 5) for 40 – 45 minutes.

Ginger loaf

cooking time 35 – 40 minutes

you will need:

good ½ oz. yeast
approximately ½ pint tepid water
1 lb. white or wholemeal flour OR use 8 oz. wholemeal flour and 8 oz. white flour
1 level teaspoon salt
1 level teaspoon sugar
1½ – 2 teaspoons ground ginger
2 tablespoons black treacle
1 oz. melted margarine OR 1 tablespoon oil
2 oz. sultanas, optional

1 Blend the yeast with half the tepid water.
2 Mix together the flour, salt, sugar and ground ginger, then add the black treacle, melted margarine or oil and sultanas, if used.
3 Put in the yeast liquid and mix lightly together, adding enough of the extra tepid water to give a really soft scone-like dough.
4 Knead together thoroughly.
5 Cover and put the dough to prove until double its size.
6 Knead again and form into either a tin loaf shape, putting into a 1½ – 2 lb. loaf tin, or put in a 6 – 7-inch square cake tin.
7 Cover and prove again, then bake in the centre of a moderately hot oven (400°F.—Gas Mark 5) for 35 – 40 minutes.

Variations:

Crumble ginger loaf

Sprinkle before baking with a crumble of 1 oz. margarine, 1 oz. sugar, 1½ oz. plain flour rubbed together until it looks like coarse breadcrumbs.

Cornflake ginger loaf

Sprinkle crushed cornflakes on top of the dough before baking.

Honey ginger loaf

After baking, brush the hot loaf with a wet brush dipped in honey.

Syrup ginger loaf

After baking, brush the hot loaf with a wet brush dipped in syrup.

Malt yeast bread

cooking time 55 minutes – 1 hour

you will need:

good ½ oz. yeast
3 teaspoons sugar
approximately ½ pint tepid milk and water
2 tablespoons malt
1½ lb. plain or bread flour
1 teaspoon salt
3 – 5 oz. dried fruit, optional

1 Cream the yeast and 1 teaspoon sugar in a warm basin.
2 Add half the tepid liquid, the malt and a good sprinkling of flour.
3 Leave in a warm place for 20 – 25 minutes until the top is covered with bubbles.
4 Sieve the flour and salt together.
5 Add rest of the sugar and the dried fruit.
6 Stir in the yeast mixture and enough liquid to give a soft pliable dough. Knead well and put to prove until double its size.
7 Knead again, form into one large or two small loaf shapes and put into a 2 lb. loaf tin or two 1 lb. loaf tins. Cover and prove again.
8 Bake one large loaf for approximately 55 minutes or two smaller loaves for approximately 35 – 40 minutes. Allow 10 minutes in a very hot oven (475 – 500°F.—Gas Mark 8 – 9), then lower the heat to moderate (375°F.—Gas Mark 4). Bake the loaves in the centre of the oven.

Orange bread

cooking time 45 minutes

you will need:

½ oz. yeast
1 level teaspoon sugar
2 tablespoons tepid water
2 oz. lard
1 teaspoon salt
1 heaped tablespoon golden syrup
1 oz. brown sugar
3 oz. quick cooking rolled oats
1 orange
just under ¼ pint boiling water
cold water
8 oz. plain flour
crystallized orange slices

1 Cream yeast and sugar.
2 Bind with tepid water in a bowl.
3 Set in warm place until bubbly.
4 Combine lard, salt, syrup, brown sugar, oats and grated orange rind in a large bowl.
5 Mix the boiling water and orange juice. Make up to ¼ pint with cold water if necessary.
6 Add yeast mixture and blend.
7 Add flour gradually and mix to a soft dough.

8 Knead dough on a floured board until smooth.
9 Place in greased bowl and brush with melted fat.
10 Cover and let rise in warm place until double its bulk, about 1 hour.
11 Shape dough into a loaf.
12 Place in a greased loaf tin 8½ × 4½ × 2½ inches.
13 Let rise until double its bulk.
14 Sprinkle on a few oats and bake in a hot oven (425 - 450°F.—Gas Mark 7) for 15 minutes.
15 Reduce temperature to moderate (375°F.—Gas Mark 4) and bake 30 minutes longer or until cooked.
16 Remove from tin and cool; decorate with orange slices.

Variation:

Lemon bread

Use 1 large lemon or 2 small lemons in place of the orange.

Orange honey bread

cooking time 1 - 1¼ hours

you will need:

½ oz. yeast
2 oz. sugar
2 tablespoons tepid water or milk
2 oz. margarine
2 tablespoons honey
1 egg
4 oz. quick cooking rolled oats
7 oz. flour
1 tablespoon grated orange peel
3 oz. raisins, optional
½ teaspoon salt
3 tablespoons yoghourt OR top of milk and squeeze lemon juice
2 tablespoons orange juice

1 Cream yeast with 1 teaspoon sugar, add tepid liquid and leave to stand for a few minutes.
2 Cream margarine and honey.
3 Add egg and beat until fluffy.
4 Add other ingredients and stir in yeast.
5 Beat well and leave in a warm place to rise.
6 Knead well.
7 Place in a greased and floured loaf tin, 12 × 4 × 3 inches.
8 Cover and leave to rise in a warm place.
9 Bake in a moderate oven (375°F.—Gas Mark 4) for 1 - 1¼ hours.

Variations:

Lemon honey bread

Use 2 tablespoons lemon juice and ½ tablespoon grated lemon rind, in place of 2 tablespoons orange juice and 1 tablespoon orange rind.

Cinnamon honey bread

Use water instead of fruit juice and add 1 teaspoon cinnamon.

Plain orange bread

cooking time 35 - 40 minutes

you will need:

1 lb. flour
1 teaspoon salt
grated rind 2 oranges
¾ oz. yeast
2 oz. sugar
juice of 2 oranges
water
2 oz. margarine or butter

1 Sieve the flour and salt, mix with the orange rind and put into a warm place.
2 Cream the yeast with a teaspoon of the sugar, add the warmed orange juice together with enough water to make ⅜ pint.
3 Sprinkle the top with a little flour and leave in a warm place until the sponge breaks through.
4 Rub the margarine or butter into the warmed flour, add the rest of the sugar, with the yeast liquid and knead together well.
5 Allow to prove until double its size, knead again and make into two loaves, putting into 1½ lb. loaf tins.
6 Prove until double its size and bake in a hot oven (425 - 450°F.—Gas Mark 6 - 7) for approximately 15 minutes, then lower the heat to moderate (375°F.—Gas Mark 4) for a further 20 - 25 minutes.
7 If wished this can be glazed on top before baking, or brushed with a little sugar and water and finely grated orange rind after baking.

Variations:

Lemon bread

Use the finely grated rind and juice of 2 lemons. Increase the sugar slightly if wished.

Orange and walnut bread

Add 2 - 3 oz. chopped walnuts to the flour.

Orange treacle bread

Follow directions for plain orange bread but add 2 tablespoons of treacle to the flour at stage 4. This means you may not need quite as much water.

Orange fruit bread

Follow the directions for plain orange bread, see page 35, but add approximately 6 oz. mixed fruit or sultanas to the flour at stage 4.

Poppy-seed roll

cooking time 45 – 55 minutes

you will need:

1 oz. poppy-seeds
1¼ oz. quick cooking rolled oats, toasted
½ teaspoon cinnamon
2 oz. sultanas or raisins
grated rind 1 orange
8 oz. flour
¼ teaspoon salt
3 oz. sugar
2 oz. margarine
½ oz. yeast
approximately 6 tablespoons warm milk
1 egg

1 Prepare the poppy-seed filling by putting the poppy-seeds into a basin and covering with boiling water.
2 Cool, and strain. Repeat twice more.
3 Mix with the toasted rolled oats, cinnamon, sultanas or raisins and grated orange peel.
4 Prepare the dough by mixing the flour, salt and most of the sugar together.
5 Rub in the margarine.
6 Cream the yeast with 1 teaspoon of sugar and add 1 tablespoon milk.
7 Pour this into a well in the centre of the flour.
8 Leave until bubbles appear in the yeast.
9 Add beaten egg and remaining milk to make a soft dough.
10 Knead well and leave in a warm place to rise.
11 Knead again and roll out to an oblong about 12 × 16 inches.
12 Spread with the poppy-seed filling and roll up.
13 Put into a greased and floured roasting tin, bending into a horseshoe shape.
14 Brush over with milk.
15 Cover and leave to rise.
16 Bake in a hot oven (425 – 450°F.—Gas Mark 6 – 7) for 15 minutes then reduce the heat to 350°F.—Gas Mark 3 and cook for a further 30 – 40 minutes.
17 Dust with icing sugar if liked.

Rich fruit bread

cooking time 40 – 50 minutes

you will need:

4 oz. margarine
2 lb. plain flour
pinch salt
5 oz. sultanas
5 oz. currants
3 oz. candied peel
3 oz. sugar
good 1 oz. yeast
2 eggs
¾ pint warm milk or milk and water

1 Rub margarine into flour and salt.
2 Add fruit and all but 1 teaspoon of sugar.
3 Mix yeast with a teaspoon of sugar until liquid and add to beaten eggs and warm milk.
4 Set aside for little while, then add to the rest of the ingredients, mixing to a dough.
5 Turn out on to a floured board and knead.
6 Put to rise until twice its size.
7 Put into two 2 lb. bread tins and allow to prove for approximately 20 minutes.
8 Bake in centre of hot oven (450°F.—Gas Mark 7) reducing the heat after the first 10 minutes to moderately hot (400°F.—Gas Mark 5) for approximately 40 – 50 minutes.
9 Brush with glaze made of 2 tablespoons sugar and 2 tablespoons water on removing from oven.

Spiced fruit loaf

cooking time 40 minutes

you will need:

1 oz. yeast
3 oz. sugar
approximately ¼ pint milk or milk and water
12 oz. flour, preferably plain
2 oz. butter or margarine
2 egg yolks
good pinch salt
4 oz. candied peel

For filling:
2 oz. margarine or butter
2 tablespoons brown sugar
1 teaspoon spice

1 Cream the yeast with 1 teaspoon sugar, add the tepid milk and water, and a sprinkling of flour.
2 Allow to rise in a warm place for about 20 minutes when the surface will be covered with little bubbles.
3 Cream the butter and the rest of the sugar and the egg yolks.
4 Work in the flour, sieved with the pinch of salt, and the yeast liquid. You should have a soft yet pliable mixture.
5 Add the peel.

6 Knead lightly but firmly with your hands until a smooth dough.
7 Return to the bowl, cover with a cloth and leave in a warm place for about 1 hour until nearly double its original size.
8 Roll out to a good sized oblong shape.
9 Spread with the warmed margarine or butter, the sugar and spice and then roll up into the shape of the 2 lb. loaf tin in which it is to be baked. Prove again for 25 – 30 minutes.
10 Bake for approximately 40 minutes, the first 20 minutes in a hot oven (450°F.—Gas Mark 7) lowering the heat for the remaining 20 minutes to moderate (375°F.—Gas Mark 4).

Plum bread

cooking time 2 hours

you will need:

1½ lb. flour (with plain flour use 5 level teaspoons baking powder)
pinch salt
½ teaspoon nutmeg
8 oz. butter or margarine
12 oz. currants
6 oz. sultanas
6 oz. raisins
4 oz. glacé cherries
4 oz. mixed peel
12 oz. sugar
2 oz. yeast
1 pint warm milk

1 Grease two 2 lb. loaf tins.
2 Sieve flour, salt and nutmeg into a bowl.
3 Rub in the fat.
4 Add fruit and all but 1 teaspoon of the sugar.
5 Cream yeast with the teaspoon of sugar until liquid.
6 Make a well in centre of dry ingredients.
7 Add yeast and warmed milk gradually.
8 Stir well until liquid is absorbed, cover, allow dough to prove, then knead well.
9 Divide evenly between two 2 lb. tins, allow to prove in warm place.
10 Bake in centre of a slow oven (300°F.—Gas Mark 2) for 2 hours, covering after first hour with greaseproof paper.

Note:

Halve the quantity if only 1 loaf is required and cook for same time.

Sweet saffron bread

Follow the directions for the spiced fruit loaf or the plum bread but allow ¼ – ½ teaspoon of saffron to each 1 lb. flour. This should be blended with the tepid liquid.

Sultana, peel and walnut loaf

cooking time 55 minutes

you will need:

4 oz. margarine
2 lb. flour
pinch salt
5 oz. sultanas
5 oz. walnuts, chopped
3 oz. candied peel
3 oz. sugar
1 oz. yeast, good weight
2 eggs
¾ pint milk

1 Rub fat into the flour and salt.
2 Add fruit, nuts and all but a teaspoon of sugar.
3 Cream yeast with 1 teaspoon sugar until liquid, and add to beaten eggs and warm milk.
4 Sprinkle lightly with flour. Put in warm place for approximately 20 minutes, then add to rest of the ingredients, mixing to a dough. Turn out on to a floured board and knead.
5 Put to prove until twice its size, this takes approximately 1½ – 2 hours.
6 Knead well again, then put into two 1½ lb. warmed and greased loaf tins and allow to prove again.
7 Bake in centre of a hot oven (425 – 450°F.—Gas Mark 6 – 7) for 15 minutes.
8 Reduce heat to moderate (375°F.—Gas Mark 4) and bake for further 40 minutes.

Swedish Christmas bread

cooking time 1 hour

you will need:

5 oz. orange peel
approximately ½ pint tepid water
1 oz. yeast
3 teaspoons sugar
2 tablespoons malt
1 tablespoon treacle or molasses
1 lb. white flour
8 oz. rye or wholemeal flour
1 teaspoon salt
3 – 5 oz. dried fruit, optional

1 Put the orange peel into a saucepan with the tepid water and simmer gently until the peel is tender, about 15 minutes.
2 Chop or mince finely and save the orange liquid for the rest of the recipe.
3 Cream the yeast and 1 teaspoon of sugar.
4 Add half the warmed orange liquid, malt, treacle or molasses, and a sprinkling of flour.
5 Leave in a warm place until the surface is covered with bubbles.
6 Sieve the flours and salt together, add the rest of the sugar and the minced or chopped orange peel and dried fruit.

7 Stir in the yeast liquid and enough extra orange liquid to give a soft pliable dough.
8 Knead well, then cover, see page 9, and prove in a warm place until double its bulk.
9 Knead again, and divide into two.
10 Place in two warmed greased 1 lb. loaf tins, cover and prove till risen to top of tins.
11 Bake in the centre of a moderately hot oven (400°F.—Gas Mark 5) for 45 minutes, reducing heat slightly after 30 minutes.

Walnut and treacle bread

cooking time 50 minutes – 1 hour

you will need:

- 1 oz. yeast, good measure
- 2 teaspoons sugar
- approximately 1½ pints tepid water
- 3 lb. plain flour
- 3 level teaspoons salt
- 2 tablespoons black treacle
- 6 oz. chopped walnuts

1 Cream the yeast with the sugar, add about ½ pint tepid water and a sprinkling of flour.
2 Make a well in the centre of the flour, sieved with the salt, and put the yeast liquid into this, adding a further sprinkling of flour on top.
3 Leave in a warm place for about 20 minutes until covered with bubbles.
4 Work the yeast mixture into the flour, then add the slightly warmed treacle, and enough tepid water to make a sticky dough.
5 Knead lightly with the tips of the fingers until it makes a neat ball and leaves the bowl clean. Cover with a warm cloth or polythene and leave in a warm place for approximately 1 – 1½ hours, until double the original size.
6 Turn out on to a floured board and sprinkle with the chopped walnuts, and knead until very smooth; you can tell if sufficiently kneaded if no impression is left by your finger.
7 Divide into two pieces and put into two 2 lb. loaf tins, half filling the tins.
8 Put into a warm place for the loaves to rise, for approximately 25 minutes, then bake in the centre of a hot oven (425 – 450°F.—Gas Mark 6 – 7).
9 Leave at this temperature for approximately 30 minutes then lower the heat and cook for a further 20 minutes, depending on the size of the loaf. You may need a little longer for large loaves.
10 To test if cooked take from the tins and knock firmly on the bottom, if hollow sounding then the loaf is cooked.

Variations:

Walnut and honey bread

Follow the directions for walnut and treacle bread but instead of black treacle use 4 – 6 tablespoons honey, which should be warmed and added at stage 4 in place of the treacle.

Cinnamon honey bread

Omit the walnuts and use ½ – 1 level tablespoon cinnamon which should be mixed with the flour. Use honey instead of treacle.

Honey and orange bread

Walnuts can be added to this or omitted as wished. Add the grated rind of 3 oranges to the flour and 4 – 6 oz. chopped crystallized orange peel. Use honey instead of treacle.

Wiener striezel

Viennese fruit bread

cooking time 20 – 25 minutes

you will need:

- ½ oz. yeast
- 1½ oz. sugar
- 4 tablespoons lukewarm milk
- 10 oz. plain flour
- 2 eggs
- 1½ oz. cooking fat or butter, melted
- 1½ oz. sultanas
- grated rind ½ lemon
- ½ oz. finely chopped almonds

1 Cream the yeast and sugar together and mix in the warm milk.
2 Sieve flour into a warm bowl, then pour in yeast mixture, mixing with a wooden spoon.

3 Add the beaten eggs and cooking fat or butter, and knead well.
4 Leave covered with a damp cloth in warm place to rise until double in bulk, about 1 hour.
5 Knead well on a floured board and add sultanas and lemon peel.
6 Divide the dough in half. Roll out one portion to an oval shape about 8 inches long and 4 inches across the widest point.
7 Roll out the second portion and cut into three even lengths and form into a plait. Place down the centre of the flat dough, securing ends well.
8 Place on baking sheet brushed with melted cooking fat.
9 Brush with egg or milk and sprinkle with chopped almonds.
10 Leave in warm place to prove for 15 minutes.
11 Bake in moderately hot oven (400°F.—Gas Mark 5) in the middle of the oven, for 20 – 25 minutes.
12 Allow to cool on baking sheet, then finish cooling on a cake rack.

Tyrolean loaf

cooking time 1 – 1¼ hours

you will need:

4 oz. figs
8 oz. prunes
4 oz. dried apricots
¼ teaspoon mixed spice
¼ teaspoon ground cloves
¼ teaspoon cinnamon
2 oz. chopped mixed peel
grated orange and lemon peel
¾ oz. yeast
2 oz. sugar
2 tablespoons tepid liquid
1¼ oz. quick cooking rolled oats
5 oz. flour
1 egg

1 Wash, soak, stone and chop all the fruit.
2 Add spices and peel.
3 Cream yeast with 1 teaspoon sugar, add tepid liquid and leave to stand a few minutes.
4 Mix sugar, rolled oats, flour and yeast mixture.
5 Add egg and fruit and mix well.
6 Transfer the mixture to a greased loaf tin.
7 Allow to rise in a warm place for 2 – 3 hours.
8 Bake in the centre of a hot oven (425 – 450°F.—Gas Mark 6 – 7) for 15 minutes, then reduce heat to moderate (375°F.—Gas Mark 4) for a further 45 minutes – 1 hour.

Savoury Breads with Yeast

Cheddar cheese is very satisfactory to use for most breads but for a sharper flavour you can use a mixture of Cheddar and Lancashire, or a mixture of Cheddar and Parmesan. All Lancashire cheese can be used.
Other cheeses that are satisfactory in bread making are Cheshire or some of the processed cheeses.
It is not possible to use all Parmesan in bread making since it produces a very dry texture.

Yeast extract savoury bread

You can turn any basic bread into a more savoury one by blending a little yeast extract with the tepid liquid. You can also use chicken or other stock in place of plain liquid. The cheese and tomato breads below are particularly delicious as a basis for sandwiches or to serve with cheese.

Cheese bread

cooking time 30 – 35 minutes OR 45 – 55 minutes

you will need:

¼ pint milk	good shake pepper
2 oz. lard or margarine	3 oz. finely grated Cheddar cheese and 1 oz. grated Parmesan or Cheshire cheese OR
1 – 1½ teaspoons salt	4 oz. Cheddar cheese
1 oz. yeast	1 egg
1 teaspoon sugar	small knob butter
just over ¼ pint water	
1½ lb. flour, preferably plain	

1 Heat the milk with half the lard and salt, then allow to cool slightly.
2 Cream yeast with the sugar, add the tepid water and the milk mixture.
3 Sieve flour and pepper together.
4 Rub in the rest of lard,
5 Add the cheese, egg and yeast liquid.
6 Knead together until smooth.
7 Leave in a covered bowl in a warm place for approximately 1 hour.
8 Turn out and knead again.
9 Form into one large or two small loaves.
10 Put into one 2 lb. or two 1 lb. warmed and greased loaf tins and leave to rise again for about 20 minutes.
11 Brush with little melted butter to give a shiny crust.
12 Bake in the centre of a hot oven (450°F.—Gas Mark 7) for about 15 minutes.
13 Then lower the heat to moderate (375°F.—Gas Mark 4) for a further 15 – 20 minutes for the small loaves or 30 – 40 minutes for the large loaf.

Note:

If using dried instead of fresh yeast use ½ oz. only, proceed as for fresh yeast but allow the mixture to stand for 15 minutes before creaming.

Variations:

Cheese and tomato bread

Use tomato juice diluted with water instead of the milk and water.

Cheese and chive bread

Add about 1 tablespoon very finely chopped chives.

Cheese and ham

Add approximately 3 – 4 oz. very finely chopped boiled bacon or cooked ham.

Piquant cheese bread

Add a little yeast extract to the water.

Cheese and celery bread

Sprinkle the top of the cheese bread with grated cheese, mixed with celery salt, before baking. Or you can add a small quantity of very finely chopped celery to the dough. Do not, however, add the outside stalks as these tend to become stringy with cooking, use the inner stalks.

Tomato bread

This bread is unusual in colour, has a light texture and keeps well. It is especially good with green salads and cream cheese or for cucumber sandwiches. Attractive double decker sandwiches can be made using tomato and white breads, or triple decker with tomato, white and brown breads.

cooking time 30 – 40 minutes

you will need:

½ oz. fresh yeast or 2 teaspoons dried yeast	1 tablespoon oil or melted butter
½ pint tepid water	1½ lb. strong plain flour
1 teaspoon sugar	1 level teaspoon salt
small 5½ oz. tin tomato purée	1 level teaspoon paprika pepper
	little oil or melted butter

1 Blend yeast with ¼ pint of the water OR cream dried yeast with sugar, add ¼ pint water.
2 Mix tomato purée, oil or butter and ¼ pint water.
3 Sieve flour, salt and pepper in a large bowl.
4 Add the yeast and tomato liquids, all at once, and mix to a firm dough, adding extra flour if necessary.
5 Remove from bowl and knead lightly for 3 – 4 minutes.
6 Cover and put to rise until dough is double in size.
7 Turn the dough on to a lightly floured board, knead and divide into two.

8 Shape each piece and place in a greased 1 lb. bread tin.
9 Brush with oil, cover and put to rise to top of tins.
10 Brush with a mixture of egg, water and a pinch of sugar and bake in the centre of a hot oven (450°F.—Gas Mark 7) for 30 - 40 minutes.

Variation:

Tomato rolls

Divide the dough into small pieces at stage 7, then continue as before, baking for only 15 - 20 minutes.

Breads without Yeast

It is possible to make a great variety of breads, both plain, savoury and sweet, without using yeast.
You follow the same methods as cake or scone making.
As a rule the dough is a little plainer and therefore can be baked more quickly than a cake and the best results are given if the dough is generally a little soft.

Plain breads without yeast

These are quickly and easily made, so they are ideal if you run out of bread. They are delicious if made freshly for breakfast.

Baking powder bread

cooking time approximately 25 minutes

you will need:

- 1 lb. plain flour
- 1 teaspoon salt
- 2 rounded or 4 level teaspoons baking powder
- 2 oz. lard or margarine
- about ½ pint milk

1 Sift the flour and salt and baking powder into a bowl.
2 Rub in the fat until quite fine.
3 Mix very lightly to a light spongy dough with the milk.
4 Shape into two small loaves and place in two 1 lb. loaf tins or bake in two greased 6-inch cake tins.
5 Put into a hot oven (425 - 450°F.—Gas Mark 6 - 7), and bake in centre of oven for approximately 25 minutes.

Baking powder rolls

cooking time 10 minutes

you will need:

- 8 oz. plain flour
- 4 *level* teaspoons baking powder
- very good pinch salt
- 1 oz. lard or margarine
- milk to mix

1 Sift flour and baking powder and salt together into a bowl.
2 Rub in the margarine.
3 Add enough milk to make a sticky consistency.
4 Form into rolls, place on a greased, floured baking sheet and bake for 10 minutes at the top of a really hot oven (475 - 500°F.—Gas Mark 8 - 9).

Barley flour rolls or bread

cooking time 12 minutes OR 35 – 40 minutes

you will need:

- 8 oz. barley flour or patent barley
- 4 oz. flour
- 2 teaspoons baking powder, if using plain flour, or
- 1 teaspoon with self raising
- ½ teaspoon salt
- 1 oz. lard or margarine
- milk to mix

1. Sieve dry ingredients together.
2. Rub in the lard and add enough milk, about 1½ teacups, to make a slightly sticky mixture.
3. Knead lightly, form into one round loaf or small rolls.
4. Bake rolls for about 12 minutes near the top of a hot oven (425 – 450°F.—Gas Mark 6 – 7) on a lightly greased baking tray, first brushing the tops with milk to give a glaze.
5. Bake the loaf on a greased tin for about 20 minutes in the centre of a hot oven (425 – 450°F. —Gas Mark 6 – 7) then reduce the heat to moderate (375°F.—Gas Mark 4) for a further 15 – 20 minutes.

Bread rolls

cooking time approximately 15 – 20 minutes

you will need:

- 1 lb. self-raising flour
- ¼ level teaspoon salt
- 4 oz. margarine
- 2 eggs
- ⅓ pint milk

1. Sieve flour and salt into a bowl.
2. Add margarine and rub in until mixture resembles fine breadcrumbs.
3. Whisk eggs and milk together. Add beaten eggs and milk, keeping back 1 tablespoon for glazing, and mix lightly.
4. Turn on to a lightly floured board, roll to ⅜-inch thickness. Cut into rounds with a 3-inch cutter, moisten tops and fold over.
5. Place on a baking sheet brushed with margarine. Brush tops with egg and milk kept for glaze. Bake on second shelf from top in a hot oven (450°F.—Gas Mark 7) for 15 – 20 minutes. Remove.
6. Brush with the milk and return to the oven for 1 minute.

Variation:

Cinnamon topped rolls

Use the recipe for bread rolls and add 1 rounded tablespoon granulated sugar and 1 rounded teaspoon cinnamon. Bake as the rolls above, but when cooked remove from the oven, brush with milk and sprinkle with sugar and cinnamon, then return to the oven for 1 minute.

Hasty bread

cooking time 30 minutes

you will need:

- 1 oz. butter
- 8 oz. flour
- pinch of salt
- 1 level teaspoon bicarbonate soda
- 1 level teaspoon cream of tartar
- ¼ pint milk

1. Rub the butter into flour (this fat is not essential but helps to keep the bread moist).
2. Add the salt, bicarbonate of soda and cream of tartar.
3. Mix with the milk.
4. Knead lightly and form into a round loaf.
5. Brush with a little milk.
6. Bake on a flat tin in the centre of a very hot oven (475°F.—Gas Mark 8) for 15 minutes.
7. After this time lower gas oven to Gas Mark 5, or, if electric oven, turn off heat, and leave for 15 minutes.

Sweet hasty bread

Add 1 oz. sugar to flour, at stage 1.

Fruit hasty bread

Add 2 oz. dried fruit to ingredients at stage 2.

Honey hasty bread

Add 1 tablespoon honey to flour at stage 2. Use slightly less milk.

Soda bread I

cooking time 6 – 8 minutes

you will need:

- 1 lb. flour (with plain flour use 4 level teaspoons baking powder)
- 1 level teaspoon salt
- milk and water to mix

1 Heat griddle, solid hotplate or heavy pan slowly.
2 Sieve all dry ingredients.
3 Mix to a light elastic dough with liquid, roll out thinly, about ¼ inch thick, on a floured board.
4 Divide into four and make into neat shape.
5 Bake on a fairly hot griddle, to test shake on a little flour and it should turn golden brown in 1 minute, for 3 – 4 minutes for each side.
6 Cool in a clean tea towel or on a wire tray.

Soda bread 2

cooking time 25 – 30 minutes

you will need:

1 oz. margarine
8 oz. plain flour
pinch salt
1 level teaspoon bicarbonate of soda
¼ pint sour milk

1 Rub the margarine into the flour; this is not essential but helps to keep the bread moist.
2 Add the salt, dissolve the bicarbonate of soda in the sour milk, add to the flour.
3 Knead lightly and form into a round loaf.
4 Brush with a little milk and bake on a flat tin in the centre of a very hot oven (475°F.—Gas Mark 8) for 15 minutes.
5 After this time lower the gas to moderately hot, Gas Mark 5, or re-set electric cooker to 400°F. for another 10 – 15 minutes.

Savoury breads without yeast

These are very easy to make and are excellent for sandwiches or to take fresh on a picnic with salad.

Cheese bread

cooking time 40 – 50 minutes OR 1 – 1¼ hours

you will need:

8 oz. flour
1 level teaspoon baking powder with self-raising flour or 3 level teaspoons baking powder with plain flour
½ level teaspoon dry mustard
½ level teaspoon salt
pepper
4 oz. margarine
¼ pint milk
3 oz. grated cheese

1 Sieve all the dry ingredients together in a mixing bowl, then add the margarine, milk and cheese.
2 Mix together thoroughly with a wooden spoon until it forms a scone dough.
3 Place in a 1 lb. loaf tin lined with greased greaseproof paper, and spread evenly.
4 Bake in the centre of a moderate oven (375°F.—Gas Mark 4) for 1 – 1¼ hours.
5 This can be baked in a 7-inch square tin and would then take approximately 40 – 50 minutes at the same temperature.
6 Cool on a wire tray.

Variations:

Cheese and herb bread

Add 1 – 2 tablespoons finely chopped mixed FRESH herbs—parsley, sage, thyme and mint.

Cheese and garlic bread

Add either 1 crushed clove of garlic to milk at stage 1, or ¼ – ½ teaspoon garlic salt.

Cheese soda bread

cooking time 25 – 30 minutes

you will need:

1 oz. margarine
8 oz. plain flour
2 – 3 oz. finely grated cheese
pinch salt
1 level teaspoon bicarbonate of soda
1 level teaspoon cream of tartar
¼ pint milk

1 Rub the margarine into the flour; this is not essential but helps to keep the bread moist.
2 Add the cheese, seasoning and then dissolve the bicarbonate of soda and cream of tartar in the milk, add to the flour.
3 Knead lightly and form into a round loaf.
4 Brush with a little milk and bake on a flat tin in the centre of a very hot oven (475°F.—Gas Mark 8) for 15 minutes.
5 After this time lower the gas to moderately hot, Gas Mark 5, or re-set the electric cooker to 400°F. for another 10 – 15 minutes.

Cheddar cheese loaf

cooking time 1 – 1¼ hours

you will need:

- 8 oz. flour
- 1 level teaspoon baking powder with self-raising flour OR
- 3 level teaspoons baking powder with plain flour
- ¼ level teaspoon dry mustard
- ½ level teaspoon salt
- pepper
- 2 oz. margarine
- ¼ pint milk
- 5 oz. finely grated Cheddar cheese

1 Sieve all dry ingredients together in a mixing bowl.
2 Add margarine, milk and cheese.
3 Mix together thoroughly with a wooden spoon to form a scone dough.
4 Place in a 1 lb. loaf tin, greased and the bottom lined with greaseproof paper, and spread evenly.
5 Bake in middle of moderate oven (375°F.— Gas Mark 4) for 1 – 1¼ hours. Alternatively bake in 7-inch square tin for 40 – 50 minutes.
6 Cool on wire tray.

Note:

This is a particularly 'cheesey' flavoured bread.

Variations:

Cheddar and tomato loaf

Use tomato juice instead of milk.

Cheddar and chive loaf

Add approximately ½ – 1 tablespoon chopped chives.

Cheddar garlic bread

Sieve ½ teaspoon garlic salt with flour.

Cheese rolls

cooking time 15 – 20 minutes

you will need:

- 1 lb. self-raising flour
- ¼ level teaspoon salt
- good pinch dry mustard and pepper
- 4 oz. margarine
- 4 oz. finely grated cheese
- 2 eggs
- ⅓ pint milk

1 Sieve flour and seasoning into a bowl.
2 Add the margarine and rub in until the mixture resembles fine crumbs.
3 Add 3 oz. grated cheese.
4 Whisk eggs and milk together. Add beaten eggs and milk, keeping back 1 tablespoon for glazing, and mix lightly.
5 Turn on to a lightly floured board, roll to ⅓-inch thickness. Cut into rounds with a 3-inch cutter, moisten tops and fold over.
6 Place on a baking sheet brushed with margarine. Brush tops with egg and milk kept for glaze. Bake on second shelf from top in a hot oven (450°F.—Gas Mark 7) for 15 – 20 minutes. Remove.
7 Brush with glaze. Sprinkle with the remaining cheese and return to oven for 1 minute.

Kosher cheese loaf

cooking time 40 – 45 minutes

you will need:

- 8 oz. flour (with plain flour use 2 level teaspoons baking powder)
- ½ level teaspoon salt
- ¼ level teaspoon mustard
- pinch cayenne pepper
- 2 oz. kosher margarine
- 4 oz. grated Gruyére cheese
- 8 – 12 finely chopped olives
- 1 egg
- 6 tablespoons milk

1 Sieve flour, salt, mustard and cayenne pepper together into a mixing bowl.
2 Rub in the margarine until the mixture resembles fine breadcrumbs.
3 Stir in the cheese and olives.
4 Add egg and milk to a soft dough with a round bladed knife.
5 Place in a 1 lb. loaf tin, brushed with melted margarine, and bake in centre of a moderately hot oven (400°F.—Gas Mark 5) for 40 – 45 minutes until the loaf is golden brown.
6 Remove from the tin and cool on a wire tray.

Herb salad bread

cooking time 45 minutes

you will need:

- 3 oz. strong Cheddar cheese*
- 8 oz. flour (with plain flour use 4 level teaspoons baking powder)
- 1½ level teaspoons salt
- 1 level teaspoon dry mustard
- 1 level teaspoon mixed herbs
- 1 tablespoon chopped parsley
- 1 egg
- ¼ pint water
- 1 oz. melted butter or margarine

* Or use half Parmesan and half Cheddar cheese

1. Grate cheese.
2. Sieve flour, salt and mustard together and stir in the mixed herbs, parsley and grated cheese.
3. Add the well beaten egg, water and melted fat all at once and stir until just blended.
4. Spoon mixture into two well-greased ½ lb. cocoa tins and bake in centre of a moderate oven 375°F.—Gas Mark 4) for about 45 minutes.
5. Remove from tins and cool on a wire tray. Serve freshly baked with butter and salad.

Laver bread

cooking time several hours

you will need:

- laver, see below
- oatmeal
- fat, preferably bacon fat

Laver is an edible seaweed that is found along the western coast of Wales. It is also found in parts of Cornwall.

1. Boil the laver for several hours in water.
2. Drain and mix with enough oatmeal to blend into round flat cakes.
3. Fry in hot bacon fat and serve with meat or bacon.

Note:

The bread is also served with vinegar or spread on slices of toast and seasoned with lemon juice, olive oil and pepper.

Tomato loaf

cooking time 55 minutes – 1 hour, 5 minutes

you will need:

- 3 oz. softened margarine
- ¼ pint tomato juice
- ¼ teaspoon Worcestershire sauce
- pinch mixed herbs
- 8 oz. self-raising flour and 1 level teaspoon baking powder or 3 level teaspoons baking powder with plain flour
- salt and pepper

1. Place all the ingredients in a bowl and beat together until well mixed, 1 – 2 minutes.
2. Place in a 1 lb. loaf tin, with the bottom lined with greaseproof paper and brushed with melted margarine.
3. Bake on the middle shelf of a moderate oven (375°F.—Gas Mark 4) for 55 – 65 minutes.
4. Cool on a wire tray.

Variations:

Cheese tomato loaf

Add 2 – 3 oz. grated cheese.

Chive tomato loaf

Add 2 tablespoons chopped chives.

Ham and tomato loaf

Add 3 oz. finely chopped cooked ham.

Sweet breads without yeast

In this section are some of the very wide variety of sweet breads that can be made without using yeast; many of them can be varied by adding more spice or using a different mixture of fruits, but the basic proportions of liquid should not be altered too much. You will find, as stressed in yeast breads, however, that flours do vary in the amount of liquid they will absorb and a little more or less liquid is sometimes required.

American prune loaf

cooking time $1\frac{1}{4}$ – $1\frac{1}{2}$ hours

you will need:

12 oz. prunes
2 oz. almonds, or shelled walnuts
1 lb. plain flour
1 – 2 level teaspoons crushed caraway seeds, optional
½ level teaspoon ground cloves
½ level teaspoon ground nutmeg
1 level teaspoon bicarbonate of soda
6 oz. margarine or unsalted butter
4 oz. sugar
2 oz. chopped mixed peel
2 eggs
good ¼ pint sour milk OR ¼ pint fresh milk and 2 dessertspoons wine vinegar

1 Set aside four prunes for decorating, stone and halve these.
2 Snip the flesh off remaining prunes with scissors and discard stones.
3 Blanch almonds, set aside a few for decorating and shred remainder or chop walnuts, saving a few for decoration.
4 Sieve flour, spices and bicarbonate soda into a large mixing bowl and rub in fat until mixture resembles fine breadcrumbs.
5 Mix in prepared fruit, nuts and sugar and peel.
6 Add beaten eggs and sufficient milk to give soft dropping consistency.
7 Three-quarters fill greased $2\frac{1}{2}$ – 3 lb. loaf tin and if the mixture is too much for tin available, then put surplus into bun tins.
8 Bake in centre of moderate oven (375°F.—Gas Mark 4). The buns will take approximately 30 minutes and the loaf $1\frac{1}{4}$ – $1\frac{1}{2}$ hours.
9 The prunes and walnuts for decoration should be put on to the loaf or buns halfway through baking. This makes sure the dough is sufficiently firm for them to stay in position but that they do not get overcooked and dry.

Variations:

American apricot loaf

Use 8 oz. dried apricots in place of prunes.

American fig loaf

Use 8 oz. chopped figs in place of prunes.

Banana bread

cooking time approximately 45 minutes

you will need:

8 oz. flour (with plain flour use 3 level teaspoons baking powder)
pinch salt
2 oz. margarine or vegetable cooking fat
2 oz. sugar
grated rind 1 lemon
3 – 4 mashed bananas
1 egg
milk

1 Sieve flour and salt into a bowl.
2 Rub in margarine or cooking fat, then add sugar, lemon rind, mashed bananas and egg.
3 Mix thoroughly. If necessary add enough milk to give a sticky consistency.
4 Put into a greased and floured 1 lb. loaf tin.
5 Bake for approximately 45 minutes in centre of moderate oven (375°F.—Gas Mark 4) until golden brown and firm.

Banana loaf

cooking time 1 hour

you will need:

4 oz. butter or margarine
1 oz. castor sugar
1 egg
3 ripe, but not discoloured, bananas
grated rind of 1 lemon
8 oz. flour (with plain flour use 2 level teaspoons baking powder)
milk to mix
little icing sugar

1 Cream butter and sugar, beat in egg and well mashed bananas and lemon rind.
2 Gradually add sieved flour and enough milk to bind.
3 Put into well greased and floured $1\frac{1}{2}$ – 2 lb. loaf tin.
4 Bake for approximately 1 hour in centre of moderate oven (375°F.—Gas Mark 4). Dust with icing sugar.
5 When cold, for a special occasion, cover with cream and sliced bananas just before serving.
6 The loaf could be split through centre and filled with mashed banana and cream.

Cherry almond loaf

cooking time approximately 1½ hours

you will need:

4 oz. glacé cherries
5 oz. margarine or butter
6 oz. castor sugar
2 large eggs
6 oz. flour (with plain flour use 1½ level teaspoons baking powder)
2 oz. ground almonds
very few drops milk

1 Halve and flour the cherries, or wash off the sticky syrup, dry well and flour.
2 Cream together margarine and sugar.
3 Add the beaten eggs, the sieved flour and the ground almonds.
4 Stir in the cherries, and enough milk to give a *stiff* consistency.
5 Put into a 1 lb. loaf tin, and bake for approximately 1½ hours in the centre of a very slow oven (250°F.—Gas Mark ½ - 1).
6 Turn out carefully.
7 If wished cover the top with either marzipan or water icing and decorate with blanched almonds and cherries. The slow baking of this cake produces a lovely moist texture.

Note:

Although this is a cake and will in most cases be eaten as a cake when fresh, it is a most delicious sweet tea bread and as such you can use a week or so after baking. Cut into thin slices and butter lightly.

Cherry farm loaf

cooking time 1 hour 10 minutes

you will need:

6 oz. butter or margarine
10 oz. plain flour
4 level teaspoons baking powder
4 oz. glacé cherries
1 teaspoon vanilla essence
1 egg
1 small can condensed milk
8 - 10 tablespoons water

1 Rub butter or margarine into sieved flour and baking powder.
2 Add cherries, vanilla essence and egg and mix to a dropping consistency with the condensed milk and water.
3 Put into a greased and lined 1 lb. or 1½ lb. loaf tin and bake in the centre of a moderate oven (375°F.—Gas Mark 4) for 1 hour and 10 minutes.
4 Store for several days before cutting; serve buttered.

Variations:

Orange farm loaf

1 Use 3 oz. chopped crystallized orange peel instead of glacé cherries.
2 Use half water and half orange juice.
3 Add finely grated rind 1 orange to flour.

Sultana farm loaf

Use 4 oz. sultanas instead of glacé cherries.

Cranberry nut loaf

cooking time approximately 1 hour

you will need:

8 oz. flour (with plain flour use 2 level teaspoons baking powder)
8 oz. sugar
¼ level teaspoon bicarbonate of soda
pinch salt
2 oz. vegetable cooking fat or margarine
6 tablespoons orange juice
1 tablespoon grated orange rind
1 egg
4 oz. chopped nuts
4 - 6 oz. cranberries

1 Sift together flour, baking powder, sugar, bicarbonate of soda and salt. Rub or cut in cooking fat until mixture resembles coarse breadcrumbs.
2 Combine orange juice and grated rind with well beaten egg. Pour all at once into dry ingredients, mixing just enough to dampen.
3 Carefully fold in chopped nuts and cranberries.
4 Spoon into greased loaf pan, 9 × 5 × 3 inches. Spread to the corners and sides and make the sides slightly higher than the centre. Bake in a very moderate oven (350°F.—Gas Mark 3) for about 1 hour until crust is golden brown.
5 Remove from pan. Cool. Store overnight for easy slicing.

Note:

Ordinary berry fruit, such as blackcurrants, etc., cannot be substituted for cranberries since these are such a firm texture, but you can use coarsely grated or chopped dessert apple.

Date and apricot loaf

cooking time | hour 15 minutes

you will need:

4 oz. dried apricots
4 oz. margarine
8 oz. flour (with plain flour use 2 level teaspoons baking powder)
4 oz. brown sugar
6 oz. chopped dates
2 eggs
little milk

1 Chop apricots in small pieces, cover with boiling water and leave for 20 minutes.
2 Drain off water and shake dry.
3 Rub margarine into sieved flour, add sugar, chopped dates, apricots and eggs, together with enough milk to make a sticky consistency.
4 Put into a greased and floured 2 lb. loaf tin and bake for approximately 1¼ hours in the centre of a very moderate oven (350°F.—Gas Mark 3).

Variations:

Apricot and sultana loaf

Use sultanas instead of dates.

Golden-topped loaf

Make date and apricot loaf.
While it is baking simmer 3 oz. chopped dried apricots with grated rind of 1 lemon, 2 teaspoons lemon juice and 1 tablespoon golden syrup, for about 10 minutes until a sticky mixture. Cool, add 2 oz. chopped walnuts and spread over top of the cooked loaf.

Date and cherry loaf

cooking time 1½ – 2 hours

you will need:

4 oz. softened margarine
12 oz. plain flour
½ level teaspoon bicarbonate of soda
1 level teaspoon baking powder
3 level tablespoons golden syrup
3 level tablespoons black treacle
4 oz. chopped dates
2 oz. chopped glacé cherries
2 oz. chopped walnuts
¼ pint milk

For topping:
icing sugar
glacé cherries and angelica

1 Place all the loaf ingredients in a bowl and beat together for 1 – 2 minutes until well mixed.
2 Place in a 2 lb. loaf tin or in two 1 lb. loaf tins, with the bottom lined with greaseproof paper and brushed with melted margarine.
3 Bake on the middle shelf of a very moderate oven (350°F.—Gas Mark 3) for 1½ – 2 hours, or if cooked in two 1 lb. tins, bake for 1 – 1¼ hours.
4 Turn out and cool on a wire tray.
5 When cold sprinkle heavily with icing sugar and place under a hot grill to melt for 1 minute. Decorate with glacé cherries and angelica.
6 This may be served as bread or cake.

Date nut bread

cooking time 1 hour

you will need:

1½ oz. walnuts
2 oz. dates
12 oz. flour (with plain flour use 3 level teaspoons baking powder)
½ level teaspoon salt
3 oz. castor sugar
2 medium-sized eggs
scant ½ pint cold milk
2 oz. melted butter or margarine

1 Chop walnuts and dates coarsely.
2 Sift flour and salt into a bowl, then stir in sugar, walnuts and dates.
3 Mix to a slack consistency with the beaten eggs and milk, stirring well.
4 Fold in melted butter or margarine, then turn mixture into a greased loaf tin, about 4 × 8 × 3 inches deep.
5 Bake in the centre of a moderate oven (375°F.—Gas Mark 4) for 1 hour.
6 Turn out on to a wire tray. When cold, serve with cheese, butter and salad.

Dark date and walnut loaf

cooking time 1 – 1¼ hours

you will need:

6 oz. plain flour
large pinch salt
4 oz. chopped dates
1½ level teaspoons bicarbonate of soda
scant ¼ pint boiling water
2 oz. butter
2 teaspoons vanilla essence
4 oz. sugar
2 eggs
2 oz. chopped walnuts

1 Sieve flour and salt.
2 Put dates in a bowl, sprinkle bicarbonate of soda on top.
3 Pour boiling water over. Leave to cool.
4 Cream together the butter, vanilla essence, sugar and egg yolks.
5 Blend in the sieved flour and salt, followed by the dates and walnuts.
6 Beat egg whites and fold in.
7 Turn into greased 1 lb. loaf tin.

8 Bake on the middle shelf of a very moderate oven (350°F.—Gas Mark 3) for 1 – 1¼ hours.
9 Remove from tin and cool on a wire tray.

Date and walnut bread 1

cooking time 1 – 1½ hours

you will need:

- 12 oz. plain flour
- 4 level teaspoons baking powder (with self-raising flour use 1 level teaspoon baking powder)
- ¼ level teaspoon salt
- ½ level teaspoon bicarbonate of soda
- 3 oz. sugar, preferably brown
- 4 oz. chopped dates
- 3 oz. chopped walnuts
- ½ pint milk
- 1½ tablespoons black treacle
- 1½ oz. butter or margarine

1 Line and grease a 2 lb. loaf tin.
2 Sieve the flour, baking powder, salt and bicarbonate of soda.
3 Stir in the sugar, dates and nuts.
4 Warm the milk, treacle and butter in a small saucepan until the butter has just melted, then stir into the dry ingredients, mixing without beating, just until a thick batter consistency.
5 Immediately turn into prepared tin and bake in centre of a moderate oven (375°F.—Gas Mark 4) for approximately 1 – 1¼ hours.
6 Cool on a cake wire and do not wrap or put in a tin until absolutely cold.
7 Serve sliced and buttered.

Date and walnut bread 2

cooking time 50 – 55 minutes

you will need:

- 8 oz. flour (with plain flour use 2 level teaspoons baking powder)
- 1 level teaspoon bicarbonate of soda
- 2 oz. sugar
- 1 oz. margarine
- 12 oz. chopped cooking dates
- ¼ pint water
- 2 oz. chopped walnuts
- 1 egg

1 Sieve the dry ingredients together.
2 Put the sugar, margarine and dates into a saucepan or basin and pour over the boiling water. Stir well, allow to cool, then add the rest of the ingredients.
3 Put into a large loaf tin, measuring approximately 9 × 5 inches, which should be thoroughly greased and floured.
4 Bake for approximately 50 – 55 minutes in the centre of a moderate to moderately hot oven (375 – 400°F.—Gas Mark 4 – 5).

Variation:

Omit walnuts and add grated rind of 1 or 2 oranges and orange juice and water to give ¼ pint.

Raisin and walnut tea bread

cooking time approximately 50 minutes – 1 hour

you will need:

- 8 oz. flour (with plain flour use 2 teaspoons baking powder)
- 1 level teaspoon bicarbonate soda
- 2 oz. sugar
- 1 oz. margarine
- 12 oz. stoned raisins
- ¼ pint water
- 1 egg
- 2 – 4 oz. chopped walnuts

1 Sieve all dry ingredients together.
2 Put sugar, margarine and raisins into a basin and pour over the water, which should be boiling.
3 Stir well, then allow mixture to cool.
4 Stir in flour, egg and nuts.
5 Put into either a 7-inch cake tin or large loaf tin, well-greased and floured, and bake for approximately 50 minutes to 1 hour in the centre of a moderate oven (375°F—Gas Mark 4).

Dutch rich cake bread

cooking time 1 – 1¼ hours

you will need:

- 1 lb. white or wholemeal flour (with plain flour use 3 teaspoons baking powder)
- 1 teaspoon powdered cinnamon
- 1 teaspoon ginger
- ½ teaspoon powdered nutmeg
- 3 oz. brown sugar
- 8 oz. syrup
- ½ pint milk

1 Sieve all the dry ingredients.
2 Mix the syrup and milk and add gradually to the dry ingredients, working quickly into a firm dough.
3 Put the mixture into a well-greased 2 – 2½ lb. loaf tin and bake for 1 – 1¼ hours in the centre of a moderate oven (375°F.—Gas Mark 4).
4 Cool in the tin.

Fruit syrup loaf

cooking time 45 – 50 minutes

you will need:

8 oz. flour (with plain flour use 2 level teaspoons baking powder)
1 level teaspoon bicarbonate of soda
3 *level* tablespoons golden syrup
1 oz. margarine
8 tablespoons water
4 – 8 oz. mixed fruit or sultanas
1 egg

1. Sieve the dry ingredients together.
2. Heat the syrup, margarine and water together, add the mixed fruit or sultanas and allow to cool slightly.
3. Stir in the rest of the ingredients.
4. Put into a large loaf tin, measuring approximately 9 × 5 inches, and bake for 45 – 50 minutes in the centre of a moderate oven (375°F.—Gas Mark 4).
5. These loaves keep very well for some days.

Variation:

Instead of golden syrup you can use the same quantity of extract of malt.

Ginger bread

Although we always consider gingerbread as a cake, this was not the case in the old days. It was, as its name suggests, a bread, and you will find that when a gingerbread becomes rather stale it is delicious sliced and spread with butter.

cooking time 1 – 1¼ hours

you will need:

10 oz. flour (with plain flour use 1½ level teaspoons baking powder)
½ teaspoon bicarbonate of soda
1 – 2 teaspoons powdered ginger
5 oz. butter
5 oz. sugar, preferably brown
6 oz. black treacle
2 eggs
⅛ pint water

1. Sieve the dry ingredients together.
2. Put the butter, sugar and treacle into a saucepan, heat gently until butter has melted.
3. Stir butter mixture into dry ingredients and beat well.
4. Add the 2 beaten eggs.
5. Heat the water in the saucepan, to make sure no treacle is wasted, and pour over the cake mixture.
6. Give a final beat and pour the mixture into a lined and greased tin, a 7-inch round cake tin, or Yorkshire pudding tin.
7. Bake in the centre of a very moderate oven (300 – 350°F.—Gas Mark 2 – 3). The mixture in a Yorkshire pudding tin will need approximately 1 hour for baking, and in a cake tin will require 1¼ hours cooking.
8. Cool in tin before turning on to wire tray.

Variations:

Add a little grated lemon rind.

Add 2 – 3 oz. chopped blanched almonds and 1 oz. ground almonds.

Add 2 oz. desiccated coconut and decorate the top with a thin layer of glacé icing and desiccated coconut.

Add 1 level teaspoon mixed spice and ½ teaspoon cinnamon as well as ginger to the flour and about 4 oz. sultanas.

Honey nut bread

cooking time 1½ hours

you will need:

3 – 4 oz. margarine
4 oz. castor sugar
6 level tablespoons honey
1 egg
12 oz. plain flour
3 level teaspoons baking powder
1 level teaspoon salt
¼ pint milk, good measure
4 oz. chopped walnuts

1. Cream margarine and sugar, mix in honey thoroughly.
2. Beat in egg.
3. Sieve flour, baking powder and salt and stir into creamed mixture alternately with milk.
4. Mix in nuts and spread mixture into a greased 2 lb. loaf tin.
5. Bake in centre of a very moderate oven (350°F. —Gas Mark 3) for 1½ hours.

Variations:

Syrup nut bread

Use 4 level tablespoons golden syrup in place of 6 tablespoons honey.

Treacle nut bread

Use 2 level tablespoons black treacle and 2 level tablespoons golden syrup in place of the 6 tablespoons of honey.

Lincolnshire bread

This bread is often called Boston bread.

cooking time 50 minutes – 1 hour OR 35 – 40 minutes

you will need:

8 oz. white flour
8 oz. wholemeal flour
1 level teaspoon bicarbonate of soda
4 oz. chopped dates
4 oz. chopped raisins
4 oz. golden syrup
2 oz. chopped nuts, optional
approximately ¼ pint milk

1 Sieve together the flours and bicarbonate of soda.
2 Add the fruit, syrup, nuts if used, and milk. Blend very well. You should have a sticky consistency so a little more milk may be needed.
3 Put into either two greased and floured 1 lb. loaf tins, or into one 2 lb. loaf tin.
4 Bake in the centre of a moderate oven (375°F.—Gas Mark 4) for 50 minutes to 1 hour for the 2 lb. loaf or 35 – 40 minutes for the smaller loaves.

Malt bread

cooking time approximately 30 minutes

you will need:

⅜ pint milk
1 oz. margarine
2 tablespoons extract of malt
½ teaspoon bicarbonate of soda
8 oz. flour (with plain flour use 2 level teaspoons baking powder)
1½ tablespoons sugar
2 oz. sultanas

1 Warm the milk, margarine and malt together.
2 Sieve the dry ingredients.
3 Beat in the milk mixture.
4 Add the sugar and fruit and stir well.
5 Pour into well-greased and floured loaf tin.
6 Bake for approximately 30 minutes in the centre of a moderately hot oven (400°F.—Gas Mark 5).

Variations:

Malt and date bread

Use the recipe for malt bread, but omit sultanas and add 4 oz. dates. Chop and warm with the milk.

Malt and orange bread

1 Omit the sultanas, add 2 oz. finely cut crystallized orange peel.
2 Use ¼ pint milk and ⅛ pint orange juice instead of all milk.
3 Heat milk, margarine and malt and finely grated rind 2 oranges.

Malt fruit loaf

cooking time 1 hour

you will need:

2 tablespoons malt
2 tablespoons black treacle
5 tablespoons milk
8 oz. self-raising flour
3 oz. dried fruit
1 egg
1 teaspoon bicarbonate of soda

1 Melt the malt and black treacle with the milk in a saucepan, over a low heat.
2 Sieve the flour into a good-sized basin, adding the dried fruit and the egg.
3 Make a well in the middle of the flour, pour in the ingredients and mix thoroughly.
4 Line a loaf shaped tin with greased paper.
5 Mix the bicarbonate of soda with a little water and add it to the loaf mixture.
6 Beat well and pour immediately into the lined tin.
7 Bake in a moderate oven (375°F.—Gas Mark 4) for about 1 hour.
8 Turn on rack to cool.
9 Serve sliced and spread with butter.

Malt walnut bread I

cooking time 1¼ – 1½ hours

you will need:

2 oz. walnuts
1 lb. flour (with plain flour use 4 level teaspoons baking powder)
1 level teaspoon salt
1 heaped tablespoon brown sugar
4 oz. seedless raisins
½ pint milk
1 heaped tablespoon black treacle
2 heaped tablespoons malt extract

1 Chop nuts finely.
2 Sift together flour and salt, then add sugar, raisins and walnuts.
3 Combine milk with the treacle and malt extract and add to flour mixture. Stir well.
4 Turn into a well-greased 2 lb. loaf tin, or two 1 lb. loaf tins, and bake in the centre of a slow oven (300°F.—Gas Mark 2) for about 1 hour, then at 275°F.—Gas Mark 1 for a further 15 – 30 minutes.
5 Turn out and cool on a wire tray.

Malt walnut bread 2

cooking time 30 – 35 minutes

you will need:

$\frac{3}{8}$ pint milk
1 oz. margarine
2 tablespoons malt extract
8 oz. flour (with plain flour use 2 level teaspoons baking powder)
$\frac{1}{2}$ teaspoon bicarbonate of soda
$1\frac{1}{2}$ level tablespoons sugar
4 oz. chopped walnuts

1. Warm milk, margarine and malt together.
2. Sieve dry ingredients, then beat in the milk mixture.
3. Add sugar and nuts and stir well.
4. Pour into well-greased and floured loaf tin.
5. Bake for approximately 30 – 35 minutes in centre of a moderately hot oven (400°F.—Gas Mark 5).

Nut bread

cooking time 1 hour

you will need:

12 oz. flour (with plain flour use 3 *level* teaspoons baking powder)
pinch salt
2 oz. margarine or cooking fat
1 egg
$\frac{1}{4}$ pint, 2 tablespoons milk
2 oz. sugar
4 oz. chopped nuts

1. Sieve flour, salt and baking powder.
2. Rub in margarine or fat, add egg, then stir in milk to give very sticky consistency, but one that drops easily from palette knife. Add the sugar and nuts.
3. Put in greased and floured $1\frac{1}{2}$ – 2 lb. loaf tin.
4. Bake in centre of moderate oven (375°F.—Gas Mark 4) for approximately 1 hour. Look after 40 minutes and if browning too quickly reduce heat slightly.

Variations:

Currant bread

Use the recipe for nut bread but use 4 – 6 oz. currants instead of nuts. The bread may take a few minutes longer to cook.

Mixed fruit bread

Use the recipe for nut bread, but use 6 oz. mixed dried fruit instead of nuts. The bread may take a few minutes longer to cook.

Nut peel bread

Use the recipe for nut bread, but use 2 oz. chopped nuts and 2 oz. candied peel. If this seems rather dry and hard soak it in the milk for about 15 minutes before blending ingredients for loaf.

Spiced nut bread

Use the recipe for nut bread, but sieve $\frac{1}{2}$ teaspoon mixed spice and $\frac{1}{2}$ teaspoon cinnamon with flour.

Nutty orange bread

cooking time 1 hour

you will need:

12 oz. flour (with plain flour use 2 level teaspoons baking powder)
pinch salt
3 oz. castor sugar
$1\frac{1}{2}$ – 2 oz. walnuts
2 oz. candied orange peel
2 medium-sized eggs
$\frac{3}{8}$ pint milk
2 oz. melted butter

To glaze:
1 tablespoon castor sugar
1 tablespoon milk

1. Sieve flour and salt together, then add sugar, chopped walnuts and candied orange peel, and mix with the beaten eggs and milk to a soft dough.
2. Lastly stir in the melted butter.
3. Put into a greased and floured 2 lb. loaf tin and bake in the centre of a very moderate oven (325 – 350°F.—Gas Mark 3) for 1 hour.
4. Test to see if cooked by knocking firmly on the bottom and if it feels quite firm cool on a wire tray. If a little soft at the bottom put back in the oven on a flat baking tray for just a few minutes.
5. Brush with the following glaze while still hot. Heat sugar and milk in small pan, and use when sugar has dissolved and the mixture is slightly syrupy. This loaf is equally good for tea or for serving with a cheese salad.

Orange tea bread

cooking time 40 – 45 minutes

you will need:

6 oz. self-raising flour
pinch salt
3 oz. castor sugar
grated rind 1 orange
1 tablespoon thick peel marmalade
1 tablespoon corn oil
1 egg
2 tablespoons milk

1 Sieve flour and salt into a bowl.
2 Stir in the sugar and orange rind.
3 Make a well in the centre and add marmalade.
4 Add corn oil, egg and milk and mix well together.
5 Pour into greased 1 lb. loaf tin and bake for 40 - 45 minutes in a moderate oven (375°F.—Gas Mark 4).
6 When cool, cut into slices and spread with butter.

Variations:

Lemon tea bread

Use lemon rind and marmalade in place of orange. This is very delicious spread with butter and honey.

Orange nut tea bread

Add 2 oz. chopped walnuts or blanched almonds at stage 4.

Orange honey tea bread

cooking time — 1 hour, 5 - 7 minutes

you will need:

- 1 oz. margarine
- 3 tablespoons honey
- 1 egg
- 8 oz. flour (with plain flour use 2 level teaspoons baking powder)
- 1 level teaspoon baking powder
- 1 level teaspoon salt
- 6 tablespoons milk
- grated rind 1 large orange

To glaze:
- 2 - 3 teaspoons melted honey

1 Cream the margarine, gradually adding the honey and creaming together thoroughly.
2 Add the egg and beat until bubbles appear.
3 Sift together the flour, baking powder and salt.
4 Add to the creamed mixture alternately with the milk.
5 Stir in about two-thirds of the grated orange rind.
6 Line a loaf tin, about 8 × 4 inches, with greaseproof paper and turn in the mixture, which should be a fairly stiff consistency.
7 Spread top smooth and bake in a moderate oven (375°F.—Gas Mark 4) for 1 hour.
8 Brush top of loaf with a little melted honey and sprinkle with the remainder of the grated orange rind and bake for another 5 - 7 minutes until glaze is set.
9 Remove from oven, leave for 5 minutes, remove loaf from tin and allow to get quite cold standing on a wire tray before cutting.
10 If wrapped in greaseproof paper the loaf will keep moist for a week.

Variations:

Nut orange honey tea bread

Add 2 oz. chopped nuts with most of the orange rind.

Lemon honey tea bread

Use lemon rind instead of orange.

Ovaltine loaf

cooking time — 25 - 45 minutes

you will need:

- 10 oz. flour (with plain flour use 2½ level teaspoons baking powder)
- ½ level teaspoon bicarbonate soda
- pinch salt
- 1 tablespoon sugar
- 1 level tablespoon golden syrup
- 2 - 4 oz. dried fruit
- 3 level tablespoons Ovaltine
- ⅜ pint milk

1 Sieve together the dry ingredients.
2 Add syrup and fruit.
3 Dissolve Ovaltine in the liquid and beat into flour mixture.
4 Put into a large loaf tin and bake for approximately 45 minutes in centre of a moderate oven (375°F.—Gas Mark 4) or in two small tins for approximately 25 minutes.
5 Keep a day before cutting.

Variations:

Ovaltine date loaf

Use 4 oz. chopped dates instead of dried fruit and heat for minute or two in the liquid before adding Ovaltine.

Ovaltine coconut loaf

Omit dried fruit and mix 2 oz. desiccated coconut with the flour. Be a little more generous with the milk, adding an extra tablespoon.

Peanut butter bread

cooking time 1 hour

you will need:

- 8 oz. flour (with plain flour use 2 level teaspoons baking powder)
- 1 level teaspoon salt
- 2 oz. peanut butter
- 2 oz. sugar
- approximately ¼ pint milk to mix
- 2 oz. mixed dried fruit

1. Grease a 7-inch cake tin or small loaf tin.
2. Sieve together flour, baking powder and salt.
3. Mix in peanut butter, add sugar and mix to a stiff dropping consistency with milk.
4. Stir in dried fruit.
5. Turn mixture into prepared cake or loaf tin and stand in a warm place for 30 minutes.
6. Bake in the middle of a very moderate oven (300 - 350°F.—Gas Mark 2 - 3) for about 1 hour.
7. Turn on to a wire cake tray when cooked and allow to cool.
8. Store for 24 hours before serving.

Variation:

Peanut butter and orange bread

Add the finely grated rind of 1 orange to the flour and use 2 oz. crystallized orange peel instead of dried fruit. Measure the orange juice and add enough milk to give ¼ pint.

Prune loaf

cooking time 40 minutes

you will need:

- 4 oz. uncooked prunes
- ¼ pint water
- 8 oz. flour (with plain flour use 2 level teaspoons baking powder)
- pinch salt
- 1 teaspoon bicarbonate of soda
- ¼ pint milk
- 4 tablespoons warmed golden syrup

1. Chop the flesh from the stones of the prunes and put into a saucepan with the water.
2. Simmer about 3 minutes and cool slightly.
3. Sieve the flour, baking powder, salt and bicarbonate of soda together.
4. Add the milk and the prunes, water and syrup.
5. Beat very well and put into a well-greased and floured tin, 8 × 6 inches.
6. Bake in the centre of a moderately hot oven (400°F.—Gas Mark 5) for approximately 20 minutes, then lower the heat to moderate (375°F.—Gas Mark 4) for a further 20 minutes approximately.

Variations:

Prune and lemon loaf

Add the grated rind of 1 lemon to the flour. Measure the juice of 1 lemon and add enough water to give ¼ pint.

Prune and orange loaf

Add the grated rind of 1 orange to the flour. Measure the juice of 1 orange and add enough water to give ¼ pint. 1 - 2 oz. crystallized peel could also be added.

Dark prune loaf

Use ¼ pint of strong tea, well strained, of course, in place of water.

Prune coffee loaf

Use ¼ pint rather weak coffee in place of water.

Quick nut bread

cooking time 45 - 50 minutes

you will need:

- 8 oz. plain flour
- 3 level teaspoons baking powder
- pinch salt
- 3 oz. castor sugar
- 3 oz. chopped nuts
- 1 beaten egg
- ¼ pint milk
- 3 dessertspoons melted lard

1. Sieve flour, baking powder and salt into a mixing bowl.
2. Add sugar and nuts.
3. Mix thoroughly.
4. Combine egg, milk and lard, and use to bind dry ingredients.
5. Place in a well-greased 1 lb. loaf tin.
6. Bake in a moderate oven (375°F.—Gas Mark 4) for about 45 - 50 minutes.

Raisin plait

cooking time 15 - 20 minutes

you will need:

- 1 lb. flour (with plain flour use 4 level teaspoons baking powder)
- ½ teaspoon salt
- 4 oz. butter
- 4 oz. seeded raisins
- 2 oz. glacé cherries
- 1 egg
- ½ pint milk
- 1 tablespoon brown sugar

1 Sift the flour and salt.
2 Rub in the butter lightly with the fingertips.
3 Add chopped raisins and cherries.
4 Beat egg and milk together and put aside 1 tablespoon for glazing the loaf. Add the egg and milk to the dry ingredients and mix to a soft dough using a knife. Turn out on to a lightly floured board and knead slightly.
5 Divide the dough into three pieces and roll each into a sausage approximately 1 inch in thickness. Plait the three rolls and place on a greased baking tray. Brush with the remaining egg and milk and sprinkle with brown sugar.
6 Bake just above the centre of a hot oven (450 - 475°F.—Gas Mark 7 - 8) for 15 - 20 minutes, reducing heat slightly after 10 minutes, if becoming too brown.
7 Test to see if cooked if loaf sounds hollow. Cool on wire tray and spread with butter.

Somerset spiced bread

cooking time 2 hours

you will need:

10 oz. flour
4 oz. demerara sugar
4 oz. sultanas
2 oz. chopped mixed peel
1 level teaspoon mixed spice
1 level teaspoon ground ginger
6 oz. black treacle
⅛ pint milk
½ level teaspoon bicarbonate of soda
1 large egg

1 Put the flour, sugar, fruit, peel and spices into a mixing bowl.
2 Warm the treacle over a low heat.
3 Mix the milk and bicarbonate of soda with the treacle in the pan and pour into the mixing bowl with the beaten egg.
4 Beat thoroughly and pour into a well greased 2 lb. bread tin.
5 Bake in a cool oven (300°F.—Gas Mark 2) for 2 hours, or until firm and well risen.
6 Cool on a wire tray then serve buttered slices of the bread topped with whipped cream.

Syrup bread

Choose any of the recipes in the section of malt bread and substitute syrup. This gives a very pleasant moist texture without the distinctive flavour of malt which is not to everybody's taste.

Tea-time fruit bread

cooking time 35 minutes

you will need:

8 oz. flour (with plain flour use 2 level teaspoons baking powder)
2 oz. margarine
2 - 3 oz. sugar
4 oz. dried fruit or more if liked
1 oz. mixed peel
1 teaspoon grated lemon rind
1 or 2 eggs
milk to mix

1 Sieve dry ingredients.
2 Rub in margarine.
3 Add sugar and all ingredients, stirring in enough milk to give a sticky consistency.
4 Put into a well-greased and floured loaf tin.
5 Bake for 35 minutes in the centre of a moderately hot oven (400°F.—Gas Mark 5).

Treacle bread

cooking time 1 - 1¼ hours

you will need:

4 oz. black treacle
¼ pint milk
2 medium sized eggs
10 oz. plain flour
1 level teaspoon cinnamon
1 level teaspoon mixed spice
½ level teaspoon baking powder
½ level teaspoon bicarbonate of soda
2 oz. butter or margarine
2 oz. currants
2 oz. sultanas

1 Combine black treacle and milk, then add beaten eggs.
2 Sift dry ingredients, rub in fat.
3 Add fruit then mix to a soft consistency with the liquid.
4 Turn into a well-greased and floured 2 lb. loaf tin and bake in the centre of a very moderate oven (300 - 350°F.—Gas Mark 2 - 3) for 1 - 1¼ hours.
5 Store a day before cutting, if possible.

Variation:

Syrup fruit bread

Use golden syrup instead of treacle. A little cinnamon, sieved with the flour, gives pleasant taste.

Treacle fruit bread

cooking time 1 hour

you will need:

12 oz. flour (with plain flour use 3 *level* teaspoons baking powder)
pinch salt
2 oz. sugar
2 oz. margarine or cooking fat
1 egg
1 good tablespoon treacle
4 – 6 oz. dried fruit
¼ pint milk

1 Sieve flour, salt and baking powder. Add sugar.
2 Rub in margarine or fat, add egg, treacle and fruit and stir in milk to give very sticky consistency, but one that drops easily from palette knife.
3 Put in greased and floured 1½ – 2 lb. loaf tin.
4 Bake in centre of moderate oven (375°F.—Gas Mark 4) for approximately 1 hour, look after 40 minutes and if browning too quickly reduce heat slightly.

Walnut bread

cooking time approximately 35 minutes

you will need:

8 oz. flour (with plain flour use 2 teaspoons baking powder)
2 oz. margarine
2 – 3 oz. sugar
4 oz. chopped walnuts
1 teaspoon grated lemon rind, optional
2 eggs (1 egg could be used)
milk to mix

1 Sieve the flour and baking powder, if used.
2 Rub in margarine.
3 Add sugar, walnuts, lemon rind and beaten eggs.
4 Gradually stir in enough milk to make a sticky consistency.
5 Put into well-greased and floured loaf tin.
6 Bake for about 35 minutes in centre of moderately hot oven (400°F.—Gas Mark 5).

Variations:

Almond bread

Use 7 oz. flour and 1 oz. ground almonds in place of 8 oz. flour, and 3 – 4 oz. chopped blanched almonds in place of walnuts.

Hazelnut bread

Use 4 oz. hazelnuts in place of walnuts. Heat the hazelnuts in the oven for a few minutes until you can rub off the skins, then use in place of the walnuts, chopping them rather coarsely.

Peanut bread

Use 2 – 4 oz. shelled peanuts in place of walnuts, and orange rind is nicer with these in place of lemon.

Walnut and treacle bread

cooking time 40 minutes – 1 hour

you will need:

1 lb. plain flour
¼ teaspoon salt
4 level teaspoons baking powder
2 oz. fat
2 tablespoons black treacle
6 oz. chopped walnuts
approximately ⅜ pint milk

1 Sieve together the dry ingredients.
2 Rub in the fat.
3 Add the treacle, nuts and enough milk to give a soft consistency.
4 Put into well-greased tin or two small tins.
5 Bake for approximately 40 minutes for the smaller loaves or 1 hour for the larger loaf in the centre of a moderate oven (375°F.—Gas Mark 4).
6 Test if cooked by pressing firmly on top, and seeing if well shrunk away from the sides of the tin.

South African clove bread

cooking time 45 minutes

you will need:

8 oz. flour
good pinch salt
1 teaspoon baking powder
¼ teaspoon ground cloves and cinnamon mixed
1 oz. butter
1 oz. sugar
⅜ pint milk or sour milk

1 Sieve together the flour, salt, baking powder and spices.
2 Rub in the butter, add sugar and gradually add the milk.
3 When the dough is smooth, grease a loaf tin and put in the mixture, prick a pattern on the top, and bake in a moderately hot oven (400°F.—Gas Mark 5) for about 45 minutes until just brown and slightly crusty on top.

Scones

This chapter contains both savoury and sweet scones. You will find a savoury scone is an ideal change from cutting sandwiches, for you can serve them with cheese. They are also useful to take out on a picnic.

A good home-made scone is probably one of the most delicious of all things to make for tea. Although they appear so simple, some people have a certain amount of difficulty in getting a really good result with a scone. Here are the important points to watch.

1. Use the right amount of raising agent. As you will see from the basic plain scone recipe this is a fairly high proportion.
2. Handle the mixture as you rub in the margarine, or whatever fat you have used, very little, so that you do get as much air into the mixture as possible.
3. Always use enough liquid to make the mixture considerably softer than pastry. As you gather it together in the bowl, the mixture should leave the bowl clean but your fingers will, and should, get slightly sticky.
4. Turn on to a lightly floured board and roll or pat as quickly as possible. Over-rolling is NOT to be recommended with scones.
   Many people do not use a rolling pin, they simply flatten the dough with the palm of their hand and then cut into the desired shapes.
5. Because a scone dough is not a rich one the scones should be baked near the top of a hot oven. To test if they are cooked, press your fingers firmly on the sides of the scone and if no batter oozes out they are then ready.
6. Scones should be made the day they are to be eaten, although any left can be freshened by re-heating for a short time in the oven.

Shapes to cut scones

The dough for the scones is generally rolled to a minimum of ½ inch unless it is being cooked on a griddle, when it needs to be approximately ¼ inch in thickness.

Although there are no hard and fast rules, sweet scones are generally cut into rounds with a fluted cutter or into triangles, whereas savoury scones are cut with a plain cutter. When the round shapes have been cut, gather the pieces left, knead lightly together to give a smooth dough, and as quickly as possible roll or pat out again and cut into the same shape. The quickest way to cut out a batch, however, is to form the dough into a round, and then to mark in triangles.

A complete scone round looks most attractive and to produce this, form the dough into a round. Transfer it to the baking tray, and mark into segments but do not cut completely through the dough. In this way the segments are easily broken apart to serve but you have your complete round to lift off the tin.

Because it is more difficult for the heat to penetrate into the dough in this way, allow a little longer cooking time, i.e. nearly 20 minutes instead of approximately 10 – 15 minutes as normally allowed for scones, and since the dough is more substantial, it is advisable to put it slightly lower in the oven.

To prepare tins for scones

When you are making a plain scone there is no need to grease the tin at all.

Some people like to flour the tin lightly for plain scones which gives a floury base to the scone when it is cooked, but this is not essential.

If the mixture contains syrup, honey or treacle, oatmeal or rolled oats, rather sticky fruit like glacé cherries, or cheese it is advisable to grease the tin lightly and flour on top, because all these ingredients have a tendency to make food stick.

To delay cooking of scones

It is not a good thing to make a tray of scones and leave them in the warmth of the room before cooking, but if you wish to get them made earlier, you can do this if you cover them and put them in a refrigerator for a few hours.

Plain scones

cooking time approximately 10 minutes

you will need:

8 oz. flour (with plain flour use either 4 level teaspoons baking powder OR 1 level teaspoon cream of tartar and ½ teaspoon bicarbonate of soda. With self-raising flour use ½ above quantity, if liked)
good pinch salt
1 – 2 oz. margarine
1 oz. sugar
milk to mix

1. Sieve together flour, salt, bicarbonate of soda and cream of tartar into a bowl.
2. Rub in margarine.
3. Add sugar.
4. Mix to a SOFT rolling consistency with the milk.
5. Roll out and cut into required shapes.
6. Put on to an ungreased tin, unless cheese, oatmeal or treacle are in the ingredients.
7. Bake near top of very hot oven (475°F.—Gas Mark 8) for approximately 10 minutes.
8. To test if cooked press firmly at the sides. Scones are cooked when they feel firm to the touch.

Note:

If using sour milk, which is excellent for making scones, then omit cream of tartar, or if using baking powder use half quantity only.

Variations on plain scone dough:

Brown scones

Use half wholemeal and half white flour.

Coconut scones

Add 2 oz. finely grated fresh or desiccated coconut to the flour.

Coffee scones

Blend the dough with a little strong coffee as well as milk. You can use this coffee flavouring with fruit or nut scones.

Cherry scones

Add 2 – 3 oz. finely chopped glacé cherries to the flour. Grease the tins well as the cherries may stick at the bottom.

Cherry and pineapple scones

Add 1 – 2 oz. finely chopped glacé cherries and the same amount of glacé pineapple to the flour. Grease the tins well.

Currant scones

Add 2 – 4 oz. currants to the flour. If the fruit is rather dry soak for about 15 minutes in 2 tablespoons of the milk, which should be warmed.

Date scones

Add 2 – 3 oz. finely chopped MOIST dates to the flour. Do not soak as currants.

Ginger scones

Sieve about ½ teaspoon powdered ginger with the flour and add about 1½ – 2 oz. finely chopped crystallized ginger if liked.

Griddle or girdle scones

Use any of the recipes given, but roll out the dough to only ¼ inch in thickness. Cook as the other griddle scones, see page 67.

Honey scones

Omit the sugar and add 1 – 2 tablespoons honey before adding the milk.

Honey spiced scones

Mixed spice, cinnamon, nutmeg all blend well with honey, so sieve ½ – 1 teaspoon with the flour.

Lemon scones

Add the finely grated rind of 1 – 2 lemons to the flour. Blend with the juice of the fruit before adding the milk. Either add 1 – 2 oz. chopped crystallized lemon peel or marmalade, the sugar could then be omitted.

Marmalade scones

Any flavoured marmalade could be used instead of sugar in the scone dough.

Nut scones

Add about 2 oz. chopped nuts to the flour.

Oatmeal scones

You can use either 4 oz. medium or fine oatmeal and 4 oz. flour or a rather smaller proportion of oatmeal. Use a very good pinch extra sugar, also generous pinch salt.

Orange scones

Add the finely grated rind of 1 or 2 oranges. Blend with the juice of the fruit before adding the milk. Either add 1 – 2 oz. chopped crystallized orange peel or marmalade, the sugar could then be omitted.

Potato scones

Use 2 – 4 oz. floury sieved potato instead of the same amount of flour. Ideally the potato should be freshly cooked, it is the best texture if baked in its jacket then sieved. If using a little mashed potato then blend very well with the flour before adding the milk.

Rich scones

The dough can be made richer by adding little extra fat, using butter instead of margarine. Do not however increase the amount of fat too much otherwise you loose the light texture of the scone. You can bind with egg or egg yolk and a little milk. To use more than one egg will tend to give a rather 'cakey' texture to the scones.

Raisin scones

Add 2 – 4 oz. raisins to the flour.

Sultana scones

Add 2 – 4 oz. sultanas to the flour. All dried fruit can be added to nuts and peel.

Treacle scones

Add 1 – 2 tablespoons black treacle to the dough before adding the milk, and omit the sugar. Some people find all black treacle too strong, so you could use 1 tablespoon black treacle and 1 tablespoon golden syrup.

Wholemeal scones

Use all wholemeal (stone ground) flour instead of white flour.

Savoury variations on plain scone dough:

In every case the sugar is omitted from the dough. The salt is increased slightly, except in anchovy scones.

Anchovy scones

Either blend about 1 teaspoon anchovy essence with the milk before mixing or add 3 – 4 finely chopped anchovies to the flour.

Cheese scones

Add good pinches salt, celery salt, pepper and mustard to the flour. Add 2 – 4 oz. finely grated cheese after rubbing in the margarine.

Ham scones

Add 2 – 4 oz. finely chopped ham to the flour.

Herb scones

Add 1 – 2 teaspoons dried herbs to the flour or up to 1 tablespoon finely chopped fresh herbs.

Savoury griddle scones

Make in the same way as sweet ones, adding herbs or cheese to flavour.

Savoury oatmeal scones

Use same proportions of oatmeal as sweet scones and flavour with plenty of seasoning and herbs.

Savoury potato scones

Use same proportion of potato as sweet scones. These are particularly good flavoured with herbs.

Savoury brown or wholemeal scones

Make using either half wholemeal and half white flour or all wholemeal flour. These can be flavoured with cheese, herbs, ham or anchovy as suggested above.

Donside scones

cooking time 10 minutes

you will need:

4 oz. flour (with plain flour use 1 teaspoon baking powder)
4 oz. fine oatmeal
2 oz. butter
1 teaspoon sugar
milk to mix

Use the method for plain scones, see page 58.

Plain feather-light scones

cooking time 10 minutes

you will need:

8 oz. flour (with plain flour use 2 level teaspoons baking powder)
pinch salt
1½ oz. margarine
1½ oz. sugar
milk to mix

1. Sieve flour, baking powder, if used, and salt together into a bowl.
2. Rub in margarine, add sugar and enough milk to make *sticky* rolling consistency.
3. Roll out, cut into rounds and bake for 10 minutes on ungreased tin near top of hot oven (450°F.—Gas Mark 7).
4. Brush lightly with milk just before scones are cooked for a soft top.

Variations:

Cream scones

Use butter instead of margarine and mix with top-of-the-milk cream or fresh or canned cream. Delicious with lemon curd.

Orange scones

Add rind of 1 or 2 oranges. Mix with orange juice instead of milk *or* ½ milk and ½ juice. Serve with orange curd.

Sour milk scones

Use plain flour and ½ level teaspoon bicarbonate of soda and mix with sour milk.

Almond scones

cooking time 10 minutes

you will need:

ingredients for plain scones, see page 58
extra 1 oz. sugar
3 oz. blanched almonds
almond essence

1. Use the method for plain scones.
2. Stir a few drops of almond essence into the dough.
3. Sprinkle a few chopped almonds on top of each scone before baking.

Biscuit scones

cooking time 10 – 15 minutes

you will need:

8 oz. flour (with plain flour use 4 level teaspoons baking powder, with self-raising flour 2 level teaspoons baking powder)
¼ teaspoon salt
3 oz. fat or margarine
milk to mix

1. Sieve dry ingredients, rub in fat and mix to a soft dough with milk.
2. Roll out about ¾ inch thick and cut with floured cutter.
3. Place on a baking tin and bake in a hot oven (450°F.—Gas Mark 7) for 10 – 15 minutes.

Variations:

Fruit biscuit scones

Add 2 oz. dried fruit, raisins or dates.

Cheese biscuit scones

Add 2 oz. grated cheese.

Bacon biscuit scones

Add 2 oz. chopped cooked bacon.

Onion biscuit scones

Add 1 fried, chopped onion.

Curried biscuit scones

Sieve a teaspoon curry powder with flour.

Orange or lemon biscuit scones

Before baking press a lump of sugar that has been soaked in orange or lemon juice on to each biscuit scone.

Butter scones

cooking time about 10 minutes

you will need:

8 oz. flour (with plain flour use 3 level teaspoons baking powder)
pinch salt
2 oz. butter
1 oz. sugar
4 oz. mixed dried fruit
milk to mix

1 Sieve the flour, baking powder and salt together.
2 Rub the fat in the flour.
3 Add the sugar, dried fruit and enough milk to make a *soft* rolling consistency. The secret of good scones is to have a *soft* dough.
4 Roll out on a lightly floured board, cut into shapes, these should be about ¾ - 1-inch thick, and put on to ungreased baking trays.
5 Bake *at once* near the top of a really hot oven (450 - 475°F.—Gas Mark 7 - 8) for approximately 10 minutes.

Variations:

Raisin and treacle butter scones
Omit the sugar, use 1 tablespoon treacle and 4 oz. raisins.

Date and orange butter scones
Add 4 - 6 oz. chopped dates, grated rind and juice 1 orange.

Orange butter scones
Add 4 oz. crystallized orange peel, and top with sugar and finely grated orange rind before baking.

Butterscotch orange scones

cooking time 15 minutes

you will need:

12 oz. flour (with plain flour use 3 level teaspoons baking powder)
2 oz. butter
1 oz. castor sugar
grated rind 1 orange
1 egg
about 6 tablespoons milk

For filling:
2 heaped tablespoons orange marmalade
2 oz. currants

For topping:
1 oz. melted butter
1 oz. brown sugar

1 Sift the flour, rub in the butter and stir in the castor sugar and orange rind.
2 Add the beaten egg and milk, mixing to a soft, but not sticky, dough.
3 Turn out on to a floured board, knead lightly to a smooth ball; roll to a rectangle about 12 × 9 inches.
4 Spread with marmalade, not quite to the edge, and sprinkle with currants. Roll up like a Swiss roll. Cut into thick slices.
5 Pour the melted butter into a shallow square or round cake tin, about 8 inches across. Butter sides and sprinkle bottom with brown sugar. Arrange scones in tin, not quite touching each other.
6 Bake near top of a hot oven (450°F.—Gas Mark 7) for 15 minutes.

Variation:

Butterscotch sultana scones

Add approximately 3 oz. sultanas to the orange marmalade.

Butterscotch whirls

cooking time 10 minutes

you will need:

use ingredients for plain scones,* see page 58
1 - 1¼ oz. butter or margarine
1 oz. currants
1 oz. brown sugar

* Use any of the scone recipes with this butterscotch filling

1 Use the method for plain scones.
2 Roll out scone dough to neat oblong shape.
3 Spread with butter.
4 Add currants and sugar.
5 Roll up like a Swiss roll. Cut into ½-inch slices.
6 Put on greased baking tin and bake for 10 minutes near top of hot oven (450°F.—Gas Mark 7).

Butterscotch scones

cooking time 10 minutes

you will need:

use ingredients for plain scones, see page 58	1 oz. margarine
	2 oz. brown sugar

1 Use the method for plain scones, then roll to half the usual thickness. Cut into rounds.
2 Spread half the rounds with margarine and sprinkle generously with brown sugar. Be careful to keep away from the edges.
3 Cover with remaining rounds and press together the edges. Place on a baking tray.
4 Bake near the top of a very hot oven (475°F.—Gas Mark 8).

Honey and cherry scones

cooking time 10 minutes

you will need:

8 oz. plain flour*	1½ oz. margarine
4 level teaspoons baking powder	2 tablespoons honey
pinch salt	3 oz. glacé cherries
	milk to mix

* If self-raising flour use half quantity baking powder

1 Sieve dry ingredients into a bowl.
2 Rub in margarine.
3 Add honey, chopped glacé cherries and enough milk to bind, or make soft rolling consistency.
4 If baking in the oven roll out to at least ½ inch thick.
5 Cut into rounds.
6 Bake for 10 minutes near the top of very hot oven (475°F.—Gas Mark 8).
7 If using a griddle, then roll to ¼ inch thick and cut into rounds.
8 Cook for about 4 minutes steadily on one side.
9 Turn and cook for about the same time on the other side.
10 Split and spread with butter.

Variations:

Honey and ginger scones

Use 2 – 3 oz. chopped crystallized ginger in place of glacé cherries. A little powdered ginger could be sieved with the flour, if liked.

Honey and orange scones

Add 2 – 3 oz. chopped crystallized orange peel in place of glacé cherries. Add the grated rind of an orange to the flour and margarine. You can mix with milk and orange juice in place of all milk.

Honey and sultana scones

Use 3 oz. sultanas in place of glacé cherries.

Honey fruit whirl

cooking time 30 – 35 minutes

you will need:

1 lb. flour (with plain flour use 4 level teaspoons baking powder)	*For filling:*
¼ teaspoon salt	2 tablespoons clear honey
4 oz. butter	2 medium-sized apples, about 12 oz.
3 oz. castor sugar	6 oz. raisins (or sultanas and currants or mixed fruit and peel)
3 eggs	
approximately 8 tablespoons milk	

1 Sift flour and salt into a bowl.
2 Rub in butter and add sugar.
3 Mix to a soft but not sticky dough with beaten eggs and milk.
4 Knead lightly on a floured board and roll to an oblong of about ¼ inch thickness.
5 Spread with honey to about 1 inch from edges.
6 Peel, core and grate apples and de-seed and chop raisins.
7 Sprinkle apple and raisins over honey.
8 Moisten edges with water and roll up like a Swiss roll starting at one of the longer edges.
9 Twist into a ring, pinching moistened ends together.
10 Lift on to a greased baking tray and with kitchen scissors snip halfway through at 1-inch intervals.
11 Bake near the top of a moderately hot oven (400°F.—Gas Mark 5) for 30 – 35 minutes.
12 Serve in slices with butter.

Cheese and apple scone

cooking time 20 – 25 minutes

you will need:

8 oz. flour (with plain flour use 2 level teaspoons baking powder)
good pinch salt
pepper
2 oz. butter or margarine
3 oz. grated cheese
milk

For topping:
3 – 4 eating apples
2 oz. brown sugar
1 oz. butter
cinnamon or spice or powdered cloves to taste

1. Sieve flour, salt and pepper.
2. Rub in butter, add grated cheese and mix with enough milk to give a soft rolling consistency.
3. Knead lightly, roll out and line an 8-inch sandwich tin or small Swiss roll tin with the mixture. The tin should be well-greased.
4. Peel and slice the apples, arrange on top of the dough.
5. Cover with sugar, melted butter and a light sprinkling of spice.
6. Bake for approximately 20 – 25 minutes above the centre of a hot oven (425°F.—Gas Mark 6).
7. Serve hot or cold, but eat on day of making, topped with knob of butter.

Herb scones

cooking time 12 minutes

you will need:

8 oz. self-raising flour
½ level teaspoon salt
2 oz. margarine
1 level teaspoon mixed herbs
approximately 6 tablespoons cold milk to mix

1. Sift flour and salt into a bowl.
2. Rub in margarine, add herbs, then mix to a soft, but not sticky, dough with the milk.
3. Turn out on a lightly floured board, knead quickly until smooth, then roll out to about ½ inch thickness.
4. Cut into four rounds with a 3½ - 4-inch plain cutter or press dough to round shape and cut across into four or six triangles.
5. Transfer to a greased baking sheet. Brush tops with milk then bake towards top of hot oven (450°F.—Gas Mark 7) for 12 minutes.
6. Split open while hot and serve with butter and Cheddar cheese or with a casserole of steak or lamb.

Hot salad scones

cooking time approximately 12 minutes

you will need:

8 oz. self-raising flour
½ level teaspoon salt
½ level teaspoon dry mustard
2 oz. butter or margarine
2 oz. strong Cheddar or Parmesan cheese
1 tablespoon finely chopped onion
7 or 8 tablespoons cold milk
celery salt

1. Sift dry ingredients into a bowl and rub in fat.
2. Add half the grated cheese and the onion.
3. Mix to a soft but not sticky dough with the milk.
4. Turn out on to a floured board, knead quickly and lightly until smooth, then press to a round about 1 inch thick, shaping the round with the edges of the hand.
5. Cut across into eight or ten wedges and transfer to a baking sheet, fitting scones back into a round.
6. Brush tops with milk and sprinkle with remainder of cheese and celery salt.
7. Bake towards top of hot oven (450 - 475°F.—Gas Mark 7 – 8) for approximately 12 minutes.
8. Serve freshly baked with butter and salad.

Irish fadge

cooking time 15 minutes

you will need:

6 oz. wholemeal flour
2 oz. white flour (with plain flour use 1½ level teaspoons baking powder, with self-raising flour use 1 teaspoon only)
½ level teaspoon bicarbonate of soda
good pinch salt
2 – 3 oz. dripping or lard and dripping mixed
1 egg
1 teaspoon vinegar

1. Sieve all the dry ingredients together.
2. Rub in the dripping or dripping and lard. The mixture gives a better result.
3. Blend the egg and vinegar and mix the dough with this.
4. If the egg is small you may need a little milk, but this should be a firm dough.
5. Roll out to about ½ inch thick, cut into triangles and bake for approximately 15 minutes near the top of a hot oven (425 - 450°F.—Gas Mark 6 – 7).

Nut scone whirls

cooking time 15 – 20 minutes

you will need:

- 8 oz. flour (with plain flour use 4 level teaspoons baking powder)
- ¼ teaspoon salt
- ¼ teaspoon mustard
- 2 oz. butter or margarine
- 1 egg
- milk

For filling:

- 1 oz. butter
- 2 tablespoons chopped nuts

1. Sieve dry ingredients together, then rub in butter.
2. Mix to a soft dough with the egg and milk.
3. Roll out on a floured board to a rectangle about 8 × 12 inches. Spread with the softened butter and chopped nuts, then roll up like a Swiss roll.
4. Cut into twelve or thirteen slices, and arrange in well-greased 8-inch sandwich tins.
5. Bake in the centre of a hot oven (450°F.—Gas Mark 7) for 15 – 20 minutes. Serve hot or cold.

Variations:

Cheese nut whirls

Add 2 oz. grated cheese to the flour and butter.

Parsley cheese whirls

Add 2 oz. grated cheese and 1 oz. chopped parsley to the flour and butter.

Oatmeal scones

cooking time 10 minutes

you will need:

- 1 oz. margarine
- 2 oz. fine oatmeal
- 2 oz. medium oatmeal
- 1 teaspoon baking powder
- good teaspoon sugar
- pinch salt
- milk to mix

1. Rub margarine into the fine oatmeal.
2. Add other ingredients.
3. Work in sufficient milk to give soft rolling consistency.
4. Roll to ½ inch thick, cut into shapes.
5. Bake on lightly greased tin for 10 minutes, near top of hot oven (450 – 475°F.—Gas Mark 7 – 8).

Note:

More sugar can be added if liked, or omit sugar and add 1 oz. finely grated cheese and plenty of seasoning.

Pineapple scones

cooking time 15 – 20 minutes

you will need:

- 8 oz. plain flour
- 4 level teaspoons baking powder
- pinch salt
- 2 oz. margarine
- 1 small can pineapple chunks
- milk to mix

1. Sieve together flour, baking powder and salt.
2. Lightly rub in margarine until mixture resembles fine crumbs.
3. Strain the pineapple, reserving the juice. This can be used for jelly or a drink.
4. Chop the chunks into small pieces.
5. Add half the chunks to the mixture and mix to a soft dough with the milk.
6. Roll out on to a floured board to ½-inch thickness. Cut into rounds with a 2-inch biscuit cutter.
7. Place on baking tray. Bake 15 – 20 minutes near top of a moderately hot oven (400°F.—Gas Mark 5).
8. Cool on a wire tray.
9. Split open, spread with butter, fill with remaining chunks.

Potato scones

cooking time approximately 10 – 12 minutes

you will need:

- 8 oz. freshly boiled potatoes
- 4 oz. flour (with plain flour use 2 level teaspoons baking powder, with self-raising flour use 1 level teaspoon baking powder)
- salt
- 2 oz. melted butter or margarine
- 1 egg

1. Mash or sieve the potatoes while they are still hot.
2. Add them to the flour and salt, also the melted butter.
3. Mix well, add enough of the beaten egg to make a stiff mixture.
4. Roll out to about ¾-inch thickness, cut into rounds or triangles.
5. Put on a baking sheet or greased dish and bake near the top of a hot oven (450°F.—Gas Mark 7) until they are golden brown, approximately 10 – 12 minutes.
6. Serve hot, split, with plenty of butter.

Variation:

Sweet potato scones

Add 2 oz. sugar and 2 oz. sultanas.

Savoury potato cheese scones

cooking time 10 – 12 minutes

you will need:

- 1 teaspoon yeast extract
- good ¼ pint milk and water
- 8 oz. mashed potatoes (use when freshly boiled as they are softer and more floury)
- 4 oz. flour (with plain flour use 2 level teaspoons baking powder, with self-raising flour use 1 level teaspoon baking powder)
- 2 oz. melted butter or margarine
- 2 oz. finely grated cheese
- salt
- 1 egg

1. Heat the yeast extract with the milk and water, then stir in the mashed potatoes.
2. Cool slightly, then add the flour, melted butter, cheese and salt.
3. Mix well, then add enough beaten egg to give a stiff mixture.
4. Roll out to about ¾ inch in thickness on a well floured pastry board. Cut into rounds and triangles.
5. Brush with the rest of the egg to give an attractive glaze, and bake near top of hot oven (450°F.—Gas Mark 7) until they are golden brown, approximately 10 – 12 minutes.
6. Serve hot, split, with plenty of butter.

Variation:

Potato cheese scones

Omit the yeast extract and sieve a good pinch of salt, pepper and mustard with the flour.

Syrup raisin scones

cooking time 10 minutes

you will need:

- 8 oz. flour (with plain flour use 2 teaspoons baking powder)
- 1 level teaspoon spice
- pinch salt
- ½ teaspoon bicarbonate soda
- 1 oz. fat
- 2 tablespoons golden syrup
- 2 tablespoons raisins
- milk

1. Sieve dry ingredients together and rub in fat.
2. Add syrup, fruit and milk.
3. Roll out and cut into rounds.
4. Bake for 10 minutes in a hot oven (450°F.—Gas Mark 7).
5. Spread with butter when cold. These scones are delicious toasted and eaten hot.

Treacle raisin scones

cooking time 10 minutes

you will need:

- 8 oz. flour (with plain flour use 2 teaspoons baking powder)
- 1 level teaspoon spice
- pinch salt
- ½ teaspoon bicarbonate soda
- 1 oz. fat
- 2 tablespoons treacle
- 2 tablespoons raisins
- milk

1. Sieve dry ingredients together, rub in the fat.
2. Add treacle, fruit and milk.
3. Roll out and cut into rounds.
4. Bake for 10 minutes in a hot oven (450°F.—Gas Mark 7)
5. Spread with butter when cold. These scones are delicious toasted and eaten hot.

Walnut scones

cooking time 10 minutes

you will need:

- 8 oz. flour (with plain flour use either 4 level teaspoons baking powder OR 1 level teaspoon cream of tartar and ½ teaspoon bicarbonate of soda. With self-raising flour you can use half quantity if liked)
- good pinch salt
- 1 – 2 oz. margarine
- 2 oz. sugar
- 4 oz. chopped walnuts
- milk to mix

1. Sieve together flour, bicarbonate of soda, cream of tartar and salt.
2. Rub in margarine.
3. Add sugar and chopped walnuts.
4. Mix to a SOFT rolling consistency with the milk.
5. Roll out and cut into required shapes.
6. Put on to an ungreased tin and bake near the top of a very hot oven (475°F.—Gas Mark 8) for approximately 10 minutes. To test if cooked press firmly at the sides. Scones are cooked when they feel firm to the touch.

Note:

If using sour milk, which is excellent for making scones, then omit cream of tartar, or if using baking powder use half quantity only.

Wheatmeal and syrup spoon scones

cooking time 12 – 15 minutes

you will need:

6 oz. plain white flour
level teaspoon salt
2 oz. granulated sugar
1 level teaspoon bicarbonate of soda
2 level teaspoons cream of tartar
10 oz. plain wholemeal flour
2 oz. margarine
1 tablespoon golden syrup
scant ½ pint milk

1 Sieve together the plain flour, salt, sugar, bicarbonate of soda and cream of tartar. Blend in the wholemeal flour.
2 Rub in the fat.
3 Mix the syrup and milk and stir into the flour, mixing with a round topped knife to a heavy dropping consistency.
4 Drop spoonfuls of the mix on to an baking tray dusted with wholemeal flour. Brush lightly with milk and dredge tops with flour or rolled oats.
5 Bake towards the top of a hot oven (450°F.—Gas Mark 7) for about 12 - 15 minutes. Serve freshly baked with butter. This makes a large quantity of scones and they can be heated for a few minutes to freshen.

Variation:

Fruit spoon scones

Use a mixture of wholemeal and white flour or all white flour, with 4 oz. dried fruit.

Wheatmeal spoon scones

cooking time about 12 minutes

you will need:

5 oz. wholemeal flour
3 oz. plain flour*
¼ level teaspoon salt
1 oz. sugar
½ level teaspoon bicarbonate soda
1 level teaspoon cream of tartar
1 oz. margarine
½ tablespoon black treacle
1 egg, optional
just under ½ pint milk

* If using self-raising flour use little less bicarbonate soda and cream of tartar

1 Sieve together the flours, salt, sugar, bicarbonate of soda and cream of tartar.
2 Rub in the margarine, add the treacle and mix with the egg and milk to a thick batter consistency.
3 Dust a baking tray or trays with wholemeal flour and drop spoonfuls of the batter on to this, allowing a certain amount of space between them.
4 Brush the tops with milk and sprinkle with flour.
5 Bake towards the top of a very hot oven (475°F.—Gas Mark 8) for approximately 12 minutes.
6 These are equally good with savoury or sweet accompaniments.

Variations:

Spoon scones

Use all white flour.

Raisin spoon scones

Add 2 - 3 oz. raisins.

Griddle Scones, Pancakes and Crumpets

Any scones, as well as the ones in the special recipes in this section, can be cooked on a griddle instead of in the oven.
These are the important points to remember.

1 The dough can be a little firmer but not too soft. If it is too soft the scones are difficult to turn and they tend to spread out and look untidy.
2 Always roll the scone dough much more thinly than for ones being cooked in the oven for you are cooking on direct heat and it is very easy to brown, or even burn too much, on the outside before the scone is completely cooked through to the centre.

To cook scones and breads on a griddle

Some of the earliest forms of cooking were done on flat stones and even today there are many recipes that are not cooked in the oven, but on a griddle, a girdle or a bake stone as it is known in various parts of the country. If you do not possess this particular cooking equipment, then you can make do by using the solid hot plate on a cooker or the clean base of a really HEAVY frying pan, but as a griddle is not a very expensive item and with careful use lasts for many years, it is a good investment.

To season a new griddle

Heat gently, and rub very well with oil or lard. Do not rub this off but allow griddle to stand for 24 hours slightly greasy. Wipe off the next day and it is ready to use.

Always heat the griddle reasonably steadily so that you have an even heat. If it is too hot, you set the outside of the pancake, or scone, too quickly and the heat cannot penetrate through to the centre without burning on the outside.

To prepare a griddle for cooking

Rub over with either a greasy piece of greaseproof paper, or with a pastry brush dipped in hot melted fat or oil. Do this lightly otherwise the heat can scorch the tips of the pastry brush and the bristles will fall out. Another way of greasing would be to push a fine skewer through a piece of suet and rub this over the griddle. The heat is unexpectedly great, so be careful that your fingers do not become burnt.

To test the heat of a griddle

Shake a little flour over the griddle. If it turns golden brown within approximately ½ minute it is the right heat for the pancake type of scones, but too hot for the more solid type of scone or Welsh tea cake. The flour should take 1 minute to brown for this particular type.

To cook on the bottom of a frying pan

If a frying pan is very thick you can use the base of this as if you were frying, with the exception that you do not use a great deal of fat. If the frying pan is light weight, it will not be found satisfactory because it will brown too quickly. Should your frying pan be in very good condition, i.e. the bottom kept very clean, the most satisfactory way to use it is to turn the pan upside down and actually cook on the base of the pan. You must keep the heat very low, otherwise you will spoil the inner surface for future frying.

To wrap up pancakes

The pancake type of scone should always be wrapped when cooked to prevent the outside curling or drying. Lay a clean tea cloth over the cooling tray and as the scones are cooked lay them carefully on this and fold the tea cloth over.

Drop scones or Scotch pancakes I

cooking time 4 – 5 minutes

you will need:

8 oz. plain flour
1 level teaspoon bicarbonate of soda
2 level teaspoons cream of tartar
pinch salt
2 oz. castor sugar
1 oz. whipped-up cooking fat or margarine
1 egg
12 tablespoons milk

1. Sieve all the dry ingredients into a basin.
2. Rub in the whipped-up cooking fat until the mixture resembles fine breadcrumbs.
3. Beat in the egg and two-thirds of the milk and stir until the mixture is smooth.
4. Stir in the remaining milk to make a batter the consistency of thick cream.
5. Lightly brush a hot girdle or electric hot plate with melted cooking fat and drop the batter on in dessertspoonfuls, well apart.
6. Cook over a gentle heat and when the bubbles rise to the surface of the scones turn over with a palette knife and cook the other sides. When the second sides are golden brown and the edges are dry, the scones are cooked.
7. Cool in a folded tea towel on a cake rack.

Drop scones or Scotch pancakes 2

cooking time 4 minutes

you will need:

4 oz. flour (with plain flour use either 2 teaspoons baking powder or ½ small teaspoon bicarbonate soda and 1 small teaspoon cream of tartar)
pinch salt
1 oz. sugar
1 egg
¼ pint milk
1 oz. melted margarine, optional

1 Sieve together all the dry ingredients.
2 Beat in the egg, then milk.
3 Stir in melted margarine. This is not essential but helps to keep scones moist.
4 Grease and warm the girdle, electric hot plate or frying pan. It is best to use the bottom of the frying pan, the part that usually goes over the heat.
5 To test if correct heat, drop a teaspoonful of mixture on this and if it goes golden brown within a 1 minute the plate is ready. Drop dessertspoonfuls of the batter on to the plate.
6 Cook for about 2 minutes on either side.
7 To test whether cooked press firmly with back of knife and if no batter comes from sides and scones feel firm cool on wire sieve.

Variations:

Rich Scotch pancakes

Use 2 eggs and add 1 oz. melted butter.

Spiced Scotch pancakes

Add ½ – 1 teaspoon mixed spice and ½ teaspoon cinnamon to flavour.

Nut Scotch pancakes

Add 2 oz. finely chopped nuts to batter.

Sultana Scotch pancakes

Add 2 oz. sultanas to mixture. If you allow these to stand in batter some little while before cooking they become softer.

Crumb drop scones

cooking time 5 minutes

you will need:

2 oz. flour (with plain flour use 1 teaspoon baking powder, with self-raising flour ½ teaspoon baking powder)
2 oz. crisp breadcrumbs or plain biscuit crumbs
pinch salt
1 egg
¼ pint milk

1 Use the method for Scotch pancakes, see page 67.
2 These have a delicious 'nutty' flavour with the combination of flour and crumbs.

Soft crumb drop scones

cooking time 5 minutes

you will need:

2 oz. flour (with plain flour use 1 teaspoon baking powder, with self-raising flour ½ teaspoon baking powder)
2 oz. soft fine breadcrumbs
pinch salt
1 oz. melted margarine
1 egg
scant ¼ pint milk

1 Mix all the ingredients together to a smooth batter.
2 Allow to stand at least 15 minutes.
3 Cook as Scotch pancakes, see page 67.

Rolled oat drop scones

cooking time 5 minutes

you will need:

2 oz. flour (with plain flour 1 teaspoon baking powder, with self-raising flour ½ teaspoon baking powder)
2 oz. rolled oats
pinch salt
1 oz. melted margarine
1 egg
scant ¼ pint milk

1 Mix all ingredients together to a smooth batter and allow to stand at least 15 minutes.
2 Cook as Scotch pancakes, see page 67.

Apple drop scones

cooking time 5 – 6 minutes

you will need:

4 oz. flour (with plain flour use 2 level teaspoons baking powder)
pinch salt
2 teaspoons sugar
1 medium-sized apple
1 egg
scant ¼ pint milk

1 Sieve flour, salt and sugar.
2 Beat in peeled and grated apple, egg and milk.
3 Beat well then drop in spoonfuls on hot greased griddle or frying pan.
4 Cook steadily until mixture is golden brown on under surface and bubbles, then turn and cook until firm.
5 Cool on tea towel over wire tray. Wrap until ready to serve with butter. Excellent with jam or bacon.

Variations:

Apple sultana drop scones

Add 2 oz. sultanas.

Spiced apple drop scones

Add a little spice to flour.

Cottage cheese griddle cakes

cooking time a few minutes

you will need:

1 oz. butter
4 oz. cottage or cream cheese
2 eggs
2 oz. flour (with plain flour use ½ teaspoon baking powder)
1 tablespoon milk

1 Melt the butter and add the cottage cheese.
2 Whisk the eggs and gradually beat into the cheese mixture.
3 Stir in the sieved flour and milk, mixing to a smooth thick batter.
4 Drop spoonfuls of the batter on to a hot greased griddle, heavy frying pan or hot plate.
5 Turn to brown on the other side.
6 Serve freshly cooked.
7 These are delicious with sugar and lemon juice, or with honey or strawberry jam.

Orange drop scones 1

cooking time 5 minutes

you will need:

4 oz. flour (with plain flour use 2 level teaspoons baking powder)
pinch salt
grated rind 1 large orange
1 egg
juice 1 large orange
milk to make ¼ pint

1 Sieve flour and salt.
2 Add orange rind and egg, then measure orange juice and add enough milk to make ¼ pint.
3 Beat together until smooth batter.
4 Cook as Scotch pancakes, see page 67.
5 Serve with butter, jam or marmalade.

Orange drop scones 2

cooking time 5 minutes

you will need:

4 oz. flour (with plain flour use 2 level teaspoons baking powder)
pinch salt
grated rind 1 large orange
1 egg
2 tablespoons marmalade
scant ¼ pint milk

1 Sieve flour and salt.
2 Add orange rind and egg, together with the marmalade, and add enough milk to make ¼ pint.
3 Beat together until smooth batter.
4 Cook as Scotch pancakes, see page 67.
5 Serve with butter.

Savoury Scotch pancakes

cooking time 4 minutes

you will need:

4 oz. flour (with plain flour use either 2 teaspoons baking powder OR ½ small teaspoon bicarbonate of soda and 1 small teaspoon cream of tartar)
pinch salt
pinch pepper and dry mustard
1 egg
¼ pint milk
1 oz. melted margarine, optional

1 Sieve together all the dry ingredients.
2 Beat in first the egg, then the milk.
3 Stir in melted margarine. This is not essential.
4 Grease and warm the griddle, electric hot plate or frying pan. It is best to use the bottom of the frying pan, the part that generally touches the heat.
5 To test if you have the correct heat, drop a teaspoon of the mixture on this, and if it goes golden brown within 1 minute, the plate is ready.
6 Drop spoonfuls of the batter on to the plate.
7 Cook for about 2 minutes.
8 Turn and cook on the other side.
9 They are cooked if no batter comes from the sides and the pancakes feel firm when pressed with the back of a knife.
10 Cool on a wire tray.

Singing hinnies

cooking time approximately 9 minutes

you will need:

8 oz. plain flour
1 oz. cornflour or rice flour
½ teaspoon salt
2 rounded teaspoons baking powder
1 oz. lard
2 oz. sugar
2 oz. currants
approximately ¼ pint milk

1 Sieve together all the dry ingredients.
2 Rub in the lard, add the sugar and dried fruit.
3 Work in the milk until a firm dough.
4 Shape into a large round, not too thick, and cut into triangles if liked.
5 Grease a griddle slightly and heat thoroughly. To test if this is ready, shake a little flour on the griddle, it should turn golden brown in one minute.
6 Cook the cake or cakes for about 2 minutes until browned on the under side, then turn them and cook on the other side for another 2 minutes.
7 Lower the heat and continue cooking for a further 5 minutes.
8 Split and serve buttered while still hot.

Treacle griddle scones

cooking time 2 – 4 minutes

you will need:

4 oz. self-raising flour (with plain flour, use 1 level teaspoon baking powder)
¼ level teaspoon salt
1 level teaspoon baking powder*
1 level dessertspoon castor sugar
1 egg
1 level tablespoon black treacle
scant ¼ pint milk

* With both plain and self-raising flour

1 Sift dry ingredients into a bowl.
2 Make a well in the centre. Drop in egg and treacle, then gradually mix to a thick batter with the milk, drawing in flour from sides of bowl.
3 Beat with the back of a wooden spoon till batter is smooth and creamy, then drop dessertspoonfuls on to a well-greased griddle, thick frying pan or hot plate of an electric cooker.
4 Cook for about 1 – 2 minutes on each side.
5 Pile scones in a folded napkin as they are cooked, then serve warm with butter.

Potato drop scones

cooking time approximately 5 minutes

you will need:

2 oz. flour (with plain flour use 1½ level teaspoons baking powder, with self-raising flour ¾ level teaspoon baking powder)
pinch salt
4 oz. very smooth mashed potato
1 oz. melted margarine
1 egg
¼ pint milk

1 Sieve flour, baking powder and salt.
2 Mix flour into potatoes very thoroughly.
3 Beat in melted margarine, egg and finally milk to give smooth thick batter.
4 Drop spoonfuls on to hot greased griddle plate or in frying pan and cook steadily until surface is golden brown and beginning to bubble on top.
5 Turn and cook on second side until cooked and set.
6 Keep well wrapped in cloth on cooling tray until ready to serve.
7 Serve with butter and jam, or with bacon.

Variations:

Sweet potato drop scones

Add 1 oz. sugar to ingredients.

Honey potato drop scones

Blend 1 heaped tablespoon honey with potato before adding flour.

Fluffy pancakes

cooking time 4 – 5 minutes

you will need:

2 eggs
4 oz. flour (with plain flour use 2 level teaspoons baking powder)
½ level teaspoon salt
1 level tablespoon castor sugar
¼ pint milk
1 tablespoon melted butter or vegetable oil

1 Start heating the pan or griddle gently.
2 Separate eggs from yolks and whisk egg whites until stiff.
3 Sift the flour, baking powder, salt and sugar into a mixing bowl.
4 Beat the egg yolks lightly and add the milk and melted fat.
5 Stir this liquid into the dry ingredients, stirring ONLY until the batter is mixed; do NOT beat.
6 Lightly fold in the whisked egg whites with a metal spoon.

7 When the griddle is hot enough (a drop of water on the griddle should spit and splutter) grease lightly and drop the batter on in tablespoons, allowing room for spreading.
8 In a minute or so, when puffed up and bubbly, flip the pancakes over and lightly brown the other side.
9 Serve the pancakes spread lightly with butter and then with warmed honey, maple syrup, golden syrup or jam, or try one of the following variations.

Variations:

Strawberry stacks

Arrange buttered pancakes in stacks of three with sliced strawberries between and on top.

Banana band wagons

Add a large banana, finely chopped, to the raw batter. When cooked serve with butter and cherry jam.

Nut pancakes

Add 1½ oz. finely chopped walnuts to the raw batter. When cooked top each pancake with butter and a trickle of honey.

German potato pancakes

cooking time 6 minutes

you will need:

- 4 oz. raw peeled potato
- 4 oz. flour (with plain flour use 1½ level teaspoons baking powder, with self-raising flour ¾ teaspoon baking powder)
- pinch salt
- 2 eggs
- 1 oz. melted margarine or fat
- just over ¼ pint milk

1 Grate potatoes straight into bowl, do not allow to stand any time otherwise mixture will discolour.
2 Add flour sieved with baking powder and salt.
3 Then beat in egg yolks, melted margarine or fat and milk.
4 Lastly fold in stiffly beaten egg whites.
5 Drop in spoonfuls on a hot greased griddle and cook steadily for about 3 minutes, turn and cook on second side for same time.
6 These are delicious with butter and cheese or bacon.

Welsh pancakes

These are generally made with the same recipe as the Scotch variety, but are slightly bigger in size. They are spread with butter and jam or honey and piled high, so you can cut them in wedges like a cake.

cooking time 2 – 4 minutes

you will need:

- 8 oz. flour (with plain flour use either 2 teaspoons baking powder OR ½ level teaspoon bicarbonate of soda, and 1 level teaspoon cream of tartar)
- pinch salt
- 2 eggs
- ½ pint milk or milk and water
- little fat

1 Sieve dry ingredients.
2 Gradually add eggs and milk and beat until a smooth batter.
3 Drop spoonfuls on to a hot greased griddle and cook for 1 or 2 minutes on the under side until golden brown.
4 Turn and cook on the second side.
5 To keep moist, wrap in a clean cloth.

Variations:

Fruit and spice Welsh pancakes

Add about 2 oz. sultanas and pinch mixed spice. If the sultanas are rather dry, soak in the milk for a few minutes.

Orange or lemon Welsh pancakes

Add grated orange or lemon rind and use a little fruit juice as well as milk, reducing milk to give a total ½ pint liquid.

Honey Welsh pancakes

Blend 1 good tablespoon honey with the batter.

Ginger Welsh pancakes

Sieve 1 teaspoon powdered ginger with the flour, add 1 – 2 tablespoons finely chopped candied ginger.

Potato Welsh pancakes

Use 4 oz. flour and 4 oz. smooth mashed potato. If using plain flour, add 2 teaspoons baking powder. If using self-raising flour, use 1 teaspoon baking powder.

Chapati (*Indian bread*)

cooking time 3 – 4 minutes

you will need:

wholemeal flour
water

1 This hand made bread is made with wholemeal flour and water.
2 Work to a stiff dough.
3 Divide into lumps the size of a large egg.
4 Roll out thinly to the size and shape of a pancake and bake on a griddle or an iron plate.
5 It is pressed with a cloth before being removed from the griddle so that it fills with air and automatically punctures.

Paratha (*Indian bread*)

This is made in the same manner as Chapati, but the dough, after being rolled out, is buttered and fried in butter on the griddle.

Pikelets or crumpets

Pikelets are the name often given to crumpets. In some parts of the country the pancake scone called a drop scone is called a pikelet.

Crumpets

cooking time 6 – 7 minutes

you will need:

4 oz. plain flour
pinch salt
½ oz. margarine
approximately ¼ pint milk
1 egg
scant ¼ oz. yeast
1 teaspoon sugar

1 Sieve flour and salt into warm basin.
2 Melt the margarine, add the warm milk, then pour on to egg.
3 Cream yeast and sugar.
4 Add the tepid milk mixture with a sprinkling of flour.
5 Allow to prove for about 15 minutes, until the surface is covered with little bubbles.
6 Stir into the flour mixture and beat thoroughly. The mixture should be fairly soft.
7 Cover the bowl and put to rise for about 45 minutes, until just about twice the original size.
8 Grease a hot girdle and drop spoonfuls on this.
9 Cook until pale brown for about 3 minutes, then turn and cook until pale brown on the other side.

Devilled griddle cakes

cooking time 3 minutes

you will need:

8 oz. plain flour
½ level teaspoon salt
3 level teaspoons dry mustard
1 level teaspoon bicarbonate of soda and
1½ level teaspoons cream of tartar or use 2 teaspoons baking powder
4 oz. lean bacon, fried till crisp
2 medium-sized eggs
½ pint milk
1 tablespoon Worcestershire sauce

1 Sift flour, salt, mustard, bicarbonate of soda and cream of tartar into bowl.
2 Add finely chopped bacon, then gradually mix to a thick creamy batter with the eggs, well beaten with the milk and Worcestershire sauce.
3 Drop spoonfuls of batter on to well-greased heated griddle, thick frying pan or hot plate and cook them steadily for about 1 – 1½ minutes on each side.
4 Pile in a folded table napkin to keep warm.
5 Serve hot.

Hardanger bannocks

cooking time a few minutes

you will need:

1 pint thin cream
1 egg
approximately 1 lb. flour
pinch salt

1 Whip together cream and egg.
2 Add flour and salt to make a firm dough and roll out into thick pancakes.
3 Bake on a fairly warm griddle or solid hot plate, turning when brown on one side. Leave to cool on a cloth.
4 Serve with one placed on top of the other with sugar and butter in between, and cut into wedge-shaped slices.

Welsh bread

cooking time approximately 15 minutes

you will need:

- 2 – 3 oz. fat (butter, margarine or lard)
- 8 oz. flour
- ¼ teaspoon salt
- 1 – 2 oz. sugar
- ½ teaspoon bicarbonate of soda
- 1 – 2 oz. currants
- buttermilk or milk

1. Rub the fat into the flour and salt.
2. Add the dry ingredients and mix well.
3. Add the milk to make a soft dough and turn on to a floured board.
4. Shape into a round and roll to about ½-inch thick.
5. Because this is a little thicker than most griddle breads, heat the griddle but make sure it is not too hot.
6. Brown on the bottom side, turn and brown on the second side and then heat gently for a further 10 – 12 minutes.
7. This should be eaten well buttered.

Norwegian flatbrød

cooking time a few minutes

you will need:

- 8 oz. flour
- ½ – 1 teaspoon salt
- water

1. Sieve the flour and salt together and mix with enough water to make an elastic dough.
2. Roll out until almost paper thin and cut into very large rounds.
3. Cook on a heated, slightly greased, griddle until firm and golden.
4. The flour used is generally a rye flour.
5. A very little fat can be rubbed in if liked.

Waffles

Waffle batter I

cooking time 2 – 3 minutes

you will need:

- 6 oz. flour (with plain flour use 1½ teaspoons baking powder)
- pinch salt
- 2 eggs
- ⅜ pint milk*
- 3 teaspoons oil or 1 oz. melted butter or cooking fat

* Use a little less if dipping a waffle iron in batter then frying in deep fat

1. Sieve flour and salt, gradually beat in eggs, milk and oil.
2. Either dip iron in batter, then put into pan of deep fat and cook for 2 – 3 minutes until crisp and golden brown.
   (If using a new waffle iron brush with little melted fat and oil, but when well used you should find the waffles can be cooked in the iron without greasing.)
3. Or heat an electric waffle iron until a drop of cold water splutters the moment it drops on the iron. Pour in enough batter to come about two-thirds the way up compartment, close lid and cook for several minutes until no steam is seen.
4. Serve with butter, jam, or syrup or with bacon or sausages.

Waffle batter 2

Use the recipe above, but separate egg whites and yolks and fold in stiffly beaten egg whites just before cooking.

Variations:

Cream waffles

Use either of the recipes for waffle batters, see above, but instead of all milk use half milk and half cream. Sour cream gives particularly light waffles.

Lemon waffles

Add 1 – 1½ teaspoons finely grated lemon rind to either of the waffle batters, see above.

Nut waffles

Use either of the recipes for waffle batters, see above, and add 2 oz. chopped nuts.

Ginger waffles

Use the waffle batter recipe, see page 73, but sieve 1 – 1½ teaspoons powdered ginger with the flour and serve with butter and ginger marmalade.

Orange waffles

Use the waffle batter recipe, see page 73, but add finely grated rind of 1 – 2 oranges to flour. Use juice of oranges with just enough milk to give the full quantity.

Muffins

Muffins have the great advantage that they are easy to make, quick to cook and make a change from bread, rolls or scones.
The sweet muffins can be served hot or cold for tea. The savoury muffins are excellent for breakfast or to serve with soup or other savoury dishes.

American muffins

American muffins are unlike the British type of muffin in that they are cooked in patty tins in the oven. Some of them are rather sweet and therefore can be eaten as cakes when fresh. Others are delicious topped with butter rather than being sandwiched with butter.

Plain muffins

cooking time approximately 15 minutes

you will need:

- 8 oz. flour (with plain flour use 3 level teaspoons baking powder, with self-raising flour 1 teaspoon baking powder)
- good pinch salt
- 1 – 2 oz. fat
- 1 egg
- ⅜ pint milk

1. Sieve the flour and all the dry ingredients.
2. Melt the fat, but allow it to cool slightly, then blend with the egg and milk, and mix with the flour.
3. Half fill rather deep, greased, patty tins and bake towards the top of a hot oven (425 – 450°F. —Gas Mark 6 – 7) for about 15 minutes.

Variations:

Sweet muffins

Add 1 – 2 oz. sugar to the flour.

Cherry muffins

Add 1 – 2 oz. chopped glacé cherries.

Dried fruit muffins

Add 1 – 2 oz. sugar and 2 oz. dried fruit. This has a tendency to fall to the bottom of the mixture as it cooks, but this cannot be avoided.

Nut muffins

Add 1 – 2 oz. sugar and 2 oz. chopped walnuts or other nuts.

Cream muffins

Use the recipe for plain muffins, see above, using ½ milk and ½ thin cream.
Any of the variations can be made.

Muffins I

cooking time 20 minutes

you will need:

- 8 oz. flour (with plain flour use 3 level teaspoons baking powder, with self-raising flour 1 teaspoon baking powder)
- ½ level teaspoon salt
- 1 oz. castor sugar
- 1 egg
- approximately ¼ pint milk
- 2 oz. fat or margarine or 2 tablespoons salad oil

1 Grease about 12 – 14, 2½-inch deep, patty tins.
2 Sift the flour, baking powder, salt and sugar together into a mixing bowl.
3 Beat the egg and stir in the milk and fat.
4 Add all at once to the flour and stir lightly until JUST mixed. Do not over-mix.
5 Fill muffin tins two-thirds full and bake in centre of hot oven (425 – 450°F.—Gas Mark 6 – 7) for about 20 minutes until golden brown and firm to the touch.
6 Serve while still warm in napkin-lined baskets.

Variations:

Fruit muffins

Add 2 oz. sultanas or seedless raisins.

Nut muffins

Add 3 oz. chopped nuts.

Muffins 2

cooking time 12 minutes

you will need:

½ oz. fresh yeast
½ pint milk
1 lb. plain flour
1 teaspoon salt
1 oz. butter
1 egg

1 Blend yeast with the ½ pint tepid milk.
2 Sieve flour and salt.
3 Add yeast liquid, then melted butter and egg, mix and knead until dough is smooth and elastic. The dough will be quite soft but add as little extra flour as possible.
4 Place dough in a bowl and cover with cloth, or put in a roomy polythene bag, to prove for 1½ hours at average room temperature.
5 Knead lightly again and roll out on a floured board to ½-inch thick. Cut into 3½-inch rounds. Re-roll and cut remains until all dough is used.
6 Place on well-floured baking sheets and dust tops well with flour. Cover or put inside a large polythene bag and prove 30 minutes at room temperature.
7 Place the muffins on a greased griddle, hot plate or heavy frying pan and cook over medium heat, not too quickly, about 6 minutes on each side until golden brown. Serve immediately with butter or later by slicing in half and toasting the cut side.

Muffins 3

To make a small quantity of muffins use the recipe for crumpets on page 72.
Work enough extra flour into the mixture to make the dough firm enough to cut into rounds.
Prove on a warmed greased baking sheet for 15 minutes, then cook on a hot griddle, electric hot plate or bottom of a frying pan for approximately 8 minutes until firm and pale brown.
Serve toasted with butter.

Apple muffins

cooking time approximately 18 – 20 minutes

you will need:

6 oz. flour (with plain flour use 2 level teaspoons baking powder)
1 tablespoon sugar
1 medium-sized cooking apple, grated
1 egg
¼ pint milk
1 oz. melted fat

1 Sieve the flour and add sugar.
2 Add the grated apple.
3 Blend the egg, milk and melted fat, then beat into the flour.
4 Half fill very well-greased muffin or patty tins with the mixture and bake towards the top of a moderately hot oven (400°F.—Gas Mark 5) for approximately 18 – 20 minutes until firm and golden brown.
5 These are nicer served hot than cold.

Banana muffins

cooking time 15 – 20 minutes

you will need:

7 oz. flour, less 1 tablespoon
1 tablespoon cornflour
2 level teaspoons baking powder
¾ teaspoon salt
¼ teaspoon bicarbonate of soda
2 oz. butter
3 oz. sugar
1 egg
3 mashed bananas

1 Sift together flour, cornflour, baking powder, salt and bicarbonate of soda.
2 Cream the butter, beat with sugar until light.
3 Add egg, beat again.
4 Add flour and mashed banana alternately, starting and ending with flour.
5 Mix lightly until batter is smooth.
6 Bake in well-greased deep patty tins in hot oven (425°F.—Gas Mark 6) for 15 – 20 minutes.
7 Serve hot or cold, plain or with butter, for breakfast or tea.

Honey muffins

Use either the cream muffin or plain muffin recipes, see page 74, and blend 1 good tablespoon honey with the egg and milk.
Be careful not to exceed the stated amount of milk or cream and milk in this recipe.

Hot fruity muffins

cooking time 15 minutes

you will need:

- 8 oz. flour (with plain flour use 3 level teaspoons baking powder)
- ½ level teaspoon mixed spice
- 2 oz. cooking fat
- 1 oz. margarine
- 1 oz. sugar
- 2 oz. sultanas
- 1 egg
- 1 medium-sized cooking apple

1. Sieve together flour, baking powder and spice.
2. Rub in fats and add sugar and sultanas.
3. Mix to a soft dough with egg and peeled and finely grated apple.
4. Turn on to a lightly floured board, knead quickly and roll out to ½-inch thick, cut into rounds about 3½ inches in diameter.
5. Place on a well-greased baking tray and cook in a hot oven (425 – 450°F.—Gas Mark 6 – 7) for 15 minutes.
6. Split open, butter and sprinkle with brown sugar. Serve hot.

Variation:

Cream muffins

Bind with egg and a little cream instead of egg and cooking apple.

Rice muffins

cooking time approximately 20 minutes

you will need:

- 4 oz. flour (with plain flour use 2 level teaspoons baking powder)
- good pinch salt
- 2 oz. cooked, dried rice*
- 1 oz. melted fat
- 1 egg
- ¼ pint milk

* When the rice has been cooked, and round grained (Carolina) rice is better, pat dry on a cloth or kitchen paper

1. Sieve the flour with the baking powder and salt, add the rice and blend well.
2. Allow the melted fat to cool and blend with the egg and milk, then beat into the flour and rice mixture.
3. Beat until very smooth, and half fill very well-greased deep patty tins.
4. Bake towards the top of a moderately hot oven (400°F.—Gas Mark 5) for approximately 20 minutes until firm and golden brown.

Variations:

Cheese rice muffins

Add a little extra seasoning, including pepper and mustard, and 2 – 3 oz. finely grated cheese.

Fruit rice muffins

Add 1 – 2 oz. sugar, plus 2 oz. dried fruit.

Sweet rice muffins

Add 1 – 2 oz. sugar.

Savoury muffins

cooking time approximately 15 minutes

you will need:

- 8 oz. flour (with plain flour use 3 level teaspoons baking powder, with self-raising flour 1 teaspoon baking powder, if possible)
- ½ teaspoon salt
- very good pinch pepper
- very good pinch dry mustard
- little celery salt
- 1 – 2 oz. fat
- 1 egg
- ⅜ pint milk

1. Sieve the flour and all the dry ingredients.
2. Melt the fat, but allow it to cool slightly, then blend with the egg and milk, and mix with the flour.
3. Half fill rather deep greased patty tins and bake towards the top of a hot oven (425 – 450°F.—Gas Mark 6 – 7) for about 15 minutes.

Variations:

Bacon muffins

Reduce the milk by 2 tablespoons and the fat to 1 oz. only. Fry 2 – 3 rashers bacon until crisp, then chop finely. Add to the mixture.

Cheese muffins

Add 3 – 4 oz. finely grated cheese after blending with egg.

Herb muffins

Add 1 – 2 teaspoons chopped fresh herbs or ½ – 1 teaspoon mixed dried herbs.

Sour milk muffins

Use either the plain or savoury muffin recipes, see pages 74 and 76, but use sour milk instead of fresh milk. This means the amount of baking powder should be reduced to half and a good ½ teaspoon bicarbonate of soda added instead.

Boston puffs

cooking time 12 minutes

you will need:

- 8 oz. flour (with plain flour use 4 level teaspoons baking powder, with self-raising flour 2 level teaspoons)
- 1 level teaspoon salt
- 2 oz. fat
- about 7 tablespoons milk and water

1. Sift together flour, baking powder and salt.
2. Rub in fat and mix to light elastic dough with liquid.
3. Turn on to floured board, roll into oblong about ¼-inch thick.
4. Fold over, turn at right angles, roll out again.
5. Cut with 2½-inch cutter into rounds and bake on greased baking sheet in very hot oven (475°F.—Gas Mark 8) for about 12 minutes.
6. Serve hot with butter.

Wafers and Rusks

These are delicious with jam and cheese as a change from biscuits. Do not store with bread as they lose their crispness.

Poppy seed flakes

cooking time 12 – 15 minutes

you will need:

- 6 oz. flour (with plain flour use 1½ level teaspoons baking powder)
- 2 oz. fine semolina
- ½ level teaspoon salt
- good shake cayenne pepper
- ½ level teaspoon celery salt, optional
- 4 oz. butter or margarine
- 1 egg
- little milk
- 1 tablespoon poppy seeds

1. Sift dry ingredients into a bowl.
2. Rub in fat till mixture resembles fine breadcrumbs, then mix to a stiff dough with the beaten egg.
3. Turn out to a lightly floured board, knead quickly, shape into a ball and cover.
4. Leave in a cool place for at least 30 minutes.
5. Roll dough into a fairly thin oblong, brush lower half with milk, then sprinkle with poppy seeds.
6. Fold top half of dough over, press lightly with a rolling pin then re-roll till poppy seed 'sandwich' is again fairly thin.
7. Stamp into rounds with a 1½-inch cutter, put on to greased baking trays and bake near top of moderately hot oven (400°F.—Gas Mark 5) for 12 – 15 minutes or till crisp and golden in colour.
8. Cool on a wire tray. Serve with butter, cheese and olives.

Variation:

Nut flakes

Use 1 – 2 tablespoons chopped nuts instead of poppy seeds.

Devilled almond wafers

cooking time 8 – 10 minutes

you will need:

4 oz. flour
½ teaspoon salt
½ teaspoon dry mustard
pinch pepper
pinch cayenne pepper
1 oz. butter
1 oz. Lancashire or Cheddar cheese
1 egg yolk
1½ tablespoons water
dash Worcestershire sauce
1 egg white
1 oz. blanched chopped almonds
paprika pepper

1 Sift dry ingredients into a bowl, rub in butter.
2 Stir in finely grated cheese.
3 Mix to dry dough with egg yolk beaten with the water and Worcestershire sauce, adding a few more drops if needed.
4 Turn on to a lightly floured board and roll to thin sheet.
5 Cut into ¾-inch wide strips of varying lengths, from 4 – 6 inches, or in rounds or diamond shapes.
6 Place on greased baking tray.
7 Brush with beaten egg white and sprinkle with almonds and paprika.
8 Bake in moderately hot oven (400°F.—Gas Mark 5) for 8 – 10 minutes until crisp and golden.
9 Serve with drinks before dinner or any cream soup.

Variations:

Plain wafers

Omit almonds and paprika pepper.

Caraway wafers

Sprinkle with few caraway seeds instead of almonds.

Oatcakes

cooking time 8 minutes on griddle
25 minutes in oven

you will need:

4 oz. oatmeal
pinch salt
pinch bicarbonate of soda, optional
about 1 teaspoon melted fat
hot water

1 Sieve the oatmeal and salt through a coarse sieve, adding the bicarbonate of soda if being used. This gives a lighter cake.
2 Add the melted fat and gradually work in enough hot water to bind.
3 Roll out on a board, dusted with oatmeal, until very thin.
4 Cut into shapes, generally triangles.
5 Cook gradually on a greased griddle, making sure this is not too hot, for about 4 minutes on each side.
6 The oatcakes should be firm but not brown when cooked.
7 If preferred bake in the centre of a very moderate oven (350°F.—Gas Mark 3) for 25 minutes.

Tea-time rusks 1

cooking time 12 – 15 minutes

you will need:

6 oz. flour
pinch salt
1 oz. margarine
1 oz. sugar
milk

1 Sieve flour and salt.
2 Rub in margarine, add sugar and enough milk to make firm dough.
3 Roll out to just over ¼-inch thick, cut into fingers.
4 Bake for 7 – 8 minutes in moderately hot oven (400°F.—Gas Mark 5).
5 Remove from oven, split and lay cut sides on baking tin.
6 Cook for further 5 – 7 minutes.

Tea-time rusks 2

cooking time approximately 15 minutes

you will need:

4 oz. flour (with plain flour use 1 teaspoon baking powder)
good pinch salt
1 dessertspoon sugar*
1 oz. margarine
milk to mix

* A little more can be used if liked

1 Sieve the dry ingredients together.
2 Rub in margarine.
3 Add the sugar and just enough liquid to make a firm dough.
4 Roll out and cut into rounds about ⅓-inch thick.
5 Put on to ungreased baking sheet and bake for a good 5 minutes in a hot oven (425 – 450°F.—Gas Mark 6 – 7).
6 Remove the trays from the oven and split the rusks through the centre.
7 Put on to the trays, cut side down.

You will, of course, need more baking trays since you now have twice the original number of rounds.

8 Bake for a further 10 minutes in a moderate oven (375°F.—Gas Mark 4)
9 Cool on rack and put into a tin the moment they are quite cold.

Yeast rusks

cooking time approximately 30 minutes

you will need:

½ oz. yeast
1 teaspoon sugar
¼ pint tepid water
8 oz. flour
good pinch salt
1 egg

1 Cream yeast and sugar.
2 Add liquid and sprinkle top with little flour.
3 Leave in warm place for about 15 minutes until surface is covered with little bubbles.
4 Sieve flour and salt, add yeast liquid and egg.
5 Knead well and leave to rise in warm place until double original bulk.
6 Knead again and roll out until very thin.
7 Cut into rounds and put on a greased baking tray.
8 Prove for 5 minutes, then bake for about 30 minutes in very moderate oven (300 – 350°F.—Gas Mark 2 – 3) until crisp and golden brown.

Tea Cakes

In this chapter are tea cakes, some of which may seem a little rich to be called breads, but you will find they can be topped or eaten with butter when they are a little stale.

Apple cake

cooking time 35 – 40 minutes

you will need:

1 lb. cooking apples
2 – 3 oz. sugar
1 good teaspoon mixed spice
6 oz. flour (with plain flour use 2 teaspoons baking powder)
2 oz. margarine
1 egg
milk to mix

1 Peel the apples and cut into neat pieces.
2 Arrange at the bottom of a well-greased cake tin or dish, sprinkling with a good 1 oz. of the sugar and the spice.
3 Sieve together the baking powder and flour, rub in the margarine and add the remainder of the sugar.
4 Mix with an egg and enough milk to make a firm dough.
5 Spread over the apples and bake in the centre of a moderately hot oven (400°F.—Gas Mark 5) for 35 – 40 minutes.
6 Turn out so that the apples are on top of the cake, and serve hot.

Banana oatmeal bannock

cooking time 15 minutes

you will need:

6 oz. flour (with plain flour use 1 level teaspoon baking powder)
8 oz. sugar
½ teaspoon bicarbonate of soda
1 teaspoon salt
¼ teaspoon grated nutmeg
¼ teaspoon ground cinnamon
6 oz. butter
1 beaten egg
3 mashed bananas
4 oz. rolled oats
2 oz. chopped walnuts

1 Sift flour with sugar, bicarbonate of soda, salt, nutmeg and cinnamon.
2 Rub in fat.
3 Stir in remaining ingredients in order given.
4 Beat thoroughly and drop in teaspoonfuls, 1½ inches apart, on greased baking sheets.
5 Bake in moderately hot oven (400°F.—Gas Mark 5) until edges are brown, about 15 minutes.
6 Remove at once with a palette knife and serve hot or cold with butter.

Chelsea buns

cooking time 15 minutes

you will need:

½ oz. yeast
4 oz. sugar
¼ pint tepid milk or milk and water
12 oz. plain flour
4 oz. margarine
pinch salt
1 egg (this can be omitted and a little more milk used)
3 – 5 oz. mixed dried fruit
1 oz. peel

To glaze:
1 oz. sugar
1 tablespoon water

1 Cream the yeast with 1 teaspoon of the sugar.
2 Add the tepid milk and a sprinkling of flour.
3 Allow to stand in a warm place for about 20 minutes.
4 Rub 2 oz. of the margarine into the flour, add salt, 1 oz. sugar and the egg, if used.
5 Work in the yeast liquid, knead lightly, then prove until just about twice original bulk, about 1 hour.
6 Knead again, then roll out into an oblong shape.
7 Spread this with the remaining margarine which has been warmed, then sprinkle over sugar, fruit and peel.
8 Roll firmly like a Swiss roll, then cut into twelve equal shapes.
9 Put on to greased and warmed baking trays.
10 Prove for 15 minutes, then bake near the top of a hot oven (450°F.—Gas Mark 7) for approximately 15 minutes.
11 Either dust buns with very fine castor sugar, or glaze them immediately they come from the oven with a glaze made by mixing 1 oz. sugar with 1 tablespoon water.

Cornish splits

Cornish splits, which are very similar to Devonshire splits, are often served with cream and treacle instead of cream and jam, in which case they are known as 'Thunder and Lightning'. If you wish to have either Devonshire or Cornish splits already prepared, they look most attractive if they are split down the centre and the cream and jam inserted through.

cooking time 25 minutes

you will need:

½ oz. yeast
pinch castor sugar
¼ pint tepid liquid (2 parts milk, 1 part water)
8 oz. flour
1 level teaspoon salt
¼ oz. fat

To fill:
cream
jam or treacle

1 Cream the yeast and sugar until it is liquid, then add the milk and water.
2 Sieve the flour and salt into a bowl and rub in the fat.
3 Add the yeast liquid and mix to a smooth dough.
4 Put to rise in a warm place for 45 minutes.
5 Cut into sixteen pieces and shape into balls.
6 Place on a floured baking sheet and prove for 10 minutes.
7 Bake in a hot oven (425 – 450°F.—Gas Mark 6 – 7) for 15 minutes, then reduce to moderately hot (400°F.—Gas Mark 5) for a further 10 minutes.
8 Split and butter and serve hot, or leave to cool, then split and serve with jam or treacle and cream.

Danish pastries

Although in this country we think of a Danish pastry as a cake for tea, in their country of origin they are generally served for breakfast and the plainer ones can be eaten with butter.

cooking time 15 – 20 minutes

you will need:

¾ oz. yeast
1¼ oz. castor sugar
9 oz. plain flour
½ level teaspoon salt
¼ pint lukewarm milk
4 oz. margarine

1 Cream the yeast to a liquid with 1 teaspoon of the sugar.
2 Sieve together the flour and salt, add remaining sugar and warm slightly.
3 Make a well in the centre.
4 Pour in the liquid yeast and sufficient milk to make a soft but not sticky paste.
5 Beat thoroughly by hand then knead till smooth.
6 Turn on to a floured board, roll into an oblong ½ inch in thickness and cover all over with the margarine, divided into pieces the size of small walnuts.
7 Fold in three and seal the edges.
8 Give the pastry a quarter turn to the left.
9 Repeat the rolling, folding and turning twice more so that the margarine is well blended into the pastry. If the pastry is sticky and too elastic to roll, rest 15 – 20 minutes between each turn.
10 Wrap in waxed or greaseproof paper and leave in a cool place for at least 1 hour.
11 Form into various shapes, see below, and put on to greased baking trays.

12 Leave in a warm place to rise for about 20 – 30 minutes.
13 Bake in a hot oven (425 – 450°F.—Gas Mark 6 – 7) for 15 – 20 minutes.
14 Leave to cool on a wire rack, then coat the buns, if wished, with thin water icing and sprinkle with chopped nuts.

Suggested shapes and fillings:

Crescents

Roll out the pastry to ¼ inch in thickness and cut into triangles, put a spoonful of almond paste, see below, in the centre of each, moisten the uncovered surface and roll up to form a crescent shape.

Turnovers

Roll out the pastry to ¼ inch in thickness and cut the pastry into squares, put 1 teaspoon of cream cheese in the centre, moisten edges and fold over to form triangles.

Pinwheels

Roll pastry into a strip, brush with melted syrup or jam, sprinkle liberally with cleaned and dried currants and 1 small teaspoon cinnamon, roll up like a Swiss roll and cut in ½-inch thick slices.

Almond paste or marzipan

no cooking

you will need:

- 4 oz. ground almonds
- 2 oz. castor sugar
- 2 oz. icing sugar
- few drops almond essence
- egg yolk to mix

1 Mix all ingredients, adding enough egg yolk to make a firm mixture.
2 Knead thoroughly. Do not overhandle.

Devonshire splits

cooking time 10 minutes

you will need:

- plain yeast dough, see page 84
- jam
- whipped cream or thick mock cream
- icing sugar

1 Make the plain yeast dough.
2 When it is proved and kneaded, cut into equal-sized pieces. Form into neat rounds and put on to warmed greased baking trays.
3 Prove for 15 minutes in a warm place.
4 Bake for 10 minutes near the top of a very hot oven (475°F.—Gas Mark 8).
5 When cold, split the bun through the centre and fill with whipped cream and jam.

Quick Devonshire splits

Use plain scone recipe, see page 58, split and fill with whipped cream or Devonshire clotted cream and home-made jam.

Doughnuts

cooking time 6 – 7 minutes

you will need:

- scant ½ oz. yeast
- 1 oz. sugar
- ¼ pint tepid milk
- 8 oz. plain flour
- pinch salt
- 1 egg
- 1 oz. margarine
- 2 oz. castor sugar for rolling
- little jam
- fat for frying

1 Cream the yeast with the sugar.
2 Add the tepid milk and the flour, salt, egg, then the melted margarine.
3 Allow the dough to prove until it is just twice its original bulk, approximately 1 hour.
4 Knead well, then divide into required number of pieces.
5 Roll into neat rounds and put on to warmed and greased trays to prove for a further 15 minutes.
6 Meanwhile heat a pan of deep fat. When tested, this should be hot enough to turn a cube of bread pale brown within a minute.
7 Drop three or four doughnuts into the hot fat.
8 Turn with either a fish slice or two spoons so that they become golden brown all over. Lower the heat the moment the doughnuts go into the fat, so that they are cooked through to the middle.
9 Drain them a second on a fish slice, then roll in the sugar.
10 Reheat fat, and fry a further batch.
11 To insert jam, make a hole before proving, put in a little jam, then re-roll so this is completely covered.
12 Alternatively, split the doughnuts before serving and spread with jam.

Fat rascals

cooking time approximately 15 minutes

you will need:

8 oz. flour (with plain flour use 2 level teaspoons baking powder)
pinch salt
1½ oz. sugar*
4 oz. butter or margarine
3 – 4 oz. currants
milk to mix

* Brown is particularly good

1. Sieve the dry ingredients, then rub in the butter.
2. Add the currants and enough milk to make a firm dough.
3. Roll out to about ½-inch thick, cut into rounds, sprinkle with a little more sugar and put on to baking tins.
4. Bake in a moderately hot to hot oven (400 – 425°F.—Gas Mark 5 – 6) for about 15 minutes.
5. Serve plain or split and spread with butter.

Variation:

Use chopped dates or mixed fruit instead of currants.

Popovers

cooking time 20 minutes

you will need:

4 oz. flour, preferably plain
pinch salt
1 egg
⅜ pint milk

1. Sieve flour and salt.
2. Gradually beat in the eggs and milk, allow to stand for a while.
3. Pour mixture into about nine hot, greased, deep patty tins and bake towards top of hot oven (450°F.—Gas Mark 7) for approximately 20 minutes until firm and brown.
4. Serve with butter and jam for tea, and with bacon for breakfast.

Variations:

Rich popovers

Use the above recipe but add 1 oz. melted margarine and 1 extra egg to batter and reduce milk by 2 tablespoons.

Special popovers

Use popover or rich popover recipes and add 1 teaspoon mixed spice to flour.

Savoury popovers

Use popover or rich popover recipes and add plenty of seasoning and 2 oz. grated cheese to batter. Excellent with bacon or sausages.

Cornish tea cake

cooking time 15 minutes

you will need:

8 oz. flour (with plain flour use 1 teaspoon baking powder)
4 oz. dripping
1 oz. chopped crystallized peel
4 oz. currants
2 oz. sugar
¼ pint milk

1. Rub the dripping into the flour.
2. Add the peel and fruit together with the sugar.
3. Blend with the milk, which gives a fairly soft dough.
4. Roll out lightly on well floured board and when about ¾-inch thick cut into triangles or rounds.
5. Bake on lightly greased and floured baking tin for approximately 15 minutes towards the top of a moderately hot to hot oven (400 – 425°F.—Gas Mark 5 – 6).
6. Split and butter, serve hot if possible.

Variations:

Spiced teacakes

Sieve 1 – 1½ teaspoons mixed spice with the flour.

Saffron teacakes

Sieve pinch spice with the flour, and blend ¼ – ½ teaspoon powdered saffron with the milk.

French cinnamon tea cake

cooking time 20 – 25 minutes

you will need:

1 egg
2 oz. castor sugar
4 tablespoons milk
few drops vanilla essence
4 oz. self-raising flour
1 tablespoon melted butter

For topping:
melted butter
1 level teaspoon cinnamon or spice

1 Whisk egg white until stiff and peaky, then gradually whisk in sugar followed by yolk.
2 Fold in milk and essence and lastly the flour and butter.
3 Turn mixture into a well-greased 7-inch sandwich tin and bake towards top of moderately hot oven (375°F.—Gas Mark 4) for 20 – 25 minutes.
4 Remove from oven, brush top with melted butter and sprinkle with cinnamon.
5 Serve warm with butter, clotted cream or cottage cheese and jam or honey.

Variation:

Instead of butter and spice top the cake while warm, with soft lemon glacé icing see page 32, and finely chopped walnuts.

Gugelhupf or kugelhoff

cooking time 1½ hours

you will need:

9 – 10 oz. butter or margarine
8 oz. sugar
grated lemon rind
4 eggs
1 lb. flour (with plain flour use 3 level teaspoons baking powder)
2 oz. chopped almonds
sieved icing sugar

1 Cream butter and sugar with lemon rind until soft and light.
2 Gradually beat in eggs, taking care mixture does not curdle.
3 Sieve flour and fold into egg mixture together with the almonds.
4 Put mixture into a greased and floured, deep, fluted ring tin, about 9 inches in outer diameter.
5 Bake for approximately 1½ hours in the centre of a very moderate oven (350°F.—Gas Mark 3).
6 Cool and dust with icing sugar.

Note:

If wished, you could pour a very thin layer of glacé icing, see page 32, over, and decorate with glacé cherries, but do not have this so thick that you spoil the shape.

Yeast gugelhupf or kugelhoff

cooking time 35 – 40 minutes

you will need:

scant ¾ oz. yeast
2 oz. sugar
approximately ⅛ pint tepid milk or milk and water
8 oz. flour, preferably plain
2 oz. butter
2 oz. blanched chopped almonds
grated rind of 1 orange and/or lemon
1 tablespoon lemon or orange juice
2 eggs
sieved icing sugar

1 Cream the yeast with 1 teaspoon of the sugar, add the liquid and a sprinkling of flour.
2 Stand in a warm place for about 20 minutes.
3 Melt the butter.
4 Mix the flour and other ingredients, except icing sugar, together.
5 Add the yeast liquid to the flour mixture and then add the melted butter.
6 It may be necessary to work in a little extra warm milk, according to the type of flour used. Different flours have varying degrees of absorbency.
7 Beat the dough very well with a wooden spoon, then put into a warmed, greased and floured fluted ring mould.*
8 Allow to rise for about 30 minutes, then bake for approximately 35 – 40 minutes in the centre of a hot oven (450°F.—Gas Mark 7).
9 Dust with sieved icing sugar.

*This is often called a savarin or angel cake tin. If you do not possess one, stand a small cake tin inside a large one.

Lardy cake

cooking time 35 – 40 minutes

you will need:

1 lb. bread dough, see page 16, or plain yeast dough as follows:—	12 oz. plain flour good pinch salt 1 oz. margarine or fat
½ oz. yeast 1 – 2 oz. sugar ⅜ pint of tepid water or milk and water	*For filling:* 2 – 4 oz. lard 2 – 4 oz. sugar 4 oz. dried fruit little spice

Although this is called a cake it is very simple to make from bread dough, so when you are next making a loaf of bread you can take off part of the dough for this recipe. Eat it as a cake when fresh, or as bread cut into slices and buttered when stale.

1. Cream the yeast with 1 teaspoon of sugar. Add the tepid liquid and a sprinkling of flour. Put in a warm place until the sponge breaks through.
2. Meanwhile, sieve the flour and salt into a warm bowl, rub in the margarine and add the sugar.
3. When ready, work in the yeast liquid and knead thoroughly. Put into a warm place for approximately 1 hour to prove.
4. When the dough has been proved and kneaded roll out to an oblong shape. It may be necessary to knead in a small quantity of extra flour to make the dough sufficiently firm to roll. Divide the lard and sugar into 2 equal portions, cutting the lard into tiny pieces.
5. Put half the lard and half the sugar and fruit with a light dusting of spice on the dough. Fold in exactly the same way as for flaky pastry. Re-roll the dough and do exactly the same thing with the rest of the fat, sugar, fruit and spice. Fold again and roll into a neat shape to fit either a 7 or 8-inch square tin. The tin should have been warmed and then greased and floured.
6. Put in the dough, making certain that it comes no more than two-thirds of the way up the tin. Prove for 20 minutes in a warm place, then bake in a hot oven (450°F.—Gas Mark 7) for 15 minutes.
7. Lower the heat to moderate (375°F.—Gas Mark 4) and cook for a further 20 – 25 minutes.
8. Glaze the cake while hot by brushing with a mixture of sugar and water, using 1 oz. sugar mixed with a tablespoon water.

Hot cross buns

cooking time 15 – 20 minutes

you will need:

1 lb. plain flour pinch salt ½ oz. yeast 2 oz. castor sugar ½ pint lukewarm milk and water 1 level teaspoon cinnamon 1 level teaspoon nutmeg 3 oz. currants	1 oz. chopped candied peel 2 oz. butter 1 egg *Short crust pastry:* 1 oz. fat 2 oz. flour little water

1. Sieve half the flour into a mixing bowl, with the salt.
2. Cream the yeast with a teaspoon of the sugar and stir in the lukewarm milk and water.
3. Pour into the sieved flour and mix well together.
4. Cover with a clean damp cloth and put in a warm place to sponge for 40 minutes.
5. Sieve the remaining flour with the cinnamon, nutmeg and sugar.
6. Stir in the currants and chopped peel.
7. Melt the butter and beat the egg.
8. Add the dry ingredients to the sponged mixture, pour in the melted butter and beaten egg and mix thoroughly with your hand.
9. Cover again with a damp cloth and put in a warm place to rise for 1 – 1¼ hours.
10. Turn the dough on to a floured board and cut into sixteen pieces.
11. Shape each piece into a round bun.
12. Place on a well-greased and floured baking sheet, allowing room for the buns to spread.
13. Make the pastry by rubbing the fat in to the flour and adding enough water to make a rolling consistency.
14. Roll out the pastry and cut into narrow strips about 2-inches long.
15. Place a cross of pastry on top of the buns and put in a warm place to prove for about 40 minutes.
16. Bake for 15 – 20 minutes in a hot oven (450°F. —Gas Mark 7).
17. Five minutes before removing from oven, brush over with a little milk and sugar.

Potato cake

cooking time 30 minutes

you will need:

4 oz. short crust pastry, see page 84
little jam

For filling:
3 oz. butter or margarine
3 oz. sugar
few drops vanilla essence or lemon juice or almond essence
8 oz. mashed potatoes (use when freshly boiled as they are softer and more floury)
pinch salt
1 oz. flour
½ teaspoon baking powder
1 oz. mixed peel
3 oz. mixed dried fruit
1 egg

1 Roll out the pastry thinly, and line a deep plate or flan ring. Spread thinly with jam.
2 Cream together margarine or butter, sugar and essence, then work in the other ingredients.
3 Spread over jam, then bake in the centre of the oven, allowing 20 minutes in a hot oven (450°F.—Gas Mark 7), and the rest of the time at moderately hot (400°F.—Gas Mark 5). The filling should be firm and the pastry crisp.

Note
If the potatoes have been mashed already with margarine and milk, omit some of the margarine and egg from the recipe.

Round yeast cake

cooking time 25 – 30 minutes

you will need:

1 oz. yeast
3 oz. sugar
¼ pint tepid milk
1 lb. flour
3 oz. margarine
grated lemon rind
pinch salt
1 egg

For filling:
1 oz. melted margarine
1 tablespoon sugar
2 – 3 sliced apples
2 oz. sultanas or raisins
2 oz. rolled oats
grated lemon rind

For topping:
1 egg yolk
1½ oz. chopped almonds

1 Cream yeast with 1 teaspoon sugar, then add the tepid milk and a sprinkling of flour.
2 Leave in a warm place until mixture bubbles, approximately 20 minutes.
3 Cream margarine, sugar and lemon rind and work in the flour sieved with the salt.
4 Add the yeast mixture and beaten egg.
5 Knead until smooth, then put into a warm place to prove for approximately 1 hour, covering the bowl with a damp cloth to prevent mixture drying.
6 Knead again and then roll out to a neat oblong.
7 Spread the warmed margarine over this, then cover with the filling ingredients, which should be mixed together.
8 Roll up like a Swiss roll, then cut the roll at regular intervals to a depth of a good ½ inch so the filling shows.
9 Press ends together to form a ring and lift on to warmed, greased baking tin.
10 Brush with beaten egg yolk and sprinkle with nuts and leave to prove for approximately 20 – 25 minutes.
11 When roll has risen well, bake in the centre of a moderately hot oven (400°F.—Gas Mark 5) for approximately 25 – 30 minutes until golden brown.
12 Take out of tin while still hot and coat with glacé icing, see page 32, which should be very thin to give an almost transparent layer.

Sally Lunns

cooking time 20 minutes

you will need:

1 oz. margarine
¼ pint milk
½ oz. yeast
1 teaspoon sugar
12 oz. flour
good pinch salt
2 oz. sugar
1 egg

1 Melt the fat and add the milk and warm to blood heat.
2 Cream the yeast with the teaspoon of sugar.
3 Mix the yeast with the milk and fat.
4 Mix the flour, salt and sugar, then add the yeast liquid, together with the beaten egg.
5 Beat to a very light dough.
6 Divide into four pieces.
7 Knead each piece lightly.
8 Put into small greased and floured cake tins.
9 Prick the tops lightly and leave to rise to the tops of the tins.
10 Bake in a moderate oven (375°F.—Gas Mark 4) for 20 minutes.
11 Brush the tops with melted fat when cooked.

Swedish tea ring

cooking time 35 – 40 minutes

you will need:

12 oz. plain flour
pinch salt
2 teaspoons yeast
1 teaspoon sugar
2 oz. margarine
warm milk or water
2 oz. chopped blanched almonds, optional

To decorate:
2 oz. shredded blanched almonds

1 Make the dough as for cherry twist, see page 32, adding 2 oz. almonds if these are being used.
2 Allow to prove, then knead and form into a ring.
3 You can either place this on a flat baking tin or put into a large ring-shaped tin.
4 Scatter the shredded blanched almonds on top and allow to prove again until double its size.
5 Bake as for cherry twist.

Sweet soda cake

cooking time 35 – 40 minutes

you will need:

1 lb. flour
1 level teaspoon salt
½ teaspoon bicarbonate of soda
½ teaspoon cream of tartar
2 oz. margarine
2 oz. sugar
4 oz. sultanas
½ – ¾ pint sour milk

1 Sift flour, salt, bicarbonate of soda and cream of tartar into a bowl.
2 Rub margarine into flour.
3 Add sugar and fruit.
4 Make a well in the centre and pour in ½ pint of the milk.
5 Mix with a knife to a soft dough, adding more milk if the dough seems dry.
6 Knead lightly to a round shape.
7 Turn smooth side up and place on a lightly floured baking tray.
8 Cut a cross on top and bake in a hot oven (425 – 450°F.—Gas Mark 6 – 7) for 35 – 40 minutes.
9 Cool on wire tray.

Tea ring

cooking time 30 minutes

you will need:

4 oz. butter or margarine
8 oz. flour (with plain flour use 3 level teaspoons baking powder)
2 oz. semolina
pinch salt
2 oz. castor sugar
1 egg
milk

For filling:
3 tablespoons marmalade
3 oz. mixed fruit
3 oz. chopped dates

For topping:
glacé icing
chopped nuts

1 Rub the margarine into the flour to resemble fine breadcrumbs.
2 Add the semolina, salt and sugar and mix thoroughly.
3 Add the beaten egg and enough milk to mix to a soft but not sticky dough.
4 Roll to an oblong on a floured board.
5 Mix the filling ingredients. Cover with the filling.
6 Roll up lengthwise, shape into a ring and place on a greased tin with a small tin in the centre so that it will keep its shape.
7 Snip half way through from the outer edge about every inch with scissors.
8 Brush with a little milk.
9 Bake near the top of a moderately hot oven (400°F.—Gas Mark 5) for 30 minutes.
10 Cool. Pour a little glacé icing, see page 32, over the top and sprinkle with chopped nuts, or brush with butter while hot and sprinkle with sugar and cinnamon.
11 Serve freshly baked, with or without butter.

Yorkshire tea cakes

cooking time 15 minutes

you will need:

12 oz. plain flour
good pinch salt
scant ¾ oz. yeast
1 teaspoon sugar
approximately ⅜ pint milk
1½ oz. butter
1 egg

1 Sieve the flour and salt and put to warm.
2 Cream the yeast with the sugar, then add the tepid milk, use a little less than the full quantity at this stage.
3 Stir in the melted butter and the beaten egg and let this yeast mixture stand for about 10 minutes until bubbling on top slightly.
4 Pour on to the flour and knead well, adding extra tepid milk if needed.

5 Cover and allow to prove in a warm place until double its size.
6 Knead well until smooth then divide into four or six portions.
7 Form into rather flat cakes and allow to prove on warmed greased tins.
8 Bake towards the top of a hot oven (425 – 450°F. —Gas Mark 6 – 7) for approximately 15 minutes.

Welsh cakes

cooking time 10 minutes

you will need:

4 oz. margarine
8 oz. flour (with plain flour use 2 level teaspoons baking powder)
4 oz. sugar
4 oz. dried fruit
1 egg
milk to mix

1 Rub the fat into the flour.
2 Add sugar, fruit, egg and enough milk to make a firm dough.
3 Roll out.
4 Cut into triangles or rounds.
5 Put on to moderately hot and greased griddle, bakestone or solid plate of electric cooker, or if these are not available you can use the base of a very solid frying pan.
6 Cook steadily for 5 minutes.
7 Turn and cook for 5 minutes on the second side.
8 Do not cook too quickly or make cakes too thick otherwise the outside will get very brown before the inside is cooked, Although normally eaten as a cake, these can be served with butter when stale.

To use up Bread

This section gives ways of using up bread that are interesting and appetizing.
Some of them are ideal for picnics or to serve for supper.

Barbecue bread

cooking time 25 – 30 minutes

you will need:

4 oz. soft butter or margarine
1 tablespoon prepared mustard
3 oz. grated Parmesan cheese
3 tablespoons chopped parsley
1 loaf French bread, see page 19

1 Combine first four ingredients.
2 Slash bread diagonally in 1-inch slices, cutting to, BUT NOT THROUGH, bottom crust.
3 Spread butter mixture generously one one side of each slice.
4 Wrap loaf in foil and heat in very moderate oven (350°F.—Gas Mark 3) for 25 – 30 minutes or until hot through.

Bread and cheese kebabs

cooking time a few minutes

you will need:

bread
butter
cheese
anchovy fillets

1 Thread alternate cubes of buttered bread and cheese on skewers.
2 Criss-cross anchovy fillets over the top.
3 Rest edges of skewers over edges of heatproof dish.
4 Place under steady grill until bread is golden and cheese begins to melt.
5 Serve at once with salad.

Cheesey bread cubes

cooking time a few minutes

you will need:

4 thick slices bread
2 oz. butter or oil
grated cheese or crumbled blue cheese

1 Cut bread into small cubes.
2 Fry until golden in butter or oil.
3 While still hot in the pan sprinkle liberally with grated cheese.
4 Spoon on top of creamed fish or chicken or vegetables, or serve with soup.

French herb bread

cooking time a few minutes

you will need:

- 4 oz. butter
- good squeeze lemon juice
- 1 tablespoon finely chopped parsley
- 1 level teaspoon mixed dried herbs, or other fresh or dried herbs to taste
- 1 French loaf, see page 19
- little oil or water

1. Mix butter, lemon juice and herbs.
2. Slice French loaf diagonally, leaving base intact.
3. Spread each section with herb butter.
4. Brush top with oil or water.
5. Crisp for a few minutes in hot oven (425°F.—Gas Mark 7)

Spreads

1. Spread bread with condensed milk.
2. Blend two tablespoons condensed milk with any of the following and spread on the bread or toast and heat under grill:

1. 1 dessertspoon lemon juice
2. ½ teaspoon cinnamon
3. 1 dessertspoon coconut with or without lemon juice
4. 1 teaspoon cocoa, beaten in well

Seed bread slices

cooking time 7 minutes

you will need:

- 1 French loaf, see page 19
- 3 oz. butter
- 1 egg yolk
- sprinkle celery or poppy or sesame seeds
- extra butter

1. Cut loaf into thick slices.
2. Cream butter.
3. Work in egg yolk and seeds.
4. Butter bread liberally.
5. Heat in moderately hot oven (400°F.—Gas Mark 5) until sizzling and beginning to brown, about 7 minutes, or toast under grill.
6. Serve hot with soup or salad.

Index

cinna
allspice

Jams, Pickles and Chutneys

All about jam making

Utensils for making jam

The right utensils are a help in producing good jam with the minimum of bother. Obviously if you only make small quantities of jam some of them would be unnecessary, but these are the things you should have:

Preserving pan – this is described on page 5 but a good big saucepan could take its place. Whatever utensil is used remember that copper or brass can spoil the colour of red fruits but help to keep green fruits green. Zinc or iron pans spoil both colour and flavour. Aluminium or copper pans do not spoil the colour or flavour, but one tends to lose any vitamin in fruits containing a high percentage of vitamin C.

Wooden spoon – choose a long handled spoon, so that you can stir without fear of the hot jam splashing on to your hand.

Jars – ordinary jam jars are not obtainable in shops so you must retain them from year to year. You can use bottling jars, etc.

Metal jug or heatproof glass jug – this is the easiest way of filling the pots. Have one with a handle so you can scoop up the jam without burning your fingers.

Perforated metal spoon – this is the best way of skimming the jam.

Large funnel – not essential, but if you fill the pots through this you keep them very clean.

Sugar thermometer – for testing the temperature of jams etc. See page 7.
Muslin – for tying peel, pips etc., in certain jams.
Covers – use proper jam pot covers to make certain the jam keeps well.
Labels – the stick-on-labels should be put on the jars when quite cold.

Preliminary preparation of fruit for jam making

The way in which you prepare the fruit will make a lot of difference to your finished jam.

1. Look over the fruit carefully – discard any bruised or damaged portions. With large fruit you need only cut away the spoilt part – with soft fruit discard the whole fruit.
2. Unless you have picked the fruit from your own garden after a spell of very fine weather, so you are certain that the fruit is very clean, it is wise to wash it. The best way to do this is to lay the fruit on fine sieves and gently pour water over it. If you actually immerse the fruit in water, it absorbs too much and will, in consequence, make your jam watery.
   (a) With soft fruits, transfer to absorbent kitchen paper to dry.
   (b) With firm hard fruits, dry with a cloth.

   Try to avoid washing those fruits that are deficient in pectin, i.e. strawberries in particular, since the extra amount of water is not required. Strawberries however grow near the ground and are sometimes extremely dirty. Never wash in hot water as this softens the fruit too early.
3. In some recipes one will need to 'top and tail' the fruit, i.e. in the case of gooseberries. The easiest way to cut off the stalk and flower end (which is what is meant by the term 'top and tail') is to use a pair of sharp kitchen scissors. Ideally, one should 'top and tail' blackcurrants, but if you are prepared to soften the fruit well, this is not essential, although it obviously gives a less perfect jam. In jellies where the fruit is being put through a jelly bag, do not bother to do this.
4. To remove stones from hard fruit, cut with a stainless knife and take out the stones. If the fruit is slightly under-ripe you may find this difficult in which case leave the stones in and take them out after the fruit has softened.
   To stone cherries, insert a fine new hairpin into the fruit with the bent end going into the cherry. Move this around until you feel it lock around the stone, then pull sharply and you will find it brings the stone with it. Do this over the preserving pan as you tend to bring juice out with the stone. Or use a cherry stoner.
   If you are following a recipe where it says 1 lb. stoned fruit and you have left the stones in, allow an extra 2–4 oz. fruit.
5. When peeling fruit, use a stainless knife and peel as thinly as possible to waste the minimum of fruit.
   If you wish to skin fruits, such as peaches, immerse for a few seconds in boiling water to loosen the skin, lift out, place in cold water to cool the fruit rapidly, and then skin.

Note

These preparations should be done just before making the jam as the moment you wash, stone or peel the fruit it is inclined to deteriorate.

Setting quality of fruits

Some fruits set more easily than others – due to the amount of pectin and acid they contain. It may seem that some recipes are a little out of proportion, but this is not the case. The amount of water and sugar has been carefully calculated so that you will get a jam that sets in the minimum of time. With fruits, that are lacking in setting quality, such as ripe cherries and strawberries, it is essential to use rather more fruit than sugar, with the addition of extra pectin and acid in the form of lemon juice or redcurrant juice.

Your preserving pan in jam making

This should be of sufficient size so the jam can boil rapidly without fear of it boiling over. A wide pan allows for rapid evaporation of the liquid, so reaching setting point more quickly. Use copper or aluminium but never use chipped enamel pans in jam making. A proper preserving pan has a handle from which the pan can be suspended when not in use which ensures that it has a good air circulation to keep it fresh. If you shut pans away in tightly closed cupboards and do not use them for some months, they often have a rather musty smell which can affect the taste of your jam.

Sugar to use in jam making
Special preserving sugar is the best, but you can use loaf or granulated sugar.

Brown sugar does not give such a good set to the jam. It does, however, produce a very delicious flavour, so you may like to try using 25% brown sugar and the rest white.

Honey in jam making – honey gives a splendid flavour to jam, but it does not allow the jam to set firmly. You can, however, use 25% honey and 75% sugar for a firm set, or 50% honey and 50% sugar for a softer jam.

Golden syrup in jam making – golden syrup gives its special flavour to jam, but used alone it will not give a good set. You can, however, use 25% golden syrup and 75% sugar for a firm set, or 50% golden syrup and 50% sugar for a softer jam.

Stirring the sugar in jam making
You will notice that a lot of stress has been laid in the various recipes on stirring the sugar until it has dissolved. This is very important because the undissolved sugar could burn on the bottom of the pan or give you a slightly crystallised effect in the finished jam. You can always tell if the sugar is undissolved if you tap the bottom of the pan with a wooden spoon. There is a faint 'crunch' if there are any grains of sugar left.

Using acid or lemon juice in jam making
Because some fruits do not set well, you will find the juice of a lemon included in some recipes, or mention made of citric or tartaric acid. The acid can be used in place of the lemon juice. Substitute ½ level teaspoon for 1 average sized lemon.

Amount of lemon to use in jam making
If the recipe includes the juice of a lemon, choose one of average size, which will give a good yield of juice. Should the lemon be rather dry, use a second to make certain of a set.

Scum on preserves
Most jams and jellies form a scum as they cook. It is very wasteful to try and take this off a number of times during cooking. It is better to wait until the jam has reached setting point and then give a very brisk stir which may disperse the scum. If any remains, take this off with a metal spoon. A knob of butter put in while making helps to prevent scum forming. There is nothing harmful in this, but if you are entering jam for a competition it could spoil the clarity of the preserve.

Filling jam jars
Fill your jars to about ⅛ ¼ inch from the top. This not only saves space, but the jam will keep better. If you have any half-filled jars, use these up quickly.

Many people expect that from each pound of sugar and pound of fruit, etc. they will have 2 lb. jam, and indeed it often happens and the jam tastes delicious and keeps well.

It is, however, a proved fact today that perfect jam (by this I mean jam that will keep throughout the season) should contain 60% sugar. This means that from your pound of sugar you get less than 2 lb. jam.

In a preserve or conserve where the fruit is poached in a thick syrup, you may get a little more than 1⅔ lb. jam.

With jams using commercial pectin, the yield per pound of sugar is rather more than the table below, which gives an indication of the yield.

Pounds of sugar	Final weight of jam
1 lb.	1⅔ lb.
2 lb.	3⅓ lb.
3 lb.	5 lb.
4 lb.	6⅔ lb.
5 lb.	8⅓ lb.
6 lb.	10 lb.
7 lb.	11⅔ lb.
8 lb.	13⅓ lb.

Importance of testing jam
On page 7 are the methods of testing whether your jam or jelly has set. Many people leave this testing rather late and they then find that the jam does not set. Often they think it is because it has been *under boiled* whereas in actual fact it has been boiled for such a long period that the setting point has been passed. With some fruits when once this has happened you cannot get them to set properly afterwards. The only remedy would be to mix with other well made jam.

Storing preserves

You must be careful where you store your preserves. The cupboard should be very dry. Dampness, or condensation of steam can cause the formation of mould.

If your house is centrally heated, the jam may become too dry and hard with storing. To prevent this, put your jam into proper bottling jars and you will find that it is not affected by the heat. To keep jam a good colour store away from a bright light.

Using preserves

While well made jam keeps for a very long time there will be a tendency for it to ferment if you fill only half the jar for this allows air to come into contact with the jam, in time, causing evaporation.

20 points for perfect jams, jellies and marmalades

1 Select firm – ripe – but not over-ripe fruit.

2 Follow recipe carefully for amount of sugar to fruit. Many people think all fruits need 1 lb. sugar to 1 lb. fruit – this is quite wrong. Where a fruit has little natural pectin (setting quality), i.e. sweet cherries – you need *more* fruit than sugar, and in addition it helps to add acid in the form of lemon juice, redcurrant juice, or commercial pectin.
Where a fruit is rich in pectin, e.g. blackcurrants, you get a better jam if you use more sugar than fruit.

3 Select a large enough pan, to allow jam to boil hard without splashing.

4 Use preserving, loaf or granulated sugar. Warm the sugar slightly as this will make it dissolve more quickly.

5 Do stew the fruit *slowly*. This is very important for it:
(a) extracts pectin (natural setting substance).
(b) softens skins – test most carefully; the skin *must* be soft before you add the sugar.
(c) helps to keep jam a good colour.

6 Stir until sugar has dissolved, to make certain the jam does not burn or crystallise during cooking.

7 When the sugar has dissolved, boil jam RAPIDLY WITHOUT STIRRING. The quicker the jam or jelly sets, the better the yield – flavour and colour.

8 Test early for setting. Some jams are ready within 3–5 minutes, others take 10–15 minutes, or even more. Many fruits will lose their setting qualities if boiled too long and then the jam NEVER sets.
There are several ways of testing:

Weight

The table on page 6 gives the ideal yield you should obtain from the recipes.

If you have sufficiently large and strong scales weigh the preserving pan before cooking. If you feel jam or jelly is ready, weigh again. Deduct weight of pan from total weight and if it is more than the table suggests the jam needs boiling a little longer.

Temperature

If you make a lot of jams or jellies it is worth investing in a sugar thermometer – stir round in hot jam – jam has reached setting point at 220°F – 222°F; and jelly at 220°F – 221°F.
Be careful not to put thermometer on cold surface or it will break.

Forming a skin

Put a little jam on an old saucer and allow to become quite cold, then see if it forms a skin and wrinkles when pushed with a spoon or finger.
Take pan off heat while waiting for jam to cool on saucer.

Forming a flake

Stir wooden spoon round in jam so that it becomes thoroughly coated, then allow to cool. Hold horizontally and inspect jam. If it hangs in

a firm drop or flake then it has reached setting point.
Take pan off heat while waiting for jam to cool on spoon.

9 When you are satisfied that the jam is ready, take pan off the heat, and remove the scum. If there is not much scum, most of this will disappear if stirred steadily. For competitions it is wise to remove the scum with a strainer, and then stir. When making jelly remove the scum with a strainer and by drawing a piece of *white* kitchen blotting paper quickly across the surface of the preserve.

10 For a jelly or jam that contains no whole fruit:
(a) Pour at once into *hot – dry – clean* jars. Tap jar as you fill to bring air bubbles to the surface.
Fill to at least $\frac{1}{8}$ to $\frac{1}{4}$ inch from top of jar. The jam or jelly will shrink a little as it cools. This also makes certain there is less air space in the jar and, therefore, less chance of it becoming mouldy. Jars filled to the brim also look more attractive.
(b) For a jam containing whole fruit, allow jam to cool in pan until it stiffens slightly, then stir to distribute peel or whole fruit and pour into hot jars.

11 Put on waxed circles *at once* – put final transparent cover on at once, or wait until jam is quite cold. Tie down firmly or use rubber band.

12 Store in a cool, dry *dark* place.

13 If a jam shows signs of mould, it is due to:
(a) Damp fruit.
(b) Insufficient boiling – giving too low a proportion of sugar in the finished jam.
(c) Bad storage conditions (e.g. damp).
(d) Not filling jars sufficiently or covering well.

14 If jam crystallises it is due to:
(a) Either using too much sugar in proportion to the amount of fruit, or too little sugar, which necessitated over-cooking to stiffen jam.
(b) Not stirring thoroughly to make sure sugar has dissolved before boiling.
(c) Too long cooking.

15 If jam shows signs of fermenting and has a 'winey' flavour, it is due to:
(a) Using over-ripe fruit.
(b) Bottling before the jam has reached setting point.
(c) Using too little sugar or not boiling jam sufficiently to give the right proportion of sugar in finished jam.
(d) Bad storage conditions.
(e) Not covering jars correctly.

16 If jam or jelly is hard and dry, it is due to:
(a) Over-boiling.
(b) Bad covering so that jam dries out in storage. (With central heating it is always advisable to put jam or jelly either into bottling jars or use tightly fitting caps over waxed circles – not just paper covers.)

17 If jam or jelly is syrupy and not firmly set it is because:
(a) The fruit juice was lacking in pectin (not enough natural setting quality).
(b) Not boiled sufficiently, or over-boiled. Jam which is boiled PASSED setting point gives sticky, syrupy texture.
(c) Fruit juice in jelly left too long after straining – use as soon as ready.

18 If jam or jelly is a poor colour, it is due to:
(a) Poor quality fruit.
(b) Not stewing fruit slowly enough to soften it sufficiently.
(c) Over-boiling, or boiling jam too slowly up to setting point.
(d) Storing in bright light.
(e) Using a poor quality preserving pan.

19 If jam or jelly has disappointing flavour it is because:
(a) The fruit used was too ripe or under-ripe.
(b) Too much sugar was used, giving over-sweet taste.
(c) Boiling too slowly or over-boiling, takes away fresh fruit flavour.

20 If jelly is cloudy in appearance it is because:
(a) It was badly strained – use proper jelly bag (see page 30), or several thicknesses of muslin over a hair (not wire) sieve.
(b) The pulp was *forced* through the jelly bag or muslin – allow to drip by itself without pressing or encouraging it through with a spoon.

Hints when entering jams and jellies for competitions

Marks are given for

(a) Appearance of the jar:
Is it clearly marked?
Is it filled to the top? (see point 10a in 20 points for perfect jams and jellies on page 8).
Is it neatly covered by:
(*a*) wax circle? (the correct size).
(*b*) top covering? (point 11).
It pays to polish jars well since this helps to make them look attractive and gives a chance for the judge to admire the colour of the jam.

(b) Contents are judged on colour – it should be bright (points 5 and 7). In the case of jellies it should be crystal clear (points 5 and 7). Where whole fruit is included, this should be well distributed (point 10b).

(c) The judge will then open jars and look at the *condition of the jam or jelly* – obviously many points are lost if jams have even faint signs of mould (point 13), if slightly sugary (points 6 and 15), or have a fermented taste (point 15).

(d) Consistency – this is important. A good jam is firm but not over-stiff (point 16), a good jelly is firm but not hard and sticky and never syrupy (points 16 and 17).

(e) Flavour – this is the most important quality of all. Read points 1, 2, 5a, 13, 14, 15, 16, and 19.
The jam or jelly should have the smell and taste of fresh fruit.
When mixing fruits try to get a good proportion of each – e.g. strawberry and rhubarb – equal proportions allows one to taste both fruits, but when mixing raspberry and rhubarb, because raspberries have a strong flavour, use a little more rhubarb.
Under the heading of flavour will come points like the taste of fruit peels or skins (point 5b). If these are tough you will lose marks.

(f) Originality – in an open class you may win if you have used a less usual recipe, so look out for new ideas.

Jams, cheeses, conserves and preserves

In this chapter you will find a very varied selection of jams of every kind.
The instructions will, I think, be easy to follow, but before making a recipe, may I suggest you read through the 20 points for perfect jam making (see page 7).
You will also find cheeses, which are based on a jam recipe; conserves and preserves, which are no more difficult to make than jams, but which enable you to make something that is a little out of the ordinary.

Making a cheese
A cheese is the name given to a preserve where all the fruit is sieved before adding the sugar. They are particularly useful in the case of fruits containing a lot of pips and stones such as blackberries or damsons. If you have a small child or someone on a gastric diet, this is the type of preserve to make. Measure the fruit pulp after cooking and sieving, and allow 1 lb. of sugar to each lb. or pint of the fruit pulp.

Rub the fruit very hard through a sieve otherwise you can waste a great deal.

Making a conserve
The difference between a conserve and jam, or a preserve, is that you add additional ingredients to give a more unusual flavour.

The method of making is, however, quite usual, and not at all difficult.

Making a preserve

The difference between a jam and a preserve is that for a jam the fruit is cooked to a purée. This light cooking will retain pieces of the fruit. In the case of a preserve, however, the fruit is purposely cooked to keep it whole. This is done in two ways:

1 By 'poaching' the fruit in a sugar and water syrup, or
2 By sprinkling the sugar over the fruit and stewing gently.

Note

Do not expect the syrup in most preserves to set, as firmly as in a jam.

Apples in jam making

While most cooking apples are good in jam making, a rather cheap apple such as a Bramley Seedling retains most of its flavour. The weight given in these recipes is after peeling and coring. The peel, core and pips can be tied in muslin and simmered together with the fruit, for these give flavour and help the jam to set.

Apple and cherry jam

cooking time: 30 minutes

you will need:

1 lb. cooking apples (after peeling and coring)
¼ pint water
2¼ lb. ripe dessert cherries
3 lb. sugar

1 Simmer the apples with the water until they start to get soft.
2 Add the cherries and continue cooking until these are softened but unbroken.
3 Remove as many stones as possible.
4 Add sugar and stir until dissolved.
5 Boil rapidly until set.

Apple ginger jam (1)

cooking time: 30 minutes

you will need:

1 lb. cooking apples (after peeling and coring)
1 lb. sugar
1 teaspoon ground ginger

1 Cut the apples into neat cubes.
2 Sprinkle over the sugar.
3 Tie cores and peelings in a muslin bag, and place this in with the apples and sugar. Leave to stand overnight.
4 Put into a saucepan or preserving pan.
5 Simmer gently, stirring all the time, until the sugar has quite dissolved.
6 Add ginger.
7 Boil steadily until the cubes of apples look transparent and the syrup has set.
8 Remove cores and peel.

Apple ginger jam (2)

cooking time: 30 minutes

you will need:

2½ lb. cooking apples (after peeling and coring)
½ pint water
1–2 teaspoons powdered ginger
2 lb. sugar

1 Peel and core the apples.
2 Tie peel and cores in muslin bag.
3 Simmer the fruit with the water and ginger until a very smooth pulp. Remove muslin bag.
4 Add the sugar, and stir until dissolved.
5 Boil steadily until set.

Apple lemon jam (1)

cooking time: 30 minutes

you will need:

2 lb. cooking apples (after peeling and coring)
½ pint water
grated rind and juice of 2 lemons
2 lb. sugar

1 Simmer the apples with the water and grated rind of the lemons.
2 When quite soft add lemon juice and sugar.
3 Stir until the sugar has dissolved.
4 Boil rapidly until set.

Apple lemon jam (2)

cooking time: 20–25 minutes

you will need:

2 lb. apples (after peeling and coring)
grated rind 2 lemons
½ pint water
2¼ lb. sugar

1 Slice apples thinly and simmer with lemon rind and water until soft.
2 Stir in sugar and lemon juice, until sugar is dissolved.
3 Boil until set.

Apple orange jam

cooking time: 30 minutes

you will need:

2 lb. cooking apples (after peeling and coring)
½ pint water
grated rind 3 oranges
pulp 3 oranges
2¼ lb. sugar

1 Simmer the apples with the water and grated orange rind.
2 When quite soft add the pulp and juice of the oranges and sugar.
3 Stir until the sugar has dissolved.
4 Boil rapidly until set.

Apple and pineapple jam

cooking time: 35 minutes

you will need:

1 lb. cooking apples (after peeling and coring)
1 lb. pineapple (weight after peeling)
⅛ pint water
2 lb. sugar

1 Dice fruit.
2 Simmer the apples and pineapple with the water until soft.
3 Stir in the sugar until dissolved.
4 Boil rapidly until set.

Apple date preserve

cooking time: 30 minutes

you will need:

2 lb. cooking apples (after peeling and coring)
juice 2 lemons
2 lb. sugar
12 oz. dessert dates

1 Peel the apples and cut the fruit into neat slices.
2 Leave for several hours with the lemon juice and sugar.
3 Put into preserving pan.
4 Stir over low heat until sugar has dissolved.
5 Add the quartered dates and continue cooking until jam has set.

Apple and plum jam

cooking time: 30 minutes

you will need:

1 lb. cooking apples (after peeling and coring)
2 lb. plums (after stoning)
¼ pint water
3 lb. sugar

1 Simmer the fruit with the water until soft.
2 Stir in sugar until dissolved.
3 Boil until set.

Apple and rhubarb jam

cooking time: 30 minutes

you will need:

1 lb. rhubarb
1 lb. cooking apples
⅛ pint water
2 lb. sugar

1 Dice the rhubarb and chop the apples.
2 Put into a saucepan with the water and simmer until soft.
3 Add the sugar, stir until dissolved.
4 Boil rapidly until set.

Apple cheeses

cooking time: 30 minutes

Any of the apple jam or preserve recipes can be made into a cheese.

1 Simmer the fruit and water until soft.
2 Rub through a sieve and measure the pulp.
3 Allow 1 lb. sugar to each 1 lb. or pint of pulp.
4 Stir until the sugar has dissolved.
5 Boil rapidly until set.

Note
There is no need to peel or core the apples.

Apple and damson jam

cooking time: 30 minutes

you will need:

1 lb. cooking apples (after peeling and coring)
1½ lb. damsons (stoned)
½ pint water
2¼ lb. sugar

1 Put the fruits with the water into a pan.
2 Simmer until soft.
3 Remove as many damson stones as possible.
4 Stir in the sugar.
5 Boil rapidly until set.
This jam will be enjoyed by the people who find damsons rather 'biting'.

Apple fig preserve

cooking time: 30 minutes

you will need:

2 lb. cooking apples (after peeling and coring)
juice 2 lemons
2 lb. sugar
¼ pint water
8 oz. dried figs

1 Peel the apples and cut the fruit into neat slices.
2 Leave for several hours with the lemon juice, sugar, and water.
3 Put into preserving pan.
4 Stir over low heat until sugar has dissolved.
5 Add the dried figs cut into neat fingers and continue cooking until jam has set.

Apricot jam

cooking time: 30 minutes

you will need:

1 lb. fresh apricots
2–3 tablespoons water (if fruit is under-ripe, use ⅛ pint)
1 lb. sugar
¼ level teaspoon citric or tartaric acid or juice ½ lemon

1 Cut the fruit into pieces.
2 If desired, crack the stones and take out the kernels.
3 Put into preserving pan with the water and simmer until the fruit is soft.
4 Add the sugar and lemon juice or acid and stir until dissolved.
5 Boil rapidly until set.

Apricot conserve

cooking time: 35 minutes

you will need:

1 lb. ripe apricots
juice 1 lemon
1 lb. sugar

1 Halve small apricots or quarter large ones.
2 Put into the pan with the lemon juice and sugar.
3 Heat very gently, stirring all the time until the sugar has dissolved.
4 Boil steadily until set.

Apricot and almond conserve

cooking time: 30 minutes

Use apricot jam recipe, but add 2 oz. blanched chopped almonds when jam has set.

Apricot jam (dried fruit)

cooking time: 1¼ hours

you will need:

1 lb. dried apricots
3 pints water
3 lb. sugar
1½ level teaspoons citric or tartaric acid, or juice 2 lemons

1 Soak the fruit in the water for 48 or even 72 hours.
2 Simmer gently until the fruit is soft.
3 Add the sugar and acid or lemon juice, stir until dissolved.
4 Boil rapidly until set.

Apricot conserve (dried fruit)

cooking time: 1½–2 hours

1 Follow the recipe for dried apricot jam (see above), and allow 2 oranges and 2 oz. seedless raisins to each lb. dried apricots.
2 Soak the slices of orange with the apricots, tying the pips in a muslin bag.
3 Add the dried fruit to the apricots and oranges.

4 Simmer until soft.
5 Remove the pips and continue as for dried apricot jam.
6 When this has reached setting point, add 2 oz. chopped walnuts or brazils.

Apricot and cherry jam

cooking time: 30 minutes

you will need:

2 lb. apricots
1 lb. cherries
⅛ pint water (if fruit is very firm, use ¼ pint water)
3 lb. sugar
juice 2 lemons

1 Simmer the fruit with the water until soft.
2 Add the sugar and the lemon juice.
3 Stir until the sugar is dissolved.
4 Boil rapidly until set.

Banana and apple jam

cooking time: 30 minutes

you will need:

1 lb. cooking apples (after peeling and coring)
¼ pint water
grated rind 2 lemons
2 lb. bananas
juice 2 lemons
3 lb. sugar

1 Simmer the apples with the water and lemon rind.
2 When soft, add the mashed banana and lemon juice.
3 Cook for a few minutes only.
4 Add the sugar and stir until dissolved.
5 Boil rapidly until set.

Banana and lemon jam

cooking time: 1¼ hours

you will need:

6 bananas
3 lemons
1 lb. castor sugar

1 Peel and cut up the bananas as small as possible.
2 Grate the lemon rind and squeeze and strain the juice.
3 Put the bananas, grated rind and juice in a china or glass bowl.
4 Cover with the sugar.
5 Allow to stand for 1 hour for the sugar to dissolve.
6 Place the contents of the bowl into a pan and bring very slowly to the boil. This should take about 1 hour.
7 Boil until the jam sets.

Banana and orange jam

cooking time: 1¼ hours

you will need:

6 bananas
3 oranges
1 lb. castor sugar

1 Peel and slice bananas.
2 Put into preserving pan.
3 Pour the strained juice over, and add grated rind and pulp of the oranges.
4 Add the sugar.
5 Leave to stand for 30 minutes.
6 Bring to the boil very slowly.
7 Boil rapidly until set.

Blackberry jam

cooking time: 25 minutes

you will need:

2 lb. blackberries
juice 1 lemon
sugar

1 Simmer fruit and lemon juice.
2 Sieve to remove pips.
3 Allow 1 lb. sugar to each pint pulp.
4 Reheat fruit.
5 Stir in sugar until dissolved, and boil steadily until set.

Blackberry cheese

cooking time: 30 minutes

you will need:

1 lb. cooking apples (unpeeled)
2 lb. blackberries
¼ pint water
sugar

1 Simmer the sliced apples, blackberries and water until soft.
2 Rub through a sieve and measure the pulp.
3 Allow 1 lb. sugar to each lb. or pint of the pulp.
4 Stir until the sugar has dissolved.
5 Boil rapidly until set.

Blackberry and apple jam

cooking time: 25–30 minutes

you will need:

1 lb. cooking apples (after peeling and coring)
⅛ pint water
1 lb. blackberries
2 lb. sugar

1 Put the sliced apples and water into the preserving pan.
2 Cook gently until the apples become soft.
3 Add the blackberries.
4 Continue cooking until all the fruit is soft.
5 Stir in the sugar.
6 Continue stirring until sugar is dissolved.
7 Boil rapidly until jam has set.

Blackberry and elderberry jam

cooking time: 25–30 minutes

you will need:

1 lb. blackberries
1 lb. elderberries
2 lb. sugar
juice 2 lemons

1 Simmer the fruit until soft. There should be no need to add water unless the fruit is very under-ripe.
2 Stir in the sugar and lemon juice.
3 Boil rapidly until set.

Blackberry and pineapple jam

cooking time: approximately 35–40 minutes

you will need:

1 lb. fresh pineapple (peeled)
2 large cooking apples, peeled and cored
little water
1 lb. blackberries
3 lb. sugar
juice 3 lemons

1 Dice pineapple and mix with slices of apple.
2 Simmer gently for about 15 minutes adding as little water as possible.
3 Add the blackberries and continue cooking for a further 5–10 minutes until soft.
4 Stir in the sugar and the lemon juice, and stir until sugar is dissolved.
5 Boil rapidly until set.

The secret of tender blackcurrants in jam

1 Simmer the fruit very gently – and *never* add sugar until you are certain the fruit is tender.
2 After cooking gently for about 15–20 minutes, try one or two currants. The skin should be so soft you can nearly 'rub it away' with your fingers.

Blackcurrant jam (1)

cooking time: 40 minutes

you will need:

1 lb. blackcurrants
¾ pint water
1¼ lb. sugar

1 Put the fruit and water into preserving pan.
2 Simmer very slowly until the blackcurrants are quite soft.
3 Stir in the sugar.
4 Boil rapidly until set.

Blackcurrant jam (2)

Use recipe and method as Blackcurrant jam (1) but use only ½ pint water. This gives a thicker jam with a stronger flavour.

Blackcurrant and apple jam

cooking time: 40 minutes

you will need:

1 lb. blackcurrants
½ pint water
1 lb. cooking apples (after peeling and coring)
2¼ lb. sugar

1 Simmer the blackcurrants and water for approximately 15 minutes.
2 Add the sliced apples and continue cooking until soft.
3 Stir in the sugar, and stir until dissolved.
4 Boil rapidly until set.

Blackcurrant and rhubarb jam

cooking time: 40 minutes

you will need:

1 lb. blackcurrants
½ pint water
1 lb. rhubarb, sliced
2¼ lb. sugar

1 Simmer the blackcurrants and water for approximately 15 minutes.
2 Add the rhubarb and continue cooking until soft.
3 Add the sugar and stir until dissolved.
4 Boil rapidly until set.

Blackcurrant cheeses

cooking time: 30 minutes

Because many people find the pips of blackcurrants rather troublesome, a cheese made from this fruit is very delicious. Use any of the recipes. Rub through a sieve. If you like a rather sharp jam, use only 14 oz. sugar to each pint of pulp. Most people will like just over a lb. of sugar to each pint or lb. of pulp.

Blackcurrant and redcurrant jam (1)

cooking time: 35–40 minutes

you will need:

1 lb. blackcurrants
1 lb. redcurrants
¾ pint water
2¼ lb. sugar

1 Simmer fruit with water until skins become very soft.
2 Add the sugar and stir until sugar is dissolved. Bring to the boil rapidly.
3 Test very soon after boiling point is reached, as this jam sets very quickly.

Blackcurrant and redcurrant jam (2)

cooking time: 40 minutes

you will need:

2 lb. blackcurrants
1¼ pints water
1 lb. redcurrants
3 lb. sugar

Use method for blackcurrant jam (1) but simmer blackcurrants with water for 10 minutes, then add redcurrants.

Blaeberry jam

This is another name for blueberries, see below.

Bilberry jam

This is another name for blueberries, see below.

Whortleberry jam

This is another name for blueberries, see below.

Blueberry jam

cooking time: 20 minutes

you will need:

1 lb. blueberries
1 lb. sugar

1 Simmer the fruit for 5 minutes only, using no water.
2 Add the sugar and stir until dissolved.
3 Boil steadily until just set.

Note
This jam sets quickly and boiling too rapidly will spoil the shape of the blueberries.

Black cherry preserve

cooking time: 35 minutes

you will need:

1¼ lb. black cherries
1 lb. sugar
juice 1 lemon

1 Sprinkle the sugar over the cherries and leave to stand for several hours.
2 Put into the pan with the lemon juice and simmer gently until the sugar has dissolved, stirring well.
3 Boil rapidly until a little of the syrup is fairly firm.

Note
This jam should never be very stiff.

Cherry jam

cooking time: 20–25 minutes

you will need:

1 lb. cherries* (stoned) or nearly 1¼ lb. before stoning
12 oz. sugar
juice ½ lemon or ½ level teaspoon citric or tartaric acid

*If using red morello cherries use only half the quantity of acid. Use black cherries for Swiss jam.

1 Tie the stones in muslin, and add to the fruit in the pan.
2 Simmer until the skin of the fruit is soft.
3 Stir in the sugar, and add lemon juice or acid.
4 Continue stirring until sugar is dissolved.
5 Boil rapidly until set.

Cherry conserve

cooking time: 20–25 minutes

1 Use recipe and method for cherry jam, but add 2 oz. raisins to each lb. cherries and simmer these with the fruit.
2 When jam has reached setting point, add 2 oz. chopped walnuts to each lb. fruit.

Cherry and apricot jam

cooking time: 25 minutes

you will need:

1 lb. stoned morello or red cherries*
1 lb. fresh apricots (stoned)
⅛ pint water
2 lb. sugar
juice 2 lemons

*Use just over 1 lb. if you want to remove stones as they rise to the top during cooking.

1 Put the fruit and water into pan and simmer gently until tender.
2 Add sugar and lemon juice, and stir until sugar is dissolved.
3 Boil steadily until set.

Clove and apple jam

cooking time: 30 minutes

1 Use recipe and method for apple ginger jam (see page 10) but omit ginger and allow 3–4 cloves per lb. of jam.
2 Tie cloves in muslin and remove when jam has set.

Cranberry jam

cooking time: 35 minutes

you will need:

1 lb. cranberries
¼ pint water
1¼ lb. sugar

1 Simmer the cranberries with the water until skins are soft. If the fruit is very firm you may need to add a little extra water.
2 Add the sugar and stir until dissolved.
3 Boil rapidly until set.

Cranberry conserve

cooking time: 35 minutes

1 Use the recipe and method for cranberry jam (see above), adding grated rind of 1 orange and 2 oz. currants to each lb. of cranberries.
2 When setting point is reached, add 2 oz. blanched chopped almonds to each lb. of conserve.

Cucumber jam

cooking time: 30 minutes

you will need:

2 lb. cucumber (after peeling)
⅛ pint water
juice 2 lemons
2 lb. sugar

1 Simmer the diced cucumber in the water until soft.
2 Add the lemon juice and sugar.
3 Stir until sugar has dissolved.
4 Boil rapidly until set.

Variation

With colouring – this jam tends to be a little pale in colour and you may like to add a few drops of green colouring. Or you can simmer the cucumber with a little of the peel left on and rub it through a sieve. The peel helps to give a cool green colour: too much peel will give the jam a bitter taste.

Cucumber and ginger jam

cooking time: 30 minutes

Use the recipe and method as cucumber jam, adding a little powdered ginger to taste.

Damson jam

cooking time: 25–30 minutes

you will need:

⅛ pint water (if fruit is ripe)
1 lb. damsons
1 lb. sugar

If fruit is very under-ripe, use the following quantities:

1 lb. damsons
½ pint water
1¼ lb. sugar

1 Put the fruit and water into a preserving pan.
2 Simmer until soft, removing as many stones as possible.
3 Add sugar and stir until dissolved.
4 Boil rapidly until set.

Damson cheeses

cooking time: 30 minutes

As it takes such a long time to remove the stones from damson jam, a cheese is a very good way of avoiding this. Use any of the damson jam recipes. Rub the fruit through a sieve. Allow 1 lb. of sugar to each lb. or pint of pulp. Stir until the sugar has dissolved and boil rapidly until set.

Damson and marrow jam

cooking time: 35–40 minutes

you will need:

1 lb. damsons
1 lb. marrow (peeled)
⅛ pint water
2 lb. sugar

1 Put damsons, diced marrow and water into a preserving pan.
2 Simmer until soft.
3 Remove as many stones as possible.
4 Add the sugar and stir until dissolved.
5 Boil rapidly until set.

Elderberry jam

cooking time: 25 minutes

you will need:

1 lb. elderberries
1 lb. sugar
juice 1 lemon

1 Crush the elderberries in preserving pan.
2 Simmer until soft.
3 Add the sugar and stir well until dissolved.
4 Add lemon juice.
5 Boil rapidly until set.

Elderberry and apple jam

cooking time: 30 minutes

you will need:

1 lb. elderberries
1 lb. apples
¼ pint water
2 lb. sugar

1 Simmer the fruit with the water until tender.
2 Add the sugar and stir until dissolved.
3 Boil rapidly until set.

Fresh fig preserve

cooking time: 45 minutes

you will need:

1 lb. fresh ripe figs
1 lb. sugar
juice 1 lemon

1 If the figs are very small, they can be left whole. If large, halve or quarter them.
2 Put into the preserving pan with the sugar and lemon juice.
3 Heat gently, stirring all the time until the sugar has dissolved.
4 Boil steadily until set.

Green fig preserve

cooking time: 45 minutes

Use recipe and method for fresh fig preserve, using green figs.

Fig and lemon jam

cooking time: 1–1¼ hours

you will need:

2 lb. dried figs
1½ pints water
3 lb. sugar
juice 2 lemons

1. Soak figs in water for 12 hours.
2. Rinse in fresh water.
3. Cut into small pieces, removing any hard pieces of stem.
4. Put into a preserving pan with 1½ pints fresh hot water.
5. Simmer until tender.
6. Stir in sugar and strained lemon juice.
7. Continue to cook, until the preserve is thick.
8. Pour into jam jars while hot.

Four fruit jam

cooking time: 20–25 minutes

you will need:

8 oz. blackcurrants
⅛ pint water
8 oz. redcurrants
8 oz. raspberries
8 oz. strawberries
2 lb. sugar

1. Simmer blackcurrants in the water until nearly soft.
2. Add the rest of the fruit.
3. Continue cooking for a further 5–10 minutes.
4. Add the sugar, stirring until dissolved.
5. Boil rapidly until set.

Fruit salad jam (dried fruit)

cooking time: 1¼ hours

Use recipe and method for dried apricot jam but substitute dried fruit salad.
The taste of this jam is most pleasant.

Gooseberries in jam making

People are often disappointed with the colour of their gooseberry jam. If you want a really green jam, then you must use the firm green fruit. Ripe gooseberries, even if they have not turned red, give a pinky coloured jam.

Gooseberry jam

cooking time: 25–35 minutes

you will need:

1 lb. gooseberries
⅛ pint water (if fruit is ripe)
1 lb. sugar

If fruit is very under-ripe use the following quantities:

1 lb. gooseberries
½ pint water
1¼ lb. sugar

1. Put the fruit and water into a preserving pan.
2. Simmer until soft.
3. Add the sugar and stir until dissolved.
4. Boil rapidly until set.

Gooseberry and cherry jam

cooking time: 25–30 minutes

you will need:

1 lb. firm gooseberries
¼ pint water
1½ lb. cherries
2 lb. sugar

1. Put the gooseberries, water and cherries into the preserving pan.
2. Simmer until soft, removing as many cherry stones as possible.
3. Add sugar and stir until dissolved.
4. Boil until set.

Gooseberry and loganberry jam

cooking time: 25 minutes

you will need:

1 lb. ripe gooseberries
⅛ pint water
1 lb. loganberries
2 lb. sugar

1. Simmer the gooseberries with the water for about 10 minutes.
2. Add loganberries and continue cooking until these are soft.
3. Add sugar and stir until dissolved.
4. Boil rapidly until set.

Gooseberry and orange jam

cooking time: 25–35 minutes

you will need:

1½ lb. gooseberries
¼ pint water
2 oranges
1½ lb. sugar

1. Simmer gooseberries gently until tender with water, orange juice, and grated orange rind.

2 Add sugar and stir until dissolved.
3 Boil until setting point is reached.

Gooseberry and rhubarb conserve

cooking time: 30 minutes

you will need:

1 lb. rhubarb
1 lb. gooseberries
2 lb. sugar
juice 1 lemon

1 Cut the rhubarb into pieces about ½ inch in length.
2 Put into the pan with the gooseberries, sugar and lemon juice.
3 Leave to stand for several hours.
4 Heat gently, stirring all the time until the sugar has dissolved.
5 Boil rapidly until the jam has set lightly.

Gooseberry and strawberry jam

cooking time: 25 minutes

you will need:

1 lb. ripe gooseberries
⅛ pint water
1 lb. ripe strawberries
2 lb. sugar

1 Simmer the gooseberries with the water for about 10 minutes.
2 Add the strawberries and continue cooking until these are soft.
3 Add sugar and stir until dissolved.
4 Boil rapidly until set.

Gooseberry and strawberry conserve

cooking time: 30 minutes

you will need:

1 lb. strawberries
1 lb. gooseberries
2 lb. sugar
juice 1 lemon

1 Leave the strawberries whole and put into the pan with the gooseberries, sugar and lemon juice.
2 Leave to stand for several hours.
3 Heat gently, stirring all the time until the sugar has dissolved.
4 Boil rapidly until the jam has set lightly.

Gooseberry cheeses

cooking time: 30 minutes

Any of the gooseberry jam recipes will make a good cheese. As you will sieve the fruit for this, there is no need to 'top and tail' the gooseberries. Rub the fruit through a sieve. Allow 1 lb. of sugar to each pint or lb. of pulp. Boil rapidly until set.

Greengage jam

cooking time: 20–25 minutes

you will need:

1 lb. greengages (stoned)
use no water if fruit is ripe (⅛ pint water if under-ripe)
1 lb. sugar

1 The stones of the fruit can be cracked and the kernels included.
2 Simmer fruit until soft, adding water if necessary.
3 Add sugar and stir until dissolved.
4 Boil rapidly until set, adding kernels at the last minute.

Greengage and apple jam

cooking time: 35 minutes

you will need:

2 lb. greengages (stoned)
1 lb. cooking apples (after peeling and coring)
¼ pint water
3 lb. sugar

1 Simmer the fruit until soft. If the greengages are very ripe, they can be added after the apples have started to cook.
2 Add sugar and stir until dissolved.
3 Boil until set.

Greengage and red plum jam

cooking time: 25 minutes

you will need:

1 lb. greengages (stoned)
1 lb. red plums (stoned)
2 lb. sugar
⅛ pint water

Use recipe and method as for greengage jam.

Green grape jam

cooking time: 15–20 minutes

you will need:

1 lb. sharp green grapes
1 lb. sugar

1. Simmer the fruit, for a few minutes, using no water unless necessary.
2. Add sugar and stir until dissolved.
3. Boil rapidly until set.

Black grape jam

cooking time: 15–20 minutes

you will need:

1 lb. black grapes
juice 2 lemons
1 lb. sugar

Use method for green grape jam, adding the lemon juice with the sugar.

Grape cheese

cooking time: 15–20 minutes

Since many do not like the pips and skin of grapes in a jam, simmer fruit until soft and then rub through a sieve. Allow 1 lb. sugar to each pint or lb. of pulp and if grapes are ripe add the juice of 1 lemon. Stir until sugar has dissolved. Boil rapidly until set.

Guava jam

cooking time: 25–30 minutes

you will need:

1 lb. guava pulp
$\frac{1}{8}$ pint water
1 lb. sugar
juice 1 lemon

1. Simmer the pulp with the water until very soft.
2. Stir in the sugar and lemon juice.
3. Stir until sugar has dissolved.
4. Boil rapidly until set.

Huckleberry jam

cooking time: 25 minutes

you will need:

1 lb. huckleberries*
water
2 lb. sugar
juice 2 lemons

*Blueberries can be used instead.

1. Simmer the huckleberries with very little water.
2. Add sugar and lemon juice, stir until the sugar dissolves.
3. Boil until set.

Variation

With apples – if preferred you may use: 1 lb. huckleberries, 1 lb. cooking apples (after peeling and coring) and 2 lb. sugar. As huckleberries are lacking in pectin, you MUST put something in to help the jam to set.

Japonica jam

cooking time: 40 minutes

you will need:

1 lb. japonica (unpeeled)
1–$1\frac{1}{4}$ pints water (depending on ripeness of fruit)
pinch ground ginger
2 lemons
sugar

1. Do not peel or core the japonica.
2. Cut into halves and simmer in the water until pulp.
3. Add ground ginger.
4. Sieve and to each pint or lb. of pulp, add lemon juice and 1 lb. sugar.
5. Stir in the sugar until dissolved.
6. Boil until set.

Lemon and melon jam

cooking time: 30 minutes

you will need:

1 lb. melon (after peeling)
1 lb. sugar
grated rind and juice 2 lemons

1. Dice the melon.
2. Allow to stand overnight, with the sugar.
3. Next day put into a preserving pan.
4. Simmer gently, stirring well until the sugar has dissolved.
5. Add the lemon juice, and lemon rind.
6. Boil steadily until set.

Loganberry jam

cooking time: 20 minutes

you will need:

1 lb. loganberries
1 lb. sugar

1. Simmer fruit until soft.

2 Add sugar and stir until dissolved.
3 Boil rapidly until set.

Loganberry and cherry jam

cooking time: 25 minutes

you will need:

1 lb. cherries*
1 lb. loganberries
2 lb. sugar

*If cherries are very ripe, allow 1¼ lb. cherries.

1 Simmer fruit until soft, removing as many cherry stones as possible.
2 Add sugar and stir until dissolved.
3 Boil rapidly until set.

Loganberry and raspberry jam

cooking time: 20 minutes

you will need:

1 lb. loganberries
1 lb. raspberries
2 lb. sugar

1 Simmer loganberries until nearly soft.
2 Add raspberries and cook for a further few minutes.
3 Add sugar and stir until dissolved.
4 Boil rapidly until set.

Loganberry and redcurrant jam

cooking time: 20 minutes

you will need:

1 lb. loganberries
1 lb. redcurrants
¼ pint water
2 lb. sugar

Use method for loganberry jam.

Loganberry cheeses

cooking time: 20-25 minutes

you will need:

Use any of the recipes for loganberry jam, but rub through a sieve. Allow 1 lb. sugar to 1 lb. or pint fruit purée. Boil rapidly until set.

Lychee jam (fresh fruit)

cooking time: 15 minutes

you will need:

1 lb. fresh lychees (when removed from their shells)
just under 1 lb. sugar
juice 1 lemon

1 Simmer the lychees with the sugar and lemon juice. Remove stones.
2 Stir well until sugar has dissolved.
3 Boil steadily until set.

Lychee preserve (canned fruit)

cooking time: 15 minutes

1 Drain off syrup from can of lychees.
2 Weigh the fruit and allow 8 oz. sugar to each 1 lb. fruit.
3 Simmer the syrup from the tin with the extra sugar until this has dissolved.
4 Boil rapidly for a few minutes until a thicker syrup is formed.
5 Put in the lychees and simmer steadily for about 10 minutes.
6 If a firmer syrup is desired, add the juice of another lemon with a little extra sugar.

Marrow in jam making

The best flavoured marrow for jam is the late vegetable; a large marrow gives the best result.

Marrow and ginger jam

cooking time: 20-30 minutes

you will need:

1 lb. marrow (after peeling), cut into cubes
1 lb. sugar
1 level teaspoon ground ginger, or 1–2 oz. crystallised ginger
juice 1 large lemon

Use method for apple ginger jam (see page 10).

Marrow and lemon jam

cooking time: 25 minutes

you will need:

1 lb. marrow (after peeling), cut into cubes
juice and grated rind 2 lemons
1 lb. sugar

1 Put the marrow, lemon rind and sugar together and leave to stand overnight.
2 Simmer gently, adding lemon juice and stirring well until sugar has dissolved.
3 Boil steadily until set.

Marrow and orange jam

cooking time: 25 minutes

you will need:

1 lb. marrow (after peeling), cut into cubes
1 lb. sugar
pulp and grated rind 2 oranges
juice 1 lemon

Use the method for marrow and lemon jam, adding orange rind, orange pulp and lemon juice.

Melon and ginger jam

cooking time: 30 minutes

you will need:

1 lb. melon (after peeling)
1–2 oz. crystallised ginger
1 lb. sugar
juice 2 lemons

1 Dice melon.
2 Cut the crystallised ginger into small pieces.
3 Allow the melon, sugar and ginger to stand overnight.
4 Put into preserving pan and simmer gently, stirring until sugar has dissolved.
5 Add the lemon juice.
6 Boil steadily until set.

Mulberry jam (1)

cooking time: 30 minutes

you will need:

1 lb. mulberries
$\frac{1}{8}$ pint water
1 lb. sugar

1 Simmer the fruit with the water until soft.
2 Add sugar and stir until dissolved.
3 Boil rapidly until set.

Mulberry jam (2)

cooking time: 30 minutes

you will need:

1 lb. mulberries
8 oz. cooking apples (after peeling and coring)
$\frac{1}{4}$ pint water
1 lb. sugar

1 Mix mulberries, apples and water in a preserving pan.
2 Simmer together until tender.
3 Rub through a sieve.
4 Add sugar to the pulp, and stir until dissolved.
5 Boil rapidly until set.

Mulberry cheese

cooking time: 35 minutes

you will need:

mulberries
water
sugar

Because mulberries are so 'woody' in the centre it is even better to make a cheese.

1 To each lb. fruit, allow $\frac{1}{8}$ pint water.
2 Simmer steadily until soft, rub through sieve.
3 Allow 1 lb. sugar to each pint or lb. of pulp.
4 Stir well, adding the sugar.
5 Stir until sugar has dissolved.
6 Boil rapidly until set.

Passion fruit jam (fresh fruit) (1)

cooking time: 15 minutes

If the passion fruit is very ripe, allow the juice of 1 lemon to each pint of pulp.

1 Scoop out the pulp and allow 1 lb. sugar to 1 pint pulp.
2 Simmer the pulp with the sugar, stirring well until dissolved.
3 Boil rapidly until set.

Passion fruit jam (canned fruit) (2)

cooking time: approximately 15 minutes

Use canned passion fruit pulp. If sweetened allow 8 oz. sugar to each pint of pulp.
Use method for passion fruit jam (1).

Peach jam

cooking time: 30 minutes

Use recipe and method for apricot jam (see page 12).
Small under-ripe home-grown fruit could be used, in which case allow ¼ pint water to each lb. of fruit.

Peach conserve

cooking time: 35 minutes

you will need:

1 lb. ripe peaches
juice 1 lemon
1 lb. sugar

1 Halve small peaches or quarter large ones.
2 Put into the pan with the lemon juice and sugar.
3 Heat very gently, stirring all the time until the sugar has dissolved.
4 Boil steadily until set.

Peach jam (dried fruit)

cooking time: 1¼–1½ hours

Use recipe and method for apricot jam using dried fruit, see page 12, but use dried peaches instead.

Peach conserve (dried fruit)

cooking time: 1½ hours

1 Follow the recipe for dried peach jam (see above) and allow 1 lb. dried peaches, and 2 oz. seedless raisins to 2 oranges.
2 Soak the slices of orange with the peaches, tying the pips in a muslin bag.
3 Add the dried fruit to the peaches and oranges.
4 Simmer until soft.
5 Remove the pips and continue as for peach jam.
6 When setting point is reached add 2 oz. chopped almonds to each lb. of jam.

Peach and pear jam

cooking time: 30–35 minutes

you will need:

1 lb. ripe firm pears (after peeling and coring)
1 lb. peaches
¼ pint water
2 lb. sugar
juice and grated rind 2 lemons

1 Cut the pears into neat cubes and quarter the peaches.
2 Simmer gently with the water until soft, but do not reduce to a pulp.
3 Stir in the sugar and lemon rind and juice.
4 Stir until sugar has dissolved and boil rapidly until set.

Peach and pear conserve

cooking time: 30 minutes

Use ingredients as for peach and pear jam.

1 Boil sugar, water and lemon rind together for about 5 minutes until it becomes a thick syrup.
2 Add the pieces of fruit with the lemon juice and simmer steadily until these are transparent. The syrup should be thick to set firmly.

Pear and clove jam

cooking time: 30–45 minutes

Use recipe and method as for clove and apple jam (see page 16), using firm cooking pears instead of apples.

Pear and ginger jam

cooking time: 30–45 minutes

Use recipe and method as for apple ginger jam (see page 10), using firm pears instead of apples.

Note

If very hard pears are used, you may need a little extra water and a further 15 minutes cooking time.

Pear and lemon jam

cooking time: 30–45 minutes

Use recipe and method as for apple lemon jam (see page 10), using firm pears instead of apples.

Note

If very hard pears are used, you may need a little extra water and a further 15 minutes cooking time.

Pear and pineapple conserve

cooking time: 45 minutes

you will need:

3 lb. pears
1 medium can small pineapple cubes
1 orange
sugar
¼ pint bottle maraschino cherries

1 Cut pears into ½-inch cubes.
2 Add the pineapple, grated rind and orange juice.
3 Weigh the fruits and to each lb. add 12 oz. sugar.
4 Leave to stand overnight in a bowl.
5 Place in a preserving pan and simmer until thick.
6 Cut the cherries in half.
7 Add cherries and liquid from the bottle to the fruit.
8 Stir well but do not re-cook.
9 Pour into wide necked bottle and seal at once.

Pear preserve

cooking time: 25–30 minutes

you will need:

1 lb. ripe pears
1 lb. sugar
½ pint water
juice 2 lemons

1 Peel and cut the pears into neat pieces.
2 Simmer the sugar and water until the sugar has dissolved.
3 Add the pears and the lemon juice.
4 Cook slowly until these are soft.

Pear and ginger preserve

cooking time: 25–30 minutes

you will need:

1 lb. ripe pears
2 oz. preserved ginger
1 lb. sugar
½ pint water
juice 2 lemons

1 Peel and cut the pears into neat pieces, together with the preserved ginger.
2 Simmer the sugar and water until the sugar has dissolved.
3 Add the pears, ginger and lemon juice.
4 Cook slowly until tender.

Pear and orange jam

cooking time: 30–45 minutes

Use recipe as for apple orange jam (see pag 11), using pears instead of apples.

Note

If very hard pears are used, you may need a little extra water and a further 15 minutes cooking time.

Plums in jam making

Many people are inclined to use over-ripe plums in jam.
For a perfect flavour they should be firm, ripe, but not too soft.
Do not worry if there is a slight 'waxy' substance round the stone of the plum – that is completely harmless.
It is worth mixing plums with other kinds of fruit; each will give distinctive flavour.

Plum jam (1)

cooking time: 20–25 minutes

you will need:

1 lb. plums (stoned)
1 lb. sugar
use no water if fruit is ripe ($\frac{1}{8}$ pint if under-ripe)

Use method as for greengage jam (see page 19).

Plum jam (2)

cooking time: 25–30 minutes

If whole fruit jam is required, proceed as follows:

1 Cut plums into halves. Remove the stones.
2 Put into a bowl and sprinkle with the sugar.
3 Leave to stand overnight.
4 The next day proceed as usual, simmering until sugar has dissolved.
5 Boil *steadily* until set.

Plum jam (3)

cooking time: 20–25 minutes

you will need:

1 lb. plums (stoned)
12 oz. sugar
use no water if fruit is ripe ($\frac{1}{8}$ pint if under-ripe)

1 Simmer the plums with the water, if used, until fruit is soft.
2 Add sugar and stir until dissolved.
3 Boil rapidly until set.

Note

This gives a very good flavour for people who do not like jam which is very sweet, but it may not keep so well and it should be used fairly rapidly.

Plum conserve

cooking time: 20 minutes

1 Use recipe for any of the plum jams (see before), but allow 2 oz. stoned raisins to each lb. plums.
2 Simmer the raisins with the fruit.
3 When the jam has reached setting point, allow 2 oz. walnuts to each lb. of jam.

Mixed plum conserve

cooking time: approximately 25 minutes

you will need:

1 lb. cooking red plums (stoned)
1 lb. golden plums (stoned)
1 lb. Victoria plums (stoned)
no water if fruit is very ripe ($\frac{1}{4}$ pint if under-ripe)
3 lb. sugar

1 Simmer red and golden plums until softened slightly with the water, if used.
2 Add halved or quartered Victoria plums and continue cooking until these are tender.
3 Add the sugar and stir until dissolved.
4 When dissolved boil rapidly until set.
This is a particularly delicious jam since you have the pieces of Victoria plum in a golden purée.

Plum cheeses

cooking time: 30 minutes

Use any of the recipes for plum jam (see before) and rub the fruit through a sieve. Allow 12 oz.–1 lb. sugar to each lb. or pint of purée. Stir until sugar has dissolved. Boil rapidly until set.

Victoria plum conserve

cooking time: 15 minutes

you will need:

1 lb. sugar
⅛ pint water
1 lb. Victoria plums (stoned)

1 Boil the sugar and water together, stirring well, until the sugar has dissolved.
2 Put in the halved Victoria plums.
3 Cook steadily until the jam sets.
4 Add some of the kernels from the stones.

Prune jam

cooking time: 35 minutes

you will need:

1 lb. dried prunes
1 pint water
sugar
lemon juice

1 Soak prunes overnight in the water.
2 Simmer the prunes in this water until soft.
3 If necessary you can add a little extra water.
4 Remove the stones and measure the pulp.
5 Allow 1 lb. sugar and the juice of 1 lemon to each pint or lb. of pulp.
6 Stir until the sugar has dissolved.
7 Boil rapidly until set.

Prune conserve (1)

cooking time: 35 minutes

you will need:

1 lb. dried prunes*
1 pint water
1 lb. sugar
juice 2 lemons

* It is better to use rather small prunes in this preserve.

1 Soak the prunes overnight in the water.
2 Next day, lift out and drain, keeping the liquid.
3 Boil this prune liquid with the sugar and lemon juice, stirring well until the sugar has dissolved.
4 Add the prunes and simmer gently for approximately 25 minutes.

Prune conserve (2)

cooking time: 35 minutes

Use recipe and method for prune jam, but add 6 oz. chopped walnuts when this has reached setting point. The grated rind of 1 orange and lemon may be simmered with the prunes.

Pumpkin jam

cooking time: 40 minutes

you will need:

3 lb. pumpkin, peeled and diced
grated rind and juice 2 lemons
4 oz. crystallised ginger or 2 oz. root ginger
3 lb. sugar

1 Boil the pumpkin until it is tender.
2 Drain well and mash thoroughly.
3 Add the grated lemon rind and juice.
4 Add ginger cut into neat pieces. If dried ginger is used, this should be bruised, put in a muslin bag, cooked with the jam and removed before putting into jars.
5 Bring to the boil.
6 Add sugar and stir until dissolved.
7 Boil for 20 minutes or until thick.

Pumpkin and lemon jam

cooking time: 40 minutes

Use the recipe and method for pumpkin jam but use 3 lemons and omit the ginger.

Pumpkin and orange jam

cooking time: 40 minutes

Use the recipe and method for pumpkin jam but use 3 oranges and 1 lemon. The orange rind should be grated and the orange pulp added with the grated lemon and orange rind and lemon juice (point 3 in pumpkin jam).

Quince jam

cooking time: 35–45 minutes

you will need:

1 lb. quinces
⅛ pint water if fruit is ripe (¼–⅜ pint if fruit is very firm)
1 lb. sugar
juice ½ lemon

1 Peel, core and cut up the fruit*.
2 Simmer with the water until soft.
3 Add sugar and juice, stir until dissolved.
4 Boil rapidly until set.

* If desired the fruit could be grated instead of cut into pieces.

Quince and apple jam

cooking time: 35–45 minutes

you will need:

1 lb. quinces
1 lb. cooking apples (after peeling and coring)
⅜ pint water
2 lb. sugar

Use the method for quince jam.

Quince preserve

cooking time: 35–40 minutes

you will need:

1 lb. quinces
1 lb. sugar
½ pint water
juice 1 lemon

1 Peel and cut the quinces into neat pieces.
2 Simmer the sugar and water until the sugar has dissolved.
3 Put in the quinces with the lemon juice.
4 Cook slowly until the fruit is soft.

Quince cheeses

cooking time: 45 minutes

Use either of the recipes for quince jam and rub the fruit through a sieve. There is no need to peel or core the quinces if using this recipe.

1 Measure the pulp.
2 Allow 1 lb. sugar to each lb. or pint of purée.
3 Stir in the sugar.
4 Stir until dissolved over a steady heat.
5 Boil rapidly until set.

Raisin and cranberry jam

cooking time: 35 minutes

Add 3 oz. raisins to each lb. cranberries and proceed as for cranberry jam (see page 16).

Raspberry jam

cooking time: 8–10 minutes

you will need:

1 lb. raspberries
1 lb. sugar

1 Heat the fruit until boiling point is reached.
2 Stir in the hot sugar – heated for a few minutes in the oven.
3 Boil rapidly until the jam has set. If the fruit is firm and fresh, this should take only about 3 minutes of rapid boiling.

Raspberry and blackcurrant jam

cooking time: 25–30 minutes

you will need:

1 lb. blackcurrants
½ pint water
2 lb. raspberries
3 lb. sugar

1 Simmer the blackcurrants with the water until soft.
2 Add the raspberries and cook for a further few minutes.
3 Add sugar and stir until dissolved.
4 Boil rapidly until set.

Raspberry and redcurrant jam

cooking time: 10–15 minutes

you will need:

1 lb. redcurrants
⅛ pint water
1 lb. raspberries
2 lb. sugar

1 Heat the redcurrants with the water for about 5 minutes.
2 Add the raspberries and continue cooking until these are boiling.
3 Add sugar and stir until dissolved.
4 When dissolved boil rapidly until jam is set.

Raspberry and strawberry jam

cooking time: 10–12 minutes

1 lb. raspberries
1 lb. strawberries
juice 1 lemon
2 lb. sugar

Use method for raspberry jam.

Uncooked raspberry jam

you will need:

1 lb. sugar
1 lb. fresh raspberries

1 Put the sugar to warm in a cool oven.
2 Mash the raspberries and stir in the warmed sugar.
3 Continue stirring until sugar has quite dissolved.
4 Put into pots and seal down.
This jam may not appear very stiff when first made, but the flavour is wonderful and it does stiffen with keeping.

Note

This recipe is suitable only for perfect fruit which is dry and freshly picked.

Rhubarb in jam making

The best flavoured rhubarb for jam is the second crop in the autumn. You can use spring rhubarb, but the flavour is not so good.

Rhubarb jam

cooking time: 25 minutes

you will need:

1 lb. rhubarb*
1 lb. sugar

* If rhubarb is very ripe you need the juice 1 lemon: if under-ripe lemon can be omitted.

1 Simmer the rhubarb with no water until soft. If the rhubarb is very hard, you may need 1 tablespoon water.
2 Stir in the sugar and lemon juice, and stir until sugar is dissolved.
3 Boil rapidly until set.

Rhubarb conserve

cooking time: 30 minutes

you will need:

2 lb. rhubarb
2 lb. sugar
8 oz. stoned raisins
1 lemon
1 orange

1 Cut up the rhubarb into 1½-inch pieces.
2 Cover with the sugar and leave to stand overnight.
3 Boil rhubarb, raisins and sugar gently for 20 minutes.
4 Add the juice and rind of the lemon and orange.
5 Boil until the syrup is thick and jelly-like but do not boil until jam forms a thick wrinkled surface.

Rhubarb preserve

cooking time: 25 minutes

Use recipe for rhubarb jam (see before), but sprinkle the sugar over the diced rhubarb, leave for several hours and then cook and stir steadily until sugar has dissolved. Add the lemon juice. Boil until syrup is thick.

Rhubarb and angelica jam

cooking time: 20 minutes

you will need:

1 lb. rhubarb
1 lb. sugar
juice 1 lemon
1 oz. angelica, chopped

1 Cut rhubarb into pieces.
2 Cover with sugar and lemon juice and leave to stand overnight.
3 Add angelica.
4 Stir well.
5 Boil all together until set.

Rhubarb and dried fig jam

cooking time: 1 hour 20 minutes

you will need:

1 lb. dried figs
1 pint water
2 lb. rhubarb, chopped
3 lb. sugar
juice 1 large lemon

1 Soak the figs in the water for 48 hours, or even 72 hours.
2 Simmer until the figs are nearly soft.
3 Add the rhubarb.
4 Continue cooking until a thick pulp is formed.
5 Add the sugar and lemon juice, stir until dissolved.
6 Boil rapidly until set.

Rhubarb and ginger jam

cooking time: 25 minutes

you will need:

1 lb. rhubarb, chopped
1 teaspoon powdered ginger, or 1–2 oz. crystallised ginger
1 lb. sugar
juice 1 lemon

1 Use the recipe for either the rhubarb jam or rhubarb preserve.
2 The ginger should be chopped finely. If using powdered ginger it should be sprinkled over the rhubarb.

Strawberry jam

cooking time: 15 minutes

you will need:

1 lb. strawberries – good weight
14 oz. sugar
juice 1 lemon or ⅛ pint redcurrant juice

1 Simmer the fruit until soft.
2 Add the sugar and lemon juice and stir until sugar is dissolved.
3 Boil rapidly until set.

Strawberry jam (whole fruit)

cooking time: 12–15 minutes

Use ingredients as for strawberry jam, see above.

1 Pour sugar and fruit into pan.
2 Heat very gently until sugar has dissolved, stirring occasionally.
3 Add lemon or redcurrant juice.
4 Boil steadily until set.

Strawberry preserve

cooking time: 10–12 minutes

you will need:

1 lb. sugar
juice 1 lemon or ⅛ pint redcurrant juice
1 lb. firm strawberries (medium sized)

1 Boil the sugar and lemon juice until the sugar has dissolved, stirring all the time.
2 Turn off the heat – leave the strawberries in the syrup for about 15 minutes.
3 Return to the heat and boil steadily for approximately 5–7 minutes.
4 The syrup does not set very firmly, but you have a wonderfully flavoured preserve.

Three fruit jam

cooking time: 20 minutes

you will need:

8 oz. raspberries
8 oz. redcurrants
8 oz. strawberries
1½ lb. sugar

Use method for raspberry jam (see page 27).

Red tomato jam

cooking time: 20 minutes

you will need:

2 lb. tomatoes
2 lb. sugar
4 tablespoons lemon juice

1 Cut the tomatoes into quarters.
2 Cover with sugar and stand overnight.
3 Simmer gently, stirring well until sugar has dissolved.
4 Continue simmering until tomatoes are soft.
5 Add lemon juice.
6 Boil rapidly until set.
7 You can alter the flavour by adding a little powdered or crystallised ginger.

Green tomato jam

cooking time: 30 minutes

Use recipe and method for red tomato jam. Green tomatoes are a good substitute for greengages.

Tomato preserve

cooking time: 15 minutes

you will need:

1 lb. sugar
¼ pint water
1 teaspoon powdered ginger
1 lb. firm red tomatoes
juice 1 lemon

1 Boil sugar and water with the ginger until sugar has dissolved.
2 Cut tomatoes into quarters.
3 Put into the syrup, together with the lemon juice.
4 Cook steadily until soft.

Jellies

You will find some helpful hints on making jellies on page 8.

Many people think that jelly making is more complicated than making jam but the method is nearly the same. The preparation of the fruit takes less time than for jam, and this compensates for time taken to drain jelly.

Clarity depends on draining the pulp properly.

How to use a jelly bag

A proper jelly bag is made of heavy duty calico or flannel. It has a very close weave so that the juice only drains and none of the pulp comes through. This is important as even a small amount of pulp will give a cloudy jelly. Jelly bags are expensive to buy, but with care they will last for a very long time. If you cannot buy a jelly bag you could make one yourself if you buy flannel or calico.

Use a square 18–24 inches by 18–24 inches.

1 Form into a triangle and machine firmly down the seam, being particularly careful at the tip so that this is well joined.
2 Attach 4 pieces of tape to the top.

To hang a jelly bag

Tie the pieces of tape on the 4 'legs' of an upturned chair with a bowl underneath so that the fruit can be put into the bag and allowed to drip through gently.

If you have no jelly bag

You can make do without a jelly bag, by using several thicknesses of fine muslin and hanging them from an upturned chair. You may also drain through muslin over a fine (not wire) sieve. But remember not to push it through, in any way, but allow it to drip in its own time.

Using the fruit twice in jelly

When using fruits such as cooking apples, redcurrants, damsons, gooseberries, blackcurrants, all of which have a high setting quality, you can produce a greater yield of liquid by boiling the fruit twice.

Follow the recipe as given and when the juice has dripped through the jelly bag, return the pulp to the preserving pan. Put only half the first amount of water over the fruit, boil again. Strain, and mix with first amount of liquid.

Dissolving the sugar in jelly

By the time the juice has gone through the bag it will, of course, have become quite cold. Reheat this, but do not boil for any length of time before adding the sugar, then stir until the sugar has dissolved.

To fill pots with jelly

Fill jam jars while the jelly is still very hot, so it does not begin to set in the pan.

Apple jelly

cooking time: 25–30 minutes

you will need:

cooking apples or crab apples (unpeeled)
1 pint water to each 2 lb. fruit
sugar

1 Simmer the fruit until a pulp; there is no need to either peel or core the fruit.
2 Put the pulp through thick muslin or a jelly bag.
3 Leave to strain overnight.
4 Measure the juice.
5 Allow 1 lb. sugar to each pint of juice.
6 Stir in the sugar.
7 Boil rapidly until set.

Apple and geranium jelly

cooking time: 25–30 minutes

Follow the recipe and method for apple jelly, but allow 2–3 fragrant geranium leaves to each lb. of apples.

Apple and lemon jelly

cooking time: 25–30 minutes

you will need:

2 lemons
1 lb. cooking apples (unpeeled)
½ pint water
sugar

1 Squeeze juice from lemons and pare off yellow part of rind.
2 Chop up apples, but do not peel or core.
3 Put apples, lemon rind and water into pan.
4 Simmer until soft.
5 Place the fruit in a jelly bag and leave to strain.
6 Add lemon juice.
7 Measure, and to each pint of liquid add 1 lb. sugar, stir until dissolved.
8 Boil rapidly until set.

Apple struper

cooking time: 45 minutes

you will need:

2 lb. cooking or crab apples (unpeeled)
1 pint water
sugar
honey (if liked)
grated nutmeg
mixed spice or cinnamon

1 Wash, but do not peel the apples.
2 Divide large ones into pieces keeping the core and pips as these help the jelly to set.
3 Simmer gently until a thick pulp.
4 Strain through a jelly bag.
5 Measure and allow to each pint of juice, 1 lb. sugar or ¾ lb. sugar and 4 oz. honey. These proportions will give the consistency of jelly.
6 If you wish, instead of putting the apple pulp through a jelly bag, the whole of the purée can be rubbed through a sieve so that you have more of a juice.
7 Allow to each pint of juice or purée, ½ level teaspoon grated nutmeg (up to 1 teaspoon could be used), and ½ level teaspoon mixed spice or cinnamon.
8 Add spices when sugar is added and boil until setting point is reached.

Apple and orange jelly

cooking time: 25–30 minutes

Follow recipe and method for apple and lemon jelly, but use the grated rind of 2 oranges.

Blackberry or bramble jelly

cooking time: 25–30 minutes

you will need:

1 lb. blackberries
⅛ pint water
1 medium sized cooking apple*
sugar

* Instead of using an apple you can use the juice of one lemon to each pound blackberries. Add this with sugar.

1 Put blackberries, water and apple into a pan.
2 Simmer until soft.
3 Strain the pulp through a jelly bag.
4 Measure juice and allow 1 lb. sugar to each pint.
5 Stir in sugar and continue stirring until dissolved.
5 Boil rapidly until set.

Spiced blackberry jelly

cooking time: 25–30 minutes

Use recipe and method for blackberry jelly but add 1 level teaspoon mixed spice to each pint juice. Stir in with the sugar.

Blackcurrant jelly

cooking time: 40 minutes

you will need:

2 lb. blackcurrants
1 pint water
sugar

Use method for redcurrant jelly (see page 35).

Blackcurrant and redcurrant jelly

cooking time: 40 minutes

you will need:

1 lb. blackcurrants
1 lb. redcurrants
1 pint water
sugar

Use method for redcurrant jelly (see page 35).

Cranberry jelly

cooking time: 30 minutes

you will need:

2 lb. cranberries
¾ pint water
sugar

1. Simmer cranberries with the water until soft.
2. Strain through jelly bag.
3. Allow 1 lb. sugar to each pint of juice.
4. Stir sugar until dissolved.
5. Boil rapidly until set.

Cranberry and grape jelly

cooking time: 30 minutes

you will need:

1 lb. cranberries
1 lb. white grapes
¼ pint water
sugar
lemon juice

1. Simmer the cranberries and grapes in the water until soft.
2. Strain through jelly bag.
3. Allow 1 lb. sugar and juice of 1 lemon to each pint of juice.
4. Stir in sugar until dissolved.
5. Boil rapidly until set.

Cucumber jelly

cooking time: 30 minutes

you will need:

about 4 lb. cucumbers (unpeeled)
⅛ pint water
1 lemon
1 lb. sugar
ginger

1. Cut up the cucumbers.
2. Add water and simmer until a soft pulp is formed.
3. Strain through a jelly bag.
4. Add the juice of 1 lemon, 1 lb. sugar and a pinch of ginger to each pint of juice.
5. Stir until the sugar has dissolved.
6. Boil rapidly until jelly sets.

Note

This is an extravagant jelly in that the cucumber yields little juice.

Damson jelly

cooking time: 30–35 minutes

you will need:

2 lb. damsons
¾ pint water if fruit is hard (⅓ pint water if ripe)
sugar

1. Simmer the fruit in the water until soft.
2. Strain through a jelly bag.
3. Measure the juice and allow 1 lb. sugar to each pint of juice.
4. Stir the sugar until sugar has dissolved.
5. Boil rapidly until set.

Damson and apple jelly

cooking time: 35 minutes

you will need:

1 lb. damsons
1 lb. apples
½ pint water if fruit is ripe (¾ pint water if firm)
sugar

1. Simmer fruit in the water until soft.
2. Put through jelly bag.
3. Allow 1 lb. sugar to each pint juice.
4. Stir the sugar until dissolved.
5. Boil rapidly until set.

Elderberry jelly

cooking time: 25 minutes

you will need:

4 lb. elderberries
1 pint water
sugar
1–2 lemons

1. Simmer the berries in the water.
2. When quite soft strain through a jelly bag.
3. To each pint juice add 12 oz. to 1 lb. sugar and the juice of a large lemon or 2 small lemons.
4. Stir well until sugar has dissolved.
5. Boil rapidly until setting point is reached.

Elderberry and apple jelly

cooking time: 30 minutes

you will need:

1 lb. cooking apples (unpeeled)
1 pint water
2 lb. elderberries
sugar
juice 1 lemon

1 Cut up the apples, but do not peel or core.
2 Simmer for about 10 minutes till quite soft.
3 Add the elderberries and continue cooking until quite soft.
4 Strain through a jelly bag or muslin.
5 Measure the juice and to each pint add 1 lb. sugar and the juice of one lemon.
6 Stir well until sugar has dissolved.
7 Boil rapidly until set.

Gooseberry jelly

cooking time: 25 minutes

you will need:

1 lb. sharp green gooseberries
½ pint water
sugar

1 Wash fruit and put into pan, with water – do not 'top and tail' fruit.
2 Simmer gently till fruit is very soft.
3 Put into jelly bag to drain.
4 Measure the juice, allowing 1 lb. sugar to each pint juice, stirring until sugar has dissolved.
5 Boil rapidly until set.

Gooseberry and redcurrant jelly

cooking time: 25 minutes

you will need:

1 lb. ripe gooseberries
1 lb. redcurrants
½ pint water
sugar

Use method for gooseberry jelly.

Greengage jelly

cooking time: 30 minutes

you will need:

2 lb. greengages
½ pint water if fruit is ripe (¾ pint if firm)
sugar

Use method for Victoria plum jelly (see page 36).

Guava jelly

cooking time: 25–30 minutes

you will need:

2 lb. guava pulp
½ pint water
sugar
juice 2 lemons

1 Simmer the fruit with the water until very soft.
2 Put through a jelly bag.
3 Allow 1 lb. sugar to each pint juice.
4 Stir until dissolved. Add lemon juice.
5 Boil rapidly until set.

Leveller jelly

This is the name given to the very large dessert gooseberries and they make wonderful jelly.

cooking time: 25 minutes

you will need:

1 lb. fruit
¼ pint water
sugar

Use method for gooseberry jelly.

Medlar jelly

cooking time: 30 minutes

you will need:

1 lb. medlars
¼ pint water
sugar
½ level teaspoon citric or tartaric acid or juice ½ lemon

1 Simmer fruit and water until soft.
2 Strain through a jelly bag.
3 Measure juice, allow 1 lb. sugar to each pint.
4 Stir in sugar and acid or lemon juice.
5 Continue stirring until dissolved.
6 Boil rapidly until set.

Medlar and lemon jelly

cooking time: 30 minutes

you will need:

1 lb. medlars
⅓ pint water
grated rind and juice 2 lemons
sugar

1 Simmer fruit, water and lemon rind until soft.
2 Strain through jelly bag and proceed as for medlar jelly.

Mint jelly (1)

cooking time: 5 minutes

you will need:

Syrup
8 oz. sugar
½ pint water
¼ pint vinegar
1½ dessertspoons powdered gelatine
2–3 tablespoons mint, chopped

1 Make a syrup of the sugar and water, by boiling together.
2 Add the vinegar and the powdered gelatine.
3 Stir in chopped mint.
4 Pour into jars.
5 Seal down most thoroughly.
6 Store in a cool place.

Mint jelly (2)

cooking time: 30 minutes

you will need:

2 lb. sharp cooking apples (unpeeled)
or
2 lb. crab apples (unpeeled)
1 pint water
sugar
2 tablespoons vinegar
mint

1 To each pint of juice allow 1 lb. sugar and 2 tablespoons chopped mint.
2 Wash the apples and if large cut into pieces, but do NOT peel or core them.
3 Cover with water.
4 Simmer gently until they form a thick pulp.
5 Put through a jelly bag or since this may not be available, several thicknesses of muslin and leave dripping overnight.
6 Measure the juice and to each pint allow 1 lb. sugar.
7 Heat the juice and when boiling stir in the sugar.
8 Continue stirring until sugar has quite dissolved.
9 Boil rapidly until setting point is reached – without stirring.
10 Add the vinegar and the mint. If you are not very fond of the flavour of vinegar, it may be omitted.
11 The jelly will be a better colour if a few drops of green colouring are added.
12 Pour the jelly into jars.
13 Seal down as for jam.

Pineapple and mint jelly

cooking time: 15 minutes

you will need:

1 pint sweetened canned pineapple juice
juice 3 lemons
12 oz. sugar
1 tablespoon mint, chopped

1 Put the sweetened pineapple juice into a pan and bring to the boil.
2 Add lemon juice and sugar, stirring until sugar is dissolved.
3 Boil rapidly until set.
4 Stir in the chopped mint.

Mulberry jelly

cooking time: 45 minutes

you will need:

1 cooking apple (unpeeled)
1 lb. mulberries
¼ pint water
sugar

1 Cut up but do not peel or core the apple.
2 Simmer with the mulberries and water until soft.
3 Strain through a jelly bag.
4 Measure juice, allow 1 lb. sugar to each pint.
5 Stir together until sugar has dissolved.
6 Boil rapidly until set.

Quince jelly

cooking time: 50 minutes

you will need:

2 lb. quinces
2 pints water with ripe fruit (use 3 pints for under-ripe fruit)
sugar

1 Do not peel or core the quinces, but just cut them up.
2 Simmer with the water until very soft.
3 Strain through a jelly bag and allow 1 lb. sugar to each pint juice.
4 Stir until dissolved.
5 Boil rapidly until set.

Note

If the quinces are very ripe, you can allow the juice of 1 lemon to each pint of juice to make certain it sets well.

Quince and apple jelly

cooking time: 50 minutes

you will need:

1 lb. apples
1 lb. quinces
sugar
1¼ pints water if fruit is ripe (1½ if under-ripe)

Use method for quince jelly. There is no need to use any lemon juice.

Rhubarb and strawberry jelly

cooking time: 20–30 minutes

you will need:

1 lb. strawberries
1 lb. rhubarb, sliced
2–3 tablespoons water
lemon
sugar

1. Simmer the strawberries and rhubarb in the water until very soft.
2. Strain through a jelly bag.
3. Measure the juice and allow the juice of 1 lemon and 1 lb. sugar to each pint of juice.
4. Stir in the sugar until dissolved.
5. Boil rapidly until set.

Raspberry jelly

cooking time: 20–25 minutes

you will need:

raspberries
¼ pint water to each 1 lb. raspberries
sugar

1. Simmer fruit and water until soft.
2. Place in a jelly bag and leave to drain. Measure juice.
3. To each pint of juice add 1 lb. sugar, stir until sugar dissolves.
4. Boil rapidly until set.

Redcurrant jelly

cooking time: 25 minutes

you will need:

1 lb. redcurrants
¼ pint water
sugar

Use method for apple jelly (see page 30).

Redcurrant and loganberry jelly

cooking time: 20–25 minutes

you will need:

8 oz. redcurrants
8 oz. loganberries
½ pint water
sugar

1. Put fruit into pan with water.
2. Simmer gently until fruit is soft.
3. Put into a jelly bag and leave to drain.
4. Measure juice, allow 1 lb. sugar to each pint.
5. Heat and stir until sugar has dissolved.
6. Boil rapidly until set.

Rose hip jelly

cooking time: 50 minutes

you will need:

1 lb. rose hips
water
2 lb. apples
sugar
lemon juice

1. Simmer the rose hips with ½ pint water and apples with ½ pint water, separately.
2. Put both lots of fruit through separate jelly bags.
3. Mix together.
4. Allow 1 lb. sugar and the juice of 1 lemon to each pint.
5. Stir over low heat until sugar has dissolved.
6. Boil rapidly until jelly has set.

Rowanberry jelly

cooking time: 30 minutes

you will need:

4 lb. rowanberries
1 pint water
sugar
lemons

1. Simmer berries with the water.
2. When soft strain through a jelly bag.
3. To each pint of juice add 12 oz. of sugar (for sharp jelly), or 1 lb. sugar for a sweeter jelly. Add the juice of 1 large or 2 small lemons.
4. Stir well until sugar has dissolved.
5. Boil rapidly until setting point is reached.

Spiced jellies

Spiced jellies are excellent if a small amount of spice is added to the juice of the following. This makes them particularly suitable for serving with cold meats.

Spiced apple jelly – follow previous suggestion.
Spiced gooseberry jelly – follow previous suggestion.
Spiced cucumber jelly – follow previous suggestion.
Spiced rosehip jelly – follow previous suggestion.

Strawberry jelly

cooking time: 25 minutes

you will need:

1 lb. strawberries	2 tablespoons water
8 oz. redcurrants	sugar

1 Simmer the strawberries, redcurrants and water together.
2 Strain through a jelly bag.
3 Measure the juice and allow 1 lb. sugar to each pint of juice.
4 Stir until sugar dissolved, then boil rapidly until set.

If you have no redcurrants:

1 Simmer the strawberries by themselves.
2 To each pint of strawberry juice allow the juice of 2 lemons and 1 lb. sugar – put the lemon juice in with the sugar.

Strawberry and gooseberry jelly

cooking time: 25–30 minutes

you will need:

1 lb. gooseberries	sugar
½ pint water	lemons
1 lb. strawberries	

1 Simmer the gooseberries with the water until nearly soft.
2 Add the strawberries.
3 Continue cooking until very soft.
4 Strain through a jelly bag.
5 To each pint add 1 lb. sugar and the juice of a lemon.
6 Boil rapidly until set, stirring until sugar has dissolved.

Red tomato jelly

cooking time: 30 minutes

you will need:

2 lb. ripe tomatoes	sugar
½ pint water	lemon

1 Halve the tomatoes and simmer with the water until a smooth pulp.
2 Strain through a jelly bag.
3 To each pint of juice allow 1 lb. sugar and juice of 1 lemon.
4 Stir until sugar has dissolved.
5 Boil rapidly until set.

Green tomato jelly

cooking time: 40 minutes

Use ingredients as for red tomato jelly, but allow double the amount of water.
This recipe can be flavoured with a little spice if wished.

Victoria plum jelly

cooking time: 30 minutes

you will need:

2 lb. Victoria plums	lemons
½ pint water	sugar

1 Simmer the plums in the water until soft.
2 Strain through a jelly bag.
3 To each pint allow the juice of 1 lemon and 1 lb. sugar.
4 Stir over heat until sugar is dissolved.
5 Boil rapidly until set.

Marmalades

Before making a marmalade, read through the directions for perfect jams, etc. see page 7, because the same rules apply.

There are, however, certain other points to remember:

1. In order to distribute the peel evenly in the marmalade, you must allow the preserve to cool slightly after cooking, then stir briskly, and pour into pots.
2. Times of cooking are given, but these may vary somewhat depending on the size of your pan, speed of cooking, etc.
3. To test if the peel is soft, take a piece between your finger and thumb. If you cannot rub the peel almost to nothing, you must continue cooking before adding the sugar. If you add the sugar in a marmalade before the peel is soft, you tend to toughen the peel and this will spoil the marmalade.
4. Although citrus fruits, such as lemons and bitter oranges, have a high degree of setting quality, this is very quickly passed, so do test your marmalades very carefully for setting (see page 7).
5. Although you must simmer the fruit for a long time to soften the peel, do not over-cook, otherwise you tend to spoil the colour (see page 8, point 18).
6. Remember the more of the white pith you put into the marmalade, the more bitter it will be, so if you do not like a bitter marmalade, remove some of this pith. However, since it has a high degree of setting quality, tie it with the pips in muslin.

To prepare fruit for marmalade

It is possible to prepare the fruit peel by putting it through a really good mincer. Or as many people prefer peel to be chunky it is preferable to shred it with a sharp knife. On an electric mincer, there is a special attachment that allows one to put the peel through the shredder.

Carrot marmalade

cooking time: 1½–2 hours

you will need:

3 lemons	1 pint water
2 lb. carrots	2 lb. sugar

1. Squeeze out the juice from the lemons.
2. Shred the peel as for a marmalade and soak for several hours or overnight.
3. Tie the pips in a muslin bag.
4. Cut the carrots into neat pieces and simmer with the lemons until tender.
5. Stir in the sugar and lemon juice, removing bag of pips.
6. Boil rapidly until set.

Carrot orange marmalade

cooking time: 1½–2 hours

Use recipe and method as before, but use 2 sweet oranges and 1 lemon instead of 3 lemons.

Clementine marmalade

cooking time: 1½–2 hours

Use the recipe and method for tangerine marmalade (see page 41) using clementines instead of tangerines.

Dark marmalade

cooking time: 1½–2 hours

1. Use recipe and method for Seville orange marmalade (1) (see page 40).
2. Boil oranges whole.
3. When adding the sugar, put in 1 good dessert-spoon of black treacle* to each lb. of sugar.

*This gives a rich flavour and a dark colour.

Four fruit marmalade

cooking time: 2 hours

you will need:

1 Seville orange*
1 grapefruit*
1 sweet orange*
2 lemons*
3½ pints water
3½ lb. sugar

*all medium sized fruit.

1 Prepare fruit as for Seville orange marmalade (2) (see page 40).
2 Cook in the same way, adding fruit juice with the warmed sugar.
3 Continue as instructed in this recipe.

Ginger marmalade

cooking time: 30 minutes

you will need:

3 lb. sharp cooking apples (unpeeled)
1 pint water
sugar
8 oz. preserved ginger

1 Wash apples.
2 Slice – without peeling and coring.
3 Put into pan and simmer gently with the water until the fruit is well pulped.
4 Strain through jelly bag.
5 Weigh the juice.
6 Put into preserving pan with equal weight of sugar.
7 Add ginger, cut in pieces about ½ inch square.
8 Boil briskly for about 10 minutes.
9 Test for 'jelling' and if necessary continue to boil for a little longer.
10 Put into hot sterilised jars.
11 Cover with waxed circles and tie down immediately.

Grapefruit marmalade

cooking time: 1½–2 hours

you will need:

2 medium sized grapefruit
2¼ pints water
2¼ lb. sugar
juice 1 lemon

Use method for Seville orange marmalade (2) (see page 40).

Jelly marmalade

cooking time: 1½ hours

Note

Use the recipe for lemon marmalade (see page 39) or lime marmalade (see page 39), or orange marmalade (see page 39). While the ingredients are the same as these recipes the method is very different.

1 Shred half the peel from the oranges very finely indeed.
2 The other half of the peel need not be shredded but tied in a bag of muslin.
3 The pips, pith and pulp of the fruit should also be tied in another bag of muslin.
4 Put the shredded peel and the 2 bags to soak overnight, in the water.
5 Simmer gently the next day for about 1 hour.
6 Take out the 2 bags and discard.
7 Add sugar and lemon juice. Stir over low heat till sugar is dissolved.
8 Bring to the boil and boil until set.

Note

If, by chance, you do not want any peel in the marmalade at all, as would be the case with someone suffering from an ulcer, then all the peel is tied in a bag.

Apricot and lemon marmalade

cooking time: 1½ hours

you will need:

1 lb. lemons
1 lb. dried apricots
3 pints water
3 lb. sugar

1 Prepare the lemons as for orange marmalade (2) (see page 41) tying the pips in a muslin bag and squeezing out the juice.
2 Soak overnight, together with the apricots, in the water.
3 Simmer next day until soft, removing pips.
4 Stir in lemon juice and sugar, stirring until sugar has dissolved.
5 Boil rapidly until set.

Lemon marmalade

cooking time: 1½–2 hours

you will need:

1 lb. lemons (4 medium or 3 large lemons)
2½ pints water
2½ lb. sugar

Use method for orange marmalade (2) (see page 41).

Lime marmalade

cooking time: 1½–2 hours

you will need:

1 lb. limes
2½ pints water
2½ lb. sugar

1 Cut or mince the limes finely, removing pips.
2 Soak the peel and pulp overnight in the water, together with the pips, which should be tied up carefully in a piece of muslin.
3 After soaking put the fruit, water and pips in a covered pan.
4 Simmer slowly for approximately 1½ hours. until peel is quite soft.
5 Take out the bag of pips.
6 Stir in the warmed sugar, until sugar is dissolved.
7 Bring the marmalade to the boil.
8 Boil rapidly in an uncovered pan until set – approximately 20 minutes.

Mint marmalade

cooking time: 1½–2 hours

Use recipe and method for lemon marmalade, and when setting point is reached, add 1 tablespoon chopped fresh mint to each lb. marmalade.

Orange and lemon marmalade

cooking time: 1½–2 hours

you will need:

1 lb. sweet oranges
3½ lb. sugar
1 lb. lemons
3½ pints water

Use method for Seville orange marmalade (2) (see page 40).

Quince marmalade

cooking time: 45 minutes

you will need:

1 lb. quinces
½ pint water
1¼ lb. sugar
juice 1 lemon

1 Peel, core and cut the quinces into fairly even slices.
2 Put into the water.
3 Simmer gently until tender. If the quinces are very hard you may find you need a little more water.
4 Add the sugar and lemon and stir until sugar has dissolved.
5 Boil until set.

Orange peel marmalade

cooking time: 1½–2 hours

you will need:

5 oz. orange peel
juice 3 lemons
2 pints water
2 lb. sugar

Use method for Seville orange marmalade (2) (see page 40).
This is a very economical way of making marmalade, since it allows you to eat the fruit of the sweet oranges.

Orange peel and apple marmalade

cooking time: 1½–2 hours depending on thickness of peel

you will need:

peel from 1 lb. oranges
3 pints water
1 lb. cooking apples (peeled and cored)
3 lb. sugar

1 Soak the peel overnight in the water.
2 Simmer until nearly soft.
3 Add the apples.
4 Continue cooking until fruit forms a smooth pulp.
5 Stir in the sugar.
6 Boil without stirring until setting point is reached.

Rhubarb marmalade

cooking time: 1½ hours

you will need:

3 lemons	3 lb. rhubarb, diced
1½ pints water	3½ lb. sugar

1 Prepare the lemons as in method for orange marmalade (2) (see page 41) and soak overnight in the water, with the pips tied in a piece of muslin.
2 Simmer gently until the peel is nearly soft.
3 Add the diced rhubarb and continue cooking until tender.
4 Remove bag of pips.
5 Stir in the sugar and lemon juice, stirring until sugar has dissolved.
6 Boil rapidly until set.

Seville or bitter orange marmalade (1) (coarse cut and bitter)

cooking time: 2 hours

you will need:

1 lb. Seville or bitter oranges (3 medium sized oranges)	2 pints water 2 lb. sugar

1 Wash oranges thoroughly.
2 Put whole oranges into covered pan with the water.
3 Simmer slowly for about 1½ hours or until a blunt wooden skewer will easily pierce the skin.
4 Remove oranges from liquid.
5 Allow to cool.
6 Cut up neatly.
7 Put pips into liquid and boil steadily for 10 minutes to extract the pectin from them.
8 Remove pips with a perforated spoon, and replace the cut orange pulp.
9 Bring to the boil.
10 Stir in the warmed sugar.
11 Continue stirring until sugar is dissolved.
12 Bring to the boil and boil rapidly without stirring until setting point is reached. It is advisable to start testing the marmalade after about 15 minutes.

Seville or bitter orange marmalade (2) (a sweeter variety)

cooking time: 1½–2 hours

you will need:

1 lb. Seville or bitter oranges 3 pints water 3 lb. sugar	juice lemon or 1 level teaspoon citric or tartaric acid

1 Cut or mince oranges finely, removing pips.
2 Soak peel and pulp overnight in the water, together with the pips tied up in a piece of muslin.
3 After soaking, put fruit, water and pips into a covered pan.
4 Simmer slowly until peel is quite soft. This should take about 1½ hours, but the cooking time will vary with thickness of peel.
5 Take out the bag of pips.
6 Stir in warmed sugar and lemon juice or acid.
7 Bring marmalade to the boil.
8 Boil rapidly in an uncovered pan until setting point is reached. This will take about 20 minutes. Start testing with small quantities after 10 minutes.

Scotch marmalade

cooking time: 1¾ hours

you will need:

2 sweet oranges 2 lemons 1 grapefruit **or** 2 bitter or Seville oranges	water sugar

1 Wipe fruit with a damp cloth.
2 Quarter, and cut through again.
3 Slice finely with a sharp knife, removing the pips which place in a small basin.
4 To each pound of cut fruit add 3 pints water.
5 Cover pips with some of the water.
6 Set aside for 24 hours.
7 Boil the cut fruit until soft (about 1–1¼ hours), adding the juice from the pips before boiling.
8 Put aside until cool enough to weigh.
9 To every pound of boiled fruit allow 1¼ lb. sugar and stir until sugar has dissolved.

10 Boil until it jellies. A period of 15 minutes fast boiling should be enough.

Variation

Using less sugar—allow only 1 lb. sugar to each lb. of boiled fruit if you prefer more 'bite'.

Sweet orange marmalade (1)

cooking time: 1¼–1½ hours

you will need:

1 lb. sweet oranges	2 lb. sugar
2 pints water	juice 1 lemon

Use method for Seville orange marmalade (1) (see page 40) adding lemon juice at step 10. The peel tends to soften more quickly with Seville oranges.

Sweet orange marmalade (2)

cooking time: 1½–2 hours

you will need:

1 lb. sweet oranges	2 lb. sugar
2 pints water	juice 2 lemons

Use method for Seville orange marmalade (2) (see page 40).

Seville or bitter orange and tangerine marmalade

cooking time: 1½–2 hours

you will need:

6 bitter oranges	3 tangerines
1 lemon	6 pints water
3 lb. sugar	

Proceed as for Seville orange marmalade (2) (see page 40).

Tangerine marmalade

cooking time: 1½–2 hours

you will need:

1 lb. tangerines (5 medium-sized tangerines)	1½ lb. sugar
1½ pints water	1 level teaspoon citric or tartaric acid or lemon juice

1 Cut the tangerines finely, removing the pips.
2 Soak the peel and pulp overnight in the water, together with the pips, which should be tied up carefully in a piece of muslin.
3 After soaking, put the fruit, water and pips into a covered pan.
4 Simmer slowly for approximately 1½ hours, until the peel is quite soft.
5 Take out the bag of pips.
6 Stir in the warmed sugar and lemon juice or acid, and stir till sugar is dissolved.
7 Bring the marmalade to the boil.
8 Boil rapidly in an uncovered pan until setting point is reached. This will take approximately 20 minutes.

Three fruit marmalade

cooking time: 1½–2 hours

you will need:

1 Seville orange or grapefruit*	1 lemon*
1 sweet orange*	2¼ pints water
	2¼ lb. sugar

*all medium sized fruit.

1 Prepare the fruit as for orange marmalade (2) (see page 41).
2 Cook in the same way, adding the fruit juice with the warmed sugar.
3 Continue as instructed in recipe for orange marmalade.

Tomato marmalade

cooking time: 1½ hours

you will need:

3 lemons	3 lb. green tomatoes
1½ pints water	3½ lb. sugar

1 Prepare lemons as for orange marmalade (2) (see page 40) and soak overnight in the water, tying the pips in a piece of muslin.
2 Simmer gently until the peel is nearly soft.
3 Add the quartered tomatoes and continue cooking until these are tender but unbroken.
4 Remove bag of pips.
5 Stir in the sugar and lemon juice, stirring until sugar has dissolved.
6 Boil rapidly until set.

Using jams and jellies in cooking

Jam glaze for cakes

This is enough to cover a 6–7 inch sponge or 12 small cakes and makes a change from icing.

you will need:

- 6 tablespoons sieved jam*
- 1 teaspoon arrowroot
- 3 tablespoons water
- ½ tablespoon lemon juice

***Any jam may be used for this but apricot or raspberry are particularly good.**

1 Put the jam into the saucepan.
2 Blend the arrowroot with the water and lemon juice.
3 Boil together, stirring from time to time, until clear.
4 Cool slightly then spread over the cake or cakes.

Redcurrant glaze

This can be used for a thin coating on cakes but its chief purpose is to coat the fruit in flans, etc.

you will need:

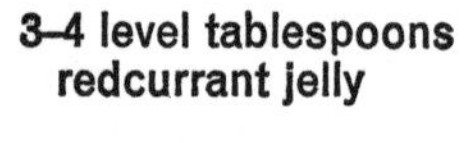

- 3–4 level tablespoons redcurrant jelly
- 1 level teaspoon arrowroot of cornflour
- ¼ pint syrup*

***from the cooked, canned or frozen fruit.**

1 Put the jelly into the saucepan.
2 Blend the arrowroot or cornflour with the syrup, put into the pan with the jelly.
3 Boil steadily, stirring from time to time, until clear.
4 Cool, but do not allow this to become too stiff, then brush or spread over the fruit in the flan.

Variation

Apricot glaze – follow the recipe for Redcurrant glaze, but use sieved apricot jam instead.

Jam sauce

you will need:

- 4–6 tablespoons jam
- 1 teaspoon arrowroot or cornflour
- 8 tablespoons water

1 Sieve the jam if wished, put into a saucepan.
2 Blend the arrowroot or cornflour with the water, add to the jam.
3 Boil steadily, stirring from time to time, until clear.
4 Serve hot with steamed puddings or cold with blancmange or ice cream.

Variations

Apricot ginger sauce – follow the recipe for Jam sauce, using apricot jam and 1 tablespoon syrup from preserved ginger in place of 1 tablespoon of the water. When thickened add 2 tablespoons thinly sliced preserved ginger.
Delicious hot or cold on ice cream.

Berry sauce – follow recipe for Jam sauce, but use a mixture of redcurrant jelly, raspberry and strawberry jams.

Coconut jam sauce – make the Jam sauce, then add 2 tablespoons desiccated coconut just before serving.

Chocolate apricot sauce – follow the recipe for Jam sauce using apricot jam. Blend 1 *level* tablespoon cocoa with the arrowroot or cornflour and water and add.
Delicious on steamed chocolate pudding.

Coffee apricot sauce – follow the recipe for Jam sauce using apricot jam. Blend the arrowroot or cornflour with fairly weak coffee instead of water and add.
Delicious on steamed chocolate or coffee puddings.

Lemon marmalade sauce – follow the recipe for Jam sauce, but use lemon marmalade instead of jam and 6 tablespoons water and 2 tablespoons lemon juice instead of all water.
Other marmalade can be used instead.

Marshmallow jam sauce – make the Jam sauce, add about 8 halved marshmallows to the hot sauce.
Serve over ice cream while sauce is warm.
Mock Melba sauce – recipe as Jam sauce but use 3 tablespoons raspberry jam and 3 tablespoons redcurrant jelly and 5 tablespoons water only.
Spiced jam sauce – Jam sauce, page 42, is delicious if ½–1 teaspoon mixed spice is added just before serving.
Tutti fruitti sauce – follow the recipe for Jam sauce.
When the sauce has *just* thickened add:
1 tablespoon blanched almonds
1 tablespoon halved glacé cherries
1 tablespoon sultanas.

Jam filling

To fill 6–7 inch sponge

you will need:

1 oz. butter
1 oz. sugar
1 tablespoon water
4 tablespoons jam
4 tablespoons fine sweet biscuit or sponge cake crumbs

1. Heat the butter, sugar and water in a pan.
2. Add the jam and heat very gently.
3. Stir the crumbs into the hot mixture and blend thoroughly.
4. Cool before using as a filling.

Variations

Apple ginger filling – follow the recipe for Jam filling but use crushed ginger-nut biscuits and apple jam or apple jelly. A tablespoon diced preserved ginger may be added, if wished, with the crumbs.
Lemon crumb filling – use lemon curd in place of jam in the Jam filling; omit sugar if wished.
Macaroon filling – follow recipe for Jam filling but use macaroon crumbs and apricot jam.
Orange filling – follow recipe for Jam filling but use 1 tablespoon orange juice in place of water plus finely grated rind of an orange and 4 tablespoons marmalade.

Jelly frosting

This is enough for the top of a 6–7 inch cake.

you will need:

2 level tablespoons redcurrant or other jelly
1 egg white

1. Put the jelly into a pan and warm until melted then cool slightly.
2. Whisk the egg white until very stiff.
3. Gradually whisk in the melted jelly then pile on the cake.
   This remains quite firm and is very like marshmallow in texture.
   Sieved jam or marmalade could be used instead of jelly.

Variation

Lemon frosting – follow the recipe for Jelly frosting but use 1½ tablespoons warmed lemon curd in place of jelly. Add ¼ teaspoon finely grated lemon rind to the curd for extra flavour.

Jam and jelly icing

Blend icing sugar with a smooth jam or jelly instead of water to coat cakes; the following are particularly suitable. You need about 2 tablespoons jam to each 8 oz. icing sugar. The jam or jelly should be warmed so you can mix the ingredients easily. Remember you never have a completely firm set icing, but a rather soft one.

Try:
Sieved apricot jam to coat the top of gingerbreads.
Apple jelly for gingerbreads or plain sponges.
Raspberry jam for sponges – top with chopped nuts or desiccated coconut.

Coconut almond topping

3 tablespoons sieved apricot jam
3 tablespoons desiccated coconut
2 tablespoons finely chopped almonds

Blend 3 good tablespoons sieved apricot jam, desiccated coconut and finely chopped almonds. Spread over a plain cake and brown lightly under a low grill.

Variation

Coconut raspberry topping – use recipe for Coconut almond topping but substitute raspberry jam for apricot and chopped walnuts for almonds.

Jam in cooking

Jam may be used as a flavouring and sweetening ingredient in cakes and puddings. Never use more than half jam and half sugar and reduce the amount of liquid slightly, e.g.

In a gingerbread – instead of 4 oz. sugar use 2 oz. sugar and 2 oz. apricot jam or jelly marmalade.
In a family fruit cake – instead of 4 oz. sugar use 2 oz. sugar and 2 oz. bitter marmalade.
In a sponge pudding – instead of 4 oz. sugar use 2 oz. sugar and 2 oz. apricot, raspberry or other jam.
To flavour a sweet white or custard sauce
With lemon curd, jam, jelly or marmalade; reduce or omit the sugar. Stir about 2–3 tablespoonfuls into the sauce when thickened.

Jams and jellies in savoury dishes

(a) Add a little jam to a **curry sauce**; plum jam is particularly good.
(b) Stir a little redcurrant or apple jelly into the **gravy of game** or other casseroles or stews.

Jams, jellies and marmalades using commercial pectin

The object of using commercial pectin in jams is to give an easy set and this is particularly useful in the case of fruits that have little natural setting quality. Also by using commercial pectin it is possible to make a good jam, jelly or marmalade without being too extravagant with fruit.
The jars are filled and covered in the same way as for ordinary jams.

Apple and apricot jam

cooking time: 30 minutes

you will need:

1¾ lb. canned apricots
12 oz. cooking apples (after peeling)
3¼ lb. sugar
1 lemon
1 bottle commercial pectin

1 Drain syrup from canned apricots.
2 Core and slice apples.
3 Cook until tender in ¼ pint of syrup from the apricots.
4 Turn apples into preserving pan.
5 Add apricots, sugar and lemon juice.

6 Heat gently, stirring occasionally, until sugar has dissolved.
7 Bring quickly to a full rolling boil.
8 Boil hard for 2 minutes.
9 Remove from heat and stir in commercial pectin.
10 Stir and skim by turns for 5 minutes to prevent the fruit from rising.
11 Pot and cover in the usual way.

Apricot and pineapple jam (canned fruit)

cooking time: 15 minutes

you will need:

1¼ lb. canned pineapple
1¼ lb. canned apricots (or a mixture of these fruits to make 2½ lb.)
2¾ lb. sugar
1 lemon
1 bottle commercial pectin

1 Chop the pineapple finely.
2 Put into preserving pan with apricots, sugar and lemon juice.
3 Heat gently, stirring occasionally, until sugar has dissolved.
4 Bring quickly to a full rolling boil.
5 Boil hard for 2 minutes.
6 Remove from heat and stir in the pectin.
7 Stir and skim by turns for 5 minutes to prevent fruit rising.
8 Pot and cover in the usual way.

Banana and pineapple jam

cooking time: 15 minutes

you will need:

5 ripe bananas
1 20-oz. can crushed or chopped pineapple
3¼ lb. sugar
1 bottle commercial pectin

1 Peel the bananas and mash thoroughly.
2 Put into a preserving pan with the crushed or chopped pineapple and sugar.
3 Heat gently, stirring occasionally until the sugar has dissolved.
4 Bring quickly to the boil.
5 Boil hard for 1 minute, and continue as previous recipe.

Dried apricot jam

cooking time: 40 minutes

you will need:

8 oz. dried apricots
1½ pints water
3 tablespoons lemon juice (1 lemon)
3 lb. sugar
1 bottle commercial pectin

1 Wash fruit.
2 Leave to soak for at least 4 hours in the 1½ pints water.
3 Cover and simmer for about 30 minutes to break up the fruit.
4 Measure 1½ pints prepared fruit pulp, making up the amount with water if necessary.
5 Add lemon juice and sugar.
6 Heat slowly, stirring occasionally until the sugar has dissolved.
7 Bring to a full rolling boil and boil rapidly for 1 minute and continue as Apricot and pineapple jam.

Blackcurrant and pineapple jam (canned fruit)

cooking time: 20 minutes

you will need:

1 orange
1 16-oz. can pineapple titbits or chunks
3 16-oz. cans blackcurrants
2 lb. sugar
½ bottle commercial pectin

1 Wash orange and grate rind.
2 Crush pineapple titbits or chunks.
3 Put blackcurrants, crushed pineapple, juice and orange rind into a saucepan with sugar. Do not use fruit syrup from cans.
4 Heat slowly, stirring occasionally, until sugar is dissolved.
5 Bring to a full rolling boil.
6 Boil rapidly for 2 minutes, and continue as previous recipe.

Cherry jam

cooking time: 25 minutes

you will need:

- 2½ lb. morello cherries (stoned)
- ¼ pint water
- 3 tablespoons lemon juice (1 lemon)
- 3 lb. sugar
- 1 bottle commercial pectin

1. Simmer the cherries in the water and lemon juice in a covered pan for about 15 minutes.
2. Add the sugar.
3. Heat slowly, stirring occasionally, until sugar has dissolved.
4. Bring to a full rolling boil.
5. Boil rapidly for 3 minutes.
6. Stir in commercial pectin.
7. Continue boiling for 1 minute.
8. Remove from heat and skim if necessary.
9. Cool slightly.
10. Pot and cover in the usual way.

Variation

With almond essence – for cherry jam with a stronger flavour add ¼ teaspoon almond essence before potting.

Black cherry jam

cooking time: 25 minutes

you will need:

- 2½ lb. black cherries (stoned)
- ¼ pint water
- juice 2 lemons
- 3 lb. sugar
- 1 bottle commercial pectin

1. Put prepared fruit in pan with water and lemon juice.
2. Cook gently with lid on for 15 minutes.
3. Remove the lid and add sugar.
4. Stir over low heat until dissolved.
5. Bring to rolling boil.
6. Boil rapidly for 3 minutes.
7. Remove from heat.
8. Add pectin and stir well.
9. Cool for 15 minutes, stirring occasionally to prevent fruit rising.
10. Pot and cover in the usual way.

Gooseberry jam

cooking time: 25 minutes

you will need:

- 4 lb. gooseberries
- ½ pint water
- 6½ lb. sugar
- 1 bottle commercial pectin

1. Put gooseberries in a large saucepan or preserving pan with the water.
2. Bring to the boil.
3. Simmer, covered, for 15 minutes, or until the skins are soft, stirring occasionally.
4. Add sugar.
5. Heat slowly until sugar is dissolved, stirring occasionally.
6. Bring to a full rolling boil quickly.
7. Boil rapidly for 2 minutes, stirring occasionally.
8. Remove from heat and stir in commercial pectin.
9. Skim if necessary.
10. Allow to cool slightly.
11. Pot and cover in the usual way.

When making half the quantity the fruit and sugar need to be boiled for 1 minute only.

Plum jam

cooking time: 28–30 minutes

you will need:

- 5 lb. plums (whole)
- ¼ pint water
- juice 1 lemon (if fruit is sweet)
- 6½ lb. sugar
- ½ bottle commercial pectin

1. Wash the plums and cut into pieces, removing as many of the stones as desired.
2. Put the fruit and water into a large pan.
3. Add lemon juice if used.
4. Bring to the boil.
5. Cover and simmer for 15 minutes, stirring occasionally.
6. Add sugar.
7. Heat slowly until the sugar has dissolved, stirring occasionally.
8. Bring to a full rolling boil.
9. Boil rapidly for 3 minutes, stirring occasionally.
10. Remove from heat and stir in commercial pectin.

11 Skim if necessary.
12 Allow to cool to prevent fruit floating.
13 Pot and cover in the usual way.

Raspberry jam

cooking time: 12–15 minutes

you will need:

4 lb. raspberries
5½ lb. sugar
1 bottle commercial pectin

1. Crush the berries.
2. Add the sugar.
3. Heat slowly until sugar has dissolved, stirring occasionally.
4. Bring to a full rolling boil quickly.
5. Boil rapidly for 2 minutes, stirring occasionally.
6. Remove from heat.
7. Stir in pectin.
8. Skim if necessary.
9. Pot and cover in the usual way.

Rhubarb jam

cooking time: 15–20 minutes

you will need:

2 lb. rhubarb
¼ pint water
3 tablespoons lemon juice
½ oz. bruised root ginger
2 oz. crystallised ginger
3 lb. sugar
½ bottle commercial pectin

1. Chop rhubarb very finely.
2. Place in preserving pan with the water.
3. Add lemon juice and the bruised root ginger in a muslin bag.
4. Bring to the boil and simmer gently for a few minutes until rhubarb is tender.
5. Add chopped crystallised ginger and sugar.
6. Heat slowly until sugar has dissolved.
7. Bring to full rolling boil quickly.
8. Boil rapidly for 3 minutes.
9. Remove from heat and take out muslin bag.
10. Stir in commercial pectin.
11. Allow to cool slightly to prevent fruit floating.
12. Pot and cover in the usual way.

Strawberry jam

cooking time: 15–20 minutes

you will need:

2¼ lb. small strawberries
3 tablespoons lemon juice
3 lb. sugar
knob butter or margarine
½ bottle commercial pectin

1. Put fruit in pan with lemon juice and sugar.
2. Stand for 1 hour, stirring occasionally.
3. Place over low heat, stirring occasionally.
4. When sugar has dissolved, add small knob of butter or margarine to reduce foaming.
5. Bring to full rolling boil.
6. Boil rapidly for 4 minutes, stirring occasionally.
7. Remove from heat.
8. Add commercial pectin and stir well.
9. Cool for at least 20 minutes to prevent fruit floating.
10. Pot and cover in the usual way.

Gooseberry jelly

cooking time: 30 minutes

you will need:

3 lb. gooseberries
1½ pints water
3½ lb. sugar
½ bottle commercial pectin
green colouring

1. Wash the gooseberries (there is no need to top and tail them).
2. Put them in a pan with the water.
3. Simmer, covered, for 20 minutes, or until the fruit is soft enough to mash.
4. Strain through a jelly bag.
5. Measure the juice into a pan and if necessary add water to make up to 2 pints.
6. Add the sugar.
7. Heat gently, stirring occasionally, until sugar has dissolved.
8. Stir in commercial pectin.
9. Bring to a full rolling boil.
10. Continue boiling for 1 minute.
11. Remove from heat.
12. Skim and stir in colouring if desired.
13. Pot and cover in the usual way.

Grape jelly

cooking time: 18–20 minutes

you will need:

3 lb. ripe black grapes
¼ pint water
3¼ lb. sugar
3 tablespoons lemon juice
1 bottle commercial pectin

1 Use only fully ripe grapes.
2 Crush fruit thoroughly and put in a saucepan with the water.
3 Bring to the boil.
4 Simmer, covered, for 10 minutes.
5 Place the fruit in a jelly bag and leave to drain.
6 Measure the sugar, lemon juice and 1¼ pints grape juice into a large saucepan.
7 Heat slowly until the sugar has dissolved, stirring occasionally.
8 Bring to the boil and stir in commercial pectin.
9 Bring to a full rolling boil and boil rapidly for ½ minute.
10 Remove from the heat.
11 Skim.
12 Cool, pot and cover in the usual way.

Orange jelly

cooking time: 20–25 minutes

you will need:

6 oranges*
1 large lemon*
water
2 lb. 10 oz. sugar
1 bottle commercial pectin

*approximately ¾ pint fruit juice.

1 Wash the oranges and the lemon.
2 Cut in halves and extract all the juice.
3 Cover the orange peel with water.
4 Bring to the boil.
5 Cover and simmer for 10 minutes.
6 Strain the liquid.
7 Add sufficient to the fruit juices to make 1 pint in all.
8 Place in a heavy saucepan with the sugar.
9 Stir over a low heat until the sugar has dissolved.
10 Bring to full rolling boil and boil rapidly for 2 minutes.
11 Remove from heat and stir in commercial pectin.
12 Bring back to boil and boil for 30 seconds.
13 Skim if necessary.
14 Allow to cool.
15 Pot and cover in the usual way.

Quince jelly

cooking time: 1¼ hours

you will need:

2 lb. quinces
2½ pints water
sugar
½ bottle commercial pectin

1 Cut up the fruit.
2 Simmer in the water for about 1 hour in a covered pan until tender.
3 Strain through a jelly bag.
4 Measure the juice and add 1 lb. of sugar to each pint.
5 Heat slowly, stirring occasionally, until the sugar has dissolved.
6 Add commercial pectin and boil rapidly for 1 minute.
7 Remove from heat and skim if necessary.
8 Pot and cover in the usual way.

Pineapple jelly

cooking time: 10 minutes

you will need:

1 20-oz. can pineapple juice
2½ lb. sugar
1 teaspoon lemon juice
1 bottle commercial pectin

1 Put the pineapple juice, sugar and lemon juice into a saucepan.
2 Heat gently, stirring occasionally, until the sugar has dissolved.
3 Bring quickly to a full rolling boil.
4 Stir in the pectin.
5 Boil hard for ½ minute.
6 Skim.
7 Pot and cover in the usual way.

Strawberry jelly

cooking time: 25–27 minutes

you will need:

3 lb. strawberries
¾ pint water
3¼ lb. sugar
3 tablespoons lemon juice
1 bottle commercial pectin

1 Put the strawberries into a saucepan and crush thoroughly.
2 Add the water.
3 Bring to the boil.
4 Cover and simmer for 15 minutes.
5 Place in a cloth and allow the juice to drain.
6 Measure the juice and if necessary add the water to make up to 2 pints.
7 Put the juice, sugar and lemon juice into a preserving pan.
8 Heat gently, stirring occasionally, until the sugar has dissolved.
9 Bring quickly to a full rolling boil.
10 Boil hard for 2 minutes.
11 Remove from the heat and stir in commercial pectin.
12 Boil rapidly for a further minute.
13 Remove from heat.
14 Skim if necessary.
15 Pot and cover in the usual way.

Dried apricot and orange marmalade

cooking time: 1–1¼ hours

you will need:

4 oz. dried apricots
1½ pints water
2 Seville oranges or 3 sweet oranges
1 lemon
¼ level teaspoon bicarbonate of soda
2½ lb. sugar
knob of butter
½ bottle commercial pectin

1 Soak the apricots overnight in ½ pint of the water.
2 Peel the rind from the oranges and lemon, being careful not to include any pith.
3 Remove the pith from the fruit also.
4 Shred the peel, and simmer it in the remaining pint of water with the bicarbonate of soda.
5 Slice the oranges and lemon and discard the pips.
6 Add the pulp, juice, apricots and 'soaking' water.
7 Boil for 20 minutes.
8 Add sugar and knob of butter.
9 Stir over a gentle heat until sugar is dissolved.
10 Boil for 5 minutes as fast as possible.
11 Remove from heat.
12 Stir in commercial pectin.
13 Skim if necessary.
14 Pot and cover in the usual way.

Orange ginger marmalade

cooking time: 1¼–1½ hours

you will need:

3 lb. oranges
2 lemons
1½ pints water
1 level teaspoon bicarbonate of soda
4¾ lb. sugar
4 oz. crystallised ginger
knob of butter
1 bottle commercial pectin

1 Remove skins in quarters using a sharp knife.
2 Shave off and discard about half of white part (pith).
3 Shred skins very finely.
4 Place in preserving pan with water and soda (this helps to soften skins).
5 Bring to the boil.
6 Simmer, covered, for about 30–40 minutes stirring occasionally, until the skins can be crushed easily between thumb and forefinger.
7 Cut up the peeled fruit, discarding the pips and tough skin.
8 Add pulp and juice to cooked rind.
9 Cover and simmer for 20 minutes longer.
10 Put sugar, chopped ginger and 3 pints of prepared fruit into a large preserving pan, making up the quantity with water if necessary.
11 Heat slowly, stirring occasionally, until the sugar has dissolved.
12 Add a small piece of butter or margarine.
13 Bring to a full rolling boil.
14 Boil for 5 minutes.
15 Remove preserving pan from heat and stir in commercial pectin.
16 Stir and skim in turns for just 7 minutes to cool slightly and to prevent fruit floating.
17 Pour into clean hot jars and cover in the usual way.

Orange and grapefruit marmalade

cooking time: 1¼–1½ hours

you will need:

3 lb. citrus fruit (4 oranges, 2 grapefruit and 1 lemon)
1½ pints water
1 level teaspoon bicarbonate of soda
5 lb. sugar
knob of butter
1 bottle commercial pectin

1 Wash fruit.
2 Remove skins by cutting in quarters using sharp knife.
3 Shave off and discard about half of white part (pith).
4 Shred skins very finely.
5 Place in preserving pan with water and soda (this helps to soften the skins).
6 Bring to the boil.
7 Simmer, covered, but stirring occasionally, for about 30–40 minutes, until skins can be crushed easily between finger and thumb.
8 Cut up the peeled fruit, discarding the pips and tough skin.
9 Add pulp and juice to cooked rind.
10 Simmer, covered, 20 minutes longer.
11 Put sugar and 3 pints prepared fruit into large preserving pan, making up the quantity with water if necessary.
12 Heat slowly, stirring occasionally, until the sugar has dissolved.
13 Add a small piece of butter or margarine.
14 Bring to a full rolling boil.
15 Boil for 5 minutes.
16 Remove preserving pan from heat and stir in commercial pectin.
17 Stir and skim by turns for just 7 minutes to cool slightly to prevent fruit floating.
18 Pour into clean hot jars and cover in the usual way.

Seville orange marmalade

cooking time: 1¼ hours

you will need:

8–10 bitter oranges
2 lemons
2 pints water
1 level teaspoon bicarbonate of soda
5 lb. sugar
knob of butter
1 bottle commercial pectin

Make as previous recipe, steps 1 to 18.

Using your pressure cooker for jams and marmalades

With fruits that take a long time to become tender, it is an excellent idea to use your pressure cooker to soften the fruit for jams or the peel for marmalades. Do not cook for too long a period because one minute under pressure is the equivalent of several minutes cooking in an ordinary saucepan. If you over-cook, you lose both the colour and the flavour of the fruit and you tend to destroy the natural setting properties.

When the fruit has been softened in the pressure cooker, you *must* allow the pressure to drop gradually. You then take off the lid and from then onwards you use your pressure cooker as an ordinary preserving pan.

Lemon marmalade

pressure cooking time: 15 minutes
cooking time in open pan: 25 minutes

you will need:

1 lb. lemons (4 medium or 3 large lemons)
1¼ pints water
2½ lb. sugar

Use method for sweet orange marmalade (see page 51).

Seville or bitter orange marmalade (coarse cut and bitter)

pressure cooking time: 15 minutes
cooking time in open pan: 25 minutes

you will need:

1 lb. oranges or 3 medium sized oranges
1 pint water
2 lb. sugar

1 Wash the oranges well.
2 Put into the pressure cooker with the water.
3 Fix the lid and bring to pressure.
4 Lower the heat.
5 Cook for 15 minutes.
6 Reduce pressure gradually. Remove lid.
7 Remove oranges from the liquid.
8 Allow to cool.
9 Cut up neatly.
10 Put the pips into the liquid.
11 Boil steadily for 10 minutes to extract pectin from them.
12 Remove and replace the cut orange pulp.
13 Bring to the boil.
14 Stir in the warmed sugar.
15 Continue stirring until all the sugar is dissolved.
16 Bring the marmalade to the boil rapidly without stirring until setting point is reached.

Sweet orange marmalade

pressure cooking time: 10 minutes
cooking time in open pan: 25 minutes

you will need:

1 lb. Seville or bitter oranges
1½ pints water
3 lb. sugar
juice 1 lemon or 1 level teaspoon citric or tartaric acid

1 Cut or mince oranges finely, removing pips.
2 Soak peel and pulp overnight in the water, together with the pips, which should be tied up in a piece of muslin.
3 After soaking, put fruit, water and pips in a pressure cooker.
4 Cook for 10 minutes and allow pressure to drop. Remove lid.
5 Take out bag of pips.
6 Stir in warmed sugar and lemon juice or acid. Stir until sugar is dissolved.
7 Bring marmalade to the boil.
8 Boil rapidly until setting point is reached.

Blackcurrant jam

pressure cooking time: 3 minutes
cooking time in open pan: 10 minutes

you will need:

1 lb. blackcurrants
⅜ pint water
1¼ lb. sugar

1 Put fruit and water into pressure cooker.
2 Fix lid, bring to pressure.
3 Lower heat.
4 Cook for 3 minutes.
5 Allow pressure to drop gradually. Remove lid.
6 Stir in sugar.
7 When dissolved boil jam rapidly until set.

Dried peach jam

pressure cooking time: 10 minutes
cooking time in open pan: 10–15 minutes

you will need:

1 lb. dried peaches
1½ pints water
3 lb. sugar
1½ level teaspoons citric or tartaric acid or juice of 1½ lemons

1 Soak the well washed fruit in the water for 48–72 hours.
2 Put into the pressure cooker, without the rack.
3 Fix lid, bring to pressure.
4 Lower heat.
5 Cook for 10 minutes.
6 Allow pressure to drop gradually.
7 Stir in sugar until dissolved and add lemon juice or acid.
8 Boil rapidly for 10–15 minutes.

Green gooseberry jam

pressure cooking time: 1 minute
cooking time in open pan: 10 minutes

you will need:

1 lb. gooseberries
1¼ lb. sugar
¼ pint water

Use method for blackcurrant jam allowing 1 minute only pressure cooking time.

Diabetic preserves

It is possible to make diabetic preserves at home. Samples of these are given and any mixture of fruits can be used. Because you cannot use sugar, which is the ingredient that preserves the fruit in ordinary jam, you must either make small quantities of jam that can be eaten up quickly or you must sterilise the fruit (see page 73).

Sugarless or diabetic jam (using gelatine)

cooking time: 8–15 minutes depending on kind of fruit

you will need:

1 lb. fruit
little water*
8–10 saccharine tablets
1 tablespoon hot water
½ oz. powdered gelatine

*Use ⅛ pint with soft fruit – ¼ pint with firm fruit.

1. Simmer fruit with water until soft.
2. Crush saccharine tablets dissolved in the tablespoon of hot water.
3. Add to the hot but not boiling fruit.
4. Add the gelatine dissolved in the ⅛ pint of hot water.
5. Stir briskly for several minutes.
6. Pour into small jars with firmly fitting tops and seal down.
7. Stand in cool place. This will keep for some days.

Note

To make jam that keeps, pour very hot jam into hot bottling jars. Seal down, giving screw band half turn back. Stand in pan of boiling water and boil briskly for 5 minutes. Lift out and tighten screw band. Test for seal next day by seeing if lid is tight.

Sugarless or diabetic marmalade (using gelatine)

cooking time: 1 hour

you will need:

2 Seville oranges
2 lemons
1 pint water
8 saccharine tablets
¼ oz. gelatine to every ½ pint pulp

1. Cut the rind from the oranges and lemons (being careful to remove no white pith with the rind) and chop it.
2. Cut up the pulp.
3. Place it in a preserving pan with the rind and 1 pint water.
4. Boil gently for about 30 minutes, test carefully.
5. Cook until pulp and rind are tender.
6. Add saccharine.
7. Stir in gelatine dissolved in a little of the hot syrup.
8. Remove from heat.
9. Bottle while still hot.
10. Cover at once.

Do not make large quantities as this will not keep unless you sterilise (see page 73).

Diabetic jams (using glycerine) with firm fruit

cooking time: 45 minutes

you will need:

3 lb. firm fruit, e.g. plums, damsons, gooseberries
¾ pint water
45 saccharine tablets
2 pints glycerine

1. Cook the fruit in the water until softened.
2. Remove as many of the stones as possible, with a perforated spoon.
3. Add the saccharine tablets and glycerine.
4. Boil until jam thickens.
5. Pour into jars and cover as for other jams.

Note

This jam will keep better because of the glycerine content.

Diabetic jams (using glycerine) with ripe fruit

cooking time: 35–45 minutes

you will need:

3 lb. ripe fruit, e.g. fresh apricots, peaches, etc.
¼ pint water
45 saccharine tablets
2 pints glycerine

1. Cook the fruit in the water until softened.
2. Remove as many of the stones as possible.
3. Add the saccharine tablets and glycerine.
4. Boil until the jam thickens.
5. Pour into jars and cover as for other jams.

Diabetic jams (using glycerine) with soft fruit

cooking time: 20–25 minutes

you will need:

3 lb. soft fruit, e.g. raspberries, strawberries, etc.
45 saccharine tablets
2 pints glycerine

1. Gently heat the raspberries.
2. Dissolve the saccharine tablets in the fruit and add the glycerine.
3. Boil until jam thickens.
4. Pour into jars and cover as for other jams.

Diabetic jams (with Sorbitol) using commercial pectin

This is another method of making diabetic jams, using a Sorbitol product.

cooking time: 25–35 minutes

you will need:

2½ lb. fruit
¼ pint water with firm fruit – damsons, hard plums, etc: ⅛ pint water with moderately soft fruit – ripe gooseberries, etc: no water with soft fruit – raspberries, etc.
2½ lb. Sorbitol powder
knob butter
½ bottle commercial pectin
5 saccharine tablets
½ oz. gelatine

1. Put the fruit and water in the preserving pan.
2. Simmer until soft, removing stones with a perforated spoon.
3. Stir in the Sorbitol and bring to the boil, adding the butter.
4. Boil hard for 1 minute.
5. Remove from the heat and stir in the commercial pectin, saccharine tablets and the gelatine dissolved in ⅛ pint very hot water.
6. Stir thoroughly until blended.
7. Pour into jar while hot and seal down.
   In order to keep, this jam must be covered immediately with a very good seal, either a bottling top or melted paraffin wax.

Fruit curds

It must be remembered that you are adding eggs to very acid ingredients in a fruit curd. This is why stress is laid on the fact that the curd must thicken *slowly*. If by chance it shows signs of curdling, lift the mixture off the heat and whisk very sharply for a few minutes. This should get rid of the curdled effect and you can then replace over heat to finish cooking. Remember the mixture thickens quite a lot as it cools, so do not over-cook.

Lemon curd

cooking time: 30 minutes

you will need:

rind 3 lemons
juice 2 large lemons
8 oz. sugar
4 oz. fresh butter
2 eggs

1. Grate the rind carefully, removing just the yellow 'zest', but none of the white pith. If using loaf sugar, rub this over the lemons until all the yellow has been removed.

continued

2 Squeeze the juice from the fruit.
3 Put all the ingredients – except eggs – into double saucepan or basin over hot water.
4 Cook stirring from time to time, until butter and sugar have melted.
5 Add the well beaten eggs.
6 Continue cooking until the mixture coats the back of a wooden spoon.
7 Pour into jars and seal down in the usual way.

Apple and lemon curd

cooking time: 1½ hours

you will need:

2 large cooking apples
8 oz. sugar
rind 3 lemons
4 oz. fresh butter
2 eggs
juice 2 large lemons

1 Bake the apples in their jackets so that you soften them without adding any water.
2 Remove the pulp and beat until smooth.
3 Mix the lemon rind, etc., and proceed as for lemon curd.

Note

This has a slightly lower percentage of sugar in the completed preserve, so is not meant to keep quite as long. To keep indefinitely, increase amount of sugar to 1 lb. It does, however, make a more economical preserve than lemon curd.

Grapefruit curd

cooking time: 30 minutes

you will need:

grated rind 2 large grapefruits
juice 2 large grapefruits
8 oz. sugar
4 oz. fresh butter
2 eggs

Use method for lemon curd.

Orange curd

cooking time: 30 minutes

you will need:

rind 3 oranges
juice 2 large oranges
8 oz. sugar
4 oz. fresh butter
2 eggs

1 Grate the rind carefully, removing just the yellow 'zest' but none of the white pith. If using loaf sugar, rub this over the oranges until all the yellow has been removed.
2 Squeeze the juice from the fruit.
3 Put all ingredients – except eggs – into a double saucepan or basin over hot water.
4 Cook, stirring from time to time, until the butter and sugar have melted.
5 Add the well beaten eggs and continue cooking until the mixture coats the back of a wooden spoon.
6 Pour into jars and seal down in the usual way.

Orange and lemon curd

cooking time: 30 minutes

you will need:

rind 1 lemon
rind 2 oranges
juice 2 large oranges
8 oz. castor or loaf sugar
4 oz. fresh butter or margarine
2 eggs

Use method for lemon curd.

Marrow curd (1)

cooking time: 45 minutes

you will need:

To each lb. cooked marrow pulp *add*
grated rind and juice 2 lemons
1 lb. sugar
4 oz. butter
2 eggs

1 Peel the marrow and remove skin and seeds.
2 Put into a pan with just enough water to cover the bottom.
3 Cook until quite soft.
4 Measure the pulp and add other ingredients (proportion see above).
5 Put altogether into a double saucepan.
6 Cook until very smooth.

Marrow curd (2)

cooking time: about 45 minutes

you will need:

marrow
lemons
sugar
butter

Peel vegetable marrow, remove the seeds. To each 1 lb. of marrow, allow the finely grated rind of 1 large lemon, the juice of 1 large lemon and 1 lb. of sugar and 1 oz. of butter, see note. Steam the marrow until nearly soft, put into a preserving pan or saucepan, add the lemon rind and cook over a very low heat until very soft, adding the butter. When very soft add the sugar, stir until dissolved, then add the lemon juice and boil steadily until set.

Note

If you wish to double the amount of lemon and butter you can do so.

Marrow lemon curd

cooking time: 30 minutes

you will need:

8 oz. cooked sieved marrow	8 oz. sugar
rind 3 lemons	4 oz. fresh butter
juice 2 large lemons	2 eggs

1 Simmer the marrow so no water is added, strain and beat or sieve until smooth. Add to lemon rind, etc.
2 Continue as for lemon curd.

Tangerine curd

cooking time: 30 minutes

you will need:

grated rind and juice 6 tangerines	5 oz. fresh butter
juice 1 lemon	3 medium sized eggs or 2 large eggs
10 oz. sugar	

Use method for lemon curd (see page 53).

Parsley honey

cooking time: about 1 hour

you will need:

2 large handfuls of fresh parsley (about 4–5 oz.)	1½ pints water
	1 lb. sugar
	1 dessertspoon vinegar

1 Wash and pick over the parsley.
2 Chop up with stalks, roughly.
3 Put into a pan with the water.
4 Bring to the boil.
5 Boil gently until the water is reduced to 1 pint.
6 Save this pint. Rinse out the saucepan.
7 Pour in the strained parsley water.
8 Add the warmed sugar.
9 When dissolved bring to the boil.
10 Add the vinegar and boil slowly until a little, when tested on a plate, is of a clear honey consistency, which will probably take about 30 minutes.
11 Pot and seal in the usual way.

Fruit butters

1 To make a fruit butter follow any of the directions for jam up to the point when the sugar is added.
2 Rub the fruit purée through a sieve.
3 Measure and add 8 oz. sugar to every lb. or pint of pulp.
4 Boil until thickened.
5 Allow to cool.

Fruit butters are generally served as a sweet with ice cream, etc., and because of the low content of sugar will not keep like a jam or a cheese. If you wish it to keep, then add extra sugar when, of course, it becomes exactly like a cheese. Alternatively, you can pour it into bottling jars and preserve it like pulped fruit (see pages 73, 74).

Apple butter – follow method for fruit butter.

Apricot butter – follow method for fruit butter.

Greengage butter – follow method for fruit butter.

Gooseberry butter – follow method for fruit butter.

Peach butter – follow method for fruit butter.

Plum butter – follow method for fruit butter.

Raspberry butter – follow method for fruit butter.

Strawberry butter – follow method for fruit butter.

Pickles

1 Always use very good quality vegetables – firm and not discoloured.
2 Use pure malt vinegar – white vinegar if preferred.
3 Cover well – see point 5 in chutneys (see page 60).
4 Never use copper, brass or iron pans.
5 You must see the vegetables are completely covered with vinegar.
6 It is essential to put vegetables in brine before covering with vinegar. (For brine recipes see this page and page 57.)
7 You should boil vinegar before using, even when allowing it to become cold afterwards – see spiced vinegar, this page.

Pickled beetroot

cooking time: 10 minutes for beetroot
15 minutes for vinegar

1 Cut the cooked beetroot into slices or cubes as desired.
2 Put into boiling salted water (1 tablespoon salt to 1 pint water).
3 Simmer gently for about 10 minutes being careful not to break slices.
4 Drain and pack into jars.
5 Cover with hot spiced vinegar, i.e. white malt or ordinary malt vinegar boiled with pickling spices. Use 1 tablespoon pickling spices to each pint vinegar.
6 Seal down at once.
7 Store in a cool dark place.

Pickled capers

1 Put the capers into brine made with 2 oz. kitchen salt to 1 pint water.
2 Leave for 24 hours.
3 Drain but do not wash.
4 Put into jars and pour over hot spiced white vinegar.
5 Cover thoroughly.

Pickled red cabbage

cooking time: 15 minutes to make spiced vinegar

1 Cut the cabbage into shreds.
2 Put into a basin with a good sprinkling of salt between each layer.
3 Leave for 24 hours.
4 Drain thoroughly.
5 Pack into jars and pour over the cold spiced vinegar. For quantities of spiced vinegar, see pickled cucumbers.
6 Seal at once.

Pickled cucumbers

1 If the cucumbers are very small, they can be left whole, but otherwise cut into convenient sized pieces.
2 Put into wet brine, or cover with salt (dry brine) and leave overnight.
3 Prepare spiced vinegar.
4 Strain spiced vinegar and cool.
5 Remove the cucumber from the brine and rinse well under the cold tap.
6 Drain thoroughly.
7 Pack into jars.
8 Pour over the cold vinegar and seal carefully.

Wet brine

Always use household salt, not the free-flowing table salt. Unless stated to the contrary, use 2 oz. salt to 1 pint cold water.

Spiced vinegar

Unless stated to the contrary, this mixture of spices and vinegar gives a very good result for most pickles. Buy the pickling spice from the grocer and you will find they consist of a mixture of chillis, peppercorns, cloves etc. To each pint vinegar: 1 level tablespoon mixed pickling spice. Boil together for 15 minutes, strain then use as directed in the recipe.

Dry brine

You will have a 'crisper' texture for pickled cucumbers if you use dry brine, but many people prefer the softer texture given by soaking in wet brine. Sprinkle layers of kitchen salt between layers of shredded cabbage or sliced or whole small cucumbers – leave for 24 hours, then shake away surplus salt.

Sweet pickled cucumbers

cooking time: 15 minutes to make spiced vinegar

Use the method for pickled cucumbers, but add 1–2 teaspoons sugar to each pint pickled vinegar.

Pickled cauliflower

cooking time: 15 minutes to make spiced vinegar

1. Break the cauliflower into neat flowerets.
2. Leave in brine (see before) for 24 hours.
3. Drain well and rinse in cold water.
4. Cover with cold spiced vinegar.

Sweet pickled cauliflower

cooking time: 15 minutes to make spiced vinegar

Use recipe for pickled cauliflower but allow 1 teaspoon sugar to each ½ pint of spiced vinegar.

Pickled damsons

cooking time: 25–30 minutes

you will need:

- 2 pints vinegar
- 1 tablespoon pickling spice
- 3–4 lb. sugar, preferably brown
- 8 lb. damsons

1. Boil the spices and vinegar for about 10 minutes.
2. Strain them, or tie the spices in muslin bag and put into the vinegar.
3. Stir in the sugar and when dissolved add fruit.
4. Simmer *gently* until very soft, but quite unbroken.
5. Lift out the fruit, remove spices and pack fruit into jars.
6. Boil the vinegar and sugar until slightly syrupy.
7. Pour over the fruit and seal down.
8. Store for several months before serving.

Pickled gherkins

cooking time: 15 minutes to make spiced vinegar

When gherkins are obtainable, pickle in the same way as cucumbers (see page 56).

Pickled marrow

cooking time: 10 minutes

you will need:

- 2 lb. marrow (after peeling)
- 4 oz. salt
- 4 oz. sugar
- ½ oz. ground ginger
- ½ oz. curry powder
- 6 peppercorns
- ¾ pint vinegar
- ¾ oz. mustard

1. Cut up the marrow, sprinkle with salt and allow to stand overnight.
2. Add other ingredients to the vinegar.
3. Boil for 5 minutes, then add drained and rinsed marrow.
4. Cook until tender.
5. Pack pickle into jars and seal.

Pickled mushrooms

**cooking time: 5 minutes mushrooms
5 minutes for vinegar**

you will need:

- 1 lb. small button mushrooms
- 1 oz. salt
- 2 pints vinegar
- 1 level teaspoon black pepper
- ¼ teaspoon ground mace

1. Peel or rub off the skin of the mushrooms with the help of a little salt.
2. Throw into boiling water with plenty of salt and boil for 5 minutes.
3. Pack into jars and pour the vinegar over them while boiling, the pepper and spice having been boiled with the vinegar.
4. White vinegar is the best for this purpose and the mushrooms will keep for a fairly long period.

Mixed vinegar pickles

cooking time: 15 minutes for spiced vinegar

Choose small onions, flowerets of cauliflower, green beans, pieces of cucumber or gherkin, green tomatoes. Prepare as for pickled cucumbers (see page 56), arranging an attractive assortment of the vegetables in the jars. It gives both colour and extra flavour if the chillis are left in the spiced vinegar.

Pickled nasturtium seeds

cooking time: 10 minutes for boiling vinegar

you will need:

to each pint vinegar add ½ oz. salt and 6 peppercorns
nasturtium seeds
vinegar to cover them

1 Boil the vinegar, salt and peppercorns together
2 When cold, strain into a wide necked bottle.
3 Gather the seeds on a dry day.
4 Put them into the vinegar and cork closely.

Note

These pickled seeds form an excellent substitute for capers. They are ready for use in about 3 months but may be kept for much longer.

Pickled onions or shallots

cooking time: 15 minutes to spice vinegar

1 Remove outer skins from the onions or shallots, using a stainless knife to prevent them discolouring.
2 Soak in brine for 36–48 hours. For quantities see page 56.
3 Then proceed as for pickled cucumbers (see page 56).

Piccalilli

cooking time: 15–20 minutes

1 Use exactly the same ingredients as for mustard pickles.
2 Chop the pieces of vegetables rather smaller than for mustard pickles so that you get a greater blending of these in the mustard sauce.

Mustard pickles

cooking time: 15–20 minutes

you will need:

2 lb. mixed vegetables, e.g. cauliflower, marrow, onions, cucumber, small green tomatoes, beans,
brine (see page 56)
1 pint vinegar
1 tablespoon pickling spice
1 tablespoon mustard powder
½ tablespoon turmeric powder
2 oz. sugar
1 tablespoon flour or ½ tablespoon cornflour
1 dessertspoon ginger

1 Cut the vegetables into neat pieces.
2 Soak overnight in brine.
3 Wash well under the cold tap and drain thoroughly.
4 Boil the vinegar and pickling spice together for 10 minutes.
5 Mix all dry ingredients with a very little vinegar until a smooth paste.
6 Pour over the strained hot vinegar and stir well.
7 Return to the pan and cook until just thickened.
8 Put in the vegetables and cook for 5 minutes.
9 Put into jars and seal well.

Pickled cocktail onions

cooking time: 15 minutes to spice vinegar

1 Choose very tiny onions indeed and pickle as for pickled onions.
2 Some people like to add a little colouring to the spiced vinegar to colour the onions, but this is a matter of taste.
3 To keep them very white, use a white wine vinegar and you may like to add 1 or 2 teaspoons sugar for sweet pickled onions.

Sweet pickled onions

cooking time: 15 minutes for spiced vinegar

Ordinary or cocktail onions can all be put into a sweet vinegar. Allow 1–2 teaspoons of sugar to each ½ pint of vinegar.

Sweet pickles

cooking time: 15–20 minutes

you will need:

- 2 lb. mixed vegetables, e.g. cauliflower, marrow, onion, cucumber, small green tomatoes, beans
- brine (see page 56)
- 1 pint vinegar
- 1 tablespoon pickling spice
- 6 oz. sugar
- 2 level tablespoons flour or 1 level tablespoon cornflour

Follow Mustard pickles recipe, steps 1 to 9.
If desired, 4-6 oz. sultanas can be added with vegetables for cooking.

Pickled walnuts

cooking time: 15 minutes to spice vinegar

1. Be certain nuts are not over-ripe.
2. Prick deeply with a silver fork in 2 or 3 places.
3. Soak in wet brine (see page 56) for at least 3 days.
4. Remove from brine and place on a tray or cloth in the sun, moving occasionally.
5. Slowly they will turn black, this will take 2 or 3 days (if very hot 24 hours may suffice).
6. When quite black, pack into jars and cover with cold spiced vinegar (see page 56).
7. Tie down and leave to mature for at least 1 month before use.

Sweet pickled walnuts

cooking time: 15 minutes for spiced vinegar

Use method for pickled walnuts, but add 1–2 teaspoons sugar to the spiced vinegar.

Pickled hard-boiled eggs

cooking time: 15 minutes for eggs

1. Hard-boil eggs by placing in cold water, bringing to the boil then turning out the heat, covering the pan and leaving for 15 minutes.
2. Take out the eggs and immediately plunge them into cold running water so that they cool rapidly.
3. Shell eggs and remove any skin.
4. When quite cold place the eggs in an ordinary glass jam jar and cover with cold vinegar.
5. Leave for a day or so before using.

Pickled fruits

cooking time: 15 minutes to make spiced vinegar, then further 10–25 minutes

you will need:

- 1 dessertspoon pickling spice
- ½ pint white vinegar to keep the colour of the fruit
- 1 lb. sugar
- 2 lb. pears, peaches, crab apples, damsons, plums or apricots

1. Tie spices in muslin and simmer in the vinegar for 10 minutes.
2. Strain.
3. Add the sugar to the vinegar.
4. Bring to the boil and simmer until the sugar has dissolved.
5. Put the fruit – peeled and cut into quarters or halves – into the vinegar syrup and simmer gently until just tender. Crab apples and damsons should be left whole.
6. Take out the fruit and pack into bottling jars.
7. Boil the vinegar (with the lid off the pan) for a few minutes to thicken liquid.
8. Pour over the fruit and seal down at once.
9. Do not use metal tops next to the vinegar otherwise they will rust. Bottling jars are ideal.

Spiced fruits

cooking time: as pickled fruit

1 These are particularly good when pickling apples and pears.
2 Use recipe for pickled fruits, but use ordinary malt vinegar and add little mixed spice, cinnamon bark and nutmeg to the vinegar and sugar.
3 Cut apples into fairly thick slices and halve pears.
4 Sliced lemons can be pickled in the same way and are very good with cold duck or pork. Do not remove peel but take out pips.

Spiced dried fruits

cooking time: 10–15 minutes to make spiced vinegar. Approximately 1 hour for fruit

you will need:

- 2 lb. mixed dried fruit (prunes, dried apricots, peaches, figs)
- 2 pints spiced vinegar (see page 56)
- 8 oz. sugar

1 Wash the dried fruit and soak overnight in the vinegar.
2 Add the sugar.
3 Simmer until soft but unbroken.
4 Pack into jars and seal down.

Chutneys and relishes

1 Do not attempt to cut down on the quantity of sugar or vinegar in a chutney recipe as this is the preservative.
2 Don't put in all the vinegar at once as this rather takes away the flavour of the ingredients – put in about ¼ of the vinegar, then add rest gradually during the cooking period.
3 Cook chutney with lid OFF pan so it thickens – stir from time to time.
4 Pour the chutney into jars while still hot – filling to neck of jar.
5 Cover very well – bottling jars are ideal as they have glass lids. Never put metal tops directly next to the chutney otherwise the vinegar in the chutney will spoil both taste and colour and will make the lid rust and be very difficult to remove. You can buy special pickling jars or instead put a round of waxed paper on chutney – then a thin layer of melted wax (paraffin wax) then the final cover *or* put the waxed paper then several thicknesses of brown or parchment paper over this – tying it down tightly.
6 Always use pure malt vinegar – white vinegar can be used for light coloured chutneys if desired and to retain bright colour.
7 Store in cool dry place – preferably in dark – to keep well.
8 Never use copper, brass or iron pans; aluminium is excellent.

Apple chutney

cooking time: 40 minutes

you will need:

- 1 lb. onions (grated or finely chopped)
- ½ pint vinegar
- 2 lb. apples (after peeling and coring), chopped
- 2–4 oz. dried fruit (if liked)
- 1 teaspoon pickling spice
- 1 teaspoon salt
- 1 teaspoon ground ginger
- 12 oz. sugar

1 Put the onion into a saucepan with ⅛ pint vinegar and simmer until nearly soft.
2 Add the chopped apples, dried fruit, spices (tied securely in a muslin bag), salt, ground ginger and just enough vinegar to stop the mixture from burning.
3 Cook gently until the fruit is soft, stirring from time to time.
4 Add remainder of the vinegar and thoroughly stir in the sugar.
5 Boil steadily until the chutney is thick.
6 Remove pickling spices.
7 Pour into hot jars.

Apricot chutney

cooking time: 50 minutes

you will need:

8 oz. dried apricots
1 pint vinegar (white vinegar is good but not essential)
4 oz. raisins (stoned), chopped
4 oz. sultanas
3 teaspoons pickling spice
1 good teaspoon salt
2 cloves garlic
juice and peel 1 lemon
1 lb. apples (after peeling and coring)
1 lb. brown sugar

1 Cut dried apricots into small pieces and soak for 2–3 hours in cold water.
2 Drain and put into saucepan with a little of the vinegar and all the other ingredients except apples and sugar.
3 The pickling spice should be tied in muslin.
4 Boil steadily for 30 minutes, adding vinegar, then add grated or chopped apples and sugar.
5 Stir until sugar dissolves.
6 Boil for about another 20 minutes or until it thickens.
7 Remove pickling spices.
8 Put into hot jars and cover as directed.

Apple and mint chutney

cooking time: 40 minutes

Use recipe and method for apple chutney but allow 1 dessertspoon of chopped mint to each lb. chutney. Stir this in just before putting into bottles.

Aubergine chutney

cooking time: 1 hour

you will need:

2 teaspoons pickling spice
2 lb. aubergines (unpeeled)
12 oz. onions
1 lb. cooking apples (after peeling and coring)
2 teaspoons ginger
1 teaspoon salt
½ pint vinegar
1¼ lb. brown sugar

1 Tie the spices in a muslin bag.
2 Wipe and cut aubergines into thin slices.
3 Put all the ingredients except the sugar into a saucepan – chopping the onions very finely.
4 Simmer gently until tender.
5 Remove the bag of spices and stir in the sugar.
6 Boil until thick.
7 Put into hot jars and seal down.

Variations

With lemon – a little grated lemon rind gives a good flavour.
With peppers – a mixture of aubergines and red and green peppers instead of all aubergines is excellent.

Aubergine and capsicum chutney

cooking time: 30 minutes

you will need:

4 medium sized aubergines (peeled)
4 medium sized capsicums (or sweet red peppers)
salt to taste
little turmeric or saffron powder
1 dessertspoon good Indian curry powder
¾ pint malt or wine vinegar
2-inch piece cinnamon
1-inch piece ginger
1–2 bay leaves, if liked
little olive oil
4 oz. peeled sliced shallots
1 or 2 small cloves garlic (peeled), finely sliced
little brown sugar or two peeled chopped apples, if liked

1 Cut the aubergines and peppers into slices lengthwise and then into smaller pieces.
2 Rub these over with salt and saffron.
3 Dissolve and mix the curry powder into a tablespoon or two of the vinegar and put in the cinnamon and ginger and bay leaves.
4 Leave for 15 minutes.
5 Heat the olive oil and fry the cut vegetables, sliced shallots (or onion) and garlic for about 10 minutes in a large frying pan or saucepan, stirring and turning it over every now and again; add sugar or apples, if used.
6 Add the curry mixture and blend all together well and cook over a low fire for about 10 minutes, stirring gently a few times.
7 Add rest of the vinegar, simmer for a few more minutes until thick.
8 Taste for salt and if liked 'hot' add a little cayenne pepper or paprika.
9 Put into dry, wide mouthed jars when slightly warm, first removing cinnamon, ginger and bay leaves.

Autumn fruit chutney

cooking time: 1½ hours

you will need:

2 lb. plums (stoned)	½ teaspoon mace
2 lb. cooking apples (after peeling and coring)	½ teaspoon mixed spice
2 lb. tomatoes	2 oz. root ginger
2 lb. onions	1 lb. sultanas
1–2 cloves garlic	1 pint vinegar – good measure
1 oz. salt	1 lb. Demerara sugar
½ teaspoon cayenne	

1 Chop all the fruit and vegetables. Add spice, etc.
2 Boil in the vinegar until tender.
3 Add the sugar and continue cooking until thick.

Beetroot chutney

cooking time: 40 minutes

you will need:

1 lb. onions, chopped	2 teaspoons salt
1 pint spiced white vinegar	1 lb. apples
3 lb. cooked beetroot	1 lb. white sugar

1 Cook the chopped onions for a short time in a little of the vinegar.
2 Add the rest of the ingredients and proceed as for apple chutney (see page 60).
The beetroot should be diced in very small pieces.

Variation

With sultanas – 8 oz. light coloured sultanas could be added to this recipe.

Blackberry chutney

cooking time: 1½ hours

you will need:

1 lb. cooking apples (unpeeled)	1 teaspoon powdered mace
12 oz. onions	1 pint vinegar (preferably white)
3 lb. blackberries	1 lb. brown sugar
3 teaspoons salt	
½ oz. mustard	
2 teaspoons powdered ginger	

1 Peel, core and chop the apples and onions.
2 Put into a pan with the blackberries, salt, spices and ½ pint vinegar and cook for 1 hour adding rest of vinegar gradually.
3 Rub through a sieve to remove the pips.
4 Add sugar and cook until the desired consistency is obtained.

Blackberry and apple chutney

cooking time: 1½ hours

Use ingredients for blackberry chutney, but use 2 lb. blackberries and 2 lb. apples. Proceed as for blackberry chutney.

Cherry chutney

cooking time: 40–60 minutes

Follow the recipe and method for damson chutney, using rather tart cherries – morello cherries are ideal. When the chutney is thick, add approximately 8 oz. chopped nuts.

Cranberry chutney

cooking time: 40 minutes to 1 hour

you will need:

1 lb. cooking apples	1 teaspoon salt
1 lb. cranberries	½ pint vinegar
6 oz. raisins	2 teaspoons pickling spice
1 teaspoon mixed spice	8 oz. sugar

1 Put the chopped apples, cranberries, dried fruit, spices tied in muslin, salt, in a pan with just enough vinegar to stop the mixture burning.
2 Cook gently until the fruit is soft, stirring from time to time.
3 Add the remainder of the vinegar and the sugar.
4 Stir until the sugar is dissolved.
5 Boil steadily until thick.
6 Remove pickling spices and pour into hot jars and seal down.

Damson chutney

cooking time: 1¼ hours

you will need:

3 lb. damsons
2 pints vinegar
1½ lb. cooking apples (after peeling and coring), chopped
1 lb. onions (peeled), chopped
2 teaspoons ginger
1 oz. pickling spice
3 teaspoons salt
1 lb. sugar

1 Simmer damsons in 1 pint vinegar until tender enough to remove stones.
2 Add chopped apples, onions, ginger, pickling spices (tied in muslin) and salt.
3 Continue cooking until fruit is completely soft.
4 Add rest of vinegar and sugar.
5 Boil steadily until thick.
6 Put into hot jars and seal down.

Quick date chutney

cooking time: 10–15 minutes to make spiced vinegar

you will need:

1 lb. dates
1 small onion
seasoning
about ¼ pint spiced vinegar
good pinch ginger and/or mixed spice

1 Chop dates finely.
2 Add little finely chopped onion, seasoning.
3 Pour over enough hot spiced vinegar to moisten.
4 Stir in good pinch ginger and/or mixed spice.
5 Stir well until the dates are softened.
6 Use fresh, as this does not keep.

Elderberry chutney

cooking time: 40 minutes to 1 hour

Use recipe and method for apple chutney (see page 60) but use 1 lb. apples and 1 lb. elderberries.
This is very pleasant if a little cayenne pepper is added.

Gooseberry chutney

cooking time: 40 minutes to 1 hour

you will need:

2 lb. gooseberries
8 oz. cooking apples
1 teaspoon salt
½ pint vinegar
1 teaspoon pickling spice
1 lb. onions (grated or finely chopped)
12 oz. sugar
1 teaspoon ground ginger
2–4 oz. dried fruit (if liked)

Use method for apple chutney (see page 60).

Lemon chutney

cooking time: 1½ hours

you will need:

4 large or 6 small lemons
8 oz. onions
1 oz. salt
¾ pint malt vinegar
1 lb. granulated sugar
4 oz. seedless raisins
1 oz. mustard seed (well crushed)
1 teaspoon ground ginger
½ small teaspoon cayenne pepper

1 Wash lemons.
2 Slice thinly and remove all pips.
3 Peel and chop onions.
4 Put on to a dish with the sliced lemons and sprinkle with salt.
5 Leave for 24 hours.
6 Put in a preserving pan, add all the other ingredients.
7 Bring to the boil.
8 Simmer until quite tender and of the consistency of chutney.
9 Turn into dry jars and tie down when cold.

Mango chutney

cooking time: 50 minutes

you will need:

2 teaspoons pickling spice
12 oz. onions (peeled), sliced
2 lb. mangoes
1 lb. cooking apples (after peeling and coring), sliced
2 teaspoons ginger
1 pint vinegar
1½ lb. brown sugar

1 Tie the spices in a bag.
2 Chop the onions in very small pieces.
3 Put all ingredients with a little vinegar into a pan, except the sugar.
4 Simmer gently until soft, adding vinegar gradually.
5 Remove the bag of spices.
6 Add the sugar and boil until thick.
7 It is advisable to keep the pieces of mango fairly large.
8 Some people may like a little salt in this chutney, but it is generally a sweet, rather hot chutney.
9 Turn into dry jars and seal when cold.

Marrow chutney

cooking time: 40 minutes

Use recipe and method for apple chutney (see page 60) but use marrow instead of apple and increase ginger to taste.

Orange chutney

cooking time: 1½ hours

Use the recipe and method for lemon chutney (see page 63), but allow 4 really large oranges instead of lemons.

Orange and lemon chutney

cooking time: 1¼–1½ hours

you will need:

3 large lemons
2 medium oranges
1 pint spiced vinegar (spiced white vinegar may be used to give a clearer colour)
8 oz. onions
6 oz. light coloured sultanas
1 teaspoon powdered ginger
salt to taste
1 teaspoon cinnamon
little pepper
1 lb. castor sugar

1 Wash lemons and oranges and squeeze out the juice.
2 Mince or shred peel and pulp, etc. of fruit (as for marmalade) and discard pips.
3 Soak for 24 hours in the cold spiced vinegar.
4 Next day add juice and thinly sliced onions.
5 Simmer very gently until peel and onions are tender.
6 Add sultanas, seasoning, etc. to taste, together with sugar.
7 Cook until thick.

Plum chutney

cooking time: 40 minutes

you will need:

2 lb. plums
2–4 oz. dried fruit (if desired)
1 tablespoon pickling spice
1 teaspoon salt
1 teaspoon ground ginger
½ pint vinegar
12 oz. sugar

1 Simmer stoned plums, dried fruit, pickling spice (tied securely in muslin bag), salt and ginger in a saucepan with just enough vinegar to stop the mixture from burning.
2 Cook gently until the fruit is soft, stirring from time to time.
3 Add remainder of vinegar and thoroughly stir in sugar.
4 Boil steadily until the mixture is thick.
5 Remove spices.
6 Pour chutney into hot jars and seal.

Plum chutney (minted)

Add ½ tablespoon chopped mint to chutney before putting into jars.

Pear chutney

cooking time: 1½ hours

Use recipe and method for autumn fruit chutney (see page 62) but use pears instead of plums.

Red pepper chutney

cooking time: 50 minutes

you will need:

- 2 cloves garlic
- 4 capsicums (sweet red peppers)
- 2 aubergines (eggplants)
- 2 good sized cooking apples (peeled and cored)
- 8 oz. onions
- ¼ oz. root ginger
- 6 chillis
- ½–1 tablespoon curry powder
- 1 teaspoon saffron powder
- 1 pint spiced vinegar
- salt to taste
- 2 oz. brown sugar
- 6 oz. raisins (optional)

1. Crush the cloves of garlic well.
2. Slice the peppers (removing the seeds) and the aubergines, apples and onions.
3. Tie the root ginger and chillis in muslin.
4. Blend the curry powder and saffron with a little vinegar.
5. Add other seasoning.
6. Proceed as apple chutney (see page 60).

Red pepper relish

cooking time: 30 minutes

you will need:

- 12 capsicums (sweet red peppers)
- 12 green peppers
- 12 onions
- 1¼ pints vinegar
- 12 oz. brown sugar
- 2 tablespoons salt
- 2 tablespoons celery seeds

1. Chop the peppers, discarding all seeds, and chop the onions.
2. Simmer in the vinegar until tender, adding sugar, salt and celery seed tied in muslin.
3. Pour into jars and seal as chutney (see page 60).

Rhubarb chutney

cooking time: 35–40 minutes

Use recipe and method for apple chutney (see page 60) but use 3 lb. rhubarb instead of apples, but if liked the quantity of dried ginger can be increased to 2 level teaspoons.

Rhubarb chutney (minted)

Make as before and stir in ½ tablespoon chopped mint before pouring into jars.

Spanish tomato chutney

cooking time: 25–30 minutes

you will need:

- 3 lb. green tomatoes (skinned)
- 1 red pepper
- 1 lb. onions
- 2 tablespoons salt
- 1½ pints vinegar
- 1 teaspoon mixed spice
- 1 teaspoon peppercorns
- 1 teaspoon mustard seed
- few chillis
- 1 teaspoon cloves
- 12 oz. sugar

1. Slice the tomatoes and red pepper, and chop onions finely.
2. Sprinkle with salt and leave for several hours.
3. Drain well.
4. Put into a preserving pan with the vinegar and spices tied in muslin.
5. Simmer steadily for 10 minutes.
6. Add the sugar and continue simmering for another 15–20 minutes.
7. Pour into jars and seal down.

This is less soft than an ordinary chutney.

Tomato chutney

cooking time: 40 minutes with ripe tomatoes, 50–55 minutes with green tomatoes

you will need:

- 1 teaspoon pickling spice
- 8 oz. finely chopped onions
- ½ pint malt vinegar
- 8 oz. apples, peeled and cored
- 2 lb. tomatoes, green or red
- 1 rounded teaspoon mustard powder
- ½ teaspoon ginger
- ½ teaspoon salt
- ¼ teaspoon pepper
- 8 oz. sultanas
- 8 oz. sugar

1. Put the pickling spices into a piece of muslin.
2. Put the onion into a saucepan with 2–3 tablespoons vinegar and simmer gently until nearly soft.
3. Add the chopped apples, skinned sliced tomatoes, spices, salt, pepper, mustard, ginger and sultanas.
4. Simmer gently until all the mixture is quite soft, stirring from time to time.
5. Add the remainder of the vinegar and the sugar.
6. When the sugar has quite dissolved boil steadily until the chutney is the consistency of jam.
7. Remove the little bag of spice.
8. Pour the hot chutney into warm jars and seal down at once.

Green tomato chutney (1)

cooking time: 50 minutes

you will need:

- 8 oz. onions, grated or finely chopped
- ½ pint vinegar
- 8 oz. apples (after peeling and coring)
- 2 lb. green tomatoes (skinned)
- 1 teaspoon pickling spice
- ½ teaspoon salt
- 8 oz. sugar

1. Put the onion into a saucepan with ⅛ pint vinegar.
2. Simmer until nearly soft.
3. Chop the apples and add the chopped tomatoes, spices (tied in a muslin bag) and salt and just enough vinegar to stop the mixture from burning.
4. Cook gently until tomatoes and apples are soft, stirring from time to time.
5. Add remainder of vinegar and stir in sugar.
6. Boil steadily until the chutney is thick.
7. Remove spices, pour into hot jars and seal.

Green tomato chutney (minted)

Follow previous recipe and stir in ½ tablespoon chopped mint before pouring into jars.

Red tomato and apple chutney

cooking time: 40 minutes

you will need:

- 1½ lb. red tomatoes
- 8 oz. onions, grated or finely chopped
- ½ pint vinegar (brown or white)
- 1½ lb. apples (after peeling and coring)
- 1 teaspoon pickling spice
- 1 teaspoon salt
- 1 teaspoon ground ginger
- 4 oz. dried fruit
- 12 oz. sugar

1. Skin the tomatoes.
2. Put onion into a saucepan with ⅛ pint vinegar and simmer until nearly soft.
3. Chop apples and tomatoes, add spice (tied securely in a muslin bag), the salt, ground ginger, dried fruit and just enough vinegar to stop the mixture from burning.
4. Cook gently until the fruit is soft, stirring from time to time.
5. Add the remainder of the vinegar and thoroughly stir in the sugar.
6. Boil steadily until the chutney is thick.
7. Remove the bag of pickling spices and pour the hot chutney into hot jars.
8. Seal down at once.

Quick pineapple relish

cooking time: 5 minutes

you will need:

- 1 tablespoon onion, chopped
- 1 oz. butter
- 4 tablespoons pineapple, shredded
- 1 tablespoon parsley, chopped
- 2 tablespoons mild mustard

1. Gently fry onion in the butter until soft, but not brown.
2. Add pineapple, chopped parsley and mild mustard and mix well.
3. Use with any hot meat or poultry.

Mustard relish

cooking time: 30 minutes

you will need:

- 1 lb. onions
- 3 lb. apples (weight after peeling)*
- 1½ pints vinegar
- ½ oz. mustard seed
- 1 tablespoon salt
- 8 oz. sultanas, washed
- 3 teaspoons dry mustard
- 1 lb. sugar

*or 1 lb. tomatoes, 2 lb. apples.

1. Simmer the chopped onions and cored apples with half the vinegar, until tender, adding mustard seed tied up in muslin.
2. When soft put in remaining ingredients, blending the mustard with vinegar. Stir well until the sugar has dissolved, then boil steadily until thick, stirring from time to time.
3. Take out the bag of mustard seed. Pour into clean hot jars and seal.

Variation

Apple and red pepper relish – follow the recipe for mustard relish, but add one or two diced red peppers (capsicums) and use 2 lb. apples.

End of season relish

cooking time: 1½ hours

you will need:

- 2 lb. green tomatoes (skinned)
- ¼ head white cabbage
- 2 small capsicums (sweet red peppers)
- 2 medium onions
- 8 oz. ripe tomatoes (skinned)
- 2 small green peppers
- 2 medium stalks celery
- ½ medium cucumber, peeled
- 3 rounded tablespoons salt
- 5 oz. brown sugar
- 1½ pints mild vinegar
- 2 level tablespoons mild mustard
- 1 level teaspoon paprika

1. Chop vegetables.
2. Place in pan in layers, sprinkling each layer with salt.
3. Stand overnight.
4. Drain and press out all liquid.
5. Add sugar, vinegar, mustard and paprika to vegetables.
6. Cook for about 1½ hours, stirring often.
7. Pour into clean hot jars and seal.

Tomato and horseradish relish

cooking time: 40–45 minutes

you will need:

- ¾ pint vinegar
- 1 dessertspoon pickling spice
- 4 lb. ripe tomatoes (skinned)
- 2 large cooking apples
- 1 large onion
- 1 dessertspoon salt
- ½ teaspoon pepper – preferably cayenne or paprika
- horseradish*
- 1 lb. sugar

*The amount of horseradish added depends entirely on personal taste, so add it gradually, tasting as you do so.

1. Boil the vinegar and pickling spices together for 10 minutes.
2. Cook the tomatoes, apples and onion until a thick pulp, stirring to begin with so that it does not burn.
3. Add vinegar, salt and pepper, remove spices.
4. Cook in an uncovered pan until it becomes thick. This will take a fair time.
5. Add 2–3 tablespoons grated horseradish and the sugar.
6. Boil again for about 10 minutes.
7. Put into boiling bottling jars.
8. Seal down and sterilise by standing these (with screw tops loosened) in a pan of boiling water and boiling rapidly for about 10 minutes.
9. Lift out jars carefully and tighten screw tops.

Salting beans

you will need:

- 3 lb. beans (runner or French) – should be young, fresh and tender
- 1 lb. kitchen salt (*not* free-running table salt)

Failures are often due to the use of too little salt, so it is better to adhere strictly to these quantities.

1. Wash, dry and remove strings.
2. French beans can be left whole, runner beans should be sliced.
3. Place a layer of salt in a glass or stoneware jar and on this a layer of beans.
4. Continue to fill the jar with alternate layers, pressing the beans well down and finishing with a layer of salt. If preferred, some salt can be used for the bottom and top layers and the rest

mixed with the beans before they are packed into the jars.

5 Cover and leave for a few days.

6 The beans will shrink and the jar should be filled up with more beans and salt, again having a layer of salt at the top. The salt does not remain dry, as it draws moisture from the beans and forms a strong brine – this should not be thrown away otherwise air pockets may be left between the layers of beans in which bacteria and moulds may develop.

7 When full, cork the jar securely.

8 If the beans become slimy and do not keep, insufficient salt has been added or the beans were not pressed down sufficiently when packed into jars.

To use the beans

9 Remove from the jar, wash thoroughly in several waters.

10 Leave to soak for 2 hours in warm water.

11 Cook in boiling water, without salt, until they are tender (25–35 minutes). Drain and serve in the same way as fresh runner beans.

Storing new potatoes

These can, of course, be stored by bottling, but you can also keep some to be used for Christmas Day by burying in sand in the garden in a sheltered place. They will not store for a very much longer period than this.

Storing nuts

The nuts should be gathered when they are mature, otherwise they will not store well.

Almonds – make certain that you are using the sweet almonds, because bitter almonds should not be eaten, although very small quantities can be added to cakes for flavouring.

1 Spread the nuts out in one flat layer to dry.

2 When dry put in containers, filling with a layer of nuts and a layer of salt and some kind of packing such as is used round grapes, if desired. If you cannot get this, use a layer of salt and a layer of nuts.

Chestnuts – store in boxes in a dry place.

Cob nuts – lay out in flat boxes in an airy space. Turn once or twice during storage.

Walnuts – remove the green husk before storing. Clean away any pieces of the husk, dry the nuts and store as almonds.

Nuts, to salt

Almonds, cashews, cob nuts, peanuts

Shell the nuts, then heat in butter or olive oil until they are a faint golden colour, and then toss in salt.

Store in airtight jars or tins. Almonds should be blanched and dried before salting.

Mint, preserving

Chop the washed mint finely and put a layer into a jar with an equal depth of sugar. Continue to fill the jar in the same way until full, finishing with a layer of sugar. Seal down.

Herbs, to dry

To dry herbs, wash them, after picking in hot weather. Dry well in a cloth, then lay them on baking trays padded with plenty of paper and a piece of muslin over the top. Dry very slowly in the airing cupboard or very low oven 200°F.– Gas Mark ¼ (with the door ajar), until brittle. Crumble and put into jars.

In hot weather they can be dried in the sun. Parsley is a better colour if dried for a few minutes in a hot oven.

Herbs, to freeze

Chopped fresh herbs may be preserved packed in ice cube containers in a home freezer. You can also store a number of bouquets garnis by placing sprigs of herbs between small squares of polythene in the freezer.

Chutneys made with a pressure cooker

A pressure cooker is ideal for softening fruits, etc., for chutney. You can do this in a very short time and make quite certain the skins really are soft before the sugar is added. Here are two recipes:

Green tomato chutney (2)

cooking time: 20 minutes

you will need:

3 lb. tomatoes
1 lb. sour apples
8 oz. onions
8 oz. sultanas
1 teaspoon salt
½ oz. root ginger
½ pint vinegar
8 oz. sugar

1 Remove skins of tomatoes, peel and core apples cut into very small pieces. Chop onions, tie ginger in muslin bag.
2 Put all ingredients except sugar into cooker (remove trivet) adding vinegar. Stir well, cover and bring to 10 lb. pressure. Pressure cook for 10 minutes.
3 Reduce pressure with cold water.
4 Stir in sugar and simmer in open cooker until chutney is of a thick smooth consistency. Remove ginger.
5 Put into warm jars, do not overfill, and seal.

Apple and marrow chutney

cooking time: 25 minutes

you will need:

2 lb. apples
1 lb. marrow
1 lb. onions
4 oz. crystallised ginger
¼ teaspoon cayenne pepper
2 cloves garlic
½ tablespoon salt
½ pint vinegar
allspice
1½ lb. brown sugar

1 Peel, core and cut up the apples and marrow into small pieces and slice onions finely.
2 Put vinegar and all ingredients, except sugar, into cooker. Stir well, cover and bring to 10 lb. pressure. Pressure cook for 15 minutes.
3 Reduce pressure with cold water.
4 Stir in sugar and simmer without lid on cooker until chutney is of a thick consistency.
5 Put into warm jars and seal.

Ketchups or sauces

When tomatoes, etc. are cheap, it is well worthwhile making your own sauces or ketchups. Bottled correctly they keep for a long period and can be used as a 'short cut' to flavour any salad dressings, sauces, or as an accompaniment to meat, fish and other savoury dishes.

To fill and sterilise bottles of ketchup

1 You can use ordinary bottles providing you have corks that fit and the bottles are made of sufficiently strong glass to withstand heat.
2 Sterilise bottles by putting into pan of cold water and bringing up to boil – lift out on to WOODEN board – do not put on cold surface.
3 Pour *boiling* ketchup into the jar while hot – a funnel is the easiest way to do this.
4 When filled to within about ¾ inch of the top, stand bottles – lightly corked – in pan of boiling water with padding at base and boil steadily for 10 minutes. Take care bottles do not fall over.
5 Lift out and coat with wax – see below.

Note

If using bottling jars, proceed as for fruit pulp, see pages 73, 74.

Using wax on bottles of ketchup

If bottling ketchup in old lemonade or ketchup bottles, you MUST ensure that they are airtight.

1 To do this the filled sterilised bottles should be sealed down with clean corks as soon as they are lifted out from the steriliser.
2 Have hot melted candle or paraffin wax avail-

able and brush round the cork to make an air-tight seal.

3 If necessary repeat with second layer of wax, then cover with foil or paper.

4 If wished a tiny round of waxed paper can be put over the ketchup in the bottle – the moment it comes from being sterilised – then a teaspoon of melted candle or paraffin wax poured over the top. You can then cover with ordinary metal bottle tops.

Blackberry ketchup

cooking time: 45 minutes

you will need:

3 lb. blackberries
½ pint water
sugar
vinegar
salt

1 Simmer the blackberries in the water until tender.
2 Rub through a sieve very firmly, leaving only the pips behind.
3 To each pint of purée, add 2 oz. sugar and ½ pint spiced vinegar (see page 56).
4 A little salt may also be added if you wish.
5 Simmer steadily until fairly thick.
6 Put into heated bottles and sterilise as for tomato and horseradish relish (see page 67).

This ketchup is delicious with cold meat.

Damson ketchup

cooking time: 55 minutes

you will need:

3 lb. damsons
1 pint water
sugar
vinegar
salt

1 Simmer the damsons in the water until tender.
2 Rub through a sieve very firmly, leaving only the stones behind.
3 To each pint purée allow 4 oz. sugar and ½ pint spiced vinegar (see page 56).
4 A little salt may also be added if you wish.
5 Simmer steadily until fairly thick.
6 Put into heated bottles and sterilise as for tomato and horseradish relish (see page 67).

This ketchup is delicious with cold meat and corned beef hash.

Grape ketchup

cooking time: 50 minutes

Use recipe and method for blackberry ketchup, using grapes instead of blackberries. When adding sugar a better flavour is produced by using 4 oz. to each pint of purée.

This ketchup is very good with cold chicken.

Mushroom ketchup

cooking time: 2½ hours

you will need:

3 lb. mushrooms
3 oz. salt
½ pint spiced vinegar (see page 56)
1 level dessertspoon onion, chopped (optional)

1 Mince or break up mushrooms.
2 Sprinkle with salt and leave for 24–36 hours.
3 Add spiced vinegar to the mushrooms and liquor (with chopped onion if liked).
4 Simmer gently for 2½ hours.
5 Strain carefully through muslin while boiling.
6 Bottle in sterilised jars and sterilise them (see page 69).
7 Seal at once, coating corks with melted wax.

Spiced apple ketchup

cooking time: 1 hour

you will need:

4 lb. apples (after peeling and coring)
2 large onions, peeled
2 cloves garlic
¾ pint brown vinegar
2 teaspoons pickling spices
2 teaspoons salt
1 teaspoon curry powder
½ teaspoon cayenne pepper
1 teaspoon turmeric
8 oz. sugar

1 Chop the apples, onion and garlic, and cook with the pickling spices, vinegar and seasoning until the apples form a thick pulp.
2 Rub through a sieve, adding the sugar.
3 Boil rapidly until set.
4 Pour into hot bottles and sterilise (see page 69).

Tomato ketchup

cooking time: 1–1¼ hours

you will need:

¾ pint vinegar	2 large cooking apples (peeled and cored)
1 dessertspoon pickling spice	6 oz. sugar
4 lb. ripe tomatoes (skinned)	1 dessertspoon salt
1 large onion, peeled	¼ teaspoon paprika or cayenne

1 Boil the vinegar and pickling spices together for 10 minutes.
2 Then strain the vinegar.
3 Cook the sliced tomatoes, onion and apples until you have a thick pulp, stirring well to prevent mixture burning.
4 Rub through a sieve taking care not to leave any pulp behind, otherwise it will not thicken.
5 Put pulp into pan with vinegar, sugar, salt and pepper.
6 Cook steadily until thick.
7 Pour into sterilised bottles while boiling and sterilise for certain keeping (see page 69).
8 Seal down and if using corks paint at once with hot wax (see page 69).

Tomato and chilli ketchup

cooking time: 45 minutes

Use recipe and method for tomato ketchup, but add 2 chilli peppers, one chopped sweet red pepper and 1 clove of garlic.

18th century catchup

1 'Take mushrooms and wipe them very clean.
2 Put them in a crock and strew salt between every 2 or 3 handfuls.
3 Let them stand for 2 or 3 days.
4 Strain them off and boil up ye licker with cloves, mace, nutmeg and pepper, a pretty while.
5 When it is cold put it into a bottle and stop it very close.'

To make this today you might care to chop up the mushrooms coarsely and keep them in the liquor, after letting them stand. Adjust the spices to taste, but as mushrooms have a definite though delicate flavour, don't be too sparing.

Apple sauce

cooking time: 30 minutes, plus time for preserving

you will need:

1 lb. cooking apples (after peeling and coring)	1 oz. margarine or butter
¼ pint water	2 tablespoons sugar

1 Slice apples thinly.
2 Put into small saucepan adding about ¼ pint water, the margarine and the sugar.
3 Allow to simmer steadily until a smooth mixture.
4 Beat well with wooden spoon when apples are cooked, to give a good smooth appearance.

Spiced apple sauce

cooking time: 30 minutes, plus time for preserving

Use recipe and method for apple sauce, but add 1 teaspoon of mixed spice.

Bottling sweet sauces

You save a great deal of time if you prepare a large quantity of cranberry or apple sauce and preserve it for use at any period in the year. These are recommended recipes, and you must sterilise as for pulped fruit (see page 74).

Apple and cranberry sauce

cooking time: 30 minutes, plus time for preserving

Use recipe and method for apple sauce (see above but use 8 oz. apples and 8 oz. cranberries.

Cranberry sauce (1)

cooking time: 30 minutes, plus time for preserving

you will need:

2 tablespoons water
3 oz. sugar
12 oz. cranberries
1 tablespoon port or sherry

1 Heat water and sugar together.
2 Add the fruit and cook until tender.
3 Add port or sherry if wished.
4 Having prepared the sauce, pour boiling sauce into boiling hot jars and then proceed as for pulped fruit (see page 74).

Cranberry sauce (2)

cooking time: 30 minutes, plus time for preserving

you will need:

8–12 oz. cranberries
¼ pint water
2–3 oz. sugar
knob of butter

1 Simmer the cranberries in the water.
2 Rub through a sieve.
3 Add sugar to taste and the butter.

Mint sauce

cooking time: 5–15 minutes, plus time for preserving

you will need:

½ pint vinegar
4 oz. sugar
8 tablespoons mint

1 Boil the vinegar and sugar until sugar has dissolved.
2 Add the chopped mint.
3 Put into the smallest size preserving jars available.
4 Sterilise as for pulped fruit (see page 74).

Orange and raspberry sauce

cooking time: 30 minutes, plus time for preserving

Use recipe and method for apple sauce (see page 71), but use 8 oz. oranges and 8 oz. raspberries.

Redcurrant sauce

cooking time: 20 minutes, plus time for preserving

you will need:

1 lb. redcurrants
¼ pint water
3–4 oz. sugar
knob butter

1 Simmer the redcurrants with water and sugar until soft.
2 Rub through a sieve. Add butter.
3 Reheat with the pulp.
4 Proceed as for pulp fruit (see page 74).
This sauce is excellent with lamb or mutton.

Bottling fruit and vegetables

In order the have the best results, it is important to prepare the fruit carefully. The look of the bottles depends a great deal on the time you have given to preparing the fruit.

To prepare soft fruit

If this requires washing, place the soft fruit on a sieve and run cold water very gently over the fruit. Leave to drain.

To prepare hard fruit

If possible, try to wipe rather than wash the fruit as using too much water will tend to spoil the flavour.

Apples – peel, core and slice, and immediately drop into a bowl of salted water, i.e., 1 level tablespoonful kitchen salt to each quart of cold water. Let the apples stay there for 10 minutes, with a plate on top of them if desired, but this is not really necessary. This prevents the apples from becoming brown in colour.

Peaches – drop the peaches into boiling water and leave them there for ½–1 minute. Remove and put into cold water, then skin them. Leave them in water until ready to pack the jars. This prevents their discoloration.

Pears – preparation of pears is similar to apples. If using hard cooking pears, simmer these until soft. If pears are ripe, then remove from the salt water and put for 1 minute only in boiling water or boiling syrup. Pears treated this way should remain absolutely white in colour.

Tomatoes – If desired to peel the tomatoes, then drop them into boiling water for ½ minute, then put into cold water. The skins will immediately come off.

To sterilise fruit in the oven

The temperature of the oven is very important. With a gas oven use gas mark ¼, if the pressure is very good, or gas mark ½. Set an electric oven 240°F.

Stand the jars on either an asbestos mat, several thicknesses of paper or cardboard, or a wooden board. Cover the tops of the jars with an old, clean tin lid.

While the jars are in the oven, put the glass lids and rubber bands on to boil, and boil these for 15 minutes. If using metal tops, just drop them for 1 minute into boiling water so that the lacquer is not damaged.

Here is given a table of the length of time to leave the fruit in the oven:

raspberries, loganberries (Do not pack these fruits too tightly, otherwise they form a solid block of fruit which is very difficult to sterilise.)	45 minutes
rhubarb, redcurrants, blackcurrants	50 minutes
plums, apples, blackberries, damsons, greengages and cherries	1 hour
whole peaches, whole apricots, halved peaches, halved apricots, pears	1¼ hours
tomatoes	1½ hours

At the end of the given time, first check up that everything is handy, for the important thing about the oven method is speed when the jars are brought out. Have ready a kettle of boiling water or pan of boiling syrup. Remove jars one at a time from the oven. Place on to a wooden surface, pour over the boiling liquid, tapping the jar as you do so, until it completely overflows. If using a screw top jar, put on the rubber ring first, put on the top, hold on to this tightly, then either screw down, clip down or put on weight. Do not handle the jars any more than necessary for 24 hours. After this time, remove the screw band or clip and test to see if the lid is firm. It should be possible to lift the jars by the lid. When the jars have sealed there is no need to replace either the clip or screw band, and these can be used again.

Note

If the screw band is put on the jar, do this only loosely, and it is advisable to lightly grease the inside of the band. The oven method is suitable for all fruits, but not for pulping or tomatoes bottled in their own juice.

Tomatoes

These are improved in flavour if salt and sugar are added. To each 1 lb. tomatoes allow ½ teaspoonful salt, ½ teaspoonful sugar. Sprinkle into the jar before pouring on boiling water.

To bottle in a steriliser

Ideally one should have a deep steriliser so the jars can be completely covered or at least covered up to the neck. If you have not a proper steriliser, a bread-bin or very deep saucepan can be used.

Prepare the fruit. See instructions for doing this on pages 72–73. Pack the fruit into the jars, packing as tightly as possible. Fill the jars to the very top with COLD water or COLD sugar syrup. Put on the boiled rubber bands and the lids. If using the screw-band jars, turn these as tightly as possible, then unscrew for half a turn, so allowing for the expansion of the glass. If using the clip tops put the clip into position. When using the skin covering, put this and the special string first of all into hot water for a few minutes, then tie on the skin as tightly as possible. Put some sort of padding at the bottom of the steriliser; a wooden board, several thicknesses of paper or an old cloth will do.

Stand the jars on this, being careful they do not touch the sides of the pan, or each other. It is always preferable to completely cover the jars in the steriliser with cold water, but if this is not possible, fill the steriliser with cold water up to the necks of the jars, then either put on the lid or cover with a board or tea cloth, so keeping in the steam. Take 1½ hours to bring the water in the steriliser to simmering, i.e. 165–175°F. for all fruits except pears and tomatoes, in which case the water should be brought to 180–190°F. With all fruits (but the following exceptions) maintain these temperatures for 10 minutes: with pears, peaches and tomatoes maintain for 30 minutes. Before lifting out the jars bale out a little water so that it is easier and safer to lift them out. Stand the jars on a wooden surface and if using jars with screw bands, tighten these.

To test if jars have sealed

Leave the jars for 24 hours, then test by remov- the the clip or band and seeing if the lid is tight. If it is, and the jar can be lifted by the lid, then the jars have sealed.

Pulping fruit

Imperfect fruit can be used for pulping if the bruised or diseased part has been cut away, leaving the rest of the fruit perfect. You must not use over-ripe fruit for pulping since this could cause fermentation during storage.

Method of pulping

1. Stew the fruit, adding little or no water, and sugar to taste.
2. With tomatoes add ½ teaspoon sugar and ½ teaspoon salt to each lb. tomatoes.
3. The tomatoes can be skinned if wished.
4. Rub through a sieve if a very smooth purée is desired.
5. If sieving, bring to the boil once again.
6. While the fruits are cooking put tops of jars to boil for 10 minutes.
7. Drop in the rubber bands for a minute too.
8. Sterilise the jars also by heating well.
9. Put the boiling pulp into the very hot jars.
10. Put on the rubber bands and the tops.
11. Put on the screw bands or clips.
12. If using screw bands give ½ turn back to allow for the expansion of the top of the bottles.
13. Stand the jars in a steriliser or deep pan filled with BOILING water.
14. Boil for a good 5–8 minutes in the case of fruit pulp and a good 10 minutes for tomato pulp.
15. Lift out and tighten screw bands.
16. Test as all bottled fruit after 24 hours.

To make syrup for fruit bottling

Obviously the strength of syrup you use will depend very much on personal taste and also the fruit to be bottled. Peaches for example are best in a heavy, to very heavy, syrup. Plums on the other hand are best in a light to medium heavy syrup.

Light syrup	4 oz. sugar 1 pint water
Heavy syrup	8–10 oz. sugar 1 pint water
Very heavy syrup	12 oz.–1 lb. sugar 1 pint water

The lighter the syrup, the better the appearance of the fruit, so for show purposes, bottle fruit in a really light syrup. To make the syrup, boil the sugar and water together until the sugar has dissolved. If syrup is slightly cloudy, strain through very fine muslin.

Bottling fruit without liquid

A less usual method of bottling fruit is to add no liquid at all, so that when the jars are opened they contain only the fruit. Obviously the flavour of fruit bottled by this method is much the best, for it is not diluted by water or syrup. This method is particularly suitable for **tomatoes**. Other fruits that can be done

this way are **raspberries, strawberries** (although these bottle less successfully than any fruit), **peaches** and **halved plums**. Do not try to use other fruits containing less juice.
To prepare the jars, wash them thoroughly and boil the rubber rings for 10 minutes. Skin tomatoes, then, if large, cut them into halves. Pack the tomatoes into the jars tightly, but being careful not to break them. Add ½ teaspoon salt and ½ teaspoon sugar to each lb. tomatoes. With other fruits simply pack the fruits into the jars with a sprinkling of sugar here and there in the jars. When the bottles are completely filled, put on the rubber rings. tops and clips or screw bands.

Note carefully

These jars may not now be sterilised in the oven, but **must** be sterilised in a deep pan, so loosen the screw bands and proceed exactly as given in the directions for bottling in a steriliser, giving exactly the same time and temperatures. When the jars are removed from the steriliser it will be found that the fruit has sunk down the jars a little; these cannot be filled up, so simply tighten the screw bands and test after 24 hours as usual.

Fruit bottling in a pressure cooker

If you have a pressure cooker, it is a very good idea to use it for bottling fruit. You must, however, be certain that you have a special 5 lb. weight to go on the cooker. Your pressure cooking book will probably give you instructions. However, here are some points that should be followed very carefully:

1 Prepare the fruit, see pages 72–73.
2 You cannot use other than proper bottling jars or the special clip tops that go over jam jars, in a pressure cooker.
3 Fill the jars as for the steriliser method (see page 73).
4 Pour 1 pint hot water into cooker, add 1 tablespoon vinegar to prevent cooker staining. Stand jars on inverted trivet. Do not allow jars to touch one another or side of cooker, Use paper between jars if they are likely to touch. If using ordinary jam jars, put cloth or layers of newspaper on the trivet to prevent breakage. Add extra ¼ pint water to allow for absorption by cloth or paper. When using electricity bring to pressure on low heat.
5 Fix cover, place on heat and bring to 5 lb. pressure in usual way. Process for time stated in table below.
6 Turn off heat and leave cooker on stove to reduce pressure at room temperature. When using an electric stove, move cooker gently away from heat. Do not reduce pressure with cold water as sudden cooling will crack jars. Open cooker, remove jars one at a time on to a cloth or wooden surface. Tighten screw bands and allow to cool. Test seal after 24 hours by inverting jars. If seal is not perfect re-process.

Timetable for bottling fruit (use 5 lb. pressure control)

Apples	3–4 minutes
Apricots	3–4 minutes
Blackberries	3–4 minutes
Blackcurrants	7 minutes
Cherries	7 minutes
Damsons	3–4 minutes
Gooseberries	3–4 minutes
Loganberries	3–4 minutes
Peaches	7 minutes
Pears	3–4 minutes
Plums	3–4 minutes
Raspberries	3–4 minutes
Redcurrants	7 minutes
Rhubarb	3–4 minutes
Tomatoes	7 minutes

Bottling fruit for show purposes

1 Check before leaving the jars that the seal is still airtight because carrying sometimes breaks this seal and your jams will be automatically disqualified.
2 Make certain that the jars are well polished on

the outside. This helps to show off the fruit inside to advantage.

3 When bottling fruit use a fairly light syrup for this gives a better colour and prevents any possibility of the fruit rising in the jar.
4 See that the jars are labelled very carefully.
5 Pack very much more carefully and in a more original manner than you would for home bottling.

Suggested ways of packing fruit in bottles

Apples
These look very good cut in rings rather than slices and the rings packed round the outside with a blackberry in the centre of each, where the core has been removed.

Whole apples
Peeled and cored these look most interesting. If slicing apples make sure the slices are all turned to face the same way.

Apricots
Turn halved apricots with their cut side towards the jar and put a cracked kernel in the centre of each.

Blackberries
Fill jars with alternate layers of blackberries and sliced apples.

Cherries
These form a very attractive jar when mixed with halved apricots.

Gooseberries
Take care to select gooseberries that are the same size and degree of ripeness.

Grapes
Pack alternate black and white grapes in a jar.

Grapefruit
Arrange the sections to form a very definite design round the sides of the jar.

Greengages
Be very careful to choose fruit that is of even size and not over-ripe.

Oranges
Whole oranges are most effective bottled and these can be bottled in water rather than syrup.

Pears
Take great care with the colour of pears. It is quite a good idea, for show purposes, to put a little lemon juice into the syrup to make certain that the fruit keeps particularly white.

Small pears
These look very effective if peeled, cored and packed whole. This means turning some one way and some the other.

Peaches
The yellow cling peaches are the best for bottling and look wonderful when halved.

Pineapple
This can be bottled as whole rings, or halved rings with cherries to give contrasting colour.

Raspberries
These are most effective if a white or redcurrant is put into the centre of each and this turned towards the outside of the jar.

Rhubarb
The right way to pack rhubarb for show purposes is to make sure every piece is exactly the same length.

Strawberries
The best way to keep the colour of strawberries is to let them stand in cold syrup overnight, take out of the syrup, pack in the jars, add the syrup and use the steriliser method.

Fruit salad
Another most attractive pack of fruit for competition is a mixed fruit salad but do remember to sterilise this for the time required by the fruit wanting the longest period.

Bottling strawberries

Strawberries can be bottled by any of the methods given, but they tend to lose their flavour very easily. The way that seems to retain it more than any other is to put the strawberries into a boiling syrup with a little lemon juice to flavour, if wished. Allow to cool in syrup, then bottle by steriliser method.

Bottling fruit in brandy

1. All fruit can be bottled in brandy, but since it is a very expensive method, only the very luxurious fruits are generally used.
2. Use fruits suggested.
3. Prepare the fruit (see page 72).
4. Where the fruit has a firm skin, e.g. damsons, prick once or twice with a needle so that the brandy syrup can penetrate the fruit.
5. Pack the fruit into jars.
6. Make a fairly heavy syrup (see page 74).
7. To each pint of **cold** syrup, allow ¼ pint brandy.
8. Cover the fruit with the brandy flavoured syrup.
9. Proceed using the steriliser method or you can use the oven method for suitable fruits (see page 73).

Peaches in brandy – see previous method.
Pears in brandy – see previous method.
Dessert cherries in brandy – see previous method.
Raspberries in brandy – see previous method.
Damsons in brandy – see previous method.

Bottling vegetables

Remember it is *unsafe* to bottle vegetables other than in a pressure cooker. Always follow the special instructions for your own make of pressure cooker. Below are the main points to remember.

1. Wash thoroughly to free vegetables from all traces of soil. Pre-cook or blanch by immersing in boiling water for the time stated in table below, then dropping into cold water. Drain well and pack into clean jars to within 1 inch of top. Do not pack too tightly.

TIMETABLE FOR BOTTLING VEGETABLES

(Use 10 lb. Pressure Control)

Vegetables	Preparation	Minutes to blanch in boiling water	Minutes to process at 10 lb. pressure
1 Asparagus	Wash, trim off scales, cut in even lengths, tie in bundles, pack upright	2–3 minutes	40 minutes
2 Beans, Broad	Pod, choose very young beans	5 minutes	55 minutes
3 Beans, Runner	Wash, string and slice	5 minutes	40 minutes
4 Beetroot	Cut off top. Blanch before slicing or dicing	15–20 minutes	40 minutes
5 Carrots	Wash, scrape, slice or dice. Young new, leave whole	10 minutes	45 minutes
6 Celery	Wash, cut in even lengths	6 minutes	40 minutes
7 Corn	Strip from cob	2–3 minutes	50 minutes
8 Peas	Wash, shell and grade	2–3 minutes	50 minutes
9 Potatoes, New	Wash, scrape carefully or peel thinly	5 minutes	50 minutes

2 Still leaving 1 inch at top, cover vegetables with a hot brine solution, made by dissolving 2–3 oz. salt to 8 pints water, boiled before using. Work out air bubbles by quickly twisting the jar from side to side. Adjust rings and lids.

3 Process jars of hot food immediately. Pour 1 pint hot water into cooker, add 1 tablespoon vinegar. Stand jars on inverted trivet. Do not allow jars to touch each other on the sides of the cooker. Use paper between jars if necessary. Fix cover, place on LOW heat. Do not put on pressure control; allow air to be expelled through centre vent for 5 minutes. Put on 10 lb. pressure control valve, still at low heat, bring to pressure. Process for the times stated before. See that there is always a steady flow of steam from the pressure control as pressure must not drop below 10 lb.

4 As point 6 in fruit bottling (see page 75).

5 The loss of liquid does not interfere with the keeping quality of the food. Jars should never be opened, after processing, to replace liquid that has boiled away. When opening a jar of bottled vegetables do not taste the cold food. If the contents of the jar do not smell right and the food is soft and mushy, discard it at once. As a safeguard, heat bottled vegetables at boiling temperature for 10–15 minutes before tasting or using.

Bottling vegetables for show purposes

The same points apply here as were given under bottling fruit (see page 75), but the following points will help you to produce perfect jars of vegetables.

1 Choose vegetables of all the same size.

2 Potatoes should be put in a little salt water with lemon juice added to make certain they keep very white.

3 A few drops of green colouring can be added to the brine for peas and beans, but some judges do not approve of this.

To make certain screw top jars are easy to remove

When you have tested the jars and you are satisfied they have sealed properly, you should then grease or oil inside the metal bands. Replace the bands, but do not attempt to screw down very tightly. If using clip tops to the jars, grease the under-side of these very lightly and just lay to one side of the tops so they do not fit too tightly.

Home freezing

Never attempt to freeze foods (except ice cream and ice and frozen desserts) in the ordinary freezing compartment of a domestic refrigerator. A home freezer, which has a much lower temperature, must be used.

General rules for home freezing

1. Food

Only first-quality foods should be preserved by this method. Fruits and vegetables should be frozen directly they are picked. Meat and poultry should hang for the correct minimum length of time before freezing.

When this is not possible, all foods should be put in a cool place or household refrigerator for not longer than 12–24 hours before being prepared for the home freezer.

2. Packaging

Moisture-vapour-proof packaging materials are essential for freezing and storing produce.

Food will lose moisture by evaporation unless well packed and sealed, because of the low humidity inside the freezer. The food will become dry, the texture and colour deteriorate and the flavour will disappear. Badly packaged strong-smelling food may spoil other produce stored in the same freezer.

Therefore, choose packaging material with care and leave as little air as possible inside the containers before sealing.

3. Equipment

Quality of frozen food depends on speed, i.e. speed in preparation and quick drop in temperature when in the freezer.

4. For freezing set freezer at –20°F. to –30°F. For storing set freezer at 0°F.

To freeze small quantities quickly

(a) This method, by restricting the size of the ice crystals formed from the natural juices in food, minimises any change in its cell structure.

(b) With the shorter freezing time, there is less time for the separation of water in the form of ice, so less mineral salts are lost through seepage as the foods defrost.

(c) In this rapid freezing process there is quick cooling of the food to temperatures at which bacteria, moulds and yeast cannot grow. Therefore, foods are protected from the possibility of deterioration during freezing.

N.B. Do not overload the freezer, i.e. for the best results do not freeze too much food at one time.

To store

The lower the temperature, the longer the food can be kept stored and remain nearly perfect in flavour, colour and food value.

Loss of nutrients in frozen food

–40°F.	none
–10°F.	negligible
0°F.	very slow
10°F. or higher	much accelerated and in a comparatively short time the frozen food becomes rancid and unpleasant flavours set in.

Freezing already cooked food

A great variety of cooked foods can be frozen e.g.:

Bread

This enables you to cook a large batch of loaves and freeze them until required.

Cooked meats, fish and savoury dishes

Allow food to become quite cold, then freeze immediately while they are still very fresh. Where the wrapping may be placed on to the cold, cooked food, wrap before freezing. If, however, the wrapping would spoil the appearance of the cooked food, freeze then wrap. Once frozen you can lift puddings out of their basins to save space; or line the basin with foil before cooking, lift out the foil and food after freezing.

Cakes

Sponges – rich layer cakes – all freeze very well. Allow to cool and freeze while still fresh. Wrap as meat, etc.

Use your frozen food cabinet to save valuable time when planning menus.

Home freezing of raw foods

Meat

1. Choose only the best quality young tender meat for home freezing. Cut the meat into portions suitable for the purpose. It is wise to ask the butcher to do this.
2. Wrap larger pieces of meat, or portions, or joints, in moisture-vapour-proof covers, e.g. cellophane. Expel the air, turn in the edges and seal down with tape or by heat.
3. Smaller cuts, e.g. chops or steaks, are separated by two pieces of grease-proof paper in order that the required number may be removed without defrosting the rest.
4. Place in container, e.g. plastic bag and squeeze to expel the air. Seal by heat, sealing tape or bag fasteners. Turn in the sharp ends to avoid piercing packages.
5. After sealing over-wrap with mutton cloth or similar wrapping to protect from damage while in the freezer. Mark each package with date and weight of meat.

Poultry

1. Before freezing prepare poultry for cooking –

wrap sharp ends of the bird to protect the container. Wash and wrap giblets separately in moisture-vapour-proof materials.

2 Place the bird in suitable container, e.g. plastic bag. Place the giblets with it in container, expel the air and seal. Label with weight of bird and date frozen.
3 Pack carefully jointed poultry in a special tray. Separate the portions – if not to be used all at once – by two pieces of grease-proof paper.
4 Wrap poultry and tray in moisture-vapour-proof cellophane. Expel the air, turn in the edges, seal. Record weight and date on package with a chinagraph pencil.

Vegetables

1 Blanch all vegetables by immersing in boiling water. Bring to boil again. Time boiling according to the size of vegetables, e.g. boil for 1 minute. Cool, pack and seal.
2 Blanched and cooled vegetables may be packed in various types of containers, e.g. polythene bags. All vegetables **must** be blanched before packing and freezing.
3 After blanching in boiling water, the vegetables should be drained and cooled. Place in bag, expel air and seal.

Fruit

1 Place clean, freshly picked fruit in a polythene bag. Cover with cooled syrup. Expel air and seal bag by heating.
2 The syrup should be poured to within half-an-inch of lid to allow for expansion during freezing. Alternatively, sugar can be sprinkled over the fruit.

Sealing containers for home freezing

Whether you are freezing raw or cooked foods, the containers must be firmly sealed. You can buy small strips of plastic for the tops of bags, or use adhesive tape.

Fruit syrups, glacé and crystallised fruits

All fruit syrups will keep well – they tend to have a better flavour as well as a thicker texture if sugar is added – but they can be preserved without if it should be necessary for medical reasons.

1 Put the fruit into the top of a double saucepan or basin over hot water, adding the water if required. Press down the fruit to squash it well and cook for about 1 hour until you are sure all the juice is extracted. Press down during cooking.
2 Strain through a jelly bag, or through several thicknesses of muslin over a fine sieve.
3 Measure the juice and add sugar, heat together until the sugar is dissolved, stirring well during this time. **Do not continue boiling** when sugar has dissolved.
4 Pour the hot syrup into hot bottling jars or use cordial bottles with well fitting screw topped lids, which should have been boiled before using.
5 Allow syrup to cool in the bottles, which should not be quite filled.
6 Stand them in a steriliser or deep pan with a rack at the bottom, or several thicknesses of cloth or paper.
7 Loosen screw bands ½ turn, then take 1 hour to bring water to simmering (170°F). Retain for 30 minutes for large jars or bottles, or 20 minutes for smaller ones.
8 Lift out carefully, stand on a wooden surface and tighten screw bands.
9 Tie adhesive tape around the corks or caps of cordial bottles.
10 Dilute with water to serve.

To use fruit syrups

Fruit syrups can be used diluted with soda water in cold drinks, with milk for milk shakes, or used as a sauce poured over ice cream, or cold desserts of many kinds.

Variations of fruit syrup

Blackberry syrup

cooking time: 1 hour, plus sterilising time

you will need:

¼ pint water to each lb. fruit
8–12 oz. sugar to each pint of juice

Use method for fruit syrups (see page 80).

Blackcurrant syrup

cooking time: 1 hour, plus sterilising time

Allow ¼ pint water to each lb. blackcurrants
To each pint of juice allow 8–12 oz. sugar

Use method for fruit syrups (see page 80).

Cherry syrup

cooking time: 1 hour, plus sterilising time

you will need:

¼ pint water to each lb. very ripe juicy black cherries
8–12 oz. sugar to each pint of juice

Use method for fruit syrups (see page 80).

Damson syrup

cooking time: 1 hour, plus sterilising time

you will need:

⅜ pint water to each lb. fruit
12 oz. sugar to each pint of juice

Use method for fruit syrups (see page 80).

Elderberry syrup

cooking time: 1 hour, plus sterilising time

you will need:

1 lb. elderberries
¼ pint water
8 oz. sugar to each pint juice

Use method for fruit syrups (see page 80).

Lemonade syrup

cooking time: 5 minutes, plus sterilising time

you will need:

8 lemons
½ pint water
8–12 oz. sugar to each pint of juice

1 Peel the lemons very thinly to remove rind only.
2 Put peel into a pan with the water.
3 Simmer for 5 minutes.
4 Strain and add to the lemon juice.
5 Measure and add the sugar.
6 Proceed as step 3 in fruit syrups (see page 80).

Loganberry syrup

cooking time: 1 hour, plus sterilising time

you will need:

1 lb. loganberries
2 tablespoons water
8–12 oz. sugar to each pint of juice

Use method as for fruit syrups (see page 80).

Orangeade syrup

cooking time: 5 minutes, plus sterilising time

you will need:

10 oranges
½ pint water
8–12 oz. sugar to each pint of juice

Use method for lemonade syrup.

Raspberry syrup

cooking time: just under 1 hour, plus sterilising time

you will need:

8–12 oz. sugar to each pint of raspberry juice
no water required

Use method for fruit syrups (see page 80).

Redcurrant syrup

cooking time: 1 hour, plus sterilising time

you will need:

¼ pint water to each lb. of fruit
8–12 oz. sugar to each pint of juice

Use method as for fruit syrups (see page 80).

Rhubarb syrup

cooking time: 1 hour, plus sterilising time

you will need:

½ pint water to each lb. fruit	12 oz. sugar to each pint of juice

Use method for fruit syrups (see page 80).

Rose hip syrup

cooking time: 5 minutes, plus sterilising time

you will need:

1 lb. rosehips 3 pints water	8–12 oz. sugar to each pint juice

To preserve the maximum amount of vitamin C, this is the method to use:

1 Grate or chop the hips quickly and use immediately after grating.
2 Put into the water when boiling.
3 Simmer for 5 minutes only.
4 Stand for 15 minutes.
5 Strain and measure.
6 Add the sugar and proceed from step 3 in fruit syrups (see page 80).

Strawberry syrup

cooking time: just under 1 hour, plus sterilising time

you will need:

8–12 oz. sugar per pint of juice	no water required

Use method for fruit syrups (see page 80).

Fruit juices

These are made and bottled in exactly the same way as the fruit syrups (see recipes), but are meant to be served undiluted, so only 2–4 oz. sugar is used to each pint of juice.
Fruit juice is delightfully refreshing and makes an ideal drink when served with ice in summer.

Glacé fruits

Fresh fruits: Oranges, Pears, Grapes, Cherries.
Canned fruit: Mandarins, Pineapple pieces, Pears, Lychees.

Fresh fruits

Sections of oranges and halved small pears and grapes are suitable.

1 Choose firm fruits, wash and divide into neat segments.
2 Cook gently in water until just tender. Grapes need no cooking – they should be put into the dish and the syrup poured over.
3 For each lb. of fruit allow ½ pint of syrup. Make this up by using ½ pint of the water in which the fruits were cooked, and 6 oz. sugar.
4 Put the fruit into a fairly shallow dish and pour the syrup over while warm. Leave for 24 hours well covered: put a plate on top of the dish.
5 Pour off the syrup and re-boil, adding another 2 oz. sugar. Pour over fruit again and leave for another 24 hours.
6 *Repeat* this another 3 times – each time adding an extra 2 oz. sugar.
7 Drain off the fruit, return the syrup to the pan, this time adding 3 oz. sugar to the original ½ pint syrup. When boiling, add the fruit and boil for 3 minutes. Return to the dish and leave for 24 hours.
8 Repeat step No. 7. The syrup should then take on the consistency of thick honey. If thin, repeat once again.
9 Drain off the syrup and place the fruit on a wire cake rack to dry – leave a plate underneath to catch the drips.

Canned fruits

1 Drain the fruit from the syrup.
2 Measure the syrup, and to each ½ pint add 2 oz. sugar. Boil together, pour over fruit and leave for 24 hours. Continue as for fresh fruit from step No. 4 to end.

Note

The syrup can be coloured if desired.

Crystallised fruits

Fresh fruit: Oranges, Pears, Grapes, Cherries.
Canned fruits: Mandarins, Pineapple pieces, Pears, Lychees
Follow instructions for *Glacé fruits*, steps 1 to 9, then

10 Put the fruit into the oven (225°F. – Gas Mark ¼) with the door slightly ajar. Leave until crisp. (An alternative is to roll and coat in granulated sugar.)

Crystallised angelica

1 Choose stalks that are young, firm and tender.
2 Cut off the root ends and leaves, then place the stalks in a basin and pour over a boiling brine (make this with ¼ oz. kitchen salt to 4 pints water).
3 Allow to soak for 10 minutes then rinse in cold water.
4 Place in a saucepan of fresh boiling water. Boil for 5 minutes if very tender – a little longer if somewhat older.
5 Drain well, then scrape off outer skin.
6 Continue in exactly the same way as from step 3, Crystallised fruits. Store in dry jars – the colour will keep better if kept in a dark place.

Crystallised flowers

Flowers: Roses, Violets, Primroses, Polyanthus.
Blossoms: Plum, Cherry, Apple, Pear, Heather.

Note
Non-edible flowers are those which come from bulbs – in many cases these are poisonous.

you will need:

1 oz. gum arabic
rosewater (triple strength)
flowers
castor sugar

1 Cover the gum arabic with the rosewater and leave for 24 hours to melt.
2 When properly melted, paint each petal of the flowers all over on both sides, using a fine paint brush, then hold each flower by the stem and sprinkle with castor sugar all over it.

Candied peel

Candied orange peel

you will need:

peel of 8 sweet oranges
½ oz. bicarbonate of soda
water
1½ lb. granulated sugar

1 Well wash the oranges.
2 Remove the skin in quarters and discard as much pith as possible.
3 Dissolve the bicarbonate of soda in 2 quarts boiling water and soak the peel for 20–30 minutes.
4 Strain and simmer gently in fresh water until tender.
5 Take out peel and immerse in a hot syrup made from 1 lb. sugar dissolved in 1 pint water brought to boiling point. Leave to soak for 2 days, covering with a plate.
6 Drain off syrup and add 8 oz. sugar. Bring to the boil and simmer peel until clear. Put on a rack to drain and dry (this can be done in a cool oven).
7 The next day, boil up the remaining syrup and dip pieces of peel in this, then dry again and store in covered jars.

Variations
Candied lemon peel, Candied grapefruit peel – follow the same procedure as for Candied orange peel.

Flavoured vinegars

Flavouring vinegar by the use of herbs or fruit provides an excellent variety, so that when you make salad dressings you can give a new flavour. Some people like to drink fruit flavoured vinegars and many people consider that in winter they are very beneficial.

Fruit vinegar

cooking time: 10 minutes

1 Allow 1 pint vinegar to each lb. of soft fruit, unless otherwise stated.
2 Add the vinegar to the fruit.
3 Leave for 3–5 days – stirring occasionally.
4 Strain off liquid.
5 Add 8 oz.–1 lb. sugar to each pint, depending on personal taste.
6 Boil for 10 minutes and bottle.
7 Use these fruit vinegars as the basis of dressings with salads or many people like a little mixed with sugar and hot water as a winter drink.

Blackcurrant vinegar

Use recipe and method for fruit vinegar, but use ordinary malt or white malt vinegar. Rather small blackcurrants can be used for this.

Elderberry vinegar

cooking time: 10 minutes

1 Allow 1 pint white vinegar to each 12 oz. fruit.
2 Add the vinegar to the fruit and proceed as for fruit vinegar (see above) adding 12 oz. sugar to each pint of vinegar.

Horseradish vinegar

you will need:

horseradish
white vinegar

1 Scrape and shred the horseradish with a coarse grater.
2 Pack into jars, half filling each jar.
3 Pour over cold vinegar.
4 Store for 6 weeks, shaking the bottles daily if possible.
5 Strain the vinegar through very fine muslin.

This is excellent for salad dressings to serve with cold beef.

Mint vinegar

Use recipe and method for thyme vinegar, but use whole mint leaves. This is ideal for mint flavoured dressings.

Raspberry vinegar

Use recipe and method for fruit vinegar – preferably use ripe dry fruit – but this is a good way to use up any fruit that might be 'squashed' at the bottom of the basket. White malt vinegar gives a better colour.

Redcurrant vinegar

Use recipe and method for fruit vinegar, but use ordinary malt or white malt vinegar. The rather small redcurrants can be used for this.

Sage vinegar

you will need:

sage leaves
malt or white vinegar

1 Bruise the sage leaves by crushing with a rolling pin to extract flavour.
2 Pack them into jars, half filling each jar.
3 Pour over cold vinegar.
4 Store for 6 weeks, shaking the bottles daily if possible.
5 Strain the vinegar through very fine muslin. Ideal for mayonnaise or dressing to serve with cold pork or duck.

Tarragon vinegar

you will need:

tarragon leaves
malt or white vinegar

1 Bruise the tarragon leaves by crushing with a rolling pin, to extract flavour.
2 Pack them into jars, half filling each jar.
3 Pour over cold vinegar.
4 Store for 6 weeks, shaking the bottles daily if possible.
5 Strain the vinegar through very fine muslin. Use for fish salads and in béarnaise sauce or hollandaise sauce.

Thyme vinegar

you will need:

thyme – lemon flavoured thyme particularly good
malt or white vinegar

1 Bruise the thyme leaves by crushing with a rolling pin to extract flavour.
2 Pack them into jars, half filling each jar.
3 Pour over cold vinegar.
4 Store for 6 weeks, shaking the bottles daily if possible.
5 Strain the vinegar through very fine muslin. Ideal for mayonnaise or dressing to serve with cold chicken or turkey.

Savoury butters

Flavoured butters

Anchovy – cream butter and add a few drops anchovy essence.

Chutney – cream butter and add a spoonful or two of chutney.

Curry – cream butter and add ½ teaspoon curry powder to 2 oz. butter.

Herbs – cream butter and blend in chopped thyme, marjoram, mint, sage or parsley, etc.

Lemon – add grated lemon rind and a little lemon juice to creamed butter.

Mustard – blend in made-mustard and chopped watercress.

Watercress – chop watercress and blend in.

Barbecue – add a few drops of Worcestershire sauce.

Seasoned butter

1 Rub bowl with a clove of garlic.
2 Cream 4 oz. butter until fluffy.
3 Beat into butter 1 tablespoon mild mustard, 1 tablespoon finely chopped parsley, 1 teaspoon finely chopped onion or chives.

Devilled mustard butter

Blend 4 oz. butter or margarine with ½ tablespoon made-mustard, ½ teaspoon curry powder, 1 tablespoon lemon juice and ½ teaspoon finely grated lemon rind. (This is excellent with fish sandwiches, hot or cold.)

Ham butter

Mince 2 oz. lean ham or bacon and mix into 2 oz. butter or margarine to form a smooth paste.

Index

D

E

F

L

M

N

O

P

Q

R

S